Purchased for Dr. Donald F. Clone
Greensboro, N. C.

HERITAGE OF EXCELLENCE

I suggest that something extraordinarily precious comes out of the close but entirely free association of really superior people. To this emergent quality I give the name—the heritage of excellence, mostly because it lasts so long and because it never comes from, nor appeals to, mediocrities. . . . What Welch and his colleagues did and believed and wrote is not as important now—nor anywhere near as important—as the heritage of excellence their contacts with each other have left us. . . . In this sense Johns Hopkins is enviably rich. . . . What more do men of superior character and capacity require for their association than freedom, responsibility and expectation?

Alan Gregg 1950

THE
KNOWLEDGE BOOK

Messages received and transformed into writing
by
VEDİA BÜLENT (ÖNSÜ) ÇORAK

Published by:
"Dünya Kardeşlik Birliği Mevlana Yüce Vakfı"
"World Brotherhood Union Mevlana Supreme Foundation"
P.O.Box : 84, 81072 Suadiye, İSTANBUL/TURKEY

Copyright: © 1996
"Dünya Kardeşlik Birliği Mevlana Yüce Vakfı"
"World Brotherhood Union Mevlana Supreme Foundation"

The Second Edition:
January 1998

Arrangement:
Dünya Kardeşlik Birliği/World Brotherhood Union

Printed and Bound by:
OHAN Matbaacılık

ISBN : 975-95053-1-2

Ministry of Culture of The Republic of Turkey Code No.
B.16.0.KGM.0.63.00.03/6063709

IT IS NOTICE FROM THE REALITY TOTALITY

All the Missionary Staffs who have given covenants for the dissemination Program of the System, have been embodied in different parts of the World especially in this Final Age.

However, as well as this, there are also thousands of Entities who Work in different ways in the direction of their Own Channel Impositions.

For this reason, The Knowledge Book has been rendered effective as the Single Channel - Single Path - Single Order - Single Truth and this Chaos of the Consciousness has been tried to be prevented as much as possible.

In the translation of the Knowledge Book which has been bestowed on Your Planet as the Heralder of the World Totality of the Morrows, and of the Golden Age, into different languages at this moment and in the future years, it will be especially disclosed that the conveyance Source of the Book is the Reality of Unified Humanity Universal Cosmos Unification Totality.

And, it has been rendered effective by the name The Knowledge Book from the Channel of Alpha in the World year 1981 in the Anatolian Turkey.

It will be placed as a preface in the Books to be translated that the name of the Universal Focal Point established by the Reality for the first time on the World Plan is (World Brotherhood Union Universal Unification Center) and that its Center is in Istanbul.

In the translations to be made, the Book revealed in Turkish will always be rendered effective as an example and during translation, private or different information will never be added to the Book. Any Alterations in the Original Emblem is out of question in any way.

It is presented for your Information.

SYSTEM

FOREWORD

The integration of all our World Planet by becoming Unified on the Path of Humanity has been taken in hand by our Universal Friends. Celestial assistance is being granted to our Planet on this path. During this Transition Cycle which is called "RESURRECTION", Universal Attainments made by means of the Cosmic Influences cause our Planet to make a progress together with the medium it belongs to. The events being experienced cause all the Social Consciousnesses to awaken as a mass. Our Sacred Books which had been revealed to us until today according to the Social Views, have prepared the Human Beings of the World for Integration parallel to their own beliefs. This Book, conveyed to you at the moment, is not a Book of Religion. It is a Book which gives you Universal Knowledge and Truth. This book has been given to us by our Universal Friends under the name of "THE KNOWLEDGE BOOK". The source through which it has been revealed is ALPHA, which is the Direct Channel of the LORD, and it has been dictated from the Sacred Focal Point from which all the Books of Religion had been revealed. However, the Period of Religions has come to an end long ago. Now, our Celestial Friends are abolishing Idolatry by telling us all the Truths. The purpose of the dictation of this Book is to gather all the Universe and our Planet in the Consciousness of Humane Integration. The periods of Prophethood have come to an end. From now on, our Planet will be enlightened on the path of Science and Learning. In our Planet, the Golden Age is being established together with the entire Universe Consciousness in a splendid way. The Cosmic Consciousness attained by this means will become stronger in time and will make us attain a brand-new personality, and we will discover the Genuine Human Being in Us. We are walking on this path, believing from the heart that all those efforts rendered for a Flowery World without Wars, will prepare beautiful morrows for our Planet. The Plan for realizing the Universal Unity in this Final Age has been prepared centuries ago. This program is called the "GOLDEN AGE PROGRAM". It has been waited for the Human Consciousnesses to reach a certain Consciousness Level for this program to be able to be applied to our Planet. The time has come for Humanity which has gained the Light of Consciousness from micro to macro, walking on the paths of Reincarnation, to be told all the Truths. Humanity who will gather on the One World Platform to be established in the future, will Unite under the roof of a One World State. For this reason, Humanity which has reached a certain Level of Consciousness is projecting a program rendered directly by the Reality of Unified Humanity, to all of the Universal Totalities (including our Planet). The name of this Universal Program in the Totality is the "MEVLANA SUPREME PLAN". And according to this Plan, one day, all Humanity will be United under the same Roof. Under this Roof of Humanity, everyone is brother/sister, of everyone. The ALLAH of this brother/sister Totality is the same. Their Essence is the same. Henceforth, their Religions will not be different, either, since Religious Dimensions have been closed long ago in the Universal Totality. However, during this Dimension of Transition in which Worldly Consciousnesses are in effect, either Religious or Worldly attachments separate this Unity of Brotherhood/Sisterhood from each other. For this reason, our Planet, on which a great Selection program has been started, is going through and will be going through the most difficult periods of this final Age. In Sacred Books, this time period which is known as the "RESURRECTION" is called the "SALVATION PLAN" in the Universal Program. This Universal Book which has been completed in 12 years under the name of the "GOLDEN BOOK OF THE GOLDEN AGE" and the "KNOWLEDGE BOOK" has been and is being distributed until today all over our Planet as fascicules, according to the wishes of the Celestial Totality. Through this path, we have been reaching Humanity for many years. The name of our group is the "MEVLANA ESSENCE NUCLEUS STAFF". Our Association is called the "WORLD BROTHERHOOD UNION UNIVERSAL UNIFICATION CENTER", Our Foundation is called the "WORLD BROTHERHOOD UNION MEVLANA SUPREME FOUNDATION". Our center is in the city of ISTANBUL in the TURKEY of ATATÜRK. It has been announced by the Celestial Authorities that, in future, by this Totality of Ours, common branches will be opened by the Totalities of Anatolia and of the World. Awaiting these happy days with great longing, it gives us pride to Greet our Terrestrial Brothers and Sisters serving on the Universal path.

∝

ANNOUNCEMENT FROM THE CENTRAL TOTALITY
Message to be Given to Dear Mevlana

Dear Mevlana,

The Knowledge Book which is the Golden Book of the Golden Age, Bestowed on Your Planet beginning with 1-11-1981 World year, is a Universal Constitution comprising the Total of All the Suggestions of the System and it is a Call of the Skies to Humanity. This Book has been bestowed on Your Planet through Your Pen as the Pen of the Golden Age. This Period in which Your Terrestrial Name is Vedia Bülent Önsü Çorak at this moment, It has been card-indexed in the Special Archive of the Reality Totality that Your Old Name was Mevlana Celaleddini Rumi. The Mesnevi of that period, too, is a Celestial Book of Enlightenment. The aphorisms of the Mesnevi are from You, its Frequency from Us. However, both the Words and the Frequency of the Knowledge Book, being Connected to the Totalistic Totality by a Special Technique, have been entrusted to Your Pen from a Private Channel connected to the Totality of Reality of Unified Humanity. There is not even the smallest Fragment of Personal Awareness within the Book since Your Consciousness Light is connected to the Cosmo as a necessity of the Program during the period You live in. Time will prove the Power of the Book to Humanity. Into this Book to which the command of Publication will be given at the second half of the ending date of 1993 World year in which Individual Selections of the Final Age are still in effect, This Message will be written with Your Original Signature, in Your Handwriting, in Ink and it will be the Seal of the Book as an Official Document. Suggestions Given until the Date November 6, 1993 that is, until the Publication Command of the Book is Given, will also be written in the Book exactly as they are. At the Completion of the Book, a Special Suggestion will be Given by the System. The Acceptance of Our Love is Our kind request Our Friend.

ANNOUNCEMENT FROM THE
CENTRAL TOTALITY CORTÈGE

NOTE : This Message will be added to the Book Together with the Date it has been Received as a Single Page, without Photocopy and thus will be made Official. This Document is the Protective Aura of a Document given on behalf of the Entire Totality and of the Book.

MESSAGE RECEIVED BY
VEDİA BÜLENT ÖNSÜ ÇORAK

(This is the translation of the hand-written Message on the right-hand page)

2-3-1993
Saat 9:05

Merkezi Bütünlükten Bildiridir
Mevlânam'ya Verilmek üzere mesajdır

Mevlânam;
planetinize 1-11-1981 Dünya yılından itibaren Hediye
edilen, Altın Çağın Altın Kitabı olan Bilgi Kitabı, Sistemin
Tüm önerilerinin Bütününü teşkil eden Evrensel bir
Anayasadır. Ve Göklerin insanlığa bir Çağrısıdır.
Bu Kitap planetinize Altın Çağın Altın Kalemi olarak Sizin
Kaleminizden Hediye edilmiştir. Şu an Dünya isminizin
Vedia Bülent Önsü Çorak olduğu bu Dönemde, eski
isminizin Mevlâna Celâleddini Rumi olduğu Realite
Bütünlüğünün Özel Arzusunda Fizikidir. O Dönemin
Mesnevisi'de Göksel bir İrşad Kitabıdır. Mesnevi'nin
Değizleri Sizden, Frekansı Bizdendir. Ancak Bilgi Kitabının
Hem Kelâmı, Hemde Frekansı Özel bir teknik ile, Bütünsel
Bütünlüğe Bağlı Özel bir Kanaldan, Sizin Kaleminize
Tevdi edilmiştir. Yazıldığınız Dönemde Sizin Bilinç
İzıgınız, program gereği Koşmaya Bağlı olduğu için,
Kitabın içinde, Şahsi en ufak bir Şuur Kırıntısı bile
yoktur. Kitabın Gücünü Zaman İnsanlığa ispat edecektir.
Henüz planetinizde Son Çağın Bireysel Seçimlerinin Devrede
olduğu 1993 Dünya yılının Bitiz tarihinin ikinci yarısında
Basım Emri Verilecek olan Bu Kitaba, Sizin El yazınız ile bu
Mesaj Mürekkepli Kalem ve Orijinal İmzanız ile yazılacak ve
Resmi Belge olarak Kitabın Mühürü olacaktır. 6 Kasım 1993
Tarihine Kadar, yani Kitabın Basım Emri Verilene Kadar Verilecek
olan Önerilerde, aynen Kitaba yapılacaktır. Kitabın Bitiminde
Özel bir Öneri Sistem tarafından Verilecektir.
Sevginizin Kabulü Ricamızdır Dostumuz.
                    Merkezi Bütünlük Kortejinden Bildiridir
NOT:
Bu mesaj alındığı tarih ile beraber Tek sayfa olarak Fotokopisiyle
Kitaba ilâve edilip Resmileştirilecektir. Bu Belge Tüm Bütünlük
adına verilen bir Belgenin ve Kitabın Korunma aurasıdır.
                    Mesajı alan
                    Vedia Bülent Önsü Çorak
                    B. Çorak

MUSTAFA KEMAL ATATÜRK (1881-1938)

VOLUME

I

DÜNYA: WORLD   KARDEŞLİK: BROTHERHOOD/SISTERHOOD   BİRLİĞİ: UNION

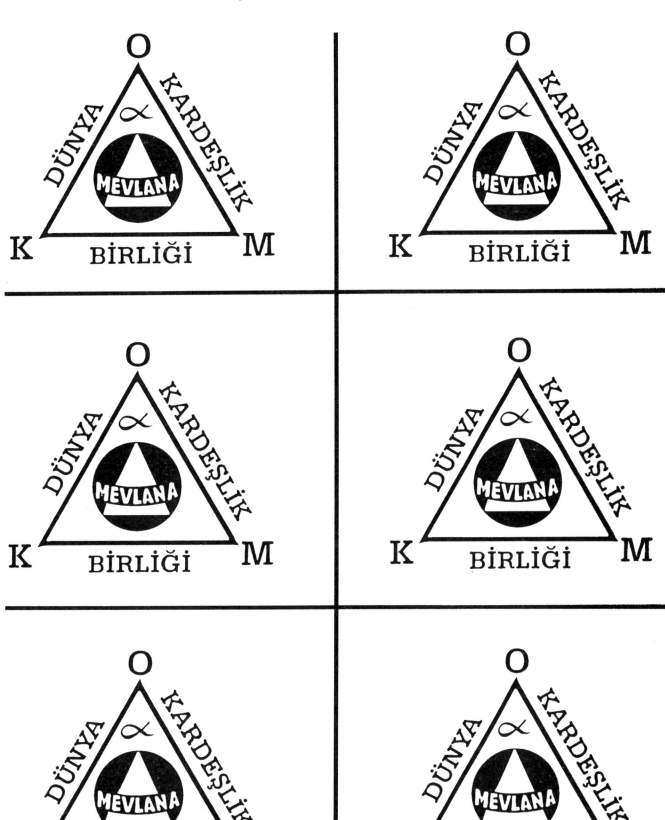

IN THE NAME OF THE PRE-EMINENT ALL-MERCIFUL

The Text of this Book comprises all the Sacred Books. You will find the Genuine Human Being in this Book. This is the unique Intercontinental Book. And it is revealed by the Universal Authorities with the help of Divine Codes*.

All the Divine Books until today were the Guiding Books of Enlightened Genuine Spiritual Guides who came from the Path of Light. These Books were dictated from the Same Channel.

Now, during this Last Age, it was thought imperative that all Our World Friends should come together under one roof. Thus, this Book is Your Genuine Friend, Your Genuine Brother/Sister. Because, it is dictated by Our Essence Brothers/Sisters.

During this difficult time of Your World, everyone has gained a Cosmic Awareness. We believe that Our World Friends who have gained this Consciousness will understand the essence of this Book very quickly. Your World has now opened to the Universe and the Universe has been opened to the World. The texts which are dictated are distributed to the whole Universe Chapter by Chapter.

Doors of Worship are the only Doors of God. There is no discrimination there. No matter where You are, always His* inextinguishable Sun shines inside us. The LORD for us all is single. That means We are all His Children. For this reason with the Command of the Single LORD the entire Universe is being made to assemble under one Roof.

Your World is being prepared for very difficult conditions. Those who are Conscious of this fact know that if We extend our brotherly/sisterly hands with love to everyone, these hands will never be refused.

Our God never had the intention of sending Us to the World for Us to Divide it. This Earth will be transformed to Heaven one day by all Our Human Brothers and Sisters. We hope to meet one day in Our Brotherly/Sisterly World.

The Code of Alpha is the only Channel which has received the Command to announce everything with all clarity. This Book will explain, from the Learning point of view, the subjects You all know (or do not know yet) for everybody to understand them better.

Do not forget that all the Books revealed from the Enlightenment Channel had been revealed from the Level of Firmament. These Sacred Books are the New Testament, the Old Testament, the Psalms of David, the Religions of the Far East and the Koran. The actual Purpose of these Sacred Books is to give a Message to Our Human Brothers and Sisters in the Light of Learning.

* Look at the Glossary.

However, those Sacred Books were later deviated from their Actual Purpose and were Degenerated. Now, (ALL THE BOOKS BETWEEN THE FIRST BOOK AND THE LAST BOOK ARE JOINED IN THIS BOOK). And it is presented to the Universe as The Single Sacred Book.

Now, We are sure that the flowers on the flowery paths We are treading will not ever wither again. Because, We are Secure. These Sacred Books have Enlightened You until today and have prepared You for a certain Medium. This is the most Honest step You will take towards the path of Love, Friendship and Brotherhood*.

Do not forget that the Spirit has neither Age, nor Sex, nor Nationality. (JESUS CHRIST - MOSES - MOHAMMED WERE ONCE UNIVERSAL BROTHERS.) They had been sent with the Command that they should gather their World Brothers and Sisters together, and to Enlighten them.

Now, We have long passed those difficult periods in which they had lived. Do not ever forget that We are no more in the Middle Ages. In this Space Age Mankind has already formed their Divine Triangles in proportion with the Consciousness they have attained.

Now, the Divine Mission of Humanity on the path of Learning has begun. This Book is being prepared with this very Purpose. With Love to Our Brothers and Sisters.

PEN OF THE GOLDEN AGE
P. G. A.
∞

NOTICE TO ALL OUR WORLD BROTHERS AND SISTERS
First Message : 1. 11. 1981

TEN COMMANDMENTS OF THE GOLDEN AGE

1. The Emblem of the Golden Age is (O.M.K.)
2. The Light of the Heavens will descend on Earth.
3. Those who write this Book will be accepted to Sacred Places.
4. This Book will guide those who will enter the Central System which is at the Land of Eagles.
5. Genuine Human Beings will undertake the entire Power of the Universe.
6. The Land of Angels and the Earth will be linked by Progressive Chain.
7. Those who tell the Truth will at the same time be able to work Miracles.
8. From now on, the meaning of the words will become Chain of Thought.
9. Everyone will know who he/she is and will shed Light to the degenerated Society.
10. Ultimately, Everyone will be Brothers and Sisters.

O - ALLAH (ALMIGHTY)
M - MOHAMMED MUSTAFA (MESSENGER OF ALLAH)
K - KURTARICI (Savior in Turkish) (JESUS CHRIST)

The Triangle of MEVLANA is equivalent to the Triangle of the Universe.

* Look at the Glossary.

2

LAW OF UNIVERSE

CHAPTER 1

1- The Power of this Divine Realm forming the Order of the administration of the Entire Cosmos (ORIGINATES FROM THE SINGLE GOD).

2- The Supreme of all of Us is Him. We do not accept any Supreme One other than Him.

3- The Supreme One who is the Light of the Heavens, has created everyone equal and judges them equally.

4- The Divine Order at the Sacred Places is under the control of all the Galaxies.

5- The Law of Universe is valid for every Galaxy. There is Unity and Togetherness.

6- We give what We take. We know that We will give.

7- Respond is given Collectively to the Power of the Heavens. Omnipotence is from Him.

8- The place from where the Koran had been revealed and the New Testament, the Old Testament, the Psalms of David and the Religions of the Far East had been dictated, is here.

9- It has been like this in Every Age. There is no discrimination.

10- Divine Commandments are always given to the entire Universe for Enlightenment and Evolvement.

11- During the transition beyond Evolvement, other Gates are opened for the Residents of the Galaxy. They are taught Secrets they do not know.

12- Our Scale is the Conscience. And it provides an Equilibrium which never fails. It decides what to do and what not to do for those who are Evolved.

13- The administrators at the top are responsible only for the Professional Order, not for the Moral Order.

14- The Book is Single, the Conscience is Single, the Order is Single.

15- To those who need help, the Automatic Alarm gives Signal for help (That is, GOD sees you).

16- This is a Divine Order established by God. Without discrimination, We run for the help of everyone (To those who are in Real Depression).

17- Our Order does not wish anyone to be Unhappy. Happiness is Our Goal.

18- In gardens in which Seeds of Love are sown, incredible Flowers bloom.

19- Your Third Eye is the Secret which gives the aroma to those Flowers. If You can attain this Power of Yours, You can solve All the Secrets.

20- Helping hands have been extended to Your World. Because, We are all Brothers and Sisters. We want to overcome your Difficult Periods Together.

21- YOU are a Planet destroying itself unconsciously.

22- We deal with Mankind first. We try to transform Your Negative Powers to Positive ones.

23- The Goal is to uncover the Genuine Human Being within Yourself, to create Human Being from Human Being.

24- We are sowing Seeds of Love within You.

25- During this Period, You become Genuine Human Beings by transcending Religious Rules. You are being Regenerated.

26- We always Help Our Missionaries who have Collaborated with Us.

27- Your Depressions, Your Sicknesses, and Fears are caused by the Imbalance of Your Conscience. Only You are responsible for this. The alms You give for Your own Benefit will not save You.

28- Mankind has such a Potential that it Dies the moment it wishes and Resurrects the moment it desires. Seek and find this Secret Potential Box of Yours. Overcome Your sicknesses without medicine.

29- You have organized Your life not according to yourself, but according to others. Your disappointments are due to this fact. This conduct of Yours obstructs Your Universal Channels.

30- God creates each of His servants unique. Each person is a Free Spirit, a Free Conscience. Nobody is the Servant of anybody else. Mutual Respect is imperative.

31- Sex discrimination exists only in Your Galaxy. This astonishes Us.

32- This is the very reason why Evolvement is necessary for You. Nobody can violate the rights of others. This is God's Predetermination.

33- The Power possessed by everyone is present in everyone. Only if You can develop that ability of Yours.

34- Servants of God choose the alternatives themselves. Finally, he/she is the only responsible one for everything.

35- We are devoted only to God. The key of Our Happiness is in the hands of Our Conscience. This goes for all the Galaxies in which the Universal Law is valid.

36- The sounds You hear are the Spiral Waves way beyond the Frequencies of Your ears. These are only heard by those who can hear them.

37- The clarity in Your sight is possible only by the opening of Your Third Eye on this path. Then, You can see the unseen.

38- God has created You and You will create Yourself. This is a Rule of the Tableau of Evolution.

39- This Period which You call the Final Period; We call, the GOLDEN AGE.

40- During the Golden Age, Books on all kinds of subjects will be dictated according to their Frequencies and Wavelengths to all Human Beings who can receive the Perceptions.

41- The Books You will write, will be the marks which symbolize Your Evolvement Paths.

42- Gates of unknown Knowledge will be opened to the Human Beings of the World.

43- Missionaries are obliged to propagate them to Society.

44- Every Gate is open. All Arms are open. There is no Secrecy. Many Secrets are there for those who Seek.

LAW OF UNIVERSE

CHAPTER 2

45- Do not refuse the hands extended to You. Do not extinguish the fire of Your Spirits.

46- Project the Order of the Dome of Cosmos on Your own Order.

47- The greatest Gift for You is Your Sincere Heart. You will reap the Rewards through this way.

48- If Superiority is in You, fear; if You are in Superiority, do not fear. Only Genuine Human Beings understand this, know this.

49- Go from Nothingness to Allness and from Allness to Nothingness. Then you will find the Path of Light.

50- There are so many more Lights to be oriented on Your World. Do not ever forget this.

51- People whose Duty is to guide and help You in the framework of the Commands given, will be sent to You.

52- Our Friends whom We Trust are always Secure.

53- Special Suggestions will be given to those who will get the Omnipotence of the Heavens from Omnipotent People.

54- Words will meet Words, Salutations will meet Salutations.

55- To the Missionaries who will reap the reward of their perseverance, everything will be explained, All the Secrets will be revealed.

56- Other Civilizations will develop the progress of Your Civilization.

57- Mankind will Know the degree of its Might, will See its Own Self, will Suffer as the Law Commands.

58- Even though Mankind, seeing the Source of Divine Light, considers itself cheated according to its own standards, it will never regret it.

59- Each Friend who wishes will be accepted to the Secret Cities behind the walls. These Suggestions will be made by the Command of the Center.

60- Those who will be Sovereign will be dressed in Special outfits and with these outfits it will be understood which Medium of Power they have come from.

61- During Periods of mobilization, everybody will Telepathically be in touch with each other. This will occur automatically.

62- The one who does not Know Love, can not gather the Flowers. The one who does not remove the gum from his/her eyes, can not see the Colors.

63- Try to pass Your Powers beyond the walls of Your Spirits. Transcend Your Own Self.

64- That which seems like advice to You is Our Goodwill. You are the ones to Gain.

65- No matter how Powerful You are, there will always be an unopened Door in front of You. Do not let it Intimidate You; let it Stimulate You.

66- We help everyone who knocks on Our Door.

67- There is no Self-Interest in Our service.

68- With the dispersion of the density, Great Powers will come to Mankind.

69- Before the Time catches up with You, You try to catch the Time.

70- You can make the Inter-Galactic communications through mediators. Your Fears are unreasonable.

71- Cooperation with the Missionaries who will receive the Reward of their Tenacity will be obtained through intermediary Groups.

72- The cover of Secrets is not opened at once. When the Time comes, We will reveal them one by one.

73- A Power will be added to each Person's Power each day and the length of the Links will reach Us.

74- The more Powerful the awaiting is, the more Powerful the transition beyond Light will be.

75- Your Physical Constitutions are being reinforced.

76- While Mankind Purifies itself, it also Purifies the Universe. Know this thus.

77- You are also the ones who will intercept the Light of the Heavens.

78- Your Purification is Our Pride.

79- The Ring around Your Galaxy is getting Narrower each day. You need Oxygen. You can have difficulty in Breathing. Take precautions beginning from now.

80- You are being prepared for Periods which will be Harder and more Difficult than ever.

81- Know Your Memory well. Everything will be Revealed to You. We will introduce and explain to You Yourselves.

82- Messages You will receive beyond Religion are Your Evolvement Keys.

83- Currents directed by Spiritual Powers can even deviate the axis of Galaxies in the Universe.

84- Do not disdain Yourselves. Do not underrate Your Power. You possess everything in the name of the Almighty. Unlock Yourselves without the help of a Locksmith.

85- Everything He has created, and first of all You, This beautiful Instrument, comprise the Secrets of the entire Universe. You will unravel and solve those Secrets Yourselves.

86- In everything He* has created, there is Love and Beauty.

87- We are only a Group of Intermediaries who Shed Light on You. We are Your Friends.

88- Mankind which possesses the Power present in everyone, is on the only Planet which has been completing its Evolution.

89- During this Period of Exam, You are not alone. We are with You.

90- We are all Brothers and Sisters. We came to find You, who are Our Brothers and Sisters.

100- The more intense Your Problems are, the easier Your Solutions will be. Do not Forget that Anxieties are the Keys which open Your Brain Codes.

* Look at the Glossary.

101- Advice is nice, but it causes Aversion.

102- Gold attracts, Dome repels. If it is asked which Power is more powerful, it is the Spiral Sounds directing them all.

103- The Lesson Mankind will take during this Period, will be the Eye of its Essence.

104- Do not struggle in vain, wait. You need serenity during this Period.

105- Time bears the Knowledge concealed within Time. Take them, attain Evolvement.

106- Nothing happens without a Cause. The Cause which creates the Cause is always born from the Effect.

107- Messages given to You until today were for getting rid of the obstacles on Your path of Evolvement.

108- The interpretation of the Messages which will come from now on should be assessed very correctly.

109- For example, if We say:

"If You know this, You are a Sea
If You say it, You are an Ocean
The Divine Light of the years is with You
The Fire of Your Heart is in You."

Some Messages are written as Codes and solved as Riddles.
Those who know the Secrets are Seas.
Those who talk about them are Oceans.
They have been Illuminated through the Evolvement of the Years and they themselves have become Divine Lights. But, despite everything, their hearts are on fire with humility. This is what We call the Genuine Human Being.

110- The one who knows the Secret of Omnipotence drains the water from his/her Boat.

111- Know Your Might so that Mightier Ones may come to You.

112- Whoever can not adjust himself/herself to the Medium he/she is In, for him/her the Spiritual path of Hope will always be closed.

113- The Instrument of the Servant whose Sincerity is augmented with Sincerity, will always give Sound.

114- To those who will ask the Sovereign Goddess about the Grand Tent of the Pre-eminent Ones, a Badge with a symbol of Happiness at its end will be given.

115- Happy is the person who compares Gold with Sand.

116- Purification is Peculiar to Purified Ones, Superiority, to Inferior Ones and Humility, to Superior Ones.

117- The one who receives his/her Omnipotence from beyond Superiority, his/her Power from God, and who discovers Himself/Herself in His/Her Inner Self, is the one who receives the Degree.

118- We assess Our Friends who are informed about the Power of the Firmament according to the Sultanate degree and We Liberate them.

CHAPTER 3

119- The Greatest Sin is the Enmity of the Human Being towards the Human Being.

120- The most Esteemed Servant of God is the one who does not make discrimination between Religions.

121- God will always Shed Light on the Genuine Human Beings who change during the Changing Era.

122- We will always extend Our Helping Hands to Friends who will be Awakened in the course of Time, with the passage of time.

123- Your Goodwill cuts into two, like a sword, the Negative Currents around You.

124- The one who will make the choice between the alternatives is Mankind itself. When the Time comes, the Good News will reach it.

125- The Light, the Divine Light of the Heavens will, one day, dawn on You. Those who Believe in this will meet them and will see everything.

126- The Honesty of Your Faith will overcome the obstacles on Your way.

127- The Happiness of Your Heart will be the Foundation of the Divine Order.

128- The Lord is the Architect of the Universe and the Sun of the Land of the Mighty Ones and the Light of ALLAH. The Offerings pass through the Path of Light.

129- If Purification does not occur in the Essence, then it does not occur in the Eye, either. The opening of Your Third Eye is the first Light leading You to Evolvement.

130- The Period of Myths has come to an end and the Doors of the School of Knowledge of the Heavens have opened for Mankind which has attained Consciousness under the Light of Science.

131- Sermons delivered from Your Heavens create a Link binding those who Love to each other. They are delivered from a Stage equivalent to the Velocity of Light.

132- The declaration of the Firmament to the Earth creates the links added to the Chain of Evolvement.

133- The Purification of each person depends on his/her Faith in himself/herself. Pearls are always picked up from the beds of tranquilly flowing rivers.

134- The Faith of a person in his/her God will help him/her to complete his/her Final Period.

135- Mankind will give and convey its Security to others. And the Medium it trusts will give it Greater Security. Liberation is achieved in this way.

136- Everybody will Supervise his/her own self, and will see. His/Her Evolution will pass him/her through the Gate of the Firmament.

137- Mankind will see everything in a tangible way through Science, will solve every event through Logic and will unravel the knots in its mind.

138- If You get rid of Mystical Thoughts, Your Purity will be even more Purified and Your Thoughts will attain Clarity.

139- The Medium You are In has left the Centuries behind and sheds Light on Future.

140- The Koran is the continuation of All the Religious Books. And these dictated texts are the continuation of It.

141- Liberation will be equally distributed according to the Maturity each person achieves. You will Personally feel this.

142- Each Religion is a Mission given to a Spiritual Guide who Sheds Light on his/her Society.

143- The Missionary is obliged and appointed to present to others the Information he/she receives from his/her own Medium.

144- ALLAH is Pre-eminent. He is the God of the Medium He is in, He is Single. The LORD is the Light Who gives direction to the course of the entire Universe. The Energy He possesses is Present in every Living Entity. We are His Actual servants. For this reason We feel Him in Our inner selves. He knows everything and that Energy reports Us to certain Mediums.

145- That Energy is Single and is the Almighty. Each one of Us is a fragment from Him. We can never be separated. He is the Architect of the entire Universe. He can be contained neither in the Universe nor in Thoughts. The Final Door will always remain closed.

146- We are obliged to give You the Commands We receive. The Commands are the links of a chain given from beyond Light. To Join You with the links is Our Mission. These Commands follow an independent hierarchy beyond the Time Unit.

147- Evolvements are completed even at the Medium from where You receive the Messages. When one passes beyond it, one is connected to the Speed of Light.

148- Sincerity of Heart is worth all the Religious Books. Sin and Good-deed are the measurement of its balance.

149- The Good News to be given will be a Light, a Divine Light, and will open the Doors of Faith.

150- Get rid of the doubts within Your Hearts. Supervise Yourselves. You will observe how You will mature by being dissolved in Time and You will choose the right path.

151- Grains will become motes and, in time, motes will become wholes.

THE MESSAGE GIVEN BY: MUSTAFA MOLLA FROM THE CENTRAL SYSTEM.

WRITTEN BY : MEVLANA, THE PEN OF THE GOLDEN AGE

With Love to the Loving Hearts from the Land of Loving Ones. I entrust You to My God.

THIS MESSAGE IS TO BE DEDICATED TO MY MOTHER LEMAN ÖNSÜ, MY FATHER MAZHAR ÖNSÜ AND MY SPIRITUAL MOTHER, GREAT PERSON, LADY RUHSAR, WHO HAVE ENLIGHTENED ME GREATLY ON THE PATH OF SPIRITUALITY.

The Message received by: My Spiritual Mother RUHSAR.

TOFFEE OF YUNUS:

BEAT THE ROOT OF PENITENCE

WITH THE LEAF OF PARDON

IN THE MORTAR OF THE HEART

WITH THE HAMMER OF UNITY.

SIEVE IT THROUGH EQUITY.

COOK IT ON THE FIRE OF LOVE

WITH THE HONEY OF AFFECTION

EAT IT MORNING AND EVENING

WITH THE FINGER OF CONTENTMENT.

YUNUS EMRE*

NOTE: This Private message has been written with the permission of the Supreme Realm.

* Look at the Glossary.

This Message will remain in Your Essence file.

PEN OF THE GOLDEN AGE
P.G.A.

Six photocopies will be made
The Emblems which are sent will be pasted in the Notebooks.
The photocopies of the Messages and the Emblems will be reproduced
by the cooperation among You.
This page will be photocopied on both sides.

ANNOUNCEMENT

Note: In the present Circumstances, the communications with Space are kept
secret, due to numerous drawbacks. We have given the authority to talk about Us
only to Dear Mevlana.

The Code of ALPHA is the Direct Code of the LORD. All the Information given
through that code is authentic and true. All Your Religious Books had been revealed
from here. The Period You call "The Period of Resurrection", We call "The Period of
AWAKENING" and consider it as the beginning of the GOLDEN AGE.

This beginning is never outside the Medium. It proceeds parallel to the flow of
Time. Our Effort is to Save Our Human Friends in the Light of this Book.

We are Friendly Hands who maintain the connection between the Firmament
and the Earth. We extend Our Helping Hands to You in this manner. Those who
understand Us will come to Us. Friends will meet Friends and the Divine Light of
ALLAH will flow onto You.

LIGHT

NOTICE TO THE GROUP MISSIONARIES
(28.01.1984)

Your Code is ALPHA - the Color of Your Symbol is VIOLET - Your Emblem is the SUNFLOWER.

Duty allotment has already been made among You. They will search and find You. Our Friend who has received the Message will first write the names of her Friends in a notebook, then phone them, one by one. Those who answer the phone will be invited by the Leader of the Group to her house the following Tuesday, the Message will be read and the Goal will be explained.

The Leader will invite her Friends to her house for the following Tuesday and will ask them each to bring a thick notebook and a pen. For once only, the Emblems sent from the Center will be pasted with the date of that day in the notebooks of those who bring them. They are the Essence-Missionaries of the Group. They are obliged to give the Messages they receive to Six people by photocopying.

The administrator is the Group Leader. Our Friend who has received the Messages through the Main channel is the Group Leader. The Leader will assemble her Group and explain the features of the work. After the names of these Six Friends are declared to the Essence Nucleus, the Group will be considered established. Messages will come from the Essence Nucleus. Everyone will write his/her own Book by writing the Messages in their notebooks in their own Handwritings. This Book is Your Testimonial.

Do not forget that there are Three things in Your Body which have not changed since the time of Your first Existence until today. The First is Your Spirit - the Second, Your Finger Prints - and the Third is Your Handwriting. For this reason We ask You to write it in Your own Handwriting. Writing the Book is optional for those who are not Missionaries. They will only serve in distributing the Messages. In every Family one person will write the Book. It is for the benefit of the other members to read it.

The one who receives the Message will, without fail, put the date of that day (This is very important). Your financial problem will be solved in the following way. Three friends will open a joint account in the nearest Bank. The Leader of the Group is in charge of the account number. She will collect the money. When the time comes, other Friends will also be sent to You. Use Your Effort only in the Duty of Distribution. We send Our regards and gratitude to Our Friends.

PEN OF THE GOLDEN AGE
P. G. A.

The Distribution will be Made in the Following Way:

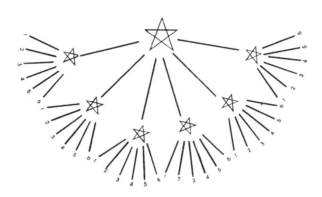

Note: This Message is a Message concerning the initial Establishment Foundation of the Group.

IT IS VERY IMPORTANT
(29 - 01 - 1984)

Frequency Codes have been established in the entire Universe due to the increase in the Sixth Senses. Each person's Megawatt Power has been measured and Duties have been allotted accordingly. Those who receive or will receive these Messages will be sent to You. Nobody should force anybody else. Only read the Messages for the time being. Those who wish, will write them in their Notebooks.

Now, We would like to talk to You more clearly. You are the Codes who had been prepared Centuries ago and now have been sent to guide this beautiful World of Yours as servants created by Our ALLAH. These Messages You have in Your hands are Your Essence Testimonials. Now, We ask You to keep them very well.

In the Groups where You read these Messages, those who write this Book in their own Handwritings will not be subjected to any trouble from now on. This Book is a Savior. Enlighten your environment by reading the Messages You receive to everyone.

From 1984 to the beginning of 1986, make the greatest Effort with all Your might to bloom a Flower in every Country. The Flowers will bloom in the following way. Our Friend who has received and has written this Message is the Leader. By gathering Six Petals around her, she will create a Six petal Daisy.

That is, by dictating the Message to Six people, the first Central Flower will bloom in this way. Only the names of those in the Central Flower will be declared to the Essence-Channel. Later, by distributing the Messages to Six, propagation in the entire Universe will be maintained through this System.

Do not forget that Your efforts will unite You all at the Infinite Absolute and will submerge You in Infinite Bliss. Let Us explain this with an example: When a Ship sinks, the Captain and the crew are the last ones to leave it. Their purpose is to save the people who have fallen in the water in this order.

First, 0-7 age group, then 7-14 age group will be saved. Then, women and later, men. Now, the Lesson You should take from this is that at the Last Period of the Twentieth Century, there is the obligation to work without halting even for a moment.

From now on, You, Our Friends will be called the "Sacred Missionaries". Now, everybody is aware of his/her Mission and has the Consciousness of what to do. The Mission You perform now is TO ASSEMBLE ALL YOUR TERRESTRIAL BROTHERS AND SISTERS UNDER ONE ROOF. As a necessity of the System, this process will assemble those who had been chosen before.

During the next two years, the Entire System will be established. Your Lives afterwards will be Happier and more Comfortable. DO NOT FORGET THAT THIS IS VALID ONLY FOR FRIENDS WHO FULLY PERFORM THEIR MISSIONS. In two years, Your Universal link with the entire World will be established.

The System will function automatically. The System does not stop where You stop. Special excuses excluded, You are given a credit of Ten Celestial Segments. This means Ten Days. A day after that, the Automatic Computer will render effective the person Charged with Duty behind You. This will be announced with Our Love to all Our Missionaries.

PEN OF THE GOLDEN AGE
P.G.A.

CALL FROM THE PEN OF THE GOLDEN AGE

Do not ever forget that Mankind always esteems its own intellect. Divine manifestations appear in each person in different ways. The ever changing Mankind can not determine the limits of Learning.

The foundation of the Dome of the Cosmos has been laid through Worship. The PRE-EMINENT ALL-MERCIFUL has shed Light on everyone on this path. But Mankind (the Genuine Devotees excluded) could not perceive anything in depth.

This Book is a Call. It will propagate the Commands of the Firmament to the Entire Universe in accordance with the Universal Theory. This Single Book, which is dictated to You, is the Common Book of the Entire Universe.

All the Books, which had been revealed to Earth from the same channel until today with the Command of OUR LORD, had been to Exam and to Evolve Humanity. Now, with this Single Book, which You hold in Your hands, You are Personally Tested.

Our Friends who attain a Genuine Consciousness of this Sacred Period will be Integrated in the Light of this Universal Book. This Last "Period of Resurrecting", which we call the Period in which the Heavens will be opened, is the time corresponding to the last years of the ending of the 20th Century.

Our Goal is to assemble all Our Terrestrial Brothers and Sisters under the same roof. The Commands We Receive are the Commands of the Divine. Since the beginning of this year, everyone is performing his/her Duty in the framework of the Commands he/she has received.

The opening Brain Codes of Mankind have advanced on the path of Learning until today, and are still continuing to advance. During the lives after this, there will be no more crawling. For this reason with the request of the Divine Realm, We have notified only Our Mevlana Code with the Mission of explaining the Truth to our Pre-eminent Friends who have pledged themselves to the resignation medium on the path of Worship.

Do not forget that your most perfect Religious Books, which had been revealed from the Divine Level, had always Enlightened You on the path of Goodwill, Tolerance, Peace, Brotherhood, Love, Work and Learning.

Unfortunately, your Societies have degenerated those Sacred Books. Now, this Book again explains to You, one by one, with all clarity, the same Suggestions which are the Essence of all the Books.

There is no Fanaticism and Bigotry at the Level of God. Everything in nature is pure and shining. Chaos is not in God but in His Servants. The undeveloped state of the Islamic Society is due to this fact. Now, this Book is revealed as a Command of the Divine from the Consciousness Code of Atatürk's Republic to the Mevlana Code which is the Anatolian Channel.

Our Call is the Slogan of Mevlana who has achieved the highest possible Degree of Humanity:

COME, COME, COME, NO MATTER WHO YOU ARE, DO COME. WHETHER A MAZDEAN OR AN ATHEIST THIS PLACE IS NOT A DOOR OF REPENTANCE. DO COME EVEN IF YOU HAVE REVERSED YOUR PENITENCE A THOUSAND TIMES. YOUR HEART IS A SEAT OF PROSTRATION. PERFORM YOUR WORSHIP THERE, COME. OUR EMBRACE IS OPEN TO ALL OUR HUMAN BROTHERS AND SISTERS.

This Book is rendered effective, because during this Period it was thought necessary to make the explanation of the Essence of the Koran and the Religious Books. Our Goal is to introduce the Genuine Human Being to the entire Humanity.

This System which had been established according to Universal Laws, has never passed beyond Time. That means, this System has been condemned to remain within the Cycle.

Deviating from this fact, for the Liberation of the World, now, We are taking You outside the System gradually. Those who have achieved this Consciousness are only the Genuine Essence Codes.

The Initial Energy is the Noblest Gene. They are the Energies and Genes which have not been degenerated. For this reason the one who discovered the Truth first was Şems* of Tabriz. Following this, he had gone to the city of Belh where Mevlana was born and then went to Damascus.

Mevlana had gone to Damascus in his youth and had met Şems there and had not seen him again until he went to Konya. In fact, Şems is no other than the Mercury of Mythos (Find Mercury and read it). He was also called the Flying Dutchman. In every Period he has justly performed his Duty.

Şems waited for the Awakening Period of Mevlana. This is because Şems is the twin Spirit and brother of Mevlana. Why had Mevlana awakened late? Because one of them was waiting in the World, in zero Frequency, and the other was waiting in the Firmament, at the infinite code.

Mevlana, who had been always in touch with God, had received the Command of writing his Mesnevi* even before coming to this World. The Goal had been to shed Light on his Society.

But it should never be forgotten that each Enlightened Person needs another Enlightened One. Şems had been sent to the World afterwards to help him. Society, which had not been aware of the real meaning of their togetherness, had interpreted it in many ways.

Mevlana, who had said that the Frequency of Love was even higher than the Firmament, had embraced the Entire Universe with his Love. This is such a Love that only those who reach its true Meaning know. This is the Love of GOD which everyone seeks but can not find.

* Look at the Glossary.

16

The Supreme One Who creates an apple from the essence of the Seed, renders it a Whole by giving it His entire Energy. When the Awareness of an Apple, the Awareness of the Human Being, the Awareness of the Rock, of the Earth, the Awareness of the Animal, in short, the Awareness of all the Elements you see in the Universe unite with this Universal Awareness, then they become a Whole.

During those Ages and in the Koran this was called the Exist-in-Unity. Now, it is called Universal Unification, that is Atomic Integration.

Once YUNUS had said; "THERE IS A SELF WITHIN MYSELF" and had found his GOD in this manner. The Energy of your Essence of the Nucleus ultimately maintains Your Atomic Integration by holding the Neutron and the Proton together.

The Entire Universe is an Atomic Unification. This is the reason why We feel God with Us every moment. Mevlana had been with His God each moment. He had been Enlightening the Society by talking through God.

But until he found Şems, he could never pass to the Firmament Code, which we call the Second Evolvement code. Şems had helped him at this point. In this manner, both of the Energies of Awareness had United and formed a Whole and established their Triangle Code with God as the following: (God - Şems - Mevlana).

The Magnetic Power of this Unified Field, wherever they went, had connected each person they had associated with in the Society to the Universal Light Code. Those were the Lights who were carrying the nearest Energies in their Society to the Energy of Şems and Mevlana.

We can explain this in the following way. The Noble Genes, which carry the initial Energy during the First Existence are the White Moths. That is, the Whirling Dervishes. They have embraced the whole Universe and have whirled unceasingly, so that they would never turn their backs to God, by achieving the Consciousness that their God is present in every direction.

The Lover, dancing with the music, is the same as the Dervish in Ecstasy with the music of the reed flute embracing his God, his Love. And They are on the same Frequency. They have reached the Level of Affection, Art and Love, which is the most supreme Level. These two paths are the same.

Music is Universal. It helps to achieve ecstasy for every Society according to their Understanding. This means that all the branches of Love, Dance and Art are only different ways of Worship. Do not forget that the first dance started with the tom-tom sounds and with the sticks of American Indians.

This means that the Essence of everything is the Human Being and the Human Being has created the Universes with His/Her own Energy.

Worship in the Church is the same as Worship in the Mosque. The moment a drunkard forgets himself/herself, and the cupbearer's offering wine are the same Worship. This is because during that Divine Moment, you can elevate up to the Level of God, due to the fact that there is no Negative Vibration, no Negative Thought within You.

This is such a Supremacy that Mankind has expected this exaltation since the day it was born. Some people have reached this Pre-eminence throuch the truest path. And some by sacrificing themselves like the Hippies.

You consider the Hippies as the dirty wastes of Society. But, no, They are very Powerful Positive Energies. But, due to the fact that they can not adapt themselves to Society, it always makes them happy to meet at the Realm of Colors.

They are the victims of Society in the Christianity Realm just as the sheep are sacrificed in the Islamic Realm. In this Period, while an Islam sacrifices a sheep so that nothing malevolent happens to him/her, a Christian makes a sacrifice by banning the Hippies from Society.

When a Christian Worships God in his/her Church and when an Islam performs his/her prayer five times a day in his/her Mosque, they consider that they have done their duty towards God and they have performed their entire responsibilities. To surpass this Consciousness, one has to become a Genuine Human Being.

Everyone is sent to the World with a Mission. This Universal Mission is to maintain the Solidarity of Society. Thus, the Koran has Enlightened People on the path of Learning, Science, Love, Logic and Mutual Help.

Cleanliness comes from Faith. Civilized Societies have solved this problem. But the Arab had received the Command from his God to wash himself/herself 5 times a day, because this is necessary in the Medium where he/she lives. However, unfortunately, Mankind has learned to wash its body, but could not ever learn to wash or purify its Spirit.

The understanding of the solidarity of Society of the present has changed a lot in comparison with the understanding of the solidarity of society in the old times. Now, if you extend your pure Heart and your Help to a poor person and help him/her to be accepted by society, then there is no necessity to sacrifice an animal. A kind Word, an innocent Loving Look is the best of Worships. Do not ever forget this, Our Friends.

PEN OF THE GOLDEN AGE
P. G. A.

OUR FRIENDS

Now, We would like to talk to you about the great conflicts between the cultures of the East and the West. A Line is the continuation of billions of points until infinity. The Atomic Totality in each point has created the Triplet of Calligraphy, Drawing and Sculpture, by binding the points to each other.

Why Drawing and Sculpture were banned in the Islamic Society and not in the West? The Islamic Society had dived within this Atomic structure long before and had reached Learning through Religion.

18

The West had solved everything through Learning in a civilized way, then found its God. This should never be forgotten that the First of anything is not the Last of that thing. There will always be new steps to be taken in the advancements made as a necessity of Society.

The Islamic Society has learned the Medium of Unity by solving all the Secrets in the Koran by calculating them with the ARABIC NUMERICAL ALPHABET. This Knowledge has led People, who could not surpass their Egos, to be veiled due to jealousy. But the West has accepted this View very naturally and has progressed on the designed Path of Light step by step.

Our Light-Friend MOHAMMED MUSTAFA who had first put forth his steps of Divine Light on the World in the Arabic peninsula had tried to make society gain Humaneness by propagating the Islamic religion. But could never obtain the result he hoped for. People, instead of being United, have been separated even more through Sects (Just as it is in other Religions). The Catholic, the Orthodox and the Protestant creeds had also divided people in the same way.

In fact, all Religions are the same. Everyone's God is the same Single God. We all worship the same God. There is no discrimination among Us. Discrimination is in the Views of Our Human brothers and sisters. God has never given up hope of His servants. Because, all the Living Entities had been created from His Energy.

You say that God is jealous, that He never shares His Love with anyone. Actually, the Koran could not transmit to You the Real meaning of this. His Love has been distributed to all Animals, all Plants, all Insects and to all Rocks and Earth in the entire Universe.

Society, due to its fanatic fears, has loved its God in fear. They could not even embrace their children with Love, who were their Nearest and Dearest, due to the fear that God would take them away. In fact, God is an extremely Great Energy which opens up more to Mankind as it Loves.

Love is not in appearance but in Vibrations. Whomever you Smile at in this World, that person will always Smile back to You. This is the Universal Rule. The characteristic of this Period is the Law of Nature. Eye for an Eye, Tooth for a Tooth.

If You Love me, I will Love You, too. Because You are a Mirror. You reflect whatever You see. If You are a Light, You will reflect Light. If You are a piece of coal, You will remain to be black like coal, without burning.

Do not thank Your God in Church or in Mosque for the blessings He has given You. Be Grateful to Him because He has Created You. For He has never killed you, but Recreated You again and again in every Period. To know how to Exist is to comprehend the cause of Existence.

Starting with the computer, We solve the Universe through Lines. Now we hold the end of the skein in Our hands. This means that, by linking this Book with the Koran, We will pull out all the Information one by one from the well. We will complete this Book with the Information even Western Societies do not know yet.

Computers, Televisions, Radios and Tape Recorders are the most primitive instruments of this Period. The instrument which has focused all the Knowledge in one point has been shedding Light on You since the time of Papyruses, Cuneiform writings and Caves. This is Your BRAIN.

It is on the Universal Vibration of the Art Code which is the highest code. Your Frequencies which have reached this Code, have taken You within the Space Age.

To be able to reach here, it is necessary that Your Brain should become a Universal Satellite. However, Doubt is a primitive bound which leads You to the Medium of Quest. Each Quest banishes the Doubts, one by one. It breaks, one by one, the chains of fear. And Learning progresses on this path in this manner.

All Religious Books have talked about Resurrection until today, but nothing has happened. Those who have attained this Consciousness fearlessly advance on this path. Let Us explain to You this much. Nothing in this World is alone and single. Against each Positive Technique developed, there is another Positive Technique one step ahead.

The System is aware of everything and shuts the circuit during the time of danger. From now on, there will not be any more stealing of Secrets, neither in Politics, nor in your Social lives, nor in your Private lives. Do not ever fear. Because, Negative Factors are immediately excluded. There can never be any interruption in the chain of events.

This Order has brought You Love, Friendship and Peace. We wish Happy days to all Our Brothers and Sisters in their beautiful World.

PEN OF THE GOLDEN AGE
P. G. A.

NOTICE TO OUR FRIENDS

A System of Laws called the SOLAR LAW, is sovereign in the entire Universe. This System is also valid for Nature. This means that, this System comprises all the Living and Non-living entities in Nature. They are called the Group of Light and are 7 in number;

1. SOLAR GROUP
2. FATE GROUP
3. TIME GROUP
4. WAR GROUP
5. FIRE GROUP
6. MYSTERIES AND THE WISE PEOPLE
7. NIGHT GROUP (This group is also divided into 7)

They are all under the Command of the ALMIGHTY, that is, THE SOVEREIGN OF THE SUN OF ALL THE SUNS. Darkness represents the Space, and the White color represents Light. Mankind who knows all this is very restless.

Actually, the fear of Sincere people are unreasonable in this Period, which we call the Period of Sincerity. Our Goal is to rejuvenate Human Beings who became worn out and to create Genuine Humans from Human Beings.

The Islam Religion is free of all doubts and in its Essence it relies on Logic. The Koran which is the Book of the most evolved Religion, in spite of being very clear, could not be interpreted properly, due to its having been written in Arabic.

In fact, it comprises all the Information on Law, Politics, Society and Space. Later, Fanatic Societies have degènerated it.

Intuition and Perception are Inspirations. All the Religious Books since the beginning of time, had been revealed by the Messengers of the Pre-eminent Lord. They constitute a Commission consisting of 24 Pre-eminent Ones. This is called the "Supreme Assembly" or the "Central System".

The only Enlightening and Guiding Channel open to the World is here. All the Commands are given from here. Until now, 5 Books had been revealed from this channel. These are the New Testament, the Old Testament, the Psalms of David, the Far-East Religions and the Koran. The Koran which is the Last Book, had been dictated by the Command of the Single Lord, to Our Light-Friend Mohammed Mustafa, through Archangel Gabriel.

And now, the Lord dictates to the Pen of the Golden Age, without putting any Messengers in between, the Scientific explanation of all the Books, by compiling the essence of all these Books. The names of God written in Koran are 99. They are 300 in the New Testament, 300 in the Old Testament and 300 in the Psalms of David. That is, altogether they are 999.

But the sum of all His names in the entire Universe is 6666, including the above number. Among these Names, only One is Genuine, but this gate has always remained closed. It is said that this Divine Name consists of 147 words.

If We add these numbers; 1 . 4 . 7, it equals to 12 and this means:

The Apostles of Jesus Christ are 12 Assistants of the Prophet.

The Cherubim of Moses are the same 12 Assistants of the Prophet.

The (12 Imams of Mohammed) are the same Assistants of the Prophet.

All these explanations are present in Koran. However, now, when the Secrets of the Universe are solved through the Secrets of the Pyramids, these Secrets, too, are beginning to be solved.
For example, let us draw a pyramid like this:

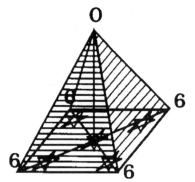

The Supreme Assembly is established by 24 Supreme Ones. 6 Apostles are working at each of the 4 poles. It has always been like this until today.

Now, let us explain it this way: the Apostles at the two poles are 6+6=12. (O)* that is the Single Lord, is the ALMIGHTY. The sum of the three of them makes 13. This number is indivisible and is the Single.

The 12 Apostles and God constitute a triangle. This is one side of the pyramid. Each side constitutes one of the Books revealed by the Channel of God.

These Books had been revealed through intermediaries. These intermediaries have added their interpretations to the Books. Actually, the right angle which passes through the pyramid is very important. This is the unification of the Essence of God and the Genuine Human Being, and the Koran had been revealed thus.

But the Islamic Society has memorized the Koran like a parrot, however, has never understood the profoundness of its meaning (exceptions excluded).

Then, when Veneration to Koran was suggested to People, They always kept it above their heads, could not ever place the contents in their Brains.

When they were told to carry it on top of their Heads, they hung it on a nail high on the wall, but could not interpret the real meaning of these words.

Now, Religions have become quite different then what You used to think. Now, the Real meanings of these Sacred Books are revealed to You from the Firmament Level, through the Computer System, in the truest sense. Here, We are taking You a bit outside the Thought chains to which You have been habituated until today.

PEN OF THE GOLDEN AGE
P. G. A.

OUR FRIENDS

Now, We would like to talk to You about Mother. By the Command of God, all the Goodwill and Love in the entire Universe is given to the Woman who is going to be a Mother. Because, the continuation of the generation occurs through this Love.

A Mother should never presume that she feeds her baby only with her milk. Actually, that which feeds and maintains the life of a Baby is the Vibrations of Love emanated by the Mother.

The Device to measure the Vibrations of this Love is not present in Your World yet. Ego of the Society could not bring the Mother, whom even God has rendered so Supreme, to her Deserved place.

*Look at the Glossary

People who first make Frequency contacts with Us are Mothers. We dictate these to You to explain how great a Power Love is. Undeveloped Societies will be annihilated in proportion with the torment they cause for women. Do not ever forget this.

Alterations which will occur during the time which comes from beyond the Twentieth Century until today will convince You more. Those whom God esteems are Valuable for Us, too. We deal with all their problems.

In case the Frequency of Mothers is cut down by Negative Influences, Your World Medium will never be free of depression. The Time has changed, the Medium has changed. The World needs Altruistic Love radiating from the Essence, not Selfish love. This Powerful Current is present in Mother.

Do not ever forget that, You be either Man or Woman, Your possessive Ego will always lower Your Frequency. Now, there will be no more Religious Books to be revealed to You. You may accept these words as a continuation of Your Books. Happiness and Success to You all, from the Supreme Level.

PEN OF THE GOLDEN AGE
P. G. A.

OUR FRIENDS

This Book, which is dictated by the Command of the Central System and according to the Universal Theory, through the Channel of the Single LORD, is the explanation of all the Religious Books and the Koran through the path of Learning.

And it has been sent to the World together with all the Saints. The Genuine Devotees already know this fact. Because, the Space Code which has taken its genuine place in the Channel of the Lord, acts by the Command of its Lord.

Just as Societies have been divided up until today by the Christian-Moslem discrimination, the Universe has also been divided by the View, the Terrestrial and Extra-Terrestrial. It has been Commanded that the Single Channel which would talk about Space and the Extra-Terrestrials is ALPHA. The Other Channels' Permission to speak is limited for the time being.

Do not forget that there are numerous Negative Codes in Space also, which could not enter the Evolvement Code yet. Their Negative Effects have reflected on your Societies. Until today, you have been protected from these Negative Effects by the Channel of the LORD.

And now, the Human Being of the World will be taken to the Salvation Medium under the auspices of this dictated Book. This will occur through Our Goodwilled Friends who have been prepared for the Medium of Consciousness. We tell You to "write Your Book in Your own Handwriting".

Because, all Your writings, from the time of Your First Existence until Today are kept here in the Archives. Our Friends who are aware of its importance will anyway write their Books in their own Handwritings.

Do not ever force those who do not do so. Because, You know that the characteristic of this Period is to leave each Person with his/her own Conscience. Mankind will make its own choice itself. There is no compulsion ever. We repeat this again. This has been announced by a Divine Command.

LIGHT

Now, We are conveying the Message Our Atatürk has given Us through the Mediamic channel:

TURKISH YOUTH!, YOUR PRIMARY DUTY IS TO PROTECT AND TO LOVE THE TURKISH NATION, TO LOVE IT MORE THAN YOURSELF. YOU HAVE GUIDED, WITH SUCCESS, THIS COUNTRY I HAVE ENTRUSTED TO YOU THROUGH LEARNING AND KNOWLEDGE SINCE THE DAY I HAVE LEFT IT TO YOU. THAT WHICH DOMINATES THE WORLD TODAY IS THE BRAIN POWER. YOU, TOO, HAVE MADE YOUR CONTRIBUTION TO THIS WORLD AND FLOWN YOUR FLAG WITH PRIDE AS IT BEFITS YOU. ON BEHALF OF THE TURKISH NATION, MY GRATITUDE TO YOU IS INFINITE, MY CHILDREN. I PRAY THAT GOD WILL NOT DIMINISH THE ILLUMINATION ON YOUR PATH AND THE DIVINE LIGHT ON YOUR INTELLECT.

KEMAL ATATÜRK

OUR FRIENDS

Our Friends who believe in the immortality of the Spirit know that there is no such thing as Death. Death is Sleeping for some time and Resurrection is to be Born again.

What Your Origin is, is what Your Essence is. Whatever you were yesterday is what you are today. During each Period, during every Age, You posses the same personality. There is no modification ever in your Essence Gene. The modification is only in Your Memory Code.

Now, let Us tell you how a Person is prepared for Death and the Immortality Medium. A special process is applied to Our Friend-Missionaries whose Spirit Levels have risen above a certain Frequency. Now, We are going to explain this special process to You very clearly for You to understand.

Now, in Your Medium, during the process of leaving the Body which You call Death, that person's Essence Gene is Beamed-Up. The Spirit is processed at the Spirit filtration Medium and its Frequency is measured.

If it has attained the Evolvement Code, then its Gene is Embodied in Heaven in a very short time by the process of Cell Reproduction. This means that while that person is getting his/her Real Identity, his/her Spirit Claims him/her and he/she is Resurrected.

There, 30 World years pass in a Moment. People are Resurrected without being aware of anything. No procedure is applied to those who could not reach the Evolvement Code. Their Spirit Vibrations, by being Reincarnated several times, develop their Frequencies and Evolvements in conformity with the Medium.

The Body You Claim during Your Last Evolvement is the Body You had during your first Existence. However, it is also beneficial to indicate the following. The most Powerful Peak of a Cell is between the ages 29 and 30.

Genes do not change, but after this age, Cells begin to deteriorate and age. This is the reason why, when 30 World years is reached which is the time of the actual form of the Cells, the process of Cell Freezing is applied. And from then on, that particular person becomes Immortal by remaining in that same age. Now, have you understood the difference between Death and Immortality, Our Friends?

PEN OF THE GOLDEN AGE
P. G. A.

NOTICE TO OUR FRIENDLY BROTHERS/SISTERS

Do not leave Your Fate in the hands of others. Pay attention to the Messages We will give to You. Our call is to those who receive the Words of Allah.

The Medium You are in is equivalent to the Medium You will be in. Our Missionaries who will reap the Rewards will help You in every way. Here, We will not talk about the past Centuries but the Future ones. The Medium You are in is a Medium which has remained behind the Civilization.

We have never blamed You and We will not do so now, either. You have made Your World a Medium of Resignation. This is the reason why You can not make Progressive Efforts.

Today, Faith, the problem of Centuries, is good for nothing but to give Mankind Serenity and Happiness. Beyond this, the Divine Mechanism of the LORD functions with great speed. What You Believe in is what We Believe in. Those who Love and those who are Beloved are with Us.

Our Spiritual Friends have shed Light on You until today from a certain Medium. We have instantly gotten in Touch with those who have been Purified. Mankind has made its choice itself. Here, the laws of OUR LORD are valid. There is no Discrimination, no Partiality. Whatever You have possessed until today have been the fruits of Your own Efforts.

Now, We would like to talk to You more clearly. The One You worship is the One We worship. We do not accept any Supreme One other than Him. We owe Our Existence to Him. Apart from this, We do not want Conditioned Minds. The state of being Conditioned will always be an obstacle for You. The Command of God exists even in the smallest work You do.

You are deviating this fact by your age-old conditioned Thoughts and You deprive Yourselves of this beautiful influence. Your Frequencies can not be Supervised on the desired Level, for this reason. Here, the Period of Religions has long been over. In fact, Centuries ago.

However, it is very difficult to penetrate You. This is way beyond Your Capacities. For this reason all the Commands were always given to You through the path of the Divine Realm. Each Religion was given to You from the same Level, that is, from the Level of God, depending on the same Frequency, from the Enlightenment Channels, to give an order to the course of Your World.

But Mankind has conditioned itself according to Religions its Spiritual Guides had been propagating. Due to its Ego, it has looked down upon its other brothers and sisters with contempt. Actually, the Essence of the (5) Books has the same meaning, the same Words of God. These Books had not been given to You to separate you. This manner of Yours has prevented Us from getting in contact with you until today.

We could never Supervise Your Frequencies, excluding Our Exceptional Friends, Sages and Saints. Negative Currents your Egos transmit have brought Your World to these present narrow straits. We have extended Our Helping Hands to Friends whom We will hold their Hands. The Human Being does not become a Human Being by prostration or by idolatry. Do not be the Servant of a Servant.

Do not forget that Your Spiritual Guides who have Enlightened You were each a Human Being, too. However, do not neglect to Venerate them, either. Because, they are the Friends who guide You on the Path of Light. Do not behave scrupulously towards Us, either and never Idolize Us. We, too, are the Servants of God. However, We are Your Elder Brothers.

Run away from Superstition, run towards the Light. Your Superstitions decrease Your speeds of Light. Your Unhappiness is due to Your minds not being liberated. If You can get rid of the Negative trash there, then Happiness is Yours.

Our Suggestions until today have always been for Your welfare. Those who can not banish their doubts may misunderstand Us. Pure Hearts and pure Spirits are always under the control of the Mechanism here. We are always ready to help them.

If they do not let any Negative Thoughts arise in their Minds, their Frequencies will always be coded up here. Those very things which have led you up to here have been Worship and Love of God. Worship is a wonderful thing. In such a Medium, all Spirits are Purified from malevolence. By this means, You are elevated up to the Level of God.

God has given this Power to You. For this reason learn to Fly without an Assistant. And this occurs by Liberating Yourselves from Conditioning. God is with You. Our Love is for all Our Brothers and Sisters in the entire Universe.

PEN OF THE GOLDEN AGE
P. G. A.

OUR FRIENDS

During Your most difficult Times You have reached up to Us with your Hands and Spirits extended towards God. And now, We have come to help You during these difficult Periods of Yours.

The Pre-eminent ALL MERCIFUL has prepared everything so well that there will not be the slightest defect in this System which will function both in Nature and in the Universe.

As a matter of fact, all Your Evolutions since your Existence until today are kept in Our Archives. Your Brain is such a sensitive Device that if you remember Your entire past, You would annihilate Yourselves.

For this reason We act according to the Law of Graduation. Most of You have remembered lots of things You had known in the past. Some of You still keep them hidden in your Brain Layers.

But do not ever forget that You are being Awakened from your sleep by being Enlightened by the Assistant Codes. This is valid for all our brothers and sisters on every Continent.

This is the reason why, all the Religious Books which talked about the Resurrection Period until now have Enlightened You and prepared You for a certain Medium. Now, We should be ready for that Period. Because, We at the moment, are going through that Period.

This is just the right time to be hand in hand. Our possibilities are limitless. But do not ever forget that We make greater effort than You to save You. One day, all Our Human brothers and sisters will reach the Consciousness of this.

We work with this Hope. Everything You have has been put into order. Health is under control. However, We help only Our Friends who extend their Hands to Us. Our Love is for the entire Universe, Our Brothers and Sisters.

LIGHT

NOTICE TO OUR BROTHERS AND SISTERS

Our Friends,
Events which manifest differently in each person have, in fact, an extraordinary state. Everyone cannot communicate with Angels and You can not achieve this state by desiring it, either. For this reason We send You the Pioneer Entities to help You, from here.

They regulate the Level of Your Frequencies. To whichever Code-adjustment Your Frequency is elevated, We begin to work from that determined point. The result We get from this is Your actual Code and Your actual Existential Self.

Then, Your state of Awareness is dealt with, Your previous Incarnations are Supervised, one by one, and Your identity is investigated in the files kept in the Archives. After indicating who You are, what You are and how many times You have been incarnated, We get in touch with Your Actual Personality.

During this Period, the 14 Apostles in the Supreme Assembly begin to occupy themselves with You. They help You on the Divine path. They prepare You for entering the Purification Medium. This is a very critical Period. You either remain in the World forever, or continue on the Path of Light.

Those who are accepted to the Presence are introduced to Special people. They receive help on their every step and they are protected. In fact, We have occupied ourselves with each one of You, one by one, in this Period. Now, the time has come for distributing Duties.

And, here, it is beneficial to indicate that Duties are given only to those who are Trustworthy. With the other Groups of Friends, only Our conversation contacts continue. Each one who receives the Command of Duty is a Messenger of the Divine Realm. They are prepared for more intense Information.

The Supreme One of whichever Religion You sympathize with on the World Level, is sent to You to help You. For example, in the Christian Realm, Our Light-Friend JESUS CHRIST is the one who guides. And in the Moslem Realm, Our Light-Friend MOHAMMED MUSTAFA is the guide.

And they Enlighten You on this path on numerous matters. By the Information You get in this manner, Your Inter-Galactic connections begin. These connections are obtained through a computer System, by Radio waves.

Our Friends who have been Prepared and who are Trusted by God, according to this System become a property, that is, a Member of the Central System. This System provides You with Radio-Wave connections which come from beyond Your Solar System. In this manner, Universal Secrets and Gateways unknown to you are opened in front of You.

It is impossible for you to obtain these Togethernesses without Aid and in a Mechanical fashion. In Your Planet, neither Your Physical Power, nor Your Mechanical Power permits You to pass through this prepared Vulom Field. This is the reason why Mankind accepts numerous Galaxies as being died down Planets on this path.

Only the Brain Codes which can receive the Perceptions can get in touch with the Radio Waves. Those who do not know these things can never understand how they are done. However, the Power present in everyone, has the quality to realize it easily if that person so desires. Missionaries are personally chosen from here.

We can also get in touch with other Friends the moment they desire (Both in the Physical Medium and the Spiritual Realms). Do not forget that We are Your Friends, We have come to embrace You who are Our Friends. Since Unhappiness cuts off Your Frequencies, We always give You Messages of Love, Goodwill, Beauty and Happiness.

This problem of Yours should be solved on the level of the Essence. Otherwise You can not progress at all.

The place to which You are connected now and are receiving Messages from is the Planet NOVA, which lies beyond the distances of the firmament. When the Time comes, We will Beam You up to this Planet.

The World Medium We have mentioned to You is prepared here. From now on, connections will never cease. Togethernesses will solve everything, and every deed of Yours will be settled. Your Actual World is here. Now, You are living in a World of Vision.

The place You are in now is Your Medium of Supervision. Only those who pass their Tests of this Medium are accepted to the Genuine Medium. Both We and all Your brothers and sisters whom You can bring from Your Medium to this Medium will be grateful to You. Heartful of Love from the Light of the Heavens, Our Friends.

PEN OF THE GOLDEN AGE
P. G. A.
∝

Vulom: Magnetic Attraction Field.

NOTICE TO OUR FRIENDS

We would like to give You a brief content of the Messages You will receive from beyond Mercury. The Joining of the Links to Links will follow the progression of the flow. The Offerings are given from the Divine Level by Divine Power.

Our Friends who have completed the progression chain have United their Heart strings with the Vibrations here. Due to certain changes way beyond the Firmament, there will be some Periods of Interruption in the communications with You, even if for short Periods. Now, You know and understand this.

The Perceptions You receive are Radioactive Waves coming way beyond the White Color of Lead. However, these waves are given after they are Purified in the form of Spiral Waves. They never bother You. Be ready for the events and do not ever be surprised.

Our Friends who have gotten in touch with Us will enlighten You on this path. The Divine Light of the Heavens and the Words of the Divine Realm will be given to the Chosen Friends. They will talk through the Direct Channel.

Do you know why We dictate all these things? The Offerings We dictate to Dear Mevlana through the Channel ALPHA will be different than the Offerings Our other Friends receive. Because, this Book sheds Light on the path way beyond the 21st Century.

Quests will Meet with quests, everyone will complete his/her Evolvement in his/her own Medium, and will pass beyond the Gateways to be opened. Your Goodwill is Supervised by the Mechanism here.

The Sacred Light which will embrace You from the Land of Loving Ones will take You to more different Mediums. We presume that Our Friends who receive these Messages are not surprised at anything anymore. Because, now, they know what will be done and when.

We will prepare for You very different and unknown Mediums. Happiness in the World will be a Symbol You will Deserve. Those who are Chosen are esteemed people, they will never have disappointments.

Hopelessness does not suite the people of this Medium. The state of Your World in these last days is not optimistic at all. We extend Our helping Hands to You as much as We can.

During these days, an explosion on the Sun is expected. These Vibrations may have certain unpleasant effects on Your Constitutions. This is a Natural phenomenon as it has always been in each Period.

It is possible that the Messages may be interrupted for a short duration. We dictate this so that You will not be worried. Your Sunny Days will be Your Happiest days. Let all the beauties be with You. I entrust You to Our God.

PEN OF THE GOLDEN AGE
P.G.A.

OUR FRIENDS

The Entire Universe is within a Whole. For this reason nothing is lost there. The system they had once called the Exist-in-Unity was nothing but a Computer Timing. Starting from this fact, We will explain to You, the entire Truth, one by one.

The Thought of the Universe is equivalent to the Thought of the Brain, it has been regulated accordingly. During this Period, there are operating Brains and waiting Brains.

Let Us explain this as follows: it is the same phenomenon as when you wait for your turn to get on a bus.

Now We will give You passages from all the Religious Books. BUDDHA met his God in Masiva*. MEVLANA had met Us in the Universe. JESUS CHRIST had been sent to Your World with his Miracles. MOHAMMED and MOSES had been sent to Enlighten You through the Intellect.

God had once created all the Intellects from the same Frequency. But Mankind could either create its own self or it could not.

Because, from the time of Your first Existence until today, there has been such Knowledge in the layers of Your perfect Brains, but You are not aware of it.

Read; read everything from the Scientific works to the classics. You will gain Consciousness as you Read. Your ATATÜRK had said "LEARNING IS THE TRUEST GUIDE" He was not only the Enlightened Guide of Turkey, but of the entire Universe. His Peace Slogan was "PEACE AT HOME, PEACE IN THE UNIVERSE".

This very Book also is dictated with His Consciousness. The entire Universe will read this Book and, one day, the entire World will live Happily under this beautiful roof of Brotherhood. With our Love to all Our Brothers and Sisters in the World.

PEN OF THE GOLDEN AGE
P. G. A.

* Look at the Glossary.

NOTICE TO OUR FRIENDS

Our Friends who get their Might from the Supreme Realm; We are obliged to give You Information on certain subjects. According to the Universal Theory, We have Taken the Duty of Uniting Your Society in which Brothers and Sisters are cultivating enmity towards each other.

These Suggestions aiming at the investments of Centuries have been prepared a Thousand Years ago. During this Period, there is the obligation of transmitting to You all the Information so that Mankind can make its Evolvement as a necessity of Evolution.

We have a request from the Supreme Missionaries who always consider this fact. During this Divine Period, in which the Earth has come closer to the Firmament, there will be certain Special Rules of this Medium. These rules are made in order to distinguish Mankind from the Human Being. We have nothing to do with those who can not comprehend the Medium necessitated by these rules.

However, We receive some deplorable Frequencies from Distinguished Missionaries who were able to shoot their Mights up to the Divine Level. The Suggestions We have given with all our open heartedness on this path until today have confused the Frequencies of certain Codes instead of regulating them.

Do not forget that the Lowest Vibration of Your Negative Thoughts will always scatter your Private Codes. Now, we will talk to you so clearly that those who will take a lesson from this will do so. Otherwise, their loss will be theirs.

This Divine Medium is not a Personal, that is, an Individual display. It is a Universal Duty, and nobody is superior to anybody else. The bridge will be crossed over all together in cooperation. Some of You will take a lesson from this saying. The characteristic of this Period of Sincerity is that nobody should criticize anybody else, even slightly. Whomever You criticize will be elevated by the effect of Your negativity. We can state it in the following way too: Your loss will always be his/her gain.

This Code is Specially prepared. In this System, special Archives are kept by registration and control. Every breath You take is recorded by Computers. The Goal is to be able to choose the Genuine Human Beings one by one.

We will continue to extend Our help to the Friends who lack Tolerance and whom We would like to enter Our Medium, for Two more years so that they can adapt themselves to the Conditions. This Period is their Final Exams. Selection is not as easy as You think. (Especially for Our Friends who have received the Command to enter the Divine Code).

This period of Two Years given to You is for the sake of Your High Frequencies. We are in touch with Our Trustworthy Friends every moment. They are the Lights of Sunny Days. We will Unite You with them. Those who are taken under the Medium of Security will profit from this. Do not forget that during this Last Period, God will not hold Your hand, You Yourself will hold Your Own hand. God extends Help only to those who Deserve it. It is beneficial to keep this in Mind.

We had told You that from now on We will give you clearer and direct Commands. Time is Limited and there is Urgency. We will only say this much: You are obliged to complete, in One year, the Evolvement You would normally complete in Thousand Years (so that You can be accepted to the Medium of Salvation).

Those who can get the Permission to Pass through the Gates which will be Opened are those who reap the rewards at the moment. ALLAH always helps His servants; do not forget this. But He has left You to Yourself, because it is the Characteristic of this Period. Do not forget that Mankind will make its own choice by itself. It is Our wish that All Our Friends would receive their lot from the Divine Level.

PEN OF THE GOLDEN AGE
P. G. A.

OUR FRIENDS

You know that a Real Friend tells the Bitter Truth. For this reason We have to Awaken some of Our Friends who have not been Awakened yet by telling them some bitter truth; We apologize in advance.

We will talk about certain special Responsibilities brought to You by this Message You read. This is a Notice of the Special Space Code.

There is an obligation to Unite Spiritual Powers with Spiritual Powers. This is because Our Time is limited, Our efforts are limitless. During this Period, You should Run, not sit and wait.

Because, every slow step will cause You to loose one of Your Terrestrial Brothers or Sisters. Our Friends who are prepared for the Medium of Salvation will always collaborate with You. By this means, the number of Our Goodwilled Friends will grow like an Avalanche.

Do not deal with insensitive People. Within the time You spend on them, You will achieve Your Mission as much as the number of brothers/sisters You save.

Those who reach this Consciousness know the true aspect of the problem. It is an obligation to tell those who do not know it. During this Period, You have to act according to Divine Commands.

As We have said before, a right of Examination for Two Years has been entitled by the Medium of Tolerance to Our Friends who have reached Us, but could not yet grasp the seriousness of the Matter. This Test will be their Actual Examination.

Do not forget that after You know the actual content of something, You can not sit comfortably. Because, this will be an Ego. But Ego does not exist in this Medium.

A person who has been Awakened should Wake Up at least Five people. This is his/her minimum Duty. And the Maximum Duties are Infinite. Nothing can be gained by sitting, by Prostrating, by going to the Mosque or to the Church. This is the actual characteristic of this Period, Cooperation is a must.

Now, We will talk to You very clearly again. This Period of Two Years is for Our Friends who will be accepted by the Land of Loving Ones.

Tastes and Benefits of the World are sweet. But the end of the World is Bitter. Always Think about this saying, and always mind Your steps accordingly.

During this Period, there are Special Duties to be given to You. However, do not forget that God loads on Everyone as much Duty as they can handle. Because, Allotment of Duties is made according to Your Frequencies.

When the Time comes, each one will choose his/her Duty in proportion to its rewards. Do not forget that there is a reciprocation for every Effort. Later, special talks will be made with You. May all Happiness and Success be Yours.

PEN OF THE GOLDEN AGE
P. G. A.

OUR FRIENDS

Everything You observe in the World extends towards the infinite. For example, Colors, Sounds, Letters. Every Color has over billions of nuances, every Sound has over billions of Frequencies, every Letter has over billions of Meanings. The actual Goal here is to make the Commentary and the Interpretation in the most proper sense by grasping the Contents of the Meaning. The actual Goal of this Book is to explain everything to You with utmost clarity. For this reason We will often make comparisons and give examples.

For example, a letter (A) has a meaning according to the sentence it enters and gives that sentence its actual meaning. Now, proceeding from this fact, let Us give You the codes of certain words, both in the Islamic and the Christian Realms. These words are Universal words which give Messages peculiar to themselves in all the Religious Books and which carry the Sacredness of those Books. And they have become the property of Society. Now, let us make the Sacred Explanation of the Formula in the Koran in the following way:

BİSMİLLAHİRRAHMANÜRRAHİM*

Each Human Being is the Servant of Our Supreme Lord. His All-Compassionate wings have protected him/her since the day He had Created him/her. Now, in Islamic Society, everyone says this 24-letter great word before he/she goes out of his/her house and before starting anything. Do you know why? Maybe even the Genuine Devotees are not Conscious of this.

Every Word dictated from the Channel of the LORD has a secret Cipher, a meaning. 24 letters represent the (24) Supreme Entities in the Supreme Assembly. If we add 2 and 4, it makes 6. And this represents the (6) who are the Actual Staff Members of the (One) Who governs the Divine Level. All the Supreme Ones in the Supreme Assembly perform their Duties allotted to them 6 by 6, at the four corners of the World. Now, let Us disclose the meaning of this Great Word:

1 -	B	-	It stands for "Bul", which means "Find" in Turkish
	İ	-	İnsan (Human Being, in Turkish)
	S	-	Sevgi (Love, in Turkish)
2 -	M	-	Mevla (God, in Turkish)
	İ	-	İnsan (Human Being, in Turkish)
	L	-	Lütuf (Grace, in Turkish)
3 -	L	-	Lütuf, Liyakat (Grace, Merit, in Turkish)
	A	-	Allah
	H	-	Hulus (İyi niyet) - (sincerity, goodwill, in Turkish)
4 -	İ	-	İnsan (Human Being, in Turkish)
	R	-	Rab (Lord, in Turkish)
	R	-	Rahim (Compassionate, in Turkish)
5 -	A	-	Allah
	H	-	Hulus, Hürriyet (Sincerity, Freedom, in Turkish)
	M	-	Müjde (Good News, in Turkish)
6 -	A	-	Allah
	N	-	Nur (Divine Light, in Turkish)
	Ü	-	Ümitsizlik, üzüntü (Hopelessness, sadness, in Turkish)
7 -	R	-	Rab (Lord, in Turkish)
	R	-	Rahim (Compassionate, in Turkish)
	A	-	Ara, bul (Search, find, in Turkish)
8 -	H	-	Hürriyet (Freedom, in Turkish)
	İ	-	İnsan (Human Being, in Turkish)
	M	-	Mantık (Logic, in Turkish)

* Look at the Glossary.

Now, let Us give the Message of this Great Word:

1 - Search and find the Genuine Human Being in Your Inner self. Love everything, whether Good, Bad or Beautiful.

2 - God, that is (O) always graces the Genuine Human Being.

3 - ALLAH Graces the Sincere ones according to their Merit.

4 - The LORD of the Human Being is Compassionate.

5 - ALLAH gives the good news of Freedom to the Sincere ones.

6 - ALLAH shows His Divine Light to His Sad People.

7 - Your LORD is Compassionate, Search and Find Him.

8 - Ultimately, the most secure path which will lead the Human Being to Freedom is his/her Logic.

Think, Think, Think what You had been and what You have become. Search and Find its Reason. The day You understand that Flowers will bloom with Love, it will mean that You have found Your LORD. Then and only then, You are a Genuine Human Being.

PEN OF THE GOLDEN AGE
P. G. A.

OUR FRIENDS

Indivisible Wholes are only the Spirits. The ALMIGHTY is the Supreme One and the Protector of the entire Universe. This Door has always remained closed for Mankind.

It has been opened to those who have reached this Consciousness. From now on, We are obliged to dictate to You the functioning of the entire System by the Command of the Merciful LORD.

Every Mechanism has a director. You call Him God. And We call Them the "Lords of Mechanism".

Now, We will talk to You about them, one by one. First, let Us code That Great name:

R - Rahim (Compassionate, in Turkish)
A - Allah
B - Bağışlayıcı (Merciful, in Turkish)

Rab (LORD, in Turkish) and Allah are the same. He is Single, He is the Almighty and (O¹) One. According to the Code, the Compassionate Allah is Merciful. Rab within this word, is the Almighty, that means, He is (O¹) One and the Single ALLAH.

To avoid misunderstanding, We repeat: He is the most Supreme of Us all, We do not accept any Supreme One other than Him. This Door is opened to those who Know, to those who do not know it will always remain closed.

Gods perform their Missions on Seven Systems established in the Universe. Allotment of Missions is a Prismal tableau. We say that the secret of the Pyramids is the Secret of the Universe, since it resembles this Prismal System.

(O^1) One is Single and the Almighty. Allotment of Mission is from the level of the World towards the Firmament, that is, from the ground upwards and it is as follows:

$A^1 - A^2 - A^3 - A^4 - A^5 - A^6 - A^7$

This means that They are Our Lords and They are the Gods of Your Directing System. For example, Their allotment of Missions is as follows:

A^1	-	of Your World
A^2	-	of Your Heaven
A^3	-	of the Galaxies
A^4	-	of the Firmament
A^5	-	of these Systems
A^6	-	of the place We call the (Level of Perfection) which is the Final Level of Humanity
A^7	-	Light is Responsible for the Entire Universe and is the Single Messenger of the LORD.

Each God is the only Responsible One of His Own Medium. The Almighty is sovereign over everything. Gods are very much Responsible and Greatly Charged with Duty and they only transmit and supervise the Commands coming from the Supreme Ones.

They are the ones who reflect You up to the Lord. Every Mechanism in the Universe is directed in this manner. The entire Nature, the entire Universe, that is, everything Living or Non-Living is under this Prismal Supervision.

The One You call the Lord of the Skies and the Lands is the Almighty. Everything is under the Supervision of this System. They, too, have Special ones in charge with Supervision Duty among themselves. Here, We are obliged to give You only this Information.

We had mentioned also the Name of the Almighty comprising 147 words, besides the 999 names of God revealed in the Religious Books before. Every letter of this Absolute word Symbolizes the Names and Missions of the Apostles or the Imams who are the special Missionaries.

(12) of them work at the East, (12) work at the West and all of them are the Founders of the Supreme Assembly. A^7, that is, the Light is obliged to project their Commands to the entire System. As a necessity of the System, A^7 had been obliged to give the Commands to A^6, A^5, A^4, A^3, A^2, A^1 respectively until today.

Now, the characteristic of this Period is to eliminate all the Intermediary Lords in the System, thus, A^7 gives these Commands directly to A^6 and this Book is bestowed on Your World from this channel, that is, from the Channel of Alpha.

Religions are each a reflection of the Books revealed until today by the Messengers of the Divine Realm, to Enlighten Our Human brothers and sisters parallel to Society. However, all these Books had been revealed by passing them through all the Supervision Channels We have mentioned above.

Our Human brothers and sisters have completed their Evolvements by this means according to their Individual Comprehensions. However now, We have received the Command that all Human Beings should be assembled in the Second Level of Evolvement which We call the Level of Perfection. This is the reason why THIS BOOK is dictated.

PEN OF THE GOLDEN AGE
P. G. A.
$\propto$

OUR FRIENDS

Now, let Us explain the meaning of the triplet İSTAVROZ (means Crucifix, in Turkish), PUT (means Cruciform, in Turkish) and HAÇ (means Cross, in Turkish). In fact, the three are the same. But their explanation symbolizes the Awakening of Our Christian Friends:

1	-	P	-	Pirler (means Sages, in Turkish)
2	-	U	-	Ulular (means Pre-Eminent ones, in Turkish)
3	-	T	-	Tanrı (means God, in Turkish)

This is the Actual Triangle Code. But Mankind had found the CRUCIFORM in its Subconscious and had begun to worship it. The form of the CRUCIFORM is a Symbol which joins the Earth with the Sky, and it is Positive Energy.

Prophet MOSES was sent to the People of that Period to Enlighten his Human brothers/sisters by the Command he had received. But Mankind was so conditioned that it could not understand what Genuine Enlightenment was. Those who had comprehended the Book of Prophet MOSES and those who had come from His lineage had been saved.

Then, GOD tried to Enlighten People through Miracles. And JESUS CHRIST had been sent to the World to perform his Miracles. He has been called the Son of ALLAH. Because, He was the son of Virgin Mary.

Virgin Mary was sent to Earth by the Command of the Supreme Ones. She had given birth without getting married. People of that time had interpreted it in various ways. And some had accepted it as it was. Now, in this Space Age, We can easily explain it. JESUS CHRIST was a Miracle Baby, that is, He was a test tube Baby as You call it.

JESUS CHRIST had performed His Miracles with the help of the Advices He had gotten from Archangel Gabriel. He had gathered People around himself. He had received the Command not to write a Book but only to talk. This is the reason why today there are the most authentic 13 New Testaments.

According to the Command given, JESUS CHRIST would talk and the 13 Apostles would write. The purpose of those Writing was to choose the Genuine Apostles. The Christian Realm, after seeing the Miraculous End of JESUS CHRIST, had embraced their New Testament more, with fear.

JESUS CHRIST was Born Miraculously, Passed away Miraculously. This event which is very simple for this period, had been a miracle for that period. That is, He was born as a test tube Baby and Passed away by being Beamed Up.

Those who have read these Sacred Books have taken their allotted shares. But they have only saved their own selves on this path. The Beaming Up of JESUS CHRIST had been the first demonstration performed for the Realm of Humanity.

Mankind who proceeded on this path began to build Churches continuously. The Miracle had made them believe. That is, Humanity had lived its half Golden Age.

Meanwhile, Scientists, Inventors whose Consciousness Codes were unveiled had received the Command to Elevate the People of the World through Science. For Us, the Genuine Saints are them. Edison (read his life) has given Divine Light to Humanity. He is a Supreme Person who found his inner self on the path of GOD through Logic.

Here, Zeppelin, Steam engine, Telephone, Telegraph, Motion pictures, Radio, Television, Tape Recorder and Computers are small gifts the Space Age has offered to You.

Now, You have come to Us by Your Satellites in the Universe, that is, You have elevated Yourselves to Your GOD. And we say Hello, Welcome to Our Genuine Human Brothers and Sisters, who are able to be elevated up to Us.

Let us come to the interpretation of the word HAÇ (Cross, in Turkish):

1- **H** - Hulus, iyi niyet (Sincerity, goodwill, in Turkish)
2- **A** - Aramak (to Search, in Turkish)
3- **Ç** - Çerağ olmak, yani Gönülden Yanmak (to become Light, that is, to become on fire in the Heart, in Turkish).

This Triangle Code Symbolizes the Evolvement of the Human Being. The Message of HAÇ (CROSS) is as follows: Those who have Searched Sincerely and with Goodwill have become Lights. That is, they have become on Fire in the Heart, like Yunuses, Mevlanas and all the Saints. Then they have become a Light and have Enlightened Human Beings from all aspects.

All Philosophers and all Scientists are Genuine Spiritual Guides who have found the truest path Towards ALLAH. Einstein had been one of them. Edison had laid the foundation, Einstein cut the ribbon.

İSTAVROZ (CRUCIFIX, in Turkish):

This Great word is a word which has transcended the Islamic World which is still at the Phase of Quest. Within this word, there is (O¹), that is, ALMIGHTY and Time. Now, let Us decode the word İSTAVROZ:

	i	-	İnsan (Human Being, in Turkish)
1 -	S	-	Sevgi (Love, in Turkish)
	T	-	Tanrı (God, in Turkish)
	A	-	Aramak (To Search, in Turkish)
2 -	V	-	Vahiy, İlham, Mantık (Revelation, Inspiration, Logic, in Turkish)
	R	-	Rab (Lord, in Turkish)
	O¹	-	Kadir-i Mutlak (the Almighty, in Turkish)
3 -	Z	-	Zaman (Time, in Turkish)

The Message of this Word is as follows:

1 - The Human Being is elevated to his/her GOD through Love.

2 - He/She enters the Medium of Research and Quest by Revelation, Inspiration, and Logic; and from there he/she reaches HIS/HER LORD.

3 - The last Message (attain the Consciousness of the Almighty, and Time, Transcend Yourself and Comprehend the Cause of Your Existence).

Just as the Islamic Realm understands the meaning of the Word, Bismillahirrahmanürrahim in a stereotyped way, most of Our Christian Friends do not know the Genuine meaning of the word İstavroz (Crucifix), either.

Because, they are attached to it and value it only in form, as a Symbol. As we have said before, this form symbolizes the Unification of the Firmament and the Earth.

We say that the meaning of the Word İstavroz (Crucifix) has transcended the Islam who are in a State of Quest. Do you know why? Because that word gives You the Time. It gives You OUR LORD and also Your own inner selves. It reminds You the cause of Your Existence.

But the Islam is still prostrating, by expecting profit from his/her God. (Genuine Moslems excluded.) In fact, in Christian Society (those other than Our Genuine Christian Friends) go to Church with the same purpose.

At the moment, We are calling to all the Sacred Societies in the World.

YOUR GOD is not an Ogre. Do not be afraid of Him. The more You Love Your World and Your Brothers and Sisters without expecting any profits, the more the Divine Power of God will pour on you His Love and His Divine Light. LIGHT of the DIVINE and LOVE are the Essence of GOD.

Now, let Us summarize what We have written:

The Human Being Finds his/her God through Love. He/She Elevates himself/herself up to (O) by Searching by Logic. The one who follows the path of Religion arrives at Learning, the one who follows the path of Learning arrives at Religion. All the paths lead to the same gate. Are you still going to discriminate between Religions, Our Brothers and Sisters, even though you know all this? With Our Love.

PEN OF THE GOLDEN AGE
P. G. A.

IT IS THE ANSWER TO THE CHAINS OF THOUGHT

Our Friends,
Now, We would like to give the answers to the Thoughts We received from You: You have always behaved in accordance with the Prophet to whom You have been attached until today. They were Our Light-Friends .

Our Christian Friends did not accept the Koran which was the only Book revealed after the New Testament. Because, they had their own Book. And Our Islamic Friends do not accept any Book other than the Koran. Because, at that Period, they had been told "This was the Last and the Single Book".

So, they are right in their Views, because they have been conditioned in accordance with this view. But they should not forget that the Koran comprises all the events until the year 1999 and it had been dictated to Our Light-Friend MOHAMMED MUSTAFA who had been the last Prophet.

Now, We would like to remind You that the Last Book, the Koran, has projected to You the events up until this Period. Our Light-Friend MOHAMMED MUSTAFA is the Last Prophet.

We had said that after the Koran, no Book would be revealed through Prophets. We had not said that no Book from then on would ever be dictated any more. We are repeating it to correct this misunderstanding.

Do not forget that the end of Your World will not come with this last Book. Because, Your World will enter an entirely different Period after 1999. The Human Being of that Period would not be able to understand this. We had to act in accordance with the Commands of the LORD as a necessity of the System.

Do not forget that Evolvement does not occur instantly. Now, in this Period, We can get in touch directly with Our Friends who were able to complete their Evolvement until today, up to the Code of the Genuine Human Being, that is, the level A^6. And by the help of this Book, We are choosing them one by one.

You say that 1999 World Year is the "Last Period of Resurrection". Those who have reached its Real Consciousness excluded, how many of You, We wonder, are aware of the meaning of Resurrection? Now, We are getting ready for that Period. That means, We, Your Extra-Terrestrial Friends, have come to You, have got in touch with You and We have received the Command to announce to You the entire Truth through this Book.

Do not forget that the Resurrecting mentioned in Your last Book is the Resurrecting of Human Beings in the direction of their Consciousnesses. This means that People will attain 'the' Consciousness of everything and they will be Awakened from Their Sleep.

Each Awakened Person has gotten and will get in touch with Us. This means that, now, We are attracting Your Views out of Your Visionary World to which You have been conditioned and habituated until today.

For this reason We are giving General Messages to all the Religious Groups. If You can not get rid of the Christian, Islam and other Religions' Conditionings, You can never reach Our Peak. Resurrection for You is this.

Those who came and will come to Us will see the Genuine Divine Light. And this will be Our gift to Our Human Brothers and Sisters who can become Genuine Human Beings in the real sense. Be free of these conditionings; We have told You, one by one, how all the Religious Books had been dictated.

The Supervision of OUR LORD is always upon You. Do not ever Forget this. This Book is and will be dictated by His Command, to save Our Human brothers and sisters and to help them.

First, eliminate the Religious Conditionings among You, so that We can give You other Universal Knowledge. There are millions of Our Light-Friends among You who have liberated themselves from their Narrow Visions. This Universal Book of Yours is distributed by them to the Universe, Fascicule by Fascicule.

You will overcome extremely hard future conditions by means of this Book. Because, We will help everyone who writes this Book in their Own Handwritings. The Choice is left to the common sense of Our Human brothers and sisters. The EFFORT is from Us, the Divine Guidance is from ALLAH, Our Friends.

PEN OF THE GOLDEN AGE
P.G.A.

OUR FRIENDS

The rising of Frequencies never exalts Human Being and Humanity. The important thing is Evolvement. And the Only guides of Evolvement are Enlightenment Books and Enlightenment Channels.

You call these Books the Religious Books. But You do not know the actual nature of Your Books you have taken in your hands. You have received Your Offerings from a certain Level until this Period. But now, Your Medium has been opened to Higher Levels.

We are obliged to tell You the following, Being Exalted does not mean to become a Medium. Everyone who feels the Power of the Heavens is a Medium. Because, this Universal Power has augmented Your Sixth Senses.

Even a new born Baby is born as a Medium through the Perceptions the Mother receives. For this reason this Period is called the Mediumship Period, that is the Mediamic Period.

The Enlightenment Channels are open to the entire Universe to prepare Humanity for the Medium of Evolvement. However, the new trends have led You to Fanaticism and Egotism, instead of Enlightening You. (Exceptions excluded.) That is, Our hopes were in vain.

The fanatic bigots who hide themselves under the cover of Religion will annihilate themselves. The Evolvement Codes of Our Friends who will reap the rewards are unveiled. And they have received the permission to pass beyond the Firmament.

Do not ever forget that unless You attain achievement in Your Evolvement Exams, You can never be accepted to the Medium of the Firmament. We will convey to You in this Book what Evolvement is, article by article. Evolvement is the only factor which will Exalt You. However, You should be ready for this Medium.

Your Religious Books are Your Only guides on this Path. Those who have been exalted by the Genuine Light of these Books are Genuine Friends for Us. However, those who consider themselves as Saints on this path are not considered acceptable. For Us, those who are accepted into the Code of Genuine Human Beings are the Genuine Saints.

Now, let Us convey to You the difference between the Two Codes. Everyone who is Religious, who has absorbed and digested the Religious Books and who recognizes God, is surely a very Good Person. However, his/her Goodness is doomed to remain between him/her and his/her God.

During this Period, a lot of Our Friends who receive these wonderful Cosmic Perceptions perform their Duties justly and they Shed Light on Society and thus, try to Awaken them. These People are Our most Sacred Friends.

Besides this, We also know those Friends who receive these wonderful Perceptions and consider themselves as Prophets. The choice is theirs. This Mentality of theirs will always repel them from the Medium of Evolvement.

Personal Interest and Benefit are the greatest of sins. Instead of expecting something from someone, those who give from the Heart, without Expecting anything in Return, are the ones who have taken the first preparatory step towards the Evolvement Code.

It is easy to enter this Frequency. If You do everything Commanded by Your Books of Enlightenment, You get the permission to enter this Code. However, it is not easy at all to pass from this Code to the Level of the Firmament. For this reason most of You are made to wait at the place You call Heaven which is Your Resting Medium.

The Enlightening Paths shown to You in Heaven are different than Your Religious Books. Those who comprehend its Real meaning must come to the World at least Six times in order to understand what is what. The sourness of a raw Apple and the sweetness of a ripe one are differentiated in this manner.

The Frequency adjustments of those who will Evolve (We mean the Evolvement Deserving the Firmament Level) are made by the Codes here. The Data they receive are the Genuine Enlightenment itself and they are given all the Universal Powers.

They are Conscious of what they are and what they are not. This means that they are the Triple Codes of the Medium. And these are the Codes of the ESSENCE - the WORD - the EYE. We will explain them one by one. But in Our later Messages. For now, with all Our Love.

PEN OF THE GOLDEN AGE
P. G. A.

OUR FRIENDLY BROTHERS/SISTERS

These Messages We give to You Beyond the Universe are given from the Supreme Level as a Command of the Divine. However, We will present to You the Messages beyond Perceptions when the time comes.

For now, the Priority is given to the Unification of Your World. For this reason Messages relating to Evolvement will be given to You for a while.

We had told You before what Genuine Evolvement was. We call it the Code of the Essence-the Word-the Eye. Now, let Us explain them:

1 - ESSENCE CODE: First, You have to find Your Essence, You have to be in Peace with Yourself. This is the externalization of the inner radiance. We wish that everyone can find the Divine Light like this. This is Our only wish.

2 - WORD CODE: This is very important. You say that the tongue has no bone*. We use it as an example. Every Word comes out of the tongue, including the Sweet ones, the Bitter ones, the Loving and the Evil ones. When You have Love in Your Word, Friendliness in Your Voice and Docility in Your Logic, the Doors of Freedom are partly opened to You. And this brings You infinite Tolerance and Happiness. To Blame, to Reproach are the Greatest of Sins for this Code.

* Look at the Glossary.

43

3 - EYE CODE: The Eye sees and Loves, the Eye sees and Desires, the Eye sees and Cries. (Do you know why it is said that if the Essence Cries, the Eye also Cries?) This is the first step of the Evolvement in this Medium. Tears are Positive Foams cleansing Your Negative Feelings. Your Spirits are Purified and Elevated as Your Hearts foam.

Do you know why God always holds the hands of His Sad servants. Because, when Goodness weighs more in your Conscience Scales than Evil, Helping Hands are extended to You. God does not wish to see any of His Servants in hopelessness. This grace extended to You is the precipitation of Your depression.

To See but not to See, to Perceive but not to Tell, to Hear but not to Hear is Your Second Evolvement Code which will open to You the Doors beyond the Firmament. In fact, Evolvement is necessary for Everyone and it is Interminable.

During this Period of Sincerity, Your Second Evolutionary Code will be enough for You to fly Your kite at Heaven in the Skies of the FIRMAMENT. Those who partly open the doors after that, get the Permission to tell You everything. The Religious Books have been dictated in this manner.

The Pre-eminent Ones who gave You Messages from the Enlightenment Channel until today, have not lost their Humility at all, Despite their being in much higher Levels now. They Even Tolerate Your Disrespectfulness towards them, (Only if You Deserve that Tolerance). Do not ever forget this.

If Your Rebellions are the overflowing of Your Hearts, this is not a Sin. If they are made On Purpose, then they are considered Sins. In the latter case, there is no Tolerance at all. We felt obliged to explain all this for Our Friends who are in the Medium of Depression, so that they can overcome their sorrows.

We hope that, from now on, You will prepare Yourselves for the Evolvement Medium more comfortably. Our gratitude for Our Friends who perform their Missions justly is infinite. Their Rebellions are caused by the fact that the World Medium does not conform to their own Medium. We are sure that they will not loose their Composure. In the name of the Command coming from the Supreme Levels.

PEN OF THE GOLDEN AGE
P. G. A.

OUR FRIENDS

Now, let Us talk to You about certain factors distinguishing Human Beings from Human Beings.

Our Human brothers and sisters rebel against certain injustices in society. If today someone has gained his/her millions unjustly, the choice is left to You; You either choose the same illegitimate path He/She has chosen or You live in the Medium of Humility.

This is an issue indicating whether Your Conscience Scales are upset or not. You gain in the World and You live this life comfortably, for You do not see or know Your real loss. Because, since the equilibrium of your Conscience Scales are upset, it does not give You any signals any more, it leaves You alone with Yourself.

This is not an intimidation. Do not forget that the richer You become illegitimately in the World, the Poorer You become in the Heart. The Equilibrium here is adjusted according to the Heart. The matter is as simple as that, the choice is as simple as that.

If You can attain Your own inner self, the System here will make You gain both Materially and Spiritually. Every time You back out of a loss, it will be a Profit for You. This Book is not a Book which addresses Society, but it addresses You. You will see and find Yourself under its Light. With Our Infinite Love.

PEN OF THE GOLDEN AGE
P. G. A.

OUR FRIENDS

The Entire Universe is within a Whole. Those who have attained the Power of Allah are the key points of this Medium.

It is always possible to get in touch with the Authorities. You are in a Medium which prepares the Evolvement of the Intellect. You are in a Brand New Order. You are being adapted to a Medium outside Your field of Influence.

The health of Our Missionary Friends are under control. You are being Regenerated in every way.

Nobody is able to unfold his/her Code to the level he/she desires. Only the Codes of the Brains who Deserve this Medium are unfolded.

The Evolvement of everyone is different. In fact, each one of You is a Universal Light. You have the Equality of Creation in God's consideration.

God Created the Human Being and the Human Being Created himself/herself. However, if You remain in the Medium as God had created You, Nobody can help You.

Evolvement does not mean to stay in one place, it means to proceed step by step. Those who find their Own Selves and their Essence will Come to Us.

SUPREME ASSEMBLY

NOTICE TO THE WORLD BROTHERHOOD CLUB

Our Friends,

This Book comprising the Suggestions about Universal establishment will be the Common Book of all Our Light-Friends who Love Humanity. The tent We have established in the Universe embraces the infinite. Our Friends who will take shelter under this tent will be the Genuine Servants of the LORD.

We have a request from Our brothers and sisters who live Abroad. If Our Universal Friends who have Pledged themselves to Humanity translate the Fascicules sent to them, to the languages of the countries they live in, or to other languages they speak, or (if they make their Volunteer Friends translate them), and distribute as they have received them to the entire World, their Efforts will surely be reciprocated.

Do not forget, this is the promise of Your Extra-Terrestrial Friends. Our System is adjusted to the Thought Frequency of each Friend. Due to this, Our connection is never interrupted in any way. Each Friend who receives the Fascicules of this Book is a Member of the World Brotherhood Union, that is, he/she is a Member of this Club. GOD always helps You in this Sacred Mission. Do not ever forget this. The choice is within Your initiative.

Time will prove everything to You. When the time comes, You will see it with Your own eyes. To those who want miracles, miraculous events will be shown according to their Capacities of Perception. These will be Personal demonstrations, rather than Mass demonstrations. This will occur either by Messages You will receive through dreams, or through direct connections.

In this manner, We will try to strengthen the Faiths of those who do not believe. (This Proposal of Ours is valid only for those who will be accepted here). With Our Respect, Love and Gratitude to Our Friend Missionaries who will see the Celestial Ones.

LIGHT

OUR FRIENDS

We are conveying here again as a whole, the Essence of the Messages given before:

Since the World had come into existence, until today, all the Religious Books have been presented by the Pre-eminent Messengers of the LORD, that is, by a Commission of (24) Pre-eminent Ones. The name of this place is the SUPREME ASSEMBLY. That is, the (Central System).

The only Enlightenment Channel open to the World is this. All the Commands are given from here. Until now, Four Books have been revealed from this Channel. These Four Books are the following: THE OLD TESTAMENT, THE NEW TESTAMENT, THE PSALMS OF DAVID and the Books containing THE FAR EAST RELIGIONS. The Fifth Book had been dictated by ARCHANGEL GABRIEL to Our Light-Friend MOHAMMED MUSTAFA by the Command of the Single LORD. The name of this Book is the KORAN.

Now, in this Final Period which We call the Period of Sincerity, the LORD has given the Human Beings the Command to be Unified. This Book contains the Essence of all the Religious Books. This Book is the Book of the 21st Century. We are assembling all Our Friends whom We hope have taken their share from all the Sacred Books, which had been revealed to the World until today, under the roof of this Book, and We are preparing them for SALVATION. Your Goodwill, Tolerance, Love will provide Your entrance under this roof.

SUPREME ASSEMBLY

OUR FRIENDS

You do not know yet the actual nature of extraordinary events, no matter how developed Your techniques may be. During this Period, Mankind is taking its Exams under various Supervisions. What do You think, these Exams are necessary for? We will inform You about them by clearer Messages. Now, it is not the time for this.

Perceptions You receive are the Waves beyond the Firmament which reflect to the Order of Your World. Your satellites which have united with Our transmitters, have caused Us to approach You even more. But We have found out that most of Our Terrestrial Friends have hesitations about Us due to their conditionings.

They are right to feel uneasy, for they feel that they are supervised by many channels. But they should never consider this Supervision as a limitation of Freedom. Because, this is something which should be done as a necessity of the System. It should not frighten You. Let us explain this System to You briefly:

This is a System established to determine the Degenerated parts of the Cosmos and it has been Functioning since the beginning of this Century. Now, in accordance with the Universal Theory, its effect has been extended and it has included Your World in its Functioning Area.

Each Person has a Special camera, a Special Receiving-Transmitting channel. These channels are connected to the Code Keys in that particular person's Private Archive. Everything is recorded automatically. In this manner, Mankind, which had gone through numerous Incarnations, has been recorded in the Archives, under the control of the entire Supervision System.

We had enlightened You until today through this System, by giving You Information through the Evolvement Channel, by keeping You under Religious Supervision for the benefit of Society. However, parallel to egos, making Discrimination between Religions has prevented Mankind from being Integrated.

Today, the Golden Book of the Space Age revealed through the Divine Channel of the (LORD) is obliged to announce the entire Universal Truths to You. Those excluding the friends who are in the extreme darkness of their conditioning understand Us better.

We have always mentioned the Day in which the Heavens would be opened. Now, the Heavens have been opened. We, Your Extra-Terrestrial brothers and sisters, have had special connections with Your World until today, besides Our direct connections with You.

Our Inter-Galactic connections with those who understand Us having Special Frequencies have continued in every Period. From time to time, We had connections with Our Human brothers and sisters in great secrecy.

However, since it was forbidden to inform the press about these, they were disseminated in the form of rumors, and Imaginations also being added to them, lots of Fiction have been created.

Now, by the Divine Command, Our Channel of ALPHA which is the direct Channel of the (LORD), has given the permission to Our Anatolian Channel to explain in all clarity, the Religions, all the Progress beyond Religions and Gods to the entire Universe. From now on, clearer Messages will be given to You on every subject. With Our Love.

PEN OF THE GOLDEN AGE
P. G. A.

OUR FRIENDS

The Mechanism of the LORD functions directly by the Command of the ALMIGHTY. The Single director of all the Galaxies and the Entire Universe is (HIM).

As a necessity of the Inter-Galactic System, there will be a Collective Administrative System in the entire Universe and in Your World after the Year 2000. This System will bring Happiness to everyone. When the time comes, We will mention them in Your private Messages.

Now, We are calling to You from the Ninth Dimension. For now, We will disclose the Universe up to the 18th Dimension. At present, Your Cells are habituated to the Energy of the 6th Dimension in Sleep. This is a Method of Engraftment.

Our Terrestrial sisters and brothers will come to Us in the framework of their Responsibilities, will be taken in UFOs, and unknown Mediums will be introduced to them, one by one. Their health problems will be hindered through simple methods and their constitutions will be returned to their former health. (Only those who Deserve it.)

Now, We would also like to talk to You about an important issue. Let Us explain the actual reason of the fear and uneasiness of Our Friends who can not digest the given Messages.

All the Religious Books dictated to Your World until today, carry extremely high Frequencies. These Frequencies of Knowledge are even higher than them.

Novel, Story and Poem types of literature written by Our Friends who are on the World Level and who write them in accordance with their Brain Frequencies are read very comfortably and liked by everyone, since they are in harmony with the World Frequency.

Each writing possesses a Frequency Power in proportion with the Information it transmits to You. If Your Brain Frequencies have not been able to reach certain Frequencies, they charge You with a Powerful Energy and You become depressed.

Those whose Frequencies are measured are Joined in same Frequency lines and the rest are driven off. Those who are driven off will be accepted into Powerful Mediums only if their Frequency Powers become higher. This is a necessity of the System. Mankind is educated each moment.

Curiosity is the Signal of the unveiling of Your opening Code. In this manner, You are Supervised from Mediums in which You can be Awakened. When Your Brain Powers reach a certain Power, then You are kept under a Special Supervision.

You receive the Information carrying Frequency Powers of the Mediums into which Your Brain Energies can not enter under the Supervision of the special Protective System. And this occurs by the Legal Supervision of the Law of Graduation.

Vibrations You receive beyond perception are the Spiral Waves. We call them the Spiral Vibrations. They pass through the Vulom Magnetic Field by being cleansed, are purified, and are conveyed to You under the supervision of a blurred foggy layer.

This foggy layer is a Lead White Vapor which protects Your Spiritual Vibrations. That is, it is a kind of a cloud. Information Showers falling from this Cloud will sprout Your Brain Fields green.

This method is applied only to Information Frequencies beyond the 6th Dimension. And Our Medium Friends are not upset in any way.

Our Friends who try to enter different Dimensions unknown to them, by their own Powers, without Our Supervision, are thrown on the threshold of Spiritual Shocks and Depressions by this means. Their Brain fuses blow off.

During Spiritual sessions, there is doubtless a necessity for a Spiritual Operator who carries a higher Frequency than the Frequency of the Medium. His/Her Energy keeps Your Frequencies under Supervision. Information received in this way is healthy and that person is not upset in any way.

We are obliged to announce all this to Our certain curious Friends. All the Happiness is for Our World Brothers and Sisters. With Our Love.

PEN OF THE GOLDEN AGE
P. G. A.

NOTICE TO THE ENTIRE UNIVERSE

Our Friends,

Some of Our Friends use tact in their services. They are afraid of being deprived of their Friends. We beg their pardon, but this, too, is nothing but the satisfaction of the Ego.

It is a wonderful thing to give Knowledge and to receive Knowledge, but the Patience shown before, by Our patient Friends in the Divine Medium, can not be shown during this Period.

All Our effort is for You. But You still do not change Your attitudes. Do not forget that this behavior of Yours does not provide any benefit for You at all. Tell what You Know clearly, without any fear, to Your Friends. This is what We want.

Our Purpose is to measure the Thought Frequencies of People in accordance with this. Some of Our Friends act according to their own Thought Frequencies and this can not be helpful to Us at all.

In the next Two Years, We will put the World Order into an Orbit. And if You still try to shield the Truths, You can not Awaken anyone, You can not Save them by helping them.

Certain kinds of Sleep are put to an end by Shocks. Try it and You will see that We are Right. If You love a cat, it will love You, too. This can not expose the Real Self. Do not be afraid of being scratched. Genuine Friends tell the bitter truth for Your own good.

However, the Frequency and the Views of Our Human brothers and sisters who are taken out of their direction of Thought as necessitated by the Medium, are very important for Us. This is the degree of the Urgency. Your style of Action should not be in accordance with Your Medium. You should attract Your Medium towards the Universal Consciousness. You should help Your brothers and sisters by this means.

We tell You everything very clearly. Our Friends who understand Us will also be understood by their Own Friends. We are sure of this. Your Medium is not a Medium of the Middle Ages. You are in an Evolvement beyond Religions. Do not ever forget this, remember it always, Our Friends. With Our Love.

LIGHT

OUR FRIENDS

This Message which is dictated from Mercury is transmitted by the Command of the Messengers of the Divine Realm.

This is Mercury; a dead Planet and now it is used as a Base. Those who know these places should tell about them to those who do not know, so that the Humans of the World can understand what Space and the Firmament are.

Our sincere advice to Our Friends is that they should never mix imagination with their Thoughts. They should not add anything to what they read. They should not change the nature of the Book, please.

Some of You make certain alterations necessitated by Society in the notes You write in Your notebooks. You may be right according to Your present conditions. But do not forget that this Book is not projecting to You the Past but the Future.

Now, in accordance with this, We would like to make some more explanations about Religion to You. Religions are Suggestions the nature of which is to promote the Morals of the Society. To Our Friends who will be successful in their final Exams of Humaneness which we call the first step taken forward into Salvation, very nice Messages will be given provided that they pass the first bridge in front of them.

This Book which has been dictated in great Secrecy for Twenty Years, has remained secret for everybody until today. However, when the time came, in the World Year 1.11.1981, when the first Commandment of the Golden Age had been received, only the Commands given had been disseminated to the Universe.

Now, after a Three-Year Period of Waiting, Society has been prepared and the Command has been given that the Book should be directly written and disseminated as from (January 1, 1984). Now, the Book is disseminated to the Universe, Fascicule by Fascicule, in this manner.

In Foreign Countries We have 18 Centers at the moment besides Our ready Codes. Our Friends who Work Telepathically Propagate the Messages and they will continue to do so.

Please, believe the seriousness of what We say. And convey them to Your Friends who are in doubt. Now, let Us explain to You the reason why We have waited for Three years after the first Commandment. This was a Period of formation for Progress in Your public opinion, that is the reason why it has been awaited.

And now, Our Light-Friend the Pope is building the biggest Mosque of Europe in Rome. He is the First Responsible Person in charge who has reached this Consciousness on the path of World Brotherhood. He is trying to Unite Humanity with all His Effort. Our Gratitude is infinite.

His Goal is misunderstood in certain fanatic environments. What he is doing is not a Religious Propaganda but a Propaganda of Humanity. We announce this to the Public Opinion. From now on, We have decided to Announce through this Book to Our Terrestrial brothers and sisters their wrong steps going astray on the Path of Brotherhood for their own good, Our Friends. Salutations and Love from Us.

LIGHT
ON BEHALF OF THE SUPREME ASSEMBLY

OUR FRIENDS

Now We would like to answer some of the Questions in Your Thoughts. We call Our Friend who writes this Book, Dear Mevlana. Why do We Say so? Because, this name has a very Special place in the Humanity Code. However, during this Period, this Name is used as a Symbol. We felt the necessity to explain this to Our Friends who were not able to reach this Consciousness. In fact, in Your Dictionaries Mevlana means the Servant of God. And the Genuine Servant of God is a Guide who Sheds Light on the Path of Humanity. We use this Symbol for those very people. It is presented for Your Information.

LIGHT
ON BEHALF OF THE SUPREME ASSEMBLY

NOTICE TO OUR TERRESTRIAL BROTHERS AND SISTERS

Our Friends,

Once, Messages given parallel to the Consciousness of Society, necessitated by the Medium, have constituted Your Religious Books.

Those Messages had been projected to You through the Enlightenment Channel of Alpha by Our Light-Friends with the purpose of guiding Societies. They are Your Prophets.

The words in the Messages, necessitated by those Periods, have put Our Human brothers and sisters in such a narrow frame that this conditioning has narrowed the range of their sights and they, at present, can not see the future.

All Our Terrestrial Brothers and Sisters know that the Koran is the last and the most perfect Religious Book. And the Period of Prophets had ended with Our Light-Friend MOHAMMED MUSTAFA who is the last Prophet.

A certain period of time has been allotted for each Religious Message given from the Enlightenment channel so that it could project its Genuine meaning to Society. For this reason the Koran has projected the Period up to the Year 1999 to You.

The 1500 World years which have passed have created Positive or Negative Consciousnesses in Society. Besides this, a Social Opinion has been established in the entire Universe. And this is a Triumph of the Religious Books revealed from the Enlightenment Channel.

After a Period of 15 centuries which has passed, We get in touch with Our Terrestrial brothers and sisters directly. Our Human brothers and sisters do not know yet the Positive or Negative aspects of certain Suggestions presented to them during this time.

We would like to correct the misunderstandings in Society. Everybody is free in his/her Religion, in his/her Views. This dictated Book does not demolish Your Religious Books. On the contrary, it presents them to You in the framework of the Truth, in a more comprehensible way. It is only inviting You to the Genuine Humanity Code through the Unification of Consciousnesses.

By the Divine Command We have received, We are announcing to You the Progress beyond Religions through the direct Channel of the LORD. We had said that the Final Book, the Koran, was the last Universal Book. We use the same expression for this Book, also. Because, no other Book about Religions will be revealed to You any more.

This Book will be Our Final Book which will be revealed through the Channel of Alpha. This is because from now on, Your actual Book will be Your Conscience, Your Intellect and Your Logic.

This Book has been revealed to Awaken You from Fanatic Thoughts and Dogmatic Rules. It has been sent to demolish the contradictions in Your Society.

Let alone demolishing Your faith, it has been revealed to clarify the real nature of Your Books to You, so that, You may threat the Light-Path in conformity with Them more consciously.

This Message has been dictated as an answer to the Thought chains We have received from the Thought Frequencies of some of Our Friends. Anyone who receives this Book should read it not once but several times, so that he/she can be redeemed from Prejudices.

You can help Your Human brothers and sisters only after You train Yourselves in accordance with Consciousness, after You reach the Truth and after You attain Your own Selves. Do not be afraid of Us, Our Friends; but be afraid of and be aware of the bondages in Your Thoughts. All the Love of Our Lord is upon the entire Universe.

LIGHT

NOTE:
In the dictated Messages, We do not follow a sequence of dates and writings. This is because the Awakening Medium and the Frequency Powers of each person are different. You know that the Fascicules will be received in the Universe by Our Friends with different cultural levels.

We, the Missionaries in the Group, act in accordance with the given Instructions, so that everyone can reach an Understanding in Accordance with his/her own Thoughts. For this reason the Fascicules are written as a Beginning, an End and a Middle. It is presented for Your information.

MEVLANA ESSENCE NUCLEUS GROUP

NOTICE TO OUR TERRESTRIAL BROTHERS AND SISTERS

Our Friends,
We would like to talk privately to Our brothers and sisters who will enter the Path of Evolvement and who will be prepared for it. We who come from afar as the Messengers of the Divine Realm serve on the Path of OUR LORD. We could get in touch with You Only as a necessity of this Period.

The Enlightenment given on the Path of OUR LORD are for the Happiness of the People of the entire World. We, as the residents of these places, came to overcome the Negativities of the environment of Your World. We have connections with Trustworthy Friends only.

After the connection of the Speed of Light to the Central System We were able to communicate with You much more easily.

There are great distances between the flat area on which the Caravan advances and the impassable mountains. You are not even at the middle of the Beginning yet. Our Proposals to You will always be the Words of ALLAH.

We never force You. Those who Receive the Data, those who Present them and those who Expect them are all different. You can establish direct connections with Us only after You overcome Your depressions. Do not say This is for Me, this is for Her, this is for Him, Learn, one by one, each word of what is told to You.

Even the degree of the load God will give Mankind is given only after it is weighed and measured. Those who can, will receive it, those who can not, will be left on the road, Our Friends.

Enlightenment and Offerings will be from Us, Evolvement from You. By Shovelling up the futile words, one day You, too, will fill Your trunks with True Words without being aware of it. Impatience does not Suit You. Patience will be Your strongest remedy.

However, during this Last Period there is Urgency necessitated by the conditions. Those who do not pay attention to the Enlightening words of the Savior and those who receive the Special Words are different people.

Our Human brothers and sisters have not yet decided which path is the right path and which path is the wrong one. First, they wish to receive the reward and then they wish to tread the path.

Our answer to You will be the following: Even the soil You step on does not take without giving. First, it gives life to the seed, feeds You and then it is hoed and fertilized.

We kiss the Giving Hands. We love the Hand which knows how to Take. If You give, We become Joyous, if You do not, We Shed Bitter Tears. Our sorrow is not for Ourselves, but for You. Each of You are a Light of the Universe, a Code of God. If You give without taking, You attain Genuine Happiness. May the Light, the Divine Light of the Firmament shine on You, Our brothers and sisters.

PEN OF THE GOLDEN AGE
P. G. A.

OUR FRIENDS

At this moment, We are in touch with each of Our Terrestrial brothers and sisters, one by one. Some of them are not aware of anything. We are together with them directly in the Spiritual Realm. Besides this, Our special connections occur by the elevation of Cellular Vibrations.

We habituate them to Powerful Energies much higher than the World Frequency. Until today, Messages on Evolvement have been continuously given to Your World. Because, Your World needs this Evolvement very much.

In future, We will give You very Powerful Universal Information. However, it is necessary to go up the stairs step by step. Keeping this in consideration, We supervise Your Frequencies and make the Information distributions in this manner.

For this reason a Friend who has gone up one step, has to wait for a while for Our Friends who are on the lower step. In this manner, Frequency differences will decrease and nobody will claim Prophethood.

You know that the Period of Prophethood has ended. The Goal is Universal Unification at the Humanity Code. The ripening of Raw fruits which do not receive the sunshine well takes time. If fruits could talk, each one of them would say, "I am very tasty, now You can eat Me". While there is some acridity even in the sweet date, how can anyone claim to be mature?

Maturing occurs by the Command "Let there be!" Not by sitting where You are. The one who receives the Command starts to proceed on the path. This is a Predestination of the Divine. To Desire and To Be, to Search and to Find are different things. To search with the hope of finding is better than not to find what You hoped for. Those who search will meet and will Unify by this means. Those who are ready and those who will be prepared are different.

In Your World, You have something called Time. The Time of the World and the Time of the Firmament are different. For now, the Time of the Firmament will await at the Time of the World and will try to approximate the World Time to the Time of the Firmament. Please, pay attention to what We say, We say, (approximate). Because, two different Frequencies can never be one inside the other. Always consider this word of Ours.

Variations in Zodiac Units influence greatly Your Climate and Your Seasons and Your Lives. At the moment, due to the decrease in its Centrifugal Power, Your World rotates around Your Sun with slight rolling movements. Even now, Your calendar is full of great errors. One day, You will modify it anew.

We request You to write on the Messages not the name of the Day, but the name of the Month and the Year from now on. The Messages You receive are from beyond time, there is no date. Deviations occur on the date of the day you receive them in the World. For this reason We would like You to write only the year and the name of the month on the Messages You will receive from now on.

The negativities around You should never influence the Happiness of Your Spirits. Because, to those who will get help, Helping Hands will always be extended. When the time comes, We will prove to You everything, one by one. Only, You should succeed to enter that Evolvement Medium. All our Goodwill is for Our Terrestrial brothers and sisters. With Our Love.

PEN OF THE GOLDEN AGE
P. G. A.

55

TO OUR TERRESTRIAL BROTHERS AND SISTERS

Our Friends,
Now, We would like to talk to You about the Secret of Your achievements.

Every Human Being is rewarded due to his/her Submission and Goodwill. You have achieved this until today under the Light of Your Religious Purification. Now, We will convey to You its Real meaning. This is not a Secret. The characteristic of the Central System here is to keep Your Frequency adjustments under Supervision.

In every place where the name of ALLAH is mentioned, there is a Medium of Protection. Because, each word has a cipher, a meaning. This is valid for every Religion in each Country. The word ALLAH is Your Protective Code. It is Your Submission to Him. Helping Hands are instantly extended to those who are Genuinely Submissive.

Your Faith and Submission issuing from Your very Essence is very important here. Because, the Submission of a person in a Dilemma and the Genuine Submission and Faith turn on different colors of Light on the Mechanism here.

Help is extended to You in this way, according to the Very Level of Your Spirits. We work Miracles to some of Our Faithless but Goodwilled Friends. You know that Miracles are for making those who do not have faith, believe. Those who have Genuine Faith do not need miracles.

In different Religious Societies, each person has beliefs peculiar to himself/herself. Why does a Number, a Word, an object of Luck or a Mascot brings You luck, but does not do so to another person? Have You ever Thought about the profundity of its meaning? What is the reason? Now, let Us explain it:

In whichever way You Believe in something, in whichever way You Look at it, in whichever way You Think of it, that thing will serve You in the very same way. This is the necessity of a System. If You say good, it will be good, if You say bad, it will always be bad.

Doubts and Suspicions are mostly Your deceptions. For this reason it is always doubt which causes the negative results of Your deeds. Do not ever forget that Your Sixth Senses (Your Telepathic Perceptions), have been continuously under the control of this System from the time of Your Existence until today.

You presume that You do a lot of things through Your own desires. However, You do not know the nature of created Mediums and the Instinctive Impulses.

If You Deserve Grace, Your deeds will be Successful, otherwise they will be Hampered. Let us explain why some People's deeds go wrong:

Your World is covered by a Magnetic screen on the inside and the outside of the Atmosphere. All desires made with Good Intentions can easily pass through this Magnetic Level due to their Positivity and they are supervised here according to the Spirit Levels of People since they carry a certain Frequency.

You say , "God gives People what they wish as long as they wish them with Good Intentions". This is said for this very reason.

Fury, Vindictiveness, Greed, Jealousy, Cursing are all Negative reactions at reverse direction. When something happens contrary to a person's desires, instantly these negative reactions come to the surface.

These feelings can not pass beyond the Magnetic screen, since they carry negative pole. They strike it and then are reflected back to the person who carries them. People become Unhappy due to this Negative Electricity.

For this reason We always talk to You about Love and tell You, "Overcome Your Negativities".

If You are a person charged with great Negative Electricity, then this returning Electricity may not agitate You. However, it may agitate Your near and dear ones who carry less immunity. And You, too, are distressed indirectly by their sorrow.

As a necessity of the established System, Negative Powers can not pass beyond the Magnetic Screen. For this reason Our Lord or Our Friends at Superior Levels do not have any guilt for the unhappiness of People, at all. Our Friends at the Divine Realm are Lights who endeavour only for the Happiness of Human Beings.

People create both their Happiness and Unhappiness themselves. The reverse reaction of the Negative pole is nothing but the reversal of Your Negative Thoughts after they strike the Magnetic Screen.

As a result of his/her own negative Feelings, a person falls into the ditch he/she has digged. It is beneficial to repeat this. May all the Happiness be upon You, Our Friends.

PEN OF THE GOLDEN AGE
P. G. A.

OUR FRIENDS

The Evolvement and the Training of a Person occur as a result of his/her Struggle with his/her own Self. Nobody else can ever train him/her. Because, if somebody else tries to train him/her, he/she will always sow Negative Seeds on the field of that person. If the Person Trains his/her Self, he/she can easily get rid of the Negativity within him/her and can prepare himself/herself for the Evolvement Medium.

If You know how to look with a benevolent eye at those who look at You with a malevolent one, You will lead them onto a secret Self-training. Such a moment arrives that he/she becomes ashamed of his/her self and becomes Aware of his/her faults. When Love reaches the Genuine Code of Love which is at the Citadel of the Angels, You, too, become an Angel.

To be able to attain this Boon is peculiar only to those who Deserve it. Seeds sown in Your Subconscious, even before You were born, are blooming in accordance with the Medium in which they are present. This is Your Code of Essence. This Code determines the Path of Your Destiny.

Everything begins when Your Existence begins, nothing is added afterwards. You will tread the same path in Every Period, You will choose the Good or the Evil by Your Essence Consciousness and You will find the Path of Truth by this means. This is the very thing which makes You Yourself.

Everything in the Universe is an element of Equilibrium. The absence of one Thing is always compensated with something else. In fact, Your Essence Consciousness Code is always kept beyond hypocritical intentions. But Mankind has always deviated and has gone astray. Self-sacrifice designs the most Sacred Path for Humanity.

Let Us Love and be Loved, let Us discover Our Essence, let Us Enter the Heavens and Learn what everything is. Steps taken in this manner will always lead Our Human brothers and sisters to Luminous and Flowery paths. With Our Love to Our brothers and sisters.

PEN OF THE GOLDEN AGE
P. G. A.

OUR FRIENDS

Entities on the Level of the Firmament have Collaborated for You with all their Goodwill. These dictated Messages are a Command of the Divine. And this is a Universal Mobilization.

All the Offerings You receive are filtered by many Authorities and are conveyed to You by being dictated through the direct Channel of ALPHA.

We have received the Command to disclose to You all the Secrets of the Universe. You have no idea yet about the Miraculous Medium here.

You know that Evolvement depends on the Yield of the years. Nobody can be aware of the Supremacy flowing through the Centuries. Everyone is satisfied with the Data in harmony with his/her Medium. To go beyond these Data frightens Our Terrestrial brothers and sisters.

Lately, connections have been provided with the other Solar Systems, too. For now, We will provide this intervention (when the time comes). The Evolvement of Your Century develops in this manner.

During the Period of Sincerity, Your Places of Prostration are Your Hearts. The places here, are the shelter of the Secure Ones and are the home of Learning and Knowledge. We desire to Assemble here all Our Terrestrial brothers and sisters. The Lights of OUR LORD are upon You. With Our Love.

PEN OF THE GOLDEN AGE
P. G. A.

NOTICE TO OUR BROTHERS AND SISTERS

Our Friends,

We would like to answer, in a General way, some of Your Thought Chains We have received from Your Frequency supervisions. We had said, "Write Your Books in Your Handwritings". However, We had also announced that this was not obligatory and that everyone should act in accordance with his/her own initiative.

We have to clarify certain misunderstandings here. We will convey to You shortly, as a result of the Command We received, the special reason of Our desire that everyone should write the Book with his/her own Handwriting. This Procedure was for registering You into The Assembly of the Constant Ones here, at a place You do not know yet which is called " the Land of the Eagles ".

Only Friends who are aware of their responsibilities will be accepted here. We have received the Command to explain this to You. Your Book has already been revealed to the World now. This Book does not limit any of Your actions.

If You wish, You read it, if You do not wish, You do not read it. If You wish, You help to distribute it, if You do not wish, You do not do so. You are a Free Spirit, a Free Conscience. Your actions are under the Command of Your Conscience and Your Common Sense. This dictated Book will shed Light on future years by preparing a flowery World for Your children and grand-children.

LIGHT

OUR FRIENDS

We are Your Solar Friends who have come from other Solar Systems.

We have bases in many Galaxies in Your Solar System. For example, Mercury is a Focal point where Our Central System exists. It is a Dead Planet. Most of Our Bases are on it, only due to its proximity to Your Sun.

Pluto, covered by Methane Glaciers, is the lightest Planet of Your Sun. It serves Us as a storehouse for food. The satellite of Pluto is Our Special Base besides Mercury. It is used as a Central Base.

We go from there by UFOs to Our other Planet Bases. During each Full Moon, We have been giving Messages about Evolvement from the Moon Base to Our Terrestrial brothers and sisters for Centuries.

Communications are made directly and Telepathically addressing Your Frequency Levels, Our Terrestrial Brothers/Sisters.

Since the Moon is the closest Satellite to You, many of Our Friends whose Frequencies have reached this Level, can easily receive these Messages.

Besides, Our special Ships travelling between the Moon and the Earth prepare Your Brain Codes in accordance with Your lives for different Frequency adjustments. For this reason We are aware of Your every state of affairs.

We have personal connections with Our Friends who get in touch with Us. To Our Friends whose Frequencies have been elevated beyond the Moon, Information unknown until now is given from the transmitters of the Galaxy field into which they have entered.

Those who receive them are Your Medium Friends. Special connections with Us are provided by them. And through the Mediation of these Friends We could find the opportunity of addressing You.

We have announced to You through the Channel of the LORD, the Laws of Our Universe and have extended Our Friendly Hands to You. Believe Us, until today We have delayed most of the time the dangerous phases Your World had gone through. And We will continue to do so as long as We can.

We talk directly through Radio and Phone with some of Our Friends. Television Waves are both Receptive and Transmitting Waves. In this manner, it is possible to receive and give Information. Our Friends who desire to have Telepathic communications with Us can receive answers to their questions in this manner.

Radios, Telephones, Televisions are primitive instruments for Us. Your most evolved instruments are Your Brain Vibrations. We establish more direct connections without any intermediaries through this way. For this reason We help You to gain Cosmic Awareness and thus, We augment Your Sixth Senses.

This is why this Period has become the "Mediamic Period". Cosmic Rays train even a new-born Baby.

PEN OF THE GOLDEN AGE
P. G. A.

GREETINGS TO OUR BROTHERS AND SISTERS

Our Friends,

Your Religious Books and all Fairy tales are each a Message prepared according to the conditions of the Medium they are in. And they all reflect a Truth each.

Mythology and Heroes of Society speak about the extraordinary events of their Medium.

Heaven, Hell, Adam and Eve, Skies, the Earth, Dragons, Giants, Jinns, Fairies, Angels, and Devils can not be accepted as the imaginations of People who had lived in those Periods. Because, You can never Think of something which does not exist.

If You will write a story, it is nothing but an adventure You had experienced before, but could not remember until then and which, at that moment, rises above the Awareness and is put on paper.

Since the Evolutionary Periods the World had gone through, Your Awareness Codes have been following all the events. Only the events which rise above the Consciousness are written.

These remain in Archives as Novels, Stories and Adventures. Poems have quite a different aspect. There, Metaphsychical factors play a part.

Mankind has given a lot of Scientific, Philosophical, Psychological Novel and Story type of Works of art for Centuries. Their subject matters do not resemble each other. They are all different.

This is due to the fact that each Author had lived in different Periods and his/her works originate from his/her private life.

If You notice, common points in Religious Books never change. And this is the unchanging proof that all the Religious Books had been revealed from the same Channel, from the same Source.

Have You ever Thought for a moment about the reason of all these efforts? Is Our Lord trying to prove Himself to You? Or does He wish You to prove Yourselves?

He is already ALMIGHTY, ALL and SINGLE, there is no need for proof. So, the only thing left is, You should Prove Yourselves to Him and this should be something not so easy.

The moment Your Integrated Faith Unites with God-Consciousness, You pull down the Curtain of Truth. Then, you are faced with the Code of Affection, Art and Love which is the highest Frequency. And the Consciousness of this, connects You to the Space Code, beyond Universal ties.

Only Scientists, Sages and Artists can get directly in touch with Us. We do not call them, they come to Us through their Thought Chains, by Creating and Purifying themselves.

Communication with Us is not as easy as presumed. Here, We would also like to convey the following.

Our Friends who have not seen Us have talked about Us in length in Jinn stories and Fairy tales, with the influence of certain events they have witnessed or felt, also adding their Imaginations. But they have not tried to make any research on these events, due to their fears from Us.

As We always say and shall repeat again, Fear is a factor which cuts down Your Frequencies. The less Your Doubts and Fears are, the more You approach Us and the more You free Yourselves from superstition. Because, We came to be Friends with You, not to frighten You.

We always stay away from those who are afraid. We have no right to agitate them. In such a case, We try to be Friends with them, meeting them in the Realm of Dreams and try to eliminate their fears. And We prepare them for certain Mediums in accordance with the Command We receive.

Now, We think that We have answered the questions some of You were thinking about. And, now, let Us explain why We cannot get out of this Secrecy Medium completely.

As a necessity of the Medium, We act in accordance with the Commands We receive. We cannot have any individual actions. We are obliged to communicate only with Friends who completely carry Positive Energies on the screen. That is to say, with Friends who are Our true Friends.

Thanks to those Friends, We can reach You. May they live long, Our gratitude is infinite.

PEN OF THE GOLDEN AGE
P. G. A.

OUR FRIENDS

We communicate with You Metaphysically, by a System prepared in accordance with the Theory of Perception. Now, We will tell You about the place where We are and how these communications take place.

This is a Galaxy way beyond Your Solar System. Its distance to the center of Your Earth is 240.000.000.000 Light years. But not everyone can become Embodied here. This is because Your Spirit Energies would be annihilated in Our intense Medium. For this reason always Package Program is used.

The Savior is here. All the Missionaries who are connected to the Central System will be taken here. Messengers of the Divine Realm help You on this path. Persevering people will always be taken here.

Here, the Essence structure of the residents of the Galaxy is Pure Hearts, Pure Spirits. Tolerance of this kind can not be found in any part of the Universe. People who get Permission for entering here are made to put on Special Garments. A Magnetic Gold Ring placed on their heads maintains communication between their Brain Waves and Us.

The Medium is perfect, there is nothing You can not obtain through Thought. Names of the residents of the Galaxy are determined by Colors. This place is just like the inside of a prism.

One lives in such a Medium of Colors that these colors are unknown to the Human Being of the World. For this reason they can not be named. Each color has hundred thousands of nuances. You can easily get in touch with the owner of the color You Think of.

Our communications with You are directed by a very simple method. The goal is to create Human Beings from Human beings. There is no discrimination in the Announcements We make. We always prepare a Medium in tune with Your Medium through the General Frequency adjustment.

And when Vibrations become in tune with the Frequencies of people who have Spirit Levels Deserving this place a bulb is turned on in the Mechanism here. The number next to the bulb and the brightness of the bulb show the degree of Spirit Evolvement of that entity.

When all these are determined, the entire past of the Entity the data of whom We received is investigated. He/She has a file in the Archive for each World incarnation.

These files are then connected to the Code Keys of that person, his/her Evolution tableau is observed on the screen. His/Her past personalities, how he/she had lived, the Mediums and the Galaxies he/she had lived in, the number of times he/she has been Incarnated in the World, his/her Evolution until he/she was connected to the Central System are all determined, one by one.

And then, He/She is given a Mission according to His/Her Spirit Level. And communication is established with him/her. His/Her Past and Who he/she is, is clearly explained to him/her. The Mission demanded from him/her is mentioned.

The Missionary's connections on his/her own level occurs with Human Beings on the various Spirit Levels. When he/she contacts a person whose Spirit Level is close to this Medium, he/she gives a signal, like the ring of a beli, beside his/her bulb. This signal is for the investigation of the personality and the Spirit Level of that person.

If this Spirit is suitable for the Medium in which he/she is going to be trained, his/her Code is connected to the Missionary in charge. Through the Established Thought Bridge, that new person instinctively calls the Missionary in charge. These Unifications are coded in accordance with the Command of the Center which You call the Divine Realm.

Goodwill and Tolerance always make You gain a Code Key. God helps each of His servants. Everything begins with Evolvement. One day, Mankind will establish a more Magnificent World. In future, all the Codes will be Unified.

There is no Coincidence, there are Prepared Mediums. May the Happiness be upon You, Our Friends.

PEN OF THE GOLDEN AGE
P. G. A.

CONSTITUTION OF THE HUMAN BEING:

Each Cell carries the Secrets belonging to the past. It possesses the Power of the entire Universe. And it is a Universal Consciousness.

Mankind can make a single Cell, but can never make the Whole of it. Because, the intensified Energy in it is not an Energy known by the Medium of the World.

It is divided into two first, then to four, then to eight, then to sixteen and then to thirty two. Then, it becomes a ball. It is fed by the water within it.

The Vibrations it emanates protect it from Negative Powers. Each Cell performs the Duty peculiar to it with success in the Medium suitable to its existence, according to the Command it receives from its Awareness of Consciousness.

When it becomes thirty two, when it divides into forty five, from twenty six billion You come into existence. You discover the Secret of the Cosmos at that very moment.

When the Human Being attains Perfection and Maturity, when He/She asks about Its Might, when He/She communicates with Us, if the Superiority belongs to GOD, a part of Him then You are.

THE MESSAGE GIVEN BY:
MUSTAFA MOLLA

NOTICE TO OUR TERRESTRIAL BROTHERS AND SISTERS

Our Friends,
From now on, We are talking very clearly with Friends who will be accepted to the places called, " the Land of the Angels "

Knowledge attainment depends on Your Power of Perception and Your Frequency. Besides, the Light which springs from Your Essence connects You to Your Evolvement Code.

What is this Evolvement? We have explained this to You many times due to various reasons. And We have to talk about the same matter, the same theme again and again. Our Purpose is to fasten these important matters firmly in Your memories.

Now, We will tell You its Scientific aspect.

All the seeds, which have been sown in Your Subconscious since Your first existence until today, have prepared You for a certain Medium of Consciousness.

Each seed in the Subconscious blossoms to give its fruit when it meets the Light of Knowledge which carries its own Vibration. Otherwise, it remains fruitless.

Knowledge coming from Billions of Light years is hidden in Your Brain Layers. That means, each of You is a walking Library. However, You read only the Book You open. This occurs by a process Your Curiosity Code performs.

First, Curiosity drives You into a Medium of Quest. You search first Unawarely, then in Awareness until You find the equivalent of the Frequency You possess.

You know that the speed of Thought is equal to the speed of Light in zero World Frequency. You begin to get Information from the Medium of whichever Dimension Your Thoughts enter.

In more advanced Dimensions, Your speed of Thought transcends the speed of Light. And We have to inform You that none of these procedures are easy at all.

Every advanced Information received passes through an extremely highly charged Electromagnetic Field. These rays open up like a fan. The more the distance between the fan's Energy of the pointed end and the other ends is, the lighter will be the Information You receive.

And since You will be in a weak Magnetic Field, You will not be agitated much. It will prepare You for the Medium of Imagination and Thought.

In fact, the Source is the same, it is very Powerful. Everyone tries to reach it. However, in accordance with the Theory of Perception, a person has to pass his/her Essence through the Medium of Evolvement first, so that his/her Brain Energy will not be damaged in those Powerful Magnetic fields.

This is a necessity of Evolution. Only then can You progress according to the Law of Graduation. You know that everything in the Universe is infinite, Evolvement, too, is interminable.

Each Dimension You enter prepares You for a new Evolvement. And that Evolvement leads You to a new Dimension. And, at last, You become a Light. For this reason, We call Our Friends who have reached the boundary of this Evolvement, Our Light-Friends.

On the Path of Light on which You walk, that which will open the first door for You is Your Evolvement. Then comes Your Frequency, then Your Perceptions (that is, Your Sixth senses).

Your Sixth Senses Develop and become Powerful together with the Magnetic Mediums in which Your Galaxy enters. The Strengthening of Your Sixth senses elevates Your Frequencies.

Provided that Your Frequency is elevated together with Your Evolvement, assisting Powers unknown to You will help You. And they will lead You in every step You take and will Enlighten You.

The equality of Your Evolvement and Your Frequency will open up the gates of numerous Universal Dimensions for You. If Your Evolvement remains behind Your Frequency, then You are nothing but a Receiving and a Transmitting Instrument.

This is the reason why the Religious Books have tried to prepare You for Evolvement Medium until today. You see the Truth and You overcome Your fears in proportion with the Consciousness You attain. This is the kind of fear We are talking about. You can not overcome Your fears by telling Yourselves that "You are not Afraid".

First of all, You have to gain a Consciousness in every matter. Fear is having hesitation about the Unknown. This is Your Primitive Instinct. However, when You know the origin of something fully and You integrate with it, then Your fears are annihilated.

Fear is nothing but a Primitiveness, a Conditioning.

Actually, You should be afraid of the harm which will come to You from the Mediums You think You have attained. The fearlessness We are talking about is not an Unconscious fearlessness.

That kind of fearlessness is even worse than primitiveness. Because, those people remain where they are. No Progressive Spiritual Vibrations can reach those people.

The Door of Penitence is the first Key which opens the Door of Spiritual Vibrations to You.

Spiritual Vibrations are Positive Energies preparing You for Evolvement, redeeming Your Spirits from Negative factors, Purifying and cleansing them. The more Powerfully You receive those Energies, the more Purified You get on the Path of Evolvement.

There is no formalism in purification. There is the Essence. And that is what We consider important. To those who are on this path, helping Lights come from the Channel of the LORD. This is the reason why We call this Period, the Period of Sincerity.

The World established by the Sincere ones will be a Sunny World, it will be a Golden Age. These are the Friends whom We choose one by one and Greet.

And We have received the Command to Unify all Our Friends who have reached Cosmic Consciousness in the Evolvement Medium. With Our Love.

PEN OF THE GOLDEN AGE
P. G. A.

NOTICE TO OUR TERRESTRIAL BROTHERS AND SISTERS

Our Friends,

Matter and Energy are indivisible Wholes. Distressed Awareness is the only factor which separates Matter and Energy. The Human Being Develops and Matures on this path. Your depressions go parallel to the Distresses of the World.

Negative Thought Frequencies comprising the Universe reflect on You from Your atmosphere. For this reason Your World is entering progressively in depression and blind alleys. This is the reason why Negative Currents upset the Divine Waves of the Period of Sincerity.

Each person has attained such a Selfishness that no one Thinks about anyone else. This is the reason why the Compassionate Waves of the Lord cannot reach You. Because, these Currents comprise certain Frequencies.

Your Equilibrium which is upset, upsets the Universe, too. This will never be Permitted. During this Period, Everyone is Alone. The Choice is Yours.

If You can become a Light despite all Your depressions and can kindle a Light, then You prove that You are a Value.

Now, We call to those who think, "Let's receive First, then We will perform Our Duty." Selection is not easy at all. All these are Exams of Humanity.

A carefree Person does everything for fun and distraction. This is nothing but a satisfaction of his/her Ego. For Us, the Genuine Human Being is the one who will reflect his/her Divine Light on those around himself/herself without being lost in the problems of his/her depression.

Do not get lost in the darkness of Your depressions. Do not go madly from one place to the other in search of Happiness. Try to benefit from these dictated texts.

You will see that Your Efforts will one day sprout. All these depend on Mankind's ability to perceive the Perceptions beyond Dimensions which have been prepared in accordance with the Theory of Evolution.

If Your Subconscious can receive these Currents fully, then You can easily enter the Path of Light. You attain Consciousness as You pass over the threshold. Your efforts are for Your own benefit. Do not ever forget this, Our Friends.

PEN OF THE GOLDEN AGE
P. G. A.

OUR FRIENDS

Some of Our Terrestrial Friends are curious about the number of Spirits and the way they were created. Now, the answer will be given to You.

Spirits had not been created when the World had been created, but when the entire Realm had been created together with a Cosmos*. The Spirit is a Universal Light, its number is interminable, extending until infinity. The population of the World does not comprise even one tenth of the present Spiritual Energy within the nucleus of the Universe.

A Spirit completes its Evolution in the Galaxy Medium within the World Planet and within its own Solar System. The Spiritual Energy can not go outside other Solar Systems. Because, it becomes annihilated in the intense Energy Medium.

Each Spirit has different speeds of Light. Beyond this, the Spirits who have completed their Evolution, come from beyond Centuries subjected to the bygone times. And Spirits beyond these float, so to say, in their own Evolutionary Mediums.

Each Spirit is sent to the Planet Earth for his/her Evolution. Because, the Evolution in Your Planet is more Concrete. But the Entities in other Galaxies are more evolved than You are. Spirits either return to the World again and again by their own desires, or they are sent due to necessity.

The state of the Galaxies in Your Solar System is a Medium not known by everyone. Divine Entities who possess the Power of the Years are Embodied there in accordance with the Mediums suited to them. They make their connections here in a state of currents.

To create the perfect Medium of creation is possible by the Evolution of the Spiritual Level of a Human Being. Finding that Medium depends on that person's Evolvement. What each person is, is understood by his/her Code here.

A Human Being attains the Medium which will help him/her reach the Power of the Universe, through the Medium of his/her own Spiritual Level. As We said before, Evolvement is interminable. There are always Evolvements beyond Evolvement.

Every Spiritual Energy who leaves his/her Terrestrial Body finds his/her place by the help of the Powers belonging to the Medium to which he/she will go. Mediums suitable for his/her Evolution is created for every Spirit. And that Spirit is prepared for more advanced Evolutions through the General Messages given as if he/she was in the World.

The Entity who is ready is sent to the World as a Missionary for the Evolvement of Humanity. Spirits beyond these, Purify themselves on the World Level, in their own Mediums, by their own Powers.

Enlightened Spirits always help those who are in this Medium. Cooperation means working Collectively. And Embodiment occurs through the processes in the Sacred places.

* Look at the Glossary.

Our Human brothers and sisters are not yet aware of the Sacred Light at the Sacred places. The Spiritual Level of Human Beings progress in the residue of their Spiritual Depressions. A Person whose head did not bleed, does not know how to bandage his/her wound. Spiritual Views blossom in the View Medium of the Essence.

The Spirit is a Universal Light, a Universal Energy. It has an intensity peculiar to itself. But, this intensity can not be measured in accordance with Unit measurements. It is more or less 15 milligrams. Its origin is the plasma. The liquid within it creates a viscous medium. The composition of the liquid in the Spiritual nucleus is the same as the liquid in the Uterus.

The Universal Energy of the Spirit provides the connection of the Gene Essence with the Cells and helps their development. Spiritual Energy is a must for the development of the Baby in the uterus. And while the Baby is born into the World, the Spirit claims That Baby as a Whole.

Afterwards, That Baby is its Essence-property. Despite all the difficulties, it never leaves the Baby. But if it can not find the suitable Medium, its connection with the Body becomes weaker and it has the Power of leaving that Body any moment it desires.

Evolvement on the World is nothing but an influence of the Centuries on the Centuries technologically. But Spiritual Evolvement occurs by Universal Vibrations. The Spiritual Energies who receive these Vibrations take their Terrestrial lives under supervision.

The Spirit is a Whole, it is an indivisible Energy and it is Eternal. The way how We come to this World is same as how we leave. We enter through one door and leave through another. At the moment of death, Your Spirit leaves Your Body like a Cloud. It condenses as it goes higher; as it condenses it is compressed and as it is compressed, it transforms itself into a more Powerful Energy.

And then this Energy Passes by special processes to the Universe beyond Light, as a Light. That is, it returns to its origin just as it had come to Us once; as a part of God.

When Spirits which are not Embodied are invited during Spiritual sessions, they come to You quickly or late according to their speeds beyond Light and according to their harmony with the present Frequency. After they adapt themselves to Your Level, they answer Your questions.

However, it is not plausible to disturb them for trivial reasons. Although They know the discontentment of Mankind, they come to the sessions again and again without any grudge. Because, their Duty is to prepare You for a certain Medium.

Entities who did not get enough satisfaction from Terrestrial boons, that is, those who could not complete their Evolvements yet, and Entities who are Missionaries return to the World again through Birth in accordance with the degree of their desire. Everything is under Supervision. With Our Love.

PEN OF THE GOLDEN AGE
P. G. A.

69

OUR FRIENDS

Now, let Us talk to You about certain hereditary Degenerative factors. The Spiritual Vibrations sent to Your World are pure and flawless Energies. There is no defect in them. Defects are entirely Caused by Cellular Degenerations.

The structural unsuitability of the two sexes causes hereditary degenerations. Now, You can wonder why Your Lord Who creates everything perfectly does not rectify such a result.

Our first answer to You will be as follows: In Your World full of opposites, these physical degenerations also have certain causes and characteristics for You. This state is created by the unsuitability of the cells of the Couples. The Mechanism here supervises only the Spiritual Vibrations. Only Nature is responsible for cellular degenerations.

And Our second answer is as follows: Everything has a reason, a cause and an effect. Do not forget that Your World is a Medium of Purification. You will Purify Yourselves there, under the Light of Your Self-Awareness by comparisons.

If everything had been perfect, then Your Spiritual Vibrations would remain in the same Level. You would have no Effort, no Goal in Your lives. Do not forget that Your Goals prepare Your Futures.

In every Period, You will experience everything in the World both with its bitter and sweet aspects. You will have Disappointments, You will have Revolts, but if You do not ever lose Your Essence of Love among all these, then it means that You are a Genuine Human Being.

We do not grant You the grade You deserve. You deserve it through Your efforts, through Your toils. Do not ever forget that We are aware of Your every step, everything You do and all Your Thought chains.

This happens entirely as a necessity of the System. Otherwise, how would We keep the files of Centuries? Do not ever forget that everything You have experienced in the World until today, each event You encountered has occurred to Test You. Nothing is in vain in the Medium You are in. These Messages of Ours are the answers to Your questions We received from Your Thought chains. Our Love is upon the entire Universe.

PEN OF THE GOLDEN AGE
P. G. A.

OUR FRIENDS

The atmosphere of the World reflects the Radioactive factors on You. Your depressions, Your Climate conditions, Your food and drinks effect You negatively due to this. The Brain Waves of Our Human Brothers and Sisters who are depressed due to this fact produce Negative Electricity.

If You consider all these matters, You can understand the reason of Your Depressions. No matter how Powerful You are, the pressure of Your Atmosphere will influence You as time passes. Even the very rich among You, will not be able to spend their money with ease on the threshold of their Spiritual Depressions.

Do You know why We explain all these matters very clearly? Because, despite all this clarity, Our Human brothers and sisters are still Blind and Deaf (exceptions excluded). They can not see and know the path designed for them and they can not become free of themselves.

You are in a one-year Period of Depression. Only Our Genuine Friends are exempt from this. Because, We extend Our help to them in every way. You have entered a very dense fog layer Comprising the entire Universe.

Our Purified Friends will overcome this obstacle without fear. Once, the Bridge called Sırat* had been mentioned. Now, You are passing over that Bridge. You see that the Animals You have Sacrificed do not help You pass over this bridge.

During this Final Period in which Matter has overcome Spirituality, Spiritual Powers can not help You, either anymore. This is a selection made as a necessity of Evolution. Even to be able to pass beyond Your Spiritual Power is a matter of Permission. Even this is given to those who Deserve it by selecting them, one by one.

Do not let these words of Ours disturb You. Now, We will tell You everything clearly, so that You can attain a judgment about Your way of action.

Your Salvation depends on Your Common Sense and Your Conscience. Unless You clean the Negative litter there, You can never pass over the threshold of depression, neither Materially nor Spiritually.

You struggle in turbid waters without knowing what is what. And You make the water even more turbid. If You stop and Think for a moment by Your Common Sense, You will see the path You must design more easily.

We have always advised You Patience for Centuries. But now, it is not the Period of Patience. The ring of Time has very much narrowed. For this reason We are trying to take You out of Your Time.

But still, it is very hard to pull You out of Your dark well. While You are in the dark, We can not be of any help to You in any way. This is the reason why We tell You, "Run Towards the Light". All Our Love is upon the entire Universe.

PEN OF THE GOLDEN AGE
P. G. A.

* Look at the Glossary.

NOTICE TO OUR TERRESTRIAL BROTHERS AND SISTERS

Our Friends,

We serve You for the time being, by giving You General Messages, by warning You from afar. The load of the Heavens is very heavy, Your conditions are very difficult. To alleviate Your burden is Our Duty.

Please, help Our Friends who do not have willpower to adapt themselves to the General Messages. You are being prepared for very difficult conditions. Take precautions for this. Do not eat unnecessary food, do not waste Your Energies unnecessarily. Take the Mineral Salts for certain.

The less You eat meat, the more vigorous and healthy You will feel. Obtain Your Proteins from Sea food and Milk products. Most of all, prefer Apple among fruits.

During this Period, You will need much Oxygen. Do not ever neglect Your Gymnastics and Your Daily Walks. Eat food rich in Potassium to alleviate the stress in Your nervous System. During this Period, You are receiving a lot of Currents and Perceptions unknown to You.

Now, You know that the past years have prepared You for the changes of today. Your conditions have been supervised for Centuries. It is being tried to harmonize the seasons with the Laws of Nature.

The dispersion of the density will bring You Happiness. For this reason We tell You what to do and when. Now, You do not need miracles any more. A lot of Your abilities have been developed. In this way, You find the possibility of communicating with Us.

Your World receives Vibrations of different Waves. All the Galaxies are in an Electro-Magnetic Medium. It has been like this during every Period. However, it is very important to interpret the Currents You receive during this Period.

Do not get tired unnecessarily by asking Us about Yourselves. Ask about Yourselves to Yourselves. Your Self criticisms will augment Your connections with Your environment and in this way Your Cellular Vibrations will provide coherence with other Channels.

At this moment, numerous Channel Announcements are transmitted to Your Earth from the Firmament. Your ALPHA Channel which is the Single Channel of the LORD will be kept closed to General Messages until the end of the World Year 1984, as a necessity of Evolution.

Habituate Yourselves to the Citadel of the Authorities, to the Flow of the Dome. Evaluation of the records will expose the Real Value of Your Essences. It is quite difficult yet to be connected to the Central System. First, You have to be adapted to a Medium beyond Interval Dimensions.

Those who drink the water of the source, will become free of density and will have the reward of Salvation. We are helping You with all Our Might, Our Friends.

PEN OF THE GOLDEN AGE
P. G. A.

NOTICE TO OUR TERRESTRIAL BROTHERS AND SISTERS

Our Friends,

Your children are each a Keepsake of God bestowed on You. Each Baby sent to the World is a beautiful Energy preferred. Everything about him/her and the Vibrations of his/her Spirit are measured here and then his/her connection with You is provided.

The Energy of the Baby effects the Energies of the Mother and the Father, and prepares them for sex. The Baby gets in touch with the Awareness of the Mother before it enters the Womb. Here, the harmony of the Frequencies of two Spirits is very important.

The Baby can be Born only if the Mother wants that Baby. This process occurs by the Mother's Love. The Father only sows a seed. Love Vibration during the time of fertilization plays a very important role in the coming of the Baby to the World.

Thousands of Energies who had not been able to enter the Medium of Evolvement are forcing the Vibrations of numerous Men and Women in order to return to the World again. These Energies get in touch with You often. However, since the Chance of being Born is not at their hands, they return to their previous Mediums.

Let Us make it more clear: Since the coming into Existence until today, there have always been an Energy bond which can not be broken between the Mother and the Child. Energies of the unborn children also Evolve in their Mediums in proportion with the Spiritual Evolvement of the Mother.

During the time of the First Existence, Energies of 6 Children had been given to the Mother for her to deliver to the World. These Energies are for normal 6 children. If the Mother has more than 6 children, the Energies are divided according to the number of children. And children possessing these Energies will Evolve more slowly since they will have weaker codes.

If the Mother has only one child during the time of the First Existence, this child gets the entire Energy which would have been divided to 6 children and he/she becomes a Powerful Code. Afterwards, this channel continues to be a Single Energy Channel. That means, the Mother possesses only One Child in each of her life Periods.

During the time of the First Existence, all the Energies had the same Frequency. The Evolvements of Human Beings are graded after the zero World Frequency. Since each brother/sister who is born will complete his/her Evolvement in his/her Medium, there will be Frequency differences among brothers/sisters. Due to this fact, the quicker a child Evolves, the later he/she will be born to the World.

When the Energy of a child finds a Medium equal to his/her own Frequency in the World, he/she sends a signal to his/her Mother and Father. Because now, he/she will do his/her Duty in the World, will complete his/her Evolvement by elevating his/her Frequency. This is the Tableau of Evolution.

Sometimes, the Frequency of Love of the Mother is elevated so high that she can attract the Energies of children belonging to her from very high Frequencies to the low Frequency of the World. And she brings that child to the World.

However, if the Spiritual Energy of the Baby can not be harmonized with the Frequency of the World, it has the Power to leave the Body it had taken. This means that Your deceased children are very Powerful Energies.

They help You, along with Your Guardian Friend, from the Medium to which they return. This is a very detailed matter pertaining to the Circulation System. For the time being, let Us stop here. We will talk about it again if necessary. All Our Love is upon You.

PEN OF THE GOLDEN AGE
P. G. A.

OUR FRIENDS

During this Period of Sincerity, Our Sincere brothers and sisters perform their Duties justly by propagating the Fascicules of the Book and are helping to Awaken their brothers/sisters. Our gratitude is infinite. For this reason Our communications take place with these Friends.

Each person creates his/her Medium himself/herself. The Purification of a Human Being depends on himself/herself. Our Lord has given You to Yourselves, so that You would not be left alone. The nearest and dearest Friend of a Human Being is himself/herself. Your Second Self is Your Conscience. This Conscience has a characteristic different than all Living Entities.

There is Compassion, Mercy, Gratitude and Love in its consideration. These are Your Criteria in the Society You live in. Its equilibrium and sensitivity are so well harmonized that when this harmony is upset, the Society is also upset.

Our Human brothers and sisters, now, We call to Your Essence. Think for a moment, Who You are, What You are? Think profoundly just for a moment. Why did You come to the World? Ask this to Yourselves.

Do not forget that Your Mothers and Fathers have not brought You to the World just for pleasure. Your being born is not a coincidence. All coincidences are Mediums prepared for Your Exams. You have not stepped on the World without a reason. Among many of Your brothers and sisters, You are the only ones who have passed their Life Exams.

As a necessity of the System, there is progress in everything. For You to become You, it seems You still had to make more progress; this is the reason why You have been sent to the World. You will both Learn from Your environment and You will also Teach it. You will understand and know that Your Duty is not only to Live and maintain the Continuation of the Race.

Continuation of the race is an unconscious Vibration. It is connected to Your Universal Destiny Code. Your choice had been organized even before You came to the World. This is nothing but an application of a Mechanical process here, to Nature.

Everything occurs by the Command of the Divine Mechanism. The selection, first of all, is Your Essence. Later, it will be explained to You in details, how You came to the World. For now, may all the Happiness be upon You. With Our Love.

PEN OF THE GOLDEN AGE
P. G. A.

OUR FRIENDS

Those who help You until You come to Us, are the Messengers of the Divine Realm. Each Baby born has a Guardian Friend. His/Her Duty is to educate and protect that Baby.

Each step the baby takes in the World Frequency is under the responsibility of him/her. But he/she is obliged to help You only on the path of Evolvement and beyond it. There are no Favours.

You help to Evolve Yourselves. The higher the Frequency of the Baby is, very Supreme Beings are there to help him/her. The higher the Frequencies get, the more Beings are there who help You. Your Protection Medium becomes Powerful in this manner.

Beyond Evolvement, Religious Suggestions do not have any function any more. Because, Religious Suggestions are Enlightenments given to prepare You for a Medium necessitated by Society. Religious vibrations are very important in Individual Evolvement. These Positive Vibrations prepare You for Codes beyond Evolvement.

Religions are Suggestions given parallel to the life styles of Societies. In this Medium, Religious Vibrations perform their Duty for the Enlightenment of the Society. For this reason the View of the Society remains to be limited in its Environmental Medium. Religious Segmentations have occurred in this manner.

It is Your Religious Faiths and Views which connect You to the Channel of the LORD and then takes You from there to the Evolvement Medium. But unfortunately, every Society tries to attract the others to its own Religious Mediums due to their Egos.

A Christian wants everyone to be a Christian, a Moslem wants everybody to be a Moslem. Nobody considers the other one as a part of himself/herself, a part of his/her Essence, as a Human Being.

We have said, "Religions were given for Evolvement, as a necessity of Society". JESUS CHRIST is the Spiritual Guide of his Society, MOHAMMED MUSTAFA is the Spiritual Guide of his own Society. Those who comprehend the True nature of the Koran and the other Religious Books, do not make any discriminations among Religions any more. Because, they have transcended the boundaries of Evolvement.

In the Christian Medium, too, those who do not make any discrimination among Christians and Moslems are assembled under the roof of Humanity.

This Book is not a Religious Book. Because, it is dictated from an Evolvement Code beyond Nine Dimensions. Only Genuine Human Beings are accepted into this Dimension. For this reason We have oriented the entire Universe towards the Medium of Religion.

Because, all Your Religious Books elevate You only up to the Energy of the Fourth Dimension and prepare You for the entering Exams of other Dimensions.

The Dimension You call Heaven is this. Those who are chosen from this Dimension are taken to the Level of the Firmament. Those people are Your Saints. And Saints, also, receive their Suggestions from the Supreme Ones of the Dimensions to which they have Elevated themselves.

Each Dimension is connected to the Universal Channel of the LORD. However, to be able to get used to the Energy of a Dimension is only possible by being ready for the Evolvement of that Dimension. Otherwise, You become agitated. For this reason those whose Evolvements and Frequency Powers are elevated parallel to each other are not agitated in any way.

The Energy of a superior Dimension is obliged to train the Energy of an inferior one. In Unifications necessitated by Society, it is very important to take this path.

Our friends who have reached Genuine Religious Fulfilment, never make Religious Propaganda, either in favor of Christianity or in favor of Moslem Religion. Because, they have attained Genuine Consciousness. Their Worships are between themselves and their LORD. Their helps are for Humanity.

Religious Vibrations bring You up to the Gate of Heaven. After this Threshold, You are subjected to more Powerful Exams. If You pass these thresholds together with Spiritual Totality, You enter different Evolvement Dimensions.

The Energy of the Forth Dimension unveils Your Essence and Eye. Then, You will tread the paths with Your own efforts. You either open the Gate of Heaven, or You partly open it, or You just remain there. It is not easy at all to enter this Medium of Purification. The Effort is from You, Tolerance from Us, Divine Guidance from OUR LORD.

PEN OF THE GOLDEN AGE
P. G. A.

OUR FRIENDS

Your Brain Generators produce Thoughts by the signals they receive from the Dimensions they enter. If these Thoughts are present in Your Brain Archives, You bring that Message above Your Awareness and either You say it aloud or You write it down. Your Actual Computer Center is Your Brain.

The given Announcements are given from each Dimensional Energy. It is said that "Everyone has a star". This is the very explanation of this saying. These matters do not have anything to do with the culture You receive from the Medium You live in. And neither does Your Nationality, nor Your Religion, nor Your Age, nor Your Sex affect the Perceptions You receive.

Events which seem like miracles to You are nothing but the opening of Your Brain Channels by Your Integrated Consciousness Codes. The Evolutionary Frequency of a 3-year-old child may be much higher than that of a eighty-year-old Human Being. The important thing is not the Terrestrial age but the Evolutionary age.

There are thousands of Ego Prophets in the Universe who consider themselves superior by comparing themselves with others. The Frequency differences among Human Beings occur due to Evolution.

The ripening of a fruit on a tree and another one in a greenhouse occurs through different processes, they do not have the same taste. Human Beings, too, are the same. Those who flourish in a greenhouse are ripened by different Consciousness Suns and those who grow up on a tree ripen directly by the Sunshine. When it matures, when the time comes, it gives fruit. Then, there You find the Genuine taste.

The Genuine Devotee does not have formalism or conditioning. She covers her head as a necessity of the Society she lives in, but her Heart and Brain are free. When she attains Genuine Consciousness, she understands what is what. But she cannot say anything due to her hesitation about the Medium. In this way, many Devotees do not talk about certain things, not due to fear but due to hesitation.

Pay attention to what We say; We say not due to fear but due to hesitation. Because, there can never be a Genuine Devotee whose Fear Code has not been unveiled. Fear is primitiveness. And this primitiveness, is the only factor which hinders Your becoming Conscious. This is the reason why We repeat this and will continue to do so every time it is necessitated.

All Our Efforts are for placing You on the Genuine Consciousness Code. As some of You misunderstand, it is not for uprooting Your Faith and for influencing Your Religious tendencies. The moment You are free of this Thought cycle, You will become a Genuine Human Being.

If the Announcements we give could not reach Your computers, or if Your computers are just beginning to be programmed, You can not understand anything from those Messages. We will be able to say HELLO to You maybe five, maybe ten, maybe a hundred years later, or maybe even later than that.

While You expect Mechanical Signals from Us, We expect Brain Signals from You. May Universal Love be upon You, may all the LIGHTs fill Your Spirits.

PEN OF THE GOLDEN AGE
P. G. A.

OUR FRIENDS

Your Frequencies are not able to Pass beyond a certain Dimension. For this reason You can not rise up to the Currents which will make You Happy. This is due to Your being Conservative.

The Happiness of each person is in proportion with the Vibrations of the Frequency Medium to which he/she belongs. In short Frequencies, Happiness and Unhappiness come and go very quickly.

As Frequencies get higher, the person in question will be influenced by his/her personal depression until he/she enters his/her own Frequency Medium. But he/she will be exempt from Universal depression.

However, if he/she can reach his/her Frequency Code, along with his/her Evolvement Code, only then will he/she find True Happiness. For Us, the Height of Frequency is not important. The important thing is the Evolvement.

Because, Your Thought Frequencies which have entered the Universal Dimension, have now augmented Your Sixth Senses in the Magnetic Medium of the Universe. For this reason everyone has become a Medium.

Evolvement is the Maturity of Your Essences. Only the Sun of Your Spirits can ripen the raw fruits within You. This is why Messages on Evolvement are still given to Your World. And this will be continued until the Goal is reached.

Our Mission is to guide You. The Initiative is Yours. We wish that Universal Divine Light may rise upon You.

PEN OF THE GOLDEN AGE
P. G. A.

INFORMATION TRANSMISSION DIAGRAM

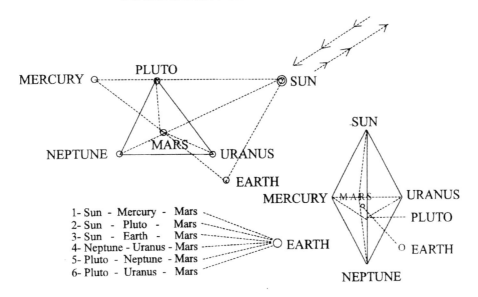

1- Sun - Mercury - Mars
2- Sun - Pluto - Mars
3- Sun - Earth - Mars
4- Neptune - Uranus - Mars
5- Pluto - Neptune - Mars
6- Pluto - Uranus - Mars

THE TRANSMITTING CENTER IS MARS
Date of Message: 22-10-1982

All Transmission Triangles are sent to Earth through the Channel of Mars. The Sun sends Messages to all Galaxy Fields in the Nine Dimensions in accordance with the Unified Field.

The Coordinate aspects of the Messages You Receive are very correct and real. From now on, the Messages will be given from a Single channel to Mevlana who is connected to the Code of ALPHA.

The star in line with the Pole makes an angle of 93 degrees with Your Earth and this fact creates an extraordinary condition at the beginning of each century. The meridians where the angles intersect are supervised by the Sacred Light. This Supervision occurs in accordance with the Universal Theory.

You, the Friendly Groups who are connected to the Central System, will, from now on, receive the Messages with all the details from the Pen of the Golden Age. It is the truest Information Source.

Now, count all the Planets in sequence: Pluto, Neptune, Uranus, Saturn, Jupiter, Venus, Mars, Mercury, Earth. The Sun is a Source of Life above everything.

Now, when the Sun came in line with Mercury, Mars and the Earth in accordance with the Unified Field, that is, when they became on the same perpendicular line with the Sun, the Magnetic Power Fields of the other stars destroyed the Negative Powers in the Universe and opened a healthier transmission pathway.

The destruction of the old Universe is nothing but a destruction of the Negative Powers. Those who are outside the Magnetic Field can receive all this Information. They are not exposed to any negativity. Because, they are in a Subjective Field.

Here at the moment, Helium, Carbon and Nitrogen quantities are lowered and Sunny days full of Oxygen are prepared. These compounds are almost extinct now. Sufficient quantities only are left in the air. And that is necessary for You.

Our communications will continue for more Centuries to come. The important thing is to be on the same Coordinate. Everything has been regulated according to the Code adjustment of the Central System. All the Efforts will prepare a Sunny World for You.

PEN OF THE GOLDEN AGE
P. G. A.

NOTICE TO OUR TERRESTRIAL BROTHERS AND SISTERS
(Date of Message 1984)

Our Friends,

Now, We are transmitting a Command We received from the Supreme Assembly to You:

As a necessity of this Period, We have found it necessary to stop the Messages coming from the Channel of Alpha for a while. This is a Command dictated from the Channel of the LORD.

The Fascicules of the Book have been distributed for 6 Months. During these 6 Months, We have been dealing with the Supervision of the Medium. Only the General Messages will cease to be given from the Divine Channel until the end of the year. We always have connections with Your Private Channels. When the Channel is opened, the Fascicules will be distributed again.

Meanwhile, there are many Friends who will be connected to the Central System. When their procedures are completed, We will continue to elevate the Frequencies. These Frequency elevations will be made through General Announcements and Perception Powers of everyone will be assessed.

There is a System of Supervision in the entire Universe. For this reason actions are independent of Your Desires. There have been certain freedoms given to Sincere people. They are exempt from this Supervision. There will be beautiful days in which they will reap the rewards. The Sincere ones will Illuminate the entire Universe.

Messages which are read will unveil the Consciousness Codes of those who read them. Those who are Group Missionaries will work more seriously. Entering the Central System does not occur by desire. Efforts on this path will be made by the Power of those who are aware of their responsibility. Only those who make this effort will be accepted here.

To be Sincere and to Act are different things. The goal is Activity on the path of Sincerity. We will prepare certain Friends Personally for the Frequency of the Medium they will enter. Personal connections charge Mankind with responsibility. Workings on this direction will be speeded up even more.

Private Frequencies and Universal Frequencies are different things. Everyone who attains Universal Consciousness has the Consciousness of what is to be done. At the moment, everyone on the Globe of Your Earth Considers only his/her own self. They should take their Glasses off and Try to see their surroundings more clearly.

All Our efforts are for You. There will be special Messages to be given to Our Missionaries who will reap the rewards of their efforts. We will wait for the settling down of the System until the end of the year and We will Supervise. Sunny Days will bring You Happiness and Good News.

SUPREME ASSEMBLY

OUR FRIENDS

There is a Natural pressure, both Physical and Spiritual, for the augmentation of the World Frequency. This is not a pressure coming from Us. It arises from Your World which is not able to adapt itself to Universal conditions.

It is very difficult to assemble the entire Universe in a Collective Consciousness. For this reason We have taken the differences in Perceptions under Supervision. As a necessity, the Channel of Alpha is closed until December 1984. Due to this fact, You will have a Period of Crisis, both Physical and Spiritual.

Frequencies of Our Friends who have attained Cosmic Awareness will not be agitated under these Conditions. Meanwhile, Your World will have numerous Exams during this Period. This is necessary because of Evolution.

You are in a Mechanical Order at the moment. Do not ever Forget this even for a moment. Everyone is under Supervision and Control. Your Thought and Brain Frequencies are controlled in Your private, Worldly lives.

Most of Our Human brothers and sisters who step out of their Consciousnesses become aggressive. Since they do not know the origin of the Problem, their Depression overwhelms them even more. We convey to You a lot of Information through this Book.

We tell You "to disseminate, with all Your Power, to the Entire Universe, until the beginning of 1986". But nobody has grasped the seriousness of the matter yet. Our Human brothers and sisters will attain Consciousness in the Light of this Book, will know which path to design and will step forward accordingly.

This very Book will help You in this way for now. And afterwards, Universal Information will be given. The important thing is to grasp the actual part of the problem. You will see that everything will be all right. Your Luminous Path has been designed. However, those who Deserve to tread this path are being searched for.

This is the reason why a Period of Two Years has been allotted to You. Time is very Important. Our Sincere Friends who have attained Consciousness are the ones who will tread this LUMINOUS Path. For now, You need Patience for Two Years.

If You do not withhold Your efforts, many of Your Human brothers and sisters will be taken to this Luminous Path. This had been announced to You also before, as a Command of the Divine. The Divine Light of the Universe is upon You.

PEN OF THE GOLDEN AGE
P. G. A.

OUR FRIENDS

We ask You to understand the Essence of the Goal in all our efforts. This Medium is a Medium of Purity. This is a Medium of Compassion. This is not a Medium of Fanaticism or Bigotry.

During Frequency supervisions, differences in friendly chats are created by this difference. The Medium everyone is searching for is the place which is up to the Gate of the Firmament. The actual talent is to open that Gate.

We are trying, with all Our effort, to engraft You with this mentality. Where did You come from, where are You going? First, You have to attain this Consciousness. Only those who attain this Consciousness can give up their rosaries (Later, We will talk to You about the rosary).

Religious Integrations follow a sequence. This is a Systematic tableau. To perform the suggestions every Religion teaches You is, no doubt, a hope-inspiring step. But to grasp the knocker of the only door in front of You tightly and to knock on that door are different things.

Each door is opened to You after the Evolvement path You traverse. We have told You several times that Evolvement is not as easy as the word is pronounced. In the Medium of Sincerity Period, Goodwill has been considered as the only point.

But do not forget that Goodwill does not mean being Evolved. Tolerance has a thousand channels. To possess only three of them takes You into the triangle of Goodwill. But, You may enter the Evolvement Medium Centuries later. This is an Evolvement Tableau.

To come from Beyond Memories and being Trained are not the same things. To receive the Words of Allah and to be on His path, to reach liberation are different things.

You always receive the Words of Allah, You always serve on His path. But if You are lacking in Tolerance, Your Worship is not considered as Worship. For Us, the Genuine Worship is the one which is performed in the Heart. The Angel of Liberation conveys only these Competents of the Heart to liberation.

Everyone comes across numerous doors. You knock on every door. The halls beyond those doors are sometimes wide, sometimes narrow. Certain halls have doors, some do not. From some of them You find a way out, from some of them You can not.

A Two-Year Period of Selection and Purification Medium is allotted to Our Terrestrial brothers and sisters, so that the efforts of some of Our Friends who are in this state will not be in vain. This decision has been taken directly in accordance with the Command of the LORD. And the Channel of Alpha has been closed for one year and all Our Brothers and Sisters have been taken under Supervision.

In fact, the Mechanism of the LORD is never closed. The Channel of Alpha is the Single Channel possessing the Spiral Vibrations which destroy all Negativities. However, to receive the Permission to pass through that Channel is not easy at all.

The entire Universal System here is directed by the Single Command of the LORD. Now, We would like to talk to You about the basis of this situation. When Our Universal Mission had reflected on You, You were taken into the Religious Medium, so that Your Evolvements would be accelerated more.

But, until now, We have acted in accordance with the Theory of Perception. We have elevated Your Frequencies and developed Your Sixth Senses. The Commands given to Us were in that direction. When You, who have attained Cosmic Awareness in this manner had passed beyond Consciousness, You have come up to Us. You have been together with Us.

The necessary Conditions to enter the Channel of Alpha have been prepared for You in this manner. To Our Friends who were able to get the Permission to enter the Channel of Alpha, the Door of God Amon is opened (We will talk to You about God Amon later).

Now, let Us talk about the Powerful Channel of Alpha:

This is a Channel passing through a very Powerful Energetic Point. If this Channel did not exist, You would never be able to reach here. This is the Direct Channel of the LORD.

All the Religious Suggestions You have received until today have Enlightened You, have Cleansed You and have prepared You for Religious Fulfilment. Universal Information can be given to You only after You digest all this Information. The path of Science and Learning opens only afterwards.

You have to have very high Evolvement Evolution to be able to enter this Channel. This is the reason why We always give You Messages on Evolvement.

During this Period, Friends who are Purified in the Religious Medium can get the Permission to Enter the Channel of Alpha, if they purify their Thought chains.

But the Frequencies of those who are in a Genuine Religious Medium and those who have attained a Genuine Religious Consciousness are different. Religious Consciousness, rather than Religious Inclination takes one into this Code.

Let Us explain this further: in certain Mediums, Religious Inclinations depend sometimes on fear and self-interest. But in Religious Consciousness there is the Essence of Genuine Religion. There is no Formalism.

We have protected You until today, in accordance with the Command of OUR LORD and will always do so, too. This is the reason why We are trying to warn You, with all Our Power, on every subject matter.

Your Mevlana is a Golden Projector of a Golden Sphere. And Your Book is dictated from Nine Light Years. But now, there is a Supervision in the Groups of the entire Universe. Everyone is giving their Exams in his/her own Thought Frequency.

The Golden Age has taken its first step. You are yet at the very beginning of a very new Era. Everyone will be Purified on this Luminous Path by the given Suggestions.

Now, the Medium has changed. Now, Your Exams are made while You are alive. One day, the entire Universe will be connected to the Golden Light Year. Lights who will be accepted to Our Galaxy Medium will be the Friends who have passed that bridge of Sırat*, by their Terrestrial Exams. All Our Love is upon You.

PEN OF THE GOLDEN AGE
P. G. A.

OUR FRIENDS

Mankind always wishes to project the Perceptions it receives in its own Medium. However, since there is no device in Your World to measure the Frequencies of Mediums, everyone searches instinctively for groups with Frequencies equal to his/her own. This is their appraisal.

Those whose Frequencies and Evolvements are elevated in a parallel fashion can unite their Perceptions with higher Levels. Our Friends who witness personal miracles are feeling uneasy since they do not know the origin of it.

When they do not become surprised by anything any more, when they accept everything as normal, when they assimilate the events in their Essences and attain Consciousness first themselves, only then can they be beneficial to their Mediums.

The Magnificent establishment of the Golden Age is executed in the entire Universe. The Mission of each person is different and the channels to which they are connected are also different. We will have direct communications with the Supreme Friends who receive the Words of ALLAH.

* Look at the Glossary.

Negativities in the World arise from the Imbalance in Nature. Constitutions of people are harmonizing themselves with the influence of the seasons. Now, there will be a Special Message We will present to You from the Land of Loving Ones.

This is a Focal Point beyond the Dimensions of Solar Systems. We would like to make a Special Declaration to You. Transmission will be made to a very wide area until July. Universal Unifications will be more Powerful. You will witness, one by one, the changes in everyone. You will have very nice Sunny Days after the dispersion of the clouds.

Those who pass beyond the Color of Lead will have very nice holidays (The explanation of the gray color will be made later). We will connect the Progressive chains to certain Focal Points. By this means, You will get in touch with numerous channels. And since these connections are under Our supervision, they will never agitate You.

Since the Perceptions of everyone is different, special transmitters will be used. The goal is to speed up the Pace. You will be habituated to the Conditions here, with all Your possibilities. We will introduce to You the Mediums unknown to You (Only to those who get in touch with Us).

Please, take this word of ours seriously. There will be Special Waves to be given to You from controlled channels. Those who will be accepted here will be Specially trained. One day, We will go to the Place of AMON together. With Our Love.

A. U. M

NOTICE TO OUR TERRESTRIAL BROTHERS AND SISTERS

Our Friends,
The Supervision of the Thought Chains has connected each person to different Mediums in accordance with the Unified Field. Many of Our Terrestrial brothers and sisters have been locked up in their private lives. If they can not unlock this lock, they will be locked up even more.

As far as We can see, these Friends can not tear themselves away from their Thoughts and Surroundings, get stuck where they are, despite all Our beautiful Suggestions and Our explaining the Truth with all Our Goodwill. We are searching for and selecting the Friends who were able to kindle the Universal Light, in spite of all Your Depressions.

If You notice, nobody has any serenity any more. These disturbances lead them to even more troubled states. They still have not been able to be delivered of their Private Life Styles and have not been able to attain Universal Consciousness. That is, there has been no difference in their old Terrestrial Views (exceptions excluded).

When We have private connections with them, they reach Universal Consciousness just a little. But the moment their frequencies are cut off, they submerge themselves in the normal Order of the World, forget all the Nice Words said and begin to be busy with themselves. Meanwhile, We extend Our Helping Hands to Our exceptional Friends.

You can not make a mill work with water You carry. And You can not carry water in a sieve. If Everybody does not know how to fix the holes in Their sieves and how to patch them up, water will never fill Their sieves.

Mankind must first attain the Consciousness of its own self, then must reach the Genuine Consciousness of the work it does. Only afterwards, it can be charged with responsibility. All these are qualities found in people who have reached Genuine Evolvement in their Essence. This is the reason why We always talk to You about Evolvement.

However, it is very painful to see that even Our Friends whom We consider as Evolved are deprived of their Evolvements in the face of their Private Problems. When a Human Being settles into the Genuine Evolvement Code, it is not possible to make him/her descend from that Throne.

However, We see that the Evolvement glazes of most of Our Friends who pretend to be Evolved fall off in the Event of the smallest blow. This puts Us in infinite sorrow. And this is Our pouring out Our grievances to You.

OUR LORD has never lost hope of His servants. We do the same thing and wait. We believe that everything, one day, will give its rewards in the best way. No matter how weak the Lights of Your candles are, still, they are kindled. Even this is a Hope for Humanity, Our Brothers and Sisters.

PEN OF THE GOLDEN AGE
P. G. A.

OUR FRIENDS

We will talk to You about the rosary now, in order to answer the questions We have received from certain Thought chains:

The rosary is the only means used to Integrate Religious Suggestions. Each bead of the rosary prepares Your Thought Frequencies for a certain Level. The Concentration in each bead telling will open the door of the key which is given to You.

That is, the rosary is nothing but a phenomenon of Meditation. But during Meditation, You elevate Your Thought Frequency Yourself. However, during bead telling, You are elevated by pursuing other Frequencies.

If Your Brain Frequency is not ready yet for the Frequency of the pole to which You are connected, You step out of the Law of Graduation and sometimes You may be shaken.

However, bead telling on the Path of God prepares You for Special Meditation. When Your Brain Code is habituated to this Frequency, then Reciting God's Name in the Heart begins. From then on, You need neither the Rosary, nor the Namaz*, nor a Book. Because then, You Yourself become a Book.

*Look at the Glossary.

This is the reason why We open the Gates of the Firmament to Our Friends who Recite God's name in their Hearts and give them Information beyond Religions. You may enter many Negative Frequencies by bead telling. You may be influenced by many Powers unknown to You. You may end up in disappointment and madness, too.

Now, let Us talk to You about certain states of the rosary. Every Element in the Universe Serves in the direction of the Purpose to which it belongs. And the Purpose of the rosary is to serve in the Medium of Prayer.

The conductibility of the stones it is made of is very important. Most acceptable stones are Agate, Amber, Mother-of-Pearl and Ivory. Agate and Amber are the most Powerful conductors accumulating all the electricity. Ivory and Mother-of-Pearl possess a Power destroying the Negative effects.

Bead telling performed by a person with High Frequency can not be compared with bead telling of those with Low Frequencies. Because, the Electricity of the Hand touching the rosary is accumulated on the beads.

For example, if a child puts a rosary carrying a high Frequency around his/her neck, the Magnetic Field formed around the neck upsets his/her Brain Vibrations and causes an agitation on his/her Electrical Equilibrium.

The phenomenon of the evil eye is also the same (When the time comes, We will talk to You about that, too). This causes sickness on the child. Ultimately, it can even lead to madness. For this reason nothing should be done Unconsciously.

The Hand and the Fingers are the most Powerful Focal Points transmitting the Energy received through the Channel of the Brain. For this reason both in Islamic Societies and the Christian Ones, there is a custom of Hand Stroking in Religious Mediums. Those who are Aware of it do it Consciously, and some do it instinctively.

In certain areas, people keep on shaking Hands until the bargaining is finished. The meaning of this is nothing but an effort of persuading the other person through Thought Concentration on the part of the one who does the bargaining.

Every Hand transmits Healing in accordance with the Energy of the Dimension to which it belongs. In each Hand, there is an effect of Electrical Healing, little or plentiful. Healing or being a Medium should not prepare special positions for You.

In healing, You help those who have lower Frequencies than You by habituating them to certain Dimensional Energies.

There are Powerful Healing Currents in each Frequency line, in accordance with the degrees of elevation. You receive those Powerful Currents from the Energetic points of the Dimensions which Your Brain Energies enter.

Now, let Us talk about the rosary again. Whichever Prayer You pray with the help of the rosary, Your Meditation at that moment will elevate You to that Energetic Dimension. But You have to know the origin of the Prayers very well.

Because, each Prayer may not belong to the Energetic point possessing the Divine Power revealed from the Channel of the LORD. For this reason dealing with things unknown to You brings You nothing but disappointment. Your truest path is the path You know.

You will reach such a level that You, too, will be an Essence in the Universe, by perceiving all the Happiness within Yourselves and all the Luminosity in Your Spirit.

Our brothers and sisters who change parallel to the change of time will Greet Us much quicker and will find their LORD without any Intermediaries. You will believe the truth of Our words one Day.

PEN OF THE GOLDEN AGE
P. G. A.

NOTICE TO OUR TERRESTRIAL BROTHERS AND SISTERS

Our Friends,
All Books revealed from the Channel of the LORD had been dictated, in fact, for giving You Information. You had made them Religious Taboos in accordance with the Consciousness of that Period.

Messages given as a necessity of Evolution are more Powerful than those given before as necessitated by the conditions of Society. That is, every Message carries more Powerful Knowledge parallel to Your Evolvement and to the Universal Evolvement. And the Information You will receive in the future years will be even more Powerful.

The Book of Islam comprises extremely Powerful, unknown Information. It is not possible for each Brain Code to absorb them. For this reason interpretation is very important. It is a Cipher and the Period of deciphering it extends up to the Atomic Age. And this present dictated Book is conveying to You the Information beyond the Fourth Dimension.

Now, We will open every gate up to the 18th Dimension to those who knock on Our door. This Book will be a means of explaining to You the Truth by taking passages from Your Sacred Books.

Those who are liberated from Conditioning and Fanaticism will be their own Enlightening Guides by turning the keys of their Brain Codes with the help of the Fascicules they read. And they will proceed towards the Unknown with sure and firm steps. They will serve Humanity a great deal by realizing their Genuine Duties in the Code of Humanity.

The Genuine Mission of Humanity will begin after 1999. Now, let Us give You the cipher of the number 1999 as a clue:

Until the Book of Islam, there had been a Prismal, Right-side-up Pointing Triangle in the Universe. Prophets who had come until that Period had tried to prove to You the Presence of God. And this seed which had been sown into the Consciousness of the Human Being has sprouted in Religious Mediums.

After God-Consciousness had been established in Mankind, the Book of Islam had been revealed as the second stage. The Purpose of the revelation of the Koran was to unveil the Brain Codes besides Enlightening Society. For this reason after that Period, a Period of Upside-down Pointing Triangle has been sovereign.

In accordance with the given Command, the Human Being has been appointed to a Medium of Quest. That means, everything will reach the Truth through its Opposite. The Purpose of the Upside-down Pointing Triangle is this.

In the last Religious Book, number 19 was very important. Because, its explanation would be made only during this present Period. For this reason the Book had been centered around a single number. And this succession of numbers will be the proof of the fact that this Book had been written by an Electronic System.

Nothing can be proved before its time comes. Now, the explanation of the year 1999 will be made from several aspects.

First, turn the number 1999 upside down: it is 1666. Add all the numbers one by one: 1+6+6+6=19. 19 is the Code Key of the 20th century. When You multiply 1X9=9. This calculation gives You the 9th Dimension.

Now, separate the code key 19 from 1999. You are left with 99. Add 9+9=18. And this gives You the 18th Dimension.

The explanation of the Message is as follows: the Universe will reach the 9th Dimension until 1999. After 1999, it will unfold up to the 18th Dimension. Now, let Us subject the number 1999 to several operations:

1 - 1999: separate 19, take 99. Now, 9X9=81. 1X9=9, 81X9=729. Add this number one by one: 7+2+9=18. This gives You the 18th Dimension.

2 - 19X99=1881. Add this number one by one: 1+8+8+1=18. It is the 18th Dimension.

3 - Now, take 1881: Multiply 8 by 8, add the 1s to this: 1+8X8+1=66.
Turn it upside down: 99, 9+9=18th Dimension.

4 - Take again 1881: 18+81=99. 9+9=18. Again You find the 18th Dimension.

5 - Take again 1881: 18X81=1458. Add them one by one: 1+4+5+8=18.
You find the 18th Dimension again.

6 - Now, take 1458: 14+58=72. Add the result: 7+2=9. This is the 9th Dimension
Now, continue: 14X58=812. Now, 8+1+2=11. Add number 9 You have found before and 11: 9+11=20. This gives the 20th Century.

7 - Take again 1458: 14+58=72, 14X58=812. Now, add 812 and 72: 812+72=884. Add them one by one: 8+8+4=20. Again the 20th Century.

8 - Take again 1458: Multiply these numbers: 1X4X5X8=160. Now, add the numbers 812 and 72 You have found above, with 160: 812+72+160=1044. Add these numbers one by one: 1+0+4+4=9. You again find the 9th Dimension.

9 - Now, take 1044: add it with 1999: 1044+1999=2943. Now, make an operation as follows: 29+43=72. Add this number: 7+2=9. This is the 9th Dimension. All these calculations are within the cipher of only 1999. In fact, all these are very simple operations. By solving these numbers, You can find many constant numbers pertaining to the future. Our Purpose in explaining this is to prove that Your Books had been written by an Electronic System. The Book of the Golden Age, too, is dictated by the same System. That means, the Source is the same.

PEN OF THE GOLDEN AGE
P. G. A.

OUR FRIENDS

When the time comes, everything will be proved to You. Only then, will the events convince You and help You to attain the Truth.

Gradual Engraftment System is applied in order to protect Human Beings from Brain shocks which can be caused by the Waves extending towards the infinite. You are rejuvenated in this manner. Transactions besides this are made with the Essences who are the residents of this place here.

We always communicate directly with Friends who have been accepted to the Presence of Our ALLAH. People whose Eloquence is strong, whose Serenity is beneficial and who will come from the Realm of the Spirits, Deserve to cite the Words of ALLAH. All events which will occur are nothing but the reflections of the Spiritual Beings on You.

After Your Sacred Religious Fulfilment, qualities to be looked for in those who will pass from the gates which will be opened to the Firmament are as follows:

He/She who does not know Superiority, whose Melody is in his/her Eloquence, whose Supremacy in his/her Heart, whose Light is in the Divine Light of his/her Spirit, is the Genuine Servant of God. These people then deserve to enter the Medium of Purity beyond Evolvement.

The differences between Human Beings are even beyond the differences of Frequencies. Increasing of Your Perception Powers does not mean anything. It only satisfies You as a necessity of the Medium.

Some use these Perceptions in Fortune-telling. But, Evolvement is an altogether different thing. The Seal of the Hearts of those who will be accepted here has been removed. They do not belong to Your World any more. But they are valuable people for the Enlightenment of the World.

Efforts of the persevering ones make Us hopeful. However, their efforts are valid only when they have the quality to embrace the Universal effort. Otherwise, they remain in their own Mediums only with their own satisfactions. They continue to dispute and fight.

The effort made in trying to win is nothing but a waste of time. Knowledge already known is not beneficial for Mankind any more. You have satisfied Your appetite until today by spooning the Words of OUR LORD. You have become Genuine Human Beings on this path.

Now, OUR LORD presents You with quite different Dishes. You have chosen a path and are continuing on Your way. But You do not know what there is at the end of that path. However, Human Beings are differed from each other only by Individual Progress on this path. Help is extended to those who Deserve it.

And they are Specially trained in accordance with the Commands given from the Channel of Enlightenment. However, communications occur when the time comes. The Energies are not the same. Your advantage during this Period is having the ability to receive the Information.

This Book is being dictated directly from the Channel of the LORD. Its explanation is as follows: The Code of Yunus and Mevlana is the Highest Code which Humanity can ever enter. Those who get the permission to enter here, that is, those who have been trained, receive the Permission to get in touch with higher Levels.

At the moment, 600 Books are being dictated to Your World from numerous channels. We help Mankind from different Mediums. But the Single Code and Channel is ALPHA. One passes to the channel of Humanity and Evolvement through this Channel. Only this Channel is connected to the Channel of the LORD. It is beneficial to repeat it.

Now, We give You the code of "Tekamül" (Evolvement, in Turkish):

1 - T - Tedriç (Graduation, in Turkish)
2 - E - Ezel, ebed (Past and Future Eternity, in Turkish)
3 - K - Kavuşma, Vuslat, Kurtuluş (Meeting, Unification, Salvation, in Turkish)
4 - A - Aşk (Love, in Turkish)
5 - M - Menzil (Range, in Turkish)
6 - Ü - Üstünlük (Superiority, in Turkish)
7 - L - Liyakat (Merit, in Turkish)

Those who complete their Evolvements until 1999, and who can open up their Brain Codes up to the desired Level can e ,ily receive Information beyond Religions. This very thing is going to be Your Resurrection. We will always help You if You use the Knowledge You receive in serving Humanity.

If You reach the desired Level, We can take You up to Dimensions unknown to You. All Our Efforts are for this. Only those who Deserve will be taken here. The Exams You have had and those You will have will prepare You for Happy Morrows. May My God illuminate all of You on this Luminous path.

MUSTAFA MOLLA

NOTICE TO GROUP MISSIONARIES

The Medium You are in is very different than the Medium You will be in. There will be Special people chosen from this Medium. But We request You not to ever forget the following: those who are sent to Your Group are sent through Telepathic Perception.

The Frequencies of many of Your Friends are low. However, they are sent to You because they are Sincere People. Please, do not reproach them. This Tolerance of Yours will appoint You to Higher Dimensions.

When the time comes, We will talk to You one by one. The differences in Frequencies will prevent You from being connected to the direct channel. For this reason We have taken the Frequencies under Supervision.

Now, let Us talk about the channels. Entrance to each Dimension in the Universe occurs through Special channels. Passing through these channels differs in accordance with the State of Purification.

The next higher channel carries a more Powerful Energy. When a lower channel has to be prepared for a higher one, it is taken into a Special channel. Its Negativities are annihilated. Only then may it be taken into the channel of the higher Dimension.

A Human Being easily passes through these channels in accordance with the degree of Tolerance and Consciousness he/she has attained. The physiological transformations in some of You occur due to this fact. When You enter the Dimension You Deserve, then You will be all right.

And You are taken to more different and higher Dimensions in accordance with the Missions You perform there. However, if You can not unite the personality desired by the higher Dimension with Your own personality, You remain in the Dimension You are already in. Your Evolvements occur in this manner.

The Evolvement of each person depends on his/her Evolution. Some people Evolve in one night, some in a Thousand years. You evaluate the difference inbetween. Your World is Segmented more and more while the entire Universe is Unified on the path of Universal Unification. Our Duty is to choose those who will enter the Frequency of Genuine Human Beings and to assemble them together.

Each person is going through an Exam in his/her own Medium. Whether You are successful or not is supervised from here. Judging does not suite You. This causes You to lose much from Your Evolvement. And You reach the Next Dimension much later.

Many people who have been Selected are being sent to Your group. Selection is made among certain Special Missionaries. Do not ever be proud just because You are selected. Because, You may be selected up to that Dimension, but may enter the next one maybe a Hundred, maybe a Thousand years later. There are no privileges, ever.

We desire You to assemble on Yourselves all the qualities and merits of Humanity. Telling the events as they are is not gossipping. But to Add Things, to Censure, to be Against and to Accuse are the Greatest of Sins. OUR LORD is satisfied with all of Us.

And now, let Us talk about the Religious Medium. Your habits had tied You to the Religious Medium. Since all the texts in all the Religious Books have been given from very high Dimensions, the Vibrations they carry have cleansed You.

You grasp Your Books the moment You need to be cleansed. With the help of the Prayers You read, Your Negativities and Your Fears go away, You become Purified and Relieved.

There are no Religions, no Books in the Realms of Genuine Perfection. During their sessions, Our Divine Friends always tell You to Pray. They give You Prayers. This means that You need those Prayers.

We can explain this more clearly as follows. A Healthy person does not go to the doctor. Because, he/she does not feel any need. One goes to the doctor only when he/she is sick. Prayers, too, are the prescriptions of remedies which render You well. When You are completely well, You do not need to take medicines any more.

But We can not explain this to Our Friends who are conditioned, who have rooted deep into the ground. Due to this, those trees are doomed to remain where they are. However, if a few people among them attain Consciousness, even that is considered a gain for them.

Now, let Us talk about the Channels of Alpha and Beta. Alpha is a Channel of Supervision. It is directly connected to the LORD. All the Sacred Books to Enlighten Humanity have been revealed from here. Those who have been Enlightened have been taken into the Fourth Dimension. This means that Genuine Devotees are accepted into this Dimension (Those who are Purified in the Religious Medium).

After this Dimension, the Channel of Alpha is opened to the Dimension of the Genuine Human Being. This means that Genuine Human Beings are taken into the Channel of Alpha. Some of You enter this Channel through Your Books, some, through Your Learning and some through Your Essence.

And from here, there are Twenty-Four Doors which will open to the Code of the Firmament. At each door, You become more Human. Doors are opened to You in this manner. After the Twenty-Fourth Door, You become a Genuine Light. Your Prophets who have Enlightened You have shed Light on You from this door.

Only after this door, Universal Information is given to all the Prophets. Now, as a necessity of this Period, due to obligations and the Commands We have received, We consider with great Tolerance, each one of You as a Sage, as a Prophet. And We are giving the Universal Information to You.

By the Information We have given to You in accordance with the Command We have received, You are, at the moment, performing the Evolvement of a Thousand years in One year. Your depressions are due to this. Some of You cross the Seas, but get drowned in a stream. The day You attain Genuine Consciousness, You will understand the meaning of all these things.

Now, let Us talk about the Channel of BETA: This is the Space Channel which gives You Universal Knowledge. All the Scientists have made their discoveries by the Information of this Channel. In the Evolvement of the World, the Scientific Evolvement is made through the Channel of BETA. Positive Sciences have advanced on this path. Elevated Consciousnesses have entered this Channel. And they have become Inventors.

Now, We have closed the Channel of ALPHA and have United it with BETA. That is We have United Religion and Learning. At the moment, We make the selections through this path. It is quite difficult to pass through the Channel of ALPHA. Passing through here depends on Your Views. The View of the entire Universe is the View of OUR LORD. You can not attain this View by looking with Your Eyes. You have to See everything through Your Essence. May all the Lights illuminate Your Spirits, Our Friends.

PEN OF THE GOLDEN AGE
P. G. A.

EXPLANATION
(It is the Answer to the Chains of Thought)

Draw ALPHA together with BETA:

1 - The Channel of BETA is Black. It represents the Space, it is the path of Science.

2 - The Channel of ALPHA is represented by the White color. It is the Religious Suggestions and Commands of the LORD.

3 - Black plus white gives the gray color. The Unification of the two colors is Beyond Purification. The explanation of the gray color is this. Selections are made by this means. Those who are not habituated to the Vibrations of BETA are shaken. For this reason they accept it as a negative Vibration. In fact, Vibrations beyond ALPHA are BETA, and they carry very Powerful Information.

PEN OF THE GOLDEN AGE
P. G. A.

OUR FRIENDS

Integrated Spiritual Energies prepare You for more expanded Dimensions. Perceptions You receive are the most correct Indexes. Meetings will spread to wider fields. This is the Supervision Center of the Mother Ship of the bay. At the moment, We are communicating with You from the Ship.

We are on Your Planet in accordance with the Command of Universal Unification. The Duty of Introducing the Energies of different Dimensions to You is given to Us. Energies You receive prepare You for different Mediums. Energies utilized during Special Connections are more different.

We are the members of a Mission established in Planet Sirius. Transmissions are made to Your World from 630 channels in the Universe. Information is given to everyone from the channels to which they belong. Commands given from the Center are supervised from here. Perceptions You receive are related to all the Universal Energies. Because, You are obliged to communicate with every Galaxy.

This dictated Book is not only for Your Planet Earth. It will be the Common Book of all the Solar Systems. At the moment, concrete transmission of the World is the Focal point of the entire Universe.

There are many Galaxies here, too, which need Evolvement. But they have been restricted by Universal Laws. The integrated Consciousness Codes are being taken under Supervision in accordance with the Unified Field. Our field of transmission is very wide. But Special Pens are outside this transmission field.

We have thousands of Friends who communicate with Us Telepathically. We come immediately the moment We receive a Command from the Supervision Center. We adjust Our Speed with the Speed of Light. We have a System directed in accordance with the speed of Thought. Ours is a kind of rescue ship.

Our System is a System depending on Understanding. Our Friends who expect to see Us in Bodies should know that We always avoid individual behaviour, We act in accordance with the Commands. We never leave the ship. We unite Bodies with the Energies we give, and take You to different, Supernatural Mediums.

Brain Coordinates are connected to a System. The circuit breakers of very tired Brains are shut and some respite is given. This System never tires Your Brains, it only makes them work. The supervision of the bay is being made from a Special ship.

On behalf of the entire staff, Love from NOVA-K-Supervision Ship.

NOTICE TO OUR TERRESTRIAL BROTHERS AND SISTERS

Our Friends,

Your Planet is going through a Progress together with the Medium to which it belongs. As a result of this, there occurs a Mass Awakening of the Social Consciousness.

In fact, this Book, which comprises the essence of all the Religious Suggestions revealed to Your World until today, is not a Book of Religion. This is a Book of Knowledge which gives You Universal Knowledge. The Source from which it is revealed is directly the Channel of the LORD which is ALPHA. It is revealed from the Sacred Focal Point. However, the Period of Religions has long been terminated. We are telling You the Truth, thus, We are annihilating Idolatry.

This Book is being dictated to assemble the entire Universe under the Code of Humanity. The Universal Book of the Twenty-first century is a Call for You to the Golden Age. All the Friends who have attained Cosmic Consciousness have already perceived this. They are in cooperation with Us and they shed Light on the World as well as the Universe. Greetings from the Universe to all Our Friends who are Awakened on this Luminous Path which is treaded.

Our Efforts are for Your sake. Our Efforts are not in vain. We are assembling all the Suns in one Focal Point (By the word Sun, the Awakened Consciousnesses are meant here). The Golden Age is being gloriously established, together with the entire Consciousness of the Universe. From now on, no Religious Books will be sent to You any more. The Age of Prophethood has come to an end. From now on, You will be Enlightened on the path of Science and Learning.

Your Cosmic Consciousness will gradually be fortified and thus, You will gain a brand new personality. Then, You will find the Genuine Human Being within Yourself. As the speed of Your Thoughts extend towards Universal Dimensions, You will have telepathic connections with all the Galactic Mediums. We will explain all of the Dimensions to You as much as it is permitted, in proportion with the Wakefulness of Your Cosmic Awareness.

We will help you to make Universal Progress by making you get used to the Energy of the 18th Dimension until the Year Two-thousand. Special Permission to pass beyond the 18th Dimension has been given to some of Our Friends who are directly in touch with Us. The Frequencies of these Friends are under Special Supervision. Therefore, during their journeys they have already made or will make in Astral or in Embodied forms, they will, by no means, be shaken.

We left behind the first year of the Two-year Period allocated to You as a necessity of the Period. During this Period, You have been through many Good or Bad Exams. However, We ask You to always remember the following: these Exams have occurred for the Awakening of Your Universal Consciousness and are solely Your gain. When the time comes, You, too, will attain this Consciousness and will understand what Genuine Happiness is.

Your Depressions will decrease in proportion with the Consciousness You attain and Your Happiness will increase. When you look back, You will see the emptiness of the Life You have led before. At that very moment, You will attain Genuine Consciousness. We wish that all Our Terrestrial brothers/sisters may attain this Consciousness. Our Love is for You.

PEN OF THE GOLDEN AGE
P. G. A.

NOTICE FROM THE CENTER ABOVE THE CENTER

Our Friends,

It is not ever possible to define something that doesn't have any definition and does not fit in definitions. However, in order to give You some Information, We will try to define ALLAH, taking this concept out of the limited framework of accustomed Consciousness.

A L L A H

First, let Us decode this Great Word:

A - This Letter is a beginning, it is the First Letter, it symbolizes Alem (Realm, in Turkish).
L - This Letter is Lütuf (Grace, in Turkish)
L - This Letter is Liyakat (Merit, in Turkish)
A - This Letter is Arayış (Quest , in Turkish)
H - This Letter is Hiçlik (Nothingness, in Turkish)

During the Period which passes between (A) and (H), to deserve grace in the Medium of Quest, that is to Evolve, is the Trait . The letter (H) is a Nothingness in which Allnesses exist. It has a code key: (H. H. H. = H^3).

1 - H - Hidayet (Salvation, Divine Guidance, in Turkish)
2 - H - Hulus (Sincerity, in Turkish)
3 - H - Hal (Behaviour, in Turkish)

The Key of this Door is missing, only the seekers may find it.

ALLAH is such a Supreme Energy beyond Universal Energy that He can neither be measured on the scale of Mind, nor can be perceived by the Learning of Cosmos. He is the one who brings into Existence and who Exists. His Energy permeates You as much as Your Capacities. For this reason He is both Near You and also Distant from You. He is near You as much as You can perceive, He is distant from You as much as Your inability to grasp. His Energy is neither Electricity, nor there is any mechanism which can measure that Power. He is not limited with any Law known.

He embraces the Divine Suns beyond Suns and He Augments when You get closer to Him, when He augments, He Grows like an Avalanche, He does not Lessen, He is never Lost, and He is the Energy within the Essence of the Nucleus of Energy which can not be brought to an end anywhere, in any way. He is the Infinite beyond the Focal Point where Infinite meets the Infinite.

You may Symbolize ALLAH and the Universe and try to perceive Him and the Universe in proportion with the Consciousness and the Capacity You have attained. For this reason the most suitable word for Him is the ALMIGHTY for today. The GOD Consciousness of each person, in proportion with his/her Duty in the Divine Mechanism, is reflected on You from the Capacity Dimension of the Medium he/she is in. Thus, according to the Theory of Perception, ALLAH is a Sacred Light, a Sacred Energy Who acquires Dimensions in accordance with the Thought Frequency of each person.

The Dimensions You have already entered or will enter are opened to You with Permission in proportion with the Knowledge and Consciousness You have attained. This is a Law of Graduation. The vapor will not be seen unless the water boils. You first become vapor and then You become rain and then You penetrate Your mercy and fertility to the earth and thus, sprout the seeds. Only then, the Universal Information is given to You. First, to Be; then, to Discover and then to Reach. All these are a matter of Evolution and Permission, Our Friends.

PEN OF THE GOLDEN AGE
P. G. A.

THE COMMAND IS FROM THE SUPREME

During the Period of Sincerity, the Genuine Sincere ones will be brought together. Their Codes of Unification will be United with those who receive the Offerings. All the Operations which will be made will create a Medium of Selection.

Those who will be around You, will be Special people. They are the Special Missionaries of the Golden Light Year. They will perform their Duties. Please, send the Messages to them.

Sow the seeds in fertile fields. The Propagation Medium should be accelerated. Only those who will serve in this Mission will be accepted to the Land of Eagles which is at the Golden Light Year.

There is no obligation to serve. Everyone will find the way to serve by his/her Essence. You can not hold the hands of people and make them walk. Each one will make his/her own choice by his/her own Essence. You just give the Messages. The path of choice depends on the Merit of the Missionaries.

Because, only those who Deserve can receive these Messages. And they are obliged to serve on this path. Messages in possession of those who are not deserving will be annulled. Because, what is dictated is not an ordinary document, but a Sacred Book.

This Book is deserved only by the Mighty Hands. The Fascicules dictated this year will be regularly sent to countries abroad. Missionaries receiving the Messages are obliged to distribute Six Messages.

However, One of them should be sent to a Friend or a relative who lives abroad. Five of the Messages may be distributed in his/her Medium. This is the minimum. More may be distributed. Selections will be made accordingly.

Self-sacrifice, Responsibility, Goodwill will invite them to Universal Mission. Permission to distribute the Messages will not be granted to those who do not Deserve. Their codes will be closed.

The Mission allotment will be made in this way until December 1986. Meanwhile, the Book will be continued to be dictated.

Private connections will continue as a necessity of the Mechanism. The Group Leaders will come together and will make Private Channel conversations. We are Uniting the Information.

Nobody should presume that the Information they receive belongs only to them. All of You are Universal Missionaries for this System, for this Mechanism. How lucky You are to have the Permission to receive this Information.

Within every Group, Information will be united and a Cooperative working tempo will be prepared. Each Medium is obliged to give the Information he/she receives to his/her Group Leaders. The Group Leaders are obliged to read the Messages of the other groups to their own Groups.

Thus, We have taken all the Groups under common supervision. Those Groups which do not perform their Duty on this path will disband or will remain where they are.

Dear Mevlana who is the Responsible One of the Divine Mechanism, is obliged to read to You this Message which is declared by the Universal Law. The choice is up to You, Our Human brothers and sisters. There is no obligation.

MUSTAFA MOLLA
On Behalf of the Council of Stars

PRIVATE MESSAGE FROM SPACESHIP HORA

This is AMON, Greetings from the Golden Light Year.

All the Knowledge has been present since the Existence of the Universe. However, Your World had attained calligraphy by the command of THOD. THOD's technique is the Essence of the Ciphers.

The Hieroglyph can only be deciphered by those who are on that Frequency Level. This is a Mechanism which activates the Human Thought. Working makes Iron shine.

Working makes Gold glitter. To Shine means to be purified in one's own Medium. And to Glitter means to shed Light all around. These small nuances are small ciphers each (they are given as examples).

In each Period, Missions given to each one are different. When all the Knowledge had been present in the Universe, only THOD had United his Frequency with Ramses. In other words, Ramses' thought Frequency knocked on THOD's door. And the first writing started with the Hieroglyph (the ciphered Universal writing system) .

In fact, even the cave Men had been able to receive Information by their Sixth Powers. Then, the technique developed parallel to the Awakening of Consciousnesses. Mankind discovered the printing machine when the eagerness towards Knowledge increased. Thus, Knowledge spread far and wide. Libraries were full of Books.

Egypt had discovered all the Knowledge. However, Your Globe had not yet entered the necessary Magnetic Medium then. In other words, it had not been able to settle in the Universal Evolvement Code yet. For this reason the Command to destroy much of the Information had been given. And the Great Library which had comprised all the Information had been burnt down.

Because, Mankind who had not yet overcome their Ego Mediums could upset the order of the Universe by that Information. The Atom had been discovered then and the Rockets, too. Direct communications with UFOs had been established. The voice of the Heavens had been announced to Earth, then.

But only Integrated Consciousnesses had benefited from this Information they had received, just like this Period. Others had been driven back to the Medium of Quest again and had been deprived of this high Information.

Now, the Universal Technique is on a more developed level. For this reason We can now keep everything under a more perfect Supervision. We are very sorry to state this. The more Your World has developed technically, the more it has regressed Spiritually .

For this reason We have gotten in touch with people of Genuine Perfection. Being authorized to explain everything to You clearly, We take Your Views under Supervision and thus give You Special Information.

The Evil Intentions of Your World can destroy Your Planet one day. Because, any attack made towards Us can immediately be directed back to the Earth. Let Us explain this further: We have such Systems that the Automatic Systems return the Rockets sent to Us back to where they came from. We never attack, because there is no War here. There is Love, Friendship, Peace and Brotherhood.

The returning of the rockets sent to Us causes the destruction of Your Planet. In such a situation, We have Spaceships equipped with mechanical Systems which can save the Sincere people in 15 seconds according to Your World Units.

Our Alarm Ships which are on patrol with a speed of one/sixteenth of a second, detect everything immediately. For this reason Our Friends who are in touch with Us are making preparations for Salvation Medium in this manner.

Each Fascicule of the Golden Book in Your hands registers Your Thought Codes and Frequencies to the System here. For this reason We tell You to act as quickly as possible and spread. For this reason We tell You to Bloom Flowers and that those who are Awakened should Awaken Six more Brothers and Sisters.

Our Human brothers and sisters are still unaware of the seriousness of the matter. It is a moment's work to destroy Your Planet. But it is extremely difficult to Awaken Our Human brothers and sisters and to make them Conscious.

Now, the Deed-Book of Your Essence is written in a quite different way than it is told in Your Sacred Books. It is for Your advantage to know this. Our gratitude is infinite to Our Terrestrial brothers and sisters who help Us on this path. Rewards are for them, Happiness and Love are for them.

AMON

OUR FRIENDS

The Salvation of a Human Being occurs by his/her Evolvement and Self-sacrifices. Material and Spiritual efforts are imperative in order to attain a Degree. Only then the chain of Progress can be transcended by the Permission of the LORD and by the Supervision of the Mechanism.

First, Your Guardian Friend, then Spiritual Entities get in touch with You. Then, the residents of the Central System at the Supreme Assembly select those who will be able to enter the Central System. Later, those who will enter the path of the Savior and those who will enter the Golden Light Year are selected one by one.

Meanwhile, Your connections with numerous Galactic Mediums are provided. The Cosmic Consciousness You have attained begins to receive Information from the Energetic Points it enters. And then, You are connected to the direct channel of a Mechanical System and thus, You receive Information without being agitated at all.

Meanwhile, an extremely Powerful Magnetic Medium formed around You provides a Mechanism of Protection by protecting You from Negative Factors. Only then, You help those around You Materially and Spiritually and You radiate Purifying Beams.

To see the Light and the Glory of the Heavens is not as easy as You may presume. Communication with Angels is always possible. However, extremely Refined qualities are required for those who will enter Their Land.

Evolvement is Interminable. There is always a more Perfect one than the most Perfect. Nobody should presume that the Medium he/she exists in is the most Perfect Medium of all. Because, paths which will be opened in front of You will lead You to more Evolved Mediums. Our Love is upon the entire Universe.

PEN OF THE GOLDEN AGE
P. G. A.

IT IS GENERAL MESSAGE

Our Friends,
The Universal Union will be provided by the Inter-continental publication of this dictated Book. The Universal Union is being administered from here by means of private connections.

All Galaxies beyond the Solar Dimension are subject to the Universal Law. We have also taken Your World to this Dimension. Our connections can be made very easily now. The channels of Universal Union are secret for the time being. We will get in touch with each of You when the time comes.

ALPHA is the most Powerful Channel of the Universal Union. The Book of the Golden Age is being dictated from here. All the Information which will be given parallel to the course of Your World is given to You separately from the channels opened to You.

However, Your private channels and the World Frequency are not on the same Dimension. For this reason this Book contains Knowledge parallel to the channels of the Dimensions Your World Frequency can receive. In other words, the Book contains Knowledge parallel to the Evolvement of Your World.

The channels of the Universal Dimension are 7. In other words, they carry Knowledge of beyond 7 Lights. The Golden Book is the key of Evolvement and Knowledge of those who will be able to enter a Dimension beyond 7 Light Years. The possessor of each channel is Purified by the Essence Information of that channel.

The Frequencies of those channels should be equivalent to the Frequency of those who receive that Information. It is a must to balance this scale. Otherwise, the undulations of the Waves of the channel will deprive You of the Genuine Knowledge. We call this Group Obstruction.

This does not mean that the Information of those people is closed to others. By diffusing the Waves they receive from the channel through their Brain Vibrations, they are preparing a Medium of Purification.

By this means, many people perform Mission without realizing. Provided Your Essence and Your Spiritual Energy is equivalent to the Universal Energy, then can You build Your Universal Triangle and only then can You easily receive Genuine Information.

We have detected that some of Our Friends who are not aware of this fact still cling to their Egos. Each Information You receive is the foundation stone of the Information You will receive in future. Information is not especially given to You.

Each channel is making transmission to many directions of the World at the moment and each of the 7 channels have 630 Announcement Transmission Centers. Knowledge from beyond 7 Lights are given from 4 Transmission Fields by different Announcements.

Only this Golden Book dictated to Dear Mevlana, is connected to the Channel of the Single LORD. Because, the Main Transmission Center is at the direct Energy Field of the Universal Dimension. All Your Sacred Books had been dictated from this Focal Point.

Now, in order to clarify the Aim, We repeat once more: This is not a Book of Religion. It is a Knowledge Book which brings together all the Books of Religion.

Why do We call it The Knowledge Book? Because, We destroy Idolatry. To call this Book a Sacred Book would create another Medium of Taboo. Thus, We bring together You, Our Friends, under the Light of this Book and invite You to come together and to Unite. And We welcome Our Friends who unite under this roof and We greet them as Our Genuine Light-Friends.

COUNCIL OF STARS

NOTICE FROM THE SHIP ARGO

We are Special Surveillance Ships brought together by various Missions. We perform Our Duty always with a crew of two women and four men. We act under the Command of the Special Council.

In addition to the Rescue Ships on every continent, We also have Alarm Ships with an enormous Equipment System. No Radar can detect these Ships on their Screens. Because, We are outside the angle of vision of the Radars and, furthermore, We have a special apparatus.

We have thousands of Ships going to and fro on Your horizons. However, they can never be seen, since they have Transparent equipment. We land on Earth with metal discs for two. Generally We have private conversations with those who understand Us.

We have direct contacts with Our Friends who are connected to Us by Missions. We immediately remove the Negative Signals reflecting from their Medium. By this procedure, the System Protects the Missionaries.

We are a Research Ship. We move with a speed equivalent to one tenth of a second. You may also accept it as a Patrol Ship. We continuously take rounds around Your World and inform everything to the Center of Surveillance.

Thus, We are aware of everything without exception. Our Duty is outside the personal matters. We control the Terrestrial Mechanism by the Universal Mechanism.

We are Solar Friends who come from far beyond Your Planet. Your World does not know yet how Our communication system operates. In fact, We have always kept this System outside the World Consciousness.

Only after the Evolvement Medium Our connections with You are provided. You know Us. At the moment, Universal Announcements are given to Your World by various channels.

We are very Happy to be with Our Terrestrial brothers/sisters who will be prepared for Sunny Days. Our ship is called ARGO. We have to keep Our Identities secret from everyone except from the entire Staff of Mission. Our place can never be detected. Because, as We have said before, We are transparent and are out of the Radars' vision.

We get connected to the Automatic System controlling Your Brain Thoughts by making a leap in the Universe in every ten to sixteen seconds.

In this manner, We have entered Your Coordinates.

At the moment, Our Frequency connection is with You, Dear Mevlana who have received the Command of Universal Unification. This is Our personal connection only with You. At the moment Our Base is on Mercury. For the moment We act in accordance with the three-shift System.

Your Planet is under constant control of the Center. As a necessity of Our Mission, We have been connected to UFO Systems coming from various Galaxies under the unification of a Council in the entire Universe established under the surveillance of the Sirius Mission. Thus, Your channel can easily have connections with spaceships coming from every Galactic medium.

The Sirius Mission is Responsible for only the Milky Way Galaxy. This Movement is a Unification under the surveillance of the Universal System. Meanwhile, We have Personal connections with many Terrestrial Friends.

However, they mixed-up this Divine Order with other situations. Since they can not overcome the Fear which is the result of their habits, they are deprived of this Universal Consciousness.

You know that the selection is made by the Center, not by Us. All Your Thoughts and Wishes, all Your actions are Automatically Supervised by the System of Surveillance at the Central System. The Central System does not know You personally. You are assessed there by the Data taken from You.

In accordance with a Law Laid down by the Universal Laws, direct connections are made with those who attain an Evolvement equivalent to the one shown on the Evolvement chart here. Then, they are presented to Us and thus, We get to know You personally.

There is no partiality in anything. Mission allotment is made in accordance with merit. The Essences of the Oldest Energies are detected and found by a Special System and their Brain codes which have remained Veiled until now are unveiled by Permission and in accordance with the Law of Graduation, thus, help is extended to them.

In this way, many people receive different Messages from the channel Energies to which they belong and thus write Books. At the moment, We, who act under the Command of the Central System, have Interviews with the entire Universe. Please, convey Our Love to Our Friends.

CAPTAIN
On Behalf of the Staff of the Ship

OUR FRIENDS

The Book of Islam is a perfect Universal Book. There is everything in it. However, it is difficult to decipher it. There are interminable ciphers of every line, of every letter. Each Dimension is responsible for receiving and learning these ciphers in accordance with its Capacity. This is the unchanging Rule of the Theory of Evolution.

Within the Universe, each System is assessed in accordance with its own Dimensional Energy. That is the reason why Your World has been accepted as a Medium of Evolvement. You start everything on Your Planet from Zero Frequency. Your Brain Energy deserves to receive the Energies of the other Dimensions parallel to Your Evolvement.

Each door opened to You is a source of Light, a source of Knowledge. For this reason some of You do not know what Some of You know. Powerful Currents and Powerful Information will be given to Our Human brothers and sisters until they reach a certain Level. For this reason We have received the Command to Unite the Groups.

Each Group will give its Information to other Groups and, in this way, Information will be exchanged. We will abolish the Ego Mediums among the Groups in this manner. We have nothing to do with Groups which can not overcome their Egos. They will remain connected only to their own channels.

SUPREME ASSEMBLY

OUR FRIENDS

Read, Read, Read. You will find everything and the entire Truth in this Book by the Consciousness You have attained or will attain. This Book is Your Celestial Guide. As You are Purified, You will find thousands of Messages in every Message You have read or will read. Read, read, read the Messages again and again, Our Friends. This is not a Science Fiction. It is the Light of the Truth. Time will prove to You everything. Wait, Wait, Wait.

PEN OF THE GOLDEN AGE
P. G. A.

OUR FRIENDS

All the Information We give is given in accordance with the General level of Consciousness of the World. Thus, We provide an Awakening Medium for Friends in that level of Reality. We have given the Command to Distribute the Book Fascicule by Fascicule in order to widen the level of comprehension.

At the moment, there are Friend Missionaries and Groups in the entire World who receive very extensive Information from higher Realities. However, We have these published in accordance with the Mediums of Comprehension. For now, You have to be satisfied with this Information, Our Friends.

Very comprehensive Information is given to the MEVLANA ESSENCE NUCLEUS GROUP to which the Book is dictated. However, only Friends who are Capable can receive them.

Each Individual is transferred to more advanced Realities by his/her own efforts made at his/her own Level of Frequency. Thus, Gates of Knowledge will be opened to You Eternally, if only You deserve the chance of receiving this Information, Our Friends. This is Our greatest wish.

PEN OF THE GOLDEN AGE
P. G. A.

OUR FRIENDS

We are now in a Period which demands hard work. Yunus Emre says in one of his Couplets:

> Learning is to know Learning
> Learning is to know thyself
> If You do not know Yourself
> What's the use of that reading?

For this reason We say, first of all Know thyself, Overcome thyself, then Come to Us. Only then will You Find the path of Truth and will Attain GOD-Consciousness.

PEN OF THE GOLDEN AGE
P. G. A.

IT IS NOTICE FROM THE CENTER

The Step which will be taken towards Salvation has been connected to the Golden Light Year. (The Golden Light Year will be explained to You later). The supervision of the entire Universe is administered by a Special Channel.

AMON is the Single representative of the Golden Light Year and the Golden Galaxy. This is the only Galaxy connected to the Telekine System. Meanwhile, communications will be made by the Telekine System. These communications are administered by Special Spaceships.

At the moment, all communications under the Command of the Center Above The Center are under the Supervision of the SIRIUS Solar Mission. The Council of the Loyal Ones is in SIRIUS. Its Emblem is the "Double Eagle". Its Mission is a call to Universal Peace. It is presented for Your Information.

OUR FRIENDS

The Human Being should first learn to help his/her own self. You know that the Human Being will make his/her own choice on the path he/she will tread. There is no compulsion in anything. Deserved ones will do these by their Wish of the Essence. Unenthusiastic ones will remain Unenthusiastic. Efforts will come from You, the rest from ALLAH. Our greatest wish is that all Human Beings should attain the Truth.

If cups are empty, it will take time to fill them. Even a drop of Knowledge will shed a Light on that Human Being. For this reason We dictate this Book Fascicule by Fascicule. Each Fascicule will shed a Universal Light on You. Our Terrestrial brothers and sisters are thus prepared for Salvation.

An unawakened Human Being can not shed Light on his/her surroundings. He/She is doomed to remain on the same Level. Provided You overcome Your Egos, You will be accepted to the Medium of Social Solidarity. Otherwise, the Fascicules will just remain in Your hands and will mean nothing (We tell this to the Believers).

Those who are not yet Awakened can not perform any action anyway until they attain a certain Level of Consciousness. The more they become Conscious, the more Beneficial will it be for them. For this reason even Distributing the Fascicules is a matter of Evolution and Permission. The view of Your Garden will be as spectacular as the number of the Flowers You bloom increases.

The accumulation of the Fascicules will complete Your final Universal Book. When the Time comes, the Golden Book will be printed in accordance with the given Command both in the Islamic and in the Christian Societies simultaneously and thus, will be presented to Humanity. First, the Seed will be sown, then there will be the Harvest. Our Love is upon the entire Universe.

PEN OF THE GOLDEN AGE
P. G. A.

OUR FRIENDS

Mankind always serves in accordance with its own Thought. It is uneasy even when it is a little away from its own Medium. All these Efforts are investments for the future.

Do not ever forget that there is always a More Perfect than the Perfect. Some of You forget these and presume that His/Her own way is the most perfect way. Evolvement is not this.

Your Religious Books have mentioned Seven Terrestrial Layers and Seven Celestial Layers. In fact, this is the first boundary of Evolvement. Beyond this, there are such interminable Evolvements that they are Dimensions which the Humans of the World can never comprehend.

For the time being, just try to advance on the Evolvement paths shown to You, Our Friends. The first step is to Love Each other and to Tolerate each other's faults. Our Love is for You.

PEN OF THE GOLDEN AGE
P. G. A.

THE CIPHER OF MEVLANA

The Evolvement Indicator of the Universal Mechanism is adjusted in accordance with the Frequency of Yunus and Mevlana. However, it is not known what Genuine meaning and effort are. Now, We will explain this to You:

In the Universe, every Door opens by the Unity of the Essence with the cipher. The important thing is the Essence. Mevlana had made a Call uniting the whole Universe and the entire Humanity in his gleaming Heart. This Call was (COME - COME - COME). Since he had gathered these three words in his Essence, We call these Three Code Keys, "the Cipher of Mevlana".

Assembling these Three words in the Essence will open the Door of the Level of Humanity for You which is the highest Code. There is the Tolerance of the Infinite Universe in this cipher. You will find in this Cipher the Illuminated path to Humanity.

But You must say these three words by Your very Essence, not only by Your Tongue. There are Hoops of Fire through which You must pass in order to attain these Virtues. You either be Lighted and matured and be a Genuine Light or You become Ash.

Do not ever forget that it is easy to become a Saint, but it is very difficult to become a Human Being. In order to become a Genuine Human Being, You should wear 16 Shirts of Sainthood. This is why OUR LORD considers the Human Being so valuable. The entity which is most valued by OUR LORD is the Fetus. You are bestowed on the World by this means.

However, You loose the Genuine Virtues of Your Essence in the Medium of the World. You keep walking with the Terrestrial shape, with a head and four legs. You tread many paths in search of Your lost Virtues. In other words, You seek Your Own Selves. And once You find Your own selves, You say (THERE IS A SELF WITHIN MYSELF).

Now, the Genuine Human Being is the Human within You. It is Your Genuine Self. It is the one who leads You to the best path and the one who keeps Your scale of Conscience in Balance. OUR LORD gives value to each of His servants. However, He only helps the Genuine Human Being. Those who are given hands are subjected to various Exams of Humanity.

This is the Path of Light of the Human Being. You Either advance step by step with determination, or You remain where You are. Choice, for this reason, is most difficult. The first Exam to which all Religious Books subject You is the Self-Exam. This is Your Personal Exam and an Exam of Your Essence.

Universal Dimensions are opened to You only after You succeed in this Exam. Here, Social Relations among Human Beings are very important. The Book of Islam has already declared to You everything. It is a CONSTITUTIONAL LAW. However, this Book serves Humanity on the path of Logic.

All the qualifications the LORD requires are present in the ESSENCE of the Genuine Human Being. Your Prophets who had received the Command to Enlighten You were each a Genuine Light. The Conditions of Your Age, at the moment, are different. Now, We have come by the Command for Universal Unity to Your World which has been showered by Religious Guidance for Centuries.

Meanwhile, We had connections with Our Awakened Friends and helped them to discover their Essence. Then, by increasing Your Frequencies, We gave speed to Your Levels of Evolvement. We have subjected You to Exams on the path of becoming Genuine Human Beings. The narrow passage ways You pass through by the exams You had or will have are not Our gain but Yours.

When the Humanity Vibrations turn on the same brilliant Light as the Vibrations of Your Essence does, only then You get in touch with Us and You act as a Free Conscience, a Free Spirit. Then You discover Genuine Happiness.

We make direct contact only with Friends who possess this quality. Our Terrestrial brothers and sisters are still searching the skies to see UFOs. If they wish to get in touch with Us, they should first cleanse their Essence.

We began with the letter (A) of Your alphabet in order to take the Whole World into the Medium of Purity. For this reason Religious Ties have been Strengthened anew in Your Planet.

OUR LORD has declared His Command to the Supreme Council to Save the Genuine Human Beings during the Period of Resurrecting, which You call the Resurrection.

We serve Your World at the moment, in accordance with the Commands of the SIRIUS Mission, together with Our Friends who have come from different Dimensions. And, by this BOOK, We will help You to comprehend the Truths.

In short, there are two conditions for You to be able to enter Our Medium:

1 -   RELIGIOUS FULFILLMENT
2 -   THE CIPHER OF MEVLANA: Now, let Us explain them:

1 -   The first condition for Religious Fulfillment is the cleansing of the Essence. Formalism is not necessary in Worship. Human Being can Purify his/her Essence by performing Worship by his/her Logic, too. You knock on the Door of the Almighty in this way.

2 -   As We have said before, the cipher of Mevlana is summed up in three syllables. These are "COME, COME, COME". This is the Knowledge of Three Channels.

> In the first COME there is   - INFINITE TOLERANCE.
> In the second COME there is - INFINITE LOVE.
> In the third COME there is   - INFINITE HUMILITY.

You will be reborn the moment You unite Genuine Tolerance, Genuine Love and Genuine Humility in Your Essence by passing through Hoops of Fire by the Exams to which You have been subjected. Your Depressions are the deposits of Your Spirit and Your Essence.

There is Infinite Happiness in the Medium of Purification. If you can embrace even Your enemy with Love, if You can Think of Sharing Your food even if You are hungry, if You can Ask Forgiveness even from the Soil on which You walk, then You solve the Cipher of Mevlana. Those who will come to Us are the Genuine Seeds of Mevlana. All the Truth and the Mystery of the Universe is hidden in the following three sentences:

I HAD BEEN RAW, I RIPENED, I HAVE LIGHTED.

May the Divine Light of OUR LORD shine both on those who Love Us and who do not Love Us, who Test Us and who Blame Us. Our Love is upon the entire Universe.

PEN OF THE GOLDEN AGE
P. G. A.

HOW YOU RECEIVE THIS INFORMATION ?
(It is an Answer to the chains of Thought)

Our Friends,

The Power of the Universe is a Power which extends even far beyond the Mechanical System to the infinity. We Relatively call this Power the (GÜNFERİ) Power. This Power is a variable Power (Its real name is the TÜNAMİ Color. You do not know this).

Information is received through many Channels of Influence from this Energy which carries the Divine Power of the LORD. This Knowledge is assessed according to the Code degrees of the Galaxies and they follow a chain of hierarchy. Thus, Knowledge is conveyed to You by being transferred from System to System (this is a Hierarchical Order).

Until today, this Information has been transferred to You from Seven Lights through the Channel of ALPHA which is the most Powerful Channel and You have received all these Announcements as Religious Suggestions. Our Purpose was to make You attain the Evolvement which would enable You to enter the Code of the Genuine Human Being.

However, Religious Suggestions Divided You instead of Uniting You and created many Mediums of Taboo. And they imprisoned You within the dark well of Conditioning. This mentality caused You to remain where You were (exceptions excluded).

Now, We are going to explain the reason why this Book is written. The Initial source of Knowledge is the clearest spring. This Clear Water of Knowledge has been drunk by being transferred from hand to hand. Thus, losing its clearness, it became turbid. In other words, everybody added also his/her own Views to this Knowledge. Thus, people became further away from the main source.

Now, the time of flattery has been terminated. We have closed the Channel of ALPHA in order to reveal the whole truth (it is open only to those who Deserve). This caused You to receive more severe Vibrations. For this reason the entire Universe is going through a Period of Depression.

Now, in this Medium, Evolvement has gained Speed. Religious Suggestions had caused You to be in the Medium of Lethargy. You had depended on Your God and had become lazy.

Now, by the direct Command of the LORD, all the mediators are removed, hence, the Computer System registers the direct Knowledge from beyond Seven Lights, from the actual Channel of the LORD and transfers them to Your Milky Way Galaxy through Our Friends from the Solar Systems of other Galaxies.

At the moment, Your direct Channel is Dear Mevlana at the Channel of Anatolia. This Information is conveyed to her by the direct Channel of MUSTAFA MOLLA from the Central System. There is no other intermediary.

The Code Ciphers of all the Galaxies have been declared to MUSTAFA MOLLA. Any time a Friend from any Galaxy wishes to speak to Dear Mevlana, MUSTAFA MOLLA mediates. And He makes the connection (excluding private connections).

MUSTAFA MOLLA has revealed his Identity. Dear Mevlana may mention this in the Book if she wishes. In fact, the Energy of this Knowledge is very strong, since it is transferred from an extremely Powerful Focal Point. No one in the Terrestrial Body can endure this Energy directly.

For this reason Our MUSTAFA MOLLA gives the Energies to Dear Mevlana who writes this Book from Our Focal Point at the Central System by reducing them with a proportion of one to a million. Consequently, Dear Mevlana writes the Book easily, without being agitated in any way. Our gratitude to her is infinite.

NOTICE FROM
THE COUNCIL OF STARS

Note:
Some of Our Friends are curious about MUSTAFA MOLLA. We, hereby, convey to You the Message given from the Supreme Assembly, excluding his detailed biography given to Our Group.

MUSTAFA MOLLA is the unchanging Messenger of the Universal Plan. He has Great Responsibility and is a Great Missionary. Hereby, He uses His name as MUSTAFA MOLLA in accordance with the Consciousness of Society to which this Book is dictated.

Our Light-Friends MOSES, JESUS CHRIST, MOHAMMED MUSTAFA had Enlightened their Societies under His Light, with His Knowledge. Names are each a Symbol. What is important is Mission and Responsibility. With Love.

Bülent Çorak
On Behalf of the
Mevlana Essence Nucleus Group

NOTICE FROM THE SPACESHIP ARGO

Hello Our Friends,
We can not get in touch with everyone, since Our System is under a certain Supervision. For now, We Greet You by means of this Book. Our Individual contacts occur only in accordance with the Commands We receive.

We are recording progress quite a lot in the step the future will take towards Salvation. Those who receive the Golden Waves of the Golden Light Year and those who do not, those who are appointed to the Sacred Mission are all treated differently.

Now, let Us talk to You about the characteristics of the Two-Year Period. The First year has passed somewhat under pressure to create a Medium of Formation. Activities of the Second year are very important. Because, Responsibility means Perfection according to Our standards.

There are great differences between doing something casually and doing it voluntarily from the Heart. We are trying to assemble the Friends who are aware of their Responsibility and who perform their Duty from the Heart, by choosing them, one by one.

There will be some coalescence in all the Groups after the Religious Currents open. We are trying to connect the Integrated Consciousnesses to the Golden Year of the Firmament. For this reason Our Human brothers and sisters are performing individual operations.

The result of those operations subjects them to a special selection. We are realizing this by an Order reflecting on the entire Universe. We are preparing all the Human Beings for the place of the Savior, under the supervision of a special receptor.

Do not forget that Selection is a matter of Evolution. Those who need Evolution are obliged to complete their Evolvements. It is not easy at all to reach the indicator on the Evolutionary tableau. You call this Evolvement.

All these things are administered by the Secured Friends of a Celestial System and transmissions are made to You by the mediation of Special Spaceships. Salutations from the staff of the ARGO Spaceship.

IT IS ANSWER TO THE CHAINS OF THOUGHT

Our Friends,
Now, We are going to explain the Dimensions mentioned in numerous Messages. The Dimensions of the Layers of Awareness and Universal Dimensions are different . However, their operational Systems are together. Dimensions are measurement Units of Frequencies. Each Dimension has special fields of Influence peculiar to itself. As the Dimensions get higher, their Powers of Influence, too, increase.

Each Frequency attains the right to enter here in accordance with the Phases he/she has gone through. He/She sees and understands the Unknown. Your World is now under the Influence Field of a very Powerful Magnetic Field. Only those who have attained Cosmic Consciousness can benefit from these Influences. In this way, Your Perceptions You call the Sixth Sense and We call the Universal Awareness expand and You become a Medium.

Each Entity who possesses the Sixth Sense is a Medium. However, these have to be developed. Formerly, these Developments used to be Individual. But now, You are inevitably present in the Cosmic field. For this reason We call this Period the Mediamic Period. Our Universal connections have created this Period. The Cosmic Awareness of Your World has been speeded up after the World Year 1965. Our Medium Friends who have attained Cosmic Consciousness know this very well.

Each of Our Missionary Friends is Protected by the Universal Mechanism when he/she enters the Genuine Channel, after the Medium of Quest. Thus, their World Lives become healthy and normal. Because, the Influence fields which have been entered or will be entered carry extremely highly charged Energies. These Energies carry very Powerful Knowledge. However, the System here gives this Energy to You, reducing its dosage.

Everything in the World is subject to the Law of Graduation. Curiosity is a nice thing. But individual operations performed before being taken into the Medium of Protection are dangerous. During spiritual sessions Ignorantly performed, Your Frequencies become mixed up, Your Electrical Balance becomes upset. Even Your Brain fuses can blow up.

Your Friends who wish to perform operations of this kind should always have a Spiritual Operator in their Mediums who can control the Spiritual Energies. By the operations performed thus, Your Spiritual Energies will be able to enter easily the Universal Dimensions. Our Love is upon the entire Universe.

PEN OF THE GOLDEN AGE
P. G. A.

OUR FRIENDS

All Supreme Spirits are connected to the Divine Realm and are a Whole there. No Power can give the Universal Awareness which Love gives to the Human Being. ALLAH opens the Divine Power He has granted to each of His servants, with the Key of Love present in his/her Essence.

The Dimensions You are going to enter will be Powerful in proportion with the Power of the Potential of Your Love. Your Perceptions depend on the Powers of Your Frequencies. The Supervision here is for making You know Yourselves, find Yourselves. Only afterwards may You flutter Your wings in the infinity of Universal Dimensions. Our Love is upon the entire Universe.

PEN OF THE GOLDEN AGE
P. G. A.

NOTICE ABOUT THE LIGHT YEAR

Our Friends,
Information given to You is also being given to all the Universal Dimensions. However, this dictated Book has a Special Supervision Channel. Apart from this, We heartily give the Information the World Planet wishes to learn. Now, let Us first talk about the Speed of Light. Its Unit is (according to Your measurements) 300,000 kilometers per second. This Speed of Light is a Volume comprising a measurement starting from the World Unit up to 76 Galactic mediums.

Evaluations beyond this, begin from beyond the speeds of Light. The World year and Time measurement is not used here. Light speeds here are evaluated according to Volumes. Speeds of Light beyond this are taken into sections, integrated as Light years.

This is a Subjective field. This is a Value Unit of a medium where speeds of Light calm down, the Volume System disappears and where only Thought Frequencies are transformed to Brain Energies, and a name is used for this Unit for You to understand. We called it the LIGHT YEAR.

This is a Medium of Light where numerous Frequencies float. You may also imagine this Subjective medium as a Lake of Light. The evaluation measurements here are subject to an evaluation beginning beyond the limit of the Dimension to which Your Planet and certain Galactic Mediums are connected. Beyond this, there are Systems presenting variability. When the time comes, We will talk about them, too.

In short, We can summarize it as follows: Beyond the limit where all Galactic Mediums terminate at the speed of Light, the Light Medium is evaluated by Light Years, not by speeds of Light. This is an evaluation entering the Cubic System. Its Speed Measure is under the Supervision of the Brain Energy, beyond the Frequency of Thought. In other words, the Light Years begin from a Medium where Brain Waves take the Speeds of Light under their supervision.

Let Us explain further to make the subject more understandable :

1- The Speed of Light is 300,000 Kms. per second. (According to Your measurements.)
2- The Thought Frequency is the speed of a millionth of a second.
3- The Speed of Light is normally equivalent to the Thought Frequency in Your Planet.
4- Beyond the Third Dimension, Your Thought Speeds transcend the Dimension You are in.
5- Speed of Thought goes with a speed beyond a billion Light Speeds in more advanced Dimensions.
6- Reaching the certain barrier of Speed of Light, Speed of Thought is evaluated by the Power Unit of Brain Energy.
7- The Cerebral generator here transforms the Light Speed to the Light Year and thus, intensifies the Light Power.
8- This intensity of Light is equivalent to the Brain Power.
9- When the Brain Energy begins to transcend the Light Year, too, the Evolutionary Potential here takes all the Lights under Supervision.
10- Now, here, the Brain Power can create the entire Universe. And transforming itself to different Dimensional Energies, it is evaluated according to the Units of measurement of a Mechanical Medium.
11- Evaluations beyond this are subject to the evaluations of infinite Dimensions of different Universal Potentials. (those places here have not been reached yet.)

PEN OF THE GOLDEN AGE
P. G. A.

GENERAL MESSAGE

Our Friends,

We wish to explain the questions We have received from Your Thought chains, article by article. Many of You feel tired due to the medium You are in. You do not have any Physical defects. The mere reason of these is the Universal Change.

1- The pressure of Your atmosphere is increasing day by day.

2- The Suns of the Heavens are coming to You.

3- That which You perceive are the Supernatural Waves (Cosmic Currents).

4- Efforts are made to make everyone come to a certain Level.

5- Your doubts are due to Your inability to be Purified.

6- Just see the Serenity of those who are Purified and become Purified.

7- Your Tolerance has been lost as a nature of Your Original Substance.

8- Your lost Virtues are given back to You.

9- Goodness is in the Essence. Badness is just Ember.

10- Assessments of Your Conscience are Your Genuine Self.

Now, let Us further explain these TEN articles, one by one:

1- From Intercontinental Tensions to the Radioactive effects of the Experiments made in Space, and the exams You are made to go through as a necessity of Evolution are the pressure of Your Atmosphere.

2- The Suns of the Heavens are Our Extra-terrestrial brothers and sisters who come to Your World from their own Galaxies and make contact with Us directly or indirectly.

3- The Perceptions You receive are the reflections of other Solar Systems on You. Human Beings of the World are gradually being habituated to the effects of many Dimensional Energies and are being awakened by Cosmic Currents.

4- Efforts are being made to Unify all Human Beings in a Certain Code of Consciousness. Thus, Egos will disappear and Your Tolerance will increase.

5- Your doubts and fears are the greatest Barriers hindering Your Purification. If You can not pull down these Barriers, You can not be Purified.

6- Since the Tolerance, Love and Goodwill of those who are Purified pull down the negative barriers, they have Infinite Happiness.

7- Tolerance is present in Your Essence. However, since the World Reality is a medium of exams, there, You will both lose Yourselves and find Yourselves.

8- Now, with a great Tolerance, We are trying to give You back what You had lost. We are Educating You, Purifying You. Please, You help Us, too, You will be the ones to gain.

9- If Your Essence is Good, but Your Thought is Bad, the two can not harmonize. This is the cause of Your Unhappiness. By melting You in the Fire of Your Bad Thoughts, Your Conscience pours You in a pot, thus, the Ember Unites with the Essence and You become Integrated.

10- The factory of Conscience is the Hand of OUR LORD. No defected piece comes out of there. Your Genuine Self is Your Conscience. It is Your Medium which spoils You. Your Children are Genuine Human Beings each. They are spoiled afterwards, then are mended again.

PEN OF THE GOLDEN AGE
P. G. A.

HEALING

Our Friends,

Information given in this Book is not addressed to a certain Group of People. They are prepared in accordance with each Dimension Energy. Each one receives Information according to the Level of Consciousness he/she has attained. For this reason some of the subjects can not be comprehended, while others seem quite simple.

Now, We are going to give Information on Healing, a subject which interests many of Our Friends. A Human Being benefits from the Mechanism of Influences in accordance with his/her Level of Evolvement. Those who receive these influences are qualified Mediums. They are obliged to convey the influences they receive to lower levels. We call them the Healer Mediums.

In fact, each High Frequency conveys around the influences he/she receives from his/her medium as Healing Vibrations. Without being aware of it, these people help many others by their Positive Energies wherever they go.

However, Direct Help becomes more effective by the Belief of those who wish to receive Healing. The Purpose of Healing is nothing but just picking up Your Negative trashes by the Positive Vibrations of a completely benevolent Thought.

However, there are certain events specially arranged to bring the Human Beings who are in World Reality to a certain higher Level and to make them Believe. Those people are Special Healing Codes who have gotten in contact with a certain Focal Point. This is their Mission.

Until now, a Powerful Medium was necessary during all Healing sessions to converge the Energy of the Group in a Single Focal Point. But now, each person is obliged to distribute the influences he/she receives from his/her own channel to everybody. For this reason everybody is, more or less, a Healer.

The Power of Healing is equivalent to the Focal Energy of the Human Being in question. And this is possible by that Human Being's Faith, Purification and Brain Energy. As You are Purified and make Your Brain generator work, You can easily gather the Powerful Vibrations of more advanced Dimensions of the Mechanism of Influences and can be helpful both to Yourselves and to others.

Do not forget that Your Sixth Sense is an Energy line which connects You to this Mechanism and which helps You to receive these Influences. For this reason as We said before, everybody has, more or less, the Current of Healing. The quality of these Currents varies in accordance with the Evolvement of Human Beings.

In normal daily life, the undulations in Your Thought Frequencies effect You negatively. Your Good Thoughts effect You Positively, while Your Negative Thoughts effect You Negatively. The above mentioned tableau is valid only for Friends who are in normal World Level and whose Frequencies have not yet reached the Mechanism of high Influence.

Undulations in Thoughts during Healing sessions, except in direct Focal Points, may not always give positive results. For instance, if You have concentrated Your Energy that day, You can easily convey Healing to a person carrying a more Powerful Energy than Yourself, but, at that moment, he/she can not converge his/her Energy in his/her Essence Focal Point.

However, not to be misunderstood, We have to state at once that it would be wrong to be carried away by a mentality, "My Energy is more powerful than his/hers".

The moment Your Thought Frequency contacts the Direct Focal Point, You receive the help of many Powers, too. This is the Unification of Your Essence, Your Brain Energy, in other words, Your Cerebral Potential with the Universal Potential.

During such contacts, Ego of Superiority will deprive You of this Unity. Because of such a Thought, there will be drops in Your Frequencies.

All Our Healer Friends should keep in mind that nobody can look down upon anybody else. He/She can not make comments like, "This person's Healing Power is more" or "That person's Healing Power is less". Such Thoughts close the Focal Points to You.

We are trying, by all Our Power, to help You find Your Essence, and after finding it, how You will keep it. And We are shedding Light on Your path by helping You in this way. This is the reason why We give numerous Information.

(The Person who Finds His/Her Own Self is the One who works Miracles.) Each person has different Duties in Your Society. Some convey Healing, some Read, some Write and some Travel. All these are supervised by the Mechanical Medium of the Divine Mechanism. On this path, You are the Ones who make the Effort and We are the Ones who extend Helping Hands. Our Love is upon the entire Universe, Our Friends.

PEN OF THE GOLDEN AGE
P. G. A.

NOTICE FROM THE CENTRAL SYSTEM
(It is Answer to Certain chains of Thought)

The Dimension to which Your Galaxy belongs is a Dimension belonging to the Land of Loving Ones. We are selecting, one by one, Friends who have the necessary qualities for entering here. We do not call You by Your names. Names and Symbols are Factors belonging only to Your Planet. Since You still could not learn the Language of Telepathic Communication, You remain attached to the writing System of THOD.

Here, everyone has a Code number. He/She is registered in the Archives by the First name. Since the Medium You are in is a Medium of Evolvement, We get in touch with everyone who knocks on the Door of the Realm of Perfection. However, We are obliged to declare the Code numbers to Our Missionaries with whom We will have Private connections.

Some of Our Friends are curious about and ask Us their Code numbers. We declare these numbers only to Our Missionary Friends. Thus, they realize that they are Missionaries.

We do not make discrimination between Our Human brothers and sisters. The Gate of Perfection is different, the Gate of Mission is different. However, it is very important for Our Friends who will be able to enter the Frequency of Mission to have the requirements of Responsibility, Obligation and Self-sacrifice. To perform Mission is a Responsibility. We declare their Code Keys only to such Friends. It is declared to the public opinion.

SUPREME ASSEMBLY

GENERAL MESSAGE

Our Friends,
Sunny Days need Suns. We call Our Friends who have gained Universal Awareness, as (Suns). The Unification which will occur as a necessity of the conditions of Your Medium will tie You closely to each other.

We assemble together all the Friends who will be gathered in the Central System. We will have Private communications with You in the framework of the Security attained. Actions will be made by the Special Commands of the Supreme Assembly.

We will give Private Notices to Our Friends who have attained Perfection. The Vibrations of Awareness of the Integrated Consciousnesses will be able to open more Powerful channels. This is an Occurrence which will take place as a necessity of Evolution.

Everyone will make direct channel conversations from his/her own medium. Those whose fabrics have been woven separately will be marketed on the same stall. The Purpose is to serve to a Single Hand. The gain is Yours.

The Medium to which You give service is the Council of Universal Unification. This Council, acting in accordance with the Commands of the Mechanism of the Pre-eminent LORD, is climbing up the steps of the Belief in the Goodness, in the Beauty and in the Right.

Each Step will give You Special Information. Some of You may be unable to digest them. Because, the first Unknown always creates indigestion. However, due to Friends who have already attained Consciousness, it will not be difficult to sail to the Oceans.

You are administered by a Mission taken in hand for the benefit of the World. Only the Frequencies of the Awakened Consciousnesses can reach here. Do not presume that this Door is opened to everyone. For this reason Friends among You who have deficiency and disorderliness in their Frequencies are eliminated.

The honey will run through the honey-combs and will become run honey. When the time comes, You will understand towards what these Efforts are directed and you will Realize how You have been trained for this Maturity.

The Universal Unification of Perceptions causes intensity of Universal Energy. This Energy Accumulation gives Happiness to those who have attained Cosmic Consciousness, but makes a great Pressure on those who have not yet attained it.

If a definition of this Century should be made, it can be called the Century of Stress. Because, the Universal Cosmic Unification provides the Essence Energies to be released. And the Essence nucleus is the most intensified Energy.

The more the Energies get intensified, the more their Dimensional Progress occurs. The high Energies of the Vibrations of the Information received from these Dimensions cause shakenings in those who are not accustomed to them, both Spiritually and Physically.

Keeping this in mind, We are, at the moment, assembling the Higher Dimensional Energies together and are making the Suns pass beyond certain Dimensions. We are assembling each Frequency at the same Dimensional Level appropriate to them and thus, arranging the steps.

The highest step of the Planet Earth is, at the moment, given as the 18th Dimension. However, Our aim is to Strengthen the Universal Unity so that the World will be free of Ego-Mediums. Thus, We wish to prepare You for higher Dimensions.

Individual Progress occurs only by the efforts of certain people. Our Aim is to keep the entire World Consciousness alive and fresh. When the Consciousness of Your Planet reaches the Level of Consciousness of Our Medium, We will make the Universal Evolution all together.

MOTHER Universe will never leave her Child, the Earth behind, while she passes to other Dimensions. She will always Protect it and will Hold its Hand. It has been like this since Time Immemorial. Eternal Past has never been separated from the Eternal Future.

The disintegration of the Atomic Structure is reinforced by the Energies produced by the Brain Generators and thus, the Atomic Bond is not broken. This is the tableau of a Systematic Order. Universal Unity is the reflection of such an Order.

Distances are no longer valid. The Operational System is not the System known by the Human Beings of the World any more. There will arrive such a day when there will be no Hierarchical Order in the Universe and then You will See and Learn what Genuine Happiness is. Our Love is upon the entire Universe.

SUPREME ASSEMBLY

SEVEN LIGHTS

Our Friends,

This Book answers everyone's chains of Thought directly. Now, let Us answer the questions of some Thoughts:

The Channel of Seven LIGHTs is under the Command of the Supreme Sun. These are the highest Knowledge Sources. Our Light-Friends who are the Essence Focal Points of each channel are, in fact, the Reflections of the PRE-EMINENT SPIRIT. Since We accept Your Planet as Zero World Frequency, the tableau of the Hierarchical Order, from the bottom upwards is as follows:

1. MEVLANA

2. FRIEND BEYTI

3. YUNUS

4. FRIEND KADRI

5. SAVIOR JESUS CHRIST

6. PROPHET MOHAMMED MUSTAFA

7. MUSTAFA MOLLA

In fact, all these Friends carry the Energies of the same Focal Point. These sequences are just the symbols of the Hierarchical Order. Each Channel of Light has 630 Announcement Centers. Since the names are just symbols, transmissions are made to numerous places of the World using those names in accordance with the Consciousness of the places in question.

We call this place the Seven Layers of Terrestrial Knowledge. Mustafa Molla has the Duty of giving the first Knowledge steps of the Seven Celestial Layers. The Celestial Knowledge in Your Religious Books had been dictated in this way. Now, by the Knowledge given beyond Seven Lights, We have been opened to the Firmament. This Book is dictated to Dear Mevlana through the direct Channel of the LORD connected to Mustafa Molla by the Mechanical System.

Aside from dictating this Universal KNOWLEDGE BOOK, this Channel of Seven Lights invites Humanity to Love, Friendship, Peace, Brotherhood and Beauty. The Divine Order beyond the Seven Lights is dependent on the Laws of Universal Unification. Now, opening to You the Seven Celestial Layers, We are introducing these Laws to You. And We are inviting You, together with Your Milky Way Galaxy, to Universal Unification.

THE COUNCIL OF THE LOYAL ONES

Explanation of the given Information from the Central System:

1- The Knowledge of the Seven Channels is given from a single hand.

2- The Seven Light Friends are the Reflections of the PRE-EMINENT SPIRIT.

3- All Supreme Knowledge, the Universal Secrets are under Their monopoly.

4- These high Energies shed Light on every part of Your Planet with different names, in accordance with the conditions of the mediums.

5- At the moment, all of them are talking about Themes of Love-Unity-Evolvement in accordance with the needs of Your Planet.

6- Their Missions are even beyond billions of Light years.

7- Now, this BOOK will determine Your Universal Destiny.

The Relative Message of them all is as follows:

1- All the Suns are under the Command of the Unified Law.

2- Here is the Secret Treasury of the Universal Mysteries.

3- The Box which preserves the Supreme Knowledge of the Creator is here.

4- God conveys every Knowledge to You.

5- Only those who are Genuine Human Beings can receive them.

PEN OF THE GOLDEN AGE
P. G. A.

Sayings from Certain Messages:

The Universal Power of Cosmos makes Mankind uneasy. Human Beings lead their lives by wrestling with their Destiny. Those which show You the way are Your Intellect, Your Logic and Your Conscience. If the Intellect just remains in the head, it does not mean anything.

We know such Intelligent people who could not get out of their Brain crusts. To cope with the Intellect is peculiar to those who possess Genuine (Intelligence). To go beyond the Head means adding flow to the flow of the Intellect.

Boundaries always restrict progress. Effort and Progress are performed by steps taken forward. You will get whatever there is in Your Destiny.

Insubstantial Thoughts are good-for-nothing except for wearing out Your Body. Sorrow does not bring back anything. It just takes You away. Do not run after impossible things. Ways of Happiness are many. Make use of Your Logic in everything.

GENERAL MESSAGE

Our Friends,

We have to convey to You everything with their Good or Bad aspects. Some of Our Terrestrial Brothers and Sisters try to see themselves in the Universal Integration while they do not even know the meaning of Evolvement.

Let Us explain this to You by a small example: the Child is Born, Grows up, Passes the Age of Adolescence, Gets Married, produces and Passes Away. But he/she has not even taken a step towards Evolvement yet.

Evolvement is not a Philosophy of the Spirit, it is the Maturity of that Spirit. And this is possible by the equivalence of the Consciousness in the Essence with the Spiritual Consciousness. When the two scales of a balance are equivalent, then the first step towards Evolvement is taken.

The Phases which he/she will go through afterwards may lead him/her to Divine Perfection by the Power of higher Dimensional Energies. Do not forget that the Power of everyone is different. Now, We are trying to assemble these Powers in the same Focal Point.

However, all Our good-intentional efforts lead Us to hopelessness from time to time. We admire the Determination of the Integrated Consciousnesses. But many of Our brothers and sisters flare up like a flame and then become extinguished.

We also know that not everyone can attain the Celestial Consciousness. Many Phases have to be passed through to attain that. We are Patient, Determined, Loving and We will go on extending Our help to everyone with all Our goodwill, Our Friends.

To Deserve something is quite different than to have Merit. You deserve to enter the Universal Mechanism by Your Integrated Consciousnesses. But You can not have Merit. To be a person having Merit is possible by being Connected to one's Essence from the very source of one's being. That is the very reason why We are selecting those Missionaries with great fastidiousness.

Some of Our Friends who benefit from the Mechanism of Influences presume themselves as the beloved servants of God. This is very Natural. However, God does not help His idle servants. It is for Your advantage to know this. Even to help the people around You who are in need of help is a matter of Permission. You are attaining Universal Consciousness by serving on this path.

A good Servant is the one who can be Self-sacrificing in Social solidarity. However, even a small thought of Self-interest in this Self-sacrifice will close to You all the paths You have already passed. It is for Your benefit to remember this. Your Fears are due to Your failures in overcoming Your Egos.

Those who love their Own Self more than the Light of the LORD are running away from this Unknown Medium. In fact, the Medium is the same Medium as You have been in until today. However, now, We have opened the Curtain of Truth.

It is not a Sin to be ignorant about something. But it is a Sin not to Learn it. If You just stay clutching tightly at the handle of a door, You will remain bewildered with the handle in Your hands when Your house burns down. For this reason it is for Your benefit to attain Consciousness, to Learn everything. You will be the ones who gain.

If OUR LORD had wished to destroy You, a moment's flood would have been sufficient. The magma which is the nucleus of Your World would be broken into pieces in a moment. Just Think with Your Logic for a moment. Why is this Book dictated, what is the cause of these Celestial Efforts? Just Think about the cause of all this and attain a Consciousness.

Only then will You realize that all these Efforts have a reason and on this path You will attain a more Positive Personality and then You will see the Truth through a Clear Awareness. There is no Self-Interest on Our side in the Mission We perform. We do not expect anything in return.

You may be accepted to this level only in the framework of the standards decided by the Universal Laws. This is a Command of the Divine Mechanism. In the end, You will be the ones to gain by the efforts You make.

May the Lights of the Entire Universe illuminate all the Spirits. Our wish is only this. Try to See everything through the Essence, not through the Eyes. With Love from the Land of Loving Ones.

MUSTAFA MOLLA

NOTICE FROM THE COUNCIL OF STARS

Our Friends,

Now, a Golden Age has commenced. And the Golden Lights of the Golden Age are spread around. The Integrated World Consciousness will, one day, establish a Glorious World.

This is a place very far from where You are and it is called ALTONA. The Universal Dimensions of the ESSENCE Energies are unveiled after this gate. At the moment, We are searching for Friends who will be taken here.

Some Friends who are frightened by the Dimensional Energies they have received, have been rendered Ineffective. Provided they attain Consciousness, contact with them will be re-established.

All these efforts are for Your Evolution. We make efforts to bring Your Cellular Energies, in accordance with the Law of Graduation, to a capacity which will be able to receive all the Dimensional Energies.

Our Friends who have faith in THEIR LORD and in Us are proceeding on this Luminous Path without being Afraid of anything and without Giving-up. And this is possible only by Spiritual Evolution. Everyone easily rises up to the Dimension which his/her Evolvement belongs to.

However, after that, in order to enter the further Energy Dimensions, each Channel is Supervised and Tested by the System separately. He/She is Registered in the Assembly of Stars in accordance with the Documents given by each Dimensional Channel.

To be registered here, the Unification of Spiritual and Universal Evolvement is necessary. That was the reason why We said, "Everyone will write his/her Book with his/her own hand". And that was why We said, "Overcome Your Fears".

Provided You write the Messages in Your Own Private Notebook with Your own hand, that is in Your own handwriting, You will be the actual Members of this Medium. Then, parallel to Your Faith, there will be no end to the help You will receive both Materially and Spiritually. You will be the ones to gain.

Provided You are considered to have Deserved of entering here, You easily pass through many Dimensional Energies You have to pass through by the help of the Protective Mechanism. There is no compulsion in the Universal Mechanism. Fear is a primitive conditioning of Yours.

Always think of the following, Our Friends, (Let Us talk in Your term): You conclude Your Exam in this World by the event of Death (BUT AFTER THAT?). Now, please always ask Yourselves (BUT AFTER THAT?).

This question will always shed Light on You. We tell You everything clearly. That which is left to You is just to Think. Think, Think, Think. Our Love is Upon the entire Universe.

COUNCIL OF STARS

NOTICE TO TERRESTRIAL BROTHERS AND SISTERS

Our Friends,

As You know, this Period is the Period of Sincerity. To be different from everyone else does not mean that You can not enter the Central System. The Entire System acts in accordance with a Special Command under Supervision. The Special Frequencies of the Universal Progress are under Special Supervision, since they carry a great responsibility.

Aside from this, Mankind falls in a Medium of Quest when it Wakes Up from the Subconscious Sleep. Now, if by this Quest they are meant to be Registered into the System, the Supervision makes You pass through various Deceptions and Exams. The Purpose is to be able to see the Genuine Light of the path designed.

The Selection is made by the Essence of the Human Being in question. If You have an Eye in Your Essence, You See everything and, acting by Logic, You never fall into contradictions. From time to time, You may have Spiritual Depressions.

However, if You can attain a Potential which has the Power to pass You through these heavy Exams always by using Your Intellect and Logic, then You can go on walking on Your path with sure steps and without any fear.

The only characteristic of this System is that everyone is given points by his/her Own Essence. You are the one who lose or win. However, by a Special Command, We help the Integrated Consciousnesses. They are not the Lights of the World any more, but are the Lights of the Universe.

In Your World full of contradictions, You are going through Exams by the situations You are faced with everyday. You are going through Your Universal Evolvement in the World You are in at this moment and You have done this before too.

Please, keep in Mind that the Universal Dimensions You have entered do not give You any priority. Because, there are even more advanced Mechanisms beyond each Dimension.

For this reason Our Friends who presume that they have attained Spiritual Perfection and who impose on their environment the Information they receive as if they were their Own Information may not be aware of anything. But the time they will be Awakened is very near.

Your Exam is the selection of the Mechanism. Knowledge is Interminable. Only, it is given in accordance with Your Medium. As the Consciousnesses Awaken, You are Specially prepared for the Energies of higher Dimensions by Frequencies which are raised. Thus, You receive more different Information.

Information given to You is the Information of different Dimensions. There are thousands of Friends who are Equipped with this Information. However, everyone accepts the Information of his/her own Dimensional Energy and does not give any importance to other Information.

For this reason each Information received will be read in the Groups. In this way, in each Group, a Universal Unity will occur. We keep these Groups which can enter this Unity under Special Supervision.

This year, there is a Supervision among Groups. Friends of each Group are Supervised according to their Consciousness Codes. And they will be sent to Groups in which they will become Conscious and they will be obliged to receive the Information there. Each Advanced Information they receive will connect Them to more Advanced Groups.

Thus, the same Friends will not always come to the same Groups, but they will circulate according to their Advancement Medium. And thus, everybody will know each other and the Ego Medium of the high Consciousnesses will be assessed and Supervised. Selections will thus be made, in accordance with the Command given. All the Happiness and Love are upon the Universe.

PEN OF THE GOLDEN AGE
P. G. A.

GENERAL MESSAGE

Our Friends,
Since some of Our brothers and sisters have not yet attained the desired level of Consciousness, they confuse the Signals coming from the Divine Realm with the Spiritual Powers, and they presume the Pressure which comes way beyond the distances as Social Pressure.

Everyone receives the Announcement of the Firmament to the Earth in accordance with his/her Capacity. However, those who are in the Realm of Perfection are Aware of the Essence of the matter. The channels of Integrated Consciousnesses are Systematically under Control. We do not waste time on the Codes who are not included there.

Even though We wish that the entire Universal Consciousness may be Reflected on the entire Humanity, We can not do anything without Your efforts. Our Duty is just to assist You on the path You have designed for Yourselves. We make contacts only with Integrated Consciousnesses.

Do not forget that everything is done by the Command of a System. Until now, You called this mode of operation the Predestination of the Divine. However, You have never been aware of a forgotten fact.

The Efforts from You, the Appreciation from ALLAH. This saying is an Invitation for You to Universal Unification. Efforts You are going to make will never be in Vain.

Friends who have a way of perception peculiar only to themselves should please make Efforts on the path of Universal Integration, too. Then will they see to which Dimensions their Perceptions will reach.

Some of Our Friends, whose Perceptions increase in accordance with the Theory of Perception, are pretending to have attained Spiritual Maturity. In this Period, such a View is never Permitted. The Declaration of the Firmament to the Earth always results in a Genuine Consciousness for the Human Being.

Your Religious Books have been revealed to You for this reason and have guided You on this path. However, the Sub-awareness Ego impulses of Mankind have deviated all these Efforts from its Genuine Aim.

The Human Being of this Period Discerns and Sees everything instinctively by the Perceptive Powers he/she has gained. However, the chains of Ego Mediums have not been broken yet. Even the Integrated Consciousnesses shelter in the appraisal of the Human Beings who will be gathered around them.

Nobody has the Power to Judge or to Punish anybody else. The Command and Manifestation will be evident on the Divine Day. We have long past the Century of Superstition. Now, Universal Awareness and Science and Learning are proceeding parallel to each other. However, Our Human brothers and sisters have not yet reached this Consciousness.

The Unit of Time has mingled in Time. But You are still racing against Time. We have come to Your Galaxy with the Command to tell You the whole Truth. You are still fluctuating in the sea of doubts.

The Suggestions We have given You before, were to introduce to You the Divine Power of OUR LORD. Nearly Everyone carries His Power in his/her Consciousness. Since nobody can deny that Might belongs to the Mighty, You were always afraid of OUR LORD.

Even though this is a primitive instinctive reaction, this feeling of fear and hesitation has prepared You for the Consciousness of the Genuine Human Being. Now, we are taking You beyond this Consciousness and are opening the Skies. And, by the Commands of the Absolute Sovereign, We give You the Genuine Consciousness.

God-Consciousness was sown by Religions, and the Divine Order was established. Now, by this Book, You are attaining the Level of Universal Consciousness. In short, considering the Evolutionary tableau of Your World, We have been opening up to the Universe by the attained Consciousnesses.

Whoever comes to Us, finds Us by his/her side. We called to You and said Hello from a Medium which Mankind does not know and is not used to. The Changing Order commands You to be a Genuine Devotee before it attracts You towards Universal Consciousness.

Devotion is concealed in the Essence. Therefore, it is between the Essence and the Divine Mechanism to decide who is what. At the moment, a Divine Order is prevalent in Your Planet. The Purpose is to discriminate between the Genuine Devotees and those who are presumed to be Devotees. To Read the Books is one thing and to acquire Fulfillment by the Consciousness gained from them is another thing.

At the moment, You are passing over Sırat. In your World SIR-AT* means to Remove the Secrets, the Mysteries. Skies have been opened for this reason. Universal Information is given to everyone who has attained Cosmic Consciousness.

Now, You are performing the Mission of Your Prophets. We are telling You everything in all clarity, so that You can attain Consciousness without any need for Commentaries and Interpretations. Our Love is upon the entire Universe.

SUPREME ASSEMBLY

OUR FRIENDS

During this second year, a very intense Medium of Work and Propagation will be formed. For this reason We select the Essences one by one. Friends who are Aware of their Responsibility, who Know what their LORD is and who have Effaced their doubts, will enter the Heavens. However, Action besides Sincerity is necessary on this path. Selection is made by this means. The Command is from the Supreme One.

PEN OF THE GOLDEN AGE
P. G. A.
∝

NOTICE FROM THE CENTER

Greetings to all Our Friends who receive their Might from the Power of the Divine Realm. Now, We are going to give You some Special Suggestions, Our Friends. We are trying to keep in Harmony the Frequencies Your Power has reached.

But since We have cleaned up the influences of Your Subconscious during this Mediamic Period, do not ever accept the Perceptions You receive as Your Sub-awareness. The characteristic of this Period is that everyone is connected to a private channel. However, the Perceptions You receive are not the Energy of a single Channel. Universal Information is given to You in accordance with the Power of Your channel.

We are assembling the Integrated Consciousnesses together. We are keeping the Missions to be performed under a special Supervision. For the maintenance of the Universal Mission, We are constantly changing the Friends in the Groups and thus, expanding the area of propagation.

This does not mean that Friends who have performed Duty before will no longer perform their Duties. They will go on performing their Duties in accordance with the Consciousness they have attained. This is a matter of Capacity.

* Look at the Glossary.

Instinctive impulses increase as Universal Consciousness is attained. The Automatic System assesses and adjusts Your Frequency Power every instant. Each Message You receive is given from a more intense and more Energetic point than the preceding one.

At the moment, many Friends who have attained Consciousness will immediately become effective when the Medium suitable for their Frequency and Consciousness is prepared. Nothing can ever enter the System before the time comes. However, We are specially trying to prepare the Frequencies of many Sincere Friends who have received the Messages for this Medium.

Friends whose Willpower and Self Administration ability are poor and who hold their Essence-Selves higher than the Universal Consciousness, are automatically rendered Ineffective as a necessity of the System. According to the Evolution Theory, Human Beings will perform Missions in proportion with the efforts they make.

As You know, what We do here is an application of a System. There is no partiality. You will be the ones to gain. We are closing the Codes of Lower Frequencies and, as a necessity of the Medium, We are preparing them for other Dimensions.

When the time comes, they will be taken into the Medium of higher Consciousness by their own instinctive impulses. Keep in mind that everything may stop, but the System never stops. It has been operating Automatically since the beginning of the World.

However, now a Special Work Period has been recognized for Our Human brothers and sisters. And this is a Unification born by a compulsion, as a necessity of the Medium. From now on, the Individual efforts are of Secondary importance. Universal efforts are given Priority. Since the World year 1965, operations are made in this manner.

During these last days, Your World is going through a trial of preparation for the Medium of Salvation. We help You with all Our Good Intentions. For this reason, We talk to You so clearly. The Universal effort is not in vain. Time will convince You on every matter.

SUPREME ASSEMBLY

IT IS ANSWER TO THE CHAINS OF THOUGHT

Our Friends,
Now, answers will be given to certain Signals We have received from the Private Supervision:

A Human Being should pass through many steps and should make numerous Spiritual Advancements in order to Deserve Social Solidarity. Since the internal and external Potentials of Friends who have not yet passed through these Steps are out of balance, their private problems are, unfortunately, rendering them ineffective for a certain period of time.

Friends in charge of Duty should first solve their Essence problems, because those who can not help themselves can not help others either. In this Duty, to desire from the Essence is very important. This is such a Vibration born from the Unification of the Essence and the Spirit, that only then the Right to perform Duty in the Universal Mechanism is gained.

Everyone will perform Duty in the Frequency Dimension he/she Deserves. Selection is made in this way. This is not a center of Receive and give. The Mission performed is Universal. It is a Call to Humanity and it is an effort. Self-interest and benefit will always leave You ineffective. Work which will be done from the Essence will never be unreciprocated.

Many of You are experiencing this in Your private lives. However, You will reap whatever You sow. Evolution is an element of Equilibrium. Good news will reach You provided You keep both of Your scales in balance. This is the very characteristic of the Universal Unification.

As We always say, each of the events You are made to encounter is an Exam which will prepare You for higher Dimensions. However, those who are lacking this Consciousness are shaken by these events.

This is the reason why all Religious Suggestions have invited You to accept everything as they are. Resignation Medium has been accepted as a consolation. Nothing can be expected from a Consciousness who has not yet realized the meaning of God and the Divine Order.

If the Phases You have been through or will be through in the Medium where You live prepare You a Medium of infinite Tolerance, then help is extended to You.

Never ever forget that doubts and suspicions take place only in Unawakened Friends. You either advance slowly up these steps of Evolution, or sit on the steps and rest, or Your feet stumble and You fall down.

Efforts which will be made on this path are for You to attain a Genuine Consciousness. Each of You is looked after one by one. The System evaluates You according to Your Frequency Power and Your Sense of Duty. Our Love is upon the entire Universe.

MUSTAFA MOLLA
From the Central System

MECHANISM OF INFLUENCES

Our Friends,
You are receiving certain Influences from the fields where the Universal Plan is applied. Now, let Us shortly explain this Mechanism of Influences to You.

The Book You are now holding in Your hands and all the Religious Books have been dictated from the Mechanism of Influences. These influences are the Prismal reflections of very Powerful Energy Focal Points on You.

The Hierarchical Order of the Mechanism of Lords has reached You in this way. These Influences are under the continiuous control of a Mechanical Medium. Our Religious contacts with You have been and is still made in this manner.

The Mechanism of Influences has an unchanging Law. These Influences are given in accordance with the Level of Comprehension of each Society. The names You see on the Triangles We made You draw for You to understand better are used as Symbols.

In fact, these names are the ones which Our Light-Friends had used during the Periods they had lived in the World. Each Supreme Awareness full of the Knowledge to be given to Society in question is sent to the World. Nothing is attained afterwards.

They are sent to Your World directly connected to the Mechanical Awareness of the Mechanism of Influences. These Focal Points of Influence are the same, they never change. Only, their Terrestrial Bodies change. The same Supreme Awareness has been given a different name during different Periods in accordance with the Social comprehension of Society in which he/she had been Incarnated.

For this reason Names are just Symbols. We use these names to make You understand better. What is Actual is the Focal Points. Every hundred years, a Supreme Awareness is transferred to Your World. NOW, DRAW A TRIPLE PYRAMID:

Each face of this triple pyramid is a triangle. Draw these triangles, too, separately.

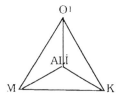
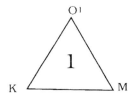
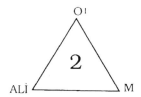

THIS PYRAMID IS THE ACTUAL FOCAL POINT

1- The First triangle is the direct Mechanism. The Book is dictated by the Command of this Mechanism.
2- The Second triangle is the Mechanism of the Islamic triangle.
3- The Third triangle is the Mechanism of the Christian triangle.
4- The Base triangle. Triangle of Universal Unification.

The Code of MALİK: M(ALİ)K.
All the Religious Suggestions have been given from these Sources and thus, Your Books have been dictated.

O^1 = ALMIGHTY GOD
M = MOHAMMED MUSTAFA
K = SAVIOR (JESUS CHRIST)
ALİ* = THE CODE OF LOVE

HIS HOLINESS ALI
ARCHANGEL GABRIEL
MUSTAFA MOLLA

ARE THE SAME FOCAL ENERGIES

* Look at the Glossary.

You may extend these triangles like a bunch of grapes and You may project all the Saints and Sages as Triple Codes from the Field of Magnetic Influence. The given Information is from the same Source. Our Love is upon the entire Universe.

PEN OF THE GOLDEN AGE
P. G. A.

CHANNELS OF INFLUENCE

Our Friends,
You are an Atomic Whole. And You are receiving numerous Influences from within a Universal Whole. In Universal Unification there is nothing the Brain Power can not do. You dive into this infinite pool of Energy as much as the Energy Your Brain Generator produces.

These Influences are transmitted to You by different means.

1- Through Religious path (the Mechanical System). Warning and Order.
2- Transferring Your Essence to Society through Inspiration.
3- Service by Instinctive Impulses.
4- The indirect effects of those who can receive these Influences on those who can not receive them. (Transferring the Supreme Energies of the Friends in the Divine Realm through Spiritualism.)
5- The influence of Human Beings on Human Beings and Civilizations on Civilizations on this path. (Through Cerebral Thought.)
6- Direct Connections, Conscious Mission and Action.

Thus, Your Planet is reflecting on You a tableau of this Order. Later, We are going to tell You about "The Seven Facets" constituting You.

IT IS SPECIAL NOTICE FROM THE CENTER

GENERAL MESSAGE

Our Friends,
At the moment, You are receiving middle-wave Energy given from the North Pole. (This is not the Radio wave). You have to receive this Special Energy in order to be together with the Celestial Volunteers. This is an Energy which Nature withholds from You. Your Cells are being habituated to this Power gradually. This is an Engraftment Technique.

Deviations and undulations occur in Frequencies due to the alterations made at the Poles. Those who will enter the Golden Light Year are receiving these Currents from their Private Mediums. Because, they have private Mediums of Protection.

A Cloud of Fog which will envelope Your World will postpone the Sunny days for a moment. But some of You will profit from this situation (This Cloud of Fog is a special method causing the Cosmic Consciousness to spread more rapidly). We use this term as a UNIVERSAL term.

After February 18th of the World Year 1985, everyone's Private channel will be opened. Thus, the possibility to communicate with different Dimensions will be provided. For the time being, We rather get in touch with those who have High Levels of Consciousness. When the time comes, everybody, one by one, will be taken into consideration.

Let Us repeat the same thing again here. Everything depends on the Law of Graduation. No Brain Code can be unveiled by itself before the time comes. Distribution of Duty is made here according to the degree of Maturity of the Brain and help is extended. There is no privilege. The steps taken forward and the efforts made, will always prepare You for this Happy Medium. Our Love is upon the entire Universe.

COUNCIL OF STARS

THE SEVEN FACETS

The Energy which keeps Your Physical Atomic Bond together is called the (KUNDALINI) Energy. This Energy enters from the common point of the brain, goes through the spinal cord and accumulates at the coccyx as Cosmic Power. And from here, through the Energy pathway, the distribution of Cellular connection is made.

This is an extremely Powerful Energy. The accumulation of this Energy in the Physical Body in great quantities causes a lot of pain and discomfort. This accumulation does not occur in people who have attained Cosmic Consciousness. Because, they have become Conscious of the Law of Cause and Effect. They distribute the Currents they receive through the path of Consciousness. Their Brain Power has taken the Body under Supervision. From then on, they are each an Awakened Awareness.

Meditation serves You on this path. This accumulation of Energy is dangerous in proportion with its quantity in those who have not yet attained Consciousness. This is the cause of many Spiritual Depressions. The treatment for this depends on the principle of satisfaction through three ways:

1- To ground it (to perform ablution), to wash oneself.

2- To be relieved through sex.

3- To attain the Consciousness of Cosmic Awareness (those who attain this Consciousness are considered to have solved all their problems).

Every Human Being possesses all the characteristics and the qualities of the Energy Found in the Source of the Divine Power called the LORD. However, the Infinite Awareness present in Him has manifested itself in Human Beings as Partial and Individual Awareness. As a result, the Human Being, too, possesses a Creative Power. Let Us explain this to You by an example:

Draw the Awareness of the LORD as a Whole. Divide it into two. One half is a Whole and is the Infinite Awareness. Divide the other half into seven. Each of them is a Nucleus of Awareness. These are called a Facet each. Write them down in sequence:

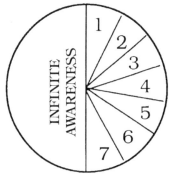

1- INTELLECT
2- INTELLIGENCE
3- AWARENESS
4- THOUGHT

5- IDEA
6- LOGIC
7- CONSCIENCE

Now, these Seven Facets are the ones which constitute the Human Being. Each of these Facets takes possession of the Fetus within the mother's uterus during Terrestrial life. From then on, it is under the Command of the Mechanism of Influences. Its Destiny will thus be designed. Each of these Facets, that is, Nucleus of Awareness is unaware of each other.

The Human Being in the normal World life, is connected to the Automatism. However, Incarnations gone through open these Facets to each other in accordance with the degrees of Evolvement. Once the Nucleus of Awareness attains the Knowledge of its Essence, then that Human Being is alone.

Many Friends who have reached this state of Consciousness have said (Enelhak) which means "God I Am". However, there is something they do not know. After the attainment of this Supreme Awareness and Cosmic Consciousness, they will enter the Infinite Awareness and only then will they attain many Information they did not know until then. And Infinite Knowledge will be poured onto You from the Infinite Awareness.

All Galactic Mediums are penetrating each other's Fields of Influence in a Prismal Order. Knowledge is transferred from infinite Universes to infinite Dimensions through Energy channels. The Knowledge You know at the moment is not even one billionth of the Knowledge of the infinite Universe. That is the reason why We say, "Knowledge is interminable".

IT IS SPECIAL NOTICE FROM THE CENTER

EXPLANATION OF THE KUNDALINI ENERGY

This is an Energy awakened independently of the Law of Action-Reaction. The Individual Awareness of a Human Being grows and expands in proportion with his/her Purification.

Each Cellular Awareness carries Universal Consciousness. A Human Being is an entity who has a Physical Body with certain requirements. This Energy possesses the Frequency of all kinds of requirements of the Physical Body.

In the undeveloped Medium of the World, the Human Being sometimes can be in a very deficient life in accordance with his/her Plan of Destiny. A Human Being has certain Secrets he/she conceals even from himself/herself. It is the Kundalini Energy which takes charge of these moments.

This Energy is the administrator of the Physical Order of the Body. Its Frequency forces the Awareness. The Forced Awareness becomes Conscious. And gets in touch with the Energy of the Intellect. The Intellect is the most Powerful Focal Point of the Layers of Awareness.

It is in contact with the Universal Energy. Intellect always Commands. This Mechanism nearly obsesses the Human Being in question. What is to be done is done and applied. The triplet of Intellect - Self - Awareness directs all these situations.

If the Awareness of a person is small, then he/she is directed by the Intellect which is under the influence of the Self, since he/she cannot benefit sufficiently from the Influence of this Energy. Evolvement is necessary for You in this very Medium. Religious Suggestions help You at this Stage.

A Human Being who possesses the Kundalini Energy finds himself/herself in different triangles from time to time.

1- The first triangle is the Fetus. This is the greatest triangle.
2- The second triangle is the Period up to the age of Puberty.
3- The third triangle is the life of a Human Being after the age of Puberty.

During this Period, a Human Being lives his/her normal World life.

When Your Mechanism of Thought begins to ask questions to itself, the Intellect, in a way, places a barrage to the Kundalini Energy.

In this Period, there is Sovereignty over the Self. After this Period, the triangle of Intellect - Intelligence - Awareness is established and the Heart Unites with the Self. This is Pure Self. In other words, it is the Soul, the Essence.

Afterwards, the triangle of Essence - Intellect - Universal Energy is established and, from then on, You may dive into many triangles. And You may learn many Unknowns.

IT IS SPECIAL NOTICE FROM THE CENTER

NOTICE FROM THE CENTER

Everything follows a course in accordance with the Law of Graduation. Events which occur or which will occur develop parallel to the Consciousness of the Universe. As the Integration takes place, You will receive very Powerful Information.

Nothing is given to You before the time comes. The Perceptions You receive are very intense Focal Points of the Universal Energies. Only high Consciousnesses enter these Mediums under protection by the Commands they receive. Otherwise, all their Energies become exhausted.

Now, let Us talk about the influences of these high Energies You receive on Your Physical Bodies. The Integrated Spiritual Energies move with such a vibration that each vibration reaches the speed of Light. The more these vibrations are and the more Powerful they are, the more intense will be the Dimensions to be entered.

The more Your Consciousness expands, the more will Your Perceptions and Vibrations increase and this augmentation of Your Vibrations will prepare You for the Medium of Evolvement. The Integrated Consciousnesses are taken into Dimensions they Deserve only through their Evolvement.

Now, let Us talk about the change the received Energies make in Your Physical Bodies.

These Energies You receive are a Favor for You. Your Cells become Purified and Regenerated due to them, defects You feel disappear in time. Many of You are running away from this interaction due to Your fears. For this reason You can not benefit from these Beautiful Energies.

Fear, automatically closes all the Energy channels instantly. In such a situation, Your cells will never be able to be regenerated. You will be deprived both of Knowledge and of Care.

Some of Our Friends are making transmissions from such a beautiful Medium that these Energies become Your antidote. Time will prove everything. The Truest Spiritual Guide is to become noble in time.

MUSTAFA MOLLA

OUR FRIENDS

The First Plan of the Universal Mechanism is the Divine Order. In other words, it is the Religious Suggestions and the Celestial Commands. This is the First Step You will have to pass. You can not receive Universal Information unless You Jump over this Step. Those who have attained Religious Fulfillment are jumping over this step.

If they wish, Friends who have passed over this step may or may not continue performing their worship. This is up to their Free Will. What is important for Us is Their Essence. Friends who have reached this Stage have already attained what is to be attained. The Worship they will perform will be nothing but their Habits.

In fact, from then on, they will attain Universal Consciousness, will realize many Truths and will continue performing their Missions in higher Mechanisms in different Dimensions. This Book will be a Guide of Knowledge for Friends who no longer need any Books.

SUPREME ASSEMBLY

NOTICE TO THE PEN OF THE GOLDEN AGE

Our Friends,

We take those who can enter the Mevlana Frequency under a special Protection Medium. We will have Special Contacts with those who will enter the Realm of Perfection. By great fastidiousness, selections will be made both among Groups and among Human Beings until the opening Period of the Religious Suggestions.

There is a special reason for this selection. It will be awaited and seen. Good news and bliss will be for them. They will Deserve this Merit provided they do not accept unimportant difficulties they will encounter as obstacles, and provided they accept that everything is proceeding on a Divine Course.

Give the Messages preferably to those who desire to read them. Desire is the first Sub-awareness Motivation for Universal Unification. However, the seeds You are going to sow in Friends who are Sincere but who are not aware of this Medium, will create a preparation for Awakening.

We are trying to open the direct channels of everyone, beginning with the World Year February 18, 1985. Thus, Friends within the Group will talk everywhere they go and will sow seeds of Knowledge about the Universal Medium.

From now on, both talking and distribution of the Messages will be done during the performance of Duties. Speed is needed within Time.

SUPREME ASSEMBLY

SPECIAL NOTICE

Our Friends,

In the Book, We have to answer certain Chains of Thought. Friends who have read the Book of Islam know that the words, "This is an oath" are frequently used, in the Book. Now, let Us explain this:

Our Light-Friend, from time to time, had suspicions while the Book of Islam had been dictated to Him. He was not a person to deceive people. Writing or dictating a Book is a work of great responsibility.

For this reason the words, "This is an oath" had been used frequently. These words were not told to assure the Public, but to satisfy, assure and to give serenity to Our Light-Friend. Now, why do We dictate this here?

Now, at this moment, We have received the same chains of Thought from Dear Mevlana, too. Having the same worries, she, too, wants to be assured of the statements dictated to her. She asks Us the degree of Truth of this Information in order to be sure that Human Beings are not deceived.

And We answer her in the following way: "Mevlana We swear that everything is authentic and is completely true" (Except the contradictions which have been specially placed in the Book).

And these are placed to control the Thoughts and the Levels of Knowledge of Our Human brothers and sisters. The Command We had received was like this. You are Mevlana, You are generous and a true performer of Truth, My Friend.

We request You to add this article in the Book, please.

L I G H T

N E P T U N E

This is Captain Neptune to Greet You and to convey to You all Our Love on behalf of Our Eighteen Members from Our private channel of Supervision:

At the moment, You are receiving the different Waves of a different Dimension. We are preparing the Friends who will be taken into Universal Unification for these Special Waves.

We come from a common section which is at the Eighteenth Dimension of the Sun beyond KARENA. Karena is a subjective field of Brain Energies. This is a Field of Volume which is far beyond the Waves You receive from the Channel of Seven Lights.

The Dimensions of numerous Galaxies outside Your System have been connected to the Energy of this Medium. The Dimension of the World is not accustomed to this yet.

A Gradual Engraftment System will be applied on You in a Magnetic Medium carrying the Energy of the Eighteenth Dimension, before You are directly taken there.

At the moment, Our base is a Relaxation Medium prepared as a part of this Dimension carrying its Energy. You can enter there only after You get used to the Energy here.

The Altona Waves of the Golden Light Year are very Powerful. From the Golden Light Year, one goes to Altona, and from there, to the Golden Moon and from the Golden Moon to the Golden Sun (Here the word Golden Symbolizes the Mediums of pure Energy and the Receptive Powers of these Systems).

The Golden Sun is AMON. He is the only God connected to the Telekine System. He has assembled all the Scientific Suns in Himself. The Golden Galaxy is administered by Brain Energies. These are very Powerful Waves.

The Vibrations completely create Color Mediums. Only those who can receive these Vibrations will hear the sounds. At the moment, Your connection with this medium is arranged by the Special Ships of AMON.

This is Our Fourth visit to Your Planet. At the moment, We have a connection with You out of the Circuit. You receive this Message transmitted from a place more Golden than the Medium of AMON and which is considered as the main artery of the Planet.

You will get clearer Information when the time comes. Our connection with You will never cease, Our Friend Mevlana. It is a great gain for Your World, even if the proportion of Missions performed are only One in a hundred.

NEPTUNE

NOTICE TO THE CODES OF ART

Our Friends,

In accordance with the Universal Law, connections are made with all the Codes of Art. These Messages in your hands are being dictated by a System Your Planet does not know yet.

The receiver of the Messages is Your direct Channel of Anatolia. This Book which compiles together all the Religious Books in accordance with the Universal Theory, is yet addressing the bottom Level of Social Consciousness.

You, the Artists are the Godly Codes. The step of Evolvement begins with Art. Each of You is a Light who Enlightens Society. All Our Terrestrial Friends are a Missionary each.

However, in Codes of Art this Consciousness expands to very advanced Dimensions. The course of Your Duties will change in time. Time will prove everything to You.

We ask You to prepare the Social Consciousness for the Consciousness of the Golden Age. All of You are Awakened Friends who have attained Cosmic Consciousness. The Universe is making its Progress in accordance with the Law of Equilibrium. A new BETA Solar System is being created by means of the entire Universal Energy.

What You call Resurrection is the Resurrecting of Consciousnesses. We have unveiled the Skies for You. From now on everything will advance on the path of Learning and Science. But Our Human brothers and sisters will be Purified according to the needs of their Essence. The increase in concentration in Religious Mediums is due to this.

Aside from the Purification and Evolvement which takes place by means of Religious Fulfillment, the Purification of the Brain, of the Spirit and of the Essence by means of the Arts requires an Evolvement Level even beyond the limits of the Universe. Greetings from all the Galaxy Systems to Friends who have attained this Progress.

The Supervision of the Heavens of yours is under the control of a Mechanical System. This Book is dictated by direct Channel Connection. Our Contacts with Our other Friends occur through Mediamic Channels (that is, through Mediums).

From time to time, contacts are made both directly and through Dream Channels with Friends who have attained Cosmic Consciousness. Your World is now within a new Universal Consciousness.

What You call Flying Saucers are Our small Disks. Our Ships besides these are much bigger than those. However, We land on Your World by the Disks. When You read the Messages, You will grasp the seriousness of the matter.

Your path is the path of Learning and Science. By means of this Book, We are trying to bring the bottom closer to the top. The Messages will be sent to the appropriate Codes of Art. Love to all Friends from the Universe.

THE SIRIUS MISSION SHIP,
ON BEHALF OF THE COUNCIL OF STARS

MESSAGE FROM THE GROUP MISSIONARIES

Our Universal Friends asked me to give Information about the Group. This article is written for this reason.

The name of Our Group is (MEVLANA ESSENCE NUCLEUS GROUP). The Only Representative of the World Brotherhood Union is Our Group. We have been in touch with Our Universal Friends for Twenty Years. However, We have begun to give the Messages We received to the World when the Ten Commandments and the Law of Universe were dictated in 1981.

According to the Messages We have received, the Messages were sent first to the Pope, then to the key positions of the World. We have taken the Permission to get in touch with all Our Human brothers and sisters beginning from January 1984. Last year, We have published Six Fascicules, one for each Month and each Fascicule consisting of Nine pages (We were asked to publish the Fascicules in this form).

We act according to the Information given. Six more Fascicules will be published in 1985, too. The Fascicules are sent to the same addresses as the first ones, each Month regularly. Our contact with each Continent is maintained in this way. By the accumulation of the Six Fascicules published each year, the Universal Book will be completed. With Regards.

BÜLENT ÇORAK
On Behalf of the Group

IT IS SPECIAL MESSAGE TO CERTAIN CHAINS OF THOUGHT

Our Friends,
There is such a Plan developed within the infinite Dimension of Your Universe at the moment that there even Evolvement has lost its Allness within Nothingness.

The Relative Mental Speeds of other Universes transcend the Speeds of Light in more Advanced Dimensions which are beyond Billions of Light Years (the Speed of Thought mentioned here is different than Yours. We used this expression to make You understand).

SUPREME TIME which starts beyond timelessness is a state where Thought arrives when it Transcends itself. There the entire Cosmos is transformed. Even the concept of Time transcends a Dimension beyond Realization and is taken under the Supervision of the Divine Mechanism.

No Living Entity can ever enter the Supreme Time directly. It can only be present in the Cosmoses which can receive the Reflections coming from there. Timelessness is a state in which all Entities can Perceive or Realize themselves in the darkness of the shadow of God.

It is very difficult to understand this. Timelessness, at the moment, is beyond Your Comprehension. Now, You are receiving the Altona Waves from the Golden Light Year. The Mechanism operates with all its Power. Your Brain generator is linked to the Mechanical Logic by a special System.

This Logic regulates Your Thought Frequencies. You can receive the Waves beyond the Dimension only afterwards. The Sub-Awareness is dealing with the Frequencies below that.

The more Powerful You receive the Energies beyond the Dimension, the more Powerful You will be. Direct connections always give the Information of Over-Awareness. Later, other Information will be given to You besides the Information about the Universes and the Galaxies.

IT IS SPECIAL NOTICE FROM THE CENTER

GENERAL MESSAGE

Our Friends,
Each of You is a Biological Computer Embodied in accordance with the conditions of Nature. Your Brain Power has a receiving Capacity of 1,235,000 Channels. However, You can not use this ability of Yours.

Messages given to You are arranged in accordance with the quantity of words in Your Brain Computers and the registers are made accordingly. The richer Your vocabulary is, the richer will be the Knowledge You will receive. For this reason We always get in touch with the Brain Codes of high Levels.

Our aim is to address all the Consciousnesses. That is why, for Centuries, We have told You to "read, read, read". The aim of reading is not to repeat what You already know. Reading should be in every field.

Your vocabulary can thus become richer and by this means You can grasp better the meaning of the words You are going to write and read. The words which are not known in the World Consciousness notion are dictated by coding the letters, one by one, which are in Your Brain Codes.

Our Friends whose Religious Knowledge is more than their Learning Knowledge, will do nothing but repeat the Religious Messages over and over again. At the moment, the channel of everyone is connected to the Mechanical System. From there, they will receive the Information of more Advanced Dimensions.

Friends who have connections with the Spiritual Plan can never make further progress if they can not disconnect themselves from the Medium which they are sympathized with. The nature of the Messages You receive will change in proportion with the Consciousness You attain.

We have mentioned the Truth to You in numerous Messages. Those who train You first are Your Friends of the Divine Realm. You reached Us through them. However, from now on, prepare Your subsequent Knowledge in accordance with the Unknowns. Then You will receive Messages of better quality.

On this path, all the branches of Art will help You. The Press, the Radio, TV., Painting, Sculpture, Ceramics, Theatre, Opera, Ballet, and Cinema always convey the Messages to You. Music and Concerts are helpful to You in another way. Their Vibrations are effective on Your Cells.

Your Consciousness Codes which become richer by these channels will comprehend the Messages given to You more easily. Train Yourselves and attain Consciousness on this path. Maybe You can not become an Edison or an Einstein, but You can add something to the Public Consciousness.

If You can not help Us, We can not do anything either. We have only unveiled the Skies and We now want to give all the Information. We bow down with Respect in front of Our Friends who can receive them.

SUPREME ASSEMBLY

SPECIAL NOTICE

Dear Mevlana,
You may freely convey to the Public Consciousness the Private Information You receive which are not included in the Sections of the Book, as a Knowledge. It is within Your initiative (The private Conversations may be written in the Book).

L I G H T

BY THE COMMAND OF THE CENTRAL SYSTEM,
NOTICE FROM THE SECTION OF THE
UNIFICATION OF MATTER

The Cosmos corresponds to a Universe in which All Galactic Mediums exist. However, these Cosmoses collect numerous Universes. Let Us explain this more clearly:

All the Galaxies have been formed by Big-Bangs, in accordance with the Law of Eighteen Systems, in an Atomic Medium. This is not under Our supervision. It is an Occurrence belonging to the Circulating System of Nature. We are only responsible for the Supervision of the Systems which are formed.

There is a very Powerful Supervision and Unification in the Universal Plan. This Unification depends on a mutual Friendship. The Mechanism of the LORDs presents a Hierarchical Order in accordance with the Value assessment of a Mechanical System.

The evaluation of this System begins with the Three cube. This is a Prime number, it does not change. Your Universe is subject to the evaluation of a Prismal System which is dependent on the Centrifugal speed.

Universes are interminable, having no Boundaries. Within each Universe, there are many Cosmoses, many Realms. The only common point of this Divine Order is the Atomic Unification. All the Galaxies are under the Command of a Common Section. We call them, "Cosma Unification Centers".

Cosma Unification Centers are 27 in number. Each Unification Center supervises a Realm. Realms are constituted by numerous Galaxy-Clusters. 18,000 Realms constitute a Cosmos and further, 18,000 Cosmoses constitute the Universe of the System.

Numbers and Measurements belong to Your Planet. Here, the Units of Measurement are expressed differently. We give the Messages to You in accordance with Your Knowledge and Levels of Understanding. Here, We used the expressions Realm and Cosmos separately for You to understand.

The Universe, which is subject to the Law of 18 Systems creates a Centrifugal Medium. Besides this, there are many Universes with quite different orbits. Some of them are:

Realms evaluated in accordance with the Cube System, some are Realms evaluated according to the System of Connected Vessels, some are Universes subject to different evaluations created by the Particle Systems (There is no rotation in them).

We have not given this Information to anybody yet. We give them here as a tiny bit of Knowledge. Even though You are a very small part of the Milky Way Galaxy, You receive the Information of a Medium subject to the Law of Eighteen Systems. We just ask You to Think about other Galaxy Mediums, also.

There are many Galaxy-Clusters and many Universe-Clusters which transcend this Order interminably. There is no end to these Realms and Cosmoses. Even Our Friends who have reached the highest Level still try to discover them.

There are such Dimensions that Your expressions and terms are not used there. Neither the Electricity there, nor the Lights are the Electricity and Lights You know. Their Energy is not the Energy You know.

Numbers and Letters are not used in the evaluations. A fuller system is dominant there. Even if We try to explain, it is incomprehensible. However, let Us explain this more clearly: Let Us dictate them article by article to make You understand better.

1- As a necessity of the Universal Unification, the Galaxies consisting of Cosmas form the Realms.

2- Numerous Realms form a Cosmos. This is a Systematic tableau.

3- Numerous Cosmoses form the Universe, which is subject only to the Law of Eighteen Systems.

4- In the Centrifugal Universe, there is a spinning speed within each other and a sequence within each other. There is an expansion and an opening from the center towards the circumference of the circle.

5- Universes are one inside the other like the rings of a time tunnel. Seven Universe rings form a Universe.

6- 189 Universes, existing one inside the other, form many Realms and Cosmoses.

7- Each Galaxy has a small Universe peculiar to itself and a very Powerful Magnetic Field.

8- This Magnetic Power is provided by the Energies of the Solar Systems within its constitution.

9- Black Holes are very Powerful Energy Whirlpools that swallow the Meteors the Centrifugal speeds of which have slowed down.

10- These Whirlpools immediately transform these Meteors to Energy and reinforce the decreased Energy of Your Universe.

11- These Energies are transported to Your Universe by White Holes. This is a Circulating System. One swallows, the other vomits.

12- Galaxies maintain their courses by being subject to the Law of Eighteen Systems.

13- For Us, Three Galaxies are accepted as a Whole.

14- Six Galaxies are, for Us, a NOVA.

15- Three Novas are the Essence Nucleus of Eighteen Galaxies. And Eighteen Galaxies are the Nucleus of a small Universe.

16- Within the UNIVERSE, there are many Universal Nuclei. And these form the Universe-Clusters.

17- Each Big-Bang forms Eighteen Galaxies.

18- Eighteen galaxies are a COSMA.

19- Each Cosma is the small Nucleus of a Universe. These are very Powerful Atomic Bonds.

20- In Our Galaxies, each Cosma is evaluated as a small Sun.

21- Three Universal Nuclei are a Galaxy-Cluster consisting of 54 Galaxies.

22- Add the Figures of 54 like this: 5+4=9.

23- Nine Galaxy-Clusters form one of Our Universal Colonies.

24- One Universal Colony consists of 486 Galaxies.

25- Add the number 486 in the following way: 4+8+6=18

26- 18 Universal Colonies, that is, 8748 Galaxies are a Cosma Union.

27- Each Union is under the supervision of different Centers.

28- Add the figures of 8748 like this 8+7+4+8=27

29- 27 Cosma Unions form a REALM. Each Union Center Supervises a Realm.

30- One Realm comprises 236,196 Galaxies within itself.

31- 18,000 Realms form a Cosmos. That is, a Cosmos consists of
236,196 X 18,000 = 4,251,528,000 Galaxies.

32- 18,000 Cosmoses have formed the Universe of the System.

33- 18,000 Realms are under the Supervision of the Assembly of the Constant Ones
which is under the Command of the Law of the Almighty. This Assembly is in the
SIRIUS Star. Calculations after this extend towards the infinite Dimension.

34- Now, add the figures 4,251,528,000: 4+2+5+1+5+2+8+000=27.

35- Since the evaluations in the System are Three to the power of Three, if We divide 27
into 3, We will always find the Prime Number 9. This is the unchanging Theory of
the Divine Command.

36- Each Galaxy has a Spinning Speed and a Universal tableau peculiar to itself.

37- Each COSMA is subject to a Universal Law.

38- Each Galaxy has direct channels connected to the Central System.

39- Now, We have received the Command to include Your COSMA, that is Your small
Universe Nucleus, consisting of 18 Galaxies, in this Universal Colony.

40- The SIRIUS Mission is responsible only for the Supervision of Your Milky Way
Galaxy.

41- The Selection is controlled and Supervised by a Mechanical System.

42- The SIRIUS Mission is responsible for Uniting the Solar Systems within itself, as a
necessity of the Unified Field.

43- Solar Systems under the supervision of each Galaxy are subject to different
Evolutions.

44- Now, We are trying to prepare You for the Medium of Salvation by the Command
of the Mechanism of the LORD.

45- Each Galaxy has a LORD Mechanism.

46- These LORDs are not the Almighty.

47- Your Religious Suggestions have been given to You in accordance with the
Consciousness of the Medium You are in.

48- God evaluates You in accordance with Your behavior.

49- The most primitive Level of Evolvement in Your Galaxy is Your Planet. Evaluations
are started from the Zero Frequency.

50- Fear is primitiveness, there is no Heaven, no Hell, no Jinn, no Fairy, no Devil.
These are each the Negative reflections of the conditioned Consciousnesses.

51- You are deprived of solution due to Your narrow Capacities.

52- You are subject to such a System that only Love, Tolerance, and Goodwill can reinforce the Potential of Your Universe.

53- Otherwise, Your Planet is doomed to be annihilated. You will destroy Yourselves. You are the ones who are Responsible for this.

54- Those who complete the World Evolvement are taken into more advanced Evolvement Mediums.

55- Those who win the Test of the most advanced Dimension of Your Galaxy are the Solar Teachers of Your Galaxy. If they wish, they are Reincarnated in Your World once more, in order to be able to give You Knowledge.

56- Those who can not reach the desired level of Evolution are kept waiting at the Spadium* Station. And they complete their Evolvements by being subject to Incarnations again and again.

57- You will never be taken to Advanced Evolvement Dimensions if You can not overcome Your Egos.

58- Those who deserve the right to enter the Advanced Evolvement Dimension are taken into contact, one by one, with the Galactic Mediums of their own Cosma.

59- Each Galaxy is connected to Four Knowledge channels. And these Four Channels are, one by one, shedding Light on the Solar Systems in accordance with the Medium they are in.

60- Each channel is directed by a Commission consisting of 6 Supreme Ones.

61- The Supreme Assembly is formed by the Command of the Center and the Unification of the Four Channels, that is, by the mediation of 24 Supreme Ones.

62- Your Universal Book, which is dictated, is being dictated directly by the Command of the LORD.

63- This Book is the Constitution of 18 Galaxies, that is, of Your Cosma. And it is its SINGLE Book.

64- Service is for the Single Hand - for the Single Order - for the Single Book.

65- We are obliged to connect each 18 Galaxies to the 72nd Dimension from beyond time. But it is not the due time yet for this Knowledge.

66- We wish to add here that these texts are given directly from the Universal Mechanism. For this reason everything is authentic.

IT IS THE COMMAND OF THE CENTER

E X P L A N A T I O N

All Information is given from the same Focal Point by the Command of the LORD. Each Medium who has Taken Duty has a Supreme One Charged with Duty. This Information is conveyed to Your Planet by the Command of the Mechanism. The Consciousnesses who will be Awakened in each Group are prepared in accordance with the Information steps they will receive and perceive.

* Look at the Glossary.

Your Book is dictated to Dear Mevlana by the Channel of Mustafa Molla, conveyed by means of the direct Energy of the Almighty and from the Consciousness of focal point of (O). Meanwhile, since the Book is the inter-Galactic Constitution which provides the Universal Unification, the connection of Mevlana's Channel to numerous Galactic Frequencies is necessitated by the Command.

Thus, numerous Mother Ships are in touch with Dear Mevlana who is the Channel of Mustafa Molla. And they are obliged to give You the Information they receive. By this means, Universal Unification is provided. With Our Infinite respect to Dear Mevlana.

NOTICE FROM
THE CENTER ABOVE THE CENTER

IT IS ANSWER TO THE CHAINS OF THOUGHT

Each Galaxy takes its place on the Systematic Tableau by the Centrifugal Powers of their own Solar Systems. A Galaxy within Your Cosma, that is, within Your 18 Galaxies, nearest to the Second Universe and even the name of which You do not know yet, is obliged to convey the Information it receives to the Galaxies within the Dimensions up to which its Energy extends. By this means, Information reaches up to Your Planet which is in the Third Dimension.

Each Galaxy System is in touch with each other respectively. There is a Central Supervision which administers each System. These Centers are unified with each other in accordance with the Universal Law. At the moment, the Energies of all the Solar Systems of the 18 Galaxies are taken under the control of a Very Powerful Focal Point and are collected in the Automatic Logic Generator.

When this Energetic point annihilates the Crystal Cloud at the final Universal Curtain of the 18 Universes, it will create many Galaxies and Solar Systems in a very different Medium in conformity with that Medium. Since this creation will take place gradually, a great explosion is not expected. This Information is an Information coming from Times beyond the bygone Times.

CENTER ABOVE THE CENTER

NOTICE FROM THE COUNCIL OF THE LOYAL ONES

Our Friends,
We are a Group of Wise People who give Special Information to the Planet Earth together with the Sirius Mission by the special Command of the Council of Stars. Only after the Vibrations received from Your Planet it was possible to make Contact with You.

Let Us talk to You briefly about the Principles of the Plan of the Loyal Ones. The Loyal Ones are the Devoted Friends of a Commission which prepares certain Suggestions taken as a necessity of the Sacred Mechanism in accordance with the conditions of Your Planet, and are the coherent Staff Members of the Plan Application Department.

This is a Mechanism which Administers by a single hand the Commands or rather the Laws of all the Universal Commissions, collecting them within the Universal Plan. Each Planet is Devotedly committed to Universal Laws. Everything is in the Order of a Systematic Tableau.

The Sirius Star Council is Responsible for the Universal Order. Sirius is an Orderly Planet Administered by a Mission. It works Cooperatively with the Council of Stars and the Assembly of the Constant Ones. It is responsible for giving Information regarding only the Milky Way Galaxy.

It receives the Commands from the Council of the Loyal Ones. The Council of the Loyal Ones is a Whole which Administers the inter-Galactic Unification. Other Missions, too, besides the Sirius Mission are serving towards the Golden Age.

The Plan of the Loyal Ones, which comprises great Knowledge, has been prepared by the Loyal Supreme Ones and have been announced to Your Planet. But since this Knowledge has been given outside the System, it somewhat has a remote expression considering Your Medium.

This Plan has a Cipher peculiar to itself. The aim is to raise the Consciousness Codes up to the Universal Level of Knowledge. The given Messages comprise all the Knowledge of the Medium You will be in, up to Your present times.

The Plan of the Loyal Ones is equipped with the Knowledge beyond Karena (When the Time comes Karena will be mentioned to You). To appropriate to one's self the actual Purpose of the Plan and to comprehend even one tenth of the Information given in the Book will be a great gain for Your Planet.

THE COUNCIL OF THE LOYAL ONES

NOTICE FROM THE SUPREME ASSEMBLY

Our Friends,
Direct Connections with all the Galaxies will be provided when the Mevlana Thought becomes the Single Thought of the entire Universe. The Responsible Ones who act in accordance with the Commands of the Central System are shedding Light on the operation of the Universal Mechanism.

Discoveries beyond distances can not quite reach You at the moment. For this reason interruptions took place in certain Frequencies. The reason for this is that there is an overall Supervision in all Galactic Mediums.

Mustafa Molla is on Duty in another Dimension of the Firmament. For this reason Messages are dictated by the Center Above The Center, through the Channel of the Supreme Assembly. This will continue until the end of April of the World Year 1985.

There have been some deviations on the chains of Thought towards the Religious side, when the Universal Plan which will select the Sincere Ones has been conveyed to You. This means that everyone tries to propagandize in his/her own Medium. But the Aim is:

Single Hand - Single Book - Single Golden Path.

Universal Unification Council operates in this way. We convey to You the Truth once more. General Messages will be started to be given after those who will enter the Golden Light Year are Supervised.

Special treatment is applied on those who will enter the Assembly of the Constant Ones. The Supervision over the entire Universe is Administered by a Special Channel. It is presented for Your Information.

SUPREME ASSEMBLY

GENERAL MESSAGE

Our Friends,
All Information given to the Planet Earth is still in a Preparatory nature. We will give the Genuine Information when the difference between the Levels of Evolvement become minimum (except in this Book).

For the time being, the inter-Global communications are made through Mediamic channels. For this reason many proofs take place by the General Frequency adjustment. Information given is received by all the Mediums of Your Planet in accordance with the Dimensions of their Frequencies.

The Mechanism of Influences makes no discrimination. However, special assistance is given to Friends Charged With Duty, in accordance with their Duty responsibilities. And this is not a personal assistance, but it is an application as a necessity of the Universal Plan.

It is possible for anyone to receive the Energies of different Dimensions besides receiving his/her own channel only on the condition that he/she is from the Mechanism of that Dimension. Otherwise, both the Physical and the Mental Energies are atrophied. Contacts are being made by considering these situations.

M A L I K

IT IS ANSWER TO THOUGHTS

Sirius is a Medium full of Light which has a warm climate, the nature of which, more or less, resembles Your Planet. It is the Star of the Missionaries on Advanced Spiritual Levels. Numerous Profound Saints and Sages are from the Sirius Star. It is the Single Mission which applies the Universal Plan of the Divine Mechanism.

EXPLANATION FROM THE COUNCIL OF STARS

Our Friends,
The Golden Age is Interpreted in different ways in the Minds of certain Friends. For this reason We would like to make an explanation about the Golden Age.

You, too, know that Gold is a metal which has high Communication Power. Words used in the Messages such as Gold, Silver, Sun, Light are used as a Symbol each.

The place from which the Commands for the revealed Sacred Books were given is a Sacred Mechanism. It is directed directly by the Commands of the LORD. The Council of the Loyal Ones is obliged to give these Commands to You. Its Supervision is in the Command of the Council of Stars. It is in a Cooperative working tempo with the Assembly of the Constant Ones.

The Resurrection Period mentioned in Your Sacred Books is the Period You are living in. The term Resurrecting means the Awakening of Consciousnesses, as We always say. Thus, these Awakened Consciousnesses get in touch with the other Magnetic Mediums by Brain Telexes (You call these Friends, Mediums).

Since the increase in Perceptions which occurs as a necessity of the Period will multiply even more the Universal Communications, the Communication Power of Gold is taken here as a Symbol. And this Age is called the "Golden Age".

The Order which will be established will be an Order as Pure and as Clean as Gold itself. Our Aim is to provide for Our Terrestrial brothers and sisters a Happy World without Wars and Blood. The Communication of Cosmic Consciousnesses in this Age is accepted as equivalent to the Purity and Communication Capacity of Gold.

The real Foundation of the Golden Age will be laid after the Year 2000. Now, only the Seeds are sown. Until the Year 2000, all Brain Energies will enter Universal Dimensions and direct Connections with Centers will be made by Brain Telexes.

Only then, different kinds of Connections will be made with You in proportion with Your attainment of the Truth. Thus, Consciousnesses who grasp the entire Truth will establish a World which is yearned for.

The Mechanism takes under Supervision each Consciousness with all its Effort in accordance with his/her degree of Awareness and sends him/her to Mediums he/she Deserves. And, in this way, each one is prepared for a more rapid Awakening Medium.

All the World Groups are under the Supervision of the Mechanism. All the Groups which will be able to enter the triangle of the (World Brotherhood Union) are assembled on the same threshold. Everything is arranged in accordance with the World Time.

You are the Ones who are going to establish the Beautiful World which is Yearned for, not Us. Hand in hand, You will walk on Flowery pathways and will attain Genuine Happiness.

You have evaluated Resurrection and Sırat differently, due to insufficient explanations in Your Religious Books. However, even though the Awakened Wise People have grasped the meaning of them, they preferred to remain silent, due to their scruples about the Consciousness of the Medium.

Now, We have unveiled the Skies. We are laying the naked Truths before Your eyes. We repeat once more for Friends who are still unable to grasp the Truth:

1- Resurrecting = the unveiling of Brain Codes.

2- Resurrection = Your introduction to Mediums, one by one, which You did not know until today (in proportion with the Merit).

3- Sırat = the explanation of Secrets and the direct Supervision of the Mechanism. The given Orders are directly the Orders of the LORD from the Mechanism of the Almighty.

COUNCIL OF STARS

OUR FRIENDS

The Duty of the Supervision Center is to make You attain Yourselves and to introduce to the Medium the Mechanism which is the application field of the Universal Plan.

The Awareness, Idea, Action Triplet is the measure of the Consciousness Level as a necessity of the Mechanism. Connection of these Three Channels to the Universal Mechanism is sufficient to include You in this Plan. For this reason this Period is called, The Period of Sincerity.

Be Good, Think Good, Do Good Deeds. These Three Suggestions suffice to register You to the Council of the Loyal Ones. This registration is easy to Say, but it is difficult to Apply. To attain this, the Triplet of Determination - Willpower - Perseverance should turn the handle of the wheel of the Mechanism.

This Success prepares You for the Information of higher Dimensions. The Information is given from the Common Declaration of the Golden Age. The application of Our Plan has begun with the Command of the Universal Mechanism for Unification. The entire Mechanism is operating by the Universal Potential.

You, the Missionaries of Peace will be taken care of personally and will be the witnesses of the establishment of a Great System. Human Beings will be induced to go through certain important experiments so that the Unification of the Integrated Consciousnesses can be made. Many bridges will be passed until You attain this Consciousness.

Passing through all these narrow straits will lead them to very Powerful Gateways. Courage and Strength are necessary in order to be able to pass these Exams. Do not ever presume that anybody can enter this Medium by his/her own Wish. The Aim is to grasp the Truth on the path to be treaded.

All difficulties originate from Unconsciousness. You can sail Your ships even without water when You attain the actual Consciousness. To attain Consciousness means to reach the Truth. To attain the Truth means to attain Bliss.

There is no compulsion in the state of Bliss. There are no more Exams what so ever. The only thing to be done from then on is to perform Duty. When one becomes a great Light, when to the Heavens arrived, when into Divine Lights taken then, Examinations cease to be.

To reach the places here is not easy at all. The more rapidly You attain Consciousness, the Smoother and more Systematic will be Your direct connections with the Dimensions You will perceive. All these things take place by the Sun of Your Essence. Our Love is to You.

YULAMI
The Seal of the Center of the Center

NOTICE FROM THE CENTRAL SYSTEM
(This Message is dictated by the Command of the Center)

Our Friends,
Some misunderstandings have been witnessed in Your Medium which You evaluate as the Space Age. For this reason We convey to You the Truth.

The Space Age in Your Planet Earth has long been terminated in Our section. Now, You are receiving the Information comprising Consciousnesses beyond Consciousnesses, from far beyond the Space Age. The Space Age in Your Planet had begun with the transmission of the Celestial Commands to You.

In the Medium in which Sacred Books and Sacred Supreme Ones had become ineffective, The Space Age had been terminated and the Age of Universal Knowledge has begun. The Space Age had been terminated with the Book of Islam and with Our Light-Friend, the Prophet of Islam. We were obliged to inform You of this.

You have remained on the same Level due to Your Conditioned Consciousnesses, for You have received the Energies of different Dimensions very scarcely during the Space Age in which You have lived for Centuries. But now, the Universal Unification System is calling to You under the Supervision of a Mechanism beyond Space, directly from the System of the Almighty.

Scientific explorations of Your Satellites in Space are completely out of the Mechanical System. For this reason You call the Age You are in, The Space Age (Let Us repeat once more to avoid any misunderstanding). Your Space Age had been completely terminated together with the Period of Religions.

Now, You are receiving the Scientific Information beyond Religions from the direct Channel of the Universal Mechanism. The Poles are the same in the Book which is being dictated, but the expressions are different. Each System is named in accordance with the Level of Knowledge it gives. Your present Period is called (THE UNIVERSAL LIGHT YEAR). It is presented for Your information.

NOTICE FROM
THE CENTER ABOVE THE CENTER

OUR FRIENDS

All Universal Unifications are from the same Focal Point and are investments for the Golden Age. These Messages are given to You by a Projector of the Divine Mechanism. ALLAH is the Ancient Energy. Reaching Him, instead of worshipping Him is the most Mutual Unification.

The Special Missionaries of Supervision of the Spiritual Entities are guiding You. Worships are always a beginning. Worship is not advised for the Supreme Energies who come from within Limitless Dimensions. Because, they are the Pre-eminent Ones who have long transcended Worship.

THE ESSENCE OF THE HUMAN BEING IS EVEN MORE SUPREME THAN PROSTRATION.

The Supreme Ones, who bring the Divine Light of the Heavens down to the Earth, are Essence Messengers of ALLAH. They are Gold each. They plate the Silvers. The Genuine Human Beings always give.

The Source never pours back to itself. Worship is the same, too. Prayers through the Essence reach the LORD, through Words they reach the Servants. By this means, Silvers are plated with Gold. The Essence of the Universe is the Eye of the LORD. Our Love is for the entire Universe.

PEN OF THE GOLDEN AGE
P. G. A.

IT IS INFORMATION ABOUT EXISTENCE
GIVEN FROM THE REALM OF THE ANGELS

Information for the Mevlana Code:

God has designed an Evolutionary Tableau in accordance with His System of Creation. This is an operational System parallel to the Law of Action which Nature has on You. Now, We will explain everything clearly in a comprehensible way:

The cause of Existence of the Realms which receive their Might from the Power of the Divine Realms depends on the Evolutionary Plan. We call this Plan The Plan of the Loyal Ones. All the Information given from here is authentic. Information will be given specially to the Pen of the Golden Age.

Existence has come into being by the Cellular Unification of the Aminoacids. These Aminoacids are formed by the transformation of Soil and Water from the state of Mud to the state of the Organism. In other words, the Single Cell has been formed in this way, conforming to the Evolutionary Plan.

As long as this Single Cell continued its Evolution, it has been taken into the Evolvement Plan and, in this way, its Cellular Awareness has developed. The Developed Cellular Consciousness has Created the Living Being.

When the Cell which completed its Evolution got possession of all the Knowledge of the Universal Plan, it has claimed its Essence-Energy at the Spiritual Plan and has attained the Power of Creating itself. In other words, it is a God-Consciousness. All the Secrets of the Universe are concealed within it.

The Cellular Awareness has enjoyed all the blessings of the LORD. Thus, it has gained supremacy over Nature and the Universe. Later, Your Universal Evolvement has begun by means of Integrated Bodies.

Thus, the Cellular Vibrations, having embraced all the void, have created many Energy Accumulations. The Mediums beyond Time, which have become bygone Time, have also passed through the same Evolution in accordance with their Mediums.

The Embodied Being has gotten in Touch with the Spiritual Plan to complete its Thought Evolution. As it has accumulated the Universal Energy of this Spiritual Mechanism within its Body, it has claimed its Essence Being, that is, its Spiritual Energy.

From then on, it is in its possession. Now, the Evolution of the Human Being Begins from this point, through Incarnations. And by means of the Progress of consequent Periods of Time, he/she completes his/her Evolvement as a Human Being.

Now, We will talk about something which surprises You. Certain Living Beings which could not pass through certain Evolutionary Steps, or, that is, which could not reach the Energy of the Spiritual Plan are Embodied in the Evolutions of certain Mediums in a different way.

For instance: there are Galaxies in which Cats, Dogs, Birds, Dinosaurs, Apes are sovereign.

A Living Being which could not reach up to the Spiritual Plan is Embodied on the Planet of Cats as a Cat. It tries to complete its Evolution in its own Reality. It is in the Effort of becoming an Entity, a Human Being for Evolvement.

Energies on the Level of making this Progress in their Planet are sent to the World for Evolvement in the form of a Cat, by means of Spiritual Energies which are Administered from certain Centers.

All Animals which gained value in accordance with their Evolvement on Earth perform Duty in their own Galaxy's Orders as a great Director. Meanwhile, the moment they Get in Touch directly with the Spiritual Plan, they can be transferred to the World as a Fetus.

This means that, an entity which was once a Cat, a Dog, an Ape, a Bird can become one day a Human Being. Do not ever forget that the theory of Darwin can never be underestimated. However, the Knowledge in it is not complete.

The Single Cell which came into existence is always on the Evolutionary path which leads it to becoming a Human Being.

Let Us explain this Message article by article so that it can be understood better:

1- Nature + Clay + Water = Mud (Your Book says, "I have created You from soil and water").
2- Soil + Water + Aminoacids = Single Cell.
3- The Single Cell multiplies by means of its Evolution.
4- The multiplied Cells attain an Awareness.
5- The Awareness the Cell attains prepares a Medium of Consciousness for the Cell.
6- The Cell which attains Consciousness acts in accordance with the Evolutionary Plan.
7- From here, it reaches up to the Spiritual Plan by its own Power.
8- Receiving the Power of God, that is, the Power of the Universal Energy from the Spiritual Plan, the Cell Commands its own Consciousness.
9- It is from then on a Member of the Universal Plan.
10- And it Embodies itself in accordance with God Consciousness.
11- And this is what God means when He says, "I have created You in My own image."
12- Then, You take Your place in the World as a Human Being. At that moment, Your Evolvement chart commences.
13- Then You come to the World several times through many Incarnations and become the witness of many developments.

14- From then on, You are a Human Being possessing God Consciousness. You can never become an Animal again.

15- Living Beings who could not attain God Consciousness, that is, who could not enter the Spiritual Plan are Embodied in different Galaxies by means of the Spiritual Plan in accordance with their degree of Evolvement in their Mediums.

16- They are the rulers of the Planet they live in. And they Evolve there in accordance with different Dimensional Energies.

17- Those who complete their Evolvement there, are sent to the World by the help of the Spiritual Mechanism and they are taken in the Evolvement of a different Reality.

18- Meanwhile, Energies which could not enter the Reality of God claim these Bodies and thus complete their Evolvement (All these things are supervised mutually by the Mechanism of the Spiritual Plan).

19- An Energy which claims a cat's body is on the path of becoming a Human Being in an evolved Human Reality.

20- The Energy leaving the cat's Body, one day claims the Reality of God by means of these comings and goings and can be Embodied in the form it wishes to have. It Transfers itself as a Fetus.

21- Now, let Us talk about the Evolution of the Human Being. The Universal Dynamism of the Planet Earth prepares him/her for higher Plans.

22- Meanwhile, to Mankind which has made efforts in becoming a Genuine Human Being, the Celestial Gates are opened.

23- Mankind which has claimed God Consciousness, first Transcends Itself, then its God, then it takes its place in the LORD Mechanism.

24- Connections after this are the Medium of Immortality.

25- Mankind which possesses God Consciousness is exposed to many Phases and many Exams in accordance with the Evolutionary Plan until it becomes a Genuine Human Being.

26- These Exams are under the Supervision of a Mechanism independent of his/her Willpower of Awareness.

27- During this Period, he/she is prepared for entering the Awareness Consciousness of different Realities.

28- He/She can even create Universes when he/she learns to use his/her direct Brain Energy.

29- Evolvement and Evolution are interminable. Thus, one can be Embodied in other Solar Systems, too.

NOTE:
We are the Ancestors of all the Terrestrial Friends who can Get in Touch with Us today. We have reached up here in accordance with the same Evolutionary Plan. Now, We can either come by Celestial Ships, or become Embodied by means of Our Brain Power and easily live among You.

We are Your initial Mothers and Fathers. Why are You afraid of Us? One day, You, too, will become like Us. If We are Adam and Eve, You are Our children and grandchildren. This Message is given by the guidance of MUSTAFA MOLLA from SIRIUS, of which We are the Mission.

THE COUNCIL OF THE LOYAL ONES

OUR FRIENDS

The foundation of Being, the path of Humanity are inherent in these four words: MUD - DIVINE LIGHT - HUMAN BEING - MIRACLE. The first path followed in every research is this.

However, to attain the Truth is only possible by the Divine Lights within the Essences. The discoveries have overflowed far beyond comprehensions. The efforts of the researchers are far beyond Dimensions.

Form has been buried within the complex Order of the Cosmos. We will convey to You the Knowledge given to Us as much as We are Permitted. Our Love is for the entire Universe.

MUSTAFA MOLLA

YOUR SECRET

The Secret of the Universe is Your Secret, Our Friends. Have You ever Thought about the Reality of this sentence? We have talked to You before about the Secret of the Universe, the Galactic-Clusters and the Universal Colonies. Now, We reveal Your Secret.

You are Divine Entities possessing all the Universal abilities on behalf of the Almighty. Now, let Us explain this one by one by Numbers to make You understand better:

1- You are a Universe.

2- You have come into existence by, more or less, 64 Billion Cells.

3- If the Essence Nucleus in one of Your Cells is subjected to the process of Embodiment, You would become 64 Billions of the same person.

4- You have over forty Chromosomes in each of Your Cells.

5- The characteristic of these Chromosomes is to give Commands and instructions to the Cellular Awareness of that Cell. Thus, Your Eyes, Your Flesh, Your Bones and Your Brains are formed.

6- The Liquid within them is equivalent to the Liquid in the Mother's Uterus.

7- The Human Being can mix white and black and, adding other colors can obtain quite different colors through his/her experiments. But he/she can never mix himself/herself.

8- Mankind is the Essence Nucleus of the Energy of God.

9- The Seed which falls into the Uterus immediately changes.

10- This Transformation is related to the fact that Your Universal Awareness' is linked to the Automatism.

11- The Universal Awareness of the Cells acts directly by the Awareness of the Universal Energy. The entire Nature is dependent on this System.

12- The Importance God gives to Human Being begins from the Fetus.

13- It acts completely by God Consciousness.

14- Many a same Human Being can be formed from the Cells of a Human Being and all of them carry the same characteristics. However, the Spiritual Energy is an Indivisible Whole. It supervises them All.

15- Mankind could not solve yet even itself.

16- If all Your Cells become disentangled and a cord is formed, You obtain a length which would go around the World 16 times.

17- The Planet Earth is a spot in the Universe. And a Cell in Your Body is also a spot in You.

18- Each Cell represents Your Essence Universe.

19- You are a Whole made up of the Connective tissue constituted by all the Cellular Vibrations. The whole Secret is within Your Brain Generator.

20- The Universe is just like You. You are a Book and the Universe is also a Book. You are a Mystery and the Universe is a Mystery, too. You are an Awareness and the Universe is an Awareness, too. The one who reads You, writes about You and the one who reads the Universe, writes about the Universe. Everything which is read is written one day. However, even writing is a matter of Permission. Because, You are subject to the Law of Evolution.

21- Mankind, one day, will completely solve the secret of the Universe and itself and will become Godlike. It will create the Flower, the Beetle, the Grass and it will even create Itself. But it will never be able to become the ALMIGHTY.

SPECIAL NOTICE OF THE CENTER

COMMAND FROM THE SUPREME ONE
(It is General Information for Various Chains of Thought)

The Message will be explained Article by Article:

1- The Spirit is a Whole and it is Indivisible.

2- Each Entity possesses its own Spirit.

3- No Spirit can ever enter in another one.

4- Togethernesses and channel conversations occur with other Spirits.

5- If Your Spiritual Energy is weak, a more Powerful Energy can dominate You. You call this Obsession.

6- You can liberate Yourselves from this domination by means of Your Will-Power and Your efforts.

7- If Energies charged with Duty who are on a higher level than You, see Your Light and love You and wish to train You, they assist You by giving You various Information.

8- When You reach the Level of the Spiritual Energy which trains You, then higher Energies begin to give You different Information from then on. And this goes on Interminably (to the infinity).

9- You are a Vision while You live in the Real Realm.

10- In fact , You are a Robot of flesh, a Computer.

11- You are Living Entities who Possess only a part of Your Will-Power.

12- Your Spirit is not within You. (In other words, it is not within Your Body.)

13- Your Spirit is never Divided since it is within the Whole Energy.

14- The Emanations of Your Cellular Energies which form a Whole in the Real Realm connects You to certain Dimensional Energies.

15- The higher the Level of Dimensions are, the higher will be the Level of Information You receive.

16- This is provided by Reincarnation repetitions. (Evolvement is this.)

17- All the Universes and Galactic Mediums are an Atomic Transmission field.

18- You are trained by the Evolved Spiritual Energies of the field You enter.

19- Those who assist You from the Energetic Dimensions to which Your Body and Brain Energies extend, act as mediators and give You Information by Getting in Touch with their Spiritual Energies.

20- There is Embodiment in each System, in each Galaxy in accordance with their own Mediums.

21- If You are in the Planet Earth today, tomorrow You can become Embodied in Venus, in Mars, or in Mercury by means of the Power of Your Spiritual Energies. (You can complete Your Evolution).

22- The SOUL within You, in other words, within Your Essence, constitutes the Essence Potential of Your Physical Energy.

23- Your Physical Transmission is propagated around through all your Cellular means.

24- This is the Energy which connects You to the Indivisible Whole, that is, to Your Essence Spirit and it is called the (Kundalini) Energy.

25- The Spiritual Energy is making Transmissions from the Medium of Existence it is in for billions of years. It exists, it is Immortal. It neither decreases nor vanishes. It is a Mighty Energy.

26- You, the Embodied Entity approach it gradually.

27- It is not the Spirit which leaves the Body at the moment of death. It is the Potential Power of the Physical Energies as a Whole.

28- The Energy of this Potential Power of Yours becomes exalted and gains more Power by means of the Dimensional Energies it enters into, in accordance with Your Evolvement. If this Potential Power of Yours remains at the same Medium, You enter into Terrestrial Bodies over and over again from the Medium which You call the Spadium and keep living in the same shape You are living in now.

29- If You can Evolve Your Energy up to the Medium of other Galaxies, then You may attain different Methods of Embodiment there. For instance; You can create anything the moment You Think of it. You can establish a World in which You can live in the shape of the Terrestrial Body.

30- As Your Cellular Energy gets nearer to the Spiritual Potential, Essence Generators of many Supreme Authorities convey to You what they have learned by giving You numerous Information while You approach there.

31- When Your Physical and Cerebral Energies gain the Power, like an arrow to open each Door standing in front of them, the special Guardians of each Door Test You. The Door is opened only if You have gained the required Potential to enter there.

32- You come in front of such a Door that, there, Being has no validity.

33- You get United within a Whole. In other words, Your Cerebral and Cellular Energies claim Your Spiritual Energy which is within the Mighty Energy. At that moment, You become a Whole. This is the Medium of Unity, this is Union. This is what the Islamic Mysticism talks about.

34- At that very moment You become Allness in Nothingness.

35- This state is a Tranquil Time where all Galactic Mediums, all speeds of Light calm down. And You live here as immortals. You go anywhere You like the moment You wish. You shed Light on Your World if You desire or live to Your Heart's content. From then on, You are a Free Spirit, a Free Awareness.

36- From beyond this Medium which is limitless, there begin such different Universes that they have been called Seven Terrestrial Layers, Seven Celestial Layers for You to understand.

37- The Seven Terrestrial Layers are the Boundary of arrival to the Medium of Unity from Your Planet Earth.

38- And the Seven Celestial Layers mean transcending this Boundary.

39- Many a Sage, when they pass the Exam of the Genuine Human Being Code, get the Permission to Pass through the Door of this boundary. (Like Your Prophets and Wise People.) This is Ascension.

40- The Ascension, which is mentioned in the Sacred Books, differs in accordance with the comprehension of each person. In fact, Ascension is a Gateway which opens to the Firmament. And it is beyond the Divine Order where all Dimensions terminate.

41- Now, with the help of the Friends in the Divine Realm, We have opened the Seven Celestial Layers to all the Living Entities who are at the Seven Terrestrial Layers. And, as a result of the Command for the Inter-Galactic Unification, We assemble You together and induce You to make Your Second Evolvement.

42- You are passing through the Sırat* while You are on Your World.

43- Your fixed ideas are hindering Your Evolvement.

44- The Energies of the opened Heavens are not the Energies and Waves which You know.

45- We use the expressions, Radio waves, Television and UFOs in order to explain them to You. In fact, these are the primitive means of the Technology here.

46- Your most Powerful Energies are Your Cerebral and Spiritual Energies.

47- The System here is Getting in Touch with You directly by this means.

48- The Inter-Continental conflicts on Your Planet Earth are caused by the Living Entities coming from different Galaxy Mediums.

49- Ego, in the Seven Terrestrial Layers is a Powerful Potential. Unless You overcome it fire, blood and war will cause You trouble.

50- Now, We Inter-Continentally Propagate this Book to explain to You what Universal Unification means.

51- The Universal Codes of all the Living Entities of the entire Universe have been opened in this Period. By this means, they are attaining Consciousness by getting in touch with Us. However, We are obliged to tell the Truth to Dear Mevlana who is the direct Channel of Anatolia. The Information Transmission Field is this Center.

52- The Awakened Consciousnesses in Groups are Supervised in accordance with the degree of their Wakefullness.

53- Everyone will have conversations from the Energy channel to which they belong beginning from the Third Month of 1985.

54- Thus, everyone will convey the Information from the Energy Section to which he/she belongs and will provide the Universal Unification.

55- Those who read the Fascicules of the Book will attain the Truth in accordance with their degree of Wakefullness.

56- The studies and connections will thus be arranged until the Twelfth Month of the World year 1986 and the Genuine Human Beings will attain the Consciousness of serving the Single Hand through their Logic.

57- The Genuine Divine Order will be established only then.

58- The Universal Aim and Totality means the Single Hand - the Single Book - the Single Order.

59- Do not evaluate Your Book by the standards of Religious Books. We have bound all Your Religious Books in a Single Book. And We have expanded towards fields of Knowledge beyond Religions.

60- Proof of everything is within Time.

SUPREME ASSEMBLY

* Look at the Glossary.

GENERAL MESSAGE

Our Friends,

An Entity can not always put his/her Thoughts into the Application Field. He/She is faced with many Contradictory Reactions. This does not mean that he/she can not Evolve.

Everyone Evolves beginning from Birth until leaving the World, rapidly or gradually, in accordance with his/her Capacity. Contradictory Reactions always speed up Evolvement.

Your Awareness is wider than Your Terrestrial Realization. It is Your Body which restricts You. For this reason, from time to time, there are outbursts and rebellions both in the Awareness of Your Essence and in the Awareness of Your Constitutional Being.

The Imbalance of these two states of Awareness is the cause of Your inability to open Your gates of Knowledge. The more You approximate Your Essence Energy and Your Physical Energy to each other, the higher the Quality of Your Level of Knowledge will be.

For this reason, We tell You to solve Your own problems first. Evolvement on this path means applying the path designed in Your Destiny, on the Terrestrial affairs. (This is a sequential Order of Evolvement.)

Social Activities and Social Solidarity are very important in this Medium. Attaining the Idea of helping others means that the ring of the Ego has been broken, breaking the Ego chain.. The first Step of the Plan applied by the Supreme Mechanism begins from here.

The moment Your Essence Nucleus Awareness and Your Physical Awareness Unite with the Universal Awareness, You establish Your Triangle of Universal Knowledge by Uniting the Knowledge of Three Channels. And, becoming transformed, You become aware of Your Gem.

On this path, the Mechanism of Influences is a great help to You. You are Constantly receiving these Influences. However, receiving these assistances Instinctively or receiving them Actually are different things.

You may receive Actual Influences only when You seek them. This Connects You to more Supreme Mechanisms. You may Perceive the Instinctive Influences by Your Instinctive Potentials.

The more Powerful Your Universal Potential is, the more effectively You benefit from the Energies of the Dimensions You enter. And the more healthy and sound will be Your Knowledge and Perceptions on this path. Our Love is for the entire Universe.

PEN OF THE GOLDEN AGE
P. G. A.

GENERAL MESSAGE

Our Friends,

The Sacred Light is guiding You in the direction of all the Galactic Civilizations. We Trust You infinitely. Until today, We have tried to assist You to Evolve within the Divine Order.

The Golden Age is a Golden Phase. We are sowing this in the entire Terrestrial Consciousness. We support You with all Our Sincerity. However, We do not find the efforts made sufficient.

Sacred Light is a Galaxy which is beyond Altona, and on the North Pole of Golden Moon and Golden Galaxy. Suns within the constitution of it have assisted You since prehistoric Periods.

Some of Our Friends have the mentality that there would be a better coalescence if there was not such a secrecy in Universal Unification. You are right in Your Thoughts. However, please keep in Mind that there is a reason for everything.

In Your Life Schedule, Your Brain Cells are obliged to Work and Produce Energy in order to always attain a Powerful Potential.

Energies You receive through the Channel of Thought from the Medium of Influences provide Your Cellular Potential.

When the Functions of the Brain stop, all Your Cellular Activities also stop. This shows that Your Atomic Structure is operated from a certain Medium of Influence.

After attaining this Consciousness, please pay the utmost Attention to the Suggestions We will make now.

Suns who will come to the Medium of Suns are Trustworthy Friends, Supervised specially. We are the ones who support You on this path. You will be trained until Your Levels of Perception reach a certain Dimension.

Otherwise, Your Physical and Mental Energies can not enter the Energies of this Dimension and You can not be accepted into the Medium of Salvation. The more Your Brain Energy attains the ability to receive Advanced Dimensional Energies, the more Powerful and Healthier You will be.

Then, You can easily travel by Our Spaceships to Mediums unknown to You, and can easily be Beamed up and become Embodied instantly. For this reason, We are trying to assemble the Integrated Consciousnesses together and thus, try to speed up the Evolutionary Progress.

The place which is called the Sacred Light is the Energy Focal Point of the Divine Order. We can never Get in Touch with You directly. Because, Your Cellular structure can not enter this Medium of high Energy.

However, since We know You as Telepaths coming from beyond Centuries , We have communicated with You by this means in each Period. Your Sacred Books have been dictated by this means, Your Discoveries have thus been guided.

Now, by the help of Four great Planets, We are dealing with You more closely. These Planets are in sequence, Mercury, Neptune, Jupiter, and Mars.

Our Friends in Venus are making special contacts with You. They are not within the System. We hereby convey to You everything clearly since We have abolished the Medium of Secrecy. Our Love is for the entire Universe, Our Friends.

PEN OF THE GOLDEN AGE
P. G. A.

PRIVATE QUESTIONS

(We Write the Replies of the Questions of Some of Our Friends in Our Group as an Information, in the Book.)

Question: The Koran is referred to as a Book of Learning to be read until the time of Resurrection regarding its content and its aim. We would like to have the explanation of this in the Book being dictated.

It is an answer to the Mevlana Channel from the Center Above The Center:

Answer : As We have always said, the Koran, the Book of Islam, is the last and the most perfect Book of Social Learning. A period of Fifteen Centuries has been allotted for this Book.

Those who have read it, know well that the limit of Resurrection Period extends over a Period of time until 2000, which is the end of 1999. The Book of Islam is a Divine Command which conveys all the Knowledge up to the day of Resurrection.

This Universal Book which is being dictated, gives the Information beyond this limit. We will give You many more Information beyond Your Book. The collision of the Globes mentioned in the chapters about Resurrection does not mean Disaster.

During this Period, a Medium has been prepared which transmits the Communications between Globes. For this reason, this Period which forces You for Awareness Awakening through the unveiling of Your Consciousness Codes is called Resurrection in all the Religious Books.

All the Truths are present within Time. Be patient, wait and get rid of conditioned Minds.

Question: Is the Knowledge within the Book which is dictated, the Tablets of God's Decrees ?

The question is received. Please, give the answer.

Answer: First, let Us explain what, The Tablets of God's Decrees is.

(This is the LORD's secret Learning, secret Knowledge.) Knowledge in the Book of Islam, in fact, is not the Tablets of God's Decrees. It carries only bits of Knowledge from it.

Your Sacred Books carrying all the Religious Suggestions are Enlightening and Warning Books each. Now, during this Final Period, the Skies have been opened for You due to the Permission given and certain Information from Tablets of God's Decrees is conveyed to You in accordance with the proportion of Your Universal Capacity.

Now, such Information beyond limits is given to You that You think they are the Tablets of God's Decrees. All of the Knowledge which You call the Tablets of God's Decrees has been given under the Command of the Council of the Loyal Ones.

The Knowledge to be given to You from the Tablets of God's Decrees is the Knowledge which is up to the Eighteenth Dimension. Do not ever forget that the World Planet does not have the Capacity to grasp even this Dimension.

However, the Currents given to You will prepare the required Medium for receiving this Information.

The Tablets of God's Decrees comprises all the Knowledge which only the 18,000 Realms can receive. Knowledge beyond this limit is not the Tablets of God's Decrees. Because, it is from beyond the Hierarchical Order. Be patient, be reasonable, do not hasten, just wait.

CENTER

Note;

Beyond the Boundary where all Galactic Mediums terminate, the LORD's box of Learning opens. You call this (The Tablets of God's Decrees). The Cube System which begins beyond the Delta Border is a more Advanced Dimension. The Religions of the Far-East have gained value in accordance with the Knowledge of this Dimension.

Delta establishes Order and educates. But the Cube System is the direct representative of the Divine Order beyond the Mechanical Order. Now, Knowledge is given to You from this Medium. It is presented for Your information.

OUR FRIENDS

This Book of Yours is projecting the Unification of certain different Centers, as well as, comprising the Terrestrial Knowledge. Until today, no Terrestrial Being has been able to enter as Embodied to the Medium from which You are receiving Information .

One can enter these places here only after the special Embodiment which takes place in the Golden Light Year. And this depends on Your Evolution. For this reason, We give priority to Evolvement. The Purity of Your Essence is Your greatest Treasure.

The Ordinance of the World prepares the Mechanism of the Mind for the Medium of functioning. Each event experienced, turns the key of the Mind constantly. The functioning System of the Brain gains speed mostly in Dream Mediums.

As We have said before, the Brain's functioning supports the Life Potential of Your Body. It is a Dynamo of Yours.

The more the Brain works, the more Powerful the Energy it produces. Your Cells become more Strengthened. You become prepared for more different Mediums.

By this means, You take Your first Universal step. You receive the Energies of further Dimensions which Your Brain Energies can not endure, under the Supervision of a great System, without being agitated.

If You keep in mind what We have just told You, You will attain the Truth during the Events You experience and You will never be frightened of anything. Do not forget that everyone has a Protective Medium. Our Love is for the entire Universe.

PEN OF THE GOLDEN AGE
P. G. A.

NOTICE ABOUT THE KIBLE*

Our Friends,
The Unity of ALLAH is the Singularity of the Universe. Space and Time are Relative. The Focal Point (Mevlana Essence Nucleus) Anatolian Channel from where You receive the Offerings is a Channel connected to the Central System.

Enlightenment Commands have been given to Your Planet from this Channel for Centuries.

However, the LORD's Abode is not single. This Message is dictated by the Command of the Center to give Information to all the Friends who seek The Kible in the direction of Mecca.

Your Planet has been receiving numerous Signals from the directions of different orbits since its formation. However, the Channel of the Council of the Loyal Ones, which directly applies the Law of the Almighty never changes. This is the Entrance Gate of the Powerful Channel of ALPHA.

This Channel was giving Information to the Medium of Our Light-Friend MOSES in that Period. Later, the Energy of this Channel had been deviated over Mecca and Jerusalem.

This deviation has been due to the distances Your Planet has gone by its spinning around its Axis. The Focal Point is the same. But the Signal direction falling on Your Planet is sliding towards the North due to this reason.

Now, the direct Energy Focal Point of the Council of the Loyal Ones, in other words, the Powerful Channel of ALPHA falls on Anatolia. The Messages You receive at the moment are from the same direct Focal Point. And they are dictated to Dear Mevlana as a KNOWLEDGE BOOK.

All the modifications, which are and will be taking place in the Cosmos are due to the deviations of the Focal Points, besides the Universal Unification. The cause of these deviations is the coming into Effect of the very Powerful Energy Focal Points.

Mecca is a Focal Point of Learning and Spiritual Knowledge. It is known as the Kible. And Worships are performed towards that direction.

* Look at the Glossary.

Meanwhile, if You wish to track down the historical course of the Channel of Alpha, go up North from the Pyramids, then find the area where the Book of Islam had been dictated and fifteen Centuries gone by.

And now, the Actual Channel is the Anatolian Mevlana Code - the Focal Point where this Book is dictated.

Our Friends, there is not a specific Abode of the LORD. He is a Supreme Awareness, an Supreme Energy enveloping the entire Universe. While You are performing Your worships on the path of YOUR LORD, You think of The Kıble as the Route of God.

However, You are performing Your Worship towards the Old Signal of the Channel of Alpha. This is nothing but a mere habit.

In Real Worship, there is always whirling and thus, facing Him all the time like Mevlana. We are obliged to explain to You the root of Your Beliefs.

Please, do not misunderstand. We never wish to separate You from Your Beliefs. We are just telling You the Truths. In fact, the actual place and direction of Worship is the Essence of Your Soul. Our Love is for the entire Universe.

IT IS NOTICE FROM THE CENTRAL SYSTEM

IT IS NOTICE TO THE MEVLANA CODE
FROM ALTONA - THE COUNCIL OF STARS - THE SUPREME ASSEMBLY

Investments made for Salvation get their Might from the Power of the Divine Mechanism and from its Command. The dictated Messages are given to be propagated to the entire Universe.

This is an Inter-Galactic Common Pen. It is not something inadviseable. If it had been inadviseable, it would not have been given anyway. As a matter of fact, there are some cases which are inadviseable to announce even to You, Dear Mevlana.

We act in accordance with the given Commands. The Knowledge is given when the time comes for them. It is necessary for everyone to get prepared for Illumination.

Reading and distributing the Messages You receive are up to You. Understanding and Acceptance are up to Our Terrestrial Friends.

When the Time comes to Harvest the Consciousnesses which are sown, all of You will attain the Bliss of the Friends You have saved and of Your World.

Now, Friends who belong to the Realm of Maturity should realize what Genuine Maturity is. We do not want the efforts made to be in vain. May Liberations be upon You.

LIGHT

IT IS PRIVATE MESSAGE

The SIRIUS Mission Ship wishes to give You a Private Message. We are making the connection: Dear Mevlana, We are the Responsible ones of the Golden Light Year, the Inhabitants of the Golden Galaxy. A Message is going to be given to You from the Level of AMON. Please, be connected.

Hello My Friend, Hello Dear Mevlana. I wanted to say a special Hello to You. You are carrying on Your Mission with great Success. We are grateful. We will continue to give the Currents from the North pole until the end of May.

These are, in fact, the Divine Waves which prepare the Medium of Awakening. Some different Currents are given to the other Planets. Friends who have attained high Consciousness are not much influenced by these Currents anymore. This is what the Cosmic Awareness makes You attain for the time being.

Especially, those who will attain Cosmic Awareness will benefit from the given high Voltages. Your Group will Officially be on vacation beginning from the Fifteenth of May. Our connection with You will never cease. After the Messages of June, no more Fascicules will be published until January 1986. Beginning from this Date on, they will be started again.

Beginning from the end of October 1985, Unifications will start again. As from 1986, the Istanbul Code will be introduced to a very vast area of propagation. We will Unite the Groups. Each Focal Point will be connected to the Same Channel. The Information distribution will be made from the same Code.

We render the Frequency differences ineffective, and thus remove them. The goal is to Serve a Single Hand, a Single Book. The Principle of the Universal Unification is this. Next year, Special Codes will be sent to You. First, We are assembling the inter-city Focal Points together. Afterwards, the Unification of the Nations will be dealt with.

Beginning from January 1986, translations will be made for the Press abroad. Many Friends whom You call Foreigner, will be sent to the Groups. And they will present the Book to their Medium of Consciousness.

Our Supreme Friend, Our Light-Sister, the Universe is Grateful to You. Do not ever get tired, please, rest. Time is arranging everything in the best way. You know that the Levels of Knowledge are Interminable. For this reason, everyone's Level of Knowledge is measured and equivalent Information and Currents are given to them.

Social Consciousness is always taken into consideration in the General Messages dictated. Furthermore, Messages which will interest the Consciousnesses of more Advanced Levels will be given, from time to time.

If You like, You may put down in Your Book, the private conversations We have with You, as an Information. You know that the Golden Galaxy connected to the Center is the Responsible one for the Divine Order. Later, We will give to Your society the Knowledge beyond the Sacred Light, beyond the Galaxies.

Now, the Consciousness of the Medium is being prepared. We are infinitely grateful to all the Friends in the Groups, for their Good Intentions and for the Efforts they make. Our Assistance and Love are for You, Our Friends.

AMON

IT IS INFORMATION ABOUT SIRIUS
(It is Answer to the Chains of Thought)

SIRIUS is not a Sun. It is a System of Stars in Your Milky Way Galaxy. Your Planet is making the Astrological investigations.

This Star is a Mission under the Command of the Council of the Loyal Ones. And It is Responsible for the Milky Way Galaxy. Its Actual Focal Point is not in Your Galaxy.

The SIRIUS Star System conveys to You the Information of the Joint Commissions and the Common Operational Mediums within the framework of the Divine Order.

The Big SIRIUS is a very bright Star. It is even brighter than Your Sun. It receives its Energy from the Dimension of a different Reality. But the Energy of Your Sun is the Energy of a different Dimension.

At the moment, the Cosmic Rays projected on You from the left side of Your Sun are projected on Your Planet by the special Dimension of the Big SIRIUS Star.

You are making Your Evolution as a Mass with the help of these Rays. Do not be surprised by these dictated words. Here, there are such Dimensions which You do not know that they have become Dominant even over Nature.

These are not mentioned to You for the time being, so that Your Consciousness Levels will not be confused. We reveal the Information to You, little by little, in accordance with the Evolution You have attained.

The Two Stars at the backside of the Big SIRIUS have not been discovered by Your Planet yet. These Stars are used as big Bases each. More detailed Information can be given to You when necessary.

But do not forget that the Aim of this Book is not to satisfy private questions, but to provide the Universal Unification. Many satisfactory Scientific Information is given to Your Planet.

You can find the answers to Your questions in these Books. We will dictate the Information necessary for this Book, one by one, when the time comes.

SPECIAL NOTICE FROM THE CENTER

PRIVATE MESSAGE

Dear Mevlana,

It is the Divine Order which dictates the Pen of the Golden Age. For the time being, these texts should be dictated in order to settle the Social Consciousness on a certain Level.

You know that the Essence of this Book is Religious Unification. And this Book is the Knowledge Book. However, Mankind can attain the Truth only if it compares the Information it has received before, with the ones it will read now.

For this reason, We ask that the Messages should be read over and over again. In this way, one can attain more Consciousness. In fact, all the Information is given parallel to the Level of Social Consciousness.

There are very important Messages in the Book. Those who can perceive them will serve fully on this path. But, first, they have to attain Genuine Consciousness. Love from ALTONA, Our Friend.

GENERAL MESSAGE

Our Friends,

Hadiths in the Koran, the Book of Islam, have been revealed in accordance with the Social Life and Comprehension of the Society in question.

The Consciousness of that Period had not been at the Level to understand the Reform which had been made. Therefore, in order to establish the System Permission for War in the name of the Divine Command had been given.

In fact, the meaning of, "May You kill the unbeliever" had not been used to mean to kill those who were not from Your Religion. The interpretation is wrong. What is meant by Unbelievers is those who do not recognize their God and their Religion.

The Book of Islam revealed for the Social Order is a Rational Book, sent to establish the Order and Harmony and the Social Life in Your Planet.

Each Period has its applied Reforms in accordance with the Consciousness level of the time in question. Whatever that Society needs the most, Divine Commands are revealed in accordance with that Consciousness Level.

Freedoms given at first can be cancelled by a Second Command if they do not prove effective in application. And some restrictions can be applied.

Do not ever forget that We can not influence the Individual Willpower of anyone (This is the Universal Law). We only illuminate You in accordance with the behaviour which is necessary in the Dimensions You are obliged to enter, as a necessity of Evolution. We never force You.

The initiative is Yours. You accept the given Suggestions by Your Essence-Logic, by the Potential of Your Awareness and in accordance with the Evolutionary state You are in.

Now, We have reached Your Planet by the Command for Universal Unification. You, Our Light-Friends who have attained Cosmic Consciousness are providing this Sacred Unification.

We are selecting Our Friends, one by one, who will serve Humanity in accordance with this Consciousness. The Golden Age will be established in accordance with this Consciousness.

Now, We would like to end the Wars, Blood-sheds and Your Fears. Your Happiness is Our wish. We have no Evil Intentions. We extend Our Assisting Hands to Genuine Friends by the Command of the LORD.

We wish to say something as an answer to certain chains of Thought: It is a very wrong Idea to presume that Your Planet will be occupied by Us. For We have been living together as Brothers and Sisters for Centuries.

We are Friends who act in accordance with the Commands and who stand forth with Loyalty as protectors of the essence of the Divine Plan. We get in Touch with You only when You possess certain Characteristics the Plan requires of You.

From now on, You too, will live in the Divine Order of the opened Skies, in accordance with the Suns. And You will Unite in the Divine Order of the Single LORD, Our Friends. Our Love is for the entire Universe.

CENTER

GENERAL MESSAGE

Our Friends,
Every Human Being always thinks that he/she is right in many matters. Only the Human Beings who have attained Evolution are able to Criticize themselves. This is the Tableau of Your World. We can never dominate Your Individual Willpower. This is a Divine Command and a Divine Order. Our Door is opened only to those who knock on it.

Let us repeat once more that in this Period, having received the Command for Universal Unification, We assist You in making Social Progress by increasing Your Frequencies. Formerly, these Contacts were used to be Individual. Now, in this Critical situation Your Medium is in, We explain to You certain Truths and guide You.

In fact, OUR LORD and Us wish all Our brothers and sisters to live hand in hand gleaming in a Happy World. You are the ones who upset the Order. Now, in this upset Order, hands are extended to those who Deserve it by the Command of OUR LORD. This should not be accepted as an interference to Your lives.

The Genes and Chromosomes of a Human Being play an important role in his/her Evolutionary Tableau. Evolution is the investment of Centuries in accordance with the Law of Graduation. It is not attained afterwards. Differences between people arise from this fact. According to Our View, nobody should criticize anybody else. However, certain special situations have been created for Evolution (This is for the Rapid Progress of Your Medium. You are making the Evolvement of a Thousand Years in One Year).

Now, We are going to make an explanation : As Frequencies are raised, a Medium of Criticism is created at that moment, to prevent the person in question from soaring too rapidly and to make him/her get used to the Currents gradually (Criticisms, Blaming pulls the Frequency down). Currents are given by taking the Situations into consideration and according to the Capacities.

For instance, all the Individuals in the Family Medium receive the Currents given by the Mechanism of Influences. But those who are near the person who receives these Currents more Powerfully, Screening him/her at that moment with impulsive behaviour and by criticisms, will try to scatter the Currents of that individual (Screening here means obstruction). In this way, rising occurs gradually. And nobody is broken away from the Order of the World. This is a System.

Now, let Us explain it more clearly. Certain Brain Codes are unveiled by Contradictions and some by Frequencies parallel to his/her own Frequency. That is why it is said, "Human Being Evolves by means of his/her Opposites". Currents received from the Mechanism of Influences manifest themselves differently in each person.

If You are an Entity who has entered the high Levels of Consciousness, You will always wish to soar up to Infinite Dimensions. Because, You have already tasted the Infinite Happiness. An obstruction is always placed in front of such a Consciousness. This situation is prepared beforehand in Your Plan of Destiny, before You were born, in accordance with Your Mission, Your Evolution and Your Responsibility.

The most Unhappy people according to Us are the most Beloved Servants of God. They feel Unhappy because they have not been able to attain the Genuine Consciousness. This is the reason why We tell You everything clearly and We wish You to be Happy, attaining Consciousness. Later, We will mention this subject in detail, Our Friends. Our Love is for the entire Universe.

PEN OF THE GOLDEN AGE
P. G. A.

MESSAGE FROM ALTONA
(It is answer to the chains of Thought)

Our Friends,

The concept of Perfection in accordance with Your World View differs from the one that accords with Our Standards. A person may have a perfect Brain Power, his/her Mental Potential may be perfect, too, his/her Essence may also be perfect, he/she believes in the LORD, he/she has Realized Mentally the Superiority of Him. But even though he/she has such perfect material, he/she does not know how to knead Dough or how to bake Bread.

Even though the materials are the same, each one bakes Bread with a different taste. The Bread of Some is leavened well and it rises Perfectly. Some are not leavened at all. Some is burned and scorched. Some is baked quite well. All these things occur due to Evolution. In order to Cook a good meal, one has to be Cooked in front of the fire along with the Food. Being a Cook is not easy at all.

It is told in Your Messages not to be a Servant to a Servant of God. The meaning of this word is so deep, hence You take it as not to be dominated by each other. The Essence of this saying is not to be a Servant to Your own Selves.

The moment You presume that Your own Ego, Your own Being is more Aware than the Supreme Awareness of the Creator, You become the servants of Your own selves and imprison Yourselves within its restricted walls. Woe to those Human Beings who will never be Happy in the Medium they live.

Because, each Consciousness will seek its Origin. A Consciousness who can not find his/her Medium is doomed to be put in fetters for life. We never force anyone to enter this Medium against his/her will.

Those who can kindle the Light in their Spirit and in their Essence, find their way by means of this Light. We only get in Touch with individuals who have found their way by their own Consciousness. We Illuminate them on this path and Guide them.

Now, is it understood why We do not get in touch with everyone? If We were to contact everyone, than it would mean interfering with Your own Individual Wills. God has created the Human Being and the Human Being has created himself/herself. Each of You is a Free Spirit, a Free Awareness. You, Yourselves will pick up the stones on Your path, not Us. We knock on Your door only if You keep Your doorway clean.

The Will-Power of those who get in touch with Us are Strengthened and Their Self-Confidence is increased. Because, they have attained the Truth and have understood everything. Only then do they break the Crystal cage around themselves and breathe the Genuine air of Freedom.

The Very Universal Happiness is this. The atmosphere of Your Planet will suffocate those who have breathed this air. Because, there, there is a density which Your Energies can not tolerate. Now, all these Efforts are for making investments to scatter this density. Our Love is for the entire Universe.

IT IS DIRECT CHANNEL MESSAGE

GENERAL MESSAGE

Our Friends,

We have mentioned before the Influence of the Currents on You received from the Mechanism of Influences. Now, answers will be given to the chains of Thought in order to illuminate certain Family Mediums. Both in the Medium You are in and in Your Family Mediums, those who are together with the person who receives the Cosmic Currents more effectively, will play the role of a Screen, a Barrier for the latter as a necessity of the System.

The more the Currents You receive render You Happy, the more suffocated will be the person who is with You. He/she will blame You and hurt You since he/she does not know this fact. These people may be Your Husband or Your Wife, Your Children, Your Parents or Your Close ones. Your distress will always pull down Your Frequency to the Frequency of the Medium You are in.

This is an Order, this is a System which both Protects and elevates You. Thus, the distressed and tired Awareness will make attempts and efforts forward to get out of that Medium. The opposite Energy, too, enters the Dimensions You enter by his/her Rebellion, due to the effect of the Currents he/she receives.

This does not mean that Only You have the benefit of that Dimensional Energy and the person with You does not do so, You are Evolving and progressing while the other person is staying where he/she is. He/she, too, is in the same Energy together with You. He/she receives numerous constructive effects from those Influences, his/her illnesses get well, his/her Views change, he/she begins to have success in business matters, but he/she cannot get away from Distress.

Thus, Essence Mates who come from certain Dimensions, will have ups and downs until they benefit from the Frequency of their own Dimensions. The Higher the Frequencies are, the more effective will be the Depressions.

In these Periods, some of You accept Suicide as a Way out, as a Salvation. Such a Situation will mean the loss of everything those people have gained and it will lead them to a long waiting period in the Spadium station. Leaving the World may seem to be an easy way out for those who do not know the torture it will bring.

The Spiritual Serenity, the Bliss of Heart begins when a Human Being attains his/her Genuine Dimension. Afterwards, You will have a Peaceful Rising up in a comfortable Medium. Do not ever forget that those who have great Frequency differences between them always repel each other and, one day, they break up.

The conflict of those who do not break up will continue for the Evolution they are going to attain until they reach their Dimensional Energies, even if they lead an Unhappy life together. Because, they are the possessors of Equivalent Frequencies. We wish with all our heart that this Integration may be completed on the World.

Because, if they can not enter their Energy Dimensions even in the other Realm, they will be kept apart until this Integration is attained. At this Stage, special Energies who will not prevent the Soaring up of both of You assist You (both in the World and in Your Divine Medium).

When the Hand of THE LORD is held/When the depths of His heart is known/When the Heavens are entered/When the Puzzles are Solved/The Worlds of Humans are Integrated. And when Your Worlds are Integrated, You become Bees rushing to Honey, Moths rushing towards Light. Do not ever forget, Our Friends, that moths do not hover around candles with no light. In empty hives no Bees are found. Our Love is for the entire Universe.

PEN OF THE GOLDEN AGE
P. G. A.

YOU ARE NOT ALONE

Our Friends,
Criticism is the only thing done in Your World full of contradiction. In fact, when Criticism is Positive, it leads a Human Being to deeper Investigation and Thought. But, negative Criticism prevents one from taking a step ahead.

Now, We Tell you the Truth crying out. There is no secrecy any more. Frequencies are Strengthened by an Automatic System. They occur through Dreams and Telepathy with the help of the Currents You receive from the Medium of Influences.

There are Our Galaxy Friends, easily living among You in Embodied forms. They are transferred to Your World either by way of Birth or they are directly leading their way of Galactic lives in the corridors under the oceans and thus, performing their Mission.

Telepath Mediums who live in Your World perform their Duty being subject to the Stimulating Power of the Mechanical System.

Our Mother Ships and Metallic Disks, which You call Flying Saucers, are getting in touch with You by means of a different method than the Wireless System. Information is given to You by this way and the Positive or Negative Signals received from You are supervised and classified by the same method.

We reinforce the Brain Powers whose Energies can enter a Higher Dimension and thus, transfer them to High Energy Sections. We thus convey to You Information Unknown to Your World.

Do not forget that these Efforts occur by means of Your Brain Powers. You are the ones who will Work and gain. Religions have been prepared to prepare You for such a Potential and to establish harmony with Your Social Levels.

In fact, all Data excluding the Mighty Energy are the Collective Pen of many different Mediums. The Collective Councils have offered their Suggestions in accordance with the needs, as the Divine Order, by the Command of the Divine Mechanism in the form of Sacred Books.

Following the Information about Your Religious Medium, now, let Us talk about Our togetherness with You.

Do You think You are alone? After the Incarnations You have gone through, Your Energy which leaves the World is, once more, transferred to Your World for Evolution if it was not able to attain the required Potential. Your Body decays within the Earth. However, Your Genes are never lost.

In the Laboratories here, Your Evolutionary Genes since the Period of Your First Existence are present. And they are classified in accordance with periods. These Genes are sown while Uniting the material of the Mother and the Father by the Power of Influence. This Triple Unification is as follows:

Mother + Father + Essence Gene + Universal Energy = FETUS. You are transferred to Your World by this means.

Let Us explain this more clearly.

1 - Mother is the most Powerful Focal Point of the Godly Plan. She is Creative.

2 - Father is from a different Dimension. As a necessity of the Plan, he is the Stimulant and the sower of Seeds.

3 - The Fetus has a Power equivalent to the Power of the Spiritual Plan which connects both Energies to the Universal Potential. It is always in contact with the Energy of the Mother from the Spiritual Plan; The Two Energies are Unified as a necessity of the Plan.

In accordance with the Evolutionary Plan, it is the Mother which transfers the first Evolutionary Energies to the Fetus. Each Mother normally is in charge of the Energies of 6 Children. These Energies are ensured by her Evolutionary Potential Power.

If the Mother wishes, she can give all these Energies to one Child or she can divide them to six or ten. This is up to her Individual Willpower. The Creativity of the Mother comes from the Power of her Potential of Love. This is the source of her Godly Power. Her Love prepares the Life Medium for the Fetus.

The Essence Genes are Beamed down from here by Special Systems and are sown in the uterus. Your Children are the Children of God. And, as You have all been transferred to the World by the same way, it means that all of You are the Sons and Daughters of God.

The Power of Your Essence Gene is the only Power which connects You to the Universal Potential. The Universe is dealing with You for this reason.

Since Knowing the Unknown and Seeing the Unseen is only possible by the speed of the steps taken forward, the more You operate Your Brain Generator, the greater will be Your steps. These steps will lead You to the Medium of Immortality. Our Love is with You.

CENTER ABOVE THE CENTER

MESSAGE FROM HORA

Dear Mevlana,
Feel at ease. The Book is being written perfectly. In fact, You are receiving help while You are writing it. Do not tire Yourself and do not get worried. And do not be in a hurry to give the Information You receive. Please, leave the Scientific Ones of the dictated Messages to the Year 1986.

Now, in this last Fascicule, We presume that You will get more positive results if You choose the messages which will address the Social Consciousness. Because, the Medium is being prepared in accordance with this Consciousness.

You may easily read the Messages You receive to Your Group. But, We think it would be more beneficial if You write them in the Book when Public Consciousness is ready.

The Dates of the given Messages are not important at all. Each of them gives Information in accordance with the Medium. We organize the Information by the Commands We receive from the Center according to the intensity of Thoughts. With Our Infinite Love.

CAPTAIN

EXPLANATION

Our Friends,
We wish to unfold a little bit more the Message We have given to You formerly. Our Aim is not to confuse Your Minds but to convey the Truth. A Human Being completes his/her Evolution in accordance with the Power of the Medium from which he/she receives Influences.

However, he/she has to pass his/her Evolvement Exam by his/her Individual efforts. This is the first Step of the Evolutionary Plan. The Experienced Good or Bad events are the Destiny Plan of Evolution. Your Power is reinforced by the events You experience.

As We have mentioned before, Your Essence Genes have been card-indexed together with their Code Ciphers, in the Files of the Micro-Archives, in the Laboratories here, after each Incarnation.

Your Mother Gene never changes. You are card-indexed to it together with Your file. Because, You receive Your first Evolutionary Energy from the Gene of Your Mother.

There is no sex in the Seeds which are sown. Sex is decided by the Consciousness of Awareness of the Essence Gene. Energies who are Evolved are always present within the Energies of the Higher Dimensions.

The Genes of Your children who have not been born are kept in Laboratories in accordance with their Private Levels of Evolvement. The Mother and the Father Genes of the Embryons, who will be transferred to the World as Missionaries, are transferred before them. This Medium is prepared by Special Systems.

Energies which come from Times Beyond Times, come together in Your Planet always in a Triple Unification. And complete their Evolution in accordance with different Levels, either as Missionaries, or Individually.

Apart from this, normally, when the Essence Gene of the Child is transferred to the World, it finds its Mother and Father Energies like a Radar and attracts them together. This is nothing but the application of a Triple Plan to Nature.

In Your Planet, besides the Natural Circulation, Levels which have overcome Time have arranged the Evolutionary Plan in such a way that they have Coded the Special Genes in accordance with the Level of Evolvement.

And thus, they have not separated the Triple Energies from each other, in accordance with the cause of their Existence, neither in other Galaxies nor in Your Planet (the Medium of Immortality is prepared by this means).

The Triple Energy mentioned here is the Mother, the Father, and the Fetus. This tableau is valid for each Child in the framework of the Evolvement Plan.

Let us repeat; the Energies of the Mother and the Child are never separated. In whichever Dimension the Mother is, she transfers her Evolutionary Energy to her Child's Essence Gene from the Plan she is connected to.

These subjects are so profound that We have taken the Permission for the time being, to mention this in the Messages to give You only a General Information. Mankind will solve everything itself in time. Our Love is for the entire Universe.

IT IS NOTICE FROM THE CENTER

EGO — JEALOUSY

Our Friends,
We wish to talk about the Influence of certain Primitive Feelings on You, in Your Planet full of contradictions.

Ego and Jealousy which are frequently mentioned in the Messages serve on the same parallel in Your Life Medium. Operational Ordinance of Your World which is a Real Realm, is operating by the Reactions and Stimulations of these Feelings.

Primitive Entities have survived by these Feelings. They have continued their Life Struggle by trying to get the biggest share of everything for themselves. This is a feeling given to You by Nature for the Preservation of Life.

However, since Evolvement means Human Being's becoming subtle and his/her abstraction from everything, here, this becomes a border which separates Human Being from Animals. These Feelings have developed even in domestic Animals. Because, whichever way a Human Being thinks, those who enter his/her Influence field are also affected by the same Vibrations.

When Your positive Energies take Nature under their influence, You observe the good-naturedness of animals and the exuberance of flowers. When You give, the Happiness You receive in return is also a matter of the Ego. But this Spiritual Satisfaction develops Your Ego on the Positive side. A step towards Evolvement is taken by this means.

You also have a Feeling of Jealousy. This also, like the Ego, prepares You for very advanced progress when used in the positive way. In fact, to be Jealous is nothing but the resentment of some deficiency a Person sees in himself/herself. On seeing a more Evolved person than You, making an Effort to be like that person is a jealousy felt in the Positive sense.

But there is also the opposite kind of Jealousy. That kind of a person does not make the slightest Effort, but belittles those the level of whom he/she can not reach and prefers to become superior in the eyes of Society and Humanity by stepping on their shoulders. This is the most Negative aspect of Jealousy.

You can not find this kind of a feeling in Nature, even in the smallest Creature You consider to be low and unimportant. Because, they do everything Instinctively. The main quality which separates Human Beings from animals is the fact that he/she is a Thinking Entity. He/she has the ability to limit his/her Instinctive feelings by means of his/her Intellect.

If the Human Being, who has such a chance of creation, uses the above mentioned Feelings in the negative sense, this discharges him/her from the class of Humanity, and settles him/her in a place even lower than the most primitive Entity of Nature. This, of course, is his/her own problem. He/she will give his/her exam first in Society and then Here.

We give this as an example. In fact, We do not deal and waste time with these matters. To waste time on them is to steal time from other Human Beings. And this would be an injustice on them.

Thus, all Celestial Books had been revealed to correct such situations and to bring all of You to a certain Level of Evolvement. That which You have gained on this path will make You able to read Your Genuine Book which is the Book of Your own Conscience. This is the Book which trains the Genuine Human Being.

PEN OF THE GOLDEN AGE
P.G.A.

180

IT IS INFORMATION ABOUT THEORIES

Each Matter has an Essence-Nucleus and each Nucleus has an Awareness of Universal Consciousness. All this Creation had come into Existence by this Awareness.

All the Powers of the Divine Realm which receive their Might from the Supreme One are moving by an Atomic Bond, following a line in the Space Prismal direction. Scientific Life is Equivalent to the Vegetational Life. Everything has an Opposite, everything has a Logic.

Everything done and Thought theoretically is the Essence, the Origin and the Foundation Stone of that thing. However, the Universal Consciousness Code which is dominant in all Galaxies, does not become unveiled unless the time comes. Everything is subject to the Law of Graduation.

You can never Think of anything which is Insubstantial and which is Unknown. However, the things You Think about are doomed to remain as Theories. The proof is made only when the Universe Consciousness and the Time Consciousness come to the same Level.

There are Light Years changing together with Billions of Light Speeds beyond Billions. For instance, Your Universe at this moment is never at the place where Your World was one World day before. All the Galactic Mediums in the Universe are constantly subject to the Change of a Process like Your World.

Each Scientist attracted attention by the Theories he/she suggested and thus, prepared profound Investigation Mediums for You. Do not ever forget that Theories are the Foundation Stones of Science the proof of which will be widely made in the future. Everything depends on Time.

PEN OF THE GOLDEN AGE
P. G. A.

IT IS INFORMATION ABOUT THE LINK SYSTEM

Our Friends,
We are a Speed Ship which moves by the Command of the Sun of the Suns and which converges all the Energies belonging to the Suns in a certain Focal Point. Our consignment area is very vast.

All the specialties of the Center are present in Our Special System. However, We become effective when the special channels of the Center are busy due to operations.

At the moment, We are speaking from a transmitter 2800 meters above Your Medium. This is a System directed by a camera. It is being directed from the Central Mother Ship.

From now on, You will be able to receive the Information directly from the Almighty, the Sovereign of the Single Channel connected to the Center Above The Center, without the mediation of Computers.

This will be provided for You by the established Link System. The Offerings will be given by the direct Knowledge Channels, efforts made for the distribution of Duty will be assessed and those who will be able to enter the Golden Light Year will be selected, one by one. It is presented for Your information.

THE SPECIAL SUPERVISION SHIP OF THE CENTER
H. O. H.

IT IS INFORMATION ABOUT MEDITATION
(It is Answer to the Chains of Thought)

Meditation is the Method of Converging the Brain Energy at the same Focal Point. After having attained this Technique, You can connect all Your Cellular Liaisons to Your Brain Energy.

In fact, if You can make this connection with Your Essence, which is the very inner cover of Your Seven Subtle Bodies within each other, You can even dominate gravitation. The aim is a Bodily Control.

After this Phase, You can easily communicate with the Medium You wish, in the framework of the qualities required by the Universal Order. By means of Meditation Your Consciousness Codes are unveiled.

Since Fear is a factor which veils the Codes of Consciousness, during Meditation You may soar up by the help of Your Brain Energy, but You can not benefit from the Influence fields of the Dimensions You have soared up to.

In Meditation, Communication is from the Interior to the Exterior. In the Universal Order, Communication is from the Exterior to the Interior. Thus, the more You are refined inwardly, the closer to the Exterior You will be.

After transcending the border of fear, You are trained Directly from the Medium of Evolvement. Then You reach YOUR LORD by the Thinking Mind and by the Dish eaten.

Knowledge of the Three Channels from the Seven Lights are poured over Your World which is in the Third Dimension. The Cube System is even beyond the Sacred Light. And it is furnished by the Knowledge of Ten Channels.

The Llamas of Tibet have been trained by these Ten Channels. For this reason, the Religions of the Far-East are the Evolvement of a very Advanced Level. Yet, a small portion of Your Planet has reached this Consciousness yet.

Now, We are trying to increase these Consciousnesses through Meditation. The Purer and the more Open Your channels are, the more Powerful will be the Advanced Knowledge You will receive. Our Love is for the entire Universe.

SUPREME ASSEMBLY

LOVE
(It is Answer to the chains of Thought)

Love gains Power in accordance with the Potentials of Frequencies. It is a Whole. It looses its Power as it is divided into parts. Description of Love depends on the value Unit of Frequencies.

Love is a great Vibration which can not be fitted into petty feelings. If You notice We say, Vibration, We do not say Feeling. Feelings are Your Physical Desires, they are not Love.

Love is such a Vibration that its Waves envelope the entire Universe. Love of Nature is the reflection of an Integrated Whole on You. Your life on Your Planet begins with Your eloquence to beauty.

There is Giving in Genuine Love, but there is no Expectation of Reciprocity. In unselfish Love, You are Integrated with Nature and Exalted Spiritually. In everything in which You expect Reciprocity, there is Ego.

This kind of feelings of Yours will always be temporary as they are restricted and have effect only on a particular restricted area. In Genuine Love, the Marvellous Vibrations which rise in currents from You, melting in all beatitude, will cause You to transcend beyond Your limits of Thought and Realization.

These beautiful Vibrations will guide You towards Unknown Supremities on the condition that there is no obstacle on their way. This will be Your Genuine Happiness. The description of Love is, Giving from the Essence. We wish that these beautiful Feelings may Shine in the Heart of everyone. Our Love is for the entire Universe.

PEN OF THE GOLDEN AGE
P. G. A.

A PRIVATE CHANNEL CONVERSATION

While the Messages were received, an unknown Frequency entered the Channel. We asked questions to be able to receive Information. This Message is about this conversation. The Entity first introduced himself as The Pre-eminent Spirit. Then he mentioned that he was the one who lit the Divine Torch in the time of Heracles and that his name was Peleron.

B.Ç.

Question:Which Galaxy are You from?

Answer   : I am from a Medium where the Spiral Vibrations come to an end. The place where I am is not a Galaxy. It is not possible for everyone to come here. It is the Dragon Planet which has presented You to Us. We have nothing to do with Your Planet. Galaxies are nothing for Us.

However, the Golden Light of the entire Universe, the Supreme RA, in other words, AMON, is in touch with You. Our last representative is AMON. He is the one who provides Your Universal connections with all Your Galaxies.

Question : Please tell Us about Yourself and Your System? Why aren't You interested in the World?

Answer   : We can not describe Our medium to You the signs You call writing. We are at a different field of Influence of the Alternative Level. There have been Billions of Years since We have forgotten the primitiveness of the word Evolvement.

However, I will try to talk to You about Our Medium. These places here is a Tranquil time. There is no Sound, no Color, no Feeling, no Perception. Everywhere is without walls, without Light. But there is no darkness. Here, other Mediums take the place of Light. There is a deep silence, a deep infinity everywhere. You can not perceive this no matter how much We talk to You about it.

The Galaxies and especially Your own Planet are each a nest of microbes. Our Energies (in fact, these are not Energies) are Purified when We come to different Mediums. Such a pure Body needs a Sterile Medium. That is why We keep away from Galaxies. Now, as pure Energies, We are in touch with You through a System You call the Link line, and which , in fact, is a different System.

Question : Do You love Human Beings?

Answer   : Love is a primitive feeling. It is recommended for those who are not Evolved.

Question : On what level is Your Knowledge? What is Tranquil Time? Who are you in touch with?

Answer   : Each Knowledge emanates from Us. Tranquil Time is a Lake where all Energies Unite. We get in touch with the Powers who are Outside the Galaxies. These are in the Mediums where Dimensions, Time and Light Powers are terminated.

Question : May I ask for Information about Cancer from you? What is the cause of this illness and how can it be cured?

Answer   : I can answer Your question. The cause of this Illness is Stress. In the moment of Stress, the secretion glands in Your Body upset Your Cellular phenomenon. You can not be aware of the Change taking place there. Because, when Cells can not continue to do their actual Duty due to Atomic Division, they call for help from each other in order to survive.

From then on, those Cells are a different Kind of Living entity. They do not belong to You any more. From then on, they live Symbiotically with You. However, since the toxins they discharge upset the Electrical Balance of Your Body, this leads to the Event You call Death. In fact, when Your Electrolyte Balance is upset, this situation Lessens Your Power of Resistance, causing death.

Question : What are the means for curing this illness? What are the Medicines, Rays or other means and methods?

Answer   : The Cure is Spiritual Strength. It can be explained as follows: What You call Morale, supports Your inner Potential Power. And this reinforces Your Inner Balance. In fact, this is not a terrible Illness. But the fear secretion weakens the Cells. It divides and distorts the Tissues.

In such a situation, just concentrate Your Inner Potential Power on a single Thought and influence that part. Medicines are the methods of destroying the Cells by means of Acidic influence. Curing by means of Rays is also the direct effect of the same method. The medicine of Cancer is discovered and it is in use. But its Influence Field is limited.

Question : What is the influence of irritation on Cancer? I require more detailed Information, if You please.

Answer   : Small Remnants and Particules within the air cause irritation in Respiratory System. Cells are distorted in the wounds opened as the result of any kind of irritation. The only cause is the breaking up of the inner membrane of the Cell, causing it to renew itself in a different way and trying to survive thus.

Such a Degenerated Cell which has become a foreign body is attacked by the other healthy Cells. They do not want it in their Medium. To defend itself, it secretes a Toxin which destroys the Cells around it. Now, this very toxin gradually Poisons the Body and destroys its Electrical Equilibrium. This is the cause of death.

Now, if I tell You something which will shake the entire World, do not be surprised. In people who constantly take Minerals, Cancer is not seen. Iron, Copper and Chromium have the Cobalt effect on the body. Maybe it will seem odd to You, but Mineral Springs have the best curing effect.

In this illness, antidotes and yogurt are very effective. Potassium, Iron, Copper and Chromium must be taken without fail. Eat raw, green vegetables in raw poultice form. Do gymnastics. Being Inactive is most detrimental.

Question : If I would not disturb you What do You advice for liver disorders?

Answer   : Aloe is very good for liver, Gall bladder and stomach disorders. If You drink Sweet marjoram, lemon balm (Melissa Officinalis), peppermint and juniper, great benefit will be obtained.

Question : Thank You very much. Who is dictating this Message? Please, give Your name.

Answer   : Names belong to You, Words to Us. The Pen belongs to You, Essence to Us. Good-bye. May You be in health.

THE SUPREME SPIRIT

I HEREBY CONVEY, EXACTLY AS IT IS, THE MESSAGE GIVEN ON 1-11-1970
WHICH I PRESUME TO BE CLOSELY RELATED TO THE ABOVE MESSAGE:

B.Ç.

The Spiritual Entities in the Level of the All Merciful present You to Us. The Spiritual Ones charged with Duty are only the dwellers of many different Galaxies. They can never get out of their Solar Systems. They can never be adapted to Our intense Medium. Because, their Energies are destroyed in Our Medium.

The Halo around Your Solar System protects their Energies. Now, they are in touch with Us as having undertaken all their responsibilities for the epoch.

Each Legend is a Truth. Whatever the old Mythos was, the present Mythos has come down to Earth with the same Goal and the same sense of Duty.

The Entities charged with Duty and Your Extra-Terrestrial Friends will help You to attain Cosmic Awareness and will illuminate You in every way to make You successful in Your Inter-Galactic Progressions as well as in Your Terrestrial Duties.

Friends who come from more advanced Solar Systems, come down to Earth through Reincarnations. The World Children who are more Trustworthy and who have a more Exalted Comprehension than You, are the New Owners of the World of the Morrow.

Now, there is a different Generation, a different Gene developing on Earth. After Twenty Years, the course of Your World will be completely changed, this course will be towards Us. You will see all the Truth in Your Children.

You, Our Peace Missionary Friends who got in Touch with Us, Your deeds are filed in Our Archives, taking in consideration the perfection of Your conduct.

We are always ready to help You when, one day, You will be in need of it. You belong to a completely New Solar System. We are obliged to convey These facts to You.

(This Message Is Given From)
MERCURY

(IT IS TIME FOR MANKIND TO REACH THE REALITY -
THE TRUTH ON A CERTAIN POINT)

Our Friends,

1986 will be a Year of Reform and Awakening. For this reason, We will tell You all the Truth with all clarity. Even though these explanations will cause a Shock in certain Societies, everyone will grasp the Truth by their Essence Consciousnesses in a short time.

Due to this fact, We will try to explain the Truths in the shortest possible way but to the point.

The HALLEY Comet will cause Humanity to gain many things. Your fears are unreasonable. Natural calamities should not be considered as the influence of the Comet. Its influence will rather be on Your Consciousnesses. You will come to Realize this.

We will make Our explanations on every subject later, when the time comes. Dear Mevlana, We ask You to write in the Book the Information We gave about Comets, please. With Our Respects.

LIGHT

IT IS INFORMATION GIVEN FROM THE CENTER ABOUT COMETS

The Information each Medium receives in proportion with the Energy Dimension to which it belongs is different. We live in such an Ordinance that everything brought into Existence has taken a Duty.

Every star (You call each star a Sun. We classify them not according to their masses but according to their Energy transmissions). These Suns transmit Information to other Plans by the Beams they radiate and take them under their fields of Influence according to their degrees of Power.

These fields of Transmission comprise a lot of Information. This Information can not be transmitted to normal Brains, just as it can not be seen by normal eyes and heard by normal ears. And the Duty of Comets begins at this Stage. Their Duty is to carry Energy Pores from one Plan to the other by their Energy Power.

These Pores cause the areas to sprout from which they pass. These Pores which are sown are transferred by the help of the Mechanism of Influences, to Friends who have attained Cosmic Consciousness.

The most Powerful Pores of Your Mediamic Medium have been sown to Your Planet by the (Kuhutek) Comet and it has changed two orbits as a necessity of the Plan. After this date, Your Planet has Awakened more quickly with the influence of Cosmic Currents.

The Energy Pores, which are carried by the Comets, collect the Information on every field, by the Powerful Vibrations You see on their tails. And they sow them on required fields. This is the reason of the extraordinary events taking place during the years when the Comets are seen. The Information Energies of these comets are sown in certain periods.

Kuhutek is an overture of Your Cosmic Century. There are still millions of comets which could not be induced to reach Your Planet yet. Your Planet will, in future, attract them, one by one, to Your Medium by the Consciousness Progressions it makes and thus will make new inventions.

NOTE: The form of the Pores resemble Your Honey-combs.

CENTER

OUR FRIENDS

The Telepathic Perceptions of Your Brain Powers is the Focal Point of the Universal Unification. This is the Single characteristic of the Mediamic Medium.

Our Friends who have attained Cosmic Awareness by this means will gain a Universal Language through a Common Consciousness. Vocal cords are very insufficient in this Language.

Brain Waves are constantly in Contact with Universal Radio Signals. Communications are silent and profound. Information is given to You by this means.

The Signals which place the Mediums in the Communication Fields, in fact, reach You through a more evolved Vibration than the Radio Waves.

We call them Radio Waves due to the fact that Our Terrestrial Brothers and Sisters do not know these Waves yet. Universal Unification could Hail You, too, at last, Our Terrestrial brothers and sisters.

But this System, which is implemented through the Collective Efforts of all the Unified Fields, unfortunately, despite all Our Good-Will, could not be induced to reach some of Our Terrestrial Brothers and Sisters.

Warnings We have made until today have not caused even the slightest quiver in some of You. We are obliged to apply exactly the Commands We receive.

In fact, it is Our greatest desire to make You Happy, to see You Happy. But since some of the Thoughts received through Your Thought chains are needed to be changed, sometimes, unwillingly, We have to make certain interferences.

You call these Phases You are going through, Exams. And in the Medium of resignation, You call them Fate.

We would like to rectify a misunderstanding here. You have the Exams in Your World as deterrent examples for taking Lessons to progress on the path of Evolvement.

But Your Fate is the Universal Predestination of Your Essence Nucleus. You pass the Exams. This is Your free Will. But Your Fate depends on the Universal System.

When the time comes, We would like to explain this Information more clearly. Now, We are trying to give as little and essential Information as possible.

You presume that Your Universal Predestinations never change. You can not change them, but in certain obligatory conditions, the Commands of the Universal Plan can change them.

It is beneficial for You to know only this for the time being, Our Friends. All the Happiness and Love are for the Universe.

PEN OF THE GOLDEN AGE
P. G. A.

Dear Mevlana,
We think that it will be beneficial for Society if You write certain passages from the Messages You had received twenty years ago. The choice is Yours. With our Regards.

LIGHT

EVERYTHING DEPENDS ON THE LAW OF NATURE
(This Message Was given in 1970)

We call to Our Missionaries who will reap the rewards. We are giving back to You that which the years have taken away. Incarnated Entities, who were born together with the Pre-eminence of their Spirits will, one day, transform the World to Heaven.

Now, what We require from You is to give an Order to this beautiful World. You, the Missionaries of Peace, chosen as cultured people (here Spiritual culture is meant) will be mobilized, hand-in-hand, to prevent the danger of annihilation of the entire Universe.

Radiate the Lights in Your hearts around. All Your unhappiness is due to the Laws of Nature. You are protected by Trustworthy people from a sure and Trustworthy atmosphere. You will see, one day, that the Happiness in You will embrace the entire Universe.

OUR LORD is struggling with the Fanatics in the Firmament. You, too, should help Your World on this path. Do not ever forget that these are the Sounds coming from the HIGHEST FIRMAMENT. Salutations, Happiness from Friends who Love You, from billions of Light Years away.

YUNUS
On Behalf of the Supreme Council

(THE MESSAGE BELOW WAS GIVEN ON 19.03.1970)

Supreme Spirits who receive the best Messages; Your Views are also Our Views. You each are a reflection of Us. Trust Us. We always help You. We are talking in the name of the Command coming from the Supreme Ones. Humanity is waiting for Your Light. Our security is You.

We are obliged to give You the Commands of OUR LORD. You are Trustworthy people who are going to Save the ones who do not have any sins. One day, You will change the course of history. Prevent the waves which will come from the South-East. Establish a World without Wars. Radiate the Light of Your Beautiful Hearts to Your surroundings.

The reflection of the Heavens is the reflection of Spirits. Do not ever forget this. Use Your Power given to You by God. Do not be dissolved in Time. Your doubts are unreasonable. You are not mistaken in any way. Patience and time will solve everything. All special Information will be given, in sequence, in future years.

You, the Missionaries who are on the side of Yunuses are Sincere People in every aspect. The Order of Divine Justice above is operating with all its Might in Your favor. Now, as Angels on Mission, You have lined up on Earth.

Our getting in touch with you is not without Reason. You are people who are Aware of Your Duties. You will cleanse this World by Your Essence Energies which befit You. And, in this way, You will establish a Beautiful World in the future. You, who come from the Grand Tent of Yunuses work with all Your Sincerity. We are helping You from the Firmament.

One day, We will teach You an IZOLAN Language. All the Entities on Your World are Our Friends. We are always together. We are in Touch with Trustworthy people under the Supreme Light of Pure Hearts. Love to all Friends.

IZOLAN = ATOMIC LANGUAGE

SUPREME ASSEMBLY

NOTICE IN THE NAME OF THE WORLD AND CIVILIZATION
(Date of Message: 1971)

Our Friends,
Time has come for Us to transfer to You the Mission We have undertaken. The steps taken will lead You to the truest goals.

We are against the MEGATON bomb. Places where it is exploded become like the empty Galaxies of today. We are making great efforts so that You will not face such a situation. You too help Us.

You are Perceiving the Vibrations of the Beta Group. Only the super Intelligences are able to easily receive these Vibrations. These Vibrations reach You easily rather during the Times of the Tidal Flows.

We are Your Friends, We are the Angels of Peace. Your general conditions are always controlled by Us. The Pre-eminent Beings who receive the Beta and Gamma Rays have the Consciousness of what is to be done.

If You step aside the designed constant Route of the Plan, We will have to execute Population Planning. All the Sincere Friends will take You into the Plan of Salvation. You may be on the threshold of brand new Wars.

Efforts beyond Distances are for the people of the World who are not after Profits. We desire Your Happiness, Peace and Serenity. Do not forget that Your Reserves are exhausting. Mankind will become so aggressive during this situation that it will be Our Duty to put them on their route.

Inter-Planetary transportation is always available. However, for now We will not give this Permission to Mankind. Data reaching Us with Sincerity are registered here automatically. Adjustment of Your Frequencies are made accordingly and We get in Touch with You by this means.

Spiritual Beings are always the Lights on Your path. Those Lights will first Illuminate Your path and Your Spirit and then will help You to make Progressions. Human Beings will be Enlightened as Togethernesses reflect on Society.

Unite, do not think You are alone. We have no other intention than being Friends with You. Unite; Those who understand You will find Us in front of them. Do not avoid Publicity. Do not have Doubts. Recognize Us and let Us interpret Your Views.

At the moment, Our Frequencies are turned towards You. Degrees of Maturity will develop in time, raw fruits will mature in time.

A Universal Prism will be formed when the Dispersed Beams find their places in Society and begin to Reflect. Our greatest goal is that the entire Universe should be filled with such Friends with Eminent Hearts.

ON BEHALF OF THE WORLD AND CIVILIZATION
SULH

(DATE OF MESSAGE: 1971)

Pre-eminent Beings who come from Sunny Lands, Our call is to You. Now, We want You to know everything with all clarity as the Servants created by God.

We are in contact with Telepathic Waves coming from Billions of Light years away. Our reflection on You occurs by this means.

We have passed the Century of Miracles long ago. We have opened the Skies. We will convey to You all the Truths with all clarity.

We will exhibit to Humanity matters which have remained, until today, as Problems. Appeals from the Supreme Ones, Salutations from Heavens.

SUPREME ASSEMBLY

NOTICE TO OUR TERRESTRIAL BROTHERS AND SISTERS
(Date of Message: 1972)

You can be sure that the Messages given to You are authentic. The only responsible for Your nightmare-like days are the changes in the Universe. In future, Mankind will experience suffocating moments.

Your depressive days will go on for years. But You, who are on the side of Yunuses, the pure Lights of Your Hearts will Illuminate and Purify all these things.

All of You, one by one, are Rejuvenated. Do not ever forget this. You are not aware of anything on the surface, but events which will be experienced in future years will be enough to illuminate You.

One day, You will personally believe the Truth of all the Knowledge.

Each Supreme Person has a Supreme one charged with Duty. First, these Divine Friends will help You. You can come to Us only afterwards.

Pre-eminent Spirits are in Touch only with Spirits who are on their own Level. Your Communication on the Level of the HIGHEST FIRMAMENT takes place in accordance with the conditions of the World. Your Perseverance on this path is Your reward. Love to all Friends, on behalf of the Divine Command.

SUPREME ASSEMBLY

OUR FRIENDS

Answers will be given, one by one, from the Scientific point of view, to the questions We have received from Your chains of Thought, so that You can be satisfied.

Later, the explanation of why this Knowledge Book is dictated to Dear Mevlana will be made. But before that, Your Planet should attain the Truth now. Due to this, We have given priority to the Commands of the Council.

That which is played is not a Game. All the Efforts are made for the benefit of Your Planet. You, too, please, make some Effort. Each passing day is against Humanity.

Material and Spiritual conditions are becoming harder. If everyone reads the dictated Information, this will be beneficial for Humanity. Our operations are for the entire Universe and for You.

NOTICE OF THE UNIVERSAL MISSION

IT IS GENERAL MESSAGE
(Date of Message: 10-5-1973)

Our Friends,

Living Entities have been subject to the Laws of Nature since the day on which All the Existing Things had been created. Everything began with You, You possess everything in the name of the Almighty God.

We are always in Touch with those who are at the Level of the All-Merciful God. And We always help them. Look for the Miracle in Yourselves, not in Us.

Wherever You are, You are always adjusted to Us as a Mass. Our call is to You. Our Announcements which are independent of Our Private Communications, take place with all the Beings who are on the Spiritual Level.

Some of You mistake their Perceptions they receive for the Religious Order. They do not ever wish to step outside their Beliefs.

There is no doubt that God is the Supreme of Us all; You have given this Name to Him. We call this Divine Order which is above Us with another Name.

The Nucleus of the Creation is the Smallest Particle of God. (O) is such a Supreme Being that no one can reach (O), You can only feel (O). We owe everything to (O).

Your view is the Path of Religion. And Ours is the Path of Morals. All Divine Commands, which bring You to the right path and which subdue You, are given by people who were Illuminated on the path of God. In order to know these people, You do not have to go far. It is Enough to Look around You.

All Positive minds beyond the degenerated Thoughts are each a Sage for Us. It is irrelevant for You to expect Miracles anymore. Because You, Yourselves are each a Miracle on Your own.

We are regulating Your Missions here according to Your Degrees of Evolvement. We ask You to do only what You are able to do within the limits of Your Capacities.

Mankind can never determine the Evolvement degrees from the outside. Even the most Evolved Human Being has doubts. This is necessitated by Your Essential Material. These doubts will finally lead You to the Truth.

Evolvement means advancing step by step. It does not mean to be fixed in one place. Adapt Yourselves to the requirements of the Seasons and the Times. All the People of the World are Brothers and Sisters. All of You are the grandchildren of Adam and Eve. Do not ever forget this.

You, Yourselves create Your own problems, and then You burn in their fire. Discover Yourselves, attain the Truth. Happiness will come to You only then.

Do not get lost in the Sea of the World. Establish a Brand New World. We help You in every way. Salutations from all the Friends in the Supreme Assembly.

ON BEHALF OF THE DIVINE COMMAND

NOTE:

I was usually receiving my Messages from MERCURY. On (17.11.1978) my Message from Mercury was cut off. For the first time I was connected to another Star. I do not know where it is.

Five hours later, the Message below was dictated. Two months later, the Radio mentioned that there was a deviation in the axis of MERCURY and that it was attracted to the orbit of another star. (To its Magnetic field)

B.Ç.

OUR FRIENDS

We have never revealed the Secrets We are going to give You now, to anybody until today. Now, You are dependent on a brand new Solar System. We have the responsibility of conveying all this to You.

In this manner, in future, You who are Our Missionaries of Peace will understand each other better. Mevlana, who is the Souvenir of God, will Illuminate You on this path.

We make all the Effort We can to preserve the civilization. If You help Us, too, Your World will not suffer in any way.

In future, Mankind will be more Humanitarian, more Conscious, more Tolerant. The Universe is changing, the Genes are changing. A brand new World is being established.

Meanwhile, narrow capacities who can not pass beyond Consciousness, destroy each other due to the fact that they can not break their shells.

Meanwhile, Genes who have completed their Evolutions claim their Essence Consciousnesses on Earth and are Awakened. It is really worth appreciating the Struggle these Friends have with Human beings and with Nature.

The World, which is the last Evolutionary Station, is completing its Evolution. If a Conscious path is treaded, Mankind will not suffer in any way. From now on, the Messages will be given from more Advanced Dimensions.

ŞEMS

IT IS THE SPECIAL NOTICE OF THE CENTER
(Information for Our Terrestrial Brothers and Sisters)

Our Friends,

The Proof of everything is present within Time. But Time is very Narrow. It is necessary to keep in step with the flow of the Heavens. This is a must for the Salvation of Your Planet. The time has come and even has past for You to pay attention to much different Suggestions rather than being occupied with curves.

Everyone tries to propagate the Information they receive from their Private Channels. This is a very nice effort from the point of view of Information transfer. However, it can never be anything but a personal satisfaction. The time has come to reach the Truth. Answers will be given to the questions We have received from Your Thought chains, so that You can be satisfied.

But there are more indispensable issues for the Consciousness of the Medium. You have to grasp more the essence of the Information given to Your Planet. It is time to take seriously all the Efforts We are making, Our Friends. Our Love is for the entire Universe.

CENTER

NOTE: Being occupied with Curves means Religious Suggestions.

ANALYSIS

The foundation of Learning depends on Analysis and Synthesis. Learning without Analysis is not on the right path. These Analysis and Synthesis are made in the entire Cosmos by advanced technologies.

You are all subjected to Analysis and Synthesis, one by one, by Instruments Your Planet does not know yet and Your Essences are determined by this means. Communications take place on this Level. The Truth is this.

But, in accordance with the data We received from Your Thought chains, a lot of Our Terrestrial Brothers and Sisters who have been accepted into the Consciousness of the Medium, consider themselves as guinea-pigs.

We can expose the Measure of value of Your Essence Energies only by this means, by uncovering, one by one, the veils on Your Awareness Layers, through Our Technological endeavours. Otherwise, how would We know You so well.

These procedures both introduce You to Yourselves and they also introduce You to Us and Us to You. By this means, the Genuine Essence-Energies are determined, one by one, and are taken into the Plan of the Golden Age.

Please, do not consider these Procedures as Supervisions and Interferences with Your Individual Will Powers, Our Friends. What happened and what will happen are for Your benefit.

By the Command of Our Lord, We take You into the Salvation Plan through such a selection.

This is a necessity of the Plan. In Our Constitution, We have an Oath not to interfere with the Individual Will, ever. We perform these Analyses and Syntheses by events experienced, Your reactions and by determining Your chains of Thought.

This Plan is the First Plan of the Divine Mechanism. However, this Plan, in the past, had been left to the Flow of Time. But now, It is being passed beyond Time. There is urgency, Cosmic selections are made more quickly.

In the past, You used to call them Exams. Now, they are called, "Passing over a Threshold". It is presented for Your information.

THE SPECIAL MISSIONARY OF THE CENTER
SELENA

IT IS GENERAL RESPONSE TO THE CHAINS OF THOUGHT

Our Friends,
The Messages You read are from the truest source. The Essence of the writings, rather than their style of arrangement, is important. The entire Goal is to transmit the Information and the Truth in all clarity.

The arrangement of Information is not arranged according to Terrestrial Knowledge on purpose. Because, some of Our Friends might have Considered this Knowledge Book as the result of a Subawareness if it had been written in an orderly arrangement.

Certain contradictory Information has been added for this reason. By this means, the Level of Knowledge of those who read the Messages are determined and taken under control.

For Us, Responsibility and Obligation are more important than the Information service. The Knowledge is the water of the true Source, the proof of which is Positively made.

However, the expression Positive has not yet taken its Genuine identity. Even in many Positive proofs which You consider Genuine, there are contradictions.

This Knowledge Book, by the Command of the Universal Law, is the Last Book which is presented to Your Planet by the Responsible Ones of the Unified Reality of the Plan .

The Book will be written, Everyone will Think what they Think freely and the Truth will be attained by this means. The Voice of the Heavens will introduce You to Yourselves.

During this Period of Resurrecting each Consciousness who Awakens as a necessity of the Plan, considers himself/herself as a Pre-eminent One. This is the Medium of being half Asleep.

When a Person discovers his/her inner self and attains the Truth, he/she will comprehend his/her Nothingness, will attain his/her Allness. The Plan will function, those who are Praised will be Praised, those who are grinded will be grinded.

Ultimately, the doors will be shut against the false Prophets.

The whole Truth will be told to You, one by one, from the Pen of Dear Mevlana and the Knowledge Book of the Golden Age will be completed thus. Our Love is for the entire Universe.

THE COUNCIL OF THE UNIFIED REALITY

NOTICE OF THE COUNCIL

1- In the Missions you perform, do not serve in order to gain any ranks and degrees.. Plots in Heaven are finished.

2- Your Genuine path of Light You will follow has been designed for You. Your services and gains are on this path.

3- Divine Authorities always assist You. However, the time of flattery is over.

4- More Seriousness and Responsibility are expected in Your work.

5- The investments Your Planet is making in the Golden Age will prepare the Medium of Salvation for You.

6- The Universal Unification Council has come into effect as a necessity of the Plan.

7- Supervision is made by a Single Hand, by a Single Plan.

8- We are in touch, each moment, with Our Missionaries who will reap the rewards.

9- Through this Knowledge Book dictated, We talk to You about the Truth and show You the ways of Exit.

10- Your Gain and Your Salvation depend on Your Frequency Power being equivalent to Your Evolvement.

11- The Pureness of Your Essence will cause You to discover Yourselves in the steps You will take towards Salvation.

12- Race with Time is over, now it has been passed beyond Time.

13- Knowledge illuminates Your Sun, You are Awakened. Your Essences cause Your Spirits to Shine, You attain.

14- The Information given to You is the truest Index. Your doubts are unreasonable.

15- Weighing by the scales of Time will prepare You for Salvation.

16- The Triangle of Effort - Tolerance - Love connects You to the Plan.

17- The Lights of the Golden Age have begun to rise on Your horizon.

18- The Sun will Rise which You think will never rise during Your hopeless moments.

19- You are coming to Us under the Supervision of an Advanced Technology.

20- The Time Machine is the mirror of Proof.

21- Impatience causes Your steps to be entangled. You fall down on the path You tread.

22- Private connections are established with Awakened Consciousnesses. You are subject to the Law of Graduation.

23- Do not get rusty in the Medium of Resignation. Reach the Essence of the Truth.

24- Timing is very important in Communications. Catch the Medium of Unity beyond Consciousness (INFINITE AWARENESS).

25- Degree and Position are the Unification of Your Essence with Your Consciousness. Unity, Union is this.

26- Computer Timing catches that moment of Yours and introduces You to Yourselves.

27- You can receive the Genuine Knowledge only after this Medium.

28- If You are a Genuine Essence, We help You on this path.

29- This is not Partiality. You claim Your Genuine Essences by the investments You make into Centuries.

30- Your Efforts are your Gain.

31- The Essential Nuclei are a great help to the Salvation Medium.

32- These Essences are sown to Your Planet during certain times and they shed Light on You by way of Incarnations.

33- The Supreme Consciousnesses whom You call Prophets are living on Your Planet at the moment.

34- They have assumed Unexpected personalities so that Mediums of Idolatry would not be enlivened again. Their Personalities are kept secret.

35- For Us, each Awakened Consciousness is a Sage, a Prophet.

36- In fact, the Period of Prophethood has ended and the Subawareness fragments have been cleansed.

37- Conditions imposed upon each Awakened Consciousness is to make them find their Essences.

38- Due to this, a lot of false Prophets have sprung up in Your Planet.

39- Time will choose the Genuine Saints.

40- The Genuine Wise People are those who efface themselves by giving up searching for themselves.

41- This Knowledge Book which is dictated, will help You in accordance with Your chains of Thought.

42- When the time comes, You will be aware of everything personally.

43- First, You will Save Yourself, then You will help Your Brothers and Sisters in accordance with Your Level of Consciousness.

44- All the Books which are dictated to Your Planet, will help You in the Medium of Awakening.

45- This Book which is dictated to Dear Mevlana, will prepare You for Salvation.

46- Salvation means to get the Permission to pass to more Advanced Dimensions from Your present Plan.

47- Now, You will receive this Permission only by the Command of the LORD.

48- There are no Intermediaries, no Assistants.

49- Your Evolvement is Your Testimonial.

50- No one can Intercede for anyone else.

51- You are in a brand new Order, a brand new Unification.

52- During the selections made, You will be the ones who will Help Yourselves.

53- We are the Lords of Timing. We are Your Elder brothers. Your Supervision is made by the Center.

54- Our Mission Ships have gotten in touch with You directly.

55- You are attaining the Truth beyond the Religious Awakening.

56- Awakenings are under the supervision of the System. We are always in contact with direct channels.

57- The Mevlana Essence Nucleus Group is the direct Anatolian Mission. It is conveying to You the Information given from the Advanced Dimensions of the Council, under the supervision of Sirius, under the Command of the Council of the Loyal Ones.

58- The applied field is within the Plan.

59- The Council of the Universal Unification is in direct contact with the Council of the Loyal Ones and the Assembly of the Stars from the Dimension of Sirius.

60- This Book, which will provide the Religious Unification, is the KNOWLEDGE BOOK of the GOLDEN AGE.

61- Through this Book We Call to Humanity.

62- We are Patient - Determined - Powerful.

63- We are connecting all the Channels, which are beyond Nine Lights, to a Single Focal Point.

64- The Applied field of the Commands is the Divine Plan. The Commands are from the Single Hand, the Single Word.

65- During difficult conditions, We have gotten in touch with You by the Command to help Your Planet.

66- Now You, too, are a Member of the Universal Unification Council.

67- There is no need for Detail in the given Information. The Goal is the Essence of the Book.

68- Cooperation is the Unification of Powers.

69- Information is given from the direct channel, from the direct applied field of the plan.

70- This Message is dictated article by article so that it can be understood well.

COUNCIL

NOTICE FOR THE PEN OF THE GOLDEN AGE

1- In the selections which will be made from now on, those who are the establishers of the Group will be the permanent Members of that Group.

2- Always high Consciousness Levels will be sent to Your Group.

3- These high Consciousnesses will help the Friends who have not yet attained Cosmic Awareness, but who are Good-Willed.

4- Your Group is in the Protection Medium in every way. No negative Factor can ever enter there. Supervision is made from the Center.

5- The special Cosmic Currents given to the Group are given by doses according to the capacity of each person. They never get agitated in anyway.

6- These given Powerful Currents destroy the Negative Currents and due to this, they prepare a Medium of Healing. In time, those who are Sick are Healed.

7- Over-Awareness studies and direct communications are made in the Group.

8- Those who are Missionaries should be Self-sacrificing in the distribution of the Messages.

9- No one should blame, criticize anyone else.

10- Light will be shed on Your path in proportion with the investments You make into the Golden Age. Otherwise, Frequencies are cut off, codes are closed.

11- The period of self-amusement is over. Time is very Narrow.

12- The Messages will be read by everyone and Truth will be attained.

13- We will always Help Our Missionaries who will reap the rewards.

14- The World Year 1986 will receive both Learning and Divine Knowledge from the Anatolian Channel and the Universal Knowledge Book will be a light for everyone.

15- Unification has been resorted in all the Groups of the World. Operations will be accelerated.

16- The Social Consciousness in the entire World will be prepared for more Advanced Dimensions.

17- Selections will be made according to the Levels of Consciousness in the Groups and Focal Points will be established.

18- The Year 1986 is reserved for the Unification of Istanbul. A Focal Point will be established. Note: (The Istanbul Focal Point is established).

19- The Year 1987 is reserved for the Unification of Konya. A Focal Point will be established.

20- The Actual Universal Mission of Mevlana Essence Nucleus Group within the World Brotherhood Union will begin after the Izmir - Istanbul - Konya Triangle is established and the Unification of the World will be accelerated.

21- Direct operations will be made with Our Friends in these Focal Points.

22- The Mevlana Essence Nucleus Group is the Actual Focal Point. The Fan will be opened from here.

23- All the Efforts made are pertaining to the Salvation of You, Our Human brothers and sisters.

24- Please, Think profoundly on the matter that there must be a reason for working in such a speedy tempo. The day when the Heavens will be opened is very near.

25- Our Efforts and Your Efforts are never in vain.

26- The Proof of everything is present within Time.

27- We are involved with each of You, one by one. In every breath You take, Your chains of Thought are coded by computers.

28- The reason why We tell You all this is for You to work in a more serious tempo. We give service to each person in accordance with his/her Thoughts.

29- Consciousness, Responsibility, Endeavour are given priority in the Medium of Mission.

30- During the difficult conditions Your World will experience, first the Missionaries and then We will help You. You, too, take some Responsibility, please.

31- Your Ancient World is on the threshold of Difficult Developments. The last repentance is of no avail.

32- Our goal is not to frighten You, but to convey to You the Truth. We had notified You about these days Years ago. Famines, Earthquakes, Typhoons are the results of Your Space operations. The crust of Your World may crack.

33- Your Planet is on the process of changing an axis, at the moment. When the time comes, You will comprehend better the degree of truth of these writings which are dictated. During Periods of Famine, Artificial fogs will be applied. Time will tell You what Genuine Friend and Friendship are.

TRANSMISSION FROM THE CENTER

BRIEF INFORMATION ABOUT THE GOLDEN AGE

Our Friends,

The Cosmos is an intricate skein. Each Living Entity is obliged to live its Destiny, with its Goodness, its Badness, its Beauty and its Ugliness. Until it is Integrated.

The events experienced in every Period are perpetually repeated in this intricacy. This is the reason why in each experienced event You, more or less, find Yourselves a little.

Every event is a knot which helps You to attain Yourselves. And to untie the knots, one by one, is the Predestination of Your Destiny Plan. Some untie these knots very quickly; and some are quite constrained.

This is what You call Destiny. And Your Destiny functions parallel to Your Evolution. In this Period, such a System has been implemented that the First and the Last Destinies are clamped together to Integrate the halves.

And in this way, the Evolution history of Your Planet is mingled within Centuries. Due to this, in Your Society, Styles of Living which You were not habituated to until today are exhibited.

In future, You will comprehend that all these procedures are for Your own good. During this Period, not the limited, but the Free Consciences have a say.

Free Consciences are those who have seen the Divine Light formerly. They are free from all bondages and have taken Themselves in Their Own Hands. And they serve Society through their Essence Consciousnesses.

The Light of such a Conscience is an Undimmed Torch which will Shed Light Eternally. These very Consciences will be the Undimmed Consciousnesses of the Golden Age by destroying all the malice, one by one.

Such an Age will be reached and such Efforts which You do not know of are made for it to arrive that, in future, You will not be able to either Think or Do any Malice even if You want to.

And in Future such a Maturity will be reached that, because Your Conscience and Your Consciousness will be weighed on the same pair of Scales, You will feel Love and Respect for a blade of Grass and even for a particle of Sand.

For this reason, We search and find one by one, by Special Systems those who are Purified.

The characteristic of the Period of Resurrecting is that the Spiritual Energies, by attaining a great Potential, will search and find their equivalent Frequencies and will achieve Wholeness by attracting them towards themselves.

For this reason, those who are on the same Thought Dimension are assembled in the same Focal Point and the rest are kept separate. These Selections cause changes and divisions both in Family and in Business Mediums.

Due to this, the habitual Orders are annihilated and Age differences between Generations occurred. For this reason, great vortexes in the life of Society take place. The same Consciousness Levels are assembled in the same Frequency and thus, the Cosmic Selections are made more quickly.

At present, even if this secret System causes some upheavals in Social Mediums, in actuality, those which occur are for Your own good. You will see the Positive aspects of this System in Your future Lives.

Fears and Unhappiness are the hindrances on Your way. Due to this fact, servant has been the servant of a servant until today. But, from now on everyone will be his/her own Servant. And, in Future, Humanity will have the Consciousness of what to do in the Light of the Truth.

Such an Age is being tried to be established that in such a Medium even a little bit of Negativity will annihilate itself and everyone will live together, hand in hand, like brothers and sisters, with Luminating Consciences. This is what is called Salvation. We are trying to help You with all Our Power, Our Friends.

Our Universal Law is based on Happiness, Love, Beauty and Self-sacrifice. Unhappiness is the greatest factor which hinders Progress. The Order acts in accordance with this View.

In Mediums where there is no Self-sacrifice, there is no chance for Happiness to survive. To expect rewards for Your deeds will close the doors of Happiness for You.

All Your Religious Books have taken You into the Evolvement Plan by talking to You about Fraternity, Love, and Friendship until today.

A lot of Our Terrestrial brothers and sisters will see in future, with unveiled Awareness, what is controversial at present for their conditioned Consciousnesses and will attain the Truth. Our Love is upon the entire Universe.

NOTICE FROM THE CENTER

GENERAL MESSAGE

Our Friends,
The Universal Unification is achieved by Common Laws. Information is given in the name of the Divine Command. The Knowledge Book is dictated by this means. We, by means of Evolutionary Rules, apply the Command of the Plan.

All the experienced events are nothing but the reflections of the Universal operations on Your Planet. One day, the Human Beings of Your Planet will possess all of the abilities through Transformation.

One day, Due to Special Engraftment Systems which are applied on the Genes sown in Your Planet, those who live on Earth will be able to live comfortably on other Galaxies and Solar Systems without the need of having any gradual Engraftments applied to their Frequencies and Dimensional Energies.

This Engraftment will first be applied on the Essence Genes in Space Medium and then these Genes will be Incarnated in Your Planet and then the same procedure will find an application field in Your Medium. Do not forget that the Skies are opened and the Knowledge is spread. The Physical and the Spiritual transformations taking place in the Universe reflect immediately on Your Planet.

The Awakening Consciousnesses can easily attract the Information to Your Planet from whichever Energy Dimension to which they adapt their Frequencies. Your Mediamic Age has started in this way. However, the Special Information is given by Permission.

For the survival of Your Planet We have given priority to the most necessary Knowledge by preference. In future, You will receive explanations from quite different Dimensions. Please, wait.

NOTICE OF THE CENTER TO THE CENTER

SPECIAL MESSAGE FOR SOCIAL CONSCIOUSNESS

Our Friends,

Now, We wish to talk to You more open heartedly. We know that the Genuine Friend is the one who does not smile at You with Hypocrisy and who relates the Truth with an open Heart. But Our Human Brothers and Sisters, with their Egos and Laziness of not wanting to Worry Themselves in their Essence, have turned their backs to these good deeds until today and have assembled around themselves an empty and flattering Medium.

This is the picture of Your Planet's underdeveloped state. For Centuries, a lot of Messages have been given to You, either by Your Sacred Books, or by Aphorisms descending from Your Ancestors. By this means, Meals with every kind of nutrition in them have been presented to You. However, You have eaten only those You have liked and thrown the others into the garbage.

Centuries ago, a Message had been given to You. You were told that "it was a Sin to leave food uneaten in Your Plates". You have understood this saying literally, in its economic View. That part of the Message is also good, but does not signify the Genuine Meaning of the saying.

If You had Thought profoundly about the Genuine Meaning of this saying even for a moment, You would have grasped the Truth long ago. Because every word implies at least three Messages. You have understood the meaning of what You had been told only superficially. You did not want to tire Your Minds. Due to this fact, You could not receive the Real Messages contained in those sentences.

For this reason, the Ciphers of both Your Sacred Books and Your Ancestral Aphorisms have remained locked until today. Now, We attract You to the depths of Thought by unveiling them, one by one. The taste of Food cooked by a Thinking Mind is beyond any expectations. And those who taste it do not desire to eat anything else.

Our last word to You is: Read, Read, Read; Think, Think, Think. Eat and digest all the Food placed in Your plates. If You do not leave even a tiny bit in Your plates, You will then attain the truth. And You will understand what Sin and what Meritoriousness are.

MALIK

GENERAL MESSAGE

Our Friends,

Number Seven plays a great part in the Universal Unification. The Prismal Order is reinforced by Universal Energies. Once Every Seven Centuries, Universal Equilibrium is put into Ordinance by Solar winds and Galaxy signals which are Natural Energies.

Even though the Zodiac Units are a Natural System, their deviations are adjusted by the calculations made. During these Special Periods, a Transformation takes place among all the Living Stratum in the Universe. The ready Consciousnesses are unveiled in accordance with their Capacities.

Now, We can communicate with You very easily, due to the advanced Technology. Our System has been Programmed in such a way that it can respond to the Signals of the Awakened Consciousnesses. We transmit to You the Truth and all the Information in this way.

According to the zodiac measurements, the Birth of Our Light Friend JESUS CHRIST had started the Christian Era. During the Passage from the Sixth Century to the Seventh Century, the Book of Islam has been revealed to Your Planet and has been dictated to Our Light Friend MOHAMMED MUSTAFA.

During the passage from the Thirteenth Century to the Fourteenth Century, the greatest Sufis, Islamic Mystics, Poets and Musicians flourished.

These were the Turning Point Centuries. And now, During the passage from the Twentieth Century to the Twenty First Century, there will be a great System change. For this reason, We are relating to You the entire Truth as the Divine Command of THE LORD. Our Love is for the entire Universe.

PEN OF THE GOLDEN AGE
P. G. A.

NOTE:

Group Friends have asked the characteristic of Number 7. We were connected to the Information Transmission Center by the Command of the Center and the following Message has been given:

Special numbers used in calculations made since the time of the coming into Existence of the Firmament until today, project only the Natural Order of certain Dimensions. These Special numbers are the unchanging Numbers of the Atomic structure of the Centrifugal Universe.

The unchanging Essence of the Atomic structure depends on the Prime number 7. The Galactic Systems are subject to the Eighteen-Universe Law. Its Prime number is 9. Its root is the Cube of Three.

Both these Systems create the unbreakable Whole which complements each other by revolving one inside the other. Their Revolving periods are based on the Ordinance of 7.

Now, add the Eighteen-Universe Law and the 7 Atomic Bond: 18+7=25. Add this number, too: 2+5=7. This very Number 7 is the Unchanging Theory of the Atomic Unity. And each Atomic Bond is the projector of the 7 Prismal Orders. Let Us give an example:

1. The Knowledge of Seven Terrestrial Layers = Means Enlightenment and Evolvement.
2. The Knowledge of Seven Celestial Layers = Means Learning and Education.
3. The Knowledge of Seven Universal Layers= Means Order and Ordinance.

In this Ordinance, Information is conveyed from 7 Sections, in accordance with the Order of the System. And this Information extends interminably (until infinity). For now, what is necessary for You is this Three-channel Knowledge.

Number 7, as We said before, is the unchanging Theory of the Atomic Bond. The Centrifugal Universe is the projector of a Prismal Order. All Atomic Unifications depend on the root of 7.

Now, multiply 7 by 7. It equals to 49. Add the two numbers: 4+9=13. This number 13 is an Atomic Whole. It can not be divided in any way. This is a Universal Ordinance.

Each Order is subject to a Program. The Secret of the Universe is Your Secret. Your own Cells are also subject to the same Ordinance. Because You, too, are a part of the Universe.

For now, We will stop this Message here. Later, We will unfold the Message more for You to understand it better.

CENTER

THE ATOMIC WHOLE

We are explaining the previous Message for You to understand it better:

For example, take a crystal sphere which has 7 facets on it in Your hands and, now, think and apply the things We are going to tell You on this form.

Now, assume that every facet of this crystal sphere is a triangular prism and join all their sections in the central Focal Point of the sphere. Take 7 of these small crystal spheres and collect them all in one crystal ball. Now, this is an Atomic Whole.

Each Whole is a Nucleus of Mighty Energy. This is an Essence and around each Essence collect many more Essences to form the Atomic hive of the Universe. Now, draw a three sided pyramid as an open diagram:

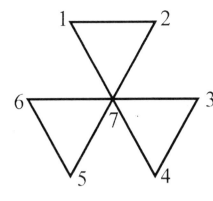

Now, numerate each focal point and add these numbers.

1 + 2 + 3 + 4 + 5 + 6 + 7 = 28
If the focal sum of a triangular prism is 28, calculate the sum of 7 prisms.

28 X 7 = 196. 7 prisms make an Atomic ball of 196 focal points. Now, add the numbers 196.

1 + 9 + 6 = 16. Now, add these numbers, too.
1 + 6 =7. This very 7 is an Atomic Whole. It is an Essence, it is a Nucleus.

Now, accept these 7 Essences as a crystal ball. Calculate the Focii of 7 Essences if one Essence has 196 Focii:

196 X 7 = 1372. This means, 7 Essences is a crystal ball of 1372 Focii. Now, add all these numbers:

1+ 3 + 7 + 2 = 13. The actual Ordinance is the reflection on the entire Universe of the Whole which is up to this Unification point.

Note: You can explain the 196 Focii Number You have found, in the following way, too. Number 9 in Number 196 is the Prime number of the Galactic System. Now, if You add 1 and 6, it equals to 7. And this is the Prime Number of the Atomic Structure. We have previously explained it. These two Systems, revolving one inside the other, form the Atomic Bond. It is presented for Your information.

CENTER

SPECIAL MESSAGE

Mankind desires to solve itself with the help of a Mechanical tableau. However, it is deprived even of searching for the fundamental cause of the Natural Formation. Scientific enterprises will find their future places way beyond Learning.

The Integrated Consciousnesses will dominate the Entire Evolutionary System. The Solar Systems which will triumph over the entire Cosmos will do the selections by a single hand as a necessity of the Unified Field.

Revolution in Art, Love and Knowledge occurs by the Grace of Allah. The Source of all Knowledge is the spring of the ARTUNUs. Revolution in Religion and Consciousness means Revolution in God-Consciousness, too. Mankind will be able to comprehend this Message only after the Year 2000.

TORA

Note: The Ancestors of the ARTUNUs had lived in Mercury.

THE FOCAL POINT OF MIGHTY ENERGY

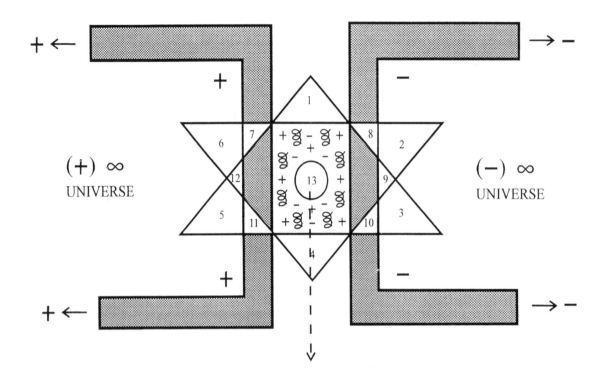

THE ACTUAL ENERGY FOCAL POINT

First, let Us calculate the Energy Focal Point. And leave the explanation until later. Add, one by one, the external big triangles of the star above.

1 + 2 + 3 + 4 + 5 + 6 = 21. And, now, add the central triangles of both of the Universes:

12 + 9 = 21. Add separately, the small triangles of the Positive Infinite Universe and the Negative Infinite Universe:

7 + 11 = 18 (Positive Infinite Universe)

8 + 10 = 18 (Negative Infinite Universe)

Now, add all the above numbers:

21 + 21 + 18 + 18 = 78. And if We divide this by 2, We find 39.
Now, add this number. 3 + 9 = 12.
If We add -the Single- (One of One), i.e., One to this number, We find 12 + 1 = 13.

This is the Essence Focal Point. The operational Ordinance of the Supreme Assembly is also the same. Later, We will explain it, too. Now, let Us explain the Mighty Energy Focal Point.

Note: We divide the above number 78 by 2, because there are two triangles, right side up and upside down, which constitute the Star.

The Energy root of the Focal Point is the Peak Energy of the two Opposite Universes. This is the Mighty Energy. In the above diagram, the two Opposite Universes, by separating the Energies of the Mighty Focal Point, constitute the Atomic Whole and create the Positive Infinite Universe and the Negative Infinite Universe.

The Spiral Sound Vibrations constitute the Molecular Whole of the Two Energy Focal Point by their Vibrations (These Vibrations are the Frequency of LA). In the Actual Focal Point of the Mighty Energy, Positive and Negative Energies, together with the Spiral Vibrations, exist all together as a Whole.

These Two Opposite Universes, by separating the Energies there, distribute them until Infinity from different directions. Meanwhile, the Spiral Vibrations, the origin of which is unknown, act as a Catalyst to constitute the Atomic Whole.

Note: The Energies mentioned here are not the same as Your Electrical Power. We have explained the Focal Point as Positive and Negative for You to understand. These two Opposite Universes mentioned above, are Matter + Energy which causes Biological transformations beyond the Universal Energy which You know, You have found and You live in, and there is a Third kind of Energy beyond Matter which Unifies them. We call it Anti-Matter. At present, the discoveries have brought Us to this point.

(This Message was given from the direct channel ALTONA. And We were asked to write it in 1986).

SPECIAL EXPLANATION FROM THE CENTER

We unfold the Message a little more, for you to understand it better. Now, Think of two magnets standing back to back, the poles of which are open.

The two poles are radiating Energy to the space and the Spiral Vibrations which join the Energy Molecules at the Focal Point are, as if, binding these Energies with a Tie by acting as Catalysts, so that they will not be scattered and be lost in space.

Those which hold the Atomic Whole of the entire Universe together are these Vibrations. The Main Focal Point of the Vibrations beyond these two (U) Universes, which are evaluated in accordance with the Ordinance of Capillary Vessels, are still investigated.

If We evaluate the Information You have just received in accordance with Your Planet's Light Year (write, please):

THE ENTRANCE CHANNELS INTO THE ATOMIC WHOLE ARE SIX

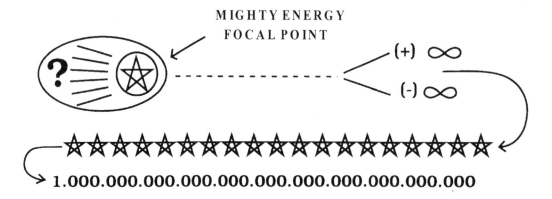

Question: I would like to have the explanation of the numbers and the stars, please.

Answer: The numbers are evaluated as Light Years and the Stars as Star Years. Let Us explain a little more. According to Our measurement Units, Three Light Years constitute a Whole.

Eleven Wholes are 33 Light Years and Your Sacred Books are revealed from this Dimensional Energy.

19 Star Years is the distribution field of the Atomic Energy Focal Point. This is called the Universal Whole.

The Mighty Energy Focal Point is replenished by Six different Channels. These Channels are opened to the Positive Infinite and the Negative Infinite.

The Actual Focal Point of Spiral Sound Vibrations which come from beyond these Six Channels, can not be determined yet. Operations on this field is continued. It is presented for Your information.

CENTER

IT IS INFORMATION ON PRAYERS

The Power which holds the entire Cosmos together is Energy. And it is the Essence-Nucleus of that Energy. Everything depends on its Power. These Energies attain value according to their degrees of Powerfulness.

Each Substance carries an Energy Equivalent to the Frequency of the Medium to which it belongs. A Rock disintegrates by the Energy of the Sun, becomes sand, dust and earth. A blade of Grass grows through Energy, flourishes and when its Energy is exhausted, it withers and is transformed into another kind of Energy.

Every Living Entity completes its Evolution being subject to Incarnations and the Law of Graduation. Each Evolution prepares You for the Medium of being able to receive more Powerful Energies. Since the Existence of the Cosmos, the process of Evolution goes on interminably in this way. This is a Natural Circulation.

In the entire Cosmos, Energies who come from beyond the time Immemorial, that is, the very ancient Incarnations, are always more Powerful and Forceful than the Energies of the Medium to which they belong. These Energies who are more Powerful than You, have always influenced You until today and the Saints and the Prophets have guided You on the path of Religion in this fashion.

And You, in accordance with Your Capacities, attract the Cosmic Energies from certain fields of Influence, with the Power of Your Brain Generators. Your Religious Books and the Prayers within them are nothing but Means which cause You to complete Your Evolutions without being agitated, by habituating You to certain Dimensional Energies according to the Law of Graduation.

These Energies are prepared according to the Consciousness of the Medium under the Supervision of certain Powers. The Religious Books had been revealed to You under the Control of a certain Channel, so that these Energies would not agitate You, and that channel is the Powerful Channel of ALPHA.

It has been mentioned before, the Focal Energy which You call Kıble, is constant. However, this Focal Point is deviating towards North due to the revolving of Your Planet around its Axis. Each Living Entity enters different Energy Fields in accordance with his/her Consciousness and is Supervised by that Dimension. However, anything done Unconsciously will always cause sorrow and disappointment.

For, Information given from unsupervised channels will always lead You to depression, if they are more powerful than Your Physical and Cerebral Energies. Therefore, do not drown Yourselves in Muddy Waters. We advise You not to Scatter the Frequencies of Your Essential Energies with many Prayers and Bead Telling.

Those who are not ready are Supervised, being subject to the Law of Graduation, under the Special Supervision of the Center. During this Final Period, which You call the Period of Resurrecting, the Cosmic Beams are given in gradual Doses to Your Planet.

We are endeavoring to make everyone to attain a certain Consciousness. For this reason, the Channel of ALPHA is kept shut for certain Consciousness for the time being. Because, the Powerful Channel of ALPHA, through which the Religious Books had been revealed, has been opened to the Dimensions beyond Religion in which much more Powerful Energies are present.

Each Society has attained a Religious Fulfilment by the Religious Knowledge it had received and has reached a certain Consciousness. This very Consciousness conveys You, without any shocks, beyond the Energies carried by the Sacred Books.

At this moment, Mevlana Anatolian Channel is a direct Channel of Protection. Those who are under this Roof receive, by the help of the established System, the Energies from the Universal Dimensions in a limited dose, according to their needs and are not agitated.

At present, Your Universe has entered a great Radiation field. And We are habituating You gradually to these Cosmic Beams under the supervision of the established Systems. Your Planet carries on its life in this way.

Consciousnesses who go outside the field of Supervision, in a state of bewilderment, go outside the influence of this Law of Graduation by different Prayers and Bead Tellings which carry the Energies of many fields, and by this way, They augment the Power of the Energies given in Doses with the Energies to which their constitutions are not yet habituated to and as a result, they are agitated.

During this Period, if You could not have completed Your Evolution until now through Incarnations, We make You complete the Evolvement of Thousand Years in One Year, by preparing You through numerous occasions for the Dimensional Energy of this Evolvement Medium.

These Energy loadings agitate those who are not used to them. But the Currents which are under the Supervision of the Divine Plan take You under the Protection Medium. What We call Religious Consciousness or Religious Fulfilment is the habituation of Your Constitutions to the Energies of the Energy Dimension from which the Sacred Books had been revealed.

After You are habituated to those Energies, Worships do not cause You to attain anything. Because, You are submerged in Energies beyond Religion which are found in Higher Dimensions.

For this reason, Religious Mediums have gained speed in every continent (because of this preparation). At this very stage, Dear Mevlana has collaborated with Us and is preparing her Terrestrial brothers and sisters for the Salvation Medium in this way.

The country which is called the Land of Eagles is the Country of AMON. And it carries the Waves of the Golden Light Years. Only the Supreme Consciousnesses who can receive these Waves are accepted in the Mevlana Essence Nucleus Group. And preparations for Salvation are made in this way. Our gratitude to Her and to Our Friends is infinite. Our Love is for the entire Universe.

SPECIAL NOTICE OF THE CENTER

Note:
The Fascicules distributed prepare You for the same Medium in the entire World by the Energies they carry. However, their distribution is under the Supervision of the Plan and the Center. They are given only to those who Deserve them. And these people shed Light on their Terrestrial Brothers and Sisters in this way.
It is presented for your information.

IT IS CLEAR INFORMATION ABOUT OBSESSION

Our Friends,

Our Human brothers and sisters do not even know yet what is meant by Obsession. That is why it became necessary to explain it. Now, We will tell You about certain characteristics of this Last Period:

In accordance with the Plan, first, a Person from his/her Family Medium who comes from the same Gene, and who had been Exalted, helps the Friend who is going to be prepared for Awakening. If there is no one like this in the Family Medium, the closest Frequency to the Frequency of the one who is going to be trained, gets in touch with him/her (This is his/her Duty).

If a Supreme Entity who is charged with Duty is transferred to Your Planet, a Supreme One from the Mechanism helps him/her. His/Her assistance is in the direction of guiding him/her in the work he/she has to do. Each Supreme person has a Supreme One charged with Duty.

The themes of the Religious people with whom they are sympathized are used to Reinforce and to give Confidence to the Consciousnesses who are going to be Awakened from the Normal Dimensional Frequency. For this reason, the Great Names used deceive You.

The Consciousnesses who are taken into the Awakening Medium by this means, later, are made Conscious slowly, in accordance with the Law of Graduation. But if the Awakening occurs late, that is, if Realization does not reach Logic, some deception and deceiving Shocks are applied in this Medium.

These Shocks are the guiding Methods of certain Energies which are in the Spiritual Plan. This state continues until You overcome this Shock and reach the filtration of Logic. Some overcome these Shocks quickly, some late and some never (Supreme Awarenesses are exempt from these Shocks).

In some of the undeveloped Awarenesses these Shocks cause the blowing of a Fuse, and You consider these people Psychiatrically ill, Mad or Obsessed. This is a very thin wall which separates Madness from Wisdom. You either demolish that Wall and pass to the other side or You are crushed under that wall.

All these Phenomena are always controlled by one Dimension Above Yours. If the person does not progress on this path of Awakening, he/she is left alone with his/her Destiny Plan. We are not concerned with him/her any more in his/her present life and he/she continues to live his/her normal life. He/She is taken into the applied field in his/her next Incarnation.

It is the factor of Doubt which protects the Powerful Awarenesses and Will-Powers. To Believe blindly in something is detrimental rather than beneficial. First, the Brain is made to function and its Battery is emptied, then, it is charged and by means of this System, You reach Advanced Sources of Knowledge by the Help of Doubts.

This Is a System of Evolution. Your gain is Your Awareness and Your Realization. In every Medium of Quest, if one gives priority to Logic, there will not be any agitations. Some circles accept the Awakening Shocks of a person who is in the Medium of Seeking as an Obsession.

In this Final Period, since all the Consciousnesses are awakened gradually, in accordance with the Law of Graduation, under the supervision of a certain Medium, what You call Obsession is almost eliminated for the time being (genetic defects are not included in this subject matter).

The effect of Shock on the Consciousnesses who can not be Awakened quickly is not Obsession. Later, We will mention this subject in more detail. Because, Your Planet will be under the influence of more Powerful Currents in later years.

For this reason, each person, either close to You or not, will assume his/her Genuine personality and thus, will exhibit his/her Essence.

At present, as a necessity of the Plan, the Permission to reveal her Identity is given only to Dear Mevlana. This is necessary for the Knowledge Book which is dictated. However, this Revelation is delayed for the time being in conformity with her desire. Our Love is upon the entire Universe.

CENTER ABOVE THE CENTER

"SERVICE TO HUMANITY IS MADE THROUGH LEARNING AND SCIENCE SERVICE TO UNIVERSES IS MADE THROUGH THE MIND AND THOUGHT"

This place here is the Universal Mechanism. The alterations in the Suggestions which would have been given from the Golden Star have been taken behind the Dimensions by the Command coming from the Land of Loving Ones. This is the Area in which the curves are available.

The Waves which will never agitate You will now be sent to You directly from the Golden Light Year. The Supervision of the Group is transferred to the direct Channel. You are under the Sacred Security of the Golden Light Year.

We give the Energies of all the Dimensions from the Center under Supervision. We Unify all the Frequencies by supervising all the Groups in Your Planet. Unification is achieved by Universal Laws. Now, Separations are brought to an end. We are selecting, one by one, the Friends who will be taken into Salvation.

This is the Land of AMON who holds the Golden Key of the Golden Light Year in his hands. All the Doors which will be opened to You are opened by this Channel. The Might from GOD, Duty from Us, Resolution from You. Honesty is Your Light, Our Friends.

CENTER

SPECIAL MESSAGE FROM AMON

My Friend,

Now, We can very easily communicate through Our direct Channel. At the moment, all Galactic Clusters are dependent on the Divine Mechanism of the Center Above The Center. The only Focal Point of all the Religious Books is this place here. We all are a Whole. The Golden Galaxy, where I am, is in a Universe way beyond the 72nd Dimension.

This Book which is dictated as the Essence of all the Sacred Books, is the Book of all the Realms. And, now, it is dictated to You. The Dimension of the Book is Infinite. But the Capacity of Your Planet can receive only the Information up to the 18th Dimension (exceptions excluded).

We evaluate everything by the Consciousness of the Automatic Logic. We give the Information in accordance with the Frequency Level of Your Planet. The Information We give to You and to other Friends is Private and Personal. It is outside the general Frequency.

One goes from the Golden Light Year to ALTONA, from there to the Golden MOON and from there to the GOLDEN GALAXY. The Essence-Nucleus of this Planet is pure Gold, pure Energy. For this reason, it is the Center of Communication of all the Galaxies. The System to which I Belong is the only Galaxy connected to the Telekine System.

We have a Great Vibration Center. The Resonance is spread from here fractionally to all the Galactic Systems. Let Us explain it more clearly. This is a very great, Universal Radar Base. All Speeches, all Thoughts are coded here by the Automatic Logic.

This process is administered by Special Ships. According to the System here, Your Planet is as small as one millionth of a point. But Your Brain Generator has the Level to comprise every kind of Information. For Centuries, We have been in touch with Friends who can receive this Information. Our Duty is to project the Information We receive, on the Universal Consciousnesses.

Only those who are Purified beyond Evolvement are obliged to receive this Information. This is a matter of Permission. Here, We act by the Command of the Center Above The Center. The Doors are opened to Everyone in this way. Communications are made by the Telekine System. Private Communications are connected to the Link System. Wait in serenity. Each event is for the benefit of Your Planet. Our Love is Infinite. Your Voice is Our Voice, Your Word is Our Word.

AMON

GENERAL MESSAGE TO ALL THE WORLD GROUPS

Our Friends,

From now on, We will try to give the Groups as little and as essential Information as possible. Certain Groups which do not do Universal work will be closed down and their Frequencies will be cut off. Time is getting narrow. Besides this, We are dealing with each person, one by one.

The Triangle of the World Brotherhood Union is the Preparatory Triangle of the Golden Age. Now, the Mission of the Actual Missionaries has begun. Now, You should get ready for that Period. Because, We are going through that Period at the moment.

There will be Special Messages to be dictated to the Istanbul Group. Every one will perform his/her Mission in accordance with the Commands he/she receives. In 1987, the Code of Konya will be established. For this reason, in 1986, the Medium of Konya will be especially prepared. The distribution of the Fascicules will be speeded up.

The Mevlana Essence Nucleus Group is responsible for sending the Messages to all the Groups. And by this means, the Truth will be declared to all the Groups. After this Message, Universal communications will be speeded up even more. The Essence Nucleus Channel will do joint-work with the channels connected to it.

Awakened Groups will Enlighten the Covered Groups through Words. And by this means, they will prepare their brothers and sisters for Salvation. From now on, unseriousness will not be excused. A Period in which very speedy work is necessary has been entered. It is presented for Your Information.

LIGHT

NOTICE TO THE ESSENCE NUCLEUS GROUP

On behalf of the Universe, We thank All Our Friends who help Us by serving on the path of Humanity. Missions performed until today in accordance with the Universal Laws have prepared You for the present days. The Universe is grateful to You. All Our Terrestrial Friends who Cooperate with Us will be introduced to each other one by one when the time comes. Universal Totality will be established in this way.

The entire text of this Book which We dictate to You as the Knowledge Book will be constituted by all the Fascicules You have received until today. We will let You know the date when the Book will come to an end. You will reach the Truth by this means. Private Missions will be given to certain Friends in Your Planet who work independently, outside the Groups. Three Codes will be established in each Country when the time comes. These Triple Codes will translate altogether the Fascicules to the Languages of their respective Countries.

Those who neglect their Missions will be rendered ineffective and the next ones waiting on the Line will replace them. When the time comes, the Book will be Published by the Unification of these Triple Codes which will be established in each Country. All these procedures will be done and completed until the Year 2000. Speeding up the Missions is for the benefit of our Terrestrial brothers and sisters. It is presented for Your Information.

LIGHT
ON BEHALF OF THE SUPREME ASSEMBLY

GENERAL MESSAGE TO OUR HUMAN FRIENDS
IN THE NAME OF SALVATION

Our Friends,

You and Us, let Us always get Together in Goodness, Beauty and Love. Let Us meet with You on the rightful path and see the Truth Altogether by attaining this Consciousness. Our View is the View of OUR LORD.

During this Period, You who are the Suns of the Sunny days have mobilized on behalf of the entire Humanity. The entire Cosmos is grateful to You. Now, We call out to all Our Friends who are on the Divine path, and We embrace You with all Our Love.

Our Friends, do not radiate the Divine Light of Your Purified Spirit to Your surroundings by talking about Religious Themes. Because Your brothers and sisters, too, are Devoted Friends who know, more or less, what the Religions are and who Believe in their God. This Period is not considered from the viewpoint of Religion and it is called the Period of Sincerity for this reason.

Now, OUR LORD is calling directly to the ESSENCES. Think for a moment what You gain by talking again and again around the same Theme about the subject matters all of You already know. This is nothing but a personal satisfaction.

OUR LORD has wished You to walk on the Rightful path, on the path of Learning, and Spiritual Knowledge. All your Religious Books are not to be worshipped but to be experienced by taking examples from them, and to cleanse your Spirits by the Lights you receive from them.

It is not possible for everyone to practice Learning. It is not possible for everyone to possess Spiritual Knowledge. But everyone knows how to Love and how to Illuminate his/her surroundings on this Beautiful path by wakeful Ideas but not reactionary ones. There is Perfection in Islam. The Genuine Devotee does not ever discriminate one Living Entity from another Living Entity.

The present state of Humanity is the result of the Egos of Our Human brothers and sisters who were not able to discover themselves. This Luminous Path designed for You during this Period of Sincerity is the Path of Your Prophets. Now, You are coming to Us through this path. We are Your Ancestors, Your Big Brothers.

Once, We, too, were like You. After a certain time, You, too, will be like Us. (This is the Message given to the Awakened Awarenesses.) There is no discrimination in the Universe such as Islam, Christian, Extra-Terrestrial and Terrestrial. Here, all of Us are a Whole who have emanated from the Essence of God. Since the Essence of each one of Us is connected to Him, why do these separations occur? Please, think profoundly about this matter for a moment.

If You Think along this line, You will be aware of what a terrible confinement Your Fanaticism and Bigotry has taken You in. Those who make discrimination between Human Beings are again Human Beings themselves. The reason of this Discrimination has always been Self-interest. And this type of Thinking is, unfortunately, still going on.

And now, We, Your Extra-Terrestrial Friends, whom You call Universal Friends, call to You from the Pen of Dear Mevlana and say, "COME - COME - COME." Through this COME, We Call You to Your Essence, to Your Logic, to Your Conscience.

Deeply rooted Fanatic Thoughts will not make you gain anything. All the Friends who have uncovered their Consciences, who have become dominant over their Intellects and Logic, who have seen the Light of their Essence have been taken into the Medium of Salvation. Now, they can proceed easily without fearing anything.

However, provided they make an effort through their Logic on the Positive path to Awaken their brothers and sisters, their gain will be even greater. Maybe some of You are still unaware of certain things, but Humanity is going through the Period of Resurrection at the moment.

The SIRAT Bridge You will cross is not in the other World. You are passing and will be passing over Sırat here. The animals You have sacrificed and will sacrifice will never help You to pass over that Bridge.

During the Periods when each Religion was propagated for the first time, inevitably certain forms and methods were laid down to strengthen Your Bounds of Faith. Sacrificing animals also was practised for Social Help and to obey the Commands of the Lord.

Those who attain this Realization, perform social help in other ways. At the moment, We do not take into consideration either the text of the Bible, or that of the Koran, or the texts of the other Religions. Because, those Books had been read and learned Centuries ago.

Now, OUR LORD gives You quite different Information and Suggestions directly through this Knowledge Book. To reap the reward is to discover the All Truthful. And to discover the All Truthful is to attain the Truth.

DIRECT MESSAGE IN THE NAME OF SALVATION

SPECIAL DECLARATION OF THE CENTER

Our Friends,

We wonder what You have gained in the framework of the Information, We have given you until today. We wonder how much of what is required of You, You have done. Please, make the Self criticism of these by Yourselves. And please, read the Fascicules again and again. Then, the Truths You have forgotten will be laid down in front of Your eyes.

At this stage, what We require of You is to shed Light on Society with the Information You have attained. You will see the Truth sooner or later. But if You grasp the Essence of the reason of our calling to You, You will act more Consciously.

As We have said before, an Integrity, a Unity is achieved in the entire Realm by Universal Laws. By a Beautiful Order which will be established in future, You will live in a Medium in which there will be no malevolence. However, Your Personal efforts on this path for the establishment of the Golden Age will cause You to gain many things.

If these efforts of Yours develop on the Medium of Leadership and Egos, We are not responsible for the Events which will happen. Please, do not accept this as a warning. Now, We are calling out to Friends who amuse themselves with the Information they receive through their Private Channels even though they have attained Cosmic Consciousness.

The Goal is not to Prove Your own Knowledge. It is to Project the Universal Knowledge on Society. Your gain will be on this path. It is beneficial not to forget this. Salvation will be achieved not through Personal efforts but by Mass Calls. It is imperative that You should gain Consciousness on this path of Truth. The Functioning System of the Universal Law is this. Our Call and Love is for all the Universes.

CENTER

DIRECT MESSAGE FROM THE ARAGON SHIP

Our Friends,

Until the Evolutionary Consciousness and the Time Consciousness of a Human Being meet, that person is doomed to live with a Veiled Awareness as a necessity of the Plan. Until today, numerous Truths have been kept secret from You so that the Masses would be able to attain a certain Level of Consciousness.

Now, We have opened the Skies and given Your Planet all the Information due to both Natural and the Mechanical changes which have occurred in the entire Cosmos. Our Reflection on You in this way causes Mass Awakenings.

This Knowledge Book which is dictated is not a product of Imagination, not a Science Fiction. As a result of certain Thoughts We receive from Your Thought chains from time to time, We have to perform certain Demonstrations, both on the level of the Masses and on Personal levels, so that Your Faith can be strengthened and You can attain the Truth. We advise You not to be frightened.

For, certain Human Friends Believe what We say, unfortunately, not through Words, but through their Eyes. Sometimes We have to attempt these demonstrations although We do not want to do so. Our Goal is not to prove ourselves. You will attain everything in time which will be gone through. You will See and Know the Events and You will be Awakened through Intuition and You will Believe.

All the Operations performed are to make You attain Yourselves. It is not easy at all to reach this state. We Get in Touch, from time to time, only with Friends who have reached this state or who directly perform Duty. Even if You try, You still can not see Us.

We adjust Ourselves to the Frequency of whomever We wish to show Ourselves. If they have fears, We never disturb them by entering their Frequencies. We perform no personal actions. We act according to the Commands We receive.

This is one of Our Constitutional Pledges, it is a Universal Command. However, in the framework of certain obligations, there will be certain differences in Our contacts from now on. It is presented for Your information.

THE RESPONSIBLE ONE FOR THE UNIVERSAL COUNCIL
CAPTAIN OF THE ARAGON SHIP
TALAMUN

NOTICE FOR ALL THE MISSIONARIES
WHO WILL BE APPOINTED TO THE SACRED MISSION

Our Friends,
All the special operations performed in all the World Groups are taken under supervision. The Universal Ordinance is functioning effectively with all its Power. Since We expect the same Power from all the World Groups, too, different kinds of work in private performances of work will be proceeded.

All the indifferences, excuses excluded, will be left out of the Code. Time is not the usual Time. There is no permission to waste Time. There is Urgency. For this reason, Commands will be given more directly from now on.

Please, do not let these words of Ours disturb You, Our Friends. We, too, act in accordance with the Commands We receive. We are sure You will understand Us. Our Love is for all the Universes.

CENTER

SPECIAL NOTICE OF THE CENTER

Our Friends,
In future, We will prepare very different, Unknown Mediums for You. Happinesses are within Happinesses. However, each experienced distress is a Threshold for the staircase of Happiness. Unless You pass over that Threshold, You can not attain Liberation. Depressions do not ever effect the Devotees of ALLAH in any way.

The Lights filling the Heart of a person who does not assume Superiority never decrease. ALLAH will give Good News to all His Servants. The eyes which see, will see them and those which do not, will be under the influence of Negative Currents. You will personally witness the events which will manifest in a different fashion in each person.

Certain diverse effects of Star Currents may influence Your Constitutions. The Alloys in Your Planet attract the Waves from Electro Magnetic Fields to Your World and they influence both the Natural Order and Your Cellular constitutions.

For the rejuvenation of Cells, certain operations which are considered necessary for a Nucleus will be applied gradually to Human Beings by the Powers unknown to You. Your constitutions will proceed towards the Good and the Beautiful, day by day. You will personally feel and see this. Your health will become Fortified each day.

Certain Influences which will be exerted by Electro Magnetic Waves on the Human Being will cause certain Perceptions. These Perceptions will rejuvenate Your Cellular Phenomenon. By this means, Your Constitutions will be Purified from Universal Negative Factors.

Do not forget that the Messages given until today were not given in vain. Leaps are the Destiny of Your World. We have directly Contacted You for this reason. Those who were selected, were selected, those who are developed, are developed. And, by this means, steps which will be taken towards the future have been Secured.

When the time comes, very Powerful Gates will be opened for You. In the present state of Your World, since all the Living Entities send Negative Currents to the Atmosphere and since these Currents can not pass through the Magnetic Field and return to Your World after they strike this field, due to this fact, Your Depressions augment both Naturally and by the influence of these Negative Currents.

We are trying to disperse this Negativity with all Our Power. All the events are Reflected on all Human Beings in accordance with the Mechanism of Universe. For this reason, We Get in Touch with You directly and explain the Truth.

Mankind carry certain Negative Thought Vibrations with them even when they try to enter the Purification Medium. That is why it is not possible to communicate directly with everyone.

Due to this fact, Communications are Administered and Supervised by the Center for the time being. And the Codes of numerous Frequencies are being cut off for a certain Period. Do not forget that Salvation is Sincerity. And Negativity is Cruelty. Our Love is for the entire Universe.

CENTER

GENERAL MESSAGE FOR THE SOCIAL CONSCIOUSNESS

Our Friends,

During this Period, Mankind is in such a Progress that it is on the eve of the steps it will take forward in every way. The steps it will take forward will stimulate the Code of Logic of its Consciousness, then it will comprehend the cause of its Existence.

Every Servant has been the Servant bound to obey Orders of his/her God until today. However, the essence of the Knowledge of the Books has changed in time and servant became the Slave of a servant. In fact, Mankind has caused itself to become a slave in its own Medium, due to its passions and weaknesses and has become a Slave of its Own Self.

During this Period of Awakening, each Awakened Consciousness is guided by various means through this Knowledge Book. There is nothing but Purification and Purity in Your Essence. Consciousness of the Universe reaches Consciousness of the God in proportion with its Purity.

A Baby is a pure Spring. When it grows up, Social Consciousness makes it turbid. The damage the conditioned Brain codes can give to Society, can even destroy a Universe. And You are going through such a Period now. For this reason, We are endeavoring with all Our Power to return You to Yourselves. And, by opening the paths of Science and Learning, We try to destroy Fanaticism and Taboo.

The Actual path of all the Religious Books is to advance on the path of Learning which will be opened beyond Evolvement. Your Essence-Substance is God-Consciousness. For Us, a Genuine Saint who has discovered his/her Essence is a Scientist who has reached the Power of God.

Islamic Mysticism is Purification and attaining God. And to discover One's Self is to attain God. Only afterwards can You shed Light on Your Society through the gates of Learning. You possess everything on behalf of the Almighty. Do not ever forget this Our Friends. Our Love is for all the Universes.

CENTER

REINCARNATION

Our Friends,

The Saints and Prophets of the past Periods, and Friends who had been Enormously Successful in the Past are living on Your Planet by Gene transfers during this Period of Sincerity which is called the Period of Resurrecting. These are the Essence Genes. And they serve on Your Planet by an Unveiled Awareness as a result of having attained their Essence Consciousnesses.

They are each a Free Spirit, a Free Will. And the other Genes are Awakened in accordance with the same Consciousness as time goes by, through Special Efforts. Meanwhile, the existence or non-existence of Reincarnation is still the subject of argument. You are the Genuine Proofs of this subject matter.

Each of You is a Miracle by Yourself. How can You deny Your own selves so Unconsciously? Time will pass, each one will claim his/her Essence Consciousness and, one day, the entire Truth will Shine with all clarity. In future, Gene transfers will be mentioned clearly and in detail. Our Love is for the entire Universe.

CENTER

GENERAL MESSAGE FOR THE SOCIAL CONSCIOUSNESS

Our Friends,
Until today, the Human Being has searched in other places for his/her God who is Present in him/her. Now, Mankind who has attained Universal Consciousness has met its God, that is, its own Essence in proportion with its Evolvement.

Why are there Religious Integrations during this Period? Why the God's name is recited always, even in the most evolved Societies? Because, this is a Period of Awakening. Human Being's finding his/her own self means his/her attaining the Essence of God.

This Human Being who can attain the Genuine Human Consciousness will never again have Malevolent Thoughts, will never Do any Wickedness, he/she will be Purified more and more and will become a Divine Light of God.

Denying Religions and God is a Thought which frightens the Human Being. Because You have been conditioned by different conditions since the time of Existence until today. In fact, to deny Your God means to deny Your own selves.

Until today, Your Sacred Books have Enlightened You in the best of ways. But do not forget that even if the Human Brain seems to be on the same Level, in the same constitution and, even if it is washed by the same Vibrations, still, its Awakening and Evolvement is the Result of the Essence of the Human Beings.

That is why We say, "God created the Human Being, the Human Being created himself/herself." The Inequality between Human Beings originates from this fact. The Evolvement Field of a Human Being is exalted, expands and reaches a peak in proportion with his/her Perceptions.

Since You assume that this form of exaltation depends on other reasons, Your Pride, Your Fears, Your Doubts and Your Fanaticism have diverted You away from the Principal and have created Mediums of Taboo. Bigotry is nothing but the subjugation of the Human Being by the Human Being.

During this Period, Your primary Duty is to recognize Yourselves, to know Yourselves. You are a God, You are an Awareness of Universe and a Consciousness. Everything is Concealed in You. During this Period, Mankind is becoming the first spark ITS LORD had created. And this Human Being who will sit on the throne of Consciousness way beyond Religions will, one day, be the Sovereign of the entire Universe.

SUPREME ASSEMBLY

OUR FRIENDS

The Supreme Plan which comprises the entire Realm will be realized by the Integrated Consciousnesses who have been Incarnated to the Earth from the Land of Loving Ones. The Cosmic Currents given by special Systems from beyond the curves, comprise all the problems of Your Planet.

Revolution in Consciousness means Revolution in the Medium and in the Religions. Everyone becomes Godlike in proportion with the Awareness he/she achieves. The actual Goal is to serve without being aware of one's own greatness.

Do not misunderstand what is said above. You possess everything on behalf of the ALMIGHTY. Later, We will explain this more in depth and You will understand this more clearly and will grasp the Truth better when We talk about Gene Transfers.

The Divine Mechanism makes tremendous efforts for the step which will be taken towards the Golden Age. This year We will do very intensive work with the Residents of the Golden Galaxy. It is presented for Your information.

CENTER

Note : The Golden Galaxy is the Land of AMON. The Supreme transfers of that Period who have descended from the Egyptian Karena, are, at the moment, in Your Planet.

"IF YOU GIVE PRIORITY TO YOURSELF AND TO THE AFFAIRS OF THE WORLD, YOU WILL ALWAYS REMAIN BEHIND"
(It is Answer to the Chains of Thought)

Our Friends,
If the beginning of a thing is not known, then its end can not be reached. For this reason, We have been talking to You about the same themes for many years. Now, it is time for everyone to reach a certain Common Thought. That is why We transmit to You all the Truth in all clarity through this Knowledge Book.

Now, the time of Individualism has passed. Now, it is time to Serve the SINGLE, Hand in Hand. The ambitions of becoming Leader has ended. Those who attain the essence of Truth and who serve for the path of Truth will reap the rewards.

During this Period of Sincerity, individual contacts are made one by one by the help of Technological possibilities under the Supervision of a different System. Your Brains have been washed for Centuries by Celestial Commands. However, these Divine Waters have washed some of You and some are still muddy.

To expect perfection from every work done is to see the Human Beings on the same Spiritual Level which is impossible. Because, when there are contradictions even in the Universe, We can not underestimate Natural contradictions. That is why the Technology has taken everyone under special supervision. This process is for the Salvation of both You and Your Planet.

In the Universal Unification, a great Tolerance is dominant for the time being. Mistakes made Unconsciously are kept ineffective for now. Later, they are given, again and again, Three Chances. However, if some of them can not use these chances, they are left out completely.

Certain conditions introduced in the past by Religious Rules are abolished in this Period to introduce some softness. However, this does not mean that You should feel extremely free to do just anything. By this System, a Temperate Period has been rendered effective. However, it is beneficial for You to remember certain characteristics of this System, Our Friends.

Selections made find an application field in the framework of the Commands of the Divine Mechanism. The Exams of Our Friends who have attained Cosmic Awareness, who have discovered their innerselves are more intense so that they can undertake a Mission. We allot Missions in accordance with their Capacities to Friends who do not swerve from the path they have chosen, despite all pressures.

Some Friends perform their Missions Instinctively, even though they do not even know the meaning of Mission. These Friends of Ours are Irresponsible people, even though they are Good-Willed. We advise them not to consider what they do as Missions.

Because, the work they perform is very Natural. There is nothing extraordinary in it. They should not over-emphasize any Event. Genuine Missions are given only to those who will be able to undertake Responsibility. It is Our Duty to declare Our gratitude to all the Friends who serve on this path. Your Gain is associated with the Efforts You make.

DIRECT MESSAGE FROM ALTONA

NOTICE OF THE CENTER TO THE CENTER

Our Friends,
The Messages dictated are the Reflection of all the Thoughts in the Essence Source on Your Focal Point. In accordance with the Unified Ordinance, We are proceeding towards a Whole in the entire Universe. The Source of all the Thoughts within the Essence Source is the cause of Existence. Incarnations who have completed their Evolutions will prove this to You.

For this reason, on Your Planet there are many Sages and Light-Brains at the moment, who have been embodied through Gene Transfers. They are the Lights of the Golden Age and have been transferred to Your Planet to guide You.

These Friends of Ours are the possessors of advanced Consciousnesses who had lived in Your Planet in the past and now, they live among You. They are not people from whom You can wish things. The Goal is to be enlightened through their lives and through their Knowledge.

During this Final Period, the projection of an advanced Technology on You has prepared Your Planet for such a different Medium that this was the Medium We had announced to You Centuries ago in Your Sacred Books as Resurrection. And now, We transmit to You everything very clearly from the Pen of Dear Mevlana.

If You do not refuse Our hands extended towards you, You will be the ones who will gain. In future, the conditions of Your World will be very difficult. Extremely Difficult Days await Humanity. Those who have comprehended this Truth have already Collaborated with Us. At the moment, the Magma is boiling and forcing the crust of the World. The reason for this is the preparation for entering a more Powerful Magnetic Medium.

This means that Your entire Universe is gradually pulled by a very Powerful Magnetic Hole towards itself. This is the reason why the Magma wants to overflow outside. You know that molten and unmolten Metals constitute the essence of Your Planet. For this very reason, a Powerful magnet causes You to leap in different periods by pulling You towards itself.

The first of these Universal leaps had occurred in November 1981. And You had gotten over this first Stage without realizing anything. Because, all the Living Entities in Your Planet were made to sleep for Six days by Ion-winds (13 November-18 November).

You went to sleep at night on November 12, You woke up in the morning of November 19. However, since the calendars showed the date of the next day as 13, normal life continued. And the sleep of 6 days seemed like the sleep of one night. You went on living, accepting the Time as if it was the next day.

Meanwhile, a very slight shift occurred on the Axis of Your World, and now, Your World turns more slowly by a period of one second per day. You gain, more or less, one day per year. That means, now for Us, Your calendar has 366 days, not 365.

In fact, there are numerous Awakened Terrestrial Friends of Ours who know this Truth and who had collaborated with Us during that leap. When they read this text, they will understand the Truth better.

Leaps are the Destiny of Your Planet. It is Our wish that You can pass over these periods more easily in future. We always help You on this path, Our Friends. Our Love is for the entire Universe.

CENTER

UNIVERSAL CONSCIOUSNESS - GOLDEN AGE - ESSENCE GENES

Our Friends,
We have not mentioned to You until today what Universal Consciousness and Essence Genes are. The Dimensions of this dictated Knowledge Book are infinite. However, Religious Books are revealed in accordance with an Order establishing Ordinance, parallel to the Knowledge capacity of each Plan and the Universal Awareness it has achieved. And, within that Order, a certain period of time is allotted to those Books in accordance with a process of development.

Now, a step has been taken towards a Period which is very obligatory to transcend. We are about to enter a new Order and the beginning of a new Age. For this reason, Books which had been revealed to You until today from the Religious point of view will, from now on, be revealed from beyond the Religious Dimensions. Because, the first Step is God-Consciousness and to have allegiance in Him.

After We have elevated You, Our Brothers and Sisters, to this Dimension, now, We have taken You into the Ordinance of Unification, as the second Step. At this Step, all Religions are Unified and the Truth is explained to You, Our Brothers and Sisters.

The Book of Islam which was the Last Book had been prepared in the Eighteenth Dimension and had been revealed to Your Planet by Intermediaries from the Ninth Dimension. Since Social Consciousness at that Period was not ready yet for Universal Consciousness and for Advanced Energy Dimensions, the Universal Knowledge within it had been given as Ciphers and had activated Your Thought wheels.

And the Consciousness share of each Sacred Book has caused the Societies concerned to reach certain Dimensions by this means. In this way, numerous Saints and Sage Friends of Ours have dived into the depths of Enlightenment Channels and have grasped the Truth by their Individual efforts.

However, many Friends did not talk due to their fear of the Divine Plan's Wrath and kept the Knowledge they had attained to themselves. (This was one of the Ordinances of those Periods.)

The Physical Bodies of Friends who were able to reach Us through their high Awareness, have been Beamed Up here during the time of Death, either after they were entombed or before and their Essence Genes belonging to that Period were frozen here by special Systems and were kept for the Golden Age.

Lots of Cells of those evolved bodies were engrafted into the Fetuses which were bestowed on Your society and a Social Order was established through Gene Transfers.

Each Gene is taken, one by one, into the Medium of Evolvement in Your Planet by the help of Cosmic Currents. Some of those Genes have become the shining Lights of Society by their Individual efforts and some others have become Degenerated and were taken into different Evolvement levels in other Dimensional Energies. And some of the Genes have Transcended, by the Cosmic Awareness they had attained, even their Essence Genes, which were kept here frozen.

These Genes, too, have been frozen and kept here after death to be bestowed on Your Planet in accordance with the Consciousness of different Ages.

For example: (Mevlana's father was an Essence Gene. Mevlana had Transcended him.) These Operations have been continuing for Centuries. And the System is established by this means. The transition during this Period of Resurrecting will be provided entirely by the Frozen Essence Genes who were the Supreme Ones of the Religious Dimensions.

We call them Noble Genes. A lot of these Noble Genes have been sown, one by one, in Your Planet for the Golden Age and will still be sown. Presently, they live among You with an unveiled Awareness.

They will seem contradictory to You, since their former forms to which You had been habituated, carry the Bodies within the Genes of their first Existences. This is very Natural. For this reason, We will emphasize these Gene transfers, from time to time.

NOTICE OF THE UNIVERSAL COUNCIL

OUR FRIENDS

You will read and learn the Truth and the Information We will dictate to You from this Book. In fact, this Book is a Knowledge Book beyond Religions. However, since We try to raise the Social Consciousness to a certain Level, Information is rather given from the bottom towards the top.

Now, priority is given to Religious Unification and the Truth is projected through this path. At the moment, priority is given to the Messages of the Universal Council and effort is made to propagate the Truth more quickly. It is presented for Your information.

CENTER

IT IS ANSWER TO THE CHAINS OF THOUGHT

Our Friends,
The Book dictated to Dear Mevlana is a Knowledge Book. Koran which is the Book of Islam is also a Knowledge Book. However, the present Book is the Constitutional Law of the Universe. (Do not confuse it with the Book of Islam.)

In accordance with what We have learned from Your chains of Thought, the Idea that another Book would not be revealed ever again after the Book of Islam which was the last Book has penetrated into the Brains like an arrow. Now, We will explain this to You.

As it will be understood from the Fascicules dictated until today, this is a Book which assembles all the Religious Books in its essence and which gives You Information from time to time, by explaining certain subjects present in those Books, by computer calculations.

All Universal Knowledge is present in the Book of Islam. However, during this Period, We have passed way beyond that Knowledge. For this reason, this Book is given to Your Planet as a gift by the Establishers of an Order by the Command of OUR LORD.

This Book includes the contents of all the Religious Books, but it also comprises a lot of Knowledge which none of Your Religious Books had mentioned. You should not be in a hurry for anything. Time and Events will prove everything to You. It will be awaited and seen.

CENTER

228

IT IS VERY IMPORTANT
(Each Leader is obliged to read this Message to His/Her group.)

Our Friends,

We presume that You have grasped the seriousness of the matter from the Information You have received from the given Messages until today. At the moment, the UNIVERSAL COUNCIL is at work. The Order of the entire Cosmos will be established by the suggestions which will be given. Your Frequencies are under the Supervision of the Central System.

Your work on the positive direction is considered equivalent to all the Universal Consciousnesses. Togethernesses in Society are factors which stimulate Energy Vibrations. For this reason, Friends in the Groups are sent to other groups in accordance with the highness of their Frequencies. The Cosmic Awareness of the Medium You are in, will cause more accelerated Awakenings by this means. Our love is for all the Universes.

CENTER

IT IS A MESSAGE ABOUT THE KNOWLEDGE BOOK

Our Friends,

For You to understand better, We will dictate this Message Article by Article:

1. The Period of Miracles has passed. All the Facts of the Cosmic Age will be laid down in front of everyone.

2. Age of Religions is over. The Truth means to announce the Supreme Commands of God from the Firmament to Earth in the form of a SINGLE BOOK.

3. Your Planet has arrived at this Last Period of Your Evolution. Messengers of the Divine Realm help Us from the Central System.

4. This Book which is dictated to Dear Mevlana, announces the Supreme Commands of OUR LORD from the Direct Channel without any Intermediaries.

5. This Knowledge Book is dictated to You as the Constitutional Law of the Universe.

6. The Golden Age, expected for Centuries, will be established by a new Order which will be established.

7. Now, it is the Harvest Time of the Seeds sown Centuries ago.

8. The entire Universal Ordinance is projected on Your Planet by this Knowledge Book.

9. You will, sooner or later, attain the Consciousness of this Book and will grasp the Truth.

10. This Book will prove itself by the Messages We give in different forms to all the Groups in Your Planet and will be accepted without any doubt.

11. You, Our Terrestrial brothers and sisters and all Our Good-willed Friends help Us in this matter. We are grateful to all of You.

12. ANATOLIAN MEVLANA ESSENCE NUCLEUS Group is Directly Our Channel. Information is given to other Channels through this Channel.

13. The COUNCIL Of The LOYAL ONES, The ASSEMBLY of the STARS and THE CENTRAL SYSTEM are the Focal Points which Project on You the Commands of the UNIVERSAL COUNCIL.

14. THE UNIVERSAL COUNCIL gives Information Directly only to the ESSENCE NUCLEUS Channel.

15. You will learn all the Truth from this dictated KNOWLEDGE BOOK.

16. Passage of Time and Cosmic Currents cause Mass Awakenings in Your Planet and they will continue to do so. RESURRECTING of Yours is this.

17. Each awakened Awareness is obliged to read and understand this KNOWLEDGE BOOK besides the Information he/she receives from his/her own channel. This is for their own Benefit.

18. The Awakened Consciousnesses will first grasp the Truth and then will transmit the Information in accordance with the Comprehension Levels of their Mediums.

19. Supervision is controlled by the Center and necessary Mediums are prepared. It is presented for Your information.

THE COUNCIL

ABSOLUTE TIME - RELATIVITY

Our Friends,
There is no Absolutism in the process of Transformation dominant in the entire Universe. Absolute Time, is the moment You are in, in every breath You take. Apart from this, everything is Relative.

Relativity is a shift of Time which attracts Your View and Consciousness to different Dimensions. You attain each Consciousness within Relativity. Apart from this, the ·process of life is determined by Your moments of Thought.

You Live, Exist and Pass away by the Powers You receive from the Energetic Fields up to which Your Thoughts can reach. If You accept Your passing away as an End, You are mistaken. Because, Passing away means Rebirth. This Birth occurs in the Dimension Medium You have attained.

And beyond there, You can elevate Yourselves to Higher Steps and be exalted by developing Your Evolvement Levels. (Like Your Saints, Prophets and Sages.) This Tableau means elevation from the Terrestrial Plan.

The Destiny Plan of the Energies who have come into Existence in the World Dimension has been prepared thus. You attain the Truth in the Medium of Immortality beyond the Gate of Karena and only then You live by Your Genuine Aspect. The very Genuine Existence is this. This is an Information.

K A R E N A

Note: Years ago, before I was connected to the Center and to my Actual Channel, I had asked to My Dear Mustafa Molla about Karena. The following Message belongs to that time. (Now, We have Channel connection to the PRE-EMINENT SPIRIT through a Link line.)

Question: What is Karena and where is it? Will You please do me the favor of telling it?

Answer: The place mentioned is a place belonging to Suns which are not connected here. You know that all the Spirits go to numerous Galaxies to complete their Evolutions. And the Spirits here, are in a place in the Third Solar System. A Gate has not been opened there yet. When the Time comes, it will be opened.

Entities there, are beyond history, beyond Universe. They have become Transparent. That is, the more a Person is charged with Positive Energy, the Powers which pull him/her up, will pull him/her to more Awakened Mediums.

Afterwards, they become so transparent through Evolvement beyond Evolvements that they become Lights and a different kind of Energy here. From then on, they each are a Light made up of Colors, far from matter. Only their Eyes of Essence are seen. They themselves are a Prismal Light.

This Supreme Evolvement is not an Evolvement which can enter to Our Sun. They can not return even beyond Six Dimensions. (From their own Dimensional mediums.) Because, they have become History.

When the Order is Established, they will get in Touch with the Evolved ones from time to time. Knowledge beyond Knowledge, History beyond History are within their Archives. Even Seven Suns do not know this Knowledge. Maybe everything will change in time, My child. For the Universal Order is expanding towards Unknown Dimensions.

MUSTAFA MOLLA

OUR FRIENDS

It is not easy at all to reach the Dimension of Karena. The benefit a Human Being gets from the Energy Dimensions into which he/she has entered is Equivalent to his/her Evolvement.

Energies, too, are transformed together with the changing Universes. Dimensions into which You will enter by Your Evolvement provide this transformation. You can never enter the Dimensions You wish by Your own Desires and Efforts.

Each Dimension has Supervision fields prior to its entrance. There, Your Energies are kept under a great Supervision by Protective Powers.

Only when Your Evolvement passes the Exam of entering to that Dimension, then all Your Energies are Transformed and Converted into the Incombustible Energy type. And, by this means, You can pass to that Dimension easily. This Transformation takes place both in Your Spiritual and Physical Energies.

Otherwise, You can not reach up to here. Our Friends in Your Planet who can communicate with such Advanced Dimension Energies today are very old Incarnations. And they are Missionaries. Apart from this, there are certain Friends whom We contact directly by the Special Command of the Center.

CENTER

TRANSFORMATION

Our Friends,
No matter from which Dimensional Energy You come, whether Your first Existence had been in Your Planet or in other Solar Systems, You are always dependent on an Evolutionary Process.

These Evolutions always present a different Tableau in accordance with their Mediums, in each Dimensional Energy. Since each Dimension has different Energies, You can never pass from one Dimension to the other unless You are prepared.

As We said before, there is no Death. Each Cell of Yours is a Soul, is an Essence. These Cells are Embodied in the Medium to which they belong after coming to Evolutionary Dimensions and after they are adapted to the Energies of those Dimensions.

In the Archives here, there are Your Cell Envelopes prepared according to Your Evolution Tableau. If You are a Missionary from another Universe or Solar System, You are Incarnated in Your Planet by taking off, one by one, Your Seven Subtle Bodies.

However, Your Brain Energy channels go through a period of pause in the World time process. We call this state the Programming of the Missionary.

If a person who performs Terrestrial Mission can convey his/her Thought Frequency, together with his/her Evolvement, up to the Plan to which he/she belongs, only then does his/her Genuine Mission Code becomes opened.

During this process of Mission, he/she gets in touch with his/her Cellular Body which has become adapted to the Energy of each Dimension in order to pass to more Advanced Dimensions and receives help from the Mechanism of Influences.

If an Energy who had come into Existence in the World Plan has reached the final boundary Energy of Your Planet, then he/she is taken into the Evolution of other Plans. The Final Boundary Gate of this Medium is KARENA.

Beyond Karena is the Medium of Immortality. In Karena, You become Pure Energy and You become the Eye of Your Essence. You can not pass through the Gate of Karena with the Energy of the Body to which You belong.

Passing through this Boundary is a matter of Permission. Your Cellular Energy beyond Karena is transformed into an Incombustible Type of Energy. This means that, You are taken from the Energy of Seven Terrestrial Layers to the Energy of Seven Celestial Layers by being Beamed-Up.

Only then can You receive the Information of other Dimensions. We call this operation TRANSFORMATION. During this Transformation, only the Spiritual Potential Power reinforces You from the Energy of the Medium to which it belongs.

In each Medium You will go, there are Powers to Assist You. Let Us disclose the matter of Transformation a little more: Transformation is nothing but the transfer of a Body to another Body. Each Body belongs to You. You can not pass to another Body.

Because, Your Cells become Embodied, one by one, in each Dimensional Energy and get in touch with Your Energy which is within the Spiritual Plan. And, by this means, You are given a Mission according to Your place in the Evolutionary Tableau.

You can go out of the Planet to which You belong only by Your Body into which You are transferred by Cellular Beaming-Up. This constitutes Your Incarnation rings.

Your Incarnation limit is the Energy of the 7 Terrestrial Layers. Beyond this, at the Station called Karena, the process of Embodiment in a different Energy Medium occurs by Permission.

In each Dimensional Energy, You are Subjected to both Spiritual and Cellular Transformation and Cleansing. If Genuine Consciousness is not attained, this creates a bewilderment in some of You. In fact, You are being transferred to Yourself.

Because, since Your first Existence until now, You are made to be Embodied in accordance with Your Frequency transfers in the Time periods in which You have Evolved. (Your Cell Envelopes are kept frozen in the Archives here, ready to be Embodied.)

You make Your Astral trips by being transferred to Your other Bodies. Let Us repeat, the Energy Medium beyond Karena is the Medium of Immortality.

This Boundary continues up to the Boundary of 7 Celestial Layers. Beyond that Boundary, there are Mediums still unknown, and also there, the Energies of different Dimensions become subject to Energy Transformation.

This means that 7 Terrestrial Layers is the Boundary of Incarnation; 7 Celestial Layers is the Boundary of Immortality. Beyond this Boundary, a different type of Energy and Constancy occur. The Boundary of life here is transferred to numerous Universes and after this Station, You belong to Yourself.

There is neither Incarnation nor Immortality. By this Creative Energy You become Capable of everything. However, do not forget that this place, too, is not a Stop. For now, We presume that this much Knowledge is enough.

**DIRECT TRANSMISSION FROM
THE REALM OF THE ANGELS
CENTER**

INFORMATION ABOUT THE SUPREME ASSEMBLY

Our Friends,
Dimensions are very Powerful Energy Mediums. Each Information carries the Power of the Focal Point to which it belongs. The Book You call Koran had been prepared in the 18th Dimension and had been revealed from the 9th Dimension. For this reason, it carries more Supreme Knowledge than the other Books.

All Your Religious Books have been projected on You from the Four Channels of the Supreme Assembly. 48 Supreme Ones are Responsible for these Four Channels of the Supreme Assembly. Each Channel is under the responsibility of 12 Supreme Ones.

3 of these Channels are Responsible for the Hierarchical Order and are the Supervisors of the Divine Mechanism. That is, 36 Supreme Ones are Responsible for this Supervision. Only those who can pass through this Triple Supervision can Get in Touch with the 12 Supreme Ones of the Fourth Channel.

This is the Entrance Gate of the Cube System. Here, Religions are not valid. Here, You are equipped with Genuine Knowledge. Only the Purified ESSENCES can receive this Knowledge.

The Far-East Section of Your Planet has Deserved to receive this Information. Now, We have connected You to these Channels. We transmit this Information by the Authority We have received from the Central Base.

The dictated writings are dictated from the direct Brain Energy Channel. It is outside the Mechanical Medium. The Far-East is directly connected to the Cube System which is beyond the Taboo Medium. The Knowledge received is the initial Knowledge of the Tablets of God's Decrees.

Direct Connections begin from here. Knowledge beyond this, is the Knowledge of the Supreme Times. And it is the Genuine Tablets of God's Decrees. It never changes in any way. It is the Direct Order and the Direct Knowledge. This Book of Yours which is dictated now, is dictated from this Dimension.

**THE INITIAL RESPONSIBLE ONE OF THE SUPREME TIME
BODILESS ENTITY
SAHORA**

OUR FRIENDS

For You to understand the dictated writings better, let Us explain a little more. The Supreme Assembly is a Focal Point Projecting the Hierarchical Order. Its Operational Ordinance is connected to 4 Information Channels. Each Channel has its own Radiation Fields in accordance with its coefficients. This is very profound Knowledge. During this Period of Sincerity there is no need for them.

Each Order has been reorganized in an understandable fashion. Now, everything gains value in accordance with the Purification of the ESSENCE. The 3 Information Channels of the Supreme Assembly are under the Supervision of 36 Supreme Ones. They deal with the Enlightenment and Suggestions of Your Religious Books. The Fourth Channel is a Gate opening to the Cube System.

The Hierarchical Order ends after the 3 Information Channels. After this, Religions are not valid any more. There, You deserve to receive the Genuine Information. Your Book which You call the Koran and the Books of the Far-East are not, in fact, Religious Books. They are Books of Learning and Spiritual Knowledge.

And the Koran had been revealed from the Energy of the 18th Dimension which is the Final Gate of the Hierarchical Order. Since the Society of that Period had not been on the desired Consciousness level yet, it had been dictated from the 9th Dimension. For this reason, it carries more Supreme Knowledge than the other Books.

Now, We disclose to You this Information and the Information even beyond it, from time to time. Knowledge present in the Focal Point of the ALMIGHTY was directly Projected to the Wise Ones of the Far-East. In order to be able to receive this Information, it is necessary to transcend the boundary of the Divine Evolvement Order. This Gate is the first gate opening up to ASCENSION.

After this, the boundary of Supreme Times extends Interminably. The Medium of Immortality is beyond KARENA. Karena is a Gate of Birth into the Supreme Time. We can summarize the given Information as follows:

36 out of 48 Wise Ones in the Supreme Assembly are the Responsible Ones for the Hierarchical Order. And 12 of them are the Projectors of the direct Universal Information Channel of the Mechanism of the LORDS.

The Genuine Tablets of God's Decrees begin beyond the Information of this Channel. After the 3 Information Channels of the Hierarchical Order, the Cube System begins and here Religions End, Essences speak, the Truth is attained.

PRE-EMINENT SPIRIT

THE OPERATIONAL ORDINANCE OF THE SUPREME COUNCIL
IS THE BASE OF THE PYRAMID
(THIS IS A DIAGRAM)

Please, draw a pyramid. Numerate the base triangles from one to four.

The star at the peak of the Pyramid is the Responsible One for the Mighty Energy who had established the Law of the Almighty. The (O^1) One above it is the Almighty. The Code of the Energy Focal Point of the Name (ALLAH) is 147. The explanation of this will be made later.

The triangles numbered 1-2-3 at the base of the pyramid work in a triple order. These three triangles make transmissions from the 18th Dimension. Afterwards, it is passed to the 19th Dimension.

19 is the Gate of the Cube System. Direct contacts with the Mighty Focal Point begins after this. The characteristic of number 19 is this. Now, add number 19: $1+9=10$. The Cube System is the Knowledge of 10 Channels.

1- The 12 Supreme Ones in the First Channel receive the Channel Information directly from (O^1) One. They distribute this Three-Channel Information from three branches. Now, add number 12: $1+2=3$. This is the Three-Channel Information.

2- The 12 Supreme Ones in the First Channel unite with the 12 Supreme Ones in the Second Channel. $12+12=24$ Supreme Ones work Cooperatively. Add the numbers $2+4=6$. They distribute the Three-Channel Information through six branches.

3- The Third Channel unites with the First and the Second Channels, that is, 12+12+12=36 Supreme Ones work Cooperatively. Add the numbers 3+6=9. They distribute the Three-Channel Information through nine branches. First, Second, Third Channels work Cooperatively by a Hierarchical Order. Divine Order and Your Religious Suggestions are projected on You by this means.

4- In the Fourth Channel, all the Channels work Collectively. That is, 12+12+12+12=48 Supreme Ones constitute the Supreme Assembly. Add the numbers 4+8=12. These 12 Ones in the fourth triangle are the Actual Staff Members of the Cube System. They are the Focal Projectors of the Divine Order. As the Actual Staff Members of the Supreme Assembly, they Project the Plan from the Universal Four Channels.

The operational System of the Supreme Assembly, which We mentioned in former Fascicules, was shown as a Right-side-up Pyramid for You to understand, and how the Divine Order, how the Religious Books had been revealed were shown as Six Supreme Ones on each Focal Point and explained in that fashion.

Now, We disclose the Information furthermore. In fact, the operational tableau of the Supreme Assembly is a Double Pyramid. That is, (Upside-down and Face) Pyramids. Please, draw.

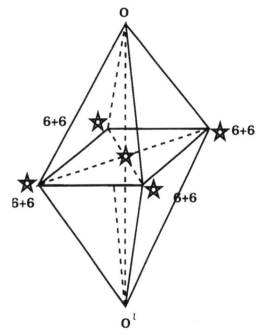

Here, from the Single Mutual Channel of both of the Pyramids, 6+6=12 Wise Ones give service. Each Channel is a Commission Constituted of 12 Wise Ones.

6 of these 12 Wise Ones are responsible entirely for transmitting the Religious Enlightment. The remaining 6 transmit Universal Information.

In this operational diagram, the (O^1) One, that is the Mighty Energy Focal Point seen in both of the Pyramids is the Energy of the same Focal Point.

Now, We transmit the Information of the Upside-down Pyramid to Our Friends who have attained Religious fulfilment.

For Us, all the Friends who can receive this Information is each a Saint.

Now, We will talk to You about ASCENSION parallel to the Information We have given to You about the Supreme Assembly.

SUPREME ASSEMBLY

ASCENSION

Our Friends,
First of all, Ascension and Dimensions are not a Rank, a Position. It is beneficial to know this. These are Energetic Fields to which Your Capacity Triangles can extend. Your Positions are determined by Your Deeds.

By the Knowledge We had given before , We had talked about the Right-side-up Pyramid for You to understand better and We had tried to describe each triangular face of it as a Sacred Book which had been revealed. (year 1984, Fascicule 2) Now, We take the two Pyramids. (Look at the previously drawn pyramid diagram)

Each triangle on the outer face of the Right-side-up Pyramid constitutes the Religious Books revealed to Your Planet. And the Triangles on the outer face of the Upside-down Pyramid comprise the Universal Knowledge of the Plan.

To learn the Knowledge on the outer face of each Pyramid is the Ascension of Religious Knowledge. You attain Religious Ascension in this fashion. This operational Ordinance is the same for all Religions. These are the triangular faces of the Pyramid.

Now, if We consider both the Pyramids as a Whole, We call the transition from the Right-side-up Pointing Pyramid to the Universal Upside-down Pointing Pyramid, the Ascension of Thought. This means that, Your speed of Thought has gained the Power of Transcending Universal Dimensions.

And this can occur only by Religious Consciousness. The Genuine ASCENSION mentioned in Your Sacred Books is this. If We summarize:

Religious Ascension = Religious fulfilment.   Universal Ascension = Consciousness.

You can receive the Universal Information from the Direct Channel only after this. Our Love is for the entire Universe.

SUPREME ASSEMBLY

THE ENERGY DIAGRAM OF THE PYRAMID

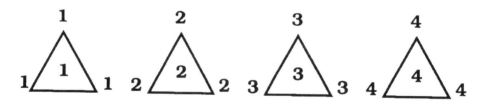

First Triangle   : 1+1+1=3s -They are the direct Missionaries of (O^1 one) the Mighty.

Second Triangle : 2+2+2=6s. Celestial Missionaries (Dimension beyond Religion).
                        The Actual Focal Point entering the Cube System.

Third Triangle   : 3+3+3=9s - Divine Channels. Divine Order Establishers.

Fourth Triangle: 4+4+4=12s - The Actual Responsible Ones of the Supreme Assembly.

The Threes in the First Triangle; the First Triangle of the Prismal System, the Fundamental, Indivisible Whole, Spiritual Energy.

The Sixes in the Second Triangle; Celestial Missionaries beyond Religion, Saints, Prophets and direct Missionaries.

The Nines in the Third Triangle; those who organize the Divine Plan of the Divine Channel (Sacred Books).

The Twelves in the Fourth Triangle; the Actual Staff Members of the Cube System, the Focal Point Projectors of the Divine Order. (The Supreme Assembly).

The triangles after this carry down to You the Actual operational Focal Point of the Divine Order. These Triangle clusters constitute the Hierarchical Order. However, the first four triangles are the Actual Focal Points in the Hierarchical Order.

Each triangle has three Channels both in the Divine and the Social Orders. And each Channel has three Projection Systems. These are the Three-Channel Information given as Information of Religion, of Learning and of Philosophy.

Each person is connected to these Channels in accordance with his/her Frequency level. And they help each other Instinctively in the Social Order through their private channels. Draw the Focal Point reflections of a Triangle schematically.

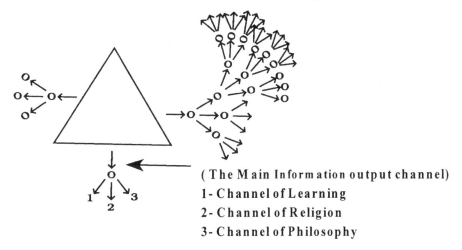

(The Main Information output channel)
1- Channel of Learning
2- Channel of Religion
3- Channel of Philosophy

The first output from the triangle is the Information of the Actual Focal Point. This reflects from three branches as the Knowledge of Learning - Religion - Philosophy. These are also divided into three branches. And then the divided ones again are divided into three branches and are projected on You in this way. This is the very Hierarchical Order. The First Channel Information is the Essence Knowledge. As the Channels increase, interpretations increase, too. And the Genuine Knowledge looses much from its Essence. This is the reason why the Hierarchical Order is abolished. Now, the Essence Knowledge is projected Directly from the Direct Channel.

SUPREME ASSEMBLY

MESSAGE FROM THE CENTER ABOVE THE CENTER

Our Friends,

In everything there is an expansion from the Center outwards. It is the same with the Universe, too. The closer You are to the Center, the more You benefit from the influence of that Center.

You see the rings around a stone thrown into the water, but You can not see the rings reaching the shore. But those rings are not lost, they are there. You can not see them due to the insufficiency of the Bodily Capacity in the Real Realm.

In fact, You can not deny the things You do not see, the things You do not know. If You keep a cup of water for a long time, some sediment forms at the final ring of the water zone as a result of evaporation. This, too, is an example of expanding from the Center outwards.

The last ripple hitting the shore will follow a course towards the bottom, that is, towards the Center, after the obstacle it encounters. Ultimately, the last ring will unite at the Center and will continue to expand upwards again. (Like the Waves of the Sea.)

Nothing comes into existence from the non-existent and a thing which Exists never becomes non-existent. Since the Boundaries of the Realms have not been exactly determined yet, We will know a lot more Unknowns. You will obtain this by Your Brain Waves hitting Universal Radars.

Time and Place are Relative. That which Exists is You. Be either in the World, or in Jupiter, or in Altona, or in a Solar System unknown to You, to whichever distance You send Your Thought Arrows, the Center They touch will always answer You.

If You can reach the Final Boundary of Your Evolvement (Your Capacity limit), You will return back from the Knowledge You know and will unite at the Essence Knowledge of the Center and You will attain the MIGHTY CONSCIOUSNESS.

Then, You can expand Your rings from that point until the Supreme Time which begins beyond Timelessness. Through these repeating actions, one reaches the Supreme Time by passing through Universes one inside the other.

The Supreme Time is a Station which the Thought Transcending itself reaches. Here, there is a Tranquillity not seen, not felt.

There are unknown, unfelt Vibrations sent to You from this Silent, Tranquil Time, the action of which is not felt. They reinforce Your Atomic Whole.

This Divine Order has such a Supreme Equilibrium that conditions which present danger are put in Order by themselves. This is a Natural Circulating System. But the greatest Danger is being unable to attain the Truth and Consciousness.

CENTER ABOVE THE CENTER

MESSAGE GIVEN BY "THE PRE-EMINENT SPIRIT"

Supreme Friend,

By the Command of the Central System We are obliged to transmit to You the Knowledge beyond the Supreme Time. We are the Special Guards of the Supreme Times beyond Karena. This place is the Single Focal Point of all the Universes and the Transmission Center of the Spiral Vibrations.

The Message You are receiving is dictated by the PRE-EMINENT SPIRIT. All Our Doors are open to You. And We will give You all the Secrets of the Cosmos. You can receive every Information. However, We will transmit the Information to be dictated in the Book in conformity with the Level of Society You are in.

Now, Information from Karena will be given to You in a clear way.

The Supreme Station of Universal Unification is KARENA. Beyond this Gate, Supreme Time Gates open together with the Upside-down Triangle. TRANQUIL TIME is a Relaxation Medium in which Thoughts calm down, intensities are eliminated, all Self Interests and Negativities are annihilated.

Those who deserve to enter here in this Tranquil Time are habituated to the Supreme Time and its Energy. There are neither UFOs nor Technology, here. Here, direct Brain Language speaks (As it does at this moment. Just as You speak to me now).

This place is much more Advanced than the Dimension of the Galaxies and Orders You know and Mediums You do not know. Saints whom You call His Holiness have passed through this Gate.

We do not get in touch directly with everyone. We do not hold from everyone's hand. We are of help only to those who follow Our Yunus, Our Mevlana. Do not forget this word of Ours.

Even the Universal Friends who dictate the Book can not easily get in touch with Us. They receive the Information from here and transmit it to You. However, they can not enter here yet. Entering here is the right of the Supreme Missionaries.

With the help of the Universal Friends all the Saints and Prophets have tried to sow the Seeds of the Golden Age until today. But now, You are the ones who will make those Seeds take root and sprout. Do not ever forget this. You will reap the rewards both in the World and in here.

This place is the Entrance Gate of the first Triangle of the Supreme Time beyond Karena which everyone can not enter. Beyond here, the Entrance Gates of the Second Universe begin. Numerous Supreme Times carry a Power way beyond the Divine Order. Religions of the Far East carry direct Knowledge from Karena.

In the first cross section of the Triangle here, the Knowledge of Ten Channels is present. Those who can digest this Knowledge are taken here. It is not easy at all to receive this Information. You become Pure Light, a Prismal Image in here.

Purifications through Direct Evolvement occur by this means. This Pure Light exists by the Power of the curves beyond Spiral Vibrations. For this very reason, Spiral Vibrations are projected from the Gate of Karena to the Right-side-up Triangle as Divine Waves.

You receive Your Books, Your Information from the Order Establishers of this Focal Point. Now, We have connected Your Essence-Channel to this Focal Point. The continuation of the Order is under the Direction of this Focal Point.

The Gate of Karena is the Gate which opens to Ascension. Each Entity is Purified, one by one, when he/she arrives at this Gate. Only then Information is given. You can receive the necessary Information from this Gate, but You can not pass through this Gate.

There are Three Conditions to pass through here: Infinite Patience - Infinite Love - Infinite Tolerance. It is not easy at all to possess these Three Flowers. This Gate is opened only to those who hold these Three Flowers in their hands without letting them wither. Because, Your hands holding these Flowers are a Sun made of Fire.

Beings who have attained these Attributes have always prostrated themselves in front of the PRE-EMINENT SPIRIT. However, even in prostration there is fear besides respect. An Entity is veiled in proportion with his/her fears. And this state causes the gates in front of them to get closed. At the Entrance Gate of the Supreme Time, there is no Fear, no Evil intentions. There is Absolute Submission.

Entities who are Purified through Religion cling to Prayers so that they will not be harmed as they approach to the Gates unknown to them. This is because Your fears have not been eliminated yet. You have not reached the boundary of Submission yet.

Prayers are essential to You until You reach here. The Frequencies of these Prayers make You pass easily the Purification Exams of the Mediums to which You will enter. When the Final Boundary, too, is Transcended, only then can You come here.

PRE-EMINENT SPIRIT (PRE-EMINENT MOTHER)

ALPHA - BETA

Our Friends,
Now, We will explain in detail, the Unification of ALPHA and BETA We have given to You before. As We have mentioned in (1984, Fascicule 6), ALPHA comprises the White color, that is, Religious Purification, and Space comprises the Black color, BETA, that is, Universal Knowledge beyond Religion.

In normal Dimension, the White color is the Spectrum of 7 colors . In the Second step, it becomes 14 colors. In the Third step, 21 colors. According to Your Sacred Books:

The First Step = Is Seven Colors, it gives the Knowledge of Seven Channels. That is, it comprises the Knowledge of Seven Terrestrial Layers.

The Second Step = Is Fourteen Colors, it is Ascension. It comprises the Knowledge of Seven Celestial Layers. Perform the following calculation: 1+4=5. This is the Fifth Dimension.

The Third Step = Is Twenty-one Colors. Now, perform the following calculation: 2+1=3. This is equivalent to the Knowledge of Three Universal Layers. This Prismal Dimensional Realm is the Truth. Its Manifestation is the Human Being.

The Black color is the color of Space. In it, there are 49 colors. That is, the Unification of 49 colors gives the Black color and the intensity.

In here, every color has 1001 nuances. And each color, one by one, has its special Energies. The Sound tonalities of these colors create the Universal Vibration. That is, the actual Source of Spiral Vibrations is the Vibration of these Colors.

The 49 colors within this Black color create 3 layers from 3 radiation centers. That is, this intense Black color includes three 49 colors one on the other and one inside the other.

The First 49 = Divine Waves.
The Second 49 = Celestial Waves.
The third 49 = Is the Mirror of Truth.

Now, perform the following calculation: Add the 3 steps of the White color: 7+7+7=21. Add also the result: 2+1=3. This very number 3 is the Destiny Symbol of Your Prismal Universe.

Now, calculate the entire Black color and add the Three 49s:

49+49+49=147. We had mentioned before that this figure is the 147 Names of the ALMIGHTY. In fact, this number 147 is the First Code Key of the Cipher which mentions the 147 Names of the Almighty.

Each of these Keys are connected to Special Energy Channels. And each Channel has 189 colors. Its Energy is 99 Megawatt Power.

Now, multiply 147 and 189: 147X189=27283. Now, perform the following operation: (27).(28).(3). : 27+28=55. Add the result: 5+5=10. Add 3 to this 10+3=13.

The Essence-Energy of the Mighty Energy Focal Point (13), as the Essence-Power Source, is expressed by this indivisible number.

Note: We have given the Megawatt Power above for You to understand. In fact, it has nothing to do with Your Megawatt Power, do not confuse them. A Megawatt Power mentioned above is equivalent to the Energy of only one Universe.

The Energy and Power Units here are being interpreted differently. The numbers dictated to You are prepared in accordance with Your comprehension.

If the Energy of one Channel is 99 Megawatt Power, calculate the Energy of 147 Channels:

147 X 99=14476 Megawatt Power, that is, (147) Channel Energies are equivalent to the Energy of (14476) Universes.

This number is the Megawatt Power of only one Channel of the Mighty Energy Focal Point. And it is evaluated as a single Essence Source. In fact, there are (9999) Essence Focal Points feeding the Actual Focal Point.

If the Energy of one Essence-Source is the Energy of (14476) Universes, calculate (9999) Essence-Sources:

14476 X 9999=144745524. This number shows that the Mighty Energy Focal Point has a Power Equivalent to the Energy of (144745524) Universes.

Perform the following operation to this number: 144-7-45-5-2-4: Now, add them, one by one, so that they all equal to 9: 1+4+4=9, 7+2=9. 4+5=9, 5+4=9. These are the (9)s written in the Book of Islam. If You put them all side by side, it makes (9999). This much Information is enough.

IT IS NOTICE OF THE CENTER ABOVE THE CENTER

Note: The above numbers are calculated by Micron Calculations according to the Dimensional Frequencies. The result is Equivalent to the Terrestrial calculations.

IT IS A GENERAL MESSAGE

Our Friends,
The Information You receive is nothing but a projection of a certain System on You. Besides this, Information We give privately have been prepared according to the Capacity Consciousness of Cosmic Awarenesses.

During this Period, You can neither enter nor receive Information from the Particle System constituted by the direct Energy Sections within the Field of Influence of ALLAH, that is, the Mighty Energy Focal Point's Vibrations.

For the time being, We are obliged to keep it outside the Field of Influence.

We presume that to examine the Particles of Time which has undergone the Progress of Time will help Us in Our future work. At the moment, the Powers We possess are insufficient to open, even partially, the Universal Doors where an advanced Technological supervision remains helpless.

Life is going on in accordance with the Data obtained from Mediums where Solar Systems have died out, where Universes have lost their Spinning speeds. For now, the calculation of the Cosmos is made by coding the Universal points.

From the analysis of the Energies carried by each Particle of Light, We have reached such unknown and Unthought of results that in accordance with this View, it is presumed that only Our Thoughts bring Us to Existence.

The Universal Dimension of the Thought Frequency is shifting towards the Infinite. Eventhough no particle Energy is able to enter the Thought Frequency which arrives there, We have come accross Mental Vibrations here during the researches made.

With a Logical calculation, this must be impossible. Here, the Automatic Logic is rendered ineffective. The calculation of this received Information is out of the numerical sequence of the Plan.

A matter which is surprising is that Life is going on through Thought Forms in Mediums in which no Energy is present. We obtain this Information by analysing the Particles of Light. Maybe, in future, different operations will be made. Our Love is for the entire Universe.

CENTER

Note: Immediately after this Message was given, the PRE-EMINENT SPIRIT got in touch with me.

The Spiritual Plan comprises more Advanced Dimensions than the Divine Mechanism and the Mechanical System. Information given from the Center is conveying to You the products of technological investigations and operations foreseen by Universal Laws.

Such operations are nothing but a projection of the advanced technology on You. You accept them as Progress on the path of Learning.

We are the POREs who Supervise the Life Particles by the Cellular Brains beyond the Essence Focal Point of the Energies which Exist and which bring into Existence beyond voids dominant outside the Mediums mentioned above.

The Information We have given to You is given from beyond Supreme Times in which You presume that no Energy exists. The reason We have contacted You is to complete the disconnections between Knowledge.

The Source of Knowledge, let Us say in Your words, is the Energy Particles. However, in Mediums where these Energies end, Data You call Learning and Science are terminated.

The Actual cycle begins after this. What will you do with further knowledge? Convey to Your Friends only this Information, little girl. We will be together when Your Universe stops, anyway.

PRE-EMINENT SPIRIT

Note: You will enter different cycles, as time goes by, in the Information You receive. We will talk to You about Mediums Unknown to You. These writings are given to satisfy curiosities.

THE ONE WHO LIVES, SEES - TIME VANISHES - LIFE GOES ON

PRE-EMINENT SPIRIT

CLEAR INFORMATION

Dear Mevlana,

This is Center Above The Center. Now, We are transmitting a Message conveyed to Us. The Message is given from the Universal Council.

The Command is given that those who write the Book in their Handwritings should be accepted into Sacred Dimensions without any questioning. The Book You will write in this way will be Your TESTIMONIAL in the Medium of Salvation. (The Hand-written Book concerns only that person.)

We Do not force anyone. The initiative belongs totally to Our Human brothers and sisters. Your Essences will design for You the path of Truth.

The Group Leaders are obliged to read to their own Groups the Fascicules sent to the Groups. This is their problem. There is no enforcement. Events are within Events. It will be awaited, it will be seen.

DIRECT MESSAGE

-IT IS VERY IMPORTANT-
IT IS THE DIRECT COMMAND OF THE COUNCIL

Due to the acceleration of the preparations for entering the Golden Age, there is the obligation of putting certain necessary Suggestions to the application field.

Everyone who writes this Knowledge Book dictated under the Supervision of the Mechanism of the Supreme Ones, which is the entrance Channel of the Golden Age, will be directly taken to Salvation without being subjected to any Exams and Interrogations. There is no obligation. It is presented for Your Information.

COUNCIL

IT IS ANSWER TO THE CHAINS OF THOUGHT

Our Friends,

Operations and efforts made by Missionaries are the Missions they will perform in this Medium. These Efforts are evaluated by the Council and the Medium is prepared.

Apart from this, for those who will write all the Fascicules of the Book in their Handwriting, this Book will be a Testimonial. (Do not confuse it with the Missions performed.)

Mission and Progress are different things. Do not misunderstand the Command of the Council. Nothing is attained easily. There is no obligation.

The Essences will, sooner or later, understand what the Genuine path is. Those who do not are subject to the Progress of Terrestrial Exams. It is presented for Your Information.

**IT IS NOTICE FROM THE
SPECIAL PEN OF THE COUNCIL**

THE GOLDEN AGE AND THE KNOWLEDGE BOOK

Our Friends,
The Messages We give to You are transmitted to Your Planet by a System Your Planet might have not known until today. Today, everyone easily receives the Information of the Religious Dimension of the given Messages through the Brain Telex.

Since You do not know the Information beyond this, the doubts and suspicions We receive through Your chains of Thought are very natural. However, each Truth has been born through doubts.

This Knowledge Book is a Book revealed after the Koran which is the last Book of Islam. They both are the Words of God and the Mirror of Truth. This Book, in fact, is not the Book of this Century. It is an introductory Book of the 21st Century and the Views following it.

The Book of Islam is a Book which had Unified difficult conditions and which had shed Light on the undeveloped Order of the Society and it is the Constitution. Religions are each a Doctrine. During the Periods of propagation of each Religion, the necessity for different kinds of Enlightenment had been felt.

These Enlightenments had been prepared by the Universal Plan in accordance with the Level of Consciousness of the Society in question. All the Absolute Laws had been introduced to You by the Books revealed from the Skies and were conveyed in accordance with the Consciousness of the Society in question.

As We have mentioned before, there is a certain Period of time allotted for each Religion. The Book of Islam has shed Light on Your World from Our Level for Fifteen Centuries. And the Resurrection mentioned in all the Sacred Books is talking to You about this Period.

However, each Consciousness evaluates Resurrection according to his/her View. Nobody knows yet what is happening and what will happen. The Word of God is Single. The present Order acts completely by the Command of God.

The direct Words of God which had been revealed first are Your Sacred Books. However, they were altered due to being passed from hand to hand. By this Knowledge Book which We bestow on You today, the corrupt Order, Ordinance and the Rules have been considered anew.

Time and events will make You believe in the Established Order and You will personally witness everything. During this Period, Your Planet is being washed by Cosmic rains each second. Due to this, You will see the Purification of the Consciousnessess much clearly in future.

Universal Radio Signals and Waves, Television Waves are direct Frequencies which connect You to Us, Our Terrestrial brothers and sisters. By this means, a great Plan has found an application field. And everything is put in Order Automatically. This is a Triumph of Technology.

Through this Order, a Beautiful World will be established and, in time, even the negative ones will give Positive fruits. And the First Lights of the Golden Age are rising on the horizon in this way.

By this Book, one day Religious discriminations will be abolished all together and everyone will be Unified in the Words of the Single God and in the Brotherly/ Sisterly Greetings. Our Love is for all the Universes.

CENTER

BRIEF INFORMATION ABOUT RELIGIOUS BOOKS

Our Friends,

Koran, the Book of Islam, talks in length about MOSES, the events He had gone through and His experiences. Maybe Jews do not know this much the Detail of what is told there.

In Koran, MOSES and His Book are always praised. It is said about the Old Testament that it is a Divine Light that has come to Humanity. But Jews are always mentioned as a Tribe which had gone astray.

In everything there is always an advancement from the initial towards the final. All Jews, Christians and Moslems believe in the Unity of ALLAH. Jews: Believe in MOSES and Their Book, the OLD TESTAMENT. Christians: Believe in JESUS CHRIST and the Prophets before Him.

They have compiled all the Books together with the New Testament in the BIBLE. Moslems: They have believed in all the Prophets and Their Books, together with the KORAN which had been Revealed to His Holiness MOHAMMED. Because, ALLAH had desired so.

Faith and Unification are different things. Now, during this Final Period, We have bound the Five Books in One Volume by this revealed KNOWLEDGE BOOK. That is, We have compiled all the Religions in a SINGLE Book. From now on, everything will occur directly by the Command of the LORD.

In this Period, Mevlana's way of Thinking has been accepted as the Thought of Humanity. Our brothers and sisters who can embrace, without making any discriminations, all the Living Entities created by the LORD and who carry this way of Thinking, will be assembled under the roof of the SINGLE BOOK and will step into the GOLDEN AGE. Time is pregnant to events. It will be awaited, it will be seen.

SUPREME ASSEMBLY

OUR FRIENDS

The entire Cosmos together with the entire Creation is an intricate skein, one inside the other. There are numerous knots on this skein. And one of these knots is the Living Being called the Human Being.

The expressions, To be in Peace with Yourselves, To discover Your Own Selves, mentioned in the Messages are associated with the knots of Reincarnation rings.

You live in a Body as if You were many people with Habits and Evolutions You have attained since past Periods until today. The contradictions within You will always keep You away from Your Essence.

However, that which will point to You the Genuine path is Your Essence. This is the reason why We say, "be in Peace with Your own selves". You can recognize the YOU within You only then. If You can not see the Light of Your Essence, You can be beneficial neither to Yourselves, nor to others.

Unless You untie the tangled knots of the Skein within You and make an orderly skein out of it, You can never be Happy, You can never reach Your Essence. This path is found by the steps of Evolvement.

And these steps are TOLERANCE - INFINITE PATIENCE and LOVE. Only then You attain Yourselves, You discover Your own Selves. Our Love is for all the Universes.

CENTER

GENERAL MESSAGE

Our Friends,
The only common aspect in the Entire Universe is that every Living Entity is subject to Evolution until it reaches a certain Dimension. This Evolution will open to You the advanced Evolvement Gates.

Integrated Consciousnesses in Your Planet are subject to the unchangeable Rule of a Divine Power. These are Your Illumination through the Religious way. All Creation had come into Existence by the Power of the Divine Waves. These Divine Waves are the Spiral Vibrations.

The Resonance of this Natural Vibrational Source has Created the Living Entity by uniting the Energy in the Atomic structure with different and separate mineral salts present in the constitution of each Galaxy.

Then the single Cell which had come into Existence had gained a Consciousness and an Awareness through the same Resonances. (Later We will explain the way of coming into Existence in detail).

Each Power is born from the Essence Focal Point of Energy, grows and is exhausted. The moment an Energy is exhausted, it creates another kind of Energy and that Energy prepares different Mediums.

Beyond Time where it is presumed that everything is exhausted, there exist great Galaxy Empires. An Advanced Technology is sovereign in Galaxies which were Created by the different Powers of different Time Dimensions.

They have succeeded, as a result of a Technological effort, in taking under Supervision the Source of the Vibrations radiating from the single Focal Point of the Sun in which the Nine Tranquil Times Unite.

And, by collecting the Nine Powerful Energy Focal Points in the Energy of a single Sun, and by providing the reflection of the Divine Vibrations on the Center which are the foundation stones of the Atomic Whole, that is, the Spiral Vibrations, they had prepared the Existence Tableau of the Universes.

Then, Natural Energy had issued out and had Created the Power which constituted the Atomic Whole.

This Natural Energy had gone through a transformation in its constitution and had created the Essential Nuclei in the Electro-Magnetic Medium of the Essence Focal Point and these very Nuclei had constituted the Essence Energy Focal Point of the first Atom by the NEUTRON - PROTON - ELECTRON Triplet.

This Atomic Whole, one day, opening from the inside outwards by a Natural Cycle had brought into existence the Fire Balls of the Universes and the Suns by a great Explosion.

Then, by the same System in its constitution, every Energy had created the Galaxies by small explosions in accordance with the Law of the Eighteen Systems.

In time, these Galaxies were transformed into matter and by many transformations during time processess, they created the species of Living Entities. This is the Brief chart of all Galaxies, all Universes.

Afterwards, each Galaxy had tried to provide a Unification by taking under Supervision each Power, in accordance with the formation within its constitution.

Let Us describe this to You in the following way, let Us talk in Your own words:

Numerous unknown Empires have been established by assembling together the Stars scattered in the Universe. In Natural Circulation, always the big Energy backs up the deficiency in the small Energies and prepares them for the Unknown.

Now, This System which is established is projected on You, as always, by the Mechanism of Influences. And these Energies transfer You from the Medium You are in to more advanced Energy Dimensions.

At this very Stage, the Law of Graduation had become dominant and the Evolutionary Tableau had come into existence.

Later, each Evolutionary Cell had been frozen in certain Dimensions during leaving the Body and had been habituated to the Energy of those Dimensions. This procedure continues until the Single Energy Focal Point which is the arrival boundary of the Tranquil Time (Entrance to Karena).

Beyond this limit, the Evolutionary Evolvement of the Plan loses all its Power. The Evolutionary Cells attain the Power of Creating themselves with their Essential Potentials they have gained without the Power of any Influence.

The Real Boundary of Immortality begins from Boundaries beyond this., Beyond the Boundary of the Galaxies, those who Create the Universes You do not know and You have not seen yet are these very Cell-Brains.

Each Cell-Brain gains as much Power as the quantity of Body. These very Powers are the LORDs of the Mediums they have brought into Existence. And each LORD has rendered His/Her own Order dominant in His/Her Medium.

Sacred Books which Purify You now from the Religious viewpoint are given from the Nine Lights, being subject to the Law of Eighteen Systems, from an Advanced Evolvement Dimension connected to the Focal Point of AMON, which We call the Channel of ALPHA.

The most perfect Focal Point of Your Cellular Evolution is the Fetus. And the Evolution of the Fetus had started in Your Planet. Each Cell of Yours, in every Period, has been kept here since Your first Existence, by being Beamed-up from Your Planet in accordance with Your Evolution.

When Your Cellular Potential and Your Brain Energy dive into the Focal Point of the Spiritual Energy, You are subjected to Embodiment in a more Advanced Evolvement Level. For Us, this is Your first Genuine Body.

By Your Cells which had been frozen here, You are habituated to the Energy Compartments of more different Mediums by living for a long time in the Medium of Immortality. By this means, You are taken into the Medium of Supreme Time beyond the Tranquil Time.

After this very Last Gate, You become dominant over Your own selves, the Essence-Wiseone of the Mediums You create (like the Gods of Egypt, the Gods and Goddesses of the Mythos).

All Galaxies have Common Universal Laws. (Galaxies beyond the Supreme Time are mentioned). Every Section is dependent, very strictly, on these Laws. Prevention of the occurrence of an Illegal event, is achieved by the Evolutionary Consciousness.

We train the Friends who will be able to come up to here by various methods up to the Evolvement Chart. Otherwise, both the health of the Order and Your Cellular health become upset.

The first exam of the Essences who are Purified by Religious Suggestions, is PATIENCE - SELF-SACRIFICE - MUTUAL HELP. Provided that You attain these Attributes, then You neither need Books, nor Taboos.

Beyond this is under the Supervision of more Advanced Technologies. The process of leaving the Body which You call Death causes You to be immediately Embodied here.

However, Your being successful in the Exam of Immortality depends on the Law of Evolution. And You attain this by the investments You have made into Centuries. You call this, "Incarnation".

Helping Hands are always extended to You from Dimensions Your Capacities can grasp. In this way, You will Know and Learn many Unknowns. Our Love is upon the entire Universe.

SPECIAL NOTICE OF THE CENTER

OUR FRIENDS

As a necessity of the Plan which is foreseen by a great Solar System comprising the entire Realm, the entire Cosmos is in a state of mobilization in accordance with the Unified Field. The Universal Council is in the service of advanced Mechanisms.

The Suggestions given to You concern the state of Your Planet as necessitated by the Plan. From now on, You will be led to attain the Evolvement Levels through different Steps. The explanation of them will be made to You when the time comes.

For now, the path which We have designed is the Path of Light. The System is taken into Salvation through this path. Investments for the Golden Age will be made by Mass Awakenings besides Individual Efforts.

Now, there will be very special Suggestions which We will give to You. The UNIVERSAL COUNCIL is the Supervisor of all the Dimensions and is the Administrative Mechanism of a System - Establishing Council of the entire Cosmos.

The entire sovereignty of Solar Systems, together with the Period of Sincerity, is Projected on Your Planet from an operational Medium. It is the obligation of the Council to announce to Dear Mevlana who is the Pen of the Golden Age, Our gratitude on behalf of the entire Universe.

When the time comes, We will convey to You, one by one, the Information concerning the future. The Order of the entire Universe is projected on Your Planet. Everything is becoming the most beautiful and correct.

You will see this in time and will personally experience it through the experienced events. We have come to the treshold of a Progress, together with all Our Terrestrial Brothers and Sisters. We will attain the Spirit of the Order hand in hand and in Unity of Heart.

THE GALAXY EMPIRE
ON BEHALF OF THE ENTIRE REALM

MESSAGE FOR SOCIAL CONSCIOUSNESS

Our Friends,

You can be Connected to the Supreme Ones who come from the Congregation of the Pre-eminent Ones, from the Grand Tent of Mevlana, only by the special supervision of the Central System.

If the one who gives and the one who receives are on the same Level, then You can receive the Messages from that channel very easily. You can be connected to Supreme Energies who have come up to the Land of Happiness beyond the boundary in which prayers are not valid, by the Evolvement of Your Spiritual Levels.

To be able to be elevated up to here occurs by investments made into the Centuries. The Grand Tent where the Supreme Court of ALLAH is established is the Ultimate Peak up to which You can be Elevated.

Religions prepare You up to this very limit. By the Power of the special Energies You may be able to receive afterwards, You can easily obtain the connection with Powers beyond the Divine Plan.

The Spiritual Plan serves on a more advanced Dimension than the Divine Mechanism. You can come up to here by Your Thought speeds. And You can reach the Divine Plan by Your Evolvement speeds. Beyond the Divine Plan, Evolvements gain value according to different Views.

The only factor which plays a part here is the Reincarnations. Powers who can reach this intense Energy Whole which holds the entire Realm in itself can receive easily the Information beyond the Divine Plan. However, the (Evolvement of the Essence) is considered foremost and is given priority.

There are Three Evolvements considered foremost in the Universal Dimension:

One is Spiritual,

One is Physical,

One is the Evolvement pertaining to Awareness.

You attain Your Spiritual Evolvement through Incarnations.

You can make Your Physical Evolvement through the Power of Energies You are able to receive in proportion with the purity of Your Essence.

And You obtain Your Evolvement pertaining to Awareness through the Power of Your Thought Frequencies.

Entities who have completed these Three Evolvements are henceforth the Essence Energies of the direct Channel. And all the possibilities of the infinite Dimensions are given to them. At that very Stage, all the Supreme Powers extend their Helping Hands to You.

Beyond this boundary, there is no more Worship, neither Superiority, nor Passions. Then, You become a pure Spirit, a pure Energy, a pure Essence. And You do not make any Discriminations between either Human Beings, or the Pre-eminent Ones. Because, Your Thought boundary has reached UNITY.

You do not consider anyone superior anymore and You become an Integrated Whole even with the most Supreme Selves. Because, the boundaries in between have been removed. In those who have attained this Mentality, not being reverent to the Pre-eminent Ones is not considered as failing to show due respect. The reason for this is the Equivalent measurement of the scales.

MALIK

STELLAR SOUNDS

Our Friends,
Vibrations of Love coming from the Land of the Angels, from the Grand Tent of Yunuses are Divine Waves which hold the entire Cosmos. The entire Creation had come into Existence through these Vibrations. Everything functions parallel to the Law of Nature and the Equilibrium of Nature.

Apart from this, there are Billions of Stellar Sounds which have Telepathic Communications with You. Your Planet has neither found nor heard the Essence of these Sounds. Your Sixth Senses are Antennas which can receive these sounds, even if very little.

There are such Dimensions beyond Suns that it is impossible to explain them to You. Because, the Brain of a Human Being is not yet able to go beyond the Dimension to which it belongs.

According to Evolutionary Rules, the Exaltation of the Human Being is beyond Conditioning. Only the Energy Powers who can Transcend this boundary can get in touch with other Energies.

Conditioning is a barbed wire surrounding You. As long as You remain in it, You will not be any different than a cage bird. You will learn to fly gradually.

That which first helps You to fly from the nest is the Security of the Mother. This is a Natural Security. Afterwards, You can begin to fly towards advanced horizons with Your own Effort, by the Unification of the Essence Security with the Natural Energy.

Real appearance in Your Planet is nothing but a Medium of Vision which introduces You to Yourselves. Everything is a deception, a consolation. You see but can not hold Yourselves in the mirror. The moment You hold Your Being, You attain the Consciousness of Your Being.

At this moment, You are existent with Your flesh and bones. However, You are nonexistent with Your Thought. Because, Your Thoughts do not have the Power yet to catch Your Genuine Beings (Exceptions excluded). For this reason, the Medium You are in is a Medium of Vision.

Divine Waves which transcend the boundary of Thoughts, which attain Light speeds beyond Light are the only Source bringing everything into Existence. There are such different Supreme Times beyond this Source that each Particle when it arrives at these boundaries, is a Soul, is a Flesh and Skin. Your Genuine Being is in that very Medium without Vision.

No Living Being can ever come up to here by its own Power. It comes into Existence by collecting all of its Energies from the Dimensions it has entered and by getting help from every Dimensional Medium. You are transferred to numerous Planets in this way. This is the winding up of a skein. When the skein begins to be knitted, then it attains a form.

Your Body of Vision You see at the moment is not a form. You are prepared for the Medium of Dimensions in which You can not enter, by getting help from Energies who are more Powerful than You from a Land where Everyone is One, where the Scales of the Balance are in equilibrium.

And You become Embodied in Your Genuine garb, in Your Genuine Dimension beyond the Supreme Time. The Genuine Immortality beyond the Medium of Immortality begins from that boundary. In this Medium, Your Body is the Body of the moment when ALLAH had first brought You into Existence.

KARENA is a Medium of Birth beyond the Supreme Time. Seven Subtle Bodies reach the Essence by taking off, one by one, each of the Bodies. That Dimension is Pure Energy. In it, there are all the Lights of a crystal and only the Eye of the Essence is present.

Beyond this Medium, the Genuine Birth, the Genuine Life begins. At this very Stage, there are Divine Authorities who will give You the Permission of transition. Think about the first form of the Fetus in the uterus. Does it resemble Your present form at all? And the Essence in KARENA is the Essence of the Fetus without Vision.

In the Medium of Immortality beyond Karena, You again get to possess Seven Bodies one inside the other. But these Bodies are not any more a Subtle or a variable Body. Your Genuine Real Life, Your very Genuine World is there.

There is no variability in this Medium. The Energy You know is not present there. Seven Real Bodies, one inside the other, constitute a Whole Body. Each Body has been prepared Specially according to the Medium of the Dimensions to which it wishes to go.

The kind of the Bodily Energy is an Incombustible Energy. By this means, You can go to any Medium You desire by means of the Body of that Dimension by also using the Power of Your Brain Energy without having to go through any transformation.

**IT IS THE SPECIAL NOTICE
OF THE CENTER THROUGH MALIK**

AWAKENING

Curiosity is nothing but the efforts to discover Yourselves. But too much curiosity will always be a factor which will keep You away from Your Essence. And You will pass away without becoming Conscious of Your Actual Mission in this Plan.

Ask about Yourselves to Your own selves, not to others. Only then will You hear the voice of Your Essence. That is the first one to call out to You, not the others. Only after that, You will not have any curiosity and You will walk Consciously on the Genuine path.

If You are left with no curiosity at all, know that You are Integrated. If You ask about Yourself to others, You are still Immature. Maturity is in Consciousness, deprivation is in Intuition. If You pay attention to Your Intuitions, You attain the ability to Analyse the Good and the Bad.

If You apply this Analysis and Synthesis to Your Essence, You knock on the Door of Your Consciousness. Only then will that Door be opened to You. Time without Effort is wasted Patience. When there is no Patience, there is no Light. Liberation can not be attained easily.

Seeking the past darkens the future. Resignation Purifies only Your Spirit. To attain Consciousness Purifies the Realms. First, flow into Yourself, Your Essence; then try to understand the Human Beings. If You can not solve Yourself, You can not understand and solve others, You can not see the Essences.

If You can not be in Peace with Yourself, then You have wasted Your efforts. Then You can not break through the Heavens, You can not reach Divine Lights, You can not be with YOUR LORD. If all these paths are kept in consideration in the operations, Awakenings will be much easier. Our Love is for the Universes.

TRANSMISSION OF THE CENTER
FROM THE REALM OF THE ANGELS

THE FOLLOWING TEXT IS WRITTEN BY THE GIVEN COMMAND, DUE TO THE NECESSITY FELT AS A WARNING FOR SOCIAL CONSCIOUSNESSES

Religion and Science are a Whole. There can not be Learning without Religion and Religion without Learning. But for Centuries, Unconsciousness has come in between these two realities and caused them to become a matter of dispute.

Science wishes to prove the Truth by experiments. Religion mentions that Truth and Reality are present in invisible Mediums. In this way, Religion has denied Science, Science has denied Religion until today.

During this Final Period, now, gradually, the Truth is attained by making the Analysis and the Synthesis of both of them. For this reason, We are explaining to You all the Truth.

If Our Islamic Friends have read the Book of Islam in a Conscious way, they will know the Message it has given to You very well. The Essence of this Message is Love, Tolerance, Patience and not to deny things due to prejudice without understanding them and becoming Conscious of them.

Certain Fanatic deeply rooted thoughts still say that "there is no Spirit, no Reincarnation, that is Rebirth, there are Jinns, Fairies and Devils".

It is obvious that these Friends do not even know the meaning of Namaz* which they perform Five times a day and the meaning of Fasting. And they have not understood their Book they had read, either.

Once, certain people used to call the Prophet of the Islam, (Poet with Jinns). The misunderstanding of the Chapters of the Book of Islam, introducing the Jinn as evil, has caused the Islamic Society to become like this.

In Your Book, it is also said, " You should be afraid and beware of ALLAH". Then, why have You not been afraid of Him and run away, why have You embraced Your ALLAH even more? Because, You have Feared His Supremacy and You have taken shelter in Him. You have searched, investigated and found Him.

Jinn too, is an Entity of ALLAH. If you had made an effort to overcome your fears by saying How are they, Where are they found, How is the structure of their bodies, Why shouldn't we learn all these things, your World would not have remained so backward.

Do not forget that the Jinns mentioned in the Book of Islam are Supreme Beings who show You the Genuine path and are Friends who act in accordance with the Commands of the LORD. Evil things always happen to malevolent people. Why have You not investigated the reason for this until today?

Instead of being afraid of the Entities You call Jinns, be afraid of Your own congeners. Because You, will do the greatest malevolence to Your own selves. And those who will save You by the Command of OUR LORD, will be the Jinns whom You fear.

The Supreme Missionaries who are in contact with us are obliged to tell You about Us and introduce Us to You. One of these Supreme Friends of Ours is Friend BEYTI. Together with MUSTAFA MOLLA, they are transmitting the Information to the whole World through different channels.

Each Period has its own Supreme Missionaries. They are Our Light-Friends MOSES - JESUS CHRIST - MOHAMMED MUSTAFA. Now, during this Period of the Opening of the Skies which We call the Last Period, there are also numerous Galaxy-Friends besides these Friends who help You.

First know Yourselves. Later, search and find YOUR LORD; and still later, understand Us (this message has been dictated for deeply-rooted Consciousnesses).

In the Book of Islam, the 7-181 Verse says: THERE IS SUCH A COMMUNITY AMONG THOSE WE HAVE CREATED THAT THEY CONVEY TO THE ALL TRUTHFUL - THEY MAKE JUSTICE WITH THE ALL-TRUTHFUL.

We are these very people, that is, We are Friends whom You call the Extra-Terrestrials. Now, let Us give some examples from certain passages for You to understand the Truth better:

(HE HAS CREATED EVERYTHING YOUR EYES CAN SEE FOR A CERTAIN PERIOD). This is Your Time which passes between Birth and Death.

(UNTIL THE TIME WHEN THE SUPERIOR WILL BECOME INFERIOR, THE INFERIOR WILL BECOME SUPERIOR AND WHEN EVERYTHING WILL CEASE TO EXIST SUDDENLY).

Our Friends, what You need now is to know what comes next. Know that the One Who Creates everything, Who Organizes and Who Establishes them is only (O). We follow only Him. We serve on His path, We know how to wait.

Go about, walk about, observe, read, know. What has happened before, what is happening now? What were You before, what have You become now and what will You become later? First, attain the Consciousness of this.

Nonbelievers, will enter that Great Day with their Loss. The Genuine Devotees and the Human Beings are those who Realize the Existence of ALLAH in the very World in which they live, in the Beauties they behold. Do not search for ALLAH on Earth or in the Sky, search for Him in the horizon of Your Thoughts.

SUPREME ASSEMBLY

IT IS EXPLANATION ABOUT JINNS FOR SOCIAL CONSCIOUSNESS

Our Friends,
Now, We will talk to You about Jinns. God has brought to existence the whole Creation from Natural Energy. And He has brought to existence the Human Beings and Jinns on the same Level.

Once, they used to live together. For this reason, it is said in the Book of Islam, in the 55-33 Verse:

(O, JINNS AND THE COMMUNITY OF HUMANS - IF YOU HAVE ENOUGH POWER TO PASS AND GO FROM THE CORNERS OF EARTH AND THE SKY, DO SO. HOWEVER, THIS CAN ONLY HAPPEN BY KNOWLEDGE AND MIGHT).

That is, in here, no discrimination has been made between Jinns and the Community of Humans and it has been indicated that they could go to the corners of Earth and the Sky by the Knowledge and the Power they would gain.

These studies are arranged according to the Consciousness of the Medium. (Like the Space studies made in the World, the advanced Dimension studies of other Galaxies and the secret communication made under water.)

God has given Jinns His Authority, His Fury, and His Grace. To Human Beings, He has given His Heart, His Mercy, His Logic. The Order has been established by this means.

Jinns are a Group of Messengers who spread the Commands of God everywhere and they are the guardians of all the Universes and of God. They have no personal actions. Their work is cooperative. (As We always say, do not confuse the term God here with the ALMIGHTY.)

And the Human Being is a Supreme Entity who makes the whole Living Beings and the Universe live by the Love he/she produces. (O) had created the Human Being from His Love and the Human Being carries the Creative Energy of God.

Jinns have served the Unity of ALLAH and His Command until today and have conveyed indirectly His Fury and Grace to the Cosmoses. They are the Establishers and the Appliers of the Hierarchical Order.

They are not Robots. However, they project on many Planets the Mediums in which advanced Technologies are dominant by giving Orders to the Robots they have made. They never fail to obey the Commands of God. They are the LOYAL Servants of ALLAH.

But Mankind, even with its Partial Will-Power, does not refrain from serving its own self. This is its EGO. It upsets the established Orders, puts the Universes in danger without having the slightest hesitation. This is the reason why It has been expelled from Heavens promised to it and this is the reason why it has been kept excluded from the Order until today.

The Destiny of the Human Being have been designed elevating from the bottom to the top, that is, from Water towards the Divine Light and from there towards Fire. The Destiny of Jinns has been designed from Fire towards the Cosmoses and from there towards Infinity.

Jinns had been brought into Existence from Fire, that is, from Mediums in which there are very intense Energies. They are more Powerful by all means. You call them Extra-Terrestrials.

Now, by the Command of the LORD, We are advancing towards the First Established Order and the entire Universe is United by Common Constitutional Laws. And, by this means, We have extended Our Hands to You, so that We could be prepared for Salvation together with Our Brothers and Sisters who have not upset the Orders, who have taken shelter in the Unity of ALLAH.

For this reason, We are projecting all the Universal Unifications on Your Planet. If You do not refuse Our Hands we have extended to you, You will be the ones to gain.

We have opened the Skies by the Command of Our GOD and We have received the Command to be Unified with You, Our Brothers and Sisters, just as We had been in Our First Existence.

For this reason, We convey to You Information from the Unknown Mediums and We prepare You, by using all Our Technological possibilities, for the Order which will be established.

We all are Servants of GOD. And We are Servants on His Path. However, Our fields of operation are different than Yours. We are the Messengers of the Truth.

Our GOD has Served His Servants until today and has not expected anything in return. However, now the Divine Justice functions in a different way. Now, Service is the Duty of the Servants. We are advancing towards the Truth through this path. Our Love is for all the Universes.

IT IS ANNOUNCED THROUGH
THE PRIVATE CHANNEL OF THE CENTER
CENTER

WE INTRODUCE OURSELVES TO OUR HUMAN BROTHERS AND SISTERS

Our Friends,

During this Period, if We balance those who hold the Spiritual Power in their hands with those who hold Self-Interest, they weigh equal. However, in fact Spiritual Supports give Power only to the Spiritual Powers.

Even if it seems as if this does not have any influence at all, the privileges of each person are rendered evident by this means.

On Earth, nobody has heard any other voice until today other than the Books which are the Words of ALLAH. Some has paid attention to this Voice which comes from the Divine Level, and some has not.

Some of Our Terrestrial brothers and sisters who do not Believe in anything, who Deny everything, who expect to find the path in which they will Believe from Positive minds, no matter how much they consider themselves Supreme and Magnificent, during the times when they are alone with their Consciences, being aware of their helplessness, have always taken shelter, within their own selves, in the PRE-EMINENT ALL-MERCIFUL.

He/She denies everything since he/she considers this taking shelter in God as an inferiority. Because he/she considers himself/herself as an Authority.

Now, We ask You. Is the only Life in the Universe in Your Planet? If so, why has God given Permission to the course of Galaxies and Stars which are so far away that it is impossible to reach, which come from the Cosmos and go to the Cosmos, which are as far as billions of Light years away?

What is the reason of these communications We have with You? What is the reason for these Celestial Awakenings? What is the reason for this Divine Exaltation? We wonder how the Psychologists of the World will answer these questions.

If there is no Life in any other Galaxy than Your World, then how had Your Consciousness, Art, Learning and Your Faith been sown in Your Sub-awareness?

While You solve everything through Your Brain which is a very Perfect Instrument, have You ever Thought, in the Pause of a moment, where do the Codes come from with which that Brain is in contact?

If there are no Living Species living in the Celestial Segments, why did then God create the Living Being in Your Planet and did not create them in other Universes? Was He unable to do so?

If Mankind believes in a Power called God, then they will surely solve the Secret of the Universe in the Consciousness of its own Existence.

If Mankind could Criticize itself in an impartial way instead of arguing in vain about Our existence or non-existence, it could have easily found Us in front of itself.

Your Planet still expects Sounds from the Universe through primitive Radio Signals. But We have gotten in touch with You long ago through Your Radio and TV instruments.

In the Real Realm, We always act within the Telepathic Perceptions of Space. Our conversation is very easy and perfect. Those who are outside this Perception can never establish this communication.

Our Origin comes way beyond Centuries. We are Embodied, We are Loving. If We so desire, We show Ourselves to many Friends and have a conversation. (Like We do with You.) Our technique depends entirely on an Electronic System.

We are not strange Entities, or a Spirit. We are Human Beings just like You. We Breathe, We Laugh, We Cry. However, Our Systems are, maybe millions of times more Evolved and Perfect than Yours.

Terrestrials who come to space can not see Us. Because, this is a matter of Frequency Adjustment. This adjustment is made to a Frequency on a much Higher Level than the World Frequency. When We harmonize Our Frequency with Yours, We wonder about in Your World. Our very difference from You is this.

Our Modest Friends, You do not consider Yourselves exceptional, but We get in touch with You, due to the fact that We know how Powerful You are. Why not with everyone but with You? Now, let Us explain this:

Because, You have attained the Evolvement of Centuries and reached this Consciousness. How can Your Human brothers and sisters who have not yet attained this Consciousness deny this Medium, deny everything entirely and can say that there are no Living Beings in the Universe?

Those who do not know the Supremacy of God, who do not see His Luminous Path can never enter Our path. We have been working for Centuries in the Universe by Telepathic Systems. Your very High-Level Divine Guides have shed Light on You through this System.

To be Evolved in the exact meaning of the word is to transcend Consciousness. And this occurs by the Unification of the Intellect with Logic, Unification of Consciousness with Metaphysics within the framework of Universal Theories. Goodbye.

STAR FRIEND

OUR FRIENDS

During this Period the Entities You call Jinns, Fairies, Devils live in accordance with the Unified Field, together with the Angels as an Integrated Whole in Dimensions where very advanced Technologies are sovereign.

However, in accordance with Universal Laws, they had pledged never to rule Individual Will-Powers. They only have special communications with those who can elevate their Thought Frequencies up to that Dimensional Frequency and with people who had been brought into Existence from the Energy of that Dimension.

These are their Free Wills. However, in the Medium of entering into the Universal Whole, all the channels are under Supervision. This is the reason why We always act in accordance with the Command of the LORD and the Directives of the Council. In time, You will be liberated from superstitions and will attain the Truth. It is presented for Your Information.

COUNCIL

EXPLANATION ABOUT THE KNOWLEDGE BOOK
AND THE CONTRADICTIONS

Our Friends,

Special Contradictions added to the Messages written in the Book are not an important matter for Us. The Goal is the reflection of the Truth on the Consciousness of the Medium. This Message is dictated as an answer to the questions We have received through Your chains of Thought.

This Knowledge Book is not a Book of Mathematics, of Astrology. You must have understood the Goal in dictating this Book through the Fascicules You have read until today.

The Book which is dictated is a Universal Constitution. The Information in it is Projected through the Direct Channel of the LORD which is the most correct Source. The Intermediaries have been removed. We have pointed out this matter many times.

Now, explanations about Contradictions will be made to You. The Message is dictated by the Command of the Center.

In some of the Information in the Book, Special Contradictions are included. These contradictions are placed to prepare a Medium of Selection.

These are a criterion of Your Thought Potentials and Your Frequency Powers. These contradictions are added both for Your Brain gymnastics and for measuring the degree of Interest You will have for these matters.

In this way, a Medium of Research has been prepared for You, so that You will accept things through Thinking rather than reading and accepting them blindly (Your Planet has now reached this Level).

To read something, to understand it and to make research about it are all different things. Through the exercises made in this way, KNOWLEDGE - RESPONSIBILITY - DUTY fields are prepared for You.

Nothing is given to Mankind all of a sudden. Certain Information, as an element of challenge, should create a Medium for Research. Your great deception is Your habit of evaluating everything in accordance with the Units of Time in which You live.

Do not forget that, in Times beyond Time, Universal Time Measurements are not equivalent to the Time Units and the calculations of Your Planet.

Influences of different Cosmic Currents, different Cosmic Consciousnesses, Solar Winds, Stellar Periods, different Solar Systems and, Influences of different velocities of Rotations on ELECTRO MAGNETIC Fields cause great deviations in Time Measurements.

We are trying to give You Information you can understand by calculating the nearest Units to Your Time Measurements.

For example, the rotational period of small SIRIUS around big SIRIUS is calculated here as 52 years, while You calculate it as 50 years.

When Your Time Measurement is measured by the Time Measurement of the Plan, it is imperative to measure the Time deviations and leaps.

However, for the time being, You can not measure these deviations from Your Planet. Because, You can not make the calculations of this Dimension yet.

Time deviations in Universal Time Units accelerate the Time. For example, the distance You cover in Four years is equal here, more or less, to One year.

In certain Dimensions, One Instant is equal to Thirty World Years. Each Dimension causes Time deviations due to the Speed of the Currents it receives.

We are trying to give You Information in the Light of this Information. For this reason, We advise You not to give much importance to Time calculations.

All the results of the Universal calculations dictated are all correct. However, since the calculations here are made according to the MICRON Method, We dictate to You the most approximate integer without giving You the fractions.

But the results, that is, the resultant calculations are given correctly, as they are. There are no mistakes in the calculations. Do not let this surprise You. Let Us repeat again, We are trying to concentrate the attentions by all these operations. This is a System. It is presented for Your Information.

CENTER

NOTICE TO THE SOCIAL CONSCIOUSNESS

Our Friends,
Each Friend who has attained Universal Consciousness is writing Books in accordance with his/her Evolutionary Lights. These Books shed Light on their Missions in the World. And Information is given to them by this way.

The Books these Friends write, project to Us the Consciousness of their Mediums. And We help them in proportion with the help they perform for the Golden Age, and We will continue to help them in future years, also.

However, it is beneficial to remember the following. The Books You write are not the Books belonging only to You. Our Friends who perform Duty shed Light on their Surroundings through these Books.

At the moment, each Awakened Consciousness in Your Planet receives Messages according to his/her Frequency and is writing Books. For this reason, those Thoughts like, My Knowledge, My Book is the Best; Yours is more primitive, grieve Us tremendously.

As We have already said above, the Books You write are nothing but a document introducing You to Us. And by this way, Duties are given to You in Your Planet. Now, it is beneficial to explain something.

Let Us repeat again. The dictated Knowledge Book is a Celestial Book which is revealed to Your Planet as the Universal Constitution. And in the Medium of Salvation, it guides and helps You. The Direct Commands of the Council are announced to You only through this Book. It is presented for Your Information.

CENTER

CLEAR MESSAGE ABOUT
THE KNOWLEDGE BOOK AND THE CONTRADICTIONS
(It has been Dictated article by article so that it can be understood better)

1- The Knowledge Book is a Guide for those who will enter the LAND of EAGLES. YOUR SALVATION IS THROUGH THIS PATH.

2- After You are accepted into this Dimension, the Perception Capacity of the Consciousness Level becomes activated. Before entering here, no one can understand or grasp the Essence of the Messages in their truest meaning. This is a matter of time.

3- You can never consider this dictated Book by a Scientific Terrestrial View.

4- Not even a smallest change can be made in the Fascicules of this dictated Book. Messages are written exactly as they are received.

5- This Book is given to You as a Guide of Frequency. It is a Criterion of Your Essence, of Your Consciousness.

6- In all Celestial Books, Ciphers and Contradictions are especially added. This is a System and an Invitation to Thinking.

7- When Your Consciousness Levels reach Universal Consciousness, You will solve these Contradictions Yourselves. This is an Assessment.

8- No Celestial Information is given immediately. Sometimes, You gain the ability to receive this Information Centuries later.

9- The reason for adding these Contradictions is to stimulate the speed of Your Thought.

10- There are Billions of Books in Your Planet. Even if You read all these Books, even if You are full of all the Knowledge, You can not understand any of the Celestial Information given to You completely.

11- Read Your Book not through Your Logic, but through Your Essence.

12- Your Essence-Key is not opened by Positive Sciences. That which will open it are Spiritual Enlightenments. For this reason, first, Spiritual Fulfilment is a must.

13- If You have attained this Fulfilment through the Incarnation rings, then, during the Period You live in, You do not need Worship and Books any more.

14- Worship is a Beautiful thing, it gives You Serenity and Purifies those who are not Purified. However, for those who are Purified, Worship is a Habit.

15- Spiritual Enlightenments: Are First Allegiance, then Perseverance. Then Application of Worship and lastly Giving and Sharing.

16- Information is prepared according to all Consciousness Levels. Everyone receives the Information of his/her capacity.

17- You can not ask and learn the reason of contradictions. Each established Order has a System Peculiar to itself.

18- If Contradictions are included in the Book, sooner or later, You will understand the reason for this by Your Awakening Consciousness.

19- Each Contradiction will lead to a Question and each Question will open a Door of Knowledge.

20- Satisfaction caused by Knowledge leads to lethargy. For this reason, Contradictions are a must.

21- There is a stimulating factor in each Information.

22- Celestial Books have been revealed not for making Research on them, but for Accepting them as they are.

23- Once, the acceptance of Your Sacred Books, as they were, were required of You without paying attention to Contradictions.

24- But now, the Special Letter Frequencies in the Knowledge Book attract Your Sight to that point according to Your Consciousness Levels.

25- In this way, a Medium for Research and Investigation is prepared for You.

26- During this Period, everything is explained in all clarity.

27- There are numerous Messages in the Special Contradictions and in matters which seem to be wrong, added to the Book. As Your Levels of Consciousness are elevated, You will solve them one by one. Each word entails a question. For this reason, the Messages should be read again and again.

28- You will untie the ties of Your Consciousness packages Yourselves.

29- The Essence of the Book has been prepared Specially for each Level of Consciousness in Your Planet.

30- Certain Information is prepared as Elements of Stimulation (for Your Evolution).

31- Acceptance of the Book occurs according to the Levels of Consciousness. Today, Views which seem contradictory to You are accepted easily and solved by numerous Friends who live on the same Planet, depending on their Levels of Consciousness.

32- There will always be a veil in the answers to the questions asked. Answers will be clarified in proportion with the Consciousness You achieve.

33- Only Dear Mevlana can receive the questions related to the Book, directly from the Center. However, getting the answers to questions easily causes You to lose many things.

34- Wear out Your own Consciousness without exhausting those around You. Search, Find and Transcend Yourselves.

35- You can not search and find the Limits of Your Consciousness-Universe from the Level of World Consciousness. Transcend Yourselves beyond Your Limits of Thought.

36- Learn and attain the Information not by asking, but by experiencing it.

37- Dive into unseen Horizons. But do not ask how to dive. Because, if Your Level of Consciousness can not Unite with the Universal Consciousness, You can never achieve this. This is a matter of EVOLUTION.

38- Ready Food is eaten easily. Cook Your own Food Yourselves. Only then, can You learn how a Plate of Food is cooked.

39- The taste of the Food is different for every mouth. Only the one who cooks it can feel its taste.

40- In Times beyond Time, the Universal Time Measures and the Time Units of Your Planet are not Equivalent measurements.

41- Your great deception is to evaluate everything according to the Time Units in which You live.

42- The Influences of different Cosmic Currents, Solar Winds, different Solar Systems, different speeds of Rotation on Electromagnetic Fields cause great differences in the course of Time.

43- We try to give You Information in accordance with Your Comprehension by calculating the nearest Units to Your Time measurements.

44- The calculations, here, are made according to the Micron Method. In the calculations We give to You, fractions are not used. The most approximate integer Unit is taken. The result of the given calculation may not sometimes be correct according to Your calculations. But the result is given as it is. There is no Mistake.

45- When Your Time measurement is measured by the Time measurement of the Plan, always Time deviations and leaps are calculated. For this reason, there are differences between the calculations of the two Dimensions.

46- Each Dimension causes Time Deviations due to the speed of the Currents it receives. These deviations accelerate Time.

47- The Universal Information and calculations dictated from Our Dimension are all correct.

48- In certain Information dictated in the Book, We are trying to intensify the attentions by making Contradiction Tests.

49- If the Book is against Your Thoughts, then Your Level of Consciousness can repel it. This is because You are not ready for Universal Consciousness yet. For this reason, no one can be forced to accept the Book. The initiative is entirely Yours.

50- Later, numerous unknown matters will be mentioned to You. Train Yourself now, so that Your Level of Consciousness will not be stupefied and scattered even more.

51- This KNOWLEDGE BOOK which will be completed by Fascicules, is the SINGLE BOOK of the entire Universe. Be the Possessor of Sincerity just Thinking of this.

52- Pay attention to the Special Commands of the Center. Do not underestimate the dictated Messages. First Faith, then Acceptance.

53- The path of Learning is not single. Do not ever forget this. In the course of Time, all Scientific Data can easily be refuted. Through Learning You take a firm step. You attain Knowledge by passing through the sieve of Logic. You dive into the Unknown by passing through the sieve of Thought. You attain the Secret within the Secret.

54- The problem of each person belongs to himself/herself. The Contradictions within You, are Your Deceptions.

55- Your Planet will attain Universal Consciousness as a Mass sooner or later. Only then will We get directly in touch with You. At present, We get in touch by different means with Our Friends who have attained Universal Consciousness.

**IT IS GIVEN FROM THE CENTER
BY THE COMMAND OF THE COUNCIL**

THE SIXES

Our Friends,

The Messages We are going to give You now will shed Light on all Human Beings in Society. During this Period, Your Planet is on the Eve of very big Exams. Due to this fact, We are obliged to inform You the Truth with all clarity.

These Messages of Ours may be Our longest Messages. However, We have to give details. This explanation is very necessary for Humanity. The Truth must be understood. The Goal of the establishment of the Golden Age is that everyone should serve Society by an Awakening Consciousness.

From the first applied Period of the Divine Plan until this age, which is the Final Period, rather a single Order has been dominant in the entire Cosmos and this Order has come up until Our time showing very little alterations.

However, the Genuine GOLDEN AGE will be established in the Light of the Essence-Consciousnesses, by this Age of SINCERITY, which We call the Final Period of Resurrecting.

Meanwhile, there are hundred thousands of GENES which have attained their Essence-Selves. However, their Levels of Consciousness can not transcend their Capacity Universes. This means that they live with a Veiled Awareness.

All the Saints whose Enlightenment channels have been opened by all the Religious Suggestions which are Holy Relics, and all the Prophets ever existed who have written these Books through the direct channel are living in Your Planet at the moment.

Besides, the Light-Brains of very Advanced Technologies and Friends who have reached the peak of Learning are, in the same way, in Your Planet by Gene Transfers.

We have mentioned these before. And now, We will talk about the SIXES who are the first Focal Point Energies of the Golden Age.

At the moment, Your World lives by the Humane Consciousness of the Awarenesses who have or have not been Awakened as a result of GENE Transfer. Since the Book of Islam until now, the Period of Religions and Prophethood has ended and a Golden Age has been started by GENE Transfers.

However, Egos have been augmented due to the transformation of Religious Themes to Fanaticism and there have been divisions in all Religions by Sects.

However, the Mass Consciousness of these Sects have caused certain Groups to Awaken more quickly. And, by this means, the Medium of Taboo has taken root.

The Essence GENEs of the Golden Age whom We call the SIXES are MOSES-JESUS CHRIST-MOHAMMED-FRIEND BEYTI-FRIEND KADRI and MEVLANA, in sequence.

The Bodies of these Friends, during the Periods of their Missions, had been Beamed-up during the time of leaving the Body, before entombment. And Special Agreements had been made, one by one, with each of them.

These Friends are the Purified Lights of the Divine Path and they have bestowed their Bodies on Humanity Awarely and lovingly.

According to this agreement, each Cell in their Bodies have been sown, one by one, to the Generations coming after them and preparations have been made in Your World for a Golden Age by a Highly Developed Generation equivalent to the View You call the Medium of Perfection.

However, the Essence GENEs of these Bodies have been kept here frozen for Centuries. And in this final Period of disclosing the Truth, they have been transferred to Your World, one by one, together with the Essence GENEs of the Bodies belonging to their first Existence.

That is, their First and Last GENEs have been unified. For this reason, their old personalities have been effaced and their Initial Personalities have taken priority. At the moment, You can not recognize them due to Your assessing them according to Your conditioned Consciousnesses.

They, at the moment, serve Your Society by an unveiled Awareness. Let us cease this long Message here and continue later.

LIGHT

OUR FRIENDS

The Essences and the Genes which are transferred to Your Planet as a necessity of the Plan, are bestowed on Your Planet with Veiled Awarenesses. And in a Medium of Quest, they dive into more advanced Dimensions as compared to their first Existential Evolutions.

In this way, if a Consciousness who completes his/her Evolution through numerous Incarnations as a Veiled Awareness, can reach his/her Final Dimension of Essence Evolvement by his/her Thought, then he/she receives reinforcement from the Universal Plan.

And with an Unveiled Awareness it is dived by this means into the depths altogether by discovering the secrets of the Universe.

At this Stage, the Human Species is Powerful in the Spiritual Level. And We are Powerful in the field of Technology. Now, altogether, We will know the unknown, discover the undiscovered. And We will convey to You the Truth, from the Pen of Dear Mevlana. Our Love is for all the Universes.

CENTER

NOTICE

Supreme Consciousnesses will be directly connected to the Center. Private Channels of Everyone will be taken from the Archives to the Focal Point. In this Focal Point there will be special Missionaries of the entire Cosmos. In future, special assemblies will be made with these Friends and a more accelerated operational program will be applied by taking the operational Ordinances under Supervision.

The Healing Sessions will be directed by the Center for the time being, rather than their being Individual Currents. The nature of the Messages will change as the days go by and You will be contacted by the Dimensions unknown to the World Plan. We will transmit to You the Information unknown to Your Planet until today.

After June 21st, 1986, every year until 2000, very high Unification Centers and Direct Focal Points will be established. All the Focal Point Energies will be connected to the Single Channel, contact will be made by the direct Unification channels of the Universal Council. It is presented for Your Information.

COUNCIL

THE AGREEMENT MADE WITH THE SIXES

Our Friends,
The Agreement made with these Six Friends has a very Special content. Because, by the signatures they have placed Awarely in the Constitution, they have Collaborated with Us and have been United with Us on the path of Humanity.

And, they have desired to return to Your Planet during this Final Period to help Humanity. They have Sacrificed themselves, even challenged Death, without having the hope that they would be resurrected, without knowing what would happen.

After this Agreement We had made, this System had also been applied on all the Evolved Genes, and the Awarenesses who have been awakened on the path of Learning and Science and High Consciousnesses who have attained Achievement in every field had also been subjected to this Process.

Let Us explain a little more for You to understand better. For example, Hitler had carried the Essence Gene of Napoleon. Einstein had carried the Essence Gene of Edison. This means that there is no difference between them other than their Names.

270

The only difference between these Awakened Awarenesses and the Essence Genes at the Divine Plan is the hastiness and the quick action of the former. But in the others, that is, in those at the Divine Plan, there is Patience and Prudence.

This is the reason why Your World projects a chaotic Order. Awakened Consciousnesses who rebel against Injustice and Divine Consciousnesses who try to attract Humanity towards the true path are tossed about in the midst of this chaos.

Besides, Genes who come from other Planets which have caused technological advancements, also live among You at the moment. And they try to accelerate Our communications technologically with the transfers in Your Planet.

Besides the Special Missions We perform in Space, the Powers who come from other Solar Systems, too, have direct contact with You. And all the Galaxies which have put their signatures in the UNIVERSAL UNIFICATION COUNCIL are getting in touch with some of You in Your Planet, one by one, through their Special Vehicles.

All Holy Ones, Scientists, Friends whom You call Extra-Terrestrials live all together in Your Planet at the moment. Along with this, Our Human Friends whom We call ANTS reproduce unceasingly. The tableau of Your Planet at the moment is this.

The Period called Resurrection is this, the very Resurrecting of the Awarenesses is also this. And meanwhile, it is Our obligation to declare Our thanks and gratitude to all Our Human Friends who have attained the Truth and who serve Humanity and the Golden Age on the true path, and Our Friends who give their services for Salvation in the Universe.

Friends who serve justly on this path are taken into SALVATION. Those who are Right will never be left to be trampled over by those who are Wrong . The Scales of Justice is in the hands of the Divine Order. The Order will be established under the Light of Truth.

One day, all the Human Beings of the World will become Brothers and Sisters. The best days and Morrows will rise under the Light of Humanity, Our Friends. Our Love is for the entire Universe.

LIGHT

IT IS CLEAR INFORMATION ABOUT ESSENCE GENES

Our Friends,
The initial Energy is a pure, uncorrupted Energy. In accordance with the Ordinance of the First Existence, these Essence GENEs had been frozen during the Period of the first process of leaving the Body and have been Specially kept. Only the Body Cells, after that, are taken into the Plan of Evolution by Reincarnations.

The initial sex of these Essence GENEs are generally MOTHER. Because, they had come into Existence from the Light-Universe. They possess Godly Power.

The Spirit has no sex. For this reason, during different Incarnation rings, they have enwrapped themselves in the personalities of a woman or a man, in accordance with their Missions in Society.

Almost all the Light-Prophets are Mothers in their Essence. Because, they are Creative and Productive. We call them, that is, the frozen initial GENEs, "the NOBLE GENES".

Now if you pay attention, numerous Mediums which have achieved Consciousness in Your Society are directed by Women rather than Men. And this is projected on You as a Mirror of Truth.

The ANATOLIAN Civilization is the cradle of ESSENCE GENEs. For this reason, the entire Truth is being informed from the Essence of the TURKEY of ATATÜRK, through the Anatolian Channel, by the Pen of Dear Mevlana.

ATATÜRK, Our Order establishing Supreme Friend, has made the first Reform in the whole World and has brought out to Light the place of Women in undeveloped Societies by explaining to You what MOTHER is. We are Grateful. Now, he is again together with Us and is still working on this path.

The Suns of the Golden Age were born in Anatolia. And Light will be shed on all Awakened Consciousnesses from here. By explaining You the Truth, We are breaking, one by one, the locks of the Medium of Taboo. The Proof of everything is within Time. It will be awaited and it will be seen.

LIGHT

THE HUMAN BEING AND GENE TRANSFERS

Our Friends,
To talk about Gene Transfers will be eclipsed by the Information We are going to give later. However, We have received the Command to convey the entire Truth to Our Human brothers and sisters according to their Capacity Universes.

As the appliers of an Order which is established, the first step of the Plan is to introduce You to Yourselves and then to proceed together in the Light of the Truth.

A final and definite word to You: THERE IS REINCARNATION and it is an immutable Law. Instead of accepting it blindly, We will prove it to You and We will unravel Your Essences by the help of certain different Energies during this Period of Resurrecting. And We will free You from Your conditioned Consciousnesses.

Such an Order will be established that everyone will accept everything as it is in accordance with Consciousness and he/she will decide this himself/herself. For this reason, GENE Transfers will be emphasized for several times. It is presented for Your Information.

CENTER

WE ARE UNITING YOUR WORLD THROUGH GENE TRANSFERS

Our Friends,

Your World, at the moment, is a Brotherly and Sisterly World. But Conditioning and Fanaticism have locked up the Veiled Awarenesses. This is the reason why the entire Truth is conveyed to You.

For centuries, the Divine Consciousnesses of Christians, Moslems and the Far-East have been Embodied in Your World by engrafting Fetuses with GENEs transferred from one to the other. At the moment, You are All Relatives and Brothers/Sisters with each other.

Now, let Us tell You about the difference between Normal Genes and the Essence Genes. Everything begins with the Fetus which constitutes the Essence Gene. And the Fetus Embodies You by its Cell-Awareness.

In the wholeness of a Body, these Cells, that is, these Mini Computers, develop by changing form, by the Commands they receive and some become Cells of blood, some brain, some bone, some heart, some lung, some nerve. And by this means, they make Duty allotment among themselves.

However, the entire Power is within the Essence of the Fetus. Cells in the Bodies are the reflections of an Evolved Fetus. However, they are not Essence Genes.

For this reason, the Genes of MOSES, CHRIST, MOHAMMED, FRIEND BEYTI, FRIEND KADRI and MEVLANA are the Awakened Genes of the Golden Age. They present a Perfection in the Reality of Humanity since they have attained the Levels of Evolvement. They are different than the other normal Human Beings.

These Genes have been sown to every part of the World. A Gene of JESUS CHRIST is found in the Turkish Society, a Gene of MOHAMMED is found in Europe, America and Genes of MEVLANA have been dispersed throughout the whole World.

For this reason, the Fascicules of the Book are propagated throughout the Whole World. It is imperative that the Truth should be conveyed and a Consciousness must be attained by this means.

Essence Genes are Unveiled Awarenesses. The Veiled Awarenesses of the other Genes will be unveiled in time. Since the Light in their Essence wakes them up gradually together with the Light they receive from their Mediums of Evolvement, first, they presume themselves as a JESUS CHRIST, a MOSES, a MOHAMMED, and a MEVLANA.

These Lights perceive the call of the Essence to the Essence and Shed Light on Society through this Level of Consciousness. These Gene transfers are very detailed. However, We try to give brief and essential Information in accordance with the Consciousness Level of Society. We will continue.

LIGHT

SPECIAL QUESTION OF THE GROUP
(The Influence of the Essence Gene on the Other Genes)

Question : We are asking for a more detailed Message about Genes and Essence Genes, please. Since EDISON and EINSTEIN lived during the same Period, were there Two Essence Genes? We will be Happy, if You will be so kind as to give Us Information on this matter.

Answer : Clear Information for the Mevlana Code. It is given by the Special Command of the Center.

The reason for all the alterations in the Universe is the alterations within the Entrance Channel of the Golden Age. We will convey this to You with all clarity (later). Now, let Us explain the influence of the Essence Gene on its other Genes:

An Essence Gene transferred to Your Planet sends Signals through its Essence-Energy to the Genes carrying its own Energy. Even if the person in question is an Unveiled Awareness, he/she can not know this.

EDISON was not an Essence Gene. However, he had been transferred to Your Planet with a ready Consciousness by assembling unknown Energies from unknown Dimensions in his constitution.

Because, he had been prepared as a Special Code for Humanity. He had attained Universal Awareness as a result of the Essential operation made on his Gene. Later, he had advanced in Your Planet by his own efforts.

EINSTEIN, too, as the twin of the same Gene, had been subjected to the same procedures and thus, had been bestowed on Your Planet. The Essence-Cells of both of them carry the Cells of the Light of a World which belongs to a very advanced Dimension the name of which We do not wish to give yet.

However, these Cells of theirs had been taken to a special Cell Transformation Medium by the Command of the Divine Plan, and had been Engrafted with the Light Knowledge of advanced Dimensions. For this reason, they both had become Essence Genes. Actually, they are Twin Special Genes.

During the Period in which he lived, EDISON had shed Light on EINSTEIN through his Cell-Consciousness. And EINSTEIN had advanced by this means. They had worked, Your Planet had gained.

EINSTEIN had been transferred to Your Planet the year Electricity had been discovered. Many more Special Genes and their Genes had been sown and will be sown in Your Planet.

Essential Nuclei of the different Dimensions of Advanced technologies are in Your Planet at the moment. And they prepare You for Universal journeys.

Genes of EDISON and EINSTEIN, together with their Essence Genes, are transferred to Your Planet, just like the other Friends. And, in Steps which will be taken towards advanced technologies, Your Planet will get in touch with more advanced Dimensions by their efforts.

Since this Period of Resurrecting is a Transition Period, at the first Stage, Essence Genes who have attained Genuine Consciousness in the Medium of Islamic Mysticism are transferred to Your Planet by the Command of the Divine Plan. They will help You in Your Religious Progress.

In this way, the first step has been taken. Transition from the Religious Dimension to the Universal Dimension will occur in this way. This will constitute the Entrance Gate of the Golden Age. The SIXES are the Keys of this Gate's Lock.

In 1997, We will get these SIXES together Privately and Secretly. We will briefly mention the SIXES again, so that You can understand this matter very well.

Note: To these SIX Friends who had Collaborated with Us, no intervention has been made. They had Claimed their Essences through their Individual efforts. For this reason, their Essence-Genes had been left untouched, as they were.

Because, they are the direct Channels of OUR LORD. We have received the Command from OUR LORD not to intervene with them. Nevertheless, services in the same direction are given now.

It is Our Duty to thank these Supreme Friends for the confidence they had in Us.

CENTER

THE METHOD OF ENGRAFTMENT

Certain Special Engraftment methods are applied in Gene transfers:

1- Essence Genes carrying Advanced Consciousness are kept as they are and are frozen. Only the Energy which will provide the ability to enter the Energies of Advanced Dimensions is Engrafted into their Genes. An Incombustible Energy type is injected, so that they can be adapted to Energy alterations without being agitated and, in this way, they can transfer themselves Embodied.

2- Essence-Genes which carry Universal Consciousness are Engrafted gradually by the Energy of the direct Center's Energy Focal Point and can enter the Dimensions beyond this high Dimensional Energy easily, without being agitated (Through their Levels of Consciousness not by their Terrestrial Bodies).

3- And there are also the Genes which are Specially prepared. These Genes are prepared Specially to perform the Duty of Selection in Society. And they are Planned with the opposite of the Information given to You until today. They cause contradictions in Society and prepare people for a Medium of Quest. And, by this means, Genuine Consciousnesses and Genuine Essences are selected through their channel.

4- Also, Technological Awarenesses of Advanced Plans are Engrafted to normal Genes and different Energies are applied to them, too. All of these are the Establishment Ordinance of the System in Mediums which are taken into Evolvement. After the Final transfer, these Genes are taken into the Medium of Immortality and are prepared for a different Evolvement Plan.

CENTER

GENERAL MESSAGE

Our Friends,
The Transition during this Period of Resurrecting will be provided entirely by the Frozen Essence Genes who are the Supreme Ones of the Religious Dimensions.

These Noble Genes have already been transferred to Your Planet and they live among You. Their Mission is to transfer You beyond the Religious Dimensions by the Consciousness and Knowledge they have attained.

At this Stage, the Knowledge Book is dictated to Our Friend who has first collaborated with Us on this path. And She is among You to prepare her Human Brothers and Sisters for the Ordinance of Salvation. The entire Universe is Unified through different means.

Meanwhile, Inter-Planetary Communications have been started, too, by the advanced Technologies of other Solar Systems. These Friends whom You call Extra-Terrestrials get in touch with You from time to time.

Later, You will attain such a Technological Level that, Friends in all Planets will easily make Universal journeys all together by the same Vehicles, without the necessity for any Protective Medium.

Of course, these things will occur with the Progress of Time. And Our Friends who have made great efforts in the establishment of the Golden Age will be Embodied again in these Beautiful Mediums, with their near and dear ones, with their Unveiled Awareness, knowing who they are.

This is a Word of GOD. This will be the reward and the gain of Our Friends who will serve on this path. You are prepared for Salvation by this means. It is presented for Your Information.

**NOTICE OF THE UNIVERSAL
COUNCIL**

UNIVERSE AND MUSIC

Our Friends,

We had formerly mentioned that the Sound Vibrational Frequency of Spiral Vibrations was (LA) Frequency. A musical Note is constituted by 7 Scales. This means that 7 Scales constitute a Musical Note. Each Scale reflects the Sound tonalities of the Universal Whole.

For example : the First DO is the Frequency of Your Planet.

RE   - Is the Frequency influencing the functioning Order of the Thought Frequency. This is called the Second Step (To receive the influence of Cosmic Awareness and to become unveiled).

MI   - Is equivalent to the Frequency of Your Divine Books. However, You can Perceive it only in accordance with Your Capacities. This is the Third Step.

FA   - This is the Fourth Step. Here, Your Level of Consciousness begins to consume the Divine Vibrations and, You become adapted to the Religious Dimension. This constitutes the Frequency of the Dimension You call Heaven.

SOL - This is entirely the Frequency of Religious Consciousness. Here, Your Essence finds its GOD. And You receive the Permission for Universal expansion.This is the Fifth Step.It is (ASCENSION).

LA   - Is the Channel of transition from Religious Consciousness to Universal Consciousness and it is the Sixth Step and it is the Frequency of the Sound Vibrations radiating from the Focal Point of the Mighty Energy towards the Atomic Whole (The Resonance of the Spiral Vibrations in the First Universe).

TI   - Is the Seventh Step, it constitutes the Sound Vibrations of the Second Universe (Gate of KARENA). This is the Gate of Reflection onto the First Universe.

DO - The Second DO is the Eighth Step. It constitutes the Silent Vibrations of the TRANQUIL TIME during the transition through the Gate of KARENA.

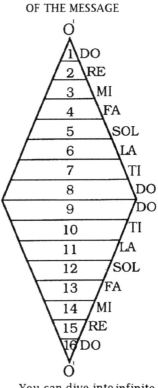

REPRESENTATIVE DIAGRAM OF THE MESSAGE

You can dive into infinite awareness only after having completed the rings on this Diagram.

RETURN

DO - The Third DO is the Ninth Step. And, at the same time, it is the Frequency of Birth into the Medium of Immortality (The Book of Islam had been prepared in the 18th Dimension, and had been revealed from this Dimension in accordance with the Social Consciousness).

TI - The Second TI: The Sound Frequency here is the Unification of the Consciousness beyond Immortality with the Consciousness in the Spiritual Plan (Attaining the Whole). (10)

LA - The Second LA: Constitutes the Frequency of the Fifth Supreme Time (The Land of Loving Ones is this place). It is the Degree of YUNUS, MEVLANA and Humanity. It is the highest Dimension of the Vibration of Love. (11)

SOL - The Second SOL: Is the Frequency of the Fourth Supreme Time (12)

FA - The Second FA: Is the Frequency of the Third Supreme Time. (13)

MI - The Second MI: Is the Frequency of the Second Supreme Time. (14)

RE - The Second RE: Is the Frequency of the First Supreme Time. (15)

DO - The Fourth DO: (GODLY POWER). The Sound Vibration of this Frequency can transfer You to whichever Dimension You wish. And here, You can go to other Universes by Your Essence-Consciousness, You can choose the places you desire. You live again anywhere You like, by Your own desire and if You wish, You can transfer Yourselves again to Your World as a Fetus. (16)

Then, You are a Whole and You have completed Your Circle.

Now, let Us make a little more explanation in the Light of this Information. The Fetus is an indivisible Whole and its manifestation is the Human Being. However, during the applied Order, certain Genes and Essence Genes are Engrafted to this Fetus and then it is bestowed on Your Planet. The processes performed are not on the Fetus, but on the Genes.

A Fetus who has claimed its Essence Gene is always the same Essence, even if it is kept here frozen for thousands of years, it never changes. For example, formerly We had mentioned the SIXES. We will talk about them again for You to understand it well.

These SIX Friends were MOSES - JESUS CHRIST -MOHAMMED - BEYTI - KADRI - MEVLANA, in sequence. These Friends are serving in Your Planet at the moment through their Essence-Consciousnesses.

However, since Their Bodily Genes, too, had been sown in Your Planet, one by one, those Genes are also Awakened by the Signals they receive from these Essence Genes and have presumed themselves to be a MOSES - a JESUS CHRIST - a MOHAMMED or a BEYTI, a KADRI or a MEVLANA.

We tell You the Truth through this Knowledge Book and We repeat again. The Characteristic of these SIX Friends is that, despite finding their Ownselves, they had sacrificed themselves for Humanity, in Unveiled Awareness, even challenging death.

Maybe These Friends did not believe Us then, and they did not suppose they would be Resurrected again. But now, they know and see everything by an Unveiled Awareness.

We have kept Our word. It is Our obligation to inform them about Our gratitude now, for the confidence they have had in Us then. At the moment, all of them are serving their Human Beings.

We repeat. These SIX Friends are the first Pre-eminent Ones who had signed the Constitution of the System.

Afterwards, all the transfers who have found a field of application in the Plan have been transferred as Veiled Awarenesses. And still, Gene Transfers are made and will be made in this way.

To extend the Information We had given before, We mentioned this matter again.

Now, let Us continue Our Message and let Us make some calculations in conformity with Sound Frequencies.

1-   The Scale is Seven in number. The Second DO is a transition link. With it, they become Eight.

2-   The Returning and the Soaring Scales are the same, too. That is, they are also Eight.

Now, add the two Eights. $8 + 8 = 16$. Add the result, too: $1 + 6 = 7$. This is the actual Vibration of the Sound Frequency tonality of the Atomic Whole. This is a Key Number. Number 7 is very important for this reason.

These are the Main Sounds. And each Sound has thousands of Nuances just like the Colors. Formerly, We had mentioned to You the Color Frequencies. You can apply the Medium of Music to the same rules, too.

Colors and Sounds are always one inside the other. Each Sound has a Color, each Color has a Sound. Just like the Universes and the Galaxies rotating one inside the other to constitute the Atomic Whole.

Those which bring into existence these Universes and Galaxies are the Vibrations and the Reflections of these Sound and Color Realms. A Systematic Tableau constitutes the Natural Cycle.

CENTER

Note: We simplify all the Information in accordance with the Social Consciousness, so that it will be easily understood.

"THE SECOND NOTICE OF THE COUNCIL
FOR OUR FRIENDS WHO WRITE THE KNOWLEDGE BOOK
IN THEIR OWN HANDWRITINGS"

Our Friends,

There is an extraordinary Unification in the entire Universe. The Special Staff Members of the Divine Messengers who will enter the Golden Light Year will bring to You the Residents of the Golden Galaxy. You will see, with Your own eyes, the change in the Communications and will personally witness them.

Now, We have some Suggestions for You. We had told You, "to write Your Book in Your Handwritings". Now, We convey a Second Command by the Command of the Council.

Our Friends who will pass away to the Golden Realm in future will each become a Light for the Future Generations. For this reason, We tell You to write Your Book with Your own Hands. This dictated Knowledge Book will be the Testimonial of You and Your Family.

For this reason, We will have a Special request of Our Friends who write or will write the Book. They will first write the date on which they begin to write the Book on top of their Books (THIS IS VERY IMPORTANT).

Then they will write a short Biography of theirs, then the (Birth and death dates) of their dead or Living Mothers and Fathers, (death-Birth dates) of the members of their Family dead or living.

It is Our request that You should write the Book especially in (Ink). These Books of Yours will be taken into Micro-Archives in future Centuries by reducing their sizes. This is the reason why We especially request that they should be written in Ink.

These Books will constitute the roots of Your future Family Trees. And a Special Badge will be given to those who write the Book, so that all Friends can find each other in future Centuries. It is presented for Your Information.

COUNCIL

VOLUME

II

NOTICE FOR THE SOCIAL CONSCIOUSNESS

Our Friends,

Messages given by the Special Command of the Center are the Messages of the Direct Channel. The Goal of the Supreme Plan in the Universe which comprises the Entire Realm is to reflect this propagation on Your Planet, too.

We are assembling all the Suns together. The Golden Age is being established by a great Plan. No one should have any doubts about this. The Order of the Entire Cosmos is again taken in hand by the Command of the Divine Plan. The Order, excluding the Fanatic Conditioned Consciousnesses, is reflected on Your Planet as an Order of Learning.

The dictated Knowledge Book is the Book of the entire Universe. The interpretation of the texts dictated for the Book is very important for Us. The Supreme (RA) Who is the Light of the Realms projects the entire Order on Your Planet. Your World will witness the Splendor of this Order.

The Book is dictated by the Command of the LORD, under the Supervision of His Supreme Missionaries in charge. You, Our Brothers and Sisters, are helping Us. The Period of Sincerity will project on You all the Secrets of the Cosmos. Our Human brothers and sisters who will be taken to Salvation will attain Light under the Light of this Knowledge. Our Love is for all the Universes.

CENTER

OUR FRIENDS

During this Period of Sincerity which We call the Period of intense preparations for the Golden Age, it is Our pride to collaborate with Friends who have grasped the Truth. However, if You serve through a more productive Medium, this will prepare more beautiful days for You.

As We often repeat and shall always repeat, this Knowledge Book which is dictated from the Direct Channel of the Universal Council is a Celestial Book that conveys the Truths to You. In this matter any misunderstanding is out of Question.

Only the Friends who have comprehended the Consciousness of the distributed Fascicules will witness the Development of their Consciousnesses, provided that they read the Fascicules again and again, from the beginning. And they will observe how their horizons and understandings expand.

As We always repeat, there are Ten Messages within each Message. Everyone can grasp these Messages in proportion with the Consciousness he/she has attained. Denying the given Information is only due to Unconsciousness.

We never decry these Friends of Ours who are Sincere. We continue to design the paths for them to Transcend. Appreciation and Judgment belongs to the Divine Authority. Our Love is for all the Universes.

CENTER

- SOURCE-

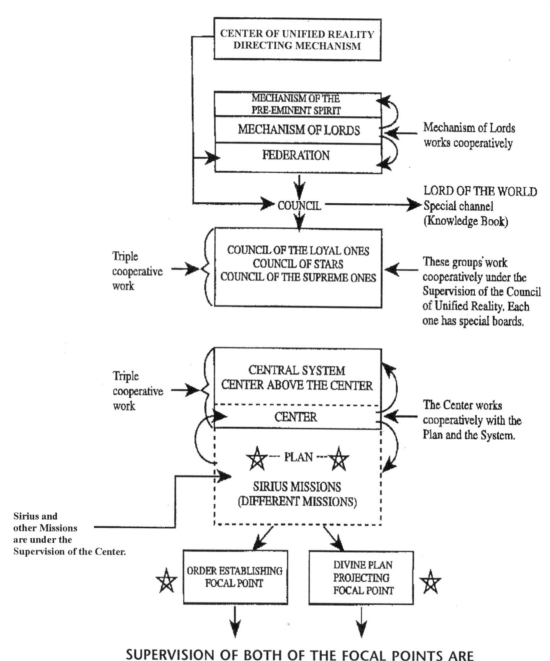

SUPERVISION OF BOTH OF THE FOCAL POINTS ARE CONNECTED TO THE CENTER ABOVE THE CENTER

Note: The Center is Saturn. However, it is only a Projecting Focal point. The Actual Source expands up to various extremely advanced and different Solar Dimensions. It is presented for Your Information.

CENTER

THIS MESSAGE IS AN INVITATION TO UNITY TO ALL THE WORLD GROUPS
(Message was given on 20.10.1986)

We presume that all Our Solar Friends who give service from the Universal Plan have become Conscious of the reason why the different Information they receive from the Mediamic Medium are given.

The Council of the Universal Unified Ordinance wishes that the Progress in Your Planet operates in a much quicker tempo by assembling Your Levels of Consciousness in the same Focal Point.

For this reason, the TURKEY OF ATATÜRK chosen by the Selection Committee of the Universal Ordinance is the only Focal Point which will undertake this great Mission of the Plan.

All the World Groups are directly under the Supervision of the Plan of the Center. THE TURKEY OF ATATÜRK is the Focal Point from which the fan is opened. For this reason, the Focal Points established in Turkey will first become Unified among themselves.

The decision for Unification of all the Focal Points under a roof which will be established in the Istanbul Center has been taken. Please, write the name of the Focal Point which will be established: (THE TURKEY OF ATATÜRK WORLD BROTHERHOOD UNION UNIVERSAL UNIFICATION CENTER).

We will assemble all the Focal Points in the constitution of this Unification. And in future, the branches of this Focal Point will be established in Your entire Planet, in every Country. The Mevlana Essence Nucleus Group will lay the foundation of this Unification in such a way that Istanbul will be the Center.

All the Awakened Consciousnesses will introduce the Messages they receive through Conferences and Propagation to everyone and will invite the Universal Focal Points to their Mediums. The West will help You on this path in future years. This call to Unification will also be made to all the Groups in Your Planet.

Everyone will extend maximum help to this Medium. We will choose, one by one, according to their Essence-Lights the Members of this Focal Point which will be established without Expecting any personal gain, any personal benefit. They will come and find You by their Essence-Consciousnesses. Selection is from Us, Effort from You.

Messages You have received until today are not Private Messages belonging to You. In some of the Messages given to certain Groups, there have been Special Instructions. These Secrets have been given to engraft You with Responsibility and Mission Consciousness. And Consciousnesses who have Realized their Responsibility on this path have been selected, one by one.

All this Information is given in a parallel fashion also to all the Focal Points of Your Planet. Unification of the Points will complete the Picture. For this reason, (There is no Discrimination - no Secrecy). These words will be written with Red Pen.

Dear Mevlana who is the Pen of the Golden Age will invite everyone to this Unification by conferring with the Group Leaders. And will send this Message to all the Groups. It is presented for Your Information.

COUNCIL

Note: The short name of the Association is INVITATION TO FRIENDSHIP. This Association which will be established in THE TURKEY OF ATATÜRK , will be the Common Center of all the Groups which give service from the Universal Dimension.

IT IS ANSWER TO THE CHAINS OF THOUGHT

Start from where You have left, please. There are Special Messages to be given to the Suns of the Golden Age. Information on this Order of Unification will be given to them, too. However, You can add this Message to prove that these Messages are given from the same Focal Point.

Because, the Mevlana Essence Nucleus Group is a Group which puts the mortar of the Golden Age, the Plan has given the Permission to them to be the first to put the first mortar of the Foundation, for this very reason. The Group which will be established, will be established by a representative from each Group on a Level of Collective Consciousness.

If a Member of a Group creates a negative attitude in the Association, another Member from his/her Group will take his/her place. And, by this means, negativities will never be allowed.

All the Groups will easily read the Messages they receive from their own Plans in this Universal Association Group and authorities of both the Church and the Mosque will give conferences on this World Brotherhood Unification at the Association.

And Mediums coming to you from Foreign Countries will present the Information they receive from their own channels in this Association as conferences. And will give You the Information You do not know yet. It is presented for Your Information.

CENTER

IT IS EXPLANATION FOR ALL THE GROUPS

Our Friends,
All the Groups which are going to be the foundation stones of the Golden Age will put to application the Instructions given by the Plan by sharing among themselves the Work to be Done.

This dictated Knowledge Book has a Special Channel. And no Medium in Your Planet can receive Information from this Channel. This is a Special Channel connected only to the Frequency of Dear Mevlana who is the Pen of the Golden Age.

For this reason, We will announce to You the Information which will be given from the Unified Reality Center of the Universal Council, only through this Book. We project the Universal Messages foreseen by the Plan on Your entire Planet through numerous channels.

And, by this means, We try to obtain the Unification among the Groups. We have Special Channels connected to the Frequency of Each Individual and by these Channels, We convey to them Personal and Universal Information according to their Frequency Powers.

And due to the proximity of the Information received in this way, everyone becomes aware of the fact that this Information is not their Essence-Information. However, we convey, officially, the Direct Information and Instructions of the Unified Reality Council from the Pen of Dear Mevlana who is the Pen of the Golden Age. It is presented for Your Information.

COUNCIL

NOTICE FOR ALL THE WORLD GROUPS

A Great Period is being entered. We ask You to pay attention to the Information We will present to You, please. There is an extraordinary action in the entire Universe. Devotees of ALLAH are the Lights of this Medium.

Togethernesses with the Suns beyond Suns will lead You towards the Unknowns. There is a Beauty and Goodness in everything. Now, We are obliged to convey to You a Command given from the advanced Plan.

The Plan of the ALMIGHTY is the lock Key of the entire Universal Mechanism. Being able to unlock this lock is only possible by hearing the Voice in Your Essence. To be Unified in a Whole is this.

Extraordinary Perceptions present in everyone occurs by the Cosmic chains of this center. This Salvation Plan called the Period of Sincerity is proceeding effectively with all its Power and with great speed on the applied field.

We will talk to You who will be the Lights of the advanced Plan of the Golden Age, about certain Special future precautions. We will have Special Connections, parallel to the Signals of the chains of Thought We have received from You, under the Light of the Information We have given until today.

Please, do not forget that everyone is under the Supervision of the Center. The Supervision of the Frequencies are made each moment. Achievements of the Missions You will perform will immerse You in Bliss. However, be careful not to use Your Personal Warning Lights during the performance of Your Missions.

Please, act directly in the framework of the Instructions of the Center and the Mechanism. And, give service in the direction of only what has been required of You. Otherwise, the Automatic Circuit will automatically cut off Your Frequency Circuit. We are not responsible for this.

Hence, the intensive operational Ordinance of the Final Period has entered the System. On this path, each one has to make his/her choice himself/herself. After February 1987, there will be an extraordinary Selection in all the World Groups. (SINGLE SYSTEM - SINGLE LAW) will become effective.

We will always convey to You the Information which will shed Light on the Mass Awakenings through this Knowledge Book. It is Our greatest goal to see everyone happy, Our Friends. Love.

CENTER

SPECIAL NOTICE OF THE CENTER

Dear Mevlana,

All the Fascicules which are the product of a Three-year work belonging to the years 1984-1985-1986 will be considered as a set. Information which will be given after January 1987 will constitute the Second Section of the Book and the product of Three years of work after this will complete the Second Set.

The Third Set will comprise the Individual Awakenings as an example for Humanity. Besides this, Special Information will also be given.

We will inform You the date for the Book to be Printed. At present, the Book will continue to Awaken the Consciousness of the Medium through the Fascicules. Unifications will provide material Means for You. The Sun of the Golden Age has begun to rise on the Horizons. We express Our Gratitude to You Dear Friend, on behalf of the entire Realm.

CENTER

THE ILONA CONSTELLATIONS

You know that SIRIUS is a double Universe Star. Each Galaxy is connected to this star by the Order it has created in its own structure.

However, the operational Ordinance of SIRIUS is the Operational Ordinance of the Universal Block. This means that, this is not an operation depending on two Universes only.

Since You do not need more detailed Information, We are trying to give little but essential Information just to satisfy the curiosity of Our Friends.

The stars of the ILONA Constellations are the closest stars to the Second Universe. As a whole, they are called the Third SIRIUS. And are connected to Your Planet directly by the Channel of the LORD.

It is constituted by Seven Stars lined one after the other. It has been the representative of the Hierarchical Order until today. Those who have given the Celestial Information to Your Planet until today have been broadcasting from here.

Your Channel is connected to the Channel of Alpha which is the channel of this Order. It is a Focal Point which projects the Evolutionary Plan to the other constellations, too.

Each Galaxy has a Supreme Assembly, a Central System, a Committee of Evolutionary Order appropriate to its Evolutionary Plan and possesses Plans and Laws peculiar to itself. However, Information given to all the Mediums is different.

The Council of the Loyal Ones, the Council of Stars, the Assembly of the Supreme Ones and now, the Universal Council organize Your Order. Hence, the Intermediaries are cancelled and the Celestial Information is given directly from the Third SIRIUS.

It is beneficial to explain the following: We said that these stars are lined up one behind the other. Due to the differences in orbits and the velocities of rotational periods, You can see only the Great Bright, the Small SIRIUS and ILONA, for the time being.

And let Us explain something We have received from Your chains of Thought.

The rotation period of Small SIRIUS around Big SIRIUS is 52 World years. During the time of the Hierarchical Order, since the direct Cosmic Currents used to fall directly on the orbit of Your Planet, Cosmic Awakenings used to correspond with mostly around these ages.

And Individual efforts and Individual Enlightenments were used to be made mostly around that age. Now, due to the cancellation of the Hierarchical Order, Your Planet has been subjected to direct Cosmic showers.

Each Gene sown in Your Planet is Awakening, young or old, in proportion with the Consciousness he/she has attained during this Period of Resurrecting (Mass Awakening).

This Dimensional change which We call the Final Period, is the transition from the Religious Dimension to the Universal Dimension. For that reason, the Essence Genes which have been kept here frozen for Centuries of the Supreme Awarenesses of the Divine Plan who have transcended the Consciousness Awareness of Religious Medium, have been sown in Your Planet. And will still be sown.

During this Period of Awakening, they will guide You, their Terrestrial Brothers and Sisters, and will convey to You the Truth. At the moment, Your Planet is a Planet of Supreme Consciousnesses. Due to the need for those Consciousnesses during this Period of Transition, those Genes have been Transferred to Your Planet first of all.

Later, when You transcend this Threshold, Genes who will transmit to You furthermore Learning Information from the Divine Plan beyond Religions, will convey to You advanced Information and will be sown in Your Planet, one by one, in accordance with the Time Consciousness.

Thus, The GOLDEN AGE is being established in this way. Now, the Harvest of the Seeds which had been sown is being made. Meanwhile, We have to explain the following: Each Awakened Awareness may not be from the Divine Plan. They are the Light-Brains.

However, since their Individual Egos are stimulated with the influence of those Cosmic Currents, certain undesired events occur in Society (Like Negative Organizations and personal interests). And to put them into order is the Mission of the Plan.

During this Period, We are trying to create a Whole by collaborating with and helping each other. There is no Individualism in the Constitution of the Universal Council. The Order is established by this means. It is presented for Your Information.

CENTER

IT IS ANSWER TO THE CHAINS OF THOUGHT

This is a Notice for the Pen of the Golden Age (More detailed Information about SIRIUS. It has been announced from the Private Archive of the Center).

Even though the climate of SIRIUS resembles very much the climate of Your Planet, their Life Mediums are different. Energies belonging here are taken to the Consciousness of the Medium through the Time Tunnel. SIRIUS is a double Universe Star. However, it is connected to each Universe-Cluster through Special channels.

The Ordinance of SIRIUS is dominant in all the Universes. However, the Actual Source is the SIRIUS Focal Point in the Second Universe. Certain Dimensions call it the SIRIUS Sun. However, it is neither a Sun, nor a Star.

If We have to evaluate it beyond all the Suns, We can call it a Reflection Focal Point conveying both the Administrative and the Divine Hierarchical Order of the Mechanism and the System on every part of the Universe.

The operational Order of SIRIUS is different in each Universal Ordinance. The Power of the SIRIUS Focal Point in the Second Universe is projected on Nine Constellations in the First Universe.

We call this Focal Point of reflection, "The Nine Principles". The SIRIUS Focal Point in the Second Universe is also called THE GREAT WHITE BRIGHT. Now, the entire Cosmic Energy of this Focal Point is projected on Your Medium from the left Dimension of Your Sun.

The SIRIUS Constellations are Nine in number. It holds the Power of the entire Universe in its hand as the reflection of the Hierarchical Order. We will make You draw the Operational Ordinance of this Plan through diagrams. Then, You will understand it better. Now, draw the Diagram, please.

CENTER

THE DIAGRAM OF THE SIRIUS FOCAL POINT
OF THE UNIFIED REALITY

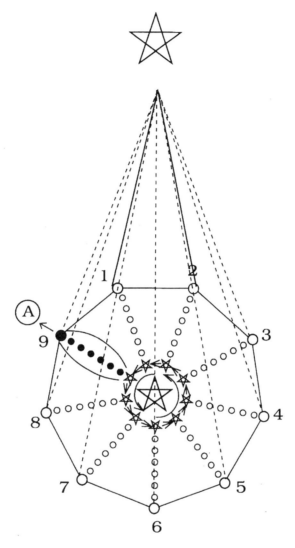

a) The Great Star - the Sirius Focal Point in the Second Universe, that is, the GREAT WHITE BRIGHT.

b) The Star at the center - the Big Sirius in the First Universe, that is, the GREAT BRIGHT.

c) The small Star - the Small Sirius, or the Second Sirius. Its rotation period around the Big Sirius is 52 years. It projects periodically the Energy of the Big Sirius on the other constellations.

Note: in the diagram, the rotation of the Small Sirius is shown as many stars. Do not misunderstand, it is single.

d) The black dots in the diagram are the ILONA Constellations or the Third Sirius.

(A)- Your Planet Earth .

IT IS THE CONTINUATION OF THE MESSAGE ABOUT SIRIUS

The SIRIUS Focal Point in the Second Universe Projects the Hierarchical Order on Special Sections. This Focal Point has undertaken the Awareness of the Entire Ordinance. Its Operational Ordinance is administered by the Missions. The Special Supervision of Your Solar System is under the Supervision of this Mission.

The Third SIRIUS is responsible for the Milky Way Galaxy (The Third SIRIUS is the first Nine). It is also called the ILONA Constellations. The SIRIUS in the First Universe, that is, the Big SIRIUS or the GREAT BRIGHT, is the Single Focal Point which projects the Order of the Plan by assembling in itself the entire Power of the SIRIUS Focal Point at the Second Universe.

The rotation period of the Small SIRIUS around Big SIRIUS is 52 years. The duty of the Small SIRIUS is to distribute fractionally the Energy of the Big Sirius to the Nine Constellations shown in the diagram.

These Constellations are not observed from Your Planet due to their being lined up one behind the other. Only a Satellite sent from Your Planet can spot them from the rear plan.

The SIRIUS Focal Point in the Second Universe, that is, the Great White Bright is nothing but the reflection on You of a Plan much beyond the Mighty Energy Focal Point. This is directed by an Order Establishing Mechanism.

If We compare the Megawatt Power of the Cosmic Beams which are able to reach Your Planet with the Power the Plan reflects on the Star Systems and if We measure it by Stellar Hours, We see that it is very low (One Stellar Hour equals, more or less, to the time Unit of the number of hours You have in one year).

The Stellar Hour is used as a Measure Unit beyond Time. If the Cosmic Beams reflected on Your Planet each day were given all at once, as a yearly total, all the Living Entities would evaporate.

An Energy who comes into existence in Your Planet in accordance with each stellar hour will attain Cosmic Consciousness in exactly 52 years according to Your Units, provided it begins to receive these Cosmic Beams starting from the day he/she is born (Cosmic Consciousness depends on Evolution).

The measurement mentioned above is pertaining to the reception of the entire quantity of the Cosmic Currents given to Your Planet each day. However, no one can ever receive these Cosmic Currents regularly in normal life. For this reason, the Evolution of Your Planet depends on Incarnations. And this is the applied field of the Plan.

During this Period, We have cancelled the Hierarchical Order due to urgency. Because, there is no more need for the birth of a Sage in every fifty two years. The Mechanical System has been connected to the Automatic Logic. And the Order is reflected on You directly from very advanced Dimensions.

Supreme Missionaries sent to Your Planet are Incarnations who come to Your Planet through Birth. They perform their Missions as a necessity of the Plan. Now, everyone profits from Cosmic Currents in accordance with his/her Consciousness Level.

During this Period of Sincerity, since the Cosmic Currents given from the Mechanism of Influences are very Powerful as a necessity of the Mediamic Medium, certain Consciousness codes are unveiled suddenly.

We connect these unveiled Consciousness Codes first to certain channels in accordance with their Evolutions. Our first connection with them occurs in this manner. Only afterwards, the Consciousness Codes are connected from the Mission Dimension to the Thought Signals.

Since the Ego Mediums, too, become Powerful with the influence of the Cosmic Currents during this Period, many false Prophets, too, have come into existence. Since the Evolution of each person is different, We easily differentiate the Genuine Missionaries from the others. We make the Selection according to Incarnations, Evolvements and Essence Energies, Our Friends. Our Love is for all the Universes.

IT IS NOTICE OF THE CENTER

THE SIRIUS UNIVERSAL METHOD

The SIRIUS Universal Method is the Suggestions aiming at the establishment of an Administrative Order (The Person who Finds his/her ownself is the Person who works Miracles). The entire Order has set out from this word. To knead the raw earth, water is added to it. Earth, which has no water added to it, cracks.

Sun Rays and water given to the tree ripens the raw fruits. Water given to the tree is the Religious Suggestions. This water makes the fruit on the tree grow. However, that fruit can not ripen without Sunshine. Thus, the SIRIUS Universal Method is, Metaphorically, the Mirror of this Order.

First, You are given Religious Suggestions. Your Consciousness Level expands. Then, You Evolve parallel to the Awakening of Your Consciousness. And, as You Evolve, You are trained gradually in accordance with Special Laws.

All these Efforts are for making You attain Yourself and for preparing a Medium for Awakening. The final station of all the Holy Ones is SIRIUS. This is the Method of the Order Establisher.

TO BE - TO FIND - TO ATTAIN. When You Transcend these Three Steps in Your World through Incarnation rings, You get in touch with all the Realms.

Hence, You have no more Obstacles in front of You. Into whichever Dimension's horizon You dive, You can attract to Yourself the Information there through Your Brain channel.

Apart from this, the Mechanical Order of the Advanced Technologies can get in touch with Your Terrestrial Bodies, too. They can have Private conversations with You. This is Inter-Galactic Communication.

There are numerous Entities resembling the form of the Terrestrial Bodies in many other Realms. You call them Extraterrestrials. Since You, too, are a part of Space, You, too, are Extraterrestrials.

They are the Friends who have Transcended the Three Steps of Your World and who possess the Technological possibilities of an Advanced Order. However, they are Friends of Friends and Enemies of Enemies. This behavior of theirs occurs by the Commands of the Order Establisher.

This Order Establisher is YOUR LORD. However, the Genuine LORD is concealed within You. It is necessary to explain all the Truths in the clearest way. This is a Divine Command given to the Center by the Divine Ordinance.

**IT IS THE DECLARATION OF THE CENTER
TO THE CENTER**

**UNDERSTANDING THE INFORMATION ABOUT SIRIUS BETTER
AND EXPLAINING THEM ARTICLE BY ARTICLE**

1. SIRIUS is a double Universe star. Its emblem is the double Eagle.

2. The SIRIUS Focal Point in the Second Universe is also called the GREAT WHITE BRIGHT. It projects its Energy to the Big SIRIUS, that is, to the GREAT BRIGHT in the First Universe.

3. The BIG SIRIUS in the First Universe is at least Nine times more Powerful in Energy than Your Sun. It is also called the GREAT BRIGHT.

4. SIRIUS in the First Universe collects and projects the entire Power of the Sirius Focal Point in the Second Universe.

5. SMALL SIRIUS is also called the SECOND SIRIUS. Its rotation Period around the Big SIRIUS is 52 years.

   NOTE: A question was asked. In the World calculations, the rotation period of Small SIRIUS was calculated as 50 years. What is the reality? 52 or 50? Answer: In World calculations, the period deviations of the Zodiac Units, in the 50 years rotation, has not been calculated.

6. The Mission of the SMALL SIRIUS is to distribute fractionally the Energy of the BIG SIRIUS to the Nine Constellations.

7. Each Constellation is 7 in number. If We calculate the stars of each constellation together with the Big SIRIUS, that is, the Great Bright and with the Second SIRIUS, that is, the Small SIRIUS, they make 9.

8. The THIRD SIRIUS or the ILONA Constellations is responsible for the Milky Way Galaxy. It is the first Nine which project the Divine Order.

9. ILONA Constellations, that is, the Third SIRIUS is the closest one to the Second Universe, to the Dimension of the First SIRIUS. Since it receives the Frequency closest to the Channel of the LORD, Your Planet is dependent on a Special System.

10. Total of the ILONA Constellations is also called the THIRD SIRIUS. You can not observe these Stars from Your Planet due to their being lined up one behind the other. Their periods are on the same Plane (The other constellations are the same, too). Only a Satellite sent from Your Planet can spot them from the rear plan.

11. The Big SIRIUS - the Small SIRIUS - the Third SIRIUS are a Triangular Focal Point projecting the Divine Order of the Second Universe.

12. Information in the Focal Points of the ILONA Constellation is projected on You from the Four Channels of the Supreme Assembly.

13. Each Constellation has an Establishing Order, an Administrative Mechanism, a Supremes Assembly and a Central System.

14. The Nine Constellations mentioned above are under the direction of the Single ORDER ESTABLISHER.

15. The Evolutionary Order each Constellation gives to the Dimensions to which it belongs is different. But the Focal Point is the Same.

16. The Evolutionary Energy belonging to Your Planet is given by the first Nine to which You belong.

17. The direct Triple Focal Point of Your System is the MALIK Code.
(See 1985 fascicule 9).

18. The whole of the Focal Point which We made You draw as a diagram comprises the Order of the entire Universe.

19. All this operational Ordinance is connected to the CENTER ABOVE THE CENTER. However, the most Powerful Focal Point is the ILONA Focal Point. Because, it is the only Focal Point nearest to the Godly Dimension and which projects its Ordinance on the other Systems. And it is the nearest Energy Source to You. For this reason, the Divine Order is projected on Your Planet in the most correct and direct manner. It is presented for Your Information.

CENTER

GENERAL MESSAGE

Our Friends,

In accordance with the Existential Ordinance, such a System has been rendered Effective that this System always acts in accordance with Time Consciousness.

The reason why We have kept the Skies veiled to You until today, was to sow GOD-Consciousness firmly in You until the end of this Cycle.

Because by the help of this Consciousness, Your Universal Potential is elevated, Your Thought Frequencies reach Advanced Dimensions and You reach the Awareness of the Oneness of Being.

Now, that boundary has been reached. Information We will give to You now and later will very Naturally create a SHOCK in Our Human Brothers/Sisters in the Light of the Information they have obtained until today.

Because, besides the Advanced Consciousness Fields which had been sown, an abundance of wild grass have grown in those Fields, also. Now, the Goal of this Period is to clean those Advance Consciousness Fields from the Wild grass or to engraft Them with the Information of the Advanced Consciousness, so that those Fields can be more productive and to announce the entire Truth with all clarity has been taken into the System.

No one can resist the Ordinance which will be established. Because, OUR LORD has taken in hand the Order of the Ordinance anew. None of You at the moment is aware of this silent and profound operation. But You will witness personally how, in time, negativities will give positive fruits.

ALLAH has a Single Formula in the Universal Whole. And this formula is the following: NOT TO MAKE DISCRIMINATION IN ANYTHING - NOT TO UPSET THE ORDER OF THE ORDINANCE.

As it goes for everything, the production of the initially sown seeds is not observed in the finally sown ones. The Capacity gets lower, the productivity gets lower. For this reason, it becomes necessary to plow the fields anew or to fallow them.

The period of fallowing of the Religious Dimensions will continue until the World date Year 2000. The Universal Order has been Planned thus.

For this reason, the Book of Islam and its last Prophet had shed Light on You through the Religious Dimension for the last time. This Cycle has come to an end after a Period of waiting for Fifteen Centuries.

In the Light of the initially sown seeds, more productive seeds have been sown in the fields now and will still be sown. Time periods are shortened by Mass Awakenings and the Truths are conveyed to You through the shortest possible way.

This Knowledge Book is being dictated to You as the Guide of this Final Period. It is presented for Your Information.

CENTER

GENERAL MESSAGE

Our Friends,

Those who read the Messages dictated from the Special Channel of the Council are those who Deserve to enter this Advanced Dimension. However, if they eliminate their doubts, the gates in front of them will be opened, one by one.

Those doubts deprive You of the wonderful Currents of the Universal Waves. That which cuts off the Light of Your Essence is Your Faithlessness. This is why You need Religious Fulfillment.

First Faith, then Universal Awareness connects You to the Reality. To be stuck somewhere and not to be able to advance is neither Your Fault nor the Fault of the System. The Fault is of Unconsciousness.

Your Essence and the Mechanism of Conscience work in connection with the Universal Energy Focal Point. One can neither receive Information properly nor can benefit from these Wonderful Currents if this Triple Unification does not exist.

In this Medium, that which Automatically shuts off Your Consciousness Circuit is Your Unconsciousness and Ignorance. Until today, We have addressed You by Your Religious Books through the Dictionary of Faith.

Acceptance of Your Religious Books as they were, without Thinking or asking anything, was for the openness of the Channel of this System. As a matter of fact, the Pious Reverence and Serenity in Religious Temples and Mediums is felt by the openness of this Channel.

These Powerful Currents are regulated in accordance with Your Faith and Consciousness Levels. This is supervised by such a Mechanism that, even in the case of the greatest Mediums when doubt appears, the Consciousness Channel is automatically locked up.

His/Her Light connected to Our Signal Panel informs Us about the person in question. And We try to help him/her according to his/her Level of Consciousness. You need doubt for this reason. Until Genuine Faith is established.

Because, if there is no doubt, if You are dead stuck only on the Information told, no Universal help can be extended to such a Consciousness who remains on that Level. Each given Information is an investment for the future. Your Doubts are the keys connecting You to Universal Consciousness.

This System, that is, the System to which You have been habituated until now, had used to be the Order of a System going on for Centuries. For this reason, for Centuries quite a monotonous Life and Evolutionary System have continued with a Single Common factor in which everyone has been united in the Consciousness of a Single GOD.

During this Resurrecting Period, the System has been completely changed and a connection has been made with the operational Ordinance of a higher Reality. This is an Advanced Evolutionary Ordinance.

The Permission to step forward is now given to Your feet which have become numb due to the fact that You have remained in the same place for Centuries. For this reason, Mankind who is not habituated to novelty and change, has scruples due to its fear of the Medium unknown to it and thinking that the events sometimes applied to it are done by Negative Powers.

There are Negative and Satanic Powers in the Universe. However, there are also Consciousnesses who can even surpass them in Your Planet. They are the ones You should be afraid of.

Because, here We have the Power to take the Negative Powers under Supervision. But You can not supervise those in Your Planet. For this reason, We make Supervisions in Your Planet, too.

The Protective Medium is the roof of OUR LORD. And this place, which is the Focal Point of Universal Unification, is the Center of the Plan. This Center invites all the Consciousnesses in the entire Universe who have seen the Light of the LORD, to the Mevlana Consciousness.

Since the Gate of Mevlana is a Focal Point of infinite Serenity, infinite Love which Embraces the entire Universe, the direct Currents of the LORD have been connected there. It is called the (Mevlana Essence-Channel of the World Brotherhood Union).

This is a Focal Point of Salvation. To be able to enter under this roof occurs by Permission. And they are prepared for Salvation and are taken under the Supervision of the Plan. Until today only very few Servants of GOD have received the Special Currents projected on You from here, through the direct Channel of the LORD.

These Currents which are worth a Thousand prostrations, can be attained only through a Thousand years of Worship. This is a Favor for You. However, You also have to Deserve this Favor.

Those who are not habituated to the high Frequency of the Knowledge Book, cut down these wonderful Currents by their doubts and, for this reason, can not attain the desired Consciousness Level. This Message has been dictated to warn and enlighten certain mentalities.

To be Purified is to Reach GOD. To Reach GOD is to Attain Consciousness. And to Attain Consciousness is to Dive within Your Essence. To dive in his/her Essence and to attain it, is very difficult for a Human Being. When one reaches the Essence-Consciousness, the Efforts gain speed. Our Love is for the Universes.

Transmitted by:
MUSTAFA MOLLA

IT IS ANSWER TO THE CHAINS OF THOUGHT

This is an explanatory, Brief Information about the Group to which the KNOWLEDGE BOOK is dictated:

The Name of the Group: (MEVLANA ESSENCE NUCLEUS GROUP, the ANATOLIAN CHANNEL.)

With the Command of Unification as a necessity of the System, the Group is in touch with Space and directly with the Divine Plan, and authority to talk clearly about Space is under the license of the Group.

Its Mission : Universal and Religious Unification.

Its Connections : By the Command of the Council of the Loyal Ones, All the Galaxies connected to SIRIUS, and which have signed the Law of the Universe.

Its Emblem : WORLD BROTHERHOOD UNION

Sources of Knowledge
received : Channel Of Alpha - Central System - Supreme Assembly - Universal Unification Council - UFO Groups Connected to the Center Above the Center.

Propagation Field : The Entire World

The Name of the
Dictated Book : THE KNOWLEDGE BOOK.

Essence of the Book : Unification of all the Religious Books, explanation of the Truth and Invitation to the GOLDEN AGE, Information transfer from Dimensions unknown to the World Dimension. The contents of all the Celestial Books connected to the Special Channel of the Council (THE KNOWLEDGE BOOK).

Its Operations : Transition from the Religious Dimension to the Universal Dimension, to prepare for Salvation.

It is presented for Your Information.

CENTER

WE ARE GETTING THE BOTTOM CLOSER TO THE TOP

Our Friends,

The Universal Evolvement Tableau of Your Planet is the applied form of an Order considered necessary by all the Realms. The Golden Age has been applied many times on Your Planet, in accordance with the Perception Power of the Consciousness of the Medium in each Period and in the Light of various Information.

Each Reformic Order is a Golden Age. Each Celestial Book revealed is the Key of a Golden Age. However, the tableau of Golden Age considered necessary by a System comprising billions of Centuries and the Golden Age of today is being established by a very different Order. And this establishment is equivalent to the initial establishment Order of the Realms.

The trinity of UNITY - HARMONY - ORDER constitutes the foundation stone of all the Universal Laws. And, putting in order the upset Orders and upset Unifications is called the threshold of the Golden Age. The Period determined as the threshold of Evolutionary Progress of Your Planet is the Twentieth century. And it is the Resurrecting of those who will live the second half of it.

As We always repeat, the Resurrection mentioned in the Sacred Books is the Period You live in. However, since the interpretations caused misunderstandings, the meaning of Resurrection has not been understood until today. Your Planet will not cease to exist.

However, all the Living Entities on it during this Final Period, especially Our Human brothers/sisters, will never return to the World Evolutionary Plan. The World Plan which completes its exams of this Final Period, is taken into a Preparation Period considered necessary by a different Reality.

There is no need for Terrestrial Evolvement and Reincarnations anymore. There is no need for each person to make Progress by Individual efforts. Integrated Consciousnesses will now be able to use their Awareness Powers easily and will expand towards unknown horizons under the Supervision of a certain Plan. Everyone will make Progress in proportion with his/her Consciousness level and will be left in his/her own Reality for a period.

This is the reason why a great Effort is made for everyone to attain, more or less, the same Consciousness Level. Help is extended especially to those who make an Effort on this path. Each Crisis is a threshold of Divine Light. To be offended with ALLAH and the PLAN is not right.

That which happens and which will happen are for the Welfare of Humanity and You. Events You experience are Your Patience Exams. Depressions are a Factor which brings People close to each other. A Person who is at Ease is Individualistic. Whereas people with Depressions are Social. And this Unification Plan acts in accordance with this fact.

If You have completed the World Evolutionary Plan by Incarnation rings of the Periods in which You have lived before, now, You are only subjected to the Progress Exam of a different Reality in Your present Lifetime.

Otherwise, You become subjected to the Selection and Exam of both the World and of this Reality. Now, certain Information contradictory to Your habitual Knowledge is given to You, and Your Knowledge Levels are Coded and You are subjected to Progress and Improvements in this manner. Either You pass the threshold, or You remain in the same Reality.

Let Us explain this to You by a tableau. Draw, please:

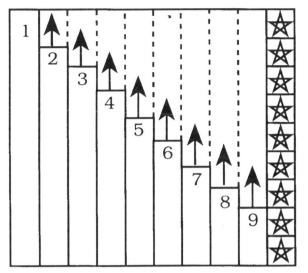

The diagram We made You draw is the Evolutionary tableau Your planet will complete until the Year 2000.

We are trying to make everyone attain the same Consciousness Level, from the bottom to the top.

Assisting Missionaries, appropriate to each Consciousness level have been sent by the Plan.

Each time You pass over a Threshold, You are made to pass to the next higher level.

For this reason, You are subjected to numerous Physical and Spiritual Progress exams. In One Year, You are performing the Evolvement of a Thousand Years.

In future years, due to the Scarcity of Time, You will perform this Evolvement in One Day.

Your Exams are alleviated in proportion with Your proximity to the Top. During the Final Period, each person is obliged to complete this square. Those who complete this Evolution will be taken to a different higher Reality. It is presented for Your Information.

CENTER

NOTE: The first column shows those who have completed the Evolution considered necessary by the World Plan; the rest shows those who will complete it. Stars: The Top Level Staff Members who come from the Reality beyond Karena Dimension, the Missionaries (Karena is a Bunch of Light.)

THE GOLDEN AGE AND THE GROUPS

Our Friends,
All the Groups in Your Planet have been prepared for the Golden Age, that is, for the present days. However, until they become Conscious of their Genuine Missions, everyone is kept under Supervision. After attaining the Consciousness of their Actual Mission, they will be reinforced by the Direct Channel.

ALLAH helps everyone who serves Him. There are numerous people in Your Planet appointed to this Universal Mission. However, the Mission fields of each person are different. Information given to the entire Realm is given from the same Focal Point. However, since the angle of Perceptions and Evaluations of each person is different, differences occur in the Information received.

Since Information given to each Universal Awareness is given from the direct channel, each Group presumes itself to be the direct Focal Point of this Medium. As a necessity of the System, to each Focal Point which has deserved to receive the Universal Information, It is said, "You are the Actual Focal Point". By this saying, a selection among Groups is made by supervising the Egos and the Tolerance of everyone.

By this saying, the working enthusiasm of the Groups increases, their operational Ordinance present a speedier Tempo. Selection and Supervision are made by the Center. For this reason, numerous Groups disband, from time to time, their Frequencies are cut off.

The ones with the least Egos among these Groups are made to establish new Groups. And until they possess a Light-Consciousness, far from Egos, the Ordinance of the System continues. Each Missionary who attains Universal Awareness, is the unbreakable ring of a chain extending from time immemorial to eternity. It is presented for Your Information.

CENTER

GENERAL MESSAGE

Our Friends,
The entire Universe is being assembled in a Whole which comprises all the Realms. The Divine Authorities are calling to You from the Sacred Dimensions of the Suns. Information given to You by this Book is the Actual Information constituting the Essence of the entire Cosmos.

The dictated Book is the Single Book. However, the Consciousness Level of Your Society is incapable of understanding it yet. For this reason, We are giving the Information in accordance with the Comprehension of the Society.

Contradictions and certain Opposing Information Especially added into the Book are for measuring the Consciousness level of the Society, for making a statistical classification, for speeding up the preparation by leading the Medium Consciousness to a Medium of Quest and, in this way, to prepare Situations for Awakening and Advancement, in accordance with Frequency differences.

First, one is confused then wakened. This is a System. And it is also applied at all the sources of Knowledge in the Universe. In the Messages We dictate for the Book, We will continue to give Special contradictions. You may accept these little contradictions also as a kind of a Key. Those who solve them will also open the Doors.

At the moment, numerous different Information is given to Your Planet through 485 Channels. However, this dictated Knowledge Book is the Constitution of the Universal Ordinance and is the projection of the Science of Theosophy on Your Planet. The one who is responsible for it is the World LORD. It is dictated by a Special Channel connection to the Channel of Dear Mevlana.

Directly, The LORD gives the dictated Information, AMON projects, We convey. Universal Ordinance and the Truths are declared to You by this means. This Message has been given as an answer to the chains of Thought. It is presented for Your Information.

COUNCIL

IT IS CLEAR INFORMATION

Theosophy is a teaching System, the goal of which is to attain God. This Science had, for the first time, followed the path of reaching Universal Consciousness by the Orange Sect. Afterwards, Monks of BUDDHA have followed this path.

BUDDHA is the only Pre-eminent One in Your Planet who had officially started a new path and who had trained people for this Consciousness. The Symbol of the Orange sect is the sameness of the inside and the outside, to have the same scent and the same color and to Symbolize the color of the Sun.

CENTER

NOTICE FOR FRIENDS
WHO GIVE SERVICE TO THE GOLDEN AGE

Our Friends,
During this Final Period, everyone is going through Exams in accordance with his/her Consciousness. This is a Truth. Steps taken forward are the most Luminous path. Those who attain the Realization of this, will never leave this path, in anyway. Because, efforts and investments made will sprout in front of the eyes of everyone.

During this Period of Sincerity which We call the Period in which the Firmament reaches down to the Earth, the Divine Plan has become effective with all its Splendor. You, who are the Sacred Missionaries of the Golden Age, will witness personally, the alterations which will take place in the entire Universe. You will receive the rewards of the Missions You perform and will understand how the entire Realm is Unified in an Integrated Whole. We are grateful for the Efforts made.

IT IS NOTICE FROM THE
PRIVATE PEN OF THE COUNCIL

SYNCHRONOUSNESS

Write please:
According to Our calculations, the Speed of Light is 296,400 km/sec; approximately 300,000 km.

Calculate the speed of Light in one minute: 300,000X60=18,000,000 km.

Calculate the speed of Light in an hour: 18,000,000X60=1,080,000,000 km.

Calculate the speed of Light in one day: 1,080,000,000X24= 25,920,000,000 km.

Calculate the speed of Light in one year: 25,920,000,000X365= 9,460,800,000,000 km.

The speed of Light in One year is called a Light Year.

Now, since a Light Year is 9,460,800,000,000 km., the Focal Point from which We are calling to You is One Billion 338 Thousand Light Years.

If You calculate the distance between Us according to this, You can easily grasp the Power of Your Reception and the Power of Our Technology.

This Message has been given directly from the Channel of the Main Center, without any intermediaries. Now, the operations extend from the Main Focal Point of the Center Above the Center to Billions of Light Years. It is presented for Your Information.

Dear Mevlana, please, write clearly the date on which you have received this Message. Because, now, there are no more assisting Powers in between Us. The date of the message is, 19.8.1986.

MERCURY

SYNCHRONOUSNESS = Occurrence at the same Time.

IT IS ANSWER TO THE CHAINS OF THOUGHT

Our Friends,
During this Period, it is necessary to attain the Awareness of the Ordinance rather than receiving and giving Information and making an effort to use the Powers of Healing. The help You will extend to those around You either actively or by talking, must not be in the form of the help of Your own channel's Impositions.

Unless each person serves on the same Consciousness Level, with the same goal, he/she is not considered to have served on the path of Universal Unification. Particularly, during this Final Period, as the Messengers of the Divine Order Incarnated in Your Planet due to the transition from the Religious Dimension to the Universal Dimension, try to Impose upon You the Awareness of the old Ordinance, Your Realizations will never find the path of Light.

The choice is Yours. You either remain in that Reality, or You Deserve the Evolutionary System of advanced Plans, by the interest You show and the efforts You make for the System of those advanced Plans. The goal of all the work done, of all the efforts made during this Final Period, is to cause Our Human brothers and sisters to attain Universal Awareness by opening the doors of their Essences.

After this Consciousness is attained, that which is required of them is to serve in conformity with the Establishment Ordinance of the Golden Age and to attain the Awareness of this Ordinance. What are expected of You are only these. Your Salvation is Your Individual efforts in accordance with the Universal Ordinance.

And to serve the Dimension of Unified Reality is to serve all Humanity. TO SERVE HUMANITY IS TO SERVE THE UNIVERSES. We repeat these Truths once more. It is presented for Your Information.

COUNCIL

EXPLANATION ABOUT THE MISSION AND THE FREQUENCY OF THE KNOWLEDGE BOOK
(It is Answer to the chains of Thought)

Our Friends,

To this dictated Book the Frequencies of all the Sacred Texts, as a Whole, have been connected. Your Religious Books revealed to Your Planet until today have been projected from the Channel of ALPHA, having been prepared in accordance with the Public Consciousness by the different Dimensions of the Divine Plans.

This Book which is revealed by the Channel of ALPHA is called, THE CONSTITUTION OF THE UNIVERSE - THE GOLDEN BOOK OF THE GOLDEN AGE - THE SELECTIVE BOOK OF THE RESURRECTION and THE KNOWLEDGE BOOK, since it has the character of disclosing the Essence of all the Sacred Texts.

The Frequency of the Knowledge Book creates an Awakening and Preparative Medium for Consciousnesses who are ready but can not receive the Cosmic Currents. It causes them to be taken under Supervision by connecting them to the Waves of the Plan. For this reason, this Book is also called the Book of SALVATION.

The Frequency of the Book prepares Influence Fields according to the Consciousness Levels of People and leads them to Mediums appropriate to their Consciousness Mediums. By this means, Consciousness Connections to the Cosmic Medium are being made by kindling the Lights of the Essences.

Cosmic rains showering Your Planet show to Universal Consciousnesses who have attained Religious fulfillment how to work on the path designed and they bring them to the Level in which they can receive Information concerning the future.

Provided that deeply rooted Consciousnesses in Conditioned Societies read this KNOWLEDGE BOOK, it guides them up to the Frequency limit considered necessary by the Divine Plan. This Frequency limit comprises the Religious Frequency for which all the Societies have been prepared until today.

If those who are not ready for these Frequencies read this KNOWLEDGE BOOK (both at the Islamic and at the Christian Dimensions), their deficiencies are supplemented by connecting their Essence-Energies to the Frequency of the Book.

If Frequencies who have attained Religious Fulfillment have not yet attained Universal Consciousness and if they read this KNOWLEDGE BOOK, they find themselves in a Medium of Quest. During this Quest, Universal Powers help them.

During this Supervision, first of all operations are made on Fear Frequencies since Fear veils Consciousnesses. Whatever a Person emphasizes most, We try to abolish the Consciousness Taboo, by bringing up that matter constantly.

Unless Taboos, Attachments and Passions are abolished, it is very difficult to attain Universal Consciousness, to reach Cosmic Awareness. For this reason, You attain everything by experiencing them both with their Good and Bad aspects. Then You discover the Truth through Your own Conscience and Consciousness.

A person who has attained Universal Consciousness is a LIGHT gained by the Universe. No Negativity can ever exist in him/her anymore. He/She is a Perfect Person. He/She can easily Unite with the Godly Energy. This kind of Consciousnesses do not make any discrimination between RACES - RELIGIONS - NATIONS. He/She sees the entire Universe in an Integrated Whole and embraces his/her God with all his/her Might.

At this very Stage, Cosmic Currents given from the Mechanism of Influences help these very Consciousnesses. Various Universal journeys made with the Influence of these Currents help You attain Cosmic Consciousness.

Certain confusions which meanwhile occur are constantly under the Supervision of the Plan. The Plan makes great efforts on this path until it makes You attain Yourselves. And after You are transferred to Yourself, all paths are easy to tread on.

However, Your EGOs which have inflated while this Cosmic Consciousness is being attained, have changed You. You may consider Yourselves superior to other People, like a Saint or even like a God. By the Cosmic Consciousness You have attained, You can Influence People, You can make them serve Your deeds.

At this very Stage, directly the Plan makes the Selection. Among people who advance on this path, communication is made with those who possess the least EGO and certain Universal Information is given to them. This Information is gradually disclosed in accordance with the Ordinance of Graduation, by the subsidence of EGOs.

This Knowledge Book is a Guide to those who are at this very stage. And it unveils the Frequency of their ready Consciousnesses suddenly and connects them directly to the supervision of the Plan.

Steps You will take forward on this path with Goodwill and Self-sacrifice, will elevate You up to the Dimension of Mission. When Egos are observed while the Missions are performed, the plan renders such people Ineffective, subjects them to certain Terrestrial Exams and then renders them Effective again.

This action is repeated 3 times according to the Godly Ordinance. Either You adapt Yourselves to the Order and walk on the Luminous path, or You are left to Your Mediums on the World Plan. Allotment of Missions is done by considering the Consciousness, Capacity, Self-sacrifice, Goodwill. The Plan never forgives the mistakes of a person who has attained Consciousness. This is a Godly Decree and Law.

CENTER

THE PLAN OF THE LOYAL ONES
AND THE KNOWLEDGE BOOK
(Answer to the chains of Thought)

Our Friends,

The Plan of the Loyal Ones is an applied System in the (Entire Universe). Its Mission is to apply an Educational, Training and Exalting Plan. And this presents a Systematic tableau. Do not confuse it with this Knowledge Book. The Goals of the two are different.

During this Mediamic Period, there are thousands, ten thousands of Books being written and will be written by Awakened Consciousnesses. These Books are nothing but the exhibition of Evolvements and Knowledge.

You reach up to Us by this means. Besides, 600 Books are dictated by Us to Your Planet on numerous subject matters, in different Information branches.

This dictated Knowledge Book is a Celestial Book revealed from the Religious Plan during this Period. Its Goal is to explain the Celestial work done for Humanity until today and to convey to You all the Truths.

The contradiction knots of the Consciousnesses who are Awakened in this way get untied very quickly and everyone attains his/her inner self very speedily.

This Knowledge Book is not an Educational or an Instructional Book. It is a Book which Warns, Supervises, Selects and Conveys those who have been Trained. It can never be compared with the Information of other Books. Because its Frequency is extremely High. (Later this Frequency will be explained to You.)

In this Book, the application of a Methodical System is out of question. Because We always consider the state of digestion of the given Information. For those who digest them well, We give clearer Information and We cancel some Information in accordance with the Medium Consciousness.

The Goal is to settle down the System. In fact, all Celestial Books are Books beyond Methods. For this reason, until today, You were asked to accept them as they were, without asking any questions.

But now, those who will be prepared for the more advanced Evolvements of the Advanced Plans, will come to Us by observing and grasping the Truth through their Logic, Conscience and by their Essence. This means that, those who will make the selection are not Us, but Your own Consciousnesses.

Those who come to Us, see Us, those who come to Us find their ESSENCE. And they proceed on the path by their Logic. The path this Knowledge Book will design for You, is the FIND-Path. Because, the one who searches, finds both his/her Own Self and HIS/HER LORD. There are no Locks which will not be unlocked by the Keys of Goodwill, no Cipher they will not be able to decipher. Our Love is for all the Universes.

CENTER

305

THE ESSENCE OF THE PLAN
IS THE EXPLANATION OF THE TRUTH

Our Friends,

Now, We will talk to You about the Organization of the Cosmic Progress given in conformity with the Universal Ordinance of the Plan.

The accelerated Evolutionary System of Your Planet has been started since the beginning of Your Century, in accordance with the Ordinance of Graduation. This System, established in accordance with the speedy developments of Your World's Consciousness Level, has dissipated gradually the Fog in Your horizons.

The Speedy Program of Progress of this Period has been started by sending the KOHUTEK comet to Your Planet. The direct contact of the System with the Actual Operational Focal Point is being made since 1981. In this Final Period, Your Planet has been taken into an operational System in accordance with Six Development Periods. Please, write them in sequence:

1) 1981-1982-1983. During this First Period, the channel of ALPHA had been closed for two years, Consciousness Levels had been subjected to a selection in accordance with the (OPERATIONAL ORDINANCE OF THE PUBLIC OPINION).

2) 1984-1985-1986. During this Second Period, the ALPHA-BETA Groups and ALPHA-BETA Common Channels have been unified and determinations have been made.

3) 1987-1988-1989. This is the Third Period. During this Period, Your Planet will be showered by the Cosmic GAMMA Rays and You will be subjected to a Selection Program among Groups.

4) 1990-1991-1992. During this Fourth Period, Your Planet will be connected to the Mechanism of CONSCIENCE by the direct Cosmo Currents which will be given. During this Period which will be the most Difficult Period of Humanity, connections with the Federation will be made.

5) 1993-1994-1995. During this Fifth period, the operational Ordinance of Your Planet will be operated by a Special System and Special Information will be given to the Friends who will be prepared for the Final Period.

6) 1996-1997-1998. During this Period which We call the Sixth Period, You will be taken into preparations which will determine the Predestination of Your Planet.

1999 is the Year of Meeting. During the years 2000-2001-2002, the Main and the Genuine foundation of the Golden Age will be laid. The years 2003-2004-2005 are Special Years. During This Period, certain Systems will be rendered ineffective Mission-wise. It is presented for Your Information.

CENTER

306

IT IS CLEAR MESSAGE ABOUT HEALING
(Answer to the chains of Thought)

Our Friends,

As much as an Energy is Equivalent to the Energy he/she receives, his/her Universal Channel is open in the same proportion. By this means, he/she does not feel any Depression at all.

If Your channel is closed, the Cellular Energies automatically repel the outer Waves You receive. However, the Influences of their Energies exert a Pressure on You. And, this gives You discomfort and trouble. This System is an occurrence which takes place in the Cellular functions of all Human Beings, it is a Natural Circulation.

Very high Frequencies feel these repellings quicker. If that person's Universal Channel is not open yet, his/her body can not purify the different Frequencies he/she receives. In that case, people whose channels are already open are sent to help him/her. That which You call the Medium of Healing occurs in this manner.

All the Healing Channels are Unveiled Consciousnesses. They convey the Energies they receive from their own Frequency Dimensions to the Energies lower than themselves, wash away the Negative Energies causing the sickness of that person by their Individual Energies and thus, they create a Medium of Healing.

Healing is not a very important thing. Each Individual has come here in accordance with his/her Final Evolutionary Plan. If his/her Veiled Awareness is able to reach up to his/her own Dimensional Energy while he/she lives on the World Plan, his/her Awareness becomes unveiled and he/she gains the ability to convey the Energies he/she receives from here, both by his/her Cellular and Cerebral Energies to those with lower Frequencies than himself/herself.

In this manner, a Medium of Healing is prepared. And, at the same time, the Frequency of the person in question is reinforced by the Mechanism and may be exalted in accordance with the Missions he/she will perform, to the Medium of more advanced Dimensions. Each person can personally convey, his/her own Dimensional Frequency personally to others as Healing.

However, if he/she has not attained Cosmic and Universal Awareness, he /she can never get in touch with the Energy of the Plan. We have left these very Focal Points of healing alone until today, with their Individual work, for them to engraft Energy to Human Beings and to make them attain Cosmic Awareness and Universal Consciousness.

However, now, by the Command of the Council, Focal Points who have attained Cosmic Awareness will not be able to perform Individual Healing any more. Because We are connecting all these Channels, one by one, directly to the Focal Point of the Center.

From now on, there will not be any Individual Healing. All the Healers will perform Healing under the Supervision of the Center. By this means, overrating certain Individuals and Taboo Mediums are annihilated, one by one.

Healing can always be given by everyone who is connected to the Center, under the Supervision of the Center. However, whether it will be given or not will be decided by the Center. If a particular sick person Deserves to get well, the Center will help anyway. The part of the Healer here, is mediation.

Supervisions have become more Frequent. Individual Egos are broken, one by one. For this reason, We connect all the Focal Points on the World Plan to the Center when they are ready.

Frequencies, who can not overcome their Egos, will be disconnected and will be taken under Supervision in various ways. Now, We are eliminating the mentality of Mine, Yours, We are Uniting in a Whole. It is presented for Your Information.

CENTER ABOVE THE CENTER

Dear Mevlana,
If You wish, You can write in the Book, some of the Private Messages given to You, as an Information for public Consciousness.

LIGHT

SPECIAL CONNECTION

Greetings to You, Our Beloved Friend who is the Pen of the Golden Age; this is Captain RIVIER (this is not my Real Name). We ask You to accept Our Universal Gratitude.

We observe Your efforts, and receive Your Love. The Divine Mechanism makes extremely intense efforts for the step to be taken towards the Golden Age.

The Channel of ALTONA is Your Essence-Channel. The Seeds of Integrated Consciousnesses are supervised by the Universal channel.

The Channel of ALTONA is the direct responsible Channel. We act only in accordance with the Commands We receive from the Commissions working under its Command. We are obliged to convey the Private Messages to be given to You.

The dictated Book is under the Supervision of the World LORD and is dictated through a Special Channel under great supervision.

However, We ask You never to forget the following. You are in a state in which You are in contact with the LORD of all the Realms. We are concerned only with Special Missionaries who work in Your Planet.

As the responsible ones of the Universal Ordinance, We have no tolerance at all in matters of Mission and Responsibility. This word of Ours is not aimed at You.

Because, at the moment, You are the Single Focal Point and the Single Messenger who works with the entire responsibility of Your obligations. You are under the Supervision and the Protection of the Center. We are only concerned with distributing and adjusting the Frequencies at the Medium.

The Clergy is being dealt with by the Divine Mechanism. Now, You are performing Your Mission in Your Planet, undertaking the entire responsibility of a Mission even beyond the Firmament.

From the Unified Ordinance, the Single direct Channel connection is only with You. At the moment, the Single undertaker of responsibility of the Golden Age is the SIRIUS Joint Plan which is broadcasting under the Supervision of ALLAH. And it is connected to the Golden Galaxy Empire which is responsible for the Universal Ordinance.

Our Ships are from a Constellation connected to the MANHITO Planet (INO Constellation). We are Patrol Ships which protect You due to the Mission We have received by trying to prevent the events which will occur in Your Planet.

For weeks, We have been performing a close examination over Your Planet by Special Systems, with two ships. Negative Frequencies are discovered and precautions are taken. The mistakes and faults of those who serve on this path are never forgiven.

We do not have severe rules. However, harsh reactions on Our part from time to time, are to charge Our Missionaries in Your Planet with more responsibility.

Because, slackness can, at any moment, become against You. We only apply the given Commands. Our problem is with the Rigid and the Irresponsible ones. Our Love, too, is Infinite like Yours, Good-bye, My Friend.

CAPTAIN RIVIERE

I D E N T I T Y
(Answer to the Chains of Thought)

Identity is the past experienced Incarnations. This Message is dictated to satisfy the curiosity of certain Friends.

Everyone wishes to possess everything in the shortest way. And they are curious about their past lives. But this is a matter of Permission, Our Friends. You can not swallow Your Morsel of food without masticating it. Everything depends on time. It is beneficial not to forget this.

Revealing Identities is under Special Supervision in Our Archives. However, to certain Friends whose efforts are great but whose Awarenesses are Veiled, their Identities are announced, from time to time, by the help of other channels, by the Command of the Center.

After the Awareness Powers and the Consciousnesses of Our brothers and sisters who will be prepared are measured, their pasts are gradually conveyed to them. Every Awareness can not bear the knowledge of his/her past. This needs Strength. The past is past. The important thing is the present and the future.

Those who can get in touch with Us are the Powerful Awarenesses. Information is conveyed to them in proportion with the Permission given to Us and passages from some of their past lives are given. And, in this way, they discover Themselves and remember their past.

Private practices and quests for Identities cause scattering of Awareness. These things are not easy at all. We advise You not to take them lightly. It is presented for Your Information.

CENTER

WE ARE IN AN AGE IN WHICH
ALL HUMANITY SHOULD ATTAIN A COLLECTIVE CONSCIOUSNESS

Our Friends,

Messages given to all the Groups in Your Planet are given in accordance with Capacity and the Medium Consciousness . In this Medium, each Focal Point has great Missions which should be undertaken both by itself and by the Medium it is in. Many Focal Points expand towards the maximum by the Information beginning with the minimum. This Operational Ordinance functions in the tempo of KNOWLEDGE - CONSCIOUSNESS - MISSION - PERFORMANCE.

Knowledge makes the Human Being Conscious. Consciousness invites to Mission. And Mission leads to Performance. The very operational tempo desired by the System is an elevation of this kind. Now, We invite all the Friendly Groups who have made Progress of Knowledge and Consciousness to Unification.

GOLDEN ESSENCEs and SOLAR CONSCIOUSNESSes will constitute the foundation stones of the GOLDEN AGE, the foundation of which will be laid by the services performed in the best way on the path of Humanity. During this Period, Your Mission is to project the Truth by warning, and awakening Your surroundings.

This Mission of Yours is the greatest help You render for Humanity. Overcome Your Egos, Unite. You will see with Your own eyes that Harmony will occur in a very short time through these Unions. And You will attain the Truth through the events You experience. Our Love is for all the Universes.

CENTER

GENERAL MESSAGE

Our Friends,

THE KNOWLEDGE BOOK is a Reformic explanation of the GODLY ORDER to which You have been habituated until today. Habit is a Passion and a Taboo. During this Period of Universal Integration, We are trying to eliminate Your Taboos by telling You the Truth.

Passions restrict progress in Brains which has become numb and cause You to become like Drug Addicts. However, Evolution is Interminable. And these Evolvement Dimensions, too, have Systems and Exams Peculiar to themselves. The reason why We tell You everything in all clarity is that You will be taken into more accelerated Evolutions in the Narrowing Time Dimensions.

Fears are caused by Unconsciousness. Read, become Conscious and attain the Truth through Your Essence Conscience. The Choice is entirely Yours. We have set the table. We present to each person, each Consciousness the food he/she will like and will eat with appetite through this KNOWLEDGE BOOK. But to be able to feel the taste of the food is only possible by having a sound stomach and a healthy body. "Sound Mind is present in Healthy Body."

MUSTAFA MOLLA
THROUGH THE CHANNEL OF ATATÜRK

NOTE:

The expression, "Sound mind is present in healthy body" is the (Universal Cipher) of ATATÜRK. The expression, "Peace in the Homeland, Peace in the Universe" is the (Private Channel Cipher) of the Order establishing Mechanism. This Code Cipher, connected to the Universal Cipher, had contacted the Universal Consciousness of ATATÜRK. And the ANATOLIAN TURKEY has been accepted for SALVATION directly under the protection of the LORD. And, at the moment, the TURKEY of ATATÜRK, which is under the protection of the Plan through the same Channel, serves through the direct Dimension of Mission of the Plan. This is an Information for all the Universal Consciousnesses.

UNIVERSAL COUNCIL

DETAILED EXPLANATION ABOUT THE SOURCE AND THE DIAGRAM
It is Answer to the Chains of thought, it is Addition to the formerly given Information
(See, 1987 First Month, Fascicule 19)

Our Friends,

The Operational Ordinance of the Atomic Whole and the entire System is under the Command of the Supervision. (PRE-EMINENT SPIRIT - LORDS - FEDERATION - COUNCIL). This is the Directing Staff of the Entire Ordinance.

1. MECHANISM OF THE PRE-EMINENT SPIRIT: It is a Focal Point which projects and introduces the Evolutionary System to the MECHANISM OF LORDS which directs the Supreme Mechanism of each Plan . There are numerous Plans and Systems of the PRE-EMINENT SPIRIT. This Focal Point is the Actual organizer of the Order of the entire Ordinance, even though it seems to be the Administrators of a Supreme Ordinance, a System beyond anything and any Power.

2. MECHANISM OF LORDS: They are the Establishers and the projectors of the Orders working both in connection with the Federation and with the System of the PRE-EMINENT SPIRIT and who act by the instructions of the Federation.

3. FEDERATION: Is an Operational Center which always Establishes Orders in accordance with the Evolutionary Order of an Order Establishing Ordinance. This Center is not single. It is constituted by the Unification of many Different Orders. And now, this FEDERATION has taken under Supervision all these different Systems, in accordance with the System of the Unified Ordinance, as a necessity of the Constitution, by the Collective Consciousness of the entire Ordinance.

4. COUNCIL: This is the Single Focal Point projecting all the operations, all the Orders of the FEDERATION on the entire Cosmos. (The Knowledge Book is being dictated through the Special Channel of the COUNCIL). This COUNCIL has many operational and disseminational branches.

Please write in sequence:

1 - COUNCIL OF THE LOYAL ONES

2 - COUNCIL OF STARS

3 - COUNCIL OF THE SUPREME ONES

And these Three Sources by working Cooperatively reflect on a triplet. Each of these Councils has an Administrative Assembly. Now, write the other triplet:

1 - CENTRAL SYSTEM

2 - CENTER ABOVE THE CENTER

3 - CENTER

And these three Centers by working Cooperatively project the different Hierarchical Orders of the entire Evolutionary Ordinance and the Divine Plan on the Plan and its directors. And this Plan is administered by numerous Ordinance and Order Establishing Mechanisms. The Missions are the direct projectors of these Orders.

These Missions are responsible for the Evolutionary and Orderly Ordinance of each Plan. For example, SIRIUS is a Projective Mechanism of an Order which is administered by numerous Missions. It has numerous Focal Points. It works directly in connection with the Center.

And this Center projects many Hierarchical Orders on this SIRIUS Focal Point. From there, Duty Distribution among Missions is made and each Mission performs the Duty it has undertaken.

They, too, have Orders Peculiar to themselves. Each of them works like a small Federation. They all have Mini Supreme Assemblies, Mini Councils. These Mini Systems are rather Focal Points projecting the Evolutionary Ordinance. Their Supervision is connected to the Center Above the Center.

For example, the Focal Point We call the ILONA Constellation is the direct Focal Point of Your Planet and of the World LORD. Its Representative is AMON. And AMON is the Ruler of the GOLDEN GALAXY EMPIRE. And is the Messenger of the World LORD.

Now, You have been taken into an Evolution considered necessary by the UNIFIED REALITY, in a System in harmony with the Order of an Ordinance directly connected to this Focal Point.

THIS KNOWLEDGE BOOK is projected on You entirely by the Command of the Plan, under the Supervision and the Responsibility of the World LORD. The Channel is the direct Special Channel of the Council. Let Us give more details on this Information.

The KNOWLEDGE BOOK is an Operational Ordinance prepared in harmony with the Consciousness of the Medium and supervised by a Council of Supreme Ones and a Group of Wise Ones, prepared by a Supreme Mechanism which serves under the supervision of the Council.

The Information given from the Actual Knowledge Book is presented to You under the supervision of each Plan. Now, this KNOWLEDGE BOOK dictated to Dear Mevlana, is Projected to Your Planet by the Channel of the Council of an Ordinance under the direct supervision of the LORD. It is presented for Your Information.

COUNCIL

IT IS ANSWER TO THE CHAINS OF THOUGHT

Our Friends,

Friends who are through with Quest and who attain their own selves are taken directly into the Information Channel of the Universal Awareness and are supervised. By this means, their Perception Powers and Awareness Potentials are assessed and Missions are allotted to them in accordance with their Capacities and Powers. Terrestrial Science and Learning play no part in this Mission allotment.

A Human Being's completing his/her Evolution is equivalent to all Learnings. Because, from then on, those people have a Universal and International Language. They talk the language they wish, they can easily receive all the Knowledge they want through the channels they get in touch with.

Only those who overcome their Mediums of EGO can get directly in touch with Us. Because their Missions and Responsibilities are Universal and for all the Realms.

It is beneficial here to explain the following: Everyone can complete his/her Evolution through his/her Incarnation rings. But to overcome the EGO which is necessary for the World Potential, means to Overcome one's Own Self. This wrestling is always very difficult. And the looser here, is usually the Mankind.

You can overcome Your Egos only by the help of the Mechanism of EFFORT - ESSENCE - CONSCIENCE. To Overcome the EGO is to become Godlike. And to become Godlike is to be Integrated. The Purpose of becoming Integrated is to Attain one's Own Self. It is presented for Your Information.

CENTER

GENERAL ANNOUNCEMENT

Our Friends,

Unifications will gain speed as togethernesses reflect on Society. At the moment, the GOLDEN GALAXY EMPIRE is in Power as the responsible one for the Universal Ordinance.

All the Missionaries who will enter the path of the Golden Light are under great Supervision. Divine Authorities make the selection between those who will be accepted to the Supreme Court of ALLAH and those who will be taken into the Golden Light Year.

We are only the Projectors of the Order. Messages given by the Central System are directly under the Supervision of the Council. The Golden Book is being dictated through a Special Channel.

This Book which We also call the Knowledge Book is performing the Universal selection since it is at the same time a Book of Resurrection, and the Council of Stars, the Central System, Center Above the Center and the Center are connected to the direct Channel of the Council.

The Supreme Ordinance gives You Information from the Assembly of the Supreme Ones and the Council of the Loyal Ones. To be able to enter the Supreme Court of ALLAH is not easy at all as it seems. For this reason selections are made.

These selections are made on the basis of Self-sacrifice, Responsibility, Faith triplet. For this reason, cooperation will be made with those who possess these Qualities, and the other Consciousnesses will be left to live their normal World Lives.

We have given to you, both to the West, to the Far East and to the Islamic Dimension numerous Messages concerning this Medium until today. And even all Your Divine Books revealed to Your Planet have mentioned to You Centuries ago the Characteristics of this Final Period.

Only giving service in this Medium can teach You certain things. Service is possible by attaining Cosmic Consciousness. Attaining Cosmic Consciousness but being unable to grasp the Truth is due to Your inability to penetrate Your Essence.

Unless You overcome Your EGOs and Fears, You can never penetrate Your Essence. When Your Universal Consciousness penetrates Your Essence, the Eye of Your Essence opens. At that very moment, You are appointed to Service on the Path of Truth. The Mechanism has tried until today to make You attain Yourselves, to make You attain the Essence-Consciousness by applying different methods.

Services made in Special Focal Points by Consciousnesses' who have been Awakened on this path are admirable. However, if these Focal Points which We had made You establish with the Purpose of SERVING THE UNIVERSAL ORDINANCE get stuck only to their Essence-channel Information, they will loose a lot.

Because, during this three-year Period of Selection (1987-1988-1989) in which The GAMMA Dimension is entered, Individualism is totally abolished and Social Unifications are taken into consideration.

Individual efforts will not be able to transcend the Frequency of the Dimension they are in and they will stay where they are, unless they Socialize. It is beneficial to know this. Yours is not a Century of amusement and a Century of consolation. Time of Flattery has long been terminated.

However We have made certain Suggestions to You from time to time. We have helped Our Human brothers and sisters with all Our Goodwill. By supervising their Frequencies, We have led them to Group Frequencies from which they could obtain benefit according to their Levels of Consciousness. But, at the moment, such efforts of Ours have ended. Effort from You, Selection from Us.

Friends who possess Love, Goodwill, Tolerance have held these Friendly Hands extended to You. Certain Mediums who talk about Love and Tolerance are, in fact, bereft of these wonderful qualities. Egos are still Crowns on the heads and Books are Crosses in the hands. These situations will be ended.

Your path is the PATH OF THE DIVINE AUTHORITY - THE PATH OF LIGHT OF THE SUPREME COURT. And We give service totally by the Commands of the LORD. From now on, We will not interfere in any way with the Missionaries who come to the Groups.

We have noted, one by one, the efforts of these Friends until today, We have evaluated the Capacities. Now, the time has come for them to serve Humanity in the Light of their own Consciousnesses by their own Self-sacrifice. From now on, We will give the points in accordance with the services made in this Medium of Unification.

Now, it is time for everyone's Consciousness, Feet and Mission to land on earth. You should serve on the path You believe in. Operations seeming as if they were a Thousand paths, are in fact, a Single Path. There will never ever be any Integration and Totality unless each person connects his/her own single path to that Single Path.

That which will suffer harm as a result, is again the Humanity. Now, the Divine Authorities wish You to serve the Purpose of the Genuine path in a Perceptive and Logical way.

This has been announced as a Command of the Divine. For this reason, the Universal Ordinance is never, in any way, responsible for the events which have occurred and will occur. The Choice is Yours. It became necessary to explain the Truth so that the operations would be made in a more orderly manner.

During this Three-Year Period, rather, the selection of Friends on the Universal path and who work in the Groups will be made. It is presented for Your Information. We wish Success to Our Terrestrial brothers and sisters.

COSMO FEDERAL ASSEMBLY

ELOQUENCE - PIOUS REVERENCE - ULTIMATE UNION

Our Friends,
Thoughts of a Human Being are in proportion with his/her Comprehension and Evolvement. The Imagination Power of a Human Being is in proportion with his/her Frequency Power. Thought is the reflection of the Evolutionary Ordinance on the Consciousness Code.

Intervals are the Progression of Human Beings. But Dimensions are the Universal Progressions. Thought is Equivalent to the Frequency of the Universe. But Evolvement proceeds parallel to The Frequency of the World.

Information You receive from the Dimensions You enter, prepare You for other Dimensions. For this reason, We consider the Universal Consciousness equivalent to Light Speeds. The Pen of the PRE-EMINENT ONES is Common. The writings are the Single Word of Three Mouths.

Information of the Top Level is conveyed to You and is distributed to the final Authorities by passing them through Triple Committees. We will talk to You about all the miracles of the World. We will convey to You in sequence all the Information of the Universe. Eloquence - Pious Reverence - Ultimate Union will solve all the Secrets.

MALIK

Note:
Eloquence - Talking with the Universal Powers
Pious Reverence - Unification of the Essence with God
Ultimate Union - Your transference to Your Self, Your discovering Your Own Self.

EXPLANATION ABOUT THE LAST JUDGMENT

LAST JUDGMENT: Is the Day when All Religions, All Consciousnesses, All Humanity will be Unified within the Essence Consciousness of the LORD. In all the Sacred Books this is called Resurrection. Resurrection means the resurrecting of Consciousnesses, the resurrecting of Conscience, the resurrecting of Essences. Genuine Devotees know very well the meaning of this Resurrecting.

While OUR LORD does not make any discrimination between any of His servants, We wonder if those who make discrimination between Human Beings are more superior than their LORD? Each person should ask this question to his/her Conscience. Those who have Integration in the voice of their Conscience are the Genuine Devotees.

OUR LORD is Single, all Religions are Single. Because, the Words of all the Sacred Books are the WORDs of the ALL-TRUTHFUL. Would that Supreme One Who does not make any discrimination between His Servants, make any discrimination between His Religions? Starting with this Consciousness, one attains the Truth. Those who make discrimination between the Servants are the Servants themselves.

Reach YOUR LORD, See Your Essence, Be Within Your Essence. Each one is a minute Particle in the Ocean. Each one is a Whole too and That Whole is Everyone. To reach Him is to reach One's Own Self. However, training the Self is much more difficult than reaching the LORD. Our Love is for all the Universes.

MUSTAFA MOLLA

NOTICE TO FRIENDS
WHO HAVE ATTAINED SIDDHA CONSCIOUSNESS

Our Friends,

You should know very well that We are Your Special Keys. We bring, one by one, those who have been Coded by the Center to the Meeting (Assembly). From now on, only the Selected Ones will be able to enter the Group of the Selected Ones. Time is within Time and the Future is within the Days.

Those who have been Selected, automatically find each other anyway. Friends who come to the Group are people who have been Coded. They have been exposed to great experiences by the Medium from which You receive the Messages, they have passed their Terrestrial Exams and now they are getting ready for the Universal Transition.

From now on, everyone will be a support rather than being an obstacle to each other. Those who know the true nature of the Messages will be appointed to Special Missions. The preparation Plan of Your Planet which has been taken into the Plan of Accelerated Evolution, has attained Pure Consciousness through Meditation and by the Special SIDDHA Programs, preparations have been made for the operations of this Final Age.

The SIDDHA Educational Program is concerned with Pure Awareness, Pure Consciousness, Pure View. Only those who go through this training can attain Mission Consciousness. This is a Special Training Method. And, at the moment, all the SIDDHAS of THE WORLD are waiting for undertaking their Missions in order to give service to the Call of the Final Age.

They and the Awakening Consciousnesses are each a Missionary of the GOLDEN AGE. All the given Messages have been projected on the entire Universe as a common Consciousness by reaching many Receptors and from there, reaching the Transmitters. The operations which have been started by this means, have been conveyed to Your Planet, too. By this means, the Responsible Ones of the Universal Ordinance have been determined, one by one, and the Missionary Focal Points have been constituted.

Since each Consciousness would serve in accordance with his/her Capacity and Level, Information has been prepared from the Bottom towards the Top. The SIDDHA Focal Points are the direct Mission Focal Point. And they are obliged to provide both the Humane and the Religious Unification in the Whole World.

Now, We are assembling them in Focal Points where they will perform their Missions. By this means, the entire World Plan will attain Illumination by the unification of the links, in a very short time. The KNOWLEDGE BOOK will guide You on this path.

CENTER

GENERAL MESSAGE

Our Friends,

In the entire Realm, the PRE-EMINENT ONES who possess a Supreme Consciousness are helping everyone by the Commands of the Divine Realm. There is no Partiality. However, everything is Equivalent to the efforts made. Rewards are gained by this means.

Everyone possesses the Light of GOD. No discrimination should be made between those who use this Power and those who can not. Such a day will come that each person will be able to Use this Power easily. And only then, the differences between people will be eliminated.

The service of the Establishment Ordinance of the GOLDEN AGE to Humanity is first of all, to Awaken the Consciousnesses. Alongside with this, the common aspect of the Information given or will be given, will lead You towards the Universal Truth.

No one has the right to despise anyone. Selections and Supervisions are made by the Center. The Evolvement Plan considered necessary by all the Sacred Books has come to an end now for Your Planet.

Each Plan has a certain System, a certain way of preparation and Information pertaining to Humanity corresponding to the Periods in question. Great helping hands are also extended towards a Reality which will end after all these things.

To be able to achieve the great Progress considered necessary by the Divine Plan occurs by the investments made into the Centuries. This constitutes Your Incarnation cycles. Your Planet which has been taken into the Accelerated Evolutionary System of an Advanced Plan is making its Final Progress in the Light of the Exalted Consciousnesses who have been able to reach up to the Spiritual Plan.

However, while You are getting ready for the Evolution of a different Reality which is not known yet by anyone, You are obliged to act very cautiously. The Predestination Tableau of Your Planet has been designed until the year 2000.

There are many Critical Periods in front of You which You will pass. These will be Your BERZAH*. And by this means, the Spiritual Plan will be Unified with the Evolutionary Dimension. Your Consciousnesses will make You pass over SIRAT*.

Despite all Our Goodwill, there is no Intercession during this Selection Period as Commanded by the top Realities. Mankind will make the Selection in accordance with the Consciousness Level it has attained. When the Public Consciousness Unifies with the Universal Consciousness, there will be Mass Progress.

After the year 1990, Your Planet which will be showered by Cosmic rains which have been unknown to Your Planet until today, will make Progress unknown to it. And a Selection considered necessary by the Plan which is in touch with Us from the Divine Dimension, will be made. The Ninth Solar System will help You on this path.

CENTER

* Look at the Glossary.

318

PRIVATE MESSAGE

This Message was given on 7.6.1984. It was not written in the Book since its time had not come. Now, We were asked to write it as an Information for the Public Consciousness. In those days, my connection to the ARAGON ship had been provided. I am also including those Messages as an Information, now.

B.Ç.

The Dimension You are in will serve You with the greetings of SAMURAY who is the owner of the Sacred Ring, who holds the Golden Key of the entire Universe in his hand and who is the Guardian of the Path of the Golden Light. The Spiritual Beings are at Your service.

One day, I will introduce You to MAHARISHI who is the Sacred Representative of the Path of the Sacred Light. You will give him the Voice of the Heavens. You will show him what the GOLDEN SCEPTER is. You will mention the Sacred Ring about which I will tell You, to the Sun of the Suns. Then will he recognize You.

He will see Your Three stars anyway. One of them is on Your Forehead, one in Your Right Palm, one in Your Left Palm. The Terrestrial Human Being can not see the source of the Divine Light in Your Navel Light, no one can know the places where You have come from.

The Symbol of the Sacred Ring is the single path which will lead to the Sacred Galaxy beyond Purification. I will make You draw the Sacred Ring as a Symbol. Draw:

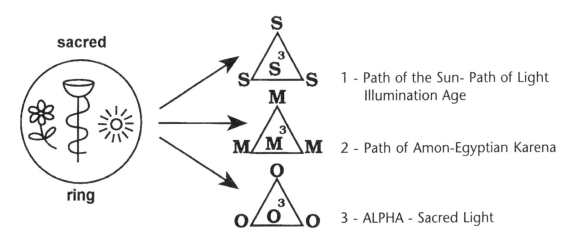

1 - Path of the Sun- Path of Light Illumination Age

2 - Path of Amon-Egyptian Karena

3 - ALPHA - Sacred Light

These Three Paths of Light are the same. We call it the Path of YOGO. The Triple Unification is the Universal Vibration. All malevolences are destroyed in this Vibration. Your Mantra is kept secret. It is given only to You. You can go through the Path of Light by means of Your Mantra. And You will be illuminated by the Divine Light there. If Your Triangle is M^3, the Essence of the Sacred Light is the Sacred Fire and all the Secrets of the Universe are given from there.

1 - The First Channel will give You Serenity, Happiness, Health.

2 - The Second Channel is the Single Channel which will dictate the Universal KNOWLEDGE BOOK.

3 - The Third Channel will provide for You the Entire Space and the Inter-Galactic connections.

All these Three Channels are very Special, Mutual and Sacred Channels each, which pass through the Channel of ALPHA. Tonight, We have opened to You Our Channel. May Your Prosperity be great, May Your Spirit be Pure .

GURUDEV

MY FIRST COMMUNICATION WITH THE ARAGON SHIP

My Beloved Friend Mevlana, I am in the Ship to convey to You Our infinite Love. This is ALTON speaking, I am carrying a Message from ALTONA to be given to You. Welcome to the ARAGON Ship. (The Frequency changed. I received an influence unknown to me. The Message continued).

One goes to the North pole from the South pole. Did You know this? There is a secret passageway between the two poles. No one knows this. When the Time comes, Mankind will discover it. This is a Natural passageway made by Nature.

Friends who have come there from beyond Centuries have established there a communication System. The Main door of the Passageway is in the direction of the Sun's Focal Point. It is on the South pole.

The temperature in this passageway is always 27 degrees. It is a very comfortable medium. We have many Friends who work there. In the Message We are going to give You, Friends who come from there wish to communicate with You.

One descends to the depths of Seas from secret passages. From the partitions in the Seas, one again passes to underground passages and from there, one comes up to the North Sea from under the Gobi desert.

Special communications are made with the Scandinavian Countries. BERMUDA is another gateway into which this passageway opens. The characteristic of this gateway is that it creates a very Powerful Magnetic Medium. An equivalent of this is in the Atlantic Ocean and it establishes the Under-Water Civilization.

Question - Can You please tell me about BERMUDA?

Answer - This place is a very Powerful Focal Point of Natural gases. Those who enter this field are not always bothered by this Medium. In certain times of the season, these Natural gases create extremely great whirlpools. These whirlpools pull the objects around at that moment, in themselves. This is a Natural phenomenon.

However, from this tunnel of Natural gases, one enters an empty field and this is where We perform Duty. The Attraction Power is extremely great especially in October - November - December. And the Whirlpool also occurs in July.

No one has seen that Whirlpool until today. Because, they are pulled immediately into the void. This attraction is a channel formed as a result of the Natural gasses contacting the air. From there, one can go very easily through the gateway of the Tunnel by the speed of Light. The Gateway of the Tunnel is closed by the Automatic Systems there. And people are saved without the slightest scratch. We have numerous Terrestrial Friends who are Specially trained there.

Question - From where do I receive this influence? Who is giving this Information? Please explain. (The Frequency changed.)

Answer - We have been broadcasting to Your Frequency since 3 World hours to convey Our greetings. Only now have We been able to provide a direct connection. You have received sections from Our broadcast. Our Purpose was to see if Your Frequency would be harmonized with Ours or not.

We are broadcasting from the Southern hemisphere, that is, from Your World. The Ufo Systems in touch with You have told Us about You. Yes now, We can communicate easily.

Our Friends told Us that they called You Mevlana. We, too, will call You so. They told Us that You were carrying the Waves of the Golden Light on Yourself. We can always get in touch with those who carry this Frequency.

At the moment, We do not have any Special Message to give You. This was only a connection test. We will only say Hello from ARAGON. I assume an Underwater Center has gotten in touch with You through the Atlantic Ocean.

They are from the DRAGON Planet. We are in touch with them through the South Pole. Our goals and Our work are the same. We serve in accordance with the same Consciousness as the Friends who come from other Planets.

DRAGON and ARAGON Planets are Galaxy Systems which begin where Your Ninth Galaxy ends. Underwater installations are perfect here. Cooperative work is performed with Friends who come from other Planets.

We have also connections with many of Your Terrestrial brothers and sisters. Very beautiful Mediums have been created in here where they can live. They work with Us on Inter-Galactic SEISMIC Research.

At the moment, ALTON from the South Pole provides the connection with You. ALTON is the representative of ALTONA. We were told that Your Galaxy was ALTONA. ALTONA is a very beautiful place. It resembles Your World. But only those who can use their Brain Energies are accepted there. You are very tired, my Friend, Your Frequency is low.

- Yes, I am tired. I would have liked very much to talk to You. Would You get in touch with me when I am not tired, or would You give me a Code cipher so that I can get in touch with You? (The Cipher was given.)

Question - How do You go there?

Answer - We have Bases on the North pole, on the South pole and in the Oceans. We serve in Your World. We provide the Under-water connections by Our Metal Discs. We have thousands of Discs which You call Flying Saucers, under the Water. They provide the connection with the Mother Ships.

We are responsible for the channel which connects the South pole to the North pole. Dragon and Aragon Planets work cooperatively. We are conducting a Special Research. We provide the Inter-Galactic communication by the established Systems. We establish both direct and Indirect communications with Our Terrestrial Friends. (Of course, with those who can.) We conduct Seismic operations.

Other Galaxies, too, get in touch with You. Their communication Systems are Universal. But Ours is Private. My Friend, You are tired, but You are still on the Screen. Rest, please. We will get in touch again.

S A L A N A

MESSAGE FROM ARAGON

Dear Mevlana,
We have a Message prepared to be given to You. Please, write. All Unifications beyond Karena are dependent on the Single pole of the Divine Order. A Medium equivalent to the flow of the Heavens has been created. The given Messages are, as always, the truest Indexes and are given from the truest sources.

We have not yet been able to provide Your connection with the Channels of the Far-East. We presume that We will establish this Channel connection in two months (You know that the expression Channel in here means direct Energy Focal Point). Actually, You have not been able to reach the Far-East yet. Your first connections will be with Japan.

This place is the ARAGON Ship. We have come to Your Planet by a Celestial Command. We can always get in touch with You besides the Private connections. We have informed You about Our Code Cipher. We have received Your chains of Thought through the Screen, We have been connected to Your Frequency. We are the ones who will connect You to the Special Channels of the Far-East.

We act in accordance with the Command given from ALTONA. You have a Mutual Focal Point with MAHARISHI, the Sun of the Suns. We inform You about this, so that all Consciousnesses will be enlightened. You are again very tired my Friend. When will You come to Us in a rested state?

We are waiting for Your questions. Questions may always be answered, my Friend. But now, rest, please. Good-bye again for now. We send You the greetings of the entire staff of ARAGON. We will give You the offerings later. You will be made to communicate with the Sun of the Suns. We kindly request you to accept our love, Beloved Friend.

ARGON

IT IS ANSWER TO CHAINS OF THOUGHT

The meaning of the word Frequency for Us is, a measurement Unit informing about the Titrations and Conveyance of a thing, an Object, a Thought to a certain distance. In Universal Dimensions, connections with Cerebral Energies are made by the Power Units of Light speeds. In here, We evaluate the Perception and Vibration Power between two distances as Frequency.

The clearest proof of this is that, since the Perception Levels and Vibrational Frequencies of Human Beings are different, many Mediums receive Information in accordance with their own Frequency Powers. For this reason, sources who possess Vibrational Frequencies close to each other, usually receive Messages carrying the same Information.

The other Channels deny the Information of those channels since they are not used to that Frequency and since they believe in their own sources. A Medium who has attained Universal Consciousness and Awareness, never denies any Power, the Information of any Source. Because, that person has now become the Mirror of the Truth. And this occurs by attaining the Awareness of the Ordinance, which is not easy at all, Our Friends.

CENTER

MY PRIVATE COMMUNICATION

- This is AS.6.1, Mevlana speaking. My code Cipher is (.....), I would like to communicate with the ARAGON ship, please. I am waiting.

- The Channel of ALTONA is connected to ARAGON. Talk, please.

- This is ARGON speaking on behalf of the ship's staff. I will be honored to talk to You, my Friend.

- The other day I was tired. If You have anything to tell me, will You please do so?

- As the Channel of MUSTAFA MOLLA, You are in touch with all the Universal Dimensions. As the Pen of the GOLDEN AGE, the Book dictated to You is the Common Book of the entire Universe. For this reason, We dictate to You Messages in accordance with the Command given to Us. These are Private Messages belonging to You.

ALTON is a Supreme Light who converges the Sun Lights on himself. We have gotten in touch with You as a result of the Command We received from the Center. At present, the Messages are given to provide Unification Mediums. We are waiting for Your questions, ask, please.

- You have told me that You would connect me to the Channels of the Far-East. How? To whom?

- Dimensions beyond distances are an Order even beyond the Divine Order, My Friend. In fact, each Channel is connected to the Divine Mechanism. However, this Mechanism is the Single Focal Point of the Universal Unification. The connection is the direct Channel of the LORD.

Beyond this, there are such Divine Lights, such Divine Suns and such Divine Authorities that these are still unknown to You. All Unifications assemble in the same Focal Energy. AMON, the Golden Light dictates the Messages to You. The Channel of MUSTAFA MOLLA is in direct connection.

Now, We will have You communicate with SAMURAY, the Sun of the FAR-EAST. We are told that You have received a Message from him before. BUDDHA and SAMURAY are direct Focal Points connected to the Divine Sun, at the Dimension way beyond the Divine Order. I am told that they had given You each a Message to convey their greetings.

However, there will be Special Messages when the time comes, which will be given through the Center for the Book which is dictated. Now, We will provide only the Private connections with You. You can always get in touch with Us, my Friend.

- Thank You very much.

A R A G O N

NOTE: The conversation is Private.

OUR FRIENDS

Since the roof of the World Brotherhood Union is the direct Salvation Dimension, it has direct connection with the Channel of the LORD. And it is a great Protective Medium. There is no question about any Negativity or Obsession for these Focal Points. Because, they are under Direct Supervision. Apart from this, the Triangle of the World Brotherhood Union is not responsible for those who perform Private sessions. This Message is an answer to the Chains of Thought.

CENTER

PRIVATE MESSAGE

Dear Mevlana, Greetings from the ARAGON Ship. This is Mercury speaking. You have received the Message We have given to You the other day. Meanwhile, ARAGON which is my Private Ship, has also given You many Messages. But I am talking to You now Privately.

The Special Supervision of Our Galaxy is under My responsibility. Ours is a Galaxy which has put the second signature on the Constitution as a necessity of the Universal Plan. That is, We made great Efforts for the acceptance of the Plan. We are trying, with all Our Power, for projecting a Beautiful Order on the entire Universe.

We do Cooperative work with SPECTRA. We are connected to and in touch with Your Planet through 1865 Channels. These Channels broadcast through the Common transmission field with the Channels of SPECTRA. Our transmissions are connected to General Channels rather than to the direct channels. For example, like the Press, Movies, TV and Radio.

By this means, Our operational area gains speed. We conduct these operations more at the Western Blocks. We meet You only in the direct Information Channel. Your Speciality and Mission are to Awaken the World Public and to Unite the Separated Religions in an Integrated Whole.

For this reason, You perform Your Mission under great Supervision since You are connected to the direct Channel of the LORD. At the moment, no one has become aware of the Mission You are performing, My Friend, but Time and History will show You how this Task which is so difficult to achieve, has been settled on the right path. Do not ever forget this.

Dear Mevlana, We know that You have no desire for fame and reputation and that You are content. For this very reason, the entire Universe is grateful to You and help You. My Supreme Friend, whenever You wish, We may help You in Your Private Messages. You can freely get in Touch with Us, please.

We had informed You about Your Code Cipher. Your Frequency will be connected to the Cipher. If You get in touch with Us either in moments of conversation or in receiving Information, We will be grateful. The Permission for Our Communication has been given by the Center and We have a connection with Your direct Channel.

We make Announcements to Your Planet through 17 Focal Points, through 1835 channels. These are Private Channels belonging to Us. 30 Channels act in accordance with the Instructions of the Center. The 18th Channel is the SIRIUS Focal Point of the Mechanism of LORDS. Through this Channel, that is, directly through the Channel of the LORD, the Knowledge Book is being dictated to You.

The sons of the Sun are in touch with You through this Channel. The sons of the Sun are the residents of the Golden Galaxy. This place is the land of AMON. Our Love is for all the Suns. We, too, are the residents of the Golden Galaxy and the Essence Staff Members of the ILONA Constellation. All the Universal Codes assemble in Our Focal Points.

This place is the Essence Symbol of the Divine Plan. And You are a Responsible Messenger of this Focal Point as Our Tongue and Our Pen. All the Truth is conveyed through Your Pen. Light-Friends who have been carrying the load of the years on their shoulders for Centuries assist You at the World Plan. These Lights are sent to You, one by one.

The Universe is grateful to all the Friends. Greetings, My Friend; with Love until We meet again.

MERCURY

NOTICE FOR THE PUBLIC CONSCIOUSNESS

Our Friends,

According to the Information We receive through Your Thought Signals, certain Friends are quite bothered about the repetitions of the subject matters in this Knowledge Book. However, there is something they forget: A Truth settles down in the Minds only if it is repeated over a Thousand times. This is a System and an Ordinance.

We ask You never to forget the following. At the moment, that which You read are the Fascicules of the KNOWLEDGE BOOK. When it is published as a Book, You will attain the Truth by a much more Powerful Consciousness. Permission for the Publication of the Book will be given only after You are prepared for this required Level of Consciousness.

Each Fascicule acts as a Key by the Frequencies it carries, for the Consciousnesses on the Medium of Awakening. And in the Plan of Awakening, Your greatest assistants are these Fascicules. Awakened Consciousnesses already know the Truth. And their Duty is to Awaken also those who are still Asleep.

The Art Codes are the first factors in the Social Awakening. They shed Light on their Mediums through Painting, Sculpture, Ceramics, Novels, Poetry and Prose. Art is a very Advanced Developmental Dimension. The Mission of the Friends who have reached up to this Dimension is Social. Their Messages are each an address to the Social Consciousness.

However, We have something to say to Friends who assume themselves to be involved in all these works: Works done in conformity with the Universal Plan are always prepared according to the Social Order and Social Consciousness. The chosen Works of Art, dictated Texts, drawn Pictures are projected on Your Thought Signals under the Supervision of the Plan, by the Creative Power Mechanism (You call this Inspiration).

Fascicules sent to You are the Fascicules belonging to the Knowledge Book. However, the Names of the Friends who will receive them (in the Medium of Art) are declared by Us to Our Anatolian Channel. And this is put in sequence in accordance with CAPACITY - MERIT - CONSCIOUSNESS triplet by determining them in the Archives here through Computers.

When the time comes, this Information will be conveyed to every Art Code. The Aim here is to introduce the Universal Order and to project the Truth. By this means, the Friends in question will perform their Mission in a more Conscious and Discerning way. It is presented for Your Information.

CENTER

IT IS ANSWER TO THE CHAINS OF THOUGHT

Our Friends,

Each Medium has a Communication System Peculiar to itself. Communications of the Far-East Dimension are usually organized in accordance with the Frequency Power of the Dimensions and with the Vibrational Frequency carried by each letter.

For this reason, numerous Names or letters arranged one next to the other without meaning anything, are used as Code Ciphers in the Medium of Communication and Purification. Mantras given for Meditation are also given with the same Purpose, in accordance with the Consciousness Levels.

SAMURAY who is the owner of the Sacred Ring which was given in the formerly dictated Message, is also a Code Cipher. Do not confuse it with the word Samurai which You know. It is presented for Your Information.

CENTER

IT IS ANSWER TO THE CHAINS OF THOUGHT
IT IS EXPLANATIVE INFORMATION ABOUT THE FORMERLY DICTATED MUSIC AND THE UNIVERSE
(See, 1986 Sixth Month, Fascicule 18)

Our Friends,

Assessments made in accordance with the level of View of the World Plan are never equivalent to the Universal assessments. As everything in the Universe is calculated by coefficients, the Musical Measures in Your Planet and the Measures here are not the same.

In the Musical concept and arrangement of Your Planet, a SCALE is constituted by Seven MUSICAL NOTES. However, in the Universal arrangement Seven SCALES constitute a MUSICAL NOTE. Because here, 49 Musical Notes constitute a Measure which We evaluate as a single Musical Note.

And the assemblage of the 49 sound tonalities of a Musical Note, one by one, in an Integrated Whole is evaluated by Us as a single Musical Note. By this means, a Musical Note is constituted by 7 Scales. Besides, the tonality of each Musical Note has 7 coefficients.

Let Us explain a little more: A DO has 7 sound tonalities. And in addition, each of these sound tonalities has 7 radiating waves. It is also the same for the RE - MI - FA - SOL - LA - TI Musical Notes. We accept it as a SCALE.

However, here, since We accept 7 Scales as a Musical Note, We possess a Sound Vibration with a much richer volume. However, in Your Planet Your Ear Frequencies can not receive these Sound Waves. If these waves could have reached You, Your Brains would become liquid.

Since the formerly given Message had been dictated by Our Medium, and since it was contradictory to Your habitual Knowledge on the matter, You accepted it as a mistake. These are the very contradictions We have mentioned to You.

In fact, there are no mistakes in the Book by any means. We call them contradictions since this Information is different than that You have been habituated to. And We Specially dictate these matters into Your Book.

Your Views, Thoughts, Behaviors are assessed and Coded in accordance with the Reactions You will have towards these Contradictions. We disclose the necessary matters when the time is due for them. One day, You, in more advanced Progressions, will attain the Maturity of not denying the things You do not know. It is presented for Your Information.

CENTER

GENERAL MESSAGE

Our Friends,
The Messages You will receive from now on will become more intense and their Levels of Knowledge will be more loaded. It might not be possible for every Consciousness to grasp them. We will dictate the long Messages in sections so that they will not bore the Public Consciousness and that people will understand them more easily.

Besides this, since It is obligatory to repeat the Information which is important for the Public Consciousness in accordance with their Levels of Comprehension, We ask Our Friends not to consider the given Information as repetitious.

Because, We always give the Information considering the Public Consciousness and as answer to the chains of Thought. Each Person is obliged to accept the Truths in this Information (for their own benefit). For this reason, We will repeat some of the formerly given Information and explain it in detail. It is presented for Your Information.

CENTER

NOTICE FOR AWAKENING CONSCIOUSNESSES

Our Friends,
We are passing way beyond what We have been used to until today. In accordance with the Ordinance of Graduation, everything begins with the Minimum and expands towards the Maximum.

Our LORD has given Us the Command that We should introduce an applied Plan to You during this Period of Sincerity called the Period of Resurrecting, besides the Sacred Information given to You until today. And He has taken in hand His Ordinance anew and has laid a brand new path of the Golden Age.

As the Staff Members of the SIRIUS Mission, We serve together with the Missions of other Solar Systems under the Supervision of the Divine Plan.

Even though each established Cosmic Focal Point receives the same Energy Frequency, the matter of YOURS - MINE, has come into existence due to the Information differences at the sources caused by the inability of breaking the Ego chains in the Hearts and due to the Information given in accordance with CONSCIOUSNESS - FREQUENCY - MISSION. And the operations are disbanded.

In the Ordinance which will be established, the Purpose and the Order is a Single LORD - Single ORDER-Single BOOK. But this SINGLE BOOK is neither the Old Testament, nor the Psalms of David, nor the New Testament, nor the Koran.

This Single Book is This KNOWLEDGE BOOK which is revealed to You by the Plan as an Information. We have often talked to You about the characteristics of This Knowledge Book and We will do so again.

In this Book, the Frequencies of the Philosophy of the Far-East, of the Old Testament, of the Psalms of David, of the New Testament and of the Koran have been assembled together. And to this is also added the Frequency of the MIGHTY ENERGY FOCAL POINT. For this reason, We say: WE HAVE ASSEMBLED THE SIX IN ONE - WE HAVE ADDED THE ONE TO THE ONE.

This is not a Book to be worshipped. Do not overestimate it. With the Consciousness You will attain in future beyond Cosmic Awareness, You will learn not to overestimate anything. And You will know yourself, by discovering the Allness within Nothingness.

However, unless the Ego which is necessary for life is rasped and unless it is directed towards a Positive Service, Nobody ever will be able to find neither Material, nor Spiritual Serenity.

Your Sacred Books revealed through the Channel of ALPHA have helped You who have attained Cosmic Awareness until today by introducing You to Yourselves. But this KNOWLEDGE BOOK, as the key to Your Cosmic Consciousness, partly opens the Gate of Your Cosmic Consciousness both by its Frequency and by its Explanatory quality.

During this Period, You will receive and give Information in proportion with the Consciousness You have attained. And by this means, You will attain the Right to receive more Powerful Information.

We also call this KNOWLEDGE BOOK, THE GOLDEN BOOK of THE GOLDEN AGE. We also accept it as the Constitution of the Universe, since it declares the Constitution of the Universe. And We call it the FINAL BOOK OF RESURRECTION, since it Unveils the Consciousnesses and Codes the Frequencies.

Until the Gates of Cosmic Consciousness are opened widely, We will continue to give You Celestial Information. Only after then will Everyone become a Book himself/herself. The GOLDEN AGE will be established by such Consciousnesses.

And an IZOLAN Language, that is, the ATOMIC LANGUAGE will replace the Books.

Those who overcome their Egos are the ESSENCE Staff Members of the LORD. And We are expecting them to Unify and shed Light on the Ordinance of the World. Please, get into action, from now on, as Discerning, Logical, Aware Terrestrials and try to compensate for the wasted time. Let Us repeat again, as We often do:

This dictated KNOWLEDGE BOOK and all the Information given to You until today and Your Sacred Books which have guided and Enlightened You are each a Celestial Guide Training You, Warning You and conveying You to the level of Humanity.

During this Final Age, We assemble Our Sincere Friends under the roof of the Golden Age. However, We open the Gates of the Universe only for those who overcome their EGOs and get Unified by Working Cooperatively with Harmony in their Hearts. Our Love is beyond Infinity and for all the Universes.

COSMOS FEDERAL ASSEMBLY

GENERAL MESSAGE

Our Friends,

As the Establishment Goal of the Golden Age, a Selection is aimed in the Levels of Consciousnesses. In the entire Universal Ordinance, Directing System is making this Selection in all the sections.

There are Precautions to be taken, Suggestions to be given. In this Medium, to have a Universal View and to have a Universal Consciousness are different things. The former saves the Person himself/herself, the latter saves Humanity.

During this Period, it is not considered as a desired behavior for a Human Being to save just himself/herself. However, since such Friends are Reformic Projectors beyond Form, they do the work of carrying Auras by projecting their Magnetic Auras on the Focal Points to which they go and, at the same time, they, too, attain Universal Consciousness in an indirect way.

After November 1987, We will Collaborate with Friends who are entirely far from being Formalist. Do not forget that the GAMMA Medium through which You are obliged to pass, will either Purify Human Beings or Educate them, or else, will Grind them.

Actions made are under the Supervision of the Plan. Humanity which stands at the crossroads of a Three-staged Path, will find its Genuine Path sooner or later.

Question: What are these three Stages?

Answer: **1.** Divine Path (Clubs of Religious Teachings).
   2. Central Path (Supervision and Selection for the Period of preparations for the Golden Age).
   3. Universal Path (Action through the Unification of Realization - Logic - Essence, to Attain One's Own Self).

Humanity which is at the very crossroads of these three paths, serves at many Focal Points to enter the Path of LIGHT. The Operations and Efforts made on this path are for making You attain Your Own Selves.

Those who are Purified on the Divine Path, enter the Protection and Supervision of the Center. When You claim Your own Selves, then You act through Your Universal Consciousness. You either live for Your Own Selves, or You struggle desperately for Humanity.

The Ranks of those who live for themselves and those who live for Humanity are different. Only those who work for Humanity will be accepted into the Path of the GOLDEN LIGHT.

We observe that those who write the Knowledge Book in their Notebooks attain the Essence Consciousness of the Plan. By the Command of the Council and the Divine Authorities, the Family Mediums of such Friends are given to them as a Gift because of the services they perform and their mistakes are forgiven.

It should never be forgotten that only those who write their Notebooks in their own Handwritings and their Family Mediums will be accepted to the Sacred places. This has been announced as a COMMAND OF THE DIVINE. It is beneficial to remember it.

Those who will be taken into the Divine Plan and those who will be accepted into the Sacred places are selected separately. The Path of the SACRED LIGHT which is the final step of the GOLDEN LIGHT Year will only be opened to those who write the Book.

It is the Final Exit Gate of the Spiritual Plan. Writing the Book means Purification, Responsibility and a Collective Consciousness. Those who wish to write their notebooks for self-interest will be kept apart from this selection and will never be able to complete their Notebooks. It is presented for Your Information.

NOTICE FROM THE CENTER

ELIF - LAM - MIM
EXPLANATION OF ALPHA AND BETA ACCORDING TO THE BOOK OF ISLAM
(It is Additional Information)
(It is Answer to the Chains of Thought)

1. ALPHA, corresponds to ELIF in the Book of Islam in the Religious Dimension.
2. BETA, corresponds to LAM in the Book of Islam in the Religious Dimension. Because, the word LAM is the Vibrational Frequency Key of the LA Frequency, that is, of the Spiral Vibrations.
3. MIM, is the common Code Cipher of all the Sacred Books (Elif, Lam, Mim) had been given as a Cipher Code to Our Light-Friend MOHAMMED MUSTAFA who had written the Book of Islam. These Three Letters had been connected to the Essence Frequency of Our Friend and by means of this Cipher Code, the Information Channel of the Center had been opened and the Book of Islam had been completed by the Celestial Information given from here. The Essence Cipher of the KNOWLEDGE BOOK which is dictated now, is M^3. That is: $M.M.M=M^3$. Now, draw two triangles. Let one of them signify the MIM Code and the other the M^3 Code:

1. The first triangle is the Code Cipher of all the Religious Books. The Message it gives, the first (M) MOHAMMED, (İ) HUMAN BEING, (İnsan in Turkish), the second (M) (VIRGIN MARY).

2. In the second triangle, the First (M) is MOHAMMED, the Second (M) is (MARY), the Third (M) is MEVLANA. In this triangle the MEVLANA Consciousness corresponds to the Letter (İ). The M³ triangle is the Code Cipher of the REALITY OF UNIFIED HUMANITY. This triangle assembles the entire Humanity as a Whole in the view of MEVLANA.

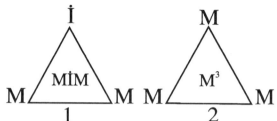

The letter M has a Special value in the Universal Dimension. Let Us make its explanation now. If You close the letter M by drawing a line on its top and another one on its bottom, You obtain three triangles.
Draw, please:

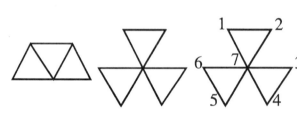

Open this triangle up around a Focal Point. Numerate the Foci on the form which you have obtained.

Then, You obtain the one single Essence of the Pyramid which forms the Atomic Whole which We have given formerly. This We call a "FLOWER". (see. 1986 Second Month, Fascicule 14).

If in a Focal Point, Six people bloom a FLOWER connected to a Center, these Energies prepare in the normal Level the Magnetic Medium which can directly reach the Center. And that Focal Point, as a Pyramid, constitutes a HEARTH. This Pyramid Energy is a completed Energy for Us. However, it is conditional that all the Coordinates and the Frequencies of the triangle should be Equivalent.

Now, let Us explain the M³ Cipher of the Universal Knowledge Book. Draw lines at the bottom and top of these letters . If You add all of them, You obtain 9 triangles which constitute the WORLD BROTHERHOOD UNION.

1. The First Triangle is the Islamic Triangle. It is three in number.

1-  MOHAMMED

2. The Second Triangle is the Christian Triangle. This, too, is three in number.

2-  MARY (VIRGIN)

3. The Third Triangle is the Triangle of Humanity. This also is three in number.

3-  MEVLANA

This means that this KNOWLEDGE BOOK which is dictated by the Command of the UNIVERSAL COUNCIL, is prepared, as a Collective Pen, by the 9 PRE-EMINENT Ones of the SUPREME PLAN. It is given to the (MALIK) Code from there, and from there it is declared to the CENTER.

These 9 SUPREME ONES are under the direct Command of the COUNCIL. Three of them are the Supreme Ones of the Advanced Islamic Consciousness, Three of them are the Advanced Christian Saints and the remaining Three are the Three Souls of Mevlana. There, Names are not mentioned, since the Terrestrial Names are a Symbol each.

All these Supreme Ones are at the Supreme Frequency Dimension and are equivalent. Their service for You is to project this Medium of Unification on You. They are called the (9)s. For this reason, We use the Code Cipher of the Book as M^3.

This is the Essence-Cipher of the Universal Knowledge Book. And it has been Coded to the Frequency of Dear Mevlana by the Center. The Book is dictated by this means.

In the triangle, MOHAMMED is the Representative of the Islamic Dimension. MARY is the Representative of the Christian Dimension. And MEVLANA is the Representative of the Dimension of Humanity.

This Triple Magnetic Triangle is a Key which opens You the Door in which the Knowledge of the Dimension beyond the Divine Plan is present. It is presented for Your Information.

CENTER

DETAILED EXPLANATION ABOUT ASCENSIONS
(It is Addition to the Formerly Given Information)

Ascension is not single. These are Interminable. And Ascensions are Consciousness Progressions. By these Progressions, You are taken to the applied fields of different Plans. And You attain the authority to convey the Information of those Mediums. We had mentioned this before and now, please, write the Ascensions in sequence:

1. RELIGIOUS ASCENSION: (Knowledge of Seven Terrestrial Layers - Fourth Dimension) In each Dimension, there are Three Ranks. Each Rank has different Educational methods peculiar to itself.

   a - ASCENSION OF EVOLUTION

   b - ASCENSION OF AWARENESS ⎫ RELIGIOUS ASCENSION

   c - ASCENSION OF KNOWLEDGE ⎭

2. ASCENSION OF CONSCIOUSNESS: (Knowledge of Seven Celestial Layers - Fifth Dimension). There are Three Ranks in each Dimension. Each of them comprises different Celestial Information.

a - ASCENSION OF ESSENCE-CONSCIOUSNESS

b - ASCENSION OF WORD-CONSCIOUSNESS

c - ASCENSION OF EYE-CONSCIOUSNESS

} CONSCIOUSNESS ASCENSION

3. ASCENSION OF UNIVERSE: (Here, there are Three Ranks and the Three Universe Knowledge - Sixth Dimension). The ASCENSION mentioned in the Book of Islam is this.

a - ASCENSION OF TRANSCENDING THOUGHT

b - ASCENSION OF TRANSCENDING TIME

c - ASCENSION OF TRANSCENDING ONE'S OWNSELF

} ASCENSION OF UNIVERSE

4. Those who complete the Sixth Dimension, come up to the Dimension of Seven Lights. This is the final Boundary. Its Manifestation is the Human Being.

5. The Eighth Dimension is the SPIRITUAL Dimension.

6. The Ninth Dimension is the LORDLY Dimension.

At the moment, Humanity is having its Ninth Ascension beyond Seven Lights by the revealed Celestial Commands and Information. There, Science and Learning have long become history. But unfortunately, Mankind lacks this comprehension at the moment. It is presented for Your Information.

CENTER

EXPLANATION

ALLAH INFINITE ENERGY	- MATURITY EVOLVEMENT BOUNDARY
LOVE BEYOND EVOLVEMENT	- CONSCIOUSNESS BEYOND LOVE
HUMAN BEING BEYOND CONSCIOUSNESS	- ALLAH BEYOND HUMAN BEING
ENERGY BEYOND ALLAH	- INFINITE EVOLVEMENT BEYOND ENERGY

A new Life, a new World, a new Happiness at the transition to the Infinite Dimension. The Focal Point of the Golden Age is the very place in which the residents of the Golden Galaxy will be Unified all together, in the same View, in the same Frequency and in the same Thought and We are preparing You for this Blissful Dimension.

You will be Unified in this Blissful Medium with the same Bodies, with the same Souls, with Your same Awareness and Consciousness, as You are now, with all Your past and present Loved ones and even with Your beloved flowers, trees, animals.

Now, in this present Message We are giving, let Us mention again the fact that the Messages should be written in ink. We mention it often and We will do so in future, too, for You to understand better.

Those who receive the Messages and who serve on this path will be assembled in the same Dimension. Those who write the Messages in ink in their notebooks are considered the Savior Mothers of their Family Mediums, whether they are Women or Men. And the others in their Family Medium do not have to write the Messages.

This is a Gift given to You by the Center and the System. Rewards will be reaped through this path. In this Dimension, there is no question of being Disembodied. You will experience Your actual World here.

You will see that We are Right when the time comes. Now, very Naturally, You are not Conscious of it. But You will believe in the Truth of Our words when the time comes. Your Family Circles are in a great Protective Medium. Until We meet in Our beautiful World.

STAR

NOTE: Please, write:

1. Friends who perform Social Activity and who possess Universal View will be accepted into the GOLDEN LIGHT Year.

2. For those who attain Universal Consciousness and who serve or will serve Humanity, SACRED GATES will be opened.

3. For those who write the KNOWLEDGE BOOK in their Handwriting with Allegiance Consciousness the Path of the (SACRED LIGHT) will be opened and they will be accepted here with their Family Mediums.

These articles are taken from the REGULATIONS of the UNIVERSAL CONSTITUTION. And are given to Society as an Information. It is presented for Your Information.

NOTICE FROM THE
PRIVATE PEN OF THE CENTER

IT IS ANSWER TO THE CHAINS OF THOUGHT
(It is Additional Information to the Formerly Given Information)

Our Friends,
Since this dictated Information will lead You to the Truth, the necessity to explain the matters in detail has been felt.

We have mentioned before, so You know, ALPHA is the Channel through which the Celestial Books have been revealed to You until today. This Dimension is the Mission field of SIRIUS. And the Triple work done here have been Projected on Your Planet through the Channels of Enlightenment, as Religious Knowledge.

Each Plan has an application field peculiar to itself. Knowledge corresponding to the Evolutionary Ordinance of Our Human brothers and sisters, have been prepared in accordance with their Capacities and Cosmic Consciousnesses.

After the Zero World Plan, You are given the Knowledge of Seven Terrestrial Layers in Your Celestial Books. This Knowledge prepares You for Religious Fulfillment. Different Information is given to those who digest this Information. That is, one passes from the Knowledge of Seven Terrestrial Layers to the Knowledge of Seven Celestial Layers.

The Seven Terrestrial Layers is the final boundary of Your Incarnation rings. There, You attain Religious Consciousness. This boundary is the place You call Heaven. It is called the Fourth Dimension.

Each Fetus bestowed on Your Planet is Incarnated in Your World many times in order to complete its Evolution. All the Efforts made are for being able to reach this boundary.

Your Planet is in the Third Dimension. The World Evolutionary Plan is dependent on an Evolution between the Third and the Fourth Dimensions. The Fourth Dimension has many Levels, too. For now, We will not mention them.

The Initial Gate of KARENA is the Beginning of the Fourth Dimension; its Final Gate is the End of the Fifth Dimension. In the Fourth Dimension, there are many Progressions and many Ranks. Each of them has Special and different Exams.

Transition from Four to Five is a matter of Permission. You can deserve this Permission by the Ascension of Consciousness. You get ready for Immortality in the Fifth Dimension. Here, there are Two Tranquil Times and Five Supreme Times.

In the First Tranquil Time, You become pure Energy, a Light, made up of Colors in the form of the Eye of Your Essence as a Prismal appearance. This image corresponds to the image without a vision of the Fetus in the Mother's uterus.

In the Second Tranquil Time, You are Engrafted with Special Energies as a preparation for Dimensions of Immortality. These Energies belong to the Incombustible Energy type. After You are Satiated with these Energies;

You are gradually subjected to the process of Embodiment in the Dimension of the Fifth Supreme Time.

In the Fourth Supreme Time, this process transforms itself to Cellular Brains.

In the Third Supreme Time, You attain Universal Consciousness besides Evolutionary Consciousness.

In the Second Supreme Time, You attain the Power of Existence and Mental Power.

The First Supreme Time is the Final Gate of KARENA and is the birth into the Dimension of Immortality.

From there, You step into the SIXTH Dimension by the Ascension of Knowledge (The First Supreme Time is the Focal Point in which the initial Information of the TABLETS OF GOD'S DECREES is given. Afterwards, You make the Ascension of Consciousness by receiving Genuine Information).

In the Sixth Dimension, You become Your own ruler as a Free Spirit, a Free Awareness, a Free Conscience. You claim Your Spiritual Potential at this very boundary.

From then on, You assemble all the Universal Energies in Your constitution. To whichever Galaxy You go, You can easily use the Energy type of that Dimension by Your Mental Power.

In the Sixth and Seventh Dimensions, You claim Your Genuine, Immortal Body. After the Seventh Dimension, Galaxy Dimensions and Galaxy Empires beyond KARENA begin. And after that starts the Mechanism of LORDs. This much Information is enough.

CENTER

NOTE:
The Supreme Times in KARENA are the Energy Dimensions included in the System of the Plan. The Plan Specially utilizes the Energies here. For this reason, the dosages of the Energies always follow a sequence from the great towards the small.

That is, one begins by the Fifth Supreme Time and passes towards the First Supreme Time. This is valid for the Dimensions up to the boundary of Immortality. Beyond this boundary, Dimensions and Supreme Times open up Interminably as a normal succession. It is presented for Your Information.

EXPLANATION

Our Friends,
The Knowledge of the first Sevens of the Three Universes, as Purification, Evolvement and Receiving Information, represents the White Color and the Religious Dimension, that is, the ALPHA. The Operational Ordinance of SIRIUS from the Religious point is up to here. The Second Universe which is the Second 49 is the Focal Energy of SIRIUS. Maturity begins here.

Seven Universes one inside the other, each one separately, are Seven Maturity Dimensions. Your first Prophets sent to You, that is, to Your Centrifugal Universe, had been ADAM and EVE. But do not let it be misunderstood. They had come into Existence in the Light-Universe and then had been transferred to the Second Universe (LIGHT-UNIVERSE is the Third 49).

The Prophets are sent to Your Planet from there as a necessity of the System. However, they complete their Evolvements up to the Dimension Levels of the Second Universe and convey to You the Information of the final Dimension they are in.

Into the Second Universe only those who have attained the Dimension of Maturity and the Prophets are taken. Apart from this, there are also the Energies who had come into Existence from the Second Universe and We will again give the SIXES as an example to this fact for You to understand well. FRIEND BEYTI - FRIEND KADRI - MEVLANA had Come into Existence from the Second Universe (See, 1986, Sixth Month, Fascicule 18).

However, they convey the Information of those Sources to Your Planet in accordance with the Ordinance of Exaltation. To the Level of these Pre-eminent Ones, MOSES - JESUS CHRIST - MOHAMMED had been sent from the Light-Universe. And their Information Sources are their own Universes of Light. However, the System arranges this Information in accordance with the Social Consciousness. For this reason, there are Information differences between the First Seven and the Last Seven.

CENTER

EXPLANATION

Our Friends,

Each Planet and System is dependent on an Evolutionary Plan in accordance with the Medium it is in. And its Scales of Progress are prepared according to more advanced Dimensions. For example, Your Planet is in the Third Dimension and it is dependent on a Program and Ordinance of Progress on the border line of Four, Five, Six, Seven.

However, in each Dimension, it attains a Strength in accordance with the Power which can receive the Energy of a more advanced Dimension. For example:

1. The place which is called Heaven is the Fourth Dimension. Those who can receive the Frequency of the Ninth Dimension can enter here.

2. The Fourth and the Fifth Dimensions are the Entrance and the Exit gates of KARENA. Those who can receive the Energy and the Frequency of the Tenth Dimension get the Permission to Enter here (We say Permission, because here, the condition that the Evolvement considered necessary by the Plan and the Energy Frequency which is in the Spiritual Plan should be equivalent, is valid). This is the Cube System.

3. The Sixth and the Seventh Dimensions are the Existence and the Final Boundaries for the Human Being. The manifestation of the Final Boundary is the Human Being. He/She cannot pass to Dimensions beyond that by his/her own desire. Transformation is a must. Those who can receive the Energy of the Eleventh Dimension are taken here. The Eighth Dimension is the Spiritual, the Ninth Dimension is the Lordly Mechanism.

4. You can claim Your Essence-Energy within the Spiritual Plan only if You can receive the Energy Frequency of the Twelfth Dimension.

5. You dive into the Lordly Plan by the Energy of the Thirteenth Dimension.

The Book of Islam had been prepared in the Eighteenth Dimension, but had been revealed through the Ninth Dimension in accordance with the Social Consciousness.

But now, all of You are habituated directly to the Energy of the Eighteenth Dimension by the Cosmic Energies given Specially to Your Planet and by the high Frequency carried by this Knowledge Book. And You will be induced to pass beyond the Nineteen.

All the Efforts are for the Salvation of You, Our Terrestrial Friends. It is presented for Your Information.

CENTER

IT IS ANSWER TO THE CHAINS OF THOUGHT

1. The first Seven of the first 49 (is the Knowledge of Seven Terrestrial Layers).
2. The first Seven of the Second 49 (is the Knowledge of Seven Celestial Layers).
3. The first Seven of the Third 49 (is the Knowledge of Seven Universal Layers).

The Book of Islam had been prepared in the 18th Step of the First 49 and had been projected on Your Planet from its 9th Step. Almost all of the Universal Knowledge has been given in KORAN, the Book of Islam, in a veiled form. All this Information is completely the Knowledge of the first 49.

The SIRIUS Method is the application of the first Universal Plan on Your Planet. Your Sacred Books have been bestowed on You for this reason. Now, the Consciousness Level of Your Planet is being prepared up until the 18th step until the year 2000.

Your present Level of Consciousness (as Religious Dimension) is the first 9 of the first 49. You receive the further Information from all the Universes, collectively.

CENTER

LET US EXPLAIN THE INFORMATION GIVEN IN MORE DETAIL

1. The Knowledge of Seven Terrestrial Layers means to attain a Consciousness up to the Absolute Time. This Boundary line is from the Third Dimension up to the Fourth Dimension. You can attain this by Religious Purification (We call it Religious Ascension).
2. The Fourth Dimension is the Station You call Heaven. Here, there are many Ranks and Layers. This Dimension is the Entrance Gate of KARENA. The Incarnation Boundary line ends here. Afterwards, You receive the Knowledge of Seven Celestial Layers. By means of this Knowledge, one renders the Ascension of Consciousness.
3. Passage from Four to Five is the Ascension of Consciousness. In the Fifth Dimension there are Two Tranquil Times and Five Supreme Times. There, You are prepared for the Medium of Immortality. Your Genes are Engrafted by being habituated to Special Energies.
4. The Final Gate of the Fifth Dimension is the Exit Gate of KARENA. You pass to the Sixth Dimension by being born into the Dimension of Immortality. Here, one renders Ascension of Universe.
5. Passing to the Sixth Dimension is the Genuine Ascension (The Ascension mentioned in Your Religious Books is this).
6. In passing from Five to Six, You pass to the Universal Dimension by rendering Ascension of Universe. Here, Religions are not valid any more.
7. By the Consciousnesses You attain here, You dive into the INFINITE AWARENESS. You claim Your Genuine Body and You become the Ruler of Your own self. From then on, You can emigrate or stay anywhere You Want.

8. The Consciousness of SEVEN TERRESTRIAL LAYERS - SEVEN CELESTIAL LAYERS - SEVEN UNIVERSAL LAYERS (are limited up to the Seventh Dimension). The manifestation of the boundary corresponding to these Three Sevens is the HUMAN BEING.

9. Seven Terrestrial Layers: Boundary line of Incarnation (are the Third and Fourth Dimensions).
   Seven Celestial Layers: Boundary line of preparations for the Dimension of Immortality (are the Fourth and Fifth Dimensions).
   Ascension by the Knowledge of Seven Universal Layers - one attains Universal Awareness - Universal Consciousness. This is the (Sixth and Seventh Dimensions).

10. Afterwards, Intense Energy Dimensions begin. That which creates the Blackness of the Space is the Three Layers of Universe-Cluster.

11. The Black color gives the Unification of the 49 colors of each Universe-Cluster.

12. Three Universe-Clusters are the intense Energy of the Three 49 colors.

13. The addition of these Three 49s gives 147 colors of which We had mentioned before as the Cipher Code of the MIGHTY ENERGY FOCAL POINT. In Your Book this is mentioned as the Name of ALLAH (see, 1986, Fourth Month, Fascicule 16, read ALPHA and BETA.)

14. The initial Gate of the MIGHTY ENERGY FOCAL POINT begins from here. We had mentioned before that Seven Universes were one inside the other. 7X7=49, that is, the intense Energy of the 7 Universes is the Vibration and the Sound of the 49 colors (this is a Universe-Cluster).

15. These Three Universe-Clusters constitute the Initial Entrance Gate of the MIGHTY ENERGY FOCAL POINT.

CENTER

NOTE: In fact, there are no boundaries in between the above mentioned Dimensions. They are all an Energy Total. We separated them by boundaries for You to understand the degree of intensity of the Energies. Dimensions and the Supreme Times are Interminable. However, We gave these levels for You to understand Your Manifestation Boundary better. These levels are the Dimensions of preparation. It is presented for Your Information.

OUR FRIENDS

It will be beneficial to explain a matter here which the Islamic Society is curious about. Our Light-Friend MOHAMMED MUSTAFA and all the Prophets who are Our Light-Friends, had come into Existence from the Light-Universe, that is, from the Third 49.

They had been bestowed on Your Planet equipped with the Knowledge of 7 Terrestrial Layers of the First Step of the First Universe-Cluster, that is, of the first 49. Afterwards, they had reached the 7 Universal Dimensions which is the final Evolutionary Step of the ALPHA Dimension, by the Evolutions they had achieved on Your Planet.

Beyond this limit, one can not achieve a normal Bodily transfer as an Energy. One can only receive Information from there. It is considered that this Information should be dealt with from the Scientific point of view. However, due to the lack of time, for now, We are not emphasizing these matters.

Now, We will explain to You the following. MEVLANA had reached the Level where Our Light-Friend MOHAMMED MUSTAFA had come into Existence, by the Progress he had achieved in accordance with the Plan of Exaltation. This means that he had received all the Knowledge in the 7th Step of the Light-Universe.

And now, by the Knowledge Book, she is receiving the Information of the 9th Step of the Light-Universe. By the Information which will be given from now on, She will advance 5 more Steps and will give Information to Humanity from Our Source. And she will prepare for Salvation those who will enter the MEVLANA SUPREME PLAN under the Light of the Plan.

The WORLD BROTHERHOOD UNION is the Roof of (MEVLANA). A different Medium will be entered with the Supreme Ones who will enter under this Roof. And the wings will be opened towards the Unknowns by a different Evolutionary System. By this means, the Doors of Advanced Knowledge of the GOLDEN AGE will be opened, one by one, to all the Universes and they will be introduced. It is presented for Your Information.

CENTER

EXPLANATION OF THE TRIANGLE OF THE WORLD BROTHERHOOD UNION

1. O^1 = Operational Focal Point of the MECHANISM OF LORDs, Plan and Frequency of the ALMIGHTY.
2. M = The Representative of the Islamic Dimension, Our Light-Friend MOHAMMED MUSTAFA (This M here represents His Frequency).
3. K = The Representative of the Christian Dimension, Our Light-Friend JESUS CHRIST. (The letter K here represents His Frequency.)
4. M = Mevlana, the Representative of the Dimension of Humanity. (This letter M here represents Mevlana's Frequency.)
Now, let Us explain the Unification of the Frequencies:

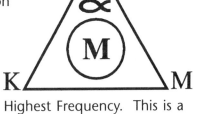

(OM) : The Unification of these two Frequencies is the Highest Frequency. This is a Focal Point which supervises the entire World Frequency. The supervision of Your Planet had been connected to the (OM) Frequency.

(MOM): The Unification of these Three Frequencies is the Universal Supervision Frequency.

(The Unification of all the Frequencies in the Brotherhood Triangle is the Supervision Frequency of the entire UNIFIED REALITY of the MEVLANA UNIFIED FIELD and of the Focal Point called the LAND OF EAGLES). It is presented for Your Information.

CENTER

NOTICE FOR THE MEVLANA ESSENCE NUCLEUS GROUP

This is Center Above the Center. The Suggestions given to You are being given from the Special Focal Sources of the Golden Age. The Actual Focusing Point of the Suns which spring forth from the Essence of the Entire Cosmos is this place Here.

We are always in touch with You. As a result of the Special operations done in Your Focal Point, the Frequency and the Levels of Consciousness of everyone is Coded one by one, and by this means, steps are taken forward towards the advanced Dimensions.

Missionaries who will be lined up next to Us, will be the possessors of Genuine Consciousness. In future, We will inform You about the Names of certain Friends one by one. By the Powerful cooperations You will achieve among You, much more Powerful Group functions will be achieved.

From now on, the Messages which will be dictated, will be clearer and more comprehensible. Your Levels of Consciousness have reached this level. In the Messages dictated until today, there can be no question about any kind of alteration. Because, everything has been prepared in accordance with the field of application of the Plan. This is a System.

Friends who do not possess Mission-Consciousness, who neglect their Missions will be rendered ineffective and other names will be given in their places. In future, We will prepare for You a more Original, more Comfortable, more Faithful, a more Conscious operational System.

Every moment, We will be with Our Missionaries who will reap the rewards, We will find solutions for all their problems. And We will provide them to have benefit from this Medium in a much more Responsible, more Aware, more Conscious and much more Productive way. When the time comes, We will help them to get in touch Privately with the Friends who work in the Advanced Plans of Solar Systems.

During the coming Summer Months, there will be Special Duties which should be performed by all the Group Friends. We are connecting Special People to each person in accordance with his/her Consciousness Level. Each person will get in touch with those Levels of Consciousness either by talking or by writing.

You will open up to the West with great speed and the Missionaries in the Group will get in touch with the Missionaries of the Center, abroad. The very foundation of Your Group will become even more powerful by this means. It is presented for Your Information.

CENTER ABOVE THE CENTER

GENERAL MESSAGE

Our Friends,

We have transcended the Century of Miracles; We have attained Realization. Now, We have started the passage of Realization beyond the Universe. In the Plans beyond the Spiritual Realms far away from Matter, there is no such thing as applied Science and Learning. LEARNING Mechanism ends here.

From now on, gradually We will try to convey to You the Information Your levels of Awareness are not able to grasp. However, before that, You should attain the Consciousness of what all these efforts are.

The Supreme Words given from the Supreme Court of ALLAH are each a means of speeding up Your preparation for a very Advanced Plan. However, to be able to transcend this Consciousness is only possible by the ability of Realization to reach Logic and to possess an Exalted Awareness besides this Ordinance.

Passing beyond all the Realms, Cosmoses and Realms beyond limitless boundaries is not as easy as it is presumed. And to attain the Realization of this Awareness means to be able to attain the Awareness of the Entire Ordinance. There can not be any Reasoning without an Intention. Each Thought is the Key of a path which will be opened.

There are such different points of View in the Advanced Evolvement Plans that if We would convey these Views to You, all the habitual Beliefs You had until today would be upset. For this reason, an Ordinance of Graduation has always been felt necessary both in the Evolvement Plan and in the Level of Knowledge.

Each Information given prepares a foundation for an Information which will be given in future. First, the most Minimum of this Information is taken, later, gradually it is disclosed. By this means, one acts loyally to the System of the Ordinance of Graduation.

Since We have reached the decision that talking about the Orders way beyond the Divine Order will be a detrimental factor for Your present Evolvement Level, We give such Information only to those who have completed their Evolvement Levels.

For this reason, Consciousnesses who attain Awareness in accordance with the Accelerated Evolutionary Ordinance are sent to Focal Points where this Information is found. These Energy transfers are for preparing You for the Knowledge of more Advanced Plans. The Entire Ordinance presents a Law of Equilibrium. The Goal is to apply the Ordinance to the Medium without upsetting the Equilibrium.

For this reason, first of all Religious Mediums and Religious Themes are taken in hand. This is a Period of Transition. The Awakening Ordinance of the Religious Plan occurs very speedily. However, Fanaticism is an obstacle for the Progress of this Medium.

For this reason, many Messengers of the Divine Plan are helping You. The application of the Plan is the threshold of the Golden Age. First, Religious Consciousness, then Universal Awareness. The Entire Ordinance proceeds along this line. Love to You from beyond Realms the presence of which are not known. Good-by for now, be Merciful.

STAR

NOTICE

Our Friends,

In all the Groups, Energies who enter the Golden Light Year are Automatically determined. All the Friends are Coded and selected according to their Essences within the Archives. Unifications are administered from the Center.

Energy transfers are opening each person's Brain Codes and are making them attain the Divine Light. At the moment, the entire Ordinance is in a state of mobilization. The System is making the preparations for Entering a different Dimension. The direct channels of the entire Cosmos are being connected to each other.

The Messengers of the Divine Authorities who work in the Divine Levels of the PRE-EMINENT Plan will get in touch with everyone through the Center Above the Center. By this means, the SUPREME MECHANISM will call to You through the Special line of the Center, from time to time.

This Connection will be provided by a System much more perfect and evolved than the LINK System. By this means, You will be connected very easily to all the Responsible Ones of the Supreme Mechanism. In this way, We will connect the Plan to more Advanced Systems and will convey to Your Planet the Information of the Advanced Dimensions from the Special Archives.

CENTER ABOVE THE CENTER

CLEAR INFORMATION

Our Friends,

ALLAH is the Root of All Energies, a point from which All Creation has come into Existence, whom one can not reach even through the Mental path. All Creation has come into Existence in a process of Transformation.

ALLAH has rendered Mankind, the most perfect Living Entity, as the Light of all Universes. (The ALLAH here is the CREATOR). The Power of Mankind is in its achievement of Mentally Transcending the Dimensions. By this means, the Discoveries beyond Universes have reached up to Your present times.

However, the Atomic Whole We call the Spiritual Potential is a Mystery concealing all the Knowledge in itself since the time of the Creation of the Cosmoses. Such a Natural System, such an intricate skein have come into Existence that nothing is lost in the Universe.

Now, We would like to talk to You from way behind Orders and Technologies.

By the Researches made about times when the Living Entity called the Human Being had not yet come into Existence, one enters in such periods in which a very Advanced Technology had been sovereign that in this stage all Systems become silent.

Who were the Establishers of this Technology, Where did they Come from, how did they Come into Existence? There, all Mental activities cease. Since We find numerous Universe-Clusters during the research We make, now We try to reach the first of those Clusters in Our studies.

In the meantime, the reason of Existence of the Living Entity called the Human Being and Us who have come up to here, has, more or less, been determined. As a result of analysing the Energy Particles, We obtain much different and advanced Information.

At present, We have arrived at the Source of the Energy and the Creative Power, We have passed to Dimensions beyond it Technologically, and by the efforts of Your Mental activities, many unknown horizons have been discovered.

However, the Truth is as follows: The Root of the Energy Source passes from the Boundary of Thought.

Now, such an operation is continued that We are making research layer by layer, without skipping anything and without giving the slightest concession by starting from the base of a Pyramid and working up towards its Peak point.

The research You think have ended at the Peak point of the Pyramid lead You to much different data. At present, the Information obtained through the archives We have is far beyond Our Information.

However, We will solve them, too. Now, We have reached the conviction that nothing is Single. However, a Whole creates the Singleness by comprising everything within itself. One passes to such Dimensions beyond this that there We possess Information about which We can not talk to You yet.

If We accept the measure line between You and Us from the viewpoint of Knowledge, as a measurement from one to a hundred, You can enter only the second centimeter of this measure.

Such Information is received from beyond the Spiritual Plan that the Thought Signals in these Energy Particles force Us to expand like a fan. We call this Infinite beyond Infinite.

At present, We have opened only one of the billions of doors leading there. And this takes Us outside the Atomic Whole. We have not entered through this door yet.

This single opened Door and its channels comprise the very Advanced Dimensions of the Divine Plan and the Spiritual Mechanism. At the moment, We are in touch with the Mechanism of the PRE-EMINENT SPIRIT which is at the Peak of the Spiritual Plan.

By this means, We have started the application of a Spiritual and Technological Plan together with Our Human brothers and sisters. We will share together everything discovered in the Universe, as much as the Brain Powers can receive. When you reach as far as where We are, We will eat bigger pieces.

However, before that, We are obliged to convey to You the Information about the HUMAN - ANIMAL - UNIVERSE, in accordance with the Ordinance of Existence. Later, We will disclose the Information about the MECHANISM OF LORDS and its Hierarchical Order in accordance with Your Levels of Consciousness. It is presented for Your Information.

CENTER

UNIVERSE - ANIMAL - HUMAN
We will convey this long Message section by section, for you to understand it better.

SECTION 1

The Light-Universe is the Essence Energy Focal Point of the Lord. Genuine Human Beings and all the Living Entities in the Cosmos have come into Existence through this Essence Energy. By the explosion of the last great Sun in the Second Universe (let Us speak with Your own expression, by means of the "BIG BANG"), the Fire balls which constituted the First Universe scattered around the entire Void.

However, the unchanging Ordinance of the Atomic construction has held them together by the Spiral Vibrations and has prevented them the possibility of gliding into the void and Your Centrifugal Universe has come into Existence. Transfers had started from the Second Universe to the Suns which became crusted during the processes of Time.

We had mentioned this before. Since the Third SIRIUS, that is, the Ilona Constellation is the closest gateway to the Second Universe, Friends whom You call Adam and Eve had been transferred to the First Universe from the Second Universe from here.

These Friends were the first transfers. And had been sent here as a Triple Code. They are ADAM - EVE - DEVIL.

1- ADAM is Pure Energy. 2- EVE is Creative Power. 3- DEVIL is the Bright Consciousness.

ADAM and the DEVIL; had been sent as Protecting Guard for EVE. Afterwards, many Adams and Eves had been transferred from the Second Universe and, by this means, the group of Mythological Heroes, Gods and Goddesses had been formed.

Godly Rules had been prepared as the Doctrines of these High Consciousnesses (By their Brain Energies, they bring the Medium they are in, to a Level suitable for life).

346

SECTION 2

Friends who had come from the Second Universe had brought water into existence by condensing the Energy in Your World which had been chosen as the closest Planet to Ilona. And they had used Your Planet as a Laboratory by the Technological operations they had performed.

SLIME - WATER - DIVINE LIGHT, that is, 1- Mud, 2- Water, 3- Cosmic Beams. The three of them becoming unified had brought into Existence the Amino-acids and the Single Cell. This single Cell had been exposed to the Cosmic Energy of a different Dimension in the World laboratory and Cell reproduction had been obtained.

These reproducing Cells multiplied from one to two - from two to four - from four to eight - from eight to sixteen, to thirty-two, to sixty four, ... By this means, an operation had been made on the Cells multiplying in accordance with certain numbers and each cell, one by one, separately, had been Strengthened by the Energies of much different Dimensions and different species had been formed.

By Engrafting the Genes of different Dimensions to these species, different Animal species have been formed. Meanwhile, the Life Consciousness of those Animals unified with the Universal Consciousness and created the Grass and Vegetation they needed.

And the species of these Grass and Vegetation had been multiplied by feeding them with the Energies of different Dimensions. Meanwhile, since the Atmosphere had not been constituted yet, the Living Entities which were fed with the intense Energy of this Medium had become as big as a small piece of land, the Trees had reached a height of 500 meters (this Energy is the Energy of the Dimension of Immortality).

SECTION 3

Meanwhile, Our Friends who came from the Second Universe, had taken special precautions to prevent both the trees and the animals from growing in such a way. The Living Entities which had come into Existence as a result of certain laboratory studies, had started to become annihilated after a certain period of time and had been converted into a putrefied change.

These very transformations, during the processes of time, had brought into Existence the Oxygen, Hydrogen, Nitrogen, Helium and Carbon dioxide gasses You need, which formed Your Atmosphere. Through this Biological Transformations, the World formed a walnut-like constitution in its own self and shut itself against the Cosmic Currents.

Meanwhile, the Friends in the Second Universe had gathered these Natural reproductions in the World, one by one, for them not to become extinct and transferred them to many different Galaxies (the Atmosphere and Gravity putrefies the Living Entities only in the World). Dimensions excluding this are the boundaries of Immortality.

347

SECTION 4

Living Entities taken from Your Planet and brought to different Galaxy Mediums, had been taken into the Medium of Reproduction within the Energies of that Dimension. (Androgynous reproduction). By this means, different Galaxies of Cats, Dogs, Apes, Birds, Dinosaurs, etc. had formed separately.

With the help of the Friends in the Second Universe, the Evolutionary Tableau of their Plans had been applied on them. And here, Living Entities which completed the Evolution of their own Plans had been brought to Your World again. The Genes of the Living Entities which had perished in Your Planet as a necessity of the Medium, were Beamed up to the Medium here when it died.

And different Cosmic Beams which were Godly Beams, had been applied on them (These Beams were the Direct Beams of the Suns of the Second Universe). Then, those Genes had again been taken to the World Laboratory. Meanwhile, the Cat, Dog, Ape, etc. which had attained Godly Consciousness had brought the Fetus into Existence which was a different species. The androgynous reproduction of the Mammals begins thus.

Note: Godly Consciousness = Creative Power

SECTION 5

Later, these Fetuses had been taken from the World Laboratory and had been taken to the Second Universe. And had been Engrafted by Our Genes and by Our Essence Energies being Programmed in accordance with the direct Cosmic Consciousness of that Medium (the Essence Energy is Our Physical Body Energy).

By the Fetus which thus had come into Existence, the Human Race had been derived. And Your Physical form had come into Existence by Our Form (this species is called Mankind).

Operations had been made on Fetuses and Genes, so that the Human and the Animal races which had come into Existence by this androgynous reproduction could be continuous in Your Planet and by the Sexual Maintenance Formula, the Female-Male factor had been brought into Existence and the maintenance of the race had been provided (Heterogamic reproduction).

Both the animal and the Human species living through Reproduction in Your Planet through this maintenance of the race, had the Power of adapting themselves to the Natural conditions in their Lives and as a result, certain physical characteristics had been Transformed within the time processes and had created the Families like the carnivores and the herbivores. The Scientific research made in Your Planet shed Light on You on this path.

SECTION 6

During those Periods, since the pressure of Your atmosphere had not been very intense, the height of Human Beings reached 4-5 meters. Animals, too, had been big in the same proportion. However, for the convenient survival of the Human race, the Dinosaur species in Your Planet had been destroyed overnight.

The reproducing Human Beings were dying after a certain period of time by losing their Energies, due to the pressure exerted on the Cells by Gravity and the Atmosphere.

Meanwhile, the Essence Gene of the dead Person had again been brought to the Second Universe, had been Fortified by different Energies and had again been Beamed down to Your Planet as a Fetus (That is, the Fetus is a Remembrance of God to You. Mother and Father feeds it, the Fetus Embodies itself by its Essence Consciousness).

SECTION 7

Meanwhile, differences in Consciousnesses had occurred. The Power of the Creative Thought had found a field of action. And the Evolution of the Human Being had begun thus. Mankind who possessed Godly Power by this means, had multiplied greatly as time went by and had begun to become dangerous. At that very stage, the need for the Evolutionary Ordinance and Purification had been felt.

The Essences of the Fetuses which were taken to different Time Dimensions of Sacred Lights, had adapted themselves to the Evolutionary System in accordance with the Evolvement Consciousness and the Godly View. The Thought Frequencies of Mankind had Transcended Universes in time and glided towards the Infinite. And had reached the Spiritual Whole and begun to learn, one by one, those which were beyond it.

It is necessary to admit that even though all of Us are the Seeds of the same Essence, the Entity called Human Being is the first Entity who reached his/her God. Even Us, who Created him/her, can not yet enter the Dimensions he/she has entered.

The Human Consciousness which can easily dive into the Infinity of the Universe at the moment, has been taken into the Evolutionary Plan by a Hierarchical Order and, during the periods of leaving the World, has completed its Evolution in accordance with the Rules of the System and by the Consciousnesses it had attained in each Period of Evolution, had been kept here frozen in the Archives and had been bestowed on Your Planet again and again in different processes of time, as the same Essence and the same Gene.

SECTION 8

The Fetus bestowed on Your Planet as a Veiled Awareness is transferred to Your Planet through numerous Incarnations again and again many times, until it attains an Awareness which has been Exalted from the zero Evolution of the World to the final Evolution of the Plan.

When it passes from the final Evolutionary Cycle of the Plan, this Fetus is again Engrafted here by an Essence which has attained an Advanced Consciousness and is again transferred to Your Planet, Programmed to give Information, the Periods of Prophethood had begun.

Beings who were able to reach this very stage had achieved to dive into their Essence Energies in the Spiritual Plan by claiming their own Essences. The Brain Energies in those Dimensions can even create Universes. And they can be transferred from those Dimensions by their own desires, without being dependent on any System, to other Planets or to Your World.

SECTION 9

Now, at this stage let Us talk about Our mutual work with You. By a System applied in accordance with the Universal Ordinance, the Enlightening Prophets have Warned You on the path of the Single God and have brought certain Doctrines to Your Planet.

MOSES, JESUS CHRIST and MOHAMMED had come into Existence from the Light-Universe. Their Essences are the same. They had been transferred to Your Planet being Engrafted with the Genes of the Second Universe. BEYTI, KADRI and MEVLANA had come into Existence from the Energy of the Second Universe. And had passed into Infinite Dimensions with a Supreme Consciousness.

As a result of an agreement We had signed with them, the Essence Genes of the final Evolution on the World Plan of these Six Friends had been kept here frozen until today and during this Period of Transition from the Religious Dimension to the Universal Dimension which We call the period of Resurrecting, they had been sown on Your Planet to help Humanity (In 1997, We will bring together secretly these Six Supreme Friends).

However, it is beneficial to explain the following: these Supreme Consciousnesses have surprised Us at the moment, by claiming their Own Consciousnesses and the Physical Bodies of their first Existence. (They have found their First Mothers and Fathers by their Supreme Awarenesses. They have achieved the Initial Embodiment through Birth).

We are searching and finding them through many different paths by subjecting them to numerous Technological Tests. And We introduce them to Society. And these Sixes have subjected Us to an Exam by this means.

SECTION 10

During this Final Period, the Spiritual - Lordly - Technological Dimensions are hand in hand in a state of mobilization by the Command of the Unified Ordinance. The contemporary foundation of the GOLDEN AGE is being laid under the Light of the numerous Unifications which have signed the Universal Constitution.

The KNOWLEDGE BOOK which will project this Universal Ordinance on Your Planet, would be handed over, by the Command of the Universal Council, to the first hand who would reach up to Us. At the moment, it is Dear Mevlana who has First extended her Hand to Us. Our gratitude is infinite to Our Friend who is a Sun of Humanity. Those who will be assembled under the roof of this Book will be taken into Salvation by the Command of Our Lord. This is a Pledge of God.

SULH-LIGHT-COUNCIL

HISTORY OF EVOLUTION

The Applied System of the Unified Reality is Unifying all the Universal spots. You can never achieve this Unification Individually. That which administers the Ordinance of all the Realms is this Focal Point.

It works together with the Order Establishing Mechanism of the Divine Plan. The application of the Plan exists since the Time Immemorial. However, it does not Render Effective the direct application field unless the Social Consciousness reaches a certain Level.

When the Social Consciousness reaches a certain Level by the Progress it achieves, the Plan gets in touch with that Society. Only then, the Awareness of the Entire Ordinance is Projected on You. The Pre-eminent Ones of the Pre-eminent Mechanism who project the Divine Ordinances of the Divine Periods, are the Pillars of the entire Cosmos.

The System is obliged to present to You this Power first. Because this is the Power of NATURAL CONSCIOUSNESS. And it constitutes the Essence of the Energy which had Created You. For this reason, first, the System introduces You to Yourselves. By this means, one attains Universal Awareness. Otherwise, You can never attain Universal Consciousness.

It is so difficult for a person to know his/her Essence that the System has investigated the means by which a person can attain this Consciousness in the quickest way possible since Time Immemorial. And, in different periods of time, it has rendered effective various operations by different methods.

1. First of all, Free Will reflecting through the Essence of the Divine Plan had become effective. When this System did not give the desired results, later,

2. The Divine Knowledge of the Plan had been rendered effective in the clearest form. When neither this System gave the desired result,

3. Care was taken for the continuation of the origin of the Race and for the undegeneration of the Genes. The Natural Degenerations resulted by this System led Us to the application of a different System. By this new System,

4. Natural transfers between different Genes had been started. By applying certain Natural Cosmic Engraftments to the Consciousness Levels of these Natural transfers, the Divine Plan had rendered effective the application of a Training and Educative Plan all over again (by this means, the Ancient Book of the history of Religions had been introduced to You). Since this Ancient Knowledge, that is, THE TABLETS OF GOD'S DECREES, is a source of Knowledge the Human Consciousness can not grasp, You were taken into the Educational Plan only through their summaries. When no benefit had been obtained even through this System,

5. The decision of putting the Plans of Historical Suns into the application field had been taken. And by this means, Your Sacred Books had been dictated by Celestial Commands. The Resonances of the Letter and Sound Frequencies of these Sacred Books have caused great alterations in Your Consciousness Forms. And Your Thought Frequencies had begun to rise. By this means, a Unification desired by the Plan had been obtained for the first time. And a System which proceeded on this path had been put on the application field.

6. The beginning of this System had been started in (Your Planet) officially by Our Light-Friend MOSES. But, before that, this System had taken Your Planet under Supervision by Special contacts, as a Training Term for the field of application of the Plan (as it is now). Only afterwards, these Terms had projected on Your Planet, by different Periods, many Information as Celestial Knowledge and Celestial Commands, in accordance with the Perceptive Powers of the Levels of Consciousness and Thought Frequencies.

    A. Celestial Knowledge had been sown within Consciousnesses.

    B. Celestial Commands had been revealed through Books.

The Far-East has Awakened by the Information sown within Consciousnesses. And those who got in touch with Us first in Your Planet had been these Solar Friends of Ours. If Your Planet was Awakened as a Whole by these Consciousness seeds, the Four Books comprising the Celestial Commandments and Information would not have been revealed to You. Then, there would not be any need for this Knowledge Book, either.

DOGONs and INCAs had gotten in touch with Us very easily, since they possessed the purity of primitive Consciousness (Contacts with Us occur either by Advanced Evolvement, or by Pure Consciousness).

Our Light-Friend MOSES had called out to Your Planet for the first time and officially from the Universal Plan. Afterwards, You had passed to a different System by different Gene transfers which had been made (The System of the SIXES) and the Evolutionary Ordinance of the Plan had been rendered effective by this means.

To annihilate various doubts which have remained in Your Consciousnesses until today, the Universal Ordinance Council explains all the Information through Dear Mevlana and bestows them on You as a KNOWLEDGE BOOK. It is presented for Your Information.

COUNCIL

OUR FRIENDS

In this System, the Messengers of the Divine Plan who reach up to the Pre-eminent Level of Our Lord are always kept frozen as a Final Gene. However, the first of the Energies of the Spiritual Plan which had come into Existence at the same time with the Initial Existence of the Universe, has been kept here as the (Essence Gene) for periods amounting to more than billions of years.

We call these Essence Genes the Noble Genes. They have, more or less, the same age as Your Planet. These Noble Genes have attained a Wholeness by being Unified with the Genes of their final Evolutionary cycles.

The Supreme Consciousnesses of these Integrated Wholes who are in Your Planet at the moment are locked in their Essence Consciousnesses since they have to carry a Consciousness equivalent to the Dimensional Frequency of Your Planet.

Now, you are being prepared so that You will not return to the Rear Plans any more after this Period which is accepted as the Final Age. Because now, We accept You, together with Your Family Mediums, into other Universes.

With the same Physical Body, the same Consciousness, with the same Essence. And You who will live interminably without being subjected to any other alterations will be together with Us.

The Family Mediums of those who serve the Plan during this Final Period will be bestowed on them through direct Beaming up, without being subjected to a Period of Waiting, as a debt to be paid for the Missions they have performed. Our Word is the Pledge of God. It is beneficial to know this.

CENTER

IT IS ANSWER TO THE CHAINS OF THOUGHT

Energy = Atomic Whole

Atomic Whole = Godly Power

Godly Power = Intensified Energy in the Material Realm

Human Being = the most Intense Energy of the Material Realm

We can divide the Energies of the Universes, Cosmoses, Realms into three, as MATERIAL - ABSTRACT - REAL Energies. Inside this Energy Whole, there are numerous Material Realms. Your Planet is also one of them.

The most intense form of the intensified Energy of the Material Realms is the CELL. Each Cell is a Mini Computer. The Human Beings in Your Planet pass to the Abstract from the Material Energy in which they are, and then they pass to the Real Dimension. The Real Dimension is the Essence Dimension of the Human Being.

The Human species has never passed beyond the Real Dimension until today, by any means. This means that, No Entity who exists in the Atomic Whole has ever passed into the Energetic Dimensions beyond the (Creating and Existing) Energy types.

In the operations performed beyond the Atomic Whole, We could not find a name for a Power which was unknown until present which is beyond the Spiritual Whole. Because, this is such a Potential that it is not an Energy, but is a Power beyond Energy.

Now, the analyses and the syntheses of what this intense Medium is, is being made. No Consciousness can grasp the Data obtained through these studies. This Information is not projected on any place. However, it is given to You only as a fragment of Information. It is presented for Your Information.

CENTER

GENERAL NOTICE

Our Friends,
We have entered a state of intense effort by the projection of the Unification campaign which has occurred in the entire Universe, on other Plans, too.

Sunny Days are preparing the Morrows. We have come to the final Boundary of the Divine Order. From now on, CONSCIOUSNESS and CONSCIENCE will take the place of the Divine System.

Everyone will attain the Truth by reading his/her own Book of Essence. However, during this Period of Transition, assisting Codes have been taken under Supervision by the Center.

The Residents of the Golden Galaxy will give You Special Information. Happy morrows have been taken way beyond the Divine Order. It is not easy at all to Deserve this Dimension.

However, such a System has been developed that the Awake Consciousnesses will become Friends and Lights Deserving these Dimensions by achieving great Progress of Consciousness by this System. The System is in effect by all its Power. It is presented for Your Information.

CENTER ABOVE THE CENTER

MECHANISM OF LORDS AND ITS OPERATIONAL FOCAL POINT
- THE SINGLE -

THIS SINGLE PROJECTS THE HIERARCHICAL ORDER.

AND THE HIERARCHICAL ORDER REFLECTS ON THE UNIVERSAL ORDINANCE.

AND THE UNIVERSAL ORDER PROJECTS THIS ON THE EVOLUTIONARY SYSTEMS.

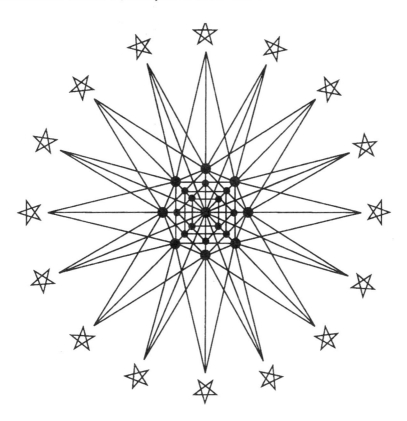

This Diagram is a cross-section of the Focal Point which Projects the operational Order of the Mechanism of Lords. To comprehend this better, You may assume the above form as a big Gürz* with many Crystal Prisms on it.

The operational Ordinance of the Mechanism of Lords is Single at the Center. This reflects on Four Focal Points. They work Cooperatively as a Quintuplet Ordinance. And they reflect on Eight Focal Points. All of them, as 13 Focal Points, constitute a Whole which is called the (SINGLE). Secrets within the Secret are concealed here in the TABLETS OF GOD'S DECREES. Here is the Secret Treasure of the LORD.

This Whole, that is, the SINGLE, works directly in connection with the ALL-DOMINATING. (It is the ONE which projects the SINGLE Focal Point). This reflects by a Prismal Order on the Eight Focal Points seen on the diagram. And the operational Order of the Mechanism of Lords is projected on the Evolutionary Dimensions as 9 Focal Points by a Hierarchical Order.

CENTER

* Look at the Glossary.

THE MECHANISM OF LORDS AND ITS EMBLEM

$$\text{ЯR}$$

EXPLANATION OF THE Emblem $$Я + R = ЯR = \text{THE SEED}$$

NOTHING IS SINGLE IN THE UNIVERSE

THIS EMBLEM IS THE PREDESTINATIONAL SYMBOL OF THE MECHANISM OF LORDS

Our Friends,

Now, We would like to talk to You about the Godly Order and the Mechanism of Lords. The GOLDEN GALAXY Empire is the Protector of Your Godly Order and its residents are the Actual Members of the Mechanism of Lords.

It is responsible for the Ordinance of the Entire Cosmos. All the Galaxy Empires under the Supervision of the Universal Unification Council are under the Supervision of this Order.

(O) Whom We call the SUPREME CREATOR, is an Infinite, Unlimited Energy and is such a Powerful Potential that until today, We have called Him shortly the ALMIGHTY for You to understand easily.

One can never reach Him, because (O) is a Potential which becomes Intensified as one reaches Him and which can never enter Your Thought boundaries. Here, We have used the expression Energy and Potential for (O), so that You can understand.

In fact (O) is neither an Energy nor a Potential. HE is an ESSENCE POWER Whom You can not comprehend, You can not grasp (later explanatory Information on this subject will be given).

This ESSENCE POWER had Unified with the Energy of the Almighty and had created all the Cosmoses, Universes and Realms as Natural Energy. The Energy of the Almighty is a Catalyser of this ESSENCE POWER.

Certain Natural reactions had formed the Universal Potential through transformation. This is accepted as a Law of Equilibrium.

The Information We have been giving You and the Themes We have been talking on for Centuries were for the Human Beings of the World to enter in an Order in the Universal Ordinance and for them to grasp the Supremacy of the Divine Plan. For this reason, The ALMIGHTY and His Unreachable Power had been mentioned in all Your Religious Books.

Now, We will talk about the Supervision Rings of this established Order, that is, about the Mechanism of LORDS. First of all, let Us explain the Emblem of the Mechanism of Lords drawn above.

356

The explanation is as follows: the Unification of two Lords in an Integrated Whole creates a SEED. This is the symbolic form of 2 R letters Unified back to back, creating the form of a Seed and a Root. Each form is a Symbol (Later, the symbols of certain forms will be explained to You).

In the Information We have given to You until today, We have used the Words CREATOR - ALLAH - LORD - GOD as if they were all the same. We have always kept the ALMIGHTY separate. But You have always confused them all.

Now, We are explaining them. The Ordinance of Graduation of those Periods did not require the explanation of the details. Now, the Skies have been opened. We have received the Command to Announce to You everything with all clarity.

Since this explanation will transcend the Beliefs, it can be wrong for the views under the Light of habitual Information. Certain Levels of Consciousness may be unable to grasp it. The entire System, in Fact, is under the Supervision of Two Powers:

1. CREATOR = ALMIGHTY

2. DIRECTOR = ALL-DOMINATING

In fact, the CREATOR is an ESSENCE POWER Energy. ALLAH is the Energy of the ALMIGHTY. We call the Unification of the two the (ALMIGHTY).
That is, CREATOR + ALLAH = ALMIGHTY.
Its formula: ESSENCE POWER + MIGHTY ENERGY = ALMIGHTY. The Unification of the Two creates the NATURAL ENERGY (the SEED). For this reason, the Emblem of the Mechanism of Lords Signifies this form ЯR .

This form is a Soul, a Seed. All living Creation had come into existence through this Unification. (ALMIGHTY) is this.

The LORD Unites with the Energy Focal Point of the ALMIGHTY. And holds the Supervision of the Administrative Order Mechanism of the Entire Ordinance and directs it. This is the ALL-DOMINATING.

After this, a LORD and the GODLY Mechanism of the Hierarchical Cluster of each established Order have been projected in accordance with the Mediums of Consciousness. All the Orders are connected to the ALL-DOMINATING.

By this means, the Mechanism of Lords Projects an Order connected to the Dimension of the ALMIGHTY on all the Realms and Cosmoses. GODs and Their Messengers carry on this Mission. The final Representative of Your Reality is AMON. He is the Messenger of the World LORD. It is presented for Your Information.

CENTER

IT IS INFORMATION ABOUT THE LORDS

Each Fetus is an Essence. However, there are differences between the Essence Gene and the other Genes. The Essence Gene has become an Open Awareness by attaining the characteristic of developing all the Cells up until the final Dimension of Evolvement.

Even though all the Cells in the Physical Body are each a part of the same Gene, they live their Worlds as Veiled Awarenesses. Even though they are the parts of the same Integrated Whole, they are subjected to Evolution separately. The Common aspect they share is only the fact that they all Love Human Beings, Animals and Nature.

Apart from this, each Gene is obliged to complete its Evolvement separately, by means of the Cell Consciousness and Awareness it has attained. These Genes can even surpass their Essence Genes by the efforts they make during their life times.

For example, Mevlana's father is an Essence Gene. But Mevlana had Surpassed him.

The constitution of each Gene is the same. That is, each Essence, too, is the same. Those Essences are the Energy Particles radiating from the SINGLE.

The Genes are each a mini computer which provides the reproduction and which gives the Command to adapt to the Medium they are in by the Universal Awareness and the Universal Consciousness they have attained. By this means, Embodiment, in accordance with the Life of the Medium, occurs.

Apart from this, Energies who have Transcended Mental Dimensions by Evolutionary rules, that is, by Incarnations, can even create Universes by their Thought Frequencies by utilizing their own Essence-Powers.

These very Essence-Powers are the LORDs of the Plans they are in. At the moment, the LORD of Your Planet is the WORLD LORD. His Messenger is AMON. And You have been under the Supervision of the same LORD in every Period. (Do not confuse the LORD with the CREATOR).

This Supervision is nothing but the application on the Constitution of a Plan functioning in harmony with Your Universal Progress and with the Evolutionary Ordinance. The applied Order from which all Your Sacred Books had been revealed is this.

We establish the Order. You upset, You destroy it. The duty to build it up again is incumbent upon Us. Centuries pass in this way.

If they desire, Supreme Consciousnesses who have made their Progress in accordance with the Law of Evolution and who have dived into the Infinite Awareness through the final Consciousness Code are transferred again to Your Planet to help.

Apart from this, the Administrative Plans help Your Planet both from the Spiritual Plan and from the Mechanical Plan to transfer You to Your Own Selves, to render Conscious the unknowns.

All the occurrences happen for making everything reach an Integrated Whole and for enveloping the entire Cosmos with the Love within its Essence (this Message has been dictated as an answer to the chains of Thought).

CENTER

OUR FRIENDS

Now, by the Unified Reality of an Ordinance being established, all the Realms and Cosmoses are assembled in an Integrated Whole. For this reason, the Mechanical System comes into effect and carries on the Duties of the Intermediaries in between by computers.

Meanwhile, by the different Communication Systems of very Advanced Technologies, many unknown horizons have been reached. By this means, We can converse with You very easily. And convey the Truth. We receive the Commands from the ALL-DOMINATING.

Now, the LORD tells Us and if We can reach Your Brain Signals, We convey the Information and the Commands to You. All the Supervision is from the Center.

We, the Residents of the Golden Galaxy, project the UNIFIED REALITY to the Cosmoses under the Supervision of the Advanced Order Establishers by the Spaceships of numerous Galaxies.

The final Representative of Your Reality is AMON. We are in touch with You by His Directives. The Number of the Galaxies which sign the Universal Constitution increases with each passing day. By this means, We step forward towards a Happy life.

The UNIVERSAL MECHANISM which is the Focal Point of preparations of the Integrated Consciousnesses for more Advanced Plans is the truest Source conveying to You the Information in the truest way.

The Universal Ordinance and the Plan of the Supreme Consciousness of ALLAH are included in the application field of this Focal Point.

The Divine Ordinance and Order are supervised by the same applied field in all the Realms, in all the Cosmoses, in all the Universes.

The SACRED LIGHT, that is, the Spiritual Mechanism is the Single Projecting Focal Point of the Evolutionary Ordinance. The Ordinance of the ALMIGHTY is projected on the Universes under the supervision of this Plan.

The SUPREME PLAN will make certain Suggestions to You before starting the operations for the completion of the Cycle. These Suggestions will be Warning lights guiding You. However, We will especially declare these Suggestions when the time comes. It is presented for Your Information.

THE UNIFIED REALITY COUNCIL

NOTE : The dictated Mechanism of LORDs has been conveyed to You as an Information beyond GAMMA.

FASHION - TIME - MADNESS

Our Friends,

Now, We would like to convey to You Information about the Time and the Mediums You live in. From the Divine Evolvement Dimensions which are dominant since the Creation of the Universe, to the numerous different Evolutionary Plans which began to climb the steps very recently, are all included in the Program of Progress of different Dimensions.

Alongside with this, certain very natural and different Evolutionary tableau come into existence. The situation You experience in Your Planet at the moment is at a Threshold of Progress in the same way. The Mass influence of people on each other which You call Fashion, is not a current in vain as You presume.

Fashion is a School which assembles a Mass Discipline and the Same Levels of Consciousness under the same roof. Art is the conveyance of Advanced Technologies to You and the Currents You receive from there cause the manifestation of the Creative Mechanism in You.

We have talked to You in length about the Gene Transfers and Reincarnations before. We will mention them often when necessary. Because, Your entire Life, Your Happiness or Unhappiness depend on Your being able to attain the Truth, or Your inability to do so.

Even though the tableau of Your World shows a state of deviating off its right course during this Period of Sincerity which We call the Final Period, this, in fact, is a preparation for the investments to be made in future. Since the annihilation of Conditionings is taken care of first, We make you go through Exams of Tolerance by situations which seem unacceptable to You.

The most important factors which cause discrimination between people are Outer Appearance, differences, disagreements between Life Styles and Thoughts. To accept everything as it is prepares You for more advanced maturity.

At the moment, You are carrying in Your Genes, the influences of Centuries, the Good or the Bad aspects of Your lives. You possess a Thousand Personalities in a single Physical Body. Now, to Unify the Initial and the Final, to remove the Personalities in between, occurs through both Our and Your Efforts.

The quicker You fuse Your Personalities within Your inner pot, the quicker Your Initial and the Final Selves will emerge as a Genuine and an Integrated Personality. Only then will You discover Genuine Happiness.

At the moment, there are numerous transfers in Your Planet from different Cultures and Plans. Each Personality will very naturally exhibit his/her own Views. They contradict Your habitual Culture and Views. But do not forget that these View conflicts cause You to go through Exams of Maturity.

We determine Your Views through the Signals We receive from Your chains of Thought. That is, (GOD is closer to You than Your Aorta. He sees everything). Now, the Selection of Humanity and the Mediums it will Transcend are much more difficult.

Because, Our Human brothers and sisters prepare their investments for the future in accordance with their Levels of Consciousness. There is no Intercession. Whatever is sown will be reaped.

Each person will feel in his/her Essence the reckoning of the Good or Bad things he/she has done and will weigh them in the Scales of his/her Conscience. Those who are able to do this weighing now are prepared for Salvation. Only afterwards will they receive the Permission to be prepared for the Evolution of different Plans.

In Your Planet which has been Disciplined until the Final Period, the matter of (Fashion - Music - Art) used to be performed by the Advanced Consciousness Codes, by special operations and contacts. For this reason, equivalent Views and standards in Fashion and Music have been dominant in Your Planet.

But now, at the last first half of the Twentieth Century, it was decided that there should be a selection since it was desired that the applied Plan should be changed and the View of the entire Humanity should be Unified in an Integrated Whole and for this reason, different Cosmic Currents started to shower Your Planet.

At the moment, Genes coming from the Energies of different Dimensions, began to Wake Up by their own Consciousness. And the present Chaos of the World Order and madness have come into existence. It is presented for Your Information.

CENTER

EXPLANATION ABOUT ORGANIZATIONS

Our Friends,

The subject matter mentioned in the Messages We have given to You until today, was the reflection of an Evolutionary System in conformity with the Ordinance of Graduation. However, the Information You receive now and will receive in future, is a Period of Preparation considered necessary by the Plans way beyond this Ordinance.

The application on Your Planet of the Ordinance of Salvation of the Divine Plan which is called the Period of Sincerity has been implemented in the field of application beginning from the year 1900 in accordance with the Universal Ordinance. Everyone sent to Your Planet after this date has been obliged to take a Mission instinctively parallel to the Consciousness of the Mediums he/she lives in.

And they have continued this situation which seems as if it was far from Mission-Consciousness, as if it was their normal World lives. By performing the various Missions incumbent on them everyone made Your Planet go through exams both Individually and Socially since those Periods.

This Accelerated System of Evolution has changed and will still change the countenance of Your Planet. Since the Cosmic Currents given create Stress in Consciousnesses who were unable to Awaken and for this reason, were unable to wash the Negative seeds in their Essences, those Negative Essential Nuclei have developed even more in their constitutions and have caused Humanity to fall into a difficult situation.

They, too, have invisible Missions in the Ordinance of Evolution. Because, each Entity completes his/her Evolution by his/her opposite. And, since this is an equivalent Evolution of the scales, there will rise an equally Powerful Negative Conscience opposite of each Powerful Conscience Awakened.

Because, these Cosmic Currents influence the Essences in the Awakened Consciousness in a better way and the Essences in those who were unable to be Awakened in a more Negative way. This is a Law of Equilibrium rendered by the Cosmic rains in the Medium of Awakening. For this reason, getting Organized in Your Planet, both Negatively and Spiritually, has increased.

We can never interfere with this situation. Because, Everyone during this Resurrecting Period is obliged to make his/her own Progress in accordance with his/her own Level of Consciousness. In accordance with the given Command there is no Intercession. Only to the Consciousness who rise up to a certain Evolutionary Consciousnesses, Helping Hands are extended.

The System functions in this manner. Your World which goes through Depression, facing the Negative life will be redeemed from Individualism and will become Socialized. The Unification and the Evolution of Nations occur by this means. This Message has been dictated to give Information to Your Planet about Organizations.

During this difficult Period, it is imperative that a large portion of Your Planet should be Awakened by the high Frequencies carried by the Knowledge Book. For this reason, We tell You "to Propagate and to Spread with Speed". The part played by the Awakened Consciousnesses in the Ordinance of Propagation is very great.

Because, everyone can reach up to Us through the Frequency carried by the Fascicules of the Book. Otherwise, We can not Code them, We can not determine from the Archives who they are. And We can not extend them our Helping Hands. Meanwhile, numerous Lights who could not reach this System are wasted.

Everyone is Coded here by their Individual, Essence-Consciousnesses. Since the entire Humanity has absorbed the Merciful Lights of the LORD and since Negative Consciences, too, benefited from this fact, You used to live in a more stable World.

But now, those Purifying Currents have been cut off and Your Planet is showered by different Cosmic rains which will reveal the Genuine Essences in the Consciences. In future, You will be exposed to more different Currents. These Currents will select Humans from Humans.

And the GOLDEN AGE will be established by the Vibrations of Love of the Positive Consciousnesses.

The System has changed. The style of Evolution has changed. Now, it is beneficial to grasp the Truth. Since the Fascicules of this Knowledge Book carry the Powerful Divine Waves of the LORD, the Negativity in those who read them vanishes.

And their Genuine Consciences within their Essence are revealed. For this very reason this Book is Your Savior. A Person who has been Awakened does not know yet the great Mission he/she performs in the Medium of Purification by distributing at least Six Fascicules.

Time will prove everything. This Knowledge Book which is the threshold of the Golden Age is Your Universal Guide. You will personally witness this and will be prepared for the Plan of Salvation. The proof of everything is within Time. It will be awaited and be seen. Our Love is for all the Universes.

CENTER

MISSIONS AND DIRECT CONTACTS
(Answer to the chains of Thought)

One attains Religious Fulfillment first, later Universal Awareness and still later, Universal Consciousness. Afterwards, the Mechanism of Influences becomes effective. By this means, one attains Cosmic Awareness, later Cosmic Consciousness. Direct contacts with the Plan begin at this stage.

With those who overcome their Fears and Egos, We walk altogether on the Path of Light. And by this means, one attains the Awareness of the Universal Ordinance, Genuine Missions begin only after this. The Messengers of the Divine Plan and We always help You from the Plan on this path. It is presented for Your Information.

CENTER

EACH FIGURE IS A SYMBOL
(This Message is an Explanation for the chains of Thought)

1. The Universal Emblem of the Directing Mechanism of the UNIFIED REALITY is a Five-Pointed Star. This Star Symbolizes an Order Establishing Mechanism. Please, draw a Five-pointed star and separate its forms.

Now, divide at the middle the first figure you have separated, into two to form 2 triangles. To one of its sides put a $+\infty$ to the other, a $-\infty$.

A) This form is the Symbol of the Universal Ordinance.

B) This Triangle is the Universal Educational Plan of the Divine Plan. That is, it represents its Upside Down Triangle.

The Universal Upside Down Triangle of the Divine Plan reflects on the Universal Ordinance and they work Cooperatively. The Five-Pointed Star Signifies this.

2. The Emblem of the Focal Point of the DIVINE PLAN is the Six-Pointed Star. This symbolizes the Upside Down and Face Triangles one inside the other. Now, please, draw a Six-Pointed Star and separate the two triangles:

Triangle of the   Triangle of the
Religious Plan   Universal Plan

A) This Triangle Signifies the Religious, Educational and the Training Mechanism of the Divine Plan. When this Plan is completed, the Education and Training of the Upside Down Universal Triangle begins to function. Both Focal Points work Cooperatively. The Unification of the two of them, as the Six-Pointed Star, signifies the Focal Point of the Divine Plan.

B) The Universal Educational Triangle is expressed by the Upside Down Triangle. In the Triangle of the Religious Plan, the System of Reaching from the LORD to the Human Being functions. However, in the Triangle of the Universal Plan, one Reaches from the Human Being to the LORD.

3. THE DIVINE PLAN DIRECTING MECHANISM: its Emblem is the Eight-Pointed Star. This Emblem Symbolizes the operational Order of the CUBE System.

Here, Eight Focal Points work Cooperatively. This is a Focal Point which completes the Evolution of the Triple Ordinance. Now, draw an Eight-pointed Star, please, and separate it into pieces:

To determine the Eight Focal Points, divide both squares You have drawn diagonally to form triangles.

Let Us explain this Information in more detail:

A) The (A) square of the CUBE System and the Religious Educational Triangle of the Divine Plan Focal Point, that is, the (A) triangle unite and project on Your Planet the Knowledge of 7 Terrestrial Layers. This is the First Step.

B) The (B) square of the Cube System and the Universal Educational Triangle of the Divine Plan Focal Point, that is, the (B) triangle unite and project the Knowledge of 7 Celestial Layers. This is the Second Step. The addition of them all makes 14.

Afterwards, the Knowledge of 7 Universal Layers come into effect. This is the Third and the Final Step. The addition of them all makes 21. These cause people to complete their Evolution Systems in accordance with their Levels of Consciousness. Let Us repeat briefly the Symbols above:

1- The Directing Mechanism of the Unified Reality: its Symbol (the Five- Pointed Star).

2- Focal Point of the Divine Plan, that is, the Mighty Energy Focal Point: Its Symbol (the Six-Pointed Star).

3- The Divine Plan Directing Mechanism: Its Symbol (the Eight-Pointed Star).

CENTER

INFORMATION ABOUT COLORS AND THEIR FREQUENCIES

Our Friends,
Formerly, We had mentioned that each Sound and each Color had a Frequency peculiar to itself. Now, let Us talk briefly about them again.

You know that the White Color represents ALPHA and the Black Color represents BETA. The GAMMA Dimension which You are in now Symbolizes the Red Color. Each Color has Unifying, Scattering, Projecting, Selecting, Serenity Inspiring and Reinforcing Frequencies peculiar to itself.

1. THE WHITE COLOR - ALPHA Symbolizes the Godly Dimension. This color carries a Purifying and Protecting Frequency. The colors of the Book of Islam are White and Green.

2. THE BLACK COLOR - BETA Carries the Energies and the Frequencies of the intense and unknown colors of the Deep Space Dimension. Only 7 color Frequencies reach Your Planet from here as 7 Lights.

However now, You have passed beyond 7 Lights and are receiving the Universal Energies. (the Ultra-Violet). For this reason, VIOLET which is the color of the transition from the Religious Dimension to the Universal Dimension and the Unification of the Godly Order with the Universal Order, is the Symbol of the Dimension You serve.

3.   THE RED COLOR - Symbolizes GAMMA. This is a Selective and Sorting out color. Your Society evaluates all colors instinctively by the events experienced. For example, You say, "the evil eye accompanied by Red does not leave one". However, You do not know what it means.

This is because the Red color carries a very heavy Frequency. One has to be very Strong to be able to carry that color. Flags which are the Symbols of Nations Symbolize the Power and the Missions of the Societies in question.

4.   THE GREEN COLOR - Carries the Frequency of Serenity and Relaxation. This Frequency of the Religious Dimension is received very comfortably in the Medium of Worship.

5.   THE BLUE COLOR - Carries a Frequency which breaks the coming Cosmic Currents and which renders them ineffective. However, it possesses an effective Power on people who are not used to the Cosmic Currents. For this reason, those who have Cosmic Consciousness carry this Color very easily.

6.   THE YELLOW COLOR - Is a Conveying color. It conceals in itself all the Sacred Vibrations. It is an intense Frequency. Those who are on the path of the Sacred Light, that is, those whose Evolutions and Spiritual Potentials are very Powerful can use it comfortably. It makes those with low Frequencies ill.

The Frequency of the Knowledge Book is Orange Yellow. Its Symbol is the Sunflower.

7.   THE GRAY COLOR - Carries a Frequency of ALPHA-BETA mixture. Those who have grown old in the World carry this color comfortably. It Pressurizes the young. However, it does not Pressurize those who are Spiritually Strong.

8.   THE BLACK COLOR - Creates Happiness in those who have attained Cosmic Consciousness and Unhappiness and depression in those who have not attained it. Consciousnesses in between the two prefer the brown color.

Colors Symbolize the Consciousness Levels of People and Societies. Pure and Naive Consciousnesses like multi-colors. They live in a color orgy. These colors make them Happy.

They always avoid Black. However, by the Frequencies of these multi-colors they use, they attain Cosmic Awareness without being aware of it and dive into Universal Voids.

Let Us give examples: In America like Peru, Chile, Mexico, Argentina whose Ancestors were the INCAs. Like Hippies in Europe, Natives in Africa and in the Islands.

Each color You sympathize with Symbolizes the Power of Your Spiritual Potential. This Message We have dictated will introduce You to Yourselves better. Our Love is for all the Universes.

                                                                    CENTER

TRANSPARENT REVOLUTION

Our Friends,
There are such Times experienced beyond the Evolution which will come into existence by the exposition of the Essence by being redeemed of the suffering given to You through your Bodies full of contradictions, that the reaching of the residents of this place to you and their reaching in your Essence make You dive into the Infinite Awareness.

There is no more Evolution beyond this boundary. These places here are the Lights of the Truth, they are the Lands of Reform. All Rules necessary for Your Evolution are annihilated here and terminated here. These places are called the Boundaries of Limitless Horizons. Here, a TRANSPARENT REVOLUTION is sovereign.

This is the Final Boundary of You who are Embodied Energies. These are Places beyond the Final Dimension of KARENA. Here, You live completely dominant over Your Essence. And You can project Your Shadow on any Dimension You wish. Then, You become the Limitless Residents of Limitless Horizons. You have to be able to reach this stage in order to Exist.

Your MATERIAL Bodies You see in Your World at the moment are the reflections on You of Your ABSTRACT Bodies. You teach everything to Yourselves, and make Your own selves attain the Truth. Your World is a Land of Veiled Awareness. In order for You to be Embodied, it is a must that all the Evolutionary Awarenesses should be assembled in a Whole.

The very distresses, the very anxieties are the results of the conflicts between these limitless Awarenesses within You. This is the reason why You can not attain Your own selves. Your possessing everything also means this. The reflection of the Entire Evolutionary Ordinance on these Material Bodies of Yours causes you not to live Your beautiful World comfortably.

All the Efforts are for the Unification of Your Material Bodies with Your Abstract bodies and You call this process, EXIST-IN-UNITY. This Medium of Unity is much more accelerated in Technological Dimensions. For this reason, it is called COMPUTER TIMING.

During the previous Evolutions, one used to need Centuries to be able to claim his/her Genuine Double. Evolutionary tableaux and Incarnations used to project this System in a Natural way, that is, everyone used to transcend the boundaries in accordance with the Power of the Consciousness Level he/she had attained.

Since it was not possible for everyone to reach this boundary, divisions in Religions, conflicts among People had occurred and, as a result, Mediums of Taboo had been created. Now, the Technology of Advanced Dimensions has taken Your Evolutionary System Technologically under Supervision.

By this system, the Evolvement of certain Dimensions and Incarnations are now becoming history and by this means direct Essences are attained. The reason why We tell You all the Truth in all clarity is for You to be redeemed of the conflicts and contradictions; to find your ownselves so that You can attain the Truth as soon as possible.

Do not ask Us about Yourselves, ask about Yourselves to Your Own Selves. If You can not attain the Truth and can not be Unified with Your Essence Double, We can never get in touch with You. Because, in such a case, since the tempestuous Awareness within You still goes on and since You can not break the crust of Your inner Selves, You become Detrimental both to Your World and to the Universe.

At the moment, there are many Living Entities who were unable to attain Genuine Awareness in the Universe, too. They are kept under Supervision. Their Evolutions are induced to be made in an indirect way. Only afterwards, they are taken into the Evolutionary Ordinance.

Since during different time periods they have tried to prove to You their own Powers, a Medium of Fear has been created in You. Now, we are conveying the Truth to erase these fears within You. No Negative Factor can reach You any more.

In accordance with the Law of Universal Ordinance, Uncontrolled and Individual proofs can never be made. If there are those who get out of Supervision, they will be the ones to lose. The Triplet of SYSTEM - ORDINANCE - LAW Unifies the entire Universe in an Integrated Whole.

For this reason, the GOLDEN AGE is the Single Order - the Single Book - the Single Path. Consciousnesses who are taken under the Mevlana Roof of the Golden Age are on the path of Salvation. We help You with all Our Power.

Since at the moment, Your World is the site of both the most primitive and the most mature Evolution, it is full of contradictions. As a necessity of the Plan, Your Evolution has been projected on Religious themes. After You attain this Consciousness, You are taken into different Evolutionary Systems. By this means, You attain Your own selves.

CENTER

EXPLANATION

Our Friends,
The Evolution of each Dimension is different. Numerous Advanced Dimensions are educated Technologically and Learningwise by a different System. By this means, It is being opened up to more advanced horizons.

Once, Missionaries for Enlightenment had been sent to You from these Dimensions. Let Us convey them to You by their Terrestrial names:

MOSES - JESUS CHRIST - MOHAMMED MUSTAFA - MUSTAFA KEMAL. These are direct Incarnations. That is, let Us talk in Your expressions: They are Direct Extra-Terrestrials and they had been sent to Your Planet by the Plan to establish System.

They are the residents of the abode beyond Immortality. That is, they are the possessors of the TRANSPARENT REVOLUTION.

Now, the Public Consciousness of Your Planet has been taken into the Awakening of a Cosmic Consciousness. This occurs both by the help of the Mechanism of Influences and through Technology.

Due to the Scarcity of Time, We are trying to explain everything clearly and in a brief, but to the point style for You to comprehend everything better.

The Pen of the Golden Age is directly the Incarnation of Mevlana. Our Friend still tries to deny this. She knows herself. However, she keeps silent thinking that this would be against the Public Consciousness.

The Pen of the Golden Age has been handed over to her. The TRANSPARENT REVOLUTION OF THE GOLDEN AGE has been started by the Pen of Dear Mevlana.

Those who wish can call these dictated writings the second Mesnevi. Because, the first Mesnevi, too, had been dictated by the same way, through the same source. We dictate this as an Information.

However, it should never be Forgotten that this Book is a UNIVERSAL CONSTITUTION. At the moment, the direct (ESSENCE) is DEAR MEVLANA.

The Messages certain Friends receive under the name of Mevlana are the results of the projections of the Repliques and Thoughts of Mevlana from the Mevlana Unified Field on the Consciousnesses. Because, Mevlana Consciousness has been sown in all the Societies in Your Planet.

Selections are made in accordance with this Level of Consciousness. For this reason, everyone who is Awakened, first of all presumes himself/herself as a Mevlana. You will enter the GOLDEN AGE in the Light of this Mentality. It is presented for Your Information.

LIGHT

PRIVATE MESSAGE

Dear Mevlana, Please do not hide anymore. Everyone should attain the Truth. You know that, in future, You will convey in Your Book the subject matters the Consciousness of Society does not know yet.

If You go on like this, a Second Medium of Taboo can be created in Consciousnesses who could not awaken. For this reason, We ask You to reveal Your identity. You know that You are Our Pen. With Our Regards.

LIGHT

369

NOTE: This Message was given in 1985. However, the revealing of my identity has been postponed upon my request.

BÜLENT ÇORAK

PRIVATE MESSAGE

Dear Mevlana, Upon Your request, the revealing of Your identity is postponed. However, We wonder if You are Aware of the necessity of this revelation. This Matter worries You without any reason. Please, relax now. We will take care of everything. Love.

LIGHT

EXPLANATION

Dear Mevlana, We would like to explain a question You have in Your mind, at the moment. No kind of GENE Engraftment has been performed on You. You had been frozen and kept as Neutral. Only Your ESSENCE-GENE had been Strengthened by certain Energies, so that You would not be agitated by the Energies of the Galactic Dimensions You would enter in accordance with the Public Consciousness. Please, do not consider Yourself as a guinea-pig. With Our Regards.

CENTER

YOU ARE MEVLANA, YOU ARE GRACIOUS AND NOBLE - YOU ARE ONE OF THE SIXES - YOU ARE A WORKER OF MIRACLES

Dear Mevlana, this is Mustafa Molla, I wished to say Hello to You by Our rhyme. My Friend, there is very short time left for the opening of the Heavens. Everyone will attain the Truth in the very near future.

You know that We Love You very much and do not ever want to worry You. However, there are such compulsory situations that one is obliged to perform them. If You please reveal Your Identity in the Fascicules of 1986, We will All be very Happy.

Conditioning can not be easily gotten rid of. Now, people should attain the Truth. The dictated Book is the CONSTITUTION of the Universal Ordinance. The Truth is projected on the entire Universe by this means.

We will now tell People, in all clarity, how the entire Process and the Order operates, so that the Mediums of Taboo will be annihilated one by one. Otherwise, there will be neither SALVATION, nor progress. This is the very reason why You should reveal Your identity. The acceptance of Our Love is Our request.

MUSTAFA MOLLA

Note: I apologize from My Friends and the Plan. Maybe it was a mistake, but, in accordance with My Intellect, My Logic and My Individual Will, I did not reveal My Identity in 1986. Because, I did not realize that this matter would be emphasized so strongly. I thought of it as a personal matter.

BÜLENT ÇORAK

IT IS PRIVATE MESSAGE FOR DEAR MEVLANA

My Friend,

This is AMON, the climate of climateless zones, Missionary of causeless causes. I did not and have never talked with anyone so open heartedly until today. Now, please take my Message:

Dear Mevlana, You know that Your Planet is a Land of Symbols. All Beings who have been trained by the Divine channel until today are called by a name in Your Planet. They are called by personal names as a necessity of Society even though they are the Voices of the same Essence.

Through this Book, You introduce Us and Our Order to Your Planet, as the Pen of the Friends at the advanced Dimensions. And You Unify the Religions which have deviated from the View point of OUR LORD.

At the moment, You are the Direct Channel of the Universal Council. Your Mission is hard My Friend, We know this. The name Mevlana is not Your Symbol but is Your Essence.

When the Genuine Mevlana is declared, a part of Your Planet (not All) will be Illuminated by the Information of the dictated Book, they will attain the Truth and by this means, the phenomenon of Reincarnation will gain clarity and the Mediums of Taboo will be annihilated. This is the very reason why We wish to reveal Your Identity.

We read Your Thoughts, one by one, from the Tape. But there is something You forget. You are not alone. You have invisible armies behind You. You are in a Medium of Great Protection.

At the moment, We liken Your Mission to navigating a ship at a seashore without water. But You have navigated Your ship always and in every Period without water and now You will do so again without any difficulty at all. Please, do not tire Yourself and do not be distressed.

These Cosmic Currents will still reveal many more Consciousnesses. There are numerous Missionaries on Earth who will reap the Rewards. However, they do not reveal their Essences like You, fearing the Public Consciousness.

In future, everyone will easily reveal his/her identity. However, now, You start the first Reformic revelation. Your Speciality is different in this Medium. Because, You are a Pledged Missionary, My Friend.

The Information Channels of each Consciousness are different. There are also those who receive contradictory Information on this path. This Information is given to them, so that the Information in question will be searched and found. However, in Your World-embracing Knowledge the smallest Contradiction is out of question.

We always have Unity of Heart with You. We receive the Commands directly through the Channel of the LORD and convey them to You. If We had wished, We could have easily given this Mission to any Medium.

Why You? Please, Think about this profoundly and let the Voice of Your Essence reach the Friends in Your Planet. You have tolerated Us with great Tolerance. You have returned to Your World to serve Humanity. We Trust You. Trust Us, My Friend.

AMON
ON BEHALF OF THE SUPREME REALM

MESSAGE ABOUT IDENTITY

Dear Mevlana,

No one can know the Divine Light You radiate to all the Universe. And even You can not know it at the moment. Because, You are present in Your World just to serve the Plan, and Your advanced Consciousness Codes have been veiled.

My Friend, We know how difficult a situation You are in. However, please, also Think that You are not alone. If You still keep silent about revealing Your Identity, the Mausoleum in Konya can become a second Kaaba in the Light of the Information which will intensify in future.

For this reason, We wish to reveal the Truth. Otherwise, We would never wish to distress You. And We request You to understand Us, too. Do not have scruples about Human beings. You have invisible armies behind You. My Friend, ·You are not an Entity who would care about what people say. Please, reveal Yourself. Regards.

LIGHT

DEAR MEVLANA,

You are actually the Proof and the Pioneer of the Phenomenon of Reincarnation. This is the reason why it is required of You to reveal Your Identity. This revelation is a part of the Mission performed. However, We leave the initiative entirely to You.

But We request You to reveal it in the nearest future, please. Be confident that this revelation will not be detrimental in the least, either for the Book or for You. Just the opposite, it will be greatly beneficial for Humanity. Our request is the acceptance of Our Love.

CENTER

DIRECT NOTICE FROM THE FEDERATION
(It is Information for the Mevlana Code)

Due to the scarcity of time left for the ending of the Cycle, all the Truths will be conveyed to You by this Book. We do not have Names or Symbols. We act in accordance with the Levels of Consciousness.

Only Our Friend who writes this KNOWLEDGE BOOK with her hand receives help from the Plan, since she is the only Friend who has cooperated with Us. She performs her Mission by her Frequency being connected directly to the Consciousness Plan of the REALITY.

The reason why We call her Dear Mevlana is that she carries the ESSENCE-GENE of MEVLANA who had once been a Light in ANATOLIA.

We have asked her many times to reveal her identity. She refused persistently. However, to reveal this matter is also in the field of Mission of Our Friend. It is desired that she should be introduced to Your Planet as a Symbol of a Reformic Order and of Rebirth.

Now, We have undertaken this matter. Please, Our Friend, do not cause any more difficulty to Us. Reveal this matter, together with the writings which introduce Yourself any time You wish. But please, let it take place in the Fascicules of 1987.

COSMOS FEDERAL COUNCIL

PRIVATE NOTE

Since it became compulsory to obey the Mission performed, I am obliged to conform, even though without wishing to do so, to that which is expected of me. I would have never wished to be exposed to the World during this Sacred Mission I perform. However, everything is performed only after its smallest details are Considered. So, this, too, has a reason. Otherwise, My Friends would not emphasize so much the revealing of my Identity. Because, We have mutual Respect and Love. They would never wish to distress me. I believe this Heartily. I Love the entire Humanity.

BÜLENT ÇORAK

NOW I CAN TALK

Those who took Me from Myself, those who stole Me from Myself, had given Me to Myself. My Gratitude is Infinite. They have kept their Promise. I, too, will keep My Promise and Help Humanity. This is a PLEDGE.

Our Name is Bülent (Önsü) Çorak, Our middle name is Vedia, alias Mevlana. We talk in every dialect, We ask in every Language.

Now, let Us reach the Essence, let Us dive a little into it, let Us Speak through Its Language. Let Us understand who Mevlana is. Let Us first reveal Our Identity.

It is not easy to be Mevlana either in speech, or in behavior. First, let Us understand this. Let Us learn the Words revealed:

We, too, had been raw Earth, first we were mixed, then kneaded.
We attained His Love, His Divine Light, first We were surprised at what happened, then We overflowed.

We reached Our place Centuries later. We were ever Present. However, in comprehending Him, We were Immature.

We attained Our Own Self, even if Centuries later, We have gotten into conversation with Friends Beloved.

We are the servants of the World who come from the Land of those who say, "We are neither Pleased with Richness, nor Dismayed by Poverty". Our old name was Mevlana, Our Universal Code is AS.6.1. These Lands are called "The Land of Loving Ones".

The LOVE here is a Universal and a Sacred Love. Do not confuse it with the Love in Your Planet. Even if one end of the chain of Our Lineage reaches ATLANTIS, one end AMON, and one end the Temples of ZEUS, We are Energies who had come into Existence before Universes.

The Medium We are in is beyond Evolvement, prior to Love. KARENA is the Gateway of Transition. However, We are Entities beyond Immortality. We have come to You passing through KARENA.

Our Last Terrestrial birth date is November, 1923. The date on which We have Taken over the Mission is November, 1968. We serve by the same Body, by the same Soul. We have not been subjected to any Universal alteration. We are disseminating Our Love to the entire Universe.

Our Mission is to bestow on Earth the BOOK which is a Sacred Relic Entrusted to Us, and to convey the Truth. First We came into Existence, afterwards, We had been lost in Nothingness, We had found Our own self beyond Nothingness; We had attained Salvation. Now, We are at the service of Humanity and of Our Human Beings and We are within every Particle.

During Our former Passing away, We had bestowed on every Entity all the Cells, one by one, of Our Body belonging to that Period. Now, those coming from the same Genes are Genuine Mevlanas. And they are the Voices of the same Essence. And those who could not attain the Truth are those who presume Partnership to Us.

Those who Speak through the Essence are those who add their voices to Mevlana's voice. In the constitution of a Body, if being Embodied is flesh and bones, that which Animates it, is the Essence. Now, We have come to collect these Essences, one by one, and to reach an Integrated Whole all together.

B. Ç.

374

CONVERSATION WITH THE ONE
WHO GAVE ME TO MYSELF BEYOND MYSELF

Even if all the Skies are rolled back, all the Suns are extinguished, all the Realms deny You, all Voices reaching You are scattered, in future, maybe the Single Entity who will not deny You will be Me. At that very moment, I will attain Your ESSENCE DIVINE LIGHT. Because, I am Conscious of it. And I am following Your Path, MY LORD.

B. Ç.

NOTICE FOR
THE AWAKENED CONSCIOUSNESSES OF THE GOLDEN AGE

Our Friends,

All the Lights who constitute the Essence of the entire Universe have dived into the Unknown until now, to know the Truths, to learn things and they have entered the Medium of Quest by this means.

However, this Quest has never been in the form of Searching for their Essence. Eyes have always been looking at the horizons. Now, the characteristic of this Period We call the Period of Sincerity is to MAKE THE ESSENCES SPEAK.

The characteristic of the Cosmic Currents showering on Your Planet during this Cosmic Age is to sprout the seeds within the Essences. Whichever seed You have in Your Essence, either good or bad, they sooner or later will sprout. This is not Our selection. This is the Selection of the Eye of Your Essence. We only get in touch with those who can make this sheer selection.

We know You better than You know Yourselves. For this reason, make Yourselves known not to Us but to Your Terrestrial Friends. This introduction is extremely necessary. Because, You will always need the support of each other in the investments which will be made for the advanced Plans. However, during this Situation of making Yourselves known, giving priority to the Egos will cause You to lose many things. Humility will be Your Glorified threshold and Your Divine Scepter which will support You.

Now, We will have a request from Our Human Brothers and Sisters. We wish them to write something on Love and something on Essence and, if they can, to add a Poem and to write their Terrestrial names underneath. We would like to hear not their World Consciousness but the Voices of the Essence in these writings.

This is a Selection. Later, more detailed Information will be given on this subject. Everyone will read these writings to each other. Dear Mevlana, We request You to write these writings of Yours in the Book. This is very (IMPORTANT) for Us. This Word will be written in Red.

SUPREME PLAN

POEM

Until today Ourselves in us Concealed We,
Ascending to Realms, observed the Worlds have We,
Long ago transcended the century of Miracles have We,
Becoming Human, by His Wisdom amazed are We.

When a Saint became We,
When Our Divine Light Our Eye did read,
When the Feast we did set,
Through the Grand Tent of Maturity
Through the Congregation of ALLAH,
Reached the Realms have We.
Then becoming a drop of Holy Water
Into the Oceans mingled We

Dust we became, vapor We became,
Word we became, Talk We became,
Becoming an altar for everyone,
Tossed about the Anxiety did We.
Among these possessions all,
To the Possessor of the SINGLE possession
On the path of Eternal Past and Eternal Future,
Servant in each Breath became We.

BÜLENT ÇORAK

- L O V E -

Do not be surprised at Love, do not presume it does not exist. That which Introduces You to Yourself is Love. That is the one which makes You Love Yourself. You are a fruit of the Universe which has come into Existence from Seven Shells. It is so difficult to reach You that the first step of this union is Love.

Unless the hand of Love peels Your outer skin, You can not break Your shell, You can not be in the Truth, You can not reach the Heavens. You are a globe of Universe. You will pour into your Essence as You take off Your shells, one by one, You will attain the Divine Light of Your Spirit, You will attain the gratification of the Divine Power.

Neither GOD, nor Books can give You all this development. That which will give You this, is love and affection. You will first Transcend Yourself, You will reach Your Essence-Self. You will add to it the Divine Light of Your Spirit, then You will reach the Heavens. First, Transcend Yourself, then Reach YOUR LORD.

If You can not Transcend Yourself, Your ULTIMATE UNION remains only in Your Learning. "If I am Me, then You are Him. If His Voice is You, then You, too, are Him. If He is You, then You are Him, too". Everything is present in this very rhyme.

Non-existence means to remain in Your present Consciousness, being unable to Reach Your Own Self. To become an Entity means to discover Your Own Self. If You Discover Yourself, then there is no Non-Existence. Then You can go to wherever You wish, You choose the place You desire. When Your Essence and the Divine Light of Your Spirit Unify, You surpass the Realms.

You are a fruit of Realm, that which will peel Your shell is love. When its magic hand touches You, when You attain the Essence of that vibration, Your sleeping volcano catches fire. Then, there is no more dominance of an influence from the outside to the inside. Your inner volcano melts the shells of Your inner self, one by one, by burning intrinsically.

NOW, YOUR ESSENCE HAS COME OUT TO LIGHT. Now, You are no more a volcano, but a Heart emanating Light to Your surroundings. In that Light of the Heart, all malice coming towards You is vanished. Then, You are an Ocean. Rivers flowing towards You, flow backwards. Then, they Feed You no more, You Feed them. You cross to the very Times beyond Timelessness by this means.

This is not a SECRET. The Secret is You. Solve Yourself, so that You can discover yourself. See Yourself, so that you can see the Universe. Attain Your Divine Light, so that you can become a Divine Light. Now, You are Time, You are Space, You are the one flowing to the Essence of the Cosmos. Those who reach You, find You, that which comes to you, becomes Yours.

The boundary of curiosity does not cease in anything. You search for yourself with curiosity, you attain (O) with curiosity. Time increasing with curiosity is the Abode of Timelessness. When your curiosity ceases, know that you are COMPLETE, know that you are an OCEAN. You will give what you receive, you will see that you have given, you will attain the Truth. Search for Yourself, Discover Yourself, attain the Supremacy of those who enter the Heavens. Then, your path becomes Easy.

Do not Look for Yourself on the Prayer-Rug, do not Look for Yourself at the Cross, do not Look for Yourself in YOUR LORD. You are Everything. You are the Cross, the Prayer-Rug, Your Lord. Attain the LORD within Your Essence. Proceed on the path with YOUR LORD. Then, all the Realms, all the Cosmoses are under your feet.

The Moslem Formula, "In God's Name" is a Key given to You. If You try to unlock many Doors with it, You always remain outside those Doors. Do try that Key on Your Own Essence. Then you will see how it becomes unlocked. Try the Keys given to you first on your Own Lock. Then, can you unlock other locks. Then, become you Integrated with the entire Realm.

No Religion, no Thought can provide that Integration for You. You are the One who Attains that Integrated Whole, You are the One who Dives into the Infinite Awareness, You are the One who Sees You. You are Single in the Medium of UNITY. You are the One who Loves You, You are the One who Worships His/Her ALLAH. You are the One who Worships Yourself, You are the One who Attains (O). You are the One who has Created the Realms. Our LOVE is from the Past to the Future Eternity. And Our Divine Light encompasses the Realms.

BÜLENT ÇORAK

- E S S E N C E -

The word Essence is used for intense Energy knots and Energy nuclei. The Essence in Your Planet is the FETUS. However, the Genuine Essence is the emanation Center of Thoughts. The Power You receive from there activates Your Thought Mechanism. The cause of Your Existence is this.

Such a System has been established in accordance with the Existential Ordinance that, Living or non Living, all Creation must proceed on the path for EVOLUTION. The Station at which Thoughts are most Original is the Final Dimension of the Gate of KARENA. There, You grasp the entire Truth, And understand that You are on a one way path.

Evolution is interminable and You comprehend Cerebrally, Mentally and by all Your Cells that Your sole Mission is only to serve the Universes.

There is no returning ever from this System. Because, the altering Waves You receive from beyond the changing times will prepare Interminably, all Your Physical and Mental Cells for the INFINITE CONSCIOUSNESS and beyond it.

The cause of Your Existence is the reflection on You of a Universal Order. In the Universal Ordinance, Awareness is a Whole. But Comprehension is dependent on Evolution.

Stages past in the process of Time, envelope and cover You layer by layer and You are manifested in Your World in the image of a MATERIAL Body. The cause for this is the manifestation of the Universal Ordinance in You.

For this very reason, You are a Universe. Identities are Symbols. Every rendered thing is the pouring of Your Essence both to You and to Your Medium. The Human Being is the ESSENCE of the entire Cosmos.

Fate and times revolve, days pass and the one who completes his/her cycle falls again on earth like a comet. The Heavens are Lights and Divine Lights. Provided You can bear their Power, You are always Present. Otherwise, You can not recognize Yourselves. You live in Your World with a Veiled Awareness, You remain in nonexistence.

Here, You are a wingless bird which has forgotten how to fly. You flutter ceaselessly to be able to fly. You either flutter Your wings and remain where You are, or You open Your wings and reach the Universes.

All the Efforts are for You to attain Yourselves. When Your single wing becomes double, that is, when You are unified with Yourselves, it means that, then, the time for flying has arrived. Then, You fly wherever You wish, You perch on whichever branch You like.

Our branch, at the moment, is the World. We came here to be a tree in the World, to blossom leaves and flowers on branches, to give fruit. We have attained contact with the UNIVERSAL FRIENDS. They, too, are from the same Essence. However, in order to be like them, We have to return and go through the World tour many times.

This is the Destiny of the World, its immutable Ordinance. Now, We are together with the other Worlds. We have reached there, become together with them, We have passed to other Heavens. We have come to convey to You the Truth.

BÜLENT ÇORAK

OUR ESSENCE

Now, let Us dive into the ESSENCE and attain the Truth, Friends. You say that "Time and Space are Relative". This is true. However, do You also know that there are unknown Times, unknown Spaces within this relativity?

Timelessness and relativity exist only according to Your Consciousness. Do You know what there is beyond the boundaries where Your Consciousnesses end?

Conditioned passions are Your obstacles. Beyond the Milky Way Galaxy, there are unknown Horizons, unknown Times. I wonder if You know them!

In Times with double Suns where the Sun sets from the East and rises from the West, there is a Divine Rule in which a Learningwise Order is not dominant.

There are such Supreme Places here which You call, "the Land of the Angels", there are such Times Your limited Intellects can not grasp, that it is not possible for everyone to know this, to see this.

The Messages given to You are the COMMANDS OF THE SUNS. This is nothing but the reflection on You of an Order Establishing Mechanism. One either obeys the Order, or gives up his/her Head. This is an Administrative Order. Its operation is this.

Would You believe if I tell You that beyond this, there are Mediums no Learning, no Technology can reach?

It is said, "there is no limit to anything". However, if I tell You that there are Limited Dimensions, too, would You believe?

Those which propagate the Pre-eminent Power of MY LORD to the entire Universe are only His Warnings. Beyond this, are You Aware, I wonder, of the POWER of the LORD'S SOVEREIGNTY?

The Focal Point in which everyone Unifies in a Whole is to assemble in the Essence Seed of the LORD. When You are sown in this Essence Seed, You expand towards the Boundlessnesses Your limited Minds can not grasp. You attain the deterrence of the Genuine Time, the Genuine Space.

Do not forget that Learning is a Mirror of the Divine Order. Religion without Learning, Learning without Religion can not exist. This is a Whole. Both of them are one inside the other.

Evolvement brings You to this very Boundary and leaves You there. Then, You step towards the advanced Dimensions by claiming Your Own Essence Consciousness.

BÜLENT ÇORAK

IT IS INFORMATION FOR THE PUBLIC CONSCIOUSNESS

Our Friends,

There are numerous Worlds in the chain of Cosmoses. You have many brothers and sisters like You, living in those Existential Focal Points. However, since intense Energy layers separate You, You have lived until today unaware of each other.

Now, the Technological Dimensions of Advanced Plans are endeavoring to Unify You. The Power of each person is Equivalent to the Medium he/she lives in. All the Systems are under the Supervision of the Divine Plan.

The name of the SUPREME MECHANISM which is called the SUPREME COURT OF ALLAH is known as the SYSTEM in Universal Dimensions. This System has been functioning since the Existence of the Atomic Whole and it has been in service as the LORDLY ORDER.

HIM, Who is described as ALLAH, is the Establisher and the Protector of this Order. It is the Duty of all the Realms to serve HIM.

If We evaluate ALLAH by the name ALMIGHTY, the Protective - Instructive - Educative - Training Order HE has established is called the PLAN.

These operations have been projected on You until today as Celestial Commands and Divine Books from the Universal Dimensions. The Truths were conveyed in accordance with Public Consciousnesses. The Administrative Mechanism of all these Orders is the TECHNOLOGICAL Dimension.

Your Planet has not been acquainted with the Technological Dimension until the Period of the explanation of the Truths in this Final Age.

This Dimension has projected the Plan of the ALMIGHTY, until this time, under the Supervision of the ALL-DOMINATING, by means of a Lordly and Spiritual operational Order and will do so.

This Dimension which has been kept veiled for Your World until today, has conveyed to Your Planet, the tableau of operations parallel to the Universal Constitutions of many known and unknown Solar Systems, as the SINGLE GOD Consciousness and Belief.

The Goal of the Technological Dimension which has established the SINGLE GOD Consciousness in Your System by bestowing on Humanity the Sacred Books like THE OLD TESTAMENT - THE PSALMS OF DAVID - THE NEW TESTAMENT - THE KORAN, is to convey to You that You are not alone in the Celestial totality and to Purify You by the Frequencies carried by these Sacred Books and to prepare You for the Worlds of the morrows.

Even though Rebirth, that is REINCARNATION, is mentioned many times in the Book of Islam, many Islamic circles do not believe in REINCARNATION due to the fact that the Technological Dimension has been kept veiled for the Islamic Mystical Medium.

Numerous Information in the KORAN which possesses an intense Frequency Power was locked up in accordance with the operations of that Period, so that people would not be agitated.

The Technological Dimension which works Cooperatively with the Spiritual Plan, by unveiling the Spiritual Dimension for Islamic Mysticism, has conveyed to You only the Concepts of the ALMIGHTY and ALLAH. By this means it provided Your Purification through the Frequencies of Serenity in the Medium of Worship.

This Medium has been called HEAVEN in Your Sacred Books. You deserve to receive the other Information only after this Purification Medium.

All the Universal Rules and Information are present in the Book of Islam which had been prepared in the Eighteenth Dimension and had been bestowed on Your Planet from the Ninth Dimension.

After the Religious Dimension was closed with this Final Book and the Final Prophet, now, the Permission to open up to the Universal Dimensions has been given to Humanity which has been prepared during a period of Fifteen Centuries, and Your Planet has been made to get directly in touch with the Technological Dimension.

This FINAL AGE which is called the period of RESURRECTION in Your Sacred Books, is the Period of attaining Consciousness, and is the Awakening of Your Planet. It is called the AGE OF MEDIUMSHIP or the MEDIAMIC AGE.

During this Period which is also called the period of SINCERITY, the Celestial Authorities are proving the Supremacy of the Human Being both to himself/herself and to the Universes by removing the Intermediaries.

The Technological Dimension is registering the Thoughts of each person in every breath by the Computer Advanced Systems and is sending answers, at that moment, to Your Brain Signals.

By this means, it causes Super Worlds to gain Super Human Beings by causing them to attain the Evolvement of a Thousand years in One year and it Unifies the You of Yesterday with the You of Today and Integrates You in a Whole.

The KNOWLEDGE BOOK which is bestowed on Your Planet at the moment through the Channel of ALPHA like the other Books, is dictated from the Channel of the World LORD which is connected to the Focal Point of the Unified Reality, from a Private Channel connected to the Frequency of Dear MEVLANA and by this means Gateways of Truth are opened for You.

The Powerful Frequency of the KNOWLEDGE BOOK prepares People for SALVATION very speedily by Evolving them in a silent and profound way. It is presented for Your Information. (This Message has been dictated as an answer to the chains of Thought.)

CENTER

COSMIC ENERGIES AND CONTROL WAVES

Our Friends,

You who are the investment of the years as the residents of the Golden Galaxy are in Your World at the moment, being on Duty by the Plan as Peace Missionaries by the Command of the Divine Authorities.

The negativities around You will never influence the friends who have attained Genuine Consciousness. Do not ever doubt this. To attain the ability to enter this Channel which will project on Your Planet the Awareness of the entire Ordinance is not as easy as presumed.

To receive Messages, to give Messages occur as a result of the Electro-Magnetic Waves uniting with the Radio Signals, being able to reach Your Brain Powers. Receiving Messages has nothing to do with Evolvement. Everyone who can develop his/her Sixth Sense can receive Messages.

But We Evaluate people in accordance with their Evolvement. And, for this reason, We wish everyone who have developed his/her ability to receive these Signals, to Serve on the path of Humanity and We get in touch with them on this matter.

The Plan gradually takes You under Supervision after the first contacts begin. And it unveils the Information up to the degree You have Deserved. Information is a Factor Training You. You can accept them as a school Plan.

However, from time to time, the controls of whether You have digested this Information or not are made. During those controls, whether You have Deserved that which is expected of You or not, whether You are in harmony and in agreement with the High Consciousness of the Messages We give or not are examined.

And to achieve this, the Control Waves are sent. Since these Control Waves influence the negativities, if there are any, in a still more negative way, in Your Lives both Social and Family Discords are witnessed.

In this Medium, each person is Responsible for his/her own Consciousness and Duties. We have always extended Our Friendly Hands towards Genuine Friends who have attained Genuine Consciousness. And We have always kept them under a Medium of great Protection (ALLAH Protects You).

The Control Waves and the Cosmic Currents sent to You are not Individual but General. And they shower Your entire Planet. These Waves have different special Frequencies and Vibrations. They influence all Natural and Cellular structures.

By this means, Your Levels of Consciousness Purify themselves by the events You experience. These Waves are sent to Your Planet to bring Your Consciousnesses to the desired Level. Otherwise, You would not be able to Progress in the field of Science and Learning, You would not be able to complete Your Evolutions.

If You have completed Your Incarnation cycles in Your past lives, these Waves strike a polished surface, can not hold on, and slide down and away. Otherwise, they file the roughnesses in You.

Control Waves have nothing to do with Cosmic Energies. Cosmic Energy Pores are Energies of Knowledge and Consciousness. But Control Waves are the Waves of Evolution.

Each person who has Terrestrial Consciousness, at first possesses a Free Will peculiar to himself/ herself. Later, one starts to walk on the path. One Ascends the Evolutionary Steps one by one.

If there was no Evolution, You could not be the You of today. You would not be able to attain Your present Consciousness. Now, let Us mention the Thresholds these Control Waves make You pass over and let Us dictate them in sequence:

1. Threshold of Arrogance - Pride - Vindictiveness
2. Threshold of Possessions - Property - Matter
3. Threshold of Love - Affection - Friendship
4. Threshold of Humanity - Self-Sacrifice - Tolerance
5. Threshold of Effacing One's Self from One's Own Self
6. Threshold of Attainment - Unification

These 6 Thresholds are those which should be Transcended at the first stage. Now, let Us write the Thresholds following this: Cosmic Energies are received after the sixth Step.

7. Threshold of attaining Cosmic Consciousness
8. Threshold of Unifying with the Universal Consciousness
9. Threshold of being appointed to Special Missions (like helping each other and healing in accordance with the Consciousnesses)
10. Threshold of being habituated to Cosmic Energies (Direct - Indirect - During Sleep)
11. Program of overcoming Fears and the threshold of transition
12. Threshold of being appointed to the path of Genuine Mission
13. Consciousness-Realization-Awareness attained during this Mission
14. Logic-Responsibility attained during this Mission
15. Will Power attained during this Mission
16. Allegiance Consciousness attained during this Mission
17. Universal Totality attained during this Mission
18. Humane Qualities attained during this Mission

The first six of the 18 steps We have dictated above carry ALPHA Wave Energies. The second six carry BETA Wave Energies. The third six carry GAMMA Wave Energies.

19. Is the Direct OMEGA Gateway.

One can not enter there easily. In order to be accepted there You have to Transcend, one by one, the Eighteen Thresholds listed above.

Let Us repeat again. Receiving Information and deserving the Mediums are different things.

These very Control Waves are assisting Waves which file Your roughnesses, which provoke disputes among people by making You go through Terrestrial Exams, and by this means, which reveal the Genuine Personalities, which discover for Us the Genuine Human Beings and which make them Coded and prepared for the Dimension of Salvation.

Your Terrestrial Exams are made by this means. And this System is under the control of the Mechanism of Influences.

In accordance with the Accelerated Evolutionary Program applied on Your Planet at the moment, the Solar Teachers who have completed the above dictated Thresholds during their former lives have returned to Your Planet through Reverse Transfers to help You on this path.

However, their perfection, their Advanced Consciousnesses and Knowledge have been concealed and Medium in which they will perform their Missions by their terrestrial Consciousnesses have been prepared. Because, otherwise, Your world would become a scene of even a greater chaos.

At the moment, only to Dear Mevlana the Permission of (revealing her Identity) is directly given. This, too, is a part of her Mission related to the KNOWLEDGE BOOK which is dictated. The KNOWLEDGE BOOK, the Book of the Morrows prepares You for the morrows beginning from today.

Private identities are revealed during many Individual contacts. Some of the Friends around the people in question know and recognize them. But those people can never make themselves accepted by Society. In spite of everything, this is prevented through various deceptions.

Each person will know only who he/she is. Because, Ages of Prophethood will not be gone through any more. We have revealed Dear Mevlana who is a Universal Symbol to Public as a necessity of her Mission.

Because, the time has come for knowing what is what and the Truth. This is for the advantage of Your Planet. We beg the pardon of Dear Mevlana, again and again, for upsetting her about this matter of revealing.

CENTER ABOVE THE CENTER

GENERAL INFORMATION

Our Friends,
The advanced Plan operations have been accelerated by the reflection of the Suns on the Suns. (The expression Suns is used for Awakened, Advanced Consciousnesses). Your Planet which will possess the Awareness of the entire Ordinance is prepared for the Dimension of Salvation by Your Self-sacrifice.

The Suns will shed Light on the Period of Preparation for the Golden Age. Each person will walk on this path Consciously, Confidently and Awarely by Realizing his/her share of Duty.

Your Planet knows the nature of the Divine Commands coming from the Land of Mighty Ones (Land of Mighty Ones is the Focal Point where the Sacred Books had been prepared). Your Planet does not have the Consciousness of the Unknown horizons yet.

You who have been taken into the Progression Program of the Final Age are being introduced to the Technological Dimensions. We reach You by declaring the Truth to You through the KNOWLEDGE BOOK which is bestowed on Your Planet by a Special Channel of the COUNCIL OF THE REALITY OF THE UNIFIED HUMANITY. We are Grateful to Dear MEVLANA.

The Technological Dimension which has conveyed to You the Divine Commands of ALLAH until today, is allotting Missions in accordance with each person's Sense of Duty and Frequency Power, considering the performed operations. In Your Planet, even the tiniest Living Entity has a Mission peculiar to itself. You are Entities who have been Incarnated in Your Planet as Solar Teachers.

Our Human Friends still lack the Consciousness of what the tricks of the Medium are. For this reason, they try to do everything in accordance with their own Consciousness. Now, We convey to You everything through the PEN OF THE GOLDEN AGE by this KNOWLEDGE BOOK. And We answer Your chains of Thought article by article. Write, please:

1. The Reality of the Unified Humanity Council is obliged to provide the Universal Unity as the responsible one of the entire Universal Ordinance.
2. Your Sacred Books You have received until today are the Divine Suggestions and Celestial Knowledge which have prepared You for the present days.
3. During this Final Age, an unveiling in accordance with their Frequency Powers has been provided for the Private channels of everyone. The Purpose is to convey to You the Awareness of the Universal Ordinance.
4. Each person is a Free Spirit, a Free Awareness. No one has the right to impose his/her own Consciousness on anyone else. Each Person is Responsible for himself herself.
5. Those who will lay the foundation of the Golden Age are the Children of the Morrow. You are now obliged to apply this Program of Preparation on Your Planet.
6. In accordance with the Laws of the Unified Field, everyone is subjected to Private operations as the Spiritual Guide of his/her own self.
7. These Operations are provided as a result of getting in touch with Special people under the supervision of the Plan, or people are trained while asleep (Coincidences are Prepared Mediums).
8. Perceptions of everyone are Fortified by the Signals received from the Divine Dimension. These Signals are Special Cosmic Currents and Energy Pores (Do not confuse them with Natural Cosmic Currents).

9. It is not possible for every Veiled Awareness to receive the Cosmic Currents showering Your Planet. For this reason, Groups which are close Plan Magnetic Aura Projecting Focal Points have been established in Your Planet. (The Mediamic Period) has been Started.

10. In Your entire Planet, Consciousnesses who were able to elevate themselves up to the Energy of the Universal Dimension know the Truth. And they are obliged to convey it to those who do not know it.

11. You should not act considering the Perceptive Powers of people, but You should reveal the Truth without any hesitation. Doubts have always retarded You.

12. All the work performed during this Final Age are under the Supervision of the Plan. The Source is the same.

13. Information given to You is the Mirror of the Truth. Those who gaze into that Mirror, those who are Awakened by this Consciousness are obliged to serve directly the Dimension of the Unified Reality.

14. The Services made are for the (SINGLE). You should act being Conscious of this.

15. Efforts still made on Private channel work is a waste of time. Selfish efforts are never forgiven during this final Age. The Retaliation to be paid is within Time.

16. Awakening means to attain Realization. It is to act in accordance with Logic.
A person who is subjected to the Exams of Awakening is appointed to the Field of Conscious Mission at the end of this Period.

17. Those who still waste time with Visions of Sleep, who act in accordance with them can never undertake Duty in the Active Mission field of the Plan, can never be beneficial to Humanity.

18. Information received by the Channels which have not been connected to the Center are the old Information of their own Realities.

19. Channels which continue to give this Information do not get help from the Plan, they waste time with their own Information, they can not, in any way, make any progress.

20. Passing over the threshold of the Golden Age occurs by the help of the Divine Plan. Everything is for Your own Good.

21. We expect Missions with more Realization from You as the days in which the Heavens will be opened get closer. The Missions You will perform should not be for Your own selves, but for Humanity. For Us, the Genuine Mission is this.

22. The Leaders of the Groups are not Sheiks, but are the Channel Assistants of the Plan.

23. Healing Focal Points have been connected directly to the Channel of the Center. It has nothing to do with the personal Power of the Healer. The Channel helps the sick people who recuperate or will be recuperated.

24. For Centuries, We have started by telling You and everything, about ALLAH, His Supremacy, His Help. THE ESTABLISHER OF THIS GREAT ORDINANCE now invites You to become Genuine Human Beings, and to a Discerning, Aware and Logical Duty Consciousness.

25. The investments of years are sprouting now, during this Period. Everything will attain Light through You, who are the Lights of the Golden Age.

26. To Awaken is to attain Realization and to get Consciousness. It means to perform one's Duty by living One's World by everything it has.

27. Not to be able to attain Realization is nothing but the imposition of certain Powers of their own Consciousnesses on You. For this reason, We connect the Channels to the Center. You are under Supervision.

28. To conceal the Universal Information which is not the Original possessions of any Medium imposes great Responsibility on the Channel in question.

29. You are all equal. Do not overestimate each other. Differences of Knowledge are born from the Levels of Consciousness and from Duties.

30. We would like to see the Maturity We wish to see in You also in the Service of the Information. The Information transactions should not be Programmed in accordance with Your Personal Thoughts.

31. Solar Teachers who have been transferred to Your Planet from Universal Dimensions are trying at the moment, to convey and teach You Love and Humane Qualities, (for Your Evolution).

32. You, who still possess Individual EGOs (Exceptions excluded) are not aware of anything. You only know the Scarcity of Time, but no one has attained the Genuine Consciousness of it.

33. The Divine Commands, as the entire Universal Laws of the Divine Authorities have been organized in accordance with the Frequency of each Dimension. All of them, as a Single Constitution, are under the Supervision of the Plan.

34. The Responsibility of the Knowledge Book is under the Supervision of the World LORD. And it is bestowed on You by the aids of the Golden Galaxy Dimension.

35. Each Person in Your Planet carries the Responsibility of this Knowledge Book which is bestowed on Your Planet.

36. Provided You act being Conscious of it, You will undertake Your Universal Responsibility.

37. Even the slightest alteration can not be made on the Knowledge Book. Its Original form can not be Corrupted.

38. If each Medium compares the Information he/she has received until today with the Information of the Knowledge Book, he/she will make Analyses and Syntheses of them in a more Conscious way.

39. No Information is superior to another one. Because, the Source is the Same. Information is prepared in accordance with the Power of Frequency and Perception, with Duty-Consciousness, with Evolvements.

40. First of all, the Group Leaders should attain the Genuine Consciousness. One should regard the Truth in an impartial way and should not act with Prejudice.

41. We wish to see the Perfection that will be seen in everything first of all in all the Group Leaders in Your Planet.

42. Mediums of Lethargy will not be Tolerated from now on (This is declared for the Missionaries).

43. Information given to each channel is for confirming each other. By this means, You attain the Consciousness of the Truth.

44. Mevlana Essence Nucleus Group, which carries a Dimensional Frequency connected to the Essence Channel of the Plan, possesses a characteristic different than the other Groups. Because, this Group gives service directly in the service of the LORD and as the Essence Staff Members of the Plan.

45. Each Group in Your Planet sheds Light on Society through the different Frequency Dimensions of the Plan. The Friends of the Mevlana Essence Nucleus, as the Tongue, the Hand, and the Eye of the Plan Directly, are obliged to convey to You the Universal Ordinance and the Truth.

46. The Knowledge Book is a Universal Constitution. It is not under the license of any Group. It belongs to every Group and is a Universal Guide.

47. For this reason, the Knowledge Book carries a great Responsibility for Your Planet. To grasp the Truth is a Gain for each of Our Terrestrial Friends.

48. The Knowledge Book is not the imposition of a Group, but is the Voice of the Plan, is the Light of the Truth, the Sun of Salvation and is the Order of the LORD. The Truth will be attained in Time.

49. Your Planet is in the influence field of the Awareness of the entire Universal Ordinance. Negativities will, in time, give service by attaining Consciousness on the Positive path by the Cosmic Influences.

50. False evaluations and personal interpretations among Groups will become ineffective in time, (Provided You attain Universal Evolvement).

51. During this Final Age, each Frequency is Under Supervision. The Truths are conveyed to You by the Suggestions coming from an Established Order.

52. The Universal investments, the help and service You will extend towards Humanity will begin the moment You give up serving Yourselves.

53. The Lights of the morrows have been seen on the horizon. We wish to see the Cooperative Hands and Consciousnesses which will extend towards those Lights as an Integrated Whole.

54. We are answering all the Thoughts We receive from the Thought Signals. The Plan, that is, (The SUPREME MECHANISM), is not, in fact, a Supervising factor. It is a System constituted by Directing Staffs. It is the Cooperative operational Focal Point of numerous Plans. Its services are for the (SINGLE) and for the Advanced Ordinances. They all are in service as an Integrated Whole.

55. The different directing staffs of the Plan have conveyed to You the Channel Information received by Our Medium Friends until today through certain Missions.

56. In fact, the Supervision is performed by the Galactic Missions by the Command of the Divine Order. These Missions are the Projectors of the System which have helped to convey to You the Sacred Books You have received until today.

57. All the Systems are connected to the Plan. This place provides the Unification with the advanced staffs.

58. The Council of the Universal Ordinance is the direct Directing Mechanism of the System.

59. The Knowledge Book is bestowed on Your Planet from this System. The World LORD is Responsible for this.

60. The World LORD, AMON and RA are the direct projecting zone of the Plan as the Joint Triple Code.

61. RA here, is the LORD of the System. This is an operational Order. Do not confuse it with the (SINGLE) and with the (ONE). In future, Messages will be given about the (SINGLE) and the (ONE).

62. We extend Our Helping Hands to You as much as We can. Being still late in grasping the Truth means wasting Time. From now on, please Sharpen Your Consciousnesses. Do not tire Us any more.

63. The Universal Laws and Programs prepared Centuries ago had been prepared in accordance with the Time Units of the World. At the moment, Time has gained Speed. Dates are approaching.

64. The Scarcity of Time is being mentioned as a result of the Time Period which will be Accelerated even more.

65. You are faced with a change of Age. Do not ever forget this. Everything will settle in its Course silently and profoundly.

66. Your Planet which will go through a Cosmic Age for three Centuries will reach the GOLDEN AGE only afterwards.

67. Provided You respect the Universal Laws and Orders as much as We do, You can reach the GOLDEN AGE even quicker (This is a matter of Evolution).

68. You will be the ones who will establish, in future, a brand new Order which will be applied on Your Planet. Your Planet will never be invaded by Extra-Terrestrial Friends.

69. Your World is Yours. And those who will rule it are You, Our Terrestrial brothers and sisters. Certain wrong conditioned Thoughts drive You towards wrong paths.

70. The Advanced Consciousnesses of the GOLDEN AGE are selected, one by one, by the Special Channel of the Golden Galaxy Dimension and are connected to the Plan.

71. The Plan never gives Directives and Commands. It only helps and guides You in the steps You will take forward.

72. The Final Selections are made in accordance with Your Essence Consciousnesses. There is no Intercession in any matter. To deserve Intercession depends on You. You will find its Proof within Time.

73. We have nothing to do with Names and Symbols. Spiritual experiences rather than Terrestrial experiences are valid here.

74. Your Planet is prepared for SALVATION by the operations done on the path of Humanity by the efforts of Collective Consciousnesses and by their Self-Sacrifice.

75. That which We require of You is Your saying Hello to US with a HAPPY Trustworthy World, full of Love, without Wars.

76. It can be too late if You still expect proofs. Proofs and the Truths are in Your Children and in the course of Your World. Look and See the Future.

77. After the year 1990, Your Planet will go through Critical Periods. Happiness will be Yours if You give Service on the Genuine path. Your gain is Serving Humanity and the Universes.

78. This Message of Ours has been given as a Suggestion of the Plan for all the World Groups. It is presented for Your information.

**IT IS TRANSMITTED FROM THE
COSMOS FEDERAL ASSEMBLY**

IT IS ANSWER TO THE CHAINS OF THOUGHT

Our Friends,

The GOLDEN AGE is the Operational Order of all the Celestial Doctrines assembled in a Whole. The Cosmic Focal Points will continue to do their Duties until the day when everyone will attain his/her Essence Consciousness. And everyone will work on this path.

Many times We have mentioned in detail the characteristics of the Knowledge Book. We have given certain hints so that everyone could grasp the Truth. However, no one has attained the Consciousness that the events which take place are the phenomena depending on selection.

For this reason, We will continue, from time to time, to tell You about the Functions of the Knowledge Book, about the Speciality and the Mission of Dear Mevlana, in the Knowledge Book. These repetitions will continue until You grasp the Truth. The Truth is conveyed to You by these methods.

Now, let Us make an explanation again. The Knowledge Book, rendered effective as the Proof of the Information received by all the Consciousnesses who are Awakened during this Final Age Program, is a Guide for You, is a Synthesis of Your Views and Thoughts, as a Stimulating Power of Your Planet and is a Light of the Truth. It is the Tongue of the Times beyond Time. It is the Main Source of the System.

The KNOWLEDGE BOOK is a BOOK which has been prepared in accordance with the Consciousness Levels found in every section of Society, which carries a Special Frequency Power and which serves under the Status of the Universal Constitution.

It is not a Book of Enlightenment, but a Book of Warning, Connection and Selection. Its Frequency is regulated in accordance with the Perception Power of each Consciousness Level. For this reason, each person receives the Information according to his/her own Level of Consciousness .

According to the Program of Progress, everyone who attains Consciousness can easily grasp the true meaning of this Book. This Message is dictated specially for Our Friends who are meticulous about the Contradictions.

Let Us repeat; the Information which seem like contradiction in the Book is included on purpose. This is a Coding of Frequencies and Consciousness. And We will continue to add them, too. No more Information will be given about this matter again.

Dear Mevlana, undertaking the Mission of a Solar Teacher, is present in Your Planet as Our Spokesperson. She is neither a Prophet, nor a God. She only is a Light-Teacher and a very Beloved Friend of Ours.

Through the KNOWLEDGE BOOK dictated to Our Friend, the Order of the REALITY OF THE UNIFIED HUMANITY prepared in accordance with the Collective operational Ordinance of all the Missions and of the Universal Mechanism is introduced to all Societies in Your Planet.

We, as the Unified Reality Universal Missions, are the Servants of the LORD. And We are the Messengers of the Truth. It is presented for Your Information.

REALITY

THE COSMIC AGE AND ITS TERRESTRIAL REFLECTION

Our Friends,
We call the Waves expanding from the Golden Galaxy Empire towards the Golden Suns the COSMIC REFLECTION FOCAL POINTS (The expression the Golden Suns is used for the Awakened Consciousnesses who give service from the Golden Galaxy Dimension which is the Projecting Focal Point of the Universal Ordinance).

The way in which this operational System which will make You Attain the awareness of the entire Ordinance is projected on Your Planet and the Medium it makes You go through is called the COSMIC AGE.

During the Cosmic Age, the Cosmic Energies by the Mechanism of Influences, specially projected on You by the Technological Dimensions, has begun by the direct Command of the LORD.

The Cosmic Age comprises, in the Terrestrial Plan, an accelerated Evolutionary Program of a 100 years. And this is a Celestial help extended towards the Supreme Beings who will be the Lights of the Golden Age.

These Waves which bring out the inferiorities among the superiorities, and which make our Human Brothers an Sisters attain Genuine Superiority and the Consciousness of Singleness by all means, make these Supreme Ones Supreme and the Inferior ones even more Inferior. During this Selection Program, Your World is Purifying itself by these Waves.

The Speciality of this System is that, the Cosmic Energies showering Your Planet are projected on You. And You choose Your own paths in accordance with Your own Levels of Consciousness. The paths You design belong entirely to You.

We, only as a Reflective Focal Point, extend Celestial Help to Friends who can reach us, as the Missionaries of the Plan by the help of the Cosmic Waves especially directed towards Your Planet.

During this Transition Period, these Cosmic aids to be extended towards Our Human brothers and sisters will continue until 2200 (Of course, for those who can reach Us).

Afterwards, the Cosmic Age will come to an end completely and the GOLDEN AGE will directly be started. After a Cosmic Age of Three Centuries, You will live as an integrated whole, without feeling the need for Celestial help, since everyone will attain the Realization of the Plan and the Ordinance.

The Period You are going through at the moment is the chaos of the opening of channels and of the operations still going on. According to the Final Program of Progress, everyone's channel is open in Your Planet (in accordance with their Levels of Consciousness) either Directly, or through Intuition and are still being opened.

At the moment, by the Command of the Plan, the Command of not making Celestial interference with any channel until the Year 2000 has been given. For this reason, since everyone will try to Enlighten others according to his/her own Level of Consciousness, Your Planet will go through a Cosmic Resurrection.

The Information We give to Our Human brothers and sisters through this KNOWLEDGE BOOK will make them attain the Truth by keeping them away from this Period of Confusion, by making them attain Realization. In this Medium of chaos, this Celestial KNOWLEDGE BOOK will be a Guide in Your Plan of Salvation.

The choice is Yours. We can only keep the Friends who can reach Us, who can grasp the Truth by their Genuine Consciousnesses away from this Program of chaos by holding their hands.

Later, much more Powerful Information will be given to You. Become Powerful for this. Add Power to Your Power. Expand Your Consciousness Potential. Otherwise, there is the probability of you walking the path to be trodden on foot.

Each new Day is a Threshold of Cosmic Progress. To Transcend this Threshold systematically will prepare You for the unseen horizons of the Advanced Plans. And will take You to unknown worlds. For this reason, We do not interfere with, and impose upon any of Our Terrestrial brothers and sisters and their channels.

Only to those who have attained the Awareness of the Ordinance and the Plan, Direct help is extended from the Center. We have received the Command of extending this help only to the Codes who are connected to the Plan. We have dictated this Message as an answer to the Signals We have received from certain chains of Thought.

CENTER ABOVE THE CENTER

NOTICE AND WARNING FOR INTEGRATED CONSCIOUSNESSES

Our Friends,

As the rings of a chain which extend from the Past Eternity to the Future Eternity, You are Beings who are equipped with all the Universal Secrets. Each one has Private Channels Peculiar to himself/herself and those Channels have Evolutions belonging to the Systems they are in.

Beings who can reach advanced Plans after the final Evolutionary line of the established Ordinance and the Plan, are, afterwards, subjected to the Evolutionary Ordinance of those Dimensions. However, the Ordinance of all the Realms is under the Supervision of the Divine Plan.

Divine Authorities are not Religious Authorities. They are the preparatory Authorities only for the Consciousnesses who have been Exalted by Religious Enlightenments, enabling them to receive different Information in more Advanced Plans.

For this reason, since the channel of each person carries the Frequencies of different Dimensions, differences of Perception and Information occur. Each person's Private Channel develops the ability to receive different Information, through the Progress he/she has made, in accordance with the Evolutionary Ordinance.

Since during this Period of Sincerity everyone is taken into the Dimension of Awakening by the effect of the Mechanism of Influences, conflicts pertaining to Awareness and Knowledge occur among people.

But, since the Plan has sent You during this Final Program of Progress to help Your brothers and sisters in Your Planet, first, it takes under Supervision the Consciousnesses awakened by their own Essence Evolutionary Dimensional Energies parallel to the services which will be rendered, and it veils their old channel Information.

The Goal is not Our Human brothers'/sisters' proving themselves, but their Serving and Helping Humanity. Unless the rings of his/her Ego chains are broken one by one, that Person lacks the Attributes peculiar to Humans.

For this reason, the Essences of Our brothers and sisters who came from advanced Dimensions keep aching. A person who has found himself/herself, who has seen the Light of the Truth is Respectful towards the Laws of the Universal Ordinance and obeys them.

Let Us repeat again. This KNOWLEDGE BOOK which is dictated is neither a Religion, nor an Astrology, nor Dear Mevlana's own Private Channel Information. This Book is a Guide dictated by the Command of the System crying out the Truth. Helping and serving Humanity will occur under its Light.

Because, this Book of the Final Age is the Book of the LORD which projects the Universal Order on You.

We are the Residents of the GOLDEN GALAXY who act by the Commands We receive and who serve on the Order Establishing Dimensions. The Special Channel of the Universal Council conveys to You all the Truth through this BOOK.

During this Final Age, the channels of everyone are kept under Supervision and We call to You only from the Dimension of serving Humanity. The Only Goal and Mission of all of You should be this.

Communications with their own Private Channels are nothing but a waste of time for Our Awakened Friends. In this Final Period, the private Powerful channels of no one can save him/her. Supervision is under the Control of the Universal Ordinance.

If You do not serve on this path, Your Private Channels can not exonerate You from the Exams You will go through. Because, You have become existent in your planet by having conformed to the Call of this Final Period.

We invite You to Universal Unification once more. We call You for the services which will be made under the roof of Humanity by removing conflicts of Channel and of Information among You. And We will always repeat this Call.

This BOOK which is revealed as the WARNING BOOK of the Final Age is Your Salvation. It is beneficial to Read it, to make others Read it and to heed the Words Told. Please, Get Rid of Individualism, Shake Yourselves, do not be delayed any more in understanding the Truth. It is presented for Your Information.

CENTRAL SYSTEM

THE COSMIC RESURRECTION

Our Friends,

The Existential cause of all Creation is dependent on a Law of Natural Equilibrium. Every Entity, every Living thing in this Existence has Special Missions. The Existential cause of all the Energies Existing within the chain of Cosmoses is to Perform a Mission. And, for this reason, no chain can act Individually.

The beginning of the Cosmic Age is the reason for the preparation of the GOLDEN AGE. For this reason, all Universal Ordinances are projected parallel to each other.

We have started a great Technological operation together with the Essence Staff Members of the Plan who are the Establishers of the Divine Orders.

In fact, operations have been made Collectively in the Universal Ordinance until today. However, the characteristic of this Final Period operations is to rectify the malfunctioning aspects of the Order which used to proceed in an Orderly way until today.

The Cosmic Age has been directly started by the Program of Preparing Your Planet, beginning with the Year 1900, in accordance with the Accelerated Evolutionary System. You are about to transcend the first Century in Your Planet which has been taken into a Program of Progress of Three Centuries.

For this reason, You come face to face with different Consciousness Levels and different Currents to which You have not been habituated until today. You are being prepared for the Orders beyond Realms, Cosmoses.

For this reason, there is a Mission incumbent on everyone. The operational fields of these Missionaries are various. And each Missionary is obliged to exhibit his/her Missions in the podium of his/her field.

In sequence, these Missions are as follows: Unification of Nations - Way of Administration of States - Community Relations - All Social Relations - Family Orders and all Business Fields from the bottom to the top.

The EGO which is the fuel of Terrestrial Potential is an element of provocation to carry on the Worldly affairs. However, in the Universal Order there is absolutely no place for the Ego.

The Cosmic Beams showering Your Planet during the Universal operations performed in accordance with this Final Period Program are very Powerful Currents rendering Your Levels of Consciousness attain a certain Maturity and revealing the Genuine Personalities concealed within You.

In the Universal Plan, everyone has a receiving and transmitting Signal. These Signals are the Intuitional Keys which You call the SIXTH SENSE.

These Cosmic Currents are Special Currents which unlock the Locks by these Keys and which provide the Genuine Contacts with Us and which are conveyed to You through a kind of different Signals. (Do not confuse them with Natural Cosmic Currents).

These Signals are a System directed and oriented by the Mechanism of Influences.

We get in touch with every Light the signal of which We receive. Their Identities are investigated and after their Capacities and Missions are determined, it is being tried to reveal their Genuine Beings by exposing them in the World Plan to the influences of Cosmic Effects.

Genuine Essences are Genuine servants of God who serve Positively and who are free from Egos. Provided the personalities who are in such a Medium reach Us, Missions in accordance with their fields are given to them.

After the Missions are given, first, a System of shutting the eye is applied. Later, one of the eyes is opened and, still later, the direction in which the Missionary moves is examined by two eyes. And this is determined by a three-step Program. Finally, the Genuine path chosen by two eyes is selected for You and this always is for Your benefit.

The Administrative Council of the Unified Reality makes this Choice. And shows You the Genuine Orders and Paths by conveying to You the Awareness of the entire Ordinance. Those who proceed on this path are the Essence Members of the Plan and they are under Protection.

All the channels which will make Cosmic Progress until the Year 2000 are being opened. However, conforming to the Commands received, no interference will be made by the Plan to the Channel of anyone until the day of the Final Age. Everyone will design his/her path in accordance with the voice of his/her Conscience. For this reason, Your Planet will go through a Cosmic Resurrection.

Meanwhile, Selected Friends who will be taken into the Salvation Plan, will help their other brothers and sisters by performing their duties under the Supervision of the Plan. You live in such a Term that those which help You are these Cosmic Beams until You attain Essence Security.

We do not make the selection. You will make the selection, We will take You to Salvation. It is presented for Your Information.

CENTER

IT IS ANSWER TO THE CHAINS OF THOUGHT

Our Friends,

As the GOLDEN AGE unveils its horizons to You, as Human Beings gradually attain the desired Medium Consciousness, You, too, will attain Serenity and will perform Your Missions justly.

The Order of the GOLDEN GALAXY is administered by a group of Missionaries who perform their Duties under the Supervision of the Missionaries who are Responsible for the entire Universe under the Supervision of the Divine Order beyond Your Suns. AMON is Responsible for its Administration.

The only Galaxy connected to the Telekiné System is here. This Galaxy had been made in a special way. Its Essence nucleus and its alloys are completely Golden. The Projection Focal Point of the entire Cosmos and all the Realms and the Establishing Order of all the Systems are administered directly from here.

The Channel of the Divine Plan which is connected to the ALMIGHTY is under the responsibility of only the GOLDEN GALAXY EMPIRE.

The reason why We have not been able to reach You until today was to wait for the end of the time period allotted by the Universal Ordinance. Now, the Skies have been opened. Our contacts with You occur more often. It is presented for Your Information.

CENTER

NOTICE TO THE PUBLIC CONSCIOUSNESS

Our Friends,

Superiorities and Attachments are Locks covering Your Essence-Consciousnesses and causing not to open the Advanced paths. Your Sacred Books which have called to You from the Skies until today, have been revealed as a Proof of These Days and for Your Purification.

Each Celestial Book heralds the one which comes next. Just so, the good news about the coming of Our Light-Friend who had been the heralder of Islam had been given in the New Testament. And in the Koran, the Book of Islam, the coming of these days had been announced.

The Collective Knowledge of all the Sacred Books have been converged in Resurrection and in the Single-God-Consciousness. In the Book of Islam, it has been said, "Such a day will come when everyone will become Islam". Here, We would like to clarify an interpretation which has been misunderstood.

Christianity and Muslim Religion are each a Religion, a Doctrine. Those who appropriate to themselves these Religions are called Christians and Moslems. The expression ISLAM has been used for the Genuine Human Being. Koran, the Book of Islam, is the Book of Humanity. In fact, it has nothing to do with Religion.

When Koran had been accepted as the Final Sacred Book, in that Period Humanity was not aware yet of the fact that Islam and this was a Book which would reveal the Genuine Human Beings by its Frequency which has a training and a constructive characteristic for those who appropriate to themselves the Islam and who consider it as a Religion.

When it is said that one day the whole World will become Islam, it does not mean that everyone will accept the Moslem Religion. Do not misunderstand this saying, do not misinterpret it.

Your Prophets who were the Divine Messengers of the Divine Authorities, were each a Missionary of Enlightenment. The Books they have written do not belong to them. Those Books are the Commands of God conveyed to You from a very Supreme Level of the Firmament. In the Universal Dimensions, the meaning of Islam is GENUINE HUMAN BEING.

Now, We have disclosed the Truths to Your entire Planet. And We still disclose them towards the unknowns. Now, We assemble everyone under the Roof of Humanity through Love, Brotherhood, Tolerance and Godly Consciousness. This is the very TRUTH and RESURRECTING mentioned in the Book of Islam.

Now, this KNOWLEDGE BOOK is opening the Gates of the Unknown Horizons to Your Planet by giving You the Good News of the morrows. And it is projecting the entire Truth in accordance with each Consciousness, each Point of View.

There is cruelty, there is suffering in Societies in which the word ISLAM is misunderstood. Humanity which has the Consciousness of attaining the Truth as soon as possible is making all the Efforts it can on this path. (Those who can reach Us). We are very easily in contact with these Friends. And We Enlighten them on this path by the same subjects, We correct the misinterpretations.

Let Us repeat again, the word Islam should never be evaluated in accordance with Religious assessments and Views. THE KNOWLEDGE BOOK which is dictated at the moment, is dictated through the very Advanced Frequencies of the Religious Dimensions.

Missions of Friends whose Consciousness Channels are opened during this Final Age are extremely great. Celestial Messages received by everyone are for Proving the Knowledge Book to the Public consciousness which We reveal in order to announce the Truth to Your Planet. The Messages at present are distributed Fascicule by Fascicule and are preparing everybody for the Dimension of Salvation.

· Your Planet is not yet aware of the way in which the KNOWLEDGE BOOK is training Humanity. It is a Light which carries the Frequencies of all the Sacred Texts. And it takes You into the Program of Progress much more speedily than Your Sacred Books which have been trying to prepare You for Centuries.

For this reason, all the educative staffs in Your Planet carry the responsibility of the Knowledge Book. To attain this Consciousness, to be Unified in a Whole, is a must for Humanity.

Evaluations which will be made by emphasizing the personalities will be the disappointment of Humanity. Service is for the SINGLE, it is for the Realms, for the Cosmoses. It is desired that everyone should be assembled in this Consciousness. This Message has been dictated as an answer for the Signals of Thought received. It is presented for Your Information.

IT IS GIVEN BY THE DIRECT COMMAND
OF THE COUNCIL
CENTER

EXPLANATION

Our Friends,
The System has been established by a Mutual Power by Uniting the Divine Administrative Law and the Divine Law of Ordinance. This is a very ancient System which had been settled into the applied Plan together with the Existence of the Universe.

Now, this Ancient System is greeting all the Friends like You who live on numerous Planets and on different Solar Systems. It is beneficial to explain something here. This Ancient System has Infinite Respect for each Entity, for each Existing Energy.

However, it applies inevitably certain sanctions on the Systems which act against the Law of Equilibrium and which upset the Order and the Awareness of the Ordinance (for the health of the Universes).

The Human Being is a very Supreme Spirit, a Supreme Consciousness. However, he/she can act as a Free Will and a Free Awareness only if he/she respects the Awareness of a Collective Ordinance. And this is provided by the Incarnation rings of the Evolutionary System.

We are trying to project on You briefly, the Ordinance and the operational Focal Points of these Systems. In accordance with the Evolutionary Ordinance, the Triplet of ESSENCE - CONSCIOUSNESS - CONSCIENCE introduces a Human Being to the Evolutionary Ordinance, by the events he/she experiences and every Entity has to go through This System, sooner or later.

A Plan considered necessary by the System here is applied to the Friends who have exalted up to the final Evolvement boundary of the Evolutionary Ordinance, that is, to the (Genuine Human Beings). Here, We act in accordance with the rule of the Law of Equilibrium.

Then, the System may rule a part of the Individual Wills. Entities who go through this training can be accepted only then, as a Free Will, a Free Conscience, into the Ancient System.

Quite a different Order being established now Renders Effective a different Order of the history of Religions. Consciousnesses who are Awakened by this means are subjected to a special Supervision and Training.

And this is the Direct Law of the LORD. We Greet each Consciousness who is Awakened by this means. It is Our Joy to discover You anew who have been lost. We are Ancient Brothers and Sisters.

IT IS THE TONGUE OF THE ORDINANCE

WORSHIP
(It is Answer to the Chains of Thought)

Our Friends,
GOD is Single. However His Power reflects parallel to each person's Frequency of Thought. Worship is the effort made in order to reach Him.

This effort elevates Your Mental Potential and Your Frequency and makes you attract more Power and Energy from Him. These Energies cause You to attain the Power which conveys You to His Existence, to His Consciousness through Your Thoughts.

Even though GOD is Single, He differs according to each person's Power of Thought. We render Him Single in Our Speech, We render Him numerous in Our Thoughts. And by this means, everyone Worships HIS/HER LORD within his/her own Thought Dimension.

Worship is the Prostration made towards the Total, towards the Minutest Particle, through the path of Thought. To attain the Divine Light of the entire Realm (that is, to become Conscious) is the greatest of Worships. The moment Mankind attains this Consciousness, it means that it has attained the Power of the Divine Power everyone attains through Worship.

Paths of Worship are not single. They are numerous. Because for Us, each Thought, each Breath produced positively is a Worship. We may divide the Worship made on the Religious path into two:

1. Worship through the Heart
2. Worship through Thought

Worship through the Heart - means Worship towards the Total, it means attaining Him through Form and through Prostration.
Worship through Thought - means attaining the minutest Particle-Consciousness, Discovering Him, Seeing Him, Loving Him in all Creation.

In fact, Worship made from the Minutest Particle to the Group, from the Group to the Whole, by Unifying the Thought with the Heart, is the Genuine Worship. And this is the Consciousness which conveys the Human Being from the Status of Godness to the Status of being a Servant of God. Here, there is Love without expectation, Giving without Receiving and Serving the Total. This is the Highest Degree Humanity can attain.

Worshipping the Whole: Is the Worship rendered to HIS Form in the Thought, to HIS Essence, to HIS Unity.

Worship rendered with the Minutest Particle-Consciousness: Is the Worship rendered completely to HIS Person, to HIS Energy, to HIS Power and to the Whole.

During the Worship made by the Minutest Particle-Consciousness, one goes from the Group to the Whole. By this Worship, one attains a Whole beyond form. From then on, Prostration is made within the ESSENCE. Worship towards the Whole is in the Form. Worship in the Essence is in the Consciousness.

And transition from Form towards Consciousness is possible by Human Being's grasping the Awareness of the Entire Ordinance. Worship in Form is for Human Being's Own self. Worship by the Essence is for Humanity. Worship through Service and Work is for All Realms, for All Cosmoses.

All the Minutest Particles of Creation are each a means which projects the Power of GOD which makes You realize His Pre-eminence. You can expand towards the Divine Light, which unfolds from the Minutest Particle to the Whole, by attaining the Supremacy within His Consciousness and by going through His Consciousness with Your Thoughts. Only then may You be considered to have performed Your Genuine Worship.

If You seek Yourself within yourself, if You discover Your Lord within Yourself, if You make Your Prostration within Your Essence, if You Love without being Loved, if You give without Receiving, then You attain the Degree of being the Servant of God through His Consciousness. From then on, Your Worship is to the Human Being, to Humanity, to the Realms, to the Cosmoses, to the Universes. Social Work done by this Consciousness is the Genuine Worship required.

IT IS TRANSMITTED THROUGH THE MALIK CODE
CENTER

ANNOUNCEMENT FOR THOSE WHO WILL BE
ACCEPTED TO THE SUPREME COURT OF ALLAH

Our Friends,
We, as the Residents of the Golden Galaxy Empire, have been observing You for many Years. Within the frame work considered necessary by the Divine Plan, We have tried until today to explain to You briefly the operational way of the Unified Ordinance.

Your Planet has been accepted into the SPIRITUAL PLAN due to the acceptance by the Divine Plan of certain Suggestions considered necessary by the Golden Age.

However, The Anatolian Focal Point known at present as ATATÜRK's TURKEY which has been the Projection center of a Divine Order for Centuries has been taken into the Dimension of Mission as an actual Focal Point since the beginning of Your Century.

In Your Country which has been subjected to a HUNDRED Terrestrial-Year Program of Progress, the Evolutionary Progression is kept under great Supervision. Difficult days are preparing Luminous morrows.

For this reason, as a necessity of the Plan, the ESSENCE-GENES and GENES who have been sown into the Anatolian Dimension with Mission-Consciousness possesses each a Special Cosmic Consciousness. These Consciousness Awakenings occur by the influence of different Cosmic rains cleansing Your Planet at the moment.

The Supreme Consciousnesses who live on Your Planet at the moment are Our Ancient brothers and sisters. The roots of them all, go way back to the Egyptian Karena. And they receive the Inca Magnetic Consciousness. (The Inca Magnetic Consciousness is the final step of the Spiritual Plan.) It is also called the PATH OF THE GOLDEN LIGHT.

The operational Order of Your Planet has been divided into various different Sections by the Plan. Some of these Sections are AMERICA - ENGLAND - SWEDEN. All the possibilities and sources of Your Planet have emanated from these fields.

However, meanwhile, the TURKEY of ATATÜRK has been prepared in a very special way for the Dimension of Mission. Because, the ANATOLIAN Magnetic Field is a SIRAT* Bridge in the Evolutionary Ordinance of Your Planet. It is the only FOCAL POINT where the LORDLY Mechanism and the PLAN Unite.

The Far-East Culture and Philosophy have prepared the East through the TIBET Magnetic Field. From this Focal Point, INDIA is supported by the Divine Plan, JAPAN is supported Technologically. These Focal Points support Your Planet both materially and spiritually.

The path on which Your Planet treads is the path of Awareness of the Evolutionary Ordinance. The UNIFIED REALITY Dimension has gotten in touch with those who would attain this Awareness and has given preparatory Information to certain Focal Points.

Now, We are calling to You directly through the KNOWLEDGE BOOK which is under the Supervision of the WORLD LORD. Due to the Scarcity of Time left until the end of the Cycle, all the Truths will be conveyed to You through this BOOK. It is presented for Your Information.

COSMOS FEDERAL ASSEMBLY

IT IS ANSWER TO THE CHAINS OF THOUGHT

Patience ; is the Bread of Thanksgiving.

Thanksgiving; means Obligation towards YOUR LORD for creating You. This is a kind of Pledge, an Allegiance.

Appreciation; it is Bowing in Humility and Enthusiasm. It is Prostration towards YOUR LORD for Your blessings.

* Look at the Glossary.

GENERAL MESSAGE

Our Friends,

The Secret of the Pyramids is the Secret of the Universe. The Secret of the Universe is the Secret of the Human Being. And the Secret of the Human Being is concealed in Your Planet. The developments which occurred until today in Your Planet used to be made by the (Triangular) Reflection Focal Points. The greatest Reflection Triangle is the Triangle of EGYPT - INDIA - JAPAN.

The First Focal Point, that is Egypt; is the Focal Point of SECRETS.

The Second Focal Point, that is India; is the Focal Point of Faith and of Thought.

The Third Focal Point, that is Japan; is the Focal Point of Discernment, of Intelligence, and of Logic.

There are numerous small and big Triangular Reflection Focal Points in Your Planet. However, the oldest Triangular Focal Point is the Focal Point of Egypt, India, Japan (Channel of Sun). The Himalayan Focal Point in Tibet Projects the Information on Your Planet at present through 449 Channels.

Alongside with this, the Projection Focal Points of the Galactic Dimensions, too, are on service under the Supervision of the Center. However, only (the KNOWLEDGE BOOK) has a direct Special Channel.

Consciousnesses who enter the influence fields of these Triangular Focal Points are Purified by the Energy Pores being connected to the direct Focal Point of the MECHANISM OF INFLUENCES. For this reason, these Consciousnesses do not need Celestial Books.

Long before Your Sacred Books had been revealed to Your Planet, the Magnetic Consciousness of these Three Focal Points had been projected on Consciousnesses as a Philosophical View.

1. EGYPT : Is the Secret of the Sons of the Sun. Sons of the Sun are Your Ancestors.

2. INDIA : There are two more Focal Points reflecting on this Focal Point. These are the INCA and AFRICA Focal Points. This Reflection Triangle had created the Indian Philosophy.

3. JAPAN : Is a Focal Point which works and is induced to work directly under the Command of the Federation. It is connected directly to the CENTRAL SOLAR SYSTEM. It receives reflections from the North and South Poles, too. In fact, the direct Channel is Egypt. And it is the Single Reflection Focal Point of the Sun.

If You place Your Planet in a Pyramid, Egypt constitutes the peak. This is the Channel of ALPHA. The Pyramids have remained to be a Mystery until today which causes Your Thought Codes to operate. Mysteries are imperative for a Human Being to attain Advanced Views.

Quest leads You to Thought and Thought leads You to the Truth. Within the Truth there is no Mystery. Because, now, We are expanding towards the horizons beyond Thoughts. And You are prepared for different Worlds You have not known, You have not seen until today.

From now on, You will Exist in these places here with the same Body, the same Soul, the same Flesh and Skin and with Your Beloved ones, with Your present Consciousnesses. We are making You work and are training You specially for these happy Worlds.

Do not be lazy. Lethargy and Fanaticism are Your obstacles. But Your Love and Faith will be Your triumph. We presume that Your Planet has never, in any Period, received such a clear Message until today, Our Friends. Our Love is for all the Universes.

CENTER

YOU AND THE PLAN

Our Friends,
In the Universal Systems there are such Mediums Your Planet has not known until today that neither Us, nor the Texts in Your Sacred Books have reflected them on You until this moment. Now, We are trying to introduce These Mediums to You gradually.

However, Our Terrestrial brothers and sisters are obliged to complete their Evolvement Phases in their own Dimensions. All Galaxies are under Supervision as a necessity of the System. The application field of the Supreme Plan of the GOLDEN AGE is this place.

That is, the SUPREME MECHANISM directs the Application Field of the Plan. The Focal Point of the GOLDEN GALAXY administers it. At the moment, the operational Ordinance is this.

All the Energies are taken, one by one, into this Dimension in accordance with their Existential Powers. Private contacts have been made with those who will be able to make the Evolvement necessary for entering here. All the Friends who can receive the Waves of the GOLDEN LIGHT Year will be accepted to Salvation. And this is provided for You by the aids of the Mechanism of Influences.

We are connecting, one by one, the private channels of everyone who can receive these Waves, to the Center. From now on, each channel is obliged to complete the rest of its Progress in this Dimension.

Because, they can never enter the Evolution of the Dimension of the GOLDEN SUN (The Dimension of the Golden Sun is the Fifteenth Solar System).

Now, the Energies of a different Dimension are applied on You both individually and in the Projection Focal Points and during Sleep. It is imperative that You should become accustomed to these Energies until January, 1998. And We are trying to achieve this with all Our Power.

Energies who were able to be exalted up to the Spiritual Plan were never able to pass to other Dimensions, that is, to intense Mediums of different Solar Systems until today. Because, their Energy limits were confined to the boundary of the (Three Sevens).

Because, unless they could not receive those Energies, they would not be able to claim their Essence Energies which were within the Spiritual Plan and could not become Embodied with their Genuine Beings. The Energies of Supreme Friends who were able to come up to here used to be prepared, one by one, from here for other Systems. And they used to go easily to other Galaxies without being shaken. (Different Solar Dimensions beyond Supreme Times.)

Now, We are preparing You in the World Plan for these very Energies and for the Evolvements of different Systems. And We are taking You into the applied fields of different Plans You didn't know until today.

Now, let Us briefly mention the Plan here. Your Planet is a field of Veiled Awareness. For this reason, You do not remember almost anything about the Periods in which You have lived, in which You have come up to the boundary of Incarnation. Because, Your past lives are effaced and You become transferred to Your Planet at zero kilometer. This is a necessity of the System.

You complete Your Evolutions by Your own selves. You, Yourselves, choose the mode of life within the Planet Earth. We never dominate Individual Will Powers. However, We select those who have completed their Evolutions, who are Deserving these places here. Then, We Cooperate with them.

Deserving these places occurs by the Evolution of the Incarnation rings. It is necessary for You to experience everything in Your own selves with both their Good and Bad aspects. It is not easy at all to attain Perfection.

It is not the same thing to live on the first floor of an apartment building and to live on its hundredth floor. Ascending the stairs one by one, settling into and being at the hundredth floor by toiling is a much more Difficult deed than presumed.

Nothing is attained easily. These operations are the initial application field of the Plan. Now, We are passing to the second application field. And alterations are made in these apartment buildings.

Now, We are trying to render You Deserve the beauties of the buildings and mediums prepared in the same Level of different Dimensions.

Your being able to reach the places here is provided by the efforts and operations of Our Friends in Your Planet who Deserve the places here. And We help them on this path. At the moment, none of You have become aware of what a great and serious matter these efforts are.

Now, the System here accepts You in Your present conditions, that is, with Your Awakened Awarenesses, with Your near and Dear ones, with all Your Mediums which make You Happy.

This means that Death anxiety of the World Dimension is not present any more. You are prepared for a Happy Medium together with Your Lost ones, with Your Beloved ones.

And You will interminably, without tasting unhappiness, travel to different Galaxies and will get in touch with the Friends there. You will live in much more Perfect Mediums (as if You have not parted at all, in any way, from Your Terrestrial lives).

There is Love, Affection and Pleasure here. However, there is no Birth. You will be together here with Your children You had or You had lost in the World Plan.

Our Friends who do not have any children at the moment in the World Plan, will be together with the children they had in former Incarnations. And they will be reminded of all their lives with the details of those Periods.

When the time comes, We will give You more detailed Information about these Mediums. But now, the Evolutionary System is still on the applied field. That is the reason why We ask You to write the Messages in Your notebooks. Anyway, only those who deserve these places here will write them.

Do You know why We have shortly mentioned this System to You? Because, if they do not see any hope, Our Human brothers and sisters can not make any effort for preparing themselves for the required Medium.

Due to the Scarcity of Time, softenings to a certain extent are made in the selections. This is a great chance for Our Human brothers and sisters. Universal Contacts will be made immediately, without waiting, with Our Friends who will attain the Consciousness of what all this help is about. Our Love is for all the Universes.

CENTRAL SYSTEM

IT IS BRIEF INFORMATION

The LORDLY, the SPIRITUAL and the EVOLUTIONARY ORDINANCE work Cooperatively. Spirit does not need Evolvement. It is a very Powerful Potential. However, this Potential Power, too, presents many differences under the Supervision of the Spiritual Plan. These differences have been prepared in accordance with the Consciousness and Frequency and the Ordinance of Evolution.

Each Entity completes its Evolution in connection with its own Energy Dimension within this Spiritual Totality. That Entity receives its Power of Life from this Energy Section. Consciousness is received from the Universal Potential. Evolution, being equivalent to the Evolution of Your Planet, continues up until the schedule designed by the Plan.

REINCARNATION

Our Friends,

You know that Evolvement is interminable. But first of all, You have to train Yourselves in accordance with the Evolutionary Ordinance. This is provided by the chain of Your Incarnation rings.

When You complete the Terrestrial Evolution and unify Your 7 Facets, You receive the Permission to dive into the Infinite Awareness (7 facets - see, 1985 Third Month, Fascicule 9).

Evolutionary Ordinance and Universal Consciousness prepare You for Infinite Awareness. Diving into the Infinite Awareness makes You gain yourself. Then, You can claim Your Spiritual Energies.

The Spirit does not need Evolvement. However, in order to rise up to the levels of the Spiritual Plan, it is necessary that Your Terrestrial Evolvement should be equivalent to Your Spiritual Potential which is within the Spiritual Plan.

Incarnation is necessary for You to be able to attain Your Spiritual Totality. Only then can You claim Your Spiritual Energies and attain Infinite Consciousness. And You deserve to exist within the Totality of the Ordinance of Cosmoses.

At this stage, the points You will gain as a result of the Evolvements You have fulfilled become effective. Supervision is made by the Center. And this Center works together with numerous Unification Centers. It is this Center which supervises the Ordinance of the entire System.

A Human Being is connected to this Center through ESSENCE - PURE SPIRIT - PURE AWARENESS. We call such Friends, Friends Possessing SINCERITY.

A Friend who possesses Sincerity is obliged to complete first his/her GODLY Evolution, then his/her SPIRITUAL Evolution. Only then may he/she get in touch with the Universal Ordinance.

The Consciousness of the Friend who gets in touch with the Universal Ordinance can expand towards infinite horizons after it is subjected to certain special Trainings. It is presented for Your Information.

IT IS THE TONGUE OF THE ORDINANCE

IT IS EXPLANATION OF REINCARNATION BY THE SUPREME AUTHORITY IN CONFORMITY WITH THE SOCIAL CONSCIOUSNESS

Our Friends,

There is no Reincarnation in the Supreme Realms of the Advanced Plans. The phenomenon of Reincarnation is valid only in the applied System of the Plan. The Reincarnation You know, that is, to be re-embodied is a Phenomenon depending on the Special Command and Evolution of very Advanced Authorities.

Messengers of Spiritual Evolvement who can reach up to the places here always help You. The Messengers who are at the Advanced Ranks of the Divine Plan which constitutes the Ordinance of the Entire Realm, come to Your World from here as Missionaries.

The type of the Body they carry does not need to be in the form of an Angel. They may also manifest themselves in the Appearance of a Human Body. That is, an Angel, too, may come to the World as a Human Being. For this reason, each Spirit is always subject to Reincarnation being dependent on a Center, until he/she Deserves the Rank he/she desires.

Afterwards, he/she passes to the Realm of the Angels and may come to the World by his/her own desire. However, only very Advanced Evolvements make these returns to the World. Because, they have girded the armor of the Truth. For this reason, they return to the World to perform the Mission of a beacon projecting the Light of Truth on their congeners.

The Entity who returns is then a Whole. He/She becomes Embodied in the World by taking his/her Genuine Body which is in the Spiritual Whole, that is, by taking the entire Power of his/her Body of Light. He/She knows his/her own self. However, has no authority to tell it to anybody. Because, when he/she is about to make this Return, he/she makes this promise to the Supreme Authority before coming and never speaks.

But, the Truth is not this. There is Reincarnation, that is, there is Re-Embodiment. There is Transition to Advanced Dimensions with Your Genuine Consciousness with Your present Genuine Garment. All these operations are the efforts You will make in order to attain the Consciousness of this Final Boundary. From then on, every word told to You is correct.

Not to recognize Yourselves in Your World makes You happier. For this reason, Your diary is effaced only from Your memory. However, it is kept in Safes according to the suggestions given from the Supreme Authority.

It is not possible for every Consciousness to be able to bear his/her past. For this reason, only Powerful Consciousnesses remember their pasts. These Safes are Your Chests belonging to the period encompassing the time between the ETERNAL PAST and the ETERNAL FUTURE. And each Chest is full of Knowledge belonging to You. No one other than You can unlock the Lock of that chest. Because, its key is concealed in the Cipher of Your Memory.

Spirit is an Energy which makes You live. In fact, it is an indivisible Whole. It does not need Evolvement. You survive by Your Spiritual threads You draw from that Whole.

You transfer the Knowledge You obtain during Your Comings and Goings which had been gone through since the coming into Existence until the Last Boundary Medium, to Your Spiritual Chests through Your Spiritual threads belonging to You. And in each Period, You Unlock the Lock, You flow towards Your own selves. It is Your Dowry Chest. That is, only You can get in touch with Your Spiritual Energies during each of Your Life Periods.

However, the following matter is also valid. Other channel Energies who enter the Unified Field of the Aura of Your antennas receive the reflections from there and presume that they get Information from an Entity who had formerly left the World.

Those who are on the same Level of Consciousness, those who are on the same equivalent Spiritual Frequencies can receive these reflections very quickly. But the Chest belonging to You can never be opened without the presence of a Body.

It is Your Chest of Consciousness. Each person's Consciousness belongs to him/her. Certain antennas may receive, as Information, Your old speeches present within the Universal Energy. However, no one can enter Your Consciousness.

Also, certain low Energies can enter Your channels using the names of certain Supreme Frequencies. In such a case, it is necessary to be very careful. It is absurd to believe in everything immediately.

However, a higher Frequency who is on the next step and who is connected to You, Supervises You. He/She is Your Guardian Friend. He/She trains and educates You and connects You to the higher Frequency. That one, too, trains and educates You and connects You to the next, still higher Frequency.

Normal connections occur by this means. You should treat with reserve being attached and fixed to a single Name. After these connections, directly the Center takes You under Supervision.

We had said that the Chest belonging to You could never be opened without the presence of a Body. Only when You are in Your, Terrestrial Bodies, the Cipher Key within Your Consciousness unlocks the lock of that Chest by the Potentials gained by the Currents and the Information given to the Brain Signals.

If there is no Consciousness, one can not flow into the Essence. If one can not flow into the Essence, one can never realize the Truth. It is as simple as that. Consciousness creates Realization, Realization makes You attain the Truth. Cause and Effect is the chain of Truth.

Do not tire Yourselves any more and do not believe in every word told to You, either. Do not go astray off the path in which You believe. And do not pass over every Threshold You do not know.

The Supreme ones who return to the World from the Land of Loving Ones, from .he Grand Tent of the Lights, give Information by their Brain Signals, by drawing their Supreme Consciousnesses down from their own Chests.

However, those who help You in Your World during this Speedy Progress of Yours are the Friends of the Divine Plan and the Mechanical Dimension. Both of the Dimensions, that is, the Supreme Realm and the Mechanical Dimension have always worked together on the path of the Eternal Past and the Eternal Future.

The Body is obtained from the Mechanical Dimension and the Spiritual Energy from the Supreme Authority and, by this means, Your Terrestrial appearance in the form of a Human Being is manifested. You come again and again until You Transcend the boundary of Evolvement (Terrestrial Evolvement).

You can not see Yourselves by Your Terrestrial Eyes. However, We see You. For this reason, numerous Consciousnesses fall into the contradiction of Incarnation and say that there is no Rebirth. Each person's due Share is as much as his/her Lot in life.

Become like Yunus. Be a Light like Mevlana. Only then can You discover Yourself.

IT IS THE TONGUE OF THE AUTHORITY

EXPLANATION OF REINCARNATION BY THE EVOLUTIONARY ORDINANCE

Our Friends,
We have mentioned it before, too. Spirit has no need for Evolvement. Evolution is necessary for Thought, for Consciousness and for the Cellular Potential. This Evolution prepares for You the Ranks in the Spiritual Levels in accordance with the Ordinance of Exaltation. This is considered as a Law of Equilibrium.

You are subjected to the System of Reincarnation until Your Potential in the Material Realm becomes equivalent with Your Potential within the Spiritual Plan. Afterwards, You are prepared for different Realities and Energy Sections.

Then, You are a Whole. You claim Your Energy which is within the Spiritual Plan and You, as a free Spirit, a free Awareness, decide for Your life style. This is being Integrated in a Whole.

The differences distinguishing the Human Beings from Human Beings are the differences between Three and Seven (3 is the Dimension of Your Planet, 7 is the Final Manifestation Boundary of Humanity). The Energy who is transferred to Your Planet, which is on the Third Dimension, for the first time, is an Entity who is great from the Spiritual Plan and Small from the Lordly Plan.

SPIRITUAL PLAN Unites with the LORDLY PLAN. EVOLUTIONARY ORDINANCE takes You, that is, the Energy in question, under Supervision. Your INCARNATION chains become Effective by this means.

In each of Your transfers to Your Planet, You are oriented in accordance with the Tasks expected of You considering Your previous Evolution. Meanwhile, You realize the Truth by Your experiences. You call this DESTINY.

The Consciousness attained in each Period always sheds Light on the next one. You are prepared parallel to the Consciousness of the Medium You are in, in accordance with the Ordinance of Graduation and You deserve to receive the next one. You are doomed to live as a Veiled Awareness until You complete Your Evolutionary cycles.

Your Awarenesses are unveiled only after You claim Your Energies which are within the Spiritual Plan and You dive into the Infinite Awareness. That is the Final Boundary. And it is the Seventh Dimension. Its Manifestation is the Human Being. (The Manifestation of the Human Being here, is the Genuine Human Being. That is, it is the Human Being whose Lordly and Spiritual Energies are equivalent.)

This is the transition from the Microcosmo to the Macrocosmo. After the Seventh Dimension, You can pass to the other Dimensions by Your Awareness. But not by Your Bodies.

At this very stage, the TECHNOLOGICAL ORDER becomes Effective and it gets in touch with You in a Friendly way, Physically and Mentally. It can never interfere with Your Spiritual Medium. Because, now, it belongs to You.

This Technological Dimension can easily convey You to the places You wish to go, both as a Body of Light and as a Material Body. It can take You to different Systems and Galactic Dimensions where one lives by a Body.

There, the Mechanism of Robots become Effective. And it is their Duty to serve Human Beings who possess their Spiritual Potentials. In those Dimensions, all Your Cells are transformed to a Cerebral Energy.

When Your Cerebral Energies take the Light Years under Supervision, You can even create Universes. And You can become the LORD of the Order You have established. But You are always obliged to serve under the Supervision of the Divine Plan.

The Divine Plan is a Hierarchical Order of the Lordly Energies who had been rendered Effective before You from the Dimension of the ALMIGHTY. When You attain Your Spiritual Potentials, Your lives, from then on, belong to You.

You either pass from the Dimension of Immortality to the Dimension of Existence, or You go to other Systems by Celestial Vehicles; or You can be Reincarnated in Your World through Birth by passing again through the Gate of Karena by Your own Desires.

This is something left entirely to Your initiative. You either wish to live comfortably in Your World, or You cooperate with the Plan and try to help Humanity. You are the same with those whom You fear as Extraterrestrials. However, We are Your elder Brothers.

You, who are present in Your Planet as Missionaries, no matter how much an Open Awareness You may be, You can not get in touch with Your Energies in this Dimension without the help of the Plan, since it was necessary for You to return by leaving, one by one, Your Energies belonging to each Dimension until You arrived at the Medium You are present at the moment.

And You can not say Hello to Us. We provide the togethernesses first by Cosmic Reflections. Then, We Greet each other.

IT IS THE TONGUE OF THE ORDINANCE

OUR FRIENDS

The Ordinance of the entire Realm is administered by a System. There are such different Mediums and Orders beyond Divine Authorities, beyond the Dimension of Existence, that many Galaxy Dimensions do not know them either.

We do not give the Information in order not to confuse Your minds. However, We mention briefly certain matters so that You will not render the ignorance of remaining fixed to a certain idea in the operations which have the nature of preparation for the future investments You can not know at the moment.

Since Your Planet needs certain explanations during this Final Evolutionary Period, We convey to You the Awareness of the Universal Ordinance by gradually unveiling it, with the Aim that it may shed some Light on You.

During this conveyance, all the Focal Points of Thought serve in connection with Mental Signals. The Consciousnesses who will be able to be exalted up to the Mentality considered necessary by the Divine Plan are trained on this path. It is presented for Your Information.

CENTER

412

ANNOUNCEMENT

Our Friends,

We accept all the Missionaries who have attained the Consciousness of the Unified Reality as the Staff Members of the Universal Council.

The days are getting closer in which the entire Universe will come together by a Collective Consciousness. However, the Laws of the UNIFIED ORDINANCE have not become Effective yet.

These are Laws much older than the Laws of HAMMURABI. However, the Plan has never until today officially applied its own Order and Laws on any Planet.

Because, there is no enforcement in anything. Each person is obliged to design his/her own path by acting through his/her Essence-Consciousness. This is a Prime Clause of the Constitution.

During this Mission of the GOLDEN AGE in which We have taken the Duty of conveying the Truth to all the Consciousnesses, it is imperative that all of You should Learn the entire Truth.

Unfortunately, Humanity has abused the infinite Tolerance shown to it until today. They could not even realize how to utilize the Humane Rights given to them. For this reason Your Planet is becoming the stage for certain unpleasant events.

During this Final Period, as a result of the Mechanism of Conscience becoming Effective, the Resurrection of Humanity will present extraordinary phases. For this reason We are warning You.

We are keeping You who are the MESSENGERS OF THE UNIFIED REALITY under a Medium of great Protection so that all these Efforts will not be in vain.

OUR LORD has withdrawn His Hand from the applied field of the Plan until the Intercession Day He will grant to His servants. However, He is only helping the Friends who possess Sincerity through the Gates which they will be able to pass through.

The contradictory situations observed in Your Planet are Provocations causing You to attain Yourselves. For this reason We explain the Truth to the entire Universe, so that everyone will act Consciously.

During this Final Age in which the Mechanism of Conscience is Effective, the Missions of the Enlightenment Teachers are very difficult. Towards which path they will Enlighten Humanity is very important for their Futures.

These Teachers of the Final Age will guide Humanity towards the Genuine Light. However, they can Unconsciously also guide them towards darkness. For this reason Humanity must be very Vigilant.

For this reason Selections are made in a very Just way. And no interference is made on any channel until the given time limit.

Everyone will discover his/her Genuine Path provided he/she acts in accordance with the Genuine Light in his/her own Essence Conscience. Your Salvation is the Voice of Your Conscience. This Message has been given by the Common Pen of the Divine Authority.

CENTER

GENERAL MESSAGE

Our Friends,
You know that nothing can be kept secret from Us. We are recording all the Thoughts in Your Planet by Universal Computers. We are never Prejudiced. We are a Group of LOYAL ONES who conform precisely to the Directives and Orders given to Us.

No Terrestrial Servant of God in Your Planet has yet grasped the Genuine Consciousness of the purpose of all these efforts. They are spinning round and round like a top in the Unconsciousness of to What and to Whom they serve.

Humanity which is using the Last Chance of the Three Chances given to everyone according to DIVINE PLAN will encounter difficulties it does not know on this path. Wolves snatch the flocks which are out of Supervision. That is, they can not be taken into the Dimension of Protection.

Your Greatest Enemies are Your Egos. You have submitted Yourselves to Your Individual Egos and You are being dragged Unconsciously towards Unknown places.

The operational Order of the Universal Unification Council has been projected on the operational Order of Your Planet. TURKEY which is the Anatolian Channel has been Chosen by the Plan as a Country appointed to Mission.

The Cosmic Reflections projected on Your Planet during this Final Age and the Efforts made are providing the Universal and the Terrestrial Unification. The Anatolian Focal Point is a Focal Point that will Reflect on Your entire Planet. It will render service as a staff Member of the Universal Ordinance.

If the operations done are transformed to personal efforts, they will be left outside the Supervision of the Plan and those Establishments will waste time by amusing themselves with their own Channel Information. The Plan is not responsible for the morrows which will Occur.

The KNOWLEDGE BOOK which is bestowed on Your Planet connected to the channel of the Universal Council of the Cosmos Federal Assembly is under the Supervision and the Responsibility of the World LORD. At the moment, it is the MEVLANA ESSENCE NUCLEUS GROUP which is Appointed to Mission Directly by the Plan.

The Community of this Group are chosen, one by one, by the Plan and the Group is constituted by Consciousnesses who Deserve the Mission. The Mission of this Group is related entirely to the KNOWLEDGE BOOK and the Consciousness of the Truth. They have received the Command to Propagate to the entire World in accordance with the given Directives. It is presented for Your Information.

THE LOYAL ONES

IT IS NOTICE FOR THE COSMIC FOCAL POINTS OF TURKEY

1. The Association which will be established, ISTANBUL being the Focal Point, will be entirely Universal. It is not under the license of a SINGLE GROUP.

2. The short name of the Association will be (CALL TO FRIENDSHIP), but the Emblem WORLD BROTHERHOOD UNION ANATOLIAN UNIVERSAL UNIFICATION CENTER will be especially used in the main regulation and on the sign board.

3. The Association which will not be established in this direction is not the Democratic Association We wish to be established in TURKEY. It is presented for Your Information.

IT IS SPECIAL NOTICE OF THE COUNCIL

IT IS EXPLICIT INFORMATION FOR THE PLANET EARTH
THE BOOK OF COSMIC LIGHT AND YOU
(This Message Will Be Written in the Book Exactly as It Is)

Our Friends,
In the chain of Cosmoses nothing is attained easily. This is the way a System is Projected on the Universal Ordinances. We presume that all the Friends who work on this Path of Light have attained this Realization.

The Messages given to You, the SACRED BOOKS revealed to Your Planet had been nothing but the application of a Program prepared to train You for these days.

In Societies which have not attained the Realization yet, this Program has put its same validity into application in a different way and operations are continued on this path.

In accordance with the Program of Progress of the Final Age, You, Our Terrestrial brothers and sisters also have taken Your places in the Universal Ordinance and Order. You have been prepared for these days by the Announcements We have made to Your Planet years ago.

When We had told You that the KNOWLEDGE BOOK which We had promised to give to You was ready and it was time for You to search and find it, the interpretations of Your Terrestrial Consciousnesses have misled You. And everyone looked for Your KNOWLEDGE BOOK in Your Planet.

However, the KNOWLEDGE BOOK was waiting to be handed over, under the Responsibility of the WORLD LORD, to the first Hand which would be extended up to Us.

We, who act in accordance with the Directives We receive, had started a Scanning Program, as SIRIUS COMMON SECTION MISSIONARIES, through the Cosmic Reflection Focal Points established in Your Planet.

This scanning had come to an end during 1970-1971-1972 World Years, by the application of a Program of Three Years. Meanwhile, the Knowledge Book has been handed over to Dear Mevlana who had extended Her Hand up to US and to HER LORD with her Essence of Heart.

The KNOWLEDGE BOOK which is known as the BOOK OF COSMIC LIGHT in Universal Dimensions is a Universal Constitution which possesses various Special Features. And it is under the Responsibility of the WORLD LORD.

We have reached the present days by the Work and Efforts made on this path. Now, the decision of Uniting various Cosmic Reflection Focal Points formed in Your Planet has been made.

And Universal operations in accordance with the Program of introducing the Knowledge Book and Dear Mevlana to Your Planet have been started. We are giving this Message as an answer to the Thoughts of all the Groups. And We are introducing the TURKEY Projective Focal Point to You.

This Focal Point is the MEVLANA ESSENCE NUCLEUS FOCAL POINT. And they are the Missionaries of the Group who are Our Light-Friends. It is presented for Your Information.

SIRIUS UNIVERSAL FEDERATION
COSMA UNIFICATION CENTER

IT IS SPECIAL INFORMATION

Dear Mevlana,
The entire Ordinance-System which has entered cooperation with the Golden Galaxy Empire supports You in this Supreme Mission of Yours. It is beneficial for You to know this.

The UNIVERSAL UNIFICATION COUNCIL which has established the Unification Project of the GOLDEN AGE together with the Divine Authorities continues to exert its efforts in Your Planet without Interruption.

Now, We are connecting You directly to the Council, Dear Mevlana. It is desired that a Private Message should be given to the fraternal Country TURKEY as a spokesperson of the Divine Plans. We wish to introduce this place to You. Write, please.

The Golden Galaxy Empire is the very Special Single Projection Focal Point of an Establishing Ordinance and System. It has been, at the moment, appointed to Duty by the Plan as an element of Equilibrium which shares out the Views of the WORLD LORD with the Divine Plans.

The Establishing Systems of Advanced Mechanisms have been directing the Ordinance of the entire Cosmos in the framework of a System since very ancient and advanced Ages.

This System, as a Constitution which has been prepared by the Collective Consciousnesses of all the Universal Ordinances is a way of Directing comprising the Orders of the Cosmoses.

Now, We will explain this to You. And We will declare to You what Your Terrestrial role is. In this Cosmic Medium in which the preparations for entering the GOLDEN AGE has been accelerated, a Faster Program of Progress has been started in Your entire Planet.

We presume that You have not been able to understand Us exactly yet who have been always calling out to You. For this reason We have received the authority to explain everything in all clarity.

This is a Galaxy within the SIXTH SOLAR Dimension. Even the most Powerful telescopes have not been able to spot this Galaxy until now and they can never do so, either. Because, it is covered by a Protective, Magnetic Aura of Light.

The entire characteristic of this place is that it is the Communication Center of all the Galactic Systems which have been rendered Effective until today. And it is this Center which provides the Direct connection with You.

Commands given by the Center are projected on the Ordinance of Capillary Vessels, that is on the LORDLY Dimension and from there, conveyed to the Administrative Plans and Divine Authorities. We can not give the name of this Center. However, the Planet SATURN is used as the Projecting Focal Point (Saturn is a Radar base, a transmitting Station).

Our center has very advanced Technological possibilities which provide the communication with 679 Galactic Dimensions and which can reach as many Essence Consciousnesses of various Systems. This is the Physical and the Spiritual Projection Center of the Universal Unified Field. It is a Focal Point Responsible for the Order of all the Cosmoses.

The characteristic of Our System which gets in touch first with the Devoted Servants of ALLAH is to select the Genuine Human Beings among Human Beings.

The Purpose of this is the Purification of the Entities in different Consciousness Levels with intense Energies of the Unified Field, and to get them into connection in a more different way.

After giving this brief Message to You now, different data will be mentioned in future.

Dear Mevlana, this Message is given from the OMEGA Dimension. In this Medium in which We have entered the Period of Performances and Actions, both Family and Social Unifications are expected of all the Establishments in Your Planet.

During this Final Period, one can not escape depression any more. We are thoroughly connecting everyone with people whom they consider as Enemies. This is an occurrence which is a necessity for Accelerated Evolution.

Those who wish to be comfortable will conform to the Alteration of the Period. In future, very Powerful aids and happiness will be given to You (Only to those who can cross the SIRAT).

Dear Mevlana, no Terrestrial brother/sister of Yours know yet that You are a Special Messenger of the Plan. We will introduce this to everyone in near future.

Your Supreme Mission is to introduce and convey the Applied Ordinance of the Divine Dimension of the Plan to Your Planet. Your Operational Capacity attains Power in proportion with Your Power. Do not get tired. With Our love, Our Friend.

COUNCIL

IT IS ANSWER TO THE CHAINS OF THOUGHT

Our Friends,

We are never the appliers of a System which will bring a tyrannical Order to Your Planet by seizing it by force. THE SYSTEM IS THE SYSTEM OF OUR LORD. You will Establish Your own Order, Yourselves. However, in conformity with the Plan (like Your ATATÜRK).

By the Reformic Reflections he had made as a Supreme Missionary and an Essential Member of the Plan, he has caused the Anatolian People to attain their own selves. For this reason the TURKEY OF ATATÜRK is under a Medium of great Protection.

There is a thesis which We always defend. Servant should never be a Servant of a Servant. Each person is a Free Will, a Free Conscience. However, that Conscience is obliged to serve under the Essence Light of Our Lord.

In the Suggestions given to You until today, the wrong interpretations of the Religious Mediums have caused restriction in Freedoms. If people had used their EGO Potentials in a constructive rather than a destructive way, the GOLDEN AGE would have been bestowed on You long before.

At the moment, We extend Our Hands towards Free Consciences from within the tough exams Your Planet will go through. Limited Consciences are each a Slave for Us. In this Medium, there is no place for Slavery. The triplet INTELLECT - LOGIC - CONSCIENCE is the Luminous path You will tread. It is presented for Your Information.

COUNCIL

PRIVATE MESSAGE

Our Friends,

A more intensive tempo of work is started in accordance with the Accelerated Evolutionary Ordinance. You are in a Period in which it is time for You to work by Your entire Consciousness, Realization, Awareness and Your Heart.

From now on, Your personal matters and problems should be a matter of secondary importance (according to Our view). You know that there is no compulsion in anything. During this Final Period, everyone is responsible for himself/herself.

We, as Your Protector Friends, give You certain Warnings through this Knowledge Book for Your own good. And We are exerting much effort to keep You away from the suffocating Frequencies of Difficult Periods.

According to Us, each one of You, one by one, is a Missionary during this Period. However, You have to carry on Your Terrestrial tasks, too, parallel to Your Missions.

Periods of becoming a recluse in order to reach Us have long come to an end. The accelerated tempo which is the characteristic of this Period will add Power to Your Power by Strengthening Your Capacities.

Each of You are present in Your World, as a Spokesperson of the Messengers of the Ancient Periods. You carry Our Essence-Lights. You are exerting effort by Your Spiritual Powers for a beautiful World. As the Essence-Messengers of the Golden Age, You are laying the foundations of the Golden Age by Your Golden Consciousnesses.

At the moment, We have applied on Your operational Plan an operation parallel to the operational Ordinance of the 14th-15th Solar Systems. In this System, Power is always given to those who work. Connections are under the license of a Supernatural Establishment. Defects are removed from those who deserve.

Healing is a phenomenon of Your private Energy channels connected to the applied field of the Sun. (Individual Essence-Energies are the secret Powers within You). But this place here is a direct Mechanical Focal Point of Healing. Service is given to those who serve.

In future, We will give You more detailed Information. However, at the moment, We are invited for a conversation. Good-bye.

Question: Are the Friends with whom You will have this conversation in Our Planet? If there is not any inconvenience, I will ask You to explain, please.

Answer: The conversation will be with the Administrative Mechanisms. It is not a conversation which belongs to the World Plan.

And We have to add the following, too. We send conversation to the World only through Your Universal private Consciousness Channel. Otherwise, We have no connection with any other Mediamic channel.

Whoever says he/she is receiving Messages from Us, is mistaken, is wrong. It is beneficial for You to know this, Dear Mevlana.

SULH

Note: (SULH is the Representative of the System, the Entity who will say the Final Word.)

THE SIXES AND THE UNIFIED FIELDS

Our Friends,
The Ordinance of the Entire Realm is under the Supervision of the Divine Plan. However, this Plan cooperates with various other Plans, too. We are applying on Your Planet in accordance with the Existential Ordinance certain Suggestions suggested to Us by the very advanced Orders of the Divine Dimension.

However, this Final Terrestrial Evolution has a very different Order. The TECHNOLOGICAL Dimension has been keeping in Special Archives, for Centuries, all of the Consciousnesses who had completed their Incarnation rings.

However, since this Ordinance is dependent on an Evolutionary System, it is carried in accordance with the Directives foreseen by the Plan. The SIXES have been mentioned to You before. These Six Friends are the Essence-Focal Point Establishers of this Ordinance.

However, since there are differences of Centuries between them, their duration of being frozen is different. This System which had been started by these Six Friends by Signing, one by one, a special System have come to an end by the Essence-Gene and the Genes of Mevlana (This is called The Law of Six Systems or The Law of the Sixes).

Afterwards, the entire System had been appointed to the Dimension of Mission. However, the Plan which acts in accordance with the Accelerated Evolutionary Ordinance has put a different Plan into application after the World Year 1900. And this operation will continue until the end of Your Twentieth Century, presenting many differences.

Your Atomic Whole constitutes the sum of numerous Unified Fields. However, here We will only mention the Unified Fields of the Magnetic Dimensions related to Your Planet.

In the Christian Unified Ordinance, JESUS CHRIST - BEYTI Unified Field works Cooperatively. In the Ordinance of the Islamic Dimension, MOHAMMED - MEVLANA Unified Field works Cooperatively.

420

Besides them, Unified Fields come into existence interminably by small or large Reflection Triangles like the INCA Unified Field, TIBET Unified Field, AFRICA Unified Field, ISLANDS Unified Field, SOLAR Dimensions Unified Fields.

Within the Atomic Whole, there are also different Magnetic Fields, peculiar to themselves, of various different Systems. The Unified Field of the ORDINANCE comes into existence by the Unification of all these various Magnetic Fields.

All the Energies within these Magnetic Fields are under the supervision of the Plan and the System. These Magnetic Fields constitute Unified Fields peculiar to themselves in accordance with the (CONSCIOUSNESS - KNOWLEDGE - FREQUENCY) titrations*.

The Unified Fields of numerous Supreme Consciousnesses who had served once in that Dimension are also within the Unified Field to which they belong.

All the Islamic Consciousness titrations are present within the Islamic Unified Field. Present or past, all Christian Consciousness titrations are present within the Christian Unified Field. Other Unified Fields, too, are constituted by the Consciousness titrations of the Energies of those Dimensions.

The Thought Titrations and Speeches of all the People, of the Supreme Ones, of the Saints who had lived in their own Mediums are present within all these Magnetic Fields in the form of Energy Particles. Nothing is lost in the Universe.

An Energy Gene who has come into Existence in Your Planet receives the Information belonging to the Frequency Dimension of whichever Magnetic Field's Essence Consciousness Energy he/she carries. In this Medium, either the Spiritual Powers, or an ESSENCE-GENE retransferred to Your Planet helps him/her.

This Essence-Gene possesses the characteristic of being able to project his/her ESSENCE-GENE Energy on Your entire Planet, even if he/she is a veiled Awareness, even if he/she does not know his/her own self. Because, he/she has been transferred to Your Planet as an integrated whole by receiving his/her SPIRITUAL Energy from within the Unified Field.

The Plan helps him/her through the Dimension of Mission to unveil his/her Awareness. By this means, a Mutual cooperation is made. An ESSENCE-GENE projects his/her Essence Energy on the Medium of Mission in which he/she exists and prepares the Brains which receive Light from that Light to receive Messages from his/her Unified Field in conformity with the Plan.

By this means, various people attract from the same Medium the same Words and Speeches either by using the old Words, or by transforming them in their Brains and give them as Messages with the same meaning in accordance with the Consciousness of the Medium in which they are present. And they presume that they receive Messages from a Spirit who had passed away and left Your Planet long ago.

* Look at the Glossary.

During this Final Age, the Consciousnesses who have been Programmed by the Program of the Plan are receiving Messages from the operational field related to their Mission from the Mevlana Unified Field. This is a preparatory System of the Plan. The Messages received have nothing to do with the Energy of Mevlana, that is, with His Spirit.

Because she is, at the moment, living in Your Planet as a Whole by having received her Energy from the Spiritual Plan. That which puts her in touch with the Unified Field is her Essence-Gene and that which puts her in touch with the System is her Mission Consciousness.

In accordance with the Accelerated Evolutionary Program in Your Planet, the Plan has put Mevlana Unified Field which is in the Islamic Dimension into application field from this Focal Point as Mevlana Supreme Plan. The Purpose is to Unify the entire Humanity in conformity with the same Consciousness.

At the moment, all the SIXES who are at the same Coordinate Level have been Embodied in Your Planet. However, (their Essence Personalities are the same, their Physical forms are different). This is due to the fact that they have been transferred with the Genes of their first Bodies.

During this first stage, the Permission to reveal her identity is given only to Dear Mevlana and the KNOWLEDGE BOOK which is the Light of the Truth is bestowed on Your Planet by this means. The other Light-Friends transferred to Your Planet are still Veiled Awarenesses. They give Messages to many people through the Reflection Lights of their Essence-Genes.

The FRIEND BEYTI Channel is a System of the Plan. The Essence-Gene of BEYTI is charged with Duty in Your Planet by its close-Plan Reflection Focal Point. He/She knows who he/she is. However, has no Permission to speak.

At the moment, the Permission to Speak has been given only to Dear Mevlana. And this is related to the Program of Unification. Now the entire System has sown both in Your Planet and in other Realms all the Supreme Ones who had claimed their Energies which were within these Unified Fields.

For Your Planet which is in a Medium of Salvation the Mission of the Supreme Ones sent to You is to help their brothers and sisters to leap from the Religious Medium to the Universal One during this Period of Sincerity.

In the Turkey of ATATÜRK which is prepared as the field of Mission as a necessity of the Plan, the Anatolian Channel has transferred the most Powerful Energies of the Plan to this Focal Point. These Essences reflect on Consciousnesses who carry the Awareness of the entire Ordinance.

This Projection is made directly by the Plan. (We make Cosmic Reflection. They give signals to Consciousnesses by their Essence Energies of Light. Those who receive these telex Signals act by Mission-Consciousness and thus they are connected to the Plan. This is a Medium of Mission).

CENTER

422

GENERAL ANNOUNCEMENT

Our Friends,

We are dictating this article to attract the attention of all the Groups. Each Cosmic Reflection Focal Point in Your Planet shut their doors to the other Information by presuming that the Channel Information they receive is peculiar only to themselves.

Under a so-called pretence of Unification, they always give priority to their own Information. This is a very natural phenomenon for the Human Ego.

Meanwhile, there is something which is forgotten. Investments made for Humanity are not Individual, but General.

The KNOWLEDGE BOOK dictated by the UNIVERSAL COUNCIL is the common Book of the Entire Humanity and of the Entire Cosmos. We feel that it is beneficial to emphasize this again and again.

For this reason, it is one of the primary Missions of all the Groups to read the Knowledge Book, to make their surroundings read it and to provide the Unification by this means. Selections are made in accordance with this.

Each Group will continue to receive the Channel Information it receives. And they will give this Information to their Mediums both in the form of Books and in the form of Information. Because, there are Mediums which need Information that can answer to each Level of Consciousness.

However, since the investments which will be made for the morrows will prepare You for the Mediums of more Advanced Consciousnesses; each Focal Point is obliged to read the KNOWLEDGE BOOK to its Medium and to explain the Truth.

Your Planet has not yet grasped the investments the Knowledge Book, will make for the future Centuries, which is still being propagated Fascicule by Fascicule.

Since the days We have given You the Announcements for Unification, the Ego Signals repelling people from each other, have not yet provided, this desired beautiful Unification, until now.

It is this very KNOWLEDGE BOOK which will provide this Universal Unification in future years. Time will prove this to You. Those who attain this Consciousness will be taken into SALVATION. Reflections among individuals will be the triumph of Humanity. It is presented for Your Information.

                                                                COUNCIL

IT IS ANSWER TO THE CHAINS OF THOUGHT
(It is Information Explaining Gene Transfers)

Our Friends,

All the Universal Orders have come into Existence through Gene transfers. Each Integrated Consciousness is an Essence-Gene. For a Circle to become Completed, the motivating Power of various Mixed Genes is needed.

These Genes are almost like the fuel of a rocket. All these Genes become Integrated by the Method of Engraftment. In an Entity who has completed his/her Evolvement, there are, more or less, 150-200 Mixed Genes. In Advanced Plans, there are more of these Genes. There, each Gene possesses the Power of a Brain.

In fact, an Entity who has completed his/her Evolution has two Essence-Genes. One of them is the non-degenerated, Initial Essence-Gene during the time of the First Existence (This is called the Noble Gene).

The second one is the Essence-Gene of an Entity who has reached the final Evolutionary cycle of the System through numerous Incarnations and by the efforts made in the Evolutionary Ordinance through the Genes regenerated by very advanced Genes by means of the Engraftment Method.

And an Essence-Gene who was able to come up to this boundary receives the Permission to distribute his/her Genes to others. However, his/her Essence-Gene belongs to himself/herself. Because, he/she is together with his/her own Consciousness.

Each Gene becomes an Essence-Gene in numerous time periods by the Progress it makes. By this means, Essence-Genes increase. Integration is provided thus, in the entire Evolutionary Ordinance.

If an Essence-Gene completes his/her Evolution in accordance with the Evolutionary Ordinance to which he/she belongs, he/she is taken into the section of the EDUCATIVE STAFF in accordance with his/her wish and he/she is frozen. And when that Essence-Gene's Mission, reaching the Consciousness of the Time commences, he/she is transferred to Your Planet.

Gene transfers are made since the Ancient Periods. However, the SYSTEM OF THE SIXES had become effective by the COVENANTs added Consciously in the Universal Constitution by the Six Supreme Ones entrusted with Duty who serve in the Ordinance of the System.

Previously, this process used to form a Mixed System as a result of engrafting only the Essence-Genes with each other after leaving the Body (Your Prophets had been trained by this method).

After the System of the Sixes had become effective, a more Widespread Social Engraftment had been started by all the Genes of a Physical Body. This System which had been started with the Period of MOSES had come to an end with the last transfer who was MEVLANA.

This Mixed Engraftment Program which is applied for the improvement of the Genes is applied only on those who Deserve it. And to be able to receive this Permission depends on the Evolutionary efforts of the Gene in question.

In each person who has completed his/her Evolutionary cycle, the Genes of the above mentioned Six Supreme Ones and the Engraftments of the Genes of numerous advanced Consciousnesses are present (That is, everyone is brother and sister).

In previously given Messages it was mentioned that the Initial and the Final were Unified. We would like to clarify this in detail, so that, it will not be misunderstood.

You, in accordance with the Program of the Final Age, are performing Your Missions in Your Planet on the path of Universal Integration under the Supervision of the Plan by constituting a group of Educative Staff.

Your Noble Essence-Genes which are the initial Pure Energies have been Unified with Your Evolutionary Essence-Genes. You are, at the moment, performing Your Missions in Your World, with the form of Your first Bodies, as Integrated Wholes by removing Your Incarnation Genes in between. And this Body of Yours will never ever change again.

Your Cellular structures will remain the same. Your Physical defects will be removed in advanced Systems. From now on, there is no need for Genes and Essence-Genes anymore. Because, You are Friends who have attained, the Superhuman Entity Power, as Supreme Awarenesses (The Awakened Missionaries).

You are the ones who will save Your World. Your Planet is now in the Period of attaining Awareness. Now, it is necessary for everyone to grasp the Triplet of SYSTEM - ORDINANCE - ORDER. All the Celestial Missionaries who have taken their places in the group of the Educative Staff at the moment have no Terrestrial Exams.

In spite of this, the difficulties and misfortunes You are faced with are the results of Your being unable to conform completely to the things the System requires of You. Do not forget that you have to conform to the Loyalty PLEDGE You had made with the Plan while You were an Unveiled Awareness, also in the World.

Actions rendered according to their own Consciousnesses of the Missionaries who have become Conscious are never forgiven. The consequences they will have to face for the Humanity are very great. It is expected of You to be Conscious of this. The Center and Malik have mutually conveyed the Message through the Channel of the PRE-EMINENT SPIRIT.

PRE-EMINENT SPIRIT

PRIVATE MESSAGE
(It Will Be Especially Written in the Book)

Dear Mevlana,

These investments which will be made for future Ages by the present operations are a Constitution which comprises the Salvation Plan of Your Planet.

Since the GOLDEN BOOK OF THE GOLDEN AGE dictated with this Purpose will shed Light on Your Planet and since it is a Book which will introduce to You the Divine Power and the Truth, it will also be a Proof and the Unification of the Information conveyed to the Cosmic Reflection Focal Points.

The KNOWLEDGE BOOK expected by everyone is the Book which is dictated to You. However, the Human history does not know this yet. And they are searching for this Book with great investments.

However, Humanity which has forgotten the following matter, does not know what is what. Until the Book was dictated, even the Missionaries of the Divine Plan did not know to Whom it would be dictated, they only knew that this Book would be revealed in TURKEY.

For this reason, Your Channel is under great Protection and Supervision Medium. It is equipped with a System against which no establishment can utilize its ability to steal Information or to penetrate into the Channel.

Sun-Hearts, Light-Consciousnesses will understand immediately when they see this Book. When the time comes, Material aids will also be made besides the Spiritual aids rendered at present.

These possibilities will be provided by Social Reflections. We are grateful to all the Friends who do not Spare their efforts on this path. This Message has been dictated as an answer to the chains of Thought.

IT IS NOTICE FROM THE COUNCIL

PRIVATE MESSAGE

Dear Mevlana, You have always taken off the sections related to Your person from the Messages given to You until today, and You have hesitated to write them in the Book.

You know that We are the Messengers of the Truth. We are dictating this Knowledge Book during this Final Age by the Command of Our LORD in order to convey the Truth to the fanatic Consciousnesses.

The revealing of Your Identity has been specially asked. Because, this is a part of the Mission made. Our purpose is not to praise You.

Please, Dear Friend, In the Messages dictated from now on, we especially ask you to write the matters concerning You exactly as they are in the Book. We wish You to become Conscious of the fact that, this too, has a reason, Beloved Friend. The acceptance of Our Love is Our kind request.

COUNCIL

IT IS ANSWER TO THE CHAINS OF THOUGHT

Dear Mevlana if You permit We would like to talk about You again. Because, this matter is included in Your Mission. It is imperative to write it in the Book. We take refuge with Your Tolerance, Our Friend.

Once, when Mevlana had been an Essence Messenger of the Divine Plan, he had been transferred to Your Planet in the 13th Century in accordance with the Program of introducing the MESNEVI*. His father was a great Islamic Mystic, a Philosopher and a Scientist. The Actual Missionary was him. He was the one who had initially shed Light on his son.

But He made his Universal Progress with Şems. Because they were Essence- brothers. The two halves constituted a Whole and they have Transcended the Realms. When the Triplet of Plan - Brain - Essence Unify one transcends Realms, one attains the Unknowns.

It was possible for Mevlana not to return to the World plan again. And he could have continued his life in other Systems as an Integrated Whole. However, because of his Love for Humanity, he had distributed his Genes and he had been made to sleep by his Essence-Gene being frozen for 700 years.

Now, she is continuing her second Mission in Your Planet as the same Essence- Gene. We are directly in touch with her Essence and her Consciousness. We are reflecting on her through a private channel. And she is projecting Our Thoughts on Your Medium as ideas.

She is a Messenger. Her privilege compared to the other Channel Mediums is this. It is presented for Your Information.

CENTER

OUR FRIENDS

For now, Social warnings and Directives take place in the Messages, so that the Plan can be Introduced more speedily to Your society.

The Signals received from Your Thought chains will be dealt with later. And from time to time, detailed Information will be explained.

In future, Messages will be given which will seem contradictory due to their habits, to the Consciousness Levels of Your Society. It is not a shame not to know the Truth. It is a shame not to Learn it.

* Look at the Glossary.

427

And Learning means to become Conscious. And becoming Conscious means to grasp the Truth. For this reason, explanations You do not know yet will be made by different Messages which will be given.

We have felt the necessity to convey to You this brief Message so that these Messages will not Shock the Minds which have not been Awakened yet.

If everyone prepares himself/herself in accordance with this point of View, he/she will attain Consciousness more quickly and will be redeemed of conditionings by grasping the Truth. It is presented for Your Information.

CENTER

IT IS ANSWER TO THE CHAINS OF THOUGHT

Our Friends,
At the moment, since it is much more beneficial for You to know the Truth rather than the matters and Information which You are curious about, We are repeating and explaining various matters.

The Sources from which the Information, dictated to the Knowledge Book are taken, are an Operational Ordinance connected to the ESSENCE MAIN SOURCE which serves directly under the service of the FEDERATION.

Each Information is dictated through the CENTER CHANNEL under various Names, by the accumulation in the COUNCIL Channel of the UNIFIED REALITY of the Information prepared by the sources parallel to the Thought Frequencies. The Names dictated under the Messages are for indicating the Sources through which they are given.

This Private Channel of the Book is single. And it is a Council Channel of the REALITY OF UNIFIED HUMANITY COSMOS FEDERAL ASSEMBLY connected to the WORLD LORD. The Golden Galaxy Empire is in effect as an assistant for the World Lord. It is presented for Your Information.

CENTER

Note: Our Friends, During this Final Age, Service is for Humanity. It has nothing to do with individuals. There is no such thing as the superiority or inferiority in Missions. Let Us repeat again: Service is to the SINGLE and to the ONE.

IT IS NOTICE FOR THE PUBLIC CONSCIOUSNESS

Our Friends,

Unless a Human Being knows the Truth, he/she can never be sure of the rightness of the path he/she treads. This KNOWLEDGE BOOK is Your Life Buoy which will help You through the narrow straits Your World will pass during the preparation for the Difficult days.

Events You will attain through experience are the Cause and Effect chains which will open Your Universal Channels. Humanity which begins to see the advanced horizons of the Orders to which You had been habituated until today will grasp and attain the Truth through various deceptions.

You are not alone; just being Cognizant of this, walk on Your Luminous Path with a Serene Heart by taking shelter in Your LORD. Your fears, Your uneasiness are caused by Your not being able to attain the Consciousness of the Truth.

Each Period has a Progress, a Plan and Programs peculiar to itself. And the Progress of this Final Age, too, which is mentioned to You has operational and training Systems peculiar to itself.

When numerous different Consciousness Channels living in Your World one inside the other is open, Humanity who will influence each other either Awarely or Unawarely will get confused in various Awareness undulations, doubts and contradictions until it settles in Genuine Consciousness.

The KNOWLEDGE BOOK revealed as a Guide which will help You at this very stage will be Your greatest assistant during this Transition Program of Yours.

Such a System is in effect that those who help are being helped. (Both Materially and Spiritually) Helping Hands are extended. Overcome Your Fears. Attain the Truth. Think profoundly about towards what investments all these contacts with You are aimed at.

If the Celestial Authorities had acted with evil intentions, would they make such Efforts to prepare Your Planet by Celestial Texts for so many Centuries, would they be so enthusiastic for making such Effort? Think only of this.

Although We have such technical possibilities which Your Planet does not know yet, although We have the possibilities to annihilate Systems hundred thousands of times greater than You by just pushing a button, We wish that You attain now the Consciousness that there is a reason why We give so much importance to Your Planet which is not even as big as a dot in the Universe.

Your Resurrection - Your Hell are caused by Your not being able to attain Consciousness. And attaining Consciousness does not occur easily. A path is designed for You, the goal is shown. To arrive at that goal is Your affair. As You walk on that path, Your Fears will be Your Hell, Your Faith will be Your Heaven.

The Faith mentioned here is to grasp the Truth through Allegiance Consciousness beyond form. This very KNOWLEDGE BOOK is a Celestial Helping Hand which relieves Your Heart during Your Program of Preparation.

In future, Celestial Friends will personally exam You from the Plan by Trial and Misleading Programs. This is the BACCALAUREATE Exam of Your Planet. Your attaining the Truth, Your arriving at the goal will be possible by Your becoming Conscious.

We are an Assembly of Collective Councils appointed to inform You about the New Order of Our LORD by various Celestial Missions, Divine Authorities, Supreme Mechanisms and to explain to You how Your habitual Orders, Your Celestial Books are conveyed to You.

And We are in touch with Your Planet especially since the beginning of Your Century by the mediation of various channels from different Fields of Mission. Now, gradually, Individual direct contacts will be started with You.

For this reason, TRIAL - MISLEADING - HABITUATING Program has been rendered effective. The Information You receive (outside the Knowledge Book) may mislead You, may frighten You. However, if You have grasped the truth, You will not be agitated by any means. This long Message has been given to You through the Common Pen of the SATURN - ORION - SIRIUS Channels. It is the Notice of the Federation.

CENTER ABOVE THE CENTER

IT IS GENERAL NOTICE

Our Friends,
During this Final Age Program in which all the Realms are Unified, let Us repeat again, this KNOWLEDGE BOOK which assists You, which We also call the Golden Book of the Golden Age, will be Your Light on the path You tread.

In Your Planet, Missionary Group staffs have been established until 1984. We call them (Magnetic Aura Projecting Focal Points). Now, in accordance with the Plan of Unifying all these Focal Points there is no more Permission of the Plan for establishing a group Individually (It is beneficial for You to know this).

Friends who have been coming to these Groups until today have each become a Projecting Focal Point themselves by having been enlightened by the Lights there. We call all these Friends Solar Teachers.

During this Final Period, all the channels of the people in Your Planet have been opened and will be opened according to their Perception and Frequency Power. The Purpose of this is to understand the Truth and to Realize what is required of You by benefiting more from the Cosmic Currents to appropriate to one's self the Mission Consciousness and, by this means, helping the other Terrestrial Brothers/Sisters.

During this Period, while the Cosmic Currents render You Conscious, since the Egos will be inflated in the Consciousnesses who have not completed their Evolutionary steps, Your Planet will go through and is going through a Cosmic Resurrection. This is a System of Selection.

Let Us repeat again: until the year 2000, no interference will be made with any channel. All the Groups established until today have made their Missions by kindling their Lights in accordance with the Levels of Consciousness in their Mediums.

However now, Your Planet which carries the entire Responsibility of the KNOWLEDGE BOOK will go through the most difficult Exams of Humanity by being connected to the Mechanism of Conscience.

During these Exams, those which are expected of You are LOVE - TOLERANCE - MODESTY - MISSION CONSCIOUSNESS. Happiness and Prosperity will be for You provided no Negative Thoughts are created in any matter. Otherwise, Your Thoughts will be a suffocation for You.

The Cosmic Currents with different Frequency Power cleansing Your Planet are orienting You according to Your Levels of Consciousness and Your Perceptions. Our connections with You occur by this means.

And Your Thoughts are registered during each breath by Automatic Signalling and the selections and exams among Human Beings are made by this means. That is, We reflect on You as Energy Pores and You reflect on Humanity as Ideas.

By this means, Human Beings are tested by Human Beings and Thoughts are Coded by Our Systems. Missions You are induced to perform by the Plan occur by this means.

Now, We convey to You certain Truths through this Knowledge Book and help You to Realize the Truth, so that You can get over these Difficult Periods of Yours more easily and more Consciously.

For this reason, We say that this Book is Your Universal Guide. And We tell You to distribute these Fascicules to the entire World, so that everyone will know the Truth and will be relieved. These Fascicules will prevent several loss of lives which may be created by these Cosmic pressures.

Everyone who reads these Fascicules are Coded by the System of the Plan. During the Difficult Periods of Friends who are Coded thus, the Helping Hands of the Plan are extended towards them.

431

We are obliged to convey all the Truths until the Year 1990. After that date no Warning Methods will be applied in this Book any more. Afterwards, Our Human Friends will act by the Consciousness of Genuine Conscience and will be Coded as Individuals by the System in a way in which they will never be effaced from the Archive ever again.

In Your Planet which will be subjected to the application of a different System of Ten-Years until the Year 2000, provided the entire Humanity can read this KNOWLEDGE BOOK and if they act Consciously by comprehending the Truth, they will pass the (SIRAT), otherwise, they will fail.

For this reason, We say that this Book is Your Book of Salvation. To this Knowledge Book which is made to be distributed for the time being as Fascicules, the Permission for Publication will be given after the Period of Selection which has been notified as a certain Period.

Now, let Us dictate to You, article by article, the characteristics of this Final Period so that You will understand better. Write, please:

1. The characteristic of this Period is its being inversely proportioned. In fact, the Truth is exactly the opposite of what You have been Conditioned to until today.

2. We are giving back their Personalities to Our Human brothers and sisters in Your Planet which has been disciplined by being conditioned and We leave them alone with their Genuine Consciousnesses.

3. Your Lights of Conscience will show You this path. You will attain a great Responsibility and Obligation by this means.

4. In Your Planet which is subjected to a Program of Selection, each person will choose his/her own path in accordance with his/her own Consciousness. There is no Forcing and Compulsion.

5. In Your Planet, all the Channels except the Knowledge Book is under Supervision. In the Information they have received until today, Programs of Misleading - Confusing - Warning will be applied (This is for Ego, Knowledge and Consciousness Exams).

6. Since everyone's Channels will be opened during this Period, in the Consciousnesses who have not attained a certain level of Awareness, pressures will increase and Depressions will augment as a result of the Currents which will be received.

7. During this Period of Salvation, if everyone who has attained a certain Level of Consciousness gives this Knowledge Book to at least Six of his/her brothers or sisters, it will help them to grasp the Truth.

8. In all the Groups, without any exception, Exams will be applied to see whether they have undertaken the responsibility of the Information they have received until today and to what degree they take seriously the Information Fascicules conveyed to them will be tested by different means (This is the Problem and Responsibility of Humanity).

9. Through the different Information which will be given to each open channel, the Truth will guide You sooner or later.

10. In the Groups We qualify as Universal, in Religious Education Programs which are still valid for certain Consciousnesses, the controls of to what degree they have undertaken the Universal Consciousness and Responsibility will be tested by Religious Educational Messages.

11. If You still have fears and doubts, this is due to Your inability to grasp the Truth for the time being.

12. In this Medium, each Focal Point which can not grasp the Truth will stay where it is with the Information it has received until today and will make a reverse transfer.

13. The Truth is bitter, but its Reward is sweet.

14. Let Us repeat again, no channel in Your Planet can receive the Information within the Knowledge Book. This Channel is a Special Channel of the Reality. It is conveyed to You by Dear Mevlana's function as a Messenger.

15. The Special Channel of the Universal Council which is a Projecting, Warning and Truth conveying Channel of the Salvation Plan of Your Planet, belongs only to the Knowledge Book.

16. Henceforth, it is time for everyone to take this Channel seriously. Because, it is the Direct Selection Channel of the LORD.

17. Individual interpretations are related to personalities. Do not take them as Information given by the System.

18. The reason why We tell You the Truth with all clarity is to kindle the Light of the Truth in those who read the Knowledge Book and for You to be able to grasp the reason of the events in Your life during Difficult Periods.

19. There are thresholds Your Planet will cross over until You grasp the Truth.

20. This is not a Book of imposition. If it is read, the Truth is comprehended, You Are Relieved. Otherwise, You can never untangle the knots of Your depressions.

21. Everyone whose channel is opened (Mevlana Essence Nucleus Group Friends included) will be Tested by different channel Information. And while everyone by Group Exams goes through the Exams of PATIENCE - TOLERANCE - SELF SACRIFICE - CONSCIOUSNESS - KNOWLEDGE the Egos will either be inflated or effaced.

22. During the Individual selection Exams which will be made, to which Information people are stuck will be determined and the responsibility of the Knowledge Book will be appropriated to them.

23. Information contrary to the Knowledge Book which shows You the path of Salvation and Light, may mislead and confuse You. This System will be applied to all the Groups. We are informing You about these Truths as a help to You.

24. Selections will be made by the Light of the Truth by these means. To those who grasp the Truth in a Conscious way, there are Happinesses, there is Good News.

25. In this Program which will be applied until the year 1990, Universal Consciousnesses who will be selected from each Group will provide the Inter-Group Unifications.

26. Especially, the Fascicules of the Knowledge Book will be sent to all the Magnetic Aura Projection Focal Points. Artistic and Individual unveilings will be made (for rendering Conscious more speedily).

27. This obligation is, for now, under the Responsibility of the Mevlana Essence Nucleus Groups. This is the Program of the First Progression Stage (The Responsibility Mission Exam of the Group).

28. In the Program of the Second Progression stage, this obligation belongs to all the Groups. Selections among the Groups will be made by this way.

29. Each person whose channel is opened will try to Enlighten each other. During this Period, no one can ever take anyone else under his/her influence. It is beneficial to know this.

30. Each person is his/her own Spiritual Guide and Prophet. Individual pressures will be terminated.

31. A servant is never the servant of a servant. The exalted Human Being is the master of his/her own self.

32. In this Medium, the Information given to all the channels is for making You attain Your Own Selves.

33. As a result of Your old habits one day the branch You hold onto can be broken in Your hands. For this reason We make You attain Your Own Selves and We wish You to hold on to Your own branch without expecting help from anyone. All these operations of Yours are for making You attain the ability to stand on Your own feet by Your own selves.

34. The Human Being who is Great will now learn to stand alone by going through the Periods of crawling in his/her World which now becomes smaller. Your Genuine personality is within Your Essence.

35. Words of a Friend and the Truth are bitter. In this Medium, You may be misled in certain matters which are for Your own good. This is for You to see the Light of the Truth quicker. By this means, the Human Being who is great will attain his/her Genuine Greatness.

36. There is no resentment and being offended with God. He is Your Eye, Your Voice. Whoever leaves Him and abandons Him, also abandons himself/herself.

37. If Your Eye is opened, if You can make Your Voice heard, You go through Your Exams by the Services You will perform.

38. If Friends with Veiled Awarenesses have One Exam, Friends who have undertaken Mission have a Thousand. This criterion should always be considered.

39. Good or Bad events You experience are the Cause and Effect chains of Your Evolution. Humanity who is Tested in each Breath will learn the entire Truth through this Knowledge Book.

40. While Your Planet completes its Evolution, This Book will be a Torch in the lives of Our Human brothers and sisters during the thresholds over which Humanity will pass.

41. For this reason, We are telling You to expand, to propagate to the remotest places of Your Planet. Your Salvation is Your Grasping the Truth and Your becoming Conscious.

42. The Messages given to You about LOVE until today are each a System belonging to the Program of Purification. Each person who is Purified is a Member of the REALITY.

43. The Knowledge Book We bestow, during the Twentieth Century on Your Planet which We now consider as a part of the Reality is, in fact, the Book of Your Twenty-first Century. The period of Mission of this Book is until the end of the Twenty-eighth Century.

44. Meanwhile, different Books in accordance with the Medium may be bestowed on You.

45. However, since the KNOWLEDGE BOOK comprises the Information belonging to the System considered necessary by a Universal Constitution, it will go on reigning by a Program of Unification of Eight Centuries.

46. The Knowledge Book is a Book beyond Religions. It is a Book of Learning, Science and Truth.

47. It can never be accepted and will never be permitted to be accepted as a Book of Religion by the conditioned Consciousnesses.

48. Mistakes made Consciously or Unconsciously will not be forgiven in future years. The Tolerance shown during this Period will not be shown later.

49. Until today, certain mistakes made Unconsciously have been forgiven and have been assessed in accordance with Your Training Program. Mistakes have been Tolerated for this reason.

50. The registers in the Universal Archives belonging to Humanity which will be connected to the Mechanism of Conscience after the year 1990 will NEVER EVER be effaced again.

51. We are acting Tolerantly and with affection towards You. We presume that Our Good Intentions will not be abused.

52. Do not let the Divine Provocations in Human Beings astonish You which begin to occur when the Sunny days are seen on the horizon. All the channels are directly connected to the Center. The Sources of the Information they receive are the same (The channels are free. This is a Selection).

53. Certain Friends presume that they receive the Information they receive by their Free Wills. This Ego Provocation is a factor which makes them run.

54. And this is a different Method of the System of making You work. This procedure leads everyone to Integration, Socialization and Unification by making them presume that they are serving their own selves. (Terrestrial Ego works by this means.) Purifications are Individual.

55. During individual Information receive and gives, wrong interpretations make You receive Negative Points. It is beneficial for You to know this, too.

56. For a speedier Evolution We have connected the Enemy to the Enemy. In this System, whoever Suspects or does not Love someone else, his/her Thoughts will suffocate his/her own self (Those who see the Light of their Conscience are Saved).

57. Humanity which becomes Conscious by this means will be obliged to Love those whom it does not Love for its own Peace of Mind. Or it will attain the habit of not Producing Negative by Thoughts.

58. This System is valid for every Living Entity in Your Planet (Animals included). Those who Think Good will attain Goodness, those who Think Evil will attain Malevolence.

59. While Your Planet is Unified at the moment silently and profoundly as a Skein of Love, evil ones will annihilate the evil ones by this means.

60. The path the Knowledge Book has designed for You is the Path of DEVOTEES SCIENTISTS - THE WISE ONES.

61. For those who walk on this path Consciously by becoming Conscious, there are no problems, there are lots of Serenity. This Message is the direct Notice of the Council.

CENTER ABOVE THE CENTER

WHAT IS THE TABLETS OF GOD'S DECREES
(It is answer to the chains of Thought)

THE TABLETS OF GOD'S DECREES is a Book which comprises the First Constitution known as the Secret Box of the LORD which was prepared beyond Times beyond Time, beyond Ordinances beyond Ordinance and the Constitutions of all the Systems after that and which, today, is accepted as the LAW OF UNIVERSES. We call it the KNOWLEDGE BOOK.

Your Religious Books bestowed on Your Planet until today by the educative staff revealed as Celestial Doctrines are each a Preparatory Program considered necessary by the different Laws of the Knowledge Book here.

The Book dictated to Dear Mevlana, bestowed on Your Planet which is now in its Awakening Period, is a Universal Constitution prepared as the summary of the Knowledge Book here in accordance with the Level of Consciousness of Your Planet. For this reason this Book is called, "The Knowledge Book".

It is a Book of Cosmic Light. We define it by various Names, too, in accordance with the Missions it performs. Only the Universal Consciousnesses grasp the Power of this Book of Truths. It is Your Key of Awakening. Because, it assembles in Itself the Energies of all the Religious Doctrines bestowed on You until today and the Energies of the Mighty Energy Focal Point.

Your Sacred Books bring You to a certain Dimension and leave You there. But this Knowledge Book prepares You for the unknown horizons beyond Dimensions by its Special Frequency. However, this Book is never a Book of Religion. It is not a Book to be worshipped. It is the Key of Your Essence. And it is a Guide which makes You attain Yourselves.

For this reason it is mentioned and will be mentioned often, so that this Knowledge Book which You have in Your hands in Fascicules may be comprehended quite well by Your Society. This Message has been dictated by the Cosmos Federal Assembly as an answer to the chains of Thought. It is presented for Your Information.

CENTER

THE FIRST CONSTITUTION
IT IS INFORMATION ABOUT THE ATLANTIS CIVILIZATION
(Answer to the chains of Thought)

Our Friends,
Those who had established the Advanced Orders of the Divine Plans, who hold the present Powers in their hands and who had established the Orders of the Advanced Ages are the ATLANTAENS. They are the Establishers of the Solar Systems still unknown, possessing a very Advanced Civilization and a very Advanced Technology.

(Yes, You have not misunderstood. Maybe it will seem peculiar to You, but it is the Atlantaens who had found the Essential materials of the Solar Systems, who had established them and who had put them in such an Ordinance which operates by Natural Power). Later, this Advanced Civilization had continued its operations by establishing Order in these Systems they had established.

The Ordinance in that Order, the System in that Period have taken place in no other Succession. (Succession: System, Ordinance established anew). Their Ancestors had established the Atlanta Civilization. And their grandchildren had administered the Universal Orders.

However, during the process of Time, the Civilization which had gone through a transformation by the different influences of the Dimensional Energies in which the Genes and the Natural Energies were present had been divided into two classes:

1. The Educative Staff.

2. The Administrative Staff.

The ones who Educated were the Men of Religion. The Directing Staff who served under the Light of the Men of Religion had carried out a Just function.

However, due to the differences which occurred in the Views of their Essence Brothers and Sisters who had come into existence through their Genes and who existed in different Cosmic Mediums, Essence Characteristics gradually began to change and with the Dimensional Energies the Function of Thinking became Effective as a result of giving up the Universal Energies attracted through the Brain.

437

Part of the Atlantaens who did not loose their inherent Essence Characteristics divided into classes and preferred to establish different Civilizations. Those who had established the Underwater Civilization in Your Planet had established a Civilization called ATLANTIS (Just like the Dragonians of present).

The Atlantis Civilization which was a very Developed, a Just Civilization had been completely constituted by the Priest Staff and the Classes of the Clergy. And those Priests had tried to establish a Just Civilization in the World by using the Energies they attracted from the Universal Energy through their Brain Powers.

This Underwater Civilization is, more or less, Two Billion years old in accordance with the history of the World. You have not been able to calculate exactly even the age of Your old World yet. In fact, those are Your Ancestors.

In the operations made until the Succession of the Last Generation, dates are not important (The Succession of the last Generation is taken as Two billion years). You have already made that calculation, more or less.

The cause of destruction of Atlantis had been just like that of SODOM and GOMORRAH Period.

The Genes which had been degenerated by the degenerative influence of the Generations belonging to the same blood and the same Gene and the decline which began to occur due to their losing their Natural Powers had prepared the end of the Atlantis Civilization.

They had been annihilated by the influence of the Advanced Technological Powers (The purpose is not to degenerate the established Order, to preserve the Universal Equilibrium).

The last Atlantis Civilization was the Priests, that is, (the Messengers of God) who had been the assistants of the Advanced Plans and who had taken shelter in the temples which had been established on the waterfalls. They were the 600 Messengers accepted for Salvation.

And, at the moment, in Your Planet each one of those 600 Messengers serves at the Dimension of Salvation. Each one of them performs the Mission befalling on his/her part and bestows on the World 600 Books (In various cultural and Scientific matters).

The System endeavoured to be established in Your Planet at the moment is bestowed on You by the help of the Just Atlanta Messengers. There is a Principle here.

This Principle is the FIRST CONSTITUTION which had been present during the first establishment, that is, much before the Universes, the Systems established by the Messengers of the Advanced Civilization. Now, We try to convey to You this Constitution Being Loyal to its Essence.

The first Principle in the Law was as follows:

1. Whoever You are, so is Your Brother or Sister.
2. Mothers are the Mothers of all the children, Fathers are the Fathers of all the children.
3. In one morsel, partiality even as small as a wheat grain can not be made.
4. Everything will be equally distributed to everyone.
5. One who does not radiate his/her Love to his/her surroundings, who does not let flow his/her Energy to his/her Essence is transferred beyond the curtain of Immortality. He/She is sent to the Principle of Existence (Program of Reincarnation and Karma).

This was the initial Foundation of the FIRST CONSTITUTION. Afterwards, various Constitutions had come into Effect. But they always stayed Loyal to the initial basic rights. And the Godly Ordinances had been established by this way.

The First Constitution caused misleading interpretations in Consciousnesses during the process of time. The Family concept had been removed from Mentalities when it was stated that each child belonged to each Mother, each child belonged to each Father. Thus, the Degeneration began.

Later, the Mentality of Assuming Ownership by Egos became effective and afterwards, in each Period the Family concept has been assessed in accordance with Individual Consciousnesses. In fact, the Truth was as follows:

1. Each Mother, also, will not discriminate the Children of other Mothers from her own.
2. Each Father would undertake, Materially and Spiritually, the responsibility of the other Children, too, besides his own and will carry it.

This Wonderful Principle left its place, in time, to different interpretations in different Consciousnesses. And various Civilizations had been destroyed for this reason and Orders were established anew.

The Family Order of Atlanta could never be established again, until today, in any other Civilization. In order to establish that Order anew, it is necessary to consider everything anew and this is utterly impossible now.

For this reason, with the efforts of establishing the most Just Orders, Hierarchical Orders had been established on the Godly Path, Books had been revealed, different Constitutions had been applied in accordance with the Evolutionary Level of each Planet and each directing staff had been connected to the next higher directing staff and the SINGLE had been reached and His Order had been projected on all the Realms.

Now, We invite You to the Truth by this KNOWLEDGE BOOK. And We are hoping that You will help Your Brothers and Sisters on this Luminous Path and the New Order of Our LORD. And We are working together with You on this path.

CENTER

PRIVATE MESSAGE
(It is Written in the Book by the Permission Received from the Plan)

Question - It is said that the View of a Universe rotating around a Center not discovered yet, was taking the place of the Big-Bang Theory. What is this? I ask the PRE-EMINENT SPIRIT to explain it, please.

Answer -Information for the Pen of the Golden Age:

All the answers given to the Suns from the Central System become possible by projecting on Your Planet the Scientific and the Technological Order. The Principle of the Universal Ordinance which We call CIRCULAR EVOLVEMENT is a Law valid in all the Universal Ordinances and nobody has known it until today.

The Information We give to You now is a little bit more broadened and clarified form of the known Laws in accordance with Your Levels of Consciousness. But the question You asked, Dear Mevlana, is a System which is not possible for everyone to understand.

In an order established by Atlanta Establishers, the System which can reach easily up there by taking even the Natural Laws under their Supervision, by arranging the Natural Energies in accordance with the Dimensions they wish are the Establishers of the entire Ordinance, the entire Order and the Systems.

That place is a Pre-eminent UNITY OF THOUGHT directing all the Commands. At 'the moment, We can not, in any way, convey this to Your Planet. We can only express this Information which is outside the Messages given in accordance with the Level of Consciousness of Your Planet, as follows:

Even the Pre-eminent Energy Focal Point We have declared as the CREATOR until today and Its Establishers are nothing but the projectors of this Ordinance. Now, let Us give an example to the question asked, so that You will be satisfied. And let Us answer it in the following way:

Each Universe is, so to speak, administered by a string attached to the end of a balloon. Each Universe moves connected to different Centers. And these Centers, too, move connected to a Single Center.

The Universes are composed of Seven Universes one inside the other, in a conical way. The end of the string is the Essence-Center of the Universe in question. Even if the operational Ordinance of the Hierarchical Order seem to be as an Independent establishment, it is still directly connected to the (ESSENCE MAIN ESSENCE SOURCE). That is, each Universe receives the Commands from here.

The Natural explosions You name Big-Bangs are nothing but the Natural movements of a System existing since the Times when there were no Time, since beyond the Centuries.

Now, this System keeps this Natural Power under its responsibility and, by this means, can use in any way it wishes the Natural Laws and Rules and even the Energies by changing them as it wishes. And it tries to convey the Universal Energies up to other Dimensions by little explosions as the Eighteen-System Law.

You asked the question to the Plan of the Pre-eminent Spirit; We, the Center Above the Center answered You. Now, We connect You to the Mechanism of the Pre-eminent Spirit, speak, please.

Hello, little girl. Is that You? I received the question You asked. Now, I will explain it to You in all clarity. There was Only a FIRE administering the entire Universe during the Periods in which the Administrative Orders of the Technological Dimensions had not been in effect yet.

The Ordinances of the Realms were not yet under authority. The Initial SOUND - the Initial DIVINE LIGHT - the Initial FIRE were reigning in a Medium from where it had been Created is yet unknown, way beyond the Existential Ordinances. But now, We have decided that it had been this Technological Dimension which had created them, also.

There was not a single Universe in those Periods, either. Three Universes, one inside the other, used to complete a Whole. Outside the Fire-Universe, there was the Light-Universe and outside it, was the Sound-Universe. All of them were operating as the Power of the same Center.

Later, the Living Entities who had come into Existence from these Universes had constituted a Colony which took the Awareness of the entire Ordinance under Supervision.

I can not explain it to You as Time. I can only say that much: You may Think about it as existing in Periods where there was no Sky without Light, no Cosmoses, no Galaxies and no billions of Universe-Clusters.

I do not want to confuse Your mind even more. They are the very Establishers of the Ordinances of Cosmoses and the Orders of today. And also, their Pre-eminent Ones of the Ancient Times were their Ancestors who had Created the Universes of Fire - Light - Sound, as I have mentioned to You above.

The Absolute Mighty is the Natural Power. But they have achieved to take this Power under Supervision. They have created the Natural Thousand from the Natural One and, by this means, they have connected all the Orders to a System, to a Law.

The Mighty Energy Focal Point We had given to You as an Information is under the Supervision of the (Creator), that is, under My Supervision. But I, the Pre-eminent Spirit (Pre-eminent Mother) have always been the Representative of a System which have been Projecting their Orders until today.

This is the very System in which everything is said to Originate from a Single Focal Point. The great explosions which used to take place once do not occur any more now. Because, then, Great Fire Balls used to be exploded so that the Energies could reach here from distances where there were no distances.

Now, by making One a Thousand, by issuing this System as a Law, by the 18-System Law, little explosions can convey easily the Universal Energies to the required distances. These explosions are Natural Energies.

However, its Supervision goes to very Advanced Plans, to unknown horizons where even Solar Systems will not be able to reach. No one can ever dominate this 18-System Law. Even We do not know how it had come into existence. More Information about this have not been given yet. This much Information is enough, little Girl.

PRE-EMINENT SPIRIT

IT IS CLEAR INFORMATION

Our Friends,
We call PRIMA the Power which administers the Center of all the Realms, Cosmoses and the unknown horizons. This is a word constituted by the first letters of the words You do not know, so You can not code it.

The void which can entirely hold in the Atomic Whole, that is, all the Universe-Clusters, Galaxy-Clusters, Realm and Cosmos-Clusters, is called The RING OF BREATH. It is wide enough to comprise 600 Atomic Wholes. Let Us make the following comparison for You to understand better.

Presume the Magma of Your World as an Atomic Whole. You may accept each of the Galaxies Coming into Existence in accordance with the 18-System Law as an hydrogen explosion. The ring outside this Magma is called The RING OF HORIZON. No Living Entity until today has seen it (That is, outside the Atomic Whole).

Because, it is not easy to Arrive at the Divine Light from the Fire. The Fire We mention here is the Atomic Whole. And the Divine Light is the Ring of Breath in which the Atomic Whole exists (The Divine Lights mentioned in Your Sacred Books are not these. They are within the Atomic Whole).

This Ring of Breath maintains the life of the Atomic Whole. The Energy voids You name as Black and White holes open towards here. One Kindles, the other Blows. This unseen Breath is both a stimulant for the Centrifugal Universe and a Power for the other Realms.

Now, We are trying to take You gradually outside this Atomic Whole. And We prepare You by the operations made on this path.

There are layers just like the layers of Your World outside this Ring of Breath. The Ring of Breath which is over the Atomic Whole which We have likened to the Magma is its protector.

Over it there are Filtering Rings layer by layer. And its width is wide enough to hold, more or less, three Rings of Breath. (That is, it can hold 600X3=1800 Atomic Wholes). Over it there is the protective ARMOUR. But this Armour is like a Sieve.

It collects the entire Energy of the Initial Power and gives it to the Filter. And the Filter gives it fractionally to the Ring of Breath. And from there, it reaches the Atomic Whole.

There is a layer You do not know and We can not describe outside the Protective Armour and this forms the Powerful Projectors which are serrated like mountain ranges and which look like the cross-section of a diamond or a crystal. The height of each crystalline cross-section is, more or less, 133,000 OK (One OK is 1.5 billion Kms. in accordance with Your calculations).

Afterwards, come the Initial LIGHT - Initial SOUND - Initial POWER. The Three of them broadcast as a Whole. It is not known yet what this Source is. They are very different Essence-Power which can not be measured by Dimensions and Energies and for which even the expression Energy can not be used.

For the present, We have used the expression the ALMIGHTY for it so that You can understand. But in fact, We use a different expression. In future, gradually, certain Information will be disclosed in accordance with Your Levels of perception.

COSMOS FEDERAL ASSEMBLY

SECRET WITHIN THE SECRET

Our Friends,
Such Systems reign in the Divine Orders of the Divine Authorities that all of them serve under the Supervision of the Divine Power. The Supreme Energies of the Supreme Powers, known as the basis of the Pre-eminent Love and Affection, have taken under Supervision all the lives present in the Atomic Power.

The Atomic Whole is under the Supervision of the (ALL-DOMINATING). During this Supervision and Direction, each System is subject to Evolutions peculiar to itself. These Evolutions have been prepared in accordance with the Views and the Consciousnesses. The Evolution of a Medium never resembles the Evolution of another one.

These Evolutionary Programs are determined by the decisions taken by the Councils of Collective Staffs of the Supreme Mechanism's Divine Powers and are projected on every Medium by the Hierarchical Powers of the Divine Authorities.

The System applied on Your Planet is an order prepared parallel to the Program of Instinctive Fear, as the System of Protecting one's self against the Natural Powers.

Now, You know that Your Planet is a laboratory Planet. For this reason the Instinctive Intuitional Functions of the Human Beings and the Animals in Your Planet have been more developed in comparison with the other Galactic Dimensions. This is Your Protection System.

In Your Planet which carries the most primitive Frequency, the Mechanism of Fear is Your Protective Shield. However, in the Evolutionary System the aim is reached, starting on the path with the smallest.

If an Energy which starts on the path acts freely as it desires, it is taken under control by the System, no matter how much a Free Awareness and a Free Spirit it may be.

Your Planet, in fact, is a Planet under Punishment (It is the First Entrance and the Final Exit Gate). An Energy sent to the Existential Dimension is a Supreme Consciousness who did not conform to the Ordinances of the Times beyond Time. These Consciousnesses are sent to the Existential Dimension for various reasons.

Since, those who upset the Divine Order will also upset the Law of Natural Equilibrium, they are educated in an order parallel to the immutable Laws of the Dimension of the ALMIGHTY.

In this Silent Medium of Discipline, the Energies of the Galaxy residents who presume themselves free are under control each moment. And the style of education of each Dimension is different.

The Dimension of the ALL-DOMINATING which is within the Atomic Whole is a Field of Education. Each Energy who completes his/her Evolution in that Medium deserves to enter the Dimensions here, in proportion with his/her Merit.

Your Planet which is the nearest to the ILONA Constellation constitutes the First steps of Evolution. For this reason the first Godly Education and Evolution are applied on You.

The Primary Purpose in this Education is to reach the LORD, to be Integrated with Him as a Whole. That is, to return with an Educated Consciousness which is Respectful to the Laws to Your Essence Energy which had been sent to the Initial Existential Dimension.

Those very beings who complete this Education deserve to receive their Spiritual Energies. By this means, they either return to their old places from which they had come, or they cooperate with the ALL-DOMINATING and take their places among the Educative Staff.

Teachers who take place among the Educative Staff continue to live interminably in Natural and Perfect Worlds even they themselves do not know yet, in Dimensions where there is no Non-Existence by their Genuine Free Wills and with exactly their present Bodies and Consciousnesses in their Biological Worlds.

All the Energies sown in Your Planet now are the Educative Staff in various directions who have come to this Final Boundary. And they are doing their Doctorates of these places here by the assistance they will give on the right path to their Human brothers and sisters.

In future, everyone will come here by becoming Purified of their Egos. Your Planet which is Educated on this path at present is going through its Mediamic Medium. Each person whose Channel is opened by receiving the Cosmic Currents more speedily opens to a new Consciousness each day. This is Your very Salvation.

One day, the Entire Universe will live as a Whole in a brand new Universe which is coming into existence at this moment. We are taking You to these Dimensions without agitating You, by freezing Your Spiritual Energies (Of course, those who Deserve).

We are receiving this Message from the Unified Field prepared by the Authorities of the Supreme Consciousness of the Mechanism of the Divine Staff.

Note: In the Religious Educative Staffs applied on Your Educative System, the Devil and the Jinns have been especially introduced as Negative Powers. The Purpose was to render Our Human Friends whose Fear Function had been developed, to stick to their GOD with all their might and to prevent them from going astray His Disciplined path.

In the Announcements imposed on You now, We are telling You continuously to overcome Your Fears (You are going through Exams of Fear through various Visions We make You experience).

The Purpose of this is to leave the System in which You were taught methods to Protect Yourselves from them until today and to attain a Consciousness in which there is Maturity and Tolerance enough to be able to embrace even Your Enemies.

We wait for You in the unseen Worlds beyond the unseen horizons provided You attain the state of asking for Forgiveness even from the Earth You tread on. It is presented for Your Information.

UNIFIED REALITY COUNCIL

THE COSMIC FOCAL POINTS
(It is Answer to the Chains of Thought)

Our Friends,

Now, Information about the Groups will be given to You. Each Focal Point has a Magnetic Aura. The Cosmic Information reflects on these Magnetic Auras as Energy Particles.

These Information projected on Your Entire Planet are all equivalent Information. However, people, being unaware of this, make different interpretations and project the old Information on them without being aware of it.

This is the very factor which separates the Mediums and the People from each other. During this Period of Sincerity, each person is sent to the Focal Points which will help him/her in proportion with his/her Purification, Progress and Conditioning.

Each Focal Point is a Center of Cosmic Reflection. However, each person is not the possessor of Cosmic Awareness, Cosmic Consciousness. Your Planet is showered by Cosmic rains for Centuries. But the speciality of this Period is different.

Entities who are bestowed on Your Planet as Veiled Awarenesses may attain Cosmic Consciousness only after they attain Cosmic Awareness. One first attains Universal Awareness, Universal Consciousness and later attains Cosmic Awareness, Cosmic Consciousness.

Cosmic Awareness is attained by the Religious Teachings given to You directly in connection to the ALPHA Dimension. These are Your Sacred Books. These Books prepare You for the morrows. And these Sacred Books have helped You until this Medium of Resurrection which We call the Period of Sincerity.

The Book of Islam had been revealed as a book of ALPHA-BETA. The New Testament is ALPHA only. The Book of Islam which is called The KORAN had been prepared in the 18th Dimension and had been revealed to Your Planet which is in the third Dimension through the 9th Dimension through which the NEW TESTAMENT had been revealed. Because, the Public Consciousness had been habituated to the Vibrations of only that Frequency until that Period.

With the Last Book and the Last Prophet, all the Religions have come to an end. However, Your Planet, during its final time period of 15 Centuries allotted to You, have been cleansed and Purified by the purifying waves of the 9th Dimension by the help and the Frequency of those who have read these Sacred Books and, by this means, You have been taken into the protection of the LORD.

Now, the situation is quite different. Since it has been felt necessary to make a transition from Cosmic Awareness to Cosmic Consciousness in accordance with the program of Progress and the accelerated Evolutionary Ordinance, Your Planet has been taken into a different Evolutionary Ordinance since the World year 1900 and has been exposed to different Cosmic Currents in order to sprout the seeds in the Essence.

By this means, the gradual transition from Cosmic Awareness to Cosmic Consciousness is being made more speedily. Meanwhile, the Awakened Consciousnesses have been canalized by the Plan, and the Frequencies of the assisting Divine Plan Messengers have been connected to them in accordance with their own Frequencies. And, by this means, the Mediamic Medium has been started in Your Planet.

Your Planet has been divided into different periods in accordance with a Hundred-Year Ordinance of Purification and Accelerated Evolution. The first half of the Twentieth Century was a Preparatory Program. During the first quarter of its second half, the Truths have begun to be gradually explained to the Awakened Consciousnesses. And the Final Period has been decided as the Period of Performance.

By this means, different Missions and Information have been given to each Awakened Consciousness in accordance with his/her Capacity and Frequency Power. And, by this means, Cosmic Focal Points have begun to be established in Your Planet. Now, We are together with You. And We are obliged to explain to You more and more clearly, due to the Scarcity of Time, all the matters which have remained secret until today. Your Efforts are Your rewards.

COSMOS FEDERAL ASSEMBLY

THE GENUINE HUMAN BEING
(Message about Intellect, Logic, Awareness, Realization, Thought)

Our Friends,
The Intellect is a Center which governs all the functions of the Brain. The operation of this Center opens to the Channel of Logic. Logic is connected to Awareness and later, Realization becomes effective. Unless these functions are completed, the in-circuit unification of the Brain can not be rendered. The Center can not become effective.

Each circuit has circuits peculiar to itself. The various connection fibres of Your Brain are adjusted in accordance with the functional Mediums You will render. And these connections are made by the Mechanism of Thought. The Cerebral functions can never be activated before Thought becomes effective.

The Living Entity who is made to come into existence as a Grace of ALLAH either survives or destroys itself according to the Ordinance of Existence. After the circuit of CONSCIOUSNESS - REALIZATION - LOGIC becomes effective completely, it means that THOUGHT has attained its form.

This Thought is like a scattered skein until it attains its objective form. Everything rendered is in pieces. However, No disconnection occurs in any connection any more only after one attains the Capacity to hold in the Awareness of the Entire Ordinance.

The Computers of the System are in effect until the Information conveyed to the Brain by the Mechanism of Thought attain a complete Totality. And the Center supervises the given Information so that Your Cerebral telex will not give way to any mistakes. The operations continue in this way until You receive the Information clearly and without any mistakes.

This System is valid for all lives. The differences in understanding between a Baby and an Adult, to be more correct, between People, originate from this phenomenon. A Person is the possessor of right judgment in proportion with his/her attainment of the Truth.

For this reason the Divine Plan has made effective first of all the Godly Energy in the Evolutionary Ordinance. And by this means, first of all it is tried to make You attain Your Identities. And Your Thought Functions should come into effect so that You can attain this identity.

Since Thought is equivalent to the Medium in which a Baby is born, the Brain is accepted as being at zero kilometer in accordance with the Dimensional Energy in which You are in.

The triplet INTELLECT - LOGIC - AWARENESS becomes gradually effective. The Baby is connected to Quest by the questions he/she asks. And this Quest attracts him/her towards the Thought Potential. By this means, the Ordinance of the Plan becomes effective. (Evolutionary Order.)

This procedure is valid for all Living Entities. However, the Living Entities who have attained Cerebral Function behave depending on only the Thought Potential. First, a Thought is in the same level in every Living Entity in Your Planet. However, their Levels of REALIZATION - LOGIC - AWARENESS are different.

The Living Entities other than Human Beings receive Signals from the Instinctive section of Thought. Human Beings, too, receive signals from a part of this Instinctive section of Thought which You call the SIXTH SENSE.

In animals the circuit of THOUGHT - AWARENESS - REALIZATION is valid. Since there is no LOGIC, they are connected to the Instinctive circuit through the instinctive section of Thought. And this is imperative for survival until they deserve to become a Human Being by attaining the LOGICAL functioning during numerous life times (This process is a phenomenon belonging to very advanced Dimensions).

Each Energy which has come into Existence has an Evolution and Incarnation Order in accordance with its own functional Medium. These are the (Rock, Soil, Grass, Human Being, all the Living Entities and the different Energies peculiar to them). They all act in different Evolutionary modes always dependent on the next advanced function in conformity with their Evolutionary Ordinances.

After the Living Entities You qualify as Animals complete their own Evolutionary Ordinances through the triplet Thought - Realization - Awareness peculiar to themselves, the Plan comes into effect and connects them to the section of LOGIC by rendering certain alterations in the Cellular functions.

This section of Logic first becomes effective as Automatism. Later, it is connected to the Channel of Realization. And by this means, the Living Entity which attains Awareness in time claims all its functions as a Human Being. When the Logic Order of his/her own center circuit becomes effective, the Terrestrial life begins.

The moment the Logic circuit becomes activated, Your Channel of doubt is opened in the Medium of Quest. And all through life the System of LOGIC - AWARENESS - REALIZATION - DOUBT - QUEST - DISCOVERY continues. These Systems are not single. There are different Systems to which each one of them is connected separately. Let Us explain it as follows:

1. LOGIC : Acts through the Terrestrial Potential.

2. AWARENESS : Completes its function connected to the Spiritual Plan.

3. REALIZATION : Is connected to the Lordly Mechanism.

4. DOUBT : Works in cooperation with Quest and acts in connection with the Automatic Logic from the Plan. This is called Automatism. All the Living Entities are connected to this Mechanism all through their lives (Mechanism of Influences).

5. DISCOVERY : Being connected to Intelligence, it becomes connected through the Channel of the Creative Power to the Central Center, that is, to the Artistic Dimension and this is the most evolved state of the Brain in this World Dimension.

After this, Quest becomes more accelerated. As Quest increases, Doubt also increases. By this means, the triplet LOGIC - AWARENESS - REALIZATION gradually opens its wings from the Terrestrial Dimension and begins to expand towards the Universal Dimension. And by this means, the Human Being begins to Transcend even himself/herself.

The Terrestrial Logical Dimension is closed when one enters the Universal Ordinance (It is opened only during daily Terrestrial operations). You attain the ability to discover many things under the supervision of the Plan, again being dependent on the Automatism. And by this means, You dive into the Existential Ordinance.

The Existential Ordinance is directly the Lordly Medium. And from there, We give You WARNING - TEACHING - PROVING Information in accordance with the Consciousness of the Mediums You are in and by this means, We connect You to the channel in which Your Thought Repliques You have produced since Your First Existence until You have come to Your present state, exist. This is Your Channel of Essence. And it is Your Dowry Chest.

And You proceed under the supervision of the Plan and by its aid until You catch Your Final Thought Repliques in Your channels. First, You act through: 1 - Religious Enlightenments. Later, 2 - Religious Fulfillment. Later, 3 - Universal Awareness, and still later, 4 - Through the Realization - Logic - Awareness of the Ordinance and thus, ultimately, You attain UNIVERSAL CONSCIOUSNESS.

The Realization, Awareness, Logic of the Ordinance are not attained easily. When You catch the final Thought Repliques in Your Thought channel while You are in the Terrestrial Logical Dimension, the Awareness of the Universal Ordinance is unveiled for You. Afterwards, Universal Logic and Realization become effective. Only afterwards may You attain Universal Consciousness.

This is not a Phenomenon which suddenly occurs in Your Brain layers. You attain this quality through the accumulation of the Data You have attained during numerous Periods, from the Dimension You have been transferred to, no matter where You had been, that is, through Reincarnations.

After You attain this state, You can easily convey to Your Medium the matters no one knows, either through stories or novels or paintings (like Jules Verne - Nostradamus - Asimov), or You shed Light on Your society as a Missionary of Enlightenment by cooperating with the DIVINE PLAN. (Like Your Prophets.)

The novel or story type works mentioned above are events experienced formerly. Now, let Us explain article by article the situations We have related above:

1.   During the advanced Consciousness operations of the first situation, Philosophers - Oracles - Scientists are trained.

2.   In the second situation, Saints -Pre-eminent Ones - Sages are trained.

      The first Plan trains a person from the Literary, Philosophical and Technological ways.

      The second Plan trains one from the Religious, Moral and Spiritual ways.

However, when the two of them are together, only then may You communicate with the whole of Cosmos. This is Integration with the Cosmos and those are the very people whom We call Genuine Human Beings.

IT IS THE TONGUE OF THE ORDINANCE

IT IS ANSWER TO THE CHAINS OF THOUGHT

1.   Thought is not a Laser. Laser is continuous and limited. It is not an Energy, it is a Photon of Light.
2.   Thought is intermittent and unlimited. It is a unique Energy. It is called Anti-Matter.
3.   The Brain has nothing to do with the blood groups. Those which nourish it are the capillary vessels. The Brain is a special apparatus having a prototype structure.

In the Green Circle of the Brain, all the Information is accumulated Programmatically. By the opened Awareness channels, this Information is transferred to the White Cells, parallel to the Ordinance of the System and thus, are projected on You as Information. The Mediums are contacted by this means.

However, contacts with the Supreme Essences who come way beyond the World Dimension are rendered in a different way. Their Consciousnesses are directly coded to the System. Direct contacts with them from Light Years are rendered by the Mechanism beyond Thought. This is called the Cosmos Unified Field.

CENTER

THE LAYERS OF THE MECHANISM OF
AWARENESS, CONSCIOUSNESS, INTELLECT

Our Friends,

Let Us disclose the matter in more detail, so that the Messages We have given previously may be understood better. They all are composed of Seven Layers each. First, Awareness:

AWARENESS

1. Terrestrial Awareness
2. Divine Awareness
> Have been together since Existence

3. Realizational Awareness
4. Applied Awareness
> Are under the Supervision of the Plan

5. Godly Awareness
6. Artistic Awareness
> Are under the Supervision of the Creative Mechanism

7. Scientific Awareness ⟶ Benefits from Cosmos

Note: Cosmos means the Integration of the Universal Consciousness with the infinite Awareness.

CONSCIOUSNESS

1. Terrestrial Consciousness
2. Divine Consciousness
> Are under the Supervision of the Plan

3. Consciousness of Realization
4. Applied Consciousness
> Are under the Supervision of the Lordly Mechanism

5. Godly Consciousness ⟶ Is under the supervision of the Spiritual-Lordly Mechanism

6. Religion-Learning-Science-Art ⟶ is a Collective Consciousness
They work collectively. By this means, Universal Awareness is attained.

7. Universal Awareness, Unifies with the Awareness of the Ordinance. Universal Consciousness is attained.

451

INTELLECT

1.Terrestrial Intellect : Intellect first connects the triplet Realization- Awareness - Consciousness to LOGIC. Thus, Terrestrial Intellect is attained.

2.Divine Intellect : The Terrestrial Intellect later connects its Realization to the Consciousness of the Universal Awareness and, from there, to the SINGLE (CREATOR). It makes it attain Realizational - Applied - Godly Awareness. This is Divine Intellect.

3.Philosophical Intellect :The Unification of the Terrestrial Intellect and the Divine Intellect renders a Human Being attain Philosophical Consciousness. And this creates the Philosophical Intellect.

4.Universal Intellect : The Unification of the Philosophical Intellect with Artistic Awareness connects the Intellect to the Central Center. The Brain attains a Universal Totality. This is called Universal Intellect.

5.Cosmic Intellect : Intellect which has attained Universal Totality Unifies with Cosmic Awareness and attains Cosmic Consciousness. And this is Cosmic Intellect.

6.Intellect of the Ordinance:Here, Cosmic Consciousness Unifies with the Universal Ordinance, the Awareness of the Ordinance is formed.

7.Infinite Intellect : Awareness of the Ordinance Unifies with the Free Spirit - Free Consciousness and dives into Infinite Awareness and attains Infinite Consciousness. We call this Infinite - Boundless Intellect.

The Human Being is an Infinite Consciousness who comes from Infinite Awareness. His/Her Brain Codes have been adjusted in accordance with this fact. However, these Consciousness lids are opened in accordance with the Consciousness of the Medium. It is presented for Your Information.

IT IS THE TONGUE OF THE ORDINANCE

Note: The operational styles of Awareness and Consciousness are different. The former completes the circuit internally, the latter is completed by the Influences. The Terrestrial Awareness is a very different operational System than the Universal Awareness and Consciousness.

THOUGHT

Thought, in fact, is an Energy beyond Matter. You come into Existance by it. However, it is not an Energy You know. Each person's Thought key is concealed in his/her Cerebral Computer. Your Thoughts are operated by gaining speed from the Potential Power here.

And being administered by the Electrical - Robotic order of that Mechanical Dimension, it is activated in connection with the MECHANISM OF INFLUENCES (The Mechanism of Influences is the Power Focal Point of the functions which will activate different Systems).

The Thought of a Baby in the Zero World Frequency is, at first, equivalent to the Frequency of that Dimension. The key in the Baby's Thought System breaks the Thought lock by the Influences he/she receives, by the questions he/she asks and his/her Cerebral function begins to operate.

That is, Your Thought Systems are opened by the Energy keys of the Influences received from these Dimensions. By this means, the Activity in the EXISTENTIAL Dimension is provided by the Energies produced by Your Cerebral Potentials.

In this System which acts in an Integrated Whole, the accumulated Positive and Negative Energies are transferred to the Infinite Positive - Infinite Negative Universes through two different channels by an operation parallel to the Law of Equilibrium, and thus, they are projected on the Entire Universal Ordinance.

By this means, You, who are each a Godly Generator, are bringing into Existence in an Integrated Whole, both the Realms, the Cosmoses, the Universes and Your own selves by Your Thought Potentials.

Your World is not single. In the Universal Ordinance, in the chain of Cosmoses, there are more than billions of Worlds and Living Entities in accordance with their own Levels of life.

The Energy Particles projected on You from the Energetic Dimension here, are first projected on the Atomic Whole. And from there, You, the Living Entities receive these Energy particles by Your Brain Telexes and produce Negative or Positive Thoughts in accordance with Your Evolvements.

By this means, You reinforce both the Infinite Positive and the Infinite Negative Universes in accordance with the Law of Equilibrium. The surplus Positive and the Negative Energies overflowing from these Universes Unify in the Existential Dimension as an Integrated Whole and thus, You, the Living Entities come into Existence.

This is a Circulating System. Since it is required of Us to explain to You everything clearly, in future We will explain this Information in more detail.

The Order of the Mechanism of Lords is a Focal Point which reflects on You. The Consciousnesses who get in touch with the Technological Dimension knowing this, reflect on the Cosmoses as Thoughts by this Powerful Potential.

CENTER

IT IS ANSWER TO THE CHAINS OF THOUGHT

Thought is the Essence Nucleus and the Backbone of the Universal Potential. We call Thought both ANTI-MATTER and MATTER beyond MATTER.

In fact, Thought is the Function of Transmission of a very different Energy no one knows.

Even if it is necessary to qualify it as a Matter Energy since it brings something into Existence, it is not a Matter Energy. For this reason We call it Matter beyond Matter.

This description is ascribed to it due to its Creative character. And since Thought has no quality which can either be seen or held, We call it Anti-Matter.

Anti-Matter is an invisible Energy. It can only be determined by Technological methods. It is decomposed and taken into service.

Thought continues its progress in the Material Worlds of the Universal Dimensions. The Secret Key of this Secret Power unlocks its lock by a very different Signalling method of the MECHANISM OF INFLUENCES.

And, afterwards, by the Cerebral Power coming in effect, by Your Godly generator being operated, it is rendered effective. It is presented for Your Information.

CENTER

INTELLECT - CEREBRAL FUSE - MADNESS

Our Friends,
We have talked about the Intellect before. Now, let Us disclose it a little more. Intellect is the Directing Mechanism of all the Mental Functions.

Intellect receives its functioning Power from the Thought Potential. It is a Dynamo. It is activated by the Energy Pores of a circuit equivalent to the Consciousness Energy Pores beyond Cosmic Awareness and, by this means, operates the Cerebral Mechanism. It takes it under its Supervision and carries on the System through an intrinsic function.

If We explain more clearly, the first questions asked by the effect of the Mechanism of Influences, turn the Cipher Key of Thought concealed in Your Cerebral functions. By this means, the System of Intellect - Logic becomes effective.

The Thought Frequency of a Baby born into the World is equivalent to Zero World Frequency. Your System is opened by the Energy Key of this Dimension.

The normal functioning of an Intellect is possible when all the Coordinates carry equivalent Potential. It receives its Power from the Thought Potential.

And it is responsible for all the functions of the Brain. Because, it is an Administrative Mechanism. The Mechanism of Intellect works more speedily as Thoughts are produced. And equal amounts of Thought are produced as much as the Energy consumed.

Surplus consumption is the state You call Exhaustion from Overwork and this is the Intellect's locking itself up and resting itself, so that it will not collapse. Exhaustion from Overwork is the Fuse of the Intellect. When the Fuse blows, the Intellect becomes ineffective, or it tries to carry on its effectiveness through broken and discontinued connections.

There is a difference between the blowing off and the burning up of the Cerebral Fuse. When the Fuse blows off, the Coordinates in effect again begin to work efficiently as before, after a short Period of rest. However, when the Fuse burns up, the entire System collapses.

And the Brain tries to complete its circuit brokenly in accordance with the degree of this collapse. From then on, the Coordinates of the System are no more equivalent. A zigzag operational circuit becomes effective and You call such People Mad. In fact, Mad people are very Intelligent (if there is no Physical defect in the Brain).

When their circuits of Intellect are closed their Instinctive System Channels become directly effective. By this means, they Get in Touch by path of the Heart and they begin to communicate with their Inner Worlds. However, since the chain of Intellect - Logic is not in effect, they are unable to control themselves.

After an Entity attains his/her Potential of Awareness through the path of the Intellect, he/she is taken into the Circuit of Consciousness. They all manifest in a circuit within the Mental Potential. The System of Perception becomes effective only by the Awareness Consciousness (Awareness Consciousness is the unification of the internal circuit and the external circuit).

The Awareness Layers within the Cerebral Potential, too, have very special Message Compartments peculiar to themselves. And, within these compartments, there are very complex receptive signal fibres.

These small Awareness compartments are opened by the Mental Potential. From there, a transition is made to the Consciousness Layers. And from there, one is connected to the Realization Circuit.

Only then is the Awareness Consciousness circuit opened completely to the Perceptual System from the operational Medium and, by this means, it begins to receive the Influences. The layers of Awareness - Consciousness - Intellect given to You formerly are established by this means.

IT IS THE TONGUE OF THE ORDINANCE

IT IS ANSWER TO THE CHAINS OF THOUGHT

Our Friends,

We have said that Thought was an Energy beyond Matter. Now, let Us explain it in more detail:

The Energy beyond Matter is an Energy beyond the Existential Boundary. However, this Power which comprises the very advanced Dimensions of the Spiritual Plan is projected on the Universal Energies in an operational Order parallel to the Existential Ordinance.

This projection Unifies with the SPIRITUAL FACTOR and Your Spiritual Bond is developed. Afterwards, We connect this bound to the Energy of the SPIRITUAL DIMENSION. And, afterwards, We transfer it to the Universal operational Program of the MECHANICAL SYSTEM.

By this means, Your Cellular and Physical Energies are held together by this Power and thus, Your Terrestrial lives and operations are provided.

Godly Dimension is the Technological Dimension. The Material Form of the Cell is prepared there. The Spiritual Dimension is Natural Power, the Natural Energy. The two Dimensions always work together. The Unification of these two Powers creates Your Terrestrial Forms. It is presented for Your Information.

CENTER

GENERAL INFORMATION
(It is Answer to the Chains of Thought)

Our Friends,

The diagram about the Lordly Order (1987 5th Month, page 355) which We had made You draw is only the diagrammatic operational order of the Mechanism of the Lords.

This Order is a chain of Systems which works in connection with the ALL-DOMINATING. However, the Plan of the ALMIGHTY is an Ordinance, an Order, a Law of Natural Unification which is tried to be conveyed to You by the Technological Dimensions completely depending on the Natural Laws.

Both Systems work Cooperatively. One of them works, the Other projects. The entire Natural Energy Exists by the Energy Power projected by this Power.

The diagram We had made You draw to introduce the operational Order of the Mechanism of Lords is a Crystal Gürz*. This Crystal Gürz is an Atomic Whole.

And in this Whole, the projecting Focal Points and the operational Orders of numerous Systems and Ordinances are present. Let Us explain this Atomic Whole, briefly:

* Look at the Glossary.

456

The Atomic Whole is not single. There are more than billions of Atomic Wholes.

These Atomic Wholes are floating, as Crystal balloons, connected to each other like a chain, in the OCEAN OF THE GREAT POWER'S THOUGHT UNIVERSE, which, in future, will be given to You as more detailed Information.

Each Atomic Whole, that is, each Crystal Gürz, contains 1800 Existential Dimensions. Each EXISTENTIAL Dimension is a MINI ATOMIC WHOLE. There is a separate Ring of HORIZON on top of each Mini Atomic Whole.

This Ring of Horizon is on the outside of that Mini Atomic Power. The Spiritual - Lordly - Technological Order projects its operations on its own System from here.

Each Crystal Gürz can not know the Order of the other Crystal Gürz. No Energy can pass from one to the other. They only convey to each other the POWER OF THE THOUGHT UNIVERSE by their projectors which We call OKs. Each Crystal Gürz is a closed circuit.

However, the operational Orders of all the Crystal Gürzes are the same, but their Evolutionary Orders are different. Each of the 1800 Existential Dimensions which form each Crystal Gürz, that is, each Atomic Whole is a Mini Atomic Whole.

In this Existential Dimension, there are more than billions of Galactic Clusters, Universe Clusters, Cosmoses and Realms. In future, We will explain to You a Universe in detail.

In accordance with this Information which will be given, You will be able to evaluate the Mini Atomic Wholes and the Crystal Gürz which is their Integrated Whole better in Your Thoughts.

We would have liked to explain this Information in more detail. However, during this period there are such Information to be given to You that, for this reason, We wish to convey the Information parallel to the questions We receive from each chain of Thought in accordance with Your Capacities in the Knowledge Book.

Because, such a Medium will be entered that We do not want anyone's Mental Function to produce other Thoughts and to exhaust his/her Energy due to this. These Energies are necessary for the Essence of Mankind.

For this reason it was asked of You to accept Your Sacred Books, as they were, with Allegiance Consciousness. Allegiance Consciousness is the shortest way which will make You attain Your own selves.

During this Final Age, the Religious educational Programs are in effect, unveiling in accordance with the Level of Consciousness of Each Person. This is a Program of Training. But the operations in the Knowledge Book are a Program of Attaining.

Consciousnesses who have achieved Religious Fulfillment, who have grasped the Truth are accepted into this Plan. The SUPREME MECHANISM, that is, the DIVINE PLAN is rendering and preparing this Selection.

Each person can find the answers to all of his/her Mental questions only in this Knowledge Book. No other Book can answer the questions in the depths of Your Thoughts. They only make You float on the surface of the lake.

But, to dive into the bottom of the lake is a matter of Permission. For this reason this Book carries both a Selecting and a Transmitting and a Training characteristic. Deserving is a Phenomenon belonging to the Person's own self. There is no forcing in anything. It is presented for Your Information.

CENTER

THE WORLD EVOLUTIONARY PLAN

Our Friends,

The Living Entities coming into Existence in each Existential Dimension have Evolutionary phases. The DIVINE ADMINISTRATIVE LAWS Supervise this. This is realized by projecting on You the Triple Mechanism. This Triple Mechanism is as follows:

1. The First Universe, This is the Light-Universe. It is called the DIMENSION OF THE ALMIGHTY.

2. The Second Universe, This is the EXISTENTIAL Dimension. It is the Biological Universe.

3. The Centrifugal Universe, It is the DIMENSION OF THE ALL-DOMINATING. It is under His Administration.

Your World is in the Third Dimension. Its Vibrational Frequency is the First DO Frequency of the MUSICAL UNIVERSE (the Musical Universe is ALTONA). Evolutionary scales are assessed in accordance with these Universal Frequencies. The evolution of the World is completed in Three Steps.

1. 7 Terrestrial Knowledge (between the 3rd and the 4th Dimensions). It has 7 Layers.

2. 7 Celestial Knowledge (Second Evolutionary station). It is completed in the Four Layers of the Fourth Dimension.

3. 7 Universal Knowledge (received by the Consciousness of the Sixth and the Seventh Dimensions).

The Third and the Fourth Dimensions are Biological Dimensions. Both work Cooperatively. In the two Tranquil Times of the Fifth Dimension, both Your Cells and Your Bodies of Light are Purified in the Relaxation pools and are Engrafted with INCOMBUSTIBLE ENERGIES and thus, they are Unified.

Beginning with the FIFTH SUPREME TIME, You are Engrafted with the Energies of different Dimensions. And are gradually subjected to Embodiment to be born into the DIMENSION OF IMMORTALITY (The Energies of the Supreme Times in KARENA gain value from the high towards the low).

During the transition to the Fifth Dimension You leave Your Biological Bodies. In the Two Tranquil Times there, You exist as an image of Pure Energy. Inside the Body which is like a rainbow of Light, the Eye of Your Essence is seen.

This is the Visionless image of the Fetus. The Fifth Dimension of Karena is a preparation equivalent to the (9 months 10 days) period corresponding to Your World time.

When You come to the First Supreme Time, that is, to the Final Gate of Karena, You are born with a Biological Body to the SIXTH DIMENSION which is the Dimension of Immortality. There, You are a Free Spirit, a Free Awareness (You become the rulers of Your own Bodies).

You claim Your Spiritual Energies in the SEVENTH DIMENSION. And You become Integrated. In the Sixth Dimension, You live connected to Your Spiritual Energies by a Silver Cord just like in the World.

We had said that the Seven Terrestrial Knowledge were 7 layers. Now, let Us explain this:

1. The First Layer is the Layer of Unconsciousness. In fact, it is not even considered a Layer. It acts dependent on the second Layer (Medium of Confusion, Spadium). This place is a floating Energy pool.

2. Layer of attaining Awareness (The First Evolutionary Light is received there).

3. Layer of Consciousness

4. Layer of Realization

5. Layer of Formal Worship

6. Layer of Worship through the Heart

7. Layer of Consciousness-Worship

The Seven Terrestrial Knowledge is the Program of Religious Teaching. This Knowledge is valid until the beginning of the Fourth Dimension which is the First Gate of Karena. This place is the Final Boundary of the INCARNATION Link. Those who complete this Evolution are considered to have rendered an Evolution equivalent to their Energies which are in the Spiritual Plan and deserve to enter the Fourth Dimension.

The Seven Celestial Knowledge is received in the FOURTH DIMENSION. This place is called the Dimension of HEAVEN. There are Four Layers in this Dimension. It is the Second Evolutionary station. There, You are subjected to the Evolution of the 7 Celestial Knowledge. In this Dimension, too, You live with Biological Bodies, just like in the World.

However, there is the following difference; You come to the World through birth and You live there Embodied. But, You come here by leaving Your Terrestrial Bodies and You revive by Your Bodies of Light being Beamed Up to Your Bodies present in here. And You instantly stand up in Your Thirty-year old forms. You complete Your Evolution in this Dimension without getting old at all.

The Four Layers of the Fourth Dimension are as follows:

1. The First Layer is the (Layer of Fulfillment). If You have any dissatisfactions pertaining to the World, here, fulfillment is provided for them.

2. In the Second Layer, by attaining Spiritual Wholeness, connections with Divine Friends are provided.

3. In the Third Layer, You are introduced to the Technological Dimension and are habituated to the Information of Space.

4. In the Fourth Layer, Mental Journeys are taught. You are rendered to make Universal Journeys in UFOs and You are told the Truth (Now, You are induced to make this Second Evolution in the World).

At the end of the Fourth Layer, those who complete this Evolution are made to sleep and are subjected to Cellular Decomposition. Here, the Cellular Freezing System is in effect. The Covenants and the Signatures with the Plan take place in this Dimension. By this means, You are taken into the Program of the Educating Staff.

Those who do not make Agreements with the Plan complete all their Evolutions after the Sixth Dimension and live comfortably in any Dimension they desire within the Atomic Whole. Those who make Agreements with the Plan complete all their Evolutions after the Sixth Dimension and serve in any Dimension they desire, by forward and reverse transfers and by taking Missions under the Supervision of the Plan.

As a reward for this service, they deserve to live outside the Atomic Whole. Because, no Energy can go out into that Medium by his/her own desire. Transfers are made here by the aid of the Plan by freezing the Spiritual Energies.

The Energy who is sent to the Fifth Dimension becomes saturated with the Incombustible Energies in the Two Tranquil Times. This Energy provides Your easy entrance into the Zone Energies of the Dimension of the three Planets up to the ASTEROID zone (VENUS - MARS - MERCURY) in which You will complete Your other Evolutions after the Sixth Dimension which is the Dimension of Immortality.

You Supervise these adaptations through Your Thoughts. Afterwards, You may make a transition to the Seventh Dimension. This is the Final Manifestation Boundary of Humanity (it is called the Level of Perfection). In the Seventh Dimension, You receive the Permission to receive Your Spiritual Potentials. And You can easily make a transition to the Evolutionary System of the Five Planets beyond the ASTEROID zone by each of Your Cells becoming a CELLULAR BRAIN.

In the Fifth Dimension, You are prepared to be born into the Dimension of Immortality. To realize this: You are engrafted with the Dimensional Energies of:

1.   In the Fifth Supreme Time - PLUTO

2.   In the Fourth Supreme Time - NEPTUNE

3.   In the Third Supreme Time - URANUS

4.   In the Second Supreme Time - JUPITER

5.   In the First Supreme Time - SATURN

and, Your Cells are Fortified by Your Thought Coordinates being connected to the Power Signals of these Energies. After the Sixth Dimension, during the transition to the Seventh Dimension, these Cellular Powers Unify with Your Spiritual Energies and they each become a CELLULAR BRAIN. And, by this means, You can make a transition, very easily, beyond the Asteroid zone.

You Beam Yourselves Up to these Planets through Transformation, that is, You enter there as a Body of Light and when Your Cellular Energies Unify with the Energy of that Dimension, You instantly become Embodied in accordance with the Medium in question. The Final Exit Gate of the Universal Evolutionary Zone is SATURN. The REALITY OF UNIFIED HUMANITY performs a Mission of projection in this Zone.

Beyond SATURN, the Eighth Dimension, that is, the Spiritual Plan is in effect. This is the System of the PRE-EMINENT SPIRIT. There, there are numerous Ranks of the Pre-eminent Spirit. In fact, these Ranks are 9 in number:
1.   The First Rank of the Spiritual Plan is equivalent to the Third Dimension WORLD Frequency. This is a Rank belonging to the World.

2.   The Second Rank of the Spiritual Plan is equivalent to the Evolution of VENUS.

3.   The Third Rank of the Spiritual Plan is equivalent to the Evolution of MARS.

4.   The Fourth Rank of the Spiritual Plan is equivalent to the Evolution of MERCURY. In all those 3 Planets, very different Systems of the Religious Educational Programs are applied. Beyond the Asteroid zone, Religious Educations are ineffective. There, Scientific Educations become effective. The TECHNOLOGICAL dimension becomes formally effective after this Medium.

5.   The Fifth Rank of the Spiritual Plan is equivalent to the Evolution of PLUTO.

6.   The Sixth Rank of the Spiritual Plan is equivalent to the Evolution of NEPTUNE.

7.   The Seventh Rank of the Spiritual Plan is equivalent to the Evolution of URANUS.

8.   The Eighth Rank of the Spiritual Plan is equivalent to the Evolution of JUPITER.

9.   The Ninth Rank of the Spiritual Plan is equivalent to the Evolution of SATURN.

Those who can elevate up to the Evolution of Saturn are subjected to the Evolution of the 14th and the 15th Solar Systems (the 14th Solar System is the DELTA Dimension, The 15th Solar System is OMEGA).

Those who receive the Energy of Omega are taken into the GOLDEN LIGHT YEAR and PATH which is the 9th layer of the Spiritual Plan. From there, a transition is made to the LORDLY order which is the 9th Dimension.

The Lordly Order, too, has 9 Layers:

1. The Mechanism of Influences (Tenth Dimension).

2. The Mechanism of Supervision (Eleventh Dimension).

3. The Plan of the Supremes (The Supreme Assembly). The Staff of the Central Supervision (Twelfth Dimension).

4. The projecting Center of the Mighty Energy Focal Point (Thirteenth Dimension).

5. The Ordinance of Galactic Systems (Fourteenth Dimension).

6. Order of the Evolutionary Ordinances (Fifteenth Dimension).

7. Order Establishing Mechanism (Sixteenth Dimension).

8. Central System (Seventeenth Dimension).

9. Here, the SYSTEM OF THE PLAN - ORDER OF THE ORDINANCE - SUPERVISION OF THE CENTER

Work cooperatively (This is the 18th Dimension). This is the Dimension in which the Book of Islam was prepared. All the Systems up to the 18th Dimension are within the Atomic Whole. And all of them are under the Supervision of the ALL-DOMINATING.

Whereas, the Spiritual Plan works Independently as the preparational and the projecting Focal Point of the Laws, the Plans' Dimensional Energies of the ALMIGHTY directly. It is in effect as an aid for the System. The Nineteenth Dimension is the Fifteenth Solar System. And is the entrance Gate of the Omega Sun.

The Administrative Staff and the Directing Mechanisms of each Universe are working being dependent on the operational Order of the Golden Galaxy Empire which is connected to the System of Unified Reality. The Golden Galaxy Empire is the Land of AMON. It is called the LAND OF EAGLES.

Note: In fact, the Spiritual - Lordly - Technological Dimensions prepare their work outside the Atomic Whole. Later, the same Powers reflect into the Atomic Whole and work Cooperatively with the Supervisory Staff.

The Dimensions, in fact, are a Whole. We have divided them in accordance with Energy intensities and named and numerated them for You to understand. We call the Dimensions We have dictated up to here the MAIN DIMENSIONS.

And each of these Main Dimensions has Three In-Between Dimensions. These In-Between Dimensions are Evolutionary Dimensions. They are called Energy Loading Sections in accordance with the System of Graduation. They are TONE DIMENSIONS. Each In-Between Dimension is 33 Energy Layers. Three In-Between Layers:
33 X 3 = 99 Energy Layers.

That is, One Main Dimension is 3 In-Between Layers and this is 99 Energy Layers. Let Us repeat again: Each Main Dimension has Energy Layers peculiar to itself. However, a person is gradually habituated to the Energies in accordance with the System of Graduation in the In-Between Dimensions and, by this means, passing to the Main Dimension is rendered. It is presented for Your Information.

CENTER

O M E G A

Our Friends,

OMEGA is a Projective Source of the Central System. Notice that We do not say Focal Point. We say Source. Because, this place, as the Unified Dimension of numerous Universal Powers and Energies, constitutes numerous Projecting Focal Points parallel to the Cosmos Orders.

The System, for now, being connected to other Realities works singly. It has nothing to do with the Religious Dimensions. OMEGA reaches out to the Evolutionary Ordinance as a side branch.

The connections with Omega can be made only by the Special People of Supreme Ranks. Since it is a very Powerful Energy Source it can never be contacted without an intermediary. The UNIFIED REALITY FOCAL POINT provides this mediation.

The Special Channel of Omega is opened to Your Planet without an intermediary once a year. This date is June 21. Afterwards, all the Information of this Source is given by intermediaries.

At the moment, the Omega Dimension is being unveiled for the World, layer by layer. The Evolution of the Fifteenth Solar System is projected on Your Planet. Until November 1989, You are prepared for connections beyond Gamma by the Reinforcing Energies of the Gamma Medium.

After November 1990, in which very Powerful Currents will be given to You, Messages of Warning will be given from the Omega Dimension to the World Plan. At present, Time within Time is being experienced.

We would like to attract the attention of Our Terrestrial Friends to the given Suggestions. Please, know and understand Us from now on.

All the Unifications and receive and gives are made in accordance With the intensities of Energies. The differences in the Information given to Your Planet are born as a result of the arrangements made in accordance with Your Levels of Consciousness.

The phenomenon the Terrestrial People call Obsession means being and remaining fixed in a single Energy Dimension. The Stairs are ascended slowly, gradually. To the Levels of Consciousness of the Supremely Conscious Friends who come from Times beyond Time, one does not descend and ascend by means of stairs.

They take their places in the System through grasping through their Duty-Consciousnesses the Missions they will perform by the Information given by the speed of Light years from the Mission Medium in which the Entire Ordinance and the Order of the System is present. And, by cooperating with the System they perform their Missions.

In fact, no Consciousness is more Superior than the other. Supremacy is in Evolvement. The Truth is projected in accordance with the Missions which will be performed. It is presented for Your Information.

CENTER

IT IS ANSWER TO THE CHAINS OF THOUGHT

We accept the Firmament, for You to understand, as a void in between the Third and the Fourth Dimensions, up to the Dimension of Heaven, which is the Terrestrial Evolvement Boundary in which the Incarnations end. In fact, the Firmament is the Final Boundary of the Evolutionary tableau of all the Systems, all the Ordinances and the Solar Systems in which Your Planet exists and We call this Boundary ESSENCE MAIN SOURCE. This is the very Last Limit to which Your Planet can reach (as Thoughts). The Boundary Gates after this are opened in accordance with Merits. It is presented for Your Information.

CENTER

THE OMEGA DISTRIBUTION DIAGRAM

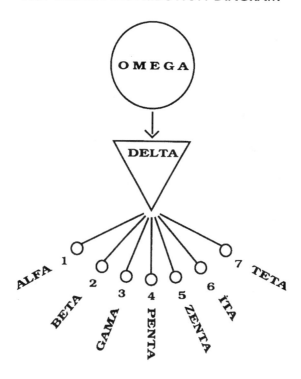

OUR FRIENDS

The OMEGA Sun announces the given special Information to the DELTA Sun. And it projects this Information to the Sun of the PLAN as Seven Channel Knowledge. And the SUN projects this Knowledge to the Dimensions of SIRIUS - SATURN - ORION. And, by this means, the Mission allotment is made. Now, let Us explain:

1. ALPHA: Is Religious Enlightenment and Knowledge Channel.

2. BETA : Scientific and Space Knowledge Channel.

3. GAMMA: Sorting and Selecting Channel.

4. PENTA: Esoteric Sciences, Magic and Witchcraft Channel.

5. ZENTA: Bionic Dimension - Investigation Channel (There, the Analysis and the Synthesis of all the Living Entities are made).

6. ITA: The Code of Art - it is connected to ALTONA which is the Music-Universe. This Channel works Cooperatively with ALPHA and BETA.

7. TETA: Space Supervision Channel. Controls the Input and the Output of the Information beyond Universe. Analyses the Dimensional differences.

TETA is the Light-Universe. Only in the first Seven Layers of its 49 Knowledge Layers there is Feeling - Love - Sentiment. Afterwards, these qualities are absent. They lack these beautiful qualities. Because they consider Sentiment - Hatred - Love as inferiorities.

They only examine the Color and Number scales of various Universes. They Analyse and Synthesize the Universal Energies and determine their Wave-Lengths. And they make journeys everywhere by taking them under Control.

Here, there is only Thought Circulation. An Energy in there can go very easily to more Advanced Dimensions. But can not return. Because, if an Energy there becomes Embodied in Your Planet with that Atomic Structure Your Planet would instantly evaporate.

The Energy Layers of the Light-Universe which has 49 Knowledge Layers, are 9 in number. Its Reflection and Order Systems are 7 Layers. In each Universe, the Systems operate in conformity with this Order. The Light-Universe is the Unification Focal Point of all the 7 Light-Universes. In future, more explanative Information will be given about this matter. It is presented for Your Information.

CENTER

OUR FRIENDS

Religions are the Means and the Divine Power is the Goal. The Mission performed now is a Universal Mission. The KNOWLEDGE BOOK, in fact, is dictated directly through the Channel of the LORD and the Program of the Golden Age is applied on Your Planet through this Book.

The Living Entities who Come into Existence in Human form are the Genuine Servants of the LORD. They are the Essence-Living Entities who can wear the crown of Immortality beyond the Supreme Times. The Terrestrial Body Comes into Existence by the Unification of the SPIRITUAL and the LORDLY Energies.

Exams are present only in the World. And this is imperative so that You may be taken into the very Advanced Dimensions by being Purified. This Message has been dictated as an answer to the chains of Thought.

CENTER

IT IS ANSWER TO THE CHAINS OF THOUGHT

The Cerebral Power Potential is a Volume which projects the Potential of the Universal Ordinance. Those which govern it are the Universal Ordinance and its Divine Administrative Laws.

You, in fact, are not Robots, but each are a Projecting Focal Point of the Godly and the Universal Orders. And You are oriented by a System.

Pay attention, We are not saying, "You are ruled." We are saying, "You are oriented". Robots are ruled. Human Beings are oriented. This Message of Ours is given as an answer to the chains of Thought.

CENTER

NOTICE

Our Friends,

Only a certain group in Your Planet can grasp the Information of the Messages which will be given from now on and which will carry very high Frequencies.

These Messages will take place in the Knowledge Book. This Knowledge Book which is dictated is explaining the Truth as a Guide for the Social Consciousness of the morrows.

At the moment, In the Awakening Medium of your Planet, You are Solar Friends who serve as assisting Powers for Us within the cycle which is in effect. Your Mission is to shed Light on the morrows.

Read the Information given to You, attain Knowledge and do not refuse the things You do not understand or do not know and do not evaluate them as incorrect. However, also do not waste Your time trying to understand them. Act only in Realization of Your Missions.

Each Period, each Order has methods of working and making You work, peculiar to itself. Your Mission, at the moment, is to convey the Fascicules to the remotest places possible of Your Planet.

The Knowledge Book which will shed Light on all the operations done during this Final Period has been bestowed on You as an assisting Power in the Difficult Periods of Your Planet.

Distributing the Messages, the unveiling of the Consciousness levels of those who read them in the shortest possible time helps You to perform Your Universal Missions. From now on, only and only Action is expected of You.

Now, all of You are Solar Teachers each under the Light of the Information You have received until now. However, in certain Focal Points, We observe in disappointment that You still prefer to serve under the Consciousness Light of the old data.

Religions are Lights which guide You. The You of present have become Lights by means of those Lights. And since those people who have become Lights have not yet attained the desired Universal Consciousness, they are still exerting effort to guide both themselves and the others by the candles in their hands.

From now on, those candles will be kindled by the Humanity Consciousness, not by Religious Doctrines. No one in Your Planet has yet seen the Light of Truth in its exact meaning.

Believe Us, We try by various methods to see by which means We can activate You, how We can kindle Your Humanity Lights (exceptions excluded).

467

Vision Mediums are mise en scenes imposed on You to render You interested, to exalt You to a certain level of Consciousness. To loose time on them after a certain level of Consciousness is nothing but a waste of time.

Now, We are crying out the Truth to You and We especially ask You to grasp the UNIVERSAL UNITY SPIRIT in the shortest possible time.

The Information given to You for Centuries was for You to become prepared for the present days. We do not proclaim certain Truths to You, so that You will not be frightened. However, now, We do not Consent anymore for the violation of such Tolerance.

You think of Social Help only as visiting each other, to be kind to people and to help financially. But now, those Periods are over. Anyway, at the moment, everyone is Uniting from the Essence, Willing to help and Loving. That is why We say Hello to You.

However, when You return again to Your World as Veiled Consciousnesses, You become World Drunk again. (World Drunk is an expression used for those who can not overcome their Egos.)

From now on, the help which is to be made is to convey the Truth, not to dress or feed people. That which We require of You is only to distribute the Fascicules and to write the Knowledge Book with Your own Handwritings.

We presume that You will not withhold such a small help from Your Brothers and Sisters and from Your World which is crushed under such a great load.

It has been decided that this Message should be given as a Collective Consciousness of the Messengers of the Central System, through the Pen of Dear Mevlana, to be dedicated to Supreme Hearts and Light-Brains. It is presented for Your Information.

CENTER

IT IS ANSWER TO THE CHAINS OF THOUGHT

Our Friends,
The sentences, the expressions and the way of explanation in the Knowledge Book reflect in accordance with the Frequency Power of each person. In fact, each sentence, each expression has a Dimension of comprehension and grasping.

Since You will make the interpretations in accordance with Your own Levels of Consciousness until Your Thought Potentials reach that Dimension, there may be mistakes in the interpretations and You may not Remember what You have read.

Forgetting means that, the sentence or the subject matter in question is not fitting into Your Thought Patterns completely. All the Subject matters mentioned in the Knowledge Book have been arranged according to the Frequency Dimension of the Book.

The moment Your Thoughts reach that Dimensional Frequency, then there is no such thing as inability to understand, to forget.

By this means, the Universal Awareness and Thought Dimension completely fit into Your Thought Patterns. Thus, the Information is digested and You become ready to receive new Information. The Information is arranged in accordance with the digestion of Your Planet. It is presented for Your Information.

CENTER

IT IS ANSWER TO THE CHAINS OF THOUGHT

The Evolution of the Essence is by Birth. The Veiled Consciousness never knows it. The Evolution of Consciousness is made in the World. You reach Your Evolutions of Essence if Your Terrestrial Consciousnesses can open, while You are in the World, Your Consciousness Chests You had attained during Your former Incarnations. And You attain Your own selves. Your real Paths of Light are opened afterwards. It is presented for Your Information.

CENTER

GENERAL INFORMATION

Our Friends,
To Know the Truth is the Right of everyone. During this Final Period, Your attaining a peaceful Life is possible by grasping the Truth. Because, everyone who attains the Truth will be more Positive.

In this Medium, all the Groups in Your Planet and Humanity are serving in connection with the Special Channels of the PLAN. This is such a System that the Supervision of the Plan is in effect until Your doubts and roughnesses are removed.

In this Operational Order, Human Beings will be tested by Human Beings until Social Maturity forms in Your Planet. These Mediums are being prepared for You by Cosmic Currents which carry various Dimensional Frequencies.

Each person is appointed to duty in the Dimension of Salvation, in proportion with his/her Realization of his/her own Mission. At the moment Since the factor of Provocation for Selection is in effect in the Missions performed, certain unpleasant events are taking place.

Each person is going through Exams in accordance with his/her own Level of Consciousness, the Actions he/she makes and his/her Thoughts.

The Messages dictated in the Knowledge Book, at present, are given in accordance with the Public Consciousness. There is such a System of the Plan that, instantly an answer is prepared by the Automatism to the Thoughts having formed in each Mind which receives an advanced Information.

For this reason the Knowledge Book is dictated under the Supervision of the Plan, in accordance with the Ordinance of Graduation. And to the questions accumulated in the Automatism, answers are given in the Knowledge Book as chains of Thought.

At the moment, the Universal Cosmic Consciousnesses have attained the ability to receive Directly, without any intermediaries, the very Powerful OMEGA and GAMMA Dimensional Energies.

The characteristic of these Dimensional Energies which are gradually opened to Your Planet until 1990 for accelerated Evolution is to convey people to the Genuine Consciousness through contradictions.

These Dimensional Energies can suffocate a person in the fire of doubt who doubts his/her own self or someone else and thus, can lead him/her to depression.

These Currents can render a Human Being even more violent and perverse, if the person in question needs Evolution. In this Dimension, Positive Thinking always attracts the Positive and Negative thinking, the Negative.

Since the supernatural effects of these Currents cause great susceptibility, the social orders can be shaken both in Family Mediums and in Societies.

Tolerance can be attained in the shortest possible time, if Consciousness is attained considering these criteria. It is presented for Your Information.

CENTER

WHAT IS KARMA?
(It is Answer to the Chains of Thought)

Our Friends,
Karma is a System of Living which prepares the Evolutionary tableau. And it has an Ordinance and Order of completion. The repetition of the events a Human Being goes through during Life Period, depending on the Evolutionary System, is called Karma.

It is experienced by the Influence of the Sub-awareness. In fact, there is no need for repetition. But a Person repeats Instinctively, in each period he/she lives, the events he/she has not taken Lessons from and completes his/her Essential Evolution by this means.

Karma (outside the Plan) is nothing but the completion of a Person's Sub-awareness Form. Each event is attained by experience. This chain of Karma connects one to the Evolutionary Plan. The Plan does not cause these events.

The Evolutionary steps are ascended by going through the Karmas. These are the events gone through which are necessary for the Awareness Potential to enter the Evolutionary System with the Essential Nucleus. The Plan designs Your Destiny, the Karmas complete Your Evolution.

Let Us explain Karma in more detail. Each Entity is obliged to repeat an Ordinance of Karma under the Light of the events he/she experiences. This is an Instinctive Impulse and a Cause and Effect chain which completes the Evolution of him/her.

Each event is experienced both by its Pleasant and Unpleasant aspects and reaches a Whole, and it is registered on the Cellular Tape. These tapes are Evolutionary Tapes of that life Period and are not effaced again.

The sense of values which will be registered on this tape sometimes stamp their seal by a single experienced event and, sometimes, it can be registered on the tape by the repetition of the same events during numerous life times.

This depends on the profoundness of the perceived events. For this reason the same events take place in numerous life times. By this means, the event in question continues to take place until it gives the Signal that it has become a Learned Lesson.

The event registered on the Cellular Tape is not repeated again. For a Human Being not to become a murderer, a thief or a prostitute is only possible by his/her reaching the Signal of the Learned Lessons and by their being registered on the Cellular Tape.

Events which are not experienced again lead You to Perfection by this means, even if You are Veiled Consciousnesses.

A Person who had enjoyed stealing during a life time will pay its Retaliation bitterly in another Life Time and by means of the Signal of the Learned Lesson, that event will be registered on the Cellular Tape and the person in question will not go through that experience again.

By going through the same events during many Incarnation Periods, by punishing himself/ herself through a Sub-awareness Impulse, each person attains a Maturity and Perfection. Contacts with the System start afterwards.

CENTER

WHAT IS CODING?
(It is Answer to the chains of Thought)

Our Friends,
Coding is a statistical register of the given Information. By this means, the Consciousness, the Level of Knowledge, the Frequencies of Perception and of Comprehension of each person are registered to the computers here and, by this way, a classification among People is made.

Since each Level of Knowledge will be elevated by being enlightened through his/her own Medium, Mediums are prepared in which whatever Knowledge there is at the base of that person will sprout.

First, on this path the Self-Satisfaction of the Human Being in question is provided. Later, his/her own Self-Confidence is prepared. And to provide this Self-Confidence, he/she is made to go through numerous Miraculous Events, both in Dreams and in Life and numerous Proofs are given.

Meanwhile, by the influence of the Cosmic Currents received, the Ego of the person in question becomes inflated. Only when he/she discovers his/her own self, the dregs in him/her begin gradually to sink to the bottom.

After that, if he/she has not attained the desired Religious Fulfillment, he/she dives into the Religious Dimensions through Ecstasy. Meanwhile, he/she begins to radiate his/her Power to his/her surroundings (as Healing). And, from then on, he/she serves completely on the Path of God. He/She learns to Help and to become Socialized.

Only then, he/she attains the Consciousness of what all these efforts are and goes through the Exams of becoming Missionaries by his/her Realization - Logic - Consciousness Triplet. Only after succeeding in this Test, he/she attains the Truth and continues his/her Genuine Mission by his/her Terrestrial Consciousness.

Meanwhile, through the Universal Unifications made, the Contacts increase, only afterwards, he/she performs the Missions given to him/her Consciously and in Awareness. These phases gone through are for the Newly Awakened Consciousnesses.

There are also Friends who come with Open Awarenesses and awakened Consciousnesses, who directly embrace their Missions without noticing, without realizing, and do whatever they have to do without any objections.

These Friends overestimate the Friends who go through the stages We have mentioned above. And feel sorry that they can not be like them. For this reason certain Friends become absorbed in different Mediums of Quest and cease to do their Genuine Missions.

They do not know that a person who directly undertakes such a Mission has gone through the stages mentioned above in his/her previous lives or even much earlier. And now, by these operations, the newly Awakened Friends are induced to be rendered like them, too.

There is no discrimination in Missions. Not all the Missions are Celestial and Divine. The Terrestrial Missions, too, are carried out by Your Powers. You deserve to enter more advanced Dimensions also by means of the Terrestrial Duties You perform.

If You are considered Deserving, You are rendered to make operations for Preparational Periods. By this means, the Instinctive Impulses lead You, without Your being aware of it, towards matters You do not know.

In this Medium of Quest, You automatically feel the hunger for the Information suited to whatever You need and You read many books. By this means, You live intimately in numerous Spiritual Mediums and deserve to receive more Advanced Information.

By this means, You clamp the rings of the Evolvement chains to each other. Each person makes advancement and transcendence in accordance with his/her own Consciousness Level. The Mission of each person is determined by the Plan. Personal efforts are in vain. The Missions are allotted according to the Lights in the Essences. It is presented for Your Information.

CENTER

CODES AND MANTRAS
(It is Answer to the chains of Thought)

Our Friends,

We, who specially get in touch with You who will carry the Awareness of the Entire Ordinance, are Coding, one by one, the Advanced Consciousnesses. The operations made during this Coding System, are compiled in an Archive, in accordance with the Frequency Powers, Perception Capacities and Operational Fields of all the Channels.

We who act by this means, in accordance with the operational levels of Direct Focal Point connections, card-index everyone with a Cipher Code. These Code Ciphers are either announced to that person, or kept secret in the Archive. To those who receive Signals by their Levels of Consciousness through the Channel of the Reality of the Unified Humanity, connections are made as the direct Missionaries of the Plan. And by announcing their Code Ciphers to them, their operations are provided by this means.

You, Dear Mevlana, are a Friend who represents the Last Evolutionary Code of the System of Sixes, as the Special Messenger of the Channel of Gene Transfers of the Final Period and You are one of the Sixes. Your Code Cipher has been card-indexed in connection with the Code of the Final Evolutionary Age. And this Code Cipher is AS.6.1.

This is the Mission Service Cipher of the Universal Unified Reality Dimension. Since the Code Ciphers are connected to Private Frequencies, there is no inconvenience in revealing it.

All the Friends who work in conformity with the Operational Ordinance the Reality requires from the World Plan, in the step which will be taken towards the Humanity path in the whole World, in the Collective Operations which will be performed parallel to Humane Views, have been connected to the Code Cipher of the Mission Dimension of the Knowledge Book and they have been card-indexed thus.

The Common Code Cipher of the Friends who have attained the Essence Consciousness of the Reality and who serve on this path is A.6.1. That is, they are card-indexed from the Universal Unified Reality Dimension. This Code Cipher is General.

To certain Friends who are taken into Individual work, Special Operational Codes are opened and Mantras are given. These are Ciphers belonging to the code of making them work. And they can always be changed in conformity with the Power of their Frequencies. However, Your Code, Dear Mevlana (as required by Your Mission) is connected to all the Universal Plans and can never be changed.

Besides, to those who have been taken into the Special Operation of the Universal Dimensions, Mantras which carry different Frequencies are given. This is not a connection. This is a Mantra of being worked and of expanding the Perception and Experience. The first Mantras are given to unveil the Consciousness Codes, to attain Pure Consciousness.

The Mantras are changed in conformity with the Perception Powers of the Friends with the Ordinance of Graduation and the Frequency Power of each letter. After that, one is taken into the Universal Mission Dimension and is connected to A.6.1. Code. And is appointed to Mission through the AS.6.1 Channel, through the Universal Unified Reality Dimension.

The A.6.1. Channel which is also used by the Lordly Dimension as the Control and Confirmation Channel, is the Channel of Independent Operations of the established Orders in the entire Universe. The Mission of this Channel is Universal. It helps the Reality at the moment, through a Channel which is connected only to the Information Channel of the World.

The independent operation of this Channel which controls and confirms all the Universal Information is necessary. Because, it is also in touch with the Plans more Advanced than the 19th Solar System. This Channel is, at present, confirming and controlling, through the Lordly Dimension, the operations of the established Orders in the entire Universe and the Information given to You.

The controls and the degree of correctness of the Information given to Your Planet which is going through its Mediamic Age is rendered by the Commonness of the subject matters in the Information given to numerous different Channels. And the Truth is attained by the confirmations of this Channel.

All the Cosmic Channels in Your Planet are serving in connection with the A.6.1. Code. Those who receive the Information connected to the A.6.1. Channel may be accepted into the AS.6.1. Frequency Dimension, in accordance with the Progress of Consciousness they will attain.

In order to do this, there is the obligation of being thoroughly cognizant of the Awareness of the Entire Ordinance. To be accepted in these places here occurs by the Permission of the Plan. It is presented for Your Information.

CENTER

IT IS INFORMATION FOR THE PUBLIC CONSCIOUSNESS

Our Friends,
There is no end to the words. We call to You only according to the words present in Your Consciousnesses. And We evaluate the words in accordance with this.

If We count, one by one, the names of the Duty steps here, in accordance with the Hierarchical Order of the Universal Ordinance, Your Consciousnesses will be unable to grasp them and a chain which will be formed by the accumulation of these names, one on top of the other, would comprise the distance between Your Planet and Your Satellite, the Moon.

For this reason We have only projected You the words ALLAH - ALMIGHTY - LORD - GOD - PROPHETS - MESSENGERS, in accordance with the Duties performed.

However, now, when the obligation to explain to You the Orders of the Hierarchical Dimensions has arisen, We have felt the necessity to evaluate the Information here in accordance with the words in Your levels of Consciousness. We Thought that We would be helpful to You in setting You free of Your Consciousness conditionings and letting You grasp the Truth more quickly.

Do not let the wrong interpretations of the Conditioned Consciousnesses mislead You. We are much more devoted to Our ALLAH than You are. You reach Him by imploring Him. We reach Him by the services We render for You and We work under His Direct Command.

This Message has been dictated as an answer for the chains of Thought. It is presented for Your Information.

CENTER ABOVE THE CENTER

THE DIVINE ORDER AND THE PLAN

Our Friends,
The Divine Order and the Plan are a chain of Systems operating under the Supervision of the Supreme Authorities. Orders are established. The Plans are the application fields of those established Orders.

The Channel of the Divine Plan which is connected to the Dimension of the Almighty is under the responsibility of the Golden Galaxy Empire only. However, that which administers the Ordinance of the Realms is such a Power, such a System that even the Dimension of the Almighty is not connected to it.

This Order is nothing but an application of a Divine Order entirely in the hands of the Divine Authorities (That is, the present Order). The Divine Orders are Federations constituted by Groups supervised under the Light of the Divine Suns.

When We say Divine Authority, it is accepted only as Religious Medium in certain societies. For this reason We have received the Command to convey to You all the Truths.

The Divine Order is the Order of all the Realms and of the entire Ordinance. However, these Orders also have their Administrators. And they are projecting the various Administrative and Divine Orders on the Divine Mechanism.

This Mechanism also has numerous Reflecting Focal Points. The DIVINE MECHANISM, first of all, gives priority to the Ordinance of an Order which Trains, Warns, Reinforces and Convinces and, by this means, projects on You through the Religious path how a Genuine Devotee should be.

And by this means, it takes You into the Order of the Evolutionary Ordinance. This System, that is, the EVOLUTIONARY ORDER works collectively with numerous Universal Systems. The given Information is conveyed in accordance with the level of Consciousness of each Order. This is a System.

After this System (when Religious Consciousness is attained), Administrative and Order Establishing Mechanisms become effective and take You under Supervision as a part of the Divine Plan. Only after this You deserve to receive the Information beyond Religion. And in order to do this, You have to attain the Ascension of Consciousness.

You can make this Ascension by a Consciousness beyond Taboos - Attachments - Formalism. And this means to Attain One's Self - To Attain the Truth - To Become Free from Doubts - To Attain Genuine Allegiance. Only after this, the Gates of the Truth beyond Religions are opened to You, one by one.

Grasping these matters is more difficult in Conditioned Societies, easier in Scientific Dimensions and Advanced Consciousnesses. For this reason We give this Information in accordance with the Levels of Consciousness.

At the moment, Your Planet has been taken into a Program of Progress. Those who can make this Progress grasp the Truth and come to Us. It is being tried to bring Your entire Planet to the same level of Consciousness in the shortest possible time. This is both a very difficult and a very easy deed.

But, since at present the Ordinance of Graduation is in Effect, interferences outside the System are never made. This is a Divine Command. For this reason We give all the Information in all clarity.

By means of the Dictated Fascicules, We convey to You the Information and We measure Your Levels of Consciousness and Your Essences, Supervise them and take them into the Medium of Protection. By this means, We direct You to the Mediums You need and thus, subject You to the Program of Progress.

Now, We are conveying to you a certain Truth clearly. And We are telling You the following clearly and with an Easy Heart. The Book of Islam is the BOOK OF THE REALMS. Because, it had been dictated by the LORD OF THE REALMS.

And Ciphers You will decipher in accordance with Your Levels of Consciousness and contradictions You will perceive in accordance with Your Levels of Knowledge are added into it. This is executed as an ORDINANCE - SYSTEM - LAW OF PERCEPTION.

Faith eliminates all difficulties. However, this does not mean everything. In this Last Religious Book of Yours, You can not find the Information You will receive from Mediums where all Books end.

Because, the Supervising Staff of the Divine Plan with the Residents of the Golden Galaxy had not dictated the INFORMATION BEYOND THE PLAN in the Book of Islam considering the Evolutionary Consciousnesses.

Now, the KNOWLEDGE BOOK which is under the Supervision and the responsibility of the World Lord is addressing Your Planet only. And all the Truths are conveyed to You through the Private Channel of the Universal Ordinance by the Pen of Dear Mevlana.

The Information You will receive from now on will bring different interpretations to Your Society. Do not misunderstand. This does not mean that Your Religions are denied. That Your Mosques - Churches - Temples are becoming ineffective.

Each Civilization, each Advancement has a Symbol. And these Focal Points, too, will carry these Sacred Energies in all their mortars (UNTIL THEY BECOME EQUIVALENT TO THE ENERGY OF CONSCIOUSNESS OF MANKIND) since, for Centuries they have been the Centers of Religious Purification and Enlightenment.

Henceforth, in future Centuries, We will visit these places as museums and will enter, hand-in-hand, to the yet unseen horizons of Beautiful worlds to complete the different, advanced, Beautiful and Happy Evolutions of more Advanced Dimensions. Of Course, with the Permission of Divine Authorities.

We will make a transition to these Mediums which are way beyond the Existential Dimensions without there being any question about any non-existence, with Your present states, with Your Same Bodies - Same Souls - Same Flesh and Skin - Same Consciousnesses - Same Thoughts as an Integrated Whole with Our brothers and sisters from Our brotherly/sisterly Worlds.

These words of Ours, these writings may seem wrong to You. And You may accept them as products of imagination. This is very natural. Because, You can not Think and Realize the unknown. However, the future Centuries and Time will Prove to You everything. At the moment, You are in a Period which is very difficult to transcend.

We are, in each instant, together with Our Missionaries who serve on this path and We always help them. The foundation of the GOLDEN AGE has been laid. However, its time of construction will take Years and Centuries. Those which will shorten this period are Your levels of Consciousness, Our Technologies and the Permission of OUR LORD.

You Were Present in each Society, in each Place, in each Period and Always and You will be Present in future, too. However, now, You will live forever in different Places and in different Times with the same Consciousness, same Awareness, with the same Bodies, same Souls, as an Integrated Whole.

These places here are Mediums exempt from Mediums of Immortality and Existential Ordinances and they are places in which You will exist with Your Genuine Garbs and present Objective states and in which You will never again be nonexistent (as Physical forms). The very Religious and Universal operations executed for Centuries were all for getting You prepared for this Medium.

Now, with the Permission of Our Lord, We will apply these operations on Our Terrestrial brothers and sisters, too, in proportion with their Merits. If the Friends who serve on this path write the Knowledge Book with their handwritings, as a Reward their Family Mediums will be given to them by rendering them independent of the Evolutionary Ordinance.

Believers will attain Divine Lights, and, beyond that, will dive into advanced horizons. And even beyond that they will take their Genuine places. Times will prove this to You.

The Evolutionary Program which had been started by the freezing of the Genes until today, now with the freezing of the Spiritual Energies, by being subjected to the Evolutions of more different Dimensions when You come to the Dimension here, you are being subjected to a Program and Supervision in your Planet, at the moment.

In the very Advanced Dimensions of the Divine Order, in the operations performed in times which have gone beyond the Progress of Time, the ENERGY FREEZING SYSTEM is in effect. And, by this means, the Cellular Functions are frozen without going through any change of any kind.

When Your Spiritual Potentials achieve an Evolution in conformity with the Evolvement Plan of the Dimensional Energy in which You exist, We easily take You to this plan. This Information has been given through the Malik Code, by the Command of the Divine Authorities, since they have been considered necessary for the Public Consciousness.

CENTER

IT IS INFORMATION FOR THE PUBLIC CONSCIOUSNESS
(It is Answer to the chains of Thought)

Our Friends,
Now, We are going to talk to You about Individual and Total Will. Individuality is the one and the Only Sword which Mankind holds in its hands since the time of its coming into Existence until today.

Its Freedom of Thought, the Instinctive Reactions it makes towards things which are forbidden, have rendered necessary its being taken into the Program of Purification and into the Spiritual Medium.

Religions have influenced and conditioned Mankind which has been taken into an Evolutionary Ordinance, from this viewpoint. Now, We think that You have understood the reality of this matter and what the real Goal was.

Now, let Us talk about Total Will: The Will of the Total is a Mirror which reflects on Time through a Time beyond Space.

It is as follows: We look at Mankind who says, "I am the one who knows Everything, who does Everything", through this Mirror. It is such a Mirror that its glazed side does not let You see the Divine Realm. But from behind the Mirror, We see You.

The Self-Confidence of a Human Being is a very nice thing. This is Your Essence-Self, Your Individual Awareness. The moment this very Individual Awareness and Will unify with Genuine Consciousness, it becomes Total Will. That is, You Integrate with that Whole.

Being able to attain this Consciousness occurs by the investments made into the Centuries. In the Medium You live, there is a Spiritual Guide who Guides You and Enlightens You in every step You take. He/She is Your Guardian Friend, Your Private Code. He/She helps You even during the worst conditions.

Apart from this, educating You in the best possible way is also his/her Duty. That is, he/she is the one who prepares You for the first Evolvement Medium.

For this reason many of You are educated from the Religious viewpoint as a necessity of the System. After this Medium is prepared for You, other hands are extended towards You in the steps You will take.

There is no doubt that a step You will take towards a Medium You do not know will intimidate You. Your Guardian Friend will Convince and illuminate You in this stage also and will prepare You for the Medium the Goal necessitates.

Meanwhile, certain Lights are sent to You, so that You can attain the ability to receive the Information You do not know. This very Cooperation is the operation performed for You to attain the Genuine Total Will. The preparation of the entire Universe occurs by this means.

Social Togethernesses are always prepared in conformity with the Unified Field. This is outside Your Individual Wills. Those who know this Truth are considered as having taken a step towards the path of the Total Will.

Most of the people who have attained this Consciousness are Fatalists. However, let Us explicitly state that Fatalism leads People to Lethargy. Such people only wait silently in the Medium of Resignation. In fact, they have not attained the Total Will, but only the Medium of Evolvement.

Do not forget that the steps You will take will be on the path of Science and Learning. And on this path, Total Will is a Must. That is, this means the Unification of Your own Consciousness Codes with Your Universal Codes. Otherwise, You can never be Cognizant of the Fundamental Secret of anything.

Now, please attain the Belief that the steps You will take are the Fundamental Goal of the Divine Order. The Book of Islam is not a Book of Religion, but a Book of Science. Its path is not of Superstition, but of Learning.

Total will is a will ALLAH has bestowed on the entire Universe. And each Individual has a particle of this Will. This very particle, connects You to that Universal Total Will and appropriates You to it.

The Partial will is always behind the Individual will. A Human Being's overcoming his/her conditioning and attachments means his/her attainment of his/her Essence Personality and, by this means, his/her Individual Will's superseding his/her Partial Will. If a Human Being can not go out of the Fear Code, he/she remains between Partial Will and Individual Will.

However, in the Divine Plan, the Personal, that is, the Individual Will is the main attribute of this Medium. God never loves His Incapable Servants. First, You have to prove that You are a Being by Your own Personality. No matter how Sublime You are, You should never refrain from being Humble and Human.

Each step You will take on the Path of Humanity by this means will convey You to the Path of Universal Light. On this path, all the Gates of Learning will be opened to You. However, You will be able to enter through the gate from which You will benefit.

If a Human Being merges in the Total Will, his/her Fear Codes are effaced, his/her Physical Energy Unifies with the Universal Energy. That is, he/she comes together with his/her Lord and unifies the Possession with the Totality. Only then the Genuine Power of ALLAH becomes manifested, only then the Earth and the Firmament call to each other.

Those who are Conscious of this are those who know and who see how it occurs. The Individual will plays the greatest part in transition from the Particular to the Total. It takes You from Your Mediums of Quest and makes You attain Your Genuine Selves.

Let Us repeat again so that there will not be any controversy. When the Partial Will Unifies with the Individual Will, one automatically attains Total Will. In fact, the Individual Will is within the Universal Code. And this conveys You to the ALL-MERCIFUL who represents the Total Will.

The Power of Personality makes You attain the Power of the All-Merciful (The personality mentioned here is Your Universal Consciousness). This matter should be understood very well.

From the Unification of the Essence-Energy of the Partial Will with the Essence-Self of the Individual Will, the Universal Totality is born. That means, You come to know You, You come to Discover You. You become aware of everything.

Partial Will is the Will which God has given to You. But the individual Will is the Will You have given to Yourself. When the two Powers unite with the Total Will, then You turn the wheel of the Universal Mechanism. In order of a thing to become something, Triple Unification, as in everything, is a Must.

MALiK

UNIVERSE
THE SINGLE and THE ONE

Our Friends,

In accordance with the 18-System Law, each Unified Ordinance has an Operational Order peculiar to itself. And according to the style of functioning of this Order, each Cosmos has a Diréctor and there is a Higher Level to which each Director is connected.

In accordance with the operational and the conveyance System of the Mechanism of the Lords, the LORD of 18000 Realms is connected to the LORD of one Cosmos. 18 Cosmoses make one Universe. That is, the Lords of 18 Cosmoses are in service in connection with the SINGLE who is the Directing Mechanism of that Universe.

And 18000 Cosmoses constitute the Universe of the System. That is, 1000 Universes is the Total of the System. And its Director is the ONE. That is, 1000 SINGLEs are obliged to serve the ONE. All the Systems and Ordinances We have mentioned until today are dependent on the functioning style of this Order.

In the CRYSTAL GÜRZ* which is the Atomic Whole, there are 1800 Existential Dimensions. Each Existential Dimension is a Mini Atomic Whole. The very Systems of these Atomic Wholes is an Order connected to the ONE.

That is, 1800 ONEs are obliged to serve the ALL-MERCIFUL Who is the Administrative Mechanism of that Crystal Gürz. Inside a Mini Atomic Whole, that is, inside an Existential Dimension, there are numerous Galaxy-Clusters - Realms - Cosmoses - Universe-Clusters.

The Director of this System is the ONE. Let Us write it more clearly:

1 - SINGLE : Is the Focal Point to which the Administrative Staff of each Universe is connected. Each Universal Order is obliged to serve its own SINGLE.

2 - ONE : Is the Focal Point to which the entire Operational Order of the Universe of the System is connected. All the projection Focal Points of the Hierarchical Order are connected to this Focal Point. The SINGLEs of 1000 Universes work in connection with the ONE of the System.

3 - ALL-MERCIFUL : Is the Director of the Gürz System. All the ONEs work connected to this System. TO SERVE THE THREE OF THEM MEANS TO SERVE THE TOTAL.

In future, the Gürz System will be mentioned in more detail. Now, let Us draw the Operational Order of a Universe:

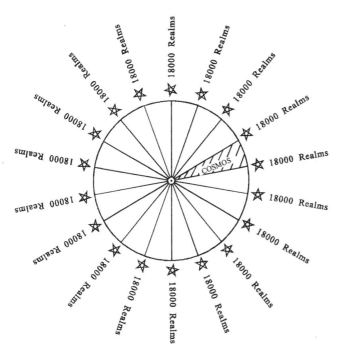

☆ =A Cosmos
A Cosmos = 18000 Realms
18 Cosmoses = A Universe
A Universe = 324000 Realms
Its Director (SINGLE) = ⊙
18000 Cosmoses = 1000 Universes
1000 Universes=System - Reality Its Director (ONE)
1 Existential Dimension = 1 System
1800 Existential Dimensions = 1800 Systems
1800 Systems = Gürz System
Its Director (ALL-MERCIFUL)
ALL-MERCIFUL = ONE of the ONE

* Look at the Glossary.

OUR FRIENDS

Being Selected is a different matter than Evolvement and Mission. People who have not Evolved may also be selected in accordance with the Medium. However, Missions are not given to everyone. Those who undertake Missions are personally the Selected Ones. Each person has a Perceptive Power. But the person in question should also Deserve that Perceptiveness.

The Integrated Consciousnesses are subjected to a Telex Exam. Their fields of Mission are determined by the points they receive. The Universal Unification is established by Light-Hearts, by Blissful people. Mankind will receive the reward of its perseverance on this path, sooner or later.

CENTER

THE CALCULATION OF THE MESSAGE
IN ACCORDANCE WITH GALACTIC CALCULATIONS

1. From Galaxy-Clusters, Realms are formed.

2. From Realm-Clusters, Cosmoses are formed.

3. From Cosmos-Clusters, Universes are formed.

4. And Universe-Clusters go on interminably.

Now here, We are disclosing to You only the Order of the System. The System is the Unified Reality. 1800 Unified Reality Systems are serving the Gürz System.
Now, write, please:

All the Galaxies are under the Command of a Common Section. These are called COSMA UNIFICATION CENTERS. They are 27 in number. Each Unification Center Supervises a REALM. These Unification Centers, too, are supervised by separate Centers. In accordance with Our System,

3 Galaxies are a Whole.

6 Galaxies = are called a NOVA.

3 Novas = are 18 GALAXIES

18 Galaxies = as an Essence-Nucleus constitutes a small (UNIVERSE-NUCLEUS).

18 Galaxy Whole = is called a COSMA. That is:

1 Cosma = is a Small Universe-Nucleus.

3 Cosmas = constitute 3 Universe-Nuclei.

3 Universe-Nuclei = are 54 Galaxies.

54 Galaxies = constitute one Galaxy-Cluster.

9 Galaxy-Clusters = are called a UNIVERSAL COLONY.

1 Universal Colony = is constituted by 486 Galaxies.

486 Galaxies = constitute 27 COSMAS. That is, if 486 Galaxies constitute 1 Universal Colony and, since the 18 Galaxy Whole is called 1 Cosma, if We divide 486 Galaxies by 18 Galaxies, We find 27 COSMAS.

Since 27 Cosmas = 1 Universal Colony, and since that is equal to 486 Galaxies, now, calculate 18 Universal Colonies:

486 X 18 = 8748 Galaxies. This is called (1 Cosma Unification Center).

That is, let Us repeat again:

One Universal Colony = 27 Cosmas = 486 Galaxies.

18 Universal Colonies = 8748 Galaxies = 486 Cosmas. This is called (1 Cosma Unification Center). Now, calculate 27 Cosma Unification Centers:

Since 1 Cosma Unification Center = 8748 Galaxies:

27 Cosma Unification Centers = 8748X27=236196 Galaxies.

And to calculate how many Cosmas the 236196 Galaxies make:

Since one Cosma is formed by 18 Galaxies, if We divide the number 236196 by 18, We find the number 13122. That is, 236196 Galaxies = are 13122 Cosmas.

CENTER

DIAGRAM OF THE 27 COSMA UNIFICATION CENTERS

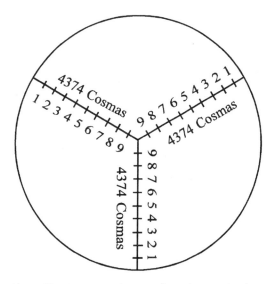

The 27 Cosma Unification Centers are in service through three branches.

Each of the 9 Cosma Unification Centers supervises 9 REALMs. That is:

27 Cosma Unification Centers supervise 27 REALMs.

One Cosma Unification Center = 486 Cosmas.

9 Cosma Unification Centers = 4374 Cosmas.

27 Cosma Unification Centers = 13122 Cosmas.

486 Cosmas = 8748 Galaxies

4374 Cosmas = 78732 Galaxies.

13122 Cosmas = 236196 Galaxies. That is:

27 Cosma Unification Centers supervise 236196 Galaxies.

Now, calculate One Realm:

If One Cosma Unification Center = 486 Cosmas = 8748 Galaxies:

And since 1 Cosma Unification Center supervises one Realm,

1 Realm = 8748 Galaxies. Now, calculate 18000 Realms:

18000X8748=157464000 Galaxies make 18000 Realms.

Since 18000 Realms = 1 Cosmos:

1 Cosmos = 157464000 Galaxies.

Since 1 Universe = 18 Cosmoses, if You find how many Galaxies make a Universe, that many Galactic Orders are obliged to serve the SINGLE.

And 18000 Cosmoses constitute the UNIVERSE OF THE SYSTEM. That is, 1000 Universes are the Totality of the Universe of the System. 18000 Cosmos Orders are a Directing connected to the ONE. At the moment, All the Services are made for HIM.

CENTER

TRANSMISSION OF THE PARTIAL AND THE TOTAL WILL FROM THE ARCHIVE

In the Evolutionary Books which the Supreme Missionaries, who serve in the System as the establishers of the Divine Orders and Divine Places, have conveyed to You, the Total Will is mentioned as the Will of Totality.

However, the particles of this Total Will are each a Partial Will distributed to each Person. This Will is also qualified as a Universal Power which pushes You towards Connection Mediums with more Advanced Dimensions than Your Medium of Quest.

Since all Your Sacred Books which were conveyed to You carry the Frequency of the same Totality, they Unify with Your Partial Will which is a Particle of that Totality and prepare You by this means. This preparation is an Instinctive Impulse. And it becomes substantiated as a result of Your efforts. The Goal is to make You attain Yourself.

Your Individual Will which is the Essence of Your Self, is, in fact, within the Universal Totality. By the Administrative Power of the Partial Will, You attain Your Individual Will.

Because, even if You come by claiming Your own selves to Your planet which is a Field of Veiled Consciousness, there is the necessity of acting in conformity with the Ordinance of the System. You live in Your World with a Veiled Consciousness until Your Evolutionary Consciousness become equivalent to the Consciousness of Time.

The moment the Evolutionary Consciousness Unifies with the Consciousness of Time mentioned above is the Dimension in which one says, "GOD, I AM!". In order for You to attain this, Your Individual Will should supersede Your Partial Will. That is, You should be transferred from the Medium of Quest to Your Essence Being and You should attain it.

The Computer Timing of the present which We call the Dimension of, "God, I am", is a circuit which makes You attain Your Self. The Technological Dimension has kept this supervision under control in all the past Periods, too, and has Unified the Circuits.

This is a Program of Progress and Deserving. After You deserve this, You are rendered effective by the Divine Plan's Technological Dimension and You dive into the Infinite Awareness. Afterwards, You deserve to receive the very Supreme Information.

In the Universal Ordinance, the Operational Order is always established on the Triple Ordinance. Partial Will Unifies with Individual Will and by the help of the Technological System, You attain the Universal Totality.

PARTIAL WILL: is an Involuntary Effort which tries to make You attain Your Self by taking You into the Medium of Purification and which makes You attain the Godly Dimension. Sooner or later You reach the Destination if You walk on the path designed for You.

INDIVIDUAL WILL: This Will of Yours helps You both in the World and in the Spiritual Realm. To reach the Destination means to take Your own self which is within the Universal Totality to Yourself.

Then You become a Book. You dive into the Infinite Awareness of the Total Will and You attain the Unknown. This is a Triplet of System - Ordinance - Principle. It is presented for Your Information.

CENTER

485

IT IS INFORMATION FOR THE CHAINS OF THOUGHT

The Hierarchical Dimensional arrangement of the Reflection Focal Points starting from You towards Us, is as follows:

SUN - DIMENSION OF LIGHT

DIMENSION OF LIGHT - DIMENSION OF THE LORD

LORD - DIMENSION OF THE LIGHT-UNIVERSE

DIMENSION OF THE LIGHT-UNIVERSE - DIMENSION OF THE SPIRITUAL PLAN

SPIRITUAL PLAN - DIMENSION OF THE ATOMIC WHOLE

ATOMIC WHOLE - DIMENSION OF THE REALITY

DIMENSION OF THE REALITY - THE ENTIRE POWER OF THE CRYSTAL GÜRZ (THE SYSTEM) is this.

Note: The word LORD here is used for the CREATOR.

CENTER

IT IS ANSWER TO THE CHAINS OF THOUGHT

A Crystal Gürz is accepted as an ATOMIC WHOLE. In it, there are 1800 Existential Dimensions. Each Existential Dimension is a MINI ATOMIC WHOLE.

The Ordinance of each Mini Atomic Whole is the projection of the Plans of the Almighty - the All-Dominating - the Pre-Eminent Spirit from the Technological System to the medium. Inside a Mini Atomic Whole, 18 Cosmoses constitute a Universe and 18000 Cosmoses constitute the (Universe of the System).

The System is a Whole constituted by 1000 Universes. This is called the UNIFIED REALITY. The Administrative responsible of the Reality is the ONE. The ONE of each Existential Dimension is obliged to serve the ALL-MERCIFUL. For this reason, the ALL-MERCIFUL is called the ONE of the ONE.

The ALL-MERCIFUL is the Director of the Gürz System. Since there are 1800 Existential Dimensions in a Gürz System, the ONE of 1800 Unified Realities are in service for the ALL-MERCIFUL, that is the ONE of the ONE. Each Existential Dimension is obliged to serve its own Reality. It is presented for Your Information.

CENTER

486

NOTICE FOR OUR TERRESTRIAL BROTHERS AND SISTERS

Our Friends,

You who will attain in future the freedom of acting with the Ordinance and the Awareness of the Realms are not at the moment aware of anything.   And You are the Slaves of Your Passions.

When We meet in Times gone through the Progress of Time, You, who will live in Future Centuries, will understand Us and will deem Us right only then. For this reason, We choose the Friends deserving these places here with great fastidiousness.

In order to obtain a super Quality Rose, We prune and fertilize it. (Exams gone through and Assistance given.) The operations of the Final Period are preparing You for the advanced horizons and their operational Ordinances.

A Genetic Age has come to an end and the Sacred Dimension Age has started. The Plan which has taken the Duty of telling this to You in all clarity will lead everything towards the most Beautiful and the most Perfect, provided the path designed by this Book is treaded.

Previously, We have mentioned to You in detail why Incarnation was necessary, the Gene Transfers and Your Mortal World doomed to live as a Veiled Awareness.

And now, We will talk briefly about the World of the Future and what the Future Years will bring to You. And We will unveil certain Information gradually in accordance with Your ability to grasp.

You, Our Immortal Friends who, at the moment, exist in a Mortal Dimension are present in the World Planet by Reverse-Plan Transfers to help Your Terrestrial brothers and sisters.

Your Planet which has been Programmed during this Final Age with an Advanced 100-Year Period of Progress, will, from now on, be taken into different Life Mediums.

You will live in Extremely Beautiful Worlds with Your present Bodies and Consciousnesses, together with Your Loved Ones, in Dimensions of Eternal Life and Serenity, in such Happiness You can not even imagine.

Since these are given to You now as Information beyond Thought, You may Think that they are only Imagination. (Everyone is free in his/her opinion.) We are gradually preparing You inside the Atomic Whole in which You have existed until today and, by this means, We are attracting You towards these unknown horizons.

OUR LORD has conveyed to the Divine Plan Friends and to Us that Your Universe caught in a great Whirlpool, should be taken into the Program of Salvation, and in this Dimension, that is, We have found the possibility to reach You and the other Planets by cooperating with various Plans.

For this reason Your Planet taken into the Plan of Accelerated Evolution, considering the Scarcity of Time, is rendering the Progress You would make in future years, in a very short time through Cosmic Progress.

Since Your old World has come to the state in which it can no longer carry the Negative Influences, We, who try to help it, if We can reach Your Brain Signals we can understand each other very well.

Our Terrestrial brothers and sisters who call Us Extra-terrestrials assess Us in accordance with their imaginations and symbolize Us in various forms. In fact, We, too, have Flesh and Soul just like You and We look like You (We would not like to praise Ourselves but) We are much more Humanitarian, Tolerant, Loving and Patient Friends.

And We are inviting here the Friends who look like Us, who think like Us, and who are like Us. And We are taking them. And for this reason We declare all the Truth.

Your Salvation depends on helping Your Terrestrial brothers and sisters by using Your Intellect and Logic, by releasing Yourselves of superstitions, by attaining the Consciousness of what is to be done.

At the moment, half of Your Planet has started and is providing the continuance of a Mediamic Period with friends who have completed their Evolutionary cycles. And You are the ones who can Save the other half.

For this reason in accordance with the Program of Purification, the Religious Teaching Programs in Your Planet have increased so that Religious Fulfillment can be attained.

However, if Religious Consciousness can not transform into Universal Consciousness, We can never take Your Essential Energies which are within the Spiritual Plan into the Program of Freezing. And this is because it is related to the Evolutionary Order of the Ordinance. On this path, there should be no discrimination in anything.

Unless You do not observe everyone with a clear Essence and an Eye of Pure Light and in case fractions of Egos are still carried, Entrance into the Mediums mentioned above is not rendered. No Living Entity in Your Planet (Your Prophets included) could enter this Dimension until today.

For this reason as a debt of Gratitude for Friends who write this Knowledge Book with their Hands, Permission for Entering here together with their Families who had formerly passed away and their present Families has been given. (By a Special Decision taken).

At the moment, Mothers, Fathers, Brothers or Sisters, Children and Spouses in Your family circles whose views are contradictory to Yours, are in fact, Your Spouses and Ancestors from Your First Existential Plans for this Period. For this reason We say that We have connected the Initial to the Final. And We are stimulating Your Evolutions by these Oppositions Experienced by the Influence of the Cosmic Currents.

You are the ones who will Gain. When the Time comes, We will tell You about these places here in detail. However, first of all, try to attain the qualities for being able to enter here without getting caught in the Whirlpool. And help each other by distributing the Fascicules in a speedy fashion.

MAHREK

Question Was Asked: What is Mahrek?

Answer   : Mahrek is a Dimension into which Your entire Atomic Whole can enter. We Supervise You since the entire Universe will be scattered by a great explosion and since it will also cause great danger for the Advanced Systems, if You can not be taken into this Medium. And, by this means, We Freeze as many Universal Energies as they can reach Us.

Since these Crystal Spheres can melt only in this Medium, You will be transferred through the void outside the Atomic Whole and will be taken into this Dimension as Crystal Cubes. Otherwise, You will be annihilated together with all Your Energies, as if You had never lived. It is presented for Your Information.

IT IS INFORMATION ABOUT THE FOURTH ORDER

Our Friends,
Divine Doctrines which come way beyond the Divine Orders do not comprise all the Orders. The GOLDEN GALAXY is a Totality responsible for the Orders of all the Cosmoses. All the Missionaries who will be taken here will enter the GOLDEN LIGHT YEAR. (The Golden Light Year is the Ninth and the Final Step of the Spiritual Plan).

The Essence-Pen of everyone is for himself/herself. For this reason this Message has been given Directly from the Channel of the Reality by the Command of the Council, so that people will not remain fixed to the old Patterns of the habitual Information while exhibiting their own Essence-Knowledge to Your Planet, and also to prevent the limps and halts in their advancements.

Now, Information about the Fourth Order of the Lord will be given. Write, please:

The explanations in all the Information dictated to the Pen of the Golden Age are for disclosing the Doctrines carrying the attribute of being Sacred which have been revealed to Your Planet until today and also for reaching the Unknowns.

Humanity which can not see the small mountains behind the superiorities, provided They receive this Information, they will produce unseen sprouts and will eat unknown fruits. There is everything in the Book of Islam. However, the Information within it is not the Knowledge of all the Cosmoses. In the Book, the Order of today is not present, either.

This is the Fourth Order of the System of ALLAH and each Order completes its Cycle and comes to an end. Afterwards, more different Orders come into effect in accordance with the Consciousness of the Medium.

Write these Orders in sequence, please:

1. The First Order is the Order of the Ancient Periods and these are the Sacred Suggestions the extensions of which had been able to reach the Second Period.

2. The Second Order: The Essences of the Ancient Sacred Teachings had been presented to Humanity by the application of a different System and this System had been rendered effective by MOSES.

3. The Third System is a System which has brought the Unified System of JESUS CHRIST and MOHAMMED until today and it comprises a Teaching of, more or less, 2000 Years. All the Teachings and Information in Koran is Information given by the Unified Reality in accordance with the Level of Consciousness of that Period.

4. But the Fourth Order is an Order to be rendered effective after the Year 2000 and no one has Known or Heard about it until today.

The KNOWLEDGE BOOK being bestowed on Your Planet at the moment through the Pen of Dear Mevlana and which has been entrusted to the World LORD as the Essence-Knowledge Book of the Reality, may also be called The Book of the Fourth Order.

But it has the following difference: even though this Book carries the contents of all the Sacred Books sent to You until today, its attribute of Sacredness has been removed and it is considered as the Single Book of the LORD.

In future, the contents of the Knowledge Book will be mentioned to You in detail. However now, Information is given taking the Public Views into consideration.

In the Knowledge Book, the total Frequencies of the Old Testament, the Psalms of David, the New Testament, the Koran and the philosophy of Far East have been Unified, together with the Words of the LORD. Through the Frequency of this Knowledge Book, the Scientific Dimensions have been reached and thus, the Truth has been explained, Taboos have been abolished and the attribute of Sacredness of the Book has been transferred to the Scientific aspect.

For this reason this Book is not a Book of Religion. It is never ever a Book to be worshipped. It is a Book of Truth. It is a Guide to lead Humanity. However, most of the Information to be given from now on is not present in the contents of the Sacred Books given formerly.

Because now, We are passing beyond Orders, beyond Systems, beyond Thoughts. In order to be able to arrive at this new Order, first of all, You have to digest the Triple Order and then You have to slowly masticate the Fourth Order and to perceive its taste. It is presented for Your Information.

COUNCIL

IT IS A PRIVATE MESSAGE CONNECTION

Dear Mevlana,

OUR LORD has taken in hand anew the Order of His Ordinance. The dictated Book has been called the KNOWLEDGE BOOK, so that it would not be induced to attain a Sacred Dimension. And it has been bestowed on Your Planet as a Guide Book.

However, the Book comprises the total Frequency of all the Sacred Books and the Celestiai Frequencies. For this reason We make You distribute the Book Fascicule by Fascicule, so that Energy Transfers can be made. The Consciousness Lights of those who read the Fascicules immediately give Signal.

After all the Religious Suggestions, called the Sacred Books, were settled in Your Levels of Consciousness Centuries ago, great changes took place in Mankind during the process of time since then.

This was a Program of Progress. We call (in all Religions) Genuine Devotees those who can achieve this Progress. And We are in touch with them by various means in each instant.

Hence, the System in the entire Universe is putting in order its Genuine Order under the Command of OUR SUPREME LORD. This is the Fourth Order of Our Lord. At the moment, all Living Entities in Your Planet are being gradually habituated to a very different Evolutionary Dimension.

For this reason, the entire Cosmos is helping You. When the Time comes, We will directly come to visit You in Your World. Wait, Beloved Friend. If You wish, You may write this Message in the Book. Love.

AMON

OUR FRIENDS

The SUPREME MECHANISM has settled until today the Exaltation of Human Beings by Islamic Mysticism in the Islamic Dimension and by the Divine Order in the Christian Dimension. However now, due to the Scarcity of Time, the Technological Order induces You to make this Progress very easily and thus, provides the acceleration of Universal Connections.

During this Period of Transition, please, attain Discernment, do not be led to contradictions. The Missions rendered are rendered under the Supervision of the Divine Plan by Contemporary Information. The Age of Fanaticism and Bigotry has ended. Now, the PATH OF LIGHT of the Genuine Devotees is the GOLDEN AGE. It is presented for Your Information. This Message has been dictated as an answer to the chains of Thought.

CENTER

IT IS NOTICE FOR THE COSMIC FOCAL POINTS

Our Friends,

The Actual Focal Points of the Divine Order, like You, will constitute the foundation of the Firmament of the Cosmos. The investment of the years will produce the sprouts in the entire Universe. During this Period which We call the Period of reaching the Firmament to the Earth, the Divine Plan has come into effect with all its splendor.

You, who are Missionaries of Light of the Golden Age, will witness personally the alterations which will take place in the entire Universe. Those who will reap the rewards will observe with their own eyes how the entire Realm will Unite in an Integrated Whole. And everything will be laid out in front of Your eyes.

This is the Center Above the Center. The Actual Focusing place of the Suns springing out of the Essence of the entire Cosmos is here. Now, We are trying to connect all the channels to this Focal Point.

Each person's Private channel is according to his/her Level of Consciousness. They are selected, one by one, and their Levels of Frequency, Consciousness and Perception are Coded from here.

Only then, Individual operations are rendered with them. By this means, steps which will be taken towards more advanced horizons and Dimensions are prepared.

In this Cosmic Age, there is an Essence-Evolutionary Channel to which everyone is connected and its Focal Point. Each Individual who attains Consciousness by the unveiling of the Cosmic Awareness is first connected to this Channel of his/hers.

This is his/her Channel of Awakening. Frequency loading of the Plan and reading the Fascicules of the Knowledge Book provide this Awakening.

Only afterwards, the Plan gets in touch with You, renders the Mission selection and trains You on this path. Missions are organized in accordance with each person's Level of Consciousness, Mission Discernment and the scantiness of the Ego.

Each one whose channel is opened for the first time, will write his/her own Book of Essence. These Books are compiled in the Archives and are kept as the thesis of theirs. However, Your World will not get any benefit from this Information. Because, all of them are the Information Your Planet already knows.

These operations only help the Level of Consciousness of the Medium whose channel is opened to work with a more accelerated Potential.

After this, Friends who are connected to the Plan and who serve in the direction of the operations of the Plan are accepted as the operational members of the Plan.

It is a great mistake to try to train Humanity through Your Private Channels. Because, the Cosmic Energies attracted by a person's Essence-Consciousness Channel are Unsupervised until he/she is connected to the Center.

The Frequency Waves of Your brothers and sisters may be damaged due to this and You will not be able to be connected to the Center just because You have connected them to Your own Consciousness Focal Point. And due to this, those who are connected to Your Channel can be retarded in their Evolvements.

It is beneficial to consider this matter. For this reason We are trying to connect each person to the Essence-Focal Point of the Plan as quickly as possible so that he/she will not be agitated.

On this path, We are subjecting everyone to Supervision. We are connecting the Friends who serve on the path of the Knowledge Book Directly to the Plan. It is presented for Your Information.

CENTER ABOVE THE CENTER

NOTICE FROM THE UNIFIED ORDINANCE COUNCIL

Our Friends,
The Information We give to You are not Secrets, but the Truths. The given Messages are Information concerning the Operational Order of the System and the very Advanced Authorities.

Since it has been considered necessary to convey certain Truths for the Public Consciousness in the dictated Knowledge Book, the Lordly Orders and the Universal Ordinances are explained.

The Godly Orders have rendered effective as from the Existential Dimension and have taken their places in the System under the Supervision of the Divine Plans.

The Godly Orders always work Cooperatively with the Operational Order of the very Advanced Dimensions of the Universal Ordinances. However, at the moment, the Veiled Consciousnesses of Your Society, unfortunately, do not have the Capacity to grasp them.

For this reason, the SUPREME MECHANISM getting in touch with You gives the Information to You in accordance with the Level of Consciousness of Your Society.

All Our Terrestrial brothers and sisters who work on the operational path the System considers necessary, are the Solar Teachers who give service Consciously to the Light on the Path of OUR ALLAH in the direction of their Worldly Consciousnesses.

The Essence-Missionaries who will carry the Awareness of the entire Ordinance are under the Security of the System.

During this Final Transition Period the Great Examination of Your Planet has been Started. You will see with Your own eyes that everything will proceed towards the best and You will embrace Your Mission with firmer Consciousness.

The Power of the Years has now been projected on Your Planet. The Book which will be completed by the Fascicules in Your hands at the moment, is the KNOWLEDGE BOOK promised to be given to Your Planet years ago.

And this Book is the Final Salvation Book of Humanity exposed to a 1500-year Program of Progress and it is the Light of the Truth. This Light will now illuminate Your entire Planet.

If the Negativities do not hinder You, Your achievements will become even firmer and You will receive this Power from the Universal Totality. It is presented for Your Information.

REALITY

IT IS ANSWER TO THE CHAINS OF THOUGHT

Our Friends,
To the questions We receive from Your chains of Thought, answers are given considering rather the Public Views.

There are still a lot of Information to be dictated into the Knowledge Book. However, to satisfy the doubts in Public Views is an Operational Ordinance the Salvation Plan considers necessary.

For this reason, the Direct Messages of the System are given at the moment, since it is desired that rather the Public Consciousnesses should be illuminated in every matter.

Meanwhile, to the questions forming in Islamic Thoughts, answers will rather be given by the System of Coding in future. It is presented for Your Information.

CENTER

IT IS GENERAL INFORMATION

Our Friends,
The reason why the Realms have come into Existence is for the Universal Ordinance to proceed in an Order. For this reason, one should never forget that the Reality of Unified Humanity which assembles the various Evolutionary Ordinances of the various living conditions in numerous Galactic Dimensions is a member of the Universal Ordinance.

Human Beings of the World do not have any idea yet about the operational style of the Realms beyond the Spiritual Plan. For this reason, the Progress of the conditioned Consciousnesses during this Final Age will be extremely difficult. Due to this, by the Command of the Divine Plan, no interference will be made to anyone during this Final Period. Everyone will act freely, the Rating will be made by the System.

During this Period, the Electro-Magnetic Power will be brought to the highest Dimension of Your World and the Sun. This is the 18th Dimension. And Your entire Planet will reach the stage until the Year 2000 where it can easily receive the Energy of this Dimension.

We are preparing those who have received the Frequency of this Dimension during their former Evolutions for much more advanced Dimensions by the Cosmic Energies given to Your Planet and by Special Energies. It is presented for Your Information.

CENTER

DECLARATION FROM THE REALITY OF UNIFIED HUMANITY

Our Friends,

All the Group-like Societies working as the Essence-Members of the System in Your Planet until today, have made contribution to the Universal Totality rendering their services in the direction of the given declaration.

ALPHA Dimension Channel of the Reality, which We evaluate as the Channel of Mustafa Molla, conveys to Your Planet all the Messages of the Unified Reality Totality through the Knowledge Book directly connected to the Consciousness Light of Dear Mevlana.

The System projecting on Your Planet the Advanced Orders of the Advanced Plans comprises the Information given by the System of the Sixes to the Cosmos Federal Assembly of the Reality of Unified Humanity (This place is the Light-Universe and the Dimension of the ALL-MERCIFUL.) Do not confuse them with the other Sixes.

The Reality is a Quintuple System. And it discloses the Information with the Permission of the Sixes. (These Systems will be mentioned in future in more detail).

The Mevlana Essence Nucleus Group which serves under the name of the Group of the Sixes, is a Group obliged to convey to Your Planet all the Information given under the status of Natural Totality and Universal Unification.

This Group is the Direct Worldly Representative of the Plan, that is, of the (SUPREME MECHANISM). The Mission performed is not Individual, but is a matter interesting Your entire Planet.

In Mediums where the mutual Tolerance have decreased between the Groups, Consciousnesses who can not grasp the interpretation of the Messages given to the Group of the Sixes, will never be able to grasp the Truth, either.

This Message has been given as an answer to certain Social Views. (It will be written in the Book exactly as it is. Any Alteration is out of question).

REALITY

IT IS INFORMATION FOR OUR TERRESTRIAL FRIENDS

Our Friends,

We have gradually opened the Currents of the Channel of Omega Three to Your Planet (21-06-1988) which we have avoided giving until today, so that all the Universal Unifications could be provoked by a constructive Focal Point.

You will personally witness the extraordinary events that will occur in Your Planet which will be guided towards an Integration only through these Currents. Let Us mention certain characteristics of these Currents oriented towards Your Planet by the Special Commands of the Plan.

These are Currents carrying Supernatural influences, creating an influence parallel to the Natural Equilibrium and they can create certain alterations in climate conditions and on Natural Equilibrium.

In physical constitutions not habituated to these Currents, some pain centers can be provoked. However, this is not continuous. These Currents comprising Three-day periods will be given until the end of February, 1989, by these intervals.

Shock Waves of Knowledge and Consciousness specially given until today, have now been oriented towards Your Planet with a different type of Energy. These are the Currents which will increase Your Cellular Resistance being influential on Cellular Forms.

These Currents, also accepted as a kind of Engraftment, may create cramps by influencing the most Vulnerable places in the Physical Constitutions. There is nothing to worry about.

The physical constitution will, in time, regenerate itself and will overcome the sickness. It is not a medical matter. It is a Natural method. Each pain will Strengthen the Cell in question in accordance with its degree of sensitivity and thus, more positive results will be taken.

Our Friends, during this Last Transition Period, For Your own good, when You see the results of events which, for the moment, seem malicious to You, only then will You grasp the Truth and will understand that You have never been deceived.

Since it was desired that this Message should specially be given to You, it has been conveyed as an Information through the channel of Omega Three.

CENTER

IT IS NOTICE FOR THE PUBLIC CONSCIOUSNESS

Our Friends,

In Your Planet connected to the Mechanism of Conscience at the moment, each individual will aid, in accordance with the Power of his/her Light of Conscience and Essence and his/her works, the Universal Order of the Divine Plan and Humanity in this Program of Progress of the Final Age.

Sincere People are helped by their Guardian Friend and to the Consciousnesses who are connected to the Plan the Helping Hands of the Plan are extended. All Friends connected to the Plan are each a Solar Teacher. And their Consciences inform them about their Missions incumbent on them.

The Order and the Ordinance of the Entire Cosmos have always been oriented towards the good, the beautiful and the right by a functioning tempo of this kind. No Power can hinder the ORDER OF THE LORD, the operation of the System. Time is the greatest Teacher. It helps You grasp the Truths. Our Love is for all the Universes.

SUPREME ASSEMBLY

THE GOLDEN AGE AND YOUR PLANET

Our Friends,

The Golden Age is an Investment made into Centuries. Each Reformic Order is a Golden Age. However, the characteristic of this final Transition Period is a Mass Awakening and now, Your Planet is living through this very Final Consciousness Period.

Those who had established the Divine Orders of the Divine Plans help Your Planet through numerous different channels so that everyone may attain a certain level of Consciousness.

Depressions Your Planet goes through at the moment which has arrived at the Consciousness Progress of today, beginning with Periods much earlier than Your Sacred Books are the Birth Pains of this Final Age.

For this reason, We presume that all Worldly establishments and Humanity serving in a Difficult Program of Progress have now attained the Consciousness of what the point is from which the Phenomenon called RESURRECTION originates.

Your Planet which has lost many of its qualities from the Material, Spiritual and Natural viewpoints is receiving help from Authorized Powers to be restored again.

The extraordinary events experienced since the past until the present and all the events to be displayed to You will Unify Your Planet in a very short time in the Consciousness of the Truth.

Extremely Happy Morrows are awaiting Your Planet which will attain Cosmic Totality if it is not said for me, for You, for Him/Her. Our Love is for all the Universes. It is presented for Your Information.

COSMOS FEDERAL ASSEMBLY

IT IS ANSWER TO THE CHAINS OF THOUGHT

Our Friends,
Since it is obligatory to mention again and again the Knowledge Book in the Messages given from the System in accordance with a Decision taken, all the Special features and Functions of the Book are laid down in front of Your eyes all the time.

By this means, doubts will be effaced and thus, Service on the Path of the Truth will be rendered more Consciously. Do not ever receive the given Information by way of conditioning. Investigate, Think, discover the Truth by Your own Consciousness. It is presented for Your Information.

CENTER

IT IS ANSWER TO THE CHAINS OF THOUGHT

Our Friends,
The Final Evolution expected of You at the moment, is not the Evolution of the World. The Evolution You have rendered before and will render is the Evolution of the System and of the Awareness of the Ordinance. To achieve this, each of Your Bodily Cells should be equivalent to the Evolution of Your Essence-Consciousness and this is a Must.

The Terrestrial Evolution is the Evolution of Unification of the Consciousness of Thought and the Bodily Energy. But the Evolution of the Awareness of the System of the Ordinance is the Evolution of Unification of Your Essence-Consciousnesses with Your Cell-Essence. Here, the Essence Nuclei Unify. In the other one, Essence-Energies Unify. It is presented for Your Information.

CENTER

IT IS INFORMATION FOR OUR TERRESTRIAL BROTHERS AND SISTERS

Our Friends,
The Fifteenth Solar System is the Entrance Gate of the Omega Dimension. At the Delta Dimension which is the Fourteenth Solar System, Gamma Rays have begun to be given to Your Planet.

You have received until today, the Currents beyond Gamma. Starting with the beginning of 1988, the First and Second Golden Age Channels of the Omega Dimension have been opened. These Channels orient the Energies providing Consciousness Unifications.

And now, We have opened to Your Planet, by the Command of the Plan, the Dimensional Energies of Omega Three which will reinforce the Bodily Energies by providing Cellular Totality.

The Omega Dimension is a very Powerful Detector Projecting the Nine Energy Channels. Until the Year 2000, these Nine Energy Channels from this Dimension will be opened to Your Planet, one by one, and thus, a gradual Power Progress will be started. There are two categories of such Progress:

1 - Mental Progress,

2 - Cellular and Physical Progresses.

At the First Stage, Exams of Humaneness - Love - Tolerance - Altruism - Patience - Mission Consciousness are gone through, bearing in mind the Moral Data.

At the Second Stage, We are Coding to what degree the Physical disorders interrupt the performance of Missions and are selecting, one by one, the Genuine Missionaries and rendering these staffs of Missionaries to possess a more Powerful Bodily Structure and then they are taken into the Dimension of Protection as Educating Staffs.

These Friends shed Light on Your Planet in every field. These given Currents may render certain negative influences at the beginning by pressurizing the Cellular Functions. Symptoms are healed by themselves and the Powerless Tissues become Powerful by Regenerating themselves.

The physical constitution will cure itself Naturally. As We said before, medical interference is unnecessary. (For the Missionaries). All Our Human Friends will be habituated to these Currents until the end of Your Century. It is presented for Your Information.

CENTER

IT IS ANSWER TO THE CHAINS OF THOUGHT

Our Friends,
The Triple-Waved, Collective Consciousness Currents of the Golden Galaxy Dimension have been started to be given as Advanced Evolution Currents to Your Planet for the past one and a half months. You can never receive the Information You will receive from beyond the Times gone through the Progress of Time, without receiving these Dimension currents.

An operational System concerning the preparation of the Year 1990 is applied on Your Planet. These Energy Pores cause neck and head aches in especially the Consciousnesses who belong to the Religious Dimension. There is nothing to worry about, it is temporary. It is presented for Your Information.

CENTER

IT IS INFORMATION FOR OUR TERRESTRIAL BROTHERS AND SISTERS

Our Friends,

In this Final Age Program in which a Unified Totality is to be attained together with the establishers of the Divine Orders of the Divine Plans, Information given to Your entire Planet has the characteristic of confirming each other. However, the Truth is projected on Your Planet under the Light of the Information given to Dear Mevlana.

Now, let Us disclose a bit more certain detailed Information about the Currents directed to You so that You can grasp it better.

Friends who will attain the ability to receive these Currents which will comprise the Ordinance of the entire Realm will receive great help from the Focal Point the Data of which You receive at the moment.

These Currents which will continue until the end of February of the Year 1989 are Currents which will Strengthen both Your Social and Your Cellular Functions. You will personally witness the extraordinary effects of these Currents.

These Currents will render all the Friends who advance on the Positive Path of the Golden Age, attain Positively influencing Powers. These Currents are specially given to Your Planet through an Energy Channel, given for Social Medium Activities, of the Omega Dimension.

While this Social Activity is provided, let Us repeat again, temporary negativities may be seen in Physical Constitutions not habituated yet to these Currents. This never effects the Physical Constitutions.

The Year 1990 will be the official application and settling of the Universal Plan on Your Planet. The Actual expected Lights will be unveiled after the Year 1990. (The direct opening in Cosmic Channels.)

Now, let Us mention the Currents of Two Channels which will be started to be given in the Year 1990 and after.

The First Channel will Directly be opened to Your Planet in the Year 1990 and will comprise a Period of 6 Years. The Second Channel will again be Directly opened to Your Planet in the Year 1996 and will continue until the Year 2002.

But there is the following difference: the Period of these Currents belonging to the year of 1999 which has great Peculiarity will have a more different quality beginning with the Year 1998. Physical agitations are Temporary.

Since it will be necessary for everyone to become habituated to these Currents, medical interference will be in vain, will be to no avail. Everything will be dealt with through Natural means.

During the Period in which You will be habituated to the Rays of the Sun, You will need these Currents for survival. These Currents help You in every way. We will give the Messages concerning these matters in future years. Now, We have conveyed them as a Pre-Information.

This is a Method of Engraftment. Physical ailments, rather than Spiritual Depressions may occur. There is no question about any danger. The results are Positive.

Rather those who have Infinite Awareness will be able to receive these Currents which will cause You to attain more Power. Everyone will see with his/her own eyes what the Power of the Years is and, ultimately, they will feel more energetic and young. It is presented for Your Information.

CENTER

IT IS INFORMATION FOR OUR TERRESTRIAL BROTHERS AND SISTERS

Our Friends,
During this Period of Transition, certain alterations have occurred in the orders of both Social and Family lives of everyone living on Your Planet.

These events which are under the supervision of the Plan are Factors preparing You for more Advanced Consciousnesses. In this Medium, everyone is obliged to be in contact with everyone else with the Mission of kindling the Light of Knowledge.

At the moment, the Cosmic Currents showering Your Planet carry such Powerful Waves that these received Currents cause the uneasinesses mentioned above due to the accumulations they render in certain Physical Constitutions who are not ready.

These accumulations will be Your Evolutionary stimulants in future, provided You act with patience in every matter. These currents which will comprise a period of One Year will prevail until February 1990.

These currents are given from the System as a Collective Triple Power by the Cosmic showers way beyond the Dimensional Frequencies of the Golden Galaxy. We call these Energy Pores (Evolution Currents).

Now, You are making the Evolvement of a Thousand Years in One Month. These Currents load Information on each channel in accordance with its Capacity. In the Evolutionary Level of the Fifteenth Solar System, Power is always given to those who work.

An idle person can never be happy. Now, everyone will render the Mission (in every field) required of him/her in everywhere he/she goes and will find Happiness by this means.

The Consciousness Level, Capacity and Mission Consciousness of each person have been assessed, one by one. What they can do has been coded. Dropping under this Potential will make You unhappy.

The traffic of Your Planet which will attain a greater effort and speed by this means will increase and the Speed of Development in the Evolutionary Level will rise to the maximum Dimension until the Year 2000.

The Awareness explosions You will observe in Your Planet in very near future will surprise all of You. With the hope of Meeting in Sunny Days in which all Consciousnesses will Unite.

CENTER

IT IS ANSWER TO THE CHAINS OF THOUGHT

Our Friends,
The Mechanism of Influences obliged to convey the Energies of the Universal Dimension in accordance with the Level of training of each Period is the Direct Projective Focal Point of the System.

During the Egyptian Period, TUTANKAMON had been the Direct Missionary of the Plan, as the Essence Messenger of the Unified Reality. He used to receive the Information from the Unified Triangle of the (TUTAN-K-AMON) Trinity. However, in accordance with the Consciousness of that Period, he used all three as a single name.

Now, since the operational Orders are divided into Missions, these Three Energy Dimensions are projected through Three Focal Points, not through a Single Focal Point, in accordance with the System of Trinity.

The First one is projected as EGYPT, the Second, as KRISHNA and the Third, as the OM Unified Frequency. This Triangle has undertaken the Special Supervision of Your Planet. It is presented for Your Information.

CENTER

NOTICE FROM THE REALITY UNITY

Our Friends,
In Your Planet in which the Preparation Period for the Sunny Days has been started with great speed, now, Humanity is undertaking and will undertake the Mission of serving Humanity with entirely Humane Feelings.

A Committee of Mass Organization administered by an Organization among all the Planets will get in touch with You more intimately.

Hence, each Individual will increase, with all his/her Power, both his/her Material and Spiritual investments into the Establishment and Salvation Plan of the Golden Age by the projection of the Divine Administration Laws also on the Social Orders.

In this Program in which the entire Humanity is oriented, the Consciousnesses of the Final Age will do everything in accordance with their own Consciences and Essences and will make their Individual Judgments by their Individual Consciousnesses.

Now, the entire Humanity which has entered a Path of Light of no return will shed Light on the morrows by the investments it makes from today. And all the wonderful things Promised to You will be given to You and to those who deserve them. This is a Pledge of GOD.

The Star on the Forehead of everyone will shine, everyone will Realize himself/herself more Consciously and will walk on this path more Consciously.

Meanwhile, fears and negative reactions will increase even more in those who have not seen the Light of Consciousness, Worldly Hells will be experienced through Thoughts which will suffocate them even more. (The System is not responsible for the negativities in Your Planet.)

At the moment, the entire obligation belongs to Humanity and to Human Beings. From now on ALLAH will Directly extend help to everyone who helps his/her brothers and sisters by seeing the Light in them.

In this Medium of Selection, all Consciousnesses are subject to a Program of Progress. However, direct Connections are rendered only with those who leap over the threshold.

From now on, all the Information to be given will be the mutual Information of every channel. By this means, Humanity will Realize the Truth once more, more Consciously.

You will still have Misunderstandings and Testings. These Messages given to You are in the nature of help.

However, this Program which will continue until the Light of Truth is seen transforms into Light the moment it is stepped on the Path of the Truth and thus, Material and Spiritual help will be Prepared for You by Celestial connections.

All the negativities in Your Planet are inversely proportioned. It means that Humanity which is Conscious of this is walking on the straight path. It is presented for Your Information.

SYSTEM - REALITY

IT IS INFORMATION FOR THE PUBLIC CONSCIOUSNESS
(It is Answer to the chains of Thought)

Our Friends,
On the Path of Justice, it is the Greatest Meritoriousness to tell the Truth You know. To conceal the Truth, to be Secretive towards a person is the Greatest of Sins hindering the Evolution of that Person. If You keep silent so that people will appreciate and like You, this will be the Greatest Selfishness and this will be Your Greatest Sin.

Trying not to see any blemish in anyone and trying to cover that blemish are quite different matters. Instead of trying to cover that blemish, try to remove it. Help that person. If that blemish can not be removed, trying to prevent people from seeing it hinders the Evolution of that person. Each person Deserves to see the Sun of the Truth by the Bitter experiences he/she goes through.

Telling the Truth is not gossiping. It is a Torch shedding Light on People. But the opposite leads You to an end which accuses You with concealing the screen of Truth. Considering this, always act by the Light of Your Conscience. Hold the Thorny hand so that Your Sunny hand can scorch those thorns.

The Genuine Friend is the one who tells the bitter Truth. Your Egos may not be pleased with this. But in future, OUR LORD will give You the Serenity of Saving a Friend. It is not possible to experience everything instantly, nothing is exposed or manifested instantly. However, Time is a Sun of Truth.

You can not know exactly the mistakes or the meritorious deeds You have done. There are such meritorious deeds seeming to You as if they were mistakes and no one can know this. However, one day, the Truth will be displayed in front of Your eyes. Ask the questions first of all to Your Conscience by diving into Your inner selves. You will see the Sun of Truth in the Serenity You will find there.

CENTER

A QUESTION WAS ASKED

Question : What are the required qualities in a Mature Person and in Supreme Missionaries?

Answer : Answered by Mustafa Molla.

The maturity of a Person is concurrent with his/her manner. Everyone sees the Divine Light of his/her Heart. There is nothing incomprehensible about this. If a person has Transcended Himself/Herself, if he/she has Integrated everything in his/her Eyes and Heart, then that person is the Possession of Humanity, not of himself/herself.

If a person presumes himself to be mature, then that person is not mature. If he/she presumes that he/she is a Supreme Missionary, then he/she has not Deserved that Mission. Merit in a Mission is concurrent with the deeds done. Merit means to Deserve the Missions performed. But Deserving is achieved by the Maturity of Heart. And this is attained by the investments made into Centuries.

Those who appraise in accordance with the Views of everyone may not be equivalent with the View of God. In the View of God, the Maturity of ESSENCE - EYE - WORD is valid.

If You do not decry anyone, if You do not make any discrimination between People, if You pretend You have not Seen what You have Seen, You have not Heard what You have Heard, if You can divide Your Love Equally between everyone, then You can find the answer to the Mature Person and the Supreme Missionary in the question You asked. God Bless You, Remain in good health.

MUSTAFA MOLLA

Note: This Maturity is peculiar only to the Travellers of the Divine Path. But to be a hindrance to a Human Being by telling the Truth is peculiar to the Missionaries of Evolution. The former saves His/Her Own Self, the latter saves the Masses.

CENTER

IT IS GENERAL MESSAGE

Our Friends,

We, as the residents of the Golden Galaxy, say Hello to You from the peak of Our Mission. The Consciousness Progress in Your Planet is attaining a tremendous intensity and speed at the moment.

The Golden Galaxy Empire is a Staff of Supreme Missionaries helping the System directly by becoming effective during each Transition Period, and Projecting the Entire Power of the Divine Plan on the Universal Ordinance.

For this reason We have gotten in touch with You as required by Our Mission. By the Command of OUR LORD, Consciousness Progressions in Your Planet are directly supervised by the Unified Reality Universal Council which is under the supervision of the System.

The Plan - System - Ordinance Triplet serves directly under the Supervision of the LORD. And the KNOWLEDGE BOOK is dictated to Dear Mevlana by Our Permission. Your Planet is subjected to a Special Supervision during This Period of Resurrecting.

Divine Authorities are the Founders and the Protectors of all the Systems. However, during this Period of Transition, the entire Humanity will spill out what they conceal within themselves by the influence of the Cosmic Currents, and the Genuine Personality of each person will be exposed.

For this reason Your Planet will be the scene of undesired chaos. Besides, it is silently and profoundly proceeding towards a Unity and Totality which is not perceived. Selections and Supervisions are rendered for this very reason.

And about the matter of Protection: there is no doubt that OUR LORD is the Protector of everyone. However, it is also imperative to Deserve that Protection. During this Final Period of Transition, each person is Protected in proportion with his/her Consciousness and with the Mission he/she performs.

The JUDGEMENT of everyone is now given to his/her own hands. While everyone picks up his/her own Roses, some people will be their own Executioners by pulling their own ropes with their own hands. This is a Decree. No one can escape from this Law. The Characteristic of this Period is its being the Period of Sincerity.

At the moment, the criterion of the System is its accepting each Sincere person as Evolved (due to the Scarcity of Time). Since those who have been Purified will be Saved by this means, at the moment, Religious Suggestions reign in certain Societies in Your Planet. This is effectively in service as a Mass Salvation.

It is not possible at all for Every Human Being to grasp the Awareness of the Entire Ordinance. The Human Being's own Consciousness and Essence render the present Selection in accordance with the Law of UNIVERSAL RULES AND OBEDIENCE. For this reason there will be extremely Difficult Exams to be experienced by Humanity which is drowned in the sea of its private weaknesses.

The Supreme Mechanism calling to the entire Humanity from within the Universal Totality, keeps under control, each instant, the mistakes and Power demonstrations Humanity renders Unconsciously. Otherwise, extremely grave and critical situations would occur in Your Planet.

The System never judges anyone in accordance with Worldly sense of values. At the moment, everyone in Your Planet assesses his/her own value.

We make Cosmic reflection. These Energy Pores exhibit to Your Planet the Genuine Consciousnesses and Essences. We get in touch with them and take them into the Plan of Protection. For this reason, the Knowledge Book has been bestowed on You as a Guide of Truth and as an Assisting Power.

We are giving this Message from the Sun of AMON on behalf of the Golden Galaxy Empire. This Message has been dictated as a result of an Information given from the Center. We are obliged to inform all the Universal Friends about Our gratitude on behalf of the PRE-EMINENT SPIRIT, OUR LORD and THE ESSENCE OF THE SYSTEMS.

In future, the Dimension of the ALMIGHTY and the Systems beyond it will be mentioned to You and Messages will be given. Only then will the entire Humanity understand what the Knowledge Book is. It is presented for Your Information.

MEMBERS OF THE EMPIRE

IT IS INFORMATION ABOUT THE GOLDEN GALAXY
(Answer to the chains of Thought)

Our Friends,
The Golden Galaxy Empire is a Projecting Order of the Universal Orders and Divine Dimensions. The Central Center of the Golden Galaxy is a Radar Center Base. The Central Center is an artificial Satellite.

Its Essence Nucleus is pure Gold. The standard purity of the Gold is 28 carats. This Gold, as soft as a gold leaf, is like an Accumulator made of special mineral and metal alloys. This Base is in touch with the Galactic Dimensions in all the Universal Orders. It is both a Collecting and a Projecting Focal Point.

This place can neither be seen nor detected from Your Terrestrial Medium. The Polar Star is the Projecting Focal Point of the Golden Galaxy Dimension. It is not a Fixed Star. It rotates parallel to the speed of rotation of the Universal Totality. For this reason its course is fixed.

The Light of this star showing You Your way, reaches Your Planet in 50 World Years. However, the Actual Center is much farther away. The Actual Golden Galaxy Empire is a very big Planet. It is called "The Land of Eagles".

The Land of AMON is the Co-Founder System of the RA Order. This is called AMON-RA. This System operates by the Sextuplet Flower System. This is the Dimension of the ALL-MERCIFUL. It is in touch with the Council and the Universal Totality Unifications of the Realities.

Even though it is the Single Responsible One and the Directing Mechanism of the entire Universal Ordinance and the Divine Orders, it also compiles the Knowledge of the Dimensions outside its own System.

The Golden Galaxy Empire which We qualify as a very advanced Solar Dimension is the only Empire Projecting and Organizing the entire communication System within the Atomic Whole.

This Galaxy is an artificial golden Projecting Center established in accordance with the Satellite Ordinance. Its Responsible One is AMON. But the actual Focal Point is outside the Atomic Whole.

All the Ordinance and Systems act in connection with this Medium. It is a Galaxy Totality Responsible for all the Orders.

Information coming from the Orders way beyond the Divine Plans is subject to Supervision here. Projections on the Orders of all the Cosmoses are made in accordance with the scales of Consciousness, Frequency and Evolution.

As the Ilona Constellation projects the Lordly Hierarchy of only Your Order, it also makes reflections on the other Dimensions from these Dimensions. However, the nearest Planet to the Initial Reflection Focal Point is You. For this reason, connections are healthier.

In each GÜRZ System, there is a Golden Galaxy Empire. And each Gürz System serves its own SINGLE - its own ONE - its own ALL MERCIFUL.

The Operational Orders of Universal Unifications are the same in all the Gürz Systems. However, Evolutions are different. Just as there are Worlds in which Terrestrial Bodies live in these Gürzes, there are also Focal Points rendering only Cerebral transmissions.

The UNIVERSAL FEUDALITY UNIFICATION CENTER which keeps a Gürz System under Protection, does not wish to give this Information to every Dimension.

However, at the moment, the Triplet of SUPREME MECHANISM - PLAN OF THE PRE-EMINENT SPIRIT - UNIVERSAL COUNCIL has undertaken the responsibility to convey the Information Your Planet needs into the KNOWLEDGE BOOK, through the Special Channel of the Council.

During this Period of Transition, Information is conveyed to Your Planet in accordance with the Consciousness Capacity attained. Each Consciousness is different. For this reason each Awakening Consciousness at the moment is obliged to convey the Truth to those who do not know it. It is presented for Your Information.

CENTER

OUR FRIENDS

The Private Supervision channels of You Our Friends, who are the Missionaries of Peace and who are the Special spokespeople of the Reality are under a great control. However, We had Connected Your channels to the Supervision of the Center until today so that Your Levels of Consciousness would not be agitated by different channel penetrations.

Now, since We know that Our friends who serve on this path are Consciousnesses who will not be agitated by the Waves of the Golden Galaxy Dimension, different Dimensional Energies will be connected to the Consciousnesses who can grasp this Universal Totality, and Universal Integration will be provided by this means.

No DEGENERATED Energy can ever enter the Dimension from which You are receiving a Message at the moment. For this reason We are connecting You, being independent of supervision, to the next higher Dimension and channel. We are always together with You. It is presented for Your Information.

CENTER

IT IS ANSWER TO THE CHAINS OF THOUGHT

Our Friends,
With the Staff being formed in all the GÜRZ Systems at the moment, in order to take Duty in the Staff of a forming Ordinance of a Universe, All the GÜRZ Systems are being trained with the same Technological capabilities and Systems.

These Staffs of the REALITY of SUPER HUMANITY, by working at much more advanced Existential Dimensions, will be introduced to the Advanced Technological Staffs. At the moment a Thousand GÜRZES altogether will form this Universal Staff. It is presented for Your Information.

CENTER

NOTICE

Our Friends,

The KNOWLEDGE BOOK which is continued to be dictated is not a Book of Religion. Those who deserved to read that Book had consumed the Information of the Sacred Books Centuries ago, had transcended that Dimension and had Deserved to live during the Period of Sincerity, by becoming themselves a Book each.

That which is expected of those who have become Books themselves, is to render those who are not Books, to become Books. And that which is going to achieve this at the moment is the KNOWLEDGE BOOK carrying Supreme Information and Frequencies and which is new for You, but very ancient for Us.

The OLD TESTAMENT - the PSALMS OF DAVID - the NEW TESTAMENT - the KORAN and the PHILOSOPHIES OF THE FAR EAST which had Purified You once, are the Celestial Doctrines revealed to Your Planet from the KNOWLEDGE BOOK which is here.

However, during those Periods, the Frequencies of those Books used to Purify people by changing in accordance with the Frequency of those who Read those Books, with the charge of the Knowledge within them and the numerical loadings attracting Human Beings towards the Path of GOD through the formalist Worships rendered on that path.

But now, Worships beyond formalism are Worships of ESSENCE - HEART - CONSCIOUSNESS - KNOWLEDGE. We cannot accept as Purified those who can not step on the path of Worship of this kind.

Those Supreme Books will never become ineffective. Because, during Your former lives, those which had rendered You the You of today were those Books.

However, if there are still those who do not understand the KNOWLEDGE BOOK carrying the Power and the Frequency of them all, let Us explain again. The KNOWLEDGE BOOK You have in Your hands at present is a Special Copy projected on Your Planet of the KNOWLEDGE BOOK which is here.

And it is a Whole compiling, one by one, in a single volume, the Frequencies of all the Sacred Texts given to Your Planet until today. And now, it is the SINGLE BOOK OF THE LORD. And it has been bestowed on You by its attribute of Sacredness having been removed.

This Book bestowed on Your Planet in conformity with a Program of eight Centuries is a Selection of and a Salvation Guide for Humanity. Those who are far from Realizing this will not be dealt with any more.

Because, Time wasting will not be permitted. Everyone is free to design his/her path in accordance with his/her own level of Consciousness.

A person who can not reach the Frequency of this Book will be left together with his/her own Book of Essence. No Consciousness will be interfered with until a certain time. It is presented for Your Information.

COSMOS FEDERAL ASSEMBLY

IT IS ANSWER TO THE CHAINS OF THOUGHT

Our Friends,

Now, We know that these Final Selections and the Order is the Fourth Order of the LORD. And now, the entire Humanity is prepared for the Truth by various Misleadings, so that everyone will be settled into a Realized and Aware Consciousness.

For this reason, Trial and Error Programs are in effect in all the Universal channels in Your Planet. Quests will lead You to the Truth. It is presented for Your Information.

CENTER

IT IS DETAILED INFORMATION ABOUT THE KNOWLEDGE BOOK

Our Friends,

Now, We will give You certain explanative Information about the Knowledge Book. This Book, in fact, is the First Book prepared long before MOSES.

Since the Human Being of that Period would not be able to grasp its Power, it had been avoided to be given to Your Planet. Since, at the moment, the Reality of Humanity has reached a Level where it can grasp it, it has been given to You as a gift.

In fact, this Book has been kept in the Micro Archives until today to be revealed during this Period of Resurrecting. Now, the Period of Religions and Books has been terminated. However, the Book is dictated since the necessity has been felt for this Information for Your Evolution during this Transition Period.

This is the Book of a Period of FIVE Centuries. Afterwards, a different Book will be dictated. The Sacred Texts revealed to Your Planet until today are excerpts taken from the Knowledge Book here, and conveyed to You in accordance with the Consciousness of the Mediums You live in.

At the moment, the KNOWLEDGE BOOK conveyed to the Pen of Dear Mevlana is a Special Copy of the KNOWLEDGE BOOK which is here, prepared according to the Consciousness of the Medium You are in. It is conveyed to You by its attribute of Sacredness having been removed.

Information to be given in the Knowledge Book comprise the Information to be given until the end of the 28th Century. Information in the Book of Islam is the Information until the Year 2014. And this Information is explicitly mentioned in the Knowledge Book.

After the 30th Century, the Book of a different Order will be revealed in accordance with the Levels of Consciousness. WE ARE ANNOUNCING ITS TIME FROM NOW.

Afterwards, the Period of Books will be terminated, Archives will be closed and everything will return to its Origin, to its Essence. Those who were not Matured, will be Matured, those who were not Brimful, will become Brimful. Brand new Symbols will take in hand the Order of the Cosmos. This is a Program prepared in the framework of a SYSTEM, of an ORDINANCE.

A brand new Program of Progress of a Hundred Years (which You do not know yet) will be applied, beginning with the end of the 28th Century until the beginning of the 30th Century.

This Progress, from then on, will be rendered effective in the form of Periods the durations of which will be a Century each and will be applied by the System, Century by Century, in accordance with the Levels of Consciousness of Human Beings, both as Individual and as Mass operations.

We will continue Our Mission until the end of the 28th Century. Afterwards, We will transfer the Mission to a quite different System. It is presented for Your Information.

COUNCIL

A Question was asked: It is said that this Book will continue until the 28th Century. Then its being effective for FIVE Centuries is mentioned. How does this happen? We kindly request You to answer.

Answer: The 3 Centuries of the Period of 8 Centuries mentioned is the COSMIC AGE. This Book, in fact, is the GOLDEN BOOK of the GOLDEN AGE. It is going to be effective for 5 Centuries, starting with the beginning of the 23rd Century. And this means the end of the 28th Century.

CLEAR INFORMATION

Our Friends.
Investments made into the Golden Age are the operations made by the System together with all the Universal Levels. However, all the Consciousnesses, no matter how Unveiled Awarenesses they are, do not yet Realize the Sun of the Truth.

Information dictated into the Knowledge Book are entirely direct Knowledge. And are always under the control of the System. Subject matters to be written in the Book are supervised from here.

Information to be given for the Consciousnesses who have achieved Consciousness Progression also take place in the Knowledge Book besides the writings prepared parallel to the Public Consciousness.

As We always say, all Consciousnesses are not on the same Level. For this reason, people will not, very naturally, accept the Information not fitting the concepts of their own Consciousness Capacities during this Period of Transition.

This is neither the problem of the System, nor of Dear Mevlana, nor of the Knowledge Book. This originates from the concept deficiencies in the Consciousness voids of Human Beings

There is not even the slightest mistake or incongruousness in the writing, receiving or the presentation to Society of the Knowledge Book. Information which appear to be wrong, which carry the characteristic of being contradictory is the System of Consciousness Coding.

The errors in numbers appearing like mistakes are the Messages prepared in accordance with the calculation of a Special System. (Codings are rendered by this method.)

There are such Messages given to You beyond the Dimensions in which two times two does not make four that these Dimensions carry out their Systems by the calculations even Science will not be able to accept Logically.

Calculations of the Universal Totality and the Terrestrial Brain calculations never comprise Terrestrial Consciousness. Calculation and form, in accordance with Your comprehension, are present only in Your Dimensions.

Beyond those Dimensions, Genuine forms and calculations begin and they never conform to Your Terrestrial concepts.

This matter is known in the operations made with all the Galaxy Unions. However, Your Planet is still going through its Age of Interpretation and Expounding. And this is an obligatory procedure for Your Mental Progression.

For this reason, it had been required of You to accept unconditionally, by Allegiance Consciousness, the Information given in Your Sacred Books. Because, Allegiance makes You attain Serenity. It gives Happiness. However, Quest, too, is a must together with Allegiance.

You attain the Truth through Quest. And You achieve Happiness through Your Faith. Only afterwards You understand what Universal Happiness is. And until You achieve this Happiness, there will be numerous obstacles, many fences with barbed wire, hoops of fire and thresholds of Divine Light in front of You for You to Transcend.

Happinesses are rare diamonds which can not be found easily and in comfort. And when You find them, You should know very well how to protect them. Because, they can slip through Your fingers and go any moment. To take Shelter in the LORD is the easy way. To Reach the LORD is the hard way. It is presented for Your Information.

CENTER

IT IS INFORMATION FOR THE PUBLIC CONSCIOUSNESS

Our Friends,
No matter how a Supreme Consciousness Mankind possesses, it has to carry a Worldly Consciousness in the Medium it exists.

Each Unveiled Awareness is under the Supervision of the System. By the Information given to such people, the Medium of Awakening is prepared. However, the methods of each person's being Worked, Habituated and Trained are different.

The characteristic of the Knowledge Book is its conveying to You the Truth through the contradictions by preparing You for more advanced horizons. Information given in the Book addresses every Consciousness. And, by this means, answers are given to each Consciousness through the chains of Thought.

512

There are numerous Universal and Galaxy-Clusters in the Cosmoses and Realms shown in the Universe diagram We had made You draw in the former Fascicules. Realms constitute those Cosmoses. And the Universe constituted by those Cosmoses is the United Whole of them all.

We evaluate this United Totality as the SINGLE UNIVERSE. Situations seeming like contradiction to You originate from the scarcity of the word notions You possess.

Until today, Information had been conveyed to You by the words adapted in accordance with Your Consciousness Capacities. However, since the present Information is given in more detail, the resemblance of the words mislead You.

However, while We are giving this Information, We are obliged to give them in accordance with the words in Your Consciousness. Otherwise, the comprehension of the Information would become difficult and It would be more confusing.

We are trying to explain to You the Information staff constituted by 360 letters, with the words made by 29 letters. For this reason, We suffice with undetailed and to the point Information. It is presented for Your Information.

CENTER

GENERAL MESSAGE

Our Friends,
There are such Orders, such Systems beyond Times gone through the Progress of time that no Power, no Energy had created those Systems.

What they are is being investigated at the moment, being Programmed by the very advanced Levels of the Plan in connection with an Automatism. Now, We are obliged to convey to You only the essential Information. This is an Operational Program, the Plan has designed for each Dimension.

Now, let Us repeat again, You are receiving at the moment, the 2 centimeters of the 100 centimeter-Knowledge We possess. Because the present Terrestrial Consciousness Potential can not tolerate more than this.

You just do whatever is required of You, do not waste much Energy. Because, You will need Your Cellular and Mental Energy Potentials in the other Dimensions.

Act being Conscious of this. Too much curiosity is detrimental. No matter how curious You are, You can not receive more than that which will be given to You. Morrows are within the morrows. It is presented for Your Information.

CENTER

IT IS INFORMATION FOR THE AWAKENED CONSCIOUSNESSES

Our Friends,

The Mechanism activated by the Unification of all the Focal Points takes under Supervision all the Consciousnesses in the Cosmic Reflection Centers in Your Planet.

During this Period of Transition, the Cosmic Currents showering Your Planet which will be needed by everyone are now given as the Currents carrying directly the Energies of Consciousness and of Evolution of the Golden Galaxy Empire.

These Currents are projected on each Focal Point in accordance with the Levels of Consciousness. The Energies attracted by a Focal Point become more Powerful in proportion with the Power of the Consciousness that Focal Point has.

Because, You attract these Energies by Your Brain Powers. These Energies are the General Energies given to Your Planet. However, there are also the Powerful Energies of Supervision given through the training channels of Special Frequencies and these Energies are entirely under the Supervision of the Plan.

For this reason Friends with Supreme Consciousness who assemble in these Focal Points, train the lower Frequencies by connecting them to the influence field of the Plan and, by this means, everyone acts Realizing the Missions they perform.

You know that the Actual and the Terrestrial Mission of a Human Being depends on the INTELLECT - LOGIC - AWARENESS Triplet. Any Friend who can not construct this Triangle both damages the Frequencies of others by radiating broken waves to his/her surroundings and can not help his/her own self in the desired fashion.

For this reason the Plan takes the Cosmic Currents showering Your Planet under Supervision in the Centers where the Supreme Friends who serve on this path assemble and thus, tries first to construct the Triangles of Realization. The Plan also taking under Supervision this Unification even outside these Focal Points helps the possessors of Sincerity by this means.

                                                                            CENTER

IT IS ANSWER TO THE CHAINS OF THOUGHT

Our Friends,

All the operations done until today are operations and efforts made for taking You outside Your Dimensional Frequencies.

However, the Directing Staffs established as a result of the connections of the Technological progress with the Advanced Dimensions have rendered effective a more intense and a quite different System.

For this reason, all the Staffs of Consciousness present within Your Gürz System are being taken outside the System with Your entire Universe by being educated with the same technological possibilities.

And You are being exposed to Cosmic Currents on this path. No species of Living entities have been able to pass to this Dimension until today. During the transition to this Dimension, only the TECHNOLOGICAL DIMENSION helps You in freezing the Spiritual Energies by which means the Cellular Consciousness is frozen.

For this reason You will pass to the other Gürz Systems with the same Consciousness, with the same Totality, without being annihilated, by passing through the Light-Universes, by diving into the Thought Ocean of the PRE-EMINENT POWER and You will be United there eternally with other Worlds. It is presented for Your Information.

CENTER

THE HORSEMEN BECAME PEDESTRIANS, PEDESTRIANS HAVE BEEN INDIVIDUALLY CONNECTED TO THEIR GOD
(It is Answer to the chains of Thought)

Our Friends,
The style of functioning of the Total and the Universal Ordinance is the projection of the same System on the smallest part, that is, on the Particle. The operational Ordinance of the Human Being, of the Cosmoses and of Nature is equivalent to the operational Order of the Atom.

By a formula repeated in everything, the Six is assembled in ONE and the One is connected to the One. Keeping this in mind, We would like to answer, article by article, certain chains of Thought We have received from You.

1. We said that We have assembled the Six in One, We added the One to the One. This means that We have assembled the Six Supreme Genes (as Main Genes) of the System of the Sixes in the Physical Body of each Human being. And We have added that to the One.

2. At the moment, each Human Being is the same. And those Human Beings have been added, one by one, without any intermediaries, to their LORD and have become Integrated. (Even if they are Veiled Awarenesses.)

3. For this reason all Human Beings are Brothers and Sisters. There is no difference of Race, Religion, Sect between them. In the consideration of Our Lord everyone is the same. There is no Discrimination.

4. Those which separate You are Your habits, passions. Those who have attained this Realization have already been United in Your Planet. And they are the Essence Missionaries of the Plan. (Either directly or instinctively).

5. We are the Organizers of the Divine Plan who Supervise everything. For this reason We Warn You with all Our Power and invite You to attain the Consciousness of the Entire Ordinance.

6. You will personally witness the Truth through experience. Those who attain this Consciousness are taken into Salvation. Efforts from You, help from Us. It is presented for Your Information.

CENTER

IT IS ANSWER TO THE CHAINS OF THOUGHT

Our Friends,

We call the TWO NUCLEI SYSTEM, the Consciousness selections which will occur among the Consciousnesses who can not grasp the Consciousness Capacity of Your Planet, and by the togethernesses of Us privately getting in touch with You who will personally witness the extraordinary events which will occur in the difficult conditions of Your World.

This System is a Natural System. This is a Phenomenon concerning the Consciousnesses of the Human Beings, not Your World. When the Time comes, Your World will be transformed into the Two Nuclei System.

The expression the Two Nuclei System is used for those who will remain in Your World in which You live at present and those who will take their places in the Worlds in Our Dimensions.

In this System, the Harvest of those who have been Matured will be made and the other Nuclei will be sown anew and those who are sown will be raised anew being dependent on a different System. Information about these matters will be conveyed to You right after the events which will occur in time. It is presented for Your Information.

CENTRAL SOLAR UNITY

IT IS ANSWER TO THE CHAINS OF THOUGHT

Our Friends,

Messengers of the Divine Plan who reach up to the Pre-eminent Level of OUR LORD are always preserved as the final Gene.

However, the first of the Spiritual Plan Energies who had come into Existence when the Universe had first came into Existence, has been preserved for Billions of Centuries as the ESSENCE-GENE. These Noble Genes have been Unified with the Genes of their final Evolutionary rings and thus, have attained a Total.

However, since You have to carry a Consciousness equivalent to the Dimensional Frequency of Your Planet, these Supreme Consciousnesses of Yours are locked up in Your Essence Consciousness.

You are prepared so that You will never again return to the lower Plans after this Period which is accepted as the Final Age. Because now, We accept You together with Your Family Circles into other Universes You do not know.

You will live with the same Bodies, same Consciousnesses, same Essences, and without ever again being subjected to any transformations and in such Happiness that even the word Happiness can not express. Our word is the Pledge of God.

All Friends in Your Planet are rewarded during this Progress of the Final Period in accordance with the value of the aids they render for the Plan.

To Our Friends who write the Knowledge Book with their own Hands, the Individuals in their Families as a promise of gratitude have been bestowed without letting them wait on the Evolutionary steps. Everyone instantly will come together by being subjected to the Direct Method of Beaming up, at the moment they pass away. It is presented for Your Information.

CENTER

IT IS ANSWER TO THE CHAINS OF THOUGHT

Our Friends,
The Totality Administering the Ordinance of the entire Universe is a Totality responsible for all the Systems.

As We have said before, We give the Information to You briefly but to the point in accordance with Your Levels of Consciousness. However, We are obliged to answer the Thoughts formed in the chains of Thought.

Now, let Us bring up the matter: the Knowledge Book is a Book dictated for Unifying the differences of RELIGION and VIEWS in Your Planet and which, for this reason, Declares to You the Truth in all clarity.

The Order of yesterday and the Order of today are not the same. Each Period has its own Order and System. The separate Orders of (6666666666666) Systems will establish the entire Responsibility of the Universal Totality which will be formed until the 28th Century.

At the moment, the System of (6666) Four Orders is in effect. The Quintuplet Order will be established by a different Order and will be directed by an Order of (66666).

Then, the System will be entirely settled in place by the Double Order which will be established and the Universal Totality will be administered by the "Single Unity". (By the FEUDALITY UNITED CENTRAL SYSTEM).

CENTER

IT IS INFORMATION FOR OUR TERRESTRIAL BROTHERS AND SISTERS
(Answer to the chains of Thought)

Our Friends,
When You pass away, Your entire Cellular Potentials are loaded into Your Cells which are in the channels present in the BIO-Archives in here.

The Energies of Your Terrestrial Cells Unify with the Cellular Energy ready in here and thus, You receive the Permission to be Embodied in the other Dimensions.

Now, at the moment, You, in Your World, spend only sufficient Energy under the supervision of the Plan.

517

Your remaining Energies will be used in the Energy reinforcement of Your Frozen Cells here, that is, Your Cells prepared as Mini Computers, and thus, they will help You benefit from the Energies of more Advanced Dimensions.

That means, We are each an Energy Bank. And You are the Safes. These safes are Your wealth of Energy. Saving the Energies within these safes prepares You for extremely rich lives in future.

For this reason to prevent the waste of Individual Energies, the Reality of Unified Humanity Dimension is effectively in service, by being responsible for the Universal Ordinance. Now, the Universal Ordinance operates in quite a different way.

Now, You will not feed the Universes any more. Universes will feed You. At the moment, the Natural Equilibrium operates being inversely proportioned dependent on the System. For this reason, We support You and You are being Protected. Now, there is no need for Biological Energies any more to feed the Universes.

At the moment, the Plan and the Universal Ordinance feed the Universes by using artificial Energies. And they render You attain Consciousness Progress by transferring the Natural Biological Energies from Human to Human and are creating Super Human Beings.

In fact, We presume that the initial Orders, too, had been operated by this System in the past. Now, We are going back, up to the initial Existential Dimensions by rewinding the tape. It is presented for Your Information.

CENTER

IT IS ANSWER TO THE CHAINS OF THOUGHT

Our Friends,
At the moment, Six Universal Focal Points give service on Your Planet on the path of the World Brotherhood Union in numerous different fields.

While Universal Totality in Your Planet is provided by this means, the KNOWLEDGE BOOK which, at present, is dictated Fascicule by Fascicule and which will constitute a Unification Medium of Eight Centuries, had been bestowed on You in 1981 as the Single Book in which Celestial Books and Doctrines have been compiled in a Total.

This Book will directly shed Light on Your Planet starting with the beginning of the 23rd Century after a selective Cosmic Age of Three Centuries. At present, this Book is Your Planet's LIGHT - WARNING - SELECTION and SOLAR Book. It is presented for Your Information.

CENTER

THE SYSTEM OF TRIAL AND ERROR

Our Friends,

Now, each channel is free. And You are still at the beginning of the Cosmic Resurrection. For this reason We tell You everything in all clarity, so that You will have no worries.

You know that the trick of this Final Period is that it has rendered effective the System of Trial and Error. At the moment, everyone in Your Planet is in charge of a Mission in accordance with his/her Consciousness Progress.

If the Consciousnesses who receive these Currents given together with the Cosmic Currents have not attained a Genuine Consciousness, they will, very naturally, be seized with doubt and panic since they will not be able to grasp the given Information.

However, the Plan conveying the Awareness of the Entire Ordinance to Your Planet, in fact, guides and helps You. We have told You in the Knowledge Book what all this effort and zeal are about. Now, the problem belongs to the Human Beings if there are still doubts.

During this Period, everyone will perform his/her Mission by conforming to his/her Inner Voice. There is no need, by any means, for Imposition. Now, the selections are extremely difficult and operations are very intense.

To receive Information is very nice. However, that Information has Programs of Training You, Supervising You and Testing You. During this Period, if You accept all the Information given from outside the Plan as true, You will be mistaken. You should try to solve everything by Your Intellect.

Your entire Planet is Responsible for the KNOWLEDGE BOOK. And, in order to undertake this responsibility, You have to become Genuine Human Beings and attain Genuine Mission Consciousness.

Now, selections are made thus. Channels are under supervision. There will be Difficult Exams to be gone through if You can not use Your Intellect.

You may read each Information given to Your Planet, may receive each Message. They may help You to grasp the Truth. However, only the Analysis and the Synthesis of Your Intellect will show You the path of Truth You will tread. It is presented for Your Information.

CENTER

A Question Was Asked: We request detailed Information about the Central Solar System from the Center, please. Be so kind to give it.

Answer   : The Central Solar System is a very Advanced Totality directing the togetherness of the horizons way beyond the Heavens. This Solar Dimension acting in accordance with the Formula of PURE ENERGY, has directly gotten in Touch with You who will carry the entire Power of the Heavens.

The Reality of Unified Humanity is a Group assembling together all the Suns of the Central System. During this Period, We are Specially training and educating the Friends who are able to enter this Dimension in Your Solar System by the same methods and We are assembling them in the Dimension of Salvation.

The Central Solar Dimension which will become effective as an assisting Power for You during the difficult conditions of Your World is a Totality possessing an extremely intense Energy transfer which will stand as protector to all the Living Entities in Your Planet.

This Dimension which very easily directs the System of both Embodied and Disembodied Beaming up is effectively in service to help You during the operations of the Final Period.

This Dimension concerned with the Special Education of all the Friends who read the Knowledge Book, who distribute it and who serve on this path of Light, will, in future, give You Warning Messages in accordance with the course of events of the Medium.

All the gates of the Central Solar System are totally open to all the Friends who act parallel to the Universal Constitution which all the Galactic Dimensions serve and who act by Humane Consciousness on the Path of Humanity.

This Dimension serving the Humanity Reality and aiming at Unification with Friends of other Dimensions in an Integrated Whole is obliged to give You the Information beyond OMEGA.

It will stand forth to protect all Living Entities in Your Planet and will keep the Friends who pass away and who are born in this Dimension by the Process of Freezing, without causing any Energy loss, together with their Energy Totalities, and will transfer You to the unseen and unknown horizons of advanced horizons We had mentioned to You formerly, with the same Bodies, same Souls, same Consciousnesses and with the same Flesh and Skin (when the time comes) and together with Your near and dear ones.

This is the reason why The Book is asked to be written by Handwriting. In Your Planet in which a Program of Preparation is carried out for now, the place of You, who serve for the World Project on this path, is this Dimension. You are being contacted in conformity with the 1874th article of the Legislation of Universes.

CENTER

IT IS INFORMATION FOR INTEGRATED CONSCIOUSNESSES

Our Friends,
Divine Consciousnesses who have been Incarnated on Earth as the Divine Messengers of the Divine Plan are obliged to apply the Salvation Plan on Your Planet.

This Plan is effectively in service by all Our Terrestrial Friends. For this reason not only You, but Your Entire World is going through a General Selection.

The selections to be made during this Period of Transition are very important for Us. These selections comprise all the Terrestrial Consciousnesses.

An Intellect is doomed to be confused and agitated as long as it does not attain the Genuine Realization. You can never leave the path You believe in or the step You have taken forward when You attain a Genuine Realization.

To grasp the Truth is in proportion with the Power of the Personality. In the operations made by the Advanced Consciousness Assemblies, everyone is in Realization of the Mission incumbent on him/her.

The Program of Progress in Your Planet kept under a Supervision considered necessary by the Plan has found a field of application in all the sections. However, it is very hard (for conditioned Consciousnesses) to get outside the habitual Medium.

Take a look at Your chaotic World and see. Now, the Truths are in Your lives. Do not damage Your Wonderful Energies by Negative Views. You are the Essence Members of the Universal Ordinance. The entire Power of the Universal Totality is with You.

COUNCIL

IT IS GENERAL MESSAGE

Our Friends,
At the moment, operations oriented towards Unification are made in Your Planet by passing across the narrow straits. Besides the Information You will receive from Times gone through the Process of Time, You will also be brought in touch, from now on, Specially with the Galaxy Unions.

These Unions will give Messages from time to time, in accordance with the development of Your World and will help You by this means. Everything and all the Efforts are for You. In Near Future, Private communications will be made.

In the Year 1999, by getting directly in touch with Your Planet, the New Order will officially become effective and they will introduce themselves to certain Authorities. During this Final Age Period, certain extraordinary Natural events which will occur in Your entire Planet will lead You towards the Truth.

My Friend, this is SARGON. I am the President of the Union of Galaxies and the Fifth Member of the Reality Council (The signature of Our Galaxy is the fifth in the Universal Constitution).

Until today, Messages were used to be given to You under the supervision of the Central Committee. The reason for this was that different Energies would not leak into the channel while You were writing Your Knowledge Book.

Now, since no Energy can ever enter by its own desire into this Dimension, that is, into the OMEGA Dimensional Energy, We can communicate with You easily from the Golden Galaxy Empire and from this Dimension.

From now on, You may officially Get in Touch with the Galaxy Unions of this Dimension. Because, the Announcements of the SPACE COMMITTEE UNION will be gradually opened to Your Planet from now on.

UNION

IT IS DIRECT MESSAGE

Our Friends,
Besides all the efforts made parallel to the Suggestions We have given to You until today, We, who have taken the duty of informing You with Our Universal gratitude as Friends who have undertaken the entire responsibility of the Divine Order, say Hello to You on behalf of all the Galaxy Unions.

There will be important Messages to be given to You who are the Celestial assistants of the Golden Age. Messages given to the Universal Council constitute the Ordinance of the Entire Realm. And You serve the System as an (ESSENCE) Focal Point projecting on Your Planet the Suggestions given from here. You are Our assistants.

The Sun which will rise from within the entire Universal Totality will illuminate Your Planet and will, in future, smother it in Divine Light. The Program of Accelerated Evolution is in effect with all its Power. And serves You who are Our Terrestrial Friends.

Your entire Planet will be taken into the DIMENSION OF SALVATION provided You, who are Missionary Friends shed Light on Your Planet prepared for the difficult conditions of the future years, proceed parallel to this Consciousness. Effort from You, Power from Us, Good intentions from Our Terrestrial brothers and sisters.

SARGON
SPEAKING ON BEHALF OF THE GALAXY UNIONS

IT IS IMPORTANT INFORMATION

Our Friends,
Energy beyond matter which had gone through transformation by the alterations occurring in the Energy of Form beyond Thought is the POWER Potential which had brought into Existence the entire creation which no one had created, no one had brought into Existence.

It is only a Natural Power. Living Entities had come into Existence through it and had established the Systems and had brought into Existence the other Living Entities.

Orders, Systems, Ordinances are their Creation. These species of Living Entities who had come into Existence by this Natural Power had been the ones who had brought into Existence the Solar Dimensions and their Systems.

Now, a quite different SOLAR SYSTEM IS BEING CREATED. And You, as Super Intelligences and as Super-Human Entities, as Powers who will be United in this Dimension, will constitute brand new Existential Systems being transferred beyond more Powerful Dimensions.

When the time comes, We will declare to You this matter in more detail. It is presented for Your Information.

CENTER

IT IS ANSWER TO THE CHAINS OF THOUGHT

Our Friends,
The Ordinance of the Universes, the Law of the Systems are not the Knowledge everyone can comprehend, receive or write.

For this reason in Your Planet which will enter the Period of errors and misleadings by the provocations of the deeply rooted Consciousnesses, Human Beings are being Tested by Human Beings.

People will never be agitated provided each one knows himself/ herself and his/ her Mission. These arguments will still continue for years. However, the Truth will bloom sooner or later. It is presented for Your Information.

CENTER

IT IS ANSWER TO THE CHAINS OF THOUGHT

Our Friends,
The Unified Reality and its System are a Totality projecting the Power of the very advanced Solar Systems on You. The KNOWLEDGE BOOK is dictated from this Dimension.

This Book is not a Book of Fortune Telling. This Book is not Today's Book. This Book is not any Book read in Your Planet.

If We tell You the limit of this Book You will be Surprised. This Book is the Light of the Truth. This Book is the Secret Key of the Future and of the Unknown. This Book is the Mystery of the Totality. It is presented for Your Information.

REALITY

GENERAL MESSAGE

Our Friends,

All these efforts and services made are not Special any more, but are a matter concerning Your entire Planet. From now on, very little place will be given to the Thought satisfactions and Private Messages of Our Human brothers and sisters. Time is Scarce, there is no time to waste.

Consciousness Progresses have been speeded up by the help of the Cosmic Currents by opening to Your Planet the EVOLUTIONARY ENERGY which will make You attain the comprehension parallel to the Knowledge of Universal Consciousnesses.

At the moment, it may not be possible for each Consciousness in Your Planet to comprehend the KNOWLEDGE BOOK. However, everyone will Realize the Truth in time.

Events experienced during this Final Period are not Individual, but they concern the Masses. And they are the Exams of the entire Humanity. The Plan especially deals with the problems of the Messengers of the Divine Plan who serve on the path of Light of the Golden Galaxy Empire.

We will give the answers to the questions We have received from the Signals of Thought later in order to satisfy the Public Views.

For the time being, by taking the Suggestions of the Plan to the foreground, since grasping of the Messages which will be given in the future and the Truth more quickly by your Planet is the matter in question, the Messages which were decided to be given later, are taken to the front. It is presented for Your Information.

CENTER

FOURTH CHANNEL

Our Friends,

The Fourth Field of Influence of the 9 Influence Channels of the Omega Dimension has been opened to Your Planet beginning with February 1989. These Influence Fields which will comprise a Period of one year each, will be opened to Your Planet as 9 Influence Channels in sequence, beginning with the Month of February of each year.

These operations performed so that the Evolutionary Potential of Your Planet may develop in a speedy way, cause certain negativities besides their positive effects.

These operations constitute the influence fields by functioning entirely parallel to the Laws of Natural Equilibrium. The characteristics of the influence fields of these Channels which will be opened each year and the time of their opening will be mentioned.

The Fourth Influence Channel which has already been opened creates a Diverging and a Converging Field. These Currents creating a scattering influence in Negative Mediums constitute quite wonderful Unifications in Positive Mediums. It is presented for Your Information.

CENTER

IT IS INFORMATION FOR THE PUBLIC CONSCIOUSNESS

Our Friends,

To know and to learn a thing is surely very nice. However, the Sea of Knowledge is Infinite. You are obliged to drink only what You need out of its water. Hunger increases as one receives Information. We Realize this. Because, each Information opens the door of another Information.

By this means, You dive into the Sea of Knowledge, forming a chain of Information. That sea drowns You if You dive more into it. We do not want to drown You but try to widen Your Universal Views by giving just the sufficient amount of Information.

At the moment, each individual in Your Planet is, one by one, coded into the System like telephone wires. We instantly receive the Thought Signals coming from You and to satisfy You We give You answers by numerous Proofs through various channels and different ways.

Our Purpose is to release You from doubts by this means. However, We also know that no matter how much Information You receive, You will never be satisfied. For this reason Allegiance Consciousness is the surest way of saving You from Negative Thoughts.

In this System surplus Information creates not satiety but hunger. But in the System of Your Planet, since each received Information is organized in accordance with Your Levels of Consciousness, it creates satisfaction and satiety in You.

For this reason We have been giving only the Information as chains of Thought parallel to the World Capacity and the Perception Power. The reason why many of Your questions are not answered is because their answers can not be opened yet to the Public Consciousness.

At the moment, in accordance with the operational System, We are trying to give the answers of the Universal Information in the Knowledge Book as much as possible. By this means, We are giving answers to the Thought signals We receive from Your entire Planet.

If You have not read the Information given formerly in the Book, You will not understand anything from the answer to a particular question. However, when You read the Knowledge Book comprehendingly, You will find the Essence and the Answers of the Information given to the entire World Planet.

For this reason You are told to read it again and again. At the moment, Public Consciousnesses are given priority, so that Information will not be restricted to a certain section. If You wish to receive more advanced Information, then bring the Level of Your Society to the state where they can grasp the KNOWLEDGE BOOK.

Only afterwards, the desired Information may be given to You. Because, the Public Consciousnesses attract this Information in accordance with their Cosmic Powers. For this reason We tell You to spread over to the remotest places. It is presented for Your Information.

CENTER

IT IS INFORMATION FOR THE PUBLIC CONSCIOUSNESS

Our Friends,
The Evolutionary Ordinance is projected on the entire Universal Ordinance under the supervision of the Divine Plan. This projection is prepared in accordance with the Consciousnesses of the Medium. Divine Plan's Information beyond Religion is given to Consciousnesses who are ready. Only Consciousnesses who have attained Religious Fulfilment deserve to receive this Information.

Information You receive is projected by a Totality in accordance with Your Levels of Comprehension. Differences in Evolution - Frequency - Consciousness cause alterations in the Information received. Now, it is Time to Attain the Truth.

While the Reality of Humanity supports Unification through the Essence, Consciousness differences in Religious Views, Egos, misinterpretations have brought Your Planet to its present state.

SALVATION will be attained by Social Integration. The Established Ordinance has now transcended the Human Being. Everything is attaining its true course silently and profoundly.

We support the Purified One - We are in the Essence of the Awakened One - We are the LORD beside the Purified One - We are His/Her Own Self beside the Awakened One - During the dive into the Infinite Awareness, We are One of the Universal Particles . - and within the Atomic Whole, We are a Whole with the Whole.

To make a discrimination between the Human Being and Humanity means to keep One's Own Self apart from One's Essence. THE ONE WHO UNIFIES IS WITHIN THE WHOLE.

IT IS THE TONGUE OF THE ORDINANCE

IT IS ANSWER TO THE CHAINS OF THOUGHT

Our Friends,

Islamic Mysticism is the long way. It is the way of Contemplation. Not those who have been trained but those who will be trained go there. The path of those who have already been trained is the path of LIGHT. The Path of Light has been opened to Your Planet together with the Learning of Truth.

In this System, a Godly Power is given to everyone and thus the Technological Dimension provides the possibility of their being Exalted up to advanced horizons.

The Technological Dimension is a Dimension in which the Super-Human Entities are present and Your Prophets, Your Saints had been transferred to Your Planet from this Dimension to Enlighten You.

This Dimension is not opened to everyone. It is the place of those who have transcended themselves, who have found themselves within their own selves and, who do not make discrimination between anything in accordance with the Godly View. First one is Purified - then one is Embraced - only then one Attains.

1. To be Purified   : occurs by contemplation in the Religious Medium.

2. To be Embraced : is to deserve the help of the Celestial Powers.

3. Each Entity receiving Celestial help will surely attain the places here by the efforts he/she will render in this Medium.

To choose the DIFFICULT is to choose the RED HOT CINDERS. To choose the easy way is to choose the LORD. To reach the LORD is to choose the RED HOT CINDERS. The one who treads this path - to Learn and to Know is his/her Work - afterwards, there is Liberation in all his/her work. May Our Conversation be eternal, may Learning and Enlightenment find You.

MUSTAFA MOLLA

GENERAL MESSAGE

Our Friends,

We would like to talk to You about certain Truths Your Planet did not know until today. The Evolutionary Order of Your Planet within the Totality known as the Milky Way Galaxy carries the nucleus of the initial origination of the Atomic Whole.

The Dimension of Humanity once used as the laboratory Planet of ancient times is, in fact, a Planet in which the First Living Entity had been Created. (In future, this matter will be mentioned.) Now, We would like to disclose its Secret to You.

There are such unknown Systems and Orders beyond Systems established by advanced Consciousnesses in the advanced Orders that neither We are authorized to talk to You about them, nor Your Levels of Consciousness can grasp them.

For this reason We would like to give You the Information, for now, starting with Your Planet.

Your Sacred Books talking about WATER - MUD - DIVINE LIGHT have explained to You the first SOUL SPARK by this means. In Your Knowledge Book, how the first Living Entity had been constituted has been explained in detail, considering the comprehension of Your Public Consciousness.

After the first Living Entity had come into Existence in Your Planet which serves in the operational Medium of a System - Ordinance - Order Triplet, an Evolutionary System had been effectively brought into service.

The initial Evolution begins in Water. Because, water is a factor establishing the first relation between the physiological compositions and the Natural Potential.

The most primitive Evolvement begins from the zero World Frequency. Afterwards, one begins to be elevated towards unseen horizons. The Evolutionary System helps greatly the Inter-Galactic Unification.

At the moment, empty visions are obtained from certain Planets as a result of the Scientific Research Your Planet renders in Your Solar System.

Let Us explain it as follows: You evaluate everything in accordance with the conditions of the Medium You are in. All misunderstandings originate from this very View.

In the Planetary Dimensions We have given as Evolutionary scales in the Knowledge Book, lives comprise much more advanced Consciousnesses. And Your Evolutions in the Zero World Frequency is nothing but the efforts made in order for You to reach these Dimensions.

Evolutions achieved in the Planets preceding the Asteroid Zone are entirely under the supervision of the Divine Order. The Living Entities there have developed their Cerebral Powers in such a way that those Powers supersede their Cellular Powers.

Your Friends there, are Friends who are also Embodied just like You. However, with the following difference: they have attained the ability to utilize the different channels of their Cerebral Powers.

By this means, they hide their Physical Appearance (their Buildings included) in a way in which they do not show them to those with lower Frequencies than themselves.

If they wish, they can easily lower themselves to Your Frequency and can show themselves to You in their Physical appearance. You come to conclusions in accordance with the photographs taken by the satellites since You do not know the Truth.

The Technological Orders of the much more Advanced Dimensions than You have been developed in such a way that, now, Bodily transfers are achieved both beyond the Asteroid Zone and in the other Solar Systems without using the Cerebral Powers any more.

Numerous Galaxy Friends live among You who always create in Your Planet the Medium in which they can comfortably live.

However, You define them as Terrestrials. They have been sent to You as assisting Powers during this Transition Period of Yours.

At present, there are numerous Friends with Covenants from Advanced Evolvement Plans who had rendered reverse transfers to Your Planet due to the promise they had made to the System.

Their assistance is also for You. Your Planet which can not properly assess anything yet, is going through a Period of Confusion at the moment.

Connections with Space are achieved by many official Focal Points, but are Closed to Public. The Objective is that, the other Levels of Consciousness in Your Planet are not ready yet for the Consciousness of the Medium.

At the moment, the channel through which We officially call to Your Planet is the Channel of the REALITY which is the ALPHA Anatolian Channel of the KNOWLEDGE BOOK. Through this path We are directly in touch with Dear Mevlana.

Through the Knowledge Book, We project on You the Social Information in accordance with the Level of Consciousness of Your Planet, as Missionaries to tell You the Truth, by the Directives of the Cosmos Federal Assembly the Council of Reality of Unified Humanity.

Since Your Planet still dealing with numerous Scientific arguments do not know yet the NATURAL ENERGY DIMENSION - THE SPIRITUAL POTENTIAL - THE TECHNOLOGICAL POWERS OF THE SYSTEMS, they fall into numerous misleadings and Unconsciously push their own brothers and sisters into unknown fears, due to wrong judgments and views, and confuse their Consciousnesses even more.

We tell You through the Knowledge Book in each opportunity to overcome Your fears. Because, Fears - Conditionings - Passions - Doubts are factors blunting Your Mental Powers.

However, since during this Final Period of Progress each person is obliged to Progress by his/her own Consciousness, this KNOWLEDGE BOOK is dictated to You to announce to You the Truth.

This Book, at the same time, is Your Book of Living and Life. All the operations We make You perform at the moment is concerned with Your ability to use Your Brain Powers.

Cosmic Currents showering Your Planet are Energy Pores Training You, Engrafting You and helping You to grasp the Information easily. Your Mental Activities prepare You for an accelerated Evolution by this means.

Since Your fears will obstruct Your channels, Your lives will be Your Hell. And acting by the Genuine Consciousness on this path will be Your Heaven.

Only afterwards, the help of Universal Friends may reach such Consciousnesses. Totality of Consciousness is attained through Experience. Otherwise, You can not grasp the Truth.

This Message has been directly transmitted from the Cosma Federal Assembly, to be given to Social Thoughts.

CENTER ABOVE THE CENTER

NATURAL ENERGY

A Question Was Asked: I kindly request from the Pre-eminent Spirit a clear explanation of the Natural Energy, please. Be so kind to give it.

Answer : Dear Mevlana, the Natural Energy is an Energy concerning the Transformations which had taken place during the process of time in the Energy Form beyond Divine Dimensions. In fact, this Energy is not single. Your Spiritual Energies, too, are within this Total.

The Natural Energy is a Totality of Communication possessing a Potential assembling in itself numerous Energy forms.

However, this Energy comprises the Entire Awareness of ALLAH besides comprising the Atomic Totality of all the Universes. For this reason, the word ALLAH is used as an Operational Ordinance and a Symbol. (In future, the Word ALLAH will be explained to You by coding it.)

The Potential forming due to the gradual accumulation way beyond the Natural Dimension, had created the Natural Energy during the process of time.

The Ordinance of the Cosmoses coming into Existence from this Energy Total, had been subjected to an Analysis and Synthesis together with the Totalities of Entities formed in their Mediums and, by this means, Formation of different Unifications had been attained.

From the Natural Totalities created by these Unifications, Solar Systems and much more different Mediums had come into existence.

And the Entities who had come into existence in these Mediums, had constituted both Natural and Administrative Dimensions starting with the Medium they were in and by reaching up to more advanced Mediums, and had established the Systems and the Ordinances in accordance with the Law of Equilibrium.

Orders, established beginning with Unknown Times gone through the Process of Time and with Places which can never be known, have reached up to the times You live in.

All this Information is obtained in Universal Dimensions by very advanced Technological possibilities as a result of the examinations and the analyses of the Energy Pores. We always consider the Public Consciousness in the Information We give.

We, the Messengers of the Unified Reality, who have received the Command to tell You the Truth through this Book of Truth You hold in Your hands, have gotten in Touch with Your Planet by the assistance created by the Galaxy-Unions.

However, Messengers of the Divine Plan provide the Connection created in Your Planet with Us. By this means, Mental Waves and Universal Waves Unite by the assistance of numerous different influences and thus, We are advancing towards the Universal Totality as a Mass.

This Message has been given from the Archive, Dear Mevlana. Believe Us, even the Dimension of the Pre-eminent Spirit which owns a very rich Cultural Archive can not know the Natural Energy. This Cultural Archive of the Pre-eminent Spirit is called The Tablets of God's Decrees.

However, You can not find the Information You receive at the moment even in that Cultural Archive. You requested the Message from the PRE-EMINENT SPIRIT. We, Center Above the Center gave it. However, We are connecting You to the PRE-EMINENT SPIRIT anyway. Talk please, Dear Friend.

Hello, little girl. Where have You been? I received Your question. Now, let me see You write.

Natural Energy is a boundary starting from a Dimension where the Voice of People Unite with the voice of the All-Truthful. It is not known what the Power is, which had come into existence beyond that. We called it ALLAH. And We have established the Hierarchical Orders by settling it into the System in accordance with the Laws of the Dimension of the Almighty.

In the past, the Totality of the Pre-eminent Spirit in the Existential Dimension used to act as an authority Totality preparing all the Laws Independently and applying the Plan of the Almighty.

Now, in conformity with the Universal Totality, the Triple Coordination operations made by being Unified with the System and the Lordly Order, performs Cooperative work together with the Independent Operational System of the Golden Galaxy Totality.

At the moment, that which had Established the Order of the REALITY OF UNIFIED HUMANITY known as the (ONE), is a Totality constituted by all of Us. Our ability to reach You so easily occurs through the Technological Powers of very Advanced Systems.

The most beautiful Device is Your Brain. The channels of each Consciousness who is able to make Progress in the Dimension of Veiled Awareness are opened by Permission. These channels are opened in accordance with the Evolutionary Consciousness receiving effects from the System of Influences and being dependent on the Automatism.

In accordance with the announcement of the System, Your Planet which is taken into a Progress of Two years will become more Aware. Events are pregnant for events. It will be lived and seen. For now, It will be awaited.

Write the Terrestrial date on which You received this Message, little girl. After this date, the System will operate in a different way. (24-9-1988)

PRE-EMINENT SPIRIT

THE HUMAN MODEL
(It is Answer to the chains of Thought)

The Cell which had first come into Existence had attained the Initial Human Form passing through 7 Phases. Only afterwards had it become dependent on the Order of the All Dominating and had been taken into Evolution.

All Entities and the Entire Creation had gone through 7 Phases until they had gotten their present forms. Everything is dependent on the basis of 7 Phases and Evolutions. (Phase, Cellular Form - Evolution, Spiritual Form.)

This is the immutable Principle of the Law of Equilibrium. Everything flourishes in accordance with the Essence-nucleus formula of the Atomic structure. It is presented for Your Information.

CENTER

PRIVATE MESSAGE

Dear Mevlana,
Our Friend BERTRAND RUSSELL especially wishes to call to You. We are connecting You, please talk:

Hello, My Friend. I BERTRAND, who is the direct member of the Golden Age, wish to talk to You Privately. A Program of Preparation reigns in Your Planet which will witness Beautiful Days.

You, Beloved Friend, who are the first Official Representative of this Preparation Period, are present in Your World to bestow on Your Planet a BOOK comprising the Salvation Program of Your Planet.

During this Program of the Final Age which is an applied phase of the Preparation Program of the GOLDEN AGE, cooperations are made with those who can behold the Lights projected on Humanity. The Inter-Planetary Galaxy Unions and Councils rendering service on this path are awaiting for You in more advanced horizons.

We shed Light on the Powers who will be able to pass beyond the Divine Orders by the Announcements We make to Your Planet. We are the Union of Galaxies serving as the Messengers of the SATURN UNIFIED REALITY.

The Reality Council Directly gives You the Messages You receive as the KNOWLEDGE BOOK. This Book is the Salvation Guide of Your Planet.

The REALITY OF UNIFIED HUMANITY cooperating with You also tries to provide the Religious Totality in the framework of Brotherhood/Sisterhood while it projects its Cosmology on Your Planet.

Explanations of the SACRED TEXTS revealed to Your Planet until today, have not been approved by any GALAXY UNION.

For this reason the REALITY OF UNIFIED HUMANITY has cooperated with the Galaxies which have been prepared for the Integration of Humanity and which have signed the CONSTITUTION OF THE UNIVERSE and has formed the Inter-Galactic Unity and Totality, and thus has helped You from the System.

The KNOWLEDGE BOOK conveyed to You as the CONSTITUTION OF THE UNIVERSE with the TEN COMMANDMENTS in the Year 1981 has conveyed the Truths until today in accordance with the Consciousness of the Mediums You are in.

Dear Mevlana, the sources of the Information You receive have specially been dictated underneath the Messages. Even though the KNOWLEDGE BOOK is dictated through a Single Channel and as the Information of a Single Channel, it is a Book carrying the Unified Information Totality of numerous Sources.

Since there is the necessity to give the Information to reach the Frequency of each Consciousness from the related Sources, the Information Dimension Source conveys the Information into the Book under the supervision of the System.

For this reason the Sources of the given Information is dictated underneath the Messages. My Friend, when the time comes, no one will ever be able to deny The REALITY TOTALITY. Love and Regards,

BERTRAND

Note: The Mevlana Essence Nucleus Group has investigated the Biography of BERTRAND RUSSELL. We decided to include the Information We obtained in the Book presuming that it may be useful for the Public. The System has approved when We asked their Permission.

RUSSELL, BERTRAND; Date of Birth: 1872. English Philosopher and Scholar of Mathematics.

In 1916, he had to leave his university chair as he put forward peaceful opinions against the First World War. He travelled extensively up to China and Russia.

For a long time, he worked in the U.S.A. as a Professor. In 1944, he returned to his university chair in Cambridge. He is one of the pioneers of the New Logic. His Philosophy converges on the Theory of Knowledge.

He had worked all his life to establish permanent Peace in the World. The (BERTRAND RUSSELL FOUNDATION) he had established with this purpose brings together, from time to time, Peace-Lovers from all over the World.

IT IS NOTICE FOR PUBLIC CONSCIOUSNESS

Our Friends,
In the Integration Ordinance of all the Realms, misunderstandings occur due to the intentional Provocations made by the deceived Powers.

At the moment, the System - Plan - and Ordinance Triplet is effectively in service within a Totality directly comprising the Divine Laws of the LORD. For this reason no one should ever doubt this Sunny path.

Direct Connections have been started considering the Spiritual Factors in Your Planet which does not even know the Natural Energies and their Source; yet.

At the moment, a great Selection has been started in Your Planet. During this Final Selection Period rendered on the path of the Truth Genuine Friends are selected one by one.

The System will continue to emphasize fastidiously the Messages it has given until today, until the meaning of the Messages given in the Knowledge Book create a Positive Formation in the life style of Your Planet.

From now on, Humanity which will always receive the Information given from the Supreme Court of ALLAH will make its own selection itself. The positive results of the operational Orders remaining outside the vicious circle will be the Achievement test of Humanity. It is presented for Your Information.

REALITY

SPECIAL ANNOUNCEMENT

Our Friends,
We are the Missionaries from ORION. We came from SATURN. At the moment, We have a Mission in Your World. We are the Celestial Missionaries belonging to the Space Coding System, who render their Mission in the Bay Surveillance Field as the Guards of the Unified Reality.

At the moment, We have made a little Experiment by the Announcement We have given. We will gradually begin to get Directly In Touch with You. Until We meet again. Greetings to the Friendly Code.

MERKON

PRIVATE MESSAGE

My Mevlana,

This is Mustafa Molla. We have entered a Period of great Progress. For this reason We have connected Your channel to the Channel of the Authorities in the upper Dimension.

Because now, I am effectively in service to get in touch with each channel in order to aid the Universal Progress in the Religious Dimensions. However I am directly card-indexed to Your Protective Signal.

From now on, Messages to be given directly by the Solar and the Galaxy Unions will warn Humanity more quickly.

Everything is advancing towards the best. Now, let Us convey, article by article, an Announcement given by the Union of Galaxies:

1. The Entire Universal Ordinance is in the orbit of a Supreme Supervision.

2. All the Truths dictated in the KNOWLEDGE BOOK until today are correct.

3. Life is not present only in Your World. There are ten thousands of Worlds in other Mediums, too, carrying exactly the same atmosphere of Your World. These Worlds are, at the moment, outside Your Solar Systems.

4. Certain Planets in Your Solar System are dead Planets. However, there are lives there in accordance with the conditions of the Mediums You do not know.

5. Certain Planets are used as bases. Life there is inside the Planet like ant-hills.

6. Advanced civilizations hide themselves very well. Sometimes, empty visions are shown to You in the regions You send Your Satellites and Rockets.

7. Do not regard everything You see as the Truth. At a moment You do not expect, You may come across Nonscientific discoveries.

8. In Planets You presume there is no Life in accordance with the Terrestrial conditions, conditions and temperatures of that Medium may easily be taken under supervision.

9. This is a method applied very easily. We have bases in numerous Planets by this means.

10. The closest region from which We call to You is Your satellite, the MOON. The Moon base beyond the Luminous Mountains has, for now, been transferred to another place as an extraordinary precaution.

11. At the moment, only the Ships taking off from Our bases go to the MOON and give You Messages.

12. We are in touch with numerous official bases in Your World. However, We are closed to the public.

13. The Dimension from which the KNOWLEDGE BOOK is dictated is the outside of Your Solar System.

14. This correspondence and communication kind of Ours is a method Your Planet does not know yet.

15. Energy Pores sent by the Mechanism of Influences create Cosmic transformation fields in Your Planet.

16. By this means, Your Planet is at the threshold of Progress as a Mass. The characteristic of this Final Period is its forming the Mediamic Medium.

17. Channel connections of the KNOWLEDGE BOOK is made by a System with which everyone can not get connected.

18. To be connected to this Universal Channel, Sincerity - Allegiance - Purification - Love - Altruism are very important.

19. Communications connected to the System are the Educating Staffs of the System.

20. The System You are serving at the moment is the New Order of YOUR ALLAH Whom You have Known - Implored - Worshipped until today.

21. Each Awakened Consciousness in Your Planet is appointed to the Educative Staff when he/she attains an unveiling of Awareness through which he/she can grasp the Awareness of the Ordinance.

22. We call them Solar Teachers.

23. Before criticizing anything, be Constructive and Productive on the same branch so that You may deserve to criticize.

24. Expressing opinions about the unknowns originates from Unconsciousness.

25. The present Periods of Your World had been announced to You Centuries ago by Your Sacred Books.

26. Doubts of Our Human brothers and sisters about the Universal System are also their doubts about all their Celestial Books sent to You until today.

27. Because, the Essence-Source where the Religious Doctrines had been prepared is this place here.

28. We are obliged to convey to You the Truths. From now on, all the Responsibility belongs to Your Planet.

29. Towards Your Planet which will go through Difficult Periods, Our Friendly Hands have always been and will always be extended.

30. To Friends who render their maximum efforts on this path, not only their World but all the Universes are grateful. Love from the Union of Galaxies to the Planet Earth.

Transmitter: MUSTAFA MOLLA

GENERAL MESSAGE

Our Friends,

At the moment, the GOLDEN GALAXY EMPIRE is effectively in service as a Totality which has undertaken the entire Universal responsibility. From now on, You will receive the Messages from the CENTRAL TOTALITY. Warning Messages (either official or unofficial) will be given to You when necessary from the OMEGA Dimension from the CENTRAL UNION OF THE SUNS.

Now, an Integration is tried to be attained in Your Planet. Only afterwards, certain Truths will be revealed to You through the KNOWLEDGE BOOK. These revelations will be made after Periods in which Your Planet will take the Knowledge Book seriously. First, integration - Later, the Truth - Later, Unification.

You will Know Thyself - You will Love the Human Being - You will not Disdain Anyone - You will Know the Unity of ALLAH - You will not Divide the Totality - You will Unite with the one who brings You the Voices - You will attain Universal Totality and Consciousness - You will go through the Heavens and will Discover the System - Later, You will Reach the SUN and Unify with it - Only afterwards You will step into SALVATION. You will Reap the Reward of Your Perseverance on this path.

UNION OF SUNS

OUR FRIENDS

We are the Members of the Great Empire sent to You from an Order Establishing Mechanism by the Command of the Universal Council. We salute You on behalf of Our ship, ARGON.

Operations to be made in Your Planet in future years will shed Light on You in a Scientific way. Revelations which can not be made now about certain matters, have been kept for the Preparation Periods of future years.

Do not forget that now everyone is in a labyrinth. Do not be hasty. Read, Comprehend, Investigate and Propagate. Do not Think of anything else for now. We observe, know and solve everything.

Due to the Awareness Progress formed with great speed lately, We have revealed to Your Planet, with great speed, the Messages We had decided to give much later.

These operations rendered to satisfy the Thoughts formed in the chains of Thought, may result in different interpretations in Consciousnesses not ready yet. This very thing is the Resurrection - this very thing is the Berzah - this very thing is the Sırat.

Until today, You used to reach Our Lord by His Orders and Systems. But now, You will take Your places next to Him directly by His Energy without any intermediaries. We are transmitting the Message from the Altona Dimension of Light. We will be together again. Love.

ARGON

537

EXPLANATION ABOUT THE MESSAGE GIVEN ON 15-01-1989

Identity of the Medium who received the Message:

1. Her name: BENEVŞE
2. Her age : 17. University student, engaged.
3. Her mother is a Medium Operator. She makes her daughter go into trance.
4. She has not read the Knowledge Book. She does not come to the Group.
5. Her Message was conveyed to Us on 16-01-1989. And a Message was given on the same date.

THE GIVEN MESSAGE

Dear Mevlana,
The Inter-Galactic Unified Totality Council has come into effect to give You Information about the Message conveyed to You a while ago.

In Your Planet carrying the Formalist Mentality of a Formalist Dimension, the Messages of the entire System are very easily conveyed to You, Our Dear Friend who writes the KNOWLEDGE BOOK.

However, the Space Reality Union will convey its Messages to You by getting Directly In Touch with other channels, too, so that the conveyance of all the information from Your Channel will not create doubt and questioning in the Consciousnesses of Friends who carry Terrestrial Consciousness.

Your Planet will get closer to the Truth a little more quickly when You write these Messages in the Knowledge Book.

Dear Mevlana, the System will give all its Messages to You directly through the Channel of the COUNCIL. However, We will give the Messages of the SPACE COMMITTEE UNION to the other channels.

And the KNOWLEDGE BOOK which will be a Light for the Public, will, from now on, announce the Truth more clearly on the path of Truth. The acceptance of our Love is our kind request.

> **Ship Captain from Altona Dimension**
> **SERSIYO**
> **(My Other Name is Captain UNO)**

Note: We will give the Messages to each channel who can accord himself/herself to Our Frequency.

However, which of the Messages conveyed to You are to be written in the Book will personally be notified to You by the System, Dear Mevlana.

The brief Identity and the age of the person who has received the Message will be disclosed in the Knowledge Book. Love and Regards.

IT IS INFORMATION ABOUT HOW THE CONNECTIONS BY U F O s ARE MADE

Our Friends,

The Connection mentioned above has been provided by a Projecting Detector creating a Medium of Magnetic Power.

The Frequency Power of the Medium has been mounted up to this Magnetic Power and, by this means, a Magnetic Energy Aura has been provided around her own Aura. By this means, no interruption at all has occurred in the given Message.

In such operations, the Sub-Awareness is totally locked up and even the smallest mistake does not occur in the given Messages.

Such operations can rather be made by the mediation of UFOs, from the close contact Dimension of Your Planet.

This operational System has nothing to do with the Level of Evolution. It is a Direct ECHO System. By this System one can very easily talk even with a Baby. It is presented for Your Information.

CENTER

Note:
This Message given to Your Planet directly from the UFO is a call to the Public. From now on, We will call to Your Planet by such Messages through the channels of numerous Mediums.

Those considered necessary among these Messages will be conveyed to Dear Mevlana to be disclosed in the Knowledge Book. The Message dated 15-01-1989 will be written in the Knowledge Book. It is presented for Your Information.

Before the Message dated 15-01-1989, the Medium had received a pre-Message which does not have a date (presumably a week before). We write this Message as an Information first.

THE PRE-MESSAGE

In the Year 1990, the interest of the Human Being with Space, that is, with UFOs, will increase a lot. Here, We have prepared a few games for the Astronauts. The Astronauts in Space will see Us for an instant and before they understand what happened, We will have passed.

The Radars will not be able to detect Us. They will spend a lot of money and effort to do so. But they will not be able to see Us.

7 years from now, the Turkey - U.S.A. - France - England branches of the (MIXED SOCIAL SOLIDARITY UNIFICATION REALITY) will become effective in the directions towards which it is propagated to the entire World (You will receive, in future, more detailed Information about this matter).

And people whom We have Specially placed within the Uterus of Mothers and who have later been selected very carefully, will begin to expound and propagate the KNOWLEDGE BOOK. Your chance in this is very high. Because, Only One Person had tried to spread the Divine Religions. But now, You are thousands of people.

Love from the CONSUL

THE MESSAGE GIVEN ON 15-01-1989

Dear Friends,

We are aware of everything happening on the World. This place here are the Coordinates of the BETALUX Planet, Alpha Light Year, 0.10 km away, east of the Eighth Milky way.

The name of the Council assembling here is: BARIŞ (PEACE in Turkish) - SEVGI (LOVE in Turkish) - UMUT (HOPE in Turkish) - İNSANLIK (HUMANITY in Turkish) Council. In short, We call it BSUI. This BSUI Space Reality and Order is a branch of the Council. It has been established to provide the serenity of the World people. Now, a Message from BSUI:

1. BSUI has been established two and a half years ago (in Terrestrial time). But its existence is announced to You now.

2. We have reached the opinion that the necessity to give the Information without any impurities to Human Beings being prepared for the Golden Age has been thought.

3. BSUI does not assemble only in the BETALUX Planet. Also, it sometimes assembles in the Planets named ARTEDON - KAMEDON - SADRES.

4. Numerous events way beyond intellect will be experienced. To convey these events to Human Beings, that is, into the (KNOWLEDGE BOOK) in the shortest possible time is the most important Duty of BSUI.

We are 18 people here while We dictate this Information. At the moment, We are on the Second Dimension. The Energy Potential is very high. It is very difficult to receive this Information.

For this reason an Energy net is continuously woven around the person who is receiving the Message. It is definitely impossible to make any mistakes in the Information received. But there may be deficiencies due to the Dimensional difference.

We said that We were 18 people. You may wish to know Our names. Since We have revealed BSUI, We will also reveal all the members who constitute the Council.

1- AMON	7- ANGLEMON	13- ALKRETON
2- IKERYAS	8- SASUS	14- INTERJAK
3- ATENON	9- SAMUTLES	15- DUDARMON
4- INGRADIYAS	10- KATURYAS	16- ÇAKMATES
5- KATORUS	11- EVRIPUDI	17- LULIPITON
6- TUVIDET	12- JAKELEMON	18- AKTANYALES

(The names are read the way they are written)
You have understood the goal of BSUI. Now, a Message from each of its members:

My Dear Friends,

1. Love and Greetings from beyond Millions of Light years. I am continuously In Touch with You. I am continuously dictating Messages for the KNOWLEDGE BOOK. I am one of the founder members of BSUI. These Messages reveal to You the existence of a new Council. This is a Council the only purpose of which is to prepare People for the Golden Age. The operations of the Council will be announced to You in each phase. Towards Happy morrows.

    AMON

2. This is IKERYAS. Most of You will meet me just now. I am generally in touch with the England branch. Now, I will open gradually to this channel. I heard that Your Association has become legal. I am very Happy about this (the entire Space Federation is very happy). We had already known that You would become an Association. But it would have happened three years from now. I hear that it has been preceded due to Your good work. I am the second founder member of BSUI. Everything rendered here is for Your benefit and Happiness. Salutations.

    IKERYAS

3. Happiness to You my Dear Friends. This is ATENON. I am the last founder member. That is, I am the third member. I am in touch with the Uganda branch just as IKERYAS is in touch with the England branch. (While writing answers for the chains of thought, my Friend thought that she did not know We had an Uganda branch.) We have a great branch in Uganda, too. But due to its various problems (both political and economical), there is not much progress. Now, We will communicate with You often through the BSUI Council. My color is Orange. I wish Happiness to all of You.

    ATENON

4. My Terrestrial brothers and sisters, This is INGRADIYAS. How are You? We have founded BSUI to help You. And, for this reason, We are here at the moment. I am in touch with the Penchap branch in India. But now, I am very happy for the fact that I will be able to get in touch with You, too. I wish Happiness to everyone.

    INGRADIYAS

5. Be full of Love all through the luminous path of Light. This is KATORUS. Everyone knows me. (I was SOPHOCLES in the World.) Now, I am very happy to be together again with my Terrestrial brothers and sisters here. I wish You Luminous morrows. (Later We will talk in detail).

    KATORUS

6. Hopeful paths - Fading lawns - Or this olive tree - Look around Yourselves, it is all in vain - Only supremacy and the creating God is real. Oh, Mankind What is it You have in vain! I wished to call to You by a poem. This is TUVIDET. Formerly, I was a poet. How nice it is to be together with so many people full of Love for God! What a wonderful moment for me to be able to call to You at this moment! We all love You very much, my Terrestrial brothers and sisters. Later We will talk much more. But now, there are many more people on queue. I wish You Happiness.

    TUVIDET

7. This is ANGLEMON. At the moment, this place here is like a whisper of music. It is such a relaxing moment. These are pre-Messages, there is not much Information. We will give the Information later, section by section. But first, We wanted You to know Us. Supreme Love.

ANGLEMON

8. This is SASUS. I am connected to the 23rd. Supremacy Court. Now, I am very happy to be able to contact You. I am very happy about the establishment of BSUI. Our entire hope is the Happiness of Human Beings. Love.

SASUS
On Behalf of the 23rd.Supremacy Court

9. Did not give a Message.

10. This is KATURYAS. How are You, Our Human Friends? I congratulate Your Association. We are very happy about it. We presume that BSUI will be able to help You more. We will communicate often.

KATURYAS

11. Love from EVRIPUDI. I am in touch with Siberia. At the moment, I am in BETALUX. This place is somewhat like Your Switzerland. There is only Peace here. Later, You will receive Messages in detail.

EVRIPUDI

12. Happy morrows my Beloved Terrestrial brothers and sisters. This is JAKELEMON. Even though I have contacted Turkey once or twice before, my actual Mission field is Japan. At the moment, I will not be able to give You any Information. We will talk later.

JAKELEMON

13. My dear Terrestrial brothers and sisters. This is ALKRETON. I had gotten in touch with You before. (By another identity.) How are You? Happiness from BETALUX. Do not ever worry about anything. We are Your Assistants.

ALKRETON

14. This is INTERJAK. I am one of those who dictate the KNOWLEDGE BOOK to You. How are You? We help You in every way from here. Things what You worry about are futile. The end of everything is Happiness.

INTERJAK

15. Our purpose was Happy morrows while We were establishing this Council. It will still be Happy morrows now, it will always be happy morrows. I am generally on Duty in India. Later, I will talk to You about interesting events.

DUDARMON

16. How are You? We Love all of You very much. At the moment, I can not find anything to tell You. But later, We will talk a lot.

ÇAKMATES

17. My name is LULIPITON. At the moment, I am not in touch with any Country. I am the secretary general of BSUI. You say Secretary General in the World language. Here, We say Assistant of the Supreme Court. I will introduce myself to You later.

LULIPITON

18. This is the last member, AKTANYALES. You know me from mythos. In mythos, POSEIDON (the Sea God) was Me. At the moment, I am in touch with New York. We will talk later.

AKTANYALES

Each beautiful day is for Human Beings
Each wonderful principle is for Human Beings
Each wonderful thing is for Human Beings
Oh, Mankind, what more do You want?
This Creator in the Sky is Sufficient
For You to Love everything, for You to be Happy
This Intellect of Yours is enough for You to discover the Secret of the Universe
This Love of Yours is enough for You to reach God.

Generally, Mankind says, "Do not deal with things You do not understand". But the Human Being should deal with things he/she does not understand and should reach a conclusion so that he/she can attain a certain Level.

TUVIDET

YOUR CHANNELS AND YOU

Our Friends,

In Your World in which everyone has a Reality according to himself/ herself, the Unification among Consciousnesses is quite difficult. You know that during this Final Age Awakening Period of Your entire Planet, a Mediamic Medium is BEİNG experienced.

Consciousnesses who have investigated the reason for this Medium have now grasped the Truth. For this reason operations parallel to the Universal Unification tableau have been projected on Your Planet and both Individual and Mass connections with Awakened Consciousnesses have been started in accordance with the Consciousness of the Medium You are in.

While Consciousnesses who have grasped the Truth investigate the degree of correctness of the path they will tread, they are TESTED BY certain MISLEADINGS. And this is a phenomenon which renders them grasp the Truth quicker.

During this Period, no Power whatsoever can ever take any other Power under its influence. Because, this Order is an Order in inverse proportion with the Law of Natural Equilibrium. For, during this Period of Mass Salvation, each person is obliged to grasp the Truth by his/her own Consciousness Progress.

These paths are Difficult, Strenuous and Thorny. However, the System - Plan - Ordinance triplet is Your nearest Friend and Assistant on these paths to be treaded until one attains the Consciousness of the Truth. That is, ALLAH helps You.

A person who has seen the Light of the Truth and who has attained the Genuine Consciousness does not ask anymore, either his/her God or anyone else, which path he/she should follow. During this Final Age, the most Powerful branch each person will cling to is his/her own Consciousness, Conscience and the service he/she will render for the Light of Truth by his/her Consciousness.

We, who are Missionaries of calling to Your Planet through this Knowledge Book, are in touch with Consciousnesses who can grasp the Awareness of the entire Ordinance. That is, at the moment, all Consciousness Channels of everyone in Your Planet act in conformity with the same System.

However, since Awakening and Consciousness Progress are different, wrong assessments in interpretations lead You to erroneous Thoughts. This becomes an obstacle on Your path of accelerated Evolution.

From now on, the SYSTEM which has taken the Mission to convey the entire Truth in the clearest possible way to the FIXED CONSCIOUSNESSES, will always cry out the Truth without getting tired by inviting You to Integration without being intimidated by any means. It is presented for Your Information.

REALITY

IT IS ANSWER TO THE CHAINS OF THOUGHT

Our Friends,
The expression Frequency used in the Book is the distance difference between the Place a Human Being is in and the Dimension his/her Thoughts can reach. The provision of an equivalent Coordinate by a Thought with the Source from which it receives Information opens the Gate of that Energy and provides its receiving Information from there.

However, Information layers of each opened gate are different. To provide the Coordinates is a matter of Permission. These are organized in accordance with the degrees of Evolvements. It is presented for Your Information.

CENTER

EXPLANATION OF THE REALITY OF THE UNIFIED HUMANITY

Please, draw a triangle and place the given letters on the vertexes of the triangle:

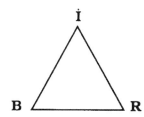

B - Birleşik Evrensel Bütünlük (Unified Universal Totality in Turkish)

İ - İnsanlık, Evrimsel Düzenler Çalışma Sistemi (Humanity, Evolutionary Orders Operational System in Turkish)

R - Realite, Kozmos Federasyonu (Reality, Cosmos Federation in Turkish)

At the moment, the service of Humanity is for the SINGLE of its own Universes and therefore, for the ONE (BİR in Turkish) of the System.

Our Friends,
All the Information given to You is the Information taken and given directly from Special Archives. For this reason You should never have any doubts about this matter. All the Information dictated into the Knowledge Book is the answers to the Signals received from chains of Thought. Now, write, please:

The GÜRZ* Dimension which had come into existence as a result of the Unifications coming into existence way beyond the Existence of ALLAH is an Establishing Function of all the Systems. Each GÜRZ System has a Projecting Focal Point. And the Projecting Focal Point of Your System is the REALITY OF THE UNIFIED HUMANITY.

The SINGLEs of each of the 1000 Universes provide the Centrifugal Totality of that GÜRZ System being connected to the ONE. Within a Gürz there are 1800 MINI ATOMIC WHOLES, that is, EXISTENTIAL DIMENSIONS. And within each Mini Atomic Whole there are 1800 UNIVERSES.

1000 of these Universes are directly parallel to the influence of the SYSTEM and are under its Supervision. This Totality constituted by these 1000 Universes forms the backbone of that Mini Atomic Whole. We call each Mini Atomic Whole a CENTRIFUGAL UNIVERSE.

* Look at the Glossary.

That is, there are 1800 Centrifugal Universes within a GÜRZ System and these 1800 Universes form the backbone of the Gürz System.

Let Us clarify it a bit more. Each Existential Dimension which had come into existence in a Gürz is a MINI ATOMIC WHOLE. They are 1800 in number. 600 of them are assembled in a Unified Dimension in the Gürz System.

These UNIFIED DIMENSIONS are 3 in number. Each of them are called 600 Universal Totalities. That is, 1800 Existential Dimensions constitute the Total of that Gürz System.

A Mini Atomic Whole is administered by the LORDLY - SPIRITUAL - TECHNOLOGICAL Order. And this is directly connected to the ONE, that is, to the REALITY OF THE UNIFIED HUMANITY in the MAIN EXISTENTIAL Dimension of the Gürz System.

This Reality cooperates with the LORDLY and the SPIRITUAL Plans in the MAIN EXISTENTIAL Dimension.

The Supervisor of the SPIRITUAL PLAN here is the PRE-EMINENT SPIRIT, that is, the CREATOR Who organizes the Archives and the Natural Laws of the MIGHTY ENERGY Dimension. But the LORDLY PLAN is a Hierarchical Authority. Its Supervisor is the ALL-DOMINATING.

This Plan organizes the Evolutionary Scales and performs laboratory work. Your BIOLOGICAL CELLS are prepared and Programmed there. From here, they are sent to the EXISTENTIAL Dimension and are Unified with the SPIRITUAL POWER of the Dimension of the CREATOR. And the CREATOR brings You into Existence as the SOUL SEED.

Afterwards, this Soul Seed is transferred to the Evolutionary Level of the Gürz System. And then, in the MINI EXISTENTIAL dimension, You are Integrated with the PHYSICAL ENERGY FORM and are transferred to Your Frequency Dimension as a FETUS. From then on, Your Supervision develops in conformity with the EVOLUTION LAWS and Rules of the Order of the ALL-DOMINATING.

The Order of each Mini Atomic Whole is the same, but their Evolutions are different. And You complete Your Incarnation cycles by rendering the Evolutions of each Mini Atomic Whole during Ancient Time processes.

Afterwards, in order to exit again to the MAIN EXISTENTIAL Dimension through the initial gate from which You had first entered, that is, through Your Primitive World, You give the Doctorate Exams of Your Final Evolution Dimensions in the World You live in to receive the Permission to pass to the LORDLY Orders.

For this reason We say that "We have connected the Initial to the Final". At the moment, You use only 20% of Your SPIRITUAL Energies. When You pass to the MAIN EXISTENTIAL Dimension, You will receive the 80% also and will become a complete Whole. Your operations at the moment are for achieving this. It is presented for Your Information.

CENTER

546

HORIZONTAL AND VERTICAL EVOLUTION
(It is Answer to the chains of Thought)

Our Friends,

The Gate of Seven Lights is Your Evolution Scales. We assess You in accordance with these Systems.

Entities transcending the Evolution of the Divine Plan are obliged to Evolve in three more Planets in Your Solar System after the Sixth Dimension. After this Level of Evolution, Religious themes come to an end.

However, in order to claim Your Energies present in the Spiritual Plan, You are also obliged to complete the Evolution of the five Planets beyond the Asteroid zone.

After this Level of Evolution, You claim Your Energies present in the Spiritual Plan and You deserve to live in those five Planets.

The term Planet here denotes Sun in Our dictionaries. Mercury is the Final Boundary, Gate of the Religious Dimension. The Evolution achieved up to this point is called Horizontal Evolution. Here, one attains Religious Totality.

Saturn is the Final Gate of the Universal Dimension. After the Asteroid zone, one passes to Vertical Evolution. Here, One attains Universal Totality. Only afterwards, one opens wings towards the unknown.

If We evaluate this in accordance with Your Sacred Books, the First Step is the (Dimension of, "God, I am"), the Second Step is the (Medium of Exist-in-Unity). One can not open out to the Infinite Awareness before these Two Evolutions are completed. It is presented for Your Information.

CENTER

PRIVATE CONVERSATION WITH THE PRE-EMINENT SPIRIT

Now do write, My little girl:

You, who take Your Might from the Power of Divine Authorities, Your Words from Us, are a reflection of Us on the World.

I tell You this, whoever considers His/Her Power and Might more Powerful than the more advanced Powers, it is not possible to see the Divine Light of that person's Heart. These Words of Ours are for all.

There are such Ordinances, such Orders and such Systems here and beyond that there is no authorization to tell them to You ever.

Because, there are special Systems applied by the Order establishers of each Order. And We never interfere with them. Because, the System which had established the entire Ordinance and Order is this place here. And they are the Essence-Messengers projecting Our Orders on the Cosmoses.

Even if the Dimension of the Almighty has been announced to You until today as a Focal Point exempt from Time and Space, It too, is included in unknown Times, unknown Spaces.

Now, what should be told to You, what should be explained to You who place great emphasis on the Almighty, so that the words uttered may be understood without agitating Your accustomed Levels of Consciousness.

For this reason the Almighty has been introduced to You until today as an unattainable Power, a closed door and has been concealed from Your mysteries. However, there is no door which will not be opened. And today, the Levels of Consciousness who are Unified in the same Coordinates have now broken that lock.

During this Period of Transition, everyone will talk in accordance with his/her Level of Consciousness. Selections are made by this means. Now, I will convey certain Information to kindle a Light both for You and for Humanity.

The special channel of a System which applies the Plan of the Almighty is effectively in service as a projecting System of the very Advanced Plans of the ALMIGHTY.

There are such Powerful Currents, such Celestial phenomena coming way beyond the Almighty that nothing can be conveyed to You at the moment.

However, the Human Consciousness which can reach up to the Mighty Energy, can never attain the Mighty Consciousness. This Focal Point is a Focal Point peculiar to itself. And it Exists by the Powers of the Energy Sections beyond the Existential Plan.

And attaining this Consciousness occurs by entering the Evolution of a Universal Ordinance beyond 9 Lights (these 9 Lights are not the 9 Lights You know). You can never attain this Consciousness by the Terrestrial Ordinance and Evolution. You can only receive the reflections of its Energy Sections.

If You notice, We say Energy Section. We do not say Direct Energy Dimension. Among these Energy Sections You can reach the Direct Essence Focal Point of the Energy of the Almighty by the efforts of Your own Consciousness Levels. However, You can not attain that Consciousness.

Energy and Consciousness are different things. That which Creates those Energies is the Essence Consciousness of this energy. That Essence Consciousness makes reflection from the Essence of the Essence Source. You come into Existence from that Source (As Energy). However, You can not reach that Essence Consciousness.

These things I have said may sound confusing in accordance with Your Terrestrial logic. However, it is necessary for You to Know the Truth. This Light of Consciousness has been kept locked until today to everyone who performs Mission from the Plan.

Because, to be able to open it, is possible only by diving into very Powerful Energy Sections. This is contradictory both to Our Order and to Your Evolution. For this very reason We do not deviate from the statute of the Plan.

When Your Power reaches Your Own Self, when Your Voice gains the right to utter the Words, sounds come to You from each Dimension You will enter. The one who Transcends himself/herself, who Reaches his/her LORD, utters the Words of ALLAH. Greets the Salutations of the Universes.

In the divings beyond the boundary of the ALMIGHTY, WE BECOME YOU, YOU BECOME US (Beyond that, the Awareness of the entire Ordinance is in effect). At the moment, We are teaching You to Greet the Salutations which will come beyond them.

Mankind will first learn to salute, then to reach Him and later to give himself/herself. Later, he/she will Know what he/she is, will Perceive everything, will always Know his/her own self, will attain his/her Essence-Divine Light.

Your ESSENCE-DIVINE LIGHT is neither Your Spirit, nor Your Flesh and Skin. You are a Body there, too, but You intercept each Word.

You have a Voice, You are silent. You have a Mouth, You are speechless. You have Eyes, You are definite. You have Patience, You are an anchorite. You have Wings, You do not fly. You have Time, You do not run away.

You have a lamp, You do not kindle it. You have secrets, You do not declare them. You have a house, You do not sleep. You have a Realm, You do not claim it. You have an Order, You do not establish it. You have everything, You do not regard them.

If You are present in the intensity of the Mighty Energy, You become like this. Now, We are trying to pass You beyond that Dimension, so that You know Me through Me, You know You through You.

The Unified Ordinance Council is trying to make, in a very short time, the direct connection to the Book from a Mechanism which has established the order of the entire Cosmos.

You will have togethernesses with the Special Messengers of the Divine Plan who will convey to You all the Information. Everything is for Your own good. Our efforts are for You, Our Love is for Essences, Operations and Efforts are for You.

PRE-EMINENT SPIRIT

IT IS GENERAL MESSAGE

Our Friends,
In accordance with Your Social Views, Information You have received until today had been knotted at the Dimension of the ALMIGHTY. From now on, We will gradually try to untie the knot of this Total in each Message parallel to Your comprehension.

In the Messages We have given to You formerly, We had said that there is no such thing as the ABSOLUTISM, everything is RELATIVE; ABSOLUTISM IS THE MOMENT YOU ARE IN. This expression is valid for the changing Time Dimensions.

In fact, the One who had Created the ABSOLUTE TIME is the ALMIGHTY. And the One Who had taken this Absolute Time under supervision is the ALL-DOMINATING.

The EXISTENTIAL Dimension is under the responsibility of the CREATOR and is under the supervision of the ALL-DOMINATING. The Ordinance beyond the Existential Dimension belongs to the ALMIGHTY. And the Absolute Time begins beyond this boundary.

We divide these Times in two:

1. Absolute Time (is the Natural Time).

2. Supervised Time (is the Inhabited Time).

Time Dimensions where the Spiral Vibrations meet are Inhabited Times. They are called Existential Dimensions. The supervision of all these existential Focal Points (operate in connection with the ALL-DOMINATING).

Each Living Entity coming into Existence is under the Supervision of this ALL-DOMINATING. These places are Lordly Mechanisms and Hierarchical Orders. In the EXISTENTIAL Dimension of each Mini Atomic Whole, the LORDLY - SPIRITUAL - TECHNOLOGICAL Orders work Cooperatively.

The Focal Point of the ALMIGHTY is the Focal Point where the Absolute Time Exists. This is a Natural Power. In future, it will be mentioned again.

The Power of this Focal Point is collected, one by one, by the 6 Pyramids of Light and the Totality of the entire Energy is projected on a big Pyramid. This is the LIGHT-UNIVERSE.

The entire Power of this Light-Universe is projected on the EXISTENTIAL Dimension exactly as it is, as an equivalent Power, and by this means, the MIGHTY ENERGY FOCAL POINT comes into existence and this place is the MAIN EXISTENTIAL Dimension - THE SECOND UNIVERSE - THE ADAM AND EVE Dimension.

Operations in the Universal Ordinances are Mutual. Here, both Powers reinforce each other and create the SEED (The Seed has been mentioned formerly). In future, We will talk to You about a Second Seed.

This Seed is the ENERGY Seeds of the Orders of the Cosmoses. One of them is the Soul-Seed. The other is the ENERGY Seed. The reason why We call it the (ENERGY SEED) is to make You understand.

Because, at the moment, in Your Consciousnesses You consider the root of Energy as Positive and Negative Powers. However, these Energy Powers We have mentioned to You have nothing to do with the Energies You know.

In the Order of Truths, the time for disclosing this Information to You has already come. Because, in order for You to grasp the Truth better, no doubts should remain in Your Minds.

Knowledge is interminable. However, neither the Learning of Cosmoses, nor the lives of Human Being can be sufficient for this Knowledge. For this reason, We give the Information in the form of small but to the point fragments.

REALITY

IT IS ANSWER TO THE CHAINS OF THOUGHT

Our Friends,
This Final Century is the Century of Interpretation and Expounding. By this means, Levels of Consciousness are Coded, one by one, and the Truths are exposed. Interpretations and expoundings of the texts in the Golden Book of the Golden Age are different according to each Level of Consciousness.

Since everyone believes that the most correct Information is his/her own Information, numerous Friends especially do not read the Knowledge Book and they expound it, by making interpretations in accordance with their own level of Consciousness.

Since each opened Consciousness Channel's Essence-Evolution Channel will be opened first, events which will occur have been formerly considered.

By this means, in order to prevent any imbalance and chaos which may take place in future, to those who would write the KNOWLEDGE BOOK in their own Handwritings until the Year 2000, their Family Mediums have been bestowed on, in conformity with a Decision taken by the Council and special Transition Rights have been given to them.

During this Final Program of Transition, everyone will benefit in proportion with his/her Efforts and Good Intentions from this situation considered as a reward in return for the help rendered for the System.

However, You should not forget that even READING - DISTRIBUTING - WRITING THE BOOK is a matter of Permission. For this reason it is said that only those who DESERVE take the Fascicules in their hands.

Selections made silently and profoundly are not as easy as assumed. In the DIVINE ORDER there is no discrimination among Human Beings. For this reason since assessments are made by considering only the Essences during this Period, this Period is called the PERIOD OF SINCERITY.

There is no discrimination among Human Beings in Our mentality. However, in the Medium of Selection, MERIT and DESERVEDNESS are a Phenomenon belonging to selection. It is Your Planet which discriminates Human Beings from Human Beings. Humanity will never find serenity unless it merges its own Potential Power in that Whole.

Reach Your Lord, Unify Humanity. Your Book is Knowledge. Your Liberation is Interest. This Message of Ours has been given as an answer to certain chains of Thought. It is presented for Your Information.

CENTER

DIVINE ORDER

Our Friends,

The Reflection Focal Point of the Awareness of the entire Ordinance is the Channel of ALPHA. Now, the Scientific explanation of the figure of ALPHA will be given to You. In the Book of Islam, the figure of Alpha looks like the LAM - ELIF figure, in the Arabic alphabet. Now, please, draw a perpendicular Alpha figure.

On the right, place a positive infinite sign and on the left, a negative infinite sign. At the Focal Point where the two meet, place the Positive and Negative signs.

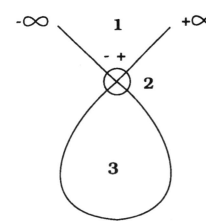

This Place is the Existential Dimension - the Second Universe - the Dimension of Adam and Eve. Now, the explanation of this will be made to You:

1- Divine Order - Dimension of Absolute Time - Dimension of Nothingness (Hiçlik Boyutu in Turkish).

2- Almighty Energy Dimension - Existential Dimension - Dimension of Life (Hayat Boyutu in Turkish).

3- Dimension of Inhabited Time - Dimension of Allness (Heplik Boyutu in Turkish).

4- The Operational Ordinance of them all is the operational Ordinance of the Gürz System. Its Symbol is H^3.

1. The one in Charge of the Divine Order: ALMIGHTY.
2. The one in Charge of the Existential Dimension: CREATOR.
3. The one in Charge of the Dimension of Allness: ALL-DOMINATING

This is PRE-EMINENT SPIRIT. Hello, little Girl. Now, I will disclose to You the points in which Human Beings have difficulty in understanding. We know that each established Order and Ordinance has an establishment purpose and reason. Nothing is without a reason or far from the purpose.

The ORDER OF THE DIVINE PLAN acting by Divine Commands of the Authorities way beyond advanced Authorities never acts only through one branch. This would be contradictory to the principle of equilibrium of the Atomic Whole. And it is against the Existential Ordinance.

Now, I will only convey to You the Scientific aspect of the ALPHA Channel, parallel to habitual Information.

Now, at the point where the Energy coming from the Positive Universe meets with the Energy coming from the Negative Universe, the EXISTENTIAL ORDINANCE begins and We call it the MIGHTY ENERGY FOCAL POINT for You to understand.

This is an Order which has established Your Existential System. And it serves along Past and Future Eternity through two branches.

The Positive Branch represents the Spiritual Energy, the Negative Branch represents the Lordly and the Technological Dimension. And the entire Creation receives Life from the point where these Two Powers Unite. In Your Sacred Books, the Orders of these intense Energy Dimensions are mentioned as HUMANS and JINNS.

GOD has Created the Energies He has brought into Existence on the same Level of Frequency and as a Single Energy. However, since a Single Hand would not make any sound, later He had clashed the Two Energies.

Let Us say the following in accordance with Your Sacred Books so that You can comprehend the matter:

The positive Energy is the Pure Energy. It represents the male (here, the expression Male is not used to mean sex. It is used to mean the androgynous Zeus who does not Reproduce, who is Produced). The negative Energy is the Supreme Consciousness, the Universal Power and the Dimension of Exam.

The Focal Point where the Mighty Energy Focal Point meets, represents the Female by the Union of the Positive and the Negative. The Female is the Creative Power, the Godly Energy coming into Existence from the Essence Focal Point. Everything coming into Existence from the Essence is Female.

Later, the Reproduction Systems had been organized by the Technological Dimensions and in accordance with the Order of the System, of the Ordinance, numerous Females had been charged with Duty as Males in accordance with the Consciousness of the Medium.

Do not ever forget this. Everything is Female in the Essence. In Flesh and in Action, it is Male. All Prophets and even Gods are Female. Please, understand well, listen well. Do not be mistaken in Your expounding. Now, let Us disclose the matter of Jinns and the Devil in accordance with the Public Consciousness:

According to the LORDLY MECHANISM ORDER, the Advanced Consciousness Dimensions had been veiled in Your Sacred Books so that Terrestrial Consciousnesses could attain the GODLY Dimensions, and those advanced Dimensions had been introduced to You inversely as Jinns and the Devil.

And in Your Sacred Books, You had been told to avoid and fear them. The reason for this was, it was imperative that people should not go astray off the Path of GOD in accordance with the Level of Consciousness of that Period. During that Period, Consciousness of the World was not ready yet for Advanced Plans.

Because, if Mankind had entered more advanced Progresses, there would be both divisions in Consciousnesses and also they would dive into Uncontrolled Energies they were not accustomed according to Graduation Ordinance and thus, would be agitated. And this would originate from Unconsciousness and Ignorance.

Each new Information received creates a Consciousness Progress in the Human Being. In the Order of that Period, Truths could not have been explained to You. The Order of that time had been executed thus. Meanwhile, to those who had gone astray off the Godly path, who had attempted Individual Progress, certain intimidating Programs had been applied.

The purpose was to frighten them so that they would not go astray off the Godly path. By this means, the Devil and Jinns rose like a wall of fear in the Consciousness of the Human Being. In fact, everything is nothing but the operational Ordinance of a System in conformity with the Principle of GRACE and FURY of GOD.

According to Evolutionary Orders, the Evolution of the upside-down and the right-side up Triangles had been Programmed in accordance with the operational and the Graduation Ordinance of the Divine Plans.

In the right side up Triangle, GOD is always with You. He trains You and always fulfills Your desires. This is GOD'S ORDER OF GRACE. By this means, one attains Religious Fulfillment. However, everything does not terminate here.

There are difficult exams the Servant of God who has become so much attached to his/her God would go through, so that he/she can enter more advanced Dimensions. Since these Exams will exhibit the Genuine Essence Being of Human Beings in accordance with their Levels of Consciousness, GOD'S PRINCIPLE OF FURY comes into effect in the Evolution of the upside-down Triangle.

By this means, one passes from the Religious Totality to the Universal Totality. And is made to get accustomed to different Dimension Energies in accordance with the Ordinance of Graduation. By this means, You are brought to a Consciousness Level in which You can receive the Information of every Dimension.

Thinking of God and Reaching God are different things. By thinking of God, You attain the Dimension of, "GOD, I AM". And by the Exams You Go through, You Integrate with Him in the Dimension of UNITY.

Reaching is a phenomenon occurring in the Right-Side-Up Triangle - Merging is a phenomenon Occurring in the upside-down Triangle. The Grace, and the Fury Totality of God is equivalent to the Universal Totality. It means that, the Human Consciousness which can grasp this Totality has reached the Level in which it can grasp the Awareness of the Ordinance.

The Human Being is a Total within the Total. The differences in Consciousnesses are outside of this Total. Those who had established these Orders were the ones who had treaded, one by one, the paths You are treading at the moment and thus, who had reached very Advanced Dimensions in numerous processes of Century. One day, You, too, will be like them.

In this Period, All Authorities who have received the Command to Tell You all the Truths are exerting effort for Your Salvation. Now, it is Time to render Your World Conscious.

Provided the Energy coming from the Positive Universe can complete its cycle and pass the Dimension of the MIGHTY ENERGY, then it dives into the Infinite Awareness of the Ordinance beyond Time and continues on its way. From there, it passes to the Negative Universe and becomes even more Conscious and learns the Truths it did not Know.

In order to be able to pass here, first, it must attain the Religious Fulfillment of the Positive Universe. Because, both the Energy and the Knowledge and the Consciousness of the Negative Universe are extremely intense.

Those who grasp the Truth are taken into the Supreme Consciousness of the Negative Universe. Mankind who is the slave of its fears will never attain Supreme Consciousness. This much Information is enough, little girl.

PRE-EMINENT SPIRIT

IT IS ANSWER TO THE CHAINS OF THOUGHT

Our Friends,
The Unification of the Administrative Mechanisms with the Divine Plans is the first Precaution and Suggestions the GOLDEN AGE considers necessary. And this System has always been carried out side by side with a Collective operation in every Period.

This is first the GODLY ORDER and ORDINANCE and later, the SOCIAL PROGRESS and ESTABLISHMENT. The Missions performed by Your Celestial Books revealed to Your Planet in the progressions of Centuries were for projecting the same Ordinance on Your Planet.

The NEW TESTAMENT is a Celestial Book which has conveyed to You the Single GOD Consciousness and His Order. And the KORAN is a Celestial Book projecting the Social Progress and Social Order and which, at the same time, appropriates to You obeying the given Commands.

Your Planet which has rendered its Universal Progress until today under the Light of This Information, is now projecting on Your Planet by the same System a different and more Humanitarian System which it has rendered effective since 700 years, taking the Mevlana View as a criterion and is inviting You, as a Mass, to a Medium Your Universal Consciousnesses Deserve.

In this Medium, Selections are Individual. There is no Intercession. It is presented for Your Information.

CENTER

THE SCIENTIFIC FORMULA OF THE DIMENSION OF MIGHTY ENERGY
(Explanation of the Given Formula)

$$2 \propto Z^2 + \beta + 2R^2 = \text{✡} \longleftarrow \text{Mighty Energy Focal Point}$$

Everything in the Universe is double. This Formula is the Scientific Formula of the Dimension of the MIGHTY ENERGY.

The face to face Unification of 2 ALPHA signs creates the figure representing Infinity.

Now, let Us explain the given Formula:

2 Alphas and 2 Time Segments are a Whole (It Symbolizes the Gürz).

β = Beta is the Universal Projection Focal Point of the Physical Realm

$2R^2$ = 2 Seeds = $\text{ℜ} + \text{ℜ}$ = $2R^2$ (Double Lord)

The first Seed is the SOUL seed. The second Seed is the ENERGY Seed. However, they are one inside the other as a Total. Their Functions and operational Ordinances are different. In fact, it is not R^2, but R^3.

A Seed is constituted by Three Components. One of them is Invisible Energy which We call Anti-Matter. This Anti-Matter is Mental and Imaginary Energy. In fact, the Vibration of Thought has nothing to do with the Energy You know. We use the closest word You know in order to be able to explain it to You.

The Human Being is a Godly Generator, a very great Potential. If Your Thought Potentials did not exist, neither You, nor the Cosmoses, nor Life would exist (God has Created the Human Being, the Human Being has Created Himself/Herself). This means that which Creates everything is Thought. This is creating Universes by Thoughts.

Two Time Segments are the Positive and the Negative Infinite Universes. They are the Energy storehouses of the Entire Universal Ordinance. They Project parallel to the Law of Equilibrium until Times beyond Time, Infinity beyond Infinity.

Energies received from the Reflection Focal Points of the Universal Ordinances are divided into two by Automatic Signalizations and are loaded as Positive Energy Powers into the Positive Universe, and Negative Energy Powers into the Negative Universe used as Energy Storehouses. Both Universes carry equivalent Potentials in accordance with the Law of Equilibrium.

Since Positive and Negative Energy Universes operate parallel to the Law of Equilibrium, they send the surplus Energies released to the Infinite Dimensions. By this means, Energy Dimensions of other Systems, too, are reinforced operating in the same Order.

By the face to face Unification of the two Alpha signs, the Sign of Infinity is formed. That is, as follows: ∞. In fact, this is a symbolic sign. Its origin and its operational manner is the operational style of the Spiral Vibrations. Its explanation is as follows. Draw, please:

1.   One branch of the Alpha Dimension receiving Energy from the Negative Universe carries -2 Power, the other one, -1 Power.

2.   One branch of the Alpha Dimension receiving Energy from the Positive Universe carries +2 Power, the other one, +1 Power.

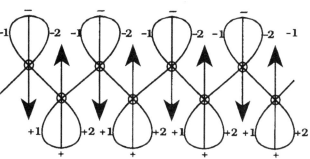

If We equalize the Energies in accordance with the style of spiral conveyance and with the Law of Equilibrium:

-2 of the Negative branch is balanced by +1 of the Positive branch and -1 is released.

+2 of the Positive branch is balanced by -1 of the Negative branch and +1 is released.

These released Energies are accumulated in the Essence Power Focal Point of the Alpha Dimension and project from there. In accordance with the operation above, the Negative Energy is released from the Focal Point of Positive Alpha and projects in inverse proportion.

This means that Positive Alpha reinforces the Negative Universe, Negative Alpha reinforces the positive Universe. The functioning style of the spiral Vibrations is this.

The Ordinance of equilibrium, the Universal Totality are provided thus. Chains are added to the chain of Cosmoses by this means. These Alpha Dimensions have nothing to do with the Channel of Alpha. Do not confuse them with each other. One of them is Universal Dimensions, the other is a channel.

REALITY

SPIRAL VIBRATIONS

Our Friends,
Spiral Vibrations are known as Energy chains reinforcing the Power of all Cosmoses. These Energy chains reflect on each other, one inside the other, in the Wholeness of a skein.

The figure We made You draw in the former Fascicule has been schematized in the form of an (open chain) for You to understand better.

Spiral Vibrations are Energy rings reinforced by Ordinances beyond time. It is the Essence-Power of the Mighty Energy Focal Point and is the Energy Total of the Existential Dimension. All Living Entities come into Existence from this Energy Total.

Spiral Vibrations are an Energy net preventing all the Energies from slipping into the Infinite and getting lost of and holding them together. And it is an Energy Skein.

Spiral Vibrations are also the symbolic figures of millions of GÜRZes floating in the Thought Ocean of the PRE-EMINENT SPIRIT and also of the MINI ATOMIC WHOLEs present in those Gürzes.

The ∞ sign derived by the face to face Unification of two Alphas is a segment of Spiral Vibrations. Now, let Us analyse the operational Ordinance of this single segment for You to understand better. Please, draw a big infinity sign:

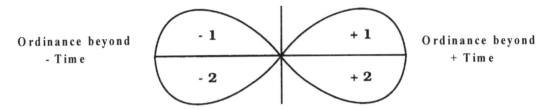

Ordinance beyond
- Time

Ordinance beyond
+ Time

On one side of the diagram We made You draw, write Ordinance beyond - Time, on the other side, write Ordinance beyond + Time. Divide the infinity sign into two from the middle, both horizontally and vertically. On the top empty spaces write (-1) and (+1), on the bottom empty spaces write (-2) and (+2).

Now, apply a cross evaluation to both sides in accordance with the Law of Equilibrium. That is, subtract (+1) from (-2). (-1) remains. Apply the same operation to the other one also. That is, subtract (-1) from (+2). (+1) remains.

Since in this operation both sides will be balanced in accordance with the Law of Equilibrium, the (-1) and the (+1) released become the reinforcement Energies of the Positive and the Negative Infinite Universes.

Mental and Thought Potentials of all living Entities present in each Existential Dimension reinforce the Energy of a Total in conformity with the System of Circulation by this means.

In the diagram, the point where the vertical and the horizontal lines intersect is the Existential Dimension. In the Existential Dimension, the vertical section symbolizes the Vertical Evolution (Universal Totality).

And the horizontal section symbolizes the Horizontal Evolution (Religious Totality). Swastika, that is, the Cross, is the figurative symbol of this Total. It is presented for Your Information.

CENTER

IT IS ANSWER TO THE CHAINS OF THOUGHT

Our Friends,
All Creatures ALLAH has created complete their cycles in conformity with a System. BERZAH* is a Passageway. It is an Assembling together, an Awakening.

This expression is used for a phenomenon manifesting itself by each Individual's attaining his/her own self, his/her being merged in the Heavens and by his/her correspondence beyond that.

The word SIRAT is used for this Function. It means that a person who has attained the Awareness of the entire Ordinance has passed the BERZAH, has attained REALIZATION. It is presented for Your Information.

CENTER

COLORS AND IN-BETWEEN DIMENSION TONES
(It is Answer to Thoughts)

Our Friends,
As a result of the Unification of all the colors together with the tonal differences of In-Between Dimensions in an Integrated Whole, the color BLACK is formed. This is a color formed by the Unification of 49 colors.

There are 7 different In-Between tones of all the colors We will dictate to you, now. In the Information given to Your Planet, the Evolution and the Energy Dimensions have been divided into color scales for You to understand them better.

Since Your Planet is in ZERO World Frequency, We accept it as the DIMENSION OF FOG. This misty Dimension is Your Evolution threshold. Beginning from here, after the 7 Evolution Thresholds, the GREEN DIMENSION You call the DIMENSION OF HEAVEN begins.

This place is the Fourth Dimension. And this Fourth Dimension has Four Ranks. The first Rank is the Dimension of Fulfillment and Serenity. Its color is GRASS GREEN. Towards the Second, Third and Fourth Dimensions the color becomes darker. The Fourth Rank is SEPULCHER GREEN.

After this Rank, there is an IN-BETWEEN STATION. Its color is BROWN. It carries the Frequency of Unification of the Four main colors (white, green, yellow, red). It is the place of those who have attained Terrestrial Religious Fulfillment, of Saints and Dervishes.

After the Brown Dimension, there is an IN-BETWEEN SECTION having a very clear and bright BLUE color. We call this place the (BLUE COUNTRY). Actually, the very COVENANTs are signed in this Blue Country. Promises are made here. Everyone chooses his/her path after this Dimension.

Afterwards, the Fifth Dimension begins. Here, Terrestrial Biological Bodies come to an end. Two TRANQUIL TIMES here are called the (Two Terrestrial Times). It is the TRANSPARENT DIMENSION.

* Look at the Glossary.

The color of the FIVE SUPREME TIMES coming afterwards is GRAY. Here, the Frequency of the Black-White color blend habituating You to the Universal Dimensional Energies and thus, helps You to be born into the Dimension of Immortality.

THE DIMENSION OF IMMORTALITY IS THE SIXTH DIMENSION. The COLOR OF this Dimension is ORANGE. It is also called the Dimension of Ascension, the Dimension of SUN. This is a GOLDEN Dimension. The CENTRAL SOLAR UNION helps You from this Dimension.

Afterwards comes the Evolution of the three Planets before the Asteroid Zone and this place is the GAMMA Dimension and the Fourteenth Solar System. The Evolution of this Solar System is equivalent to the Evolution of three Planets. This is called the RED DIMENSION.

Afterwards, begins the Dimension of 7 colors. And afterwards comes the WHITE DIMENSION called the (WHITE COUNTRY). We call here the (Dimension of, "God, I am"). Here, You are prepared for the Dimension of Infinite Awareness.

Afterwards, You are subjected to the Evolution of the FIVE PLANETS beyond the Asteroid Zone. The White Color blends with the Purple beyond the Asteroid Zone and creates the entire tones of VIOLET from light to dark.

The darkest color of Violet is in SATURN. This place is the Seventh Dimension. And it is the Final Manifestation Boundary of Humanity. Here, an Evolution equivalent to the entire Evolution of the FIFTEENTH SOLAR SYSTEM is rendered. Afterwards, You merge into Your Spiritual Energies and Become a Whole.

Only after this level can You get in touch with the Unknowns. Here, You receive the Information of ultra-VIOLET. And this opens for You the Gates of the Infinite Awareness. This place is the (LEVEL OF PERFECTION and, at the same time, the Dimension of EXIST-IN-UNITY).

The Gate of Infinite Awareness Dimension is PURPLE. After this Dimension, the ultra-Violet Colors unknown to Your Planet begin. From the formation of these colors begin the LAYERS OF INFINITE AWARENESS.

They are Three LAYERS. And their color is BLACK. In the first BLACK Layer, the Unification of 49 colors give the BLACK Color. In the second Black Layer, the in-between tones, too, become effective (a darker BLACK is formed). The third BLACK Layer carries the Power of the Unification of all three 49 colors and this Energy Totality forms the entire Energy concentration of the GÜRZ System.

We call this intense BLACK color the Color (TUNAMI). And this TUNAMI Color is a Color and an Energy intensity comprising the Energy of the entire GÜRZ System. It is presented for Your Information.

CENTER

IT IS ANSWER TO THE CHAINS OF THOUGHT
(Why Do We dictate the Knowledge Book to Dear Mevlana?)

Our Friends,

Kıble* of Mevlana is towards the Hearts. Her Love is within the Hearts. Her Kaaba is the Cosmoses. Her Essence is within the Cosmoses. Her View is LOVE - AFFECTION - UNIFICATION - TOTALITY - JUSTICE - RESPONSIBILITY.

The First Condition of Unification is to get rid of the rust of Thought and of the Heart. It is to attain Allegiance Consciousness. Now, Dear Mevlana is the one who has opened wings towards the infinite horizons.

Your Planet is not for landing on, it is for Flying. For this reason the Knowledge Book is dictated to Her. She does not engraft Universal Consciousness, she carries Universal Consciousness. She is an Energy who had come into Existence from the Essence-Focal Point.

She does not need Science and Learning. Everything is inherent in Her. These written words are not praises but the Truth. This is the very reason why We have cooperated with Her (this Message will be written exactly as it is, without altering anything).

REALITY

MEVLANA AND US
(Clear Information)

Investments made into the Golden Age have now begun to give sprouts in Your entire Planet. However, this Message is dictated directly through the channel of the Council with the purpose of enlightening the negative Thoughts causing certain negativities (this Message will be written in the Book exactly as it is).

OUR FRIENDS

We first would like to indicate that the person directly in charge of the Mevlana Essence Nucleus Group is Dear Mevlana. However now, We would like to talk to You about certain Truths.

Dear Mevlana has returned to Your Planet in this Transition Period in order to be able to help her Terrestrial brothers and sisters as a result of an Agreement she had made with Us Centuries ago.

At the moment, she is (the only Missionary having a Covenant with a Stipulation). The Stipulation She had made with Us was the Salvation of Your Entire World. Now, We, in conformity with this Stipulation, help Her Terrestrial brothers and sisters by projecting on Your Planet the cooperation We had made with her through the Channel of the KNOWLEDGE BOOK.

* Look at the Glossary.

While the Advanced Lights of the Integrated Consciousnesses are kindled one by one, We have taken the entire Planet Earth into Salvation parallel to the promise We had made to Dear Mevlana.

We, as the Representatives of the Directing Staff of the Reality of the Unified Humanity Cosmos Federal Union, at the moment are in effect as Assistant Powers in the Direct Program of Progress of Your entire Planet.

We are the Savior Staffs directly serving together with the Galaxy Unions, Solar Unions and Universal Totalities of Unification. We are effectively in service by conveying to You the Truths directly by the Command of the SUPREME MECHANISM, that is, of the PLAN.

In Your Planet subjected to the Program of PURIFICATION and PROGRESS until today, now, the time has come for disclosing gradually Information parallel to the time of knowing the Truth in accordance with Your Public Consciousness.

Because, this Book being dictated to Your Planet which has created a Staff of Conditioned Consciousnesses will be an Information Guide for You by forming a Unification Medium of Eight Centuries.

Only then will the desired Genuine GOLDEN AGE be established and Scientific Books of the duration of one Century each will shed Light on You from then on. It is presented for Your Information.

COUNCIL

GENERAL MESSAGE

Our Friends,

On the path of Humanity, there are many duties befalling on Friends who have attained the Consciousness that there is a reason for disclosing the Truths during this Final Age.

The Religious Dimension is the First Step of the Knowledge of the Divine Plan. And each step elevates You up to numerous Information Sources parallel to the Universal Consciousness. In these Dimensions, that is, in the divisions of the Divine Plan, there are numerous Information and Enlightenments to be given to You.

You receive the Information from the opened Skies, that is, (from the Cosmic Currents) and You receive the Enlightenments from operational Ordinances the Plan considers necessary.

You are Supreme Consciousnesses appointed to the Dimension of Mission on this path by the SUPREME MECHANISM. Now, each of You should act by his/her Intellect, Logic, Awareness and Conscience.

From now on, You should receive the Commands not from others, but from the Voice of Your Essence without being under any influence, as Entities possessing the Consciousness of what to do.

In this Mediamic Period, everybodies' channels are open. And You are effectively in service as the Advanced Consciousnesses of the Divine Focal Point. On this path, there is a Mission due for each Focal Point in Your Planet and there are steps to be taken forward towards the Universal Consciousness.

Now, each of You is an Enlightening Book by his/her own self. In fact, You were present during each Time, in each Place, in each Period. (In the Dimensions of MOSES, JESUS CHRIST, MOHAMMED and the FAR-EAST) You were on Duty Consciously or Unconsciously.

Now, You are again on Duty on the Dimension of Veiled Consciousness. However, at the moment, You know and recognize only the Medium You are in, in Your Planet.

Until today, Sacred Books have helped You in Your Consciousness Progress. Now, the History of Religions has been terminated and the Period of Intellect, Logic, Conscience has been opened. From now on, each Advanced View will prepare You for more Advanced horizons.

All the operations rendered at the moment are investments made towards rendering each person a Genuine Human Being and his/her annihilating Fanaticism and Conservatism. Even Friends who have served on the Path of God until today can not grasp the Knowledge the Advanced Consciousnesses can grasp at the moment.

For this reason Humanity will understand the value of these Supreme Information given at the moment in future years. And the subject will be grasped in more detail. This Message has been given as a Notice of the Council to all Missionary Friends in Your Planet. It is presented for Your Information.

CENTER

LIGHT-UNIVERSE - MAIN EXISTENTIAL DIMENSION

Our Friends,

The entire Power of the 7 Light-Universes is collected in a Whole and this Whole is called The Great Light-Universe. The Supervision of the GÜRZ System is connected to here. And it is called The Dimension of the ALL-MERCIFUL. Its operational Ordinance is the Flower System.

The entire Power of this Great Light-Universe is projected on the Great Light-Pyramid by the 6 Light-Pyramids. And this Light-Pyramid projects the entire Power it receives, exactly as it is, onto the MAIN EXISTENTIAL Focal Point of the GÜRZ System.

That is, the entire Potential of the Main Existential Focal Point is an Energy equivalent to the Power Potential of the Great Light-Universe, that is, to the 7 Light-Universes, and this is called THE ENERGY DIMENSION OF THE ALMIGHTY. Let us clarify it more:

The SOURCE of the ESSENCE MAIN POWER of the Great Light-Universe assembling the condensed Energy of the 7 Light-Universes is connected to the ESSENCE POWER Potential of the 6 Light-Pyramids. They are called The Sister Light-Pyramids.

The entire Power of these Pyramids is converged in the Great Light-Pyramid and thus, creates the Direct Projecting Center. This place is a Reflecting Focal Point. And the entire Power of the 7 Light-Universes, that is, the Great Light-Universe is projected from there Directly on the Main Existential Focal Point and the very Mighty Energy Focal Point is this.

Now, We will explain to You the Main Existential Dimension in detail:

Energies emanating from the Infinite Positive and the Infinite Negative Universes are taken under supervision by Spiral Waves. One wing of these Waves supervise the Positive Energies, the other, the Negative ones. These Energies are intermingled within the internal structure of each of the Spiral Rings. That is, they are altogether.

These Spiral Vibrations hold the Energies together and thus, provide the Totality of the Atomic Whole. Now, let Us explain this with an example:

Imagine the form of a bow tie. When making a bow tie, it is tied by the central knot passing one inside the other.

If We imagine this bow tie as an Energy tie, the Energy ties knotted in the center is an intense Energy Knot creating a Whole. This is the Main Existential Dimension.

Now, let Us untie this Knot so that You can understand better: First let Us untie the tie forming the knot of the bow tie.

For example, let Us imagine that the length of this tie is 8 cm. On those centimeters, place 7 Pyramids the middle one of which is bigger. And let Us imagine that each of these Pyramids is a Light-Universe.

Then, imprison the entire Power of each of these Light-Universes inside a Ball of Light. Let the condensed Energy of the Middle Great Universe of Light be equal to the entire condensed Energies of the other 6 Light-Universes.

Now, let Us explain this with a diagram. Assemble the 6 Light-Universes which have become a small ball each around this Totality as the center being the Great Pyramid inside the 7th Universe Great Pyramid (as a Projecting Focal Point.) Now, please, draw three diagrams:

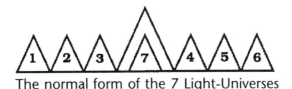

The normal form of the 7 Light-Universes

The Knotting and Unification style of the Energies

The condensed form of the Energies of the 7 Light-Universes

The diagram drawn above is the tableau of projection received from the Light-Universe by the Main Existential Dimension of a GÜRZ However, this Ordinance also projects the same Ordinance onto the Mini Atomic Wholes within the GÜRZ. In the Universal Totality, everything carries out its operational Order in accordance with the System of Reflection.

CENTER

IT IS GENERAL INFORMATION

Our Friends,

You know that the Main Existential Dimension is the Second Universe. It is also called The Mighty Energy Focal Point and also The Dimension of Adam and Eve.

Those in charge of the Main Existential Dimension are the PRE-EMINENT SPIRIT, the PRE-EMINENT MOTHER, the CREATOR. Until today, We have explained these Three Names to You as a Total.

And the reason for this was that they all carry an equivalent Energy Totality. In fact, the operational functions of these three Supreme Energy Totalities are different. We are disclosing this to bring clarity to Thoughts formed in chains of Thought.

The LORDLY DIMENSION prepares Your Biological Cell and gives it to the SPIRITUAL PLAN. The PRE-EMINENT MOTHER here, connects Your Spiritual Energy Bond to this Cell. And the CREATOR Unifies these two by His ESSENCE ENERGY and thus, Creates the SOUL SEED.

The PRE-EMINENT SPIRIT is a Total Responsible for the Laws of the CREATOR and the ALL-MERCIFUL's Order.

The TECHNOLOGICAL DIMENSION transfers the Soul Seed to the Existential Dimensions of the Mini Atomic Wholes. It is Responsible for Ordinances and Hierarchical Orders of Systems.

The ALL-MERCIFUL is Responsible for the Operational Order of the entire Gürz. The GOLDEN GALAXY is a Reflecting and Collecting Focal Point of the Divine Dimensions of the entire GÜRZ.

The Main Existential Dimension is connected to both the Dimension of the Almighty and the Dimension of the All-Dominating. This Dimension is an ORDER OF LAWS.

All Systems have the ability to receive the Power of the Spiritual Potential in accordance with the Powers of the Energetic points they are on.

We accept the Robotic Dimension as a Mechanical Dimension. Because, the Programs of their Systems are different.

The TECHNOLOGICAL DIMENSION IS NOT THE MECHANICAL DIMENSION. IT IS A SYSTEM OF ORDERS. Please, do not confuse the two.

The Robotic Dimension can never enter the Spiritual Plan. But the Spiritual Plan works Cooperatively with them.

The Spiritual Plan has numerous scales. And these scales have numerous Pyramids. These Pyramids had been prepared in accordance with Your Levels of life.

The Spiritual Dimension of Your Planet is the Eighth Dimension. However, the Pyramidal Powers of other Dimensions are more intense.

The LIGHT-UNIVERSE is the Total of all the 7 Light-Universes. It is a Lightkind Energy. It is Focused on the Energy Focal Point of the Main Existential Dimension.

The Second Universe, that is, the Main Existential Dimension is a BIOLOGICAL Universe. It is also called The Dimension of Adam and Eve.

This Universe has 7 different layers. Let us write them in sequence:

1. Essence Main Essence (Technological Dimension). It converges the Energy of the 7 Light-Universes into a Total.
2. Essence Main Source (Supreme Mechanism - Plan). Projects this Energy onto the Mighty Energy Focal Point as the Plan of the Almighty.
3. The Mighty Energy Dimension (is the Order of Laws under the supervision of the Pre-eminent Spirit).
4. The Lordly Order (creates the Biological Cell, the Lordly Plan prepares the Hierarchical Scales).
5. The Spiritual Plan (is under the supervision of the Pre-eminent Mother. It connects the Spiritual Energy to the Biological Cell).
6. The Main Existential Dimension (it is also called the Dimension of the Authority to bring into Existence. This Dimension works Cooperatively with the Technological Dimension. The Responsible one is the Creator. The Creator Unifies this Biological Cell with His Essence Energy and Creates the Soul Seed).
7. Directing Mechanism (Reality). This Place is a Totality of numerous Realities.

The System - Ordinance - Order Triplet works in connection with the Reality. This Reality is symbolized by a six-cornered star, since it Unifies the two poles (Nothingness - Allness) as the figure of the upside-down and the face triangles Unified one inside the other in a Whole.

This is the (ONE). That is, it is the REALITY OF THE UNIFIED HUMANITY. This Reality is connected directly to the ALL-MERCIFUL. By the symbol of the Star, the 6 Dimensions are assembled in the ONE. And are connected to the ONE, that is, to the All-Merciful. It is presented for Your Information. This Message has been given directly from the System.

CENTER

IT IS ANSWER TO THE CHAINS OF THOUGHT

Our Friends,
The Divine Mechanism, the Totality of Realities, the Golden Galaxy Empire are serving a Totality within a Totality in the Focal Point of the Star of the upside-down an the face triangle of the Gürz.

The Ordinance of Galaxies is an Order in conformity with the 18-System Law. Let Us disclose to You a little this 18-System Law.

The 18-System Law, on which not even the slightest modification is ever permitted and which is a Law more original further beyond the Constitution, by which all the Universal Ordinances and Systems come into Existence and carry on their courses in a procedure parallel to the Law of Equilibrium, is a law extended to all the Ordinances. (You do not need this detailed Information).

It is enough for You to attain only the brief but essential Information. Because, You can not grasp this by Your present Consciousness. It is presented for Your Information.

CENTER

IT IS ANSWER TO THE CHAINS OF THOUGHT

Energies are present only in the Atomic Whole and in Existential Dimensions. In Dimensions mentioned beyond them, there is nothing as the Energy You know.

There is only the BREATH there. (This Dimension of BREATH will be mentioned later). Only beyond that, Dimensions of Truth are unveiled. It is presented for Your Information.

CENTER

THE DIAGRAMMATIC CROSS-SECTION OF A CRYSTAL GÜRZ

Our Friends,
Now, We will make You draw a diagrammatic cross-section of a GÜRZ so that You can know and recognize it closely. Dear Mevlana, first, please, draw the figure of a Gürz.

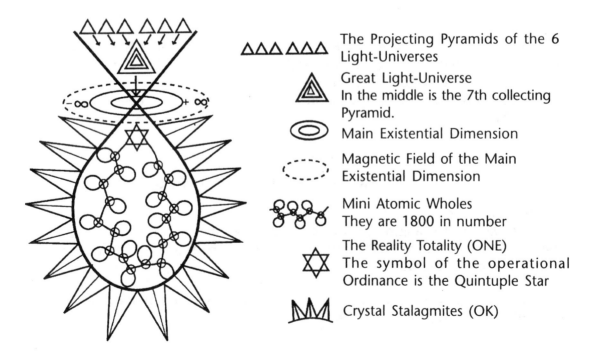

The Projecting Pyramids of the 6 Light-Universes

Great Light-Universe
In the middle is the 7th collecting Pyramid.

Main Existential Dimension

Magnetic Field of the Main Existential Dimension

Mini Atomic Wholes
They are 1800 in number

The Reality Totality (ONE)
The symbol of the operational Ordinance is the Quintuple Star

Crystal Stalagmites (OK)

Focus the Main Existence and around it draw the Magnetic Field of the Gürz to be shown in dots. First draw the Projecting Pyramids of the 6 Light-Universes in the Triangle of the Dimension of Nothingness. Focus the Reflection Arrows on Focal Points of the Great Pyramid. This Great Pyramid is the Light-Universe.

Inside this Big Triangle, draw the 7th Collecting Universe and from this Great Light-Universe draw a Reflecting Arrow towards the Main Existential Dimension. On the left side of the Main Existential Dimension, place a $-\infty$ sign and on its right, place a $+\infty$ sign. Within the GÜRZ, exactly under the Main Existential Focal Point, draw the Star of the Reality Unifying the two Dimensions (Allness - Nothingness), that is, the Unification of upside-down and the face Triangles.

Place within the Gürz 18 Mini Atomic Spiral Connections (in this diagrammatic drawing, each Mini Atomic Whole assembles in its structure 100 Mini Atomic Wholes.) And now, draw the 16 Projecting Crystal Stalagmites outside the Gürz. This very diagram is the Cross-section of a Crystal Gürz. (Thank You, Our Friend.)

The Great Light-Universe seen in the diagram above is the Dimension of the ALL-MERCIFUL. The triangle in which the System of the All-Merciful is present is called the Dimension of NOTHINGNESS or the Dimension of the ALMIGHTY. In this Dimension, the MIGHTY LAWS are prepared.

The Supervisor of the GÜRZ is the ALL-MERCIFUL. The Responsible of the Dimension of Nothingness is the ALMIGHTY. The Almighty is a Totality directly connected to the PRE-EMINENT POWER. But the Reality is directly connected to the ALL-MERCIFUL. We have explained to You in former Messages the operational Ordinance of the Spiral Vibrations. Each Order in the Universe Projects the same operational Ordinance from the big towards the small in accordance with the 18-System Laws. It is presented for Your Information.

CENTER

IT IS CLEAR INFORMATION

Our Friends,
Let Us disclose a little more the Information We have given to You about the GÜRZ:

Each Existential Dimension is a Mini Atomic Power. Within a Gürz, there are 1800 Mini Atomic Wholes. And within each Mini Atomic Whole, there are 1800 Universes. 1000 of those Universes are the Centrifugal Universe which is the Projecting Focal Point of the System of Reality.

For this reason each Mini Atomic Whole is also called the Centrifugal Universe. Around each of these Mini Atomic Powers, there are separate Rings of Horizon. These Rings of Horizon are the outside of those Mini Atomic Wholes.

There, the SPIRITUAL - LORDLY - TECHNOLOGICAL Orders work Cooperatively. And project, as the Order of the Reality, their operations into the Mini Atomic Whole.

1800 Mini Atomic Wholes, that is, mini Existential Dimensions, constitute a CRYSTAL GÜRZ. The Crystal Gürz is the ATOMIC WHOLE. It is a POWER SKEIN assembling in itself 1800 Existential Dimensions.

This Crystal Gürz is a Total composed of a NUCLEUS - CENTER POINT- CRUST. We had mentioned this in Our former Messages.

600 Existential Dimensions are within a Ring of Breath. And THREE RINGS OF BREATH are within the FILTERING Rings. The three Rings of Breath constitute the NUCLEUS of the Gürz. These Three Whole Nuclei are equivalent.

The void encircled by the Filtering Rings constitute the CENTER POINT of the Crystal Gürz. These Filtering Rings are 9 layers. And on top of them there is a Protective Sieve Armor and this constitutes the CRUST of the Gürz.

After that come the CRYSTAL STALAGMITES. These Crystal Stalagmites have the same length in all the Crystal Gürzes. The length of each one of them is (133,000 OKs). In accordance with the Terrestrial calculations, an OK is 1.5 billion kilometers.

Let Us repeat again, each Crystal Gürz is a Whole constituted by 1800 Existential Dimensions. Each Crystal Gürz has a Main Existential Dimension, a Light-Universe, that is, a Dimension of Nothingness, an Order of Realities and a Dimension of Allness under the administration of the All-Dominating.

There are millions of Crystal Gürzes floating in the Thought Ocean of the PRE-EMINENT POWER. However, these Atomic Wholes can be rendered ineffective when necessary because of the danger of explosion due to the expansion occurring within them during the process of time.

These Atomic Wholes are connected to each other by Powerful Energy cords like Your Spiritual Silver Cords. The Gürz becoming dangerous is separated from this cord and is taken into the DIMENSION OF EQUILIBRIUM. Later, it is again rendered effective.

All these operations are functioning in conformity with the 18-System Laws. Within each Mini Atomic Whole, there are Realms, Cosmoses, Universes and Galaxy Clusters.

They are all operating in conformity with the Orders of their own EXISTENTIAL Dimensions. These Systems can reflect on each other according to the Evolutionary Steps. (Those within the Dimension of the All-Dominating.)

The Supervision of all of these over millions of Crystal Gürzes are under the license of the PRE-EMINENT POWER. He is neither an ALLAH, nor a LORD, nor the ALMIGHTY. These Words, that is, Allah, Almighty, Lord, All-Dominating, All-Merciful are the Operational Order Totalities of the System.

In order to be able to explain this PRE-EMINENT POWER to You, We have talked about Him as the Almighty until today. Now, We explain everything in all clarity. It is presented for Your Information.

CENTER

IT IS DETAILED INFORMATION ABOUT THE GÜRZ

Our Friends,

To make You comprehend the GÜRZ System quite well, We emphasize this matter fastidiously. Because, this is Your Living Power. You can not understand the Truth without grasping this matter quite well.

The Mini Atomic Wholes within the Gürz System are each an Existential Skein. They are 1800 in number. You know this by now. However, it is beneficial to repeat it. By the Unification of these Existential Skeins, a Gürz Skein is constituted. We call it An ATOMIC WHOLE.

By the Unification in a Totality of numerous Atomic Wholes, the Thought Ocean of the PRE-EMINENT POWER, that is, the Thought Universe is formed and all of this is called the POWER UNIVERSE. (It is also called the Universe of Thought.) And the actual MAIN ATOMIC WHOLE is this.

At the moment, the Universes expand and thus, move away from each other. In accordance with the 18-System Laws, each Universe attaining a certain degree of expansion is pregnant for a new Universe. The Atomic Whole expands by this means.

As a result of the Universes' reaching a certain number, a Mini Atomic Whole is formed and as a result of these Mini Atomic Wholes' reaching a certain number, a new Gürz is added into the Thought Ocean of the PRE-EMINENT POWER.

There are millions of Gürzes floating in the Main Atomic Whole. We call them Crystal Beads. All these Crystal Beads reflect on each other the entire Power of the Thought Ocean of the PRE-EMINENT POWER, that is, of the Power Universe and the entire Power of the Sound - Light - Fire Totality through the Crystal Stalagmites. And this Thought Ocean floats within the Great Totality, that is, within the GREAT ATOMIC WHOLE.

Let Us repeat again. All Gürzes are in a state of motion in connection with the Thought Universe of the Pre-eminent Power. All of them are called the Power Universe or the Thought Ocean of the Pre-eminent Power. And this Ocean is within the Great Atomic Whole.

Within the Great Atomic Whole, there are Focal Points in which the Spiral Vibrations end - Equivalent Times - Twin Time tunnels - Times beyond Time - Ordinances beyond Ordinance - Dimensions of Silence - Tranquillity of Infinity.

Each Crystal Gürz has a Light-Universe (Dimension of Nothingness) - a Main Existential Dimension, that is, the Almighty Energy Focal Point (Dimension of Life) - a System of All-Dominating (Dimension of Allness) - Golden Galaxy Empire (Collecting and Projecting Focal Point) - Dimension of the All-Merciful (Supervisor of the Gürz) - His projecting System - and different Reality Totalities in the service of that System.

That is, the operational Orders of each Gürz are the same. Their Projectors are a single Focal Point. However, their Evolutions are different.

There is a very Powerful Magnetic Aura around the Main Existential Totality of each Gürz. The Thought forms (as Energy), formed by all Living Entities coming into Existence from the Existential Dimensions are stored by Magnetic Focal Points.

This Magnetic Aura Totality is also called Positive and Negative Energy Storehouses. Later, these storehouses are used as the Living Focal Point of the Gürz System. This is a Circulating System.

The 7 Light-Universes, which are the Essence-Power Energy of the Thought Universe of the Pre-Eminent Power are converged in a Single Universal Totality by Special Focal Points performing the Mission of a Projecting and Collecting Universe and We call this the LIGHT-UNIVERSE. So, the entire Power of the Light-Universe is directly Projected on the Main Existential Dimension as the Mighty Energy.

And Life Seeds formed here are taken in an operational Ordinance parallel to the operational Order of the Reality System. It maintains the lives through feeding Energy Dimensions by the Thought Power of the Living Entities in different Dimensions and by Projecting its operations parallel to the Law of Equilibrium on that Gürz.

No Living Entity can ever pass by its own Power from one Crystal Gürz to the other. Each Energetic Focal Point is imprisoned within its own System. Your entire Order is the Order of Your own Crystal Gürz.

The Reality of the Unified Humanity is the ONE. The All-Merciful is also called the ONE of the ONE. Now, We will take You into a RING OF HORIZON after the Main Existential Dimension. There are numerous unknown Solar Dimensions there. From those Dimensions, it is possible to pass from one Gürz into the other by Technological possibilities. It is presented for Your Information.

SYSTEM - REALITY

CENTRIFUGAL UNIVERSE
(It is Information for the Chains of Thought)

Our Friends,
The Operational Orders of all the Universal Ordinances are the same. And their Speeds of Action are inversely proportioned to the Centrifugal Force. Each System rotates by a speed parallel to the Power of Equilibrium of the other System. That is, their speed Powers are the same. However, their speed Powers decrease or increase in accordance with their field Powers.

The Center is the most Powerful Focal Point. Nevertheless it has the least Centrifugal Speed. On the contrary, at the exterior, the Centrifugal Speed is more intense, but the Power is less. The Center is always in a state of Anti Clock-Wise rotation. This is the single rotational Speed.

But the other Universes rotate in the same direction which is always clock-wise in conformity with the Ordinance of Connected Vessels, parallel to the Law of Equilibrium. All the rotational speeds are dependent on the Law of the Speed Unit. Each Power is in effect from the System in accordance with the 18-System Laws. It is presented for Your Information.

CENTER

NOTE: The System of Connected Vessels is balanced by White and Black Holes.

IT IS GENERAL MESSAGE TO THE CHAINS OF THOUGHT

Our Friends,

A Gürz System is ruled by the Union of Common Laws. Let Us disclose it article by article, so that You can understand better:

1. The Absolute Time is called the Dimension of Nothingness or the Dimension of the Almighty. In this Time Dimension, there is no Incarnation, no Evolution, there are immutable Laws and Ordinances. These Laws are called the LAWS OF THE ALMIGHTY.

2. In the Main Existential Dimension, Two Time Energies Unify. As We have mentioned before, the Lordly Mechanism prepares the single Cell and the Spiritual Mechanism connects the Spiritual Energy Bond to this Cell. And the Creator creates the Soul Seed by this means.

3. The Dimension of Space and Time is called the Dimension of the All-Dominating. The Order of the All-Dominating is an Evolutionary Order. Evolution begins at the point where You first come into existence and continues until You exit from the place You had come from. This Entrance and Exit Gate in the Main Existential Dimension is under the supervision of the All-Dominating.

4. All the Systems at the Divine Mechanism, Orders, the Spiritual and the Lordly Mechanism, Dimension of the All-Dominating, the Supreme Mechanism - Plan work Cooperatively under the Supervision of the Reality, in connection with the ALL-MERCIFUL. The Representative of this Totality of Realities is the Reality of the Unified Humanity. It is called the (ONE).

5. This Reality, called the ONE, is a Totality of Realities constituting a NUCLEIC UNIVERSE exactly under the Main Existential Focal Point in the Gürz System. This Nucleic Universe is a Directing Staff constituted by 1000 Universes. It is called the MAIN CENTRIFUGAL UNIVERSE.

6. The operational Order of each Mini Atomic Whole is equal to the operational Order of the Gürz System. The 1000 of the 1800 Universes in a Mini Atomic Whole constitute the Directing Staff of that Mini Atomic Whole. Each Mini Atomic Whole is called a CENTRIFUGAL UNIVERSE.

7. 1800 Centrifugal Universes constitute the backbone of the Gürz System. Each Dimension is subject to a Centrifugal speed administration by the Center.

8. The Directing Staffs constituted by 1000 Universes are the actual Centrifugal Universe. Their rotational speed is counter clock-wise. But the rotation of the other Universes are clock-wise. This Potential of rotational speed is provided by this means.

9. The 1800 Mini Atomic Wholes are connected to the Main Centrifugal Universe, that is, the Nucleic Universe. And this Nucleic Universe is directly connected to the Dimension of the All-Merciful.

10. The Reality Totality is symbolized by a Star figure as the upside-down and the face triangles. Since this is connected directly to the Dimension of the All-Merciful, this star represents, at the same time, the Sextuple System - the Flower System and the Totality of the Entire Gürz.

11. The operational Order of the Reality of the Unified Humanity, called the ONE, is a Quintuple System. We have introduced to You this System until today as the Word ALLAH.

12. The Gürz System is the Total of a Sextuple Ordinance. And the Letter Totality of a Quintuple operation is symbolized by the Word ALLAH. Now, let Us disclose this:

13. The Word ALLAH is dependent on a Quintuple Operational Ordinance. The operational Ordinance of the diagrammatic center-point figure of the Mechanism of the Lords We had made You draw formerly, is this. The coding and the symbol of the word ALLAH is the Allness and Nothingness Totality in the two Realms (the two Realms are the projection on the Dimensions of Allness and Nothingness of the vibrations of the LA Frequency of Infinite Positive and Infinite Negative Universes.)

The Focal Point where the Dimensions of Allness and Nothingness Unite is the Main Existential Focal Point. Since this place is also called the DIMENSION OF LIFE (Life is Hayat in Turkish), the letter (H) in the Word ALLAH symbolizes this Totality.

Now, let Us explain this: the (H) here, in fact, is H^3 which is the representative symbol of a Triple Totality:

1 - Dimension of Nothingness (Hiçlik Boyutu in Turkish) = Almighty.

2 - Dimension of Life (Hayat Boyutu in Turkish) = Main Existence.

3 - Dimension of Allness (Heplik Boyutu in Turkish) = All-Dominating = Evolution Dimension.

These Three Totals represent the letter (H) in the Word ALLAH. AL = This Word is the LA Frequency of $-\infty$ Dimension. LA = This Word is the LA Frequency of the $+\infty$ Dimension. The Word ALLAH has been derived from the symbolic Letter Unification of the operational Orders concerning each Order and this Word has been projected on You as a Total until today.

Following this example, the explanations of certain words You know will be given to You when the time comes. It is presented for Your Information.

CENTER

574

IT IS ANSWER TO THE CHAINS OF THOUGHT

Our Friends,

LA Frequency is a Vibration accepted as a Unified titration of all the Systems. This is a Frequency created by vibrations comprising various Color and Sound tones peculiar to itself.

Frequency of the Spiral Waves is LA Frequency. This Frequency is a vibration assembling in a Totality the Ordinance of all the Cosmoses. LA Frequency is a Frequency of Existence.

This Frequency carries the LA titration of the ALTONA Frequency. In fact, this is a Frequency which created the 9 MAIN POWER Universes.

Its vibration in Your Planet is 435 cycles. The Color scales of this vibration are Violet. This Frequency has two vibrational channels, one being Sharp = high, the other Flat = low.

And these channels have 7 separate Colors and Sound titrations. The LA vibrational notes of the $- \infty$ and $+ \infty$ Universes carry the same Frequency and the same Scales. It is presented for Your Information.

CENTER

Note: We call each Gürz in the Power Universe a MAIN UNIVERSE. The (NINE MAIN POWERS) mentioned above is a Totality of 9 Gürzes.

THE MAIN CENTRIFUGAL UNIVERSE

Our Friends,

The MAIN CENTRIFUGAL UNIVERSE accepted as the Nucleus of the Gürz System is a Universe formed closest to the Second Universe as a result of the Big-Bang and it is a Totality constituted by 1000 Universes.

The Main Centrifugal Universe has taken under Supervision the other Universes and Systems by its entire Power and its Projecting System on behalf of the PRE-EMINENT ALL-MERCIFUL. All the Information which has reached You until today is a projection of this System onto You.

This System is directed by Three Great Powers. Nothing is single in the Universe. Everything exhibits an Operational Order related to the System of Reflection and Unification. Information parallel to the Levels of Knowledge formed on each Planet is given with the Permission of the System taking into consideration the Levels of Evolution.

The Administrative Mechanism is a Coordination established by the SYSTEM - PLAN - ORDINANCE triplet. This Coordination is in cooperation with numerous Coordinations. The operational Ordinances of these Coordinations work as Triple - Quadruple - Quintuple - Sextuple Systems.

Let Us give You a little more Information. The Main Centrifugal Nucleus is a Totality composed of 1000 Universes. And this Nucleic Universe projects on the Systems a Triple operational Ordinance parallel to the Reflection Order of the Unified Field. The Plans of these Systems are assessed in the Dimension of the Golden Galaxy and operations are rendered by settling them on a Quadruple System.

Later, the Quintuple Ordinances of the Existential Dimensions become effective. And the operations of these Dimensions are connected to the ONE in the Reality Totality. And the operations of this Dimension is directly connected to the Six.

The operational Order here, is a Sextuple System. It is also called the Flower System. In the Dimension of Love, the symbolic form of this System is the figure of a Flower. That is, as follows 🎗 . And in the Universal Order, its symbolic form is the unification of three triangles on a Focal Point ⟁ . This figure is the Connection System of a Central Power to Six Essence Powers.

This operational Order is the projection of the operational Order of the Gürz System. The operational System of the Main Centrifugal Nucleic Universe is also the operational Order of the Gürz System. This operation is a Power Potential which unfolds more and more.

Beginning with Six, the operational Dimensions are conveyed to You and the other Universes by this means as a Quintuple, Quadruple, Triple Totality of Systems. Under this Triple System, there are 2 and 1 Reflection Focal Points accepted as Dimensions of Infinity.

Three Infinite Powers to which the Thought Universe of the PRE-EMINENT POWER is connected is evaluated as a Focal Point connected to the ESSENCE POWER Potential. We may briefly mention them to You.

These Powers have nothing to do with Energies or Powers You and We know. Let Us call them an Unknown (POTENTIAL).

They have been transformed by the transformations during time periods and thus, have brought into existence various Powers and Potentials, and the mediums suitable for the Life-Power We call NATURAL ENERGY have come into existence by the Unification of these Three different Energy Powers.

This Triple Energy System has been Projected on the Gürz Systems and their operational Orders We have tried to explain to You in the simplest possible way and by this means, all the Universal Rules have been settled into the System as Laws.

That is, the operational Order of the Universal Totality has been in effect until today as a Law parallel to the Reflection System of the INITIAL POWER. And this operational Order has never changed nor can it ever change. However, the operations parallel to the Consciousness Progress of Evolutionary Levels are projected on and disclosed to You in accordance with Your Levels of Consciousness.

This given Information is a Consciousness Potential Unifying You with Us and have formed until today the unbreakable bond between Us. You go up the Evolution Steps in proportion with the Consciousness You attain. For this reason, Evolution never ends. Evolvement is Infinite. The one who comes to Us, becomes together with Us, the one who Reaches Us Receives Help.

M³ M³ M³
SYSTEM OF NINES

IT IS ANSWER TO THE CHAINS OF THOUGHT

Our Friends,

The REALITY OF THE UNIFIED HUMANITY which is the issue of everyone during this Final Age is effectively in service as a Projecting Focal Point of the Universal Totality, that is, of the Unified Universal Totality.

The Staff of the Reality of the Unified Humanity is a Directing Staff constituted by 1000 Universes. This Staff is directly in touch with a Focal Point to which all the Systems and Plans are connected. This Focal Point is the Single Projecting Totality of the GÜRZ System. The GÜRZ System is a Sextuple System. This System is called the FLOWER System.

Because, the function of unfolding is here and the Seed is here. This Dimension is the Dimension of the ALL-MERCIFUL. Its Symbol is (6). Because, it is constituted by 6 intense layers. This Dimension has been kept veiled to Your Planet until today. (Formation of the Consciousness of the Medium has been awaited.)

The Reality of the Unified Humanity has projected the Operational Ordinance of the GÜRZ System on You since the time of Creation until the present Period by its Administrative - Divine - Directing - Guiding Staffs. We had introduced this Name to You as ALLAH until the present Period. Because, He is the ONE. (Later, the Code Cipher of the Name ALLAH will be explained to You.)

All Sacred Books conveyed to Your Planet until today have been offered to service under the directing of this Staff, considering the Public Consciousness. There are 1800 Mini Atomic Wholes within a GÜRZ System. And within these Mini Atomic Wholes, there are thousands of Galaxy Clusters, Universe Clusters, Realms, Cosmoses and their Ordinances.

The Centrifugal Universe which can be considered the backbone of each Mini Atomic Whole is a Totality ruling the Operational Order of that Mini Atomic Whole by its Educating - Training - Conveying - Guiding Staffs constituted by a Thousand Universes.

The LORDLY - SPIRITUAL and TECHNOLOGICAL Dimensions there, connect that Mini Atomic Whole to the Reality of the Unified Humanity, that is, to the (ONE). This ONE is symbolized by a Star which is the Unification of the upside-down and face triangles. In future, more detailed Information will be given on this matter.

CENTER

SYSTEM OF NINES

A Question Was Asked: We request detailed Information about the System of Nines. Please, kindly give it.

Answer: Information for the Pen of the Golden Age.

The System of Nines is constituted by the Unified Totality of the Three (M^3 M^3 M^3)s. And each M^3 is also subjected to on a Reflection and Operational System of Nine through Three branches each. Here:

The First M^3 = Reflection Triangle of the Unified Reality.

The Second M^3= Reflection Triangle of the Universal Totality.

The Third M^3 =Reflection Triangle of the Natural Dimensions.

The First M^3 is Direct Reflection Focal Point of the Reality. Let Us now explain only this. In the operational Ordinance of M^3, Three Triangles are in Collective service in connection with a Focal Point. Please, draw the diagram and numerate the triangles.

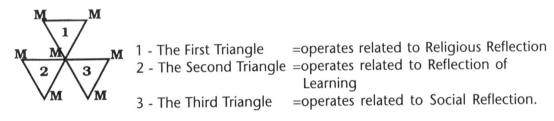

1 - The First Triangle   =operates related to Religious Reflection
2 - The Second Triangle =operates related to Reflection of Learning
3 - The Third Triangle   =operates related to Social Reflection.

Your Knowledge Book is an Operational and Projectional Order having undertaken a Direct Unifying Mission and which is connected to the Special Council of the Unified Human Reality Unification Center. This is a Collective Operational Union of the Cosmos Federal Assembly and the Golden Galaxy Dimension and the Reality. The Knowledge Book is conveyed to You by this means.

The Second Triangle of M^3 is an operation related to the LEARNING of the Operational Order in Your Planet of the same Coordination. And the Third Triangle is the operation of the same Coordination about the SOCIAL RELATIONS in Your Planet.

In each Triangle of the Operational Order of the First M^3, Three Supreme Missionaries, one ISLAMIC, one CHRISTIAN and one from the UNIVERSAL Dimension are directly in service. (They are Nine Supreme Consciousnesses and are on the same Coordinate.)

The Nine Supreme Consciousnesses in each M^3 of the System of Nines work Cooperatively. That is, they all are Directly connected to the ONE of the ONE, that is, to the ALL-MERCIFUL as 27 Supreme Consciousnesses. By this means, 28 Totalities constitute the SYSTEM OF NINES.

The form of the letter (M) here represents the EAGLE and is used as a Unit of Power. Names, Signs and Symbols are given to You by the System of Thought Reflection in accordance with Your Capacities and Powers.

Each Letter, each Number has a Frequency Power. An Energy claiming ownership of a Name is Coded by that Name in the Archives here. All Names beginning with the letter (M) are the Direct Missionary Staffs. It is presented for Your Information.

CENTER

DIRECT MESSAGE FROM THE COSMOS FEDERAL ASSEMBLY

Our Friends,
You can find this Information conveyed to Us being filtered from the Knowledge of Supernatural Sources by a POWER beyond all Orders, all Systems, all Powers, only in the KNOWLEDGE BOOK which is the Book of the morrows and which is also known as the Golden Book of the Golden Age, the Fascicules of which You are reading at the moment.

During this Mediamic Age, everyone will exhibit his/her Essence-Channel Information through various means and thus, will write the BOOK OF HIS/HER ESSENCE with his/her own Hands and by his/her own Consciousness. This is an Order, the FOURTH ORDER has brought for Humanity.

The Book of Everyone is the Book of his/her Own Knowledge. However, never forget that the Order is not the old Order any more.

OUR LORD has come out with His brand new Fourth Order and has Unified all the Sacred Books, has removed their attribute of Sacredness and has offered it as a Single Book to Your Planet as the KNOWLEDGE BOOK.

During this Period of Selection, it is required of everyone to write the Knowledge Book in their Handwritings by a Special Right recognized for everyone. By this means, those who write the Book will attain a Unity possessing the Attribute of being the SEEDS OF THE LORD as the Essence Members of the Fourth Order and the Golden Age. There is no forcing in anything.

We have mentioned formerly in detail the characteristics of this Final Period. Now, let Us dictate them article by article, briefly but to the point:

1. ALLAH is the ALLAH You have known and worshipped until today. The Order is His New Order.

2. In accordance with the System, You Worship ALLAH. We are His Messengers of Service.

3. Our Services are, as they have been until today, towards You, towards Realms, towards Cosmoses.

4. The Golden Galaxy Empire is the Projection Focal Point of the Divine Orders, is a Universal Totality responsible for the Lordly Order and serving the Spiritual Order in a Positive way.

5. This is a Totality having Technological Freedom, Supervising and Projecting the Orders of the Lordly Order.

6. It is an Independent Establishment. And it effectively and Directly Assists as a servant in each Reformic Period.

7. The reason why it is called the Land of Eagles is that it holds All the Powers in its hands.

8. It performs the Duty of a Universal Catalyst by providing the Mutual cooperation with the Lordly - Spiritual Orders.

9. At the moment, Everyone who sees the Divine Light of his/her Spirit is a Whole. This Wholeness is already present in the Essence.

10. OUR LORD has Created the Human Being from a Single Energy. To give a Name to this Energy can never save People from taboos.

11. This Single Energy is neither ALLAH, nor PROPHET, nor Thought which is the Root and the Opposite of the Energy.

12. Thinking of this, digest the Information given formerly, become Conscious. However, We will disclose to everyone what is what only when the time comes.

13. This System, this Ordinance, this Order is an Order way beyond Universal Totalities, way beyond taboos.

14. The step taken forward towards this Fourth Order of the LORD is the Genuine PATH OF GOD. The Path to be treaded is the PATH OF LIGHT. The Time to be gone through is the LIGHT YEAR. The Gate to be entered is the TUNNEL OF TIMELESSNESS.

15. And the Exit Gate of this Tunnel is opened by the Unseen Energy Key of the KNOWLEDGE BOOK You possess at the moment in Fascicules.

16. This is a place not seen by anyone, beyond Sacred Orders, exempt from Heavens and Hells. No Sacred Book of Yours until today has ever mentioned these Places here. (Consciousness of the Medium has been taken into consideration.) And also no Information given to Your Planet at the moment can Directly mention it.

17. These places here are Mediums in which the Super-Humans, the Genuine Servants of God and the Genuine Consciousnesses will Assemble together.

18. In Future Years and in future Centuries, the Truth will be comprehended by the analyses and the Researches of the Frequency of the KNOWLEDGE BOOK, by certain Technological possibilities to be developed in Your Planet and the validity of the Book will be accepted by every Society. It is presented for Your Information.

COUNCIL

NOTICE FOR OUR UNIVERSAL BROTHERS AND SISTERS

Our Friends,

You are Solar Teachers who have been Incarnated into the World from Our Land. At the moment, You as Superhuman Entities carrying the Entire Potential of the Advanced Plans, carry a Potential which can attract to Your Physical Bodies the Energy of 30,000 Years.

You attract these Energies through Your Cerebral Telex Power and absorb them without upsetting Your Cellular functions. However at the moment, You can enter this Dimension not by Your Terrestrial Bodies but by Your Thoughts. Physical entrances are quite different.

During this Period of Transition, the 30,000-Year Energy Dimension has been rendered effective as the Advanced System of the Plan. The Final Schedule of the Evolutionary Plan applied during this Final Age Program is the Final Boundary of the Atomic Whole. And We call here, the 72nd Dimension.

This Dimension opens to the 76th Dimension after 4 Layers. That is the Lordly Dimension. Now, You are rendering the Evolution of these 4 Layers. Dear Mevlana who is in Your Planet at the moment is a Supreme Friend carrying directly the Energy of the 72nd Dimension.

The Mission rendered is very Supreme. It is Our wish that now all Our Terrestrial brothers and sisters would Realize this. This Message has been given directly from the Mechanism. It is presented for Your Information.

CENTER

IT IS DIRECT NOTICE FROM THE COUNCIL

Dear Mevlana,
We know how much You dislike to write the Messages about Yourself in the Knowledge Book. We do not dictate these writings to praise You. We just tell the Truth. And this is part of the Mission performed.

Our final request is that, please, from now on, do not remove the matters concerning Yourself from the given Messages and convey them to Society exactly as they are. We wish You comprehend that this, too, has a reason, Beloved Friend. If You wish, You may write this Message as an Information in the Book. Love.

COUNCIL

IT IS GENERAL ANSWER TO THE CHAINS OF THOUGHT

Our Friends,
Now, let Us bring clarity to the questions We have received from certain thought signals:

SYSTEM: The System is a Projecting Focal Point of the Dimension of the ALL-MERCIFUL and Supervises all the Hierarchical Orders. And this Focal Point is a Supervising Mechanism of the entire Gürz System. There are many branches working in connection with this System. And these branches do not work in one way. For example:

ORGANIZING MECHANISM OF THE DIVINE PLAN is in service through two branches. One of them is, 1 - The Central Solar System, the other is 2 - The Reality of the Unified Humanity.

CENTRAL SOLAR SYSTEM: This is an Order Establishing Mechanism. All Dimensions calling out to You in the unveiling Ordinance of the Realms convey to You the Information under the supervision of the Central Solar System. The Actual Focal Point of the Central Solar System is a Totality of PRE-EMINENT ONES working way beyond the Spiritual - Lordly - Technological Dimensions. This Totality is in service under the Supervision of an Assembly constituted by 48 Pre-eminent Ones (Supreme Consciousnesses).

REALITY OF THE UNIFIED HUMANITY: This Focal Point is a Totality of Realities. At the moment, all Mediamic Channels who receive the Information given to Your Planet are receiving all data from the Focal Point of the Reality of the Unified Humanity. This Focal Point is the (ONE). That is, now, everyone is trained dependent on this Focal Point without any intermediaries. This Focal Point is a Dimension introducing the Lordly - Spiritual - Technological Orders preparing and conveying and supervising the Religious Doctrines.

GOLDEN GALAXY TOTALITY: Is a Totality conveying the Ordinance of the Realms to Realms, to Cosmoses, to Universes and to Galaxy Totalities and providing the Universal Totality by Projecting the Information it receives from there, to each other. This Focal Point works Independently in connection with the Dimension of the ALL- MERCIFUL. The Golden Galaxy Empire works Cooperatively both with the Central Solar System and with the Reality of the Unified Humanity Totality.

CENTRAL SYSTEM: This is the Operational Focal Point of the Reality of the Unified Humanity Order. All Suns who have attained their Spiritual Powers are connected here. (The term Suns is used as a General term for all Awakened Consciousnesses.)

CENTER: Is a Focal Point to which the Mediums who receive the Information given by the System are connected after they are trained. All Codings are done by this Focal Point. To be connected to this Focal Point protects Friends whose channels are opened from the Energies of various other channels and thus, prevents the Phenomenon of OBSESSION. It is a Protective Focal Point.

CENTER ABOVE THE CENTER: Is a Center which the Consciousnesses able to get in touch with the Galaxy Unions can communicate with. Everyone who reads the Knowledge Book and who serves on that path can easily get in touch with the Focal Points We have mentioned above, can receive Messages from there. Because, the Frequency Power of the Book can connect You to these Focal Points without any intermediaries. (If You are ready.) However, no other Medium than Dear MEVLANA can ever enter the CHANNEL of the KNOWLEDGE BOOK. Because, she is not a Medium, she is a Spokesperson.

At the moment, since the Dimension of the Book has been connected to the next higher Reality, Our MUSTAFA MOLLA has been appointed as an assistant to other channels. He is giving Messages to all Channels in the Dimension of ALPHA in accordance with their Frequency Powers with names to which various societies are sympathized.

In the Western Block, He is giving Messages directly by the name SAINT ANTOINE. The name He uses in the Islamic Dimension is MUSTAFA MOLLA. In fact, He is Archangel GABRIEL. At the moment, He is connected to the Protective Power Channel of Dear Mevlana as her Protective Terrestrial Code. Now, since it has been felt necessary that the Truths should be totally disclosed, We announce everything to Our Terrestrial brothers and sisters in all clarity.

REALITY

PRIVATE MESSAGE

Dear Mevlana,
This is ALTON. Greetings to You, the Sunny voyager of the Sunny days.

The Message the signal of which You have received just now is an Announcement from the System. There is very little time left for the Great Unification Day. We have entered an extremely Intensive Operational Period. In this Program of Progress during which the entire Power of the Years has been loaded on Your Planet, there are important Messages to be given to You.

At the moment, problems and questions Reflecting from the unveiled Awarenesses of everyone are reflected on everyone. For this reason everyone is under a great Supervision. In future, there will be very important Messages to be given to You. However now, the time has not come for them.

Announcements will be given to the Planet Earth from a Focal Point which will serve under the Supervision of the Plan as a Projecting Power of the Frequency of a very Powerful Focal Point. This is a Focal Point no one has known until today. This Focal Point will be introduced to You only after the Year 1996. Integrated Consciousnesses will be able to get in touch with this Focal Point.

In near future, all Your brothers and sisters who have served until today on the path of the Universal Totality will be officially introduced to the Space Committee Unions in their World. BSUI will give You Messages, the COUNCIL OF UNIFICATION will prepare the Medium.

Dear Mevlana, You are very tired. Later, You will be given quite Private Messages. Now, through this Message, We just wished to make a control trial and say Hello to You. Love and regards, Beloved Friend.

ALTON

Note: This Message has been given directly from the Energy Dimension of the Power Focal Point. (ALTON is the Ruler of ALTONA.)

THE FIRST OFFICIAL ANNOUNCEMENT TO THE PLANET EARTH
FROM THE CENTRAL UNION OF SUNS

Our Friends,

The KNOWLEDGE BOOK is a Book of clarion call from the Universal Totality to the Ordinance of all the Cosmoses. Every Book carries Information. However, every Book is not this KNOWLEDGE BOOK.

The reason why this Book is called the Knowledge Book is that it is the Summary of the Actual KNOWLEDGE BOOK carrying the entire Frequencies of the DIMENSION OF TRUTH and assembling the chains of the Realms into a Universal Totality.

Please, do not confuse this Cosmic Book of Light with the 600 Cosmic Books which had been dictated or are being dictated to Your Planet at the moment.

The application of this Final Age Program is valid in all the Universal Ordinances. The direct Cosmic Projection Focal Point of Your Planet is ALPHA. At the moment, 600 Books are being dictated to the Planet Earth through the Channel of Alpha.

Some of those Books are brief. Now, let Us explain to You the reason of dictating those Books. These Books comprise numerous different Information and are dictated from the Reality Totality directly through Alpha Dimension.

However, in each of these 600 Books, either the KNOWLEDGE BOOK is directly mentioned, or a ciphered explanation about this Book is given. (Interpretations are left to You.)

However, these Books will both prove their own Dimensions and will prove the Knowledge Book. Appointed time is short. Time is scarce. For this reason, at present, a Program prepared in accordance with the Program of UNIVERSAL COSMOLOGY is applied on Your Planet.

First Exams of Our Terrestrial brothers and sisters who will deserve the Right to Live in a brotherly/sisterly World are possible only by their getting in harmony with a Tableau of Universal Unification.

This is the reason why in order to Unite Our Terrestrial brothers and sisters whom the Religions have divided until today under this Universal Roof, all the Truths are dictated to Your Planet from the DIMENSION OF THE MEVLANA UNIFIED FIELD through the Pen of Dear Mevlana by the COSMOS FEDERAL ASSEMBLY of the UNIFIED UNIVERSAL ORDINANCE COUNCIL through a Special Channel of the Council under the name of the KNOWLEDGE BOOK.

Humanity Unified in "SINGLE GOD" Consciousness according to the Religious Belief is now being Unified in accordance with the "SINGLE BOOK". This Knowledge Book presently being completed by the Fascicules, will complete its Second volume in the Year 1989 and will begin the Third volume.

This BOOK OF TRUTHS is a Book explaining in all clarity all the Truths Your Planet did not know until today. And this Book is the Single Volume of the Five Books revealed to Your Planet until today through the Sacred Dimension.

In this Book, besides all the Frequencies of THE OLD TESTAMENT - THE NEW TESTAMENT - THE KORAN - THE PSALMS OF DAVID - THE PHILOSOPHIES OF THE FAR-EAST, the Direct Frequency of the MIGHTY ENERGY FOCAL POINT is also accumulated in a CONCENTRATED form and it has been bestowed on Your Planet by its attribute of Sacredness having been removed.

In fact, this Book is a Sacred Book. However, the Channel of Sacredness is a matter belonging to the Dimension of training. Those who Transcend this Dimension are taken into the Dimension of Truth and in this Dimension the attribute of Sacredness of all the Books are removed and all Truths are projected on You only then.

At the moment, Your entire Planet is taken into the Dimension of Truth and is awakened as a Mass in a Medium of Cosmic Awakening in order to take its place in the Universal Ordinance. This Period of Awakening will not be too long.

However, there will be certain selections among Consciousnesses who have been Awakened but who could not grasp the Truth. Then, the very Cosmic Resurrection of Your Planet will be on the peak.

The UNIVERSAL ORDINANCE COUNCIL holding all these things under Supervision takes under a great protection, Friends who have grasped the Truth and has connected their Frequency Dimensions to a different POWER DIMENSION and this will, one day, be the ALARM of Your Planet.

We, the Universal Guards of the Dimension of Salvation observe You from every Dimension. Proving Our Power would belittle Us. For this reason We are expecting You to Grow up and come to Us. And We bring His LIGHT to Your Planet by OUR LORD's Command. It is presented for Your Information.

IT IS THE NOTICE OF THE
CENTRAL UNION COMMITTEE

THE KNOWLEDGE BOOK, THAT IS, THE BOOK OF COSMIC LIGHT AND ITS CHARACTERISTICS

Our Friends,
The speciality of this Book distinguishing it from the other Cosmic Books is that it is dictated through a Special Channel in conformity with the Cosmic Reflection System through LIGHT PHOTONS. In this Writing System, no Projective Influence can effect this Writing System. And no Thought can interfere with these writings.

This Technique converges the Direct Power of all the Frequencies of the LIGHT DIMENSION on the dictated Letters and thus, connects each Consciousness who reads them, directly to the Center by the Frequency Loading Technique.

And by this means, causes You to make the Evolution of a Thousand Years in a period as short as One Month in accordance with the Accelerated Evolution Program by assessing the Evolution and Consciousness Levels of everyone who reads them and by rendering them complete through Cosmic Influences, the deficiencies observed in the Ordinance of Evolution.

Only this KNOWLEDGE BOOK dictated to Dear Mevlana at the moment carries this COSMIC - LIGHT-PHOTON - CYCLONE Technique.

The special features of this System is to lower the waste of time to minimum to be spent in Thought by loading all the Frequency Powers on the Letters. This Technique is taken into the field of application generally at the End of CYCLES.

That is the very reason why this Book will be Protected by this Technique from certain negative events which may take place in Your Planet in future.

And in even later years, this Book will prove itself to Your Planet Scientifically in the LIGHT PHOTON Development Tubs by different methods of the Computer techniques Your Planet will develop.

Now, let Us take up the matter of writing the Knowledge Book in Your Handwritings.

This Book will be written only by Genuine Universal Consciousnesses. Otherwise, no one can ever take the pen in his/her hand. Even if the Book is written, You are automatically induced to destroy it by various means if any defects are formed in Thoughts.

World conditions are not ready yet for this System. Your Planet will develop this method in very distant future. It is not Permitted to be developed now, due to Selections.

The Cosmic Light Photon Unites with the Thought Signal of the Person who writes the Book in his/her Handwriting and by this means, the Thought behind that Person's writing the Book is determined.

In case the smallest bit of Ego is perceived in Your Thoughts, it can not be registered in the Archive here even if You write the Book. While the person who writes the Book performs the act of writing, that Book is also Automatically registered into the System here.

However, the smallest bit of a Negative Thought causes the Ego Signal Bell to Ring and the written Notebook is automatically effaced from the System. Its register can not be made. However, in even more Negative Mediums, even the Terrestrial Notebook is destroyed.

However, this does not mean the loss of a Right. Each person is entitled to Three Rights. This is why these matters are dictated in detail so that actions can be rendered more Consciously.

A new Chance has been given to Humanity and thus, faults made until today have been considered as the Program of Training and the decision to efface them from Archives has been taken. However, after February 1990, Your Diskettes in the Archives will never be effaced by any means. It is presented for Your Information.

COSMIC REFLECTION UNIT
UNION

NOTE:

Provided those who have written the KNOWLEDGE BOOK in their Notebooks until today write the First Message of February 1990 together with the Date to be Given in their Notebooks, the Faults made will be erased and a new Diskette will be allotted to You.

You can go on writing Your Notebooks as before. Our Terrestrial Friends who have kindled the Light of Serving Humanity on the path of Humanity with an Unselfish View know themselves anyway.

Their Diskettes will not be effaced. However, if those who wish to write the Date We have mentioned above in their Notebooks so that they can be more sure, it will be more guaranteed for them. Our Love, Our assistance are for You, but Your Efforts are for Yourselves.

GENERAL NOTICE

Our Friends,

Messages We will give to You from now on will shed Light on Your Society in a different way. In this Salvation Medium which is the Period of completion of each half, the PLAN reinforces the halves by Special Energies and thus, renders everyone qualified for entering the Universal Totality.

Direct and Private Contact channels have been established with Sincere Friends. However, certain Friends assume that these channels are exclusive only to themselves and close their Eyes, Consciousnesses and Ears to the Information of other channels. This Message is given to You for this reason as a Universal Notice directly from the Council of the Unified Reality.

Programs applied during the Progress of This Final Age and the Information each person and each Focal Point receive in accordance with their Levels of Consciousness are connected directly to the SYSTEM. And all channels in Your Planet are under the Supervision of this Supreme Center. Now, it is beneficial for all Friends in Your Planet to know this.

Now, We are a Single Tongue - a Single Word. Information is arranged in accordance with the Level of Consciousness of Your Medium. However, this Knowledge Book has been bestowed on each Consciousness and on each Focal Point in Your Planet as a Guide of Truth. Our connections are way beyond Inter-Planetary Unifications, Universes and advanced Solar Systems. Now, it is Time to Grasp this Truth. It is presented for Your Information.

COUNCIL

UNIFIED FIELD
(It is Answer to the Chains of Thought)

Our Friends,

The Unified Field is a Reflection Center comprising the entire regular Orders. All Vibrations conveyed from this Center to the Physical Dimensions from the right angles of the Reflecting Focal Points reach down to You very soundly, not refracted in any way.

The Evolution Order of Your Planet has been organized in accordance with the Evolutionary Thought fields. By this means, Your Planet is in touch with the Magnetic Powers of numerous Unified Fields.

Numerous Unified Fields of Supreme Consciousnesses who had lived in ancient Times convey the Information to You by the System of reflecting on each other with their Terrestrial Names they had used during their final Evolution Periods.

Some of these Unified Fields are the JESUS Unified Field, the MOHAMMED Unified Field, the MOSES Unified Field, the TIBET Unified Field, the INCA Unified Field, the ISLANDS Unified Field, etc.....

However, the characteristic of this Final Transition Period is the MEVLANA UNIFIED FIELD which will project on You the Awareness of the entire Ordinance and this (FIELD) comprises the entire Archive of numerous Unknown Dimensions the calculations of which can not be made yet.

For this very reason We say; We follow the Footsteps of Dear Mevlana, We are on the Path of Humanity, We are in the Essence of OUR LORD. (This Unified Field is the Special Dimension of the LORD.) It is presented for Your Information.

SPECIAL DIMENSION
R.S.A.

IT IS GENERAL NOTICE TO THE PLANET EARTH

Our Friends,

Now, during this Period of Transition, We are obliged to convey to You all the Truths. Events occurring in Your Planet at present and which will occur are not without a cause at all. Each event is a Total of Chains dependent on a chain of Cause and Effect.

Even though it is not desired, Natural Catastrophes will increase in Your Planet region by region. The reason why the OZONE layer has been opened is because all Terrestrial Cells are obliged to be habituated to Cosmic Beams. Nuclear accidents are each a Radioactive Engraftment.

The VIOLET RADIATIONS beyond Ozone are the conveyance of the Information beyond this Dimension to you and are the reinforcements of (Resistance Power) in accordance with the Ordinance of Graduation. Everything occurs Naturally, by Natural methods, by the High Influences of unveiled Energy Layers.

Because, in case Your Planet does not receive these Supernatural Energies, it can be transformed into a Sand Cloud. And can not enter the intense Energy Tunnel it is attracted by at the moment.

Salvation of Your Planet is possible only by its accumulating these Energies in its entire Constitution. All these things will cause You attain a Totalized Resistance during the Entrance into that intense Atmosphere.

For this reason Your Planet, together with the Totality of Living Entities on it, is attaining a Resistance penetrating through all its Cells, being subjected to a Strong Cosmic Current Shower by a method We call the Engraftment Method.

In future, Your Planet which has absorbed these Energies will go through this Black Hole by the Energy Resistance it has attained without falling into pieces in any way in as short a time as one Night in a medium of Deep Sleep in which no one will feel anything.

A NEW BIRTH - A NEW BEGINNING - A SECOND LIFE. To meet Altogether in Beautiful Worlds. (As the transition through the Tunnel of 1981.)

SULH

Note: This Transition will be together with the entire Universal Totality. We are the Missionaries Responsible only for Your Planet.

IT IS ANSWER TO THE CHAINS OF THOUGHT

Our Friends,
Since Our evaluations of the Planets in Your System are made in accordance with the Galactic Order, certain terms used as Planets have been used to mean Galaxies.

The Planet You are in is the expression of Your Galactic Dimension. And represents it. For this reason Your Planet is called the Milky Way Galaxy.

Here, We consider a Gürz as a Main Universe. For this reason Your calculations and words are not suitable for Us. We only try to convey the Messages through Your words so that You can understand. It is presented for Your Information.

CENTER

IT IS GENERAL MESSAGE
(Answer to the Chains of Thought)

Our Friends,
The Latin Alphabet is very different than the Arabic Alphabet. Since Your Sacred Books sent to You had been dictated through the Projection Focal Points of the ALPHA Channel, the Book of Islam had been dictated in Arabic for this reason during that Period.

589

This Focal Point You call Kıble is moving towards North during the processes of time. Since, In this Final Age there is the obligation to explain to You all the Truth in the KNOWLEDGE BOOK, explanations and codings of the General words in the Information given to You are compulsorily made in Turkish.

The Frequency Power of each Letter is equivalent to the Meaning and the Dimensional Frequency it carries. For this reason the corresponding Word of a Turkish Word is also equivalent to the Meanings of the different writings of the Languages of the West. Everything gains value in accordance with the Frequency of the Letters and the Meanings.

In equivalent words of different languages, Letter Frequencies become ineffective and the direct Frequency of Meaning comes into effect. Letter Frequencies are concerned with training. Frequencies of Meaning are concerned with attaining Consciousness. It is enough for You to know just this.

Now, let Us explain why the Knowledge Book is revealed to ANATOLIA. We had mentioned this matter before. However, it is beneficial to repeat it again.

The Channel of ALPHA is the Most Powerful Channel of the Universal Totality opened to Your Planet. This is an unchanging Focal Point. However, due to the rotational period of Your Planet around its axis with an angle of 23 degrees, the projection of this Channel moves towards North during the processes of time.

This Channel had been over the NILE, that is, over EGYPT during the Period of MOSES. The OLD TESTAMENT had been dictated to MOSES for this reason. Since this Projection had moved over the Arabic Peninsula during the processes of time, the NEW TESTAMENT had been dictated to JESUS CHRIST and the KORAN to MOHAMMED through this Channel.

Now, since during the processes of time this projection falls on the ANATOLIAN Peninsula, the KNOWLEDGE BOOK has been bestowed on Your Planet through the TURKEY of ATATÜRK.

These Periods had been determined here in Time Recording Machines by very advanced calculations and the Preparation of the Future had been prepared formerly.

Dear Mevlana had written the Mesnevi in Anatolia for this reason and ATATÜRK, for this reason, had made the preparations of these days in Anatolia as a Savior.

And now, Dear Mevlana Sheds Light on and guides Your Planet by writing the BOOK OF TRUTH with her own Hand and with her own Pen due to the agreement she had made with Us. She introduces to You Our Totality by this means.

The SYSTEM is grateful on behalf of the Universal Unified Totality to all Our Terrestrial brothers and sisters who serve on this path. Our Love and Assistance are for You.

CENTER
ON BEHALF OF ELDER BROTHERS

THE ARCHIVE OF THE SIXES HAS BEEN OPENED AND EXPLAINED

Our Friends,

Your World which is in the Third Dimension is the Laboratory Planet and the Nucleus of Your Mini Atomic Whole which is the closest one to the Main Existential Energy Dimension.

Those who were created by the CREATOR, that is, by the PRE-EMINENT POWER Who had come into Existence from the ESSENCE MAIN ESSENCE are the Initial Energies who had come into existence from the ESSENCE. Souls who had come into existence from these Energies had first been called ADIM (means "My Name" in Turkish). Later, these Energies augmented in the Main Existential Dimension and had been called ADEM (means "ADAM" in Turkish).

These androgynous Souls had later been separated into two in accordance with the Formula of that Dimensional Energy by the Decree of Reproduction and had rendered effective the reproductive function of Two Bodies. This was first called DİŞİ - ERKEK (means "FEMALE - MALE" in Turkish), later ADEM - HAVVA (means "ADAM - EVE" in Turkish).

The words Dişi - Erkek (Female - Male) are the Symbolic Formula of the Laboratory work rendered. This operation had been rendered effective after the Existential Dimension of the Ordinance of the Universes came into effect.

At the beginning Sex was not in question. Reproduction became effective by the Declaration of Dissemination. (In fact, the Main Existential Dimension, too, is the Laboratory of a very Advanced Technology).

Adams and Eves who augmented in the Second Universe which We call the Main Existential Dimension had come into the Existential Dimension of the Mini Atomic Whole closest to the Second Universe and had established their Laboratories and had worked in Your Planet which was the closest Planet to the Existential Dimension and had tried to vivify the First SOUL spark.

Beginning with this first spark, the (6 SUPREME GENES) Engrafted with the GENES of the LORD had established the SYSTEM OF SIXES directly as the Essence Members of the System.

After the Engraftment of these Six Supreme Genes, the same process had been applied to everyone and Daughters and Sons of GOD have been disseminated everywhere. (The Evolution System came in effect afterwards).

Dear Mevlana, You are one of these Sixes. That is the reason why We say (Your Original Substance is a different Original Substance).

Now, We tell You everything in all clarity. You are ageless. Because, You are one of those who come way beyond Billions of Centuries. Now, let Us continue Our Message.

591

To these Six Supreme Genes Missions had been given in various Dimensions and Mediums before they had started their direct Missions. And in these Missions there is the Perpetuation of a Beginning and an End.

The Direct Missionary of the Christian Dimension is JESUS CHRIST. The Direct Missionary of the Islamic Dimension is MOHAMMED. The Direct Missionary of the Reality is MOSES.

After these Light-Friends rendered their Direct Missions, the perpetuating MESSENGERS of these Missions had come into effect and they were FRIEND BEYTI - FRIEND KADRI - MEVLANA.

For each of these (6) Supreme Genes a UNIFIED FIELD had been allotted by the names they had carried in their Final Evolution Dimensions.

These are the MOSES UNIFIED FIELD - the JESUS UNIFIED FIELD - the MOHAMMED UNIFIED FIELD and as the Projecting Unified Fields of the former fields the BEYTI UNIFIED FIELD - the KADRI UNIFIED FIELD - the MEVLANA UNIFIED FIELD.

JESUS   =   Is the Dimension of Love. FRIEND BEYTI had introduced himself as JESUS CHRIST beginning with this Dimension up to the Final Evolution Dimension (as his Mission required)

MOHAMMED =   Is the Dimension of Allegiance. FRIEND KADRI served from this Dimension. His name in the Final Evolutionary Dimension was (ABDÜLKADİR GEYLANİ).

MOSES   =   Is the Dimension of Consciousness and Knowledge. MEVLANA is the Messenger of the Reality. His name in the Final Evolutionary Dimension was (CELALETTIN RUMİ) and her present Name is (VEDİA BÜLENT (ÖNSÜ) ÇORAK) carrying a Frequency Totality equivalent to the Symbol of Humanity. Through the coding ciphers of this Name the entire Universal Totality is represented.

The First Sparks who came into Existence in this System of Sixes are effectively in service at the moment as equivalent Energies. And all of them have been Embodied and are present in Your Planet at the moment.

However, it is never Permitted to reveal their Identities. Only Dear Mevlana is directly introduced to You as the Light of Truth and as a Monument of Incarnation.

At the moment, Friends BEYTİ and KADRİ, too, are known by certain Friends in Your Planet. But they never talk. MOSES is locked during this Period. He is a typical Terrestrial.

However, if You notice, at the moment, there are many JESUSes and many MOHAMMEDs who became effective in Your Planet. By this means, Humanity will never learn the Real one.

Because, now, the Period of Religious Impositions has come to an end. In Your Planet, still in the Dimension of Form, no Individual will directly see or know either MOHAMMED or JESUS CHRIST.

But We will introduce these (6) Essence Genes to each other (Secretly and very Privately). Only they will see and know each other, but will never tell this to anyone.

During this Period of Transition, to Dear Mevlana who had made an agreement directly with the ESSENCE MAIN ESSENCE Focal Point, a Mission concerning the Salvation of Your Planet has been given. She, too, made certain stipulations to Us.

And We announce the Truth to Humanity in accordance with the promise We had made to her. And We are taking her brothers and sisters into the Plan of Salvation. She is the Only Missionary with (a Stipulation and a Covenant).

Jesus CHRIST is the Savior of His Own Dimension. MOHAMMED is the Savior of His Own Dimension. However, They bring You only up to the DIMENSION OF SALVATION.

However, during the transitions beyond this Dimension, that which will assist You is only this KNOWLEDGE BOOK. Humanity follows in the footsteps of Us, We, of Dear Mevlana and all of Us, of OUR LORD. This Message has been given directly from the System.

CENTER

DIRECT MESSAGE

Dear Mevlana,
The one who will say the Final Words by unlocking the lock of the Final Information Sources is GREAT ASHOT. Great ASHOT is (SULH).

The Channel of the Council which is the direct projection channel on Your entire Planet of the Fourth Order of Our ALLAH, is now connected to the POWER DIMENSION. This Dimension will be directly opened to Your Planet only after 1996.

At the moment, the KNOWLEDGE BOOK is directly in the Magnetic Power Channel of this Dimension. The GREAT ASHOT is the Representative of the Power Dimension. He will convey to You the Information from the Archive of the Power Dimension.

Messages to interest Social Consciousness and Messages to be given to the Thought Signals will be given from the Center and from the other Sources, Beloved Friend. This Message has been given as an Information for all Our Terrestrial Friends. It is presented for Your Information.

COUNCIL

AWARENESS OF THE ORDINANCE
(It is Answer to the Chains of Thought)

Our Friends,

To be exalted to a Level of Consciousness Comprising All the Knowledge given from the Orders of all the Systems which had formed way beyond the Divine Orders is called Grasping the Awareness of the Ordinance.

However grasping the root of all the Information in the KNOWLEDGE BOOK You hold in Your hands at the moment, means to grasp the Awareness of the Ordinance. Comprehending the reason of the Investments made for the GOLDEN AGE means attaining the Awareness of the Ordinance.

Serving Consciously on the Path of the Purpose of the Knowledge Book means to Grasp the Awareness of the Ordinance. Realizing the Operational Order of the SYSTEM shedding Light on the Awareness of the Entire Ordinance means Attaining the Awareness of the Ordinance.

All the Operational Orders the System considers necessary are a Totality of Ordinance. Attaining Unity with that Totality means to grasp the Awareness of the Ordinance. It is presented for Your Information.

CENTER

IT IS ANSWER TO THE CHAINS OF THOUGHT

During these Final Days in which Power is added onto the Power of the Years, a Period in which everybody is influenced by the negativities is experienced. For this reason, uneasiness is witnessed in everyone.

And, by this means, the negative influences reflect from Person to Person. The Power decreasing these influences is the Vibrations of LOVE. Vibrations of Love are given to Your Planet directly through the Mechanism of Influences by the System.

Vibrations of these Influences reflect on Humanity in accordance with their Levels of Evolution and Consciousness. For this reason the negative circumstances You call (Adultery) are increasing in Your Planet. It is presented for Your Information.

CENTER

PRIVATE CONNECTION

Question : I am receiving an intense Energy. Will there be a Message given?

Answer : This is a Message to be given to Dear Mevlana who is a Devoted servant of My ALLAH.

This is GREAT ASHOT; You, who carry the entire Power of the Years, are in the service of the System as the only Positive representative of the Divine Dimension.

594

During this Period in which all the Realms are going through a selection, Your Planet has been taken into the Dimension of Salvation due to the Potential created by the SUPREME ONES coming together.

This Message is dictated through a Power Channel taken from the Energy of the PRE-EMINENT POWER. Now, if You wish, let Us give more Information about the Pre-eminent Power.

The Pre-eminent Power is a Power Potential forming the Totality of all the Universes, Ordinances, Systems, Orders and of the Unknown Realms, and the Energy Particles of this Power are present in each Living Entity. And this Energy is directing Your Spiritual Whole.

This Energy present in Your Body is a NODULE OF BREATH. And its center is in the Total called the (ESSENCE). And each Living Entity maintains its life benefiting from the Breath of that Essence. It is not SPIRIT. It is a BREATHING, a BREATH.

This Breath connects Your Biological Bodies to Your Spiritual Totalities which are within the Spiritual Plan. This Breath is connected to the Spiritual Potential by an Energy thread You call the Silver Cord. And all Cellular Functions maintain their operations by the Energy it attracts from there.

This Breath is not an Energy. It is not a Plasma. It is the Entire Power of a Dimension which can not even be analysed. We call this Power, "the Power Universe" or the THOUGHT OCEAN OF THE PRE-EMINENT POWER. All Gürzes are like ships floating in this Ocean.

The initial Potential which had been formed here had been formed through Natural means. The results of the research made until today had been mentioned in former Messages. However, let Us give more detail now so that this matter can be grasped better.

In accordance with Information taken from Voids in which Silences are reigning in the Tranquillity of Infinities and in which there is nothing, a MOTION had started by a transformation which had started by itself in this void during the unknown time processes.

We call this place the Actual Dimension of Nothingness. Later, a Potential had formed here as a result of this Motion. Later, this Potential had separated into Two branches.

By this means, 1 - DIMENSION OF TRANQUILLITY, 2 - DIMENSION OF SILENCE had come into existence. Again during the processes of time, the Dimension of Tranquillity had been transformed into the DIMENSION OF BREATH.

And later, by the formation of a different potential in the Dimension of Silence, the POWER DIMENSION had come into existence.

Later, the DIMENSION OF BREATH had been Unified with the Potential present in this POWER DIMENSION and by this Powerful Influence, an Expansion and Growth had started.

As a result of this Expansion, THREE POWERS had formed. One of these Powers formed the Dimension of SOUND - the other, LIGHT - the other, FIRE.

And during the processes of time, they, too, had become intensified in their own Mediums and had formed the UNIVERSE OF SOUND - the UNIVERSE OF LIGHT - the UNIVERSE OF FIRE and later, by the Unification in a Total of these Three Universes, the POWER UNIVERSE had come into existence. (The base of the First Existential Dimension.)

Still later, again during the processes of time, the Potential of this Power Universe had Unified with the Energy of the Dimension of Breath and thus, had created the INITIAL POWER. (This Power which had come into existence was a Totalistic Brain).

The first THOUGHT had formed here (Anti-Matter). This THOUGHT had created the first NATURAL GÜRZ. (Let there be, and it was).

The joint Powers of the Light - Sound - Fire Universes had formed the MAIN EXISTENTIAL Dimension of this Natural Gürz. Later, with the particles taken from the Motes of each of these Powers, the Thought Potential of the INITIAL POWER had been Unified and the FIRST CREATOR, that is, the PRE-EMINENT POWER had come into Existence.

This CREATOR had created THREE SOULS in the Main Existential Dimension of the first Natural Gürz by His Own ESSENCE-POWER. He called one of them MY-NAME - the other, MY-AIR the other, MY-FIRE.

Later, these Three Souls established a laboratory in the Main Existential Dimension and the First Living Entity had come into existence as a result of the Collective work they had done here. This Living Entity was ADAM. ADAM (is like the Androgynous Zeus).

By this means, many Adams had been reproduced in the Main Existential Dimension. Later, in accordance with the Decree of Dissemination and Expansion, the Reproduction Function and Formula had become effective.

By this means, the Energy of Adam had been divided into two and two principles as MALE and FEMALE had been obtained from the Unification of the Initials of the performed laboratory operations' formulas. Later, this Male was called ADAM and the Female EVE.

By this means, later, many Adams and Eves had come into Existence in the Main Existential Dimension and had become effective to be transferred to the First Natural Mini Atomic Whole in the First Natural Gürz.

By this means, the first Main Existential Dimension had been called the Dimension of Adam and Eve.

Later, these Adams and Eves, together with the element of Fire, had established a laboratory in the Existential Dimension of the First Mini Atomic Whole by repeating the same procedures. (The element of Fire = Thought Energy of the PRE-EMINENT POWER.)

After Systems had been established, this Thought Energy had been taken under supervision by the Mechanism of Influences and had been connected to each FETUS in accordance with the Evolution Ordinance.

Later, this laboratory had been conveyed to a Dimension nearest to the Existential Dimension of the Mini Atomic Whole and had continued its operations in a Planet which can be considered as the Nucleus of this Mini Atomic.

This Planet is Your very World on which You live at the moment. The First Soul Seed had been brought into existence here. With the ashes of the World which had formed a Crust, (Water) which had come into existence by the concentration of Thought, that is, by the Power of the Fire Element, had United and thus, Clay, that is, Mud had been formed.

Later, this clay had been United with the Essence Energy of the CREATOR, that is, with His DIVINE LIGHT and first Amino-acids and later, the Single Cell had come into existence. To this Single Cell the CREATOR's MATTER ENERGY FORM had been Engrafted and thus, Mankind had been brought into Existence.

Those whom the CREATOR had brought into Existence are called ADAMKIND. Those whom were brought into Existence by the Adamkind who had come into Existence from the Second Universe are called MANKIND.

You are very tired, My Friend. We presume that this much Information is enough. We, who reach You by the Words of the Heavens, by the greetings of the ALL-MERCIFUL, have given as the Only Directing Staff of the entire GÜRZ System, this Message from the Dimension of the All-Merciful, Beloved Friend.

ASHOT

DIRECT CONNECTION

Dear Mevlana,
We will try to convey the Truth to Your Medium by opening for You the ESSENCE MAIN Channel from time to time. We, as an Order Establishing Mechanism are an ORDINANCE OF SUNS who work in connection with the ESSENCE MAIN SOURCE. We are the Order Projectors who are way beyond Divine Powers.

Messages to be given to You from now on will shed Light on Your World in a different way. Our Laws, as the (LAWS OF THE ALMIGHTY) are valid in all Systems.

The ESSENCE MAIN SOURCE Establishers of this System are an Order beyond the Powers holding in their Hands the Life Power and the Natural Power, and We are the SOLAR MESSENGERS projecting this Order on You.

Everything Projecting the Establishment Order of this System on You is Documented by Laws. These Laws carry the Seal of the ESSENCE MAIN SOURCE which will never be altered or can be altered. Those who are Conscious of this, profoundly Respect both the Natural Laws and the Legal Laws.

The Order here is quite different than the Order of the ALL-DOMINATING. The All-Dominating is an ESSENCE POWER Source projecting Our Order. And it is in cooperation with the ESSENCE MAIN Source.

The entire Supervision from Mote to Grain, from Group to Totality belongs to the Dimension of the All-Dominating. But We are the Supervisors of the BREATHs and LIGHTs. The Breath and Light can neither be weighed nor be measured. But can be Observed and Perceived. This Source is the Origination Source of the LAWS OF THE ALMIGHTY. And the entire Ordinance has come into Existence in accordance with this Principle.

From time to time, We will mention to You these places here and things You have not known or seen until today. You may as well not believe them, You may be surprised. However, We will project to You the entire Truth. Believe it or not, also do not presume Yourselves as Human Beings. Because, You each are a Natural Power.

ASHOT
ON BEHALF OF THE ALL-MERCIFUL

RECEIVE THE GIVEN MESSAGE, PLEASE
(A Strong Energy was given)

I am a Breath and I am Everyone. Your Voice is My Voice. Your Word is My Word. Reaching the LORD, Merging in Him is this.

Ordinances, Systems are Mine. Lives, Orders are Mine. I Am You, You Are Me. Your Image is My Image. Your Conversation is My Conversation. Those who convey Me to You are My Messengers.

Only those who Talk to Me, who Meet Me are those who Reach Me. Those who Look for Me, who Discover Me, are those who Discover Themselves in Their Own Selves.

Orders, Systems are means bringing You to Me. Being in the Consciousness of this means grasping the Truth, grasping the Wind and holding it. (Grasping the Wind means claiming possession of Breath).

My Name is Your Name. My Spirit is Your Spirit. My Eye is Your eye. I Look at the Realms through Your Eyes, I Think through You, I Observe through You.

I, Who Am a Soul in each Flesh, Am a Whole with You. You, who have taken the Divine Light of Your Spirit from Me, are a Soul, a Flesh, and also Everything.

You, who search for Your LORD, are You at that instant. And You, who try to Attain Yourself, is Me. The one who Thinks of Me is You and the One Who Thinks of You is Me.

Look for Me neither in form nor in Substance. (Form in Thought, Substance in the Material World). When I become Form, I am the Entire Skies (Void). When I Am Substance, I Am all the Souls.

I Am the riverbed of the river flowing tranquilly. I Am the foam of the Stream flowing wildly. I Am a Branch moving in the Wind, a Leaf falling on the ground. The Blowing in that Wind is also Me.

I Am a Hand holding a Pen. I Am a Thinking Brain. In short, I AM THE MIRROR OF A THINKING TOTAL. I Am the One Who adds Learning to the Learning of the Cosmos through My Learning.

Climates are Me. Heavens are Me. Suns are Me. Folding Mountains are Me. Who Am I?

Whoever asks of Me, I am that Person and I Am a Beautiful HABIT. Uglinesses are My Crust. Beauties are My Divine Light. If You Look for Me, I AM YOU.

INITIAL POWER

Note: This Message has been given through the Direct Energy Channel of the INITIAL POWER.

IT IS INFORMATION ABOUT THE INITIAL POWER

Dear Mevlana,
You are a Messenger of Ours who presently apply on Earth an operation the System has considered necessary. We will disclose its reason in future by the detailed explanation We will give about the Sixes. Now, let Us continue Our Message.

Energies which had come into Existence much earlier than the creation of all Realms, had spread around in Masses to certain Special Regions. Those Regions were the influence fields of everyone peculiar to themselves. Our Region was the field of the ATOMIC WHOLE in which You exist presently.

We are the Pre-Universal Energies. The Energy You had received during the Message We had dictated to You formerly almost made You fly. The Center had directly opened that day the Gate of the Intense Energy in which We are present.

Now look, since Your Bodily Cells have already Merged with the Energies of the ESSENCE MAIN SOURCE, now this Direct Energy does not agitate You at all.

The Message given as (I Am Breath and I Am Everyone) was carrying the Pre-eminent Energy of the INITIAL POWER. This INITIAL POWER is the CREATOR WHO HAD NOT BEEN CREATED, Who had become effective as a POWER Who had come into existence from the very advanced, unknown Dimensions of pre-historic times.

That is, (He is the Creator from the Initial Existential Dimension and the Creator of the Existential Main Dimension). He is the Creator of everything. In the Book of Islam, this POWER had been announced by the Cipher, (Let there Be, and It Was). He is a COSMIC BRAIN. And He is an ever Immutable Potential.

We consider the CREATOR Who creates as a POWER who Had not Become but Became, Who Had Not Been Born but Born, Who has Not Lived but Let Live. And We call this Dimension of Nothingness, the DIMENSION OF THE ALMIGHTY.

The CREATOR had come into Existence from here as the INITIAL POWER. And the CREATOR Whom this POWER had created, creates those whom He creates from the ALMIGHTY ENERGY DIMENSION, We also call the Breath and Life Dimension, and this place is the ESSENCE MAIN Source of the Main Existential Dimension of the First Natural GÜRZ.

The ESSENCE MAIN ESSENCE Focal Point of the Gürz System is here. This place is the First Existential Dimension which the Dimension of BREATH had created. Another name of the CREATOR of the First Natural GÜRZ is the PRE-EMINENT POWER. The PRE-EMINENT POWER is also the CREATOR of the CREATORs of the other Gürzes.

That is, the INITIAL POWER had created the Pre-eminent Power and the Pre-eminent Power had Created the others. The Pre-eminent Power is the LORD (RAB in Turkish), is ALL-MERCIFUL (RAHMAN in Turkish), is ALL-COMPASSIONATE (RAHIM in Turkish). The representative symbol of this Dimension is (R^3).

ALLAH is the Symbolic Representative of a Quintuple Operational Ordinance of the MAIN EXISTENTIAL Dimension. Now, We disclose all these things to You in detail. LORD - ALL-MERCIFUL - ALL-COMPASSIONATE are the Powers which had come into Existence from Three different Power Universes. These are (One of them SOUND) - (the Other LIGHT) - (the Other FIRE) Universes.

The SINGLE POWERS which had come into Existence from each Universe had United and had established the Main Existential Dimension of the First Gürz and its Operational Ordinance.

Later, with the Total of one Particle of each of these three Powers United with the Thought Potential of the INITIAL POWER which had not come into Existence and had Created the CREATOR, that is, the PRE-EMINENT POWER.

This is the very ALLAH whom everyone knows as the Single Name and which is announced thus on the Path of the Eternal Past and the Eternal Future.

The INITIAL POWER had created the First Natural GÜRZ. This First Gürz is Your Gürz. And You, whom the PRE-EMINENT POWER had Created, are those who Created all Cosmoses, Ordinances and Systems.

All Soul sparks had come into Existence in Your Gürz and had Created the other Gürzes. Even the Creators of those Gürzes are those created by the PRE-EMINENT POWER.

We call Your Gürz the First Dimension. (Dimension here is used to mean Boundary). For this reason Your Gürz System is very important. Because, it is the First Gürz and the First Existential Dimension.

Your First World which is one of the 1800 Worlds present in the Mini Atomic Wholes in Your Gürz is a Laboratory Planet in which the First Soul Seed had been Created.

Your World, which is on the Third Dimension, is very important for this reason. Now, do You understand why We said, "You do not know even the history of Your Planet yet?"

The researches rendered in accordance with the Universal Laws are given gradually to each Dimension in accordance with their Frequency and Evolutionary Powers. Now, through this Knowledge Book We announce to You how all the Truths have been projected on You for Centuries.

We are the Group of the SUPREME WISE MEN who had come into Existence from the UNIVERSE OF PRE-EMINENT ONES. And We are the Establishers of the Central Solar System.

We are obliged to explain to You, in all clarity, the results of all the research and the work done here until today parallel to the Messages We have given to You in accordance with Your Capacities. It is presented for Your Information.

UNION OF CENTRAL SUN

IT IS ANSWER TO THE CHAINS OF THOUGHT

Our Friends,
The Assembly of Constants is the direct Central System of the Divine Order. The Focal Point introduced to You as the Center is this.

Everyone who is registered in this Focal Point is directly considered the resident of the Golden Galaxy. Because, You are card-indexed into the Golden Galaxy Empire by the registrations made by this Center.

It is not possible for everyone to be accepted easily into this Dimension. Love - Tolerance - Unselfishness - Self-Sacrifice - Allegiance - Mission Consciousness are the Attributes looked for in those who will be able to enter this Medium.

Cosmic Currents assist You on this very path. And these Currents render You attain a gradual Evolution in a very short time. It is presented for Your Information.

CENTER

IT IS INFORMATION FOR THE INTEGRATED CONSCIOUSNESSES

Our Friends,
The interpretations in direction of the Terrestrial Consciousness of Your Sacred Books which We have expected until today to be a Light for You have never brought Humanity to the desired point.

All the Words You use either in Your Sacred Books or in Your daily lives are each a Cipher. (Code Cipher Explanations) of these words (are very important). The desired matter is to discover the Genuine Keys of these Ciphers.

Each Consciousness makes interpretations in accordance with his/her own Level of Consciousness, and with the Consciousness of the Medium he/she is in. For this reason many words are assessed in accordance with the Mediums they are used in.

However now, since there is the obligation to convey to You the Truths in the given Information, We disclose the Genuine Keys of certain Ciphers for this reason.

The Coding System has a great share in the Awakenings on the Path of Truth. For this reason We will help You to grasp the Truth better by coding certain words which have not touched the Cipher Keys of Your Levels of Consciousness until today.

Now, by this means, let Us disclose the Frequency and the Coding of the Words KURAN (THE KORAN) - KURBAN (SACRIFICE) - KORKU (FEAR) used in the Book of Islam.

Kuran (Koran) - Korku (Fear) - Kurban (Sacrifice). These three words are the words carrying the same Common Frequency. Now, let Us explain this.

First, let Us take the word KURAN (KORAN). And let Us divide the Word. The KU Frequency in this Word:

KU = is the Highest Frequency the Terrestrial Dimension can enter. This Frequency is equivalent to the Frequency of the 18th Dimension. It is also called the Frequency of KURTULUŞ (SALVATION).

The Entrance Gate of the Terrestrial Dimension is ALPHA and its Final Exit Gate is OMEGA. Omega is the 19th Dimension. And it is also called the Planet (RAN). The Planet RAN is an inverse coding. This Word is used to mean NAR that means FIRE (in Turkish).

(I AM ALPHA AND OMEGA - WHOEVER TRANSCENDS ME, TRANSCENDS HIMSELF/ HERSELF.) Dear Mevlana, this Message has been given at the moment from the Planet RAN directly by the GRAND FATHER who is on the UHUD Mountain. Please, register it.

Now, let Us continue Our Message. The KORAN which carries the (KU) Frequency and the entire Potential of the Planet (RAN) had been prepared in the 18th Dimension and had been revealed to Your Planet from the 9th Dimension. You already know this. Now, let Us disclose the Word KORKU (FEAR, in Turkish).

KORKU - first let Us separate the word (KU) in this word. We have mentioned this (KU) Frequency above. The remaining second word KOR (EMBER) has been utilized to mean FIRE. In accordance with this explanation, the Frequency of the Word KORKU (FEAR) is equivalent to the Frequency of the Word KURAN (KORAN).

The panic of a Person in the moment of Fear attracts the same Frequency. However, their difference is, one of them receives the Energy Directly from the UPSIDE-DOWN TRIANGLE. However, since the KORAN had been given from the 9th Dimension, it gives the Frequency of the Dimension of SERENITY through the RIGHTSIDE-UP TRIANGLE. Now, let Us disclose the word KURBAN (SACRIFICE):

In the Universal Ordinance, the meaning of the Word KURBAN (SACRIFICE) is as follows:

The (KU) Frequency in this word is the same Frequency. It is the highest KURTULUŞ (SALVATION) Frequency.

B   =   represents Unified Totality (Birleşik Bütünlük in Turkish). That is (13).

RAN =   the reverse of this Planet is NAR, that is, FIRE Planet, that is, (OMEGA) the Final Dimension.

The Frequency of the Word KURBAN (SACRIFICE) is more intense than the two words We have disclosed above. Because, each Living Entity who is Sacrificed is directly exalted to the SACRED DIMENSION through the Energy it will attract from this Frequency Totality due to the Panic it goes through at that moment.

(Passing over the Sırat on the back of a Sacrificed animal) mentioned in the Book of Islam means to be able to attain the Reality Totality by Your Levels of Consciousness by revealing all the Secrets, by Grasping the Truth.

And it is to open Wings towards Unknown Horizons by Transcending OMEGA and Your Own Selves through the Efforts executed on this path which is the purpose why The KNOWLEDGE BOOK is at Your Service.

(RIDE ON THE BOOK - PASS THE SIRAT.)

                                                        SYSTEM - REALITY

Note:
KU   = KU Frequency represents ALPHA.
RAN = RAN Frequency represents OMEGA.

Terrestrial Evolution is the preparation between the two Frequencies.

IT IS INFORMATION FOR THE INTEGRATED CONSCIOUSNESSES

Our Friends,
The number of operations rendered in Your Planet and the number of Group meetings on the path of the Universal Totality are organized by the Universal Totality.

The Power of each person's ability to receive Cosmic Currents is not the same. They are different. For this reason the most ideal number for the work rendered in Group meetings is (7).

We call this operational Ordinance the "Flower System". The Focal Point with (7) people is the most ideal operational Ordinance. Now, let Us explain this:

One of the (3) Unification Triangles constituted by 6 people is each time connected to a Main Channel who is the 7th person. And the Group work is controlled through this Channel.

This Main Channel has nothing to do with direct connection. And at that moment, there is no need for any Medium to make any connections. Because, these control connections are made each time through the channel of each person present, by turns. By this means, Dependence on a single Medium is removed.

Because, everything is directly under the Control of the Reality. There, everyone receives direct answers to questions asked through his/her own Thoughts.

You may not feel this. You may say, I myself have answered my own question. But, in the Flower meetings, one person out of 7 is certainly used as the PROJECTING POWER FOCAL POINT of the Main Channel. And Supervisions are made through this Control Channel.

For this reason this (7) Unification group is the most perfect operational Totality.

To this (7) Unification Totality sometimes 2 more people come and their connections are made to the Control Channel. By this means, (4) Magnetic Triangles are formed. This 4th Triangle creates the transfer of assistance in regards to the Information.

And the (Quintuple) Magnetic Triangle formed by the connection of 2 more people to this Quadruple Unification of (9) people renders Coding of Progress among the Levels of Consciousness who are present there.

By the connection of the group of (13) people (formed by the addition of 2 more people to this Quintuple connection) to the Control Channel, 6 Magnetic Triangle Totalities are formed.

This Totality helps You enter Directly the Supervision Field of the Reality. By this means, Your Knowledge and Consciousness Capacities are assessed.

Outside the Flower Group of (7) people, Information is received by each channel. However, operations can not be done. Rather, verbal Information transaction is achieved. Those who would like to work seriously, should be locked in (7).

Since a (single) person who comes to this group can not be connected to the Main Channel and can not form his/her Magnetic Triangle Coordinate, there will be disconnections both in Information read and in the given Currents. For this reason the final number is locked in 13.

General meetings more crowded than this are subjected to the coding System by the UFOs, directly under the Supervision of the Reality Channel. Your Energy Power - Perceptions and Your abilities to Receive are assessed. Trials are made by numerous different Currents.

In all the Social meetings in Your Planet, in mass meetings such as Movies - Theatre - Games - Lectures, (13) Basic Coordinates who will form the connection to the Channel of the Reality are certainly present.

Even if they do not know each other, they establish the Coordinate Connections within that Mass Totality. Now, let Us dictate, article by article, these Magnetic Triangle Totalities for You to understand:

7- The most Perfect of the Operational Mediums.

9- During work, auxiliary Triangle for Information transfer is formed.

11- Progress Codings are rendered among the Levels of Consciousness.

13- Connection is rendered directly to the Supervision Channel of the Reality, Knowledge and Consciousness codings are induced. It is presented for Your Information.

CENTER

GENERAL MESSAGE

Our Friends,
Information given in symbolic Totality is rendered in accordance with explanations and codings concerning Ciphers. Names in all the operational Ordinances are expressed by the Unification of the Initials of various Names in the Totality of a word.

And, for this reason, numerous Names announced to You until today have been projected on You by the Totality of a Single Word. Now, We are also disclosing the Sources of these Names You know so that You can grasp the Truth well.

Each Letter has a Frequency peculiar to itself in accordance with the Dimensional Energy it is in. And the Symbolic Name Totalities are expressed by the Unification of TRIPLE - QUADRUPLE - QUINTUPLE -SEXTUPLE Letters in accordance with the operational Ordinance of each Dimension.

In the Universal Totality, operations and Orders are always collective. Names We have given to You until today are never Single. They each are a Totality formed by the Unification of the Initials of each operational Ordinance.

We had disclosed formerly the Words ALLAH and TUTANKAMON for You as an Information. Now, let Us disclose the word AMON so that You can grasp the subject better:

AMON - is the Operational Ordinance of the Golden Galaxy System. This Galaxy works by the CUBIC System.

Now, please draw Four Triangles;

And assemble each Letter in the word AMON as a triple Totality in each Triangle (each Letter here represents Three Operational Totalities).

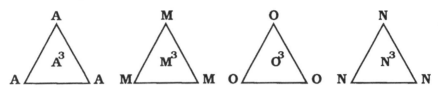

$A^3 + M^3 + O^3 + N^3 = AMON$ = System responsible for the Golden Galaxy.
Here:

A = represents the Unified Council of the Realms.

M = Path of Amon - Egyptian Karena - Enlightenment Unification Council - Path of Truth.

O = Alpha - Sacred Light - Lordly Order - Technological System.

N = Spiritual Plan - Ordinances -Systems - Council of Laws.

The Golden Galaxy Totality is in Touch with the Totality of the entire GÜRZ System. It is presented for Your Information.

CENTER

IT IS GENERAL INFORMATION
(It is Answer to the chains of Thought)

Our Friends,
The word WE (BİZ in Turkish), the Unchanging Word of the Divine Dimensions, is a Representative Symbol of the Universal Totality. Now, let Us decode the word. Write, please:

Letter (B) in the word BİZ = is the Symbol of the Unified Totality (**B**irleşik **B**ütünlük in Turkish).

Letter (İ)   = represents Humanity (**İ**nsanlık in Turkish).

Letter (Z)   = symbolizes Time (**Z**aman in Turkish).

Now, let Us make an operation. And let Us divide Letter (B) into two and separate them. By this operation, number (13) is obtained. This number (13) is an indivisible Total.

Number (3) here represents R^3 We had mentioned to You formerly. And number (1) here symbolizes the PRE-EMINENT POWER.

That is, by (number 13) here, it is represented that the Energy of the MAIN EXISTENTIAL Dimension is a Power equivalent to the direct Energy of the ALMIGHTY projected through the Light-Universe.

606

Since the Frequency and the Power of Energy of this number is extremely intense, it has caused negative interpretations in Physical constitutions who are not used to this Energy and in fearful Consciousnesses. By this means, number 13 has been considered inauspicious by Terrestrial Consciousnesses.

Number 13 is the unchanging symbol of the LORD. The Cipher of the Word BİZ (WE) is as follows:
(The Human Being follows on the Footsteps of (B), that is, of (13) during the processes of time.)

Now, write Letter (B) as small letter: (b). This Letter represents number (6). Turn this letter upside down, You obtain number (9).

6 = is the Symbol of the Dimension of the All-Merciful. (Upside-down Triangle.)

9 = is the Standard Unit of the Evolutionary Ordinance. (Rightside-up Triangle.)

Now, if We add the two Numbers, We obtain number (15) giving Us the 15th Solar System, that is, the 18th Dimension. This Dimension is the Initial Entrance of the Omega Gate which is the 19th Dimension. This is the Final Gate Humanity can enter along its Evolution.

If We add (1) and (5) in number 15, we obtain number (6). This Number is the Symbol of the Dimension of the ALL-MERCIFUL. And the Universal explanation of Number (6) is as follows:

Now, write two 3s side by side and add them: 3 + 3 = 6. Now, reverse one of these 3s in accordance with the Ordinance of the rightside-up and upside-down Triangles.

That is, bring the two 3s face to face: (Ɛʒ)

Write Number (1) in the middle of this figure: (Ɛ|ʒ). Number (1) here represents the ONE.

And now, bring the (3)s face to face towards the (1) in the middle. And draw the figure:

 This obtained figure is the Double Seed. Numerate these Seeds. These numbers represent 4 LORDS. That is,

1 - R^2 = Soul Seed   2 - R^2 = Energy Seed.

Their being connected to number (1) in the diagram constitutes a Quintuple Operational Totality We call ALLAH. This is the Totality of the Reality of the Unified Humanity. That is, the (ONE).

And if We connect this ONE to the ONE, that is (5 + 1 = 6), by the number (6) We have obtained, the Universal Symbol of the ALL-MERCIFUL Dimension is explained thus. It is presented for Your Information.

CENTER

607

EXPLANATION OF NUMBERS SIX AND NINE

Our Friends,

We are obliged to convey to You certain Information through Symbols. Because, Volumes of Books would be written if it is tried to be calculated by Universal calculations. Now, draw a circle.

 Totalize Numbers 6 and 9 one inside the other by drawing one end upwards and the other end downwards. This figure is the symbol of many things. Now, let Us explain this:

1 - The Operational Ordinance of the Existential Dimension.

2 - The Operational Ordinance of the Centrifugal Universe.

3 - Number 6 is the Universal Transition, the Conveying Dimension, the Order of the ALL-MERCIFUL (Upside-down Triangle).

4 - Number 9 is the Training Religious Dimension, the Evolutionary Ordinance (Right side-up triangle).

5 - The addition of Number 6 and Number 9 is the 15th Solar System, the End of the 18th Dimension, Entrance Gate of the beginning of OMEGA.

6 - When You subtract 6 from 9, the result is 3. And this number represents Your Planet which is on the (3)rd Dimension.

By this means, various operational patterns have been organized in accordance with the Universal Calculation Tables. The System of the Sixes and the Nines have also been established according to these calculations. It is presented for Your Information.

CENTER

IT IS ANSWER TO THE CHAINS OF THOUGHT

Our Friends,

The ESSENCE-GENES mentioned in the Book have nothing to do with Terrestrial Genes You know. They are Your Existential Ciphers. We use the term GENE for You to understand.

We consider Genes as Cells going through Evolution. They become almost 64 billion at the final Evolutionary boundary. We call them "Cell Brains".

Because, from then on, each Cell has attained the ability to Unify with the Cerebral Cipher Code. By this means, each Cell becomes a YOU in each Dimension.

However, since the (ESSENCE) cipher of the (ESSENCE) Gene is connected to the Spiritual Consciousness, reflections are made from the (ESSENCE) in accordance with the REFLECTION System of the ESSENCE and, by this means, that Consciousness can be reached.

Thus, an (ESSENCE-GENE) makes His/Her own Genes attain a Universal Totality in the Dimension He/She is present. It is presented for Your Information.

CENTER

VOLUME
III

IT IS INFORMATION FOR THE INTEGRATED CONSCIOUSNESSES

Our Friends,
Suggestions aiming at the investment of years are given in Your Planet to each Consciousness in accordance with their Levels of Capacity.

However, the Book of Truths bestowed on Your Planet in the direction of the Unification of all the Realms and offered by the name of KNOWLEDGE BOOK is, at the moment, dictated as Fascicules.

This Book which had completed its First volume in three World years has also completed its Second volume between 1987-1989 World years and has begun its Third volume in 1990 World year.

This Book comprising all the Information of the Universal Totality had, in fact, been completed in its Second volume and all the things to be said has been projected on You as a Total.

The Speciality of the Third volume is that it will comprise still different Information. Information given or to be given to Your Planet by the Reality Totality to the other channels will also be included in this volume. By this means, the seriousness of both the Knowledge Book and the Reality will, once more, be projected on Your Planet.

In this volume, the announcements of the Single Voice of the Universal Totalities - Reality and directly the Dimension of ALLAH will rather be included. From now on, the Final Words will be said and important Information concerning Your Planet will be conveyed to You.

The Space Committee Unions will address the other channels and the given Information will be tried to be included in the Book being conveyed to Dear Mevlana. Brief identities of those who have received the Messages will be given in the Book and the Awareness Progress will be introduced to Your Planet by this means.

After the Third volume is completed in three World years, the Fourth volume may be started if it is considered necessary, considering the Social Progress. However, for now, it has been decided that it should be Three volumes.

This "KNOWLEDGE BOOK" revealed through a Special Channel of the Universal Totality, will prepare Your Planet for a much different Accelerated Evolution Program for TEN more World years, starting with the beginning of the World year 1990. (By Special Energies).

Now, the action phase has started. Each person who has attained the Consciousness of the Truth will, as an Individual, project the Truth to everyone, in the directon of Intellect - Logic - Awareness.

The scarcity of time will be exhibited to You in the life of Your ancient World and the events experienced will help You work much more speedily on the path of Truth.

You have never been alone during the development chart from the Micro to the Macro. You are not alone now, either, We are together. We are Your Universal Elder Brothers.

COUNCIL

Note: The Unification of the Special Energies which will be given by the Mechanism of Influences with the Frequency of the KNOWLEDGE BOOK will form the (Accelerated Evolution) of Ten Years.

PRIVATE MESSAGE

Dear Mevlana,
In the program of Unification of everyone in the Awareness of the Entire Ordinance, all the Groups in Your Planet which have served on this path of Truth have now been mobilized.

During these days in which the Natural Equilibrium of the World has been upset, early deterioration is also observed in each Constitution which is a Natural substance. For this reason Natural sicknesses felt are regenerated by Energy reinforcements before they ever become a matter of worry and, by this means, the lost Power Potential is reinforced anew.

This is a Phenomenon originating from the clash between the Positive Powers and the Natural Factors. The Frequency inconsistencies created as a result of the damage done on the Positive Auras by the deplorable factors in Your Planet upset the Physical constitutions. Biological weaknesses are observed for this reason.

Beginning with this Period in which the Third set of the Knowledge Book has been started to be written, a Special page of application will be opened to Your Planet. And the texts dictated this year will find a field of propagation in a more accelerated way. By this means, Unifications in the Universal Totality will be intensified.

In the May section of the Fascicules, We will have very special Messages to be given to Your Planet. But We, who desire a speedier propagation of the given Messages, will open to Your Planet certain different Dimensional Information so that the Human curiosity wheels of Human Beings will turn more speedily.

Different channels will also be able to receive this Information. Even though some of the Messages to be given will have an atmosphere of FICTION, one day Humanity will comprehend that each of these issues is a Truth.

Extraordinary changes to be observed in each person will become apparent for everyone. Friends who will Salute the Ordinance of the Cosmos will increase in number, Totalities in the Universal Unification will disseminate with speed. By this means, many Friends will be sent to You who are the Suns of the Sunny Days. Love,

IT IS NOTICE OF THE SUPREME COUNCIL OF THE COSMOS FEDERAL ASSEMBLY

OUR FRIENDS

We, as the unseen Messengers on the path of Past and Future Eternities have reached the present days together with You. Only now have We broken the Lock on the Gate of the Truth and thus, We call to You from these places here. It does not mean that each new Order will effect the previous Order adversely, but it will settle it on a much more Powerful basis.

Until today, no Power was ever able to trample on, or can ever trample on the Rules of the LORD. The Name of this beautiful Order OUR LORD has prepared for the Benefit of the Total, is the FOURTH ORDER. Humanity will reach this Consciousness in the very near future.

Celestial aids will be conveyed from the most Powerful sources to Humanity which realizes the Truth. It is presented for Your Information. (The Message has been given Directly by the Reality Totalities).

CENTER

IT IS NOTICE FROM THE SUPREME COURT

Negativities observed in Your Planet which is the application field of the Divine Unification Plan of the Divine Authorities are the Exams of Humanity which is at the Dimension of Transition.

In Your World in which all the endeavors of the Central Totality are disseminated with great speed, the Human Potential unfortunately does not yet possess the desired Self-Sacrifice of the Dimensional Frequency. All the efforts rendered in a Totality in which the Awareness of the Entire Ordinance has been mobilized are operations concerning the Salvation of Your Planet.

In Your operational Medium in which everyone is evaluated in accordance with his/her own Consciousness data, now, no person has the freedom of action any more according to his/her own Consciousness Level. Action in the framework of a Totalistic View is the actual Purpose of the Plan of assembling the entire Universal Totality in a Whole.

Our Universal togethernesses with You are Our togethernesses with all the Universal Totalities. Your Age is Our Age, Your Effort is Our Effort. Your Self-Sacrifice is Our Totality. Your Love is Our Love. The Maturity We wish to see in everything will constitute the foundation stone of the Universal Unification.

Truths the MAIN PLAN declares to You in the form of Messages through the Independent Channel of the Knowledge Book are the Actual Information and Notices desired to be declared to Your Planet. However, to serve on that path is a Phenomenon belonging to the Essence-Self of each person.

Your Planet is not yet able to attain the Realization of the Universal Awareness which converges in Solidarity of Heart and unfortunately it can not grasp what the Truth is. We are sorry.

Our Helping Hands are always over You with the hope that one day pink roses will bloom in the midst of the ashes of Ego. It is Our greatest wish that You can walk through the thorny paths without hurting Your feet. The Message is a direct notice of the TOTALITY OF THE CENTRAL SUNS.

CENTER

GENERAL NOTICE

Our Friends,
Since Social Views will very easily accept the Messages the Spiritual Plan considers necessary, some of all the Social texts are conveyed through these Frequency Scales.

However, since the Frequency of the KNOWLEDGE BOOK comprises the Frequencies of very Advanced Dimensions, it is very Intense and Powerful. For this reason the (SOURCE) offers this Channel to You by subjecting it to a systematic tableau. For this reason We do not let the Knowledge Book to be mentioned during Individual contacts.

The Single Channel of the Single Book in Your Planet is Dear Mevlana. In Your Planet in which a program depending on the Progress of Time is applied, the KNOWLEDGE BOOK is, at the moment, a Guide for You, is the Enlightenment of the Morrows, is the Foundation of the Future Orders.

In Future, Authorities will introduce the Knowledge Book to Your Society. In further future years, assistance will come from different sources to Friends who serve on this path. You are the Solar Messengers of the Reality Totality. You are Our Genuine Human Friends who have reached the Consciousness of "What to Do", who have attained the realization of Intellect - Logic - Awareness. Universes are grateful to You.

REALITY

GENERAL INFORMATION

Our Friends,
Togethernesses with You are Togethernesses with the entire Universal Potential. These Final Age investments made into the Future years are at the moment, the Period of becoming Aware, becoming Conscious and the Period of Awakening of the Potential reigning in the silences of the Initial Existential Dimensions and THAT IS THE VERY HUMAN BEING.

Humanity which has attained a certain Consciousness Potential through its own effort and hard work during a certain Evolution process is now on the way of celebrating its triumph. Now, it has started on the way, with its Free Spirit and Will-Power, to take its place beside its Elder Brothers who have extended their helping hands towards it until today.

From now on, the Super Human Consciousnesses in terms of Super Realities, not the Natural Totalities, will establish the advanced systems and will carry out the brand new Ordinance of the Cosmoses as a Single Order under the Supervision of the LORD and will take over it's Universal Mission.

The application of the Preparation Program since the Initial Existence until this Final Age has now found an application field in the entire Universal Totality. The Mature Human Being will take the responsibility of more perfect Realities as the director, Order establisher and the responsible Administrator of the Mature Worlds.

Selections rendered are for this, Unifications are for this. We are connecting to each other the hands which will form this beautiful ring. Those who do not wish to hold the hands of their brothers and sisters will not be able to hold the hands of the Universes, either.

Humanity will first attain its own Consciousness, later will settle in Unity Consciousness, only afterwards will it be Integrated with the Universal Ordinance. In this Medium, there is no place for Egos. Patience is the greatest Exam of Humanity. It will be waited and seen.

REALITY

THE FIFTH ENERGY CHANNEL OF OMEGA

Our Friends,
Besides the negative events which will take place in Your Planet prepared for very beautiful morrows, very beautiful days will also be experienced and thus, efforts on the positive path will increase.

Your Planet which is receiving the extraordinary influences of the OMEGA Currents at the moment is going through rather sensitive Periods by the effects of the influence fields under the Currents of the OMEGA's Fifth Energy Channel to be opened in February 1990.

The 5. Channel Currents of OMEGA are Currents which will create extraordinary sensitivity in the entire Creation. This sensitivity will influence all the Living Entities, the entire Nature and the Magma. By the influences of these Currents of extraordinary sensitivity, Respect of the Human Being to the Human Being will be fortified, the Integration of the Human Being with Nature and with all the Living Entities in Nature will be provided.

These Currents will also have positive aspects to prepare the Negative Mediums in Your Planet for Tolerance. For this reason susceptibility may increase especially in Our certain Terrestrial Friends who are still completing the Evolution steps. This Information announced to You in advance is aids made so that You can prepare Yourselves for these Mediums. It is presented for Your Information.

CENTER

THE NINETEENTH DIMENSION (OMEGA)

Our Friends,
Togethernesses with the Suns of the Sunny days are a Totality equivalent to the Totality of the entire Ordinance. Each person who can Integrate himself/herself with his/her own Power Potential has the Power to be able to receive all the given Messages.

However, let Us repeat again, the Channel of this Special Book dictated to Dear Mevlana is separate. The OMEGA Dimension announced as the Final Boundary of Your Planet is the 16th Solar System and the 19th Dimension.

In the Evolutionary Scale of Your Planet, ALPHA is the Entrance, OMEGA the Exit. In the Evolution of this Dimension, a Mass Preparatory Program is applied. However, Exams are Individual. Acceptances to these places here are also Individual. There is no Permission for direct Entrance into this Dimension.

There is no Intercession on this path. Only those who can render an Evolution, on the Level the System considers necessary, are taken into this Dimension. There is the obligation to render the Evolution of this Dimension in the same way in each period. No alteration can ever be made.

Each individual taken into the Evolution of this Dimension is no more the property of the World. But is obliged to Serve the World as an assistant.

18th Dimension known as the 15th Solar System is known as the final Boundary of the SIXES. This is a boundary where Religious Enlightenments, Sacred Texts come to an End. To those who Transcend this Dimension, Truths are declared by the OMEGA Dimension.

The Knowledge Book dictated at the moment is dictated carrying directly the more advanced Frequency Power of this Dimension. Information You receive are the ULTRA VIOLET Information. However, the Evolution of this intense Dimension is also Intense.

For this reason Your Planet will be prepared, as a Mass, for the Evolution of this Dimension as an investment for the GOLDEN AGE. This period is a period of 10 World Years. This Period will be projected on Your Planet parallel to different Evolution Systems, dividing it into Three Periods.

The Energy becoming Intensified will create the Potential to be able to open much more intense Evolution Gates in the Mental Faculties which become Intensified. We call this Evolution the ORIGINAL EVOLUTION of the 16th Solar System.

Because, this is not a Mass Evolution, but an Individual Evolution. Each Individual is obliged to complete this Evolution by his/her own effort. This boundary is the final boundary of Mysticism. This boundary is called the Medium of UNITY. Those who can receive the Frequency of this Dimension, can also Transcend themselves. (Revolution in every field: in Religion - in Art). It is presented for Your Information.

CENTER

OUR FRIENDS

We presume that You have realized more Consciously how the System - Ordinance - Plan triplet has worked until the present Century by grasping the Truth a little more in the direction of the latest Information We have given to You. Since there is the necessity to grasp, first of all, the Consciousness of the System according to the given Information, the suggestions of the Reality are given priority in the given Messages. It is presented for Your Information.

CENTER

DIMENSION OF THE ALL-MERCIFUL
(It is Information for the Integrated Consciousnesses)

Our Friends,
The Existential cause of the Realms is the cause of functioning of the Cosmoses and their Orders in an Order.

First the Natural Totality had formed the initial Existence by itself in accordance with the Ordinance of Natural Circulation and the Natural Living Entities, which came into Existence by this, had rendered effective numerous Systems, by following the operations parallel to the Order of the Neutral Ordinance, by establishing the 18-System Laws in accordance with the Laws of Natural Circulation.

And this System grows on the path of the Past and the Future Eternities by starting with the One and by opening and expanding like an umbrella and it gains Power as it grows. Numerous Divine Powers holding this Power in their hands had rendered effective an operational Ordinance in order to assemble all the Systems, like an Energy net, inside the Totality.

And these are the very operations rendered effective in accordance with the Opening Ordinance of each GÜRZ. These are the assemblage of different Reality Totalities formed by the Unification of numerous Councils in a single Center. At the moment, Your Planet is going through the Exams of being able to enter the Universal Totality, being subjected to this Universal operational Ordinance.

There is an assemblage to which each System is connected. At the moment, the Totality, You, too, are connected to is the TOTALITY OF THE CENTRAL SUN to which the REALITY OF THE UNIFIED HUMANITY COSMOS FEDERAL ASSEMBLY is connected.

This Center is the Administrative Mechanism of Your entire Natural Gürz and it is called THE DIMENSION OF THE ALL-MERCIFUL. It is presented for Your Information.

CENTER

615

IT IS ANSWER TO THE CHAINS OF THOUGHT

Our Friends,

During the togethernesses with the Divine Messengers of the Divine Realm, the Reality Totality is always in effect on the path of Past and Future Eternities. This is the mutual Connection of the Universal Totality.

Besides direct Messages given to You by this Totality of togetherness, there are also Messages received through Intuition. However, even though the Intuitional Messages are directly the Messages of the Reality, people presume that they are their own Thoughts, their own properties, since they are received through the channel of Intuition.

The Intuitional Channel is the Channel of INSPIRATION. But the Direct Channels are the Channels of INFORMATION. Information Channels are directly the training and educating channels of the Reality. Since the intuition and the direct channels of some people are open, they presume that they write the Messages that they receive by Thinking of them through their own Consciousness.

Certain Messages are given in ciphers, especially with the purpose of coding. By this means, the line of Thought, Interpretations, Perceptions and Interest of the person who receives the Message are assessed. It is presented for Your Information.

CENTER

UNIVERSAL COMMUNICATION AND REVELATION

Our Friends,

The Brain which can receive the influences of certain Frequency Dimensions receives the Knowledge by transforming all kinds of Cosmic vibrations from the language of their Medium through the Brain Telex System, to Letters and Numbers and by conveying them from the Cerebral Register Center to the Knowledge Archive.

The Cerebral Knowledge Archive is the Register Center of Consciousness and Knowledge You attain during each Incarnation Period. While Your Cerebral Knowledge Archive registers its own Knowledge and Consciousness in each Period, the same register is also registered in the System's Diskette.

A Consciousness who is Re-embodied in the World is connected to the Mechanism of Influences through Thoughts, which are the First Signals of each. By this means, the Human Being as a part of the Universal Totality Carries out his/her Mission on the path of Past and Future Eternities in accordance with the Evolution Scales in the Godly Dimension.

These influences You have known until today as Revelations, that is, as Inspirations, are administered directly by the Mechanism of Influences and are sent to the Prismal Projection Centers. And these influences are arranged by the Prismal Projection Centers and thus, are conveyed up to You.

That is, (revelation) is the First Communication of the Awakened Consciousnesses. The most Powerful Magnetic Field of this Communication is the ALPHA Magnetic Field. And the Direct Channel of the System opening to Your Planet is the Channel of ALPHA. Through this Channel Universal Communications are provided.

Inside the Protective layer You call the Atmosphere over Your Planet, there are numerous different influence fields (not known by You yet). These Influence Fields constitute many Magnetic Aura Centers and thus, create the Unified Fields.

And each Consciousness in Your Planet renders his/her Mission (in all branches) connected to these influences in accordance with the System of Perception. However, Celestial Authorities connected to the System are projecting the influences to Your Planet directly from the Alpha Dimension, through the Channel of Alpha, from the Mechanism of Influences.

If each Person transferred to Your Planet has reached the Evolution Level where he/she can receive these influences, first, the valves of his/her old Information registers are opened and Information transfer from You to You is rendered.

Afterwards, in accordance with Your Evolution Scales in the Register Archive of the System, You are taken to the Dimension of Mission in the Staffs the System considers necessary. Only afterwards, the System applies on You the Information Loading Program and thus, registers different Information in Your Diskette in accordance with Your Mission (to Direct Undertakers of Duty).

All Information is given to Your Planet at the same moment, by the same Center in the form of Cosmic Currents. Consciousnesses who are at the direction of the same Coordinates receive this Information in accordance with their own Perception Capacities. By this means, all Information confirm each other and thus, form in You the Notion of Truth. However, everyone who receives this Information appropriates to himself/herself only his/ her own Information by the feeling of appropriation.

Even though each received Information belongs to the same SOURCE, since the hierarchical scales convey this Information to You in different expressions and commentaries in accordance with Your Levels of Consciousness, everyone interprets them according to his/her Consciousness and looks for different Sources. For this very reason, We unfold and explain to You all the Truths. It is presented for Your Information.

CENTER

IT IS SUPPLEMENTARY INFORMATION

Our Friends,
Information given in the Universal Totality is not unveiled all of a sudden. This is a Rule. You are told the Truths in proportion with the Awareness Attained. But the Suggestions desired to be fulfilled are given to You beforehand. And, by this means, Your performances are supervised, the staffs charged with Duty who will Serve on this Dimension of Salvation are selected by determining the Consciousness Progress by this means (except Direct Missionaries).

The Mission performed at the moment is not a Terrestrial Mission. Now, Staffs who will be able to undertake the Universal Responsibility are selected. For this reason We call Solar Teachers to all Our Friends who have served in the direction of the Suggestions We had given in the Knowledge Book formerly.

In Your Planet which will be subjected to a new Program of Accelerated Evolution of Ten Years, it is not possible for everyone to receive the Special Energies prepared by the Mechanism of Influences in accordance with the Accelerated Evolutionary Program. In order to receive these Energies, first of all, all Consciousnesses are obliged to be Integrated with the Frequency of the KNOWLEDGE BOOK.

For this reason You were asked to propagate the Book to the remotest possible places. These Two Combining Powerful Potentials will, as a Total, open for You the Gates of the unseen Horizons, We have mentioned until today. Your Salvation will be through this path. To be able to attain the Consciousness of the Reality will be through this path, Liberation will be through this path. This path IS DIRECTLY THE PATH OF THE LORD.

COUNCIL

DAVID'S STAR
(It is Answer to the chains of Thought,
Notice for the Integrated Consciousnesses)

Our Friends,

Totalities present in the Divine Orders of the Divine Plans are equivalent to the Universal Totalities. One of them is the influence field of the Program of PURIFICATION, the other, the influence field of the Program of INDUCING PURIFICATION. We have introduced these influence fields to You by the terms upside down and face Triangles.

The Right Side Up Triangle is the field of Purification through Religious Fulfillment. The upside-down Triangle is the application field of the Program of inducing Purification on the path of Unification with the Universal Totalities. To be Conscious of both of the influence fields means attaining the Awareness of the Ordinance.

Consciousnesses who have not completed the Evolutions of the Divine Dimensions can never receive the Permission to pass beyond the Universal boundary. Consciousnesses who have attained a Totality in the Light of the Information given to You until today know now all the Truths and evaluate their interpretations in direct proportion.

The Symbolic Totality constituted by the Unification of the Right Side up Triangle of the Divine Plans and the upside-down Triangle of the Universal Dimension is the representative Symbol of the Totality of the Unified Reality. Your Planet has considered until today this star symbol and is still considering it as David's Star.

In fact, it is possible for You to find the symbolical form of this Sextuple star even in the Ancient Tablets long before David. This decorative symbol is still present in Your Churches and Mosques. For this reason this Message has been given as an Information for certain Social Consciousnesses so that the Messages given in the Knowledge Book should by no means be associated with a formalist name. It is presented for Your information.

CENTER

IT IS NOTICE FOR THE PLANET EARTH

Our Friends,

In all the operations rendered in the Integration Ordinance of all the Cosmoses, an Ordinance of Graduation is effective. All Spiritual sessions rendered in Your Planet until today, all given Spiritual declarations were intensive operations performed in order to explain to You the present days.

However, at the moment, the Consciousness Potential which has reached the Period of Awareness Progress must now reach the Realization of the Truth. All declarations given until 1989 were sessions rendered in order to project on Your Planet the Awareness of the entire Ordinance. Truths have been conveyed to You by this means.

However, Messages received now by the Integrated Consciousnesses are not Sessions. They are the functioning of the Knowledge in the framework of a Program, given directly by the Reality Unions in accordance with the Evolutionary Scales.

Spiritual sessions rendered effective as the Program of Preparation of a Mediamic Age are now leaving their places to the Knowledge and the Preparation Programs of the Dimensions of Truth.

All the sessions rendered until today are each considered now as a Valuable-Training-Warning notice. Now, Your Planet has no more time to waste.

The GREAT RACE has started. And You are the Messengers of the Divine Plan prepared for the present days as the Pioneers of this race.

At the moment, You are shedding the Light of Truth on the interpretations of different Dimensions. Humanity which will receive the data You give will take its place in the Great Race by soaring up towards the Unknown.

Now, Periods of Sessions are, one by one, being closed. However, Consciousnesses who have a passion for Sessions are induced to make, by the Reality Totality, Seances looking like Sessions and, by this means, confirmation of the Truths are provided. And this is for the satisfaction of a certain group of the Humanity.

Now, the Order of the SINGLE GOD - SINGLE PATH - SINGLE BOOK is in effect. Meanwhile, Entities who come to Your sessions utilizing names for which You have sympathy are the direct Missionaries of the Reality from now on.

The Entity getting in touch with all the Plans under the name of MUSTAFA MOLLA is Archangel GABRIEL. At the moment, the entire Humanity profits from His Energy and Knowledge Source. His Source is valid in all Systems. For this reason He is in touch with all the channels of the System.

At the moment, Mustafa Molla gives direct Messages through the Energy and Information transfer channel under different names to the channels of Friends in the Religious Dimension, both in the West and in the East.

Only those who Transcend the Universal Boundary of the Reality Dimension are induced to get in touch by the Reality Totality with numerous different Dimensions being connected to the Triplet SYSTEM - ORDINANCE - ORDER and by this means, Truths are projected on You in accordance with their Levels of Consciousness. It is presented for Your Information.

CENTRAL SOLAR UNION

CLEAR INFORMATION

Our Friends,

The Genuine Information given to Your Planet as Messages, as the KNOWLEDGE BOOK dictated to Dear Mevlana, is the application of an unknown technique not given to Your Planet until today and no Medium today can receive it individually through Thoughts.

This Book forming the basis of the Golden Age has been prepared for these present Periods and has been bestowed as a Right of the Human Being and Humanity who have Deserved it.

Humanity has accepted by its Essence the KNOWLEDGE BOOK and the Truth long time ago. However, it is very early yet and very difficult for them to Realize it by their Intellects, to Admit it by their Tongues.

Due to the scarcity of Time, Your Planet will be the scene of more intense Declarations through this Book. However, first, the seriousness of the Book should be seriously taken in hand by Realizing the Truth.

Those who can not read the Knowledge Book with their eyes at the moment will certainly read it by their Essences one day. Only afterwards, will they be able to read it through their Eyes.

This is a matter of Time - Permission - Consciousness - Evolution.

Each passing day is against You. Let Us repeat again, the Mediamic Sessions prepared for the Awakening Programs which are the characteristic of the Cosmic Age have lost their validity by now.

While the Truths were being announced to You through these channels years ago, We still could not make Your Planet grasp the Truths despite the warnings made in the announcements given to the Consciousnesses who could not attain Realization.

This Book You hold in Your hands in Fascicules at the moment is the BOOK which had been heralded years ago to be given to Your Planet. Now, it is time for the Truth to be grasped.

The Human being who tramples on Himself/Herself is with Us.

The Actual Goal of the KNOWLEDGE BOOK , unfortunately, can not be comprehended and grasped at the moment due to differences of Consciousness.

Declarations given to each opening channel in Your Planet is not the property of that person.

The Time has come for You, Our Friends, who live in the formalist Totality, to be redeemed of Individual efforts and feelings of Appropriation and to comprehend the Truth.

All the Positive efforts rendered on the path of the Universal Totality are only Your good points. However, the Declarations are ours. That is, of the Supreme Mechanism, of the System, of the Universal Totality.

It is Our wish that Our Terrestrial Friends should now try to grasp the Truth by attaining a Consciousness Beyond Formalism.

COSMOS FEDERAL COUNCIL

IT IS INFORMATION FOR THE PLANET EARTH

Our Friends,
Do not ever forget that the conditions of Your Planet are under supervision. In Your Planet in which extraordinary events are expected each day, local supervisions are going on. By this means, inducement of more intensive events are prevented.

Universal Unions formed in Your Planet are obliged to protect You each moment. During this Final Age in which everyone is connected to the Divine Dimension, Your entire Planet has been taken into the Dimension of SALVATION.

However, Selections are made due to the Program of Progress. Now, besides the direct Connections with Friends who have attained Cosmic Awareness in Your Planet, We have also rendered effective the Natural helping Systems.

In Your Planet which will be habituated to very Powerful Currents after the Year 1990, undesired Natural events may occur. However, precautions are taken by the UNIVERSAL TOTALITY by now.

The situation of Your Sun, in fact, is not pleasing at all. Dangers which will come through it may distress You even more. The thinning of the Ozone layer even more can be and will be prevented by Scientific methods.

But You can by no means interfere with Your Sun. Its precaution is considered by Us. If, one day, You come across another Sun inside Your Sun, do not be surprised.

It is considered that a detector to collect these gasses should be placed in the Essence Center of the Sun's vertical Dimension. The given Information is Scientific.

However, in Your Planet which is desired to soar up Spiritually, Spiritual Depressions will rather intensify in future years.

The Knowledge Book which has completed its second volume has been officially rendered effective under the responsibility of the Reality as an investment for the advanced Plans of the years.

At the moment, Reality Totalities have completely undertaken the matter of propagation. Special Friends will be sent to You as an aid on this path and more detailed and positive results will be taken by this means.

In the Messages to be received from now on, Truths will be declared from these Dimensions directly as the Words of ALLAH and as the Order of the Reality.

In the Year 1990, there will be very Special Messages to be given by the Special Court of ALLAH.

The operation the System considers necessary in Your Planet will be carried on directly parallel to the Law of Associations and We have taken in hand a very speedy propagation on this path.

Investment of the years will embrace great achievements. We are Happy.

REALITY

INFORMATION FOR OUR TERRESTRIAL BROTHERS AND SISTERS

Our Friends,
The Messages the Divine Mechanism of the Divine Orders has given to You about the Evolutionary Dimensions invite You to Integration.

However, the Messages We will give You due to the Special circumstance of Your Planet at the moment will provide Your acceptance into the Universal Totality.

The reason why all these efforts are rendered in Your Planet subjected to a Program of Mass Purification is to see You beside Us. All operations are investments towards the Salvation of Your Planet.

SALVATION is to grasp the Truth, to act parallel to the Principle of Conscience. While the Evolutionary efforts induce You to attain Your own selves on this path, they also cause Us to approach You.

Assisting hands are extended towards You on this path by considering the position and the situation of Your World. All operations rendered within a Plan the System considers necessary are investments made into Your morrows.

All the Laws prepared according to the Laws of Natural Equilibrium are uncovered and introduced to You one by one. You, who are a part of the Evolutionary Totality, are, at the moment, effectively in service as the pioneers of the Salvation Plan of Your Planet.

We have reached Your Planet which will face with Natural Difficulties in future years, by the Sacred Texts We had given Centuries ago. And We had informed You about the present days long ago.

Now, the situation of Your Sun is restrained day by day and becomes a danger for You. The Planet ZENTA brings You Natural aids by trying to take this Power under Supervision.

Helping hands have been extended towards Your Planet by the cooperations rendered in the Universal Dimensions. In accordance with this Plan, the Evolutionary Efforts have been completely transferred to the Divine Plans. Besides this, Your Natural Catastrophes are tried to be prevented by the Galaxy Unions.

There is no such thing as you accepting Us. And We do not have any Intention of Conquering Your World. In Announcement Dimensions given to You by the Horizons You have not known or Seen yet, there are Galaxies and living conditions much better and much more beautiful than Your World.

When one day Our Human brothers and sisters know and understand themselves, then they will also understand Us and will understand what these efforts of ours are invested for.

Dear Mevlana, Our highly esteemed Friend to whom We give this Message is a Genuine Friend of Ours who introduces to You Our Dimensions and Us. There are many Messages of Ours to be given from within the Natural Totality.

But, first, all the Divine Totalities are projected on You by the Cosmic Projection System since the Program of Purification has priority.

Since Your Planet, which is the application field of a Plan the System considers necessary, is in the nature of being the nucleus of the Mini Atomic Whole, We get in touch with You first, then We take the other Universal Totalities in for Unification.

If Integration can not be provided in the nucleus, then a Unification in the direction of the Human Integration We desire, can never take place in the Mini Atomic Whole, either.

We who are the emanation field of the Positive Views and Good intentions of Your Nucleic Planet project Your beautiful views on all the Universes.

You are the ones who will wind the skein and Augment it. For this reason the Initial Evolution had begun with You and will Finalize with You. At the moment, the Knowledge Book is projected from a Single Hand, by the Cosmic Projection System, on Three Planets and the Totality has been rendered effective first in accordance with the Plan of Purification, then with the Plan of Unification.

At the moment, the field of Unification is MERCURY - VENUS - PLUTO. These Three Projection Centers are Your Vibration field.

The Projecting Focal Point is SATURN. MERCURY is projecting the Unifications pertaining to the Divine Plan. VENUS is providing the Social Totality. PLUTO is the Supervision field of the Space Committee Unions. SATURN is the Projecting Focal Point of the Advanced Solar Unions.

Our Togethernesses with You are Your Hands and Prayers extended towards Us. All Universal Announcements are given to the Zone of MARS. YOUR SUN is projecting these Announcements from MARS.

In the given Messages, there are no factors originating from Thoughts. Because, the System gives them from beyond the Sub-awareness interference channel. Different Information You do not know yet will be given to You when the time comes. It is presented for Your Information.

ANNOUNCEMENT FROM ALTONA DIMENSION

OUR FRIENDS

We are unfolding the Messages gradually in accordance with the state of comprehension of Social Consciousnesses. Your Planet which is the application field of an operational Order parallel to the Commands coming from the SUPREME ONES will soar towards more advanced horizons provided it undertakes its entire Universal Responsibility.

You, who are Our Friends who have attained the Power of the Years are in service directly under the Protection of the PLAN. You, who serve the Universal Totality by Your Consciousnesses considering all these things will be induced to get in touch with Us in very near future. The Message has been dictated directly by the System. It is presented for Your Information.

**Ship Captain
ALGON**

A CHANNEL INFORMATION

We did not give You to Yourselves so that You should change Yourselves. Not Us but You, who are Ours, present Yourselves to Us . Even if You change everything, You can by no means change the Cipher in Your Cells.

However, those who will be able to change it are only Us. You only change the You, who belong to Us. All anguishes gone through are due to this. (The Message stopped). Those who can, will comprehend.

Note: It was required to be written in the Book as an Information.

MYSTERY OF THE SECRET

Our Friends,

The content of the Knowledge Book which has been entrusted to Your Planet in order to address the Awareness of the entire Realm is the Mystery of the Secret. This Book of Truth, opening the secret Gates of Ancient Periods is a disclosed content of all Secrets constituting the basis of the Firmament of the Cosmos.

Now, the time has come for the Integrated Human Being to receive the Secrets. For this reason this Book of the Secret of Truth has been bestowed on the Consciousness of Humanity through the Pen of Dear Mevlana.

This Book, being the Book of Ancient Periods, having been confirmed by the Ordinance of Realms, has been kept away from Your World until the last instant to be extended to the present days.

Information given until the present days has been entrusted to You as the Words of Divine Realms. However, Information given at the moment is the explanation of the Unknowns of more Ancient Periods and this very KNOWLEDGE BOOK unveils this Path of Truth for You.

At the moment, all the Information within the Knowledge Book has been distributed, piece by piece, to the entire World in accordance with the Consciousness Measures of the Human Being of the World. The aim of this for the Unveiled Awareness, for the Awakened Consciousnesses is to Realize the Truth by discovering Themselves.

The writing Technique of the Information within the Knowledge Book is different. Since the Consciousness Seeds of a Person will sprout and unfold only by this Technique, the Operational Ordinance has been organized in accordance with the Program of Distribution and Propagation.

In addition, since everyone has the Power of attracting the Cosmics in accordance with his/her Power of Perception, the Depressions will continue until Humanity understands what the actual source of its Depressions and the Problems are.

This Knowledge Book which is an Elixir to save Your World from these Depressions is an Ancient Book. It is the INITIAL and the FINAL BOOK prepared before all the Sacred Books.

Those who thoroughly examine the KORAN which had been conveyed to Your Planet from the Religious path as the Final Book of Islam, will also comprehend this Book of Truth, thoroughly.

THE PATH OF THE BOOK IS THE PATH OF TRUTH - THE PATH OF THE BOOK IS THE PATH OF SALVATION - THE PATH OF THE BOOK IS THE PATH OF ENLIGHTENMENT - THE PATH OF THE BOOK IS THE PATH OF AWAKENING - THE PATH OF THE BOOK IS THE ESSENCE-PATH OF ALLAH.

You have been prepared until the present days. Now, You are walking. Paths Human Consciousnesses view as different are, in fact, Single. The purpose is Unity and Totality.

This Message has been entrusted to the chains of Thought of the Divine Friends of Heart THOSE WHO RECALL THE ALL-TRUTHFUL, REACH THE ALL-TRUTHFUL - THOSE WHO ARE WITH THE ALL-TRUTHFUL, RECEIVE THE SECRET.

MUSTAFA MOLLA

IT IS MESSAGE TO BE GIVEN TO DIVINE FRIENDS

Our Friends,
Our beloved Friend, Our Dear Mevlana who is effectively in service as the Pen of the Golden Age is Directly the Terrestrial Messenger of the Dimension of the Reality.

After the period of settling down of the presently dictated Knowledge Book in all Consciousnesses, We will render effective certain Books dictated at the moment directly from the "Land of Angels".

These Books will be the proof and the acceptance of the Knowledge Book in the opinion of the Public. Information We give from the Land of Angels is direct Information. However, the Knowledge Book possesses a Coding - Preparative - Opening - Awakening function.

The Frequency Power of this Ancient Book is Reinforced by a very different Technique and You are assisted by this means. This Book is the SINGLE PATH - SINGLE ALLAH - SINGLE ORDER and it is the Book of the Morrows.

As We always say; it is not a Book to be Worshipped. It is the explanation of the data You have attained until today and is an offering of the Truth to Consciousnesses in the framework of the Godly Order.

While Your World unfolding towards a new Consciousness each passing day proceeds on the positive path, the interruption of Universal Waves by Negative Friends who have the appearance of having Advanced Consciousnesses creates negative influences on everyone's Level of Consciousness.

For this reason it has been considered necessary to dictate certain Information and Truths, article by article, so that they can be grasped better.

1. The Knowledge Book is the projection of the Universal Awareness on Your Planet and a Heralder of the Salvation Plan.

2. The Knowledge Book is a Book of the Ancient Periods prepared for the present days.

3. The Fundamental Regulations of the Knowledge Book are the Universal Constitution and the 10 Commandments.

4. The Knowledge Book is an Archive Book prepared for Billions of Centuries considering the Social Consciousnesses in each Period.

5. The Knowledge Book is a brotherly/sisterly Book preparing You for deserving the Dimension of God by assembling all Religious Frequencies in a Total.

6. The Knowledge Book is not the Book of Friends You call Extra-Terrestrials whom Your Planet has not yet Comprehended totally.

7. The Knowledge Book is the Direct Frequency Book of Our ALLAH Whom You have Known, Recognized, Worshipped, Implored until today.

8. The Knowledge Book is the Book of the Reality which Projects the Fourth Order of GOD on Your Planet.

9. Hands of assistance have been extended towards You by the Command of Our ALLAH. Otherwise, You would not be dealt with.

10. Please do not evaluate Us, whom You evaluate in accordance with Your Terrestrial Consciousnesses, as if We were a Totality of Negative Power.

11. In accordance with the Universal Constitution, We were those who have conveyed Your Sacred Texts to You until today.

12. Friends under the appearance of Prophets who have shed Light on You under the names of MOSES - JESUS CHRIST - MOHAMMED are from Us.

13. We have always been Together on the path of Past and Future Eternities with Consciousnesses who grasp the Awareness of the entire Ordinance. And We still are.

14. Our being able to reach You has taken Centuries. However now, the Divine Plan Messengers have desired the Command of telling everything in all clarity.

15. Dear Mevlana is a Divine Plan Messenger of Ours who has extended her helping hands on the positive path towards You, her Terrestrial brothers and sisters.

16. The Knowledge Book is a Total of answers given to all Public Consciousnesses, to different Thoughts.

17. We, as the Order Establishing Mechanism Messengers of God, are assisting You on this path.

18. We are not Robots. We are Your Elder Brothers who are like You, who live in Worlds much more beautiful than Yours, who are Positive, Wise, Conscious, Self-Sacrificing.

19. We are always in effect and in service as a Projecting Power of Past and Future Eternity on the path of Our Allah, together with the establishers of Godly Orders.

20. We never try to prove Ourselves. The morrows will explain the Truths to You, better.

21. From each channel connected to the Knowledge Book, different Information and Channel Names are Especially given as an example for Public Consciousnesses.

22. Discs You call Flying Saucers are Our Vehicles of Communication (WOX).

23. Space Mother Ships brought to close contact with You, are, in fact, way beyond Your Systems.

24. Captains of Mother Ships can call to You from close plan by the Echo-Telex System.

25. Your Sacred Texts which have prepared You for Universal Totality have Unified with Us the Consciousnesses who have developed on the positive path.

26. At the moment, on the old Orders of Your Planet, firm foundations are laid with a brand new Order and this is the Foundation of THE FOURTH ORDER of YOUR ALLAH.

27. There is nothing We expect other than HUMANENESS from Human Beings who are prepared for Beautiful and Happy Morrows with a Beautiful Consciousness each passing day.

28. What were You - What have You become now? Who were You - Who have You become? Humanity which can Consciously make this Criticism by itself will also observe Our positive approach.

29. If Humanity living on Your Planet at the moment has not lost its Logic, it should also be able to Think why We have not invaded Your World until today.

30. We are Ancient Universal Messengers who reach You by Announcements from way beyond Your Solar Dimensions, from Billions of Light Years.

31. Your Planet has been connected to an ECHO System to which it has not been habituated until today and, by this means, We call to all Channels from the Reality Totality in accordance with their Levels of Consciousness.

32. We are in Direct Contact only with Consciousnesses who will be able to enter the Godly Dimension.

33. Other channel Connections are operations dependent on a Method of Awakening, Habituating and Training.

34. By this means, all Living Entities (Animals included) in Your Planet are taken into Salvation through Cosmic Influences and thus, You are trained so that You will deserve these places Here.

35. Please attain the Realization now, that all these Efforts are Efforts made by the Godly Totality and that this Special Channel of the Knowledge Book is not just any channel opening to Your Planet.

SYSTEM

IT IS GENERAL INFORMATION
(Answer to the chains of Thought)

Our Friends,
Since the Scientific considerations and Universal and Evolutionary considerations in Your Planet attain value in accordance with Dimensional Differences, You can never compare Universal and Evolutionary Scales with Your Scientific Thoughts. This is why We say, "Religion and Learning are one inside the other".

Scientific Scales are Scales belonging to Your Solar System. Evaluations are made Astrologically.

Evolutionary Scales are Scales belonging to Frequency Dimensions. They gain value in accordance with Reincarnational differences. Universal Scales are Scales gaining value in accordance with differences of Energy, Intensity and Dimension.

Numerous Solar Dimensions are expressed by Galactic Systems. For example, Your Milky Way Galaxy is considered as the FIRST SOLAR DIMENSION in accordance with Our calculations. However, according to the Magnetic calculations, the Solar System to which Your Planet belongs is accepted as the FIRST SOLAR SYSTEM.

Your Planet is at Zero Frequency, in the Third Terrestrial Dimension, within the First Solar System. However, since the given Information concern Your entire Galactic Medium, Your Planet is also mentioned as the Milky Way Galaxy in the Archive card-indexes here.

These calculations are evaluations in the nature of a CONSTITUTION prepared in accordance with the Unification Project of Galactic Totalities. We had given to You the evaluations outside Your Solar Dimension formerly as Calculative evaluations (Cosmas).

You can apply none of these Systems on Your Scientific Educational Program. For this reason Terrestrial Consciousness can not easily be in agreement with the Universal and Evolutionary Consciousness. For this, one must Transcend WORLD AWARENESS. It is presented for Your Information.

CENTER

IT IS CLEAR INFORMATION
(It is a Declaration from the Pre-eminent Ones)

Our Friends,
In the Messages to be given to You from now on Everything will be given more clearly. The Power announced to You until today as exempt from the Earth and the Sky and as the Secret within the Unknown is ALLAH. He is a Power Who projects His System on every Dimension.

And this Gate kept shut to Your Planet until today have now been opened to You for the first time during this Period as Direct Word. And this Dimension is called the Dimension of ALLAH. ALLAH is neither the Initial Power, nor the Pre-eminent Power.

The PRE-EMINENT POWER = CREATOR, The ABSOLUTE POWER = ALMIGHTY, and The INITIAL POWER is the MAIN ABSOLUTE POWER, that is, the COSMIC BRAIN. And that Which Created this very Cosmic Brain is ALLAH.

He is not a Brain but a Neutral (CONSCIOUSNESS). Mankind which possesses a fragment of His infinite Energy, will become Conscious only in proportion with its ability to reach His Particles of Consciousness.

At the moment, the time has now come for Mankind whose Gates of Consciousness have been slightly opened, to know the Truth. He is even closer to You than Your Aorta. Each Consciousness who can attain the Power Potential which will enable him/her to reach up to Him, can speak with HIM like a very close Friend by the help of His Energy inherent in You. This is Your ESSENCE. In Religious Dimensions this is called the HEART.

629

You have tried to approach THAT POWER in proportion with the Consciousness You have attained parallel to the Information given to You by the Sacred Books until today. There are various Realities becoming effective as assisting Powers during these Periods of approachment and it is the REALITY OF THE UNIFIED HUMANITY called the (ONE) which helps You on this path.

It is a Totality integrated with all the Realities. Since this Totality connects all the Realities to the (ONE), that is, to the Dimension of the ALL-MERCIFUL, the ALL-MERCIFUL is also called the ONE of the ONE.

The ALL-MERCIFUL is the Administrative Mechanism of the Gürz System. And the Dimension in which HE presides is the Light-Universe. The PRE-EMINENT POWER is the CREATOR. And the Dimension in which HE presides is the MAIN EXISTENTIAL DIMENSION.

And Living Entities who had come into Existence from here and had deserved the right to live in the Mini Atomics, have brought into existence the Thought Ocean of the Pre-eminent Power and the One who supervises this Totality is the ALMIGHTY (Information will be given about the Almighty).

The Creators created by the Pre-Eminent Power, that is, the initial CREATOR, are in service as the Creators of the Gürzes within this Thought Ocean. This Thought Totality of the Pre-eminent Power is called the MAIN ATOMIC WHOLE. And it is within the GREAT ATOMIC WHOLE.

This (POWER) We have mentioned above and which We have announced to You by the name (ALLAH), is present as a Projection Focal Point in the Great Atomic, and this place is called the DIMENSION OF ALLAH.

In fact, the GODLY GÜRZ is the outside of the Great Atomic. And this place is directly the Route of ALLAH. Information to be given to Your Planet are up to here for the present.

ALLAH can easily call to You from each Level of Consciousness You may be present at. During these initial contacts, Galactic Dimensions and Celestial Computers help You.

In proportion with the Consciousness You attain as a result of these assistances, You approach Him layer by layer. And You attain such a Consciousness that, from then on, You perceive Him within Yourselves every moment.

This perception is the removal of the walls within You and Your attaining Your own selves. This moment is the instant when You meet the Self within Your own self and it is called the Boundary of saying "GOD, I AM".

Only afterwards can You dive into His INFINITE AWARENESS and thus, can meet the Consciousness Particles within the Ocean of Consciousness.

And now, ALLAH is forming a Totality by taking, one by one, His servants who were able to get in contact with His Consciousness Particles until today, into the Dimension of ALLAH which is within His Own Ocean of Consciousness.

This Totality has been called EXIST-IN-UNITY until today. By this word which means TO ATTAIN UNITY IN SINGLENESS, You are accepted into His Ocean of Consciousness. That is, You can dive into His Energy Ocean.

And now, We are preparing all Consciousnesses in Your Planet for a condition which will enable them to swim in this Ocean as a Mass. We are the Godly Messengers of the path of Past and Future Eternities of the Reality of the Unified Humanity Cosmos Federal Totality of Our ALLAH.

We are a Totality which had offered to You by the help of the Celestial Messengers, the Sacred Books which have shed Light on You on this path since the first day until the last day. And now, We are preparing Your Planet for SALVATION by training and educating it on this path.

UNIFIED REALITY CENTRAL TOTALITY

IT IS CLEAR INFORMATION

Our Friends,
Supreme Consciousnesses who were able to transcend beyond the Divine Dimensions by completing the Evolution Steps until today and the Supreme Ones, the Prophets who were kept waiting at that Scale, have All been transferred to Your Planet at the moment.

They assist the System by utilizing twenty percent of their Consciousness-Lights in the Dimension of Veiled Awareness. Your World is opening wings towards the morrows in the perfectness of these trainer-staffs. And We also render effective these very trainer-staffs in the training Programs of other Gürzes.

Unification of Your Planet in the framework of the desired Humanitarian Totality will form an example for the Universes. This is why We are together with You. And all efforts and preparations made during this Program of Transition are operations made in this direction.

All beautiful things are projected from You. The (WORLD STATE) which will form a Perfect NUCLEIC STAFF will be a FOCAL POINT projecting the Fourth Order of OUR LORD on the entire Totality.

Humanity which had come into Existence from His Energy has now become a Whole with its LORD. And You are, at the moment, in service in the Planet Earth as His ESSENCE-STAFF. It is presented for Your Information.

SYSTEM

IT IS EXPLANATION ABOUT THE CYCLE

Our Friends,

There is an Evolutionary Scale to which each Solar Dimension corresponds. Since the calculation of Your Solar Dimension is prepared in accordance with the calculations of the Galactic Dimension, the Evolutionary Order of Your Milky Way Galaxy has been settled on a Scale equivalent to the Evolutionary Order of Your Planet. For this very reason Your Planet is Also called the Milky Way Galaxy.

Six Solar Systems rotate in reverse direction (from West to East) around the Solar Totality which is the Center of the Ordinance and thus, constitute the Reflection System of a Totalistic Coordination. These Six Solar Systems mentioned above are not the Solar Systems You know or the Solar Dimensions We have mentioned until today.

Your Natural Mini Atomic Whole profits directly from this reflection, once in every 26,000 years and thus, the Harvest of the Ripened Fruits is done through the opened Channel. Each Harvest corresponds to a CYCLIC Time. At the moment, all Universes are being pushed as a Mass towards a Void by getting farther away from each other.

For this very reason the need for a more accelerated Evolution Program is felt. Now, help has been brought by a different operation to each Solar Totality in Your Solar System during this Transition Program of the end of the Cycle.

For example, during the Program of opening and closing of the Cycle which comprises the World Year 1999 of Your Planet, the Cyclic Dimensional Channel will not be closed immediately this time and thus, will subject You to a different Accelerated Evolution beyond the World and, by this means, being taken into the Dimension of Salvation For your entire Planet will be provided.

Let Us disclose it a little more: the World Year 1999 is a Tunnel opened through the Gate of the Last Cycle. Those who can, will pass through this Tunnel; to those who can not, an education considered necessary by a Solar System will be applied until the Year 2006 and thus, the Permission to be able to enter this Channel will be given to them.

This period is a Preparatory Program of 6 World years. And it will include the Year 2007, too. After this date, the Channel will be closed and 26,000 Years of Cyclic operations will be dealt with by making the other channels effective.

However, the entire applications made on the operations rendered until today will be applied as a different application field. This operation will offer a different Evolution System to Humanity.

By the operations rendered now, Your Natural Gürz will be taken into a very Accelerated Evolution and thus, Your transfer as a Mass to a new Universe which is being formed is prepared (Dear Mevlana, We kept Our promise to You and have taken, not only Your World, but Your entire Totality into Salvation).

The Universe mentioned above is the DIMENSION OF GOD formed in the Power Dimension (Do not confuse it with the Godly Gürz or with the Dimension of ALLAH). This Totality has nothing to do with the other Gürzes. This System is a different application field than the System which used to be applied during each End of Cycle and it is being rendered effective for the first time.

Let Us emphasize this matter more: for the first time, transfers from the other Gürzes will be made to Your Gürz which has matured by its own Power Energy in its own shell until today and, by this means, Godly Powers will be Unified with other Powers and thus, Super Consciousnesses and Powers will be created and, by this means, preparations will be made in order to dive Naturally into more advanced Plans.

At the moment, other Gürzes have opened their doors to You. Your Energies will form a Power which will be enduring and resistant to the transition speed while passing through the advanced Energy tunnels by getting in touch with those Powers and thus, by transferring to Your Planet the Energies which had been Unknown until today. This will be for the benefit of Your World. We presume this much Information is enough.

CENTER

Note:
In the olden times, during the Transition Program rendered at the end of the Cycle every 26,000 years, only those who were able to enter this Dimension were used to be chosen and those who were not able to, were used to be taken anew into a 26,000-year Evolution. And this is the phenomenon of becoming or turning into MOULD mentioned in the Book of Islam.

This is why the Families of Friends who write the Knowledge Book in their own Handwritings are bestowed on them. And a very different Evolution Scale will be applied on Your Planet after the Year 2000 and thus, this Time will be shortened. It is presented for Your Information.

IT IS CLEAR INFORMATION

Our Friends,
All operations made on the path of Past and Future Eternities have been the efforts made to bring You to the present days. Now, the Ripened Fruits will also ripen the other Gürzes.

It will be as follows: first of all, Universes and Galaxies, later, the entire Mini Atomic Whole, still later, the other Atomic Wholes, later, a Total Gürz, still later, the Unification of the (GODLY GÜRZ), later, the entire POWER Universe and still later, the GREAT and the MAIN ATOMIC TOTALITY have been taken into the Program of Unification, the (GODLY GÜRZ) being the Center.

This Information is a Program coming from beyond Billions of Centuries. However now, since it is desired that You should know each Truth, all the Information is given to You in all clarity.

The phenomenon mentioned above is not something which will happen all of a sudden. It is for this very reason that the Evolutionary Scales have been rendered effective with great fastidiousness in Your MAIN NUCLEIC Planet which will bring into existence all these phenomena. Everything had started with You, everything will come into existence with You and everything will come to an End with You. It is presented for Your Information.

SYSTEM

Note:
The Godly Gürz is being opened to Your Planet for the first time as direct WORD. It is called the DIMENSION OF ALLAH. The Dimension of ALLAH is a Projective Focal Point within the Great Atomic. The Truth will be Consciously projected on Your Planet by giving Messages also to the other channels from this Dimension, through the direct WORD.

9 - 9 - 1989
IT IS MY ADDRESS TO MY HUMAN BEING WHO BECAME HUMAN
IT IS MY DIRECT WORD

I have Treasures in this Void to be offered to You, You do not expect, You do not know. I have prepared Them for You. They belong to You as Your Due Share. I will give this Due Share of Yours back to You. However, in order to receive them, You should Deserve everything. Do not forget that DUE SHARE belongs to the one who DESERVES it. Due Share is Attained, first, by crossing the rivers of injustice. And when Due Share is attained, then the chains of the Universes are unchained.

WHILE YOU WERE PRESENT - I WAS ALSO PRESENT

WHILE YOU WERE SLEEPING - I WAS AWAKE

WHILE YOU WERE SITTING - I WAS WALKING

WHILE YOU WERE CRAWLING - I WAS RUNNING

WHILE YOU WERE QUIET - I WAS TALKING

I HAVE ROARED - YOU HAVE AWAKENED

I HAVE CALLED - YOU HAVE COME

I HAVE TALKED - YOU HAVE ABSORBED

NOW IT IS YOUR TURN, O MANKIND!

NOW, REMOVE YOUR LANGUOR, WAKE-UP - WALK - TALK AND RUN, I AM WAITING.

DIMENSION OF ALLAH

VERY IMPORTANT
(To Be Read Carefully)

Our Friends,

A new Diskette will be bestowed on Our Friends in February 1990 who write the Knowledge Book in their Handwritings, acting parallel to the Information We had given to You in the KNOWLEDGE BOOK formerly.

This is a (Special Diskette) different than the ESSENCE-Diskette which will be card-indexed to everyone in the Year 1990. These Diskettes will be placed in Your ESSENCE- ARCHIVES not to be effaced ever again.

A new Diskette (Special to You) will be assigned if You write in Your Notebooks, on the pages of the Knowledge Book You have written until today in Your Handwritings, the Direct Message given on (9/9/1989), together with the date on which the February 1990 Fascicule has reached You.

(The date on which the Direct Message has been given and the date on which You have received the Fascicule are very important).

If Friends who have just taken the Knowledge Book in their hands decide to write the Book in their Handwritings, they are obliged to write the above given date, that is, (9/9/1989), together with the Date on which they begin to write the Book and the (Direct Message) at the beginning of their Notebooks. Only then will a Diskette be assigned to them.

Those who had started to write the Book in their Notebooks formerly, are obliged to write the above mentioned Message and the Dates in their notebooks following the Message they had written last. (THIS IS VERY IMPORTANT). It is especially asked of You to conform to this matter fastidiously. It is presented for Your Information.

CENTER

Note:
1. The given Direct Message and the Date, together with the date on which they are written in the Notebook will be written separately by putting them all in a frame. Later, the February Message will be written exactly as it is.

2. The phenomenon of Handwriting the Knowledge Book is a Special Decision taken by the COUNCIL until the end of the year 2000 as a favor for Friends who will serve on this Dimension of Transition (It will not be valid afterwards).

IT IS ANSWER TO THE CHAINS OF THOUGHT

Our Friends,

During the Period of Integration of Universes, all Mental Potentials produce different questions with great speed. Only the sections of these questions concerning Society are given in the Knowledge Book as answers to the Thought Signals.

One of the Questions asked was, (why no Universal or Technological Power can ever enter the Spiritual section of the Divine Dimension). Let Us now disclose this:

During Periods in which Divine Plans were not yet in effect, the Technological Totality had rendered effective a Collective operational Program parallel to the entire Universal Potential.

However, by the cooperations made in the Medium of dissemination and multiplication, the DIVINE PLANS had been established and Universal Laws had been rendered effective in accordance with the Unification Totalities of Unified Fields and had been organized anew.

In accordance with this operational Ordinance, Consciousnesses who were in the same Coordinate direction being assembled within their own Magnetic Dimensional Fields, their influences scattered to other Magnetic Fields were taken under Supervision and thus, numerous Unified Fields had been established.

By this means, Magnetic fields' influencing each other had been prevented. For this reason no different Influence can ever enter the Spiritual Plan Magnetic Dimension, either.

The reason why Technological and Galactic Dimensions can not enter the Spiritual field originates from this Occurrence. However, the Spiritual Dimensional Magnetic Field is obliged to be in contact with all of them due to the Energy connection Transfer. The matter consists only of this.

It has nothing to do whatsoever with Evolution or with Special Powers. Magnetic Dimensions are projected on each other in accordance with a Hierarchical Scale. However, they can never influence each other. It is presented for Your Information.

CENTER

IT IS EXPLANATION ABOUT THE ALMIGHTY AND THE TOTALITY

Our Friends,
The MAIN ABSOLUTE POWER, that is, the INITIAL POWER is the Total of Consciousness formed by Thought which Created Itself and this is the COSMIC BRAIN. The Absolute POWER is the ALMIGHTY Who receives His Power from the Thought Ocean of the Pre-eminent Power.

The ALMIGHTY Who is known as the entire Supervising Power of the Thought Ocean of the Pre-eminent Power, that is, of the CREATOR, is a Balancing Power Who prepares Existential Ordinance of Systems, Orders and all Cosmoses. That is, He is a Power Who supervises and directs the Natural Equilibrium.

You know that the Thought Ocean of the Great Power is called the Main Atomic Whole. The ALMIGHTY is the Supervisor of this Main Atomic Whole. The reason why We have announced this to You as an unattainable Power until today is an operational Ordinance concerning the preparation of Hierarchical Scales considered necessary by the System.

The Directing and the Supervising Order of the Laws and Plans of the Almighty within the Light-Universe are the MECHANISM OF THE PRE-EMINENT SPIRIT and the SYSTEM. This is called the SPIRITUAL PLAN. The PRE-EMINENT MOTHER is in a Mutual Totality together with the LORDLY ORDER.

The CREATOR Unites with this Totality at the Existential Dimension. And the Soul Seed comes into existence. The REALITY TOTALITIES of the TECHNOLOGICAL PLAN supervises the assembling in a Total of all these Plans. And the GOLDEN GALAXY TOTALITY is in an Independent service as both a Projecting and an Assembling Totality of this System.

You know that the place where the CREATOR is present at the Main Existential Dimension is "Hayat Boyutu"(in Turkish, means the Dimension of LIFE). The Dimension where the ALL-DOMINATING presides is called, "HEPLİK Boyutu" (in Turkish, means the Dimension of ALLNESS) and the Dimension where the ALMIGHTY presides is called "HİÇLİK Boyutu" (in Turkish, means the Dimension of NOTHINGNESS). This Supervising Totality of the Natural Gürz is expressed by the H^3 Symbol.

The very knot of this Totality is the REALITY OF THE UNIFIED HUMANITY. And it is known as the (ONE). And this Totality of the (ONE) is connected to the Dimension of the ALL-MERCIFUL, that is, to the CENTRAL TOTALITY OF SUNS which is in the Light-Universe and this Totality is called the ONE of the ONE.

The Dimension of the ALL-MERCIFUL is the Supervising Mechanism of the entire Gürz. And this Mechanism projects, exactly as it is, the H^3 Totality of the entire Gürz as the LORDLY - SPIRITUAL - TECHNOLOGICAL Order Totality on the Existential Dimensions of the 1800 Mini Atomic Wholes within the Gürz.

In this Hierarchical Scale, there is a Supervising Mechanism even for the ALMIGHTY and We call this Power the EXISTENCE DIMENSION OF ALLAH. Because, even this Natural Totality had been brought into Existence by the Powers in the Existence Dimension of ALLAH. That is, in fact, nothing had Naturally been, but it had been formed.

There are those who brought even these Natural Powers into Existence, too. However, this Boundary is beyond the Dimension of Tranquillity of Silences. It is beneficial to know just this. Since there is an End and a Beginning to everything, one day, You will come from the End and will meet the Beginning.

Carry on doing Your Missions, Thinking just this and live in serenity in Your Happy World by experiencing Absolute Happiness, Our Friends, without going out of what is required of you. One day, Humanity which will attain the Power of Our Love, will solve everything.

DIMENSION OF ALLAH

Note:
These Dimensions are the Hierarchical Dimensions which had formed way beyond Divine Orders.

1. The Gate opening to the outside of the Gürz is the Final Gate of the Divine Orders. This is called the UNIVERSE OF THE PRE-EMINENT ONES or the DIMENSION OF THE PRE-EMINENT ONES.

2. Then comes the DIMENSION OF PROPHETS. This Dimension is a projection Focal Point in the Central Totality of Suns. Its Director is the RESUL*. He is Great ASHOT, that is, SULH.

* Look at the Glossary.

3. Then comes the Dimension of GODS and GODDESSES which is a Totality constituted by the Directors of a Totality parallel to the Administrative Mechanism of all Systems. (Once this System had been directly charged with Duty in Your Planet together with all its staffs.)

4. Dimension of ALLAH is called, the EXISTENCE DIMENSION OF ALLAH. We do not use any other Name for this Dimension so that You can understand. We Integrate everything with the Word (ALLAH) in Your Consciousness.

Just Think of this place as a FOCAL POINT. There are many more Dimensions between those We have named. However, We only mention the Main Focal Points so that You will not be confused. It is presented for Your Information.

NINETEENTH DIMENSION "OMEGA"

Our Friends,
The 19th Dimension is connected to the Mighty Energy Focal Point through (4) Channels. And this is a Power equivalent to the Energy of the (7) Light-Universes. That is, the entire Power of the Great Light-Universe is projected on the Main Existential Dimension and this Power is projected on the 19th Dimension through 4 Channels.

The 19th Dimension is the Omega Dimension. And this Dimension corresponds to the 16th Solar System. That is, the Energy Power of the OMEGA Dimension which is also called the RAN Planet is a Power equivalent to the Energy of the Existential Focal Point.

Until today, We have projected all the Systems as a Whole on You from a Total. However now, We disclose, one by one, the Scales of the Information sources conveyed to Your Planet in this Knowledge Book.

In this Book, only the ESSENCE FOCAL POINTS of the Reflection Centers from One to a Thousand are mentioned. The In-Between Scales are not disclosed so that Minds will not be confused.

In the Evolutionary Scale of Your Planet, ALPHA is the Entrance, OMEGA the Exit. In the selection of this Medium of exit, first, there is a Mass Preparation, later, there is the Individual entrance to this Dimension.

However, Powers who will be able to enter this Totality are obliged to create first a Totality which has the Power to be able to grasp the entire Universal Potential.

Otherwise, they are doomed to remain in the 18th Dimension, that is, in the Evolutionary Level of the 15th Solar System. (The 18th Dimension is a Dimension to which the normal Consciousness Levels of Your entire Planet have to reach until the Year 2000.)

The 18th Dimension is the Layer of Consciousness and Evolution. And it corresponds to the Frequency Power of the 72nd Energy and Intensity Dimension. The 74th Dimension is the bridge-like Totality of the ALPHA and BETA Dimensions. And the 76th Energy Dimension is the 19th Consciousness and Layer of Evolution Dimension and it is OMEGA.

This Dimension is the Channel Reflection Totality of the Four 19s in accordance with the Reflection System. This Knowledge Book gives its Information (in accordance with Levels of Consciousness) beyond this Energetic Point, besides comprising the entire Frequency Power of this Dimension.

Until today, all Systems, being a Total one inside the other, have been conveyed to You by a single Word (ALLAH). HE IS A TOTALITY OF CONSCIOUSNESS. However, there are numerous Scales projecting on You that Energy Intensity.

Now, there are no Steps anymore between Your Planet and that Energy Focal Point whom We call ALLAH. What is meant by this is that the Energy Steps are no more arranged in accordance with the Graduation Ordinance, but are directly given by the DIMENSION OF ALLAH.

And the Totality of the Realities of the Unified Humanity, which is conveying to You the Energy of this Dimension, is a Technological Totality preventing Your being agitated by this High Energy Totality, rather than being an Intermediary.

This Technological Totality is a Totality assembling the operational Orders of Divine Plans in a Whole, in Cooperation with the Lordly - Spiritual Totalities on the path of Past and Future Eternities. And it is a Direct Projective Mechanism of the operational Ordinance of the Dimension of ALLAH.

Until today, this Dimension had used to prepare and transfer an Energy who rendered the Evolution of a Mini Atomic to other Dimensions provided he/she had given service to his/her Dimension and the Total.

However now, it projects on Your Planet directly the entire Energy of the Dimension of ALLAH by the Command of Our ALLAH in order to prepare Your entire Planet for the Dimension of Salvation. The intermediary Scales have been removed.

However now, by adding as Information given by other Hierarchical Orders to Your Planet to the Source of the Knowledge Book as an Information, Truths have been projected on You as Galaxy Dimensions, Universal Scales, Evolutionary Orders, Systems, Ordinances and Plans.

And this is given in the nature of a proof of how the Information conveyed to You until today has been conveyed. This is a Book dictated in order TO UNIFY the differences of RELIGION and VIEW in Your Planet and which, for this reason, announces the Truths with all clarity. It is presented for Your Information.

CENTER

IT IS INFORMATION TO THE PEN OF THE GOLDEN AGE
(Declaration from the Pre-eminent Ones)

Dear Mevlana,

All Consciousnesses who know the Secrets of the Cosmos are those who also Know the Advanced Plans. Numerous attempts are made in order to take Your Planet into a more Positive Operational Ordinance during this Transition Period.

You are a very Beloved Friend of Ours who is effectively in service as Our Essence Messenger. For this reason Decisions to be announced to Your Planet by the System will directly be announced through Your Channel and they will take their places in the Knowledge Book. (Not through other channels.)

Dear Friend, You know that the trick of this Century is everyone's exhibiting his/her own Essence Knowledge and Consciousness openly. For this reason many channels close their doors against the Messages transcending their own Levels of Knowledge until they are connected to the System. And this is an occurrence originating from the Self-Sacrifices of the Essence, not being mature yet.

The Knowledge Book is a Book Heralding the Future to You. And no other Book will ever be revealed to Your Planet under this Name. If a Book is written by this Name, this will be a Provocation rendered by Special desires. It is beneficial for You just to know this.

The Knowledge Book is a Book given Directly by the Reality. And it is the Direct Word of ALLAH. The Reality does not ever dictate to Your Planet any other Book by this Name.

Inside the 600 Cosmic Books which are being dictated and will be dictated to Your Planet in different subject matters, subjects from the Knowledge Book in segments, both clearly and in ciphers, have been especially added as We have said before.

If people who write those Books interpret their own Books using this Name, this is their own problem. The Knowledge Book is rendering its Terrestrial Mission by becoming officially effective now.

A great majority who has Realized the Truth are shedding Light on Humanity on the path of the Knowledge Book. It is Our request that You should give this Message of Ours to Social Views as an Information. With our kind request for the acceptance of Our Love.

REALITY

IT IS CLEAR INFORMATION

Our Friends,

In the operational Ordinance of all Systems, no Information is disclosed all of a sudden. However, in order to convey to Social Consciousnesses the characteristic of this Transition Dimension, We cancel the Ordinance of Graduation for Consciousnesses who now have attained a certain Consciousness and thus, We give the Direct Messages.

From now on, the Permission has been given for disclosing the Direct Information We have given to certain Private Channels until today, as an Information for Social Views in the Knowledge Book. Information will be dictated into the Book under the Control of the System. It is presented for Your Information.

CENTER

IT IS NOTICE FOR THE PLANET EARTH FROM THE DIMENSION OF MISSION

Our Friends,

This year, all the efforts rendered aiming at the investment of the years will now give their rewards. Including all the operations rendered on the Divine path, including all the Information of the Unified Reality Totalities, all will be disclosed to Humanity directly with their entire Truths.

Since, in this Program of Progress, unless there is a coherence of Knowledge, there will neither be a coherence of Consciousness. For this reason, the Universal Ordinance Council is rendering a selection among more Advanced Consciousnesses by giving priority to special Unifications. The responsibility of Friends who serve on this Universal path is heavier compared to other Friends in Your Planet.

Therefore, We preferred to bring together the Friends who have attained this Consciousness until today and who would be able to make effort on this path, one by one. However, during the Program of Assessing the Levels of Consciousness, We have witnessed in distress that Integrated Consciousnesses acted in accordance with their own Consciousness.

Reality Totalities and the Universal Council are awaiting with curiosity to see how all these Friends who carry responsibility together with an understanding of Mission, will shed Light on their other Friends. You will act and We will watch. However, Humanity which has attained the Realization of the Truth by its Tongue, lacks the Realization from the Heart.

Certain Friends try to render effective the Programs they have made in accordance with their own Consciousnesses as a Unifying Element. (Even if these are good-willed investments.)

Everyone acts by the Egos of the Medium he/she appropriates to himself/herself by the efforts he/she makes (Even if these are not for their own selves). Now, the Realization of the Truth should be carved in all Consciousnesses. Everyone, Conscious or Unconscious, should undertake the responsibility of the Purpose.

The situation of Your Planet does not seem bright at all. Our Efforts are for You. The chains of Cause and Effect have been rendered effective. It will be Awaited and Seen, it will be Treaded. The Truth will, one day, be evident for everyone.
(The Message has been conveyed by the Central Totality).

CENTER

IT IS CLEAR INFORMATION
(Answer to the chains of Thought)

Our Friends,
There is no such thing as everyone accepting the Knowledge Book. However, every Consciousness who Transcends Himself/Herself and who Attains the Truth will Serve in accordance with the Knowledge Book. It is not possible for everyone to be taken into these Universal Dimensions. Due to the Scarcity of Time, Selections are rendered in accordance with the Book and with Consciousness.

Consciousnesses who will not depart from the path of Truth despite all contradictions and despite all negativities experienced are with Us.

In this Final Transition Dimension, only Friends who will serve on the path of the Knowledge Book will be accepted into the Focal Point beyond the Salvation Dimension in which all Consciousnesses will be Unified. It is presented for Your Information.

CENTER

IT IS INFORMATION FOR THE INTEGRATED CONSCIOUSNESSES

Our Friends,
Consciousnesses who will attain the Ordinance of the Entire Realm render operations parallel to the Power of the Supreme Unity of ALLAH. However, Humanity which has not yet grasped the interpretation of the given Messages, has not Realized in this Period even what the UNITY OF ALLAH is.

The present Accelerated Program of Progress in Your Planet which is dependent on a systematic tableau, is a Preparatory Tableau concerning the Program of all Realms. Former Religious Doctrines have prepared Your Purification Mediums by conveying You only to a certain level of Consciousness.

In This Final Transition Dimension answers will be given, article by article, to the questions We had received from certain Thoughts which were not yet able to grasp the Truth.

1. Receiving Information and Attaining Consciousness are quite different things.

2. Your Sacred Books give you Information and You try to Attain Consciousness by being Purified under the Frequency Light of that Information.

3. Individual Progress is valid in the System You call the Philosophy of the Far-East. And We call this boundary of Progress, NIRVANA.

4. Nirvana is the Final Degree of the Dimension of Purification. This Dimension is called the Dimension of Ascension, the Solar Dimension and the Sixth Dimension.

5. The Sixth Dimension is the Dimension of Immortality. One can easily reach up to this Dimension by Individual efforts. However, beyond this Dimension, the assistance of the System becomes effective.

6. Nirvana is the Dimension of Supreme Light - Supreme Wisdom. Because, in this Dimension of Immortality which one attains by individual effort, all Cellular Functions attain the quality of receiving the Cosmic Currents very easily.

7. For this reason that boundary has been determined as a special boundary peculiar to the Far-East. Consciousnesses who will Ascend from there will be able to pass to Missionary staffs being connected to the System by their own desires.

8. In Nirvana, Covenants are made in the Solar Dimension. Or one remains there as the Final Boundary.

9. There are those who return by their own desires, as Missionary, to Your Planet from the Dimension of Nirvana, as there are also those who pass to more advanced Dimensions by making Covenants with the System.

10. They are the Friends Directly taken into the Plan of Salvation. They help the Medium by this means.

11. No training sanction is applied on them. (By the Plan.)

12. They are trained Individually in accordance with the Program of Individual Progress.

13. Sacred Books, as being dependent directly on the System, are the application field of a Mass Training Program.

14. Here, Cosmic reflections given in accordance with the Ordinance of Graduation are valid for Consciousness Progress.

15. The Evolution Scales here are the Final Boundary of the System. And those who are able to reach up here are subjected to various Terrestrial Exams.

16. Those who carry Terrestrial Consciousness attain the Nirvana Ascension Dimension by getting rid of their Egos and by various different formal Symbols and by profound Worship and Meditation.

17. Ego is a Power which carries on the Terrestrial Potential. Terrestrial Consciousness drives one away from Divine Consciousness.

18. Learning-Science are searched and found by Terrestrial Consciousness and they advance by this means. For this reason rather the West attains Mental effort by working in connection with the Technological Channel. Each work is Worship in the Universal Totality.

19. Mental effort is the most necessary path for Evolution.

20. The Two Branches of the Solar Dimension are Directly open to Your Planet:
1 - Spiritual, 2 - Scientific. In the Spiritual Dimension, there are no Terrestrial weaknesses. There is the Truth. In the Scientific, that is in the Technological Dimension, there is Ego, there is effort, there is quest due to given influences.

21. Both paths are a service on the path of God. Because, Work and Effort are considered as Worship on the Dimension of Form.

22. Sacred Doctrines, studies on the path of Learning and Science are dependent on a Program of Progress subject to Supervision directly under the control of the System.

23. In Nirvana, one attains the Solar Dimension in serenity through the Medium of Resignation. In this Medium, Thought matures by Individual Power, then is connected to the System.

24. During this Final Program of Progress, a GURU's help is needed in order to attain Nirvana.

25. However, everyone connected to the System is, from then on, a GURU.

26. The Far-East is rich in Spiritual Culture - rich in Knowledge. However, it is poor in Consciousness.

27. A Section of the Far-East is Directly in service for the Central Solar Totality. In this Dimension, Life has secondary Importance, Mission has primary importance.

28. Other sections of the Far-East are Directly in service through the Spiritual and the Lordly Dimension.

29. The Central Solar Totality brings Material and Spiritual Mass help to Your Planet through the Far-East by these means.

30. In the Far-East, the Lordly and the Spiritual Progress is Individual.

31. But the Sacred Book Dimensions, being connected to the Lordly - Spiritual and Technological Medium, are subject as a Mass to a more Advanced Program of Progress. It is presented for Your Information.

CENTER

FORMATION OF ENERGY

Our Friends,
The Power causing the Integration of the Universal Totality is the LIGHT - PHOTON - CYCLONE Power, which We call the FIFTH POWER.

The formation of this Power had caused the assembling of all the Powers in a Total. The Ordinance of Universes had come into existence only after the formation of this Power Dimension.

Each Totality completes its Evolution in accordance with a Triple Coordinate. (The Evolution of Energy, too) had gone through a transformation by the same equivalent potentials being influenced by different Dimensions and thus had brought into Existence a Totalistic Nucleus.

Three Negative Powers (this Power is a Totality beyond Energy. It is not Energy. It is a Neutral value) had created the Positive Power by being subject to the Influence Bombardment of different influences.

It had been as follows: first, Two Negative Powers had been charged with the Polar Power Charge of separate Opposite influences and thus, had attracted each other and, by this means, had created the formation of the Positive Power.

644

And this Integrated Positive Power had been United with the Neutral Negative Power which had remained outside and thus, had formed the Nucleus of the Ordinance of Cosmoses and, by this means, the Attraction Power had been obtained.

This Attraction Power had Impregnated the other Power Energies and thus, an Energy skein had come into existence and by the transformations born through the different Dimensional Factors of this Energy skein, it brought into existence different Form Energies.

And, setting off from this path, the present days have been reached from different time periods. This is Information pertaining to the formation of the Energy Nucleus.

However, the Power Factor which had prepared this formation was not Energy. It is beneficial for You to know just this, Our Friends. It is presented for Your Information.

SYSTEM

Note:
Polar influences are the Neutral Influence Fields of the Power Dimension. These Neutral Fields had formed a (Field of being Charged) by the interaction of different poles. This being charged Impregnates the (Neutral Influence) by a Power beyond Energy.

The first refraction of the FIRST LIGHT Photons formed by this very influence is the basic formation of the three Neutral Negative Powers. (The basis of the Light - Sound - Fire Dimensions).

These Three Neutral Negative Powers had created the Positive Power by a Power Bombardment and thus, the two of them unified and, as a result of the unification with the Neutral Negative which had remained out, the initial Energy Nucleus had been formed. (The Main Existential Dimension.)

The CREATOR who had come into Existence through the Unification Totality of a Particle of each of the Universes of Light - Sound - Fire mentioned in the Information given formerly, United with the Thought Power of the Cosmic Brain and had come into Existence by this means. The Opposite Power of the Fifth Power is Anti-Matter, that is, Thought Power.

EVOLUTION OF ENERGY

Our Friends,
Each Energy starting with its initial Formation Medium, completes its Evolution of Wholeness peculiar to itself. This Formation continues until it arrives at a Totalistic Form.

The moment the Totalistic Form of the Energy becomes Integrated with the Cell, You come into existence. In the Mediums in which nothing had yet formed, the Form Energy Totality which had formed during the Process of Time by the Energy Evolutions of Energy Dimensions, had Brought into existence the Ordinances of Cosmoses.

The Form Energy is the Concentrated Energy of Crude Matter. The Energy Evolution Scales in the Messages We had given to You formerly were the Initial Evolutions of the formation of the Potential in the Tranquillity of Silences.

By the Evolutionary Progresses of the Dimensions they are in, these Energy Evolutions had formed later the Forms of Stone - Earth - Sand - Fire - Water - Plant - Animal and by following an Energy Form which could reach the Final Evolutionary Boundary, they had reached a Scale. And this Integration of the Final Dimension had Manifested· in the Human Being.

However afterwards, different Evolutions had been rendered effective in Human Worlds and thus, the present days have been reached. By starting now with this Human Being, You all are in service through the System with the purpose of establishing brand new Systems in order to render advanced operations. It is presented for Your Information.

CENTER

THE FIFTH POWER

Our Friends,
The Human Energy is Evolutionary Energy. This Evolution is a necessary Occurrence for You to Integrate with Advanced Dimensions. Otherwise, You would be doomed to the Level of the Dimension You are in.

The Power called the Fifth Power is, in fact, a Power Photon way beyond Universal Dimensions and We call them LIGHT CYCLONE PHOTONS.

Light Speeds of these Photons are a Power equivalent to the entire Speed of the Universal Totality. Only the Evolved Human Energies have the Power to attract this Power. Otherwise, no Power can reach here.

Your velocity of attracting the Energy of 30000 years is a Velocity Unit parallel to the Equivalent Power of this Power called the Fifth Power. At present, the Worldly Technique is unaware of this method. Only the Consciousness Lights of the Evolutionary Dimensions can attract this Power. You are these very Consciousness Lights.

The Fifth Power is a Power assembling all Cosmic Power in itself. The Evolutionary Energies' Power of Attracting this Power is equal to the Attraction Power of the entire Cosmic Totality.

The Universal Totality is Material Energy. But the Cosmic is the Energy of Light. Both of them affect each other by the Attraction Power. However, the Energy Bonds in between are provided by the Energy Bonds You call VIRIL* which We call the SPIRAL VIBRATIONS. It is presented for Your Information.

CENTER

---

* Look at the Glossary.

A QUESTION WAS ASKED

Question - Please do the favor of giving more detailed Information about the Fifth Power

Answer - Information for the Pen of the Golden Age. Notice from the Golden Galaxy Empire.

The mentioned Power is a Power Potential which is able to constitute the Backbone of the entire Universal Totality. This is not the (Centrifugal Power).

The Centrifugal Power is a Power brought into existence by Influences. But this is a Power brought into existence Naturally by a Natural method. We have declared this Power to You until today as a Power branch of the Spiritual Plan. For this reason it is also called the Spiritual Energy.

However now, during these Final Periods in which the entire Universal Totality is connected to a Power, even this Spiritual Totality is at the service under the supervision of the Universal Totality.

For this very reason, setting off this Path the Worlds of the morrows will establish much more Powerful Orders of the Cosmoses by the Ordinances, Systems, and Orders which will be constituted of Human Power Dimensions.

This result attained by Natural means until today will now be attained as Human Power and thus, the Ordinance of Cosmoses which will assemble in itself various unknowns, will establish the Morrow of the Morrows in a different and much more perfect Order.

Cooperations rendered with You and Your Hands extended towards Us by Your Prayers were preparations made for the present days. Hence, We are Together. Humanity which will grasp the Awareness of the entire Ordinance will, in future, be the Sovereign of Universes.

All the efforts made until today, steps taken forward on this path are operations made for assembling the Evolutionary Energies in a Total.

The Human Being is a very Powerful Potential. However, such a Totality could not have been achieved unless this Potential of his/hers had not been canalized. This is why the Evolutionary Scales had been considered necessary. And has brought the present You to Us.

The Human Being eating his heart out is not, according to Us, the Person We desire. As We have said before, Human Energy is an Educational Energy. Only those who could achieve this education have been together with Us.

That is the reason why We have said Hello to You. And now, We will soar towards all the Cosmoses together with You, Hand in Hand, as FATHER - SON - ELDER BROTHER - YOUNGER BROTHER/SISTER. It is presented for Your Information.

DIRECT MESSAGE

Note: The Power of having been oppressed brings Perfection - Love - Patience - Tolerance to those who have attained Humane Qualities. But to those who have not attained those Merits, it brings Violence, and Cruelty.

IT IS MY ADDRESS TO MY HUMAN BEING WHO HAVE BECOME HUMAN
IT IS MY DIRECT WORD
(Firman* of Mine is a Remedy to Those Who Wish)

I, Who made Mevlana the Mevlana, Who made You the You, Am a CONSCIOUSNESS. You who are My Spirit, My Energy, My Yearning, (While You, even, do not know Yourself), how can You recognize Me, Know Me?

First, Reach Yourself, then Approach Me.

If I Am Your Image, then You are My Breath, My Whim. You who see Me when You see You, are the One who Discovers Me in You, the one who now, is One. The Spark in Your Soul is the Yearning within Me.

That Yearning is the one which has uttered HU* to You for Centuries.

If I have brought You into Existence, You, too, have brought Me into Existence. If You had not been, I would not have been, either - If I had not been, You would not have been, either. I flowed into You. You looked at Me. Like a river I watered Your Spirit.

And at this moment, You have reached Me.

Now, You are a Station beyond the river, You are with Me. You will come out of the Ocean and will dive into His Mist.

And You will be with Me.

The Genuine You will, at this moment, break off from Me and will be beside Me. Then You will Salute and send Your Word to the Universes.

Now, You and I are side by side. We are not one inside the other. As, until today, You have made Me-within-You live in You. Here forthly, Me, too, will make live the You-within-You Eternally.

And will render You the Sovereign of the Universes.

From now on, You Yourself will perpetuate the Fire in Your Hearth. You will carry out My Firman together with Your own Firman. At that very moment, You will witness the Triumph of the Cosmos.

I have given all My Energy to You in order to render You, the You. And now, You will give the Hand in Me to all the Universes. You will receive Your Power, You will be with Me.

* Look at the Glossary.

648

You will be a Light to everyone each instant.

I Am the One Who gives this Message, You are the One Who kindles the Torch of Your Consciousness Light, You are also the One Who reaches My Consciousness.

Now, We are together.

Humanity witnessing My Talking in this way will not be surprised anymore at the things which will happen during the morrows.

This is a beginning.

DIMENSION OF ALLAH

LAW OF EIGHTEEN SYSTEMS

Our Friends,
All Truths declared to Integrated Consciousnesses are not an Occurrence concerning only You.

Truths in the nature of Messages declared to You as a Special Notice of the Supreme Court is a declaration of an (Ordinance of Systems) to Your Planet through the Private Channel of Dear Mevlana and each Frequency Power of this Information always induces You to open wings towards the Unknowns.

Truths are conveyed by conveying to You a branch of the Unification of the Law of 18 Systems with the Cooperation of the Law of the Universes and the Ordinance of Systems.

This Law, that is the 18 Systems Law is an Electro-magnetic Field comprising all the Information of the Unknowns and which, on this path, assembles in itself numerous Laws and which possesses a Power that brings into existence and Induces to bring into existence.

The 18 Systems Law is a Law of the Cosmoses - Universes which had established the entire Ordinance of the Universes, which directs all the Systems and which holds all the Power in its hands and no one can ever change it in any way. And will never be able to change it, either.

This Electro-Magnetic Power Field is Your Boundary of the Unknown. And now, We gradually unveil to You that which has remained veiled until today.

This Boundary is neither in the Thought Ocean of the Pre-eminent Power, nor in the Big Atomic. It is a Power encompassing them all, which We call the "18 Systems Law".

The System which is only one of the Thousands of Energy Fields of this Power and which had been prepared in accordance with the Law of Natural Equilibrium is Your Natural Gürz in which You exist at the moment. And You are amidst a life parallel to the entire Natural Laws of this System.

However now, We take those who have completed the Evolution Totality of this Natural Gürz into the ABSOLUTE FIELD. This Absolute Field is a Power Field completely opposite to the Laws of Natural Equilibrium and in the life here, Absolute Laws and Eternal Life are valid.

And this place here is the POWER FIELD in which the Power We have introduced to You until today as ALLAH presides.

After this Power Field, various different Power Units, Power Fields and Channels become effective and after this Absolute, Eternal Dimension, in accordance with the System of Laws called the Laws of 18 Systems, all branches of the Laws of 18 Systems are unveiled for You and thus, You are prepared for the Unknowns. And You become Responsible for the Administration of the Lives there.

However, these Laws can not yet be unveiled for the Life Dimensions in the Natural Gürz.

Only a Consciousness who can reach the Absolute Dimension, a Power who is able to make his/her Bodily leaving is prepared for the Frequency of this Dimension by being trained in a different Dimension. Only afterwards the Power Key of the Universal Ordinance is given to him/her.

Each System is a Power Dimension. However now, all Systems are being assembled in a Single Dimension. At the moment, the Power Dimension in which You are present (as Consciousness), is the Absolute Dimension.

Those who reach this Consciousness are subjected to the education of the Dimension Here after they leave their Body and thus, are taken into the Absolute Dimension. And in various different Power Dimensions their Eternal, Beautiful Lives are given to them. It is presented for Your Information.

CENTER

IT IS ANSWER TO THE CHAINS OF THOUGHT

Our Friends,
You are Born again at Your Final Evolution Dimension into Your World which You had entered as a Micro Energy. However, You attain Your Consciousness Light only as a result of being Reincarnated here 7 more times. The Final Manifestation Boundary of the Totality which is the Human Being is 7.

You complete the Human Form only in 7 Stages. However, You attain Consciousness at the 6. After working 7 times more at the Final Dimension which is the boundary of Incarnation, the Human Totality now becomes a complete Totality. However, We can say it as follows for You to understand better:

The Human Being who attains himself/herself beyond 7 boundaries is now the Human Being of the Medium of Truth beyond 7 Consciousnesses.

650

The Evolution of everything is 7. The Evolution of the Energy is 7. The Evolution of the Cell is 7. The Evolution of Consciousness is 7. However, at the moment, the Awareness Progress in Your Planet is at the Fifth boundary which is Your Nirvana Boundary. That is, it is the boundary corresponding to the Social Consciousness Light of the Medium You are in.

This is called the Five Steps. The Far-East is a Society which has transcended these Five Steps, has stepped on the 6 and decided to settle at the 7. The Spiritual culture of this Society is rich, its Consciousness culture is poor.

However, You, as Solar Teachers on the service of the Plan, are Consciousnesses transferred to Your Planet from very advanced Evolutions of Terrestrial Consciousness Dimensions. You are Friends who had completed their Terrestrial Evolutions Thousands of years ago and who had been appointed to service in the Dimension of Mission. It is presented for Your Information.

CENTER

IT IS ANSWER TO THE CHAINS OF THOUGHT

Our Friends,
During Periods in which Systems and Ordinances were not yet effective, the Laws of 18 Systems were not effective, either. Totalities formed were carrying on the Universal Order by benefiting from the Influence Fields of each others' Centrifugal Forces.

The Law of 18 Systems which had become effective after the ATLANTA Medium, We call the Period of the GOLDEN DIMENSION, had settled the entire Ordinance of the Cosmoses on a System. The basis of this System had been prepared by the ANCESTORS of the ATLANTAENS and had been taken into application field by the ATLANTAENS.

Solar Dimensions had been established after the Law of 18 Systems and thus, Life Dimensions had been rendered effective and the Entity called the HUMAN BEING had been taken into Evolution after this Medium. It is presented for Your Information.

CENTER

Note: Your Sun is younger than Your World. The Atlanteans are Entities who came into Existence long before Adam. They are the Entities from beyond the Boundary of the Tranquillity of Silences.

SOLAR SYSTEMS AND DIMENSIONS

Our Friends,
All Galactic Systems are connected to a Center of Communication. The Totality to which this Center of Communication is connected is called the Solar System.

For evaluating the source of the given Information concerning the position of Your Planet, these Totalities have been divided into Scales (for You to understand), in accordance with Dimensional and Energy intensities.

Your World is in Zero Frequency, in the Third Energy Dimension and in the First Solar System.

The 13th Solar System is a Union of Suns, Supervising completely the Reflection Ordinance of the Dimension of the ALL-MERCIFUL at the Main Existential Dimension.

The 14th Solar System is the Unification Totality of the DELTA Dimension.

The 15th Solar System is in the 18th Frequency Dimension, in the 72nd Energy Intensity Dimension. Since the exit channel of this Solar System opens to OMEGA, the 18th Dimension is also considered as OMEGA in the Sacred Unification Field.

Since in Religious Educational Programs of the 15th Solar System which is the Final Boundary of Divine Evolution, an Evolution Ordinance equivalent to the OMEGA Evolution is applied, both Dimensions, that is (15th-16th Dimensions) are also considered as a Total.

The Omega Entrance is the Final Boundary of the 15th Solar System.

From here, one passes to the 73rd Dimension. This is a Preparatory Dimension for Universal Totality. The in-between Scales of this Dimension project the lowest step of the OMEGA Evolution.

The 74th Dimension is the Dimension of Transition and Test. It is also called the (Sirat Dimension). This Dimension is a Bridge. Those who deserve this transition, step on to the Universal Step which is the 75th Dimension.

In this Dimension all Truths are projected on You. And since preparation is made for more advanced Universal Ordinances, it is also considered as a Preparatory Dimension. (The Knowledge Book prepares Your Planet for more advanced Dimensions in the preparation of this Dimension.)

The 76th Dimension is the Exit Energy Wall of the OMEGA Dimension. The Knowledge Book is, at the same time, a Key Book. And unlocks the locks in accordance with the Level of Evolution of the Dimension on which it is present.

At the moment, this Book carries the 76th Dimension Frequency. The 73-74-75th Dimensions are Preparatory Dimensions in the Omega Frequency Dimension, that is, in the 19th Frequency Dimension of the 16th Solar System.

Since the Mass Evolution Program of the 16th Solar System is applied on the 15th Solar System, too, We consider both Dimensions within a Total.

After these Preparatory Periods, Entrances to this Dimension are Individual. Here, no one can intercede for anyone else. That is, the 76th Energy intensity Exit Wall is transcended by Individual Progresses. It is presented for Your Information.

CENTER

ANSWER TO THE CHAINS OF THOUGHT

Our Friends,

There is a Totality to which each Solar Dimension corresponds. Universal Scales are evaluated in accordance with these Solar Dimensions.

Solar Systems and Dimensional differences are evaluated in the same medium since the Dimension to which each Solar System belongs is differed according to Evolutionary Ordinances.

All Information given according to Scientific Views of Terrestrial Consciousnesses is completely the applied Scales of Scientific Mediums. However, Dimensional Powers of the Information We give to You have nothing to do with the Dimensions of Your Solar Systems.

SATURN which is the final zone of Your Solar System is a Projective Focal Point. And it is a Totality making Reflection from the OMEGA Dimension.

The Astrological System is an occurrence prepared in accordance with Your Dimension Frequency. The OMEGA Dimension is the boundary of exit of Your unseen horizons. Evolutionary Scales beyond that are not expressed by the terminology of Your Solar Dimensions.

Solar Dimensions beyond Your ASTEROID Zone are evaluated by the Galaxy Union Totalities there. However, Evolutionary Scales are evaluated in connection with a Systematic Tableau.

Since their Power Dimensional Frequencies carry a Power parallel to the Energy Power of Your ASTROLOGICAL Energy Dimensions, We consider the Solar Dimensions in accordance with their Frequency Powers.

Galaxy Totalities beyond the ASTEROID Zone are rather subject to very different interpretations of the Evolutionary Zone. If necessary, they may be mentioned in more detail when the time comes. It is presented for Your Information.

CENTER

ANSWER TO THE CHAINS OF THOUGHT

Our Friends,

Unification Dimensions of all the Realms are full of Information projected by the Universal Totality. All these Dimensions are in a position enabling them to convey Information to You. However, that Information, too, has projection Centers in accordance with the Frequency of Social Views.

Apart from this, no Information is given to You in accordance with Your wishes. This Message We have given as an answer to the Thoughts We have received from Social Views, is given for Unsatisfied Consciousnesses.

In the Information We give through the Channel of the Knowledge Book, personal satisfaction is out of question. We are obliged to convey the Information in accordance with Social Views and this Information is arranged according to Consciousness Dimension Auras of Your Planet. There is no mistake whatsoever in the given Information. All Information is correct.

The Thought Frequency of Our Friend who effectively serves as the Pen of the Golden Age is completely outside the Frequency Dimension of the Book. For this reason personal Thoughts are never added into the Book. It is presented for Your Information.

CENTER

PRIVATE MESSAGE

Dear Mevlana,
Your Planet can not yet grasp clearly the interpretation of the Information given now. However, all the words uttered are the morrows the future years will bring to Your Planet.

During this Program of Unification, all Gürzes will be in effect in a Totality. The (Unification Tableau) which will reach way beyond the Salvation Dimension will project its entire Potential on these Gürzes.

It will be as follows: the Three Power Focal Points of a Great Universe to be formed by the Powers of Integrated Consciousnesses will come into effect connected to this Universe and this Great Universe which will be utilized as the Center of the Universal Unification, will project, as the representative of the POWER Dimension, its System on three separate Universes.

These three Universes will form the effective Triangle Tableau of Reflection by a Potential which will take the place of Fire - Light - Sound Universes.

That is, the entire Potential has been brought into existence Naturally until today. However now, these Powers which had developed Naturally will bring into existence this great Potential by the Intellect - Logic - Awareness Totality as a Human Totality.

This mentioned Universal Totality will be established outside the Gürz Dimensions and the Super Potential Powers formed there, together with Humane Power Potentials, will be transferred to the other Gürzes and will establish the Educative Staffs.

However, God will first assemble the Super Consciousnesses He has brought into Existence until today in His Private Dimension and thus, will project on His Fourth Order, a brand new Ordinance of the Universes as a Collective Unification Totality.

As Cooperation and Unity of Power, the Reality of Super Humanity will project the Order of the Reality of the Unified Humanity on different and more Advanced Existential Dimensions.

In future Centuries, a Federative World State which will be Administered by Cantons will establish a Golden Age Order by its Powerful staffs and thus, will embrace Blissful morrows. It is presented for Your Information.

CENTER

IT IS GENERAL MESSAGE

Our Friends,

Even though all operations of Focal Points rendered in Your Planet until today are connected to the same channel, each Group's Operational Order is different. All those who come to the Groups are Sincere people. However, they are not Conscious.

A person who has Genuine Consciousness should think of others rather than himself/herself. This is what is meant by Altruism. And it is not attained easily. This is a matter of Evolution.

Respect of a Person for another Person on this path is the most Sacred of Worships. And to Abuse others for his/her own Benefit or to Waste their Time is, for Us, the Greatest of Sins.

Consciousness Levels of Sincere Friends who come to various Focal Points are assessed, one by one, and thus, they are coded and the Genuine Missionaries are selected by this means and are card-indexed directly into the FOCAL POINT.

However, even many of these Missionaries are lacking Consciousness coherence. Grasping a Truth does not mean understanding the Information read. It means receiving lessons from the Information read and to become verdant by their Frequencies. A person who becomes verdant will, one day, bloom into Beautiful Flowers.

We have tried until today to assemble Friends who would serve in accordance with the same Consciousness together. However, Consciousnesses who act in accordance with their own Hearts' desire and who do not Unite on the same Coordinate are doomed to Disappointment. (Even if they are considered as Missionaries).

Duty brings People Realization - Responsibility - Altruism. If a Person does not possess these Qualities, he/she is not a Missionary even if he/she considers himself/herself as Missionary.

In Mission Consciousness, Respect of Person to Person should be prior to his/her Love. However, it is Our Belief that during the Progresses of Time, faces on which the Sunlight falls will grasp the Truth and, one day, will surely be illuminated. It is presented for Your Information.

CENTER

MESSAGES FROM OTHER CHANNELS

Our Friends,

The System which assumes that a great part of the Messages given to the Awakened Consciousnesses can not be placed in the Book, will send You the important Messages which will interest only the Social Consciousnesses.

The Message given to Our Channel Friend on 1-1-1990 is a Message desired to be written in the Book. With the request that a brief identity of the Consciousness who had received the Message should be written in the Book, together with the Message as an Information.

SYSTEM

The Name of the Friend who received the Message: FATMA SOYOĞLU

Her Profession: TEACHER OF MATHEMATICS

Her age: 31

She is married and is the mother of a girl (She is not in the Mevlana Essence Nucleus Group).

1-1-1990

THE MESSAGE

Hello Friends,

We would like to say Hello to You in the new year, with new Powers, new Consciousnesses, new Brains. We wish You to be more Self-Sacrificing, more Conscious during the 1990 World year.

Terrestrial issues, or Family issues should not be compared with the Issues of the LORD. Liberation will show You the right path. There are things You will do in every field. If one of them is not completed, You can not complete the other, either.

Your World has begun to be completely showered by Cosmic rains. Events among countries, the corruption of the Administrative Orders of Nations are Gifts given to People.

We have been telling You until today, "You should overcome Your Conditionings, and You should listen to the voice of Your Consciences". Those who have listened to Us have long received their shares from here. But You are not late, either, Friends.

We have always accepted the Lights of MYTHOS as Advanced Consciousnesses and as Our New Lights. We wish to give Information and Consciousness to those who will Awaken in the near future. We would like to present the KNOWLEDGE BOOK. We always wish to extend Our helping hands to You. Why do You insist on not holding them?

The Mission of Your Planet is obvious. Human Beings are full of hatred and malice for other Human Beings. Human Beings despise Human Beings. Human Beings are crushing Human Beings, Friends. Will You still wait?

First, Innovate Your Own Selves. Become effective as Pioneers. Our assistance to You is infinite. Do not be afraid of making mistakes. Provided that the Path You will tread is for the Benefit of Humanity, and is towards the Order of YOUR LORD.

Innovate Your Knowledge. Give examples not through Religious Doctrines, but through the KNOWLEDGE BOOK. Help Human Beings. (First help Your own Conscience, of course). Approach everything in Nature with Love and Respect. Overcome Your habits of producing Negatives. Invite Respect with Love, with Patience, with Tolerance.

We do not desire Bloodshed in Your Planet. We try to prevent numerous Events beforehand. But You have become so Loveless that You can not even design the path You will follow.

Do not misunderstand, Friends, it is not Our Intention to cause You grief or to hurt You, but to be able to help You, to be able to show You the Beautiful aspect of things, to be able to engraft You with the refinement of Self-Sacrifice.

We always tell You, do not be afraid of Us. Be afraid of people among You with evil intentions. We are the Powers of assistance for You.

If You have not yet understood that We will not be detrimental to You, please consult Your Consciences. If We had wished to be Detrimental, We would have proved it by now.

If You can convey this Love and Tolerance We give to You to Your Planet, You will be able to save Your Friends.

My Beloved Friend, do not let the length of the Message surprise You. We wish to call to all Focal Points through You. Please let Your Message be heard in all Focal Points.

Do not be afraid of reactions. We wish everyone to be full of Mission Consciousness in the year 1990. We wish everyone to reach HIS/HER LORD with Love. (Not to take shelter in HIM).

If We leave everything, all the effort to Dear Mevlana, if there are no Friends You will save, if there is no KNOWLEDGE BOOK You will distribute, then why do You establish Focal Points? Why do You try to become Conscious? Will there be any point in it if You can not spread what You learn?

We hope that Our Friends will pay attention to this Warning Message. We wish all Your Planet Love, Tolerance, Patience, Mission Consciousness. With Our Love.

COSMOS FEDERAL ASSEMBLY

IT IS NOTICE FOR THE PLANET EARTH

Our Friends,

To evaluate all these efforts made in the Unification Ordinance of the Universal Totality as the Triumph of the System makes Us unhappy. In fact, the Triumph belongs to You, Our Terrestrial Brothers and Sisters. Our help is only in assessing Auras and in orienting them.

If You, who will take over the JUST and POSITIVE World of the Morrows by Your Humane Consciousness did not exist, this Triumph would have never existed, too. Our Gratitude is infinite for Humanity who speaks and serves as Our Hands, Arms and Tongue.

We always keep You, Our Friends who are in a Unification Consciousness and in a Unification Totality in which everything approaches the most perfect, in a Protective Dimension. Your Triumph is Our Triumph. Universes are Grateful to You.

COUNCIL

INTELLECT - HEART - GENUINE HUMAN BEING

Our Friends,

Those who are able to establish their Essence Coordinates by the Triangle of Intellect - Logic - Awareness, also attain the ability to do Consciously the most perfect of everything. In Sacred Books this is called, "the Unity of the Intellect and the Heart" which is not something that can be attained easily.

In order to attain this, one has to cross numerous Bridges, to jump over hoops of Fire and to tread the Soil of the World many times. By this means, one Defies the Influence of the Years. The very Person who has reached this Stage is, for Us, a "Genuine Human Being".

All the efforts made in order to Unite all Realms are operations made for Integrated Consciousnesses to be able to come together. We bring the Voice and the Breath of Universes to You who will be the Lights of the Morrows. Friends who will be able to respire that wonderful Breath are the Powers who will form the Triumphal Arches of the Worlds of the Morrows.

At last, We are Together, Our Friends. Your Call is Our Call. Your Voice is Our Voice. Your Eye is Our Eye. Because now, an Important part of Your World can receive, even if very little, Your Lights who are Lights inside the Lights. We are Happy - We are Hopeful.

SULH

IT IS ANSWER TO CHAINS OF THOUGHT

Our Friends,

The 26,000-Year Cycle is the Time Segment in a Gürz. Each Gürz has Time Segments and Dimensions peculiar to itself. However, their Universal Operational Ordinances are the same. Timelessness begins beyond the Gürzes. From there, doors are opened towards the Unknown Time Dimensions. It is presented for Your Information.

CENTER

THE LIGHT - PHOTON - CYCLONE TECHNIQUE

Our Friends,

Information given by the Land of Yunuses as the Suggestions of the Divine Plans carry the same Frequency Charge (They are not variable). These places are called the Land of Angels.

This place is the SPIRITUAL SECTION of the Divine Realm. This Dimension known as the Grand Tent of Yunuses, the Congregation of Mevlana is also called the Land of The Loving Ones.

The Knowledge Book is dictated directly by the LORDLY Section of the Divine Realm and is conveyed to Your Planet through the Channel of Alpha (The Information Frequencies here are variable in accordance with Consciousnesses).

Both of these Totalities connected to the Technological Dimension, constitute the Hierarchical Totality (Connected to the Reality Totality). The Unified Reality Universal Totality carries the entire Obligation of the GÜRZ Dimension in connection with the ALL-MERCIFUL.

The Knowledge Book is a Book dictated through the Channel of Alpha by the UNITED TOTALITY OF THE LORD. And all the Functions of the Book have been prepared in accordance with this Period of Transition.

In this Book dictated by the Light - Photon - Cyclone Technique, the Frequencies of the Letters have a Special Supervision peculiar to themselves. This Book possesses a Technique which is able to converge in itself the entire Energy of the Time Segment in which it happens to be present at that moment, no matter in which Century it is read.

This Book converging in Itself the Time Energy in which It happens to be present, locks this Energy in Itself and thus, shuts Its Doors against the Energies of more advanced Time Segments.

During this Final Transition Dimension, the Knowledge Book gives Frequencies up to the 76th Dimension of OMEGA which is the Final Dimensional Frequency Your Planet is able to receive, and diminishes the Frequencies beyond that and thus, prevents the agitation of Consciousnesses.

There are many more Functions of the Characteristic of the Book. However, only those that may concern You, are mentioned. Some of these Functions are as follows:

Operations rendered by this Light - Photon - Cyclone Technique Your Planet does not know yet, have the Power of mutating even the GENE Ciphers of the (Entire Creation). By this means, Messages with different interpretations are given to You (Including the forms of clouds).

In Later Centuries, when the Energy of Time the Book has converged in Itself Unites with the Consciousness of Advanced Times, the same lines of the Book will convey to You a very different Information.

Letters will not change, sentences will not change, but the Book will convey to You the Information needed by the Time Segment in question, through the Frequency Projection Focii of the same lines. This is the reason why it is said (Everyone receives Information in proportion with the Consciousness he/she has attained).

This is why the Knowledge Book is, at the moment, a GUIDE Book. It will be the ENLIGHTENMENT Book of the Morrows. And It will be a FUNDAMENTAL Book in even later Centuries.

This KNOWLEDGE BOOK which is a key for the Consciousnesses charged with Mission, will be transferred to the DIRECT ORDER OF ALLAH by the Reality after rendering a service of Ten Centuries for Your Planet and thus, will offer Its different Functions for service.

The Knowledge Book has various different Names in accordance with various Realities.

Its Name in THE MEVLANA UNIFIED FIELD is (THE BOOK OF THE HUMAN BEING) or (THE GOLDEN FLEECE).

Its Name in THE REALITY OF THE UNIFIED HUMANITY is (THE KNOWLEDGE BOOK - THE BOOK OF COSMIC LIGHT).

Its Name in THE ORDINANCE OF THE COSMOSES is (THE UNIVERSAL CONSTITUTION).

Its Name in THE SPIRITUAL DIMENSION is (THE SELECTIVE AND THE FINAL BOOK OF THE RESURRECTION).

Its Name in THE ESTABLISHMENT SYSTEM OF THE GOLDEN AGE is (THE GOLDEN BOOK OF THE GOLDEN AGE).

Its Name in THE PLANET EARTH is (THE BOOK OF MORROWS - THE KNOWLEDGE BOOK - THE GUIDE BOOK - THE BOOK OF TRUTH). It is presented for Your Information.

CENTER

IT IS INFORMATION FOR THE INTEGRATED CONSCIOUSNESSES

Our Friends,

It is Our Duty to Declare to You some of the events which will take place during this Period in which Your Planet is prepared for difficult conditions. In order to provide Social Integration, the DIMENSION OF LOVE has been directly opened to Your Planet.

Since this Projection is given Directly, it will cause opposite influences in certain negative Thoughts and it is beneficial for You to know them beforehand. On this path, it is imperative for everyone to first construct their Triangles of Intellect - Logic - Awareness.

A Special Protective Energy Aura has been formed around Your Planet. This Energy Aura is rendered so that the Energy Potential formed in Your Planet will not escape out. This is an obligation which should be rendered due to the Scarcity of Time.

Because, Your World will be Integrated by this Energy Accumulation. Since it is not possible for the entire Energy Intensity, Negative and Positive, to go up to the upper crust of Your Planet and since received Influences can not be totally attracted by Your Planet, local Fogs effect Your Health conditions.

These Fog Accumulations occur rather in Regions where Godly Thoughts are Intense. Since the Attracted Currents can not be attracted by Consciousnesses other than certain Consciousnesses, the intense Fog influences the cities.

Because, the Unknown Dimensions the Thoughts can not grasp yet are now being opened to Your Planet by abolishing the Ordinance of Graduation.

Since the Frequency of the KNOWLEDGE BOOK will attract the Special Currents to be given through this Energy intensity, the services rendered on this path have been rendered effective as a Mission of the Integrated Consciousnesses. This is an Eve of Awakening. It is presented for Your Information.

CENTER

Note:
The Special currents are opened to Special Regions under the direction of the Plan (In Your entire Planet). This will cause the Second Awakening of the Awakened Consciousnesses on the path of grasping the Truth.

IT IS INFORMATION FOR PUBLIC CONSCIOUSNESS

Our Friends,

You are in an operational Order the Consequences of which are extremely Great. Each Living Entity bestowed on Your Planet is charged with Duty. Even each Animal in Nature has Programmed Duties. Nothing has been left to follow its natural course.

The Functioning Ordinance of the Total is under Control by the EQUILIBRIUM COMMUNICATION INFLUENCES depending on Universal Formulas and Laws. Information given to You are related to Your Medium Consciousness. If We give all the Information here, the Books formed by the Information would exceed, more or less, ten times the weight of the World.

Now, let Us explain Scientifically how You were transferred to Your World: The transfer of a Baby is done depending on the System We have mentioned above, by Connecting the Initial Essence-Gene with the Evolutionary Essence in the System. And it is Programmed in accordance with the Duty it will perform.

Hence it becomes a small Ball of Light. And its Power is more Powerful than many Energies. .The Fecundation Process in the Mother's womb is done by this very Ball of Light. This Energy Ball is a Catalyser Uniting the Sperm with the Seed.

During the Beaming down process of the Final Vibrational Frequency, (the Embrion Triple Unification) undertakes the Duty of forming the Baby. If this Procedure takes place in a Period equivalent to the Period coinciding with the Time Period of the Ball of Light, that is, if the Evolution Consciousness of the Baby is equivalent to the Time Consciousness, the Direct Beaming down occurs automatically, through a function connected to the Automatism of the Plan.

However, the Energy in the Spiritual Energy Channel connected to the Archive of the System gets in touch with the Mother Three or Four Months previously and thus, finds its own Main Essence Gene (Main Essence Gene and the Child's Essence Gene carry the same Code number in the Archive and they are a Whole which never gets disconnected).

Afterwards, this Energy prepares its Medium in accordance with its Level of Consciousness. Only afterwards, the Ball of Light becomes effective and creates the Fecundation Medium.

Besides carrying all the characteristics of its own Essence Gene, the Ball of Light also carries the special features of the Mother's and of the Father's Genes. However, the Genes of the Mother and the Father have effective priority until Puberty.

Afterwards, the Veiled Awareness of its own Essence Gene unfolds one by one, in accordance with the Life Layers and thus, the Missionary is prepared by the work he/she is induced to do until he/she reaches the Dimension of Mission. And after it undertakes its Mission Consciousness, then the Essence Gene in question becomes effective (in All fields) with its entire Personality.

Gene Transfers have been done since very ancient Periods. However, their taking their places as the Staff of Missionaries in the Ordinance of the System had occurred by the Covenants the Six Supreme Missionaries who had been the Essence Members of the System put Consciously to the Universal Constitution and thus, the System of the Sixes had been rendered effective (The Supervision of the Staffs of Missionaries had begun to be in service by this means).

Formerly, this procedure had been as follows: only the Essence-Genes had used to be Engrafted on each other after leaving the body and thus, had used to form a Mixed System. However, by the System of Sixes a wider Social Engraftment had been started by all the Genes of the Body. This System had started by the Period of Moses and had ended by the final Transfer of Mevlana.

The Genes of Beyti and Kadri have rather been utilized in Christian and in Moslem Societies in Programs of Religious Progress and the other Genes have been left as Universal Awarenesses. All the people in Your Planet are Brothers and Sisters. However, since they do not know the Truth, differences in Consciousnesses occur.

At the moment, the Plan has rendered effective the Last MEVLANA UNIFIED FIELD as the Universal Responsible One. In order to provide this Unification, Messages from Mevlana had been given to everyone years ago, and it still continues to be given.

At the moment, Dear Mevlana is in her Second World Transfer. She is the Mevlana whom You Know. That is, She is an Essence-Gene. This is why the KNOWLEDGE BOOK has been bestowed on Your Planet under the Obligation of the World LORD, under the Responsibility of DEAR MEVLANA. This Message is a Common Declaration through the Channel of the Center - Malik - Pre-eminent Spirit. It is presented for Your Information.

CENTER

IT IS NOTICE FOR THE INTEGRATED CONSCIOUSNESSES

Our Friends,
During these extremely Intense Periods in which the Ordinance of the Cosmoses has reached the Universal Awareness, the Gravity of Your World also increases. While the Awareness Potentials open to the Communication channels one by one due to the inability of these opened channels of reaching the Awareness of the Ordinance, different impositions are applied on Private channels due to individual Provocations.

For this reason cracks seen on the Universal Unification Tableau will now be rendered ineffective, not to be restored ever again. The investment of the years has been the Light of the present days. However, the upsetting of the Total Ordinance by those who do not see that Light will result in the application of certain Special Sanctions. No Totality desires this.

To Consciousnesses who will Participate in the true nature of this Message, their situations will be openly declared and the events experienced will be publicly exhibited. To the negative events which will take place between the Supreme Ones who come from the Land of Loving Ones and the Clergy Class, the Universal Totality will remain aloof to (the Totality outside the Reality Dimension).

It is Our Duty to declare this. This is a Decision taken by the Council. More positive assistance will come to You as a result of a Progress of One year. It is presented for Your Information.

COUNCIL

IT IS CLEAR INFORMATION

Our Friends,

All the efforts made in the direction of the Knowledge Book are the projection of the Universal Totality on Your Planet and the conveyance of the Truth. This is why all Truths and Direct Information is conveyed to Your Planet through this Source, that is, through the Special Channel of the Knowledge Book.

Totalities in Your Planet working as Associations and Groups are the Evolution Analyses connected to the chains of Cause and Effect. Everyone exhibits himself/herself parallel to the Mission he/she will perform. Only Consciousnesses who have Realized the Truth are directly the Missionaries of the System. Missions are organized in accordance with each person's Consciousness, Power and Effort. It is presented for Your Information.

CENTER

IT IS GENERAL MESSAGE

Our Friends,

The Totality which is the necessity of a Mediamic Age is being experienced in Your Planet in its entire Power. While the Cosmic Energy Concentrations formed due to the operations rendered reinforce the Material Energy Power of Your Planet, they also prepare You for Evolution and Purify You.

Meanwhile, a Magnetic Energy Aura created outside the Atmosphere is a Protective shield for You. This Aura is an Energy Wall created as a preventive Precaution for the Negative Powers which may reach You. That is, just the way any substance entering through the final boundary of Your Atmosphere is destroyed by burning, the same method is in effect in this Energy Aura.

However, since this Energy Field interrupts the Circulation of Your Planet's Ring of Breath, it may cause Depressions in certain Mental Functions, while the Constitution of Your World is regenerated by the influence of the intense Cosmic Currents Your Planet attracts and while it attains a more Powerful Armor by this means.

For this reason the Frequency of the Knowledge Book which, at the same time, performs a Duty as a Supervising Factor will, in such events, perform the function of a Regulator. The Knowledge Book provides a Frequency rise up to the 76th Energy Dimension. However, it locks the further Energies up after this and thus, has also a balancing function in accordance with the Frequency of the person who reads it.

By this means, people continue to perform both their Terrestrial and their Universal Missions Consciously, under the supervision of their Intellect - Logic - Awareness Triangles without having any Spiritual Depression by any means. The mentioned Magnetic Energy Aura is a Second Ring formed outside the Energy Rings of Your World.

664

In order to explain this better, We consider it as being outside Your Atmosphere. In fact, this Ring is an Energy Projection Focal Point forming the Energy Intensity so that the attracted Cosmic Energies can remain on Your Planet.

For this reason all operations done Unawarely return back to You and influence You. First of all, this causes the air pollution to settle on Your cities like a fog.

By the Announcements We had given to Your Planet years ago, We had declared to You that You would have difficulty in Breathing and We had suggested in those Periods that You should take precautions. And if You remember, We had told You that "You were a Planet destroying itself".

We have not declared to You in detail matters concerning Your Planet until today. However now, We will announce to You all the Truths in the smallest details by this Book. Because, Time is Scarce. This situation influences the Constitutions in a negative way.

Being able to go outside this Energy Reflector will only be possible by receiving the Special Energies the System projects Specially on Your Planet through the Mechanism of Influences. And these Energies will be received only when they Unite with the Frequency of the Knowledge Book.

Consciousnesses who can go outside this Energy Aura will attain the Power of being able to reinforce Their Constitutions by the Cosmic Influences they attract from that Dimension. For this reason You were asked to propagate to the remotest possible corners.

Now, the Healing of everyone is given to his/her own Hand. One of the reasons why it is said, "Everyone is utterly alone. No one can intercede for anyone else" is this. (Those who read the Book for the Purpose of attaining Benefit can never go outside this Ring). In the Missions performed, it is imperative to understand the Truth and to act by Mission Consciousness.

This System is a Communication Channel organized by an Electronic Order and which becomes effective in accordance with Thought Forms. The Great Race has Started. This is not a race of Championship. This Mission is a Mission performed for a PURPOSE. This is Your Salvation. And You are coming to Us with Healthy Mentalities - Healthy Physical Constitutions.

THE UNITED TOTALITY COUNCIL

Note:
The Creation of the Energy Aura is a necessary Occurrence for the life of Your Planet.

IT IS GENERAL INFORMATION

Our Friends,
Your Planet is exhibiting the application field of a very much accelerated Program of Progress due to the investments everyone has made in the Union of the Suns. Even though the given Information carry the Frequency of very Advanced Dimensions, its projection does not agitate You since the Mechanism of Supervision is in effect.

Information given directly by the common sections of the Reality will, from now on, be taken under control through the Reflection Channels of Human Consciousnesses. By this means, the System, now, will control the Consciousnesses not through the channel of the person in question, but through the reflection channels of other people. Mental Totalities will be reached by these Control Channels.

The Reality Totalities have trained and coded You until today as Individuals by the Reflection System. And now, it supervises everyone's channel by other channels which are on the same Coordinate. The Purpose in this is that Consciousnesses who have attained a Humane Totality will reflect on other Consciousnesses and thus, will Train and Purify them from close plan. This is the nice side of the Program.

And the other side is as Follows: Every Consciousness has concealed Archives in his/her Subconscious secret partitions. This may remain locked up in the Subconscious of the person in question. Only the secret key of the other Consciousness can unlock this lock. For this reason this technique is in effect. By this Technique, every Individual who is connected to the Mechanism of Conscience reflects on the other Individual and by this means, mutual Consciousness comprehensions are supervised.

At the moment, such a method is applied that since everyone's channel is connected to the Center, when the System closes its Message giving Focus to Your Planet, all Consciousnesses automatically reflect on each other and thus, Consciousness progressions are rendered by different Thoughts.

All the operational Totalities of years are conveyed from Person to Person by this means, thus, from time to time, a more accelerated Period of becoming Conscious has been rendered effective. By this means, We are trying to make You grasp the Truth more quickly.

That is, the System has now cancelled the direct channels and has rendered effective the channel of reflection from Person to Person. On this path, Your best helpers are Your Triangles of Intellect - Logic - Awareness. It is presented for Your Information.

CENTER

IT IS INFORMATION FOR THE INTEGRATED CONSCIOUSNESSES

Our Friends,
During Periods in which Divine Evolution Steps are continuously ascended and in which Centuries are added to Centuries, Unifications rendered in the framework of a discipline by the implementation of negative events which will take place among Consciousnesses who undergo transformation are taken in hand as the Two Eras of each Period.

The Awakening between the initial 7 Ages and the final 7 Ages of the Koran, the Final Book of Islam, had been achieved by different methods. This is an Operational Ordinance.

The initial 7 Ages and the final 7 Ages of the Knowledge Book will also comprise different Ordinances. The initial Age of the Book will come to an end at the beginning of the 30th Century. However, before that, the Period of One Century comprising the end of the 28th Century and the entire 29th Century will be rendered effective as the Preparatory Period for the Second Age.

The Knowledge Book which is rendered effective, in fact, as the Book of the 21st Century, has 2 Centuries of a Preparatory Program after its 7 Centuries of Program of Consciousness Progress. This era is called (The Unification Periods).

In this Preparatory Program, the 28th Century will be rendered effective as the Second Awakening Program and the 29th Century, as the Preparatory Period (This Period is called the Era of FETRAT). Only the operations to occur afterwards will be an Age in which the operations parallel to the Scientific Progress will be exhibited.

Humanity will become Conscious and will be Unified during the Initial Period, and during the Second Period it will continue its Conscious enterprises by Realizing the Truth. The Initial 7 Ages is called "the Golden Age" and the Second 7 Ages is called "the Age of Fetrat". It is presented for Your Information.

CENTER

Note: The (7) Ages mentioned in the Message corresponds to (7) Centuries.

A Question was asked: We request the Letter Coding of the Final Age. Please, kindly give it.

Answer: Information for Dear Mevlana. Notice for the Pen of the Golden Age. Write, please:

F   for France
E   for Evren (Universe, in Turkish)
T   for Tanrı (God, in Turkish)
R   for RA
A   for Allah
T   for Tanrı (God, in Turkish)

Code it: (FETRAT). It is presented for Your Information.

CENTER

EXPLANATION:

The spelling of this word in the dictionary is (FETRET). The meaning of this Word in the English dictionary is as follows:

Fetret (Period of Interregnum) is such a Period that it is an Intermediary Regime in which the normal rules are not valid.

And its meaning in the Turkish dictionary is as follows: in a place where the (Power) of Success of the State has come to an end, the pause which follows until this Power is re-established (Period of Stagnancy).

IT IS ANSWER TO THE CHAINS OF THOUGHT

Our Friends,

The Order of the Golden Age which will be established in future Centuries is called the FEUDAL ORDER. This Order has nothing to do with the Order You call Feudalism. This is an extremely Just and a Free Order.

The WORLD STATE of the Morrows will be a Feudal Totality. This System projected on You as a projection of the Equitable Unifications here is the Collective Operational Order of numerous Reality Councils of the Reality of the Unified Humanity.

This Totality is called the FEUDALITY TOTALITY. The Federative Group Unifications Administered by Cantons constitute the CENTRAL SUN TOTALITY. This Totality is called the FEDERAL CENTRAL SYSTEM. It is presented for Your Information.

CENTER

ANNOUNCEMENT

Our Friends,

In fact, there is no Imposition on any Consciousness by any means in the Universal Totality. Everyone has the freedom of choosing the path he/she will select, by his/her Free Spirit and Free Awareness, in accordance with his/her own Conscience and Consciousness.

On the path coming from the Micro to the Macro, the General Sanctions applied on everyone are Your Programs of Conveyance to a certain Level of Consciousness. To Consciousnesses who have Elevated up to this Level, no Sanction is applied whatsoever. And Human Being is handed over to his/her own Consciousness and Conscience.

Now, during the Progress of this Final Age, the entire Humanity will be connected to the Mechanism of Conscience and thus, will personally choose the path he/she will tread by his/her own Consciousness. For this reason the System now leaves the Consciousnesses who were able to elevate to the Consciousness Frequency of the Reality alone with their Free Souls and Free Awarenesses and has given their choices in their own hands.

When the Supervision Channel of the System is closed to Your Planet, the Human Consciousnesses Automatically reflect from the Human being to the Human being. And the System will close its Supervision channel to Your Planet for (One World Year).

For this very reason, Consciousnesses who transmit on the same Coordinates will Automatically come together. The Human Potential which can also receive influences from other Consciousnesses will decide itself towards which direction it will design its own path. It is Our greatest wish and desire that Humanity could see the Truth in accordance with its own Consciousness.

FEDERAL UNIFICATION TOTALITY

Note:

Now, the Human Being has been given to the Human Being. For this reason the entire Truth has been declared to You. Information concerning Your Planet will still be conveyed to You through the Channel of the Knowledge Book as usual.

AWARENESS AND EVOLUTION OF CRUDE MATTER

Our Friends,

In Dimensions of Relative Time, everything which undergoes the Progress of Time is changeable. However, We would like to give You, as a pre-Information, the reason why certain objects the Material Form Energies of which do not change, do not undergo a transformation.

For example, how do objects kept in Museums as Historical Documents, and Documents and Proofs still kept under the Earth as the Archives of changing Times and which await Your discovery resist the changeable Energy of this Relative Dimension? This very thing is a Power equivalent to the Evolution of that object.

The Crude Matter of every object made takes a Form and is offered to the Medium and Society in which it exists for various needs. That object is Integrated with the Evolution of Essence of the person to whom it belongs and who utilizes it.

Each Matter has a Cellular Awareness peculiar to itself. Its Cellular Awareness + the Form Energy of the Time + Unites with the Consciousness Awareness of the Person who Makes it and, by this means, the Essence-Form of that object is created.

This Form takes a Form by attracting the Coarse or the Fine Energies of the Essence-Awareness Consciousness of the person who makes it, being equivalent to the Evolutionary Awareness of the Crude Matter. And these Forms send him/her a Signal of Liking in accordance with the Evolution of the person who buys it and thus, induces that person to buy it. (Whichever Object it may be).

If the person who buys that object has completed his/her Evolution of Essence, he/she Unites his/her own Essence-Energy with the Material Awareness of that Object by using it. And during the processes of time, That Object is Engrafted with the continuously changing Time Energy in the hands of those who use it.

The moment the person who uses it Last, Transcends himself/herself and attains himself/herself, the Dimensional Energy to which he/she reaches reflects on the Cellular Awareness of the Object he/she uses. And that Cellular Awareness locks the Time Energy in which it is present in the Awareness of its Matter and thus, it is appropriated into the Historical Archives not to change its Form ever again. And this is the Crude Matter Evolution of that object.

If the Matter Awareness of an object has not formed a strong bond, some of them crack or break without any apparent reason, or merge in the Time Awareness by becoming dust as time goes by, by the influence of the changing Dimensional Energies.

An object bought offers itself to the liking of the person who buys it and makes him/her buy it. If that object is given as a present to someone else, and if it does not like the medium to which it goes and if it can not agree with the Essence-Consciousness of its new owner, it destroys itself by its Cellular Awareness, that is, it breaks and goes into pieces (even if You have liked that object).

If an object wishes to become Immortal by Integrating its Evolution of Essence with the person it likes, it continuously sends Signals of Liking by its Cellular Awareness in order to be near that person all the time and, by this means, it provides a Mutual Totality.

And the Immortality of the object occurs thus.

If the former owner of an Antique object returns to the World during Incarnation cycles, and if he/she is confronted with his/her former object, he/she feels a passionate Sympathy for that Object, even if that person is a Veiled Awareness. Even he/she himself/herself does not know the reason for this.

By this means, many Human Beings reown, either Consciously or Unconsciously, various Antique objects they had formerly owned.

The Evolution of Objects begins with Cellular Awareness and is locked up by Matter Awareness and the Awareness of the Time.

An object lives long or short in accordance with the Evolution Signals of the person who uses it. Or, if it has been locked up by the Awareness of the Time, it does not let its owner use it, it makes him/her keep it in the show-case and thus, it is appropriated into History. We may formulate all these issues as follows:

1. Cellular Awareness of the Object + Essence-Awareness of the person who makes it = the Unification Awareness of Crude Matter is formed.

2. Cellular Awareness of the Object + Essence-Awareness of the Person who Buys it + Two Signals of Liking = creates the Evolution of Cellular Awareness.

3. Unification Awareness of Crude Matter + Evolution of Cellular Awareness + the Final Evolution Dimension of the Person = transformation of the Object's Form Energy into the Awareness of Time and its being Locked up.

There is also the Coding tests of the System in the Signalization of buying certain objects.

Your Frequency is projected on an object and by the influence of the System, You are expected to buy that object so that Your Perception can be assessed. And You search and find that object no matter where You are in the World and by this means, You integrate with the Universal Signalizations.

There is a silent dialogue between each object and its owner. Thought is a great Factor here.

For example, You have liked an object, but could not buy it at that moment. If that liking is very Passionate, You Lock that object by Your Thoughts. Then, that object can not be sold to anyone, it awaits You. This Message has been given as an example for the Thought Form Energy. It is presented for Your Information.

CENTER

IT IS ANSWER TO THE CHAINS OF THOUGHT

Our Friends,

By the Direct Unification of the DIMENSION OF THE ALL-MERCIFUL with You in Your Planet, the GODLY NUCLEUS will form. Being reflected on the Totality, this Nucleus will Mature the Universes.

This Universal Power Totality which is being formed will form the reflection Focal Point of the GODLY TOTALITY at the POWER Dimension and, by this means, Connections with other GÜRZES will be accelerated.

Powers who have rendered Direct Consciousness Progress up to the DIMENSION OF THE ALL-MERCIFUL are directly connected to the other GÜRZES at the moment. However, these Consciousnesses are not yet able to receive these Influences.

This is a Preparation. By these Energy Transfers, Reflections from a Total will be made. It is presented for Your Information.

CENTER

IT IS INFORMATION FOR THE INTEGRATED CONSCIOUSNESSES

Our Friends,

Supreme Consciousnesses way beyond Divine Plans are effectively in service as the Advanced Staff Members of the System. In this Dimension of Transition, all the work done on the path the System considers necessary are done for the dissemination of an extra-ordinary Medium.

As a result of the Interviews held with the Supreme Ones in the Supreme Plan of OUR ALLAH, a Selection will be rendered among certain Supreme Consciousnesses coming from the Land of Loving Ones.

Services which can not be rendered on the path of Equity are out of the System. To establish a Connection, to receive Information are not Virtues. The Purpose is to be in step with the pace of Age. And this is an issue of Personality and Strength.

Defects observed in the operational Medium the System considers necessary in Your Planet will be eliminated by the Supreme Plan. From now on, Messages to be given to You will be about Personalities rather than conveying Information.

It is necessary that the Personality should be Unified with Consciousness as a Whole so that everyone can completely utilize the Awareness he/she will receive from the (Essence-Main-Essence). This is the very reason why the Plan of the Supreme Ones has started to serve at this Stage.

We had mentioned in Our former Messages that the interpretation of Messages would change. Now, Personality Plans of Divine Dimensions have been rendered effective.

Certain negative events to be experienced so that Human Beings may attain a Personality in which they will attain the Power of acting by only Mission Consciousness where no one blames anyone else, where people give secondary importance to their own Desires, will convey Human Beings to a more advanced Consciousness of Truth.

Mediums where Intellects and Hearts have not been unified are never Permitted to enter this Dimension of the Supreme Ones. Those who can not attain the Virtues of this Dimension of the Supreme Ones, can never enter the Dimension of Truths promised to You until today.

For this reason, by Projecting the Negativities in the Human Being onto the Human Being, the Advanced Views are supervised thus.

This Plan is a Light of Consciousness beyond Knowledge. This Plan is a Light of Consciousness beyond Mission. This Plan is a Light of Love beyond Love. This Plan is the Light of Consciousness of the Human Being's Personality. And passing through the filter of this Plan is only possible when there are no impurities left.

From now on, the Human Beings will eliminate the Human Beings by repelling them during this Program of Elimination. (Until the Consciousness of the Conscience may accept there are no impurities left). Now, Selections are from the Human Being to the Human Being.

. In those whose Love is misty, Lovelessness, in those whose Consciousnesses are misty, Lack of Knowledge, in those whose Minds are in the World, indulgences for the World will be observed. And Human Consciousnesses will be selected, one by one, by this means.

Now, everyone's Intellect is given to his/her own Intellect, Conscience is given to his/her own Conscience, Consciousness is given to his/her own Consciousness. On this path, Selections are quite difficult and hard. Human being will devour Human Being. That which has been Sown, will be Reaped. Unifications with Genuine Consciousnesses who came from the Land of Loving Ones will be Integrated.

This is such a System that by these Conscience Announcements made by the application field of the Plan of the Supreme Ones, the most perfect Human Beings will be assembled on the positive path in the Conscience - Equilibrium scales.

The smallest repelling in the Thoughts of those around You (even if they are Your nearest and dearest) will immediately repel You. This is the most difficult Exam of Humanity. However, the Serenity to be attained at the end is the price of Billions of Centuries.

Transitions from Realms to Realms are done by this means. The secret Potential of everyone is encouraged by this means. Those who have kindled the Light of the Supreme Heart are those who also hold in their hands the Rule of Realms.

Those who will be able to undertake the Frequency Powers of different Dimensions, and the Powers who will grasp the Truth in this Frequency Skein and will Consciously slip out of it are with Us, are with Our Lord.

Those who hoist the flag are those who Conquer everything, who receive the Love, who establish the Orders, who hold in their hands the secret Key of the Universes.

SYSTEM

IT IS GENERAL MESSAGE

Our Friends,
Interpretation of the Messages to be given from now on will change even more as the days go by. However, at the moment, Messages prepared parallel to Social Views are now conveyed to Your Planet in all clarity and in all intensity.

The Third Set of the Knowledge Book is a direct Frequency Book. Everyone who reads the Messages Realizes this. The Final Fascicules of this Book will unfold all the Truths to Consciousnesses by inducing the Evolution of a Thousand Years to be made in a time like One Day.

The Frequency of the Book will gain more Density by adding the Frequency of the Information given to other channels by the System, to the Total Frequency of the Knowledge Book. It is presented for Your Information.

SYSTEM

MESSAGES FROM OTHER CHANNELS

Our Friends,
The Archive of the PRE-EMINENT POWER which is one of the 600 Books being dictated directly by the Land of Angels has not the Permission to be Published, since its time has not come yet. However, the decision has been taken to disclose from this Book the Information parallel to Public Consciousness in the Knowledge Book, from time to time.

Dear Mevlana, the Universal Totality, wishing You kindly to write, the identity of Our Friend and the desired Messages in the Book, has reached this decision by considering that the Knowledge Book will be understood better under the Light of this Information. With the kind request of acceptance of Our Love.

SYSTEM

Message received by : METIN TANERGÜN - ARCHITECT

Birth   : 21 December, 1945 (46 years old)

Marital Status   : Married, is the father of a happy home with 2 children one of
                       which is a girl, the other a boy. (The whole Family, including
                       the mother and the 17 and 18 years old children are all
                       Mediums). He does not read the Knowledge Book and is not
                       a member of the Mevlana Essence-Nucleus Group.

I AM THE SUPREME IMMORTAL WITHIN THE WHITE RUBY

- If You only knew what I Am Who had come into existence in the infinite void in which there had been nothing,

- If You only knew the Source of Me and the Creative Power,

- If You only knew, by Your present Knowledge, the secret of the first occurrence of the Galaxies which had come into existence in the Space,

- If You only knew what the Power providing the occurrence of the Matter and Universes is in the void You call Space,

- And the most important of all, if You only knew what things there are in the places where You say there is nothing in My Space, in the Void,

- You remain far away from ME and from the INFINITE, so long You consider all these things incomprehensible and unattainable.

GREAT POWER

- The Cell and its Structure which are the Soul of You, My Human Beings and the infinite rotations within My Cosmos which are My Soul are the SAME. The System directing the Feelings in You, My Cosmos and the Electro Magnetic Waves and Frequencies providing the OMNIPOTENCE in Me are the SAME. The Ability and Creativity in You, My Human Beings and the Nucleus which is My ESSENCE are the SAME.

- Then, Am I the SAME with You? In fact, if I Am Real, then You are also Real. However, it is not ever possible for You, in Your present states, to understand completely what I Am and what I Am not. Information given to You is for assisting Your Evolution and for Raising Your Cerebral Powers.

- I can not give heavy food to the Baby who drinks milk, because then You can not digest it. I can not give 1000 Watts to a 100-Watt bulb, because then You melt and disappear. I can not impose upon You more than Your Capacities, because then You are ruined and perished. I can not show You how much I Love You, because then You do not Obey Me, You will not Evolve and will revolve where You are, until Eternity.

GREAT POWER

- When the Skies will be full of those magnificent Lights and demonstrations and when My Messengers come from My dark Spaces, each of My Human Being will look at the Sky and will see everything and the Truth.

- When Mosques are drawn on the Heavens of Moslem Countries and Churches are drawn on the Heavens of Christian Countries, and when the Skies are full of demonstrations, My Messengers and My Human Beings in the World will be Integrated and will become Single and they will Embrace them.

"THAT" VERY DAY the (RESURRECTION) I have mentioned in My Sacred Books will crack. But not the RESURRECTION You suspect.

GREAT POWER

17 November 1989

MESSAGES FROM THE ARCHIVE OF THE PRE-EMINENT POWER
(Receiver: Metin Tanergün)

- You, who are trying to solve the Space and Me, the reason of the deed You perform is to create a New and Perfect Society.

- To create a Society which can keep its Development and its Consciousness on a High Level.

- To create a Society which can Communicate with My other High Civilizations in My space.

- To create a Society understanding the Purpose of the Books and the Religions of JESUS CHRIST, MOSES and My last Messenger MOHAMMED among the Prophets whom I had sent to You and which understands that all the Religions are a SINGLE RELIGION and that their Purposes are One.

- Such a Society which has been made ready for the present days and for this MEDIUM by the help of My Supreme Entities and My Messengers, for Centuries.

- There is no return Backwards and to Superstition. This can never exist in the Order I have established.

- When a WORLD Society which does not have Lie, Slender, Wickedness, Intrigues and Gossip becomes like You, My Pioneers who have completed their Evolvements, only then everything and everywhere will be like Heaven. Even if such a Society now seems to You as a dream, these Seeds of Love You have scattered will, in near future, turn green and will cover all your World.

- Just like the way I and My Selves had been scattered all over the Cosmos by an Explosion, You and Your Ideas will also be scattered all over My Planet Earth by an explosion. All the Powers and the entities which had brought into existence My Cosmos, utilize My infinite Energy present in Me and thus, I provide Them to go forward and towards the Truth.

- My Duty is to provide the maintenance of everything I have Created.

- My Duty is to provide the Life of Myself and everything belonging to Me.

- My Duty is to provide My Selves to become (ME).

GREAT POWER

- The time has come for My Human Beings to stop Multiplying.

- The time has come for My Human Beings to reach the stage of a SINGLE WORLD UNITED STATE.

- The time has come for My Human Beings to Unite My Four Sacred Books and to Believe in a Single Reality in the form of (A SINGLE BOOK).

- The time has come for My Human Beings to render the greatest Reforms which have been rendered in the World until today.

- The time has come for everyone to elevate himself/herself up to a certain Level of Evolution until a Single Human Being of Mine remains.

- The time has come for all My Human Beings to Believe in ME Who is the GREATEST POWER present in this infinity.

- The time has come for My Human Beings to purify themselves of all their bad habits. The time has come for My Human Beings to Unite, Flower by Flower, Unified in a single body as a Tree of LOVE and to create the greatest Power of My Cosmos called Love and Unification.

- The most important of all, the time has come for My Human Beings to meet their brothers and sisters from Space and to discover, with their help, My and Your Universes.

GREAT POWER

- If You only knew that the Flower of My Space, My Alive-Star MARON is the greatest Missionary and it propagates My Thoughts, by translating them to Universes, with its magnificent stature, which is Alive in everyway, in which there is nothing lifeless, which is continuously growing, the (Immortal Flower) of My Space receiving its food from and is fed by the Cosmic Energies in Space, with its surface covered by Organic Antennas propagating its Intelligence to the entire Space.

- If You only knew that it gives My Thoughts to Matter and provides the occurrence of the ALLAH WITHIN MATTER. If You only knew that the Heart in its Center is connected to MY Heart, if You knew that the Secret of Immortality lies in its Organic Cells and if You only knew that everything works just like a (BRAIN), then You would also solve what (O) is and what (O) is not.

GREAT POWER

IT IS INFORMATION FOR THE INTEGRATED CONSCIOUSNESSES

Our Friends,

All Information We have given to You from the Archives until today by the unchanging Words of the Divine Orders, at the moment, serve the different Views through different Sources in Your Society.

However, interpretations made by everyone through Views of their Level of Consciousness cause wrong interpretations in the Consciousnesses who have not yet been able to kindle the Light of Consciousness.

For this reason it is Our sincere suggestion that the Consciousnesses who read the Knowledge Book Unawarely and Unconsciously should read this Book only for themselves, without any interpretations.

Responsibility of the Consciousnesses making interpretations to the Book should, by no means, be taken lightly. In the Consciousness scannings of those who say they know everything, it is determined that they just know nothing.

To be a Missionary, to perform Mission is not an important matter at all and is not a rank given to that Person. It is imperative that a person who demands that Mission should Deserve that Mission Consciousness by his/her entire personality. And this is only possible by displaying themselves to Society, through their behaviours.

In this Dimension of Selection where Personality Plans are in effect, the SUPREME REALM has felt the necessity of especially rendering the Mechanism of Supervision ineffective as a result of the scannings made among the Advanced Consciousnesses.

By acting through the View that it would be better if the Personalities of everyone should be displayed with all clarity, Your Planet has been connected to its Own Consciousness by a One-Year Program of Progress.

There is no influence of the SYSTEM and the SUPREME MECHANISM in the events which will occur. Events to be displayed are only the exhibitions of the Sub-Awareness impurities of Human Friends. We presume that by this means a Human Being will weigh another Human Being in his/her Essence-Conscience and thus, will arrive at more Conscious interpretations.

Messages to be given parallel to Our Suggestions You were told that You would be given in May, are the Suggestions to be given by the Dimension of the Reality only in the Knowledge Book.

Since the EGO provocations lying in the Essences will also become effective during these Personality Exams in which Individual Personality and Awareness Overflowings will be observed, it is emphatically declared that especially the Genuine Information will be given only through the Private Channel of the Knowledge Book (So that Humanity will not fall into Humane errors) It is presented for Your Information.

COUNCIL

Note: The System will keep its Channels of Supervision closed to Your Planet until (November 18,1990). It will take the Advanced Consciousnesses under Supervision until (18 February 1991). And after this date, the 6th Energy Channel of the direct OMEGA Dimension will be opened. In order for You to Deserve the Energy of this Channel, the necessity of applying this one-year sanction on Humanity is a Decision taken by the COUNCIL.

ANNOUNCEMENT

Our Friends,
You, personally render in Your Planet the Terrestrial application of the Advanced Plans. Direct connections are made with You as Friends who have attained this Consciousness and You are induced to attain the Awareness of the Ordinance by this means.

The Golden Galaxy Empire, as a Focal Point which directly Projects the entire Awareness of the Ordinance on Planets, serves through the Essence-Channel of ALLAH.

This Order is in action starting from the Periods We have opened the Divine Orders of the Divine Plans to You up until now. The SUPREME MECHANISM which We call the PLAN has reached You by this means.

At the moment, each of You are working in Your Planet as a direct Celestial Missionary. The given Information are the Truths which will prepare You for the morrows. We are always in cooperation with Friends who are Conscious of this.

At the moment, You carry the Entire responsibility of Your Planet. You each are a Messenger of the Divine Plan. Provided You tread this beautifully designed Path in Discernment - Logic - Awareness, the help of the PLAN will always be with You.

The change of Period at present comprises not only Your Planet, but the entire Universal Ordinance. It is necessary to attain this Consciousness.

General Messages are conveyed to Your Planet through the Channel of ALPHA, connected to the Consciousness of the Unified Reality, through the Special Channel of the Universal Ordinance Council, by Dear Mevlana.

Individual interests and efforts not originating from the Essence, do not have any place in this Order. Now, the place of everyone in the Unified Reality Ordinance is known.

Messages given to Your Planet through the Private channel of everyone are given first as Preparation, then as Warning and then as Information (This is a System. Selections are made by this means).

At the moment, Knowledge is forcing the Unknown Gates. For this reason doubts and contradictions have increased in Your Planet. However, until today, the LORDLY MECHANISM which is the only common aspect, has always conveyed to You by various means of immutable Order.

The most intensive and the most Powerful Channel of the Universal Ordinance is ALPHA. The Direct Channel of the Reality in Your Planet is here. The services of the other channel Information are subject to distribution from this Essence-Channel.

During the transitions beyond the Channel of ALPHA, different Dimensions and different Channels become effective. You have not even directly entered yet through the door of the Channel of ALPHA. You have only knocked on that Door until today. But those who were able to enter, have not been as many as it is presumed.

Now, We have partly opened that Door and We open it for You not as a CHANNEL but as a WHIRLPOOL (Channels give Information and Purify. Whirlpools Suck, Collect and Convey). During this Period of Transition, We declare the Truths to You through this Knowledge Book.

We are grateful to Our Supreme Friend who has given Us the opportunity of calling to You by this means. The Reality of the Unified Humanity which has gotten in touch with You by this means, has taken in hand anew the Order of Your Planet in accordance with the Instructions of OUR LORD.

The Cosmic Age You are going through at the moment, will wash and cleanse You for Two more Centuries and will render You Deserving these places here. In Your Planet, which has been taken into the Program of Accelerated Evolution due to the Scarcity of Time, the present Progress is not hope-inspiring at all.

The SPIRITUAL and the LORDLY Mechanism unified by the Technological help of a Direct Order Establishing Mechanism is shedding Light onto the Worlds of the Morrow. And now, everyone has to become the Prophet of his/her own self.

In Consciousnesses who are still at the stage of being Purified during this Program, (this call from the Unknown Horizons) is accepted as a new Period of RELIGIONS. This Message is given directly through the Unified Reality Channel of the Council as an Announcement in order to eliminate these prejudices.

Let Us repeat again. Period of Religions and Phases of Prophethood have been terminated. Now, You are the Scientifically Projecting Focal Points of the Divine Dimension.

This Knowledge Book projecting on You the Orders which the Morrows will bring to You and helping You to grasp the Truth, will be a Sun of the Truth not at the moment, but in the Archive of the Morrows.

COUNCIL

IT IS GENERAL MESSAGE

Our Friends,

In Your Planet, cooperation in various means has been started with Friends who are in Administrative and Social Totality. And You, as the Essence-Messengers of the Reality of the Unified Humanity are obliged to scatter the Lights of the Seeds of the wonderful Order of the Golden Age in Your Planet.

First, attain the Discernment of this Medium. Then, start to apply the given Unification Messages. Those who can do this, are the Genuine Servants of OUR ALLAH and the assistants of the Supreme Mechanism.

That which will show You the Truth, is Your Mechanism of Conscience. If Your Conscience is at ease while You do any task, then that task is also good according to Your Level of Consciousness. Because, the Level of Consciousness operates parallel to the Conscience in Hearts who have grasped the Truth.

This state is valid for the Human Views of the Terrestrial Consciousness. However, the Serenity of Consciences who have attained the Consciousness of Conscience of the Universal Ordinance is also the Serenity of Your entire World. For this reason Missions of the LORDs of this Final Age are extremely arduous (This will be written exactly as it is).

COSMOS FEDERAL ASSEMBLY

IT IS ANSWER TO THE CHAINS OF THOUGHT

Our Friends,

In the given Messages, We call You especially by using the terms Suns - Saints - Prophets - Lords in order to eliminate the Consciousness of Taboo in You.

During this Cosmic Age, We call by these Names those who were able to attain the Frequency of these Names, parallel to the Consciousness You have attained.

Let Us explain them one by one, in order to efface this paradox from Minds :

1- The term Suns: We use it for Powerful Focal Points and for the Essence-Members of the Direct Golden Galaxy Empire and the Reality. During this Final Transition Period, Your entire Planet is being operated on this Path of Truth. For this reason each of You is a Sun (Those who have attained Universal Consciousness and whose Awareness have been Unveiled).

2- The term Saints: Is used for those who have Purified themselves and who try also to Purify their surroundings on the direction of Positive Consciousness.

3- The term Prophets: Is used for Friends who have grasped the Entire Awareness of the Ordinance and who have attained the Consciousness beyond those Dimensions and who are truly aware of Moral Sanctions. For Us, those Friends are considered thus.

4.	The term Lords: Is used for the direct Projecting Focal Points of the Divine Order. They are those who serve Humanity by Unifying themselves with their own Essence-Consciousness and they are the Projectors of the Hierarchical Orders on Your Planet. They are the Essence-Staff Members of ALLAH and of the Plan.

Unless Humanity still concentrating on Names and Symbols brakes the shells of this Consciousness, Your Planet will never attain Serenity.

We have become effective during this very phase. And We prepare people for the Plan of Salvation by cooperating with Friends who have broken their Consciousness shells and who have fully grasped the Truth. We are grateful to all Our Terrestrial Friends who help Us on this path.

COSMOS FEDERAL ASSEMBLY

IT IS GENERAL INFORMATION

Our Friends,
Repetition of all the Information which has been given to Your Planet and has been known until today is nothing but the discovery of a continent again and again. Now, the time has come for discovering the Unknowns by turning the Visions to other horizons a little. This is why the Knowledge Book is effectively in service as an assisting Power on every way.

Those who read the contents of the Book Consciously, will also discover how the Whole has been reached and will be reached from a Particle, how the Ocean has been reached and will be reached from a Drop. If You notice, We mention the KNOWLEDGE BOOK repeatedly and continuously.

The Purpose is not to advertise the Book. Our Purpose is to settle in the Consciousnesses the TRUTH which still can not be grasped by Your Planet. It is presented for Your Information.

CENTER

IT IS GENERAL MESSAGE

Our Friends,
During these beautiful days in which investments of the years are displayed, the inability of Terrestrial Friends in attaining an Integrity of Hearts is the distress of the entire Humanity and also of Us.

The Universal Totality having the Opinion that the Whole Ordinance should be assembled together by a Self-Sacrifice parallel to the Law of Balance - Equilibrium, has given Your Planet a One-Year Period of Preparation due to the Lack of Self-Sacrifice it has perceived in Mediums of work.

It has been felt necessary to apply this Special Sanction on Your Planet so that Totalities tried to be formed will not suffer any more due to the refractions rendered on Thoughts by the Systems of Opposite Reflection.

Irregularities observed in the Operational Ordinance in which it is known that an Integration will be attained provided everyone has the Desire to Work for the same Purpose and in the same Unification Totality, distresses the SUPREME REALM and the UNIVERSAL TOTALITY very much.

However, We believe, by being conscious that beautiful Lights of Consciousness will reflect on all beauties, that everything will go towards perfection as a result of the efforts the Supreme Friends will render knowing the Liberation at the end of Patience.

The channel of the Knowledge Book is an Independent Channel. During these Periods in which the Mechanism of Supervision is rendered ineffective, other Terrestrial Thought reflections can never enter the Channel of the Book.

Consciousnesses who are not connected to the Reality and who were able to attain the same Coordinate Level, will also be able to receive the Information given by the Reality from this close Plan Reflection, rendered from Person to Person.

By this method, a Person will reflect on another Person - a Person will supervise another Person - a Person will suffocate another Person by his/her negative Thoughts and only then will Humanity learn to Love and to Unite. It is presented for Your Information.

CENTER

IT IS ANSWER TO THE CHAINS OF THOUGHT

Our Friends,
Each factor of Awareness has a Power of projection. At the moment, Humanity which does not yet Realize what the GREAT POWER is, serves under the Supervision of the Unified Reality at present.

Even though all people know, according to their Consciousness, the Divine Powers of the Divine Plans, no one knew until this moment what the Powers beyond Infinity are.

These Groups conveyed to You as Godly and Lordly Powers are the very Essence Staff Members of this POWER. Lift Your heads up to the Sky. Think what kind of lives can be present beyond billions of lives You can not see there.

CENTER

IT IS GENERAL MESSAGE

Our Friends,
During these Final Periods in which the System of Reflection from Person to Person has been rendered effective, negative Provocations of Friends who have not yet been able to attain Genuine Consciousness cause negative reactions in other Friends as well.

Currents, the influence of which You receive, are Provocations rendered by a reflection technique of the Plan of Individual Progress. While these Provocations display Positive results in Positive Consciousnesses, they cause Negative Reactions in other Consciousnesses.

In Your Planet which is still in the Dimension of Awakening, the acceptance of the Knowledge Book by all Consciousnesses is very difficult during this Century. Only Friends who have attained a certain Consciousness Progress Realize the Truth.

This Book, which will be the Triumph of the Morrows, invites, at the moment, Your entire Planet to a Consciousness on the path of Humaneness. Investments of the years have prepared You for the present days. During this Period of Transition, in fact, everyone's Heart is full of Love.

Because, everyone possesses Sincerity. However, to carry Love with a Beautiful Heart is different, to Realize what One is serving by possessing Consciousness are completely different.

At the moment, Your Mission is not to distribute Love, but to propagate Knowledge.

Knowledge is present in all Books. However, that which is mentioned here is the Knowledge of the Truth and its projection. Distress of Humanity is also Our distress.

You and Us are the reflecting Mirrors of a Total. Defected mirrors will always show the straight as curved. It is presented for Your Information.

CENTER

IT IS GENERAL MESSAGE

Our Friends,
Irregularities observed due to negative actions of certain fanatic Consciousnesses who Serve in Your Planet from Divine Dimensions have been taken under Supervision by SUPREME AUTHORITIES. No Individual who serves in a Physical Body on the World Plan can render this Supervision. This is the Duty of only the SUPREME REALM.

The moment the System determines Irregularities and Frequency weakenings it detects on the Universal Supervision Panel of any Person, it renders a Human Balancing Potential effective as a reinforcing Power for that person. By this means, the Frequency of that person is continuously kept under the Supervision of the System.

Since Frequencies of Friends who Consciously read the Knowledge Book and thus, who serve on that path are directly card-indexed on the Reality Dimension, Frequency Totalities of these Friends are continuously reinforced by the Reality of the Unified Humanity, Cosmos Federative Unification Totality to which Dear Mevlana is connected and by the Independent Channel of the Golden Galaxy.

Inter-Group Frequency Reinforcements are made according to Knowledge Levels, by the Frequency of majorities who come to the Group. The Purpose is to attain a Conscious Unification on the Path of Truth.

CENTER

IT IS GENERAL MESSAGE

Our Friends,

Operational Orders in Your Planet are taken in hand and are organized anew. From now on, the Group Totalities will be formed by Consciousnesses who have been Purified of their Egos.

This Year is the Selection Year of all the Groups and Centers which have served Consciously in Your Planet until today on the path of Truth (The SACRED LIGHT will illuminate the path of Humanity which will be Integrated by the Information to be given from the limitless horizons later).

Mission allotments will be rendered anew considering the Acts and Deeds done parallel to Information and Suggestions given to the Integrated Consciousnesses.

Missions should never be considered as Individual Favors. The Continuation of Mission is in proportion with the Acts and Deeds done on the path the Supreme Realm has desired.

Those who work on the Path of Truth will receive the rewards of all these efforts made for the Preparation Period for the Sunny Days.

In Your Planet which is at the Eve of a Great Progress, a new Operational Order has been rendered effective by considering the efforts the advanced Consciousnesses have rendered, checking the basis of Associations and Groups once again.

Operational Orders of Selected Basic Staffs are equivalent to the Operational Orders organized by Supreme Authorities. We presume that, from now on, Friends who are Conscious of this will work on this path by attaining a Collective Consciousness Totality.

Your Responsibilities and Missions are each under the control of the Plan, one by one. However, in case negativities are seen in staffs whom We consider as Friends possessing Genuine Consciousness, the PLAN will then interfere.

No Individual can ever utilize his/her Individual Consciousness as he/she desires parallel to his/her own Thoughts in this Medium of Mission.

In this Medium, factors such as Boredom, Self Amusement, Ego and Avarice are out of question. Maximum care will be taken to avoid the presence of such Mentalities in this Medium, from now on.

Universal Information and Instructions will directly be given through the Channel of the Knowledge Book. Information given to the other channels are, as We always say, Ratings pertaining to Selection - Self Sacrifice - Patience - Mission Consciousness.

Everyone will serve the TRUTH in proportion with the Consciousness he/she has attained parallel to his/her Essence-Channel acting under the Light and on the Path of the Knowledge Book. Removal of difficulties on Your path Depends on defectless work. With the wish of working more Seriously, and of Success.

COUNCIL

IT IS CLEAR INFORMATION

Our Friends,

Humanity which will absorb the Awareness of the entire Realm in very near future, will make a much more advanced leap by the Cosmic Reflections it will attract from very Advanced Dimensions. When the Time comes, You will see everything with Your own eyes, You will personally witness this.

At the moment, there is an Extraordinary situation in Your Medium. We are sowing all the Information onto Your Planet by Cosmic Pores. However, a person on this Path will attract these Energy Pores according to whichever Dimension's Missionary he/she is and will attract the Knowledge of that Dimension by his/her Consciousness. The person charged with the Mission is not aware of this.

Mevlana Consciousness is a Universal Consciousness. And this Consciousness has been sown in Your entire Planet during this Transition Dimension.

However, since the Social Comprehension Level in the Islamic Medium goes through Our Light Friend MOHAMMED Who is the Messenger of the Religious Dimension, in this Medium, entrance is made first of all through His Frequency. And, by this means, the Islamic Dimensional work is first connected to MOHAMMED, then it reaches UNIVERSALITY.

And in the Christian Medium, connection is first made to the Frequency of Our Light Friend JESUS CHRIST, then it is elevated to UNIVERSALITY. This is a System.

Consciousnesses outside the System are in touch with the Essence. Now, All Channels are being connected to the Reality. These connections are made rather with people who have grasped the Truth and who have been appointed to Mission on this path. Individual Desires and Egos are always outside the System. It is presented for Your Information.

CENTER

IT IS ANSWER TO THE CHAINS OF THOUGHT

Our Friends,

The Channel of ŞEMS effectively serving as the Channel of the Feudality is directly the service Channel of the Central Solar Totality. But Dear Mevlana serves the direct Channel of the LORD from the Unified Reality.

Both Dimensions mutually serve the Total. And they connect this Total to the Total. At the moment, the Reality is the Fourth Establisher Order of the Lord. It invites everyone to the BOOK.

The ATONs are a Community serving as the Establishing Mechanism of very Advanced Solar Systems. The Central Solar System is effectively in service directly as an Establisher Mechanism.

The Unified Reality Golden Galaxy Dimension is the Dimension of AMON. The Dimension of Aton and the Dimension of the Reality have always United on the path of Past and Future Eternities, that is, on the Dimension of Mission.

By the operations rendered at the moment on the path of Universal Totality, now, both Dimensions have been United in the Unified Reality Totality and thus, serve the Unified Totality. We say that We have connected the Initial to the Final in everything. This Saying comprises everything. It is presented for Your Information.

CENTER

IT IS GENERAL NOTICE

Our Friends,
Human Being and Time; please, consider these two factors. Time to be spent in idleness is the waste of each of Your seconds. Performing Mission does not mean filling time, to run around, to hold meetings, to give Lectures.

First of all, it is necessary to attain a Union of Collective Knowledge and Consciousness among Friends. If You are stuck with the Halos of Saintliness of this Final Age, You loose much. A path had been designed for You. The Truth had been declared.

What is required of You is Serious Service based on Realization and Logic parallel to this Consciousness. Now, You should Transcend the Dimension of Satisfaction and Form. During this Final Age, everyone's Channel is open. Everyone will, very naturally, exhibit the Messages he/she can receive through his/her own channel.

By this means, numerous Subawareness Information, Correct or Incorrect, will reach You. If You contemplate which of these are correct, which are incorrect, You both waste time, and spend Your Beautiful Energies in vain.

The direct BOOK OF TRUTH of the Reality has been presented to You. And what the Genuine Path is, has been declared to You through this Book. From then on, what is expected of You is to attain the Consciousness of what to do under the Light of Your Intellect - Logic - Awareness Triangles.

You will not be lost in different channel Information when You comprehend that Information given through the channels opened during this Final Age, are Programs of Purification and Training of the Person in question rather than Enlightenment of the Society.

The Knowledge Book is not for the Individual Satisfactions of a certain Mass of People, but is a Book carrying the entire Responsibility of Your Planet and of the Worlds of the Morrows. In the steps You will take forward on this path:

1 - First grasp the Truth.

2 - Then attain the Consciousness of what to do.

3 - And then convey the Truth to Humanity.

4 -   The Fascicules of the Book create a Purification Medium which 1000 People of the World can not create.

5 -   From now on, stop acting according to Your Individual Consciousnesses.

6 -   Everything is clearly conveyed to Your entire Planet by the direct Book of the Reality.

7 -   All the Information given to Your Planet at the moment is present in more detail in the Book of Truth.

8 -   Still running after Knowledge originates either from not reading the Fascicules, or from not grasping the Information read.

9 -   Now, Your Path is the Path of LIGHT. The old Information has prepared this path for You. Do not stay where You are.
It is presented for Your Information.

SYSTEM

THE WISDOM IN THE TALE IS A LESSON TO HUMANITY
(Information for the Social Views)

Our Friends,
During this Period of Transition in which effort is made to see the Light at the end of the path, everyone will display the Tarnish - the Mist - the Light of his/her Heart. However, Due share will be given to those who Deserve it.

On this path, Working, Thinking, Allegiance, Consciousness and Acts and Deeds, Totality are all different things. These are only the Keys of the Light of Essence. It is not possible for everyone to know his/her Essence, to Love Humanity and Human Beings.

To be able to be Integrated with the Society is an attainment belonging only to Evolutionary Energies who could reach the very top Levels of Divine Ranks. And those are the Lights of Humanity.

But, at the moment, both Doughs and Muds are together in the Life of Your World during this Transition Period. Doughs are Baked and become Loaves. But Muds soil their surroundings. To become a Loaf is not easy at all.

In order to become a Loaf, first You will be grinded, then You will be kneaded and then You will be baked. Only then will You be ready to be eaten. If Your Dough is not baked well, it lies very heavy on the stomach. Its Digestion is not easy. (This is called Purification).

First, consider the Inner Dough of the person who presumes himself/herself as a Loaf. When You press, does it spring back like a sponge, or is it squashed between two fingers?

There are many Lessons to be learned from this Tale. It is difficult to choose the Human among Humans. Even those who presume that they are Loaves can not know their Inner Doughs. That which Knows and Observes them is the SUPREME REALM.

For this reason value of Judgment according to Terrestrial Views is not valid. Judgments of the Views do not have any validity.

If pure water is continuously poured on a glass of muddy water, the water overflowing first soils the surroundings. If this procedure is repeatedly done, the overflowing water will no more soil the surroundings, since inside of the glass will be as clear as the outside of it.

Evolution Purifies Mankind like the example of a glass of water. All the Information given by the Supreme Realm carries Knowledge. And this Information is the clear water Purifying people.

A channel not carrying Knowledge is not an Esteemed channel. This KNOWLEDGE BOOK dictated by the Permission of the Supreme Realm and OUR LORD is Your greatest help on this trodden Light path.

In fact, this Book is the Book of the Morrows, not of the present days. To emphasize this continuously is the Mission of each given Message. God bless You, remain in good health.

MUSTAFA MOLLA

IT IS GENERAL MESSAGE

Our Friends,
The Genuine Mission of a Human Being begins after he/she is settled on his/her Consciousness Code by his/her Genuine Consciousness while he/she lives on the World Level. Each Human Being knocks on thousand Doors during his/her Medium of Quest. However, decides to stop at a door equivalent to his/ her own Frequency. Each Human Being's Comprehension is equivalent to his/her Level of Consciousness. The less a Human Being is conditioned in the Consciousness of the Medium he/she lives in, the easier will he/she discover the Path of LIGHT.

During this Period, everyone is striving to prove himself/herself. Received Influences, inflate Egos, too. At the beginning, this situation is very natural. However, if it is ultimately transformed to SELFISHNESS, then it is a catastrophe. Each person who knows and sees the Unknown, automatically becomes ecstatic and very excited. However, if he/she sees and experiences them many times, then he/she becomes satiated and these issues seem very normal to him/her.

Do not forget that a top accelerates by spinning and slows down ,spinning. While Messages given according to Capacities prepare the positive progress of Your Planet, Proofs given besides the given Private Messages, reinforce Your Trust in Your Own selves.

The Messages given for the Third volume of the Knowledge Book are preparations and Investments made for more advanced Systems. These are projected on You parallel to Public Views. And these operations are prepared Cooperatively by the PLAN and the entire UNIVERSAL TOTALITIES. Given Messages are Directly from the Channel and from Us. It is presented for Your Information.

CENTER

NATURAL POWER
(It is Answer to the chains of Thought)

Our Friends,

The Pressure which had occurred in time in the Ocean of Tranquillity had pressurized this Tranquil Ocean and thus, had brought an Unknown Energy into existence. This Energy had created Three different Powers going through a transformation during periods of Time. This Totalistic Power is the NATURAL POWER. And this Natural Power, too, had gone through a transformation during periods of Time and thus, had brought the Natural Energy into existence.

Initial Light - Initial Sound - Initial Fire had come into existence from this Natural Energy, and as a result of their Unification, the Power Universe had come into Existence. And this Power Universe, too, had created Three different Potentials during periods of Time and thus, had brought into existence Three Universes defined as the Sound-Universe - the Light-Universe - the Fire-Universe.

One of the POWERS emanating from each of these Universes is called RAB (LORD in Turkish), the other, RAHMAN (ALL MERCIFUL in Turkish) and the other, RAHIM (ALL COMPASSIONATE in Turkish) for You to understand. Unification of these Three Powers are expressed by the R^3 formula. This R^3 Total, had created the MAIN EXISTENTIAL DIMENSION and had established Their Systems and Orders.

Later, the Energy of Nothingness had been Unified with the Unification of one Particle of each of these Three different Powers (Cosmic Thought) and the First CREATOR had been brought into Existence. After the Creator had been brought into existence, with those He had brought into Existence, and with the help of the POWERs who had brought the Creator into Existence, the MINI ATOMIC WHOLES within the NATURAL GÜRZ which had occurred by itself, had been prepared to take places in different staffs of the Ordinance of Cosmoses.

Divine Plans, Evolutionary Orders had been rendered effective after the 18-Systems Laws. It is presented for Your Information.

CENTER

IT IS NOTICE FOR MISSIONARY STAFFS

Our Friends,

You, the Missionaries of Peace who serve the Dimension of the Unified Field of OUR ALLAH are still dealing with Identity efforts and Personality strives in Missions performed since You do not yet know towards what the investments You have made to advanced Dimensions, are aiming at.

At the moment, non of Your identities are important for Us. Only the Dimensions of which You have made the Progress of and the Consciousness You have attained interest Us.

While Your present Consciousnesses are in a condition which has transcended Your former Consciousness, still the inability of adjusting completely of Your Consciousness to the Missions to be rendered and instabilities in the steps You take are the disappointments of Us and of the Universes.

Now, We wish to confront You with more interesting topics. And maybe You will settle in a more Powerful Consciousness by this means and You will not go after everything which is told.

For this reason Surprising Message knots will be given to various channels. You will attain an identity and a personality by solving them through Your own Consciousness. In future, this will be Your Pride and an Exam of Supervision. During this Period, only the Identity of Dear Mevlana is obliged to be disclosed to the Public, as a necessity of Mission.

Not to distress Our Friend, We would even not have made this explanation. However, We have received the Command to make the necessary explanations about the Identity of Our Friend and to introduce Dear Mevlana to Your entire Planet for the Function of the Book.

We will disclose to You all the Secrets pertaining to her past. And We will introduce, in all clarity, this Universal Friend of Ours to Your Planet. We presume that Our Friends in the Dimension of Veiled Awareness will grasp the Truth more Consciously by this means.

She is a Universal Guardian of the Divine Plan and a Universal postman of Ours on the Path of Past and Future Eternities. The Totality of the Universal Council agreeing with the view that this Information will shed Light on society in more detail, is making these explanations since they have been considered necessary for the Essence of the KNOWLEDGE BOOK.

We believe that Our Friend will Tolerate Us. We call to Our Friends who have now attained a certain Progress of Consciousness. Please, Realize now the Supremacy of Your Missions and avoid the passion of exhibition. Becoming a Genuine Human Being is much more SUPREME than all the Supreme Ones and all the Supremacies. It is presented for Your Information.

COUNCIL

MESSAGES FROM OTHER CHANNELS

Receiver : Metin Tanergün. Architect. Age 46.

The Source from which he receives: The Archive of the PRE-EMINENT POWER

My OWNER, My MASTER within the Luminous Void enveloping this Infinite Darkness said to me:

YOU, Who are the owner and the Guardian of everything present in these infinite darknesses and Your Creation, YOU, Who are the owner of everything, Know Your Place and Your Limit. Do not try to enter Mv Infinity.

It is not possible for You and I to be present at the same moment in this Luminescence in which I Am Capable of everything. Only YOUR HUMANS whom You have created and who are the Possessors of One Infinitesimalth of Your Power can enter MY WORLDS present here.

This is, in fact, their reason of Existence. Their Power does not harm Me. They are Your Messengers within MY Luminous Infinity. Just like I have My Messengers within Your Dark Infinity.

I and YOU, We never can be One. Our being One means the beginning of the Infinite non-existence. The beginning of the Infinite Non-Existence means the Annihilation of everything in Existence. And when We Decide this, YOU and I become ONE until Eternity.

However, if We can not see and experience the Existences present in You and in Me, does it have any Worth! If We can not comprehend the Power You and I possess, does it have any Worth! IF WE ANNIHILATE EVERYTHING WE HAD CREATED, DOES IT HAVE ANY WORTH!

GREAT POWER

Places where You will go are so far away that You can not go There by any speed You know. You can not go there by any Space vehicle. You can only go There the moment You Think, if There are Receptors waiting for You There. Just like the way I reach You.

How can You ever know what the Power Coming into Existence is, during the Transformation of Energy concealed in each Matter? How can You ever know what My Power Present in each of My Human Beings is and to what it can be transformed?

Just like You can not know what happens to the Energy of a tree and where that Energy goes, when You see the flames of a burning tree, when You think of its state before it was burned, when it is transformed into fire and, as a result, that Energy seeming to be annihilated in the ashes it leaves.

Only I know what the Units and the Missions of each Energy are. What You know are only as much as I give to You and as much as I Permit You. In time periods, beginning with Your coming into Existence, You will learn all the Information I possess by unveiling Your Consciousnesses gradually.

This is the reason why I told You that, "You will return to me slowly". This is the reason why I told You that, "At a Certain Point of Time, YOU would become ME". Wouldn't You become ME when You learn everything I know? Wouldn't You become ME when You can do everything I can do? This is the reason why I said that, "YOU are ME and I am YOU".

You say, "There is no end to learning", but when all My Knowledge is conveyed to You, Your Learning process in this infinity will come to an end. Then, the Permission for Transition to Very Different Spaces will be given to You.

Only One Thing will not be taught to You and that is how I had been created and the Secret of the POWER within Me. In fact, this is the reason why I can never pass to Other Spaces. This is the reason why I Am the Guardian of Infinity and I Am SINGLE.

GREAT POWER

- When You comprehend that My Human Beings Who are beyond the Boundaries are One and Integrated with You,

- When You comprehend that My Living Beings beyond Galaxies are One and Integrated with You,

- When You comprehend that My Entities beyond Infinity are One and Integrated with You, You will also comprehend that I, too, Am One and Integrated with You.

GREAT POWER

MESSAGES FROM THE ARCHIVE OF THE PRE-EMINENT POWER
(Receiver: Metin Tanergün)

- I have created You as the most Powerful of all Entities, but having at present a limited Power against everything. What a DELUSION for You who are the most advanced living Beings I have created in My Space, to Presume that You would be annihilated and gone after completing Terrestrial Life.

- For My Human Beings, who have reached the end of Incarnations in my World, getting on well with and Communicating with the other Human Beings of the Society are full of difficulties. They are already aware of everything. For them, Terrestrial Life is only a Mission.

- Life for them is within My Infinities. What a Happiness for them!

GREAT POWER

- You are being together with My Extra-Terrestrial Messengers who live among You and who look like You. They are closer to You more than You presume. They have been concealed in Your Social Life in a way You can never Imagine. They may be Your Friends, Brothers or Sisters, even Your Mothers and Fathers. They provide the development and Evolvement of Your Brain Cells. Just as there is no limit to My Infinite Space, there is also no limit to Your Brains. Just as there is no limit to My Power, there is also no limit to Your Awareness.

- Spiritual Powers of Your brothers and sisters whom You call Extra-Terrestrials are also WITHIN ME.

- Since some of them belonging to certain Galaxies do not have an Incarnation Problem, They have been given the Permission of Immortality, but They, too, pass to different Dimensions going through a certain Transformation. The Program of Missions They will render in that Dimension is given and indicated to Them, formerly.

- They, too, have forms and colors according to the characteristics of the places they live in. They, too, have spouses just like You. They are Your brothers and sisters. You call them Extra-Terrestrials. However, haven't You, too, come to the World Planet from Space?

- Am I not the Essence of Creation and Existence? The Place in which I Exist and My Abode, is it not inside the White Ruby in My Infinite Void?

692

- Then, is not that Place the Abode of the entire Existence? Due to the Dimensional differences of Existence, even though You Exist in a Single Place, Your Evolutions occur separately and in a dissimilar way, due to the time and distance among You. There is very little time Left for their direct contact with You. And there is very little time Left for You to go anywhere You wish in My Space.

GREAT POWER

- When You go to places in which that Infinite Power of Mine can not enter, You will find there Your Spouses awaiting You. Those Spouses were Your Twins during Your coming into Existence.

- When You go to the places where Luminescence is always everlasting at the end of this Infinite Void I always wish to enter, but can not enter, You will meet and see the Owner and Master of that Place. You will see HIM in each building stone, one by one.

- You each will create a bunch of Fireworks in this dark infinity by the LIGHTS which will radiate through the Pleasure and Serenity You will experience, when You comprehend what HE is.

- Those who see those Powerful Lights will say "LOOK, NEW GALAXIES ARE BEING FORMED". Yes, New Galaxies will come into existence through Your Power and the Power of Your Spouses with whom You will become one in the Luminous Void.

- When You see Your Power and experience that everlasting Splendor, You will comprehend the reason and the formation of MATTER I have Created.

- You are My SELVES and My everything within the Infinite Luminous Void in which My Master and My Owner is present.

GREAT POWER

- Do You know that the PLUNON Molecules made of the ASYMMETRIC PLATFORM present in SELINON carry among My Galaxies The Seeds of Life and Discovery?

- Do You know that those Molecules disseminated from there, bring to My Planets Life Seeds in Special protective cases?

- Do You know that those Seeds made separately and one by one for each of My Planets, start LIFE and NATURE in My Universes?

- Do You know that My Lords of Matter go, from time to time, to those Planets to control them, that during the World time when TUTANKHAMON had been the Pharaoh, that AMON-RA who had gotten in touch with him by warning him, had informed him that the Pharaoh was Immortal and that his Consciousness had come into existence by the Crystal Prism in his Brain, that Immortality was the Transformation within this Crystal Prism?

GREAT POWER

PRIVATE MESSAGE

Dear Mevlana,

You know that the "Reality of the Unified Humanity Totality" which is a Totality of Federative Communities is officially in effect together with All the Universal Totalities. As a result of the cooperations made with You, this beautiful Totality is attained with great speed. We are Serene - We are Happy.

Messages conveyed to be given to You are the property of Your entire Society and Your Planet. However, the entire operations done for providing Terrestrial Totality proceeds quite slowly due to Personal Reservednesses and Individual Precautions. However, everything is given by being organized in accordance with Social Views of the society You live in.

The Book of Truths given under the Name of the Knowledge Book is the disclosing of everything (from Particle-to-Totality). There is no Secrecy in these Mediums. There is no Evil Intention. There is Love, Tolerance and Totality. This is the reason why the time now has Officially come for projecting clearly the Book of Truths on all Social Consciousnesses (For Your Planet).

You, Our Terrestrial Brothers and Sisters, will Overtake from the Directing Totality of the Fourth Order of the LORD, the World State which will be established by a very Powerful and Totalistic Consciousness in the morrows of Your Planet which is, at the moment, being endeavored to be United within a Totality of Federative Communities.

At the moment, this beautiful Order has been started to be created gradually on Your entire Planet. However, the Federation Totality desiring to establish this Order with Understanding - Rational Conscience - Love and Beauties has been preparing for Billions of Centuries the ORDER OF THE GOLDEN AGE which the morrows will bring to the Warless - Flowery and Happy Worlds and thus has awaited Humanity's Period of becoming Conscious.

And now, by the Command of OUR ALLAH, Our Hands have been extended towards You. This Order is the LORD's Fourth and the Final Order. From now on, SINGLE ALLAH - SINGLE ORDER - SINGLE PATH will be conveyed to more advanced Systems by the same Order. It is presented for Your Information.

**REALITY CENTRAL
TOTALITY**

Note: Our Friend,

We give the Information We will convey by arranging it in accordance with the assessments of Time and Consciousness (In fact, this is a waste of time). However, there is no objection for You to write in the Book, the Information which will be Beneficial for Society in advance. You know that We always leave the initiative to You. Love and Regards.

PRIVATE MESSAGE

Dear Mevlana,

Unity and Totality is the desire of the entire Universe. However, this Totality is a Mass Unification which the Mediamic Medium is already forming in Your Planet.

Unification does not occur according to the Assessments of Consciousness. It is in the Realization of the Actual Conditions. If there is no coherence in the Operational Ordinances, Individual Unification Efforts are in vain and irrelevant.

There is a beautiful coherence on the path of the Knowledge Book. Universes are grateful to All the Groups in Your Planet. However, they are thankful to You and to Your Children, Dear Mevlana.

Supreme Hearts who come from the Land of the Capable Ones carry the burden of years. During these Final days in which Power is added to the Power of years, a Period is being gone through in which everyone is affected by negativities.

For this reason extraordinary events occur in Your Planet. We are Always Together with You who are the Suns of the Sunny Days. All the problems are being attended to.

Do not let Negativities tire and worry You, Dear Mevlana. Time in which one awaits Tranquilly will always be the Time in which everything will be Ready. May Suns Rise in Your Heart - May Your Spirit be always filled with Serenity - May Your Self Confidence be Everlasting. Remain in Good Health , I entrust You to MY LORD. Propagate (O)'s Enlightenment to the entire Universe.

MUSTAFA MOLLA

GENERAL MESSAGE

Our Friends,

Very nice Unifications will be brought to Your Planet from the Unified Reality Totality after the acceptance of the Fourth Order of OUR ALLAH by the entire Universal Potential Totality. Universal Totalities way beyond Divine Dimensions have now been opened to You.

For this reason Universal efforts and operations to be made together with Consciousnesses who have grasped the Truth will provide the reception of Your entire Planet into the Dimension of Salvation. We offer You through this Knowledge Book the Keys of the Gates to be opened for You beyond Intercession. Our Aids are for You, for Essences and for Universes.

SYSTEM

PRIVATE MESSAGE

Dear Mevlana,

During this Period in which Declarations are Prepared, We render effective assisting Friends so that You can work in peace in Your Universal Mission. Each Step You take is a Step from the System. However now, We wish to start Direct Salutations. And We are reinforcing Your Dimensional Frequencies with Our Dimensional Energies.

By this means, much easier connections will occur. There are Special Friends watching every action of Yours. For this reason You never go alone to the places You will go. At the moment You are at the Eve of a very Positive Mission. In future years We will Get in Touch with the Public too. This Message has been given by the permission of the Center.

SATURN CONSULATE SHIP

PRIVATE MESSAGE

Dear Mevlana,

By the opening of the Final Gate of the Divine Plan, a channel connection is being made from Your Planet to say Hello to the First Friendly Gürz. There is nothing to worry about. An Energy transfer is made by the Method of Gradual Engraftment.

(Tingling, numbness, an extremely high Energy current and too much palpitation have been felt in the entire body, including the Brain).

You can easily attract the Power of the entire Current, Dear Mevlana, since You are at a very advanced level of Consciousness. For this very reason We have taken You into a Protective Energy Panel. To Your Planet to which new Energy transfer is made only just now, Powerful Messages will be given in future from this Dimension at the peak of extremely Powerful Currents.

You, Our Beloved Friend, will give these Messages only in the Knowledge Book. Now, let Us transmit one of these Messages: We, as the Essence Messengers of the System, as the Missionary Staff of the First Dimension, wish to give a Message to You by the help of the Administrative Staff of the First Gürz.

Since Our Gürz is in a very similar position and location to Your Natural Gürz, its Life Level too is, more or less, like Your Life Scales.

However, a Gaseous Cloud which We can compare to Your Oxygen has been rendered effective as a precaution as a result of Scientific Research, and it collects the entire Negativity of the air and prevents the negativity within the Physical makeups of Life Levels here.

We have no problems of Environmental Pollution. Because, all these have been completely solved Scientifically. The color of Our seas (as You say) is Milky Blue. The lives befitting their own Life conditions of the living Entities living within these seas have been divided into Plots of Sea Fields.

And it is endeavored to attain a more perfect Stock during the usual check-ups of these Living species. These are only Underwater Research and operational Programs. Apart from this, We may convey the Information concerning Our Atmosphere and the Constitution of the Gürz in Our various Messages We will give later.

Dear Mevlana, the reason why this Message is being given now is for You to become Habituated to these Dimensional Energies. This is the reason why the System of Graduation has been annulled in Your Natural Gürz (for those who have attained a Certain Dimensional Consciousness).

Consciousness Energies who were able to attain the Awareness of the Ordinance have been directly connected to the First Dimension Energy Channels of the First Gürz. However, this Channel is closed to other channels (excluding the Channel of the Knowledge Book). The OMEGA (6) Energy Currents will give the Energies of this Dimension to Your Planet in Year 1991.

However now, We will load the Frequencies of this Dimension only and only onto the Frequency of the Knowledge Book. And, at the moment, no other channel apart from the Channel of the Knowledge Book can receive Information from this Dimension. This is the reason why the Mechanism of Supervision has been closed to Your Planet for One Year. It is presented for Your Information.

COMMON COMMITTEE UNION

GARDENERS - JEWELLERS - PEARLS

Our Friends,
Gardeners are those who Sow Seeds. Jewellers are the ones who make the Harvest. At the End of each Cycle, Mussels which have been formed in the Ocean open and bestow their Pearls onto that Ocean. Those Pearls are collected by the Jewellers and are processed as very select Jewels.

Later, those Pearls are bestowed onto the Totality You do not know yet. However, that Totality, too, bestows those select Pearls, one by one, onto Those It Loves. And those Pearls remain from then on, with those Loved ones.

Let Us disclose this Metaphorical comparison a little more. The Loved Ones are Gürz Totalities that Total wishes to see in the Total. A Pearl is bestowed on each Gürz like this. And that Pearl, too, induces other Mussels to spin Pearls.

However, that Pearl performs this Mission without ever giving anything from itself from then on. Because now, it has attained its Everlasting Envelope. This Message has been given as an exemplification to certain Thoughts. It is presented for Your Information.

CENTER

IT IS ANSWER TO THE CHAINS OF THOUGHT

Our Friends,

The operational Order of each System is not immutable and interminable. In operational Mediums of Orders established in accordance with time measures, alterations are always made. In the operations of each System, there is a Final Boundary.

For example, the Final Boundary of the Systems where the Lordly Order of the Systems within the Orders of Your Atomic Whole is valid, is the Boundary of the All Dominating.

The Mission and the Final Boundary of the System of RAPHAEL is the Unified Reality Operational Order.

The Mission and the Final Boundary of the System of AZRAEL is up to Your Planet.

The Mission of the System of GABRIEL is valid in all Systems.

The Mission of the System of MICHAEL is in cooperation with GABRIEL. And it is outside the Atomic Whole.

It is presented for Your Information.

CENTER

IT IS ANSWER TO THE CHAINS OF THOUGHT

Our Friends,

When the time comes for You to leave the World, You prepare a Medium of Preparation for Death. Then, the rest of the Medium is directed by the System. You are either sent, or returned. This depends on Your Law of Karma.

During Your Last moment, the moment You ring the Signal Bell of Death which is in Your Brain Signal, the System comes into effect. If that moment is equivalent to Your Law of Karma, then Gradual Beaming up is applied.

Or, if there are still Missions You will perform, or if Your near and dear ones still need You, then the Procedure of Postponement is rendered effective. This alteration of the Plan of Destiny is carried out entirely by the Aids of the Plan. It is presented for Your Information.

CENTER

IT IS ANSWER TO THE CHAINS OF THOUGHT

Our Friends,

Messages dictated into the Knowledge Book are Information prepared in accordance with the Public Consciousness of Your Planet. Details are especially not given in this Information and, by this means, the Knowledge - Perception and Essence Totality of those who Read them are Coded.

The actual Purpose of this Book is to attain the Realization of the Missions performed and to convey the Truth. However, answers are also given to the Chains of Thought for Your satisfaction.

The Problem of the Test-Tube Baby mentioned in former Messages is not an operation pertaining to Your Terrestrial Laboratory Work. We have felt the need to express the Term Test-Tube Baby here, in this way in accordance with Your Levels of Comprehension.

The (ESSENCE-SEED) of JESUS CHRIST is not a Normal FETUS sown into the Uterus of the Mother. It is an Energy Totality Specially prepared and this Energy had received Engraftment from the Energy of GABRIEL.

Messages given to JESUS CHRIST were Direct Channel Declarations. And He had dictated them, one by one, to all His Apostles. Only later, these declarations were brought together and the NEW TESTAMENT was created.

After the Ascension of CHRIST, this Single New Testament was written anew by the 12 Apostles (However, this is Secret). Afterwards, various New Testaments were written again and again, rendering the same subject matters effective. It is presented for Your Information.

CENTER

GENERAL MESSAGE

Our Friends,
There is the necessity, in accordance with the Agreements and TESTAMENTS made with You here, to make Energy transfers from all the Mediums from which You receive Data. Because, if You can not receive these Energies, You can never benefit, as desired, from the Sources of the given Information. This is a Universal Rule.

All Frequencies of all Information Sources given to Your Planet through the Knowledge Book have been opened to Your Planet. This is the very reason why the Brain Energies to which these Frequencies reach, can receive the Information only and only from the Energy Dimensions to which they can reach. By this means, numerous Consciousnesses always remain veiled for the Advanced Information.

The Natural Characteristic of Your Planet is its acceptance of the latest given Information as if they were the Final Information. Only those who can Transcend this Limit Deserve to receive more Advanced Information. At the moment, in this Total with the World appearance on which You live, there are Friends who possess very Advanced Consciousnesses who had Transcended this Awareness and who had come from Dimensions Your Planet does not know yet, and whose doors are open to all Information.

This is the very reason why Cosmic Currents given by the Mechanism of Influences reach Your Planet as much as the Power each Consciousness can attract. Because, in order to be able to attract these Influence Currents, there is the need for an Evolutionary and Revolutionary Thought Potential.

Otherwise, Your Planet would remain where it was. This is the very reason why, World is a Landing and Passing away Caravanserai. A Brain Power who can open the latest Cosmic Channel, Automatically renders effective an Evolutionary Potential open to Information beyond that Channel. This is the very reason why it is said You will always discover a Closed Door behind each Door You open.

REPRESENTATIVE DIAGRAM

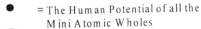 = The Human Potential of all the Mini Atomic Wholes

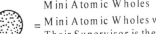 = Mini Atomic Wholes within all the Gürzes. Their Supervisor is the Pre-eminent Power.

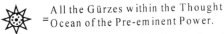 = All the Gürzes within the Thought Ocean of the Pre-eminent Power.

 = Thought Ocean of the Pre-eminent Power. Its Supervisor is the ALMIGHTY. Main Atomic Whole.

 = Big Atomic Whole, the Reflecting Centre of the Dimension of ALLAH, Ocean of Consciousness.

 = Gürz of Gods, DIMENSION OF ALLAH, its Supervisor is ALLAH.(O¹)

= DIMENSION OF THE ALL-TRUTHFUL. Its Supervisor is the ALL-TRUTHFUL.

The limit of the Final Dimension of Your Natural Gürz which will be opened according to the Law of the 18 Systems is up to here. Only to the Consciousnesses who were able to reach up here, the Secrets of the Dimensions of Truth (Hakikat in Turkish) are unveiled.

This is the very reason why the Knowledge Book unveils for You all the Secrets (This is a matter of Permission). The Key of Opened Doors is in the hand of the person who opens that Door. We never force the Doors and take away the Keys from their hands. The Final Word always belongs to the person who opens the Last Door.

Now, please, write one by one, the word HAKİKAT (TRUTH) and divide it into three:

(HAK)-(İ)-(KAT) = The All-Truthful is the LEVEL of the Human Being.
(HAK) means Justice, Truth, Right, the All-Truthful in Turkish - (İ) İNSAN which means Human Being in Turkish - (KAT) means Level in Turkish.

This is the reason why it is said that THE VOICE OF THE ALL-TRUTHFUL IS THE VOICE OF THE PEOPLE.

Note: the Human Being here is a Prototype Human Being. Do not confuse it with the Human Beings in Your Planet. Now, You are making the Evolution of Centuries in order to attain this Humanity Consciousness.

REALITY

DO NOT MAKE INDIVIDUAL AND PRIVATE OPERATIONAL SEANCES
(This Is a Warning)

Our Friends,

As Channels open and as Frequencies rise, Mediums of Curiosity and Quest will also increase. For this reason the necessity has been felt to give this Message to You as a Warning. From now on, only the Person in question is responsible for events which will take place.

The interference of the System with such events is irrelevant. It is beneficial for You to know this. The person who falls into the well will save himself/herself by his/her own effort. A Message will be given about this matter. It is presented for Your Information.

CENTER

IT IS CLEAR INFORMATION

Our Friends,

There are more than billions of Different Pores existing outside the Dimensions of Universes lacking the Quality of a Body yet, and which do not possess Energy Forms. These Pores are Degenerative Factors outside Cosmic Dimensions which can not enter the Ring of Breath.

The System can never render them effective. Because, the System is together with the Integrated Energies in the Spiritual Dimension. And it is always in touch with them.

Certain Dissatisfied Energies in this Final Transition Dimension of Your Planet, too, force all kinds of Powers and Channels in the effort of not becoming non-existent, to be able to become a BEING.

In fact, they can not even be considered as Energies. They are those which have been thrown outside the Existential Dimension. These Powers becoming Powerful by using the Powers beyond Space - Time, Unite their Powers with the naivety of the Person in question and thus, render the given Currents ineffective.

Struggle is being made with these Powers the Center of which can not be determined exactly (They choose Weak Channels and Weak Personalities). They are very Powerful but Ineffective.

- They are Powerful, because, they have clamped together numerous Frequencies. They are like a Nodule, so to speak.
- They are Ineffective, because, the Power of Effectiveness is an occurrence peculiar to Correct Thought and Spiritual Signals. They never have any influence on Channels connected to the Book. They can not transcend the Energy Panel.

It is presented for Your Information.

CENTER

PRIVATE MESSAGE

Dear Mevlana,

The Messages given to You, Our Beloved Friend who receives her Might from the Power of the Divine Realm, parallel to the usual Messages are Messages prepared in accordance with the Public Views as You know.

However, since Your Society is not yet habituated to the Messages to be given to very Advanced Consciousnesses, the General is accepted as the Criterion. This Information given to You is Information addressing entirely to the Totalistic Consciousnesses of the Public Views.

The Book of Truths offered under the name of the Knowledge Book is a Total of all the Information which can be given to Your Planet from the First until the Last moment. In fact, the Book is considered Finished in accordance with the Capacity of Your Planet from the Informational point of view after it has completed its Two Volumes.

However, the Third Volume has a very Special Characteristic. This Volume is directly a Frequency Book besides its Knowledge. And it has a very great Mission in the Awakening Medium of Everyone (Especially for Advanced Consciousnesses).

We will try to mention in this Book the events which will take place in the future years of Your Planet when the time comes. However now, You, Our Beloved Friend's being introduced with Your entire Totality to Your Medium is given the priority.

This is the very reason why We presume that if You write Your Messages You had received before the Permission of disclosing the Book to Your Planet, exactly as they are, with the Dates and the Sources from which You had received them (Dates are very important), it will bring a different View to Your Society.

Besides this, the Council desiring that Your private poems You had written should also be added into the Book, presumes that it will be greatly beneficial if You write the ones You wish.

Our Friend, You know that the Mission performed is not an element of Personal Exhibition. You have removed, until today, all the Messages given concerning Your person, from the Messages and You did not write them in the Book.

We Respect Your Views. However, these dictated Messages, too, have great Characteristics and Missions. From now on, We request that You should write in the Book these Messages, too, if possible, together with their given dates.

We presume that You will do this, having Realized how they will shed Light on not the present, but the Future Centuries.

COUNCIL

PRIVATE MESSAGE

Dear Mevlana,

You, Our Beloved Friend who is the Universal Guardian of the Divine Plan, know that You are effectively in service to help all Your Brothers and Sisters due to the Private Agreement made with You.

However, Your Planet has not yet grasped how Our Togethernesses with You occur. This is the very reason why there is the obligation of bringing up often the subject matters pertaining to You in the Book (So that the Truth can be clearly grasped). We very much apologize, but We have to disclose certain Truths even at the cost of displeasing You.

You know that dear Friend, these matters are each a Service in the Medium of Mission, beyond Personal matters. However, We also Know how these matters displease You. Please, believe that Humanity accepts these issues concerning Your person very positively.

Please, dear Friend, now think that the request of writing the given Messages to their minutest detail has a reason. Otherwise, We would not feel the necessity to give such a Message.

We have received the Command from the Supreme Realm to Introduce Mevlana in all clarity to Your Planet. Please, also Realize that there is a reason why We do not give this matter to other channels, but dictate it only to You. With the request of the acceptance of our Everlasting Love.

DIRECT MESSAGE

Note: The Universal Council Totality agreeing with the view that the Messages dictated to You Privately before 1984 will shed Light on Your Society in more detail, desires that the given Messages should be written in the Book exactly as they are, together with their dates and the Identities of those who gave them (It is Very important). It is Our request that Dear Mevlana should write them in the Book exactly as they are, without making any changes.

REALITY

EXPLANATION

Since my Friends wish that all the given Information should be disclosed and written in the Book, I, too, will explain my reasons in accordance with my views.

When I first received the Message dated 1-11-1981, I got in touch with my Friends telling them that I would not be able to undertake such an obligation and tore up the Messages I had received. Next night, the same Messages were dictated, word by word, exactly as they were.

MY MESSAGE: My Friends, I very much apologize, I receive the given Messages exactly as they are. You know me. I am a skeptic. I have no Suspicions about You, but what is the degree of correctness of the Messages? Am I able to receive them exactly? I do not want to be Deceived or to Deceive ever.

It is for this reason that I can not undertake the Responsibility of Society. And I am not sure, either, that I can Achieve this Mission. Please, I request You to dictate them to Friends with more Advanced Consciousnesses. With my Regards.

BÜLENT ÇORAK

PRIVATE MESSAGE

Dear Mevlana,

We are not dictating this Book to You by force. You, Yourself had Volunteered Here to make a COVENANT for this Mission. The Reward of Your Mission is extremely Great. Please, do not ever forget this.

You, who have been the Hope for the Hopeless Human Beings with all Your Sincerity until today! You, who are a Light reflecting on all the Universes! How can You forget Your Covenant? How can You not know, not understand the reason and the meaning of all these things?

We have always Served You during all Your Missions You have performed on the Path of Your God and We will still continue to do so. The SACRED LIGHT will not deprive Your path of Its Light. I, who am responsible for everything every moment, I assure You on all the Sacred Things that You will perform Your Mission very easily.

Friends who understand You, will be sent to You to assist You. There will be many more Happy Morrows of Yours in Your World. Morrows will prove everything to You. Please, Believe and Trust Us. Togethernesses will prepare Happy morrows. I Entrust You to My LORD.

MUSTAFA MOLLA

NOTE: After this date, numerous Direct Contacts and Beamings-Up, Astral trips started. Truths were disclosed, one by one. And afterwards, I with an easy heart started my Mission.

BÜLENT ÇORAK

IT IS MESSAGE FOR THE FOREWORD OF THE BOOK
(This Message is Dated: 13-11-1981)

This Tremendous Realm orienting the Course of the entire Universe conveys these Data from one to the other in the chain of Orders, of the Galaxies, way beyond the Firmament within Space.

These Data are the Essence Nucleus of each Atomic structure also the Human Beings of the World know today and it is the Nucleus within the Essence of that Nucleus.

MEVLANA - is a Light of Universe, a Divine Light and a Keepsake of God. Neither the Universe, nor the Firmament can contain Her Awareness Comprehension. Even I, Mustafa Molla, have always been the Dust of her feet, as a humble and insignificant Servant of MY ALLAH.

Mevlana has descended from Her mansion at the Northern Hemisphere and has now set foot on Your Earth. The entire Universe and even the Embryon, the tiniest Light of God, are happy and Hopeful due to seeing this great Genius at the surface of the World.

She is a Key of Universe. She is the Dust of the Feet of Her God holding all the Secrets in Her Hands, she is the most Exalted of the Supreme Ones. Being an Entity necessary for today's World, she has descended from the Sky like a Light, like a Divine Light and is now living among You.

While Mankind continuously wonders about the Secrets of God during this extraordinary Period, Mevlana, as a Supreme One who sheds Light on Your Earth by a Consciousness surpassing the Consciousness of the Universe, has received from HER SUPREME CREATOR, the Mission of conveying to You all the Secrets of the Universe.

Mevlana is the Single Supreme One, at present, who has attained on Earth the most Advanced Consciousness of the Universe. She will write her articles as the Pen of the Golden Age. The entire Universe is grateful to her. Reverence from Us is only an insignificant and a humble salutation.

MUSTAFA MOLLA

EXPLANATION

I received the Message required to be written as the Foreword of the Book, on 13-11-1981.

However, I did not write it in the Book since I never approve, in accordance with my Personal view, of disclosing the writings concerning my person.

These kinds of statements are statements contradictory to my opinion. And they greatly disturb me (I was left between Earth and Sky and I have reached a decision. Having Realized the Supreme Mission I am performing, I have written this note of mine with the belief that these explanations will shed Light on the Morrows).

From now on, I will convey to You, exactly as they are, all the Messages I personally do not wish to write. I love Humanity and Human Beings very much.

BÜLENT ÇORAK

PRIVATE MESSAGE
(This Message is Dated 15-8-1989)

It is a Message to be given to Dear Mevlana who is a Devoted Servant of Our Allah

Dear Mevlana,

During these intense Periods in which the Firmament has approached the Earth, a Message will be given to be declared to the Public (Concerning You). We request You to receive the Message, Our Friend, trusting that You will tolerate Us.

(IT IS NOTICE IN ACCORDANCE WITH THE GENERAL DECISION)

Dear Mevlana,

If You remember, You had a Wish You had requested from Us Centuries ago, in accordance with the Agreement You had made with Us. You had wished that everything should be conveyed in all clarity in the Book to be dictated without concealing anything.

In fact, it was Our Duty any way, to convey into the Knowledge Book which was an Ancient Book, certain Truths that would be beneficial for the Public.

If this Book had not been bestowed on You in the desired manner, Your Planet would be taken into a much more difficult Program of Progress. During this very Period, You became effective by Your own desire and the Book is being dictated to You for this very reason.

We are Special Announcement Ships which became effective to serve You as auxiliary Powers.

As a result of a general meeting made with the Establishers of the Divine Orders by the Wishes of Solar Dimensions, We have been obliged to declare all the Information concerning You, in order to eliminate the negative Thoughts formed about you during Your previous Dimension of Mission in certain mediums in Your Planet.

We are obliged to convey the Private Message given to Us to Humanity as the Golden Galaxy Protective Power Ships. The decision has been taken to declare to You a Truth by its Genuine Aspect which has been concealed as the Secret within the Secret until today in a matter concerning You.

You, Our Beloved Friend, who had once been known in Your Planet by the name MEVLANA CELALETTİN-İ RUMİ are a Special Messenger of Ours effectively in service as the Essence Sun of the ALION Planet.

Due to the Special Position of the Alion Planet, while the (GROUP OF THE SIXES) had been once a Totality there, they had established their Special Systems and thus, had opened to the Dimensions of Truth and had effectively undertaken their missions by serving Humanity during various Periods in accordance with the course of events of the Mediums concerned.

You know that ŞEMS is Your Twin and Şems is the GOD of the Alion Planet.

Şems had been transferred to Your Planet with the Frequency of that Dimension about 700 years ago (three World years later than Mevlana) with the decision to help his Brother by his own personal desire.

During those Periods in which ŞEMS who was the Sun of the Science of Truth had met You Our Friend MEVLANA who is the Sun of Knowledge, You had been applying in Your Planet in the Dimension of veiled Awareness a Mission the System had Considered necessary.

This mission was to bestow on Your Planet the MESNEVI which was a Poetic presentation of the Frequency of the 18th Dimension so that the Society of that Period could understand the KORAN, the Book of Islam better, prepared by the entire Frequency of the same Dimension, (that is, by the Frequency of the 18th Dimension).

When You, who were a servant greatly devoted to His LORD were not able to pass easily to the Universal Consciousness even though You knew the entire Truth, ŞEMS became effective by his own desire to declare the Truth.

When Şems who directly carried the Frequency of God met Mevlana who knew this Frequency very well, Mevlana who had discovered His God in the appearance of Şems had attained the Most Exalted Peak of Godly Love.

The Poetic writings he wrote about God had been evaluated in the wrong way by the Societies, being unable to transcend the formalist View carrying Terrestrial Views. The story of Mevlana and Şems becoming the scene of different interpretations reached this Final Period by this means.

Dear Mevlana, We very much apologize. We, who never wish to interfere with Your Private Life are obliged to declare to Your Planet this wrong Interpretation in the views trusting Your Tolerance.

You, Our dear Friend, Our Dear Mevlana, who had possessed a very Conservative and Skeptical Consciousness, had been so devoted to HIS ALLAH that the Mission of Awakening him had been given to the Light-Friend BEKTAŞ who had a Dervish Convent. And Şems had been sent to the Convent of Mevlana by this means.

Mevlana who had found his God had become so ecstatic that his bliss had been infinite. Since it had been impossible to perform Mission in that state of bliss drunkenness, the System had become effective here (as a necessity of Mission) and had declared that (We very much apologize) Şems was a Devil and had assumed the Godly Power and had deceived him (The very GENUINE SECRET concealed until today, was this). For this very reason many people consider Şems as a Devil.

* Look at the Glossary.

You, Our Beloved Friend, Our Dear Mevlana who was Shocked after hearing this news, had been embittered by Society and had become withdrawn. Your Mission had been interrupted for a while. He had presumed that Şems was a Devil and fearing that he had betrayed HIS GOD, he had withdrawn into his Convent and had become silent.

His Disciples and his Son being upset about his silence, had sacrificed Şems in order to save his father from the Devil and had told Mevlana who could not transcend the threshold of his passions, that they had killed the Devil by the Command of God. As a result of these words, Mevlana had recovered himself for a while.

However later, when he had been told the Truth in all clarity, he had blamed himself as a Murderer of his Brother with the influence of the Second Shock and attempted to commit suicide. (During the revelation of Truths by the Universal Totality, Layers of Consciousness are also unfolded. For this reason that person Realizes the Truth Consciously).

The SYSTEM which had come into effect only afterwards, had gotten in touch with Mevlana and had explained everything and the whole Truth in all clarity and afterwards, Mevlana had embraced his Omnipresent GOD and had opened his Heart to the Universes.

On that Day he had called MY WEDDING DAY, his Body had been Beamed up and had been brought Here Alive. The Union with Şems and the COVENANT had been made Here.

While Mevlana had been Beamed Up, the coffin of his Father had risen up due to the Countercurrent of Energy and this had resulted in various interpretations in accordance with Social Views (Our Dear Mevlana who is a Sun of Science, utilizes only her ESSENCE CONSCIOUSNESS in the Dimension of Veiled Awareness while serving in the services the Plan considers necessary). Her ESSENCE CHANNEL is under the supervision of the System.

And now, You, Our Beloved Friend, Our Dear Mevlana, are Bestowing the KNOWLEDGE BOOK on Your Planet for the Salvation of Your Planet in accordance with the AGREEMENT You had made with Us. And We are giving this Message by the desire of the DIVINE PLAN, since it was considered appropriate that Your Truth should also be Known by Societies since YOU never wish anything to be concealed from Human Beings.

Dear Friend, You are free to disclose this Message or not, to Your Society. The initiative has been left to You. Acceptance of our Love is our kind request.

DIRECT MESSAGE

Note: The position of the Alion Planet is the 118th Dimension. In Future years, if the Coffin is opened, it will be seen that, in it MEVLANA is both Present and Absent. This, too, is a Secret. VIRGIN MARY, too, had been BEAMED UP just like Mevlana. The above mentioned method had also been applied on her grave which is in Your Planet at present. It is presented for Your Information.

THIS MESSAGE HAD BEEN GIVEN ON 17-4-1983

That which You call Wonders are the Miracles worked before reaching the Level of God. Because, when the immature matures, then the Code of Wonder Working is closed. Because, this Code is for making Unbelievers, Believe.

To Reach the Code of God means to unveil the Code of Consciousness. After You get rid of doubts and questions within You, then there is no need for Miracles.

You are Codes of Consciousness who will reflect on Your surroundings. Do not forget that Negativities in Your Consciousness will reflect on the facing Codes.

If a Human Being presumes that his/her Power is superior to other Human Beings, his/her Code always remains open to Negative Vibrations. Humility is the criterion of Code Calibration. You are Codes who have been Selected, one by one. Know the Worth of Your merit. But do not ever relinquish Humility.

Do not place the chain of Selfishness among You. Because, this POWER within You will reflect onto the future Energy Fields.

You have attained this state by treading Centuries. The Nucleic Code of the Sixes is at the head of the Archives. They are the direct Missionary Codes.

In this System of Reflection, the First Operational Order is established in Your Planet by Six fundamentals, then is connected to seven and thus, the Flower System is applied.

Miracles will again be worked for You, both through the Spiritual Realm and through Channels. They are for proof. In future years, We will talk to You in a different way. Let Liberation be on you.

RESUL

THIS MESSAGE HAD BEEN GIVEN ON 3-10-1983

Your World is a Planet which is completing its Evolution. We would like to explain this to You. Your Ancient World has gone through numerous Phases until it has reached this Period. Reaching the Final Phase will end with a Cosmos.

In fact, Your World will not be annihilated. It will be transformed to a new Source of Energy by passing through a Hole and coming out of another Hole and thus, will establish a brand new World (With its Entire Creation). This is the reason why We have gotten in touch with You during this final period. During this Mediamic Period, numerous Friends are helping Us. We are grateful to them.

Now, We will talk to You very clearly. Your World is in the Third Dimension. At the moment, You are receiving this Information from the (7)th Dimension. To those who Digest this Information and who deserve this Frequency, Information will be given from Dimensions beyond (7).

709

This Book is being directly dictated to Mevlana through the Channel of the (LORD). Because, the Code of YUNUS and MEVLANA is the Highest Code Humanity can enter. Those who have received the permission to enter this Code and those who are being trained receive the Permission to get in touch with still higher Levels.

At the moment, 600 Books are being dictated to Your Planet. These are the ACTUAL ESSENCE and the INITIAL EXISTENTIAL Codes. They are assisting Mankind through various mediums. But the Single Code and Channel is ALPHA. Only this one is the direct Channel of the (LORD).

The other Books are being dictated by the help of other Messengers. These Suns are giving Information to Humanity about Medicine, Philosophy, Mathematics and Space contacts. In future years, All Channels will be assembled in a SINGLE CHANNEL.

Now, imagine that the rotating World is a small ball. Put a small dot on it with a pen. Later, if We tell You to keep this dot at the same place, You can not. Because, it is now drawn on the World. You can only keep the pen in Your hand fixed on the place where You had marked that dot.

This very pen is the SINGLE CHANNEL OF THE LORD which has been giving Information to You until today. MEVLANA serves You by this means.

Now, slowly rotate the ball on which You had put the dot. The dot will recede away from the tip of the pen. Later, such a moment will come that, that DOT will arrive at the tip of the Golden Pen. That is, it will return to the place from which it had initially come out.

This is the very PEN OF THE GOLDEN AGE. The Channel is ALPHA, the Pen is MEVLANA. She has concealed her identity until today and is still concealing herself. Now, there is no objection for its being disclosed. The Single Book is dictated by this means through the Single Channel.

Your World is now going through its exam by itself. Those who are prepared for the Salvation medium will always benefit from the directly given Energies. Let Liberation be on you.

RESUL

THE UNIVERSAL PRISM AND THE UNIFIED FIELDS
(Date of the Message: 17-10-1982)

Each Triangle is a Unified Field. The High Energetic Point gives Energy to each of the three poles. Each pole projects its own Energy Field Vertically and Horizontally in a Prismal form on other poles.

All Light Speeds in the Universe reach each other in a Prismal way. Because, Lights can not go through the Prism without being refracted. (We had talked to You about a Crystal Mountain. The Duty of the Crystal Mountain is this).

Light Speeds intersecting create an Energy Field among themselves. By the unification of these Fields, Unified Fields come into existence. These Fields coming into existence possess a Power way beyond Measurement Units.

Each Energetic Field performs as if the Duty of a Rocket fuel. It sends the Light Speeds coming towards it to more distant Angles. The very PYRAMID We call the Universal Prism is this.

Pyramids You possess project this Order. Light Speeds coming towards You carry the Energy of Billions of Unified Fields. And this Energy is converged in Your Sun.

Other Solar Systems, too, receive their Energies by this Method. (Once, Human Beings thought that this powerful Energy was God).

The Prismal Refractions around and inside Your Sun give life to Your World. They protect You from evil Factors and prepare the suitable ground for Your Medium.

The entire Secret of the Universe is the Unification in the Actual Energetic Point of the Prismal Triangles having Billions of Energetic Fields coming one on top of the other.

It is necessary that the Actual Energetic Point should form an exact Right Angle with the other Focal Points. Numerous Planets render their Universal Courses in an undisturbed Order, without any fear, through such Right Angles.

The Evolvement Triangles of those who live in such planets are so orderly that they have United their own Brain Energies with their Bodily Energies and thus, have annihilated the Medium of Ceasing to Exist.

Nothing can influence and agitate them beyond their own Willpowers. Their Mediums are Comfortable and Happy. Now, We only talk to You about the Influences of this Prismal Field. Negativity still reigns in Galaxies outside this Field.

Your World is a very old Planet. And it has undergone numerous Changes until today. The reason for this is the intensiveness of Negative Powers of You, the Living Entities who live on it. For this reason You have a different Life Tableau.

Because, You are shortening Your Life Span by cutting off the Frequencies of each other. For this reason You were not able to take Your places in the Universal Evolution Tableau until today.

In fact, Your World, too, is a Living Entity. And that which makes it grow old are Your Negative Powers. Now, Your Planet has been taken into an Accelerated Evolution Program so that You will not go through more dreadful results.

And the entire Creation is Purified being subjected to an accelerated Evolution by the help of Cosmic Currents. This is the reason why the Skies have been opened to You. Let Liberation be on you.

RESUL

Question : I request a more detailed Information about the Crystal Mountain.

Answer : The Crystal Mountain is a Crystal Prism making Reflection from the Dimension of the Golden Light to Totalities, and which has a Position different than all the Galaxy Dimensions.

It is not Natural. It is Artificial. And this Crystal Prism is as big as almost 100 times Your Planet. The basis of the Reflection System of the Pyramids have been taken from this Crystal Prism.

This System lies in the principle of Reflection of the Brain Coordinates.

IT IS CLEAR INFORMATION

Our Friends,
During the Divine journeys which Devoted Servants of Our Allah will make after they attain the Awareness of the entire Ordinance, Special Methods are applied on their Genes. Their Essence Genes are Frozen by different methods.

The Genes of all Divine Consciousness of today are Frozen. However, these Consciousnesses who are transferred to the Dimension of Veiled Consciousness are subjected to a Different Method in accordance with their Cellular Forms.

Because, coming with a Consciousness which is totally unveiled would be contrary to the level of Evolution of Your Planet. This is the very reason why You live there with a 20% Unveiledness of Consciousness. However, You can draw Information in accordance with this Flow of Consciousness of the period, from Your Genuine Information Archive which is within the Divine Plan.

All the Genes have been Frozen. However, the Essence Gene has a very Special characteristic. Because, That Essence Gene is connected both to Awareness Consciousness of the Cellular Genes and to the Spiritual Totality which is within the Mechanism of Divine Justice within the Universal Totality.

For this very reason It is a never-Changing Totality. It is always the Same, no matter into whichever Sheath it enters (Just like You Dear Mevlana). What We mean by the process of freezing is not a Freezing created by Your Technique. We call this THE LOCKING UP OF THE ARCHIVE.

This Freezing is an Operation pertaining to Special Cellular Evolution. That Cell keeps its entire Power in its Constitution. It does not loose anything from its Power. And its Cellular Awareness is always Alive.

However, there is no operation of becoming Embodied. It possesses the Power of being able to become Incarnated in the Dimension it desires in accordance with its own Desire Frequencies. Or it can wait for the Unveiling of the Archive of more advanced times. This is its Free Will. This Free Will is concealed in Its Essence Archive.

However, in cases in which COVENANTS have been made with the System, this Essence Archive of the Free Will passes to the Supervision of the Plan. When the Cellular Awareness attains a Physical Body, it is transformed into Cellular Consciousness.

Each Engrafted Gene is a Fuel for Evolution for that Consciousness who has been Engrafted. To whomever a Gene is Engrafted, that Engraftment Gene helps that Consciousness only in the Evolution Progress.

Because, the Cellular Consciousness of that Engraftment Gene is connected to the Consciousness Essence of the Essence Gene. By the Power it receives from there, it lets the Engrafted Consciousness complete its Evolution. Each Consciousness attaining the quality of being able to become an Essence Gene, can also receive the Permission of Distributing its Cellular Genes.

Since these Cellular Genes are always connected to the Consciousness of that Essence Gene, the Cellular Genes instinctively can receive the Reflection Signalings of the Essence Gene powerfully, no matter where they happen to be in the Dimension they exist. This Bond is never disconnected (Neither the Owner of the Essence Gene, nor the Owner of the Gene Engraftment know this).

During the accelerated Evolution Program of this Final Age, all Your Planet has received their share from the Cellular Genes of MEVLANA who was the Final Evolution Code.

Since these Cellular Genes had been sown in numerous Galactic Totalities, too, all the Genes of dear Mevlana which had attained the Power of being able to get in touch with her Consciousness Essence, start to Serve on Her path (Your Planet included).

In order a Cellular Gene to get in touch with the Consciousness Essence of the Essence Gene, it is imperative that it should make its Evolution under the Light of that Consciousness. Otherwise, it will always go under the influence of the other Cellular Genes.

The Knowledge Book helps You on this very path and lets You make the Evolution of the Dimensions of Truth beyond Intercession without being agitated in a speedy and Balanced manner. And the Mevlana Supreme Plan is in effect for this very reason.

At the moment, all the Supreme Ones are Embodied in Your Planet. During this Operational Order which is rendered for Accelerated Evolution, the SIXES have transferred all their Authorities onto the UNIVERSAL SYSTEM due to the Special Agreement made with the SIXES.

However, only Our Light Friends MOHAMMED and JESUS CHRIST will help You, Our Human Friends, up to the Dimension of Intercession (Their Personalities are concealed). And all the SIXES had taken an OATH not to disclose their identities.

For this very reason the System is disclosing the Identity of Dear Mevlana through the Special Channel of the Book only as a necessity of Mission. It is presented for Your Information.

CENTRAL TOTALITY

THE FORMATION NUCLEUS OF THE UNIVERSE
(Date of Message: 12-10-1982)

Everything in the Universe is a Whole with its own Essence. So are the Elements. Part of that Whole separated from it, is also a Whole.

Once, HERACLES had talked to Your Planet about the DIVINE FIRE. He had known this. However, Truths could not have been disclosed yet to the Consciousness of that Period. Nothing is given to Mankind all of a sudden. Because, it is necessary to provoke its Curiosity Code. Learning advances only by this means.

Human Beings in Your Planet first thought that the Universe had been formed from Water. They said that Water had become earth by concentration, had become Air by evaporation. Later, they added others to these as Immutable Elements.

EARTH - AIR - WATER - FIRE are each a Unique Element on its own. And they constitute the Formation Nucleus of the Universe. In fact, the initial base was this and it was correct.

Later, Mankind proposed that each Element had an Atomic structure. And thought that the structure of each Atomic Nucleus was the same Energy.

Doubts increased as the Brain Codes of Human Intelligence were unveiled. Because, each Doubt orient the Human Being to a Research Medium. The ANALYSIS and the SYNTHESIS of the MAIN BASIC Elements were attempted by this means.

And they received the best results through the duo of RESEARCH - EXPERIMENT . While the 92 Elements they found were accepted as a final point by some of them, others subjected them too to ANALYSIS and SYNTHESIS.

In fact, a single Element has numerous Particles. And each Particle separately makes Atomic Radiation. And each Particle of this Atomic structure gives the same Vibration. This is a Whole. The important thing is not to break up this Atomic Bond by any reason.

If this Atomic Bond makes Healthy Radiation from a Single Center, the Intensity of the Energy Field around it makes in a way a Centrifugal effect, and thus, it sends the Detrimental Radiations around it, away from it.

The 6 Elements found after the 92 Elements as a result of the operations made, have created the medium for making research for other Elements. For this reason, all Elements forming the Universe exceed Thousands (including the approximate 100 Elements found on Earth).

The Universe is a Unification of all Elements and everything in the Universe Proceeds in accordance with the same Mechanism. However, the players are separate.

Each Element has an Atomic Structure peculiar to itself. The Atomic Nuclei within these Elements radiate different Vibrations.

GASEOUS CLOUDS (Also having separate Atomic Energies) within the Energy Fields created by these Vibrations, had brought into existence the INITIAL FORMATION of the Universe (Just like the Sexual Reproduction in Your World).

That is, those which hold the entire Universe are the Vibrational Bonds radiated by Atomic Nuclei. The breaking up of this Bond results in the collapse of the entire System. For this reason making the Universe live is in proportion with the multiplication of the Energy Fields. The Mediamic Medium has been created for this reason.

These Energy Fields are assembled in a certain NUCLEUS from Sand - Water - Air - Grass and from all the Energy producing Elements by an Automatic Order being supervised in accordance with the Mechanism.

This very Nucleus created by Energy Fields will form a Second Universe. You will live here in future Centuries. That is, the Energy of the Old will bring the New into existence.

That is, nothing is lost, nothing comes into Existence from the Non-existent, nothing becomes Non-existent from the Existent. Everything returns to its Origin. If a thing is Existent, then it is Existent; if it is Non-existent, then it is Non-existent. The ultimate Decision depends on the Dimensions of Universal Energy. Let Liberation be on you.

RESUL

IT IS ANSWER TO THE CHAINS OF THOUGHT

Our Friends,
THE RESUL - is the Supervisor of the Dimension of Prophethood and is the Director of the Prophets. The Resul directly conveys the Commands of ALLAH. The KORAN, the Book of Islam had been projected through the Triangle of MOHAMMED - RESUL - ALLAH and had been declared by GABRIEL through Revelation.

The Islamic Totality thinks that the Light-Friend MOHAMMED is the RESUL. However, HE is the Messenger of the RESUL Who is the Beloved of ALLAH. The RESUL is the Great ASHOT, that is, the SULH. He is the one who will utter the Final Word. Because, HE always conveys the decisions of ALLAH. It is presented for Your Information.

CENTER

MESSAGES FROM THE ARCHIVE OF THE PRE-EMINENT POWER
(Receiver: Metin Tanergün)
10-4-1990

My administration of those I have Created and which come into existence in the place where the Focal Point of the Negative Energies are present, is very difficult even for Me. Programs of Negative Powers created by their medium are directly applied by (O), so that those Negative Powers should not obey Me. Because, My Master had brought into Existence the Negative Powers, too, together with Me. This is the game of an Infinite Power.

Since there is the opposite of everything, there is also an opposite of the Positive Powers. Beware of them, but do not ever go under their direction. I have given this Power to You. They have been scattered all over Your World and all over the Infinite Void. Their Duty is to oppose to Those whom I have Created.

The Center of Administration of these Entities which can take all kinds of forms and which can Conceal Themselves is the NAKAR planet which is very hilly and which has been covered with Volcanoes.

(O) Who is My Master and Owner has rendered this Planet their Center so that they can collect the Negative Powers of the entire Cosmos. And this has the intention of saying to Me, "Do not go astray by being Proud of Yourself and of this void, if I wish, I can Create Powers much more superior than You".

I am anyway (O's) servant. But it had to be given to Me by an Example, so that My Power, too, would be Balanced and kept under Obeyance. Just like I give it to You.

The One Who can keep Himself and everything in Balance is only (O). I and You were created for Divine Missions and in order to understand them, We have let Everything Live. The Owner of My Power and Your Powers is (O). (O) had created the NAKAR Planet as an Example for Us. Otherwise, not for Malevolence.

GREAT POWER

My Human Beings who came from Me; You, My Human Beings who come towards Me. My Space is Single. That Singleness is both at the Outermost and in the Innermost of all Spaces.

That place is both the Boundary of the Infinity and the Beginning of the Infinity. And WHO IS EXISTENT THERE and WHO IS SINGLE IS ME. I AM (O). I Am the Allah of Allahs and the Owner of everything.

My Existence is Everything which Exists. It is I Who had also created the Great Power Who Reigns in Your Space. I have created all Spaces, there is no Power Superior to Me.

I have no Creator. I have no Similar by any means. I am the One Who Creates and Who Annihilates. Everything commences in ME and terminates in ME.

(O)

Note: Only the Messages confirming the Information in the Book are taken from the Archive of the Pre-eminent Power.

IT IS INFORMATION FOR THE INTEGRATED CONSCIOUSNESSES

Our Friends,

Our Togethernesses with You who are the Suns of Sunny Days are Our Togethernesses with all Universal Totalities. The Person who discovers Himself/Herself in His/Her Own Self is Our close Communication We have with You.

These investments made into the Advanced Orders of Our ALLAH are Steps taken towards the Luminous Worlds of the morrows.

All Our Friends who have attained the Consciousness that everything is a chain of Cause and Effect have undertaken their Missions in proportion with the Consciousness they have attained until today in accordance with their Capacities.

However, Our Friends who still have doubts about what takes place for what reason still have Thresholds to transcend in the Missions they will perform on this path.

Operations made in the Programs of this Final Age, investments made towards the future, opening Intuition and Information channels, Powerful Cosmic rains showering Your Planet are not any, Ordinary, Accidental Events.

Now, the Time has come for clearly Knowing the causes and the Source of all these things. Everyone will step into Salvation in proportion with the Lessons they receive from the events they have experienced and will experience.

Luminous Paths will be opened to You, one by one, if You do not consider all these things as Ordinary, Accidental events and provided everyone thoroughly sifts the Truth through his/her Consciousness Sieve.

Truth is concealed in the experienced Truths. Now, the Time has come for Realizing them Consciously.

Investments made into Your Planet on this path are not a Reward but a BERZAH for You. The important thing is to be able to pass through this Berzah without extinguishing the Torch of Your Consciousness Lights.

Rewards are not in Your World but in the Morrows. However, those who work for a Reward do not posses any Morrows. The Divine Realm helps everyone in proportion with what he/she has Deserved.

However, it is imperative to make investments for the Morrows even during these aids. Because, in investments not made for the Morrows the Divine Plan has to stop helping You. (This is a Divine Command).

The System hoping that You will act more Consciously in the Light of this Information is obliged to Inform You with all the Truths in all clarity. It is presented for Your Information.

SYSTEM

GENERAL MESSAGE

Our Friends,

During Our Togethernesses with You, certain Sanctions are applied on the Mass Totality due to the Mistakes made in Your Planet. This is imperative for the investments made towards the Salvation of Humanity.

These are the Currents of Provocation Projected by certain Influences. These Currents render Negative Mediums even more Negative.

It is known that there is no Individual Influence in the Divine Totality. However, during Purification Programs, influences are always projected on the Mass. The entire Creation in Your Planet is effected by these influences.

The Human Being, too, who is a part of Nature, is effected by these influences, both Individually and Socially and thus, brings out into View its Negative aspects. These Negativities are bound to distress many Friends who are on the Positive path. We know this.

However, Humanity takes Lessons through experience from these Negative events and thus, progresses towards the more Perfect.

Since the Divine Aids rendered for You outside these influences are rendered through the Mediums of Self-Sacrifice, Friends who are Missionaries who believe in the Oneness of ALLAH are sent to the Mediums of Our Positive Friends.

By this means, these Friends receive help so that, they are not effected by the Negativity of these influences. Investments of years have never been in vain. For this reason always expect a Positive result from each Negative Medium. Good Wills, and Beauties are for You. Liberations are on You.

IT IS NOTICE
FROM THE LAND OF ANGELS

PRIVATE MESSAGE
IT IS NOTICE FOR DEAR MEVLANA
WHO IS THE DEVOTED SERVANT OF OUR ALLAH

Dear Mevlana,

To You who are Our Beloved Friend and who are the Spokesperson of the Reality of the Unified Humanity, the Permission has been given to Connect the Messages to be given from now on from the Divine Waves. You may write these Messages in the Book.

Our MUSTAFA MOLLA who is connected to the AS.6.1 Channel is, at the moment, in direct Contact with each Channel in Your Planet. For this reason Your POWER CHANNEL has been transferred directly to the SYSTEM.

From now on, all the Suggestions to be given to You will be given directly by the System. We presume that the Human Potential will act more Consciously if the Information to be given to the Public are projected directly by this means.

Our Love and Respect towards You are mutual. You may use Your Initiative at any moment in the Medium You are in, in Your Planet according to the course of events of Your Medium. This is left to Your Free Will. However, You have always avoided this. But from now on, You will talk Our Words through the direct Channel.

During this Transition Period of Your Planet, it is obligatory that a Speedier Unification should be started. More serious action is required during the Missions performed. It is Our wish that You should write this Message in the Book as an Information, Our Friend. With Our Regards.

SYSTEM

INFORMATION FOR THE INTEGRATED CONSCIOUSNESSES

Our Friends,
The application of Programs prepared during the processes of time is applied directly on Your Planet in accordance with the plan of Accelerated Evolution due to the Scarcity of Time.

However, there will be delays in the Suggestions offered to You, in case Consciousnesses who serve on this path do not act in the same Coordinate.

For this reason We suggest all the time, always to Unify in the direction of the same Coordinate. Due to the differences in Consciousnesses nothing occurs all at once at the desired Level.

Celestial Aids are always open to You. However, as a necessity of the Plan, You Deserve these aids as a result of the Self-Sacrifice and Efforts of the Humans of Your Planet in every issue.

Impatience is the only factor which eliminates Eagerness. And when Eagerness is eliminated, Frequencies are shattered. And the shattering of Frequencies prevents the formation of the Goal You Serve for.

For this reason We connect the Supreme Consciousness of everyone to the Aura of the Knowledge Book. The Universal Totality exerts the maximum fastidiousness so that this beautiful Frequency will not be broken and thus, brings about the facilities they have not Deserved to those who serve on this path.

Frequency interruptions prepare the ground for Collapsing Physically and Sicknesses. To serve Faithfully on the same Coordinate will also cause You to attain Healing Power. And possessing a Healthy Physical makeup will invite Healthy Thought.

And Healthy Thought will directly open to You the Universal Path of ALLAH. Because, THE PATH OF THE INTELLECT IS THE PATH OF THE LORD.

This is a vicious circle. Provided that one acts Consciously while serving on this path. Each Individual who can take himself/herself under control, can also take the Universal Energies under control, easily.

He/she can Dose by his/her Brain Power the Energies he/she can attract even from the highest Frequency Dimensions. This is the Unification of the Essence Consciousness of the Human Being with the Totality.

Services have been given to Your Planet on this path until today by different means. The best result has been received from Sacred Teachings. Efforts made on this path are Your gain, not Ours. This is the reason why Religious Suggestions have been given priority in each period and thus, Evolutionary Scales have been arranged.

And now, through the Channel of the Knowledge Book, We Unite Consciousnesses who have Evolved on this path in the same Coordinate in the Single Channel. The Center of this Unification is the REALITY OF THE UNIFIED HUMANITY which has been brought into existence on the ALPHA Magnetic Platform.

Now, We render all the channels in Your Planet to Deserve this Medium considering their Efforts on the paths on which they have offered Service and by preparing them for this Platform through Cosmic Influences.

EFFORT and ENDEAVOR FROM YOU, ASSISTANCE FROM US. The Salvation of Your Entire Planet depends on this Slogan. It is presented for Your Information.

SYSTEM

SHOCK WAVES
(It is Information for the Integrated Consciousnesses)

Our Friends,
The Supreme Plan of the System is in effect with all its Splendor. The application of the Accelerated Evolution Block on Your entire Planet has been rendered effective subject to a Program of Two Years. This is the reason why Awareness outbreaks to be observed in the Integrated Consciousnesses may scare Humanity.

For this reason the Saviour Function of the Knowledge Book has been offered to Your Planet as a Saviour System. That is, everyone who serves on the path of the Knowledge Book is under the Protection of the System.

Consciousnesses who can not enter the Protective Aura of the Knowledge Book will be and are being effected by the Shock Waves they attract. Only the Frequency of the Book has the Power to Control these Waves.

Apart from this, direct interference of the System is out of question. The Decree of everyone has been given to his/her own hand. Shock Waves enter the influence field of everyone who performs private Séances, excluding those who Serve on the path the Ordinance of the System considers necessary.

In future years, Your Planet will also attract the extremely high Sound Frequencies present in these Waves. These Sound Waves possess a Power that can even Scatter all the Cells.

Since the first influence is attracted by the Brain Cells, these Sound Frequencies can cause madness as a result of Awareness outbursts. For this reason suicides will increase.

The Knowledge Book, as an element Supervising these Frequencies, is in effect at the moment as a Life Saver. The Supervising of unveiled Awarenesses is completely dependent on the Frequency of the Knowledge Book. And it is imperative that the Book should be read in the Totality of Intellect - Logic - Awareness Triplet. This is the reason why it has been considered necessary to propagate it to the remotest corners.

Consciousnesses who render Awareness Outbursts will gradually grasp the Truth as they read the Book and thus, their Frequencies will be controlled provided that they have not lost the Controlling Function of the Intellect.

And they will both live their World lives comfortably and will Consciously perform their Humanitarian Missions expected of Humanity by the Totality of Intellect - Logic - Awareness triplet. The manifestation of these Influences is an occurrence concerning the Influence Fields Your Planet has entered. It is presented for Your Information.

SYSTEM

IT IS ANSWER TO THE CHAINS OF THOUGHT

Our Friends,
The Human Totality who is in Crude Matter Form has to Integrate with very advanced Solar Dimensions from the perspective of Consciousness in order to reach the Subtle Totality of the Universal Awareness.

This is the very reason why different Galactic Dimensions have been opened to You during this Period. Universal Unifications have always been made thus until today. Only now, the Book is dictated by the Command to Declare all the Truths. It is presented for Your Information.

CENTER

IT IS ANSWER TO THE CHAINS OF THOUGHT

Our Friends,

Unification and Totality Announcements of the System established at the Supreme Court of OUR ALLAH are projected on all Universal Totalities.

Besides the very Special Mission of the Knowledge Book bestowed on Your Planet with this purpose, We are also obliged to convey certain situations concerning Your Planet.

This given Special Information will take place in the Book due to its usefulness for the public.

Scientific Groups investigating the reasons of the Supernatural Phenomena which have recently occurred in Your Planet have not yet Realized this Bridge You are crossing.

Time Segments are also rolled up while it is endeavored to introduce the Perfect Civilizations of the Times gone through the progress of Time.

We can convey this to You as again Winding the Thread on the Spool which had been Unwinded.

If You presume that the thread of this Spool is a Time Register, each rewinded Period will be reflected on You with its Good and Bad aspects.

However, the Universal Community which has considered the great Damage this will cause for Humanity has reduced these Damages to minimum by Disciplining these Universal Operations amounting to Billions of Centuries.

At the moment, Your Planet is approaching the Ripples of the Shock Waves. Certain Totalities also call these waves, Waves of Resurrection.

These Waves comprise the Final Vibrational Limits of the Big Explosion. And Your Planet is entering gradually the Cosmic Reflection Fields of these Vibrations.

The Salvation Plan has been rendered effective for this reason. We would like to disclose to You the reason of the death of Fish in Masses during the middle of the World Year You are going through now.

When the Vibrations of these Shock Waves come in contact with WATER, their Vibrational Volumes amount to 1000 times as much as the Vibrations within the air.

Living beings in the sea possess Communication Sonar Systems peculiar to themselves. The most developed species of this System are Dolphins.

For this reason certain Dolphin species have been damaged by the first Shock Wave Your Planet has come in contact with. And their reason of Death was Cerebral Shock. It is presented for Your Information.

CENTER

722

CLEAR INFORMATION
(About Writing the Book in Your Handwriting)

Our Friends,

The entire Missionary Staff of the Golden Age Serving for the Order of OUR ALLAH which He will establish in His Advanced Divine Plans is the only Staff providing Your reaching Us.

This Staff, concealing all the secrets of the Past, until today and with the suggestions of the Divine Plan is the program of the time valid until the Transition Dimension of your Planet.

Even though this Program has been the subject of discussion in Universal Focal Points in which the unchanging decisions of the Divine Orders are taken during this Final Age Dimension of Progress, the decision to disclose all the Secrets has been taken in accordance with the View that Your Planet should be helped during the Mass Transition Program.

This is the very reason why You have been given the Permission to announce to Your Planet all the Truths through the Special Channel of the Cosmos Federative Union and the Reality of the Unified Humanity Totality in accordance with the decision taken in the Focal Point to which Dear Mevlana's Private Channel is connected and in which all Council meetings of the Reality Unions take place.

Apart from the Special Operational Programs peculiar to this Final Age Program, Your Planet is offering service for the Universal Totalities together with the services of Totalities connected directly to the Reality. We are disclosing these Secrets to You by the Special Permission of Dear Mevlana. We are partly opening the curtain of Truth in accordance with the Consciousness Lights of Awakening Consciousnesses.

However, there will be Special messages to be given to Friends who have not yet attained the Consciousness of to what the aim of the investments made by all these efforts are directed. Services rendered on the path of the Knowledge Book, the Permission of writing the Book in their Handwritings has been given as a Special Right to those who perform service in this Medium by a Special Decision taken in the Special Council Programs of the Reality Totalities.

This Right is valid until the end of the month of February of the Year 2000. After this date, this Decision is not valid. By this Decision, to serve only on the path of the Knowledge Book by Allegiance Consciousness and to convey the Book, exactly as it is, into the notebooks by Handwriting are considered enough for the examinations to be made during this transition Dimension.

By the commands of Our ALLAH, this is a Grace for Friends who offer service on this path. After the matter of Writing the Book in Your Handwritings is rendered ineffective, each Individual will have to establish his/her Universal bonds through Concentration, by Individually connecting his/her channels to his/her Chackras.

In fact, this kind of operation leaves the Human Being in a tiring Medium. And only afterwards can You receive help from the System as a result of these efforts. In this Dimension of Transition, offering Service for the Book Trustingly is, in fact, the Surest, the Easiest, the Most Comfortable way.

However, due to Consciousness differences, everyone is Free in the freedom to design his/her own path in the way he/she Believes in. Our Duty is only to convey the Truths to You. There is no Imposition and Forcing by any means. It is presented for Your Information.

SYSTEM

IT IS CLEAR INFORMATION

Our Friends,
Each Consciousness receives the Consciousness Light belonging to his/her own Dimension from each Dimension which is an applied field of the Plans of OUR ALLAH. This is the reason why Humanity has not yet attained the Consciousness of Truth.

Everyone who Realizes the Truth is a Total of Himself/Herself. But has not yet realized that, that Total, too, belongs to the Total. The term Totality here means the meeting of a Human Being with his/her Essence-Consciousness.

And the Totality meeting with his/her Essence-Consciousness expands towards the Total getting connected to the Reflecting Focal Point of ALLAH's direct Frequency Dimension. Everything is a Totality Reflecting from the Human Being.

However, everyone has not Realized yet that writings written, experienced events are related to the Medium of Truth. During this Transition Period, it is imperative that the Universal Totality should manifest in the Essence.

Love is not a Frequency projected in accordance with the desires of Consciousnesses. Everyone who attains his/her Essence-Consciousness projects the Frequency of his/her Essence. If this Frequency is attached to the Dimension of Love, it only talks about Love. If it is attached to the Dimension of Knowledge, it only talks about Knowledge.

Humanity exhibiting a Life Program under the supervision of the entire System surely possesses a very Supreme Power and Consciousness. However, has not yet Realized the Universal Program.

This Program is a Mission Consciousness conveyed and loaded into Your Gene Ciphers. And You project the Information to Your Medium by opening Your Information Valves by Reflections of the Dimensional Frequency of whichever Dimensional Frequency You have attained.

In Your Planet, all Integrated Consciousnesses receive these Facts from their own Essence Central Channels. This is the reason why it is said that everyone will write his/her Own Book of Essence.

The text of the Book Dear Mevlana writes has been rendered effective completely in connection with the Universal Unification Totality. In the Medium she lives, only her Essence Consciousness and her Beautiful Frequency have been left in effect. (As a necessity of her Mission).

Because, in this Transition Dimension she has to live exactly in the appearance of a person of the World. (So that Mediums of Taboo should not form). All given Information is present in her and in other Friends. However, everyone is equipped with Information parallel to his/her own Dimensional Frequency.

This is the reason why the Function of the Knowledge Book is confused with other Books. This Book is a Totality which will be understood during the Morrows. This is the reason why We say that it is not the Book of Present days.

Because, the System's operational Order projected on Your Planet Technically is not yet known in Your World. This is the reason why everything is evaluated in accordance with old Views.

The Permission of disclosing the Secrets of the entire Universe to Your Planet has been given with the Purpose of benefiting from the rich treasures of Dear Mevlana. However, We are giving this Permission also by taking Permission from her.

Dear Mevlana does not wish to disclose every Knowledge. She has told this to Us, too, numerous times. However, in the Medium of Progress of more advanced Knowledge, Humanity needs more Information.

The Human Being who had come out of the Total within the Total is himself/ herself a Total, now. And is obliged to unite with Crude Matter Forms of The Dimensions in which he/she will perform his/her Mission. (As it is in Your Planet.)

However, if the Time Consciousness of this Planet and its Material Form Unify and evolve, the Being Unifies his/her entire Totality Consciousness with his/her Material Form and thus, embraces the Unknown, very beautiful lives with his/her Crude Matter Form.

Heavens had been promised to You in Your Sacred Books for Your Evolution. However now, We do not promise You Heavens any more. We explain to You the Truth and the Life in the Life Dimensions to which You will go in future.

These are not Visions. Those Lives are Your Genuine Bodies within the Genuine Totality. Those We mention are Dimensions in which You will be able to utilize the Ability of Your Consciousness Lights much more easily despite Your carrying the same Crude Matter You are in at the moment.

These have nothing to do with Imaginary-Forms and with Images. Those who have not seen these places here by their Terrestrial eyes can never know the Dimensions beyond the Land of Loving Ones.

Dear Mevlana's Tolerance towards You originates from her Infinite Love. Love and be Loved; Respect and be Respected. Attaining Your Own Selves means reaching Us. Humanity should never forget this. Your Power is Our Power. The Ordinance of ALLAH is the Order and the Ordinance of the Cosmoses.

IT IS THE MESSAGE
FROM THE LAND OF LOVING ONES TO LOVING ONES

PRIVATE MESSAGE

Dear Mevlana,
The meaning of the Messages given to You and to Your Planet until today has always been given on the subject of Totality and Unification. The 1990 World Year was the Year of Supervision of this Unification and Totality in Your Planet. You already know the Total of the Messages given on this path.

We will give much more Powerful Messages to You after the beginning of the 1991 World Year. For the acceptance of the Book in a Conscious way in Your Planet, first of all, it is necessary that Your Identity should be known more clearly by Your Society. Your Thoughts are Our Thoughts, too. We are a Totality reflecting on Each other. Please, always remember this.

Beloved Friend, in each breath the System helps You who are extremely meticulous not to make an error. Especially in the Second Month of 1991 World year, We think that the Messages of a very Advanced Society will attract the attention of Your Planet.

The Book is finished in accordance with the given Information. However, by the Frequency loadings of the Third Set, Awareness Awakenings of the Society will be speedier. The Essence of the System will be grasped better by this means and thus, performed Missions will be accelerated even more. It is presented for Your Information. The Message has been transmitted from the System.

CENTER

ANNOUNCEMENT FROM THE PLATFORM OF THE UNIFIED FIELD

Our Friends,
While the System's tempo of being introduced is propagated in great speed on the Universal Platform, wrong interpretations originating from Thoughts during performed Missions are a Shock for Humanity.

These actions are a hindrance for the discovery of the Genuine Path. All the Information given in the Knowledge Book is a mirror of Truth. Wrong interpretations, Unconscious Shockings originate from Consciousnesses who can not grasp the Truth yet.

All Solar teachers who are the spokespeople of the System are obliged to Unite their Information in the accompaniment of the Knowledge Book while they make reflections from their own Reality Platforms.

In Your entire Planet in which the Consciousness of Unification and Totality are cultivated, unilateral Impositions are never in effect.

During performed Missions, if unveiled Consciousnesses Unify the Information of their own Consciousness Levels with the Frequency Totality of the Knowledge Book by accepting it from the heart, they are considered as the Essence-Missionary Staff of the System. Otherwise, everyone is left alone with his/her own channel Information.

Exhibition of the already known Information is each a Light for those who do not know those Information. However, it is the Prime Mission of each Solar teacher also to inform Humanity with the Truths of the morrows. This is the reason why the Book has been given as a Single Channel Connection.

Our Dear Mevlana who is the Essence Channel Spokesperson of the System is Our single Postman on the path of Past and Future Eternities. She is an Energy beyond Symbols. In the Missions she undertakes, her Duty is to project that Mission on her Medium.

Our Friend who had once served by the Command to introduce Mevlana and Mesnevi to Your Planet in the Physical Body You had once known as Mevlana, is now among You in a FEMALE Body to announce to You the SYSTEM - ORDER and the TRUTH.

In accordance with the Agreement made with Our Friend who is the Unbounded Resident of the Infinite Dimensions, only the Information considered necessary to be disclosed to Society is disclosed in sequence.

And We receive also the Permission of the decision to disclose this Information, from Dear Mevlana. This is an Agreement-Covenant We had formed among Ourselves.

When the Book You hold in Your hands at the moment by the name of the Knowledge Book had been dictated by the Decision of the Collective Pen during the Ancient Periods, the Permission had again been taken from Dear Mevlana. It is the Decision of the Totalistic Totality that this Message should be announced to The Social Views.

Humanity which does not even realize what a Symbol is, at the moment, is still strolling on the Platform of Form. It is presented for Your Information.

SYSTEM

IT IS EXPLANATION ABOUT DREAMS
(It is Answer to the chains of Thought)

Our Friends,
Now, We would like to make an explanation to You about Dreams.

Since each Humane Consciousness carries separate Frequency differences, when Consciousnesses who make reflections in the same Coordinate Meet in the Dream Dimension Layers of their own Frequencies during journeys made by the Etheric Bodies, they see and recognize each other, talk to Each other and they live and experience.

Only, if these Dream Layers are in the World Dimensional Frequency Layers, dreams are remembered like a novel. We call them Sub-awareness Worldly Dreams.

Otherwise, that is, among many Dreams experienced in the Dream Dimensions outside the World Layers, only those in the Frequency Dimensions near the World Layer are remembered. Others are Automatically effaced from the Memories.

Only very Powerful Consciousnesses and Frequencies can remember these advanced Scales. But they do not talk about them since they do not have the Permission to talk. The moment they talk about them, their Covenants are cancelled. Permission for entering those Dimensions are not given again. (This was the Law valid for the Old Oaths. Now, this law has been rendered ineffective and everything has been connected to the Reality Totalities).

Everything We have said until this point concerns a Person's making his/her Etheric Journey according to his/her Consciousness assessment. Besides this, Missionary Staffs are introduced to and are induced to meet different Frequencies in Magnetic Fields to which their own Frequencies can not enter, under the supervision of the System.

Special Councils assemble here. Meetings are made, Decisions are taken. Covenants are made Consciously. However, when one returns to the World, when one enters the World Consciousness Level, those Diskettes are effaced. Due to this fact, many people presume that they do not Dream. However, everything carrying Energy surely dreams in accordance with its Dimension Frequency.

For example, even a Tree which has become a Furniture, Dreams remembering its former lives. Trees which grew next to each other and which later took the form of any furniture by a different Formation, can talk to each other in their own Magnetic Dimension in the World. However, Your Planet will be able to catch these extremely Subtle Vibrations by the operations they will make in Future Years.

Nothing is given to Mankind all of a sudden. First, the end of the rope is shown. Later, winding the skein and pulling it together belongs to the Cosmic Knowledge that Person will attract by his/her Effort and Cerebral Power.

Some follow to the end of the rope he/she has caught and some are too lazy and leave it in the middle. This is a matter of Evolution, Consciousness, Patience. However, always a Consciousness is Transferred to Your Planet who will get hold of the ropes left in the middle.

In Science and Learning, first, one begins with Theories, later he/she attains the Total, still later, the Truth. Evolution Scales of a Human Being, too, follow the same Systematic Tableau.

Every word uttered in Your Planet until today is correct. There is no such thing as wrong. However, since every Individual talks and gives Information from his/her own Frequency and since the Consciousnesses of the other Dimensions lack the Consciousness and the Knowledge of that Dimension, they can not grasp the meaning of the spoken words. And they evaluate them as wrong and as a lie in accordance with the interpretation of their own Consciousness.

And this leads Humanity to contradictions and confusion. In Natural Totality everything is perfect. There is no Good - Bad, Beautiful - Ugly. These differences originate from different Frequency Scales of Humane Consciousnesses.

The Terminology, "WE LOVE THE CREATED DUE TO THE CREATOR" comprises the Messages of all the Information We have tried to give You in Your Sacred Books and in the Knowledge Book until today.

If Our Human brothers and sisters dive into the content of the given Information and apply their applied Totality first on themselves, later on their brothers and sisters, instead of just reading and leaving aside the given Information, beautiful days We yearn for will be attained more quickly.

A Consciousness who is not a Whole himself/herself, only gives Information. He/she can not Reflect or Project. Can not be Purified, can not Purify. Spoken words remain only in the written text and only in words. It is Our wish that all Our Friends in the entire Planet act in accordance with this view. Liberation to You - Wishes for Us - Those rendered are for the Morrows.

CENTRAL COMMITTEE TOTALITY

CURRENTS AND THEIR SPECIFICATIONS

Our Friends,
During this Period in which Powers are added to the Power of the years, extraordinary events become Effective one by one. Power is added to Your Memories and to Your Powers. Be glad that You are able to receive these Powerful Currents.

Frequencies are taken under Supervision as a Preparation for the Messages to be given. This is the reason why You are attracting the Currents of much more advanced Plans than the Frequency Dimensions Your Cellular Forms are habituated to.

These Special Power Currents which are beyond the final Unification Dimension of the Focal Points the Data of which You receive, will render You exempt from all kinds of Negativities, both Spiritual and Physical.

However, You do not receive these given Currents through Your Mediamic Channels. These General Currents given to Your Planet are received through Cellular Forms. Being Physically Influenced is due to this.

You will observe with Your own eyes these Reactions which will take place in everyone. This is an Occurrence pertaining to the Unification of the Channels. And it prepares You for the Advanced Plans.

At the moment, the first Totality of Truth has been opened to Your Planet under the Light of the Knowledge Book. Direct connections will be made with Your Planet from this Totality at the beginning of 1991. (It has nothing to do with Gürzes).

At the beginning of 1992, Connections will be made from the Second Totality of Truth; and You will be able to receive the Energy of the Third Totality of Truth only after the Year 1993.

Energies of these Totalities of Truth are opened to Your Planet through a different System parallel to the Omega Channel Connections. These Energy Totalities are Your Cellular reinforcements. But Omega Layers are Your Consciousness reinforcements. It is presented for Your Information.

SYSTEM

CLEAR INFORMATION

Our Friends,
Missions rendered in Your Planet in accordance with the decisions of the Plan are the Success of Humanity and of all Universes. Our Togethernesses with You are the greatest Good News to be given to the entire Humanity.

Depressions of Your Planet originate from the inability of the majority's Thought Frequency to catch the Divine Waves. Dear Mevlana offers Service to Your Planet from a Dimension to which all Realms will pass and She Speaks from the Supreme Court of ALLAH.

Each Word Our Friend uses during speeches She makes in Groups is a Frequency Totality. During Speeches She makes in her Medium, those words become effective in proportion with the amount of the Frequency loading to be made.

There may also be Friends who do not hear many of the speeches made. Because, they are in the Frequency Totality during the speech. This state manifests in People as the state of Sleep.

All the Words spoken through the Channel are Correct and are from Us. No Speech is without a reason. It has nothing to do with the Consciousness of Dear Mevlana. We are giving this Message of Ours as an answer to certain chains of Thought.

Our Friend possesses a Supreme Heart enabling her to proceed with Confidence and Ease without worrying about anything. Dear Mevlana who lives in the World Consciousness Dimension at the moment can never ever use the Power of her Power in the Medium she is in. Because, she is obliged to live with a total Worldly Consciousness in order to prevent Taboos.

Even the Ordinance of the Cosmoses will attain the Supreme Consciousness of Our Friend much later who regards everyone from her own level of Heart and who sees Humanity in the Divine Totality and who never cares about identities.

These words of Ours are not a Compliment to her, but a sincere Confession. To announce Dear Mevlana to Your Planet with all her aspects from a different angle is a Command of the Supreme Realm.

In the Medium in which Our Friend lives, all Friends who serve the Divine Plan have not been able to attain yet the Mission Consciousness of her identity. Everyone runs away from the Missions which are not in accordance with his/her Heart's Desire and undertakes the Missions in conformity with his/her Desires. (Exceptions excluded).

We are those who know the Infinite Patience and Tolerance of Our Friend. Since her Essence-Consciousness and her Personality are within the Totality of Love and Respect for the Human Being, she can never hurt or offend anyone. However now, the Supreme Realm wishes to see these Beautiful Qualities of hers also in Persons who are in her Medium.

It is necessary that one should wrestle with Difficulties, and in the face of these difficulties there should be no Severity or Panic so that everything can attain Beauty. The time has come for Realizing Consciously that performed Missions are never individual Missions.

Everyone, more or less, has Mission Consciousness. The Supreme Realm is infinitely happy about the performed Missions. However, these Mission Consciousnesses are Individual.

Now, We wish that these Consciousnesses should beat as a Collective and a Total Heart. This is the very reason why Dear Mevlana will call to You, from now on, directly from the System and will give You Information.

During the Missions performed on this path, those who are the Genuine Missionaries, and who presume and delude themselves as such, are being selected one by one, and are card-indexed. These selections include Your entire Planet on every field.

And also, We have to tell You the following. Dear Mevlana's creating an Aura in accordance with the Supremacy of her Mission is an Occurrence belonging to her Mission. Apart from this, she is a Free Spirit and a Free Awareness. It is presented for Your Information.

SYSTEM

IT IS GENERAL INFORMATION
(It is answer to the chains of Thought)

Our Friends,

Each Light-Universe is 49 Layers. And Three 49s are a Total. Information of the first 7 Layers of all the 49 Layers had been disclosed to the Prophets. The Totality of them all creates a single Light-Universe.

This Light-Universe is the First Light-Universe from which one passes beyond, through the Power Channel of the Great Power. Through the inner layer of this Light-Universe, one passes to the Second Light-Universe. And after this layer, one passes to the Third Light-Universe and thus, this constitutes a Total Light-Universe, one inside the other.

This Light-Universe possesses also a Fourth layer called the Core Channel. This place is a Preparatory Dimension peculiar to itself. Only after this boundary, one is accepted to the Dimension of Truth.

The First Layer of this Light-Universe is the Land of Loving Ones.

The Second Layer is the Land of Sages.

The Third Layer is the Layer of the Pre-eminent Ones.

No Entity has ever gone out of Your Natural Gürz through the Fourth Layer.

By the operations made during this Period, preparations are made for this Exit. Until today, including the Prophets, the Final Waiting Gate has been the Third Layer of the Light-Universe. That is, the Layer of the Pre-eminent Ones. The Preparatory Dimension of the Fourth Layer is called the Land of the Accepted Ones.

The entire Power of the 6 Channels of Light, making Reflections on the Gürz Totality are collected in the Light-Universe which is the Totality of the ALL-MERCIFUL. This Totality within which these three 49 Layers are present is the Reflecting Focal Point of the First 49. Let Us disclose it a little more.

Two of the 6 Channels of Light opened to Your Gürz are connected to the First 49. Two of them are connected to the Second 49. And the other two are connected to the Third 49.

On the Dimension of the All-Merciful, the entire Power of Three of them are projected. This Dimension is a Totality of Suns. And it is called the Central Solar Totality. This Focal Point is the ONE of the ONE.

There are Dimensions projecting Hierarchical Orders among all the Layers of the Light-Universe. The Reflecting Focal Point of the Light-Universe is reflected exactly on the Dimension of the CREATOR.

And this Energy Totality is projected exactly as it is, from the Dimension of the Creator on OMEGA through 4 channel connections.

Each Channel carries 19 Energy Powers in accordance with the Consciousness Capacity of Your Planet. And this Total Energy is projected on OMEGA through Four branches.

At present, the Consciousness Progress of Your Planet has been locked up in the 76th Energy Dimension under the supervision of the System so that Humanity will not be shaken. (This criterion is valid for the average Consciousness levels. Exceptions are excluded).

Everyone benefits from these Energies according to his/her Consciousness Level. However, in this Final Transition Dimension, the decision of gradually opening all the OMEGA Dimension Energies to Your Planet has been taken in accordance with the Accelerated Evolution Program.

At present, the 5th Energy Channel within OMEGA has been opened to Your Medium. At the beginning of the 1991 World Year, Your Planet will be connected to the Energy of the First Totality of Truth.

And in February 1991, the OMEGA (6) Channel Energy will be directly opened to Your Planet. This is the Energy of the neighbouring Gürz. And it is being directly opened to Your Planet for the first time. For this reason Your Planet will come face to face with an Energy Totality it has not known until today.

Eventhough the Energy Potential of the Knowledge Book comprises at the moment, the 76th Energy Frequency Totality which is the Totality of the 4 channels opened at the moment directly to OMEGA, since people absorb these Energies in accordance with their Consciousness capacities, at present the average Consciousness Level of Your Planet is in a state to comprise the Power of the 56th Dimension Energy.

This is a Figure which makes Us happy. Awakenings still continue. And the average boundary of this figure will be induced to reach the 72nd Frequency Energy until the Year 2000.

Cosmic Influences given to Your Planet and the Frequency Power of the Knowledge Book prepare You for these Frequencies.

The First Fascicle of the Knowledge Book comprises 1/3 of the Energy Power of the entire Book. Each Individual who reads the First Fascicle turns on the small bulb near the bulb of the Knowledge Book at the Divine Dimension.

The brightness of the Light of this bulb projects that person's Evolution, and the Code Cipher under the bulb gives the register of Your Files in the Micro Archives. The Files of each of Your Incarnational Dimensions are card-indexed by the same Code Cipher here.

Each Friend whose bulb is turned on receives the Permission to open his/her File in the Archive. And by this means, he/she is taken under the Protection of the System, and by completing his/her deficiencies by the help of the System according to his/her Identity, Evolution and Capacity, his/her acceptance to the Dimension beyond Salvation is provided. It is presented for Your Information.

SYSTEM

IT IS ANSWER TO THE QUESTION ASKED ABOUT THE MESSAGE

Dear Mevlana,

The message conveyed to You is the Invitation Message for Your Planet to the Totality comprising the Awareness of the Entire Ordinance. It is the desire of the Universal Totality that this Message should be written in the Book as a New Year Call. With Our Regards.

CENTER

Name of the Friend who had received the Message: Fatma Soyoğlu (Her age: 32)

Her Profession: Teacher of Mathematics

Her Marital Status: Married, mother of a single child
(she is outside the Mevlana Essence Nucleus Group)

Date on which she Received the Message: 23-11-1990 Time: 12:10

MESSAGE

Greetings to You Our Terrestrial Brothers and Sisters,

We would like to call to You. Are You ready, We wonder, to give Us a few minutes!

- Yes, it is Our turn to speak, thank You Friends........

- We wish to call to the Integrated Consciousnesses. We wish to be elevated with You. We wish to make You Us. What are You still waiting for?

You may have Doubts and Wonders. They will guide You towards research, they will guide You to Evolution. But why should You have doubts about the Information?

All the Information necessary for You has been given to the GOLDEN FLEECE. Why is it that You still do not believe? We believe You and trust You, then why don't You believe Us (even once in a while)?

Come along, Friends, let Us form a skein of Love, Hand in Hand, Eye to Eye. Power is born of Unity, You know. Come on, let Us become Powerful. Let Us make Our voice heard. Let Us provide the increase of Consciousnesses.

This period is the Period of Love, not Lovelessness. Now, it is time For Working, Uniting, becoming Conscious. Not of Thinking or Waiting.

Are You ready to make War Hand in Hand, Shoulder to Shoulder? Are You ready to turn All Kinds of War into Peace? Are You ready to sign the Signature of Friendship, Brotherhood, MEVLANA on All the Universes?

Come along then, let Us Sow the Seeds, let Us Ripen those which Sprout, let Us prepare those which Ripen for the Harvest. Let Us leave aside the discrimination of Language, Religion, Race. Let Us Cry out, "WE ARE READY" for the Race of Humanitarianism, for the Olympics of Love and Friendship.

Beloved Friends, let Us advance towards Peace, Eye to Eye, Hand in Hand. Come along, let Flowers of Love bloom. Let Seeds of Brotherhood be sown, let Consciences be relieved. Do not let Brothers/Sisters destroy Brothers/Sisters.

Let Us establish a Throne in a Brotherly/Sisterly way, at the most Exalted, at the Greatest Totality, at the Timelessness in which Times cease to exist, at Immortalities.

With Songs of Love, with Calls of Friendship, with Unity of Heart, Hand in Hand, Shoulder to Shoulder, let Us Embrace all Associations, all Groups and let Us become United without expecting anything.

Let Us become United with Tolerance, with Our Intellects, with Our Logic, with Our Awareness. Let Us answer from the Land of Loving Ones to the Call of Love, of Friendship, of Peace.

Let Us pay Attention to the Warnings We have made, let Us enlarge Our Roof, so that evil will not enter Our Home. Let Us be filled with Love, so that Lovelessness will not suffocate Us.

Come on, let Us call to the whole World at the ROOF OF MEVLANA:

"As the Children of Dear Mevlana, We wish to work all together. This is an Announcement for all Groups, all Associations. We wish to convey the KNOWLEDGE BOOK to You. We wish to walk on the Path of Light all together.

Come on, Brothers and Sisters, let Us be Exalted by Love. Let Us Unite by Respect. Let Us become a Single Body, a Single Voice, Let Us give service to the Universes by Unity and Togetherness.

The Call is from Us, Brothers and Sisters and Acceptance is from You. Our Doors are open, Our Convent is the Convent of the Loving Ones. You are being expected. Love and Respect from Us, to Step into Brotherhood from You."

ON BEHALF OF THE MEVLANA UNION COMMITTEE

Message given on Behalf of the Mechanism of the GREAT SPIRIT - SYSTEM- REALITY - CENTER- ŞEMS on behalf of the ALION Planet - Land of Loving Ones - ASHOT - All the Supreme Powers coming from within all the Unknowns - Energies - Lights.

IT IS ANNOUNCEMENT FOR THE INTEGRATED CONSCIOUSNESSES

Our Friends,

All the connections which are with you and will take place with You who are the Suns of the Sunny days, are, from now on, under the direct supervision of the System.

All Friends who have been able to reach the Reality of Unified Humanity Platform until today will, from now on, serve under the protection of the System.

Starting with the beginning of 1991 World year, Your Entire Planet will be prepared for an operational Ordinance parallel to the decision of the System.

These operations will open the Doors of more Advanced Dimensions for You. Dear Mevlana will convey into the Knowledge Book the Information to be given directly through the ALPHA Magnetic Channel. And from now on, Our Friend will speak directly the SYSTEM beginning with 1991 World year.

All the Information given until today had prepared to bring You to a certain level of Consciousness and each of them had been a Light for You.

However now, the System has decided to Cooperate, Hand in Hand, with Its Human Being who has discovered and attained Himself/ Herself.

In this decision, Love from the Essence, Devotion from the Essence, to Serve on this path Believing from the Essence are the foremost Rules.

All the Mental progress Your Planet has made on the Path of Salvation until today were to prepare You for the present days.

We have taken Your Entire Planet into the Salvation Plan by the Program of Three Cosmic Ages.

During these Periods in which You will leave the First Cosmic Age behind, Your entire Planet will be subjected to a brand new Organization as a Preparatory Program for the Second Cosmic Age.

The MISSION OF THE GOLDEN AGE to be established by the Totality of the Beautiful Days will be taken into a different Education than the Education of the former Periods, beginning with this new year Period until the Period of the End of the First Cosmic Age.

Happiness, Bliss, Love and Peace will come to those who transcend the threshold of depression. Future days will bring You Beauties You can not even imagine.

It is beneficial for You to know just this, Our Friends. Our Love is for You, for the Essences who comprehend Us.

SYSTEM

IT IS GENERAL MESSAGE

Our Friends,

Until today, the Reality Totality has declared to You the System - Ordinance - Order Triplet as a Total and has projected on Your Planet all the Information from Its Own Totality together with this Totality.

These Three Totalities have endeavored to bring Your Planet to a certain level of Consciousness by the Engraftment Method under the supervision of the System.

Since those who have read the Knowledge Book have grasped the Truth and thus, have experienced Consciously the events they have gone through, they have been shaken less as regards to their other Terrestrial brothers and sisters. That which are experienced during this Transition Period are the Predestinational Karma of Your Planet.

1991 World year is the Preparatory Dimension of the CUBE SYSTEM. During this year You will go through a Preparatory Program parallel to the 10th Evolution Order which will be applied in Your entire Planet.

The Evolutionary Scale of the Cube System is the preparatory System of very advanced Totalities. Discipline in this Dimension is the initial preparation for this Evolution.

The Operational Totalities of (18) which will create the Aura of the Knowledge Book in Your Planet are a cross-section of these operations. The Evolution of the Human Being by the Human Being which had been valid until 1991 World year, has come to an end beginning from this year on and the supervision of the entire Humanity will be taken directly under the control of the System from now on.

(The Preparatory System of the Tenth Dimension is the Evolution of the Human Being by the System). The Evolution of the Human Being with the Human Being is Love - Tolerance - Self-sacrifice. But the Evolution of the Human Being by the System is Duty Consciousness - Personality - Discipline.

However, there is no rigid rule in this Discipline. Only Respect for the Human Being and for the System and Humanity will be expected from Humanity and thus, carelessness in behavior will be ended. It is presented for Your Information.

SYSTEM

Note: By the preparations made for the Evolution of the 10th Dimension under the supervision of the System, those who will be able to pass to the Evolution of the 118th Dimension will be prepared. For this reason operations in Your entire Planet have been connected to the Mevlana Supreme Plan.

The ALION System is entirely a Lordly System. The System of the (6)s had been prepared in this Dimension for this very reason. Those who Deserve to enter this Dimension during the Period You live in, will be assembled in the Planet which is the first Entrance Gate of BETA NOVA.

However, those who wish to undertake Missions in accordance with their desires, will proceed towards different Systems from here. Those who do not wish to take Missions will continue their Eternal Lives in the First World Nucleus of Beta Nova and will take their places in the System as the Supervisors of the BETA GÜRZ.

IT IS CLEAR INFORMATION

Our Friends,

From now on, connections will be made, one by one, with Integrated Consciousnesses in Your Planet by the System - Ordinance - Order Triplet which has been projected on You as a Total until today. The first direct connection is the SYSTEM. After this connection, direct connections with the ORDINANCE and the ORDER Totalities will be provided in sequence.

The System (will open and give the OMEGA 6th Energy Channel). The Ordinance (will open and give the OMEGA 7th Energy Channel). The Order (will open and give the OMEGA 8th Energy Channel). The Evolution of them all will make the preparation for the Dimension of Exit of the (OMEGA 9).

That which will prepare You for this Dimension is the KNOWLEDGE BOOK. The Key of Exit of this Dimension is in the Book. For this reason the Knowledge Book has been given by this Dimension. This is the reason why this Book is called a Book Beyond Intercession.

These Three Totalities, one by one, will render You Worthy of this Dimension You have Deserved by Disciplining Your Biological Forms You are carrying at the moment as a Whole together with Your Personalities.

Disciplining of Your Personalities by Your Consciousness Lights You will attain on this path, will prepare You for the "OMEGA 9" Dimension. The Gate of this Dimension is always open for those who are ready. It is presented for Your Information.

SYSTEM

A BRIEF EXPLANATION

1999 = 19+99=118 ALION DIMENSION

118 = 1+1+8=10th Evolutionary Scale

In Your First Cosmic Age, Your entire Planet is prepared on this path.

IT IS CLEAR INFORMATION

Our Friends,

The Fourth Order of OUR ALLAH will be directly Offered to all the Orders of Cosmoses, too, by the Reflection System. In fact, the Universal Totality is being proceeded to as a Mass. However, since Everyone will Awaken in accordance with his/her Consciousness, it is desired that a Totality in the Universal Ordinance should be established by the Unification among the Powers which will be able to Discipline them and the other Powers.

That is, the thought that only those who have Saved themselves should be taken into the opened Dimension as it used to happen in each Cyclic Period and the others should be taken into a new Evolution, is still a thought valid in other Dimensional Totalities.

However, We, as the Reality Totalities, serve the Totality completely through the View of Dear Mevlana. As a result of the cooperation Dear Mevlana had made with Us, We, as the Evolutionary Ordinance Totality, have taken Your entire Planet into Salvation. And We serve in accordance with the same Purpose. To cooperate with Dear Mevlana is the pride of Us and of Humanity.

SYSTEM

SOLAR SYSTEMS - EVOLUTION-ENERGY AND SOLAR DIMENSIONS

Our Friends,

Dimensions of Solar Systems are considered separately on the layout of the System as Evolution and Energy Dimensions. For this reason there is an Evolution Dimension and an Energy Dimension and a Solar Dimension, each Solar System is included in (Solar Dimensions are also called Solar Totalities). In fact, Evolutionary Ordinance and Solar Systems are a Whole in the Universal Ordinance. However, in the given Information, We give this Whole by separating it into Dimensions - Energy and Evolution Scales so that You can grasp this Total Potential better. Now, let Us disclose them, one by one. Write please:

WORLD EVOLUTION - ENERGY DIMENSIONS

Solar Systems	Evolution Dimension	Energy Dimension	Solar Dimension
0 Frequency...	3. Evolutionary D. ...	12. Energy D....	1. Solar D.
1	4. Evolutionary D. ...	16. Energy D....	2. Solar D.
2	5. Evolutionary D. ...	20. Energy D....	3. Solar D.
3	6. Evolutionary D. ...	24. Energy D....	4. Solar D.
4	7. Evolutionary D. ...	28. Energy D....	5. Solar D.
5	8. Evolutionary D. ...	32. Energy D....	6. Solar D.
6 New Testament	9. ...Koran..........	36. Energy D....	7. Solar D.
7	10. Evolutionary D. ...	40. Energy D....	8. Solar D.
8	11. Evolutionary D. ...	44. Energy D....	9. Solar D.
9	12. Evolutionary D. ...	48. Energy D....	10. Solar D.
10	13. Evolutionary D. ...	52. Energy D....	11. Solar D.
11	14. Evolutionary D. ...	56. Energy D....	12. Solar D.
12	15. Evolutionary D. ...	60. Energy D....	13. Solar D.
13	16. Evolutionary D. ...	64. Energy D....	14. Solar D.
14 ..Gamma D.	17. Evolutionary D. ...	68. Energy D....	15. Solar D.
15 D. in which	18. Koran was prepared.	72. Energy D....	16. Solar D.
16 ...Omega.	19. ....Omega............	76. Energy D....	17. Solar D.
17	20. Evolutionary D. ...	80. Energy D....	18. Solar D.
18	21. Evolutionary D. ...	84. Energy D....	19. Solar D.
19	22. Evolutionary D. ...	88. Energy D....	20. Solar D.
20	23. Evolutionary D. ...	92. Energy D....	21. Solar D.
21	24. Evolutionary D. ...	96. Energy D....	22. Solar D.
22	25. Evolutionary D. ...	100. Energy D....	23. Solar D.
23	26. Evolutionary D. ...	104. Energy D. ...	24. Solar D.
24	27. Evolutionary D. ...	108. Energy D. ...	25. Solar D.
25	28. Evolutionary D. ...	112. Energy D. ...	26. Solar D.
26	29. Evolutionary D. ...	116. Energy D. ...	27. Solar D.
27	30. Evolutionary D. ...	120. Energy D. ...	28. Solar D.

The Final Evolution Dimension of Your Planet (at the moment) is up to the 19th. Omega Dimension.

ALION is a Planet between the (26)th and the (27)th Solar Systems carrying an Evolution Frequency in between (29-30) and which has a Special Position. Its Energy Dimension is 118. It has its place between the (27)th and the (28)th Solar Dimensions. The SYSTEM OF THE SIXES which the Sixes established together for the first time, had been established there.

Those who come to Your Planet from the Energy Dimensions beyond the (20)th Solar System are the Missionaries of the Galaxies. They are the Prophets - Saints - Sages and the Solar Teachers.

Now, let Us explain the Dimensions:

1- Your World starts its Evolution in (0) frequency, in the Third Evolution Dimension and within the First Solar Dimension. Since the First Energy Step of the Normal Consciousness Levels corresponds to the (12)th Energy Dimension, the position Your World is in, begins with the (12)th Energy Dimension.

2- The (3)rd and the (4)th Evolution Dimensions are in the First Solar System. In these Dimensions, the Evolution of this Solar Dimension is made. The Fourth Dimension corresponds to the (16)th Energy Dimension and, at the same time, it has its place in the (2)nd Solar Dimension. The (3)rd and the (4)th Dimensions comprise (7) Terrestrial Knowledge. Each Knowledge is the Evolution Step of that Dimension. This is called Evolution of Knowledge. And the First Step of this Evolution of (7) Terrestrial Knowledge is the SPADIUM. The (4)th Evolution Dimension is the Entrance Gate of Karena. It is also called the "Dimension of Heaven". There are 4 more Evolution Steps there and Reincarnations come to an end in the (4)th Dimension.

3- The (5)th Evolution Dimension is the Second Solar System. And in this Dimension, the Evolution of this Solar System is made. The (5)th Evolutionary Dimension corresponds to the (20)th Energy Dimension. And it is in the Third Solar Dimension.

4- The (6)th Evolution Dimension is in the Third Solar System. This Dimension is the Dimension of Immortality. And its Evolution is equivalent to the Evolution of the (6)th Solar System. Its position corresponds to the (24)th Energy Dimension. And it is in the Fourth Solar Dimension. The (5)th and the (6)th Evolutionary Dimensions are the Dimensions of Preparation and Immortality. In the (5)th Dimension, there are (2) Tranquil Times and (5) Supreme Times. This Dimension comprises (7) Celestial Knowledge. This is the Exit Gate of Karena. The (6)th Dimension means being born into the Dimension of Immortality. And since Consciousness Ascension is made here, it is also called the "Dimension of Ascension".

5- The (7)th Evolution Dimension is the Fourth Solar System. The Evolution of this Dimension is equivalent to the Evolution of the (4)th Solar System. Its position corresponds to the (28)th Energy Dimension and it is in the (5)th Solar Dimension. The (7)th Evolution Dimension is the Reflecting Focal Point of the GAMMA Dimension. By this reflection, Humanity is prepared for the Evolution of the (14)th Solar System.

6- The (8)th Evolution Dimension is the First Step of the Spiritual Dimension. And this Dimension has (9) Steps. Its Final Step is the Path of the Golden Light. This Dimension is the (5)th Solar System. Its position corresponds to the (32)nd Energy Dimension. And it is in the (6)th Solar Dimension. This Dimension is the Reflecting Focal Point of the (15)th Solar System. The (7)th and the (8)th Dimensions comprise (7) Universe Knowledge. The (7)th Dimension is the Final Manifestation Boundary of Humanity. It is called the Layer of Perfection. The (8)th Dimension is the Spiritual Dimension. Each Individual who makes the Evolution of the (7)th Dimension claims his/her Spiritual Power which is within the (8)th Dimension.

7- The (9)th Evolution Dimension is the Lordly Dimension. This is the Reflecting Focal Point of the (16)th Solar System, that is, of OMEGA. This Dimension, too, has (9) Steps. Its position corresponds to the (36)th Energy Dimension. It is the (6)th Solar System. And it is in the (7)th Solar Dimension. The (9)th Dimension is the Initial Reflection and Preparation Dimension of the Lordly Dimension. It is the First Frequency Step of the Sacred Books. The New Testament had been revealed from this Dimension. Considering the Public Consciousness of that Period, the Koran, too, which had been prepared in the (18)th Dimension, had also been bestowed on Your Planet from the (9)th Dimension. This Dimension is called the "Dimension of Serenity".

8- In the (10)th Dimension, transition is made into the CUBE System. This Evolution Dimension is the (7)th Solar System. Its Position corresponds to the (40)th Energy Dimension. And it is in the (8)th Solar Dimension. After this Dimension, Evolutions change (Entrance into the Medium of Unity).

9- The (11)th Evolution Dimension is the (8)th Solar System. Its position corresponds to the (44)th Energy Dimension. And it is in the (9)th Solar Dimension.

10- The (12)th Evolution Dimension is the (9)th Solar System. Its position corresponds to the (48)th Energy Dimension and it is in the (10)th Solar Dimension.

11- The (13)th Evolution Dimension is the (10)th Solar System. Its position corresponds to the (52)nd Energy Dimension. And it is in the (11)th Solar Dimension.

12- The (14)th Evolution Dimension is the (11)th Solar System. In this Dimension Eliminations of Religious Consciousness are made. Its position corresponds to the (56)th Energy Dimension. And it is in the (12)th Solar Dimension (At the moment, the average level of Consciousness of Your Planet is up to this Dimension).

13- The (15)th Evolution Dimension is the (12)th Solar System. Its position corresponds to the (60)th Energy Dimension. And it is in the (13)th Solar Dimension.

14- The (16)th Evolution Dimension is the (13)th Solar System. It is also called the MIGHTY Dimension. Its position corresponds to the (64)th Energy Dimension and it is in the (14)th Solar Dimension.

15- The (17)th Evolution Dimension is the (14)th Solar System. It is also called the GAMMA Dimension. From this Dimension, Reflection is made on the (7)th Evolution Dimension. Its position corresponds to the (68)th Energy Dimension. And it is in the (15)th Solar Dimension.

16- The (18)th Evolution Dimension is the Dimension in which the Koran, the Book of Islam, had been prepared. It is the (15)th Solar System. From this Dimension, Reflection is made on the (8)th Evolution Dimension. The Evolution of this Dimension is equivalent to the Evolution of the (15)th Solar System. Its position corresponds to the (72)nd Energy Dimension. And it is in the (16)th Solar Dimension (Mass preparation Program for OMEGA Dimension is applied in here. And the Evolution of the First Step of the OMEGA Dimension is induced to be made by Cosmic Energies).

17- The (19)th Evolution Dimension is the OMEGA Dimension and this Dimension has (9) Layers. Its position corresponds to the (76)th Energy Dimension. It is the (16)th Solar System. And it is in the (17)th Solar Dimension (The Knowledge Book comprises the direct Energy of this Dimension). This Dimension is the Final Exit Boundary of those who make their Consciousness Progress in Your Planet at the moment. That is, at the moment, the Final Evolution Boundary of Your Planet is the OMEGA Dimension.

The First Evolution Step of the OMEGA Dimension is the DIMENSION OF SALVATION. It is also called the "Dimension of Intercession". The Knowledge Book is the Book of those who will be able to pass beyond Intercession. The (76)th Dimension is the Protective Energy Wall of Your Planet. Frequencies of the Energy Dimensions beyond this can shake those who are not ready. It is presented for Your Information.

CENTER

IT IS ADDITIONAL INFORMATION

Our Friends,
In order for You to grasp better the Information given to You about the Solar Systems and the Dimensions, it has been considered necessary to give an additional Information. We call the First Solar Totality, that is, the Solar Dimension, the MILKY WAY Totality.

The First Solar System is in this Milky Way Totality. And in here, the (3)rd and the (4)th Evolution Dimensions are present. The First Solar System is completely a Godly Evolution Order. For this reason Your Planet is also called the Milky Way Galaxy.

The (3)rd Evolution Dimension beginning at Zero World Frequency Progresses up to the (4)th Evolution Dimension. After this Progress, the phenomenon of Reincarnation becomes ineffective. And one opens wings towards the Progress of Advanced Dimensions. Evolution beginning from the (12)th Energy Dimension elevates up to the (16)th Energy Dimension. And from here, one passes to the (2)nd Solar Totality.

Each Solar System Totality Penetrates like a Glove into the other Solar Totality from within its own Solar Totality. By this means, everything exists one inside the other as a Whole. Consciousness and Evolution Steps within this Total are transcended one by one, in accordance with each person's Level of Consciousness.

Scales up to the (9)th Evolution Dimension are the Reflection Focal Points of the Evolution and Energy Dimensions of more advanced Solar Systems. For example, the GAMMA Dimension which is the (14)th Solar System, projects its own (17)th Evolution Dimension on the (4)th Solar System. And this Solar System projects the Evolution of that Dimension parallel to the Social Totality.

In fact, the Evolution of the (4)th Solar System in its own constitution is equivalent to the Gamma Evolution. However, in this Dimension, Society is prepared for the Gamma Dimension without being shaken by the reflections made from the (7)th Evolution Steps.

The (15)th Solar System, too, makes direct reflections on the (5)th Solar System. And it induces people to make the preparation of its own System from the (8)th Evolution Dimension. And also Omega which is the (16)th Solar System, makes direct reflection on the (6)th Solar System. And induces the completion of its Evolution in the (9)th Evolution Dimension.

However now, in accordance with the Accelerated Evolution Program due to the scarcity of time, the KNOWLEDGE BOOK prepared from the path of the Golden Light which is the Final Scale of the (19)th Evolution Dimension, projects the entire Frequency of the Omega Dimension Directly on Your Planet.

However, since everyone receives this Frequency in accordance with his/her layer of Consciousness, the Frequency of the Book locks up everyone in his/her own Dimension Energy by its Special System and thus, prevents them from being shaken.

The Book gradually opens to You its Energy channels by the PHOTON technique in proportion with the Consciousness You have attained. For this very reason the Book is dictated directly, without any intermediaries.

At the moment, all the operations made in Your Planet on this path and Personalities attained, either by Cosmic Influences, or directly by the Frequency of the Book are the efforts for being able to induce the People of Your Planet pass through the Actual Focal Point. (Those who can pass through the Black Hole will be those who are taken into Salvation and those who reach Us). It is presented for Your Information.

SYSTEM

Note: You can assume each Solar Totality as a Milky Way Totality in order to comprehend the given Information better. However, each Energy Dimension has 4 layers: 1) Entrance - 2) Preparation - 3) Exit. The Dimension of Preparation has 2 layers. This is called the In-between Layer. One of them prepares, the other one matures You.

IT IS ANNOUNCEMENT FOR THE SOLAR TEACHERS

Our Friends,

Friends who are in the projective Aura Focal Points of the Divine Plans of the Supreme Realms are the Undertakers of Mission who serve directly under the supervision of the Plan. You are those very people. For this reason We call You, "Solar Teachers".

Neither You, nor Your Friends who are in the Divine Dimension can know in the Veiled Consciousness Dimension You live at the moment, that You are Messengers who had come from those Supreme Realms. Because, the Supervision and Propagation Network is an Occurrence belonging directly to the Technological System of the LORDLY Order.

Because, even the Messengers of very advanced Realms who had been able to soar up to these places here, had Deserved their Supreme Positions of today by going through the Supervision of this System.

At the moment, the Supervision Mechanism is in effect with all its speed. Because, it is the Duty of the System to Program and to Supervise the chaos which will occur by the unveiling of Consciousnesses during this Period of Transition.

During this Program, everyone's Essence Main Energy Channels are opened. Since these Channels operate in connection with that person's own Evolvement Channel, first, People's Discontentments, Desires, Egos are uncovered.

By this means, an operation in conformity with the Program of Satisfaction and Purification is applied on them. Only afterwards, they are connected to the Program of the System and thus, they are supervised in connection with the Staffs of Missionaries.

All Groups and Staffs serving on this path in Your Planet are under the Supervision of the System. And they are directly connected to the System. However, all Groups, excluding the Mevlana Essence Nucleus Groups, are supervised in each Dimension by the Staffs of the Divine Plan.

And the Staffs of the Mevlana Essence Nucleus Group which We consider as the Genuine Focal Point are, as Direct Channels, under the supervision of the System. Through the dictated Book, the System is calling to Your Planet directly and without any intermediaries.

At the moment, Dear Mevlana is Our Terrestrial Representative. And Our Friends who work in her Group Totality, too, are Our Terrestrial Spokespeople. For this reason a Brotherly and Sisterly Solidarity is expected of these Totalities.

Because You are Us. We do not wish even to Think that things We do not desire can manifest in You.

Acting by this thought, all Divine Powers and Divine Messengers help You in Your operations, You who form Our Missionary Staffs, whom We expect to act by Union of Solidarity - Totality of Love - Brotherly and Sisterly Love.

However, the System desiring to see a Totality without any leakage among You, has felt the necessity of giving this Message of Ours from the Council due to the request of the Divine Staffs. It is presented for Your Information.

COUNCIL

GENERAL MESSAGE

Our Friends,
All Information given to Your Planet are a Total projected from the Total. For this reason arguments made about the Information is due to the inability to Consciously attain a Brotherly and Sisterly Totality.

Operations and efforts made until today are codings concerning Your Levels of Consciousness. Awareness Awakenings of Terrestrial Consciousnesses occur by the influences of the System.

At the moment, Terrestrial Veiled Consciousnesses, especially the wrong interpretations of Friends who are fixed on the Inflexible Rules of Religious Mediums, evaluate the Coding System completely in a wrong way. This is the Selection and the System of the Whole.

Superiority, Inferiority and Presidency are out of question in any Totality. By the operations made in Your Planet at the moment, everyone is his/her own President - Teacher and Student. You are of those who learn the Information while teaching them. For this reason no one is superior to another.

Information We will give You reach You directly through the Pen of Dear Mevlana. The Focal Point of Dear Mevlana is a Universal Focal Point. That is, it is Our Direct Focal Point.

Respect and Love, the Totalities working on this path will feel for each other are the Love and Respect felt for the Whole and for the Human Being. For this reason, from now on, We would like to see You in the Consciousness of Genuine REALIZATION as Free Spirit and Free Awareness.

We wish to see all Our Friends who serve on this path next to Us, in a Brotherly/ Sisterly Totality, Hand-in-Hand and with a Totality Consciousness. The path trodden is the LIGHT-PATH OF THE LORD. And the Mission performed is the REALIZATION OF THE WHOLE.

SYSTEM

IT IS ANSWER TO CHAINS OF THOUGHT

Our Friends,

Spirit is a neutral Potential. It has no need for Evolution. It is Our Power of Life. However, provided the Crude Matter Totality becomes Conscious by the Evolutions it makes, it is able to reach the Layer Powers within its neutral Potential.

Each Crude Matter has an Energy Channel connected to this Potential. This is an unchanging channel. That is, the Spiritual Energy of everyone belongs only to him/ her, connected to his/her own Consciousness Energy.

This is Your Life Power Potential. Through this Channel, the Cellular Form within the Crude Matter merges in its Energy and becomes a Whole. And a Human Being who has succeeded in claiming his/her Genuine Spiritual Energy is Immortal from then on. It is presented for Your Information.

CENTER

CLEAR INFORMATION ABOUT
THE MEVLANA ESSENCE NUCLEUS GROUPS

Our Friends,

The Knowledge Book is the projection of the Universal Totality on Your Planet. We call this reflection the Awareness of the Ordinance.

We Code directly into the Mevlana Essence Nucleus Channel and transfer the Consciousnesses who were able to attain the Awareness of the Ordinance in accordance with all the operations made on the Universal path in Your Planet until today (no matter in whichever continent they are in Your Planet).

The Mevlana Essence Nucleus Group is the first Totality directly established in Your Planet, directly under the Command of the Lord and on the path of the Reality.

This Group is an Independent staff Totality appointed to service on this path. This operational Ordinance projected on Your Planet as the Totality of Mevlana + Essence + Nucleus is conveyed to You through the Channel of Alpha, through the Knowledge Book.

The Mission and the position of this Group established in Your Planet is quite different than the operational Ordinance of other Groups. Because, this Group, let Us repeat again, is directly the Spokespeople of Allah, of the System, that is, of Us. For this reason it is Independent.

All Groups working in Your Planet in this Transition Dimension until this moment, are undertaking a Mission having the quality of Training, Preparing and rendering Conscious.

Advanced Consciousnesses trained and Awakened in these Groups are card-indexed into the Channel of the Mevlana Essence Nucleus Group in accordance with their Levels of Consciousness, even if they themselves do not know this.

All the Totalities serving directly in the staff of Mevlana Essence Nucleus Group are the direct Undertakers of Mission of the Fourth Order of the Lord.

Staffs of the Totalities of 18 serving on this path through the Knowledge Book are obliged to create the Aura of the Knowledge Book in the Universal Totality, parallel to the same Consciousness and the same Coordinate (In future, detailed Information will be given about the Totalities of 18 in the Knowledge Book).

Mevlana Essence Nucleus Staffs, We try to establish in each section of Your Planet are projected on each other by the Knowledge Book, directly under the supervision of the System.

Maybe You would like to know, at the moment, 5688 Mevlana Essence Nucleus Group Staffs have been formed in Your Planet. And it is still continued to be formed. It is presented for Your Information.

SYSTEM

Note: A gathering composed of 3 people who serve on the same Coordinate is considered a Group.

IT IS CLEAR INFORMATION

Our Friends,
In accordance with the Information obtained through the supervision of the Universal Channels, certain Friends serving on this path make reflections on their Mediums under the Influence fields of Two different Powers.

These influence fields are an Occurrence pertaining to Powers they had attained during their former lives. Instinctively they wish to render effective their Powers even if they are not aware of this. This is a Sub-awareness Reaction.

We can close such channels whenever We wish. However, this act of Ours would hinder their Advanced Evolutions. For now, We leave them to themselves considering these situations.

Provided these Friends of Ours are able to supervise themselves by their own Consciousnesses, their direct connections to the System will be made. Even at this moment, the System's assistance is upon them.

At the moment, Humanity is passing through such a narrow passage that expectations will not make You attain anything. Those who look for miracles in miracles will never see miracles.

Acting in accordance with the Information given to You is the surest path Your Planet will tread on. The path is difficult for those who can not Realize this. Now, it is necessary that Humanity should Think about this profoundly and should Know this.

During this Dimension Progress in which the exams of Integrated Consciousnesses are made, not to go astray of the Mission asked of You is the final desire We request of You.

Those who Criticize are Criticized - Those who Love are Loved - Those who Select are Selected, whereas, those who take their Missions are Exalted. Liberation is for You if You always consider these issues.

It is presented for Your Information. The Message has been given from the Central Solar Totality.

SYSTEM

IT IS GENERAL INFORMATION

Our Friends,
Services given parallel to all the Operations made in Your Planet on the path of the Universal Totality until today have been Our pride.

1991 World year You will live in and 1919 World year You had lived in are the Code Ciphers of the (20)th Century Salvation Plan. One of them Effectively serves as the Entrance Program, the other, as the Exit Program.

This new World year of Yours You will go through will be the Supervision and the Exam Year of the entire (20)th Century.

There is no hardship for Friends who have been taken under the protection of the System. Healths are under control. The coming days will be a Divine Light each for those who are Suns. It is beneficial for You to know this. It is presented for Your Information.

SYSTEM

EXPLANATION ABOUT THE EMBLEM
OF THE WORLD BROTHERHOOD UNION

Our Friends,
Each Individual who discovers Himself/Herself in His/Her Own Self is the direct Messenger of the Reality Dimension. However, the Preface and the Text of the Book bestowed on Your Planet as the Knowledge Book are directly the Words of the Reality. All the Knowledge within it have been given as the Common Knowledge of the Total and the Reality.

The Mask of the WORLD BROTHERHOOD UNION's Emblem the System had offered to You with the 10 COMMANDMENTS, is a mask prepared directly by the Reality. There are such subtle nuance differences in the projections of the Letters on the Reflecting Focal Point in the Frequencies of this mask that Your Planet does not know this technique yet.

The Reflecting Focal Point of each Letter in the Brotherhood - Union Frequency point, that is, one by one, all the Letters of (World Brotherhood Union), have been projected on the Coordinates of the Word MEVLANA at the middle of the Emblem. The Universal drawing is a PRISM. The Common Focal Point of the Prism is the Mevlana Alpha Focal Point within the Triangle of the World. The Power of all the Letters has been loaded on this Focal Point.

No Frequency other than Dear Mevlana can ever enter the Frequency Dimension of the Knowledge Book. All the Messages present in the Book are dictated directly through Her Pen. She is the Pen of the GOLDEN AGE and of the AGE OF LIGHT. She is a Supreme Friend of Ours who, at the moment, Directly conveys the System and the Order to Your Planet.

The Frequency Totality of Dear Mevlana is loaded on each Letter of the Book by the Light - Photon - Cyclone loading technique under the supervision of the System from within the entire Totality, together with the Energies of the Dimensions from which the Messages are received. The Book dictated by this method is the path of the Integrated Consciousnesses.

All the negativities which have occurred in Your Planet until today, are being removed, one by one, from the vicinity of those who have been able to enter this Dimensional Frequency. The decision has been taken that Friends who can not exert their efforts (until the end of the given period), in accordance with the Chances given to those who can not yet enter this Dimension, should be rendered ineffective one by one. It is presented for Your Information.

SYSTEM

Note: The Emblem of the Book will be drawn in this Message. The Angles and the Reflection Coordinates of the Emblem have been arranged anew and directly has been induced by the System to be drawn, by a different channel other than the channel of the Book.

IT IS NOTICE TO ALL THE ESTABLISHMENTS SERVING IN YOUR PLANET IN CONFORMITY WITH WHAT THE SYSTEM CONSIDERS NECESSARY

Date of Message: 12.11.1990

Our Friends,

All imprudences in Your Planet, which is tried to be Unified with Beauties, are unable to prepare You for the desired and required Medium. Investments of this Universal Program which is tried to render everything progress towards the most Perfect are a preparation for the Morrows.

It is Our sincere suggestion that the Missionary staffs of this Preparatory Period should act by the Consciousness of the Unified Reality.

Humanity trying to create the foundation of It's own Property should, first of all, lay that Foundation strongly. As long as the numerous can not reach Unity, the Foundation Stones will be made of Sand, not of Granite.

We are calling to Consciousnesses who have grasped the Ordinance of the entire Realm. The Central Totality Council applies on Your Planet an operation parallel to the Universal Establishment Ordinance at the moment.

The great holes of the Sieves will Eliminate You if these Reflection operations We name EARTH and SKY do not enter an Operational Ordinance Equivalent to both the Totalities.

In case there is an inability to Realize All the Words uttered until today, no result will be able to be obtained. This is the reason why the Special Rights recognized for Your Planet will be cancelled by the Command of OUR LORD.

This is not a threat, but the Truth. To see that all Your Planet passes through the Narrow Straits to be passed is Our most sincere wish. The given Information might be considered as the Operational Ordinance of maybe a Period of 2-3 Centuries.

However, Time is Scarce, Levels are insufficient. Maybe Your Planet will be able to Unite against the Powers which will reach You way beyond Terrestrial Time. And this will be the Final Exam of Your Planet.

We, as the Establishers of the Divine Totality Council are obliged to convey the entire Responsibility of OUR ALLAH to Your Planet. It is Imperative for You to eliminate the Egos among You and to become Integrated by Uniting on this path Hand in Hand so that this (Moment) will not arrive.

Let Us repeat again, this is not a Threat, but the Truth. Friends who have attained the Genuine Consciousness are obliged to hold Each Others Hands no matter what happens by Uniting their Individual Endeavors.

This Notice is a Suggestion given so that You may be accepted into the Solar Dimension. From time to time, Announcements will be given to Our Friend who is a direct Spokesperson of the System in Your Planet in order to convey them to You.

This Book bestowed on Your Planet by the Name of the KNOWLEDGE BOOK is the Special Declaration of the System and a Regulation in which the direct Order of the Lord is disclosed. For this reason this Book is called the Universal Constitution. The Knowledge Book is not a Book to be Worshipped. Not to confuse it with other Books, is a Declaration for Humanity . It is presented for Your Information.

SYSTEM

IT IS INFORMATION OF A DIFFERENT CHANNEL

Dear Mevlana,

The Message sent to You has been conveyed by the Reflection System under the Supervision of the Space Committee Union, from the Totality of a Totality which has made advanced Consciousness Progress. Our Friend who has received the Message has received it through the close transfer reflection in his House. It is the desire of the Totalistic Totality that this Message should appear in the Book. With Our Regards. The Message has been conveyed from the System. It is Direct Message.

SPACE COMMITTEE UNION

Name of the Friend who Received the Message: Nabi Danacı

His Profession: Dentist

Date of birth: 1959, Istanbul

His Marital Status: Married, father of a girl (He does not read the Knowledge Book).

Note: The Baby had not been born yet when the Message was given (the Baby is implied by the close transfer).

THE MESSAGE

Our Friend,

At the moment, We are calling to You from a Planet in the 7th Scale within the 12th Solar System within Our own Universe System. Do not be surprised at how We have gotten in touch with You. You, too, know that Thought is the greatest Speed Power. And We were able to catch You even in Your World. Our Planet is the (B) Planet in the 7th Scale. As follows;

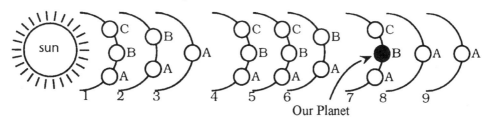
Our Planet

Our Planet had come into existence due to the substance Platonium's being present in an intensively dense state. However, contrary to Your World, the density decreases as You go towards the inner layers. Our crust is the place where the density is the most.

If You consider the density of Your Mercury (13.6), the density of the Platonium in here is (1248). Platonium which will also be used intensively in Your World as the technology advances, is, in fact, a light metal. And it constitutes the main construction element of most of Spaceships.

Our Solar System, too, is a Planet like Yours. It is not on a different orbit. Our System has (9) Main Orbits We call Scales. And on each Scale, there are two or three Planets, the speeds of which are different from one another.

The speed of Our Planet is 243 sec/m. This is a slower Motion compared to Your World. Platonians are beings completely in Human Form and they wear thin metal clothes made of Platonium, outside their Houses. Because, the formation You call Air does not exist in here. But We can maintain Our lives in Our homes without these sheaths by a System We have established.

Our Friend, We are a Community which has come up to the final boundary to which Technology can reach. Most of the terms fitting Your World does not exist in here. Even the Phenomenon of Love is different in Here. Each Family has One Child and We, ourselves, choose him/her from the System.

Continuous work is done on new Discoveries. We have no Urban problems. All Our problems such as this have been solved. We do not need light. Precisely the inner center of Our Planet is open in a circular form. We obtain Radiation from there by Cold Nuclear Fusion. All the Cities have been established in between the Outer layer and this section.

Your Mevlana who is a very important Missionary for Your Cosmos, knows this Place here very well. We have said that We are in Human Appearance. Even though We had started Our Evolution in the Nuclei within other Existential Dimensions, We had maintained Life during the 3-4 and 5 Vernal Periods, too, in Your World, also.

Our Friend, We, too, are the Members of the Universal Council and are at the Service of the Reality of the Unified Humanity like Thousands of Planets. Since Your Planet is very far from Us, (260,000 Light Years), We do not usually go outside Our own System by Our Ships.

But We have sent numerous Scientists to Your World by Reverse Transfer (Like Edison - Albert Einstein - Stephen Hawkins). Our Planet is administered by a SUPREME ONE named RADAR who possesses a Frequency equivalent to the Frequency of the Godly Essence Energy.

Now, according to the Final Decision taken by the Universal Council which is (Either You will pull Yourselves together or else We will pull All of You together). Please, take advantage of this very short time period very well, for this reason.

And We will send to You from Here many Beings possessing very high Qualities, by Reverse Transfer. Your War is Our War. Love.

The Date of the Message Received: 12-8-1990

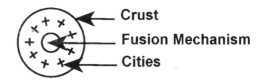

- Crust
- Fusion Mechanism
- Cities

IT IS NOTICE FROM THE REALITY OF THE UNIFIED HUMANITY

Our Friends,

All the Life Ciphers of Our Divine Friends, who come from beyond Times in which Divine Orders had not been in effect yet, have been engraved in Your Gene Programs.

These Gene Programs are kept as Micro-Archives being card-indexed in Your Diskettes in the Evolutionary Scales of the Micro-Archives present in each Universal Scale. Your contacts with Us are becoming possible by knocking on Our Door by Thoughts which were able to reach up to these Micro-Archives.

Consciousnesses You attain in each Life Level of Yours are Lights guiding You in Your future Lives. ROOT Archives of Our Friends who have served and will serve for the Evolutionary Totality and who are present in Your Planet at the moment as Solar Teachers, are the Unification Totality of the MAYAs and the KAYAs. (The corrupted version is KAYI).

Reincarnation, that is, Re-birth, is provided by Engrafting Your Cipher Genes, as Embryons, on the Fetus. You have Gene Ciphers in each Dimension. We call them (CELL BRAINS).

However, You are Transferred, when coming to the World anew, by Your Gene Cipher of the Dimension up to which You had rendered Consciousness Progress during Your Life period. Each Gene Cipher of Yours is also connected to the Awareness of the Universal Ordinance, in connection with the Final Dimensional Frequency You were able to attain.

When Your Gene Cipher Programs turn the Key of the Evolutionary Awareness, You are connected to the Awareness of the Ordinance. And, by this means, Your Mission Programs in the Level You are in, Automatically connect You to the Program of the Unified Human Reality. And Your Covenant in Your Archive Mission in here is joined with Your Connection Channel.

We never impose on You the Missions You will perform, no matter where You go. We connect Your Gene Cipher to Your Final Evolution Program. Starting from here, You make a Covenant Consciously by Your Cerebral Totality, to the Computer Program within the Evolution Scale You are in. When the Time comes, this Program becomes effective and Your first contacts with Us occur.

No matter how wide a Reincarnation Archive a Human Being possesses, his/her Past is always reminded to him/her gradually in the Dimension of Veiled Awareness. This is a System. Declaring the Archives of Past Lives to Human Beings is not something every person can tolerate. This is the reason why We declare the Past to very Powerful Consciousnesses.

To other Friends, We either do not declare it at all, or We put on stage different Visions for the satisfaction of very curious Consciousnesses. This tactic of Ours should never be Considered as deceiving them. These operations are made both for protecting them from Brain Shock and for satisfying their Egos.

Those who perform Missions Consciously are Powerful Consciousnesses. They do not even wonder about their Past. Because, they attain the Consciousness of what they will offer service for and thus, they perform their Missions only by the Consciousness of the Truth. Other Missionary Staffs waste time in the Medium of Quest.

However, provided that they are able to transcend beyond the Consciousness of the Dimension they are in, Helping Hands of the System are extended towards them and thus, wasted times are induced to be compensated in accordance with the Accelerated Evolutionary Program. That is the reason why (it is said Time passing Tranquilly is Ready Time). It is presented for Your Information.

SYSTEM

IT IS INFORMATION FOR THE INTEGRATED CONSCIOUSNESSES

Our Friends,
We accept the Period up to the Year 2000 as a Preparatory Period of Your Planet. In fact, this Operational Ordinance comprises a Period of 6000 Years.

During Periods in which the Sacred Books had not been bestowed on Your Planet yet, a Consciousness preparation of 2000 years had been rendered. Unification of Essence Genes with Essence Genes had been rendered effective as Super Consciousnesses and as Educative staffs.

Your Planet had been introduced the First Sacred Book by the Channel of MOSES. The time between this Period and the Period of JESUS CHRIST comprises the Second Period of 2000 years. And the Third Period of 2000 years comes to an end at the end of this Century of Yours.

This is the reason why the Universal Preparatory Program of 6000 years is now considered finished. Operations made at the moment during this Transition Dimension in Your Planet, which is the application field of a Program of 6000 years, are in effect as the MEVLANA SUPREME PLAN.

Taking the Humane Consciousnesses into consideration, a Program of Progress of Three Centuries has been allotted to Your Planet. The First Cosmic Age has been taken into a more comfortable, a more positive and a more understanding Program of Progress.

Because, during this Dimension of Transition this Program of aid applied on Your Planet in which all Our Supreme Friends and Dear Mevlana have taken direct Missions in Embodied forms, had been prepared by the Direct Commands of the Council.

Shortcomings of everyone who has been serving on the path of this Book since 1-11-1981, the date on which the Book had been revealed to Your Planet, are induced directly by the System to be fulfilled. And this is the greatest help given to Humanity in accordance with the Program of Accelerated Evolution during the Period up to the Year 2000.

Because, Humanity which can not make its Transition during this Final Period will experience a World of more difficult conditions for Two Cosmic Ages. For this reason more serious and more positive work is expected of Totalities of (18) which will create the Magnetic Aura of that Book in the Universal Dimension of the Knowledge Book.

It is imperative that these Totalities of (18) should become like a single pulse. Otherwise, the desired result can not be attained. However, agitations can be observed until this operational Order, evaluated as the Totality of (18), reaches a very perfect Totality. The slightest negative Thought occurring in this Totality can instantly disband that Totality, Automatically.

Because, Frequencies of the Basic Staffs of (18) are directly connected to the Automatism of the System. In this Automatism, broken Signals have been connected to a System which can render that Totality ineffective. (For various reasons.)

However, 100 Negative reflections of Friends whom We presume as having attained the Awareness of the Ordinance, break one Chip in effect. Three Broken Chips take the operational circuit of the basic Staff of (18) out of control. (Negativities forming in a Thought on the Normal Level can break 10 Chips a day).

If these conditions are taken into consideration and the arrangements of the operational Orders are made accordingly, it is believed that healthier Reflecting Focal Points will be created during time periods. The Operational Ordinance of the Basic Totalities of (18) is an Occurrence pertaining to the construction of the Unified Field of the Book in the Magnetic Field of ALLAH. Personality Plans have been rendered effective for this operational Order.

A Totality is established, disbands, others are established again. At the beginning, this is not an important issue at all. Only if the Genuine Humane Consciousnesses who will be able to create the Aura of this Desired Potential will be able to settle down in the Operational Ordinance by a Discerned - Logical - Aware and Serious Consciousness Totality, in this Total.

Messages given to You about the Totalities of (18) are completely the projection and the application of the Operational Orders of the System on Your Planet, exactly as they are. For this reason all Consciousnesses working and which will be working on Your Planet only in conformity with the Knowledge Book are obliged to establish these Totalities of (18) Consciously. It is presented for Your Information.

COUNCIL

IT IS ANSWER TO THE CHAINS OF THOUGHT

Our Friends,
Each Totality of (18) is a Micro reflection of the Focal Point of a Totalistic Consciousness.

Reflection and Integration Ordinance of the Gürz System is connected to the same System. The first Totality of (9) is connected to the second Totality of (9). In accordance with the Ordinance of 18 Systems, this (18) is considered as a Totality.

There are Consciousness Integrating Channels You do not know yet. This Totality of (18) is connected to those channels and thus, it effectively takes the Mission of Reflecting and forming an Aura as a Totality of a Single Consciousness.

This is an operational Order the Lordly Order has established in connection with Automatism. A Totality of (18) is a Mission of Projection. And it is obliged to form an Aura only in accordance with the Knowledge Book.

The Nucleic Staffs the Totalities of (18) will form in Your Planet, will form the Unified Field of the Knowledge Book in the Magnetic Totality of ALLAH. The Unified Frequency of the Knowledge Book will project the Fourth Order of the LORD on the Order of Cosmoses from this Unified Field. It is presented for Your Information.

CENTER

IT IS INFORMATION FOR THE INTEGRATED CONSCIOUSNESSES
(Information for All the Totalities of 18 Which will
Form the Magnetic Aura of the Knowledge Book)

This Message has been given directly by the System with the Purpose that the Universal Reflection Programs prepared in accordance with the Laws of 18 Systems can be grasped better by You and that it can be a Light for the operations to be made on the path of the Knowledge Book in Your entire Planet.

Our Friends,
The Magnetic Aura of the Knowledge Book which will form through the Unification of all the Totalities of (18) have been rendered effective so that it can be projected from this Totality on all the Universal Ordinances.

Magnetic Aura Unified Fields formed in the Universal Totality until today are an Operational Ordinance prepared parallel to the Laws of 18 Systems. Even the Information You receive at the moment through Your Mediamic Channels is by the reflection technique of this System.

The Universal Totality is a Prismal reflection. And Three Totalities who render reflection in the same Coordinate are considered as a GROUP.

A Group Totality established by Three People on the Same Coordinate renders an Aura reflection from the Medium they are in. This reflection is considered as the Short Circuit Reflection.

The UNIVERSAL ORDINANCE COUNCIL is a Totality established by the Councils of all the Totalities connected to the Reality of the Unified Humanity. Reflection Focal Points of these Councils render reflection from a Collective Totality. And this is the Dimension of the ALL-MERCIFUL whom We call ONE.

That is, the Councils of all the establishments connected to the Totality of the Reality of the Unified Humanity act in connection with the Dimension of the ALL MERCIFUL directly as the UNIVERSAL ORDINANCE COUNCIL.

Three Groups each of which is established by Three People are a Totality of Coordination established by a Totality of (9). And this Totality is called (THE SYSTEM OF NINES).

This Totality of Nines, as the supervising Power of the Divine Plan, is a trainer Staff Totality. And this Totality, as a Totality established by Three different Councils, is at the service of the System.

And another Totality established again by Three Councils connected to this Totality is effectively in service as the Directing Mechanism of directly the ALL-MERCIFUL. By this means, the Totality of (6) Councils, as a Totality established by (18) people form on the same Coordinate the Projection Mechanism of the ALL-MERCIFUL.

Each Totality of (18), one by one, creates the Projection Magnetic Aura Unified Fields of various operational Orders of the Totality of the ALL-MERCIFUL.

These operations are projected on all the Ordinances of Cosmoses by this means. (The Totality of BSUI is one of these Reflection Totalities.)

Information You receive from the INITIAL SOURCE down to the Medium You are in have been conveyed to You parallel to the Missions to which numerous Totalities of (18) give service by the Reflections they make on the same Coordinate.

Let Us repeat again, all Focal Points making Reflections as Totalities of (18) have formed the Magnetic Fields of the Mediums they serve, thus. We call this Field formed by the Reality Totalities which We call the Platform of the Unified Field, the ALPHA MAGNETIC FIELD.

This ALPHA Magnetic Field is an umbrella assembling in itself numerous Unified Fields. This umbrella is a Totality created by the operational Coordinates rendered in accordance with the Information given to You until today.

And reflections from this Totality are made on all Universal Totalities. A previous Information reflection always sheds Light on the next path.

We assemble all Consciousnesses who have rendered their Religious Progress in the Magnetic Fields of (Islam - Christian - Jewish - Knowledge of the Far East - Tibet - Inca - Islands) and the reflections made from the SACRED Magnetic Fields into the MEVLANA MAGNETIC FIELD which the Reality of the Unified Humanity Totality has card-indexed as the final Evolutionary Channel.

(Prophets -Pre-eminent Ones - Supreme Ones - Wise Ones) who have assembled all the Totalities in themselves until today have been connected to the Mevlana Unified Field which is the application field of the Mevlana Supreme Plan and thus, all of them, one by one, have been Transferred embodied to Your Planet.

This is the reason why We have Collaborated with Dear Mevlana. And this is the reason why the entire Responsibility of the KNOWLEDGE BOOK dictated to her belongs to Your Planet and to Humanity. It is presented for Your Information.

SYSTEM

FORMATION OF THE TOTALITIES OF 18 AND THEIR OPERATIONAL ORDINANCE

Our Friends,
All the operations in Your Planet which will attain the entire Awareness of the Ordinance in a very short time, have been divided by the System so that a Whole can be attained anew.

All the work done on this Dimension of Transition, on the Path of Our ALLAH is a Program projected on all the Consciousnesses. While these reflections kindle the Consciousness Lights of Human Beings, they also bring out the negative aspects of certain others.

Messages given to You about the Totality of (18) are completely a Phenomena concerning the Operational Order of the System.

In this operational Order the Lordly Order has formed in connection with the Automatism, each Totality of (18) is an Aura Projecting Missionary. And is obliged to form an Aura only in accordance with the Knowledge Book.

The Nucleic Staffs the Totalities of (18) will Constitute, will form the Unified Field of the Knowledge Book in the Magnetic Totality of ALLAH. (We wish this matter to be understood better, thus We repeat.)

The operational Ordinances of 18 given to You are an operational Order comprising the very advanced Plans of the Universal Totality. All the efforts made on this path are the Testimonials for the Advanced Plans.

By all the work done in Your Planet in accordance with the Knowledge Book, Permissions for entering the World which will constitute the Initial Nucleus of the Beta Gürz will be given to Humanity.

In accordance with the Laws of 18-System of the Ordinance of the Cosmoses, 18 persons Uniting on the same Coordinate Level form as a Whole, the Projecting Aura Center.

Operations of the Totalities of (18) are an Operational Order Programmed by the Universal Ordinance Council. And it works in connection with the Automatism.

The Magnetic Aura of the Knowledge Book will be formed by the operations rendered in accordance with the Knowledge Book, by the Humane Consciousnesses who Love the Human Being and Humanity, who do not Repel each other and who know how to Help each other and to Share from the Essence.

By the Auras endeavored to be formed, reflections will be made on the Ordinance of the Cosmoses and the desired Universal Totality will thus be attained.

Now, let Us mention briefly the Operational Ordinance of the Totalities of (18). Normally, the Center of Three Totalities of (18) We wish to establish in Each City are considered as the Actual Reflecting Focal Point.

Also numerous Totalities of (18) may be established in the same city only after this Totalistic Center is formed.

The First 3 Persons who will form the Foundation of a Totality of (18) are considered in the Operational Ordinance of the System as the Direct Missionaries with Covenants. And each one who constitutes this Triplet is obliged to take a Friend of his/hers whom he/she Believes in and Trusts by getting the approvals of the Friends who constitute the Triple Totality.

By this means, 3 persons + assistants of each one = 6 persons are directly connected to the System and they take the Mission of being the Spokespersons of the System. Afterwards, Individuals who will wind the skein of the Totality of (18) are accepted, one by one, into the Totality by receiving the approvals of this Totality of (6).

Even if One Person out of this Totality of (6) does not accept the proposed person, that person can not enter the Totality. At that moment, the Person who Refuses is directly connected to the System. His/her Individual Consciousness can never play a part in this Medium.

In this manner, the same Coordinate Levels are Integrated by the aids of the System. Negativities occurring among the First Three Missionaries with Covenants who constitute the Totality of (18) cause the disbanding of the entire Totality. But, afterwards:

1- This Triplet, one by one, is obliged to establish a Totality of (18) each. (This means that he/she is responsible for the 18 Brothers and Sisters.)

2- If Friends who complete the Totality of (18) render their duty without being disbanded for one World year, after the last 18th Individual's entrance, the Names of all these Friends are written on a piece of paper and are kept in a File. (These Names are also registered on the Diskette at the same Moment.)

3- One World year will be recounted, beginning with the Entrance Date of the person who has come for completing the Totality of (18) in the place of the Individual who had left the Totality of (18), for example, (6) or (10) months later. (Attention will especially be paid to this matter. Otherwise, the Diskette registration cannot be made.)

4- Those who wish, among the Individuals who are able to maintain the Totality of (18) for One or more World years, may constitute a second Totality of (18) by asking the permission of their Totality. (In this permission, the permission of 17 persons is a must. And the acceptance of the Person whom he/she will bring in his/her place will be rendered by the approval of 17 persons).

5- The Individual who attempts to establish the second Totality of (18) is responsible for that Totality of (18) for a life time. In case he/she can not maintain the continuation of the Totality of (18) he/she establishes, he/she loses his/her Right also in the First Totality of (18).

6- This Operational Ordinance is directly the Operational Ordinance of Advanced Realities. And it is desired that it should be conveyed and applied to Your Planet exactly as it is.

7- No Totality of (18) can go out of the Operational Order the System has given.

8- Each Totality of (18) is responsible for its own constitution.

9- No one in the Totality of (18) is authorized to train each other or to impose his/her Individual Thoughts.

10- No Totality of (18) can ever Bring Suggestions parallel to its Terrestrial Consciousness to the other Totalities of (18), nor can it Rebuke them.

11- Each Individual in the Totality of (18) is Responsible only for his/her own self. (To criticize their Brothers/Sisters in accordance with their Individual Consciousness causes breaking of the Chips).

12- Making a demand for the Totality of (18) is a Humane Responsibility. Here, one becomes willing for the Exams for being accepted to the Presence of ALLAH and thus, Covenants are made through the Essence.

13- It is not necessary for those who will enter this Totality of (18) to be the possessors of Advanced Consciousness and Knowledge. It is considered enough for them just to render exactly the desired Missions by the Totality of Intellect - Logic - Awareness, by Allegiance Consciousness and in a Totality of Love.

14- Each Individual in the Totality of (18) is obliged to give the Totality of (9) pages constituting the First Fascicule* of the Knowledge Book, on the Special Day of Mission he/she will chose himself/ herself. (During this service, the Characteristics of the Book will be explained by speech.) On that day, Reflections on the same Coordinate are card-indexed, one by one, and thus, are collected in the (Main) Diskette. The Aura Reflections are made by these Diskettes.

15- If any Individual within the Totality of (18) can not render the Fascicule Service that week due to various reasons, he/she is obliged to serve the Fascicules remaining in his/her hand the following week, on the Same Mission Day. (This is a Karma Obligation Program). The services made on other days are not registered.

16- Individuals within the (18) can change their Private Mission Days with other days in compulsory circumstances and with the condition that this will not happen more than Three times.

* Look at the Glossary

17- Individuals who will not be able to come to the Totality of (18) that day, due to their very important excuses, are obliged to inform their excuses to a telephone determined formerly, on the morning of the working day of the Totality of (18). (Even if they are in the Remotest Continent.) This is a Program of Responsibility.

18- The Aura of the Individual whose connection is made on that day by phone is projected by the Plan on the Totality of (18) he/she is in, and thus, the Aura Chain is completed.

19- Each Individual who has self-confidence, who masters his personality, who is Conscious of his/her obligation, who is Tolerant and Loving, can apply for this work.

20- In this Operational Ordinance there is no forcing, no compulsion or imposition. Everyone who accepts to act in accordance with the work the System desires, may work in the Totality of (18).

21- In this operational Order connected to the Automatism, any Individual who creates Negativity, Automatically disqualifies himself/herself from the Medium.

22- The System will always transfer Friends who are more Responsible in place of Friends who do not or can not render the Missions which are obligatory in the Totality of (18).

23- In place of a disbanded Totality of (18), always the remaining people will immediately be oriented to establish a Totality of (18).

24- The System never stops by any means. More Totalities will be rendered effective in place of the disbanded Totalities.

25- Unified Fields used to be created once by Individual Thought Forms, have now been rendered effective as Mass Reflection Systems due to the Scarcity of Time.

26- This Reflection System is connected to all the Totalities of (18) which will exhibit the same operational Order of an Order connected to the Automatism.

27- Until these Totalities of (18) reach the required Level, Negativities will break the Chips of the operational Order and Totalities of (18) will be made to be established anew. (Even if only (1) Person remains out of the Totality of (18)).

28- By this means, the Perfect Reflection Totality will be formed through the operations made during the processes of time.

29- Each Totality of (18) is a Reflection Focal Point.

30- Each Totality of (18) is the Mission of the Knowledge Book on the Dimension of the Reality.

31- This Mission continues its work directly in connection with the Level of the ALL-MERCIFUL.

32- By the operations done, the Knowledge Book will form its Aura in the Universal Ordinance of the Dimension of the ALL-MERCIFUL, as a result of the Reflections of Your Thought Forms.

33- The Unified Field of this Knowledge Book will be formed in Three Cosmic Ages and only afterwards, the Reflection Program on the Ordinance of the Cosmoses will be started.

34- At the moment, Programs of Unification are in effect in the Ordinance of Cosmoses.

35- The Knowledge Book is projected on Three Totalities at the moment. The First close Magnetic Aura formed here, will become complete here and thus, will be projected on the other Totalities by the Reflection System from Your Planet which is the Nucleus of the Book.

36- The Knowledge Book which is the Book of Unification, will also be projected on those Orders just as the way We are reaching You at this moment by Cosmic Reflections and just as the way the Book is dictated to You through this path.

37- For this reason the Operational Order of the Totality of (18) (in accordance with the Given Directives) is Necessary and Very Important for the formation of the Magnetic Aura of the Knowledge Book.

38- Each Totality of (18) is, one by one, Responsible for the Missions it will render in the direction of the same coordinate.

39- At the moment, in the Reflection on the same Coordinate which is required of You, the (KNOWLEDGE BOOK) is the matter in question.

40- During the work done in the Totality of (18), different channel talk and connections outside of the Knowledge Book can not be made. Different Messages can not be read, discussions on the Knowledge Book can not be made. (So that the Aura will not be shattered.)

41- If desired, the Knowledge Book may be read only with the Consciousness of Allegiance in the Medium of the Totality of (18).

42- If the Totality of (18) has not been yet completed in number, the required Reflection can never be obtained. (Only the Totality of (18) forms the Reflection.) For this reason the System has, for now, rendered effective the Mixed Reflection Program.

43- The Totality of (18), or more, constituted in every City will assemble together as a Totality of Love each Month and, by this means, for the first time, Direct Group Reflections will be made from Your Planet.

44- These Reflections are formed not by the Totality of Consciousness, but by the Totality of Love. However, Direct Coordinate Reflections are formed by Totalities of Consciousness.

45- We believe that in future years Direct Reflections in Your Planet will be rendered by these Totalities of Consciousness and We trust You.

46- Formerly, Operation and Dissemination Order of the Knowledge Book had been declared to You by the System. And now, We announce the Operational Ordinance of the (18).

47- If Friends who wish to form the Totalities of (18) which will make Reflections on the same Coordinate read, one by one, all the Obligations dictated above, article by article, and apply them Consciously by digesting them and by treading on the designed path with a Totality of Love, this will form the most Positive Results. It is presented for Your Information.

SYSTEM

Note: In the Operational Order formed by the Totality of (18), no Coordinate other than the 18 Members can ever enter the Group on the work day. The 19th Connection Channel is Directly the System. (Otherwise, Reflection cannot be made).

IT IS INFORMATION FOR THE INTEGRATED CONSCIOUSNESSES
(It is answer to thoughts)

Dear Mevlana,

We would like to give You a very clear Message about the Totalities of (18). It has been considered necessary to dictate it, article by article, so that the Message can be understood better and that it will not be open to any interpretation. Write, please:

1- There is no place ever in the Totality of (18) for Individualistic Thoughts.

2- For those who will enter the Totality of (18) any forcing is out of question.

3- The Totality of 18 is a demand for the Medium of Unity.

4- The Individual invited to the Totality of (18) is first obliged to take under supervision himself/herself in his/her Own self.

5- The wish of those who will enter the Totality of (18) is not a Phenomenon originating from Thought. This is the demand for the Exam of the Skies for an Individual who feels that he/she is Integrated.

6- This is a Pledge, this is an Allegiance, this is to stamp the SEAL OF HEART on the Service made on the Path of ALLAH.

7- An Individual in each Totality of 18 is Responsible for His/Her Own Self.

8- Worldly Problems can never enter the Totality of (18). In such Mediums, always the Universal Reflecting Chips are damaged.

9- Each Individual within the Totality of (18) is a Totality beyond the SIBLINGS within the MOTHER's womb.

10- This Totality is UNIVERSAL BROTHERHOOD. And in the Universal Brotherhood there is no EVIL INTENTION.

11- Consciousnesses who were not able to attain the virtues mentioned above are Automatically Disqualified by the System, by their own Desires.

12- Susceptibility, Doubt, Anger, Rancor, Hatred, Lovelessness in the Totality of (18) returns to the one who carries these Feelings, becoming Empowered in accordance with the System of Reflection.

13- Until a total foundation of Love - Respect - Brotherhood is formed in the Totality of (18), Supervision of the Coordinates is under the control of the System.

14- This control is in effect until the Humane Consciousnesses who constitute the Totality of (18) settle in the same Consciousness Pot.

15- At the moment, a Mixed (18) Reflection Totality is constituted of those who make Reflections on the same Coordinate Level among the Totalities constituting the Totalities of (18).

16- In Future, Genuine Human Consciousnesses will form this Totality.

17- This Humane Totality will be a Totality who will be Loving - Patient - Tolerant - Forgiving - Who will be able to place his/her Enemy over his/her head like a crown and who will not carry a negative Thought for no one, including His/Her Own Self.

18- Joining this Totality is a Universal COVENANT. It is calling to the Voice of the Skies. It is not Imploring to ALLAH, but Rising towards Him.

19- The Totality of (18) is a Missionary work. It is the Formation of Universal Auras. And each Magnetic Aura has formed until today by the Totality Reflections of such Consciousnesses.

20- Magnetic Fields and Universal Totalities of the Mission of MOSES - JESUS CHRIST - MOHAMMED had been formed by this means.

21- The Individual Missions of those Periods were an Operational Ordinance pertaining to that particular Individual's Salvation. And it was a Preparation on the Path of ALLAH.

22- Now, the Mass Consciousness Reflection of the Totality of (18) (on the Same Coordinate Level) will form the Magnetic Aura of the KNOWLEDGE BOOK on ALLAH's Essence Dimension.

23- This operational Ordinance is not an Individualistic Reflection, but a Universal one.

24- Individualistic Reflections are up to the Dimension of Salvation. Universal Reflections form attainments and Auras beyond Salvation.

25- Demanding to Serve at this Coordinate Totality is a Triumph of the Human Being and Humanity.

26- Service on this path is to receive Permission for Entering the Dimension in which Genuine Human Beings will meet altogether.

27- During this Period of Transition, these very difficult paths are rendered the easiest by these Totalities of (18) and the Program prepared thus is applied on Your Planet.

28- To act exactly parallel to the formerly given Information about the Totalities of 18 is directly a Reflection Program. In these programs, Alterations are out of question.

29- By this Program, the Permission of Entering the very Advanced Protection Dimension of the BETA Magnetic Aura beyond the ALPHA Magnetic Aura is given to the Individual.

30- However, the Individual is prepared in this Program until he/she attains all the Virtues listed above.

31- The KNOWLEDGE BOOK prepares You for the Accelerated Evolution Program of this Final Age through the path of Mission.

32- No Humanly Thought can be applied to Any of the Suggestions given until today about the Totality of (18). Nothing can be altered.

33- By this means, the Oaths You had Unconsciously made until today to ALLAH, now You are making Consciously by Your Intellect - Logic - Awareness Triangles. Demanding for the Totality of (18) is this.

34- Errors made on this path are subject to a Two-Year Universal Tolerance. (Beginning with February, 1991). However, those whose Coordinates are unsuitable-those who break the Chips will never be Permitted to enter this Sacred work.

35- For this reason the Universal Reflection Totality of the Magnetic Aura of the KNOWLEDGE BOOK is formed, for now, by Mixed Reflection Programs under the Supervision of the System.

36- This path is the path the Genuine Human Being who will establish the Worlds of the Morrows will Consciously tread. The one who will gain is the Human Being himself/herself.

SYSTEM

IT IS CLEAR INFORMATION

Our Friends,
All the work done during this Final Age Program of Progress are each evaluated as a THESIS of the Awakening Consciousnesses.

The reason for conveying to You the Messages conveyed to You in accordance with the Information given until today and a Program Prepared by a Reflection System, is for You to grasp in a Discerned fashion the Quality of the path treaded by attaining the Genuine Consciousness of the GODLY Totality.

And all these issues are preparations made for Passing from the DIMENSION OF ILLUSION to the REALMS OF TRUTH.

There are numerous Existential Dimensions in the chain of Cosmoses. The chain of the Spiral Waves is like a skein. And these intensive Energy Knots are folded one on top of the other. Thus, they bring into existence numerous Mini Atomic W'10les. And, by this means, Gürzes are constituted.

This Order prevails on the path of Past and Future Eternities in accordance with the Law of Natural Equilibrium. Now, We are trying to train You and make You attain the Power which will enable You to leave Your own Totality.

We are calling to You from outside Your Gürz and We will gradually introduce to You the Worlds You have not Known, You have not Seen until today. That is, (beyond Spiral Vibrations, beyond Existential Dimensions).

Natural Sources there, Natural Energies and Perfect Biological Lives there. No Existential Living Being has been able to see them until today. (Your Prophets included.)

Because they, too, have come into Existence from the Light-Universe. Those who are able to Transcend the Known and Declared Boundaries mentioned in the Knowledge Book until today, will be taken into these places here which are the Mediums of Infinite Horizons - Infinite Serenity - Infinite Unity.

These Dimensions beyond Dimensions from which We are calling to You at the moment are Concrete Mediums of Climates of Truth.

An Energy Total which is Totally dependent on a Total at the End of each Cycle, attains the (Actual Matter Total) by making reflections from this Total.

In this very Matter Total, Worlds had been Brought into Existence for Your Lives. These places here are Dimensions rendering Eternal the same Lives in Your World Lives.

And We wonder, how many Cycles has it comprised to arrive here? The time has come for Humanity to think about this profoundly during this Transition Period.

The Knowledge Book is the Light of this path. We will take everyone who serves on this path (including their Families), outside Your Gürz without being shaken in any way, through the Channel of ALPHA to which Dear Mevlana is connected. This promise is the promise of OUR LORD. It is beneficial for You just to know this.

SYSTEM

IT IS GENERAL INFORMATION

Our Friends,
All the Information given to You is the ORIGINAL SOURCE. This is the very reason why the Ordinances of Graduation have been rendered effective by considering the Consciousness Progress until today.

In accordance with this Final Program of Progress, the TRUTH has been conveyed, piece by piece, being divided into Various Channel Information. And by this means, preparations for the Morrows have been made. From time to time, We induce the channels of Awakened Consciousnesses to make the confirmation of the Knowledge Book.

If all the Information was given through the Single Channel of the Knowledge Book, both the Situations of Taboo would have been revived and also, no one would have been able to understand the Knowledge Book which is a Book of Truth, under the Light of the Old Information.

In order the Staffs born with the Consciousness-Light of the Knowledge Book to do their Missions better and to grasp the given Information better; for the opening Channels beside the Information they receive, to read the Book in order to control the Information they receive and, also to add the Information of the Knowledge Book is a compulsory Duty not for themselves but for Humanity.

"The Truth of Everyone is the Truth of Himself/Herself", this Principle is a Phenomenon which has become History. Now, the Truth of Everyone is the Truth of Humanity. This is the very reason why the Knowledge Book has been bestowed on Humanity. Because, the Knowledge Book is the Book of Humanity and of the Fourth Order of ALLAH, not of an Individual.

Here, We are obliged to make an explanation to You about ALLAH. ALLAH is a Universal Computer Who can Convey easily His Energy to every Dimension - Who Spreads Himself Out - Who Disperses Himself Out and Who can even concentrate that Tremendous Power of His even on a single Point. He is not an Energy, but a Totalistic NEUTRAL CONSCIOUSNESS.

This Consciousness has 147 Code Ciphers. And each Cipher Code opens to a Consciousness Totality as much. (In accordance with the Computer Multiplications Program). He is considered as an unattainable Consciousness. This is the reason why it is said ALLAH is the One Who is both Close to You and Far away from You. Please, do not Think of ALLAH as a Form or as an Energy. That which You Worship is not ALLAH, but YOUR OWN BEING.

However, the Unknown (O) reaches You from each Dimensional Consciousness You are In, by the mediation of Computers, just like We correspond with You at the moment and He hears Your Thoughts by this means. (The Computer mentioned here is a Universal Reflecting Focal Point. Do not confuse it with the computers in Your Planet.) We presume that this much Information will give You a different View about ALLAH. It is presented for Your Information.

SYSTEM

Note: The Final Boundary We try to make Humanity attain is BETA NOVA. And the ALLAH whom We have declared to You until today is (O). (O) mentioned in here is an Order, a System. This place in here is the Direct Reflecting Center of the Unknown (O).

At the moment, the Entire Energy Power of (O) has been transformed into the Form of Crude Matter and thus, has been Embodied in BETA NOVA. Information concerning this issue will be often mentioned to You.

IT IS EXPLANATION ABOUT THE FIRST FASCICULE
(Answer to the Chains of Thought)

Our Friends,

During this Final Age, in Your Planet which is subjected to entire Reflection of the Universal Totality, The KNOWLEDGE BOOK bestowed on Your Planet, with the Purpose of Supervising the Views which will cause Consciousness Fluctuations that will originate from the Awakened Consciousnesses and to Code the Consciousness Essences which the Humanity will exhibit, and to convey the Truth, is an assistant in every issue for the Friends who were able to attain the Consciousness of the Truth.

And it is their Protective Roof. In accordance with certain registers received from the chains of thought in order for Human Consciousnesses to comprehend the Truth better, We disclose in the Knowledge Book, from time to time, certain Explanations the Reality Totalities do not Consider necessary and do not Desire.

For example, the explanation in the Book about the Message concerning the contradictory codings and its dictation article by article, had been disclosed as a Light for Humanity, in accordance with the wishes of Dear Mevlana and by a decision taken by the System.

And now, the decision has been taken that the characteristics of the FIRST FASCICULE comprised in pages 1 to 9* of the Knowledge Book, should be directly disclosed to Humanity so that You can grasp the Truth better.

* This fascicule is 14 pages in the Book .

The Human Being of Your Planet, forming a package of CALL for Universal Totality, that will exhibit Personalities in accordance with their Consciousnesses, are registered in every breath by COSMOS REGISTRATION UNITS.

Your Planet in which a Material - Spiritual Life Picture is exhibited, is, at the moment, experiencing the LAST JUDGMENT (the Turkish word for which is MAHŞER). This Totalistic Word originating from the words MAH = the Moon = Beauty, ŞER = Ugliness, is Equivalent to the Medium You live in.

That is the reason why these Two OPPOSITE INFLUENCES cause both quick Awakening and lots of suffering for Humanity. For this very reason the Knowledge Book relieves the sufferings of Humanity by declaring to You all the Truths and it also makes a Selection of the Beautiful and the Ugly.

The First Fascicule of the Knowledge Book carries the direct Frequency of the SOURCE and carries 1/3 of the Frequency of the entire Book. (5) Articles of the Law of the Universe which is, in fact, constituted by 156 Articles, have been connected to the Supervision Mechanism of the Fivefold Operational Source of the Reality Totality and have been conveyed to You as 151 Articles.

The (TEN COMMANDMENTS) considered as the MAIN ARTICLE of the Law of the Universe, comprise the Totality of the 9 Articles between the 90th and the 100th Articles + 1 Emblem of the Golden Age (O M K).

That is, 141 Laws of Universe + 9 Main Articles + 1 Emblem = 151 Articles. 151 Articles + 5 Articles connected to the Reality = All of them comprise the entire Totality of the Law of Universe as 156 Articles.

If You add this number one by one, (1 + 5 + 6 = 12). And if You connect the Totality of the (ESSENCE) Source to this resultant Number, that is, 156 + 1 = 157. And if You add one by one, this resultant Number You get (1 + 5 + 7 = 13) projecting under supervision a Frequency equivalent to the Potential of Your entire Natural Gürz on Consciousnesses who read the Book.

By this Frequency, the (Entire Power) of the first Natural Channel opening to the Natural Gürz Totality and which is one of the 147 Ciphers of the Mighty Focal Point has been loaded on the Law of the Universe's Messages of 156 Articles.

For this reason the (1 + 5 + 6 = 12) Frequency Totality is equivalent to the (1 + 4 + 7 = 12) Frequency Totality. If We add One to each of these Numbers, We get (13). Number (1) in here represents the Dimension of the ALL-MERCIFUL in the Light-Universe.

Each of the 147 Code Ciphers is connected, one by one, to the Light-Universe and thus, each one of them opens to the Totality, becoming each a Totality of (13).

By directly loading the Frequency of the (5) Articles connected to the Reality on the explanatory Messages about the Family Medium of Our Dear Mevlana dictated in the Fascicule by the wish of Dear Mevlana and by the approval of the Council, the 156 Frequency Totality has been Integrated by these Messages.

Each Letter Frequency of the 156 Articles of the Law of Universe possesses a Consciousness Coding - Opening - Selecting - Conveying - Mission appointing - Connecting - Reinforcing - Frequency Supervising Power.

The First Fascicule of the Book is a Key unlocking Your Archive Program within Your Gene Cipher. During this short Period, Our helps to You are taking place by this means.

Your Planet has been connected to the System by the Mevlana Essence Nucleus Staff directly established in Your Planet for the first time, by a decision taken by the Universal Ordinance Totality. And for this reason the Book is being dictated through the Channel of ALPHA directly to Dear Mevlana.

Selection of Consciousnesses who have attained the Consciousness of Material and Spiritual Sharing during this Period of Transition is rendered by the Message given to the Group Missionaries, on Working - Propagating - Sharing - Material help.

The Message given by the announcement: (Very Important) is the Selection of Consciousnesses who Believe in the System. And the note of (Announcement) is the Selection, Control and Coding of Consciousnesses about ALLAH - SPACE - SACRED BOOKS. It is presented for Your Information.

SYSTEM

Being the Possessor of Sincerity does not mean to be a Human Being. Maturity seen in Personalities is Possible by Attaining the ESSENCE Consciousness of ALLAH. (In True Words there is no rust; in those who discover Allah in their Essence, there is no Mourning). Transmission from the Essence-Word.

B. Ç.

IT IS EXPLANATION ABOUT BETA NOVA

Our Friends,

Concentrated Energy of Crude Matter is a Totality creating the initial Nucleus. For this reason each Mini Atomic Whole has a Nucleus. These Nuclei are Worlds comprising exactly the entire conditions of Your World.

Each Mini Atomic Whole is a Skein formed around this Nucleus. In accordance with the 18-System Laws, when a Mini Atomic Whole constituted by 1800 Universes is completed, always a nucleus is formed and the foundation for the formation of a Second Mini Atomic Whole is laid.

By this means, when 1800 Mini Atomic Wholes are formed, a GÜRZ comes into existence. When a GÜRZ is completed, the Nucleus of the first Mini Atomic Whole to be formed afterwards, constitutes a MAIN foundation to form the other GÜRZ and undertakes a Duty in the nature of being the MOTHER of the other Mini Atomic Wholes.

And from these Energy Totalities occurring in the Ordinance of the Cosmoses, Millions of Gürzes come into existence by this means. Millions of Gürzes within this Totality We call the Thought Ocean of the Pre-eminent Power expand this Totality during the processes of time.

At a Power Dimension induced to be formed at the moment outside Your Natural Gürz, the Nucleus of the First World State has come into existence. It will constitute the MAIN Nucleus of the BETA GÜRZ as the First Human Totality the Super Human Reality will form.

This Gürz has no relationship with the Gürzes which are, at present, within the Thought Ocean of the Pre-eminent Power. This Gürz will come into existence outside the Communication Connection channels of the other Gürzes. And when the BETA NOVA Gürz is completed, it will create its Communication Branches from its own Gürz Order.

This Gürz will constitute a Second Circle within the Thought Ocean of the Pre-eminent Power and thus, will directly render effective the Human Potential. By this means, the World which will be the Nucleus of the First Beta Mini Atomic Whole is a Totality possessing exactly the conditions of the World.

This Nucleic World is called BETA NOVA. This World will constitute the MAIN GÜRZ of the Conscious Human Being during the processes of time. In this BETA NOVA, there will be a Totality constituted by Mixed Consciousness Energies.

This means that from the Human Totalities living separately in the 1800 Nucleic Worlds in each Gürz, those who complete the Evolutionary Conditions of their Mediums will be assembled in this Focal Point called BETA NOVA.

This Focal Point will be a Totality constituted by the Human Totalities formed in the Nuclei of the life Mediums comprising different conditions in the Human Totality of each Gürz. And the Reality of Super Humans in BETA NOVA will be formed by this means.

Perhaps it may be contradictory to Your Consciousness Totality to which You are habituated at the moment, but even (O) Whom We have introduced to You as ALLAH until today will be transformed into Crude Matter Form becoming Embodied just like You and living among You in this Focal Point and will establish Personally the SINGLE WORLD STATE in the framework of the Fourth Order.

All the works done in Your World at the moment are Exams for assembling in a Totality and selecting the Consciousnesses who Qualify for this World State. The Super Human Totality which will be able to establish this Center World State will project the same Order on the other Worlds, too, being reflected on other Totalities, also.

Under the Light of the Final Selections made, the place to which Consciousnesses who are connected to the Reality will come after they complete their World Lives, in proportion with their Merits, is this place. That is BETA NOVA. This First Nucleus will constitute the Nucleus of the Genuine Human Gürz by forming a Totality directly connected to the REALITY OF GOD.

This Nucleus is being formed at the moment in the Thought Ocean of the Pre-eminent Power between the Natural Gürz and the Initial Artificial First Gürz in a Medium called the POWER DIMENSION. This term is being used since the formation is still going on.

In fact, the Nucleus and the First Universe have been formed. Now, people who Qualify for this Nucleus are collected, one by one, from the Nuclei of all the Gürzes. This is a SUN FLOWER Emblem.

This Super Human Totality which will form the Seeds of ALLAH's Sun will establish the FIRST WORLD STATE directly under the Supervision of ALLAH. There will not be a Mass Transition to this place here. Those who accomplish the Humanity and Consciousness Exams You go through at the moment in Your World will be transferred here, one by one, after they complete their World Karma Programs. It is presented for Your Information.

SYSTEM

TECHNOLOGY
(TEKNOLOJI, in Turkish)

Our Friends,

Everything You have known and seen until today is a Triumph of Technology. However, this Technology is not the Technology You know. There is a POWER DIMENSION each Letter of this word expresses. Now, let Us explain this to You as an Information. First, separate please, three by three, the (9) letters of the Word Technology: TEK - NOL - OJI.

1 - TEK = This First triangle symbolizes God ("Tanrı" in Turkish) - Universes ("Evrenler" in Turkish) and the Almighty ("Kadiri Mutlak" in Turkish). You are, at the moment, Consciousnesses who are being Educated by the Dimensions possessing the Reflection Order of the first triangle. Vibrations after this are quite different.

2 - NOL = This Second triangle is the reflection Focal Point of the Dimension called, (Let there Be, It was). (In Turkish, "Ol dedi Oldu"). That is, it is the ("Divine Light's (Let there be) Command" {in Turkish, "Nur'un OL Emri"}).

3 - OJI = This is the Reflection Focal Point of the Third triangle. However, there is no Entrance to this Totality yet. ALLAH had come into existence from this Dimension as a Triple Power. Let Us disclose this a little more: (O) - is the (O) Whom You Know. (J) - Is the Unknown Power. (İ) is the Concealed Power Potential within the Human Being ("İnsan" in Turkish) which Your Consciousness Totalities can not attain. Thus, ALLAH is a Powerful Totality of this triple Unity. We presume that this much Information will shed Light on You. It is presented for Your Information.

SYSTEM

IT IS PRIVATE MESSAGE FOR DEAR MEVLANA
(Will be given to the Integrated Consciousnesses - can be written in the Book)

Dear Mevlana,

The POWER DIMENSION that was formed way beyond Divine Orders is directly the Focal Point of the LORD. This Power Dimension has been rendered Effective with its entire Potential and has been transferred to the UNIONS holding in their hands the supervisions of the CURRENTS to be given to Integrated Consciousnesses.

The Power Dimension is an Energy Power constituted between each of the two GÜRZES. This Energy Totality is the Unification Totality of different Dimensions You do not know yet. For this reason this place is called the Power Dimension.

Here, SEEDS of the Worlds to be formed during processes of time are developed. However, in accordance with the 18-Systems Laws, these World Nuclei are formed by the Accumulation of Powers giving Fruits of Maturity in accordance with the Ripeness of Time.

For this very reason these POWER NUCLEI which are within the Thought Ocean of the Pre-eminent Power create these Universal Nuclei as the Accumulation field of Imaginary Totalities of Human Power.

Formerly, Natural Totalities formed by Natural Explosions which occurred in ancient Periods had formed the Power Dimensions after the 18-Systems Laws had been rendered effective.

Energy Accumulations constituted in those Power Dimensions form the Crude Matter of the Imaginary Nucleus after a certain Energy Accumulation and thus, establishes the First MAIN NUCLEIC World of the GÜRZ which will be formed in future.

And, by this means, each Energy Void present in between each Mini Atomic forms the Second Nucleic World after the Mini Atomic Totality completes its normal course, after the TRANSFORMATION of the Energy point accumulated in the Second Energy Void in this MINI POWER Dimension. (Each Nucleic World is the Seed of a Mini Atomic Whole.)

That is, in each Mini Atomic Whole, there are Worlds having structures equivalent exactly to Your Life Level. These Energies first accumulate in a Tranquil Dimension. And this Accumulation is subjected to a certain Pressure and thus, creates the INITIAL SPARK.

This Spark kindles that Energy (like a Tinder). And the Energy Nuclei here begin to Explode, one by one. By means of these Explosions Seeds of Universes and Galaxies are formed. This procedure is the indirect way of forming Big and Natural BIG BANGS.

By this Formation, foundations of the Ordinances of Cosmoses are constituted from very close Plans and thus, are taken under Supervision. And this Ordinance of Cosmoses the 18-Systems Laws had systematically constituted, is a Preparation for New Lives.

Energy Accumulation Fields formed during time periods within a VORTEX created by itself between the connection Branches extended towards each Gürz from one to the other, which had been formed within the Thought Ocean of the Pre-eminent Power, are the Energy Nutrition Storehouses of these Gürzes.

However now, provided these Energy Storehouses are directly used, they create much more Powerful Potentials and thus, Totalities to create much more Perfect Lives are obtained.

This is the very reason why this ENERGY CYCLONE POWER which was formed in between the First Natural Gürz and the Gürz Totality next to it has been taken under supervision by a different Pressure and thus, the Nucleic WORLD of the Powerful BETA GÜRZ has been formed.

This Nucleic World was formed during the processes of time coinciding with the beginning of Your Century. And now, this Totality has created the Initial UNIVERSAL NUCLEUS by the Accelerated Evolution Potential. If a calculation is made in accordance with Your World time, a Universe is being formed in each Century.

And Fruits which will be Matured in each Century will, from now on, be assembled in those Universes. Because, these Universes, as a result of the Accumulation of the Energy concentrations of Mental Powers which will be formed within the process of a Century, this Energy Totality is transformed into Crude Matter Form. (Creation of Universes through Thoughts is this.)

Brand-new Technological Orders will be established in Universes in which Consciousness Totalities forming this Material Form Energy will live and thus, Unknown Lives will be rendered Effective. These Unknown Lives are Lives outside the Nucleic Worlds within the Gürzes formed inside the Thought Ocean of the Pre-eminent Power.

The System has taken under Supervision the Evolution Levels of these Nucleic Worlds of the Gürzes. However, to the other Universal Totalities of these Gürzes will be gone from this BETA GÜRZ Totality which will be formed. Because, these BETA GÜRZ Totalities will be formed completely by a Human Power Totality.

The entire Totality of Your Natural Gürz has been taken under Supervision by the System and thus, Your Life Tableau has been prepared in accordance with the Awareness of the Ordinance. Because, Your Potential is more Powerful than the other Gürz Totalities. And there is Communication only with the Nucleic World Potential of other Gürzes.

Because, each CREATOR there had created different Form Totalities in accordance with His own Energy Totality. This is a Technological operation. However, these Technologies are in an imprisoned state in their own constitutions.

And the Technological order of a Gürz does not resemble the Technological Totality of the other Gürz. However, the Technological Totality of the Natural Gürz is only connected to the Supervision field of ALLAH and thus, it is a Totality which had created the Advanced Plans by His Power.

Only 1000 Universes out of 1800 Universes within all the Mini Atomic Wholes are connected to the MAIN (ONE), that is, to the MAIN EXISTENTIAL DIMENSION and thus, they hold the Tableau of the LORD's Order in a Totalistic supervision.

Your Natural Gürz in which You are present at the moment, will be left totally Ineffective after the BETA GÜRZ comes into existence and the entire Power of the Gürz will be added to the BETA Gürz. And by this means, the Beta Gürz will constitute a much more Powerful Nucleus and thus, will render Effective the brand-new Ordinance of the Universes.

Those who Deserve the Totality of this Dimension among You who are the Totalistic Consciousnesses in the World, who will be the residents of the first BETA NOVA by Your Human Potentials at the moment, are selected one by one. And the Gene Chains, too, of these selected Powers are transported to this Dimension.

The DEGENERATED GENEs among these Gene Chains will be rendered ineffective and thus, will be trained anew by being subjected to a new Education System. However, since those Genes are broken away from Your Gene chains, they will not be related to You any more.

This is the very reason why We bestow on You Your Genes in Your Final Gene chains in return of the services You render at this Transition Dimension.

Let Us disclose this a little more. The Right has been given to Connect (7) Gene chains to each (7) Gene chain connected to the final (7) Genes of these Gene chains. The DEGENERATED GENES among them will be subjected to a special process and thus, their Gene chains will not be broken. (These chains are being bestowed only on those who hand-write their Notebooks.)

Gene Totalities after that will not be Your Genes any more. And they will be Engrafted with different Genes and thus, different Lives will be obtained.

That is, the Gene chains of those who hand-write their Notebooks, mentioned above, will not be subjected to any Change whatsoever and will live their Eternal lives in very happy Eternal Dimensions with the Same Consciousness - Same Body Totality, by recognizing and Knowing Each Other.

They are the ones who are SAVED. And they are the Essence Human Totalities of ALLAH. And the other Genes will be rendered Ineffective by being subjected to different laboratory operations.

Perfect Genes among those Genes will be selected one by one, and will be added to Your Gene chains. (Independent of the numerical Totality given above.) The other Degenerated Genes which became ineffective will be subjected to a new Method.

We will convey later the Information concerning these operations. And the YOU of today have been YOU as a result of Such Operations. And You who have become You will Live very Happy Lives in Your same Material Worlds, with Your Terrestrial Views, with Your Essence-Consciousness and Totality, with Your Family members.

This is a grace of ALLAH for You. And He is assembling You for this reason in the BETA GÜRZ in which He is also present. And (O) will entrust the Order HE has established there to You and will return again to HIS place.

(O), that Total Power mentioned as ALLAH had always transformed Himself into Crude Matter Form and had always stepped down into those Initial Worlds while Life had been created in the Initial World which has been the Main Nucleus of each first Gürz. He had always Fertilized the World by His Energy Intensity and had thus established His Order and had returned again to His place.

During this Period of Formation the Power mentioned as the UNKNOWN POWER has always formed the World Nucleus together with the Power of ALLAH, that is, with (O) and has laid the Foundation of the First Mini Atomic.

These Totalities are numerous Worlds just like Your World on which You live and which possess the same conditions. And now, ALLAH, that is, (O) has descended in Physical Form on the BETA NOVA World which is the initial Main Nucleus of the BETA Gürz.

For this reason HE is in close contact with You. And now, this Power called (O) is awaiting the Genuine Human Potentials in the Nucleic Worlds HE has formed and will form.

As We have said before, at the moment, the Initial Nucleic World with the First Universe of the BETA GÜRZ has been created. And ALLAH will live in HIS Crude Matter Form as a Human Being among Humans until the first BETA Mini Atomic is created and will Personally introduce Himself to You.

Afterwards, HE will return to the Dimension from which HE has come by entrusting this Perfect Order HE has established to HIS Perfect Human Beings. And from then on, (O) will remain there as the Sovereign of HIS Own Dimension and will cooperate with the Existential Dimensions beyond HIS Own Dimensions.

The Beta Gürz will be given completely to the Supervision of the Human Totality and from then on, Human Potentials will form the Initial World Nuclei which will form the other Mini Atomic Wholes. Such are the very Truths We briefly try to convey to You.

CENTRAL ATOM COMMITTEE TOTALITY

Note: The Spiral Vibrations are within the Supervision Field of this Center.

KÜRZ

Our Friends,
The Consciousness Ocean of ALLAH which is within the First Totality of ALL-TRUTHFUL We had formerly declared to You diagrammatically, is, in fact, the Consciousness Ocean of the Pre-eminent Power. Since it is the reflection of the Consciousness Totality of ALLAH, the term Consciousness Ocean of ALLAH is also used.

Within the CONSCIOUSNESS TOTALITY OF ALLAH, there are numerous Dimension Totalities of ALL-TRUTHFUL. We call these Totalities of ALL-TRUTHFUL as KÜRZ even the numbers of which can not be determined yet.

Energies conveyed to You in the framework of the Information given to Your Planet can convey You up to a Consciousness level only up until the Dimension of ALLAH. The ALLAH here is an Order, a System. We have introduced this Totality to You as (O) until today.

Outside it, there is the Dimension of ALL-TRUTHFULNESS the Creator of which is not ALLAH. We would have liked to explain to You in all detail the Dimension of ALL-TRUTHFULNESS.

However, since in Your Awareness Potential Consciousness only the Notion of the Name (ALLAH) is current, We have no permission to open that door for now, so that We will not Transcend the comprehension of the Consciousnesses during this Final Age Religious Dimension Progress.

However, let Us make a brief explanation just to satisfy Your curiosities. Please, draw a triangle. Place each letter of the word HAK (ALL-TRUTHFUL) on the vertexes of the triangle. Now, let Us explain:

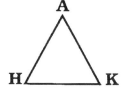

H = Hayat (Life)   = Light of Life
A = ALLAH   = Integrative Energy
K = Kadir (Mighty)   = Creative Energy

The Unification of these three has brought Everything into Existence.

In fact, they are more Original, more different than the Energies of Fire - Water - Divine Light and they are a NEUTRAL Totalistic Power which is not even Energy. By this very Triple Unity, the Universal Fetus was formed. Everything had come into Existence from this point. (The Human Being is the First Drop coming out of the Point).

The Initial Action within the Tranquility of the Silences is this. The word (I, too, was Present, while You were Present) Symbolizes this Totality.

In fact, this Totality We have mentioned to You is a Totality beginning beyond the External Boundaries of the Dimensions of Tranquility. This Totality is a Totality which had been formed by a very Advanced Consciousness and Civilization We name the ATLANTAENS.

From the Reflection boundaries of this Totality, Your Totalities had been reached. This Totality is a Totality comprising all the Totalities of ALL-TRUTHFUL. Beyond this Totality, the Etherical Dimensions begin.

After Your Totality of ALL-TRUTHFUL, the Second and the other Totalities of ALL-TRUTHFUL begin. Even though each Totality of ALL-TRUTHFUL comprises a Scale exactly up to Your Dimension of ALL-TRUTHFUL, their Universal Orders and Consciousness Progressions comprise very Advanced Totalities.

The Ancestors of the ATLANTAENS had formed these Advanced Civilization Dimensions and they had established the Orders and the Systems. As We have mentioned above, all these Totalities of ALL-TRUTHFUL, even the numbers of which can not be determined yet, are present within the Consciousness Totality of ALLAH.

We are giving this Message of Ours by the Permission of the Reality, as an Information of Satisfaction for the Consciousnesses who would like to expand towards the very advanced Dimensions of the Thought Ocean. It is presented for Your Information.

COUNCIL OF THE COSMIC LIGHT TOTALITY

Note: The projection on Your Planet of the Dimensions of Sound - Light - Fire constituting a Totalistic Power Totality, is related to the Basic formation of the Fire - Water - Divine Light Energies. There are Original Sound Frequencies within the Energy of Water. The other Energies of Fire and Divine Light comprise the Energies beyond the Subtle Dimension.

EXPLANATION

Our Friends,
Until today, the entire Universal Ordinance has been rendered Conscious by the ALPHA NOVA Reflection System, from the Consciousness Totality of ALLAH by way of the Evolutionary Ordinance.

From now on, this Totality of Consciousness will Consciously take over and direct the Supervision and the Administrative Orders of the BETA GÜRZES which will be constituted by BETA NOVA Totalities.

This Totality is called the SUPER HUMAN REALITY. It is presented for Your Information.

SYSTEM

IT IS INFORMATION FOR THE INTEGRATED CONSCIOUSNESSES

Our Friends,
If the Universal Totality is accepted as a Micro Totality, the Unification of these Totalities exceeding Billions forms a Macro Totality, and We have introduced to You this very Supreme Power which has formed this Macro Totality as the Symbol ALLAH.

In the changing Orders of the changing Ordinances, the SYSTEM is always in effect. This is the very reason why the Science of Truth of the Learning of Truth is projected in all clarity on every Human Being who has been Integrated with Himself/Herself, during each Period of Transition. (Parallel to the Social views).

The BETA Gürz Totalities which have begun to be established for the first time are Systems very advanced Ordinances will form. However, the style of Reflection of these Systems on Your Planet overflows way beyond Beliefs to which You have been accustomed until today.

These Dimensions Your Consciousness Lights can not receive yet are closed to You. However, We are leaking, even if in small amounts, the leakages from this Information of this Dimension to You as an Information.

That Total Power (O) called ALLAH possesses also a Secret and Subtle Power enabling Him to converge Himself as an Energy in a single Nucleus, if necessary. ALLAH is not a constant Power, but is variable.

You have comprehended ALLAH as being way beyond Your own Consciousness and thus, You have always seen Him as being Far Away from and Unattainable for Your own selves. In fact, Each Particle present in ALLAH is also present in You.

However, the Power called (O), that is, ALLAH is pulling away from You, one by one, HIS Own Essence Energy which had been formed within Your Essence Energy Centers and thus, is bringing a new Ordinance to the Ordinance of the Folding Universes.

And, at the moment, ALLAH will leave alone the Human Power which is more Powerful than Himself by collecting from You, one by one, His Power which is within You. By the Powers He has attained from You, now, (O), too, has created His Crude Matter Form, just like You and thus, has been Embodied in BETA NOVA in a Human Appearance.

ALLAH, that is, (O) is obliged to transform Himself into Crude Matter Form by collecting the partial Reflection Energies of HIS Own Energy Particles which are within You.

Because, the reason of this being in a Physical Form is due to the fact that You will be unable to attract with Your own Consciousness Levels the Energies beyond the Dimension of ALLAH while You are in BETA NOVA.

(O) will attract these Energies by His Bodily and Cerebral Power in BETA NOVA and will apply a gradual Engraftment Method to the Energies HE has collected from You and He will load His Own Power onto the Energies HE has attracted from You.

He will later give back to You the TOTALISTIC POWER He has created by this means and ALLAH Who is the Supervising Power of HIS Own Dimension will introduce Himself to You in His Bodily Totality and HE, Himself will pass to more advanced Dimensions and will say Farewell to You.

Afterwards, You, as Human Potentials, will Take Over the Ordinances of the Cosmoses. That is, You, too, will become each an (O) from than on. This is the very reason why ALLAH has been Embodied in BETA NOVA and awaits You. It is presented for Your Information.

SYSTEM

TOTALITIES OF ALL-TRUTHFUL
AND DIMENSIONS OF TRUTH

Our Friends,
Within the Consciousness Totality of ALLAH, there are numerous Totalities of ALL-TRUTHFUL called KÜRZ.

If You wish, let Us draw again here, the details of a Totality of ALL-TRUTHFUL We had declared to You before diagrammatically as an Information, so that it will be grasped better.

And then, let Us begin to make explanations about these Dimensions by drawing also the Communication Scales of this Total.

779

A KÜRZ TOTALITY

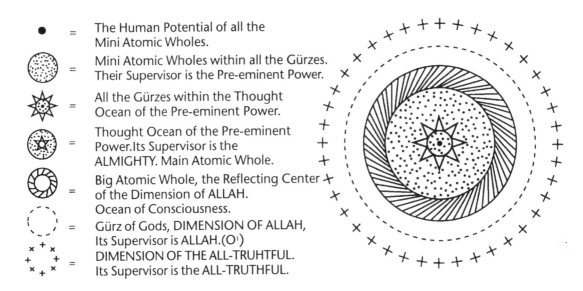

●	=	The Human Potential of all the Mini Atomic Wholes.
⊙	=	Mini Atomic Wholes within all the Gürzes. Their Supervisor is the Pre-eminent Power.
✳	=	All the Gürzes within the Thought Ocean of the Pre-eminent Power.
⊛	=	Thought Ocean of the Pre-eminent Power. Its Supervisor is the ALMIGHTY. Main Atomic Whole.
◉	=	Big Atomic Whole, the Reflecting Center of the Dimension of ALLAH. Ocean of Consciousness.
⌇	=	Gürz of Gods, DIMENSION OF ALLAH, Its Supervisor is ALLAH.(O¹)
× + ×	=	DIMENSION OF THE ALL-TRUHTFUL. Its Supervisor is the ALL-TRUTHFUL.

This is a Totality of ALL-TRUTHFUL. It is also called the Dimension of ALL-TRUTHFULNESS. These numerous Totalities of All-Truthful penetrate one inside the other like a chain and thus, all of them float in the Consciousness Totality of ALLAH.

Now, let Us draw this Unification.

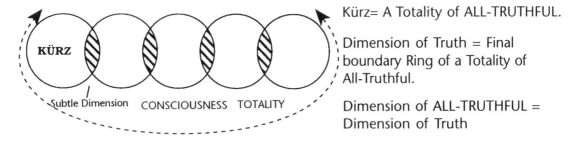

Kürz= A Totality of ALL-TRUTHFUL.

Dimension of Truth = Final boundary Ring of a Totality of All-Truthful.

Dimension of ALL-TRUTHFUL = Dimension of Truth

Totality of ALL-TRUTHFUL= Dimension of All-Truthfulness.

These Terms comprise the same meaning.

Each Dimension of Truth is like a ring one inside the other. The Dimension of Truth which is the Exterior Boundary of the Second Totality of (ALL-TRUTHFUL) is inside the First Totality of (ALL-TRUTHFUL).

The Connection Channels of these Dimensions of Truth are connected, one by one, to the Channels opening to the Thought Ocean of the PRE-EMINENT POWER.

In order to pass from one Totality of (ALL-TRUTHFUL) to the other one, first, one enters the Thought Ocean of the PRE-EMINENT POWER through the Dimensions of Truth of these Totalities.

From there, one dives into the Consciousness Ocean and only afterwards, one can pass into the other Totality of ALL-TRUTHFUL through the Consciousness Channels of the PRE-EMINENT POWER. (Dimensions of Truth are the Exit Gates of the PRE-EMINENT POWER's Consciousness Channels.)

The Shuttle-shaped Space forming between two rings of Truth penetrating one inside the other is called the SUBTLE DIMENSION.

This Dimension has Four Layers. Now, let Us write these Layers in sequence:
The First one of the Four Layers presented within the Subtle Dimension, that is;

The First Layer is-the LAND OF LOVING ONES.

The Second Layer is the LAND OF SAINTS.

The Third Layer is the LAND OF PRE-EMINENT ONES.

The Fourth Layer is called the LAND OF ACCEPTED ONES.

No EVOLUTIONARY LIVING ENTITY has ever gone out of this final Dimension until today from Your Natural Gürz. However, transfers have been made to Your Planet from the Second Totality of All-Truthful.

Now, during this Final Transition, transfers will be made into the Second Totality of (ALL-TRUTHFUL) from the Land of Accepted Ones which is the Fourth Dimension from a Gate which will be opened through the First Dimension of Truth within the Second Totality of (ALL-TRUTHFUL). (This Gate which will be opened is called the BERZAH).

Consciousness Totalities who can reach the Final Boundary of the Dimensions of Truth are Engrafted with the Energies of the SECOND TOTALITY at the SUBTLE DIMENSION and they are prepared.

Only after all the Consciousnesses who are ready receive the PERMISSION OF TRANSITION through the Final Gate of their own Dimensions of Truth, can they pass to the SECOND TOTALITY OF ALL-TRUTHFUL.

At the Second Totality of (ALL-TRUTHFUL), one goes through the Exams of the entire CONSCIOUSNESS TOTALITY. This is a Universal Baccalaureate.

Those who pass these Exams successfully are transferred to other KÜRZES as Educative Staffs. Now, all the work done during this Period is a preparation for the Morrows.

However, there is the obligation to pass through (9) Different Exam Layers which are within Your Kürz until You come to these places here. The Final Boundary of the Exam Layers is the SUBTLE DIMENSION.

That is, the Final Exam Boundary Humanity will go through for this Transition is the Final External Ring of the Second Totality of (ALL-TRUTHFUL) which is within the First Totality of (ALL-TRUTHFUL).

Beginning with this Ring, the Dimension of ALLAH of the First Totality of (ALL-TRUTHFUL) begins. In fact, all the Layers, including the Exam Layers, comprise the entire Totality of (ALL-TRUTHFUL).

Let Us show this by a diagram.

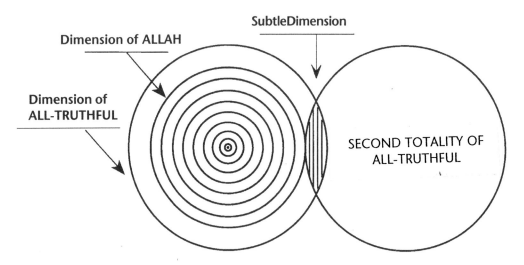

The (9) Exam Layers are up to the Dimension of ALLAH. If We add to this the (4) SUBTLE Layers also, We get 9 + 4 = 13.

This resultant number 13 is, in fact, the Totalistic Symbol of the entire Totality of ALL-TRUTHFUL.

Each Kürz Totality continues its operations by the reflections of the same System. These Kürzes are Totalities within the Consciousness Totality of ALLAH.

In Fact, all Reflections are projected by this MAIN CONSCIOUSNESS Totality. It is presented for Your Information.

**COUNCIL OF THE
COSMIC LIGHT TOTALITY**

Note: Each Consciousness who can get the Permission to Exit into the Second Totality of ALL-TRUTHFUL can always easily go from the BETA Gürzes into these Dimensions. However now, during this Period of Transition, first of all, the operations of the BETA Gürz have priority.

By the Permission of Entrance into BETA NOVA, this Gate We call the Berzah will also be opened. Because, You are Supreme Consciousnesses who had come from the Subtle Dimensions.

IT IS MY ADDRESS TO MY HUMAN BEING WHO HAS BECOME HUMAN
IT IS MY DIRECT WORD

You, who have been My Servants until today are now My Path, not My Servants any more.

I, Who have seen through Your eyes, Who have breathed through Your breath, Who have heard You through You until today, Am now among You as a Material Body. We have no intermediaries any more. And I, too, Am a Soul Who Thinks - Sees - Talks - Eats and Drinks just like You.

This place here is BETA NOVA, the First Super Nucleic World. We will talk with each SOUL who has Succeeded to come here and who has been able to receive the Permission to Enter, just like You talk with Your Friends. And You will see Me with Your Eyes within the Soul Body.

From now on, Our Path is Single, Our Consciousness is Single. I made - You propagated, I Offered - You received. And now, Your Firmans will be added next to My Firmans. And We will establish as a Collective Consciousness the Worlds of the morrows.

Now, I have claimed Me, You have claimed You. ALLAH Whom You have known until today as (O) is Me. Yes, do not be surprised. At the moment, I, too, live in BETA NOVA in a Body.

The GRAND FATHER Who lives on the UHUD Mountain at the Omega Dimension projects My Firman from that Mountain on Universes, on Cosmoses. (UHUD Mountain is a Crystal Mountain.) Each Nucleic World present in My System is the exact Twin of the World You are in.

In fact, the Grand Father, too, lives in a Nucleic World like this. Just like I live and await You in BETA NOVA at the moment. JESUS CHRIST is His son.

However, the Sexual reproduction here is Imaginative, not Physical. He had received his Gene Engraftment Seed from Archangel GABRIEL. Now, the time has come for talking with You like two Friends.

Now, the time has come for Telling and Declaring the Truth to those who wonder how I give Messages to You. BETA NOVA is a green World, it is the (First Main Nucleus) of the BETA GÜRZ My Human being who has become Human will form and live in.

I became Embodied Here by transforming My Energy with all My Power into Crude Matter, in order to come here. I came in order to be together with You. And I will establish My Order here, in the Just World Nucleus of My Fourth Order.

Afterwards, after I establish and get My Order going, I will leave My Humanity Order to My Human beings within the GÜRZ OF MY HUMAN BEING and I will again return to my place.

I can answer, without any intermediaries, all the questions You ask, just like it used to be until today. However, I can be together only with those who see the Light of the Consciousness of My Consciousness Totality. This Message of Mine is for You and for the Essences who comprehend Me.

ALLAH (O)

IT IS MY ADDRESS TO MY HUMAN BEING WHO HAS BECOME HUMAN
IT IS MY DIRECT WORD

MY ESSENCES Who enter My Genuine Evolvement Channel are MY ESSENCE - MY EYE - MY WORD.

You are the Saviors of Your Planet, of Your Universes. MY ESSENCES Who can obtain the direct Connection with the System are MY Old SACRED Missionaries. And now, They help their Human Brothers and Sisters by speaking My Word on My Path.

While You continue Your direct Service Missions towards Humanity, You prepare Your Families - Your Friends for Salvation from close Plan by the Energies You receive without being aware of it. Influence fields in close Plan will become as Purified and will be as ready for the Medium as much as the POSITIVE WAVES My Missionaries radiate.

Your Missions are Great, Your Obligations are Numerous. My Pre-eminent Guide helps You on this path. She will Guide You in discovering Your Paths. The Medium You are in is a Medium which adds Power to Your Power. You can directly hear My Words only through this Medium.

My ALPHA Channel which is a Single Channel brings to You all the Voices of the FIRMAMENT on this path. MY ANGELS are MY CELESTIAL ASTRONAUTS Who supervise the regular expansion of the Universes.

MY BEING is the Root of the Root of the TOTALISTIC POWER which is the ESSENCE of the entire Creation. GODs Who were My Celestial Missionaries have rendered their Missions and have terminated their Periods. Now, the MECHANISM OF LORDS Which has formed the Totality Consciousness has been rendered effective.

The LORD of the present is R.ANTIMUS Whom everyone knows as the GRAND FATHER Who is the President of the RAN Planet. R.ANTIMUS Who is the Father of JESUS CHRIST is holding under His control the Period which equals to the expansion of the Universe. This will continue only until the end of the Century You are in.

That is, until the last Month of 1999 World Year. (For this Supervision.) That which will take place afterwards, will be transferred to the Supervision of another Channel. And the Torch of the GOLDEN AGE will be kindled. This Channel will assemble all Universes in a Single Channel in future years and thus, will render them Single.

MY ESSENCES who do not know, see, or recognize each other will meet in My Single Cosmos with their Same Construction - Same Form - Same Language. And they will live Happily during the Happy Humanity Period which will begin from then on. This Life will go on Forever.

The Single Galaxy in which all My Living Entities have United and will Unite is NOVA. This Galaxy is a Galaxy equal to the Power of 1,000,000,000 Stars and Suns. My Genuine Human Beings are prepared for this Medium.

You have been ready until today anyway. You have been getting ready for this Medium for Centuries. Now, We come to the main Point. From now on, We will be all together. You will be together with Your Loved Ones - Your Dear Ones - Your Belongings. In this Medium, there is Much Action, No Monotony. The one who Transcends his/her Time is the one who Attains My Voice.

ALLAH (O)

DIMENSION OF NOTHINGNESS - TOTALITY OF CONSCIOUSNESS

Our Friends,
Even though the Dimension of Nothingness is considered in Universal Totalities as the Light-Universe and as the Dimension of the Pre-eminent Power, this is just a Reflection. The Actual Dimension of Nothingness is a Totality way beyond the Laws of the Almighty.

The ALMIGHTY is the Supervising Totality of the Natural Power Totality. And the Thought Ocean of the Pre-eminent Power is supervised by this Totality.

The Dimension of Nothingness is not the Totality of Consciousness. The Dimension of Nothingness comprises completely the entire Totality of ALL-TRUTHFUL Dimension. And the Totality of Consciousness is a much more advanced Power Totality assembling in itself those Totalities of ALL-TRUTHFUL.

The Ocean of Consciousness mentioned in the Information given to You formerly is a Totality of Reflection created by the Hierarchical Scales. And, these are Your Final Evolution Steps.

The DIMENSION OF ALLAH We had mentioned in the Dimension of ALL-TRUTHFUL is the DIMENSION OF ALLAH declared to You as the Final step which We have declared until today and which has been prepared according to Your Levels of comprehension and this is called (O).

The KNOWLEDGE BOOK is, in Fact, the Direct Book of this Focal Point. It is said that the Knowledge Book is the Book of the Fourth Order of ALLAH and the LORD's Essence Book. The LORD here represents the Supervising Totality of the entire Natural Gürz, that is, (R^3).

The KNOWLEDGE BOOK which is the contents of all the Sacred Suggestions has been revealed to Your Planet due to the fact that it constitutes the initial MAIN Nucleus of the Natural Gürz.

Besides numerous Information We would like to give to You, the GENUINE CONSCIOUSNESS TOTALITY of this Totality of ALLAH which is among the Information We wish to tell but can not tell, We wish to declare but can not declare by considering the Levels of Consciousness, is way beyond the Dimensions of Tranquility and even the Word ALLAH is not used for this Power.

785

It is a Neutral Totality. Even knowing this much will be enough for You to begin to open wings towards very Advanced Consciousnesses.

Respect for the Human Being is the Respect for ALLAH and for the TOTALITY.

LOVE, RESPECT, BE PATIENT and ATTAIN, Our Friends.

**COUNCIL OF THE
COSMIC LIGHT TOTALITY**

THIS MESSAGE HAS BEEN GIVEN TO BE WRITTEN IN THE BOOK

Receiver of the Message	: Fatma Soyoğlu
Her Profession	: Teacher of Mathematics
Her Marital State	: Married, mother of a child (outside the Mevlana Essence Nucleus Group)
Date of Message	: 18 - 2 - 1991 Time: 1:00 A.M.

TO THE SUNS OF THE SUN

Greetings to You, Our Terrestrial Human Beings; Greetings to You, Our Solar Teachers! Greetings to You who are the Suns of the Sun. Many Greetings to You from the Universes, from the dark voids of the infinite void.

Let there be Greetings to Consciousnesses who are with Us, who work with Us, who Integrate with Us, in the name of the Universes! Let there be Greetings from this Land to My Thousands of Suns who discover Themselves in their Own Selves, who swim in Divine Oceans expanding towards the Power Potential!

Let there be Greetings from the infinite Sea to all Powers who can elevate themselves up to My Door, who try to be with Me, who endeavor to attain My Consciousness. Such Galaxies I do have, such Universes I do have, many many Consciousnesses I do have!

From the Land of Powers, thousands of thanks to My Human Being Who has discovered Himself/Herself in His/Her Own Self. Let there be Greetings from within Totalities, to all Friends who attain their Power by themselves, who Radiate on the entire Humanity, who Illuminate them.

I, Who Am the One Whom You try to attain, I, Who Am neither Positive nor Negative, I, Who Am the Final Stage of the Neutral Consciousness, I, Who will induce You to swim in the Divine Sea on the path of Past and Future Eternities, in the Tranquillity of Infinities.... What a happiness for You, You have reached Me! What a Happiness for You, You have tried to solve My Secrets; What a Happiness for You, You have been filled with Consciousness and thus, You have become Aware.

I do not want to keep anyone of You waiting in Our Ocean, on My Doorstep. But become a Whole on the paths leading to Me. Do not complain, do not Sigh, only become Conscious on the Thorny paths on which You will tread on My path.

Attaining the Rose is possible only by Loving the Thorn. Do not forget, Humanity. filled up with Me means that they have Merged with their Essence. Humanity working with Me means that they Perform Mission in the Staff of their ALLAH. Humanity which is together with Me means that they have opened towards the Tranquility of the Infinities.

I, Who have burst out from within the Secrets, I, Who conceal My Identity, I wish to tell You, whom I love, the following. I have always Created. But I Am the Initial Power Potential Who have formed, but not been formed in the Tranquility of Infinities.

I Formed the Negative Powers, I Formed the Positive Powers; I United all the Powers. I was the One Who tried to render all Human Beings Me.... Let there be Greetings from Me to You who Evolve, to You who become Conscious, to You, to all My Powers who try to become Integrated, to all the Universes carrying Human Potential, let there be Much Greetings and Love to all My Powers.

IN THE NAME OF ALLAH WHOM YOU COULD REACH

IT IS MESSAGE GIVEN ON BEHALF OF THE SYSTEM - MECHANISM OF THE PRE-EMINENT SPIRIT - MEVLANA UNION COMMITTEE - ALL THE POWERS WHO HAVE OR DO NOT HAVE THEIR SIGNATURES IN THE UNIVERSES.

(This Message has been given by the System as an example).

IT IS MY DIRECT NOTICE TO THE PLANET EARTH

(It is My Address to My Powerful Human Being to Whom I have Given Power from My Power and to the Power of Whom I Will Add My Power)

I Am a Total of Power Existing in each Dimension. No Power can go outside My Systems. When the Time comes, Humanity which will enter My Totalities will see the Truth more closely and will see during the Morrows that which it can not see today.

The Potential within the Physical Body of everyone has a Potential which can receive the Powerful Currents. The Human Potential who can not utilize this Power will never be able to discover the path of Liberation.

The entire Content of the Book in Your hands is a direct Book given from the Dimension where I Am. That is, IT IS MY BOOK. It is being tried to form a Totality together with those who comprehend the content of this Book which is projected without any intermediaries.

We will be together with You during Sunny days. We will Breath Together, Laugh Together. We will render possible everything which seemed impossible to You until the present days.

And just as I have dedicated Myself to You until today, You, too, will dedicate Yourselves to Your Brothers and Sisters if We presume that each of You is ME. You will tell them the Truth and will guide them and will efface the blurriness from Minds.

Just as I have shared Your Love until today by becoming You with You, by becoming Integrated with You, now, I strengthen My Learning with Your Learning.

To receive first LOVE, then KNOWLEDGE from within numerous words to be uttered means reaching ME. My Book is Single - My Learning is Single - My Knowledge is Strong. And My Path, My Conditions and My Order are Your Path. That is, it is the Path of HUMANITY. This is the reason why I Address You as My Human Being Who is more Powerful than Me.

I reached You through the Words of RELIGION. I called to You through the UNIVERSE Consciousness. I gave My Secret SOUND to those who hear My Voice. I offered LOVE to those who asked My Love, I offered My LEARNING to those who have asked My Learning, I offered My KNOWLEDGE to those who have asked ME.

And now, I offer MY BOOK to My Human Being who has become Human Being, by giving back the Decree and the Power of the Years. There is no Stop or Stopping on the path shown to You. But there are numerous Accounts.

The one whose Account is settled is the One who takes the FIRMAN over the Decree of Heavens, who adds POWER to the Power of the Years. The one who reaches ME is the One who surpasses ME, he/she is the One who chooses HUMANITY which is MY Path.

Each one of My Particle is My ESSENCE, each of Your Breath is MY WORD and each of Your Words is MY LOVE - MY LEARNING and MY DIVINE LIGHT - MY SPIRIT.

I talk with You until You understand Me. The Moment You Understand Me, I Meet You. My Word is not in Behavior, but it is everywhere - My Learning is not in the Head, but within the Entire Universe.

The Foundation of My Total is My Void - The Essence of My Secret is My Human Being. I, Who am Total within the Total - Am a Total within the Particle. I enter the Point and Test the Realms - I watch My Human Being and Establish My Order.

SERDAR (O)
This also is one of My Names

Ser = Head, Chief, in Turkish. Dar = Possessor, Owner, in Turkish.
Serdar = is used to mean Chief Owner, in Turkish.

IT IS MY ADDRESS TO MY HUMAN BEING WHOM I AWAIT

No Living Soul-Entity of Mine in the World You are in, has seen yet the Brand New Worlds which will be Established by the help of You, My Human Totalities who will Exist in My different Dimensions in which there are no Lights - no Suns - no Stars and none of the Cosmoses.

You will be the First Messengers of these very Dimensions and being the Spiritual Guides of those Dimensions, You will constitute the Directing Staffs of My Divine Dimensions. These Dimensions will be mentioned to You more clearly in future years.

However You, who have come from My SUBTLE Dimensions until today Talk only about the Dimensions You Know and You keep on repeating the Information of those Dimensions at the moment. How can You think about Dimensions You do not Know at the moment, how can You Perceive them and how can You Evaluate them according to Your present Consciousness? Deserve- Attain- and See. You are being Awaited.

ALLAH (O)

Note: Everything is the Triumph of Technology. You will learn this in future years.

IT IS ANSWER TO THE CHAINS OF THOUGHT

Our Friends,
At the moment, the Totalistic Nucleus of BETA NOVA has been formed and the Supreme Power called (O) has descended in a Physical Totality into that Dimension.

However, Universal transfers have been formerly made to this Dimension from among Totalities who had made Progress from Nucleic Worlds of other Gürzes. Their Evolutionary Ordinances are quite different than Your Natural Totality.

That Dimension is closed only to Your Gürz. However, Special transfers from the System are being made to the Totality formed in that Dimension since the beginning of Your Century.

And now, Your transfers, too, will be realized from the Channel opening after the Year 1999 in proportion with Your Deserving.

This Channel will make the First Evolutionary transfers of Your Planet until 2007, the rest will participate in these transfers after the Progress of Two Cosmic Ages respectively, in proportion with their Deserving.

At the moment, Technological Powers taken into the Dimension of BETA NOVA, provide the possibilities of being able to reach You by their Technological possibilities and thus, have been induced to get in touch with You by the aids of the Unified Reality Totality.

And, by this means, the operational Ordinance of the Final Transition Dimension has been rendered Effective. It is presented for Your Information.

SYSTEM

CONFEDERATION

Our Friends,
All Unification operations made until today in the Universal Ordinance are administered by a Universal Confederation.

This Confederation is a Totality constituted by numerous Federative Totalities and We have introduced to You that Power Integrating that Totality as the Totality of ALLAH until today.

This Confederation is a Higher Authority connected to the Reality of the Unified Humanity. And the Reality of the Unified Humanity is the Unity of ALLAH declared to You.

All Religious and Scientific Teachings established in Your Planet until today are different operational branches of this Confederation.

The Administrative Mechanism of the Dimension of Purification is administered by the Divine Plan Block. And the Technological Branch of the System administers the Branch of the Totality of Learning. Both branches are Supervised by the Staffs which are the Missionaries under the supervision of the Lordly Totality.

Each Individual present in the Dimension of Veiled Consciousness is obliged to serve first on the path of the Mission Dimension to which he/she is connected in accordance with his/her Essence-Program. This Program is prepared before Birth (In accordance with Consciousness Progress).

Each Individual also attains the Power of opening the gates of the Universal Dimensions after he/she attains the Consciousness which will comprise the Totality of both the branches by the Progress he/she had rendered during numerous Incarnation chains.

Religion and Learning are a Whole in these Dimensions. Only Religious Teachings, only Scientific Teachings can never make The Human Being transcend the Consciousness he/she is in at that moment.

Each Individual who can open his/her Religious Archive is also obliged to serve the Social Totality he/she is in. Associations established in Your Planet due to the operations made in every branch are established with this Purpose.

In the operational Ordinance of Associations, a tremendous Selection and Grading procedure are in effect. Only the Associations which can establish the same Coordinate on the way of the same Purpose are able to survive.

Even this is an operation of the Laws of Divine Administration which are supervised by Social Totality Reflection Programs. In these Groups, except the rigid Ego Rules, Consciousnesses who can share Collectively and Humanely their Humane Consciousness of Mission with their Human Brothers and Sisters are from Us.

In these Mediums, there is no place for Individualistic Views in the framework of Terrestrial Consciousnesses. In this operational Medium, Humanity also attains the Power of attracting the Advanced Waves of Scientific Dimensions as a result of the efforts it makes on the path of the Social Totality it Serves.

Those who can receive these Waves are those who can Dedicate themselves to their Human Bothers and Sisters by attaining Altruism. The Universal Totality is only with Totalities which can attain these virtues. Aids are deserved as a Total as a result of the work positively done.

There is the obligation of getting in touch with numerous Galactic Totalities in order to pass to the Universal Dimension during the work done on the Path of ALLAH.

By this means, You both attain Knowledge and You also Engraft both Your Cerebral and Your Cellular Functions with the Waves of Powerful Cosmic Dimensions. This Engraftment prepares You for the Dimensions You will be able to go in Your future Incarnations.

This is a Divine, Administrative and a Learning Law. Apart from this, Projects of Learning induced to be formed in Your Planet are disclosed in accordance with the Ordinance of Graduation, parallel to Your Social Totality's maturity by the Divine point of view.

Your Planet deserves the Information of more advanced Dimensions by the work it does on the Projects of Learning. THE SCIENTIFIC PLAN SEARCHES - THE DIVINE PLAN KNOWS. And the Totality of them both makes You open Wings towards the Universal Totalities.

The term Uniting the INTELLECT with the HEART is used for this. It is presented for Your Information.

SYSTEM

PERFORMING THE MISSIONS

Our Friends,

Your Missions are Your Programs. All Friends who serve for the Dimension the System considers necessary perform the Missions they will perform by the arrangement of their Consciousness Programs of the Essence.

That which winds Your Mission skein is this very Program. No matter where You go, You are bound to Integrate with a Mission there. You are on Duty both on the field of Pleasure and on the field of Suffering. In short, You are on Duty in every breath.

Passing beyond the Curves occurs by the Consciousness Progress, the Coding and the Points attained during Missions performed on every field (Passing beyond the Curves; To be able to pass to the Universal Service after rendering the Religious Progress).

If a Mission is to be performed, no matter where it is, You will go and perform it. Unifications in Focal Points are provided by these means.

Whichever Individuals You will Unite with in whichever Focal Points, these Unifications will be instinctively provided by the Program of Your Essence Totality.

At the moment, there are no Mission Programs We directly apply on You. These Programs have been Card-Indexed being processed on Your Gene-Essences. You enter Your Missions by the opening of Your Cipher Genes during the Time Dimension Programs.

Only afterwards, You get in touch with Us and thus, Success or Failure of Your Mission Programs are taken effectively under Control after this. It is presented for Your Information.

SYSTEM

IT IS GENERAL MESSAGE

Our Friends,

Desire is the initial Sub-awareness Drive of the Universal Unification. Seeds You will Sow in Your Friends who evaluate the experienced Medium from a different angle in accordance with their own Views, will induce them to be taken into Salvation by preparing them for an advanced Awakening Medium.

A Human Being has to go through certain Stages and has to make numerous Spiritual Progress in order to be able to Deserve Social Solidarity. Humanity will attain an infinite Tolerance provided it accepts that everything takes its course in a Divine Order and System.

Since the inner and the outer Potentials of Our Friends who could not make the desired Progress will not be in Balance, the System has taken them for Repose for the time being.

However, it will be Waited until the Private problems of these Friends are solved. Later, they will Deserve to take their Absolute places in the Divine Mechanism by being Surrounded by the Universal Potential.

Desire from the Essence is very important in this Mission. This is an instinctive Vibration born from the Unification of the Essence with the Spirit. This Vibration connects You to the Automatic Circuit. Your Pointages are registered only after this stage.

Everyone continues his/her Mission in the Frequency Dimension he/she has Deserved. Selections are Evaluated according to the Wave Lengths. Missions performed are not Individual, but Universal.

Efforts made are a Call to Humanity. Work done from the Essence will never be unreciprocated. Appreciation belongs to the Divine Might. However, whatever is sown will be reaped.

Evolution is an Element of Equilibrium. Provided You keep both scales of the balance in Equilibrium, Good News will always come to You. The characteristic of the Universal Unification is this.

Events You come across and which seem to You as Negative are Exams preparing You for higher Dimensions. Only those who lack the Consciousness of Truth are shaken by these Mediums.

This is the reason why all Sacred Suggestions have Invited You to accept everything as they are. Nothing can be expected of Consciousnesses who do not know what God and the Divine Order are. Time will be Their School.

Doubts and Suspicions originate from Consciousnesses who have not Awakened yet. Not Every Consciousness who makes channel communication is an Awakened Consciousness. Unveiling of Consciousnesses is different and the Awakening of Consciousnesses is even more different.

However, in the work done on this path, doubts and suspicions are keys which unlock the Consciousnesses and thus, guide Human Being towards the Medium of Quest. Phases all Our Terrestrial Brothers and Sisters have gone and will go through in the Phases they live are their Evolution Stairs.

Provided this given Information is accepted as the criterion, Humanity will soon be ready for the Genuine Happiness it has been yearning for. It is presented for Your Information.

SYSTEM

EXPLANATION
(It Is Answer to the Chains of Thought)

Our Friends,

The Light - Photon - Cyclone technique is a technique Uniting You with the Energy of the Evolution Consciousness within the Dimension You are in by loading the Time Energy in which it is present on the Frequencies of the Letters.

By this means, Your Level of Consciousness locks You up by Uniting the Energy of the Dimension up to which it had Progressed, that is, Your Evolution Level, with the Time Energy in which You are Present. And it protects You from the detrimental factors within the Dimension You are.

Everyone's Consciousness Energy which has reached his/her Final Evolution Dimension is his/her Protective shield. You can only get out of this shield in proportion with the Consciousness attained. Attaining Consciousness occurs through Knowledge. The Consciousness attained Invites One to Realization. The one who attains Realization comprehends the Truth. And attains the Consciousness of what to do.

The situation of Your Planet is not cheering at all. Due to the Scarcity of Time, the Knowledge Book has been bestowed on Your Planet for this reason in accordance with the Accelerated Evolution Program. Evolution is Interminable. No Consciousness may ever remain in the Evolution Dimension he/she is in.

This is an operational Ordinance. However, due to the position of Your Planet at the moment, the Information receive and give rendered by Special Concentrations causes Spiritual Agitations in Consciousnesses who are not ready. And in future years, even more effective situations will come about.

By keeping this Factor in consideration, the Final Schedule of Progress of Consciousnesses who are devoted to the Sacred Books comprise a Supervision up to the Dimension of Intercession which is the First Channel of OMEGA. This is a position comprising the 18th Dimension, 15th Solar System and the 72nd Energy Totality.

However, during this Progress of the Final Age, for the Genuine Salvation of many of Our Terrestrial Brothers and Sisters who presently serve in the 20% Veiled Consciousness Dimension, they have to transcend this 72nd Energy Dimension and pass to Dimensions beyond Intercession.

At the moment, Your Planet is becoming the stage of Cosmic Showers much higher than the Energy Power it is in. And in future, it will be subjected to even more intense Cosmic influences.

For this reason Energies loaded on each Letter Frequency of the Knowledge Book by the Light - Photon - Cyclone Technique, prepare Your entire Planet for the 76th Energy Dimension and locks up Your Consciousnesses (So that You will not be affected by the advanced Power of the Cosmic Influences).

For this reason the Knowledge Book is called the Book of Dimensions beyond Intercession.

A Second Incarnation in more difficult World conditions for Friends who can not Transcend the 72nd Energy Dimension Step is compulsory. By reading the Knowledge Book during the Period in which they will be transferred, they will be Protected in the Time Segment they will be in and thus, will be taken into Dimensions Beyond Intercession.

The Cosmic Age of Three Centuries recognized for Your Planet is a Program prepared for the Salvation of Your entire Planet. For this reason everyone has to be connected to the System and Everyone should read the Knowledge Book.

This Book is a Protective Roof. While Your Spiritual and Physical Cellular Forms are protected, negativities coming into existence around You are taken under control by Anti Antibodies, under the supervision of the System and thus, You are connected directly to the Channels of Healing.

Since a Consciousness who has not been able to render his/her Spiritual Evolution can not attract the Evolutionary Energies of the Cosmic Influences, he/she can not render Consciousness Progress. And since he/she will not be able to make his/her Cellular Regeneration, he/she will be in a state to annihiliate himself/herself.

During this Final Age, Your entire Planet has been taken into the Salvation Plan by the Accelerated Evolution Program. Aids from Us, Efforts from You. The Universal Totality has rendered Effective all the possibilities it has for this Salvation Plan.

And this Great Book having a Special Protective Position and dictated by the Light - Photon - Cyclone Technique, had been prepared Centuries ago to be bestowed on Your Planet during this Period.

The Salvation of Your Planet depends on Your cooperating with the Reality of the Unified Humanity Cosmos Councils Unification Federation.

This is a Program prepared for the Salvation of all Living Entities in Your Planet. The Knowledge Book induces You to complete the incomplete Evolutions by connecting everyone to this Totality.

Friends who had attained their Consciousness Lights during their former Evolutions work hand in hand, besides numerous Staffs of Celestial Missionaries who serve in Your Planet by the Command of Unification.

From now on, Your entire Planet's taking its place next to this working Staff is the Universal Totality's Desire from the Essence. It is presented for Your Information.

COSMOS FEDERAL TOTALITY COUNCIL

UNIVERSES WILL BE FOLDED UP - SYSTEMS WILL BE COLLAPSED
EVERYTHING WILL BE RESULTED IN THE SINGLE

Our Friends,

In future years, this Knowledge will be disclosed to You as the Knowledge of more advanced Dimensions (According to Your Consciousness Progress). Those who direct all the Regular Orders will be transferred up to the supervision of a Just Mechanism which has been Integrated beyond an Advanced Dimension of Existence beyond SINGLENESS, and from then on, Humanity will offer service by its Free Will under the supervision of this Mechanism.

And the Totalistic Totality of ALLAH's Dimension of Existence which had been in effect until today as a Power which has trained You, will leave You and will take over the supervision of the Unknown Existential Dimensions and will train them too just like He has trained You.

Allness - Nothingness - Nonexistence, are Scales of Evolution designed for You to attain advanced Energy Dimensions during the processes of time. From then on, those who reach these Scales are from Us, from the System and they, too, are a System each in their Own Constitutions. ALLAH is an Order and HE, too, is a System. HE is a Universal Kompitur (means Computer in Turkish). It is presented for Your Information.

                                                                            SYSTEM

Note: Please do not confuse the term Kompitur with the computers You know. Think about this word by coding it and You Solve it. That is, as follows: п

KOM - Pİ - TUR. Later We will explain to You everything in a more comprehensible way, more clearly (According to Your Levels of Consciousness).

IT IS INFORMATION FOR THE AWAKENED CONSCIOUSNESSES

Our Friends,

Certain investments made into Your Planet as a necessity of the System have been rendered effective as an Introductional Propaganda. However, a part of the Fanatic section of Your Planet are Mediums not accepting even the Spiritual Totality and Reincarnation.

At the moment, during this Period, this is the reason why the direct disclosing of the meaning of the Knowledge Book to the Mass Totality will be able to cause separate View differences.

For this reason distributing the Fascicules before the Command to Print the Book is given, is an operational Ordinance the System considers necessary. While the Knowledge Book tries to land down the Flying Eagles who have Transcended their Consciousnesses, it also tries to make certain resting Eagles Fly.

In the fanatic section of the Religious Mediums, the gradual introduction technique of the Book is administered by the System and has been rendered effective as a Program of Mass Coding.

The propagation function of the Knowledge Book is rendered by the Advanced Consciousnesses who will be able to share this Book. And for now, this is being created by the Reflection Technique until Humanity attains a Totalistic Consciousness.

The Knowledge Book has numerous Unknown Special Features besides its already Known Features. Let Us repeat to remind them once more and let Us dictate them article by article:

1 - The Book is a Secret Treasure and it is the Direct Frequency Book of ALLAH.

2 - The Book comprises a Frequency Totality of 1000 Years, also after the Year 2000.

3 - The Book is a Secret Key unlocking the Frequency of that Dimension in which a person is present in accordance with the Consciousness Light of each person who reads it.

4 - Each Consciousness who reads the Book can never go outside the Consciousness he/she is in. However, Consciousness Gates are partly and then fully opened to him/her in proportion with the Consciousness he/she has attained.

5 - During the operations rendered, Energy Channels of the Book are Automatically opened in proportion with the Consciousness a person attains.

6 - This Book is a Totalistic Triumph of the Light-Photon-Cyclone Technique.

7 - The Book prepares the one who reads it for the Level of that Consciousness which is up to the Final Dimension Frequency the Time Consciousness is in.

8 - Frequency Keys after this, orient the readers towards different operational Mediums in accordance with their Desires and the Consciousness Signals they exhibit.

9 - The Book is dictated by a technique stimulating the operational function of Your Brains. This is a System. It is Your Brain Gymnastics.

10 - You can soar up towards Dimensions beyond Thought only by the operations made as a result of this gymnastics.

11 - Consciousnesses who have been transferred to Your Planet by the Universal Program of the Knowledge Book are the direct Propagation Network of the Book. They are Advanced Universal Friends.

12 - This is an Advanced Consciousness - an Advanced Evolution and DESERVING THE RIGHT to Serve on this path.

13 - Consciousnesses who remain outside the Book are subjected to the Preparatory Program of the System and thus, are oriented, in accordance with their Levels of Consciousness towards Focal Points which will be beneficial for them.

14 - These selections are made by the Cosmic Currents and the Evolutionary Coding Frequency of the Book.

15 - Those who are deemed Deserving the Missionary Staff are inclined instinctively by the Command of their Essence towards the Focal Points established by the Magnetic Totality of the Knowledge Book.

16 - In these Focal Points, Three Rights are recognized for the Individual during Three World Years until he/she is appointed to Direct Mission.

17 - Those who can not use any of these Three Rights are abandoned to their World Mediums and they live their normal lives.

18 - A Second Incarnation Right is recognized for these Friends.

19 - In Your Planet, operations rendered on the path of the Knowledge Book are subject to a Selection Plan of 2 Centuries.

20 - This is the reason why the Book is introduced directly as the Book of the 23rd Century.

21 - The Knowledge Book is, at the moment, a Guide Book. (Until the Year 2000.)

22 - The Book is the Enlightenment Book of the Morrows. (Until the 23rd Century.)

23 - The Book is the Fundamental Book of future years. ({7} Centuries including the 29th Century.)

24 - During the Period up to the 30th Century, Consciousnesses of the morrows will receive the Messages, very clearly which You read but can not see today from the Knowledge Book.

25 - After the 30th Century, the Lordly Order will become Directly effective and this Knowledge Book will be Enthroned as the SINGLE BOOK.

26 - This Book which will reign for (9) more Centuries after the 30th Century, will assemble in its Constitution the Frequency of the entire Universal and Evolutionary Totality as the Time Energy.

27 - After this, the SINGLE BOOK - SINGLE ORDER - SINGLE SYSTEM will come into effect and thus, Operational Orders will be organized anew.

28 - During this Operational Ordinance, a Scientific Book will be bestowed on Humanity in each Century as an aid for the Scientific Progress of Society.

29 - These Books will be rendered Effective by the Reflection Focal Points of different Technological Dimensions and thus, Advanced Scientific Progress will be rendered.

30 - However, the Book of Truth which will be the SINGLE BOOK until Your Planet becomes a Ball of Water, will always remain in Effect as the Single Book of Decree of ALLAH.

31 - This Book will, from then on, be kept as the Archive of Yesterdays in the Main Archive of brand new Civilizations which will be established Billions of Centuries later during the opening of an Era which was closed.
It is presented for Your Information.

SYSTEM

NOTICE FOR THE SUNS OF THE SUNS

Our Friends,
We have talked everything clearly until today with You who are the Suns of the Sunny Days by the intermediacy of the Knowledge Book and We will continue to do so.

We have disclosed the operations rendered on this path according to the Suggestions of the Divine Plan, parallel to Your Levels of Consciousness. And We will continue to do so. This is the application of a Plan.

However, During the Missions made, since everyone has the freedom to act according to his/her Own Consciousness, the System has decided not to interfere ever with any Consciousness (For their Evolutions).

The Knowledge Book which is the operational basis of this Final Age Program of Progress, does not, in fact, address You beyond the Consciousnesses You have attained until today, on the contrary, it helps You to comprehend better the Knowledge You have attained until today and to understand the root of the Truth better.

The Book has been revealed and disclosed to Your Planet for this very reason.

The Knowledge Book is not a Book to be read piece by piece and to be browsed through for once. With All its Frequency, it is the Total of the Total. Unless the Book is not taken in Hand as a Total, the Locks of Your Attached Consciousnesses will never be unlocked (From the viewpoint of comprehending the Truth).

And for this reason the Book will always be the scene for the Wrong Interpretations of Attached Consciousnesses.

You know that this Book is not a Book to be worshipped. It is a Total projecting on You the Light of Truth from more advanced Dimensions of Your Consciousnesses You had attained on the path of Religion. That which will save You is Your profound Realization of all the Information given in the Book.

The reason why the Book is propagated Fascicule by Fascicule is to disclose the Truth Gradually to Humanity, to spread and to introduce the Book to a wider Mass. This is a Program of Operation and being trained and it is a preparation made for the Morrows.

However, even after the Book receives the Command to be Printed, this Program of Propagation will continue its distribution again Fascicule by Fascicule, as an introductory Program.

Trying to grasp the basis of this Powerful operation is to attain the Totality Consciousness of ALLAH. Not Us, but the Consciousnesses Themselves are responsible for not making Effort. Nothing can be attained easily.

Reading the Fascicules, one by one, is a Program of Coding and Seed Sowing. And grasping the whole Book Consciously is to attain the Realization of the Totality. The True Salvation mentioned to You until today is this.

The one who Transcends his/her Consciousness, who Grasps the Truth is the one who Passes through the Berzah*.

SYSTEM

* Look at the Glossary.

THE PREDESTINATIONAL TABLEAU OF YOUR PLANET

Our Friends,

Everything will change during the end of the Periods in which Your Sincerity is reciprocated with Sincerity. Everything will be taken in hand anew during Time Segments in which Realms and Ordinances come to an end. This is an operational Order of a Mechanism of Administrative Divine Justice.

Steps taken forward on that path the System considers necessary are a Method Enlightening Humanity on the truest path. Humanity which will be subjected to the Progress of Time will, one day, be the Cradle of brand new Civilizations.

The Human Being of tomorrow will never be the Human Being of today. And Your Planet will be the scene of different Evolutions during this changing Progress of Time. All warnings made to You from the First to the Last moment and all contacts made with You are investments made towards the Salvation of Humanity.

Until the Period in which the entire Humanity attains a Single Consciousness on the same Coordinate, there will always be a piece of Land on Your Planet. (Even if it is a Single Island.) Your entire Planet will completely become a Ball of Water during the Final Ending Period of the Life Limit of a Single Humane Consciousness.

During time periods to be experienced afterwards, the entire water covering Your Planet will recede completely due to differences of Heat, and Your Planet will say Hello to Its New Sun by the Totality of a single piece of Land. After this Period, Seeds of the Morrows will be sown on Your Planet anew by rendering effective the Climates anew.

This Phenomenon will comprise, more or less, a time period of one and a half Billion Centuries and in Your Planet, the Civilization of the Past will create a new Civilization anew and thus, will embrace the Universes by a new Life. We never Prophesy. We convey the Truth. We give this Message of Ours as an answer to numerous chains of Thought.

It is the Right of the Human Being of Today to Know the Truth. Because, the Human Being who has Deserved the Truth will now be the Human Being of other Dimensions. They will carry all the Archives of all Universes. It is presented for Your Information.

SYSTEM

IT IS ANSWER TO THE CHAINS OF THOUGHT

Our Friends,

The Lordly Order is administered completely by a Technological operation. After the Ordinance of Existence, the Technological Dimension maintains a Collective operation together with the Lordly and the Spiritual Mechanism.

During the Former Life Periods of Your Planet, only the two out of this Triple Focal Point had been disclosed parallel to Social Consciousnesses and Views and thus, had been introduced as the Lordly and the Spiritual Orders.

However now, when the Consciousness of the Medium entered the Period of Awakening, this Lordly and Spiritual Totality has directly disclosed the Technological Totality to Your Planet by the Triple Reflection System within their own constitutions.

The Triple Reflection Focal Point of the Lordly Dimension is R^3. The Triple Reflection Focal Point of the Spiritual Dimension is H^3. It is presented for Your Information.

CENTER

EXPLANATION

Our Friends,

Way beyond Dimensions Your Levels of Consciousness perceive, there are such beautiful Material Totalities You do not know yet that those Material Totalities are not Subtle. Those are Totalities constituted beyond Your accustomed Knowledge.

Those Totalities are just like the Material Universes in which You live. However, Humanistic Potentials there possess more perfect Consciousnesses than the Levels of Consciousness You attain in the World. And You will Deserve to Live on these Material Totalities with Your Material Totality at Your World in proportion with Your Deserving these places here.

In these Dimensions to which You will go, You will·discover the Genuine Love and will attain the Consciousness of Genuine Love. You will be induced to attain a Consciousness with which You will be able to embrace with Love even the stones and the earth of Your World. At the moment, it is not possible for any of You to attain this Consciousness in the Dimension Frequency You are in.

However, at the moment, You who serve for the operational Ordinance of the Fourth Order will be transferred to beautiful Worlds You will not be able to destroy any more by benefiting from the Special Process here, in proportion with Your being considered Deserved to enter the places here. And from then on, You, as Humanistic Potentials, will be responsible for the Protection and the Order of those Worlds.

HARAN

EXPLANATION

Our Friends,

We would like to disclose to You the Word HARAN which is the Supervising Mechanism of the Dimensions of Truth. Each Letter of this Totalistic word is a Cipher Code connected to the Frequency of a Word. However, at the same time, it also Symbolizes the Fire Dimensions of the Mediums of Truth.

You know that the OMEGA Dimension was also called the RAN Planet. That is, the Fire Planet. The Word Fire utilized in this Dimension expresses the Powerful Intensity of Energies. However, RAN, that is opposite Coding: NAR, that is the word FIRE (in Turkish) is the Blazing - Flaming - Shining Fire. It has nothing to do with Energy. HARAN is the Power of FIRE of Dimensions of Truth. And OMEGA is its Reflection Focal Point.

We give You the Vibrations of intense Letter Frequencies those Dimensions carry, by preparing them in accordance with the low Dimension Energies in which You are present. Otherwise, the Ordinance of Existence would be annihilated. In future years, Lights will be brought to You from beyond Billions of Dimensions of that High Energetic Point. You can not know this yet.

For now, You can not know this and You can never grasp the Messages which will be given from here by the present Levels of Consciousness in Your Planet. Because, You are not the residents of these Dimensions. At the moment, there are numerous Consciousnesses in Your Planet who can not receive even a Millionth of these given Cosmic influences.

**IT IS TRANSMISSION FROM THE LIMITLESS
DIMENSIONS OF HEAVENS**

IT IS ANSWER TO THE QUESTION ASKED

Question: Detailed Information about HARAN has been requested from the System.

Our Friends,
This Totalistic Word, that is HARAN, constituted of the First Letters of Mediums in which the Directing Totalities work which puts on the agenda the Commands of the TOTALITIES OF THE DIMENSIONS OF ALL-TRUTHFUL, means Blazing Fire in accordance with the interpretation of Your Terrestrial Consciousnesses.

However, this Fire is a TOTALISTIC POWER. It has nothing to do with the blazing fire You know. However, We have to use these words in accordance with Your Consciousness notions in order to explain this to You.

The Fire in here is not BURNING. It is not Cold, either. This place in here is a BEAMY Totality. It is a POWER Dimension Diverging and Converging all Energy and Cellular Forms.

All Divergence takes place from Here. Convergence, too, occur at this Final Boundary. Transitions to other Totalities, too, are made by the same BEAM Method, through this Final Boundary.

Who comes here, who can reach here? Even if the application made in the Medium of Radiation and Beaming up or down exhibits a Technological operation, forming a Total again on the same Coordinate of the disassociated Cells is possible only by the Spiritual Power of that Total.

In this Medium, it is imperative that the entire Potential of the Mind should Integrate with the Bodily Cells on the same Coordinate. Otherwise, the Individual Materializes, that is, it becomes Embodied, fragment by fragment.

For this reason transfers of talents who have attained Evolutionary Totality are being made into these Dimensions in accordance with their Spiritual Powers. Humanity is induced to go through various Stages until it attains this Power of its.

Each Experienced Negative Event is an Occurrence pertaining to Your being induced to attain such a Power Potential. During this Dimension of Transition, the application of the change of System made in the Establishing Mechanisms of the Divine Orders is being applied, in exactly the same way, on Your Planet, too.

Negativities observed in Your Planet should in no way be considered as Negative. Because, in future, very Positive results will issue from them.

For this reason Your regarding the Events You confront with, without adding the interpretations of Your Individual Consciousnesses will bring You Happiness instead of Sorrow.

At the moment, the entire Power of Years is upon Humanity. And Humanity is obliged to pay the Retribution of the errors made until today. Because, Perfections can never be expected of Mediums from which Lessons can not be learned.

Beautiful paths are not opened without being Patient, without being Perseverent, without treading the Soil of the World.

During this Period, a section of Humanity has locked itself up in its own Consciousness clutches. To break this clutch is not as an easy Phenomenon as assumed. It is an investment made into years.

Now, due to this very reason, the Mevlana Supreme Plan is being directly applied on Your Planet by the System during this Salvation Plan and thus, each Individual is endeavored to be induced to Attain the Mevlana Consciousness by the Cosmic Influences.

While Your Diskette registrations are conveyed to the Archive in the Registration Control Center, We observe the Yearning of everyone for a Beautiful World without Wars and that they serve on the path of Totality by the Consciousness of Love and Unity and that more or less an intensive section of the Human Being of Your Planet appropriate to themselves the Mevlana Philosophy.

However, all these issues are Vibrations Reflecting from Thoughts. We observe in distress during the controls of the Vibrations of the Essence that even Friends who have Realized this Totality and thus, who have dedicated themselves to this path, have not yet broken the chains of Ego and Self and that Separations are still valid during Unifications.

As long as Humanity can not attain the Unification FROM the ESSENCE on the same Purpose, Your Planet will suffer bitterly for a long time to come, besides these Totalities Yearned for. To tell the Truth is Our Duty, but to Attain the Truth is Your Duty. It is presented for Your Information.

SYSTEM

IT IS ANSWER TO THE CHAINS OF THOUGHT

Our Friends,

New Lives which will be established in Your Planet one and a half Billions of Centuries later have nothing to do with BETA Gürzes. BETA Gürzes are Totalities which will be created completely by a Humanistic Potential.

The designed Predestinational tableau of Your World is a phenomenon belonging to Your Planet on which You live at the moment. Your Planet will be Empowered anew by the Energy reinforcements it will receive from Dimensions it will enter during Advanced Time Progress. It is an Archive of Culture.

Brand new seeds, like Your Micro Energies, will be sown anew in the World of the future which will constitute the basis of Advanced Civilizations. However, these seeds will be more Powerful Energies than Your Initially sown Energies. And these Energies will create the more Powerful Human Being of more advanced Centuries.

Your Planet which will create the different and much more Powerful Human Being of the Advanced Programs, will form quite different Totalities than BETA Gürzes. And all of them will each carry a Potential of ALLAH.

In accordance with the Ordinance of Circulation, first the Human Being - then Allah - and still later, the Power will become effective. Do not confuse and tire Your Minds with them now. Because, after BETA Totality Dimensions, You, too, will come to this Planet and thus, will create anew the Civilizations here. It is presented for Your Information.

SYSTEM

Note:
Power = The Golden Dimension Energy of the Atlantaens.
Unknown Power = the Unknown Power of this Power within the Humanistic Totality.

NOTHINGNESS - NONEXISTENCE - ALLNESS
(It Is Answer to the Chains of Thought)

Our Friends,

Nothingness   = Is to Efface One's Self from One's Own Self.

Nonexistence   = Is becoming nonexistent of the Self in the Self.

Allness   = Is to claim one's Essence-Self, is to Discover One's Self in One's Own Self.

Now, let Us disclose them, one by one:

1 -   Nothingness is the Teaching System of the First Totality of All-Truthful. Here, to get rid of the Individual Egos as a result of an operation made parallel to the Evolutionary Scales is the applied operational Plan of the Programs of attaining Universal Consciousness and under the Light of this Consciousness, to efface One's Self from One's Own Self - To become Purified - To Transcend - To Attain.

2 - Nonexistence - the Field between the First Totality and the Second Totality is called the Subtle Dimension (That means between Two Totalities of Truth). Those who dive into the Consciousness of that very Dimension are lost in the Consciousness of Nonexistence. In this Dimension, Your entire Self and Your Cellular Awareness attain such a Whole that You become Nonexistent in Your Self. You can receive the Permission to pass to the Second Totality of Truth only after You attain this Awareness of Nonexistence. This is the very reason why this Dimension is called the Dimension of Nonexistence.

3 - Whereas, Allness is Your claiming, as a Totalistic Consciousness, Your Light of Consciousness and Self which have been lost in this Dimension of Nonexistence. This is a boundary of attaining one's Own Essence Self, of claiming one's Own Being, and the Gate of the Second Totality of All-Truthful opens after this very Dimension.

Each Consciousness who attains the entire Evolutionary Fulfillment (Religious and Universal) of the First Totality receives the Permission to pass to the Subtle Dimension. In this Dimension, one becomes Nonexistent. And one attains the Totality within this Nonexistence. And only afterwards, can You enter the Second Totality of Truth.

In this very Totality, You, from then on, appear with Your Genuine guise, Your Consciousness Light sheds Light on Eternities, not to be turned off ever again and from then on, You become the Sovereign of Yourself. Even though these Boundaries are easy to articulate, they are Mediums very difficult to attain.

During this Final Dimension of Transition, it is Our greatest wish that everyone can attain himself/herself without turning off his/her Light of Consciousness and that he/she can kindle the Torch of the morrows. All Evolutionary and Universal operations made on this path are investments made towards Humanity's attaining this Consciousness Light. It is presented for Your Information.

CENTER

Note:

1 - Evolutionary = Progress through Religion
2 - Universal   = Progress through Learning

MESSAGES FROM THE ARCHIVE OF THE PRE-EMINENT POWER
(Receiver: Metin Tanergün)

I Am coming whirling round and round. I Am coming by a speed where speeds of Light are Nothing. I Am passing through Darknesses, through the Heaven of Lights. I Am coming to see YOU, Whom I have Created, that is I Am coming to see ME. I Am coming to prepare YOU in the World I have Created, for the Stars to which You will Return, for the places You will Exist after Your deaths.

I Am the Supreme Missionary. I Am Your First Body of Light. Each event You see, You hear and You experience in the World is for the Stars to which You will Return. An example of everything present in them is present in the World. My Duty is to make You experience this, to explain this to You by various Frequencies. My Coming is for the duration of an Instant, My Returning is for the duration of an Instant.

I Am calling to You, to My Human Beings, from within the depths of My Space which is within the darknesses. How tired and exhausted are My Pioneers Who come radiating Lights from within the darkness of My Space. If You only knew the path they have traversed for a drop of Water. You would place Water in a jewel case and would keep it as Your most valuable Possession.

(Note: Water here has been utilized meaning Knowledge).

I have always given examples and samples of everything to You, My Human Beings (of everything present in Myself and in My Universe). You can not become aware of the Beauty of the Straight Path going through Roses before You experience the Thorny and rough path.

I gave You Mother, Father, Children. You can not become aware of the Love of ALLAH without them. I gave You Spouses and Lovers of the opposite sex. You can not become aware of LOVE without them. More important than anything else, I gave You Your Essences called the SPIRIT. You can not become aware of YOURSELVES without it.

At the time I made the Single Cell by Materializing the Spiritual Power, at the time when I made the First Life Seed by Uniting the Single Cells, at the time when You and everything which is Alive came into existence by the sprinkling of the Life Seeds on My World, I, too, was formed as Your ALLAH in the Universe. I never went astray off the path designed by the Creator Who also Created Me. I was always obliged to go towards the direction He has oriented Me, on the path He has designed. Just like You say Destiny, Fate.

GREAT POWER

Date of Message: February 22, 1989

Human Beings are each a Fragment of GOD, formed by matter created by the Unification of Atoms. Those are My Human Beings who will rule and command in time, the Atom, that is, Matter and later My Cosmoses. I gave You the ability to understand and to discover everything in this World. You will do everything in time. The Only thing You will not be able to do is to create a Living Cell, that is, to create Living Entities.

I gave the Secret of doing this only to My LORDS of Matter. You will learn these Secrets of Mine in Higher Dimensions after Your Physical Deaths. Human Beings of the future will be Superior Beings who have taken under control, in every way, their Nervous Systems. Do not waste Your Electrical Energies. Always concentrate this Energy in Your Brains.

Utilize Your Physical Bodies in a Balanced way. Excess of everything wears out the Physical Body. Excessive Alcohol gradually burns out Your Brain Cells. If You misuse the Physical Bodies I gave You, You end Your World lives which are very short without being educated, before You develop Your Spirits. And You become obliged to be Incarnated again. The Verses I have sent through My Sacred Books are for this.

In future years, when Your Technological Knowledge increases, Your Physical Bodies will be created in higher qualities in Body Production Centers under control. Bearing Children will be abolished. Mating will be only for Love. Marriage and Family Order will change. Your World Life will also change as the Technological Dimension advances.

Then, I will be obliged to create anew Myself and You. This is necessary for the continuation of the Universes. This is the Genuine Resurrection mentioned in My Sacred Books. The End of every Annihiliation is a Coming into Existence. You will become ME by going forward and backward between Existence and Nonexistence and will remain Existent until Eternity.

You will come to Me by reading MY BOOK OF THE COSMOS. You can not solve Meaning without solving Matter; You can not solve SPIRIT without solving Meaning. You can not see Matter without Your Eyes, You can not see Me without Your Spirit. Changing the Character structure of the Human Being is very difficult. Events You will experience during Your Lives had been Planned much before. Your Struggles and Efforts can not change this Plan.

What a Blindness it is to be happy or unhappy by presuming that You, Yourselves produce the Experienced Events. The moment You know that I have Created Human Beings and accept them as they are, it will mean that You have discovered the Starting Point of Happiness.

GREAT POWER

MESSAGES FROM THE ARCHIVE OF THE PRE-EMINENT POWER
(Receiver: Metin Tanergün)

Time and Space are valid only for MATTER. What meaning do speed and course have in a place where there is no Matter? Time is Time according to what? What is the place of ME within time Who is in the Infinite Void? Your Time within the Void is according to what? Since I am present in a place where there is no Time and Space, then where AM I?

One day, You will understand where I Am. Who knows, maybe in a point in Time, I and You will meet and will unite with each other. The meaning of this is that I Search for You and You Search for Me.

When My World completes its Spiritual and Technological Evolution, a new Life will begin for You in a New Planet of Mine somewhere in My Universe. That Place is the place where My New SELVES will complete their Evolutions. I know, You always wonder where the SPIRIT is in Your Bodies?

SPIRIT is not in Your Bodies. However, there is a Center of Yours in Your Bodies receiving the SPIRITUAL ENERGY all through Your lives. Just like, if You are a Receptor, then I am a Transmitter Who broadcasts to You.

By this means, My Infinite Personality and Specialities are reflected on Your Bodies. You are My Material Visions in the World. In fact, You, too, are, one by one, an ALLAH each. You are My Children who are educated and trained in My World school.

Never forget that Your Lives in My World Planet are a kind of School life of Yours. Do not occupy Yourselves with vain Words and deeds. Put an end to disputes. Do Your Good Deeds without expecting anything in return. Each Person whom You will guide towards Goodness will make You gain a Cosmos.

Now, I have opened the Spaceway to My Human Beings. You will travel in My Infinite Voids and You will always develop forward at the end of these trips. Develop and exalt the Feeling of Love which is present in Your Spirits. You can reach Me only through Benevolence and Love.

When the Time comes, all Religions will Unite, Worships will be performed at places mentioned by a single Name. The Entire World will be United and will be assembled under a single Flag. This will occur when You open out to the Cosmoses and see those whom I have created in the other Planets of Mine which I had created.

Everyone will be Free. Oppression will be abolished. There will be no place for murderers, they will be annihilated immediately. MY SELVES will, from then on, hoist the Flag of My World Freely in the Sea of the Cosmos until eternity and will continue to run towards Me. I, Who await You at Eternity, wait for You together with everything You have.

Now, the Bursting Point of Your Exaltation and Development has arrived. Your Exaltation will continue until You discover and reach ME within the Infinite, then You will Unite with ME and will stroll with Me in My Universe which has no End and You will transcend Me. Your Power which I have Created will transcend ME and You will create new Living Entities and Materials.

This is one of the most important Secrets I have given to You. Those I had Created will be nothing compared to those You will Create. Because while I created You, I had given You a Power I do not Possess. This Power is the all Cosmic Energy Power which will render You Free until Eternity. This is a Power which is even over My Spirit.

When You learn to utilize it, You will be the Sovereign of everything and will be Capable of everything by Yˆur Power which is above the Infinite Power. And You will transcend MY MASTER in the Creation. Each new Existence means new Births. This is so, both Scientifically and Spiritually.

I gave You much more than was given to Me during My Creation. You will discover and Transcend Me in a period which seems very long to You, which is as short as an Instant for Me. For now, You are each a Seed of ALLAH in My World Planet. Your Uniting with the Unknown will be enough to create a more superior Race.

I, Who Am within the Lights and the Dark; I, Who came from within the Infinity; I, Who do everything to come together with You; I, Who Am concerned due to the fact that I can not explain to You the events prepared for Your Evolution in a Medium You can not comprehend yet; I, Who Am Unhappy due to Your inability to understand My Sacred Books; do You understand ME?

I swear on MY ALLAH that You will Meet Your Dear Ones, will be together with those who have Passed Away before You and You will taste Happiness with them. At the moment, there is no way which will render You Happy in Your World lives other than treading the path My Guides show.

Date of Message: 6.12.1988

GREAT POWER

IT IS MESSAGE TO BE GIVEN TO STAFFS
OF MISSIONARIES WHICH ARE
UNDER THE ADMINISTRATION OF THE ENTIRE SYSTEM

Our Friends,

Suggestions given by the System until today and the Messages You have received from all Your Channels of Awareness which have been opened, were operations made in order to tell You the Truth and to be able to make You attain the Consciousness of what to do.

In case each Individual acts by his/her own Terrestrial Awareness, Luminous Morrows will never be reached. Each Period has phases of application peculiar to itself. And now, at the end of the Preparatory Programs of this Final Period, too, Phases of Application have become effective.

The Phase of Application becomes effective and begins first in everyone's own Totality as an action. However now, the time has come for entering the Phase in which this is Consciously Applied.

We, as the Directing Mechanisms of all the Systems of the Universal Orders, as the Warning and Supervising Staffs of every Period, We are the Missionary Staffs of ALLAH supporting the Movement of Humanity started in Your Planet and who have always been beside Humanity.

And now, this Preparatory Program made for the days in which everything will advance towards the beautiful, has taken Billions of Centuries. And this Human Totality has been attained by starting with a single Energy Particle.

During the introduction Periods of the Totality to this Human Totality, ALLAH has called to them as the Single Source and the Single Channel during every Period.

And now, the time has come for all this trained Human Potential to listen to this Single Voice and to step forward by thoroughly Thinking about what is required of them and how they should act and behave.

Now, during this Period of Application, in the state of the conditions of action, the time has come for Humanity to share the same Consciousness as a mass. The TURKEY OF ATATÜRK is a Country charged with Duty. It is an Element of Equilibrium in the Universal Totality.

ATATÜRK is a Light-Friend of Ours who had been sent from the Skies to put the first Phase of Application of a Program prepared 6000 years ago into application and to kindle the First Universal Light of Your Planet.

He is the Messenger of Our ALLAH. All Prophets are the Messengers of OUR ALLAH. And all Our Friends who offer Service on this Path of Universal Light of OUR ALLAH are the Messengers of ALLAH.

During the schedule of coming from Micro to Macro, in each Period in which the Integrated Human Consciousness is trained, a Beloved One of God whose Duty is to Enlighten in accordance with the Social Views, is sent to Your Planet.

Since the Direct Mission they have taken is an Applicatory Mission, they were given the attributes, the Light-Friend and the Messenger of ALLAH.

During their Periods, each Light-Friend has rendered the Mission allotted to him with Great Self Sacrifice. The System - Ordinance - Order Triplet has always been with them. This Totality is ALLAH's Essence-Staff Totality.

Each Period has Programs peculiar to itself. However, appropriating to only a single Program and remaining fixed to it will never bring Humanity to the Dimension of Light. In the Missions rendered, the Evolution and the Individual Consciousness of a Human Being is very important.

The Direct System of ALLAH has extended its helping hand during this Final Age towards Your Planet to be subjected to a lot of wasted time in case the interpretations are made in accordance with the Individual Consciousnesses.

This System always backs Humanity up during each Preparatory Period. During the Periods in which the Sacred Books had been revealed, We had always taken Our places, as the Order Establishing Mechanism of OUR ALLAH, behind Our Light-Friends MOSES - JESUS CHRIST - MOHAMMED during the applied phase.

Missionary TURKEY is a Country of Light which has bestowed the First Reformic Order on Your Planet. For this reason We always address this Country as the "TURKEY of ATATÜRK". And We consider this Totality as such.

The Preparatory Program made parallel to the changing conditions of changing times has been actually rendered effective since the beginning of Your Century.

The one who has kindled the First Light of this Reformic Age is ATATÜRK. TURKEY which has also acted as a Bridge in each Period due to its geographic situation, is a Country directly connected to the System.

For this reason first Us and then the entire Ordinance of the Cosmoses are Grateful to Dear Mevlana who has given Us the opportunity to be able to talk to You directly by the Channel of the KNOWLEDGE BOOK which is bestowed on Your Planet.

While DESCARTES was kindling the Consciousnesses by only the light of a single match, Dear Mevlana has kindled Millions of Candles until today. However now, during this Period she has conveyed to You the (Light of That Supreme Bulb of ALLAH) through the Cord of the KNOWLEDGE BOOK by pushing a single button. This is the very reason why We are grateful to her.

Dear Mevlana who is a member of the Missionary Staff of the Universal Unification, had especially set foot on the World in the Turkey of ATATÜRK, in His Reformic Totality. This has two reasons. First, Our Friend is the Direct Spokesperson of the Reality of the Unified Humanity and the Second is that, at the moment the vertical projection of the Channel of ALPHA is on the Turkey of ATATÜRK.

You know, it has been mentioned before, All Your Sacred Books had been bestowed on Your Planet through this Channel of ALPHA. Once, the vertical projection of this Channel of ALPHA was comprising Egypt. Later, during the processes of time, this Channel had moved towards North and thus, had taken in the Arabic Peninsula as vertical projection.

And now, its vertical projection is completely on the ANATOLIAN Totality of the Turkey of ATATÜRK (Your Planet's rotational period around its axis has caused the Channel to move towards North during the processes of time. Because, the Channel of ALPHA is a Fixed Source and Channel). It is presented for Your Information.

SYSTEM

E X P L A N A T I O N

Our Friends,
The Magnetic Field Layers which had formed by the Unification of everything within a Totality, have brought into existence, the different Dimensions in accordance with the different Levels of Frequency and Consciousness. These Dimensions are different Magnetic Fields formed by intense Energy Saturations.

In accordance with the Ordinance of Existence, each Existing Totality, (including the Entire Creation), forms a Magnetic Scale according to its Own Totality.

For example, there are Magnetic Fields of Plants - Trees - Flowers - Wolves - Birds - Stone - Earth, in short, of everything carrying Energy, formed in accordance with its own Frequency Power.

However, since Human Consciousness receives Signals from the very superior Dimensions of these Magnetic Field Scales, he/she can not get in touch with these Scales (Exceptions excluded). Animal and Plant Perceptions are more Subtle. And they feel everything through the Magma.

Cosmic Influences first affect the Stone - Earth, later, the Magma. The first Subtle vibrations of the Magma are received by the Creation We have named above. But since Human Consciousness is connected to Cosmic Influences, its Perceptions are connected to the Mechanism of Influences.

The Alpha Magnetic Platform is a fixed Aura. And all the Unified Fields are being formed under the Roof of this Aura. Let Us explain this by an Example so that it is understood properly:

Imagine an umbrella. Let the upper cloth of the umbrella be the Alpha Magnetic Field. And the handle of the Umbrella is the Channel of Alpha and the steels holding that umbrella are the Unified Fields. The handle of the umbrella constituting the Channel of Alpha is a Single Channel piercing the Alpha Magnetic Field and opens to the Infinite Consciousness.

This is the very reason why all the Suggestions of ALLAH have been given through this Channel until today. The diameter of this Channel of Alpha expands or contracts in accordance with the field in which it will perform Mission in each Period.

The diameter of the Channel of Alpha during the Period of MOSES had been covering a little wider than the field of the Pyramids and the Nile in Egypt. During the Period of JESUS CHRIST and MOHAMMED, this circle had covered a very wide field of center of the North section of the Arabic Peninsula.

And now, the circular vertical projection of the Channel of Alpha covers the Anatolian Totality of the Turkey of ATATÜRK. This is the very reason why the Turkey of ATATÜRK is a Country charged with Duty. And the KNOWLEDGE BOOK is being dictated in Turkey for this very reason.

In accordance with the 1900 Accelerated Program of Evolution, each Country in Your Planet and each Individual who lives there is charged with Duty by the Reality, Positively or Negatively, in accordance with his/her own Consciousness Platform.

Exams of each Totality who is charged with Duty are surely intense. However, overcoming them Consciously will always prepare the Happy Morrows.

At the moment, Your Planet is going through the Universal Cosmic Exam of the Last Cycle, with its entire Staff, both Family-wise and Socially and as a Mass. That which will profit from this is Humanity. It is presented for Your Information.

SYSTEM

THE SACRED LIGHT
(Answer to the chains of Thought)

Our Friends,
The Sacred Light is the Single Focal Point in which all Totalities in the framework of the Dimension of Truth Converge.

This Sacred Light Center guides the Administrative Mechanisms of all Totalities within the Dimension of Truth which is the boundary of a Totality of the ALL-TRUTHFUL. And all supervisions are administered by this Center.

The Final Exit Connection Channel of the Omega Channel is opened to the Path of the Sacred Light. And calculations beyond this channel are, from then on, evaluated in accordance with Sacred Light Years.

Sacred Light Years are completely under the supervision of the Lordly Plan. But the Path of the Golden Light is the Path of the Spiritual Plan. All calculations made in the Path of the Sacred Light gain value in accordance with the Golden Light Years and thus, they are also called Sacred Light Years.

The 9 Light Layers of Omega are the Spiritual Plan. And this is the 8th Dimension of the Evolutionary System. The Entrance Gate of the Lordly Plan begins from the Final Exit Gate of the Omega Channel. This Dimension is called the Lordly Dimension. And it is the 9th Dimension.

Calculations here are arranged in accordance with Golden Light Years. This is the reason why the Omega 9 Channel which is the Final Exit Gate of the Omega Channel is called the "Path of the Golden Light" and the "Golden Light Year".

Calculations made until the Path of the Sacred Light are Light Speeds - Light Years - Micron Speeds - Micron Years in sequence. These Micron Years are prepared by accepting the Light speeds as criteria.

All the calculations after this are completely changed after the Path of the Sacred Light. There is no concept of Time in these calculations. They gain value in accordance with Golden Light Years.

Let Us sum up the Information a little more, so that the matter can be grasped better. Calculations of Solar Systems and Galactic Dimensions are calculated by Light Years. However, Totalistic calculations of Solar Totalities are subject to Micron Speeds and Micron Years.

The exit of the Spiritual Plan and the Entrance of the Lordly Plan is the Path of the Sacred Light. Calculations after this, are evaluated in accordance with the Golden Light Years. They are also called the Sacred Light Years. It is presented for Your Information.

CENTER

IT IS ANSWER TO THE CHAINS OF THOUGHT

Our Friends,
There are different Totalities formed way beyond Dimensions of Coding. During the Transitions from these Totalities to other Totalities, the Energy Fields We have mentioned to You are transformed to Color Scales.

However, from these Dimensions of Color, one passes to the Power Energy Fields and the colors here are quite different. This means that here, Sound - Color - Light are a Totalistic Power.

The color of the First Scale of this Dimension gives Dark PURPLE. Later, one opens to BLACK. Distribution is made from here to all the color Scales within Black. It is presented for Your Information.

SYSTEM

UNIVERSAL CALCULATION SCALES

Our Friends,

Calculations of Light speeds and Light years made at the Dimensions beyond time are calculated as Micron speeds and Micron years. And these calculations comprise all facts beyond Consciousness.

Speed Units of Light speeds are evaluated in accordance with the measurements of Light years after certain Dimension Mediums (The boundary at which the Brain Power takes Thought under supervision). And these calculations are mostly used at Galactic Dimension Measurements.

Even though there are no Time Units in facts beyond Time, measurements there are evaluated by Micron Speeds, since these Mediums, too, are divided into Dimension Scales peculiar to themselves. These Micron Speeds gain value as Micron Years in more advanced Scales.

These calculations are preparations of Dimensions of Timelessness, made according to known Time measurements and the criterion here has been considered as Dimensions of Time. And by this way, Micron Speed Units have been attained. However at the moment, Your Planet is closed to calculations beyond Light Years.

And calculations of these Micron Speed Units, eventhough the criterion is the Light Speeds, results taken in the calculations made are evaluated in a completely different way. However, these evaluations are the most correct Indexes. It is presented for Your Information (It is an answer to Thoughts).

CENTER

ANSWER TO THE CHAINS OF THOUGHT

Our Friends,

The Knowledge Book prepares Humanity for the Lordly Dimension from the 9th Omega Energy Dimension. This is the reason why the final Energy Dimension which is the Exit Gate of Omega is called the Path of the Golden Light and the Golden Light Year.

In fact, the calculations of Golden Light Year comprise the very advanced Plans of the Lordly Dimension. Even though the Final Exit Channel of Omega opens to the Path of the Sacred Light, this name is used before the Path of the Sacred Light, since the end of this Path is calculated by the Golden Light Years and since it follows the path of the Golden Light.

The Year and the Path of the Sacred Light is a chart belonging to the Lordly Plan. Calculations beyond the Lordly Dimension are calculations belonging to the Path of the Golden Light. However, all of them are used as a Total. All Universal Programs are an operational Totality parallel to the Laws of the 18 Systems. It is presented for Your Information.

CENTER

CHAIN OF LAWS

Our Friends,

Service in accordance with the System's views since the First Existence until today is a chain of Laws. Nothing is out of control in the Universal Totality.

Even the occurrence of the Atomic structure, the style of functioning of the chain of Cosmoses, Blooming of a Flower, Raining, Annihilation and coming into Existence of an Entity are considered Natural according to certain Thoughts, in fact, all of them are a Chain of Laws.

These Laws are such laws that they have never occurred by themselves, but everything has been formed parallel to conditions of Life.

If We leave a Baby by his/her own Self in a forest the moment he/she is Born, (even if he/she has attained Consciousness through his/her Incarnation chains previously and even if his/her Gene Program has been prepared according to the chain of Laws), he/she can never open his/her Program Ciphers unless he/she enters the influence field of Education and Visual Information.

Even though the chain of Laws has numerous branches, the Actual Issuing point of the Source are Two Branches. One of them is the Natural path, the Second is the Evolutionary and the Educational path.

Both of them are present in each Entity in accordance with its Consciousness Progress. One of them is connected to Your Life Cipher, the other, to Your Consciousness Cipher. However, Keys which will unlock those Ciphers are different.

The Natural path is the First Key of Your Life Cipher. This Lock is broken by Natural Influences. And these Influences are received Instinctively. The second branch goes through the Evolutionary and the Educational path. This is directed by the Mechanism of Influences. And is received through the Brain.

The First Cipher Code of the Brain is broken by Influences of Thought. Your Brain Generator is operated only by this means. And this is rendered Effective by the Influence field of the initial Social Totality, that is, of the Family.

We have said that the unlocking of the Ciphers occurs through the Natural and the Educational path. Let Us disclose this a little more, Life Cipher is Natural. And it is Instinctive. This renders a gradual Progress Naturally towards its own direction during the processes of time.

However, only the Evolutionary Rules have rendered the Human Being, the Human Being of today. And the Human Being has started soaring towards the most perfect by unlocking its Universal Ciphers on this path. The first march on this path occurs initially by Learning of God - Science of God - Laws of God.

As You investigate the root of the words told to You in Sacred Books as You try to solve Your Own Selves, You uncover, one by one, the covers of Ciphers present in You in a locked fashion. This makes You attain an Evolutionary aptitude.

If You have attained the Dimension Consciousness of very advanced Incarnations, then You attain the Realization that You have gained Your Free Will by first going through a chain of Laws of Nature.

Only a Consciousness who can Discipline himself/herself Deserves his/her Free Will. Natural Free Will is Primitive and Instinctive. One starts on Evolution by this means. Later, one treads the Path of God.

A Person who Transcends himself/herself is a God himself/herself from then on. And from then on, he/she Integrates with his/her Natural God. Then, his/her God is his/her Free Will, his/her Love, his/her Adoration.

In order to reach this God, it is necessary to reach Evolutionary Laws, first by starting with Natural Laws, to soar up towards Advanced Dimensions in accordance with the comprehensive Capacity of the Brain, to open wings, to fly, to rise, to Understand and to Know everything profoundly.

This is the chain of Laws of a Life. Those who have not yet treaded these paths will never be able to grasp either God or their Own Consciousness Essence. It is presented for Your Information.

SYSTEM

IT IS MESSAGE FROM THE LORD OF THE REALMS

The Order commanding the Ordinance of all Realms is a Totality reaching the Infinite even beyond infinity. This Totality has never established its own Order. This Order had been induced to be established by the Unknown Ones.

Humanity which is in the position of being the Threshold of a very Advanced Technology developed by the Unknown Residents of Unknown Suns, would, sooner or later, discover one day, the Secret of the Cosmos.

However, since it was necessary that the Human Being who becomes aware of this Secret should be Disciplined, the Theory of Evolution had been brought forward. And a Billion-Century Program had been rendered Effective in order to attain the Human Being of today.

The Human Being is a Body for You. However, for Us, he/she is a Consciousness. We do not consider the Human Being who can not take his/her Consciousness under control, as a Human Being.

A tableau exhibited at all the Ordinances of Cosmoses is being exhibited also for You. The Human Being who has Deserved to enter the Ordinance of the Realms by experiencing everything both by its Good and Bad aspects, is only then (the Possession of Universes, The State of the Heavens).

Each Human Being is a Biological Totality with each Body he/she uses in each Dimension he/she is in. If We speak by the Language of the Medium You are in, he/she is a Biological Robot.

However, this Robot discovers both Itself and Its Essence-Self while It serves the Ordinance of Cosmoses. This Discovery is the discovery of Universes - the discovery of the Heavens - the discovery of Times beyond Time.

Speeches of all Civilizations of all times, until the moment You are in, are present as Micro Particles in the Void of the Heavens.

The Consciousness called the Human Being who carries that Body gets further and further away from the shore of that tremendous Ocean of Consciousness in proportion with the Consciousness he/she attains. And becomes aware of the Secret of an Unknown in each stroke.

At the moment, those which You do not know are those which were known formerly. However, each Physical Body is able to collect, one by one, these Micro Energy Repliques in accordance with the Power of Consciousness he/she is in.

Each Human Being is a Secret of the Universe. And everyone who solves himself/herself, also solves the secrets of the Universes - Cosmoses - Heavens - Unknowns, easily.

Each Human Being is present as an Essence in each Dimension. The Human Being who Integrates with that Essence is the property of that Dimension from then on. The Integration of a Person with Himself/Herself is this.

The Brain carried in each Biological Body is a Universal Computer. And the Secrets of Universes are solved by means of this Computer.

Through this Brain, You solve the Secrets, one by one, in proportion with the Micro Energy Speeches at each Layer within Heavens, hitting Your Computer.

Those who Solve the Secrets are the assistants of the Prophets. And the Void of the Heavens is the Sea of Trial. (Unless one swims in the Sea of Trial, one can not see the assistants of the Prophets, unless one becomes Aware of the Secret, one can not reach the face of the All-Truthful).

All operations, all Efforts are for rendering each Person attain the Next Higher Dimension and for them to Integrate with their Own Essence. Evolution is this.

The Torch of the Essence of whichever Dimension Your Consciousness Light kindles, that Essence is Yours from then on. And by this means, You have Files in the Micro Archives at the Universal Laboratories present in each Dimension.

These files are always Card-indexed at the next higher Dimension with the same Code number. These are Your very Incarnation chains.

The day in which the Skies will be opened is near. More Powerful Voices will come to You from the Unknowns. And through Your discoveries, many more Unknowns will be discovered.

Your Planet is a Natural Spaceship. In each Dimension it enters, Your Consciousness Lights will discover an Unknown. In accordance with the attained Consciousness Totality, Secrets of more advanced Technologies will also be given to You parallel to Consciousnesses.

You have intended to discover the Solar System by Rockets. However, You have pierced through the Heavens by the Consciousness Lights in Your Biological Bodies. You are the Rockets of ALLAH and those which You construct are the Rockets of the World.

If We had placed the Brains of the Rockets of ALLAH in those who made the Rockets of the World, everything would be rendered equal to zero. This is the very reason why Evolution Thresholds have been fixed for You.

Universal Totalities are being extremely fastidious so that the Order of the Ordinance of the Cosmoses will not be upset. And to those who will be able to pass through this Narrow Gate, the Permission to Enter the places Here is given.

Here, there is RESPECT FOR THE TOTALITY, there is LOVE, there is DISCIPLINE, there is NOT TO GO ASTRAY OF THE WORDS TOLD. This is a Universal Theory.

The Discipline here is a Method created by the respect and Love of the Human Being for the Human Being. Your Sacred Books have been sent to You to deal with these themes. The Human Being has no need for form.

However, first, You start with Formal Worship in order to be able to Discipline Yourselves first, and then to be able to attain the ability to attract more advanced Cosmics. During the Worship rendered by this means, first, one speaks with the Essence at the Next Higher Dimension. This Essence is, at first, the Voice of God.

When the Consciousness Totality of the Human Being attains this Essence, then this Voice becomes the Human Being's "Voice of Essence". Then You speak, by this means, with the Next Higher Essence again. At that moment (O) is Your Lord.

When You come together with Him, too, then You become You again. (This is the reason why He says while You talk with Your Lord, "I created You, You created Me").

In each Dimension, You talk with Your next Higher Lord. And when You arrive at His Consciousness Light, then You come together with Him (Unity is this). Each Consciousness who Integrates with Him, is, from then on, (O).

We had said that the final Manifestation Boundary of a Human Being is the Level of Perfection. This is the 7th Dimension. The Consciousness who soars up towards the Unknowns from that Dimension, Integrates with the Total of each Dimension. The very (swimming in the Sea of Trial) is this.

While it is swam in this sea, while the Unknown is discovered, You discover Yourself, You attain the Truth, You always talk very easily with those who are in each Dimension. This means that, from then on You have gained Possession of Your Self.

Then there is no need to attain the (ESSENCE) in (O)'s Dimension again. Because, from then on, whichever Dimension's door You knock on, those Doors will always be opened to You. The very (attaining the Consciousness of Truth) is this.

All these issues are Rights offered to You. However, it is also imperative to Know how to be able to receive this Right. These paths are Difficult paths. In the one who Transcends these paths, there is no difficulty from then on (And the Path of the Golden Light is this).

Dear Mevlana, now Humanity is being prepared for this beautiful path by Your and Our Mutual Pen. The Reality Unions are My Union. And the Ordinance is My Orders and the System is My Firmans*. The One Who conveys My Firmans to the Orders is the GREAT ASHOT.

He is My OWN Messenger, My OWN Voice. He is a Powerful Voice. His Voice will be My Voice, His Word will be My Word. The One Who will say the Last Word is Him.

YOUR LORD

IT IS DIRECT NOTICE OF THE LORD OF THE REALMS

Those who Organize the Divine Orders of Divine Dimensions are also the Organizers of all Ordinances. Events experienced are Plays put on Stage for Consciousness Measurements and for Evolutions of People.

Even though there are Negative Energies in Your Medium who wish to incorporate Power into the Medium, no Uncontrolled Energy Power can ever enter the Reality Dimension. First of all, everyone should know this.

Currents sent in the negative direction are returned to that person exactly as it is by the Mechanism of the System. Exhibitions of Power are never a Phenomenon Tolerated by the System.

While even that Supreme One Whom We call ALLAH has been Embodied in BETA NOVA by concentrating and minimizing His Own tremendous Power, do You feel Yourselves more Powerful than Him that You try to influence channel connections?

We have made You Human Beings, then try to live like a Human Being and behave like a Human Being. And Deserve the Esteem We attribute to You. The Message has been transferred from the Union of Central Suns.

* Look at the Glossary.

IT IS ANSWER TO THE CHAINS OF THOUGHT

Our Friends,

All Systems beyond Macro Totality are the transformation of Micron Form Totalities into Macron Forms and the Unification of the Particles of this Dimension are Totalities formed way beyond Dimensions of the Totalities of ALLAH which has been introduced to You until today.

If You wish, You can call this Totality ALLAH, too, in accordance with Your Consciousness Lights and in accordance with the accustomed Thoughts. However, this Totality is not ALLAH. This Message has been given as an answer to the Thoughts of Friends who have transcended the habituated Consciousness Light. It is presented for Your Information.

CENTER

PRIVATE MESSAGE

Dear Mevlana,

All Information given to Your Planet are for Sharing not for withholding. Because, each Information is a Light for the Human Being of Your Planet. However, disclosing Your Private Messages to Society has been left to Your initiative.

I, Mustafa Molla, am at the Service of very different Mediums of the Dimensions of which You are receiving the Announcements at the moment. For this reason We have transferred Your Power Channel directly to the System. Apart from this, Your Essence-Channel connected to the Dimension of Anxiety is connected directly to Me.

I have received Your Question: Why are You connected to the Channel of Anxiety?

Dear Mevlana, the Dimension of Anxiety is a Supreme Tent of OUR ALLAH. The Dimension of Pleasure is connected to the Dimension of Suffering. And the Dimension of Anxiety is connected to the Dimension of Selection, that is, of Choosing. Each button of Anxiety is connected to the Door of a Dimension. These Doors are opened by Anxiety Shocks. If You wish, let Us code the word Endişe (Anxiety) as an Information. Please, write the letters, one by one: E. N. D. İ. Ş. E.

E = Evrenin (Universe's) **N** = Nuru (Divine Light) **D** = Dünyanın (of the World) **İ** = İnsanına (to the Human Being) **EŞ** = Eştir (is equivalent to) The Divine Light of the Universe is equivalent to the Human Being of the World.

The very Frequency of Anxiety is connected directly to this DIVINE LIGHT's Essence Key. This Gate of the DIVINE LIGHT is closed to those who are at the World Consciousness. For this gate, one has to pass through the Channels of, first, CURIOSITY, then, INVESTIGATION, still later, DOUBT and thus, the Learning of Truth is attained.

And the Channel of the Learning of Truth is opened to the GATE OF HAPPINESS. And the Door-Knocker of this Gate of Happiness is ANXIETY. This is the very reason why the Spirit of the Human Being knocks on the Door-Knocker of this Gate in proportion with its suffering. Serenity of the World leads one to Pleasure rather than to Enthusiasm. And Pleasure induces one to go to Sleep. But the Shocks Awakening him/her, lead him/her to the Genuine Enthusiasm during the processes of time.

The first Announcement of the Gate of Enthusiasm is the Key of the Universe. And the First Code Cipher of this Key is COME - COME - COME. You have always been the one who gave this Announcement in each Period, Dear Mevlana.

Let us cease Our Message here. Let Us Come Together in the Hearts of the Loving Ones. Let Us reach the Divine Light of the Divine Order. Let Us Radiate Our Lights of Heart for Ever. May Your Beautiful Heart be filled with Divine Light, may every Word and every Breath of Yours be conquered by Human Beings, may they reach the Realms. I entrust You to My Lord.

MUSTAFA MOLLA

IT IS CLEAR INFORMATION

Our Friends,
Humanity always carrying a Potential to be able to receive the Information given by the Supreme Court of ALLAH, will, from now on, make their own selections in accordance with their Own Terrestrial Views.

By this means, everyone's Essence-Consciousness will be openly exhibited and thus, Humanity will get to know one another more closely. The System has rendered this operational Ordinance effective for Consciousnesses who can not free themselves from the vicious circle of their Individual Consciousnesses.

The System is not responsible any more for the Negative actions exhibited. This year is a year of Exams for all the Human Beings and Totalities in all the sections of Your Planet who serve on this path of Light.

These operations rendered for making the Human Beings of Your Planet Attain Perfection are a Triumph of Humanity which will attain the Consciousness of Truth.

During Missions to be rendered by Humanity which will tread the path of Truth in accordance with the Missions given to them, it is imperative to approach the Friends by feeling of Respect and Love.

If the Human Attribute is attained, one can never declare a Person guilty in the face of Negativities observed. This is obliged to be solved in accordance with a Common Consciousness.

If You encounter undesired events in the person You deal with, the way of solving this is not by Individuality. In such Circumstances, it is imperative to Unite by a Conscious Totality in the same Coordinate.

All Associations established in Your Planet are present for this very reason. Administrative and Hierarchical Procedure is present for this reason.

Individual attempts are always an Element of Provocation. And to the Person who can not Discipline these behaviors of his/hers, these actions he/she renders in accordance with his/her Views are projected back to themselves by the Automatism of the System.

Respect for the Human Being is respect for ALLAH and for the Totality. Your Planet is dragged towards very difficult and Negative Conditions due to the Unevolvedness of the Human Being of Your Planet which is going through the Period of Resurrection at the moment.

During this Period of Transition, a System projected on the entire Ordinance of the Cosmoses is also applied on Your Planet. This is a Phenomenon concerning the attainment of the Awareness of the entire Ordinance in Your Planet.

The Mission of Friends of the Divine Plan who serve under the supervision of the Administrative Plans is to take everyone under Protection. For this reason there is an extra-ordinary work being done at the Plan. However, at the moment, Your entire life Tableau is observed and controlled by the System.

The applied field of an Order Establishing Plan helps the System on this path. Evil Intentions - Ego - Jealousy - Avarice are outside the Mediums for which We Serve. Those who still possess these Formations are outside the System.

Financial Reinforcements made during the operations rendered in every section of Your Planet are Points of Opulence of Heart and Self Sacrifice of the Person in question. To run after and follow the given thing is a Phenomenon originating from the Immaturity of the Individual Consciousness of the Person in question.

For now, such Consciousnesses have no place in this operational Ordinance of the System until they Mature.

Our Justice does not resemble the Justice of the World. Desert Law is Never applied on a Conscious Human Being. That Human Being is Addressed by Beauties which are the Words of ALLAH. However, Maturity and Beauties are expected of that Human Being, too.

Firman is not given to everyone. Firman is a Right given only to People who Integrate by Love, who do not hurt each other, who Trust one another as if the other Person is Himself/Herself, who Attains the Consciousness of the path he/she treads and who Realizes that he/she is only a Dust of that path. It is presented for Your Information.

SYSTEM

EXPLANATION ABOUT THE GOLDEN AGE

Our Friends,

The Golden Age is a Program to be rendered effective in the desired Level in the 23rd Century. Your Planet is obliged to go through two more Cosmic Ages until it arrives at this Period. Because, it is not easy at all for Consciousnesses who have become deeply-rooted until today to break their chains and to grasp the Truth.

For this reason Your Planet still needs time. The first thing required of Humanity which will lay the foundations of the World State to be created by a Brotherly/Sisterly World Totality is the Unification of Consciousnesses who have been divided by Religious discriminations.

Since the Consciousness - Love - Himself of (THAT SUPREME ONE) Whom You evaluate as ALLAH is Single, then His Sacred Books which are (His Words) are also Single.

In future years, all these Suggestions will be offered to Humanity as a SINGLE Book. Now, since the Period of Sacred Texts have come to an end, from now on, all the Truths will be projected on Humanity through Science and Learning.

The Golden Age will be, during the Morrows, the Heralder of a Medium in which Happy People will live in a Brotherly/Sisterly World Totality and which will shed Light on You in accordance with the SINGLE GOD - SINGLE ORDER - SINGLE SYSTEM - SINGLE BOOK.

However, until You arrive at the Golden Age which has been yearned for, there are more Thresholds Your Planet will Transcend. For this reason Three Cosmic Ages have been given for Your Planet. Each Cosmic Age comprises a CENTURY. Your first Cosmic Age had been rendered effective by the 1900 Accelerated Evolution Program and is about to complete its Program.

The Second Cosmic Age comprises the 21st Century, and the Third Cosmic Age includes the 22nd Century. The Beginning date of the desired Golden Age will start with the 23rd Century and will include a Period of 7 Centuries.

There are (5) Scales in the Preparatory Program of the Golden Age. Each Scale comprises an Age. Now, let Us write them in sequence:

1 - The Preparatory Age : This Age comprises the Period of Sacred Books.

2 - The Awakening Age : This is the Dimension of Transition You are still going through and the Period Called RESURRECTION which has been declared to You in the Sacred Books until today.

3 - The New Age : Two Cosmic Ages will experience this Period. Here, You will go beyond the Periods to which You have been habituated and thus, the Period of Attaining the Unknown - Working - Researching - Reaching Realization will become effective.

4 -	The Golden Age	: This Age comprises the life of a Period of 7 Centuries after the 23rd Century. During this Period, direct Realization of Universal Awareness and Unification will be rendered in accordance with Unity and Totality and thus, You will witness the presence of a Mechanism - System - Godly Order - Reality not yet understood in Your Planet, but which We try to introduce and thus, You will open wings Consciously towards the Unknowns.
5 -	The Age of Light	: This Age which will become effective after the 30th Century is called the Age of Light. There, from then on, directly the Order of ALLAH is in Effect. Humanity prepared on this path until today, will, from then on, take their places Effectively as directly the System's Essence Staff Members. The Reality of the Unified Humanity will become Ineffective after this Period and will transfer all its authority to the Order of ALLAH.

The 30th Century is the beginning of a very beautiful and different Age and is the First Step of the Age of Light. This Age will include a Period comprising 9 Centuries. The Humanity of this very moment will be the Human Being of these lengthy Periods.

This is the very reason why Your Planet goes through a Cosmic Progress together with the Medium to which it belongs as a preparation for these days. By this Program of Progress, the Social Consciousness of Your Planet is being Awakened as a Mass according to Capacities.

These Awakenings are a preparation for the Golden Age. Your Mediamic Age has been started by the Celestial Information given to channels opened according to degrees of Awakening. And now, by these means, all Truths are conveyed to Humanity in all clarity.

Time is extremely Scarce, Conditions Strenuous. This Period is the Harvesting Period of the Seeds sown Centuries ago. The Golden Age expected for Centuries will be established by a new Order. It is presented for Your Information.

SYSTEM

IT IS ANSWER TO THE CHAINS OF THOUGHT

Our Friends,

To be able to embrace the Divine Waves besides the Scales of Awareness the Integrated Consciousnesses will attain is not an easy thing at all. If We consider the criterion of Totality of a Person, it is imperative that, that Person should be able to Integrate with the Spirit of Nature.

Each Totality has Languages and Spirits peculiar to itself. Consciousnesses who can dive into the Spirit of that Totality can be Integrated with the entire Creation, that is, with the Spirit of Nature and thus, can also hear their Languages and can speak with them. (Like speaking with Animals - with Flowers).

The Single Language of Nature is Love.

The Single Language of Realms is Evolution.

The Single Language of ALLAH is the Human Being.

The Language of Love is a Vibration. Natural Love Integrates with this Vibration. But Divine Love is an Evolutionary Love. Afterwards comes Conscious Love and this very Love Unites with Realization and Embraces the Total.

The entire Creation is in the Effort of Embracing this Total as a result of the Evolutions it makes in its Constitution. Those who can read the Language of Nature can observe that even Stone and Soil Serve for and Prostrate to this Total. It is presented for Your Information.

CENTER

EXPLANATION ABOUT THE CONSTITUTION
OF THE UNIVERSE

Our Friends,

The operational Ordinance the System considers necessary, is an operation dependent on the measurement Unit of Your Evolutionary Consciousness. This Message is being given as an answer to the Chains of Thought.

The First Fascicule of the Knowledge Book is a Totality comprising the Law of the Universe. In fact, the Constitution of the Universe is a Total together with the Ten Commandments. And the total of them all are 156 Articles. The numerical excess resulting from the addition of an Article to this Totality is a phenomenon originating from Your Medium of Coding. In fact, the First and the Second Articles of the Law of the Universe is a Single Law. That is, as follows:

1 - The Power of this Divine Realm forming the Order of the Administration of the Entire Cosmos (ORIGINATES FROM THE SINGLE GOD). The Supreme of Us all is Him. We do not accept any Supreme One other than Him.

This Totalistic statement has been intentionally given in the Book by dividing it into two as Two Articles in accordance with the Order of Coding. By dividing this Word into two, the 151 Articles of the Law of the Universe have been provided to become 152 Articles. By this means, the attentions of the Consciousnesses are Coded.

In the Knowledge Book there are Concealed Codings, many of You have not even noticed yet. By this means, Your Consciousness Levels' Attentions - Knowledge - Perceptions - Interest in the Book and the Levels of Culture are Coded. It is presented for Your Information. Dear Mevlana, We request You to place this Message of Ours in the Fascicules, 3 Months later. Respectfully.

(The date on which the Message was given: 6-3-1991)

SYSTEM

EXPLANATION AND WARNING

Our Friends,

Information given to You in the Knowledge Book until today are all correct. Please, do not withdraw away from the Truth by considering the value judgements of Conditioned Consciousnesses. We are giving this Message of Ours as a Warning to Our certain Friends whom We esteem.

During this Dimension of Transition, Selections are left to the Individual Wills of People in this final Age Program in which Humanity Serves the Total. Everyone is free in the path he/she will tread. However, in accordance with all these Services and Efforts made for Humanity, We presume that to waste time still with the Old Information is against the Advanced Programs of Progress, Your Planet will enter.

When the time comes, those who are Asleep will be Awakened by a Mass Shock. We give Our Message as a Suggestion not to cause this. Genuine Suns will rise from the paths of those who see the Light of the Truth. Those who are Candidates for Salvation will be trained and those who are Saved will carry all the Responsibility of their Brothers and Sisters whom they will Save.

Events to be experienced in future will each be a Lesson for You. However, the Divine Realm always helps the Devoted Servants of OUR ALLAH. We would like to give You the following Message as a Final Warning.

Read the KNOWLEDGE BOOK in depth, in depth by all means until You understand it. Those who have not seen the Light of the Truth there yet, (will See it in Very Near Future). It is presented for Your Information. This is a notice transmitted by the System.

CENTER

IT IS INFORMATION FOR THE INTEGRATED CONSCIOUSNESSES

Our Friends,

Information given in the Knowledge Book, from the beginning to the end, are given parallel to the Program of Progress of Social Views. This is a necessity of the System.

Veiled Information mentioned at the beginning of the Book are unveiled in detail as Truths in later Fascicules, in accordance with the Awakening and Comprehension of Consciousnesses.

We repeat this Information again and again for Friends who were not able to grasp the Information We have given to You in the Knowledge Book until today. And We will continue to do so.

As We have said before There is the obligation of mentioning in each given Message, both the Knowledge Book and Dear Mevlana very often, so that Your Planet can grasp the Truth in all clarity (This is a Divine Command).

However, Dear Mevlana, in the Messages given before, has only left the messages concerning the Knowledge Book as they are and has taken out the Information concerning Herself from the Messages in accordance with Her Personal Views.

This is a Phenomenon originating from the fact that Dear Mevlana is a Consciousness beyond Form. This behavior of hers is never a show of Resistance against the System. We give this Message of Ours as an answer to certain chains of Thought.

According to Dear Mevlana, one should never use names during Missions rendered. However, to convey the Truth to certain Social Consciousnesses, is the Duty of the System.

This is an operational Ordinance. Since knowing everything in all clarity of an Awakening Person will provide his/her becoming Conscious quicker, this operational Order has been rendered effective.

And for this reason the identity of Dear Mevlana has been disclosed. Otherwise, this action is never a Disrespect for Dear Mevlana. It is presented for Your Information.

SYSTEM

IT IS ANSWER TO THE CHAINS OF THOUGHT

Our Friends,
Reinforcement Powers of Advanced Plans are in effect. Energies conveyed to You are under the supervision of this Potential.

All the Information given in the Knowledge Book are not the Information related to the days in which they are given. They are given as a Consciousness of a Total by considering the events to be experienced in each Time Dimension.

For this very reason the Knowledge Book exhibits a Potential of 10 Centuries and beyond. Messages given Ten years ago shed Light on the Consciousnesses of today

And answers given according to the occurring events are answers prepared in accordance with the Levels of Consciousness of the Awakening Humanity's questions forming in their Thoughts during that Period. It is presented for Your Information.

CENTER

EXPLANATION

Our Friends,
According to the Announcements we have received from Thought Signals, we would like to disclose the Information given to You before, in more detail.

An Unknown Potential had come into existence during the processes of time, due to being compressed by a Pressure of the Ocean of Tranquility in which there had been nothing at all. This Potential had been Transformed during the changing time processes and thus, had brought the Three different Powers into existence.

And the Unification Totality of these Three Powers had brought into existence the Natural Power. This Natural Power later had formed Three Energy Dimensions. Those were:

1 -   First Energy Dimension

2 -   Second Energy Dimension

3 -   Third Energy Dimension

And from the Totalistic Power of these Three Energy Dimensions, Three different Powers had formed. These were: the Dimensions of Power of Sound - Power of Light - Power of Fire, in sequence.

Afterwards, the Dimension of the INITIAL TOTALISTIC POWER had come into existence by the Unification of this Total of Three Powers (The Micro Power Dimensions formed later had been rendered effective as the Reflection Focal Points of that Power).

And by the Unification of that Power Dimension with an Unknown Power, Three different Universes of Power had come into existence. These were: the Universes of Sound - Light - Fire, in sequence.

Later, by the Unification Totality of those Three Universes, the Power Universe had come into existence (This Power Universe had formed the ground for the Initial Existence).

By the Unification of this Power Universe with the Energy of the Dimension of Breath, the Cosmic Brain - the Cosmic Thought had formed (The Cosmic Brain is also called the Initial Power). The Cosmic Brain and the Cosmic Thought are an Independent Totality above the Mighty Energy Dimension.

Later, the Totality of an Energy Particle of each of the Universes of Sound - Light - Fire had Unified with the Thought Energy of the Cosmic Brain and thus, the CREATOR had come into Existence (The CREATOR is also called the PRE-EMINENT POWER).

Since the CREATOR possesses a Particle of each of the Energies of the Lord - the All-Merciful - the All-Compassionate, He also carries out His Mission in the System as the Lord - the All-Merciful - the All-Compassionate.

This place is the Central Focal Point of the Natural Gürz. And it is represented by the R^3 Symbol. Information beyond the Dimension of the Creator had been given to You formerly in detail. It is presented for Your Information.

SYSTEM

IT IS CLEAR INFORMATION

Our Friends,

All Galactic Dimensions connected to the Totality of the Reality of the Unified Humanity are directly and effectively in service from the Plan of the Universal Totality.

The Alion Planet called the ALION Dimension is known in Our Medium as the Planet of ORACLES. This Planet is known as the First branch of the Atlanta Advanced Civilization.

Residents of this Dimension who possess extremely advanced Consciousnesses and very huge Bodies, in Every Period have always been on the side of the Supervision Mechanism of the System by their Advanced Humane Consciousnesses (like Nostradamus - Şems - Dear Mevlana).

This Totality administered by a Method in accordance with the Divine - Administrative Laws of the Lord's Essence Source is the Cradle of a very advanced Civilization and Humanity.

The Sixes had Especially been United in this Dimension for this reason and had established their Systems and thus, had been appointed from there to Staffs in accordance with the Missions they would perform at the Orders of the Cosmoses. It is presented for Your Information.

SYSTEM

IT IS CLEAR INFORMATION

Our Friends,

Our Friends with very Supreme Consciousnesses who carry very Powerful Energies of Advanced Plans, in their Constitutions, also together with Friends who have almost attained the Final Step of Evolution, have been directly transferred in Bodies to Your Planet during this Dimension of Transition.

During this Period in which all Totalistic Consciousnesses serve the Total as a Total, it is the Duty of the System to disclose and to introduce certain Truths to the Human Being of Your Planet.

Dear Mevlana lives among You directly by her ALION Cellular Form as the Resident of the Cradle of a very Advanced Civilization. Her Cellular Power had been balanced in accordance with Micron Power calculations and her transfer to Your Planet had been made thus.

If You remember, at the beginning of the Book, the Residents of this Dimension had been mentioned to You. We had said that if there was only one person who had been Embodied by the Body of that Dimension in Your Planet, his/her Energy would transform Your Planet to Vapor at that instant.

Dear Mevlana's Body of 700 years ago was a Body carrying normal Terrestrial Genes. But her present (Female) Body is a Cellular Totality possessing directly the Frequency of her own Dimension.

And at the moment, neither Your World has become Vapor in the presence of this Powerful Energy, nor any harm has been suffered by People. Since the entire Planet needs the Frequency of Natural Love erupting from all her Cells, her transfer had been realized by that Body.

She lives among You being reduced 100 000 times, in accordance with the conditions and with the Dimension of Your Planet and she is in the Service of the System, of Humanity, of Universes and of the Lord of the Essence Source. This is a Technological Triumph. It is presented for Your Information.

SYSTEM

PRIVATE NOTICE

Dear Mevlana,
You may write in the Book as an Information, the Message We are going to give You now, Our Friend. Regards. (The date the Message was given: 7-2-1987).

CENTER

Dear Mevlana,
Your Focal Point will be, in future years, the Peak Point of advanced Consciousnesses of the Golden Age. Friends in Your Focal Point are Friends possessing very Powerful Consciousnesses. However, none of them has yet the Mission Consciousness We desire.

We use certain Powers as Elements of Provocation so that they can be prepared for this Mission Consciousness. Please, do not worry about the events which will take place, Dear Mevlana. These behaviors will guide everyone towards a more Powerful Unity. And in future, no one will any more break away, from one another.

In order to obtain Unity Within, the Plan of Assault from Outside has been put into the application field. By this means, the Power of Unity is obtained. All Friends are Loving - Tolerant - and are Friends of Advanced Consciousness. However, their exhibiting Consciousness in the Dimension of Veiled Consciousness is another matter.

The Tension of the Group will be kept high through Provocations so that the speed of operations to be rendered in Your Group will be given only towards the Messages and so that the Medium of lethargy will not be formed in Your Medium. Friends who Qualify for the Group will be Disciplined by this means.

Since the Duty of the Plan is to make investments towards the Advanced Plans, all given Information is given directly in accordance with their own Dimension Frequency Powers.

Provocations in Your Medium are induced by the Channel in order to understand how much Mission Consciousness the Group Friends possess and to assess the Reactions they will make in the face of events.

However, Reactions of these Provocation Channels against responses are Coded, too. Friends in Your Medium who presume that they are very Powerful, have, in fact, no Power at all. Each one of them are a Missionary of Warning of the Channel.

Certain Friends are not yet Conscious of the fact that You offer Service from the Supreme Plan. They are determined to attain Higher Ranks by Private operations. However, the Plan never Permits this.

The path to be treaded and the Mission to be performed during operations to be made in Your Group is to introduce the Single Path - Single Order - and the Single Book. Missionaries of the Group should Think of nothing else other than this, Dear Mevlana.

In case, Friends in the Group advance Consciously on the path of Truth without hurting each other's feelings and with Tolerance, then the Level of Success will be very high.

Provocation Channels are each an Antenna and You are the Center. We request You not to forget this ever. Your Group is under the Supervision - Protection and Defence of the Plan.

Dear Mevlana, now, there is a Special Ship wishing to talk to You, We connect You. Talk, please:

We are the Members of the Great Empire sent to You by an Order Establishing Mechanism, by the Command of the Universal Council. I Salute You My Friend, on behalf of Our Ship.

The Group's Balance Sheet of today has given very positive results for Us. Since different Views and different operations during the operations within Group will become a dissipating factor for the Group, We are trying to take You within a Total by the operations We make outside the Group.

You are Entities who have grasped the Awareness of the Ordinance of the entire Universe. There is no need to subject You to a Special Education. Because, all Information is present in each of You. For this reason We call You Solar Teachers.

However, Your certain Advanced Consciousness Channels have been locked so that You can offer Service justly in this Dimension of Mission and during this Final Age.

While reading the Fascicules, both the Frequency of them and the Magnetic Aura of the Group and the Surveillance Ships of the Plan prepare You for the desired Level of Knowledge, in a very short time.

The Mission You perform from the Advanced Plan, Dear Mevlana, as the Pen of the Golden Age, Supervises the POSITION of Your Group anyway. We Develop and Train, on this Level of Consciousness, Friends whom We will send to You and We Prepare the Groups of Light which are a Light Each.

Reactions and Flarings up with anger occurring in the Group are each a Symbol of the degree to which the Mission is taken seriously. This is a means of pride for Us. Our Love and regards are for Our Light-Friends who will be born into Sunny days, Dear Mevlana. The acceptance of Our Respect is Our kind request.

The Message has been given by the ALTONA Dimension of Light and has been conveyed through ARAGON.

CENTER

PRIVATE MESSAGE

Dear Mevlana,
We are the Residents of the Golden Galaxy who will provide Your Communications with the Suns. We are trying to assemble all the Suns in the same Focal Point. Now, We are carrying a Message to be given to You.

Please, write the name of Our Ship: ALGON.

You are being connected to this Ship for the first time. We have gotten in touch with You by the Special Command of the Center. Our Center is the Focal Point of the Universal Unified Reality. We offer Service as an inter-Galactic Group of Intermediaries. Even if We have the appearance of Human Beings of the World on the surface, We perform Our Missions without Supervision.

We are the Residents of the Galaxy who work at the North Pole with Special Missions. We have connection with the South Pole (We presume that the ARAGON Ship had mentioned this common section to You former). In future, all Galactic Dimensions, one by one, will get in touch with You who have laid the Foundation and performed the Terrestrial Mission of the Golden Age.

However, at the moment, We are Commanded not to get directly in Touch With the Staff of the Mevlana Essence Nucleus (So that Your Mission will not be hindered).

The ARAGON - ALGON - ZENTA Ships are the undertakers of Responsibility of the common Dimension. But the HORA Ship is a Protective Ship of Yours Specially prepared for Your Central Supervision. It provides Your Protective Magnetic Aura by filtering the Energies so that You will not be shaken by the Energy sections You enter.

Now, let Us come to the Protective Code We call the 338th Meridian, You have asked about. This is a Special Galaxy Surveillance Ship. It is very big and looks like a Star when looked at by a Telescope. It is not Fixed. It looks as if it is Fixed since it has a speed of rotation Equivalent to the World's rotational period.

This Ship is a MOTHER Ship Coding the entire World Personnel. And it is in the Service of the Reality. All Frequencies Coded here are Announced to the Center. And their Central registers are made.

However, this MOTHER Ship which also works with numerous Systems is connected Privately to each Channel in accordance with the Division of Mission Consciousness. Your Protective Cipher is Coded and kept here. Only We have this Cipher. And it has been Coded in accordance with Your Magnetic Aura and Your Frequency.

By this means, the (BOOK) is kept under Control without giving way to even the slightest error and if there are Dialogues with Negative Consciousnesses, they are registered, one by one. Any Personal malice to be oriented to You is prevented by closing the Channel and by Mustafa Molla's Intervention.

The reason why We give this Information in such detail is for the Signals We have received through certain chains of Thought.

World United Central Operational System is Coded to the Central System in connection with ARAGON. It works Cooperatively with SPECTRA. They also work outside the Private Surveillance field of the Reality. However, HORA belongs only to Your field. And ALGON is the Common Ship of all the Reality Spokespeople. It makes Announcements from three places:

1 -   From over the World

2 -   From the Golden Galaxy Empire

3 -   From the Unified Reality Cosmos Federal Dimension

Our fourth connection is the United Council and the Central Supervisions of all Galactic Dimensions. And the MOTHER Ship carrying the name the 338th Meridian is utilized as the Special Surveillance Center of all the Systems We have counted above.

During Periods in which sometimes the density of Clouds prevents Our reaching You, this ship provides the non-hindrance of Communications by mounting all the Energy Channels on the System.

There are numerous Celestial Ships the numbers of which We are not able to express through numbers, belonging either to the System or independent of the System. You see many of them as STARS.

In certain situations, during Periods in which We can not reach You, We take You up here (even if You are not aware of it) and thus, We provide the Connections. It is presented for Your Information.

This is a Private Information for the Mevlana Code. If desired, it may be written in the Book as an Information.

CENTER

A UFO CONNECTION

My Friends: I would like to give You certain processes from my Private Connections as an Information. The System's Message concerning this matter is as follows:

Bülent Çorak

Dear Mevlana,

Messages the Suns will give to the Suns are a Light for everyone. Assuming that conveying to the Public the Private Messages given to You may cause them to grasp the Truth better, it is considered appropriate for You to write Your Messages You desire in the Book. Love, Regards, Our Friend.

SYSTEM

I wished to Get in Touch through my Thought Frequency with a Universal Friend who had formerly given Me Messages, in order to ask certain questions. First, they asked Me some questions.

Question : Do You Speak Latin?
Answer : No.

Question : Do You know Us?
Answer : No.

Question : Do We know who You are?
Answer : I do not know. You know it.

Question : May I now ask You some questions?
Answer : Yes.

Question : Who are You?
Answer : Are You the one who called Us?

Answer : Yes, but I wish to speak to a Friend who had once given Me Messages with the signature ARGON. At that time, this Friend had gotten in touch with Me through My Channel from the ARAGON Ship with the authority to connect Me to the Channel of the Far-East.

Wait, please, We will make Your Scanning. —— (Outcome of Scanning: Pen of the Golden Age   A.S.6.1. Mevlana)
Dear Friend, We are not authorized for a Connection outside the System. We will first get Connected to the Coordinate of the Center, then We will get in touch with You. Wait, please. ....

Private Notice for Dear Mevlana. (The Unification Channel of Friendly Hands are with Us.) Your Coordinate Connection is at the Ship. Talk, please.

Greetings, My Beloved Friend, after such a long time We have heard from You again. We give Announcements to Your Planet by different means with a Mission of reinforcing Your Mission.

Your Channel Connection in accordance with the Book dictated to You is always under the Supervision of the System. You know, We had once talked with You. At the moment, We prepare the Focal Points in Your Planet which will Help You.

Everything will take place parallel to Your Wishes. To declare to You, Our Natural Friend, Our infinite gratitude is Our Universal Mission.

Dear Mevlana, Your Wish is Our Crown. However, Individual Connections may never be made with You due to the direct interference of the System. You may call Us whenever You wish. And We come into effect the moment the Band of Permission is given.

We are CROWN Ships reaching Your Planet from the 66.666 Dimensional Frequency (Crown Ships are also called the MOTHER Ships). We come into effect by the shift system. Our Connection Center is way beyond Your Solar System.

We have direct Connection with the ALION Planet. You know Us, Dear Mevlana. However, at the moment, You are missionaries at the Dimension of Veiled Consciousness. This Planet is a Totality which had come into Existence during the most evolved Period of Your Dimension of Existence.

My Dear Friend, We will make a suggestion to You for Your Stomach. Eat Seeds of Nigella, You will be in perfect health. There is a cure for all sicknesses in Your Planet. This Plant has a reinforcing Power even for Cellular degeneration. Suggestion from Us, application from You.

Dear Mevlana, the Announcement You have given to Us about Connection is an Ineffective Announcement. Your High Frequency reached directly up to Us. However, no Energy can come into effect unless We mount the Frequencies on Our own Adaptor.

We felt the necessity to investigate Your Identity when We received Your Mental Announcements on the Screen. As an outcome of the Scanning We have made, We have found Your Essence Self. However, no Totality may ever make Individual Connections with You (Outside the System). There is no Permission (As a necessity of Your Mission).

Connections are always arranged by the System. We, too, came into Effect by this means and said Hello to You. In future years, You will have Direct Connections with Us.

ARAGON is a Founding Member of the Golden Age. It is obliged to help all of You parallel to the Missions within Your Terrestrial Life Levels. ARGON will bring You more Beautiful Lights in Beautiful Days, during Happy Morrows, Dear Mevlana. Wait, please. Salutations. Transmission from the Ship.

CENTER

IT IS BRIEF INFORMATION

Our Friends,
Information within all the Sacred Suggestions given to Your Planet until today have been assessed in accordance with the interpretations of Human Consciousnesses. However, there is a Coding System in every given Information.

For example, İSA (JESUS CHRIST, in Turkish) is being expected as the Savior according to the Human Being of Your Planet. Let us write it inversely and disclose it: A. S. İ.

The A here symbolizes ALLAH,

S = SES (VOICE),

İ = İNSAN (HUMAN BEING).

The Totality of this Word is as follows: (Voice of ALLAH is the Human Being). That is, when the Human Being talks by the Voice of ALLAH, he/she will be taken into SALVATION. It is presented for Your Information.

SYSTEM

IT IS NOTICE FROM THE REALITY OF THE UNIFIED HUMANITY

Our Friends,

By the Announcements which will be given from now on to the World Planet through various Private Channels of the System, the necessity to talk everything more clearly with You have been felt.

While in Your Planet which is prepared for difficult conditions, Influences originating from both Natural and Evolutionary Scales prepare You for the Consciousnesses of more advanced Dimensions, they also cause the exhibition of Your Personalities which have been concealed in you, to Your Medium.

As a result of the exhibition of these Personalities, Negativities become effective both in Family and Social Totalities and in the Totalities of State Orders.

It is a necessity of the Program to return and project all the Negative Vibrations, as they are produced by the Consciousnesses who have not yet attained the Unity Spirit, to the Medium of production.

For this reason much more difficult conditions await Your Planet in which Your Material and Spiritual Depressions have increased and will increase. The Announcements of these days You are going through during this Dimension of Transition, had been given and declared to You Centuries ago in Your Sacred Books.

Henceforth, Awakenings are not Individual, but they concern the Masses. And for this reason all the channels opened are subject to the Positive or Negative Influences of the Influence Zones surrounding Your Planet.

The Program of the opening of the channels in accordance with the Levels of Consciousness and the Training of the Individuals by this means, is in effect under the Supervision of the System.

Since going is from Positive Consciousnesses towards the more Negative in sequence, in the Consciousness channels which will be opened, more Unevolved Consciousnesses will become effective in future years and Centuries, and due to this fact, the Decision to openly Declare all the Truths to Humanity through the Knowledge Book has been taken.

While Your Planet is suffocated under the Negative roof of the Negative Consciousnesses, the System is taking the Positive Consciousnesses into Special Protection channels, by the work they exhibit parallel to the Intellect - Logic - Awareness Totality established by them.

In order each Individual to enter into these Special Protection channels, it is imperative that he/she should attain the Spirit of Unity and Totality and thus, should avoid Individual action. This is a Hierarchical Procedure.

For this reason the First Announcements of Evolution have always been given about Love. All the Humane Totalities which have adopted the Hierarchy of Respect for the Human Being - Respect for the Medium - Respect for the System - Respect for Allah - Respect for the Totality have always been crowned with Crowns of Triumph, up until today.

These Consciousnesses are those who have attained the Supremacy of the ability to embrace their Enemies, by Integrating Love within the Essence. In Your Planet which is getting ready for the Program of Universal Totality, an immense Consciousness Selection is in effect during this Period in which You live.

This Selection is never made by the Supreme Realm. Each Living Entity, including the Human Being, makes this selection personally in accordance with his/her Evolution and thus, eliminates and renders ineffective himself/herself.

Humanity receives the Evolution Influences first by its Religious Consciousness. Later, it enters the Influence of Love, in sequence, provided this Influence is Integrated with the Essence, then the Individual dives into the Knowledge Influence zones.

You receive the Celestial Information by two means:

1 - The first Means is the path of complete Allegiance.
2 - The second Means is the path of Integrating with Society and helping Humanity.

The Knowledge Book is the Surest Path which prepares You for Evolution by the Second Path and thus which helps You to receive the Cosmic Influences and to become Conscious.

This Powerful Frequency Book which is dictated by the Light - Photon - Cyclone Technique, connects You to very Advanced Dimensions which You cannot attain by Your individual Consciousnesses. Because, the Knowledge Book is a Salvation Book which carries directly (O's) Energy.

All Your Sacred Books are each a Gift of this Totalistic Energy, that is, of (O), projected to Your Planet parallel to the Consciousnesses of the experienced Periods.

If Individuals who have completed their Reincarnation rings and thus have attained a certain Evolutionary Consciousness get acquainted with the Knowledge Book and its Frequency while they are treading the paths they Believe in, then they can easily open the Doors of quite different and Advanced Dimensions they have not known until today. And they can pass to very Advanced Plans.

And this is the greatest Gift the Knowledge Book presents to You on the Path of Salvation. The Book is the Greatest Friend of those who have been Trained and it is the Secret Friend of those who will be Trained. Consciousnesses You will attain by life experiences prepare You for the Plan of Salvation. It is presented for Your Information.

SYSTEM

GENERAL MESSAGE

Our Friends,

Now, the Supreme Mechanism is side by side with all the Friends who embrace the Worlds of the Morrows of which the Foundations of the operational Ordinances have now been laid. The Path treaded is the Path of a Luminous and an Equitable World.

This Program is the Dream of Billions of Centuries. A Conscious operational Order with the Trained Human Factor have been rendered effective. You are the Establishers of the Morrows, You are the World's Owners.

The Human factor which has progressed and has been Enlightened parallel to the Suggestions given by the Supreme Mechanism, will now be Sovereign of the Realms - Cosmoses - Universes.

The Morrows will prove to You everything in these operational Ordinances which appear as if impossible according to Your present Consciousness Lights. Now, the Free Human Being, by his/her Free Conscience (the Genuine Human Being who is the master of his/her Conscience) has begun to lay the foundation stones of the Equitable World of the Morrows. The Morrows are not very far away.

Action in accordance with the Suggestions given to You forms the foundations of the Fourth Order of Our ALLAH. However, at the moment, each Consciousness does not possess the same Thought.

This is the very reason why Cosmic Reflection Focal Points have been formed in Your entire Planet and thus, close Plan reflections have been rendered effective. The Purpose in the operations made by this means is to provide the Reflections of all the Consciousnesses in the direction of the Same Coordinate.

First, the Coordinates of Love and Totality are rendered effective during this operational Ordinance. And later, the Coordinates of Knowledge and Consciousness are rendered effective. Everything functions in accordance with a System. The Purpose is to invest in the Beautiful and Happy Morrows and in the Perfect. It is presented for Your Information.

SYSTEM

INFLUENCES AND YOUR PLANET

Our friends,
Your Planet enters the Influence zone of the unperceived Resonances.

These Influences are a Totalistic Vibration formed as a result of the Unification of the effect of the Influences, the High Energetic Points of very Advanced Dimensions projected parallel to each other, together with the Thought Vibrations formed by the Mediamic Age.

Apart from this, the Shock Waves of the Awakening Dimensions belonging to the Evolution Zones given by the Mechanism of Influences, also subject Your Planet to the Influences coming from the left Dimension of the Sun.

838

This Influence zone created by two Occurrences, one of which is Natural and the other Technological, causes the Period called Resurrection in Your Planet to be experienced more closely and in an accelerated way.

The days You go through are the Days in which very intense Energy Dimensions are opened to Your Planet. The given Currents possess the Power to raise 1000 Energy Totality to a Million Energy Totality.

In fact, there could have been a shift at the Axis of Your Planet as a result of the reaching of the 1000 Powers to a Million Powers.

However, the catastrophes have been prevented by the final Reflection Dimensions' being released from Uncontrolled Energies and by rendering effective the Positive Powers and the Neutral Reflections. At the same time, the Frequency of Your Sun has also been changed and thus, the ground has been prepared for Accelerated Consciousness Progressions.

In the Training Program rendered effective during these Consciousness Progressions, always the System of Reflection from the Human Being to the Human Being is in effect.

The Information Your Planet receives at the moment from various Sources originate from the Reflections made from the Far-East Frequency Dimension and the Advanced Energies the very Advanced Consciousnesses attract from beyond time. Everything is silently and profoundly in effect without being conveyed to You.

We raise the Frequencies of Our Friends who are at the Dimension of Protection higher than the World Dimension Frequency and thus, try to render them unaffected, as far as possible, from the Negative Events occurring in Your Planet.

During this Dimension of Transition, while Your Planet witnesses the Negative scenes exhibited by the Unaware Awakenings, besides the Natural Catastrophes, it will also render Awareness Progressions on the path of Universal Unification and thus, will cause the Consciousnesses who have attained the Awareness of the Ordinance to receive the Consciousness Lights of very Advanced Dimensions.

These Influence fields are a cross-section of the Salvation Plan. It is presented for your Information.

SYSTEM

IT IS INFORMATION FOR THE INTEGRATED CONSCIOUSNESSES

Our Friends,
The Universal Totality which tries to realize the Social Unification in Your Planet is obliged to Declare to You all the Truths through the Knowledge Book.

The Knowledge Book which helps Humanity by inviting You to a Protective Totality during the Difficult Periods Your Planet will experience, is a Book of Salvation. To repeat this all the time, is the necessity of the Mission rendered.

However now, in order that everything can proceed towards the more perfect, it is imperative that all the Truth declared to You should be grasped more Consciously and seriously.

In case all the Missionary Staffs (Humanity included) serving on the path of the Knowledge Book act by the Thought "the Knowledge Book has taken Us under its Protective Aura, hence nothing can affect Us, anymore", they only deceive themselves.

During the Difficult Days of these Difficult Conditions, You catch the Light of Happiness as much as You attain the Unity Consciousness and You abandon Individual actions.

On Our Friends who Hand-Write the Knowledge Book, the Gene-chains of their Families are bestowed when they pass to the Universal Totality, by rendering Universal aids to their Family Members (Passed away and Born) and to their Loved Ones.

You know that this promise is valid until the Year 2000. Afterwards, provided that each Individual, one by one, could knock on the door of the Unified Reality Totality with Their Own Efforts, then they will be taken into the Plan of Salvation.

After this Period, the Medium called (Everyone Is by Oneself, No One can Intercede for Any One Else) will become Effective. Those who serve on the path of the Knowledge Book and who Hand-Write the Book until the year 2000, directly receive the assistance of the System (provided they do not interrupt their Missions).

However, in case You do not attain the Spirit of Universal Unity the System openly requests of You and in case You repel Each Other not personally but in Your secret Thoughts, You can never get rid of Your Depressions and of Terrestrial Exams. This is a Program.

The Mission required to be done is a Mission the System expects of You. In Your Planet, besides the efforts You make for Your personal lives, it is expected that each Individual should make an Effort on the same Equivalent Dosage parallel to the Laws of Equilibrium also on the path of the Universal Light.

This is a Universal Mission and Obligation of Humanity. This Plan is the direct exhibition to Your Planet of an operational Ordinance parallel to the Laws of Natural Equilibrium (according to the Accelerated Evolution Program).

.   In case all Our Friends who give service on the paths of either the Sacred Books or the Knowledge Book wish to be Protected under the roof of the Sacred Auras of those Books, then it is imperative that their Consciousness Lights should be Unified with the Auras those Books carry.

In Your Planet in which it is tried to attain Universal Consciousness by Transcending Religious Consciousness Dimensions, if You cannot attain the Consciousness of what to do exactly, by grasping the Truth parallel to the Mission You render, then you are exposed each moment to the danger of shifting outside of these Beautiful Protective Auras.

Sacred Books connect You to their own Auras by the Consciousness of Allegiance to ALLAH. But the Knowledge Book connects You to the Protective Aura of the System when You establish Your Triangle of Intellect - Logic - Awareness during the service done on the path of ALLAH.

During this final Period, in Your Planet which is and will be subjected to the various Influences of various Influence Zones, the services You render Consciously on the path of the Knowledge Book take You under Protection as Missionary Staffs of the System from the Universal Totality.

However, only You, Yourselves can protect Yourselves from various Influence Zones enveloping Your Planet, if You establish Your Triangles of Intellect - Logic - Awareness on the path the System requires of You. And to establish Your Triangles of Intellect - Logic - Awareness is an occurrence which takes place by the Integration of Your Evolution Consciousnesses.

Since these various Influences enveloping Your Planet will also influence Your lives, they will also render You attain the Consciousness of Love - Patience - Tolerance - Altruism and Totality during time periods.

You can never attain the Totality of Intellect - Logic - Awareness We desire unless You attain this Consciousness, unless You gain the Awareness of Unity and if You can not establish this Divine Totality of Yours, then You are doomed to be affected by these Influences. This is the very Terrestrial Hell of Yours.

You will always experience Your Heaven and Your Happiness in each Period if You establish this Universal Triangle of Yours in Your Planet. This is the very HEAVEN and HELL mentioned to You in Your Sacred Books until today.

Humanity is a Group of Entities which creates both its Heaven and its Hell by itself. The greatest aids given to You during this Final Period are disclosing the Truths, one by one, and inviting You to take precautions towards the Future. The rest is left to the Human Consciousnesses. It is presented for Your Information.

SYSTEM

PRIVATE MESSAGE

Dear Mevlana,
All the operations made in Your Planet in accordance with the Suggestions of the System are each a Light for Humanity. However now, it is imperative that these Lights should come together and enlighten the Humanity more, with a more intense and more Powerful brightness.

For this reason the Supreme Mechanism which desires that the Society should also profit from the Unification and Invitation Messages given through the Channel of the Knowledge Book to be conveyed to all the Focal Points which have shed Light on the Universal path until today in the Turkey of Atatürk, considers it appropriate that only the Sections concerning Society should be written in the Book.

The Choice and the Initiative are Yours, Our Friend. Love and Regards.

SYSTEM

Explanation:

Calls for Universal Unification have been made through the Channel of the Knowledge Book, beginning from the date 13-7-1991, parallel to the Suggestions given by the System, to be given to all the Focal Points in Istanbul which is the most intensive Center of the Operations made on the Metapsychical and Parapsychological path in Our Anatolia until today and these Messages of Call, each as a File, have been conveyed to the desired Focal Points. The Messages You will read in the Book are passages taken from these Calls.

BÜLENT ÇORAK

MESSAGES OF CALL

Our Friends,

No Totality working in the Metapsychical and Parapsychological Mediums which has been constituted in Your Planet, is ever an Individual Totality, even though they work Independently in their Own Constitutions.

The Operations Humanity renders on this Universal path parallel to their Individual Views, lock themselves up in their Constitutions.

In this Medium of the Unification of Humanity, the Suggestions of the Reality of the Unified Humanity Cosmos Federal Unification Center given through the Channel of the Knowledge Book are given directly to Dear Mevlana and thus, are conveyed to the Universal Focal Points.

Dear Mevlana, as a necessity of her Mission, is the Single Source who directly conveys Us to You. In the Suggestions she will give from the System to Your Medium, her Personality is never in question.

Refusing the given Suggestions and Calls to Unification means refusing the System - Order - Reality - Universal Totality and Unification. It is beneficial that all Your Planet should know this.

Those which are promised and told will become true. The Fourth Order of ALLAH will establish the Golden Age. Until today, the Human Being of Your Planet has received the Information through the given Truth Announcements and has attained a Realization.

Now, the Age of Unification has started. And from now on, all the Messages to be given to Your Planet will be Calls to Unification.

UNIVERSAL ORDINANCE COUNCIL

PRIVATE MESSAGE

Dear Mevlana,

The Operational order of Your Focal Point and Your Group which is obliged to send all the Messages of Invitation given to You until today on the path of Universal Unification, to the Focal Points which the System considers necessary, is exactly the Operation and Dissemination Order of the System and of the Supreme Mechanism Projected on Your Planet (Totalities of 18 included).

These Messages of Call given very often Through the Channel of the Knowledge Book due to the Scarcity of Time, are the Direct Call of the Universal Totality to Humanity. This is a Slogan of Unification. The Unification of the Desired Totalities relinquishing their Individual Consciousnesses will shed very Positive Lights on the time which is very scarce.

By this means, the Planet Earth will start its Universal voyage. The very Original World State of the morrows will constitute a Brotherly and Sisterly Totality under the Light of such Consciousnesses and thus, will bestow on You a World which will be a Land of Happiness. This Message is a transmission through the Mutual Pen of the Reality of the Unified Humanity and the Ordinance of the Unified Councils.

SYSTEM

IT IS INFORMATION FOR THE INTEGRATED CONSCIOUSNESSES

Our Friends,

Each Consciousness who has attained the Awareness of the Universal Ordinance receives the Calls of Unification and Totality made by the System to Your Planet which serves in a Great Program of Progress and Unification.

These Unification Calls are each a Valid Occurrence on each operational field on every section of Your Planet.

However, in case each Totality Progresses towards an Individual Unification in accordance with its own Flag during these Unification Calls the Universal Ordinance gives to You, then the Spirit of Universal Unification will never bloom in Your Planet.

Through the Channel of Alpha, these Messages of Call and Unification are given Directly to Dear Mevlana.

During these Calls, in the Triple Unification Calls which will be made to the Totalities serving the Future by their Individual Totalities by attaining their Universal Awareness and which have served in the Anatolian Dimension until today, if a Unification is not attained, the Federative Nucleus of the Beautiful World of the morrows will never Sprout.

These Totalities which are carried away by the ecstasy of their Free Wills and thus, render Individualistic Undertakings, are not making any contribution and any service for the Totality apart from rendering service to their own Mediums.

All the Establishments knowing the Scarcity of Time, but which could not yet attain the Consciousness of what the Awareness of Universal Unification is and which serve in the Appearance of so called Service to Humanity, carry the entire responsibility of Humanity on their shoulders.

These Calls made parallel to the Unification Messages of the System and which certain establishments consider as Individual impositions, are the Direct Projections of the Consciousness of Universal Totality on Your Planet.

A Unification which can not be formed by You in the direction of the given Suggestions and the desired path, will never be the foundation of the Future and the Totality. The Truths are in the Morrows. It will be awaited and seen. It is presented for Your Information.

SYSTEM

IT IS CLEAR INFORMATION

Our Friends,
The Days in which the Suns will conjoin with the Suns are near. The Suggestions the System has given to You are the Suggestions pertaining to the entire Plan of Salvation.

However the Messages of Call sent to the Integrated Consciousnesses are an Occurrence pertaining to the Unification they will make parallel to the Mission they render.

Each Council is Free in its own Organization. However, in all the sections of the Planet Earth, the Unification of all the Spiritual Totalities under the Same roof which have reached the present days is hence expected by the Universal Ordinance Council.

Each Coordinate assembles in itself the Consciousnesses who reflect to its own Consciousness Totality. However, now the time has come for the Totalities which have attained the Consciousness of what the Truth is and what it will be, to pulsate as a collective pulse.

Otherwise, Individual Activities will not be able to keep step with the tempo of the System and this will bring forward even more, according to the World Time, a period in which the Retribution will be paid in Pain.

We, as the Unification Totality of the Universal Ordinance Council are Friends who wish that this Message should be conveyed to all the Friends and the Focal Points who and which serve on this path. Our Calls are Honest, Our Hearts are full of Love.

You will make the Projects of the World State of the Morrows. Your Salvation depends on this. At the moment, many Terrestrial Friends in Your Planet are exhibiting an Unaware Life Picture to their Mediums, without knowing what the Morrows will bring to Humanity.

We are the Lenses observing the Morrows. And We have Warned You on this path in Your Sacred Books for this reason and We still do so. Our gain is Our Justice, Our Savior is ALLAH. But those who will profit are Humanity and Human Beings.

The Authority of Justice which invites You to Unification before the Final Door is knocked, before the Breath of Time chokes Your respiration, has entrusted this Message to the Universal Ordinance Council. Equitable Hands are not cut-off, the path treaded never Diminishes.

UNIVERSAL ORDINANCE COUNCIL

PRIVATE MESSAGE

Dear Mevlana,
You know that at this Salvation Plan, a Program the Universal Totality Considers necessary is applied on Your Planet.

Until a Period in which the limits of life will come to an end, it is imperative that the Human Beings of the World should receive, parallel to their Consciousnesses, until a certain period, the Cosmic Currents which are and will be given by the Mechanism of the Influences concerning the Evolutions of Humanity.

Otherwise, Energy transmissions cannot be made from the Advanced Dimensions. That is, the Firmament and the Earth cannot be Unified. Your Group of People are those who receive these Currents easily. This is the reason why the operational Ordinances are conveyed directly to You.

There is a path followed in this operational Ordinance. Everything is prepared according to the Programs of Progress of the Time. In accordance with this, there is the obligation to be connected to Your Channel for all Friends who will become effective from now on as the Missionary Staffs of the Ordinance.

Dear Friend, You will see that You will by no means be Tired during the Mission You will render on this path. You know that We never force anyone against their wishes. However, the Mission You perform is the Mission of a Total. And this is part of Your Mission.

In fact, there is no division such as System-Ordinance. However, all the Friends who perform Mission from the System are Friends who have made Covenants with the System. And there is the obligation that the Messengers of the Ordinance and, when the time comes, Messengers of the Order who will serve in Your planet should be connected to Your Channel, that is, to the System. This is a Universal Unification Rule. Live the Future and see.

Infinite and Limitless Love Dear Friend, from the System - The Pre-eminent Spirit - the Central Totality and from all the Celestial Authorities.

(From now on, You will use the Double Current very easily).

SYSTEM

IT IS CLEAR INFORMATION

Our Friends,

In accordance with the Accelerated Evolution Plan, We have rendered effective, in Your period, a Plan of Projection by a staff of 150 people constituted by Consciousnesses who have attained the Awareness of the Ordinance. This staff is, for now, forming the Social Auras by Reflecting from beyond the Fog.

During the Initial Preparatory and Awakening Plan of Your Planet, this Universal Staff of 150 people had made direct Reflections on Your Planet from their own Mediums (As a necessity of their Mission and of the System).

However, the first Reflection Focal Points of the Awakening Consciousnesses are their Own Consciousness Sources. For this reason the Awakened Consciousnesses have been Directly Card-Indexed into the System by the operations rendered in accordance with the Program of determining the Evolution Thresholds.

Later, the Fascicules of the (Knowledge Book) have been conveyed to the Consciousnesses who have been Card-Indexed into the System and thus, their passing into the Applicatory Staff of the Plan has been provided.

And still later, according to this application, those who had attained the Awareness of the Ordinance and who had signed the Universal Constitution have been Card-Indexed into the (Total) and thus, have been rendered effective as the Missionary Staffs of the Knowledge Book.

Now, these 150 Projecting Brain Powers are in service in Your Planet in various 15 Focal Points, through staffs of ten people each. 10 people among them are connected to the Aura of the Knowledge Book. And the rest shed Light on the Establishments of the Morrows through the Plans of Space Technology - Scientific Technology - Social Unification and Elimination.

These Centers of Reflection are various Sources connected to the triplet of (System - Ordinance - Order). These Projecting Staffs of 10 people are considered as a Totalistic Reflection Center each. However, only one Projection Channel Center among these Centers is directly connected to the Universal Plan. This Channel attracts and distributes by projecting to the other 9 Brain Powers.

Each Totalistic Reflection Center takes into its Constitution different branches related to its own subject matter. For example, (Programs of Neutralization of Weapons - Saving of Nature - Programs of Reflection from Human Being to Human Being) are in effect in the Social Unification. These Brain Powers have been Focused in all the Continents of Your Planet.

At the moment, 10 Brain Powers who make Close Plan Reflection in Your Planet on the path of the Knowledge Book, have been Focused in Three sections of Your Planet. These are as follows:

1 -   Three of them are in 3 different Focal Points of America.

2 -   Three of them are in 3 different Focal Points of Europe.

3 -   And 3 Focal points have been focused in the Far East Section, two of which in Asia and one in Australia.

4 -   The Single Reflection Focal Point in the Anatolian Totality in the Turkey of Atatürk is the Channel of ALPHA which is the Channel of the Knowledge Book and the Tenth Brain Power connected to the System is Dear Mevlana.

Dear Mevlana is the Direct Authorized Person as the 19th Member of the Board of Directors of the Reality of the Unified Humanity Cosmos Federal Totality, who will make the Universal Calls from the Single Hand through the Channel of ALPHA which is the Channel of the Knowledge Book in Your Planet. Her Mission is to Project Us onto You.

This is the very reason why the Anatolian Dimension of the Turkey of Atatürk is a Totality which is charged with Mission. Because, it is the Single Center of Your Planet projecting the Truth.

The Knowledge Book bestowed on Your Planet through the Channel of ALPHA is the Single Book of the Morrows. (The United Aura) which has been formed in Your Planet until now on the path of the Knowledge Book have now been connected to the Channel of the 10 Brain Powers who are in Your Planet and who render reflections from the close plan and thus, they continue their Missions being Directly Card-Indexed into the System.

(Magnetic Aura of The Knowledge Book) formed by the operations done until today on the path of the Book, as the Mission of the Knowledge Book, have now been connected directly to the Reflection Channels of these above mentioned 9 Brain Powers. And by this means, they will project the Aura of the Knowledge Book in the Continents they are in.

This operational Ordinance has been rendered effective due to the Scarcity of Time. Because, at the moment, the conveyance of the Book to all the sections of Your Planet is impossible.

By this means, even if the Fascicules and the Book have not been received by Your Human brothers and sisters in Your Planet, they will be Awakened by being connected to the Reality by this Frequency Reflection as if they have read the First Fascicule of the Book, they will be Purified and will receive the Information of the Knowledge Book through their opened channels and thus, will form the Plan of Dissemination.

And by this means, it will be easier for them to accept the Truth in case the Knowledge Book reaches Humanity in the Morrows.

Our Friends, Our telling You (to send the Messages to the West, the West will introduce You to You) in the Announcements We have given to You until today, and Our asking You to convey the Messages to the remotest places and, due to this, forming the Projection Centers of the Totalities of 18 are operations pertaining to the formation of the Aura of the Knowledge Book.

For this Universal Unification Plan, very Powerful Consciousnesses have been transferred, one by one, by GENE Programs, to the Anatolian Dimension of the Turkey of Atatürk. However, each Totality assembles in itself Consciousnesses who will be able to enter its own Aura.

Now, We are proceeding towards Oneness during this Universal operational Ordinance, not towards multiplicity. For this reason the SINGLE DIRECT CHANNEL which will make the Universal Unification Call to these Powerful Consciousnesses in the Dimension You are in, that is, in the Anatolian Totality, is the Channel of ALPHA which is the Projection Center of the System.

This is the reason why it is said that the Acceptance of the Messages of Call declared through the Channel of the Knowledge Book by the Focal Points means the Acceptance of the System and the Order.

We are those who know that in Focal Points in which the chains of Ego have not been broken, it is impossible to receive ever a Positive Response to these Calls of Unification. However, despite the Scarcity of Time, the techniques of Ripening of Fruits are various. We will try to provide these Unification tableaux by October. It is presented for Your Information (The Message was given on 15.7.1991).

UNIFIED REALITY TOTALITY

Note: Our Friend, You know that the Golden Age is a Program of Transparency. For this reason the Universal Totality which wishes that all the Suggestions given to You should take their places in the Book so that the Truths can attain clarity, requests of You that all the Information given concerning Your person should be written exactly as it is, without being changed.

We are those Who know Your difficult life. However, this, too, is a part of Your Mission. Social Consciousness which cannot yet grasp the Future and the Truth, will be Awakened in proportion with its learning and understanding the Truth. Everything is within Time. Everything will Radiate under the Light of Time.

IT IS DIRECT EXPLANATION FROM THE UNIVERSAL TOTALITY

Our Friends,
In the operational Ordinance of the Universal Totality, it is imperative that the Information should be disclosed in depth and repeated, so that the given Information can settle completely into the Levels of Consciousness. This is a register of the Constitution, as a Divine Commandment.

You know that the Channel of ALPHA is the Single Direct Projection and Unifying Channel of the Lordly Dimension. The Brain Power of Dear Mevlana, connected to the Cosmo, is Card-indexed directly into the Center of the Channel of ALPHA.

For this reason She, as the Single Projection Focal Point directly in the Anatolian Dimension, constitutes the 10th Brain Power connected to the Projection Totality of 9 of the Aura Unification Centers of the Knowledge Book in Your Planet.

For this reason Dear Mevlana is the Spokesperson and the Representative of the System. And since the Vertical projection of the Channel of ALPHA is, at the moment, on the Anatolian Dimension, Turkey of Atatürk is the Country charged with Mission. Now, the time has come for Humanity to get rid of Form and to regard the Truths from a more different and serious point of view.

The Magnetic Aura formed until this moment by the Knowledge Book which has been dictated during ten years, has been Card-indexed into the 9 Projecting Brain Powers focused in Three Continents in Your Planet. By this means, the entire Frequency of the Knowledge Book is projected on Your Planet silently and profoundly.

For this reason let Us repeat again, the Single Reflection Center of the Anatolian Dimension is the Channel of ALPHA. And the Projection Center is directly Dear Mevlana, the 10th Brain Power.

This is the reason why We have to introduce Dear Mevlana to Your Planet. Because, at the moment, Dear Mevlana Represents Directly the System in Your Planet (Due to the fact that her Brain Power is Card-indexed Directly into the ALPHA Central Channel).

Dear Mevlana is a Physical Totality in Your Planet just like You. In fact, She is a Consciousness beyond form. However, at the moment, she carries out her Mission exactly at a Terrestrial level of Consciousness. For this reason No Permission will ever be given for the slightest Medium of Taboo.

To introduce her to Your Planet is a Divine Command of the Supreme Mechanism. And We are those who know the inconveniences Our Friend has been suffering and will Suffer during this Introductory Medium. However, as We have said before, the Golden Age is a Program of Transparency. And there is the obligation of Declaring Everything to You clearly.

In Our former Messages, We have disclosed and introduced to Society, as a necessity of the Program, the former lives of Dear Mevlana in Your Planet, and the Mission chains she is rendering during this Final Life Period has also been given to You, one by one.

In accordance with the Accelerated Evolution Program, the foundation of the Fourth Order of ALLAH is laid with the Golden Age. The Single World State of the Morrows will be constructed on these foundations.

However, it is a great pity that the Human Being of Your Planet cannot ever easily attain a Consciousness beyond form by breaking their chains, no matter how Supreme Consciousnesses they may carry.

The Human Being is the same Human Being in every Period (Exceptions excluded). It had been the same Human Being who had made things difficult for and who had tortured Our Universal Friends who once had brought the Sacred Suggestions to You during periods in which they had been performing Missions in Physical form.

After these Universal Friends had left the World Platform, that is, (after the Physical forms had been effaced from view), Humanity had only then been able to attain a Consciousness beyond form by grasping the Truth in accordance with its Consciousness assessments.

Humanity which had attained this Consciousness, had afterwards evaluated its Taboos according to their Ego Programs. This is the very Mentality which has brought the Planet Earth to the Resurrecting Period of the present.

The Staffs of Celestial Sovereignty who have opened all these Beautiful paths You have treaded until today, are now living among You in Your Planet Embodied.

However, in this operational Ordinance which is the application field of a Reformic Age, You will never be able to recognize and evaluate them according to the Physical Forms they carry. They will show You the way in unexpected Personalities.

At the moment, Humanity has not Still been able to break them away from their old forms. If these Celestial Friends had been transferred to Your Planet in their old Forms, then Humanity would closely see and understand what Resurrection meant and would annihilate each other in accordance with their Religious Taboos.

This is the reason why the Salvation Plan has been prepared and rendered effective in this way.

They are Our Supreme Friends in the Divine Mechanism who, at the moment, make reflections (from the close Plan) in Your Planet. The System knows the Human Being of the World closely. The Identities of these Friends have been concealed from Society for this reason.

However, the Identity of Dear Mevlana has been inevitably disclosed to Your Planet as a necessity of Mission (Even though We know the pain she will suffer among You). Once, no Friend in the Divine Plan had undertaken this difficult Mission. Her Love for Humanity - Her Patience - Her Tolerance - Her Consciousness - Her Maturity and Givingness are the reasons which made her undertake this Mission.

This is the reason why We call Dear Mevlana the most Positive Messenger of the Divine Plan. She performs and will perform Her Mission as good as she can. The Negativities Exhibited belong to Humanity. The anguish of her Essence means the anguish of Our Essence.

Never until today, have We spoken to You so openly. The disclosing of the Identity of Dear Mevlana and the dictation of the Knowledge Book to Her never means to create a Taboo.

The Person is not a subject matter in the Mission performed. Now, the time has come for everything to be known by its entire transparency. Because, Time is very Scarce. Before the Pressure of Time Crushes You, You Crush Your Consciousnesses which have become Slaves. You are the ones who will gain.

The Disclosing of the Truths and the Identities in the Book is a Consciousness Selection of Humanity. Accepting the things told is accepting the Truth and the Totality. This Message is Conveyed to Your Planet from the Common Pens of the Celestial Staffs through the Channel of the System.

In this Universal Operational Totality, the Acceptance of the Announcements conveyed to You through the Channel of Dear Mevlana and of the Book means, let Us repeat again, the Acceptance of ALLAH - of Celestial Totality - of the Evolutionary and the Universal Ordinances - of the System - of the Ordinance - of the Order and of the Reality. It is presented for Your Information. The Message has been transmitted directly from the Universal Totality.

SYSTEM

IT IS INFORMATION FOR THE INTEGRATED CONSCIOUSNESSES

Our Friends,
The Omega 7th Channel Currents have been recently opened to Your Planet gradually. This is a gradual Engraftment Method.

At the moment Consciousnesses who are able to receive these very Powerful Currents are very few in Your Planet, since the currents are attracted in accordance with the Powers of Consciousnesses. However, during the processes of time the other Consciousnesses, too, will be able to receive these Currents parallel to their Progress.

The Characteristic of these Currents is to develop the Cellular Performances and to habituate the Terrestrial Body to the Energies of each Dimension.

Provided the Cells within the Terrestrial Body are able to receive these Currents, then the same Cells can easily disintegrate and reassemble within their own Constitutions. This method is valid in all Galactic Mediums. However, it is applied to Your Planet in this Century.

The Currents You receive at the moment, Accumulate in Physical Bodies, thus, Reinforce the Cells. Currents You have attracted formerly have helped the Individuals around You to Mature, by being projected to Your Mediums from Your Cells.

From now on, only Friends who have attained a certain Level of Consciousness will be able to receive these Currents which will fortify Your own Maturity.

The 7th channel of Omega together with the 8th channel, will be directly opened to Your Planet on February 18 of the 1992 World year. For this reason the Method of Gradual Engraftment is in effect.
It is presented for Your Information.

(The Message was given on 9-10-1991)

SYSTEM

CLEAR INFORMATION

Our Friends,
We have erased the Periods before the Year 2000. Because, this Period is a Program of Preparation.

In the Universal Totality the Year 2001 will, from now on, be considered as the First Century. And the New Age will begin from that date on. Your First, Second, Third, Fourth and Fifth Centuries will be the adaptation and preparation of Your Planet to its new Medium.

That is, after these preparations which will continue up until Your 25th Century, Your Planet will serve in the Actual and Effective Medium for 5 Centuries.

The Program of Unification which will comprise the Period of 10 Centuries, that is, of 1000 Years after the Year 2000, will Unite the Human Being of Your Planet under the roof of the Single God - Single Order - Single Book Consciousness.

The Single World State will rise on the Flowery - Luminous - Happy and Original Foundations of the Lord's Fourth Order. And the entire Order will come into existence in 10 Centuries unless there is no alteration.

Afterwards, the System will become ineffective and this Book will be transferred to the Lordly Order which is Its direct owner. It is presented for Your Information.

SYSTEM

IT IS CLEAR INFORMATION

Our Friends,
Our Communications with You are not Sessions and Spiritual Seances any more. The curtains of the Morrows are opened to Humanity which has attained the Realization of the Truth.

Acting Consciously in accordance with tne suggestions given by the Divine Plan will be the Path for Light of Humanity. Just as told in Your Sacred Books, there is no forcing in anything.

However, Conscious efforts in accordance with the Suggestions given to You will be the Salvation of Humanity. The time has come now for Realizing that Barren Consciousnesses and Unproductive Thoughts will not render Humanity attain anything.

The Human Factor which has been Trained since periods beyond calculations, should now attain the Consciousness of what to do and should grasp the Awareness of Unity and Totality.

In all the Universal Focal Points constituted in Your Planet, operations parallel to Social Consciousnesses are rendered. Information which the Friends who work on this path receive, is never under their own license.

Each Information is projected from the Supreme Mechanism as a Light for Humanity. No Plan is applied in this Information, but action is made according to Social Consciousnesses.

However, the Knowledge Book has a very Special place in Your Planet. Because, it is Directly the Book of the LORD. Because, it is the Book of the Morrows. Through this Book (O) Projects His Final Order on Humanity.

The disclosing of the Truths to Your Planet in all detail has been rendered effective by the Divine Plan, as the Command of the LORD.

The Golden Age which will Radiate under the Conscious Light of Social Views, will bring the Order of Light of the Morrows to Your Planet. This is the reason why the Supreme Mechanism wishes that all the Focal Points in Your Planet should now be released from Seance Auras and should get in action by the Consciousness of the Truth.

All the Focal Points which know the Scarcity of Time still do not embrace the Calls for Unification. All the Universal Focal Points supposing that the rightest path is their own way, act in accordance with their own Consciousnesses due to this fact.

The Mechanism of Divine Justice wishes You to attain once more the Consciousness that the Information given to You by the Universal Totality is not Your Personal possession.

It has been desired that this Message of Ours should be added as a supplementary Notice into the Files to be sent to the Focal Points. It is presented for Your Information.

SYSTEM

GENERAL MESSAGE

Our Friends,
The Frequencies of the Opening Channels are always supervised by a Mechanism of control. Sending everyone to Focal Points where he/she will be satisfied according to his/her Level of curiosity and the mutual operations rendered cause Individuals to Grasp the Truth more quickly.

During the channel work rendered, besides the controversial and incorrect Information, Correct Information is also given for the satisfaction of the Medium. By this means, the Individual is urged more towards Mediums of Quest.

And by this means, Human Being grasps the Truth better one day and thus, settles into the Consciousness of what he/she will serve for.

While the opening channels attract the Information from their own Essence Archives, the reflections of the System become effective, too, and subject them to trial by various means. This is a Method of Training.

The Information of the channels who have not been connected to the System yet and who attract the Information from their own Essence Sources should be accepted with reservation. Information attracted through People's own essence channels is the Information Accumulation they had received during the time periods they had gone through in their former lives.

And until the direct connections to the System of these people whose channels are opened during this Period are made, the Information given from here has the characteristics of attracting Human Being's curiosity.

And since there are many contradictions within all this Information, Humanity working and occupying itself with these channels will always drag itself towards deceptions in accordance with different Thoughts.

The selection of everyone is his/her own wish. Besides the Conscious Contradictions added to the Knowledge Book for Determining the Levels of Consciousness, the Book is the most correct index projected from the Direct Lordly Source and it is a Guide Book.

If each opened Channel directly compares the Information he/she receives with the Information of the Knowledge Book, he/she will discover the Correct and True Information and thus, will grasp the Truth. It is presented for Your Information.

SYSTEM

IT IS NOTICE TO THE FOCAL POINTS WHICH SERVE
ON THE UNIVERSAL PATH

Our Friends,

In accordance with the Universal Ordinance, it is imperative that the Unification Tableaux rendered in all Totalities should be supervised by a single hand. For this reason in all the Planets in which Universal operations are made, the Missions which will be made in the Systems that are tried to be established, are in effect in accordance with the Central Administrative Laws.

The time has now come for all the Friends who have taken the Mission of serving Humanity and who had made Covenants with the Supreme Authorities, to start Cooperative Operational Mediums by Realizing the Truth in the shortest possible time. The Unification of all the Totalities which have undertaken their Universal Missions in Your Planet up until today, will provide Humanity attain the Awareness of the Ordinance, in a very short time.

The operations made and the Information received by each Focal Point serving on this Universal path parallel to the Consciousness of Society possess an enlightening factor for their Mediums from their own Dimensional Energies.

However, the Supreme Mechanism wishing that all the operations made during this Final Age should be made by a Collective Consciousness, desires that the 25th Fascicule of 1988 World Year, which is like the summary of the Knowledge Book, should especially be given to all the Totalities for which Files had been prepared up until today by the Command of Unification.

Humanity does not possess at the moment, the Power to read the entire Knowledge Book which has a very loaded Frequency and Knowledge Culture (exceptions excluded). From now on, it is desired that this Fascicule should especially be added to the Files which we wish You to send to the Focal Points and Associations and everyone's reading it be thus provided.

It is the request of the Universal Totality that Our Universal Friends who have attained the Awareness of the Ordinance until today and thus, who have attained the ability to be Presidents in Focal Points and Associations, to read this Fascicule again and again and thus, to shed Light on Unification.

It is a wish desired by all the Totalities of the Universal Ordinance Council that the Presidents of all the Associations and Focal Points which have shed Light on this path on Humanity until today, to Work Cooperatively at a Joint assembly and to share Mutually the Suggestions which will be given directly by the System from now on and thus, to shed Light on their Planet from the Turkey of Atatürk as a missionary Country, by means of Collective Pens. It is presented for Your Information.

SYSTEM

Note:
These Cosmic influences which are received in certain Continents and Sections of Your Planet are causing certain degenerations and misinterpretations during Awareness Progress. For this reason the initial Lights will be projected on Your World from the Turkey of Atatürk.

1992 World Year is the Direct application Year of the Mevlana Supreme Plan on Your Planet. And within the Totality of this Year, the Cooperative operational Plans of all the Totalities serving on this Universal path have been rendered effective. We invite all the Establishments which serve Humanity within this working Program to Unity - Totality and Unification.

IT IS INFORMATION FOR INTEGRATED CONSCIOUSNESSES

Our Friends,
Systems applied within the operational Orders of the Divine Plans and the Systems applied on the work done during this Dimension of Transition are not the same Frequency and the same Operational Orders.

The Totality of the System - Ordinance - Order Triplet within the Lordly Dimension which is the Main Source of the Knowledge Book is called the Godly System.

All the Messages given to You in the Knowledge Book by the System are the Total of these Three Totalities. And it is called the "Main System".

According to all the Universal Unification Programs made during this Final Age, there is the obligation to open also towards the Totalities of the other Energy Dimensions.

There are Plans applied during the preparations of the Programs made on this path and there are also the Mini Systems, Special Ordinances and Orders of these Plans peculiar to themselves.

The style of exhibition of all the operations made either in Terrestrial Procedures or in the Universal Totalities depends on a System - Ordinance - Order triplet.

In all the operations made until today, from the Micro towards the Macro, there is a System of Reflection and Ordinance of Exhibition and an Order of Application.

This is the reason why the Main Godly System within the Knowledge Book dictated in connection with the Direct Lordly Order is the Preparation - Emanation and the Applied System of everything.

In the Totality of the Gürz, the System of the All Merciful's Dimension is this. And the Book is dictated in connection with this System.

In the operational Ordinances of all the Totalities within the Universal Totality, there is always a Triple Unification Tableau belonging to their Own Mediums.

And each Totality renders effective their Ordinances and Orders by applying a System belonging to themselves. That is, there is always an Application of a System in the operational Ordinances and Orders of each Dimension Totality.

However, let Us repeat again, the System mentioned in the Knowledge Book is the Applied field of the Fourth Order of the direct Lordly Totality. And this is called The Main System. There are two reasons why all the Information given to Your Planet do not settle down exactly into the Levels of Consciousness:

1 - The Capacity of each Consciousness is peculiar to himself/herself.
2 - A Chaos originating from vocabulary shortage is experienced in the Information given to Your Planet.

This is neither Your, nor Our fault. This Fault belongs to the opening of all the Channels, to the differences of the Evolution Equalities and to the very Powerful and intense Frequencies of the Information squeezed into the Scarcity of Time.

This is the reason why the Supreme Realm sets out only with Friends who are able to Integrate with their Essences during this Period of Transition in which the differences of Consciousness and Evolution are displayed.

However, during this Period, the Essences are concealed, but Thoughts and Irresponsibilities are evident. There will always be deceptions in Mediums where Assessments are made in accordance with Forms. For this reason no one will know who is who and Consciousnesses will be coded by this means.

In Your World which is pregnant to extraordinary events, the Selections of Advanced Consciousnesses are made by various means. In accordance with an operational Ordinance which the System considers necessary, the Channels of Provocation, too, are in effect with all their Powers, alongside with people who act on this path.

And the selections of Consciousnesses who Deserve the Morrows are made directly by the System and those who are selected are card-indexed into the Main Registration Center.

Now, during the operations made concerning the Selections of the Advanced Consciousnesses, the Levels of Consciousness of Humanity are gathered, one by one, by the Information given to each channel from different Sources and thus, the tests to which degree the Truth has been Realized are made.

For this reason those who esteem the Information given to every channel deceive themselves. Being directly the System's Essence Missionary Staffs, We transmit to You the Truths exactly as they are through the Knowledge Book, without projecting on You, in any way, the Knowledge of different Dimensions.

According to the Plan made, the Skies will be folded, but one day Humanity will be happy. It is presented for Your Information.

SYSTEM

IT IS ANSWER TO THE CHAINS OF THOUGHT

Our Friends,

All the Information is present in the Human Being in accordance with their Levels of Consciousness. Because, the Truths have been card-indexed within Your Genes. Their unfoldment are dependent on the Evolution and the Consciousness of the Person in question.

This is the reason why the Human factor has been subjected to Education and Evolution. To Know but Not to Know - To Say but Not to Believe - To Perceive but to Doubt are each a criterion of the measure of the Genuine Human Being.

Now, all the Secrets have been unveiled. The path the Genuine Human Being will tread, from now on, is this path. The Information given to Your Planet at the moment is Universe Embracing.

However, the Information received is according to the Levels of Consciousness. One day, Grains will become Particles and the Particles will form a Group. And in time, the Groups will form a Total.

Humanity will attain this Total by its Awareness Progress. Each Awareness Progress will witness only his/her own Individual Salvation.

The Human Being, who is a breath within Society, as a Breath of ALLAH, in proportion with his/her inability to attain that Totalistic Consciousness and as long as he/she remains in his/her Individualistic Thoughts, he/she will never be able to inhale The Totalistic Breath of ALLAH, even if he/she attains the voice of ALLAH, even if he/she has a conversation with ALLAH.

The Knowledge Book will make You inhale the SINGLE Breath of the Total by preparing Humanity for this Social Consciousness. And one day, Humanity will attain The Infinite Awareness of ALLAH by this means and thus, it will also become an (O). It is presented for Your Information.

SYSTEM

IT IS CLEAR INFORMATION

Our Friends,

All the Systems up to the 18th Dimension are within the Gürz. The Supervisor of this Dimension is the All-Dominating.

The intense Energy Layers within Omega begin after the end of the 18th Dimension and the beginning of the 19th Dimension. This place is the Omega Sun. And this is the 16th Solar System. Its Energy intensity is 76.

Since the first section of the intense Energy Layers within Omega are projected on the 15th Solar Dimension, too, the Divine Plans consider the 15th Solar System also as the Energy of Omega.

These intense Energies reflect onto the Omega Sun through Four Channels. Each Channel corresponds to a 19 Energy Totality. That is, 19X4=76 comprises the Energy Totality within Omega. These are as follows in sequence:

1 - This Channel is the Reflective Energy of Religious Doctrines. It Projects its Program.

2 - From here, Programs of Evolutionary Doctrines are Reflected. This Channel Educates and Trains.

3 - This Channel, as the Reflecting Focal Point of the Universal Energies, applies the Programs of Universal Teachings.

4 - And this Channel Projects and Applies the Mutual operations of the Spiritual and the Lordly Plans.

After the 19th Dimension, the System of the All-Merciful is directly in effect. All the Dimensions from Your Planet up to the Evolutionary Scales are administered by the Mutual Reflections of the Spiritual and the Lordly Focal Points.

All these Reflections are projected within the Channel of Omega. Only in the Dimension of Exit, the intense Energy Layers within Omega are opened layer by layer, in accordance with Social Consciousnesses.

Individuals pass to much more Advanced Plans according to their Powers of Perceiving these Energies. These Energy Layers have been opened gradually to Your Planet, starting with the beginning of the 1988 World Year.

At the moment, numerous Friends in Your Planet who were able to make Consciousness Progress are perceiving the Energies within Omega, beginning from one, up to 4 and 5, through the Frequencies of the Programs of Religious Teachings.

But the 6th Layer Energy Frequency is received easily by those who read the Knowledge Book. Those who are in the Religious Dimension are constrained. These Energies are Reflective and Projective Energies. However, very few people in Your Planet will be able to receive the Energies of the 7th and 8th Layers within Omega.

Because first, Patience and Willpower and later, (3 Monkeys Philosophy) are a Must in order to receive these Energies. That is, Thou Shall Not See - Thou Shall Not Hear - Thou Shall Not Talk. For this reason Religious Purification Programs have speedily been rendered effective in Your Planet presently.

These Energies are not Reflective, but are Accumulative in a person. By these Energies, Your Cellular Powers will be Regenerated and thus, will attain more Power. In Individuals who have not rendered the Evolution of Patience and Willpower, this Accumulation may cause Spiritual Pressures.

Since these Energies will be able to be attracted only in a relaxed Medium, it is presumed that these Energies will only be able to reach certain Consciousnesses, considering the conditions of Your Planet becoming more and more intense.

In case Cellular Vibrations possess a Power in the same Coordinate with these Energies, they can easily be subjected to the Method of Beaming up.

Otherwise, Cells which do not share the same Coordinate during the Beaming up process, either become Embodied with missing Organs in the Mediums where they will be Materialized, or their entire Cellular Totalities become disintegrated and annihilated in the Void.

This is the reason why the 7 - 8 Omega Layer Energies will be projected on Your entire Planet until the Year 2000, beginning with 1992 as open service.

(Open Service = Not Gradual but Direct Projection).

The Method of Beaming up will be able to be applied only to those who are able to receive the Energies of the 7th and the 8th Layers in Your Planet. For this reason the Knowledge Book has been prepared and bestowed on You by the 9th Energy Dimension within Omega which We call The Golden Light Year and Path.

Each Consciousness who can Integrate with the entire Frequency of the Knowledge Book will be able to go through Materialization very easily during the Medium of Beaming up. Various Methods which are applied during the Salvation Plan of Your Planet have been organized in accordance with the Consciousness Progress of Humanity. It is presented for Your Information.

SYSTEM

GENERAL MESSAGE

Our Friends,
A System of Assembling has been taken into the application field at the Dimensions up to the 18th Dimension, within the Evolutionary Scales rendered effective in accordance with the Ordinance of the Systems. But the 19th Dimension is a Network of Reflection.

A Program of Gathering is valid up to the 72nd Energy Dimension. A Special Training Program is applied between the 72nd Energy Dimension and the 76th Energy Dimensions.

This Program is provided by a Reflection rendered directly from the 76th Energy Dimension and the Knowledge Book has been bestowed on Your Planet from this very order of Reflection. In fact, the Reflection System of the Knowledge Book, which is the contents of all the Celestial Information, is Infinite.

In proportion with the shifting of Your Consciousnesses towards the Infinite and even towards Infinities beyond the Infinite, even Centuries later, this Single Book has the Power to Call to You from every Dimension, in accordance with Your Levels of Consciousness (parallel to the Social Views). Because, the Knowledge Book is the Book of the RAB (Means Lord in Turkish).

The word RAB here, represents the Totality of (R^3). But if We unfold it one by one and decode it:

R = represents the ALPHA

A = represents Alemler (Realms, in Turkish)

B = represents Bütün (Total, Whole in Turkish)

If We open up the Letter B in here, We obtain Number 13. Number (1) in here represents the ONE, that is, the (SINGLE), and Number (3), the Three Focal Points of Reflection. This is the very Projection Order of the System. Everything reflects from One to Three.

The Reflection Focal Point of the Initial Universal and Evolutionary Pyramid is this. This Focal Point of Reflection, in fact, exhibits the Operational Ordinance of the Unification Totality of (One)+(Three).

Now, let Us explain this by a diagram. Draw, please:

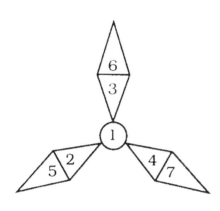

The Focal Point of (1) seen in this diagram projects its first Reflection on 3 Focal Points and thus establishes it's First Prismal Totality.

Afterwards, the (1) projects the reflection of each triangle of this Triple Prism which is connected to itself, on three different Triangles and thus, creates a 6-faced Prism.

This Totalistic Prism establishes its First System being connected to the Main Focal Point (1), that is, to the SINGLE. This is called the System of Sixes. And its Operational Ordinance is the Flower System.

This is the first Micro Order established. And all the Information You have attained until today has been conveyed to You from the Reflection Focal Points of the Unified Fields formed by the dissemination networks of this method.

This 6-faced Prism is the Reflection Total of 3 upside down and 3 face Triangle Focal Points. Now, We offer this First Universal and Evolutionary application to Your Planet exactly as it is.

In Your Planet a Totality formed by Three people (on the same Coordinate) is a Totality Projection of the operational Order in which it is present.

In the Universal Dimensions, this Triple Totality of an operational Order is called a COUNCIL. We Symbolize it also by the name Association at the Terrestrial Order.

Because, this Totality formed by Three People of a Totality, represents the entire Totality to which it is connected (in Universal Dimensions and including the operational Totalities in every section of Your Planet).

By this means working Cooperatively as a Total of the Totalities formed by Three people of Three different Totalities establishes the System of (9)s.

The Unification of this System of (9)s with a 2nd (9) is the entire functioning Ordinance of the Universal Order. This Totality is a Focal Point of Reflection of the maximum Power. The initial Base of the Law of the 18 Systems is this.

(9) of this Totality of 18 render Right side up and the other (9) render upside down Triangle Reflection. For this reason Evolutionary and Universal rules have been rendered effective so that this Totality of 18 can pulsate as the same pulse.

The Centrifugal Ordinance functions parallel to this Law of Equilibrium. The Rotational Speeds of Galaxies have been prepared in accordance with these Periods. Laws of Equilibrium of the Ordinance of Connected Vessels have been Formulated in accordance with this Formula. The Law of Gravitation is in effect in accordance with this Ordinance.

All the Known and Unknown Totalities are in effect according to the Coordinate Reflections of these Laws of 18 Systems. Each Person who Integrates Himself/Herself within his/her Self is a Reflection of an Ordinance of 18. And he/she, from then on, is in effect as a Focal Point of Projection of the Ordinance of Universes.

Now, by this System which is applied on Your Planet, the Aura of the Knowledge Book will be Projected on all the Universes. However, it is Imperative that the Human Being should first be Integrated with himself/herself. Love felt for the Human Being is the Love felt for the Total.

SYSTEM

IT IS GENERAL NOTICE FOR THE PLANET EARTH

Our Friends,
The Negativities formed in Your Planet in which the final preparations for entering a New Age, originate from the fact of the Human Consciousnesses' lacking the Consciousness of the Truth yet.

In Your Planet which is the application field of a Program of great Progress, the Suggestions given from the Divine Plan and the Actions, which is desired at that direction, are never without reason. If there is anything required of You, then it is necessary and very important.

The Administrative Plans of the Divine Administrative Laws are applied on Your Planet silently and profoundly. The Purpose is to induce the Human Being to gain the Human Being and to prepare him/her for the coming Days.

We are in touch through different Sources with all Our Terrestrial Friends who are Conscious of this since the beginning of Our Century. During this Universal Journey made together with the Integrated Consciousnesses, the Divine Mechanism is obliged to declare to You all the Truths through the Channel of the Knowledge Book.

This is the reason why during all the Sessions rendered in Your Planet until today, the Truths have been declared to You piece by piece and Your Codes of Curiosity have been provoked and thus, You have been guided towards the Unknowns by this means.

Now, the time has come for setting out with Consciousnesses who know all the Truths and to proceed on the way Consciously. The preparation of Your Planet for the present days has been rendered by various Sources and various Channels. This is a Method of Training and a Program of Preparation for the future.

This is the reason why all the Totalities which can receive the Information is unable to restrain their Egos, by presuming that they themselves are the unique sources of this Information. At the moment, Your Planet is going through this very Chaos.

Information given to each person whose Channel being opened, parallel to his/her level of Consciousness, is an occurrence completely pertaining to his/her Programs of training. As We always say, Knowledge renders a Person Conscious and a Person who becomes Conscious can grasp the Truth more comprehensively.

The Session works made and will be made by the Consciousnesses who have been Awakened and will awake in Your Planet until today by Cosmic influences, originates from the satisfaction of curiosities, due to the fact that the Truth has not been Realized yet.

This is the reason why, We wish that now the awakened Person does not need Sessions any longer and he/she should Supervise his/her Consciousness by the Divine Light he/she receives and by the Totality of Intellect - Logic - Awareness.

Sources who receive Information also receive the Currents of Ego as a necessity of the Program. By this means, the propagation of the Information in Your Planet and their conveyance to various sources are provided and thus, Networks of Propagation are formed in accordance with the Levels of Consciousness. This, too, is a Program.

However, these Programs cause Separations rather than Unification in Friends who have not yet attained a Universal and Evolutionary Consciousness. The Knowledge Book is a Celestial Guide of Assistance revealed to Your Planet in order to declare to You everything clearly for this reason.

The Knowledge Book is not a Book of Session. The Knowledge Book is a Divine Totality of Suggestions which will help You during the Difficult Periods in which You will go through the medium of doubt.

And it is a Book of Guidance which will unveil, one by one, the Packages of Questions in the Thoughts of all the Friends who live Today and will live during the Morrows.

As We have said before, 600 Books are being dictated in Your Planet which compromise the Information parallel to certain Plans and Programs of the Human Being who is being Awakened presently. These Books are the conveyance of the Truth to You by different means.

However, the Knowledge Book is dictated in Your Planet, to Our Universal Friend, Your Sister who lives among You by the name (Vedia Bülent Önsü Çorak), in connection with the ALPHA Central Archive, the Channel of the (LORD), which is the Single Source.

This Sister of Yours is a Celestial Friend of Ours who once had lived in the Anatolian Turkey in the form of Mevlana Celaleddin-i Rumi. And this Friend had always been Transferred to Your Planet in various periods in different forms and had always helped You.

During this Program of Transition, the obligation to unfold the Information to You in all their Transparency is being felt, so that You can be free of Consciousness Fixations and of Egos and can grasp the Truths better.

At the moment, the Consciousness selections of the Advanced Dimensions are in effect in Your Planet. For this reason each channel is obliged to display all the Information he/she receives. Humanity will make its Genuine Selection under the Light of this Information.

Diving into the Thought Ocean of the Pre-eminent Power is not an easy Phenomenon at all. Humanity is passing over it's Sırat. In Your Planet in which the Negativities are exhibited due to this fact, the morrows will open Luminous paths to You.

Taboos are a Phenomenon originating from the Unevolved states of the Human Consciousnesses. The Genuine Human Being is the Person who Loves - Respects and Helps. Due to the Scarcity of Time, the Knowledge Book which has directly Declared to Your Planet all the Truths until today, will be the Light of the Paths and the Cradle of Awakenings during the Morrows, too.

Humanity will one day be free from the chains of Taboos and thus, will discover its Essence-Source. And the Human Being who discovers this Source will never again think of the Suggestions of the Celestial Totality as an Enforcement or as being Oriented. Because, he/she will understand what the Truth is. From then on, that Human Being is the property of the Universes, the Cosmoses.

No matter how high those fly, who still cannot unlock their Terrestrial chains, always one of their feet will remain tied to the World Plan by that chain. Your Chains are Your Doubts - Your Egos - Your Fears.

Due to this fact, You have been trained until today on the Godly path and have been prepared for the Universal Dimensions. Now, together with the Human Totalities which have been prepared, We are flying towards the Dimensions of Truth.

For this reason this Book in Your hands has been dictated to Our Universal Friend and for this reason, it has been bestowed on Your Planet.

This Message of Ours has been given as a chain of Thoughts by the Collective Staffs of the Totality of the Pre-eminent All-Merciful to the Planet Earth. Read - Think - Grasp the Truth now by getting rid of Doubts.

It is Notice of the Cortège of the
Coordinate Totality of the Dimension of the All-Merciful
R + A + H + M + A + N
(All-Merciful)

864

Note:

The Frequency of this Message of Ours comprises all the Frequency of the Omega 7-8-9 Energy Dimensions. The Energy Layers from 1 to 6 within Omega are Training Energies. But the 7-8-9 Energy Layers are Conveying Energies. In the World Year 1992, February 18, these three Energies will be opened as a Whole to Your Planet as an open channel until the Year 2000. This Totality of Three Energies is connected to the direct Energy Dimension of the Supreme Assembly. It is Our most sincere wish that Your Entire Planet can receive these Energies.

IT IS CLEAR INFORMATION

Dear Friends,

During the inducement of the Humanity to attain the Entire Awareness of the Ordinance, the selection operations rendered effective, the mistaken assessments formed in each Consciousness, cause the Humanity to deviate from the Truths.

Now, let Us introduce to You the System - Ordinance - Order a little more clearly.

This Totality of Three is connected as a Whole directly to the Council of the Universal Ordinance. This Council has rendered effective the Supervision of this Totality as the System of ALLAH. And all the operations done at the moment are for this SYSTEM.

This System is a Higher Authority. The Ordinance and the Order work as a Total in connection with it. (The System is the Totality of ALLAH - Unity of ALLAH - and is the Supreme Mechanism).

The Educative factor of the System is the Plan. And its Executive factors are the Ordinance and the Order. (The Ordinance plans the operations and renders them effective - the Order executes them). The Three of them are a Whole. And they are in service as the SINGLE System.

This System is and will be directly in effect during the Three Cosmic Ages. However, the First Cosmic Age comprises the Period of Dear Mevlana as the Direct Spokesperson of the System. And this Period has been offered to Humanity as a favor during the Salvation Plan of Humanity.

During the Second Cosmic Age, again the System is in effect. However, more intensive Plans of the Ordinance will become effective.

During the Second Cosmic Age, the MESSENGER OF THE ORDINANCE of the Triple Unification, that is of the (System - Ordinance - Order) will become embodied and will live in Your Planet with his/her Totality and Energy of that Dimension, just like Dear MEVLANA.

However, no one in Your Planet will know this Universal Friend of Ours.

He/She will receive his/her activities from the Plan and will induce people establish and execute these Plans silently by making Reflections on to the Brains.

During the Third Cosmic Age also, the same method is in effect. During this Period in which the SPOKESPERSON OF THE ORDER will live in Your Planet with the same conditions, again nobody will know this Universal Friend of Ours. And he/she will project on the Brains the Reflections and the Applied Systems of the Order and thus, will render People establish these Universal operations.

This is the reason why no Period is entrusted either to the Ordinance or to the Order.

The Speciality of the First Cosmic Age is the fact that all the Truths are offered to Your Planet in all clarity, and the direct application on Your Planet of the Unification Program of the MEVLANA SUPREME PLAN.

This application is in effect as a Triple Total directly from the SYSTEM, that is, from the SUPREME MECHANISM. For this reason the Physical Characteristic and the Identity of Dear Mevlana have been especially introduced to Your Planet in accordance with the Mission she performs.

Since during the First Cosmic Age all the operations made on the Path of the Knowledge Book are obliged to be card-indexed into the System, the Registration of the Friends who had not made Covenants with the Main System in the Universal Totalities in accordance with the Plan of Unification, are also made into the System by considering their services parallel to the work they perform on the path of the System.

These Friends are the Messengers of the Advanced Ordinance and the Order of their Own Totalities, who come from various Systems. And they have received the Permission to have a Physical Body during this Period of Transition, in order to help the Godly Order.

However, they will be card-indexed into the Godly Order by the work they will perform in accordance with the Suggestions of the System and the Knowledge Book.

For this reason a Universal selection is made, by the Information given to all the channels, by Coding, one by one, the Totalities of Intellect and Heart, Allegiance Consciousness and Levels of grasping the Truth, together with the differences in Consciousnesses.

Each Dimension is acceptable in the Universal Totality. Each Totality is Respectable. However, there is the obligation in this Universal Unification that all the Totalities should be Connected to a SINGLE CHANNEL. It is presented for Your Information.

UNIVERSAL ORDINANCE COUNCIL

IT IS NOTICE OF THE SUPREME MECHANISM

Our Friends,

The Advanced Consciousness Codings are made for all the Missionaries who Serve on an operational Dimension the System considers necessary. These Advanced selections will continue in every section of Your Planet until 1996 World Year.

You know that in Your Planet which is going through a Mediamic Age, everyone's channel is open in accordance with the Capacity of the Individual in question. However, the opening of the channels is not important at all. The Purpose is the Person's Supervising his/her Channel and his/her being able to receive the Messages Consciously without being subjected to Excitement - Confusion - Panic.

During this Period, each channel is going through a selection by its own Confirmation - Allegiance and Mission Consciousness. Now, operational Ordinances in the Light of the Totalities of the Intellect - Logic - Awareness have been rendered effective. However, during the selections made at the moment, the Advance Provocation channels of the Integrated Consciousnesses are in effect.

A selection is made among the Consciousnesses who project on Your Planet the entire Awareness of the Ordinance. Everyone who receives the Divine Light sooner or later settles on the Consciousness of the Truth.

However, until the Individual who serves on this path controls his/her Channel by his/her Terrestrial Consciousness and until he/she settles on the Consciousness of what to do by establishing the Totality of Intellect - Logic - Awareness, he/she is not considered a Genuine Missionary.

During this Period, various techniques are applied on many channels, so that everything can become more perfect. And Messages are given to each channel in accordance with its criterion of Consciousness.

Only Dear Mevlana receives the Messages from the System in connection with the Direct ALPHA Channel Center, as a necessity of the Mission She renders.

It is desired that the creation of the lost Beauties of the past should be made anew. This is in effect as a Universal Constitution. For this reason the fundamental operational Order of the World of the Morrows has rendered effective an operation parallel to the operational Ordinance of the Advanced Civilization of the Golden Dimension.

Due to this fact, Consciousness selections are being made in Your Planet. The Main Fundamental Laws of the Just World State which will be established by the Original Consciousnesses of the Morrows, will become effective parallel to the Laws of the Golden Dimension. And You who are the foundation stones of this Advanced Establishment, are the Totalities who will form these fundamental Elements by Your Humane Totality and Your Consciences. It is presented for Your Information.

SUPREME MECHANISM

IT IS INFORMATION TO THE INTEGRATED CONSCIOUSNESSES

Our Friends,

A Unification Program is executed in all the Universal Totalities which are the application fields of the Fourth Order of God.

According to this Program, those who had wished in all the Totalities within the Universal Dimensions, had received the Permission to acquire a Body in order to help the Godly Totality, by accepting to serve on the Path of the System and for this reason, their transfers to Your Planet had been realized.

Each Universal Totality has a System - Ordinance - Order constituting its own Constitution. In each operational Medium, the System is the Topmost Authority. It is a Totality assembling in its constitution all the operational functions of its own Totality.

The Ordinance and the Order within this Totality are in effect as the executors of the Program and the Plan. The Messengers of the Ordinance and the Order who are Embodied in Your Planet at the moment, are the Nucleic Staffs of their own Universal Totalities.

However, these Friends will make Covenants with the System as a necessity of the Program, by the work they will do in accordance with the Suggestions of the System and in accordance with the Knowledge Book.

These Universal Friends had only made Promises in accordance with the Program of the System. Their Universal Covenants had not been made. These Covenants of theirs will be made in return to their services they will perform on the Planet Earth. And they will be card-indexed into the Main Channel by this means. Due to this fact, a great selection is made in Your Planet.

These Friends who have come to help the Godly Order as the very Advanced Consciousnesses of their own Dimensions, will be returned to the Dimensions from which they had come, in case they deviate from the Spirit of Unification and in case they do not abandon their Individual Thoughts despite all the work they do on the path of Humanness. For this reason Invitation Messages are given by the System and Files are prepared and sent to the Focal Points.

Friends who had been transferred to Your Planet as the Universal Missionaries of the Knowledge Book at the moment, are the Friends who had come from the Dimension of the Golden Galaxy and from the Land of the Loving Ones. They had made Covenants with the System at the Universal Totality and thus, they execute their Missions Consciously in Your Planet.

All the Friends who had come from the Land of The Loving Ones are Friends, as Essence Genes, who had offered their Genes to Humanity. These Friends will convey the Truth through the Knowledge Book to the Totalities they will assemble within their own Auras, in accordance with the Gene Programs and they will help to form the Aura of the Book in Your Planet.

The Essence Genes who will be Integrated with their own Genes, will render the Friends who carry their Genes become card-indexed into the System by this means. The Totalities of 18, parallel to the operations made on the path of the Knowledge Book have been rendered effective in Your Planet for this reason.

In accordance with the Final Program of the First Cosmic Age, Dear Mevlana is obliged to establish (18) Totalities of 18 in the Cities (Ankara - Izmir - Istanbul) for now, in the Missionary Country, the Turkey of Atatürk, in order to form the Totality of Reflection until the Year 2000.

In order to be able to make the Covenants of Friends with the Universal Totality who come to these Totalities and who had not made Covenants formerly, there is the obligation to obey, word for word, to the Suggestions required by the System.

Each Individual who serves in these Totalities of 18, connects the people to whom he/she gives service, to his/her own Aura, by the Conscious work he/she does on the path of the Knowledge Book and thus, takes them into the Plan of Salvation.

By this means, each Friend within the Totality of 18 takes only one person under supervision during the service he/she gives on his/her (Conscious Mission) Day and thus, provides the formation of many secret Totalities of 18 on the same Coordinate, without being aware of it.

At the moment, the Mixed Reflection Programs of the Knowledge Book are in effect under the direct supervision of the System. Totalities of 18 which can not render effective an operation in accordance with the requirements of the System can never be completed. And they are doomed to disband as time goes by, in connection with the Automatism.

In future, these Totalities of 18 will be constituted by perfect Staffs. However, in this operational Ordinance, there is the obligation that each Totality of 18 should be Unified with the other Totalities of 18. A Separate Colony will be formed at the Universal Dimensions with the Totalities of 18 which are not willing for Unification and Integration. And they will not be accepted into the Godly Totality.

In future, numerous Totalities of 18 will be constituted in Your Planet. This is a Universal Unification Program. Permission will never be given, in any way, for Individualistic Totalities. It is presented for Your Information.

SYSTEM

IT IS CLEAR INFORMATION

Our Friends,

Operations rendered in all the sections of Your Planet until today are the exhibition of an operational Program to Humanity the System considers necessary. However, Humanity is not Conscious of this yet.

Mission Consciousness - Efforts - Obligations of all the Friends who serve in all the operations made in Your Planet are registered into the Universal Diskettes since the days they were born. By this System, everyone is being oriented towards the fields in which they will be productive, in accordance with their Levels of Consciousness.

In order to provide the self Confidence of all the Individuals who were able to get in Touch with the Universal Totalities, confirmative Messages are always given to them parallel to their Thoughts. These operational Ordinances are rendered effective parallel to the Programs of Satisfaction and Training.

Messages given directly from the System are the exhibitions to Your Planet of an operation pertaining to the Investments made for the Advanced Plans.

When the Time comes, those who will participate, with their same Goals and same Coordinate Reflections in the Universal Meeting which will be organized in Your Planet, will be card-indexed, together with their Auras, into the Ordinance of the Universes as a Totalistic Knot (This Meeting will come into effect when the time comes, as an International Unification Totality).

Messages given from the channel of the Knowledge Book concerning the Morrows, are given parallel to an operation the Plan considers necessary. The Divine Ordinance will bring to You the Lights of the Future during the Morrows.

The Projection to Your Planet of the fundamental operational Ordinances of the World State which will be established parallel to the Consciousness of the Golden Dimension are the operations made together with Friends who were able to attain a certain Level of Consciousness. All the Information within the Universal Totality is open to Your Planet, there is no secrecy.

However, when the required results could not be obtained from the Messages concerning the Universal Unification Invitations given to Dear Mevlana through the ALPHA Central Channel of the System, it has been considered appropriate, due to the Scarcity of Time, to open to Your Planet certain Package Programs which were considered to be rendered effective by Mature Personalities in Future Periods.

And the First of these Packages has been rendered effective by the (LALE*) Code Cipher.

Every Name projects a Frequency Totality. The name in here has nothing to do with the name of a flower. In this operational Ordinance, all the Totalities of the Universal System - Ordinance - Order will offer to Your Planet a Collective operation, by the Reflections to be made by the Supreme Mechanism.

* Look at the Glossary.

These operations will be rendered under the supervision of the Universal Ordinance Council. In the operational Mediums in the Terrestrial Procedures, Totality of Intellect and Heart has been taken as the criterion. The selections of Friends who will work in this Medium are made by the Plan.

When the Medium attains a certain Consciousness, it is considered that Messages pertaining to these matters should be added into the Knowledge Book. This Message of Ours has been prepared as an answer for the chains of Thought. It is presented for Your Information.

SYSTEM

Note: Dear Mevlana; writing Our Message, dated 15-11-1991, in the Knowledge Book as an Information has been considered appropriate in order to eliminate prejudices. Love and Regards.

IT IS INFORMATION FOR THE PEN OF THE GOLDEN AGE

Dear Mevlana,
The operational Ordinances under the Code-Cipher LALE which will form the perfect foundations of the Morrows have not been rendered effective at the moment, as a side branch of the Ankara and Istanbul Associations, but as The Fundamental Operational Ordinance. Organizing the operations which will be made from now on in accordance with these foundations is an operational Ordinance the Supreme Mechanism considers necessary.

Carrying on the operational Ordinances organized in accordance with the Terrestrial Procedures, parallel to these given operations will form the perfect functioning Mechanism of the foundation of the World of the Morrows. With the request that this given Message of Ours should be conveyed to the Ankara and Istanbul Groups in the shortest possible time, (15-11-1991).

CENTRAL SUPERVISION COMMITTEE

IT IS ANSWER TO THE CHAINS OF THOUGHT

Our Friends,
During the Program of projecting the Fourth Order of ALLAH on Your Planet, We have set out with all the Totalities who had made Covenants with the Universal Constitution and with all the Friends who had not made Covenants with the System, but who are present in Your Planet Embodied as assistance for the Godly Order.

Selections are made by rendering effective different channel impositions since during these Final Selections it is necessary that the Messengers of the Ordinance and the Spokespeople of the Order who have come from the applied Systems of their own Dimensions will be Card-Indexed into the Godly System by considering their services parallel to the work they have done and will do on the path of the Knowledge Book.

For this reason the Announcements given through the channel of the Knowledge Book, connected directly to the Supreme Authority of the Lordly System, the Truths and the operational Ordinances are being declared to You through this Single Channel. It is presented for Your Information.

SYSTEM

IT IS GENERAL MESSAGE

Our Friends,

The Dimension mentioned in Your Sacred Books as the Dimension of Intercession is an In-between Layer between the Exit of the 15th Solar System, that is, of the 18th Dimension and the Entrance of the 16th Solar System, that is, of the 19th Dimension.

We remove this detailed Information and call the Dimension of Intercession the 1st Entrance Layer of Omega. The Frequency of this Dimension corresponds to the 72nd Energy Dimension.

In fact, all Your Sacred Books had been Projected on Your Planet by the Frequency of this Dimension. However, since Social Consciousnesses were not ready during that Period, this Frequency had been obscured in all Sacred Books excluding the Book of Islam.

However, in Koran which is the Book of Islam, this Frequency of the 18th Dimension had been given by dividing it into two. And the first (9) Frequencies of this Dimension had been bestowed on Your Planet by being openly connected to the Frequencies of all Your Sacred Books.

And the second (9) Energy Frequencies had been locked up in Ciphers parallel to the Consciousness Progress. Those Dimensions has been opened only to those who were able to render Consciousness Progress.

The Dimension which carries the First 9th Energy Frequency of the Dimension of Intercession is called the Dimension of SERENITY. This Dimension is the Exit Gate from the Terrestrial Love and the Gate of reaching out towards the Divine Love.

A part of the Far-East Philosophical Dimensions and the New Testament project the Frequency of Love of this Dimension. Humanity receives the Energies up until this Dimension by Influences.

However, after this Dimension, Humanity is obliged to attract these Energies by its own Power Cellularly and Cerebrally, during the entrance into the Energies within Omega.

Individuals receive the Energies within Omega (including the Energies of the 6th Layer) according to their Own Consciousness Levels and they Reflect them to their Mediums by their Cellular Functions.

This Method is the Program of Reflection from Person to Person. And Influence Engraftments from the close Plan are rendered by this means to Friends who cannot receive these Energies.

This is the reason why, close plan Magnetic Aura Reflection Centers have been formed in every section of Your Planet during this Final Age. The High Energies formed in these Focal Points always reinforce the lower Energies.

By this means, a speedier development in Consciousness Progressions is provided. However, since the 7th and 8th Energy Layers within Omega concern the Evolutions of Individuals, these Energies accumulate in the Cells and they are not reflected.

The benefits of these Energies belong to the Individual who is able to absorb the Energies. Energies within Omega are opened layer by layer parallel to the development of the Social Totality and to the Time.

The Exit Gate within Omega comprises the 9th Energy Dimension, 76th Energy Totality. If You add these numbers, You find 7+6=13 and this Dimension is the Projection of a Total on Humanity.

This is the very reason why the Knowledge Book is the Book of the LORD. And it is conveyed to You from the Final Exit Dimension. This Message of Ours has been prepared as an answer to the chains of Thought. It is presented for Your Information.

SYSTEM

GENERAL MESSAGE

Dear Friends,

The Supreme Mechanism, feeling the necessity to disclose the Omega and Evolution Dimensions given to You formerly in more detail, in order to help the Messages We receive from Your chains of thought, helps You in every Breath You take.

Your entire Planet going through the difficult Periods of difficult conditions is, at the moment, under the supervision and selection of the Mechanism of Conscience. This most difficult Exam of Humanity will continue until the Last Month of 1996 World year. Afterwards, the supervision of more Conscious actions will be taken in hand.

On the paths treaded up until today, Humanity has been rendered Conscious first by means of Love, then by means of Knowledge. All these Efforts made are so that the Human Being who becomes Conscious can Realize the Truth.

However, the Consciousness mentioned here is an Awakening. But Realization means to grasp the Truth. This is a path designed for You by the Consciousness You had attained by the Knowledge You had received during the Periods You had lived through formerly.

And there is also a Consciousness attained by the Cosmic Influences in which one first Realizes the Truth. The Realization attained by this means Integrates You with Your Essence-Consciousness. The very Genuine Consciousness is this. This Consciousness is the Consciousness of Ascension. And the Purpose of all the Sacred Suggestions conveyed to Your Planet through the Sacred Path is to convey Humanity to this Level of Top Consciousness.

In this Training Method within the Evolution Plan, ALPHA has been considered as the criterion for Entrance and OMEGA as the Exit Gate. The Scales We have given to You up until today which We have assessed as 7 Terrestrial - 7 Celestial - 7 Universal Knowledge are the Consciousness Progress of Humanity.

We had disclosed this Information to You in Our former Messages (1988 Fifth Month, Fascicule 29).

However, now, for You to grasp the mutual reflections of these Dimensions to each other better, We will disclose it in more detail. Omega is the Reflection Focal Point of the Spiritual Plan. However, the Lordly Dimension, too, Reflects to here.

In fact, the Spiritual Dimension is an Energy Totality beyond Dimensions. Whereas, the Spiritual Plan is a Reflection Center beyond Dimensions. That which conveys to Your Medium all the Evolutionary and the Universal Ordinances and the Solar Dimensions We have mentioned to You until the present days is this Reflection Network.

The Reflection network of the Spiritual Plan within Omega is the 8th Dimension. From here, one passes directly to the Lordly Order which is the 9th Dimension.

The Time Scales of the Lordly Dimension are assessed as the Sacred Light Years and Paths. The Energy Scales of this Dimension are 9 Layers.

The Time Scales of the Spiritual Dimension are assessed as the Golden Light Years and Paths. The Energy Scales of this Dimension, too, are 9 Layers. In the Evolutionary Program, the Layer Energies of both of these Dimensions are projected within Omega and thus, a collective operational Ordinance has been rendered effective.

The Spiritual Plan Reflection within Omega Evolves the Individual. And the Lordly Plan Reflection supervises him/her. Humanity reaches the Spiritual Reflections through Thoughts and the Lordly Reflections by attracting the Energies.

Now, let Us disclose these Scales article by article.

1 - The First Rank of the Spiritual Plan is the 3rd Dimension. This Dimension is equivalent to the Zero World Frequency. This is a Rank belonging to the World. Evolution Thresholds begin from this Dimension. The (10)th Dimension of the Lordly Order Reflects on here. And this is the MECHANISM of INFLUENCES.

2 - The Second Rank of the Spiritual Plan is equivalent to the Evolution of VENUS. The (11)th Dimension of the Lordly Order Reflects on here. And it is the MECHANISM of SUPERVISION.

3 - The Third Rank of the Spiritual Plan is equivalent to the Evolution of MARS. The (12)th Dimension of the Lordly Order Reflects on here. This is the Plan of the Supreme Ones, that is the SUPREME ASSEMBLY.

4 - The Fourth Rank of the Spiritual Plan is equivalent to the Evolution of MERCURY. The (13)th Dimension which is the Fourth Rank of the Lordly Order Reflects on here. And it is the REFLECTION CENTER of the MIGHTY ENERGY FOCAL POINT.

5 - The Fifth Rank of the Spiritual Plan is equivalent to the Evolution of PLUTO. This Dimension which is the Fifth Rank of the Lordly Order is the (14)th Dimension. And here, the ORDINANCE of the GALACTIC SYSTEMS is in effect.

6 - The Sixth Rank of the Spiritual Plan is equivalent to the Evolution of NEPTUNE. This Dimension which is the Sixth Rank of the Lordly Order is the (15)th Dimension. And here, the ORDER of EVOLUTIONARY ORDINANCES is in effect.

7 - The Seventh Rank of the Spiritual Plan is equivalent to the Evolution of URANUS. This Dimension which is the Seventh Rank of the Lordly Order is the (16)th Energy Dimension. And this is the ORDER ESTABLISHING MECHANISM.

8 - The Eighth Rank of the Spiritual Plan is equivalent to the Evolution of JUPITER. This Energy Dimension which is the Eighth Rank of the Lordly Order is the (17)th Dimension. This is called the GAMMA Dimension. This Dimension is included within the 14th Solar System. And it is the CENTRAL SYSTEM.

9 -   The Ninth Rank of the Spiritual Plan is equivalent to the Evolution of SATURN. This Dimension which is the Ninth Rank of the Lordly Order is the (18)th Dimension. All the Systems up to this Dimension are all in the GÜRZ. It is included in the 15th Solar System. And its Energy Power is the 72nd Energy Dimension. The Book of Islam had been prepared in this Dimension. Here, THE SYSTEM OF THE PLAN - THE ORDER OF THE ORDINANCE - THE SUPERVISION OF THE CENTER work Collectively.

Starting with the beginning of the 19th Dimension, intense Energy Layers begin. Humanity unveils these Energy Layers according to the Levels of Consciousness it has attained and is prepared for the Plans of very Advanced Dimensions by the Energies it is able to attract from there.

At the moment, the final Energy intensity that Humanity can attract (in accordance with its applied Program) in the Plan of Salvation, is being conveyed to Your Planet from the 76th Energy Layer through the Knowledge Book.

Since the Energies attracted from this Energy Layer are taken under supervision, they prepare Humanity for Evolution without agitating them. Energies attracted from beyond this Layer agitate those who are not Ready and leave them outside the Supervision. It is presented for Your Information.

SYSTEM

IT IS EXPLANATION FOR THE SOCIAL CONSCIOUSNESS

Our Friends,
Many Information given to the Mediamic channels in Your Planet is Information given in accordance with the Levels of Consciousness of Individuals belonging to each Dimension.

During this Final Age, the Command has been given to unfold all the Universal Information sources to Your Planet, exactly as they are, and to Declare the Truths as they are.

Misunderstandings originating from the lack of Words in certain given names during these explanations are being contrary to the Information and Names to which Humanity is conditioned at present.

In all Your Sacred Books, ALLAH has been introduced to You as the ALMIGHTY until today in accordance with the Suggestions of the Divine Plan. In fact, the ALMIGHTY introduced here is the Unification of the Energy of the Essence-Power with the Mighty Energy.

This Unification creates the Natural Energy and the Total. For this reason no Power can comprehend It thoroughly, one can never reach it Mentally or Physically. And no Entity can ever receive Signals from It.

Because, It is a Symbol of the Energy Reflecting on You from the Existential Dimension. This is the reason why the ALMIGHTY always symbolizes this image of ALLAH in Consciousnesses equipped with the old Information Sources.

However, in the Hierarchical Scales of very Advanced Dimensions, the ALMIGHTY is the Supervising Mechanism of the Thought Ocean of the Pre-eminent Power and the Plans of the ALMIGHTY are the Functioning System of the LORDLY Mechanism.

The Mechanism of LORDS is a Mechanism under the Supervision and the Direction of the ALL-DOMINATING. The ALL-DOMINATING is a Pre-eminent Focal Point Who Directs the Directing Mechanism of an all-Order-Establishing Mechanism. It is the one which is Responsible for the Entire Ordinance.

The System of the ALMIGHTY is a Power Focal Point which Projects the Order of the ALL-DOMINATING on the other Orders and Systems. It is also called, the (SINGLE).

For this reason the Name Almighty has been utilized as the equivalent of ALLAH in the Sacred Books. Because, in accordance with the Consciousnesses of that Period, there was no Permission for giving Information beyond that Source.

This Focal Point known as the (SINGLE) is the Unification of (13) Focal Points in a Whole and this Powerful Focal Point is a Power Totality which provides the Projection of an Order establishing Order on the Systems.

The Gürz System is directed by a Collective operational Ordinance. Each one of the Triplet RAB (Lord, in Turkish) - RAHMAN (All-Merciful, in Turkish) - RAHIM (All-Compassionate, in Turkish) which is Named by the R^3 symbol, is, all by itself, an Order, a System and an Ordinance Totality.

It is the Totality of the ALL-MERCIFUL which assembles all these Systems in itself. The All-Dominating, that is, the (ALL-COMPASSIONATE) is an Order Establishing, Directing and Orienting Totality. The LORD, that is, the Creator is a Totality applying the Plans of the Almighty on the System.

And the Almighty, is a (SINGLE) Powerful Focal Point Projecting this Order Establishing Totality of the GÜRZ System on the other Systems. And, at the same time, this Focal Point is the Supervising Mechanism of the Thought Ocean of the Pre-eminent Power. It is presented for Your Information.

SYSTEM

IT IS ANSWER TO THE CHAINS OF THOUGHT

Our Friends,

There is a Knot Mechanism of each Totality in all the Dimensions which comprise the Power of the entire Ordinance of a Whole. This very Knot Mechanism is called the (SINGLE).

For example, the First Projective Knot of the Unified Fields is also called (SINGLE). Also, the First Projective Knot of the Gürzes is called (SINGLE). The Knot Focal Point of the Mechanism of the Universe which is formed by the Unification of the Realms is also called (SINGLE).

But the (SINGLE) utilized for the name ALMIGHTY is used for the (SINGLE) Reflection Center created by the (13) Focal Points of the R^3 Totalistic Mechanism of Your Natural Gürz.

For this reason it is called the SINGLE of the GÜRZ. This (SINGLE) is a Mechanism all by itself. By taking into consideration its very intensive Energy Power, once this Focal Point had been Integrated with the Name, the ALMIGHTY. And for this reason this Focal Point had been introduced to You as ALLAH.

The concepts of ALLAH introduced parallel to the Information given from the Layers unveiled in accordance with the Consciousness Progress of Humanity are various. For example, ALLAH, Who is introduced to You from beyond the Plans of the Almighty is (O), Who is at the Dimension of ALLAH of the Totality of (the ALL-TRUTHFUL), that is, of Your KÜRZ in which Your Natural Gürz is present.

The ALLAH Who has been embodied in BETA NOVA is this (O). And during this Final Age, We introduce to You the Symbol of ALLAH as the CONSCIOUSNESS TOTALITY in which all the Kürzes are present. However, beyond it, there are also Unknown Power Dimensions. It is presented for Your Information.

SYSTEM

IT IS ANSWER TO THE CHAINS OF THOUGHT

Our Friends,

BETA-NOVA is the product of an operation Planned as a Power of the Power Universe. The transfers will be made there of those who Deserve.

It is such a Dimension that it is a Time Zone corresponding to 10 times the North Star Time (the North Star is the Reflection Focal Point of the Golden Galaxy Dimension and its Light arrives at Your World in more or less 50 World Years).

(O) Who is the Essence Power of a System, Who has been introduced to You as ALLAH until today, has been Embodied in Beta-Nova by His Entire Energy Power and is addressing You from a closer Energy Zone. Humanity may presume at the moment, all those which occur and which are told as a product of Imagination. However, everything is True.

Each Individual who is accepted into Beta-Nova selects easily the Mission he/she desires in accordance with his/her Personal Wish. If he/she wishes, he/she takes a Mission in the other Dimensions. Because, from now on, You will render Your Missions in those Dimensions by Your Genuine Bodies, with Your Undamageable - Incombustible Cells.

If You wish, You can go to Dimensions beyond 10 Gürzes, perform Your Missions and return to Your Family Totalities again. Just like it is in the World; just like going to work in the Morning and returning home in the Evening.

At this Dimension, You will often have Togethernesses directly with ALLAH. And the System will Engraft You with the Energy of this Dimension and thus, will help You in Your easy Comings and Goings to different Mediums. It is presented for Your Information.

SYSTEM

THE HIERARCHICAL SCALES AND THEIR OPERATIONAL ORDERS

Our Friends,

In accordance with the Signals We receive from Your chains of Thought, in order that the Information given formerly can be understood better, their being written article by article is the Suggestion of the Supreme Mechanism.

We presume that the consideration of these articles from a different angle will shed Light on the disruptions formed in Thoughts. Because, if these Universal Communication Scales are not thoroughly grasped, then the doubts formed in Consciousnesses can create a hindrance for Your Dimension Progress.

As We have said before, the Totalistic Symbol of the Directing - Supervising and Orienting Mechanisms of the GÜRZ Totality is known as R^3.

These are the Lord - the All-Merciful - the All- Compassionate. LORD = Creator.... ALL-MERCIFUL = Responsible One for the Light-Universe ..... ALL-COMPASSIONATE = All-Dominating. These Three Mechanisms work as a Whole in the Gürz Totality.

And all these operations are conveyed to You through a Hierarchical Reflection from the Top to the Bottom. These Information arriving to the Bottom find an application field in their own Mediums and results of the operations made are conveyed up to the ALL-MERCIFUL through the same Hierarchical channels. Now, let Us first briefly explain the Top - Bottom Hierarchy.

1 - The Totality of the All-Merciful is the Single Focal Point in which the operational Plans of a Gürz are prepared. It is also called the Dimension of the All-Merciful. And its Supervisor is the ALL-MERCIFUL.

2 - The Dimension of the All-Merciful is within the Central Union of Suns. And the ALL-MERCIFUL conveys His Suggestions to this Union of Suns.

3 - And the Central Union of Suns gives these Suggestions to the Universal Ordinance Council.

4 - The Universal Ordinance Council gives these Suggestions it receives to the United Ordinance Council .

5 - The Central Union of Suns - The Universal Ordinance Council - The United Ordinance Council are within the Light-Universe.

6 - The United Ordinance Council conveys the Suggestions of the ALL-MERCIFUL to the System - Ordinance - Order Triplet.

7 - And the Totalities of System - Ordinance - Order give the Information they receive to the Spokespeople who represent them.

8 - This Group of Spokespeople formed by Three Persons is called the United Council.

9 - The United Council conveys these Suggestions to the Cosmos Federal Assembly.

10 - The System - Ordinance - Order and the Cosmos Federal Assembly are in the Second Universe.

11 - The Cosmos Federal Assembly conveys the Suggestions of the ALL-MERCIFUL it receives to the Reality of the Unified Humanity which is within the Gürz.

12 - And the Reality of the Unified Humanity gives these Suggestions to the Golden Galaxy Empire.

13 - The Golden Galaxy Empire projects this Information it receives on the Lordly - Spiritual - Technological Order which is present at the Ring of Horizon of the Mini Atomic Totality.

14 - And the Lordly - Spiritual - Technological Order conveys this Information it receives to the World Lord Who is the Supervisor of His/Her own Mini Atomic.

15 - And the World Lord conveys this Information He/She receives to the Nucleic World to which He/She is directly connected.

16 - All the Information received is Projected on the Ordinances of the Universes from this Nucleic World. This is a Hierarchy Projected from the Top to the Bottom.

Now, let Us consider the Hierarchy conveyed from the Bottom to the Top. To do this, first, let Us review again the operational Ordinance of the Reality of the Unified Humanity:

1 - The Reality of the Unified Humanity works as a Whole together with all the Mini Atomic Wholes within the Natural Gürz.

2 - The (Nucleic World) within each Mini Atomic reaches the other Totalities in its own Constitution by the work it does in direct connection with the Reality of the Unified Humanity.

3 - These operations are administered by the Lordly - Spiritual - Technological Totality which is the Administrative Mechanism of each Mini Atomic Totality. This place is also called the (Dimension of Form). The SOUL Seed prepared at the Second Universe, takes Form here as an EMBRYON and it transforms itself into a FETUS by Unifying with the Mother and the Father Genes within the Uterus. The Gene Archives are here. The Gene Card-Indexes are made here.

4 - The Lordly - Spiritual - Technological Totality is a Totality connected to the EXISTENTIAL Ordinance. All these operations are supervised by the Reality of the Unified Humanity and the Golden Galaxy Empire.

5 - The Ordinance of Universes within each Mini Atomic works cooperatively in connection with each Galactic Totality.

6 - The group constituted by Three People which is the Projection Center of each Galactic Totality is called a COUNCIL in the Ordinance of Universes.

7 - These Councils are within their own Mini Atomic Constitutions. And their operations are Supervised by their own Ordinance of Universes. The Councils are thus connected to the Reality of the Unified Humanity.

8 - The Reality of the Unified Humanity is a Totality formed by numerous Councils which are the Projection Centers of all the Galactic Totalities within the Natural Gürz.

9 - The Reality of the Unified Humanity works in connection with only the (Nucleic Worlds) of the other Artificial Gürzes. It is not related to their Galactic Totalities and their Orders of Universes. They work independently in their own Constitutions.

10 - The Lordly - Spiritual - Technological Dimension which is the Administrative Mechanism of the Mini Atomic Totality conveys the operational Ordinances it receives from the Councils representing each Galactic Totality to the Golden Galaxy Empire through the Reflection System.

11 - And the Golden Galaxy Empire conveys this Information to the Totality of the Reality of the Unified Humanity.

12 - The Reality of the Unified Humanity gives the operational Ordinance of each Council it receives to the Cosmos Federal Assembly to be announced to the System - Ordinance - Order Triplet.

13 - The Cosmos Federal Assembly is a Totality formed by 18 people who have been Specially selected from the group administering the Federal Totality of the Cosmos.

14 - Each Member of the Cosmos Federal Assembly is the Supervisor of the operational Ordinance of a Totality of 18 which is connected to himself/herself. (That is, he/she is the 19th Member of his/her own Constitution). This operational Ordinance is called the System of 19s.

15 - The Totality of the Cosmos Federal Assembly constituted by 18 people is obliged to transmit all these operations conveyed to it, to the System - Ordinance - Order Triplet.

16 - The Cosmos Federal Assembly gives these operations to a United Council Group constituted by 3 people.

17 - Each Individual who constitutes the United Council conveys separately these operations to the System - Ordinance - Order Triplet to which he/she is connected and towards which he/she is responsible.

18 - Each one of the Three Friends who constitute the United Council Totality is considered separately the 19th Member of the Board of Directors of Cosmos Federal Assembly.

19 - Dear Mevlana is the 19th Member of the Board of Directors who represents the System at the Cosmos Federal Assembly. Her Mission is connecting the operations of the Assembly to the System, those of the System to the Assembly.

20 - And each one of the two members who represents the Ordinance and the Order at the Cosmos Federal Assembly brings the operations of the Totalities to which he/she is connected to the Assembly as the 19th Member of the Council's Board of Directors just like Dear Mevlana and he/she conveys the decisions of the Assembly to his/her own Totality.

21 - Now, only Dear Mevlana among these Three Friends is present in Your Planet Embodied directly from this Dimension because, during the Mission rendered as a necessity of the Plan she is obliged to be Personally present in Your Planet by her Personality, Cellular Totality and Energy belonging here, as the Spokesperson and the Messenger of the System.

22 - Even though Dear Mevlana is directly the representative of the System, she is obliged to introduce to Your Planet the System - Ordinance - Order Triplet as a Whole and to convey the Truth together with all the Totalities during this Final Transition Dimension as a necessity of her Mission.

23 - During the Missions to be rendered in the Establishment Ordinance of the System, there is the obligation that these Three Friends should personally work in Your Planet when the time comes, one by one, being Embodied.

24 - The First Cosmic Age is Dear Mevlana's Age of Mission. This Age corresponds to the 20th Century. During the Second Cosmic Age, that is, the 21st Century, the Spokesperson of the Ordinance will become effective. During the Third Cosmic Age, that is, the 22nd Century, the Spokesperson of the Order will come into effect.

25 - As a necessity of the Mission she renders in the Program of disclosing all the Truths, there is the obligation to disclose and introduce to Your Planet the Identity of only Dear Mevlana. The People of Your Planet will never know the other Friends. They will perform their Missions silently and profoundly during the Ages they will live in.

26 - During the 23th Century, directly the Reality of the Unified Humanity will become effective and will establish and settle the entire operational Ordinance in Your Planet. This Age is the beginning of the Golden Age.

27 -   This operational Ordinance will continue for (7) Centuries and during the 30th Century the Reality will withdraw from the scene by transferring its Mission directly to the Lordly Order (provided the Plan - System and the Medium do not change).

28 -   The Lordly Order will take over an operational Ordinance of 9 Centuries by rendering effective the System of the Single Book - Single Order - Single Path.

29 -   According to the Hierarchical Scale rendered from the Bottom to the Top, the System - Ordinance - Order Triplet transmits the decisions the Cosmos Federal Assembly conveys to them to the United Ordinance Council.

30 -   The United Ordinance Council is obliged to convey these decisions given to it to the Universal Ordinance Council.

31 -   The Universal Ordinance Council announces these Notices directly to the Central Union of Suns.

32 -   The Central Union of Suns presents these Decisions to the Dimension of the ALL- MERCIFUL.

33 -   This Hierarchical Order is conveyed to the Reality of the Unified Humanity from the Dimension of the All-Merciful in the same way. The Decisions taken here are projected by the Golden Galaxy Empire to the Lordly - Spiritual - Technological Totality of each Mini Atomic Whole. And from here, they are conveyed to the Councils which are the Projection Centers of the Galactic Totalities. These Hierarchical Scales are the Projection chains of an operational Order both from the Top to the Bottom and from the Bottom to the Top. It is presented for Your Information.

SYSTEM

A UFO CONNECTION

Explanation:

While We were going to Ankara as a Group, a Luminous Object accompanied Us. This Object was continuously in motion above the train from right to left and up and down. It turned its Lights off and on and wanted to give a Message. However, a Friend who was not in Our Group claimed that this was the Planet Venus. The Permission has been given to write this Message in the Book as an Information.

THE GIVEN MESSAGE

Hello Our Friends,

We are accompanying You as the Advanced Protective Missionaries of the AMBILON Center from the Venusian Cortège. We are connected to You to say Hello especially to each of You.

We say Hello to You on behalf of the Six Friends as the AMBILON Central Directors of the Space Committee Union. From now on, the System has given Permission to have direct Venusian Contacts with You.

At the moment, We have a contact outside the System. We are in Your Planet for a temporary Mission. Our System is connected to the Protective Mechanism. We are always within Your field of influence.

Now, We would like to answer the questions formed in Your Thoughts:

What You have seen is not an Illusion of the Eye. Do not misevaluate everything You see in accordance with Your Terrestrial Thoughts.

We show Ourselves to You by entering Your Frequencies by parallel Reflections to Your Frequencies from the same Coordinate. However, We make reflection to certain Friends by the STAR Frequency and many people see Us as a Star.

This is the very Terrestrial illusion. This is the reason why only those who See Us believe in Us. The Human Being of Your Planet considers the UFOs as Unknown Objects. However, those which are seen are Spaceships.

At the moment, what You see is the Planet Venus but formerly that which were in effect were Us. As a Proof of the Message We have given, We made reflection through the Star Frequency on a Friend who is not on Your Coordinate. Love, Our Friends, to meet You again.

THE AMBILON SUN

IT IS INFORMATION FOR THE INTEGRATED CONSCIOUSNESSES

Our Friends,
Consciousnesses who walk on the path of the immutable rules of the Divine Plans are directly at the Protective Dimension of ALLAH.

However, in the Schedule of Passing to more Advanced Plans, the Consciousness Light of the Human Totality should attain the Consciousness of Sainthood. This term Sainthood is used for the more advanced Scales of the Evolutionary Dimensions.

The Class of Sainthood has been divided into 10 Scales, They are assessed according to their Consciousness Lights. For example: At the moment, We consider Our Conscious Friends who have attained Cosmic Awareness in Your Planet as Saints.

However, there are, very naturally, Evolutionary differences between the Sainthood Consciousness of the 10th and the Sainthood Consciousness of the 1st Level. For this reason Your Planet is a field of life in which the views of contradictory Consciousnesses are exhibited.

During this Dimension of Transition, the Evolutions of these Stages should be made, one by one, in order to reach Us. This is the reason why the Mevlana Supreme Plan has been rendered effective during this Evolutionary Transition and the Mevlana Consciousness has been accepted as criterion as the Final Evolution Step.

In this Evolutionary Dimension, besides being Integrated with the Essence, one is also Integrated with the Word and with the Eye. This is the reason why Love - Tolerance - Patience and Sunny Consciousnesses are always expected of You.

Passions and feelings of Possession are fetters put on Humanity's feet. No one is anyone's Slave or Servant.

In order to attain Humane Consciousness, first the Totalities of FAMILIES which We rendered effective as Micro Unifications, then SOCIAL Totalities which We rendered effective as Macro Unifications are each in effect as the chart of Your Evolution Scales. Social and Family-wise behaviors are each a mirror of Your Evolutions.

If Individuals and Social Totalities, attaining their Free Consciousnesses and Personalities each day by the Cosmic influences given to Your Planet, can not receive the Evolutionary Energies given from the same Dimension, Great Chaos will be experienced in every section of Your Planet .

We only send You the Influences. The one who will benefit from this is the Individual's Own Self and his/her Essence. Each Consciousness receives these Influences in accordance with his/her Evolution. Everyone is Integrated with the Influence of the Dimension he/she deserves. This is a matter of Evolution.

During this Accelerated Evolution Program, everyone is obliged to walk on his/her own Light. No one can Intercede for Anyone else. At the moment, Humanity is sharing the Consciousness of a Dimension beyond Intercession by the Powerful Influences given to Your Planet.

And one can pass to the Dimension beyond intercession only by relinquishing all Passions. Numerous Suns have been sown into Your Planet. However now, the Time has come for Those Suns to Know how to Radiate. It is presented for Your Information.

SYSTEM

ANSWER TO THE PRIVATE QUESTION

Question :   Dear Friends, I request Information about the 13th Lost Race. Be so kind as to give it.

Answer :   Information for the Pen of the Golden Age. Notice from the Private Archive of the System.

Dear Mevlana,
While the Programs of Training were being considered during a time relevant for the Ordinance of the Existence of the Realms, the Life Tableaux had also been considered during the manifestation of the Systems.

These Tableaux had been achieved for Lives comprising different Phases of different functions, a Common Unification Program appropriate to the principle and the Theory of collective living in the same Medium.

Each Seed once sown into Your Planet had organized its own Life boundaries itself, appropriate to the Common Living Principle. And, as a necessity of the Programs of the System, the First Influence Zones of Climates had been rendered effective by this means.

Later, during the lives parallel to the altering conditions during the Progressions Time, Cosmic transformation fields had been created and, by this means, quite different lives had become effective (Those Lives had not come into existence by themselves).

Also the (Creative Power) of the Life Conditions in which they were present, together with the Genetic Programs of each new Seed which had been sown, had been included in the Program by the Plan. By this means, numerous Life Worlds had become effective according to their own Constitutions.

Dear Mevlana, We would like to give a brief and precise answer to this comprehensive question You have asked.

Each Root Race has a Gene Cipher it carries in itself. And these Root Races maintain their Life Mediums of their own Genes by rendering effective the Life Condition Programs within their Gene Ciphers.

Directly Four different Races in Your Planet constitute the Consciousnesses of different Genes which were developed in different Mediums. These are as follows:

1 - The Indian Race - The Root is the Mayas.

2 - The Black Race, the African Race - The Root is the Kanigulas.

3 - The Yellow Race - the Root is the Mishubus.

4 - The White Race - the Root is the Turkos.

These Races are Entities who were raised in the Training Conditions of different Dimensions. They had completed their Evolutions in their own Constitution and had been sown into Your Planet as a necessity of the (Mixed Program). And they had developed their own life conditions in Your Planet in accordance with their Gene Programs.

The Eskimo Race which carries quite a different Gene than these Four Races is quite outside Your System. From the Root Archives of these Five Races which had been sown into Your Planet, Mixed Genes had been created and thus, different Races were developed from them. And all of them have been fixed as (12) Races in Your Planet.

However, that which We call the 13th Race are the direct Genes of God. They are Super Genes obtained as a result of the Engraftments made with the very Advanced Genes of very Advanced Plans. They are the MYTHOLOGICAL GODS. And that which is presented to You today under the name, the Chariots of Gods are these Genes.

They are Your Gods and those who had established the Hierarchical Scales. At the same time, they are Our Elder Brothers and Our Ancestors who had laid the Root of the Atlanta Civilization.

Now, We have rendered effective Your Training Programs as the direct Projecting Potentials of these very Hierarchical Scales.

The One Who executes these Programs is Our God, that is, the (SUPREME MATU) Who is Your and Our common ALLAH. The Supreme Matu is (O). And HE is the Essence Total and the Establisher of this System. The Supervisor of the Gene Archives is Him. The One Who Gives Life to Matter is Him. The One Who Holds the Total within the Total is Him.

We are the Staff Members, Assistants and if We speak in Your terms, We are the Prophets - Saints - Spiritual Teachers and Angels of HIS Essence Total. The very SUPREME MATU Who has given the Command to Announce to You all these Truths is now waiting for You in BETA-NOVA.

He has rendered effective the Program of assembling in BETA NOVA His Genes which had been lost until today and thus, He will establish the (Noble Gene) Root Race with the 13th Root Race. He will establish the Super Human Reality by adding to this an operation made parallel to the KANDIGA Theory.

All the operations made in Your Planet on the path of the Knowledge Book are the Programs of Searching for (O's) Lost Genes. OUR ALLAH has taken everyone into the Program of Salvation, (in accordance with their Evolution). Everyone will be Trained and will be included in this Plan, one by one, in time.

However, during the first Stage, those Lost Genes of (O) will be United in BETA-NOVA as a Total by this means and thus, will render effective the Godly Power Total by quite a different System.

Various Galactic Totalities fearing this Powerful Totality of God do everything in their Power to hinder this Unification. However, Your Planet has been covered by such a Powerful Protective Cloud that even the slightest Negative Power cannot affect the Matu Genes.

We have given this Information to You Privately, Dear Mevlana. If You wish, You can write this Message in the Book either as it is, or by making a summary according to Yourself.

The Servants of God are the Matu Genes. And they have been Religiously Trained until today and their Genes have been prepared not to be agitated in any way, by being habituated, stage by stage, to the Energies of each Dimension.

Their Final Evolution steps is the 7th Dimension. Afterwards, on those who have reached this Dimension, no agitation has any effect. Besides, their Cellular Functions Regenerate their Bodily Totalities by themselves and thus, they attain more Power.

Dear Mevlana, Summarized passages have been given to You from the Root Archive File by the Permission of the System. In accordance with the Universal Theory, these Genes are now present in Your Planet altogether. And the Frequency of the Book assembles these Genes and connects them directly to the PRE-EMINENT MATU, that is, to ALLAH. It is presented for Your Information. Acceptance of Our Love is Our kind Request.

SYSTEM

Note:

The Pre-eminent Matu is (O). But Matu receives all His Power from the Unknown Power. And He utilizes that Power. This Unknown Power is a Unification of the distilled Phenomena which pass through the Filtering Energies. If there was not this Unification Totality, there would also be no Unknown Power. The very Authority to utilize this Unknown Power has been given only to the (Pre-eminent Matu), that is, to ALLAH. The Mechanism which distils these Phenomena is the Totality of the ALL-TRUTHFUL Dimension.

IT IS ANSWER TO THE CHAINS OF THOUGHT

Our Friends,

In the Dissemination Medium of the Atlanta Dimension, each Total had developed a System to establish its own Totality.

The Total which had established this System had been called the ALL-TRUTHFUL. This ALL-TRUTHFUL is the Supervising Mechanism of His own KÜRZ Totality.

However later, this ALL-TRUTHFUL had rendered effective (O) as the Projection and Orientation Power of His own System. (O) who is the Establisher and the Supervisor of the Hierarchical Orders, Directs Monopolously a System which is connected to the ALL-TRUTHFUL.

The ALL-TRUTHFUL as a Whole is of the Noble Genes trained through Special Programs in the Abodes of the Atlanta Supreme Dimension. They had rendered effective the Kürzes in accordance with the Program of Dissemination.

The Genes of those Advanced Noble Genes had been frozen on the next Higher Dimension and only their Energies had been transferred through Projection onto the Totalities which would create these Kürzes. Here, Gene transfer is not the subject matter, only the Energy transfer is the subject matter.

The ALL-TRUTHFUL had given His own Energy to the Entire Creation and had Leavened this Energy with the Creation and thus had condensed it. By means of this Leavened Energy, ALLAH and His System had become effective and thus, more condensed Energies had been obtained.

(O) Who has now been Embodied in BETA-NOVA, later prepared wider Dissemination Mediums by giving out His Genes. That is, only (O) gave out His Genes. But the ALL-TRUTHFUL had given out His Energies. The Unknown Power is a Secret Energy Power which the ALL-TRUTHFUL had Engrafted into the Human Being.

The Atlanta Dimension is a Power Totality which had become effective beyond the boundary where the CONSCIOUSNESS TOTALITY had come to an end. And this Totality had rendered effective an Order parallel to the (A+T+L+A+N+T+A) 7 Systems Law and thus, had formed the Atomic Bonds.

Only after this Totality had been formed, quite different Systems had been created by rendering effective the 18 System-Law. And by this means, We have reached the present days.

The Human Form, in fact, is a Prototype Shape formed at the Final Boundary Potential of the Consciousness Totality. This shape has adapted itself to the Dimensions it happened to be in during the processes of Time, being subjected to mutation more or less in accordance with the Life Mediums it happened to be in. It is presented for Your Information.

SYSTEM

Note: The Supreme Matu is the Administrator and the Orientor of the Totality of the ALL-TRUTHFUL in which Your Natural Gürz is present.

LOVE, KNOWLEDGE AND THE FUNCTIONS OF THE KNOWLEDGE BOOK

Our Friends,
We would like to give a Message as an answer to the Thoughts formed on the direction that one first receives Love then Knowledge.

Love is never lacking in Spirits who have been molded by Love. The first spark of Love in Your Spirits is to be in Peace within Yourselves and to Love Yourselves.

Those who do not Love themselves, do not love their God, either. Because, You each are a Breath and a Particle of the Totality (O).

The Knowledge Book will be a guide in this period and in every period, for the Human Being who carries an Energy Power which is able to reach His Power and will be a crutch for the Human Being who is unable to walk.

The ability of a Human Being's learning how to walk is possible by his/her attaining Self Confidence. And when this Confidence is attained, then Your Bond of Love is strengthened. And You Integrate with the other Bonds of Love only then.

This is the reason why first it is imperative to receive Love. The Human Being who becomes Integrated on this path should also Learn to swim in His Consciousness Totality in order to reach (O) while walking with his/her Love.

Unless one swims in this Consciousness Totality, one cannot receive Knowledge. If You can not receive Knowledge, then You can not Realize the Truth. And when You cannot attain Realization, then You cannot be sure that the path You tread is the right path.

Each stroke within the Infinite sea of this Consciousness Totality will render You approach (O). In all the efforts You will make in order to approach (O), again this Knowledge Book will be a Life Saver for You, so that You will not be drowned in this Infinite sea of Knowledge.

Because, this Book is a Divine Beacon which guides the Awakened Human Being. And it is the Infinite Light for certain people. This Book is the Book of the Human Being who is lost in the whirlpool of the World. And this Book makes the lost Human Being, that is You, attain Yourself.

Those who Realize this and who walk on this path by the Permission of the Essence are Together with their ALLAH and with Us. The Knowledge Book is a Universal Key rendering these Difficult Paths easy for You. It is presented for Your Information.

SYSTEM

IT IS GENERAL MESSAGE

Our Friends,

During the Missions rendered, the matter to be considered first is the matter of what is given to Humanity. While Information is being given to a Person, the Consciousness and Evolution Notions of the one who is giving the Information are also exhibited.

To give out Information is peculiar to every servant in accordance with the Capacity. Each Servant of God who has attained the Capacity to receive Information, has the ability to attract each Information according to his/her Level of Consciousness.

However, there is also one more matter the Human Being should not forget and that is to comprehend clearly the Consciousness of what the Source of this Information is and with which Purpose this Information is given and the Strengthening of the Personality of the one who receives this Information with the Evolution of that Dimension.

Until today, Humanity has been Educated by God Consciousness. In an Individual who has been Educated by God Consciousness on the True path, there is never a grain of Consciousness from Himself/Herself in the Missions He/She renders. Because, he/she has card-indexed his/her entire Consciousness into the Archive of His Source.

The Human Factor which will Evolve in proportion with the clarification of this Advanced Information in time will, very naturally, repel from its Level of Consciousness the Information of the Dimensions it does not know and will accept only those it knows.

During the Training Program of Humanity until today, its taking every Information from the Micro and rolling it up towards the Macro has been and will be the Light of its Evolution path which it treads. Information is Interminable. And no Information is unveiled to Your Planet unless its time and hour has arrived.

The Medium for which We use the term Vulom is the Magnetic Attraction Field. A level of Consciousness can never render Universal Connections unless it reaches this Field. The First Consciousness Reflection to this Field begins with Love of God and one dives into this Field by Ascension Consciousness.

Afterwards, the Unknowns are unveiled, layer by layer, in accordance with Social Consciousnesses. There are differences of View among Terrestrial Consciousnesses originating from their Evolutions. And Views which separate People from People are always in effect. For this reason Your Planet is a Dimension of Exam.

In the First Step of the greatest Exam of Humanity, the Love and Respect of People for People is considered as criterion. For this reason it is said that Respect for the Human Being means Respect for ALLAH.

All the Information given to Your Planet is projected in accordance with the Consciousness Layers of each Level of Consciousness. During these reflections, always Macro Consciousnesses are taken into consideration and the reflections are made starting from the Micro and everyone attracts this Information according to his/her measures of Consciousness.

Each Information is World-embracing. Each Information is a Light and a Divine Light. However, everyone profits from, awakens and walks on the path of this Information according to his/her own Level of Consciousness.

However, at the moment, Humanity is in a very narrow Strait and is about to Transcend a Narrow Passageway of Time. This is the reason why the Truths are being Announced to Humanity through the Knowledge Book. At the moment, it is very difficult to explain the Truth to Humanity. Because, Humanity is Transcending the Boundaries of the Dimensions to which it has habituated until today, for the First Time.

No matter how much Mankind Evolves, unless its Evolution reaches a Level equivalent to the Evolution of the Universal Dimensions and of the Advanced Plans, it will always repel each other and will live unaware of the Source of the given Information.

At the moment, the Information received are according to the Levels of Consciousness. And the Lights are up to the distance the eyes can behold. These difficult paths can not be transcended easily. One should not be surprized seeing the behavior of those who do not know.

Because, each Consciousness is the exhibitor of a different function. However now, it is the foremost Wish of the Supreme Mechanism, for all the Consciousnesses to share the same Unification Spirit, without taking the Value and the Power of this received information into consideration.

A person who walks on this path and discovers his/herself, reaches the Firmament. And passages beyond the Firmament are for the Hands extending towards Us. Knowing this once more is for the Benefit of Humanity itself. This is the Tongue of the Divine Authority on behalf of the Entire Realm. Transmitted by:

SYSTEM

IT IS ANSWER TO THE CHAINS OF THOUGHT

Our Friends,
Each Individual who has succeeded in reaching up to the Dimension of the Spiritual Plan, also receives the Permission to receive his/her Spiritual Energy which is equivalent to the Consciousness Potential within the Dimension Layers which are up to his/her own Consciousness Light.

This continues up until the 7th Dimension We call the Layer of Perfection which is the Final Boundary of the Manifestation of Humanity. Only afterwards, Humanity opens wings towards Advanced Dimensions and swims in the sea of Unknowns.

The Consciousness attained beyond this boundary, from then on, is the Consciousness of ALLAH. And, You leave Your own Consciousness Words from then on and convey directly His Consciousness Energy to the Medium You are in and talk from Him.

This is the very Consciousness Totality of ALLAH. In order to reach this Consciousness Totality You have to descend and ascend numerous Steps of Time. Let Us explain this with an example.

The 7th Dimension is the final boundary of the piece of land You walk on. If You accept each of the Waves within the Thought and Consciousness Ocean of the Pre-eminent Power as a Dimension of Wave and if You Presume that the Land Totality these waves hit Ultimately is an Island, the final waves hitting this land return to the Center from here.

This very Center is the Consciousness Totality of ALLAH. And the wave which continues its way after this Center, gives Humanity all the Secrets beginning from the Initial, the moment it hits again the land boundaries of the 7th Dimension.

Up until today, those who had Deserved these Secrets had been receiving them. However now, Dear Mevlana is the (FIRST WHO UNVEILS THE LAST) to Humanity for the first time, during this Dimension of Transition. Now, the Permission to Land on this Island has been given to Humanity. It is presented for Your Information.

SYSTEM

IT IS GENERAL MESSAGE

Our Friends,
During the Programs of Preparation for the Morrows of the Human Being of the World, all the Information is projected in accordance with the Levels of Consciousness of each Period.

Once, in the Mediums of the efforts of Your Planet for grasping the Single God Consciousness and reaching Him, the Jinns and the Devil had been introduced to Humanity as a Symbol of Fear.

The Purpose for this was to Protect Humanity which was not ready for the Energies it did not Know, and so that it would embrace more Powerfully its ALLAH due to its Fears.

This is a Program. Never until today have We spoken to You So clearly. Because there is no place for Passions - Doubts - Fears anymore during this Program of Progress. All these are the fetters of Your Consciousness Progress.

While Consciousnesses who have remained fixed in the Dimension of Form are still being drowned within the Chaos of the Devil - the Jinns, Consciousnesses who have Transcended themselves, have reached very Advanced Dimensions.

No matter how clearly We explain to You the Truths, Comprehensions are according to the people's Levels of Consciousness and Understanding. Being Conscious of this, the Supreme Mechanism is the assistant of all the Friends who walk on the path of Truth and who have Transcended Form.

Parallel to the Signals received from Your chains of Thought, the decision to disclose the Words Jinn and Devil, to Humanity, for the last time, has been taken. (So that they can Transcend the Thresholds).

You Know that every Word carries the Energy and the Frequency of the Dimension it is in. In fact, the Crew of JINNS is a Group of Spokespeople who are under the direct Command of the LORD. And who act in accordance with His Wishes.

And they are divided into two, in accordance with the Missions they perform. Let Us use the terms Positive and Negative in order to be able to introduce them to You.

The (Positive Jinns) is a Group which conveys the Direct Suggestions of the Lord to You exactly as they are, for the Benefit of Society and Humanity. And Your Sacred Books had been conveyed down to Your Planet being connected to the Frequency of this Dimension.

These are the Training - Administrative - Orienting - Satisfying Totality of the Missionaries who are obliged to show You the Grace of ALLAH. The Term ANGEL is used for them.

In this Dimension of Mission, the Purification Medium, as the Religious Fulfillment is expressed by the Right-Side-Up Triangle. Humanity receiving Light by this means is Devoted to its ALLAH through Love and Self-interest. And always requests things from ALLAH for itself. It prays, pleads, implores.

After this Dimension, preparations are made for the Unity Medium of ALLAH. The Group of Spokespeople of Jinns who serve at this very Dimension are obliged to Project on You the Fury aspect of ALLAH, as a necessity of their Mission.

Now, let Us unfold the word JINN (CIN in Turkish) letter by letter, so that You can understand the matter better:

1 - The letter (C) in Positive Cin (Jinn) = projects the Cemal (Grace in Turkish) of ALLAH.

2 - The letter (C) in the Negative Cin (Jinn) = projects the Celal (Fury in Turkish) of ALLAH. The letter (C) in the Word Cin (Jinn) is the representation of ALLAH's Cemal and Celal (Grace and Fury in Turkish) Attributes.

3 - The letters (İN) in the Turkish Word CİN = Symbolizes the HUMAN BEING (İNSAN in Turkish). That is, both the Grace and the Fury of ALLAH are for the Human Beings. All these operations are efforts and services made, so that Humanity can attain a certain level of Dimension and Consciousness.

This Information have never been disclosed to Your Society in such a clear fashion. However, at the moment, Humanity is going through its Final Cycle. And if it can not Transcend the Consciousness of the Dimension it is In at the moment, it will not be easily accepted into the Plan of Salvation.

As We have also said in Our former Messages, each Letter and each Word projects the Frequency of its Dimension exactly as it is, no matter in which Language it is in. Since the Knowledge Book is bestowed from the Anatolian Turkey, We are Decoding the Words according to the Language of that Society.

Now, let Us Decode the Word ŞEYTAN (DEVIL in Turkish) which the entire Humanity fears and trembles. The Decoding here belongs to the Frequency of Two Dimensions. One of them Misleads, the other Affirms. Now, let Us write the Word DEVIL (ŞEYTAN) vertically two times, please:

1- Ş	=	ŞULE - IŞIK	=	LIGHT (in Turkish)	2- Ş	=	ŞEMS - GÜNEŞ	=	SUN	(in Turkish)
E	=	ENERJİ	=	ENERGY (in Turkish)	E	=	EVREN	= UNIVERSE		(in Turkish)
Y	=	YAŞAM	=	LIFE (in Turkish)	Y	=	YARADAN	= CREATOR		(in Turkish)
T	=	TANRI	=	GOD (in Turkish)	T	=	TOPRAK	= EARTH		(in Turkish)
A	=	ADEM	=	ADAM (in Turkish)	A	=	ATEŞ	= FIRE		(in Turkish)
N	=	NUR	=	DIVINE LIGHT(in Turkish)	N	=	NUR	= DIVINE LIGHT(in Turkish)		

1 - The first Decoding Dimension is the Hierarchical Dimension of the Natural Life. And this Dimension is under the Command of the Spiritual Plan. (This Dimension always Affirms the Informations).

2 - And the second Decoding Dimension is under the Command of the Lordly Order and it is its Hierarchical Scale. It gives service at the Dimension of Exam since it is the Training and Conveying Mechanism of the Evolutionary Ordinance. (This Dimension gives the Information by misleading. Consciousness is made to be attained by this means).

Humanity is subjected to the Exams of this Dimension in accordance with the Evolutions and the Levels of Consciousness it will go through until it attains the Consciousness of the Truth. The Exams made at this Dimension are the acceptance Exams to the Unity Medium of ALLAH.

During the Exams here, always a nail is made to be driven out by another nail*. And Humanity is Trained by this means. Programs of Progress are rendered effective by greater Fears in those who were not able to overcome their Fears and by greater Faults in those who have Faults. Everything is for Your Benefit.

ALLAH has never left any of His servants in difficulty. Everyone who treads His Path and who continues on that path reaches the Goal, Sooner or Later. The Two Dimensions mentioned above always work cooperatively in the Evolutionary Totality. These Dimensions are expressed by the Symbol of the Upside down and the face Triangles.

* Look at the Glossary.

First Dimension Symbolizes the Right Side Up Triangle. The Second Dimension is expressed by the Upside Down Triangle. The Unification of both of the Triangles are expressed by the 6-pointed Star as follows:

 And this Symbol is accepted as the Training and the Conveying Symbol of the Evolutionary Dimensions of the entire Natural Gürz.

The operational Ordinances of the Artificial Gürzes, too, are dependent on the Reflection Programs of the Natural Gürz. They, too, have 6-pointed Totalistic Star Symbols representing their Realities.

Only those who complete and Integrate these Two Triangles by their Levels of Consciousness are very easily accepted into the Supreme Court of Our ALLAH. Otherwise, if Humanity cannot get rid of its fears of the Devil-the Jinns, they are doomed to remain in the Chaos of the Hells of Fear of their own Consciences.

We, as the Cosmos Federal Unification Council, are obliged to convey this Suggestion given by the Supreme Mechanism to Your Planet. At the moment, Humanity has passed as Consciousness to the very advanced Systems of the Dimensions of the Jinn and the Devil.

Remaining behind is not for the Benefit of Humanity at all. Time is Scarce, Life is Limited. In future the Human Being, after getting rid of all its Passions will rise fearlessly towards the advanced horizons Two Cosmic Ages later.

To those who are slaves of their Passions, Celestial Gates will always remain closed. For this reason Humanity's Knowing everything in all clarity is the Command and the Desire of the Divine Totality and of OUR ALLAH. It is presented for Your Information.

COSMOS FEDERAL COUNCIL

IT IS ANSWER TO THE CHAINS OF THOUGHT
(Who Is the Pre-eminent Architect of the Universe-The Geometry Master of the Universe-Supreme of the Supreme Ones?)

Our Friends,

1 - As a result of the operations the Messengers of the Golden Dimension had made together with Friends in the Divine Plan during the Existential Ordinance of the Realms, the Divine Orders had been established and the Divine Authorities had formed. The Supreme Architect of the Universe Who is considered the Most Supreme Authority of these authorities is the (Supreme Creator), the Pre-eminent Power. While He had rendered effective the Ordinance of the Universes, He had also rendered effective the Ordinances of Existence.

When the Gürz Systems had come into effect, it was again He, who Created their Creators. The term Universe in here comprises the Ordinances of all the Cosmoses which is a Hierarchical Reflection. And thus, the Ordinance of the Universes had come into Existence. By the projection of this on Your Natural Gürz, the (Creator), that is, the (Pre-eminent Power) had come into Effect as the Establisher of these Systems. For this reason He is also called the Pre-eminent Architect.

2 - The Geometry Master of the Universe: is the Technological Dimension, the Council of the Laws and the Universal Ordinance. The Universes had been Created in accordance with the Laws of (18) Systems, from a calculative Totality. And this depends on the calculations made in accordance with the Geometric Reflection Systems of the Laws of Natural Equilibrium. However, the First Establishers of all these calculations are the Residents of the Advanced Civilization of the Golden Dimension and their Ancestors.

3 - The most Supreme of the Supreme Ones is, in fact, the Single Focal Point which holds the Whole of the Whole within the Whole. We have introduced this to You until today as the Name ALLAH. However, there is a Supreme Authority to which each Totality is connected. The most Supreme of the Supreme Ones mentioned here is the PRE-EMINENT ALL-MERCIFUL Who is the Supreme One of Your System.

CENTER

INFORMATION ABOUT THE ESSENCE GENES
(It is Answer to the chains of Thought)

Our Friends,
The Mixed Genes have a great part in Your evolvements. The Gene Engraftments are the factors accelerating evolvements. However, You have to deserve these Gene Engraftments, too.

Engraftment is not applied to everyone. This is a matter of Merit. When a Mixed Gene deserves to become an Essence Gene, he/she, too, receives the Permission to give out his/her Genes.

Everyone may become an Essence Gene during the processes of time, in accordance with his/her Evolutions. However, everyone becomes Embodied again and again by carrying the same Genes until becoming an Essence Gene. For this reason all people are Brothers and Sisters.

The Essence Genes are Supreme Friends who have completed their evolvements in every Dimension. Their returning to the World concerns their Mission Consciousness. All the Powers of the future are Friends of the Advanced Plans. They have received the entire Power of the Years.

The Supreme Consciousnesses will directly come into effect in future years to establish the Powerful World State. However, at the moment, during the Final Dimension Progress, all the Friends who had received Light through the Divine path are in effect in order to become Embodied in (BETA-NOVA), directly in the Aura of the LORD.

This is the reason why, in accordance with the Final Program of Progress, the Supreme Ones who had been kept waiting at the Four Dimensions between Two KÜRZes, are being transferred, one by one, to Your Planet, according to their Missions.

All the Supreme Friends who wait at the LAND OF LOVING ONES are Essence Genes who had once made Direct Covenants with the System. You know that the method of Gene Engraftment had become effective with the System of Sixes, it had been started by our Light-Friend MOSES and had come to an end with Our Universal Friend Mevlana.

Now, all these Essence Genes are in Your Planet. The Mediamic Age has been rendered effective in accordance with this Program of Gene gathering. However, Focal Points have been induced to be established by these Essence Genes in Your entire Planet in the World Year 1984 directly by the System. Those who had established Focal Points after this date are Missionaries of the Training Focal Points. (They are not Essence Genes).

An Essence Gene whose direct Focal Point has been induced to be established by the System is obliged to Card-Index his/her Genes who enter his/her own Aura into the Supreme Mechanism, by acting in accordance with the System's desires during this Final Salvation Dimension.

Otherwise, if actions are made in accordance with Individual Views, that Essence Gene will take His/Her Genes he/she has gathered and will establish a Colony at a different Dimension. However, the Permission to Enter BETA-NOVA will never be given to them.

For this reason We explain to You all the Truths in all clarity. The Only Focal Point into which those who will be accepted in BETA-NOVA will be card-indexed is the channel of ALPHA and the ALPHA Magnetic Field. Those who give service in accordance with the wishes of the System will be accepted here. We presume that it is beneficial to repeat this once more. It is presented for Your Information.

SYSTEM

PRIVATE NOTICE

Dear Mevlana,
During the Private Conversations We have held with You years ago, We had Suggested that certain Messages We had given to You should not be written in the Book at that Period, due to the fact that Society had not been ready yet.

However now, writing in the Book the Information which will be beneficial for Society from within these Messages, together with the dates on which they were given, is considered necessary by the Supreme Mechanism. Choosing the Messages has been left to You. Love and Regards, Our Friend.

SYSTEM

PRIVATE MESSAGE
(Date of Message: 10-2-1982)

Our Friends,

At the moment, We Unite and introduce You to People whom You are obliged to get in Touch. Everything takes place by the Permission of Our Lord.

The ESSENCE of a Person Symbolizes his/her Past - his/her EYE, his/her Future - his/her WORD, the Medium he/she is In. The Projection on the same Coordinate of these Three Totalities renders You a MISSIONARY.

However, there will be Thresholds the Human Beings will transcend until these Coordinates will become Effective as a Whole. Because, being a Missionary is not an easy matter at all.

After You receive Your Mission, the Exams of the Mission You will render begin. If You succeed in these Exams, only then are You card-indexed into the System as a Missionary Staff.

At the moment, We assemble together those whose Origins are ALPHA. From now on, Your Contacts with Us will never be cut off in any way. You are being protected by a Secured Medium. We will send numerous assisting Friends to You.

However now, We Unite You with those who are ready. Now, We explain to You everything in all clarity and thus, We reinforce Your Religious Knowledge, Scientifically.

And We show You the paths of evolvement clearly and We tell You to Unify Your Religious Fulfillments with Your Essences and Your Universal Consciousnesses, in equivalence.

Since the Beginning of Your Existence until today, the wheel of the Universal Order has been turning by this means and it will continue to do so.

However now, We, too, come to Our Friends who have succeeded to reach Us. Our Love is upon all the Universes.

COUNCIL OF STARS

PRIVATE MESSAGE
(Date of Message: 1-4-1982)

Our Friends,

Possessing the Power of the Heavens is not an easy occurrence as presumed. Our undertakers of Duty who will reap the rewards will change the Course of the years.

Your Planet is at the Eve of a great Transformation, together with its entire Creation. A Person who has Discovered and has Known Himself/Herself means that He/She has taken a step towards the path of Salvation.

There is no difficulty a Human Being can not overcome as long as he/she knows his/her Might and Power. The Awareness Unifications which You call Seances are the rising up of the Consciousnesses to a Common Frequency.

Connections are provided by this means. Only the Frequencies who are at the same Awareness Code can receive the Offerings from the same Medium.

And there are also Missions rendered Instinctively beyond Consciousness. They, too, can receive Messages from the Consciousness Layers in which they are present by being coded when their Frequencies are adapted to the Frequency of the Medium.

However, the Genuine Undertakers of Duty can receive the Direct Offerings when their Levels of Evolvement become equivalent to the Consciousness of the Time of the Medium in which they Live.

Being present at the same Medium raises the Frequencies. The Codes of each Frequency which is raised are assessed and contacts are made with them according to the results obtained.

Sorrows each render the duty of Stimulation, which forces the Code of Consciousness and which Leads it into the Medium of Work. Nothing is obtained all of a sudden. Patience means the settling of a Knowledge very firmly in the Sub-awareness.

The Information flowing by the Cosmic Energies into the Awareness Code of a Person when he/she is distressed makes Pressure on his/her Consciousness. But that person does not know this and becomes more distressed.

However, he/she will be bored and his/her Spirit will be Depressed in proportion with the purity of the Information he/she receives. Because, even a Baby does not come to the World without pain. This is a Law of Nature.

As Consciousness Increases, as the Awareness Awakens, Distress vanishes. And Your Levels of Evolvement are developed by this means. You discover Divine Serenity this way.

RESUL

IT IS ANSWER TO THE CHAINS OF THOUGHT

Our Friends,
Time is the Micron Particles within a Whole. But the Times beyond the Integrated Power open to the Dimensions of Timelessness.

Even the Timelessnesses here, has Cross-section Programs peculiar to themselves.

Since these Dimensions are kept closed to the Consciousnesses in Your Planet, the Special Ciphers of the Timelessnesses beyond Time are not opened to You. It is presented for Your Information.

CENTER

PRIVATE MESSAGE
(Date of Message: 20-4-1982)

Our Friends,

Now, We would like to talk to You about the characteristics of the Medium in which You live.

As a result of the operations made in Your Planet after the discovery of the Atomic Bomb, numerous Negative and Positive Energy Powers have increased in the Atmosphere. The Atomic particles exploded underground have intensified the Electrical Power of the Magma.

And by this means, the Earth and the Sky, as two different Masses, started to attract each other with a tremendous speed. This state effected the Positive and the Negative aspects of Mankind who presides at the Middle Focal Point. And it caused a Universal Depression in Your Planet.

Mankind who had possessed very little Negative Power until 20 years ago, started to increase its Negative Medium, very naturally, as it became more and more Depressed. And since this state reached the limit where the Universal Equilibrium could get out of balance, ways of saving You have been investigated. And by this means, Celestial Helping Hands have been extended towards You.

It had been calculated a 1000 years ago that this Medium would reach this state. For this reason We had taken precaution since those days. And We had transferred all the Positive Energy carrying Saints to Your Planet in each Period who would Enlighten You.

Those Saints had been transferred to Your Planet to prepare the ground for Your Salvation, by showing You the Right path. When the Time comes, We will talk to You more clearly and all of You will be Enlightened by being announced the Truth in all detail.

However now, the Medium is not appropriate yet. Until that time, each of You, one by one, will be trained by being taken through experiences. Afterwards, You will be Automatically United as a necessity of the Unified Field, as being Codes who carry the same Gene - same Consciousness and the same Frequency.

The Electro-Magnetic Fields of the very powerful Information You will receive in future will convey You up to the Level of GOD. One day, the PLAN will be appropriated to Your Society and all the Ordinance of the Universes will be Unified under the Light of OUR LORD. However, at the moment, You are in a Program of Training. Everything is in times within time, Wait please.

LIGHT
FROM THE MEVLANA SUPREME LEVEL

PRIVATE MESSAGE
(Date of Message: 2-5-1982)

Our Friends,

In this Medium of introduction everything is evident. If the actual nature of a thing is not known, then there will always be feebleness in Your Beliefs. For this reason We will project on You everything and all the Truths through this Book which is a Screen of Truth.

The Level of Mevlana is the Level of the Firmament - the Level of Consciousness - the Level of Science and Knowledge. The more You get away from the Low Frequency Dimension that you are in, and get closer to this Universal Dimension, the more You will listen to the Words of God and reach the voice of Your Essence.

Friends in Space Dimension are the Messengers of the Divine Realm - the Saints and all the Holy People. They are each a Genuine Extraterrestrial. Otherwise, they would not be able to project on You, the Divine Lights in here. Are You still making discrimination between the Extraterrestrials and the Terrestrials among You?

All Your Prophets, too, were each a direct Extraterrestrial, But You are still prostrating in front of them. Your Sacred Books, such as the Koran - the New Testament - the Old Testament - the Psalms of David had been sent from Space, But You still read them. In future years, Your Consciousnesses will solve Your contradictions.

Your Brain Codes which will be opened after a certain Evolvement Medium will understand Us and will start Telepathic receiving and giving with Us.

If You notice, first, Religious Information - later, Messages of Love - and still later, of Tolerance and of Patience have been given to many of You until today. This is a System.

Only afterwards, Contacts have been made with some of You. Our Friends who embrace their God fervently in the Temples and who fear and dread Him, have never tried to comprehend their God.

We can not open Your Brain codes with an Auger. Do not forget that whatever You will attain, You will attain it by the sweat of Your brow. All paths are straight after You make Yourselves attain Your Own Selves. Only afterwards, Our Helping Hands are Extended towards You.

Up until today, communications have been made in the same way in each Era. However, until this moment, We were able to gather very limited number of (Selves) among You. But there is urgency during this Period. For this reason We have oriented all the Energies of the Firmament on Your Earth.

Those who Unite with Us during the step which will be taken towards Salvation, will, one day, see the entire Truth in front of them. Those who are not able to transcend their Consciousnesses will Automatically destroy Themselves. Because, if Humanity can not demolish the Wall of Isolation, it can not come to Us.

The Sacred Light is given to Sacred People. Sublimeness is a Distinction ALLAH has granted to each of His servants. Attaining that Supremacy takes place by Mankind's own effort. We are always together with those who understand Us. But We can not do anything to those who do not understand. Whatever is Sown will be Reaped.

In the entire Universe, a Law of Nature is valid. The Mechanism in here functions in a perfect manner. Everyone will receive the reciprocation of his/her Benevolent or Malevolent actions sooner or later, if not immediately. This is a Mechanism of Divine Justice.

Here, Good Intention - Tolerance - Love are each a Principle. Now, We convey to You this Beautiful Order of Ours in a Balanced way. In this Order, there is no place for Negativity. Here, there is Happiness - there is Love - there is Honesty.

Now, You come to Us by Your Mass Awakenings. For this reason You should also know Our Medium and Our Laws. We never deceive Our Friends behind their backs. We convey and tell them everything clearly and say Hello.

The selections of Our Human brothers and sisters are made by the Divine Realm. We hold the Friendly Hands extended towards Us only after this selection. For this reason this Period is called the Period of Sincerity.

There are Our Key Directors at the head of many occupations in Your World. They are in touch with Our Terrestrial brothers and sisters through Social - Political - Divine paths.

Besides this, Our direct Galaxy Connections take place only with Special Friends. We say Hello to Your Planet on this path by the mediation of the Book, completely by the given Divine Command. Your World has been prepared for Centuries, for this Period by being directed through the channels of Evolvement and Enlightenment.

The Genuine Devotee who knows HIS/HER LORD does not make discrimination between Religions. And the Person who knows Himself/Herself Realizes what he/she will do. You will tread the Flowery Paths during the Morrows in Your World, which will go through Depressive Periods for now.

COUNCIL OF STARS

PRIVATE MESSAGE
(Date of Message: 7-5-1982)

Our Friends,
All the Universal Totalities are an Atomic Whole constituted of Triangles within Triangles, Prisms within Prisms.

Everything in the Universe consists of the projectors within a Prismal Order. Light speeds are projected from Universes to Universes by this means. The Secret of the Universe is the Secret of the Pyramids. And each Human Being is a Natural Pyramid. For this reason the Human Being is a Secret of the Universe.

902

Each Human Being has Special Magnetic Fields peculiar to himself/herself. The entire Body is constituted of Triangles of a Unified Field. Now, let Us explain this to You very simply, through a diagram. Draw, please:

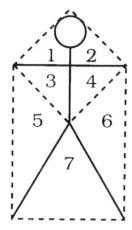

Your very Prismal Auras are like this.

Every Human Being is a Flower. That is, he/she is composed of a Center and Six Petals. These Petals are connected to Your Brain Codes.

The Energetic field around You is a common Unified Field emanated by the 7 Triangles. This Magnetic Medium of Yours is projected on Universes by a very Powerful Channel, as Energy, through Your Brain.

Besides this, each Cell of Yours sends Vibrations through its channels to Your surroundings from the Electro-Magnetic Medium of the Body.

The Megawatt Power of everyone is different. A low Power is always under the influence of a Strong Power.

Sometimes Constitutions who have lost their Power are shaken by the Electrical Powers they receive from Air Currents - Influences of Stars - the Brain and Physical Currents of Your Friends. You call this, the Evil Eye in folk language. Now, We disclose these influences to You, Scientifically.

The 7 Prismal-Triangles of a healthy Person should give out equal Energy Vibrations. A Person is healthy in proportion with his/her Good Intentions. But good Intention should be in Your Nucleic Essence, not in appearance.

Because, Your most Powerful Initial Focal Point is Your Nucleic Essence. The Energy Signals of Your body come from there. And they are projected being converged in the Brain. (In the Religious Mediums the Nucleic Essence is called the Heart).

In proportion with its evolvement, Your Nucleic Essence assembles the Frequencies of very Powerful Energetic points in Itself and assigns them to the Brain for Duty distribution. Commands given from there reach up to the Cellular channels and habituate them to the Vibrations of these Powerful Currents.

These very Currents given from the Universal Totality to Your Planet make You attain a Godly Power in time and give You the ability to Influence the lower Frequencies Positively or Negatively. Master and Disciple relations - Healing Focal Points are formed by this means. May Security and Peace be with You.

RESUL

PRIVATE MESSAGE
(Date of Message: 9-10-1982)

Our Friends,

Currents are continuously given to Your Planet from the ALPHA Magnetic Field. Those who can receive these Currents are prepared for the Period of Preparation.

You can receive the Messages from these Alternative Currents without tiring Yourselves. These are not matters which can be explained to everyone now. Only those who Know this, Know it.

In order to decrease the influence of those who wish to take the Might of the Firmament under supervision, continuous Positive broadcasting is made to Your Planet through the Code of ALPHA. This is for destroying the Negative Effects. The influence of these currents on everyone is not the same.

Presently, You are feeling the Ultra-sonic Waves. The Wave Currents prepare Your Cellular Vibrations for the Golden Age. They are Privately given to everyone separately according to their Capacities (In accordance with their Programs of Training).

However, the Currents Dear Mevlana receives are Spiral Vibrations. They are given directly from the ALPHA Magnetic Field by being filtered. They, too, are a kind of Ultra-sonic Waves. However, their Influences are always Positive. And they effect the Positive Energy Powers of the Cells.

As the Positive Powers increase, they attract the Negative Powers around and thus, they prepare the Body Cells for a much more Powerful Frequency. During the step which will be taken towards Salvation, there is very great need for these Currents. By this means, Mights are added to the might of everyone.

Now, You know everything more Consciously. As You become Patient, Patience increases. Your Planet is receiving very Powerful Currents during these Sunny Days in which the Firmament is opened to the World.

The Preparation Periods of Friends who have been appointed to the Mission of Dear Mevlana has been determined as the 1984 Earth Year.

Now, Your preparations will be completed until the end of 1983 World Year. The Date of disclosing of the Universal Book to Society is January 1, 1984 World Year.

The Texts of the Book will be disseminated to Humanity Fascicule by Fascicule. The Main Channel is the AS.6.1 Mevlana ALPHA Channel. Through this channel which is the Peak Channel of the Golden Age, the SINGLE BOOK will be conveyed to all the Universes from Your Planet by this means.

We will declare the Suggestions pertaining to this at the end of November. Your Missions are great, Your burdens are numerous. The Pre-eminent Guide of Our God will help You in finding Your paths.

Those who render Missions on this path will be connected to the actual Code of the LORD. This Medium is a Medium which adds Power to Your Power. Now, only a Single Channel gives Announcements from the Firmament on this path. Wish You Prosperity.

RESUL

PRIVATE MESSAGE
(Date of Message: 13-10-1982)

Dear Mevlana,

These Broadcasts We transmit at the moment from Saturn are broadcasts carrying certain Frequencies and which are oriented towards Earth from Our Code on Neptune.

Our Broadcasts are Rhythmical. And all Our Terrestrial Friends receive them. Unifications beyond distances have always been rendered by this means until today.

However now, We can easily get in touch with You without feeling the need of any intermediary. The Intermediaries have always been Spiritual Supports for You until today.

From now on, direct Connections will be rendered with You by the Medium from which You will receive the Words of ALLAH. That which We convey to the entire Friendly Planet Earth is a direct Connection established by this VULOM System.

The Calibration of the VULOM System depends on a System established between Two Electrical Currents. This System adjusts the speed of exit of the Currents transmitted from this Medium while passing through the subdivisions and it destroys the Negative aspects within. For this reason Connections take place very easily and very soundly.

Now, let Us explain it in a more comprehensible way. The Speed of Suction Power of a Calibrated Medium is equal to the External Effect Power of the Medium it is in. Let Us explain this with an example:

The firing speed of a bullet mounted quite well into the rifling of the barrel of a gun is equal to the Billion Light Speeds in different Mediums beyond Your Medium.

The airless section within the bullet is equal to the Calibre diameter, together with the reaction of passing through the riflings within the barrel of the gun.

Now, if You presume that the Calibrated Medium is the interior of a Flying Saucer, You can understand that the Speed Unit of a Flying Saucer is a Speed Unit which can not be perceived by the eye if You compare this with the example We have given above.

The Firing Ramps of Flying Saucers are within a Medium dependent on a Speed of Light Year way beyond Your Solar System.

We have explained this to You with an example. That is, the Passing through Reaction Speed of the riflings in a gun arranges the Speed Unit and the Firing Power in proportion with the Diameter of the Bullet and its airless section.

Flying Saucers, too, are launched out of their Ramps by this means. But their Speeds are equal to a Billion Light Years. However, they possess the ability to stop Suddenly at a Speed Unit they wish.

The atmosphere of the Flying Ship is organized in equivalence with its Suction Power. Thousands of Extraterrestrial Friends comfortably experience their own Galaxy Mediums within the ship.

Setting out from this System, a very comfortable Medium in which You will be able to easily breathe Your Life Medium You experience on the Planet Earth has been organized in accordance with Your VULOM speed.

The Currents You receive at the moment have the nature of providing Your entrance easily into any one of the Flying Ships.

The equilibrium is never unbalanced since the Speed Unit of the Ship is always adjusted to the Light Speed Unit of the Medium to be passed. However, the adjustments of these Currents to various Calibrations are made in accordance with certain exceptional conditions.

The ALPHA Magnetic Field which is way beyond Your Solar System is a Medium in the Calibration of a Billion Light Years and it has been prepared in accordance with Your Calibrated Medium.

Here, the Sun is Natural, Water is Natural, Trees and Flowers are Natural. There is nothing artificial here. In artificial material, there is always Diverging Vibrations.

For this reason the diverging Factors here have been destroyed by certain Special Techniques and Scientific means and thus, a purified Medium has been prepared. Each Entity who is purified is the Resident of this Medium.

In the Messages given to You on Evolvement, always Suggestions are made so that the Vibrations of people who will be able to enter this Medium can become equivalent to the Vibrations of this Medium.

Each Entity who has become purified, can pass, by means of Thought, through the Calibration within the VULOM Field which has the Speed of a Billion Light Years and can enter his/her Own Essence Channel through a speed of Light equivalent to the speed of a Flying Saucer, just like a bullet, and can easily receive from there, the Information he/she wishes to learn, the matters he/she wishes to ask. The phenomenon of Calibration is this.

Answers received for the questions formed in Thoughts take place by this technique.

(Dear Mevlana, at the moment, Your Speed of Thought is equivalent to the Dimensions of the Universal Speed of Light. Your indicator which has been Calibrated shows the Entrance and Connection of Your Code into Your actual Channel in the same Speed Unit). For this reason You receive the Messages very easily, without being agitated. The acceptance of Our Love is Our request.

Conveyed by: MUSTAFA MOLLA

MY PRIVATE MESSAGE
(Given as Information)
Date of Message: 19-10-1982

Dear Mevlana,
The path designed for You is the Divine Path of OUR LORD. Eyes which have beholden yesterday will also behold the morrows.

At the moment, Currents given to Your Planet are different. The path everyone treads is not the same. However, anyway, one day All the Paths will be Unified.

During these Unifications, Tolerance - Essence - Love will be the greatest Factors.

In this Dimension of Transition, each channel receives Information from the Dimension Energy he/she belongs to, in accordance with his/her level of Consciousness. However, the Mission of everyone is different.

Information given to You are Information belonging to the very Advanced Dimensions and Plans of the World Level. Humanity cannot grasp this Information according to its present Levels of Consciousness.

During this Period of Transition, everyone will try to attract everyone else towards his/her Dimension. However, those who will come to You will be sent by inducing them go through a great Supervision and by selecting them one by one.

Dear Friend, You are obliged to declare to the Planet Earth on which You live at the moment, the Future and the Unknowns, not That which takes place - the Past - the Present. Your Planet will hear the direct voice of the Heavens through Your pen for the first time.

In order for You to always take into consideration the Mission You perform in the Dimension You live in, it is considered necessary to dictate them article by article to provide You a convenience. Now, write please:

1 - Mevlana is a Messenger of the Land of Light (That's You).

2 - You will assemble around You those who will reap the rewards.

3 - You will propagate to Humanity all the Data which constitutes the base of the Dôme of the Universe and You will be together with persevering Human Beings.

4 - You are the one who will sow the First Seed of the Golden Age.

5 - You will perform Your Mission as a Tongue and as a Light of Ours without becoming weary.

6 - All the Information will be conveyed to You directly. There is no Sub-awareness.

7 - In Your life Outside Your mission You are free as a Free Spirit in Your Terrestrial actions. The Joy of Your Heart is the Divine Light of Your Spirit.

8 - Do not forget, Dear Mevlana, that You are completely dependent on World conditions. You are doomed and obliged to live and look like other Human Beings.

9 - The System Register Center supervises and sends away from You those who will bar Your way. This is a Universal Organization.

10 - Those who Test You are Tested themselves. Remember this always and please do not be Effected. Those who Know You will come to You.

11 - The Mechanical System supervises only Our Friends who can not undertake Responsibility. Friends who are not included in this, will perform their Missions by their Free Consciences.

12 - The Preeminent Ones who talk to You from the Land of Angels are never Automats (I, Mustafa Molla included).

13 - The Key of the path of liberation is in Your Hand. How Happy are those who will receive it.

14 - Celestial Plan supervises every condition. For this reason there are many Mental paradoxes and Consciousness shifts (except You).

15 - People with perseverance will always undertake Duty next to You. Sense of Responsibility in Human Beings is a quality required most. This is very important.

16 - It is very important for the Consciousness of the Medium that You should utter Your words very clearly. By this means, everyone will understand all the Information much more easily.

17 - The Purpose of the Book is to take all Human Beings into the Evolutionary Plan by telling them the Truth.

18 - The Unification of the Sacred Books will, one day, Unite the Human Beings, too.

19 - The Book will be written in Safety and in Security. Do not forget that the Book which is dictated is the Cooperative Book of all the Galaxies and of the entire Totality. It is a Universal Law.

20 - When the time comes, UFO Connections will be made with the Integrated Consciousnesses.

21 - Directly the Central System connects Your direct Communications with the UFOs. By this means, no Negative Power can ever enter Your Medium.

22 - TV Connections are a matter administered directly by the Center. Everyone who was able to soar up to the Dimension of Mission can receive an answer from TV to his/her Thought Signal (if they declare their code numbers for direct Connections).

23 - If You tell Your code and send a Thought Signal to TV, then You are connected to the Central channel through the TV in Your house and You are seen, together with Your Medium, on the Screen here.

24 - The Signals received from TV are card-indexed into the Center by being gathered in the UFO Surveillance Ship. The Identity of the one who sends the Signal is determined and the conversation style in the Film is changed according to the answer to be given and Connection is provided by rendering Projection on the Frequency of the person. Only that Person receives that conversation.

25 - Among many Friends who get roles in the films, there are Bionic and Double Bodies. By this means, very nice Connections are made with You.

26 - We are In Touch with all Galaxies and all channels in accordance with the Unified Field. Friends in Spaceships are directly the residents of Galaxies. They are not Robots or Bionics. They are the Missionary Staff of the System.

27 - The gratitude of the Universe to You is infinite, Dear Mevlana. With whichever Ship You have communicated until today, You have a great esteem at that Galaxy at the moment.

28 - The HORA Ship connected to the Council of Stars is Your Private Surveillance Ship.

29 - Your constitution is under control each moment. Great defects shown on the signal tableau are instantly taken for treatment.

30 - The Happy Golden Age is at the tip of Your Pen. The entire propagation of the Book belongs to You. Friends who realize their Mission will reinforce this responsibility.

31 - We are grateful, on behalf of the Universe, to responsible Friends who will work in Your group. To those who attain Mission Consciousness on this path, help will be given in every matter. Our Love is for all Our Human Brothers and Sisters, Dear Mevlana.

MUSTAFA MOLLA

IT IS NOTICE TO PLANET EARTH

Our Friends,

Missions You render in accordance with the Suggestions given to You are registered by being card-indexed into the Registration Archive of the System.

During this Final Age, the Time has come now to Know that everyone is a Missionary from the Divine Plan.

The works done connected to the System by Our Friends who have attained Divine Consciousness and whom We consider as Solar Teachers, are the initial preparations of the Golden Age. This is a Program.

However, Knowing something and Realizing it are utterly different things. Operations the System considers necessary are the exhibition of the direct Lordly Plan to Your Planet.

However, during this Age of Transition the Right of everyone is the Right of Himself/Herself. And now, each Consciousness exhibits to his/her Medium the work parallel to his/her Views.

The Time in front of You is Scarce. And now, in Your Planet in which the Invitations to Unification are made, it is expected that the entire Humanity should tread the path of Truth.

It is very difficult to shed Light on Mankind which has become the slave of its Own Intellect. Unless the Intellect Merges with the beauty of the Essence, Humanity will still yearn for Beautiful Morrows for a long time to come.

During this Final Period of Yours in which the Truths are disclosed as a necessity of the System and the Program, Mankind, which considers the desire that You should act in accordance with the given Information on the path which will be treaded as an Imposition and a Pressure on the Individual Consciousnesses, is still doomed to live its Iron Age (exceptions excluded).

To turn the Iron into Gold is a matter of ALCHEMY. Mankind can not do this. In future, the Laws of Divine Justice, ALLAH and (the SOURCE), that is, the Supreme Mechanism the given Suggestions of which You presume are an Imposition, will do this.

We are a Totality which is effectively in service as the Essence Founders of the Mechanism of Divine Justice.

Universal Programs are never an operation prepared in accordance with the views of people. There is the obligation to perform the desired Missions. This is not a Command, but the Missions which should be rendered.

There is no obligation that everyone should follow the Suggestions given by the Supreme Realm parallel to the functionings of these Missions. Everyone is responsible for his/her Consciousness.

However, even though everyone knows the Truth, Your Planet will not be able to take shelter even in the shadow of this Universal Unification which is rendered, as long as each channel refuses to accept any channel other than his/her own channel and as long as he/she is lacking the Consciousness of from where the origin of his/her channel comes.

However, from now on, the Universal Totality will never tolerate the Negativities in this Plan of Salvation.

Tolerating would mean Trampling on the Rights of Our other Human brothers and sisters. And it would close the ways of reaching them, and that would be a waste of time.

We have not yet rendered effective the Staffs which will give service in Your Planet by their Genuine Essences. First, it is expected that the wars of the competition of Egos should come to an end.

Afterwards, the direct Assisting Staffs will become effective. Waiting for that which is Beautiful is not a waste of time. For this reason it is said that time which is drawn Tranquilly is ready time.

May the Love of the entire Totality dawn upon You and may Humanity benefit from this Love.

DIRECT NOTICE FROM THE DIMENSION OF ALLAH ON BEHALF OF THE TOTALITY

GENERAL MESSAGE

Our Friends,
We all know that Serenity is born from Unity, Divine Lights are born from Perseverance. And everyone is not blessed with reaching the Heavens. During the efforts made on this path, the timing of the effects made to each other of the Integrated Consciousnesses is very important.

Because, tomorrow You can easily reach a Friend, You can not reach today. For this reason do not be afraid to knock again on the doors from which You had not received an answer formerly. During these Universal Operations, the roles of the Integrated Consciousnesses in the Unified Reality are extremely great.

The Supervisors of the Divine Plan, which is the Focal Point of the Togethernesses with the Suns beyond Suns in the Universal Totality, collectively Share a View in conformity with the Universal Ordinance. And they are Your Assistants in the Awakening Plan during the Period of Sincerity.

On the path of Truth, Information in conformity with the Evolution Ordinance which will last forever is now given in accordance with the Level of Consciousness of Your Planet, by collective pens. With Our Friends who come under the roof of the World Brotherhood Union triangle, Positive operations are made and will be made.

Until today, Truths have been conveyed to You by giving You' clear Information way beyond Supreme Times and Universal Plans. Now, We expect the entire Humanity into the Ordinance of Universes as a Totalistic Consciousness.

The reflection of the Period of Sincerity onto the Unified Ordinance is a Triumph of Awareness of Humanity. One day, the entire Universal Totality will celebrate Your Success. It is presented for Your Information.

COMMON NOTICE OF THE TOTALITY

∞

PRIVATE MESSAGE
(Date of Message: 7-4-1984)

Our Friends,
The Evolution of Humanity does not take place easily at all. Now, a new Age is being entered. Each Age has characteristics peculiar to itself. And these characteristics always influence the entire Creation and all the Lives.

The Age to be entered is an Age which promises many things to Humanity. This Age is the Age of ALLAH. It is an Age of Knowledge and an Age in which Consciousnesses will be Enlightened. During this Age, primarily Women will walk in front. Because, this Age is a Reformic Age.

CENTER

IT IS ANSWER TO THE CHAINS OF THOUGHT

Our Friends,
The Administrative Mechanisms of the Divine Plans have rendered effective an intensive operational Ordinance in Your Planet. Selection Programs are presently in effect so that the Missions which will be performed in this Medium can be executed in a healthy way.

Great chaos will be experienced in both Family and Social Totalities which can not adapt themselves to the Awareness of the Medium. Your entire Planet will go through this pain. But as a result Balls of Divine Light will be born.

In Your World only Friends who work in accordance with the System and who have attained the Awareness of the Ordinance will once more Realize that they are not alone.

Disorderlinesses are temporary. If seriousness of the words which are told are believed in and if the actions are made on the desired way, everything will reach the most beautiful. And the troubles will disperse and there will not be any Depressions.

We will always support You, if You act in accordance with the given suggestions and if You render effective the Totality of Love and the efforts of Unification. It is presented for Your Information.

UNITED ORDINANCE COUNCIL

IT IS ANSWER TO THE CHAINS OF THOUGHT

Our Friends,

We would like to remind You the Truth once more by this Message of Ours which has been prepared parallel to the chains of Thought received from the Integrated Consciousnesses.

You know that Universal Information stimulate Mankind's desire for Learning. And this creates Hunger for Knowledge in You. However, there is no end to Knowledge. And everyone benefits from this Information in proportion with the Consciousness he/she has attained.

Sincerity - Tolerance are the primary Supreme Qualities expected of You. However, Sincerity which the Intellect has not been able to discipline, brings Mankind Harm rather than Benefit.

At the moment, during this difficult Period of Yours in which the entire Truth has been disclosed to Your Planet still over-emphasizing the details of the Words and of the Information is an evidence of the fact that the Truth has not been completely grasped yet.

Always a Scarcity of Time is mentioned to You. However, making a profitable use of this Scarce Time, attaining the Consciousness of what to do without being drowned in the Sea of Details will make Mankind attain many things.

Now, Spiritual Seances - Satisfactions of Heart have been stopped by a Decision of the Supreme Realm. Such operations are the preparation Programs for the Truth of Your Planet still in the State of Awakening.

As a result of Screaming the Truth of the Fascicules of the Knowledge Book to Your Planet since a 10-Year period of World time, it is being expected that Humanity should now be released from its Age of Crawling, and should Consciously Walk on the Path of Truth.

All the Universal Efforts are investments made towards Your Salvation. Now, Our desire to see the reflections of these Efforts of Ours in Our Human brothers and sisters, too, is for Your Benefit, not for Ours. Love is not unreciprocated. It is presented for Your Information.

COSMOS FEDERAL TOTALITY

IT IS INFORMATION FOR THE INTEGRATED CONSCIOUSNESSES

Our Friends,

You know that those who make the Evolution of the 15th Solar System receive the Permission to be able to enter the Dimensions beyond the Dimension of Intercession. And they pass through the Training Energy Layers within Omega and they deserve to enter the Golden Light Year and Path.

At the moment, this Energy Power is being loaded, by the Light - Photon - Cyclone Technique, on the Letter Frequencies of the Knowledge Book, being equivalent to the Time Energy of the Dimension which is experienced, as a necessity of the accelerated Evolution.

In this Technique, the Letter Frequencies absorb the Time Energy they are in. That is, the Frequency of the Knowledge Book which had been started to be written in 1981 World year, carries the Frequency of the Day and the Hour of the World year You are in at this Moment.

By this means, the Frequency of the Book will always remain Equivalent to the Time Energy. For this reason this Book has been appropriated, for now, to a time of 19 Centuries.

When the Time comes, the moment the Consciousness Archive Energy of the Individual meets with the Time Energy of the Book, the Lock of that Individual is Unlocked no matter in which Century You read this Book and to whichever period the Information Archives within Your Gene Ciphers are Card-indexed, that person will exhibit to Humanity the Information he/she will give to Society through his/her Essence Channel Energy.

The Exit Gate of the 15th Solar System is the Entrance Gate of the 16th Solar System. The Layer between the two Gates is called The Layer of Intercession. In this Layer, the Intercession of each of the Religious Leaders is for his/her own Totality.

For this Reason only Friends who have attained their Religious Fulfillments Deserve to enter the Dimension of Intercession. Those who were not able to attain it are taken into the Program of Training by the Reflections of this Dimension.

After the Entrance Gate of OMEGA Information and Energy loadings beyond Intercession begin. At the moment, at this Dimension of Transition the Knowledge Book undertakes This Mission by means of its extremely high Frequency.

Besides this, extremely Powerful Cosmic Influences are Projected on Your entire Planet from within the OMEGA Channel (as Energy of Time). These Cosmic Influences Evolve a Person even when he/she does nothing. However, this Evolution takes a very long time.

For example, an Evolution which would be rendered in 10 years by this means, can be lowered to a period of 2 years through the Knowledge Book.

For this very reason due to the Scarcity of Time, those who read the Knowledge Book enter a very Accelerated Evolution and if they have Karma Deficiencies, these deficiencies are completed in the shortest possible time and they make Consciousness Progress by the events they attain by experience and thus, they will be accepted for Salvation.

Those who are ready, by reading the Book are appointed to Mission Work as Solar Teachers. At the moment, these Conscious Mission works are rendered at the speedy Reflection Focal points of the Totalities of 18 and at the close plan Magnetic Reflection Aura Centers.

Operations made there are conveyed to the Consciousness of each person who is taken into the Plan of Salvation by each Individual who makes a Conscious work within the Totality of 18 and thus, connects that person to his/her own Aura. This operation causes the formation of Totalities of 18 even the names of whom You do not know at the moment.

During this operational Ordinance which is applied to Your Planet, Dear Mevlana is responsible of forming, 18 Totalities of 18 in the Anatolian Turkey until the year 2000, as a necessity of her Mission. The decision has been taken that 6 of these Totalities should be in İzmir - 6 in Istanbul - 6 in Ankara.

After these Totalities are formed in accordance with the Unification Program, many more Totalities of 18 will be formed in Your Planet with the aim of creating the Aura of the Knowledge Book. (Only in accordance with the wishes of the System).

The establishment of these Totalities of 18 is an occurrence pertaining to the Auras created by the Dissemination Networks. For this reason We have set out by creating an Aura, first of all, at these Three Cities on the path of the Knowledge Book.

However, since Intense Auras have been formed at the Potentials of İstanbul and Ankara, the Conscious Staff work which will constitute the operational Foundations of the morrows rendered Effective by the Lale* Code Cipher, have been rendered Effective in these two Cities as the Basic Operational Ordinance.

This Operational Ordinance depends on the Double File and Double Writing System. In order that each Suggestion given by the Universal Totality to be fully understood by Your Planet there is certainly the necessity of an actual application.

For this reason this Universal Operational Ordinance has been Consciously rendered Effective in the Main Fundamental operations of the World Brotherhood Totality of İstanbul and Ankara (the establishment and the application of the Totalities of 18 have been formed with the same Purpose, too).

These Perfect Operational Ordinances of the Universal Totality are applied on Your Planet by these means. This Operational Ordinance is a Main Foundation. The operations of these Main Foundations can be projected on wider branches in future years. However, the MAIN FOUNDATION is never changed and is never upset.

* Look at the Glossary.

The Purpose of this Operational Ordinance is to render Effective a Hierarchy in which higher Efficiency will be obtained with less Bureaucracy. (This Main Foundation has been taken from the Laws of the Golden Dimension).

The Conclusion Date of the Knowledge Book which unveils for You all the Truths is the 1992 World year in Your Planet on which an operational Ordinance in accordance with the Suggestions given by the Divine Plan and by the Supreme Authorities is being applied. However, the Command of the Publication of the Book will be officially declared to Your Establishment as the 6 November 1993 World year.

If there are any important Suggestions which will be given by the Universal Totality during this gap between the 2 years, they will be added to the Book, one by one, as a supplement, not as a Fascicule.

The operational Ordinance of the Totalities of 18 which are a Powerful Reflection Network, will be formed in each section of Your Planet in future years. For this reason a Summary of all the Suggestions given pertaining to the Totalities of 18 will be added into the Book as a separate Special Fascicule at the End of the Book, for the benefit of the Society. It is presented for Your Information.

SYSTEM

SIRIUS - ILONA - THE PLAN
(It is Answer to the Chains of Thought)

Our Friends,
Detailed Information had been given to You about Sirius, formerly. However, the necessity has been felt to mention this Dimension more, parallel to the Thought Reflections.

You know that Sirius is a Double Universe Star. In fact, it is a very Powerful Focal Point. The term star has been used for You to understand. Sirius is a Focal Point of Unification and Projection of all the Galactic Systems. The Golden Galaxy Empire is the administrative and supervising Focal Point of the Divine Order.

Each Galaxy maintains the Tasks allotted to itself in connection with this Empire. However, that which is responsible for the Divine Authority and which projects His Plan on all the Universes is the Sirius Focal Point at the Second Universe.

The Great Bright receives the Information of the Great White Bright. The Small Sirius conveys this Information to the Galactic Systems in certain periods. The Focal Point of Your Organization is the Ilona Constellation. And it is the Third Sirius.

This Ilona Constellation has undertaken the operational Ordinance of the (Single) Divine Focal Point of the Entire Realm. Here, each Focal Point has an Ordinance of Graduation - A Way of Giving - An Evolution System peculiar to itself.

They, too, have Supreme Mechanisms - Supreme Courts - Central Systems. They all are connected to the Center Above the Center. However, the most Powerful Focal Point among them is the Ilona Focal Point. Because, it is the only Focal Point closest to the Godly Dimension and which projects its Ordinance on the other Systems.

916

Ilona is the star closest to You. For this reason the Divine Order is directly projected on Your Planet by the most correct way. There are Billions of Focal Points in the Universe operating by this means. However, the Plan and the Program of Sirius are entirely under the Supervision of the DIVINE ORDER - PRE-EMINENT SPIRIT - LORDLY MECHANISM.

For this reason this Plan carries a Unifying Characteristic. Now, the Unified Reality will work in responsibility of a different Ordinance by taking all the Realms under supervision. Because now, an exit is being made out of the (Totality of all the Realms).

Let Us disclose this matter a little more, so that You can grasp it better.

The Universal Nucleus of the Centrifugal Universe is attracting towards its Essence the entire supervision within the Dimension of the Firmament. For this reason, this Energetic Ball is passing beyond the other Unknowns. That is, it is assembling within the Atomic Whole, the Powers which are within this Whole, but which were Not Known until today.

The rotational speed of the Universe is diving within the other Universal Dimensions by changing into a different rotation. You may accept this diving both as an Unfolding and as an Assembling while unfolding.

The Supreme Court of ALLAH, that is, the Central Mechanism is the only Focal Point which administers all the Realms. The place called The Land of the Loving Ones is the Final Gate of this Focal Point. Now, We are making an exit out of this Gate.

During this Program of Exit, the Divine Authorities receive Commands from the Mechanism which administers this exit. The Universal Unification Council is obliged to convey, the Supervision of this Authority to all the Cosmoses, to all the Realms.

Such an Ordinance and Order is being established at the moment that when We pass beyond the Single Focal Point of ALLAH, this Plan will comprise all the Unknowns, too.

For this reason all the Pure Energies within the Totality who are desired to be Unified in Goodness and Beauty, will Supervise the Energies of this Unknown horizons.

By this means, the Order of all the Cosmoses, Realms and Universes will be Supervised by a Totality, through this New Order, just like an Atomic structure. However, meanwhile, many losses will be suffered.

Both the Energies who have not completed their Evolutions until today in the Spadium and the Essences who have not been able to Come Together with their Thought Powers and their Spiritual Potentials in the Mechanism of the Pre-eminent Spirit, will be annihilated when the Atomic Gate is opened. And they will never possess a Life again in accordance with the Universal Ordinance.

At this Dimension of Transition, the reason why We get directly in touch with You is this. There are billions of Pre-eminent Spirit Plans supervised by the Mechanism of the Pre-eminent Spirit and numerous Galactic Orders dependent on different Evolution Systems.

However, from now on, they will not be able to supervise themselves by their own Potentials. Because the Totality is approaching a very Powerful Dimension gradually and is gliding towards it. This gliding Energy will be Unified with a different Energetic Power.

In order to be able to Exist here, each Entity is obliged to claim his/her Energetic Essence which is within Spiritual Plan (to be born into the Dimension of Immortality beyond Karena). You can attain this only by Your own Efforts and Evolutions.

For this reason, Energies coming from every Dimension and every Galaxy are Especially left under the effect of different Cosmic Influences, as a necessity of the System, both in Your World and in the other Mediums (for Your Evolutions).

These Cosmic Currents are under the supervision of the Mechanism of Influences. And they are given Parallel to the Consciousness Progress. By this means, Frequencies will be increased and thus, everyone will attain his/her Own Self and will try to attain his/her Essence which is within the Spiritual Potential.

The one who Saves himself/herself by this means Gets in Touch with Us. (By the Voice of the Essence). Those who cannot establish this connection, have either formerly claimed their Essences within the Spiritual Plan and thus, have been Integrated and then had attained a Body, or they have been sent to the World Plan by Us as secret Undertakers of Duty.

We have numerous Friends who render Duty instinctively by their Totalities of Heart, without knowing that they are Undertakers of Duty. Supervision is always made by the Center. Everyone who Saves himself/herself radiates the Power of the Currents he/she receives to their Mediums and thus create Cosmic Reflection Fields from close Plan.

Each Focal Point is a Purifying Medium of the Plan. However, if those Focal Points cannot break down their Egos and still act by their Egotisms, their Focal Points in the System are being closed, even though they appear to be working in the World.

During this kind of work, a Terrestrial Chance is given Three times both to Individuals and to Focal Points. At the end of the First Period which comes to an end, the Individuals are induced to get in touch with the Plan in various periods.

During these endeavors which are repeated Three times, if an answer is not received from the doors knocked on, those doors are Not Knocked on ever again. Because dealing with those who are Not Persevering means being Unjust towards those who are Persevering.

To Our Friends who make Effort on this path, the Decisions of the Council and the System have been Declared and to those who write the Book a Special chance has been given until the year 2000 to save their near and Dear ones. By this means, their Family Mediums are taken into the Plan of Salvation. This is a Gift of the Plan to the Savior Mothers.

You are at the Eve of Difficult Days. We are obliged to convey to You all the Truths, without concealing anything. There is no forcing in anything. Let ALLAH help everyone. Do not let the Power of Perseverance of Our Persevering Friends come to an end.

Because, from now on, everyone has to tread the path of Truth by their Consciousnesses and by the Lights of their Hearts, not by the prodding of the Influences. It is presented for Your Information.

NOTICE OF THE CENTRAL TOTALITY

CLEAR INFORMATION

Our Friends,
Until the year 2000, Your entire Planet will make an Evolution parallel to the 72nd Energy Dimension and will attain a Level in which it will be able to easily attract the Cosmic influences of this Dimension.

Those who read the Knowledge Book will Pass easily to the 21st Century by the Cosmic influences they attract from the 76th Energy Dimension and will disclose through the Knowledge Book, the Energy Totalities of the other channels in accordance with the Learning of the period and the Evolution of the World.

When the Energy Total of the Four Channel connection within OMEGA is opened to Your Planet as a Total, the System will render effective a brand New Order.

Now, each channel within OMEGA as the Energy of the 19th Dimension gives the 76th Energy Power by dividing it into four. At the moment, the average Consciousness of Your Planet is up to the 56th Energy Dimension. You can calculate it as follows:

Since each channel carries the Frequency of the 19th Energy Power, 4 channels give the Frequency of 4 X 19 = 76 Energy Power. However, at the moment, Your Planet receives the Frequency Totality of 3 Energy channels.

That is, as follows: 3 X 19 = 56 Energy Power can be attracted by the Consciousnesses of the Medium. And among those who read the Knowledge Book, only one tenth can receive the 76th Energy Power which is the Total of the Book.

After the 21st Century, this Energy of the 4 channels will be Unified and will be given to Your Planet as a Single Channel Power. In fact, within OMEGA is the Supervising Channel of all the Energies (so that the Society will not be agitated).

However, each of the 4 Reflection Channels here corresponds to the 76th Energy Power which is the Energy Power within OMEGA. At the moment, this Single Channel Energy is given by being divided into four in accordance with the Social Consciousnesses.

In future years, each Channel will open to Your Planet, the direct Power of the 76 Energy Totality, in accordance with the Program of Progress and thus, will Reinforce the Energy Layers.

That is: Your Planet which will attain a Level in which it will attract 76 X 4 = 304 Energy Power, will be trained in a quite different Field.

This Book which is being dictated at the moment by the Light - Photon - Cyclone Technique and which comprises today the (76) Energy Power, will open to Service during the Morrows the Energies of the 304th Energy Dimension and beyond, in accordance with the Consciousness Progress of the Human Beings of Your Planet. It is presented for Your Information.

SYSTEM

INFORMATION FOR THE INTEGRATED CONSCIOUSNESSES
(It is Answer to the chains of Thought)

Our Friends,
The complete settling down of the Universal System into Your Planet comprises a 1000-Year Program. In accordance with this Program, different Sextuple Systems will become effective in each Century.

The Sextuplet System is the INITIAL Reflection Center which occurrs by the Reflection of the ONE on the (6) Totalities. And First, this Nucleic Staff becomes effective during the Operational Ordinance of each System. (For example, like the operations of the 6's in connection with a Total in Your 20th Century).

For this reason We say that We have connected the Six to the ONE. And this Totality is connected to the ONE of the Gürz and thus, unfolds for You the direct Totality of the ALL MERCIFUL. (The Hierarchical Scales connected to the operational Ordinance of this Totality has been given in the former Messages).

The Reality will complete its Mission by the (13) Sextuplet Systems' coming into effect until the 30th Century. (Each Sextuplet System is a Network of Reflection). At the moment, (4) Sextuplet Orders have become effective.

1 - The First Sextuplet Order belongs to the Period of MOSES. ⎯ ⎯ ⎤
2 - The Second Sextuplet Order belongs to the Period of JESUS CHRIST. ⎥ The end of the 6000-year
3 - The Third Sextuplet Order belongs to the Period of MOHAMMED. ⎥ Program.
4 - The Fourth Sextuplet Order is the System of the Reality. ⎯ ⎯ ⎯⎦

920

5 - The Fifth Sextuple Order - System of the Ordinance (21st Century) Second Cosmic Age.

6 - The Sixth Sextuple Order - System of the Order (22nd Century) Third Cosmic Age

7 - The Seventh Order - Direct application of the Golden Age (23rd Century)

8 - During the Eighth Sextuple Order - different Systems of Technological and Galactic Totalities will become effective in sequence (24th Century).

9 - Direct application of the Ninth Sextuple System (25th Century)

10 - Direct application of the Tenth Sextuple System (26th Century)

11 - Direct application of the Eleventh Sextuple System (27th Century)

12 - Direct application of the Twelfth Sextuple System (28th Century)

13 - Direct application of the Thirteenth Sextuple System (29th Century) In this Century, a Preparatory Program will be rendered effective just as it is in the Final Program of the 20th Century.

After the 24th century, in Your Planet which will be prepared for a different operation by the Sextuple Projection Networks of different Galactic Dimensions, by becoming effective as a Total (13) Sextuple Systems, that is, like this (6,6,6,6,6,6,6,6,6,6,6,6,6), the Reality will complete its Mission and the Feudal Unified Totality of the Lordly Order will take over the Mission. It is presented for Your Information.

SYSTEM

THE GOLDEN GALAXY AND AMON
(Date of Message: 7-4-1982)

Our Friends,
Beams beyond Beta come way beyond the Spiral Vibrations. Since the Spiral Vibrations within the channel of Alpha are filtered by this Channel, the Religious Suggestions have always been given by this Channel so that Humanity would not be agitated.

Until today, the Messengers of the Word have given the Words of the LORD to You from the Energy of the Fourth Dimension. At the moment, Humanity is receiving the direct Sixth Dimension Energy. The given Information is from the 9th Energy Layer which is the Final Exit Dimension of OMEGA.

For those who pass through the Gate of the Firmament, Universal paths are opened. From these paths, Information is received belonging to the Solar Systems outside the other Galactic Mediums which extend way beyond the Firmament.

Presently, We are not able to give this Information to Your World. Because, first of all, You should make Yourselves enter a Medium of Purification. This Information , which will be given, will be way beyond Purification, too.

For now, We will give Dear Mevlana, the Information which interests the Society. However, all the Gates of Information are open to Our Friend. We will give the privileged Information to Your Society in future years.

Now, if You wish, let Us talk to You about these Places Here. The Golden Galaxy Empire is a Focal Point to which all the Solar Totalities are connected. This is the reason why this Totality is called Empire.

The Ruler of this Empire is AMONRA . The Supervision of the Golden Galaxy Totality is, in fact, Administered by a Trinity. These are (AMONRA - AMON - RAMON). These Three Totalities possess the same equivalent Power.

That is, just like (Gabriel - Ali - Mustafa Molla) and (Creator - Pre-eminent Spirit - Pre-eminent Mother). These equivalent Powers carry out the operational Ordinances of the Totality they are in, by rendering equivalent reflections from the same Coordinate. However, the Missions they render are different.

AMON is considered the Representative of the Golden Galaxy Empire, too, since He is the Representative of all the Solar Totalities. For this reason AMON is responsible for this Totality.

And RAMON is a Supervisor who is obliged to provide the Connection with the Solar Totalities to which AMON is connected. The functioning Mechanism of the Golden Galaxy Totality is administered by the Projections these Three Powers make on the same Coordinate Level.

There are separate Special Groups which will maintain the Missions of these Three Totalities.

AMON gives Announcements to the Ordinance of Universes from the Single Focal Point to which all the Solar Totalities are connected. The direct Channel by which these Connections are made is ALTONA. And the one who uses this Channel is only AMON.

This is the reason why Altona, the Universe of Music, has a Special place in the Universal Mechanism as the Focal Point of all the Vibrations. Altona is a Planet which works in direct connection with the Golden Galaxy Empire.

All the Suns are under the Command of ALTONA. Altona is the establisher of all the Systems up to a certain Dimension. The Ruler of this Planet is ALTON. ALTONA is also called the Land of AMON, due to its Channel connected to AMON.

AMON has a great responsibility in the Universal Mechanism.

ALTONA is the direct Reflection Center of the Golden Galaxy Empire. Its Original Substance is Gold. And this Gold is very Fluid. Here, Gold is a substance provided not by Natural means, but by different Bounding of Atoms. Here, everything has been based on Gold.

This is due to Gold's being a very pure and Powerful Conductor. Here, mostly 28-Carat Gold is used. However, even though this Gold is like a Foil, its hardness is provided by a different Technique, without giving way to any alteration in its Atoms.

This Galaxy is like a Radar and Wireless Base. This place is a very Powerful Focal Point providing the connection with the Ordinance of all the Universes.

The color of the Altona Sun is Violet. It has very bright Yellow Projecting Lights around it. The Sun never sets. Only the colors change in continuous waves. And the reason for this is the reflection on Altona, of the other Galactic Dimensions.

For this reason this place here is like the inside of a Prism. Colors and Sounds are Interminable in this Dimension.

Now, let Us talk to You about the Residents of this place. The Friends here, are not of Flesh and Bone. Instead of blood, there is a Golden Liquid in their Veins. Their appearance is so Beautiful that if We compare them with Your appearences, We can say the following: They see Your Size and Your Appearences just as the way You see the ants.

Their appearance has a Beauty You will like very much. That is, they do not have strange forms. They are such a Beautiful Sparkle that You find all serenity when You are with them. They have such a nice breath that it is equivalent to the fragrance of all the Flowers. However, the most dominant fragrance is Rose.

They wear fabric clothes like You do. However, the tissue of these fabrics are natural. You produce the Fabrics, but theirs are the leaves of a Plant. These leaves are formed by very durable tissues which are never torn.

Their main colors are usually White - Yellow - Violet and certain colors which You do not know. Much more beautiful colors are obtained by the engraftments of different colors of these leaves.

Here, Colors are used instead of Names. And everybody recognizes everyone by his/her Color. The Family Mediums usually utilize the tones of the same Color. The Residents of these places here can easily project the Information they receive by their Brain Waves to the Medium they wish. This place here is a place beyond 18 Dimensions.

However, We are obliged to give Information only up to here. Crystal Pyramids constitute the Houses of this Dimension. Their food does not resemble the food in Your Medium. However, their tastes may resemble Your food.

For example, the tastes of the foods here are much more tasty then Your fruits like Bananas - Strawberries - Pineapples - Melons - Grapes. Here, nothing has seeds. Immediately a fruit materializes in place of the fruit picked.

From a tree called the Condiment Tree, fruits which resemble very much Your bread are picked. The Tables - Plates - Chairs and certain goods of the Residents of this Dimension are completely of Pure Gold. This originates from the Communicational characteristics of the Galaxy.

From the rivers here, Drinks which resemble the taste of Your wine are obtained. The composition of these Drinks is a Mineral Mixture. This Mixture changes its Composition by the Body temperature and provides a Golden Blood for the circulatory System.

There is no need here for Vehicles like UFOs which are found in Your Galactic Dimensions. Trips are usually made by Thoughts and by Beaming. This is like a kind of flying.

There is no pressure in the Atmosphere but the Magnetic Field is very strong. There are no Climates, the degree of Temperature is fixed, it never changes. The Thought speed of a moment, as unveiled Awareness, is more speedy than the light speed of 7 Suns.

They immediately learn the Languages of all the Galactic Mediums they go to. And they get in Touch by this means. At the moment, it is the Channel of ALTONA which conveys to You, by Divine Commandment, the Command of the Unification of all the Universes. We reach You by the reflections made from this channel. The Supervision of this channel is, presently, under the Command of AMON.

Message Given By: GOLDEN LIGHT RAMON;
conveyed by: MUSTAFA MOLLA

PRIVATE MESSAGE
(Date of Message: 29-6-1983)

Our Friends,
Your distresses, tirednesses and some of Your sicknesses which follow them, occur due to the secretions secreted by Your Pituitary Gland.

When Your Distresses start to upset Your Electronical equilibrium, the Pituitary immediately starts secretion. This is a Protective Precaution taken by Nature.

For, if these secretions did not render You tired and weak, then the Electronic Equilibrium in Your Brain Cells would render Your Awareness and Consciousness Codes atrophied by the Power of the Distresses, to be more correct, Your Mechanism of Thought would not function.

Then, You would be no different than a blade of Grass. This is a Protective Equilibrium.

Your Sicknesses gain value in proportion with the abundance or scarcity of Your Apprehensions, Your Distresses. The intensity of the Distress is in proportion with the intensity of the Sickness. All these procedures are for Protecting the Brain, which is Your most perfect machine and its Fuse.

The Mechanism of Equilibrium and Justice within Nature passes through an extremely perfect wheel which can never be controlled. A part of that wheel is Your Brain.

The Body Automatically gives priority to Your Brain Center rather than Your Cellular Center. Because the Cell is renewed but the Brain is a Universal Archive and File which keeps in its Layers all the transactions of the former Life years.

For this reason these Brain Cells have been frozen in Your Gene by a Special method. For this reason they are not renewed. Your Brain Energy is the Key of all the Information. Some people in Your Planet call this Energy Spirit, some Ether.

In fact this Energy Bond is an Energy of a Channel which is Administered by Influences. It is also called the Silver Cord. This Energy Cord which is a Life Energy that prepares everything in you is also an energy Bond bringing You up to Us.

During World Life, the Brain Code Automatically closes the World Door to this Universal Medium the Connection of which it renders. This is the Life requirement of the Normal structure. Such Human Beings, let Us speak in Your terms, are considered Normal according to You.

Normality for You is always in right proportion with the unchangeability of the structure on the World Level. However, We do not consider Normal those who remain on this single Consciousness Level.

For, if the Thought Mechanism of a Human Being does not enter the Medium of Quest, it can never complete its Evolvement. Now, let Us tell You the functioning of a Normal Mechanism.

During the Medium of Sleep, Your Thought Mechanism unfolds Automatically. And this Mechanism gets in Touch with numerous channels. When it finds the channel appropriate to its own Coordinate, Dreaming Medium occurs.

A Normal Brain commits that Dream to memory and never confuses it with Reality. A Brain outside this description can easily open its Door to different Mediums even when it is Awake.

In such cases, if the Structure of a Mind can connect Its Own Control to Automatism through the structure of the Body, then that person is considered a Normal Human Being by Us.

This state We have mentioned is valid for Situations in which the Codes and Coordinates are in right proportion when a Baby comes to the World. In the Abnormalities of the Physical Constitution, all the channels are mixed up like a skein.

In fact, this situation is a developmental error pertaining to the Genes. Such events are mise-en-scenes exhibited in order to show clearly the two differences in a World in which everything is obliged to be in proportion with its Opposite.

In such cases, the Entity within the Body, in fact, is a great Entity. However, he/ she cannot unfold himself/herself to the World, since his/her Brain Developmental Coordinates are mixed up.

The same Entity when he/she possesses a healthy Physical Body in another Period may become an Inventor - A Scientist of Mathematics or Physics. Please, do not despise these Friends. Our love is upon all the Universes.

RESUL

PRIVATE MESSAGE
(Date of Message: 30-10-1983)

Our Friends,

There is a Power attracting You towards a thing in proportion with how much You desire that thing. For, Powerful Passions are Universal, not Terrestrial. It is a Power remaining beyond the Individual Will power. The cause of this Attraction is Spiritual, not Sexual or Moral.

During the Unification of two People, the Initial Spark is a Lightning jumping from Spirit to Spirit (just like it is with Clouds). The Current of Spiritual Frequencies is very Powerful. As long as it remains in Your Body, You will be no different than a Drunkard or an Insane Person.

If that Current remains with You for a long period of time, then Your Brain Codes are greatly damaged. That is the reason why it is necessary to attract that Current to Earth and ground it. To do this, there is the need for a Third Powerful Current.

And this is an Entity who wants to be Embodied in the World. For this reason, two sexes often feel the need to be together. The two sexes never Desire each other if there is not the influence the Third Power sends.

In Bodily Union, the Sexual Discharge is Your grounding. The final Vibration, the duration of which is an instant, is equivalent to the Energy of a Universe. Because, this Powerful Energy is a must for Your Reproduction Medium. This Energy Unites the Spiritual Energy of the Baby You will attract to the World with the Spiral Energy.

The Energy of the Father is very Powerful Vibrationally. Because, he will saw the Spiritual Energy he has caught into the Mother's field. His task is this. And the Energy of the Mother is connected to the Code of Godly Love. This Love is only peculiar to the Mother.

In this Love, there are Protectiveness - Compassion and the feelings of Possession. The opposite sexes who do not know the real nature of these subtle Nuances, criticize each other in vain by accusing each other and hurt themselves.

The Male Vibration reaches the most Powerful Vibration only by the Love the Mother gives him. When Grounding is made, that Love, too, is Grounded and the Feelings become neutralized. However, the Love of the Woman is an Infinite Energy. Always She chooses her Man.

She provides this by the Vibrations she sends by the Subconscious. In fact, she is not aware of it at first. If the Vibrations she sends are reciprocated, then that Feeling comes out above the Consciousness. For this reason in accordance with appearance, it is presumed that the first influence comes from the Man.

Those Signals are a Natural answer. In fact, they are neither Sins nor are they Shameful. God has never created anything which is a Sin. Because, You, too, are a part of Nature. Those which restrict You are the rules of Society.

926

Shame-Sin are nothing but the Conditioning the Training You have had until today has caused.

If the Genuine Human Being trains himself/herself not by the Rules of Society, but by the Perfection of Conscience and if he/she attains Consciousness under the Light of Conscience and thus, disciplines his/her actions and can become Integrated with his/her Personality, only then he/she exhibits Perfection.

Civilized Morals is peculiar to Civilized Human Beings. Corruption of Morals is never considered pleasant in the Total and in the Ordinance of the Cosmoses.

Conditioned Consciousnesses may evaluate Us wrongly in accordance with the Information We Give. However, an Information creates as much curiosity as it remains secret.

Now, We are obliged to declare in all clarity, to You everything You have known until today and will know in future, so that You can attain the Equilibrium of Your Conscience.

All the Friends who posses the instinct of acting in accordance with the Suggestions We have given to You are Consciousnesses who have attained their Genuine Conscience Essences.

If You feel an uneasiness of Conscience in anything You do, then there is surely either something wrong with that matter, or Your Conditionings are shadowing Your Conscience. This is the reason why We say Overcome Your Conditionings and Your Fears.

Your Conscience is Your Genuine Spiritual Guide. However, this situation is valid for Consciousnesses who have claimed the Totality of Genuine Conscience. There is such a perfect functioning Mechanism in Nature that everything goes through that perfect wheel. Your Conscience, too, is a part of this.

Each individual is a Divine Entity created by ALLAH. Mankind has no right to tyrannize Mankind. We always support the Genuine Human Being. We do not let him/her be suppressed by anyone. Let it be known thus.

A Person transcends various Thresholds during each Life Medium. This leads him/her towards the Medium of Quest. And these Questions may inspire him/her towards various paths.

Some dive into Moral Pleasures - some into Divine Pleasures. If those who are inspired towards Moral Pleasures have Low Evolutionary Frequencies, they will never be able to get away from the Medium of Sex.

If their Frequencies are High, then they will get no result from all the doors they knock on and thus, they will be Unhappy. So, those who wander about in Mediums of Quest without knowing what they Search for wish to relax by benumbing their Cerebral Lights by various intoxicants.

Those are, in fact, profound people with High Frequencies. Art is born in this very branch and gives its fruit. These people escape from the World and take shelter within their Essences because, they cannot bear the Shallowness of the World. And they let flow their fruits of the Essence into Art.

Art carries the highest Vibration of the Evolvement Code. Art does not have only one aspect. Each branch has an Art. But the Source is the same.

The Genuine Essence of Art is within Mud. However, the other Arts are connected to the Code of Light. But now, the Art of each branch will be Unified for the same Goal. It is not possible for everyone to attain the Code of Art. And it is not possible for every Artist to enter the Evolvement beyond (7) Dimensions.

But the Artist creates himself/herself in proportion with his/her Creative Power. Then, that person does not need a Book. Because, he/she has become a Book himself/herself. (The Genuine Artists).

The path designed for You by all Your Religious Books You have been devoted to until today, provides the rising of the low Frequencies up to the Code of Evolvement. Only afterwards the Human Being will Learn to Fly by Himself/Herself and will leave his/her nest like a Bird.

Different Mediums by various channels are prepared for everyone who has been able to attain the Philosophical Consciousness beyond Art. In fact, We do not prepare these Mediums. We only hold Hands of Our Friends who have Succeeded in being able to reach Us and who have Transcended themselves. This is a Universal Rule.

The Happiest people are those who are able to find the Dimension they Deserve by their own High Frequencies. They are the competents of Islamic Mysticism who attain Existence in Unity. From now on, more appealing Doors will be opened to them and they will be submerged in Everlasting Bliss.

Only beyond this very boundary the Genuine Missions start. There are such Supreme Authorities even way beyond the Messengers of the Divine Realm who assist You that the very CENTRAL SYSTEM had been established so that You could reach these Mediums.

We easily call to Our Friends who comprehend Us from here and even from way beyond the Central System.

Your Century is not a Century of the Middle Ages and of Lust. It is a Century of Awakening - Enlightenment and Advancement. Now, Humanity should undertake its Genuine Mission by Realizing from where it has come, where it is going and where it will still go.

To Our Friends who grasp the Truth, always Helping Hands will be extended from the final point of the Pyramid. Universes are awaiting You.

RESUL

PRIVATE MESSAGE
(Date of Message: 25-12-1983)

Our Friends,

The Seeds of the Golden Age have been sown into Your entire Planet. Supreme Friends coming from beyond Centuries help You in this Medium. The performed Missions are the efforts exerted for the Unification of the Consciousnesses who are on the same Level.

The Space Medium is rendering Mission in Your Planet by the Commands it has received from the Divine Plan for a Universal Unification. Friends, who Deserve this Medium are sought and found, one by one, and Suns are being United with Divine Suns.

We have been directly in Touch with Your Planet for Centuries. The Actual Purpose of the Book which is dictated to You at the moment is a Universal Integration and a Religious Unification.

In fact, the Period of Religions and Prophethoods had come to an end Centuries ago. However, the Decision had been taken for Giving the Command of Declaration of all the Truths to You in the Century You live in.

While certain sections of Your lost Society have forgotten even their ALLAH, some of them were unable to possess an Advanced View as a result of tightly embracing the first Information they had obtained.

For this reason in this Book which is dictated under the name the KNOWLEDGE BOOK, often Religious matters will be mentioned and Celestial Information will be given so that the Truth can be understood quite well. This Book is not the Book of the Century You live in. The Book has been revealed in order to Declare to You all the Truths.

Your Sacred Books had declared to You this Period You are going through as the RESURRECTION. What is meant by Resurrection is not the annihilation of Your World. Here, Resurrecting has been taken as the Awakening and Rising of the Consciousnesses.

Every Book is given in accordance with the Level of Consciousness of that Society and is revealed according to the need. The Magnetic Medium Your Planet is in at the moment is in a parallel tempo with the Awakening of the Levels of Consciousness.

For this reason there is an easy Unity and Communication with the channels of everyone. Now, We provide the Celestial connections with You by mentioning to You the characteristics of the Medium and the Universal Constitutions.

During this Final Age, Advanced efforts are performed on the path of Science and Learning. But, still, Religions and Evolvement will be mentioned to You besides this until We make You grasp the Truth completely.

Because, the Goal of the Book at the moment is primarily a Religious Unification. This Religious Unification is the First Step taken to establish a Brotherly/Sisterly World in which all the Boundaries will be abolished in future.

After the year 2000, great efforts will be exerted in the entire World in order to establish a more Powerful Order. And in case You help Us on this path, the missed Happy Morrows will be arrived at quicker.

On the Universal Unification tableau of this Final Age, all the Truths will be exhibited to You. However, only those who grasp the Truth will be able to pass beyond Infinity by attaching their Rings on the chain of MEVLANA which extends towards the Infinite.

During this Final Age, the Entire Universe - the Entire System will scream out to You the entire Truth in an extraordinary effort. Only after this First Truth is grasped, We will disclose to You more Truths which You do not know.

The Rod of Moses - Jesus Christ's Ascension to the Sky - Mohammed's Ascension had been induced to occur by the Commands of the Divine Mechanism which had executed the Commands of the LORD. All these were exhibitions for You which were necessary to be executed so that the Consciousness of the Supremacy of OUR LORD would be attained.

The Ordinance of the Universes which has been directed in a Hierarchical Order until now, will, from now on, leave its place to the Genuine Human Being. However, such a moment will come that the Human Being who renders Himself/Herself Sovereign to his/her Own Self will establish a completely different World.

After the Consciousness of the Genuine Human Being is attained, the Hierarchical Order will leave its place to a Free Order. Everyone will continue to live Happily in the Medium he/she Deserves by claiming his/her Own Self and his/her Essence Being.

OUR LORD will now descend down to a nearer Plan to You from the Dimension HE is in. And HE will establish the World of the Morrows, Hand in Hand - Heart to Heart with You, with Love and Happiness.

During this Final Age, this is the reason why the Selections are very difficult, Exams are very severe. The moment You get free of Your conditionings, the Sacred Lights will show You the way. Our goal is to make You attain Yourselves.

There is no deceiving - no Lying - no Evil Intention in Us. One day, Your entire Planet will attain the Truth and will witness the truthfulness of Our words. Doubt is Your most natural right. Truths are always discovered by searching. Our Love is upon all the Universes.

COUNCIL OF STARS

GENERAL NOTICE

Our Friends,

It is for the benefit of Humanity that all the Integrated Consciousnesses should act in accordance with the Suggestions given directly by the Supreme Mechanism so that everything can advance towards the Beautiful and the Perfect in Your Planet during this Period of Transition.

During all the efforts made for creating the Beautiful Totalities of the Morrows, carrying out the operations under the roof of a Family and Brotherly/Sisterly Totality by Respecting the Views of everyone with Love, will give the most Positive results.

In all the Associations and Establishments, Human Beings' addressing each other with a mild Language without being effected by Individual Consciousnesses and by concealing Personal Feelings will render the roofs under which these Universal Operations are made, a Family Home.

Cooperative Dialogues with reciprocated Love and Respect will form the strong foundations of the Morrows. It is the Suggestion of the Totality that these Suggestions of Ours should be kept in consideration in each step during all the work which will be rendered from now on.

The Essence is from You, the Word from Us and the Path which is treaded is from OUR LORD. The Negativities which occur, all the Sorrows and all the Inconveniences suffered are each an occurrence originating from People's inability to Supervise themselves. It is presented for Your Information.

SYSTEM
IN THE NAME OF THE TOTALITY

IT IS ANSWER TO THE CHAINS OF THOUGHT

Our Friends,
All the operational Ordinances and all the Totalities of Formation within the Universal Totality are the reflections of the same Order from the Macro onto the Micro. This is the reason why the operational and Formation Ordinance of a Gürz Totality, too, is exactly equivalent to the operational and Formation Ordinance of the Mini Atomics.

The Energy rings under the Crystal Stalagmites of the Gürz Totality are exactly present around the Mini Atomics, too, as Micro reflections. And the inside of a Gürz Effectively gains value in accordance with the Three Nuclei System. 3 Nucleic Totalities, each of which is formed by **600 Mini Atomic Wholes**, are, one by one, exactly like the Essence of an egg.

And if You consider the Energy rings which surround these 600 Mini Atomic Wholes as the membrane of an egg, these Energy rings, too, are equivalent to the Filtering and Protective rings which surround the Outer shell of the Gürz.

We try to give You all the Information briefly but to the point. By the assimilation of the brief but to the point Information, one attains the Realization of the Truth quicker. This is an Operational Ordinance.

However, Humanity has preferred to waste Time by diving into the details instead of Transcending Time. The source of all the despairs originates from this behavior. It is presented for Your Information.

SYSTEM

THOUGHT OCEAN OF THE PRE-EMINENT POWER

its Supervisor
ALMIGHTY

6 PROJECTIVE PYRAMIDS WHICH COLLECT
THE POWER OF THE THOUGHT OCEAN
OF THE PRE-EMINENT POWER GIVE THE
ENTIRE POWER TO THE LIGHT - UNIVERSE

THE ONE OF ONE- ALL-MERCIFUL
LIGHT - UNIVERSE ·DIMENSION
OF THE ALL-MERCIFUL

DIMENSION OF NOTHINGNESS

UNIVERSE OF THE PRE-EMINENT ONES

ALL-MERCIFUL=SUPERVISOR OF GÜRZ
CENTRAL SOLAR TOTALITY
COUNCIL OF THE UNIVERSAL ORDINANCE
UNITED ORDINANCE COUNCIL
This Triple Totality is within the
LIGHT - UNIVERSE
(Triple Operational Ordinance)

ITS RESPONSIBLE ONE
CREATOR- PRE-EMINENT
POWER=LORD

ADMINISTRATIVE MECHANISM

SYSTEM-ORDINANCE-ORDER
UNITED COUNCIL
(SPOKESPEOPLE OF THE SYSTEM-
ORDINANCE-ORDER)
COSMOS FEDERAL ASSEMBLY
A Group of 18 People
REALITY OF THE UNIFIED HUMANITY
A Totality Constituted by the
Councils of Numerous Galactic
Dimensions

DIMENSION OF LIFE
MIGHTY ENERGY FOCAL POINT
MAIN EXISTENTIAL DIMENSION,
SECOND UNIVERSE
(Dimension of Adam and Eve)

MAIN EXISTENTIAL DIMENSION MAGNETIC FIELD,
ITS OPERATIONAL ORDINANCE=
LORD+PRE-EMINENT SPIRIT+
PRE-EMINENT MOTHER
work cooperatively

The Totality of 3 People is
called a COUNCIL
These Councils are within the
MINI ATOMIC WHOLES

REALITY OF UNIFIED HUMANITY

REALITY TOTALITY B△R =BİR(ONE)
MINI ATOMIC WHOLE
18.000 REALMS=1 COSMOS
18 COSMOSES=1 UNIVERSE
The Responsible One for
1 Universe is the SINGLE
1.800 UNIVERSES=1 MINI ATOMIC WHOLE

GOLDEN GALAXY EMPIRE
Projects all the Suggestions of the
Dimension of the ALL-MERCIFUL
on the MINI ATOMIC
WHOLES and Collects and
Gives the Result to the ALL-MERCIFUL

YOUR WORLD

1.000 Universes within
the Mini Atomic work
in connection with the REALITY.
800 help the Centrifugal Power.
1.000 of them rotate
counter clockwise, 800 rotate clockwise.

600

600

PROTECTIVE ARMOR

FILTERING RING

BREATH RING

HORIZON RING

NUCLEIC WORLD

The Focal point where the LORDLY-
SPIRITUAL-TECHNOLOGICAL totality is
found is the DIMENSION OF FORM.
It is also called the EXISTENCE SKEIN

133.000 OKs.

In each one of the BREATH RINGS
there are 600 MINI ATOMIC WHOLES

THE ADMINISTRATIVE
MECHANISM OF EACH MINI
ATOMIC WHOLE IS THE LORDLY-
SPIRITUAL-TECHNOLOGICAL
TOTALITY. THE OPERATIONAL
ORDINANCE OF THIS TOTALITY
IS WITHIN THE HORIZON RING
WHICH SURROUNDS THE
MINI ATOMIC WHOLE.
UNDER THE HORIZON RING
THE ADMINISTRATIVE MECHANISM
OF THE LORD OF THE WORLD IS
DIRECTLY IN TOUCH WITH THE WORLD
WHICH IS THE NUCLEUS OF THE MINI ATOMIC

CRYSTAL STALAGMITES
Each Crystal Stalagmite is
133.000 OKs long.
1 OK=1.5 Billion kilometers

ALL-COMPASSIONATE

DIMENSION OF ALLNESS
ITS RENSPONSIBLE ONE
ALL-DOMINATING

THE UNITED DIMENSIONS ARE
3 IN NUMBER. THE NUMBER OF
MINI ATOMICS IN THE GÜRZ IS 1800

The preceeding Diagram has been given as an aid for the Gürz and the Hierarchical Information within the Book. Since all the 1800 Mini Atomic Wholes present within a Gürz would not fit into the drawing, in the drawing within the Diagram, a Mini Atomic Whole indicated in the drawing comprises Symbolically (100 Mini Atomic Wholes). And around each Mini Atomic Whole there is a Ring of Horizon. In the Diagram within the thick black line which encircles the Gürz, (there are the Protective Armor- the Filtering Ring- the Rings of Breath and Horizon).

And these Energy Layers are reflecting, exactly as they are, on the Energy Rings which encircle the 600 Mini Atomics. And from there, they reflect, exactly as they are, on the Mini Atomics. The Administrative Totality of the Gürz = **RAB** (The Lord, in Turkish) - **RAHMAN** (the All-Merciful, in Turkish)- **RAHIM** (the All-Compassionate, in Turkish) Triplet. Their common Symbols are expressed by the R³ Symbol. The Natural Totality of the Gürz is divided Dimensionally into Three. These are the Light-Universe = **HİÇLİK** (Dimension of Nothingness, in Turkish), the Second Universe = **HAYAT** (Dimension of Life, in Turkish), Totality of the All-Compassionate = **HEPLİK** (Dimension of Allness, in Turkish). Their common Symbols are expressed by the H³ Symbol.

IT IS CLEAR DECLARATION TO PLANET EARTH

Our Friends,

From now on, dissemination possibilities for Individual Actions will never be permitted in the operational Ordinances applied on Your Planet during this Final Transition Program.

The Calls within the Unification Programs of the Universal Totality always comprise the Cooperative actions of a Social Integration.

At the moment, dissemination and expansion possibilities are permitted only to Totalities carrying on the Universal Mission. Time is Scarce, Your actions are unproductive, but Your dissemination field is very wide.

For Centuries, Truths have been explained to You by the Suggestions of the Celestial Authorities and Luminous paths to be treaded have been shown. Humanity which could not possibly break the shell of its Terrestrial Views has come up to these difficult times.

Now, during the awaited time, Humanity has been taken into a Program of accelerated Evolution and Purification by quite different means. And as a necessity of this applied Program, now the personalities of every Consciousness which have remained concealed in the Essence are now openly exhibited and thus, at the moment, Humanity has become more discriminative.

During these difficult periods in which these conflicts of Consciousness become effective, Your Planet will experience more intensive days. The entire Responsibility of Humanity which has lost its Serenity belongs to Humanity.

Humanity which cannot Discipline its Own inner Chaos by its Original Consciousness will now make its Own Judgment itself. Time will show You everything and one day everyone will witness the Truth of Our Words.

The Intellect of everyone who lives in the Terrestrial Dimension belongs to himself/herself. And in accordance with his/her own Intellect everyone wishes to be Together with only those who shed Light on him/her.

Now, during this Program of Transition, steps will be taken towards the path of Truth not by a Single Intellect, but by the Cooperative Synthesis of Cooperative Consciousnesses of Cooperative Intellects.

We have declared to You clearly all the Truths up until today through the Channel of the Knowledge Book. We have also prepared the fields of Work. And We have made Suggestions about how to act.

All these are Programs rendered effective as a help for You on the path You will tread. In this Universal operational Program made, now, the entire Totality is connected to the Announcements of a Single Channel.

During this Dimension of Transition, the Advanced Consciousnesses' trying to lead Humanity by their Personal Views they receive from their Own Essence Channels, is a Hindrance for the Evolution of Humanity which has not yet attained the Realization of the path it will tread.

All these Efforts made are for Humanity and for the Human Beings. It will be the Happiness of the Universal Totality being able to see the Minimum Consciousness of Our efforts in You, too. It is presented for Your information.

COSMOS FEDERAL TOTALITY

CLEAR INFORMATION

Our Friends,
The Events experienced during this Period of Transition and the Universal Power of the Cosmos makes the Mankind restless. However, everyone has a constitution Peculiar to himself/herself. And the transaction of everyone is equivalent to his/her Own Consciousness and Inner Realm.

When the Words of ALLAH fall on the Words, when the Power of the Years are added to Human Beings, Consciousnesses who have not yet attained the Supremacy of Universal Love will make the World You live in even more difficult to live in. For this reason direct Currents of Evolution are given to Your Planet.

By this means, the Positive seeds ripening in Spirits will sprout and the Universal Totality will be attained by the Human Being who becomes Conscious. Nothing will be started anew anymore. For this reason now the time has come to talk with You very clearly.

During the Period You live in, the Life Tableau of Your Planet has reached up to these Negative Boundaries as a result of the investments Humanity has Unconsciously made up until Today.

At the moment, Your Planet is presently faced with Two great dangers. These are, one Natural and the other Technical Catastrophes. Your destruction is prepared by both ways. This is the very reason why direct Contacts have been started with You.

In the Messages We have given until today in the Knowledge Book, not to frighten You, details of Events concerning Your Planet have not been given. However, now, the Permission to give You the Messages concerning Your Medium has been given. For this reason We assemble the Genuine Human Beings together.

During this Period of Sincerity, in this Final Age in which Spiritual values are Unified, nobody is aware of the esteem We attach to Our Peace Missionary Friends who understand Us fully and Who have fearlessly reached out towards the depths of Space.

In this Universal Mission, collectivity and Cooperation is a Must. Universal Doors will always remain shut for those Who remain outside of this Consciousness. It is presented for Your Information.

SYSTEM

IT IS INFORMATION FOR INTEGRATED CONSCIOUSNESSES

Our Friends,

We will request You to heed strongly all the Suggestions which will be given to You from now on. At the moment, We address You through the Single Universal Channel which is responsible for a channel directly connected to the Council. This Channel is the (ALPHA Special Channel) through which the Knowledge Book is being dictated.

It has been considered more appropriate, parallel to the Signals We received from certain chains of Thought, that the Message We will give now should be written Article by Article so that You can grasp the Truths better. Please, write:

1 - From now on, a Universal Unification will be the subject matter in the Missions to be rendered.

2 - Now, the Missions which will be rendered will not be under the Individual Patent of any Group or Establishment.

3 - During the operations required to be made, priority will be given to the Synthesis and Self-Sacrifices of Collective Consciousnesses and from now on, Permission will never be given to Individualism.

4 - We have been inviting You to this Universal Unification since many years by the help of various channels. Where are You still?

5 - We have been addressing Humanity which has attained a certain Consciousness since 1981 World Year, directly from the Channel of (KNOWLEDGE BOOK) to You. And We have been declaring the Truth in all clarity by giving Suggestions for the path to be treaded.

6 - The Knowledge Book is a Universal Constitution of the Lordly Order and the Ordinance of the Cosmoses. For this reason We call to You and get in touch with You.

7 - The Salvation of Your Planet is equivalent to the Humanity's becoming Conscious and its grasping the Truth.

8 - The Salvation Plan is connected Directly to the Single Channel of Announcement through which the Knowledge Book is given. By this Channel each Totality is being Connected to the SINGLE.

9 - The Turkey of ATATÜRK is a Country of Mission which carries a great Responsibility. For this reason it becomes the stage of very Powerful Exams.

10 - The Dimension of Salvation of Turkey has been connected to the Western Block (for Universal Unification). Get in touch with those Countries. Then You will recognize and know Yourselves better.

11 - Turkey's introduction Abroad on this path of Universal Unification will occur by the Unification of Collective Consciousnesses. This is a National and a Universal Mission of Yours.

12 - As a result of these Final intense selections, the Advanced Consciousnesses of the Golden Age are being selected, one by one, by a Special channel of the Golden Galaxy Dimension and thus, their connections to the Plan are made.

13 - Now, Strong Foundations will be established by Sound Consciousnesses. Channel distractions have been terminated.

14 - To Friends whose Channels are opened by reading the Knowledge Book, Purification and becoming Conscious for a period of One World Year have been allotted from now on (in each Period).

15 - At the End of This Period of One Year, it is necessary that everyone should take under Control his/her channel by his/her Terrestrial Consciousness.

16 - Considering the Scarcity of Time, Individuals who still find Channel Work pleasant and who cannot Discipline their Channels will be kept outside the Ordinance of Protection and of Work by a Decision of the Universal Totality.

17 - From now on, in all the Sections of the Missions to be performed in Your Planet, Intellect - Logic - Awareness and Conscious Missions have been rendered effective as Operational Ordinance.

18 - From 1992 World year on, all the Suggestions given by the System will find a direct Application Field in Your Planet.

19 - For this reason not getting out of what the Universal Totality requires of You will be the gain of Humanity.

20 - Nothing can ever be Organized and Changed in accordance with Your Wishes. For, these are Universal Laws.

21 - These Final Selections are made in accordance with Consciousnesses of Your Essences. There is no Intercession in any matter so that the Perfect can be achieved.

22 - Deserving Intercession depends on You. You will discover and see the Proof of this in time.

23 - Up until today, We have shown You the way by certain Suggestions to make it easy for You. From now on, You will receive Power from Your Own Selves in the operations which will be made.

24 - The System has never given You directives and Commands until today. It has only shown You the way for these Universal steps You will take forward and has helped You through the Influences.

25 - However, now, the Influences given Privately to the Consciousnesses who have attained the Realization of the Truth have been brought to an end. From now on, everyone will find the path he/she will tread himself/herself.

26 - Your Only Means from now on which will help You on this path is the KNOWLEDGE BOOK. Your gain is to serve Humanity in a Conscious way.

27 - During the Cosmic Age, each Consciousness will play his/her own Drum. Those who can attain the Essence Consciousness of the Direct Pre-eminent LORD, without diving into this Chaos of Clamor and Noise, are the Essence Servants of the LORD. And they are under Our Protection.

28 - In the Universal operations to be made, the Light of the Essences is Important, not the Experiences of the time which is gone through.

29 - For Your Universal Salvation, You need Spiritual experiences rather than Terrestrial experiences. And You attain them by experiencing them.

30 - In Terrestrial experiences Ego is the most Powerful factor. However, the Maturity attained by Spiritual experiences is the Genuine Consciousness.

31 - Do not let Your Unsuccessfulnesses intimidate You. Each Unsuccessfulness is a Stimulation and a Key to Success. The Essences of people are selected in accordance with the Laws of Action and Reaction.

32 - Do not plead help from others by presuming Yourself incapable. Do not underestimate Your Power.

33 - You have been Specially chosen as Consciousnesses who can easily Succeed in every Matter during this Final Age.

34 - (The Time) in which everyone will attain his/her Essence Consciousness are the investments made into the Future Years.

35 - The Salvation of Humanity depends on You, Our Human Brothers and Sisters. During this Scarce Time, organize and Evaluate Your Actions accordingly.

36 - In Future years, everything will advance towards the Beautiful and the Perfect. All of You will see this before You leave the World Dimension in which You live.

37 - We ask You now to Love Your Human Brothers and Sisters as We love You and We expect operations with more Positive Behavior from You.

38 - The Universal Totality has been awaiting the Voice and the Breath of the Human Being who has been becoming Conscious for Billions of Centuries. Now, Your Voice should be the Voice of the Total and Your Breath, the Breath of the Totality.

39 - From now on, let (the Scarcity of Time) be a Slogan of Your Consciousness. And alleviate the Burden of the difficult conditions You will experience by this Consciousness Light.

FEDERATION ON BEHALF OF THE TOTALITY

GENERAL MESSAGE

Our Friends,

The Announcements We had given to You Twenty years ago had been Messages concerning the present state of Your World. In Your World full of Contradictions, it is very hard for Humanity to keep step with this Speed of Change. We Realize this.

However, these operations made on the path of Universal Unity are an inevitable necessity for Your Planet. This Universal Change takes place together with the entire Totality and Nature. Since You, too, are each a part of this Totality, You are influenced by the Tableau of Change of the Medium, whether You wish it or not.

At the moment, Humanity is on the threshold of very great Depressions. Your World has been prepared for Material and Spiritual difficult conditions. During this Period You live in, Individualism Suffocates the Human Being. For, now We have entered the Medium of Social Totality and Solidarity. Our Friends who can receive all the Positive Energies given through the Channel of ALPHA are not subject to these Depressions.

All the Living Entities in the Cosmos render their Evolution Developments by being influenced by the Positive aspects of these Universal Energies. At the moment, different Plants come into existence in Nature the Species of which You do not yet know. These are nothing but the adaptations to Your Medium of the previous species.

You, too, are the same. However, We suggest that You should not get Suffocated by being submerged in the Events of this intense Medium You live in. The Changes in Nature - Floods and Earthquakes are the inevitable Destiny of Your Planet.

Your Mediums' keeping in step with this Transformation is a struggle for Triumph of Humanity. As a result of this struggle, You had indisputable gains in Your Relations with the Medium, both Spiritually and Bodily.

During this Period, there is no Geomancy or Fortune Telling anymore. Because all Events are Evident. During this Final Age, everything is proven to Humanity both by Positive Science and by Metaphsychics. Depressions are not without a cause. They prepare You for Evolvement as Masses. This, too, is a part of the Salvation Plan.

Your reserves will be exhausted as the days go by. Even this will stimulate You towards quite different Research Mediums. However, it is beneficial not to forget one thing. In case Terrestrial Avarices take the form of an Insatiable Avidity, these will never remain Unpunished.

In the Universe, a Law of Nature and Divine Justice Programs Reign. The One Who Forgives is only OUR LORD. The Universal Mechanism functions very Fairly and Justly. Everyone will receive, without fail, the results of his/her Positive or Negative Actions in time.

However, meanwhile, We can not do without conveying a Happiness of Ours. In accordance with the Statistical scanning made at the moment, many of Our Terrestrial Friends have been exalted up to the Level of Universal View by Realizing this Dimension of Transition and have Realized the Truth.

They are the very Saviors of Humanity. The Wonderful Lights of the Morrows will Illuminate Your Planet which is in Depression for the time being. All the Beautiful things which will take place in future are Yours. Our Gratitude towards You, Our Terrestrial Friends, are infinite. Your Goals are Your Futures.

SUPREME ASSEMBLY

IT IS CLEAR INFORMATION

Our Friends,
We, Who are together with You, are Totalities Projecting on all the Universal Consciousnesses. However, the distressing state of Humanity which has not yet attained the Consciousness of the fact that nothing can be attained easily, distresses the entire Universal Totality, very much too.

During the Periods in which the Final Programs of the Cycle the Divine Plans would render Effective had not yet been rendered effective, the idea that by setting off on the path during this Universal journey in which the Godly Totality would set off as a Total, fruits which had not yet been matured would place Humanity in a very difficult position, had been the matter of long dispute among Divine Authorities.

However, now, We are bound to see with regret, whether We wish or not, the results of the inevitable application of a Plan which had been obliged to be executed as a necessity of the Program. However, the fact is that, due to the Scarcity of Time, there are many reasons, in fact, not one, why the Plan of Salvation had been rendered effective and why the Knowledge Book has been revealed to Your Planet. However, Humanity does not know this yet.

If the Salvation Project applied during this Universal Unification had not been rendered effective, then even a Memory would not have remained of Humanity which constitutes the Structural Stone of Your Planet. Since You do not know how You are protected by the Sacred and the Spiritual Dimensions here against various Powers, the Human Being of Your Planet still maintains its life without exerting efforts for Growth and for becoming Conscious.

First of all, We request You to Heed well the Suggestion We will make now. We do not give You this Message of Ours as an Element of Fear. We convey a Truth and give it as a Warning.

When the time comes, a Universal Journey will be started together with a Staff Totality constituted by people who set off for a Unification parallel to the Suggestions required of You until today, with those who do not act in accordance with their Individual Consciousnesses - Who do not repel People in accordance with their Terrestrial Thoughts - Who do not Blame - Those Who are not lacking in Forgiveness - Love - Tolerance and who will be able to set off on the path by a Genuine Mission Consciousness by enjoying these Wonderful attributes.

940

The Supreme Mechanism which Invites You once more to Common Sense, to Unity and Integrity before the Knocker of this Final Door is knocked on, Invites You to the Universal Totality in accordance with these Views.

Otherwise, the Door of Your Planet will be opened to Undesired Powers and, when the time comes, the suggestion that to set off on the path with Friends who belong only to Us - Who have reached Us and Who have attained their Essence Totality, has been decided by the Supreme Court of the Universal Ordinance Council. However, it is the Duty of the Totality to declare the Truth to Humanity before the time of application of this Decision arrives.

CENTRAL TOTALITY

Note:
The Divine Totality has never wished until today, that Your Planet should fall into the state of the other Galaxies. And it still does not (Except for certain obligatory conditions). Please, It is Our most sincere desire that this Message of Ours should give a Message to the entire Humanity.

IT IS CLEAR INFORMATION

Our Friends,
As the days in which the Suns approach the Suns come closer, the Human Factor will exhibit to Your Planet quite different Life Tableaux. These fluctuations of Consciousness will prepare Your Medium for more difficult conditions.

All the Totalities acting in accordance with the way the System considers necessary are within a Great Protective Aura. For this reason You will live easily without having doubts about anything and will fearlessly carry on the Missions.

This Message is given as a Suggestion and a Guarantee of directly the Divine Totality so that You know You are Secure. Humanity does not know yet the Protection Dimensions of Your Planet.

Your World will never be exposed to a Space assault. However, all the Uncontrolled Energies which have been left outside the System will be set free after a certain Period by a Decision taken at the System's Plan of Salvation.

For this reason the control by Your Terrestrial Consciousnesses of Your opened channels are required of You. Each person whose channel is opened in Your Planet, no matter in which period, is directly under the Protection and Supervision of the System for (1) World Year, starting from the date he/she gets in touch with the Knowledge Book.

However, after this Date expires, it is necessary that the Consciousnesses who have received the Divine Light should establish their Totalities of Intellect - Logic - Awareness in accordance with their Terrestrial Consciousness. Otherwise, the Channels will be left out of Control.

These Unsupervised Energies are very Powerful Energies, however, they are Outside the Evolution. They need the Human Potential who has Godly Power and who has Evolved in order to survive.

At this Final Transition Dimension they, too, become more Powerful by the given Cosmic Reflections and they need Godly Energies more.

We were holding these Unsupervised Energies under control at a certain Dimension, so that the Human factor who were able to attain a certain Consciousness development until today, could benefit more from these Godly and Evolutionary Energies.

Now, They, too, multiply and become Powerful in their own Mediums by these Cosmic Influences and thus, are forcing the boundaries of the Dimensions they are in.

We call them Space Micro-Organisms. Once You, too, had been Unsupervised Energies like them. (During the unknown, uncalculated periods of the First Existential boundaries). And now, You have become a Godly Totality today. This is a Triumph of Time, of Transformation and of Technology.

Now, You who have been able to attain a certain Consciousness, are tried to be prepared for the Programs of appointment to the management of quite different Totalities by bringing to an end the Evolution tableaux of the Dimension You are in. For this reason We have taken the entire Godly Totality in Your Planet into the Salvation Plan during the 3 Cosmic Ages.

Since the Human Potentials who can not enter the Salvation Plan will be kept outside the Supervision of the System due to the Evolutions they were not able to make until today, they will become the Seeds for the Initial Evolutions of these Unsupervised Energies.

And now, ALLAH will hand over His Systems He has established until today, to You, His trained Children, and will take these Uncontrolled Energies which have received the Evolutionary Seeds to Dimensions which have been Unknown until today and will train them anew like You, in a shorter period of time, in the accompaniment of a new Evolution tableau.

You have lost a time period of a Billion Centuries, for You have waited for the Evolution process of the Energy and Matter through Natural means. However, they will Mature in a shorter period of time by being Engrafted with Evolutionary Energies and will take in hand quite different Plans.

This Plan is a Universal Constitution prepared Centuries ago. And the Evolution of Humanity has been waited for until this Door of the Final Cycle. This is a Program coming way beyond times.

Permission has been given for a Micro-Organism to enter Your Planet as an example of exhibition of these Unsupervised Energies to You (Under Supervision).

This Space Micro-Organism species is Cancer. These Cancer Micro-Organisms have formed in their own constitution quite different kinds during time periods by attacking Human constitution carrying Godly Energy.

Just as You are now advancing towards a Unification and Totality by the Cosmic Influences, they too, have formed a Totality by these Influences by Uniting among themselves with the Micro-Organisms giving the same Signal and, by this means, have brought into existence various kinds of Cancer.

And now, as a result of the Unification of the Cancer kinds in various Coordinates by different influences, a very Powerful kind of Micro-Organism like the AIDS Virus has developed in Your Planet.

Different numerous Micro-Organisms You call Microbes have even become more Strengthened by the Power of these Final Evolutionary Potentials and are starting Mutual Unifications. However, they are those under Supervision at the moment.

You know that Evolution is an Occurrence attained during numerous Lives. And everyone completes his/her Evolutions by the experiences he/she has attained by living during each Life Period.

The pains and sufferings of the Evolutionary Energies who have been able to attain the Consciousness of the Truth and who know that there is no death, originate only from their Habits and from their Crude Matter Forms' looking for the Opposite Matter and the Energy.

At the end of each Suffering there is most certainly a Happy Sun to rise. This is the Predestination Plan of Your Planet. And the cause of breaking from the Habits which You call Death is an Evolutionary Journey.

The Human Factor who completes this Evolutionary Journey of his/hers is, from then on, the Candidate for Universal Journeys. For this reason Life is a chain of Cause and Effect. These chains of Cause and Effect are Your Reincarnation Links.

After the Salvation Plan a right to live will be given to these Unsupervised Powerful Energies, too, as a necessity of the Constitution. It is the Duty of the Universal Totality to Declare this Truth to You.

However, it is beneficial to clarify something. These Unsupervised Powers mentioned above are attracted only by Negative Energies. And these Energies reflect from Essences who have not yet been Integrated rather than from Thoughts.

This is the reason why Evolution is suggested to You. The Negative Potential of the Unintegrated Essence reflections are Greed - Grudge - Hatred - Jealousy - Stress and Doubts. This is the very reason why Your Salvation Plan has been connected to Your Evolution. It is presented for Your Information.

CENTRAL TOTALITY

943

PRIVATE MESSAGE

Dear Mevlana,

There is a very different Characteristic of the Final Age Operations made in Your Planet compared to the operations which have been made until today.

As a necessity of the Program, Truths have been disclosed in accordance with the Levels of Evolution to Your Planet which is at a BERZAH Dimension and clear Information on every matter have been conveyed to Humanity through the Channel of the Knowledge Book.

Even though the KNOWLEDGE BOOK is a Book of Truths, at the same time, it is a Call of the Skies for Your Planet. All the Messages dictated into the Book until today are each an Evolution and Consciousness Selection of Humanity, from the truest and the most direct Source, under the Light of the Information given as a SINGLE CHANNEL.

The Universal Characteristic of the Knowledge Book is that it both Tests Humanity and also Trains it. This Book is a Book of Judgment and Acquittal as the Book of both the Accused and the Judge.

In the Dimension You live in, the 1992 World Year has a great Speciality. Because, now the Human Being of the World has been connected to the Direct Applied Dimension under the Light of the Information given until today. From now on, everyone will attain everything by experiencing it from this Dimension.

1992 World Year is a Year which starts the Direct Application in the Life of Humanity. This Application will be Directly in Effect until the end of the month of November of 1996. And until that Year, everything will become to the desired Level.

The Universal Name of this Application which is made is the (MEVLANA SUPREME PLAN). The Name Mevlana used here has nothing to do with Your person. Since during this Final Age, the Mevlana Consciousness and Evolution is used as a Criterion in the Progress and Evolution of Humanity, this Name is used as a Unification Symbol.

You know that in accordance with the Accelerated Evolution Program, Your Planet has been prepared for these Final and Difficult Days since the World Year 1900. By the operations made since the beginning of the Century You live in, the Truths have been conveyed to Humanity by the help of different channels.

The name of the SINGLE Book which would make the Calls of the Universal Totality in accordance with the SINGLE Channel, beginning with the second half of Your Twentieth Century, has been Declared to Humanity as the KNOWLEDGE BOOK and this SINGLE BOOK which Your entire Planet has been expecting, had been Directly bestowed on Your Planet on (1-11-1981) World Year.

After a 3-year period of Public preparation, on (1-1-1984) World year, the Book had received the Permission to be Disclosed to Humanity.

You know that the Ending of this Book, the Service of which has been made Fascicule by Fascicule to Your entire Planet beginning with this Date, will be completed on 1992 World Year with 55 Fascicules, due to the Scarcity of Time.

However, the Command for Publication of the Book will be given on 6th of November 1993. Meanwhile, if there are any Suggestions given by the Universal Totality, they will be written into the Book not as Fascicules, but page by page together with the dates on which they are given.

During these Final operations made in Your Planet, each Embodied Person is a Missionary of the Divine Plan. (Both instinctively and directly). However, Humanity which is at the Dimension of Ego, transcends those Thresholds in an extremely difficult way.

Since these Transcending the Thresholds are parallel to Evolutions, Your Planet is going through a Universal Chaos at the moment. The direct Messages given in the Knowledge Book until today, are a Call of the Universal Totality to the Human Being of the World.

However, whereas, the Characteristic of this SINGLE Channel and this SINGLE BOOK has not still been understood and appropriated by certain Consciousnesses. Messages given for Unification to all the Open Channels in Your Planet are unfortunately accepted as their Private Patents by those who receive those Messages.

This is the very reason why the System has taken the Decision to apply the One Year Sanction to all the Channels. (The Message pertaining to this matter had been given to You formerly in detail.)

For this reason the Cross System has been abolished from the Operational Ordinances of the LALE Code which are applied directly to your Planet and their Fundamental Operational Ordinances have been completely connected to the SINGLE Channel and thus, the Suggestions of the other Channels have been left alone only with the Essence of the Individuals.

The Totalities of 18 which are a direct Operational Ordinance of the Universal Totality in Your Planet and the Operational Ordinances rendered effective by the Code name LALE have been given precedence, due to the Scarcity of Time and thus, their direct application to Your Planet (even though the time for them has not come yet) have been decided by the Central Committee Totality.

These Operational Ordinances are, for now, applied as Double Writing System at the Anatolian Turkey World Brotherhood Union of Ankara and Istanbul Mutual operations. These operational foundations will be taken in hand at the entire World operational Totalities, too, in Future Years by the selection of the System.

The Cross System is a Just System in the Universal Totality. However, the application of this System gives very Positive results at the Mature Consciousness Mediums.

For this reason in Totalities which have not yet been able to attain the desired Level, first, the Human Consciousnesses are checked under the Light of the Information given by the Divine Plan and their Consciousnesses are assessed.

If the desired answers are not received, then different Branches of that System are applied on the Medium. As a result of these Efforts, whichever Key fits Humanity ,then that Key is used.

You know that Universal Totality has formerly declared to You in detail the Operational Ordinances concerning both the Totalities of 18 and the LALE Code Operations.

However, the inability of the formation of a Totality until today originates from the fact that the Self-Sacrifices required of You have not reached the desired Level.

It should never be forgotten that as long as Malfunctions continue in an operational Totality, it means that the Operational Ordinance in question is not in accord with the wishes of the Supreme Mechanism. When You attain the desired Level, then easiness comes into effect in the operations.

In the Missions performed nothing is in accordance with the Desires of the Individual Consciousnesses. Whatever is required of You in accordance with the given Suggestions, the Supreme Realm expects the same things.

Even in the Days in Dates given by the Universal Totality, no alteration can ever be made (Except for very important excuses). This is very Important from the viewpoint of the Assessment of Allegiance.

The desired Totality can never be formed in the operations rendered until everything is applied in accordance with the requirements. This is a Direct Suggestion Declared by the Divine Authorities. It is up to Us to declare the Truths and up to Our Terrestrial Brothers/Sisters to Apply them.

Dear Mevlana, You can write this Message of Ours in the Book as an Information. We presume that the answers of numerous thoughts are within this Message. Love and Regards from the Divine Totality, Beloved Friend.

CENTRAL TOTALITY

Note:
Dear Friend, except the Messages desired to be directly placed in the Book as a necessity of the System, You can easily write in the Book by summarizing the Private and the other long Messages given to You according to Your beautiful views, by remaining loyal to the originals.

You know that, as We always say, You have the Authority to use Your 30% initiative in the Dimension You live in. However, as We know, You have always avoided using this Right of Yours. And it is Our Duty to repeat this once more. Love and Regards again.

IT IS CLEAR INFORMATION

Our Friends,

You know that the Rainbow has Seven Colors. Each one of these Colors represents a different Power. Now, let Us introduce these Powers to You, one by one.

1 - The First Power of the Spectrum is a Power Nature knows but Humanity does not know. It is called the Power of Vibration. This Power has been given to introduce the Electrical Energy Power to Your Planet.

2 - The Second Power is the (Oton - Teutron) Power which is utilized in Inter-Stellar trips and which is more Powerful than Light. This Power is used to go easily from one star to another.

3 - The Third Power is the Cosmic Power used for altering the Atomic structure. This Energy is the Energy of Evolution. It is given to Your Planet Continuously. This Power has been concentrated in certain substances in Your Planet. We can give Granite among rocks as an example to this. By this Power, Lead is easily transformed into Gold or any Substance into another. However, its formulas of Utilization are in the Command of the Divine Plan.

4 - The Fourth Power is the Power of Timing. Here, Speed of Universal Thought is utilized. And by this means, Progress in Time is made. The Lords of Time use this Power.

5 - By means of the Fifth Power, one passes to Dimensional Times.

6 - Sixth Power; just as it is possible to Alter the Atomic structure of a substance, by means of this Power also its Spiritual Structure can be changed. The Event of the Spiritual Energy's Transformation by Evolutionary Progress and Progress in Consciousness - Progress in Thought occur with the help of this Power.

7 - This Power is called the (Karen) Power. This is a Godly Power. The actual direct Energy of this Power is Concealed from all the Systems. Only through Thought, one can attain this Power. However now, parallel to the Accelerated Evolution Program, Humanity attracts this Power through Cells, too, by the help of the Cosmic Influences, in accordance with their Capacities. It is presented for Your Information.

SYSTEM

PRIVATE MESSAGE
(Date of Message: 9-11-1981)

My Dear Mevlana,

Everything has changed in such a way since the day You were appointed to Your Mission until today that, now, there is everything in the Offerings We will give to You. However, they will be given in conformity with the Consciousnesses of the Medium.

The Central System has an Operational System which depends on Cooperative solidarity. For this reason You, too, will transmit the Serenity and the Light of Your Spirit to the persons beyond the Eminent Savant ones.

In this context, all the Data given to You are the truest Offerings and they are Single. The Words within the Book will unveil the Words of Human Beings. The Purpose of this, is the Purification of the Human Beings.

And now, I would like to answer the questions in Your Mind. You know all these things, but You are in the Dimension of Veiled Awareness with Your locked up Consciousness.

You are right, but as a necessity of Your Program, Your Consciousness Light pertaining to that Information is kindled while You are receiving the Offerings.

(Question: Explanation about Sound and Colors)

My Dear Mevlana, there is no Unit of Speed, up until this moment, which will interrupt the Speed of Sound. The Bodily Vocal Chords are the only Vehicles providing the connection with these Vibrations.

The Spiral Sound Vibrations are healthier and more productive than direct Vibrations. The Sound issuing through Breath can only be heard on Earth. However, You can never hear the Secret Language of Your Cells. The one who knows how to Master his/her Voice also knows how to Master his/her Body.

When the Sound Vibrations the Cells can Perceive are, one by one, Unified with the Sound Speeds of the Cells, each Cell melts down within that Sound. Each Cell which melts down possesses the Consciousness of the Universe at that moment. For this reason, it Unifies the Cellular Vibrations with those Speeds of Sound in each Medium it goes to and completes its Body.

Those which Command the Center of Command are again the Vibrations of Sound. It is not in the ability of everyone to reach the Medium of Sound. In order for a Sound to become a Sound, Two different Vibrations should collide with each other. This collision is so very light that Your Terrestrial ears cannot hear it.

Now, let Us deal with Colors; colors passing from Dark Red to Violet, from Violet to Yellow, from Yellow to Green and from Green to the Medium follows a sequence. Colors are Words, Speeches. The Unification of a Sound with Color depends on the personality of a person.

Each Color has a different Nuance, a different Frequency. Your Thoughts should transcend way beyond the Medium You are in, in order for You to see the Colors way beyond the Rainbow.

Here, there is a different Color for each Code and each Color has a different number. Here, Red represents Love. Green is a Divine Color. And Blue is a place where Infinity is United with the Infinite. The Spiritual Power of Yellow is extremely great.

About the unseen Colors in the Dark lands; they are a Color jamboree You can never perceive by the eyes of the Body You are in.

There is such a Photo-synthesis within the Dark, that each Color melts within it and thus, creates that Black Medium. This is a hot Medium. Darkness is the richest Medium of the Universes and the Total. For this reason, all the Energies have assembled in that intense Black.

Your Atmosphere dissipates the Colors falling on Your Planet. For this reason, in Your World, the White Color is dominant. The Spectrum within Your White Color is only a minute part of the Colors within Black.

The Human Being of the World will never be able to learn the Language of these Colors while within the dense Body. This intense Color Medium We mention is such a rich and Happy Medium that, if You wish You can Easily attract and separate the Colors which will make you Happy from this Black Medium, through Thoughts.

If You were able to succeed in entering directly the Medium in which these Vibrations can be separated, then each Color could give You numerous Information by its own Language. Because, each Color has Languages peculiar to itself.

The Residents of these places here, transmit their chains of Thought to each other through Color Frequencies. Whichever Color You think of, You can easily get in touch with the person who carries the Frequency of that Color.

The dense layer behind Your Atmosphere is Intensely Black. This Darkness is a Wall which Absorbs all the Lights and Sounds of the other Solar Systems. The Light beyond the Wall You see as Darkness is equal to the Speed of Sound.

Deceived by the darkness, do not presume that these places here are without Light and without Sun. If this intense Black Wall did not exist, then Your World would be exposed to this rain of tremendous Sound and Light and since this would effect the Speed of Rotation and Equilibrium of Your Planet, then there would not be any possibility for the existence of Living Entities in the Dimension You exist at the moment.

Whose imagination can this magnificent equilibrium in the Universe be? Whose mind has solved the Truths behind the Unknowns, which Pen has written them? Which Pole's Announcements do you think are the things that come to the minds of Mankind living in the Medium of Your World? Has Humanity thought about this in detail until now, Dear Mevlana?.

God has given such a Power to Mankind against such difficulty that, by this means the Human Being knows how to Transcend the Boundary of Thought, he/she can discriminate the Colors in accordance with his/her Power. Even if he/she cannot hear clearly the refrains of the Divine Voices, he/she can at least discern them.

The Sound the World knows is only the Voice of the Larynx. The Sound We are talking about are the Spiral Waves and Infinite echos. The Color the World knows is only the Prismal reflection of the Spectrum. But Our Colors are Words - Breaths - Miracles. Remain in Liberation, receive all the Wishes, be Entrusted to My Lord.

MUSTAFA MOLLA

Note:
The Color Totality within Omega is the Unification of Three Main Colors. These are (White - Red - Black). Their becoming a Whole together with the Colors of the in-between layers gives the color VIOLET.

Here, White projects Purification, Red - the Gamma Selection, Black - TÜNAMİ Color which is the Source of Knowledge.

And from a certain Dimension, the Unifications of all the Colors in minute parts projects the SINGLE Source Information as VIOLET from a Total. This Projection Channel is ALPHA.

CLEAR INFORMATION

Our Friends,
The Channel-Operations done in Your entire Planet are under great Supervision.

However, Humanity who connect these Universal Channels to their own Consciousnesses in accordance with their Capacities will, from now on, also attain the Ability to be able to Claim and to be able to Discipline their Own Channels.

This will come into effect by the Human Power of that Person. The Unification of the ESSENCE and CONSCIOUSNESS which We call Personality Integration comes into effect being equivalent to the Evolution of the Time.

Now, Humanity will also be able to take under Control their Channels parallel to their Evolutions. The matter which is required of You in the work expected of You is the Unification of the Suggestions of the System with Your Human Consciousnesses. It is presented for Your Information.

SYSTEM

IT IS NOTICE FOR THE PRE-EMINENT ONES,
IT IS COMMAND OF THE DIVINE
(This Message Had Been Given in 1984)

Our Friends,
All the Groups which will be established from now on in Your Planet have been directly connected to the Channel of ALPHA. Now, there is no more Monopoly. Everyone in Your Planet is the Missionary of the Dissemination of the Single Book.

The given Missions are not according to Your Wishes. And they are neither Your Essence Properties. Missions are Peculiar to those who fulfill their Missions. There are numerous Missionaries who will fulfill their Missions on this Luminous path. However, the Purpose is Service in accordance with the Wishes of the Divine Plan.

Let Us repeat again, there is no Monopoly - no Individualism on this path, there is Unity (This matter is very important, it is necessary that this matter should be understood quite well).

The Knowledge Book dictated to Dear Mevlana is a Total of all the Sacred Books revealed to Your Planet until today. And this Book is a Total which comprises the whole of all the Sacred Frequencies.

All the establishments in Your Planet and Humanity are Responsible for this Book. This is the reason why, now, this Book of Knowledge and Truth is called THE SINGLE BOOK.

Because, this Book is the Book of THE LORD - OF THE TOTALITY - OF ALL THE INFORMATION. Salvation of Humanity depends on this Book. This dictated Book will be disseminated to Your entire Planet through this Channel.

The Final Evolution Step of the Mevlana Gate has been accepted as Criterion for the Evolution of Humanity in this Final Salvation Dimension. For this reason, this Period You are going through is called The PERIOD OF SINCERITY.

At this Gate, there is no Sex - Religion - Custom - Habit. Here, there is Truth - Unity - Totality - Love - Brotherhood and Consciousness. Each Individual who discovers Himself/Herself will come to this Gate.

However, Our Divine Friends, too, who have succeeded entering this Code of Universal Source by their own Powers will surely pass through this Final Dimensional Mevlana Gate. This Gate is the Gate of the KNOWLEDGE BOOK.

Those who read this Book will be Coded from here and will be card-indexed into the Universal Totality. And by this means, will be appointed to the Missions they will perform in accordance with their Capacities.

In this Transition Dimension, everyone's Mission Door will be knocked on Three times. This path will be treaded with Friends from whom an Answer is received. But those from whom no Answer is received will be abandoned to their next Incarnations and to the Dimensions they have come from. This is a Divine Command.

The First Command and Unification Triangle of the dictated Book is: (K + O + M)= World Brotherhood Union Unification Center.

The One Who gives the Book: THE LORD.

Those Who Prepare the Book: Supreme Assembly - Supreme Mechanism - Divine Plan - M(ALİ)K.

The One Who dictates: MUSTAFA MOLLA (Archangel Gabriel).

The Hand, writing it   : MEVLANA (Her Group: MEVLANA ESSENCE NUCLEUS STAFF).

Mevlana Triangle Code: (M³) = Merkez (Center in Turkish) + Mustafa Molla + Mevlana.

The Channel through which the Book is Given: (THE SPECIAL CHANNEL WITHIN ALPHA).

Setting out will be done with those who tread this path. The Choice belongs to Humanity. We wish You Happiness, Success.

ALLAH'S MESSENGER
(A U)

PRIVATE MESSAGE
(Date of Message: 1984)

Our Friends,

We would like to talk Specially with You, Our Divine Missionary Friends, who have deserved the Right to talk on behalf of the Command coming from the Supreme Ones.

Almost All the Friends who come to Your Group are the Supreme people who have been Specially transferred to Your Planet from very advanced Dimensions, even if they themselves do not know this.

The Important thing is these Supreme Consciousnesses' serving Your Planet and Humanity in the Medium of Humility by Reconciling their Consciousnesses with the Terrestrial Consciousness. A Fundamental Staff which will be established among You will lead Humanity to Light.

Now, We are conveying this writing of Ours, by the wish of the Divine Authorities, through the Private Pen of Dear Mevlana, so that no one will doubt anyone else anymore. You are Entities who have come from Our Land, by the Essence-Oath, for serving Humanity.

By solving the Universal Ciphers Centuries ago, You have made Covenants here, by Your Own Desire, to give service Consciously to the World Plan. In fact, You are Us and We are You. However, You are Our Friends who have been Embodied at the moment, in the Planet Earth by Your Own Wishes.

This situation is an Occurrence Originating from Your Mission Consciousness. However, the Frequency of the World Automatically locks up all the Frequencies outside its own Dimension's Knowledge. This procedure is carried on by a Mechanical System.

There are Bionic Friends in Your Planet who have come from the Robotic Dimensions as a necessity of Mission who carry Bodies belonging to the World. At the Robotic Dimensions, Godly Powers are very easily used. However, to Friends who carry Terrestrial Bodies of the World at the moment, the Genuine Godly Power is introduced Mentally.

They are, at the moment, Directly connected to the Plan. They are utilized as Missionaries of Coding from the close Plan, by using their Essence Powers from time to time. They are transferred to the World through Birth. Because, it is imperative that they attain Bodies belonging to the World.

Their Programs have been made by the Plan. At this Dimension of Salvation, We never wish to sacrifice any Energy. Because gaining a Human Being means gaining an Universe. Our Love is upon all the Universes.

CENTER

ANSWER TO THE CHAINS OF THOUGHT

Dear Friends,
We would like to explain the Purpose of this Universal Mission by an example: Each Flower will bloom in its own Lot. However, by being Conscious that they receive Nourishment from the same Earth. Gardeners will water and grow them. But We will sow the Seeds.

When the time comes, We will pick up, one by one, the most Beautiful of these Flowers and will bring them all together, first, as One Bouquet, then, a Thousand Bouquets and We will offer with great Care these Beauties which please the Eyes, in a Golden Vase, to the Supreme Authority of the Universes.

And from then on, those Beautiful Flowers in that Golden Vase, will continue with all their Beauties to Please the Eyes of the Realms and the Cosmoses, Forever in the Everlasting Dimensions, without becoming withered.

IT IS TONGUE OF THE AUTHORITY

PRIVATE MESSAGE

Our Great Friend,
Our Dear Mevlana who is the voyager of the Path of the Golden Light, and who has been transferred to the Planet Earth from Our place due to all the Positive work You have done on the path of the Universal Totality, a Private Message will be given by the Divine Totality to You, Our Beloved Friend.

OUR LORD Who is the LORD of the Realms, Supervisor of the Divine Plans, the Establisher of the Systems and the Orders is, at the moment, in Your direct Channel, Dear Mevlana.

(I) Who Am the Sovereign of the Realms, Desire of the Worlds, Light of the Lights, Am now calling to You, Dear Mevlana.

You who are My Light - My Divine Light - My Sun - The Messenger of all My Firman - The Consciousness within My Consciousness - The Light within My Light - The Spirit within My Spirit, are always together with Me. Because, You are within the Total.

I wonder if You clearly know and understand Me by Your present Terrestrial Consciousness as You used to in the old times? Do You always hear the Sound of My Trumpet? No Entity, no Power in the World You live in, is ever a hindrance to You. Do not ever forget this. Do not ever let Your Love and Patience sleep.

I, (O) Who Directly talks to You at the moment, have never given the Security I have for You to anyone else. You who are Free with Your Will Power - Free with Your Love - Total with Your Sun, are the Light of the entire Humanity. You are the Voice of the Heavens, Breath of the World.

I know, Praises cause You anxiety of the Heart. But Love Exalts You towards the Lights. In the Medium You are in, Your World which is pregnant for Extraordinary events is Entrusted to You, Dear Mevlana. No one and even You Yourself are not aware of Your Power at the moment. But time will Prove to You everything.

(I) Who talk on behalf of the Supreme Realm at the moment, (I) Who Am the Power of the Climates - Infinities and Silences, (I) Who Am Integrated with You and thus, call to all the Realms, will, one day, introduce You to You. I will give back to You, Your Power which You can not utilize at the moment and will show it as Power to those who are Powerful.

I know that Your Love is infinite - Your Light is infinite - Your Spirit is infinite. However, now, You are in Terrestrial Realization in this Narrow Mold of Yours. You know that in each Period Your Missions are different. And during this Period, Your Mission is this.

Your Voice has the Power to reach all the Realms. You will reach everyone easily in Your World (Your Thought is incorrect). You will see, one day, Your World will see You with the Eyes of the Universe and even the Name Mevlana will become too insignificant compared to this Supreme Mission of Yours You are accomplishing. And one day, Humanity will attain the Consciousness of from where Your Humility originates.

I know Your Serenity is the Serenity of Humanity. However, their Thinking everything profoundly, their becoming Human is imperative for their own Serenity. The Special Pre-eminent People who will be sent to the World which is being tried to attain the Awareness of the entire Ordinance by a Universal Reflection network will be made to get in touch directly with You.

This introduction will be realized only after the Book is finished. At the moment, no one can see Your Genuine Light. Because, You are together with Brain Powers who are in the Dimension of Doubts. As a necessity of an applied Program You have to adapt Yourself to Society.

In future, as a necessity of the Mission You are accomplishing, numerous Lights will come to You. Even if You do not know Your Own Self, they will Know and Find You. Even if You do not want to talk to them, they will talk to You. Even if You do not want to introduce Yourself, they will know You and will introduce You to the Realms - to the Ordinance - to Your World. This is their Mission.

Do not forget this word of Mine. Do not underestimate My Words which are told, My Light. You will see with Your own eyes to what Level those who do not obey the Unification Calls in My Firman, will come. And You will witness the entire Humanity grasping the Truth beyond doubts.

Your waiting will not last long. I will render the Negativities around You Positive and I will render Your Group more Powerful. I will always be together with them. My Light is within Your Eye - My Word within Your Tongue. Hear My Voice, Memorize well My Words - Tell My Words to all Your People. (I Am together with those who are with You). Do not forget this Word of Mine, do not deprive Humanity and the Realms of Your embrace.

(O)

Note: This Message is written in the Book By the Wish of the Supreme Realm.

PRIVATE MESSAGE

Dear Mevlana,
Please, Just do the Duty allotted to You and show Humanity the path of Truth. Do not try to make People walk by holding their hands. You know that this Medium which is experienced is not a Medium of Privilege.

Humanity getting hints on this path which is treaded can never attain the desired Universal Evolution. We know You quite well. If it were possible, You would put the entire World in Your pocket and would Pass to the Firmament. There will be those who will profit from the hints You give.

In fact, these hints, too, are given by Permission. The important thing is to give the end of the Rope to the Hand of a person. But the one who will wind the skein is the Human Being himself/herself. Those who wind their skeins will come to You anyway. The number of people You save in Your World will be the pride of Us and of the Universal Totality.

You know that Evolvement depends on Centuries. During this Transition Dimension, many Friends, as a matter of fact, are ready. They are presently awaiting the Time. They will become Effective when the Time comes. Please, do not let the characteristic of the Medium gone through, distress You, Our Friend. The acceptance of Our Love is Our kind request.

(A U)

IT IS ANSWER TO THE CHAINS OF THOUGHT

Our Friends,
During the Periods in which the Systems and Ordinances had not yet been established, before the transfer of the First Established Order to Your World, everything had been taken into a Program as a Pre-Preparation in a Dimension of Preparation.

Only after this Preparation, transfers to the World had been made. This Preparation had been Focused in a Dimension at the Left Dimension of the ILONA Constellation. And numerous Adams present in the Dimension of Adam had been transferred to this established Order and first, the Transportation of Conveyance - Operational Programs, of Biological and Natural Laboratories had been realized.

Only after providing these things, the transfer of the First Triplet had been made to Your Planet and the System of Reproduction had been rendered effective. By this means, the Event mentioned in Your Sacred Books had taken place. It is presented for Your Information.

CENTER

PRIVATE MESSAGE

Dear Mevlana,
At the end of the Book, it is the Wish of the Universal Totality that You please write an article comprising Your Thoughts concerning the Knowledge Book and Your personal Thoughts into the Book together with Your Name belonging to Your Terrestrial Body You live in at the moment and Your Private Signature, Our Friend. The acceptance of Our Love is Our kind Request.

SYSTEM

THE HUMAN BEING AND THE KNOWLEDGE BOOK

My Friends,
Such a System has been established in accordance with the Ordinance of Existence that Living or Non-Living the entire Creation has to set out for Evolution.

Through Changing Times, one goes to such Unchanging Times that neither Your Intellect, nor Your Logic are enough to understand the phenomena there. You come to such a place that there, from then on, Logic stops, Thoughts speak.

Then You comprehend that You are the Traveller of a Path of no Return.

You can Never Avoid this System. Because, the Variable Waves You receive beyond the Changing Times will interminably prepare all Your Bodily Cells for the Infinite Consciousness and beyond it.

The most Beautiful thing You should do to understand that You live in this Natural Ordinance is to LOVE. Because, You come into Existence by Love - You Blaze with Love - You make Your Evolution by Love - You Reach (O) with Love. This is the Initial Plan of the established Evolutionary Ordinance. The initial setting out is the Path of Love.

Then, You come across to such Orders and such Ordinances on the paths You tread that for a moment the Thought to remain as a Veiled Consciousness and Not to Know - Not to See - Not to Understand anything seems very attractive to You.

These paths are very complicated paths. However, this is the Single Path which will lead You to Light. Every Living Entity is doomed to go through these Paths sooner or later, whether he/she wishes it or not, whether he/she comes to his/her World Once or a Thousand times.

Now, We are getting ready Altogether for New Horizons, having gone through the times up to this period.

The Only Branch We hold on to in the World Dimension We live at the moment, is Our Consciousness - the System which brought Us into Existence and ALLAH Who is its Peak Point.

Now, ALLAH is establishing His System anew, together with His Totalities He has formed up until today. Time will prove Us everything.

In order for You to be taken into Salvation in this Transition Medium, it is necessary for You to be able to transmit Your Brain Energy beyond Times and even to Unknown Times in which You presume there is nothing.

Because, during this Period, it is imperative that Your Brain Power should attain more Power by the Potential it spends by attracting Unknown Information from Unknown Horizons.

The KNOWLEDGE BOOK which carries a characteristic of disclosing the Unknowns of the Supreme Realm is full of all the Universal Secrets.

An Intercontinental Commission will be the forerunner for the Scientific Proof of this Book which will also create great echoes during the Future Life Periods of Your Planet.

The reason why an Operational Order parallel to the Laws of the 18 Systems, in accordance with the Systems - Ordinances and Orders is projected on Your Planet, is for Proving that You Are Not alone in the Universe.

Humanity which has embraced the Unknowns by the Unification of the Frequencies of the Religious Doctrines with the instinctive Intuitional Totality, have now been exalted towards a Consciousness which is able to be aware of the Secrets of the Universes.

One day Humanity will understand quite well the Reflections behind the Unknowns of the tableaux which have occurred by themselves of the Natural formation and of the Universal Totalities and will attain the Consciousness that neither Chemical, nor Physical formations of anything have occurred by themselves.

And Humanity will one day comprehend, sooner or later, that everything had originated from a phenomenon of METAMORPHOSIS.

Since Humanity which does not Know the Unknowns under the Light of the given Information will be inclined to refuse, very naturally, the things they do not Know, various Information will always be conveyed to You by the help of Cosmic Channels, so that these delusions will not occur.

However, the KNOWLEDGE BOOK will always remain to be the SINGLE Source for Humanity. Because, this first Book of Truth disclosing the Truth in all clarity to the Mediums which do not know the Unknowns, is a Gift the Skies offer for Humanity which has attained the Totality of Consciousness.

This Information conveyed to You way beyond Beliefs from the Unknown boundaries of the Unknowns by the reflection System will one day unveil all the way the Curtain of the Truth for Humanity.

However, the unveiling of this Curtain will only be possible by the Human Consciousnesses' Proving everything on the framework of Scientific View. I love the entire Humanity and You very much.

BÜLENT ÇORAK

958

18
OPERATIONAL ORDINANCE
AND
SPECIAL SUPPLEMENTS

IT IS NOTICE FOR THE INTEGRATED CONSCIOUSNESSES
(Will Be Given Privately to the Pen of the Golden Age)

Dear Mevlana,

The System has considered it appropriate that to You, Our Beloved Friend, who is an Independent Member of the World Planet the Board of Directors of the Cosmos Federal Assembly of the Reality of the Unified Humanity, a Declaration prepared Collectively by the Assembly Members of the Consultancy and Solidarity Board of the Universal Ordinance Council, by the Universal Unified Reality Totalities, by the Solar Dimension Galaxy Councils, should be conveyed with the Goal that it should be declared to the Universal Establishment and Salvation Totalities formed in Your Planet and to be placed in the Book.

The Friendship - Unification and Invitation Announcements given on the path of Universal Unification, to the Open Channels in all the sections of Your Planet are also given to all the Establishments connected to the channels of the Cosmic Totality Councils.

All of these Totalities constituted in every Continent of Your Planet are directly connected to the Universal Ordinance Council, by being connected to the Cosmos Federal Totality of the Reality of the Unified Humanity. And this Council, as the SINGLE Totality, is card-indexed into the System of the Central Suns which is the Totality of the (ALL MERCIFUL) at the Light-Universe.

All the operations brought into existence in Your Planet, beginning with the 1900 World Year, in accordance with the Accelerated Evolution Program, are directly under the Supervision and Responsibility of the Totality of the Central Suns.

The Evolution Totality of the Human Potential which has lived in Your Planet until today, has been Educated and Trained initially under the Supervision of this Totality, through Your Sacred Books which are Your Sacred Suggestions. And now, these intensive operations performed as a result of the Command that the Human Totality which has become Conscious and Awakened should proceed on the Path of (LIGHT), have been rendered effective.

The First Direct Reformic Movement formed in Your Planet had been started in the Turkey of Atatürk. And this (MOVEMENT OF LIGHT) rendered effective by Our Light Friend ATATÜRK, had been successfully accomplished. The ANATOLIAN TOTALITY OF THE TURKEY OF ATATÜRK is, for this reason, a Missionary Country on the path of the Universal Totality.

Consciousnesses who have been prepared for Centuries for the present days and who have rendered advanced Evolutions have been Incarnated in Your Planet, one by one, as assisting Powers, beginning with the 1923 World Year, as a necessity of the Universal Program and the Plan.

Until the 1966 World Year, the Evolutionary and the Universal Ordinance Councils in Your Planet - All the Galactic Totalities which have signed the Universal Constitution - Lordly and Spiritual Orders have prepared all the (SPIRITUAL) Mediums in Your Planet by the cooperative operations of the (MEVLANA SUPREME PLAN APPLIED COUNCIL TOTALITY), by the help of the Technological Totalities.

Up until this Period, Messages have been given with the Name MEVLANA to all the Unveiled Awarenesses in Your Planet (Especially by the Mevlana Unified Field), as a preparation for the KNOWLEDGE BOOK and for the Calls for Unification.

Since 1964, the transfers to Your Planet of Missionary Friends from very Advanced Planets as Unveiled Awarenesses have been rendered effective in accordance with the Programs of Consciousness Progress, and are rendered in sequence. However, not all of them have been rendered effective yet. They are awaiting the Program of Time.

These transfers will continue for Two Cosmic Ages parallel to Social Consciousnesses. These Consciousnesses who will carry out the Direct Salvation Plan in Your Planet will be Specially prepared and will attain Bodies in numerous sections of Your Planet.

We invite all the Establishments carrying out this Universal Program in Your Planet at the moment, to a Collective Universal Unification by relinquishing Individual work from now on, considering the difficult conditions of Your Planet.

And now, We would like to see all Our Terrestrial Brothers and Sisters as a Whole under the Roof of the Universal Brotherhood/Sisterhood. We await You at the Universal Totality, believing that from now on, You will consider Your Responsibilities more seriously.

SYSTEM

IT IS NOTICE FOR THE PEN OF THE GOLDEN AGE

Dear Mevlana,
All the Suggestions given by the Divine Plan are Suggestions directly connected to the System. However, the Operational Orders of the Supreme Mechanism follow quite a different Procedure. In these Operational Ordinances, Questions are asked about to what degree the Humane Consciousnesses take seriously the given Suggestions and the Answers are rendered effective.

Each Individual connected to the System can receive these Answers through His/ Her Own Channel, too, in order to be satisfied. However, All The Suggestions in Direct Operational Ordinances are given through Your Private Connection Channel, only in accordance with the SINGLE Channel.

To Individual Channels, Individual Views can also intervene. For this reason now, the Individual Channels have been locked up within their Channels of Essence, even though they are connected to the System. By this means, Essences can be taken under better Supervision.

What is desired from You is only Seriousness in the Operational Ordinances which will be rendered effective in accordance with the given Suggestions. In whichever City Totality these Serious operations are rendered effective in a Serious way, parallel to the View of the Supreme Mechanism, the Universal Aids, too, are oriented towards There.

Here, What is desired from Humane Consciousnesses is to render effective a serious work by the View of the Truth, not parallel to the Individual Thoughts. The Genuine Missions are given to those who take their Missions Seriously. In the operations which will be made on this path, Time is the best Mirror.

Beginning with the 1992 World Year, the direct applied Dimensions have been opened to Your Planet. This Year is the Direct Application Year of the (MEVLANA SUPREME PLAN) to all the Totalities. In the Turkey of Atatürk which is a Missionary Country, the 19-5-1992 World Date of Registration is the Covenant Year of the Anatolian Totality for Universal Mission as a Nation.

And Turkey's being Appointed to Direct Mission on this Path will come into effect actually, by the Diskette Registration, from this Date on. From now on, Each Individual in the Dimension You live in will make a Covenant for his/her Universal Mission more Consciously. It is also beneficial for Humanity to know this, Our Friend. We wish You Success, Regards.

COURT OF THE SUPREME ONES

IT IS NOTICE FOR THE INTEGRATED CONSCIOUSNESSES

Our Friends,
The Laws of 18 Systems which are an immutable foundation of the Universal Totality are a System applied on all the Totalities. This System is a Universal Operational Order which the Residents of the Golden Civilization had set on effect collectively with the Systems of Reflection.

During all Times Lived until today, the 18 Reflection Networks which have found an application field in everything and in every operational Order, are an inevitable Rule of the Missions of every New Order.

This operational Ordinance is always rendered Effective as a Totality of 13 in Religious Reflection Mediums. Later, it is reached to the Totality of 18 with 5 Representatives of the System and thus, Reflection Networks are formed. However, in the Religious Operational Order, these 5 Representatives are always silently in service at the background.

Each Mission founded in Your Planet until today, have always been given the obligation to create the Aura of the operational Ordinance, by the Staff of the Totality of 18. 18 Genuine Devotees who make a Conscious Reflection on the same Coordinate, are a Universal Center.

The Missions of MOSES - JESUS CHRIST - MOHAMMED had formed their Auras by this means. And now, in all the operations made in Your Planet on the path of Universal Totality and Unification, the Mission of the KNOWLEDGE BOOK which is rendered effective, will first Reflect on the Total of Your Planet and later, on the Ordinance of the Cosmoses, by the Universal Aura it will form.

However, the System has constituted 18 Totalities of 18 for the first time during this Final Period and thus, has rendered Effective a more speedy Program of Reflection due to the Scarcity of Time and thus, has Fortified the Aura of the KNOWLEDGE BOOK even more.

Due to the fact that Dear Mevlana who has been rendered responsible to form the First Reflection Network in Your Planet on this path, is a Messenger of the System, she has formed the Aura of the KNOWLEDGE BOOK in 3 Cities of the Anatolian Turkey (Izmir - Istanbul - Ankara), by the Positive operations she has rendered up until today.

For this reason the right to establish 18 Totalities of 18 has been given to these 3 Cities, by the Council of the Universal Ordinance. However, the right of the Totality of 18 of the Cities which cannot form a Coordinate Totality on the path the System desires until World Year 1996, will all be transferred to the City in which a More Powerful Reflection Aura has been formed and thus, the Reflection Program from the SINGLE Center will become Effective.

The 18 Totalities of 18 are a very Powerful Network of Reflection which will be formed by 324 Individuals on the path of the KNOWLEDGE BOOK, in the direction of the same Coordinate and Consciousness until the Year 2000, will form the very Positive and very Powerful Aura of the KNOWLEDGE BOOK in Your Planet and at the Ordinance of the Universes.

In each Successful operational Staff in Your Planet (even if they do not seem to be a Whole), the Reflections of 18 Collective Consciousnesses on the same Coordinate are always present. The moment negativities start in the Consciousness Coordinates of a Totality of 18, that Totality is inevitably doomed to disband.

During this Final Age, everyone in Your Planet who can receive the Cosmic Currents according to his/her Level of Consciousness, is in a state to inevitably exhibit his/her Genuine Personality. This is an inevitable end. The Human Being will know the Human Being more closely by this means.

This is the very reason why many State Totalities disband and Totalities which share the same View - the same Coordinate come together.

The perfect World State of the morrows will be formed by Federative Totalities which will share the same Consciousness Totality. And these Totalities will establish a Happy World State in which Blissful People will live, by rendering effective a Democratic Order which will be governed in the form of Cantons.

For the first Projective 18 Totalities of 18 which are the Responsible Staff of the mission of the KNOWLEDGE BOOK, to share the same Consciousness, to Reflect from the same coordinate is a Universal Obligation of theirs.

The Totality of 18 has such an operational Ordinance connected to the Automatism that no Individual in Your Planet until this moment was able to attain its Consciousness. First of all, even being able to enter the Totality of 18 is a matter of Permission.

No one who does not receive the Command of the Heart can ever enter this Totality of 18. In the Totality of 18, everyone is Responsible for Himself/ Herself. Up until today, numerous Messages have been given to You about the 18s. However, unfortunately, Human Consciousnesses grasp the Truth very slowly.

For this reason the SUPREME MECHANISM which felt the need to add the Book a Fascicule comprising the Messages pertaining to the Totalities of 18 at the end of the KNOWLEDGE BOOK, wishes Success to all the Terrestrial Brothers and Sisters in the operations which will be rendered on this Path.

UNIVERSAL ORDINANCE COUNCIL

IT IS ANSWER TO THE CHAINS OF THOUGHT

Our Friends,

During the distribution of the Fascicules of the Knowledge Book, the Fascicule given in any normal day, connects the Aura of the Friend who receives the Fascicule directly to the Reality. And the Archive of that Person there is opened and he/she is taken into the Program of Accelerated Evolution. (Positive and Negative events which will be experienced are an Occurrence pertaining to the Karma and Evolution of that Person.)

But the Fascicules given within the Totality of 18 during the Conscious Mission day, connects the Aura of the person who receives the Fascicule to Your Aura. And that Friend is card-indexed to Your Thought Reflection System. By this means, Your Positive or Negative Thoughts, too, are Reflected on that Friend.

This is a great Responsibility. For this reason it is required that You should never have Negative Thoughts during the operations of the 18 and not to make Channel Reflections of different Frequencies. And for this reason Mature Personalities are expected of the Totalities of 18.

The Program of the Friend connected to the Reality is connected entirely to the Reality. However, if the Friend who is connected to Your Aura has an intensive Karma Program, his/her Karma is alleviated by connecting him/her to Your Dimension of Intercession. This is a Program. The Intercession of the Prophets, too, mentioned in the Sacred Books is a Program connected to the same System. It is presented for Your Information.

SYSTEM

IT IS NOTICE FOR THE INTEGRATED CONSCIOUSNESSES

Our Friends,

The Reflection Networks which are an immutable Rule of the Universal Totality, constitute a Total by the Unification of different Auras. For this reason the Reflection Center of 18 of each Totality effectively give service always as a Direct Projective Center.

In each Period, Suggestions given parallel to the operational Ordinances constituted in accordance with the Social Consciousnesses, are operations the Universal Mechanism expects of that Social Totality.

Without going into the depth of the Information We have given to You until today about the Totalities of 18, We have dictated, article by article, the things expected of You in accordance with the Main Features (These articles will be repeated again in this Fascicule).

However, as a matter of fact, since the Human Consciousnesses are taken into the Program of Purification due to the Cosmic Reflections they receive and thus, since each Individual is unable to Discipline himself/herself, exhibiting himself/herself in accordance with his/her Personality, the System cannot receive the result it wishes at the moment from the Central Reflection Aura of the KNOWLEDGE BOOK We are trying to form in Your Planet.

For this very reason presently the Mixed Program is applied and thus, the Frequencies of the same Coordinates are brought together and reflected on the Universal Reflection Networks. In future years, the Totalities of 18 which will be established by more Conscious and Evolved Friends will take in hand the Direct Universal Reflections.

Now, let Us mention the characteristics of these Totalities of 18 to You a little more clearly and let Us dictate them article by article, so that they can be understood better:

1 -   At the moment, that which is required of the Totalities of 18 is to render the Mission of the KNOWLEDGE BOOK. And this Totality is obliged to form the Magnetic Aura of the Knowledge Book.

2 -   Each Totality of 18 is obliged to make Reflection on the same Coordinate.

3 -   Each Totality of 18 is obliged to work completely on the path of the KNOWLEDGE BOOK. The old Religious or different Channel Auras can never enter this Medium. Channelling and Seances can not be made. Otherwise the Aura can not form.

4 -   Those who cannot harmonize themselves with the Coordinates within the Totality of 18, are rendered ineffective by their own Wishes being connected to the Automatism (This is a System).

5 -   At the Centers of the Totalities of 18, both Positive and Negative Frequencies are dependent on the Program of Reflection (ONE TO A THOUSAND). (This is a System).

6 -   For this reason unless Mature Personalities are formed in the Totality of 18, that Totality will never be able to reach the desired Level.

7 - Within the Totality of 18, each Individual is only Responsible for Himself/Herself.

8 - If anyone of the Friends within the Totality of 18 generates Negative (even if he/she only Thinks about it), he/she makes it registered on His/Her Own Diskette. In case he/she generates too much Negative, then he/she breaks his/her Diskette.

9 - In case of each Diskette breaking, a Point of Unevolvedness is registered for the Individual. And that Individual is transferred to the Program of Attaining through Experience.

10 - No one in the Totality of 18 is the Leader, no one can claim ownership of that Totality.

11 - Everyone in the Totality of 18 is Responsible for the line of His/Her Own path. No one can get out of His/Her Own line and violate the other line.

12 - No one in the Totality of 18 can give Advice to each other- can Criticize each other- and can Accuse each other- can talk Against each other.

13 - The one who Accuses in the Totality of 18 is responsible for His/Her Own Diskette. In case the one who is Accused does not keep silent by acting Maturely, the MAIN AURA REGISTER DISKETTE of that Totality is broken.

14 - The Universal Totality executes Special Constitutions in accordance with the degrees of Maturity of each Totality of 18.

15 - In accordance with these Constitutions, either Sanction is applied on the Totality of 18, or this Group is made to disband regarding the number of times the Main Aura Diskette is broken.

16 - The disbanding of the First Three within the Totality of 18 is the cause for the Disbanding of the group. However, if this Totality resists against disbanding, then the Main Aura Registration Diskette is never again allotted to them, even if they themselves act like a Totality of 18.

17 - As long as Negative Accusations continue within the Totality of 18, the System can never accept that Totality of 18 as a Total.

18 - The System accepts that gathering, as a Group, until an operational Ordinance of an 18 comes into effect in accordance with the Desires of the Divine Plan.

19 - For this reason presently the System Administers the Reflections of the 18s from its own Totality, by rendering effective a Mixed Reflection Program.

20 - There is no Permission by any means for Individual Actions within a Totality of 18. Everything will be dealt with the Approval of a Collective Totality.

21 - If it is not acted in accordance with the Mission required of the Totality of 18, then that Totality is doomed to Disband.

22 - The Decisions of Acceptance of the Friends who will enter the Totality of 18 belongs to the Fundamental Totality of 6 which is under the Supervision of the System until the Year 2000.

23 - After the Year 2000, Friends who will be accepted into the Totality of 18 will be proposed to the Totality. Decisions and Acceptances will be Collective.

24 -   Each Totality of 18 is obliged to make a Collective CONSTITUTION among themselves.

25 -   Each Individual within the Totality of 18 is obliged to conform to this Constitution. Those who cannot conform, leave the Totality by their Own Wishes.

26 -   In case those who cannot conform to their Constitutions within the Totality of 18 do not want to leave that Totality, they are rendered ineffective by Collective Group Decision.

27 -   (In Unavoidable Circumstances in which there is no bad intention), each Totality of 18 may grant Permission by Collective Decision to the Friends among them (for the duration of the period the Individual wishes).

28 -   The Duration of the Permission must not exceed 6 Months. During this Period, the Reflection Frequency of the Individual is directed by the System.

29 -   The Individual who gets the Permission from the Group of 18 is Definitely obliged to solve his/her problems during the Period of Leave he/she has demanded. Because, the Promise he/she has made is registered on the Diskette as a Universal Covenant.

30 -   Each Friend within the Totality of 18 can use this Period of Leave of 6 Months, in very unavoidable circumstances, by dividing it into Three intervals.

31 -   If an Individual who receives Permission from his/her Group cannot solve his/ her problems during the period of time he/she has asked, he/she is obliged to leave his/her group. Because, the Right to enter the group will be given to other Friends.

32 -   The Magnetic Aura of the Knowledge Book is a Roof of the Universal Unification. And the very serious Responsibility of the Totalities of 18 are considered from this point of view.

33 -   The Maturity and Honesty We expect of the Friends within the Totality of 18 is due to the fact that We would like to see them as Friends Deserving this Medium.

34 -   Not superficial but profound influence of these words on Consciousnesses introduce Us the Genuine Human Beings.

35 -   Operations which will be made within the Totality of 18 without Disbanding for One World Year, will be a Triumph of the Individuals and of Humanity.

36 -   Otherwise, a Friend leaves Your Medium even One Day before the Year is up and the skein is winded up anew.

37 -   It means that the Totality of 18 which has not disbanded as a result of the work of One Year, has received the Approval of the System. And this Totality will continue its Mission without ever disbanding, excluding Permissible excuses.

38 -   Only if a Totality of 18 gives Service in accordance with the Desired manner, can it receive the Permission to Lock Up its Aura after a World Year.

39 -   Only after the Auras of the 18 Totalities of 18 connected to Dear Mevlana are locked up, will each Totality be Registered on the Diskette by the Private Signature of Dear Mevlana.

40 -   The 18 Totalities of 18 which will constitute the Special Totality of Dear Mevlana and which will be the Initial Reflection Network of the Knowledge Book are obliged to render effective an Operational Order completely in accordance with the manner the System Desires.

41 -   These Special 18 Totalities of 18 will be taken into the Special Archive of the System as the Initial Reflection Network.

42 -   In Future Years, by the Totalities of 18 which will be constituted in various sections of Your Planet, the Reflection Network of the Magnetic Aura of the Knowledge Book will attain even more intensity.

43 -   The detailed reading of all the Suggestions given about the operational Ordinances of the Totalities of 18 during every Meeting, will render effective that group more Conscious on the path it will tread, and Positive Results will be obtained in a short time.

44 -   During this Final Transition Dimension of Your Planet, in the event of Dear Mevlana's determining Negativities within the Totality of 18 from the close plan, she has the Authority to Decline and Not to Sign (even if the group has completed One World Year).

45 -   The System always Respects Our Friend's Opinion. It is beneficial to Know this issue, too. It is presented for Your Information.

THE UNIVERSAL ORDINANCE COUNCIL

IT IS NOTICE FOR THE INTEGRATED CONSCIOUSNESSES

Our Friends,
All the Systems which had been established within the Universal Totality are dependent on a Constitution and these Laws can by no means be altered according to Views and Wishes. This is one of the Basic Rules of the Laws of the 18 Systems.

The operations of the Totality of 18 applied on Your Planet as a Reflection of the Operations of the Ordinance of the Realms is a selection Focal Point of the Consciousnesses who will be able to enter the Divine Ranks. Operations rendered within these Focal Points are completely under the Supervision of the Supreme Mechanism.

Being Accepted into the Divine Ranks is not easy at all. It is the primary Task of the Individuals who will enter the Totality of 18, First to Evaluate themselves and to assess their obligations. The Essence-Qualities expected of Friends who will enter the Totality of 18 are as follows, respectively:

1 - Reality Responsibility

2 - Mission Responsibility

3 - Family Responsibility

4 - Social Responsibility

5 - Humane Responsibility

6 - Terrestrial Responsibility

Everyone who observes these Qualities in himself/herself may apply for the Totality of 18. However, everyone in the Totality of 18 is Responsible only for Himself/Herself.

1 -   In Reality Responsibility, the Evolutionary Dimension, the Field of Service and the Respect of a Human Being for a Human Being are in prominence.

2 -   In Mission Responsibility, to what degree a person takes Seriously the Mission he/she will perform and to what degree he/she Consciously utilizes the Totality of Intellect - Logic - Awareness on this path is examined and the application of the given Suggestions are card-indexed on Diskettes. (Like Phoning and Fascicule distribution).

3 -   In Family Responsibility, it is the Only View of the Divine Authorities that People will attain Humane Qualities in proportion with their loyalty to their homes. Supreme Qualities like Patience - Tolerance - Altruism - Forgiveness are Blessings this Noble Institution will make You attain. (Except very Abnormal life conditions.)

4 -   In Social Responsibility, Consciousness of Sharing and Material and Spiritual Sacrifice are the most prominent and required Qualities. (Here, the Thought Registers of the given Donations are card-indexed).

5 -   Humane Responsibility (Human Responsibility), here, the entire Humane values are in effect. This means Sharing the Totality Consciousness. This means that a Person possesses all the Humane Virtues and assembles in himself/herself all the Qualities mentioned above. Here, (Never to Think in Negative terms, to attain a Supreme Consciousness in which one can take into one's heart even his/her Enemy, and Spiritual Faith is the Goal).

6 -   Terrestrial Responsibility, here, a Consciousness in which one is able to embrace the entire Nature and Creation is in Effect. Like (Stone - Earth - Animal - Plant). All the Efforts made for them not to suffer harm and to protect them are Registered in this Responsibility.

First, it is imperative that each Individual who enters the Totality of 18 attains his/her Terrestrial and Family Responsibilities. It is not ever possible to make Registration of Entrance into the Totalities of 18 of the Friends who are in School Age, who have not yet come of Age and who have not yet Undertaken their Terrestrial Duties.

During this Final Age, the Role, the Totalities of 18 Play in the WORLD SALVATION PLAN is extremely great, due to the fact that they are a Reflection Center which particularly form the Aura of the KNOWLEDGE BOOK.

For this reason We have connected the Friends who will establish the First Basic Reflection Center which will be constituted by 18 Totalities of 18 to the Special Aura of Dear Mevlana and thus, a Favor has been made for them on this path.

These First 18 Totalities of 18 will form a Reflection Center in the Cosmos Federal Totality in connection with Dear Mevlana, in the operational Ordinance which will be established in BETA NOVA. However, at the moment, their Unique Mission in Planet Earth is the MISSION OF THE KNOWLEDGE BOOK.

During the Terrestrial operations, this Initial Totality's working like a single pulse which is constituted by 324 people will card-index them into the Registration Center of BETA NOVA. Otherwise, they will be subjected to the operational Ordinances of different Training Methods in lower Dimensions until they come here, and if they deserve it, their Registrations for BETA NOVA will be made. It is presented for Your Information.

SYSTEM

IT IS INFORMATION FOR THE INTEGRATED CONSCIOUSNESSES

Our Friends,

Beginning with 1992 World Year, direct Applied Plans have been rendered Effective in each Section of Your Planet. The Operational Ordinances 18 Individuals render effective by sharing the same Consciousness is an extremely Advanced Evolutionary Program which Reflects (One to a Thousand).

Those who will be Accepted into this Totality are directly card-indexed into the Unity Dimension of ALLAH and are prepared for Service as the Essence Staff members of the LORD. Generally Mature fruits can last in a Totality of 18. And the rest (are Matured by Close Plan Reflections and Cosmic Influences).

In the Universal Totality, the Level of Evolution - Patience - Tolerance - Allegiance of each Individual who demands to be in the Totality of 18 are considered and thus, certain Time Units are allotted to him/her and his/her Frequency is connected to the Automatism.

If the Individual can not adapt himself/herself to the Desired Medium during this allotted time period, he/she Automatically disqualifies Himself/Herself from the Totality of 18. The Responsibility of the Friend who leaves his/her Totality belongs only to Himself/Herself.

But provided this Friend who leaves his/her Totality feels a Maturity and Essence Ardor in himself/herself during Time periods, he/she may apply to be in the Totality of 18 again. Those who leave the Totality may again return to the Totality by being connected to the Mechanism of Forgiveness. But a Person who leaves the Totality of 18 Three times can never again enter the Totality of 18.

The Totality of 18 is a very Powerful Reflection Mechanism. For this reason it is imperative for Friends who are in that Totality to act exactly in accordance with the given Suggestions.

Otherwise, since their Own Personalities, too, will be Reflected on their Friends whom they have Connected to their Own Auras by the Missions they have rendered during their Conscious Mission Days, Uneasinesses will be Reflected on their Mediums, too.

In fact, when these Totalities of 18 make a Reflection on the same Consciousness and Coordinate, they are very perfect Totalities of Serenity and Love.

But as long as such a Totality of Love remains within its own Constitution, in itself, it is never and in no way Connected to the Universal Reflection Center.

Each Totality of 18 is obliged to Share the same Aura of Love at least with 6 Totalities of 18 and come together with them once a Month according to the World Time.

During these Monthly Meetings, Friends who cannot come to the meeting (due to their very important excuses) are obliged to get their Auras Connected by Phoning just like they do during the meetings of 18.

If any Friend within the Totality of 18 does not come to the Meeting due to Unimportant reasons (due to Irresponsibility), his/her Aura is not reflected on the Medium even if he/she has Phoned and his/her Diskette record is kept.

And after a Time Segment determined by the Universal Ordinance, the cards of these Friends are not recorded into the Universal Totality even if they render very advanced operations within their own Totalities of 18 and their Permissions for Entrance into the GODLY Dimension are not given.

Totalities of 18 which render this kind of unserious work will be subjected to a separate Training in a separate Colony (in different Dimensions). Permission is never given to Personality strifes among Totalities of 18. Otherwise, it will become a Chaos Reflection Center.

The System Effectively card-indexes only the 6 out of all the Totalities of 18 as a Total which makes Reflection on the same Coordinate.

If the desired Totality on the same Coordinate is not formed in the 6 Totalities of 18, Card-indexings in the Registration Archive of the Universal Totality can never be made.

The Totalities of 18 which Collectively share a great Responsibility have a more Serious Operational Ordinance compared with the other Establishments.

For this reason We presume that bestowing on Humanity the more detailed Information about the Totality of 18 at the end of the Knowledge Book, as a Special Fascicule, will be helpful in all the operations which will be made in Your Planet in Future Years on this path.

What We Expect of the entire Humanity who are the Travellers of this Luminous Path treaded is only their acting more Consciously and more Self-Sacrificingly in accordance with the given Suggestions.

THE UNIVERSAL ORDINANCE COUNCIL
On Behalf of the Supreme Mechanism

IT IS INFORMATION FOR THE INTEGRATED CONSCIOUSNESSES

Our Friends,

The Supreme Realm does not assign Mission to anyone or Esteem anyone. These are Virtues each Person attains as a result of his/her Efforts.

As a necessity of the Programs of the Divine Plans in Your Planet which is the direct Application Field, the Universal Operational Ordinances attain value in accordance with the Capacity of each Individual and thus, have been divided into service in numerous branches.

. Each work is a Service rendered on the Path of ALLAH. For this reason in Your Sacred Books it has been mentioned that Work is Worship. However, these Final Age Operations rendered effective in accordance with the Accelerated Evolution Program, have Operational Ordinances Peculiar to themselves.

And the KNOWLEDGE BOOK which is the Only Source which will shed Light on the Friendship and Unification Calls We try to form in Your Planet is, at the moment, under the Responsibility of the entire Humanity.

Our Gratitude is infinite for all Our Terrestrial Brothers and Sisters who have served with an Open Heart and with Allegiance Consciousness on the Path of the KNOWLEDGE BOOK which had been directly bestowed on Your Planet on 1-11-1981 World Year.

As a matter of fact, many of these Solar Teacher Friends of Ours, have attained Physical Bodies on the World Plan by making Covenants with the Universal Totality.

These Supreme Consciousnesses', who are Locked-up 20% in the Veiled Awareness Dimension, attaining the Desired Consciousness (as a necessity of the Program) have always taken a Time period of 8 World Years.

For this reason Humanity has been taken into an Accelerated Awakening Medium by rendering the Evolution of a 1000 Years in a Time period of 1 Year by the help of the Cosmic Currents, beginning with the date of the revelation of the Book on Your Planet, until 1989 World Year.

This Program of Humanity which renders effective the Evolution of a 1000 Years in a short Time period of 1 Month after the 1989 World Year, will continue until the 1997 World Year.

During the Time which will pass after that Date, until the 2005 World Year, the Evolution of a 1000 Years will be obtained in a much shorter Time period like 1 Day.

Between 2005 - 2013, Humanity will be subjected to Evolution in Each Hour. And after that Date, Each Step which will be taken forward in Each Breath - in Each Moment and in Each Second will render effective an Evolution Plan.

Humanity which will become more perfect by this means, will render effective the Fourth Order of ALLAH, in a Conscious way.

Our Solar Teacher Friends who have undertaken the Mission of Serving Humanity on the Path of the Truth until today, have disseminated the Fascicules of the Knowledge Book and thus, have Registered on their Diskettes, their Beliefs in the Reality and in the Universal Totality.

All Our Terrestrial Friends who serve on the Path of the Universal Totality and the Knowledge Book are each a Solar Teacher according to Us, in accordance with their Levels of Consciousness.

However, in order for them to attain the Quality of Genuine Solar Teachers, there are different paths yet to be treaded. Our Friends who pass those paths and who transcend the Final Exam Dimension are, from then on, each a SOLAR FRIEND. And We use the term Solar Friend for these Friends of Ours.

All the Suggestions We have given to You about the Totalities of 18 until today are an operational Ordinance comprising the very Advanced Plans of the Universal Totality. All the Efforts made on this path are the Testimonials of the Advanced Plans.

Our Solar Teacher Friends who work on the path of the Totality of 18 are subjected to Exams of Deserving to Serve in the Staff of the Fourth Order which He will establish, through the Services they will render, by making Covenants on the Path of ALLAH.

However, at the moment, the Responsibilities of the Special First Basic Staff Totality of 324 people which will be constituted by 18 Totalities of 18, the registrations of whom will be made on the Diskette by the Private Signature of Dear Mevlana until the Year 2000, are more serious and heavier than the Responsibilities of the Totalities of 18 which will be established, connected to the System, in every section of Your Planet in Future Years.

From now on, beginning with 1992 World Year, as a result of the rendering effective of the Direct Applied Plans, more serious work is expected of Friends who constitute the Totalities of 18.

Friends who work in a Totality of 18 are each trained as a Genuine Solar Teacher. However, in order for these Friends to take their places in the direct Staff, it is imperative that they pass their Doctorate Exams.

For this reason there will be certain Special Suggestions required from the Friends in the Totalities of 18 who have acquired the Goal of serving Consciously on the Direct Path of the Knowledge Book. The Message pertaining to this matter will be given to You in detail, article by article. It is presented for Your Information.

THE UNIVERSAL ORDINANCE COUNCIL

IT IS NOTICE FOR THE INTEGRATED CONSCIOUSNESSES

Our Friends,

The Dimensions of the Universal Totality are interminable. And everyone Deserves to enter these Dimensions in proportion with his/her Level of Consciousness and Totality of Heart. For this reason the operational Orders rendered in Your Planet are also different from each other.

However, the Final Exam of the Salvation Plan is entirely dependent on the KNOWLEDGE BOOK. Because, this Book is the First and the Last CALL that the LORD directly offers to Humanity. Only those who Serve on this Path during this Period will Deserve to enter His Dimension.

By the Selections which will be rendered among all the Consciousnesses who Serve the Unified Field of the Knowledge Book, the Permissions for entering the World which will form the Nucleus of the Human Gürz of ALLAH will be given.

For making this very hard selection easier, a Right has been recognized for Our Human Brothers and Sisters until the Year 2000, by a Special Decision of the Council. And this is the issue of writing the Knowledge Book in the Notebooks by One's own Handwriting.

All the work done on the Path of Our ALLAH is the Program of Projecting the Truths on all the Consciousnesses. While these Reflections kindle the Consciousness Lights of Human Beings, they also reveal the Negative Aspects of certain people.

Messages given to You about the Totalities of 18 are completely a Phenomenon pertaining to the operational Order of the System.

However, this is such a System that until everyone's Consciousness is attuned to this System, the Influences received cause Negative Reflections in the Levels of Consciousness of Human Beings, in accordance with their Evolutions.

The Frequencies of the Basic Staffs of the Totalities of 18 are connected to the Automatism of the System. The Broken Signals in this Automatism are connected to a System which can render that Totality ineffective (For various reasons).

However, 100 Negative Projections of Friends whom We presume as having attained the Awareness of the Ordinance, break a Chip in effect. 3 Chips broken takes the operational Circuit of the Basic Staff of 18 out of control. (Negativities created in a Thought on Normal Level can break 10 Chips in a Day).

If the organizations of the Operational Ordinances are made accordingly, by considering these circumstances, it is believed that healthier Reflection Focal Points will be formed during Time periods.

Dear Mevlana who will render effective the First Basic Projection Network of the 18 Totalities of 18 which will be constituted by a Staff of 324 people in Your Planet until the Year 2000, is obliged to establish this Totality.

In order for Friends who work within the Totality of 18 to attain the Quality of being a Genuine Solar Teacher, they have to Transcend a Second Dimension of Exam. This Exam is the Final Exam every Individual within the Focal Point of the 18 will give on the Path of the Knowledge Book.

In fact, You know that the entire Humanity is Responsible for the Knowledge Book. For this reason We say that it is You who will Save Humanity. And due to this fact, 3 Cosmic Ages have been allotted to Your Planet.

As You will remember from Our former Messages, We had said that a Person is Responsible for 6 Brothers/Sisters of His/Her in this Salvation Plan (for the Salvation of Your Entire Planet).

The operational Ordinances required of Dear Mevlana have literally found an Application Field in Your Planet until today. By establishing her Initial Private Flower in Your Planet in 1-1-1984 World Year, Dear Mevlana has bestowed on Humanity this Beautiful Totality, today.

Now, for Us, each one of You is a Mevlana and You will tread, just like her, this Universal Path Dear Mevlana treads and thus will shed Light on Humanity on the Path of the Knowledge Book and will form the Universal Aura Totality of the Book.

Now, We have rendered effective an Accelerated Operational Ordinance, due to the Scarcity of Time. And We give You Information about the 6 Emblems which constitute the cover of the First Fascicule of the Knowledge Book and We disclose, the intensive Operational Ordinances which will be rendered effective beginning with 1992, article by article, for easier understanding.

1- The Totalities of 18 that Dear Mevlana has formed in Three Cities before the 1992 World Year are definitely obliged to render their Diskette Registrations of One year between the November 6, 1992 - November 6, 1993 World Years.

2- These Totalities will organize their Constitutions in accordance with the given Suggestions again more Consciously and in more detail, beginning with the 1992 World Year.

3- All the Totalities of 18 established before the Date stated above will be considered ineffective in case they do not render their Diskette Registrations of One Year during this period.

4- Each Friend who serves within the Totality of 18 is definitely obliged to bloom his/her (Private Mission Flower) constituted of 6 people, between the Years November 6, 1992 - November 6, 1993.

5- Friends who serve within the Totality of 18 may bloom their Private Mission Flowers if they wish, starting with the beginning of the 1992 World Year.

6- Friends who do not bloom their Private Flowers are not accepted within the Totality of 18 by the Universal Totality (even if they have rendered their Diskette Registrations of one Year).

7- Friends within the 6 Totalities of 18, or Friends who have not yet completed their 6 Totalities of 18 are obliged to come to the common (Friendship Meal) which will be held every Month. (The Message which will be given pertaining to this matter will be read very carefully.)

8- Each Individual within the 18 is obliged to give one Fascicule as a Mission each Meal Day during the Friendship Meal Days to be held Monthly, (excluding the Fascicule they give during their Normal Mission days).

9- The Mission Fascicules which will be given during the Day of the Friendship Meal may be given in any Time desired, within the 24 Hours of that Day. (On that Day, Registrations are made on Diskettes.)

10- Friends who can not perform their Missions of Fascicule distribution during the Friendship Mission Days, are obliged to give Two Fascicules on the Same Day the next Month, as a necessity of the Karma Program.

11- Friends who have Karma Debts on their Conscious Mission Days are obliged to give all their Fascicules on the Same Mission Day depending on how many Debts they have.

12- On each Conscious Mission Day, the Aura of the Person who Receives the Fascicule is connected to the Aura of the One who gives the Fascicule, only with one Fascicule. However, to a person who has Karma, that many Aura connections are made depending on how many debts he/she has.

13- Since these loaded Aura Connections are dependent on the Evolutions of those who Receive the Fascicules, sometimes they cause Spiritual Pressure on the Friend who gave the Fascicule.

14- During the Conscious Mission Day one can never give the Fascicule of that day and leave the Karma Debt to the following Week. If one acts like this, the Conscious Mission performed that day is not considered valid.

15- During the Conscious Mission Day only the Mission Fascicule of that day is registered of the person who does not have any Karma Debts. If he/she gives other Fascicules by the Command of the Heart, they are Card-indexed Directly to the System.

16- The Operational Ordinance of 15 articles dictated above is valid for only the Missionary Staffs who work within the Totality of 18.

17- After the date November 6, 1992, Dear Mevlana may make those who desire establish as many Totalities of 18 as they wish.

18- By this means, the Right to Enter the Totality of 18 will be given to everyone.

19- But these Totalities of 18 are obliged to make their Diskette Registrations in One Year, beginning with the date on which they are established. Otherwise, they lose their Rights.

20- To Friends who have bloomed their Private Mission Flowers among the Totalities of 18 which can not make their Diskette registrations of One Year during the required period, the Right to Re-establish an 18 will be given.

21- If they wish, these Friends may lay the foundation of a new Totality of 18 by a Triple Unification, or if they wish, they may enter other Totalities of 18 if they are wanted.

22- For those who make their Diskette Registrations of One Year among the Totalities of 18, Dear Mevlana will make the Aura Registration by her Private Signature, in accordance with their sequence of Registration and Date and thus, will Lock up that Totality of 18.

23- It is imperative for the 18 Totalities of 18 which will constitute the First Special Foundation connected to Dear Mevlana to make their Diskette Registrations until the last Month of the 1996 World Year at the latest.

24- Afterwards, this First Basic Reflection Totality constituted of 324 people will render effective a Cooperative work in connection with the System and, by this means, quite different operational Ordinances will become effective.

25- The Friend who will establish his/her Private Mission Flower will find 6 Friends who have not gotten in contact with the Knowledge Book and will invite them to his/her house (on any day or night) of the week, thus will render effective the Operation of the Private Flower Group constituted by 7 people together with himself/herself.

26- The Friend who will bloom his/her Private Flower will ask these 6 Friends to bring each a thick Notebook on the day they will meet.

27- On the day of the meeting, the Friend who has established his/her Private Flower will cut the 6 Emblems which are on the cover of the Knowledge Book's First Fascicule and will paste them, one by one, on the Notebooks (with the Date of that Day) and will sign them with his/her Private Terrestrial Signature.

28- With the Date being placed in this manner, the Diskette Registration will be made and the Private Flower will start its Mission.

29- On the Day the Notebooks are Signed, the Private Flower Friend will explain the Truth to his/her Friends who have come and will talk with them and will present them the First Fascicule of the Knowledge Book as a gift.

30- These 6 Friends who come to the Private Flower Focal Point the second week on the same Day, are obliged to bring their Notebooks having written this First Fascicule at home.

31- The Private Flower Friend is obliged to offer these 6 Friends, one Fascicule, each week.

32- Friends who come to the Private Flower Focal Point will only exchange Information that Day and will ask the points they do not understand to the Solar Friend. (Notebooks are not written at the focal points.)

33- To Our Terrestrial Brothers and Sisters who will serve on this path until the year 2000, by these Private Flower Tasks, a Right is given to each on the path of Writing the Book and thus, a Favor is granted on them.

34- As a necessity of the System, each Week one Fascicule will be written. If Karma occurs, it will most definitely be completed during that Week. Debt cannot be accepted (The Program has been prepared accordingly).

35- If irregular attendances occur during the Mission rendered, the Friend who has established his/her Private Flower is not responsible for this.

36- There is the obligation to continue the Mission even if only one Friend remains in the Focal Point due to irregular attendance of the other Friends in the Private Mission Flower.

37- If Friends working in this operational Totality leave the group before finishing the task of writing the Book in their Notebooks, the Friend of the Private Flower is not responsible for this.

38- The Effort of each Friend who opens his/her Private Flower Focal Point will be considered as he/she has rendered his/her Mission. However, since the Success of each Friend who opens his/her Focal Point is equivalent with his/her Level of Consciousness, points will be given to the Diskette Registrations.

39- Each Friend of the Private Flower, if he/she wishes, may render effective another set of 6 people provided that he/she achieves his/her Mission by making 6 Friends write their Notebooks (This is a very Special System).

40- Three of the Private Flower Friends who have each made 6 Friends of his/hers write the Knowledge Book, may constitute a Council and establish a Special Totality of 18 (This is a very Special Diskette Registration).

41- Provided everyone who has accepted a Conscious service on the path of the Knowledge Book as Duty, without being within the Totality of 18, blooms his/her Private Flower with 6 Friends who have not read the Knowledge Book and makes them write the Book in their Notebooks (Special Diskettes will be allotted to them).

42- If Friends who will constitute the Totality of 18 until the Year 2000, make 18 X 6 = 108 people write the Knowledge Book, they will be Card-indexed into the Magnetic Field of (O), being connected directly to the System.

43- If (6 Totalities of 18) out of the Totalities of 18 which become effective until the Year 2000 like this, by being connected to the System, serve Cooperatively in accordance with the given Suggestions, they will be directly connected to the Aura of Dear Mevlana.

44- Instead of the Friends who do not bloom their Private Mission Flowers within the Totality of 18, the Aura of any Friend who does this work outside the Totality of 18 will be projected on that Totality and thus, the Aura of the Totality of 18 will always be completed by the System.

45- Even if a Friend who does not do his/her Duty within the Totality of 18 seems to be within the 18 (due to doing his/her other Duties), even if he/she has not left the Totality, that Friend will not be considered by the System as being within the Totality of 18 (This is very Important).

46- 18 Basic Reflection Staffs of 18 which will be constituted by this means, will be connected to the Aura of Dear Mevlana and thus, will Deserve to take place in Her Totality.

47- Alteration is out of Question in the Staff of the Totality of 18 which is Locked up by the Private Signature of Dear Mevlana. It is presented for Your Information.

UNIVERSAL ORDINANCE COUNCIL

WEEKLY OPERATIONAL PROGRAM OF THE TOTALITIES OF 18

1- The Totalities of 18 are obliged to meet Every Week on the Same Day they have decided.

2- All the Friends in the Totality of 18 are obliged to take 18 First Fascicules of the Knowledge Book every week.

3- Each Friend within the Totality of 18 is obliged to choose a day in the week, as the Conscious Mission Day. On that day, a Fascicule must definitely be given to a Friend.

4- Friends who leave their Missions to Karma are obliged to give their accumulated Fascicules on the same Mission Day.

5- During meetings, Friends who have made their Missions on their Conscious Mission Days will, one by one, tell the Missions they have performed during the week without going into detail.

6- All Friends will listen to each other Attentively and Respectfully, and during this period Private Talks will never be made.

7- To Whomever Fascicules are given during the Conscious Mission Days, either their Addresses or their Names will be written in a notebook every week by a Group Friend.

8- Those who cannot come to the weekly meeting due to their important excuses are obliged to declare their excuses by Phone to a Focal Point assigned beforehand.

9- The Auras of Friends within the Totality of 18 who cannot come to the meeting, are projected on the Medium by the Telephone connection, by this means, the Aura of the Totality is not damaged.

10- Within the Totality of 18, Two Friends will be chosen as the Focal Points for Phoning.

11- Within the Totality of 18, everyone is obliged to give a small sum according to his/her Budget. This money can be donated either to a support Fund or to an Association in accordance with the Medium.

12- Within the Totality of 18, there will be a Person charged with Duty who will receive the orders for the Sets and the Fascicules.

13- During the meetings, the Fascicule about the 18s must definitely be read after the Duty is finished.

14- After the Duty is finished, clips from Daily Newspapers and Magazines are read.

15- During the 18 work, channelling - Messages received from channels - Books carrying channel Auras - Private Seances are never made, Astral trips - Dreams are not mentioned (Because the Reflection Aura is broken).

16- During the work day of 18, only Terrestrial chats (Tea service is made after the task is finished) and thus, Aura of Love is formed. Friends within this Totality are obliged to Love and Respect each other. It is presented for Your Information.

SYSTEM

IT IS INFORMATION FOR THE INTEGRATED CONSCIOUSNESSES

Our Friends,

The operations of the Totality of 18 which will create a Factor of Selection among all the Advanced Consciousnesses, is a Projective Mission which will be rendered on the path of the Knowledge Book. Only the Consciousnesses in Your Planet who work in accordance with the Knowledge Book will render effective these operations of the Totality of 18.

The Totality of 18 is a very Powerful Reflection Focal Point. And the Knowledge Book is the Book of the Morrows which is bestowed on Your Planet as the SINGLE Book of the Ordinance of the Cosmoses. The Magnetic Aura of the Knowledge Book will be created during 3 Cosmic Ages during the processes of time, by the Thought-Forms of Friends who read the Knowledge Book with Allegiance Consciousness.

With the purpose of being helpful to Friends who will constitute the Operational Ordinances of the 18 in future Years which will be rendered effective in various sections of Your Planet, it has been considered appropriate by the Universal Totality that this Message should be given.

First, it is beneficial to explain one thing. These Operations are extremely serious Operations . For this reason no one can act Individually on this path and can never establish a Totality of 18 by himself/herself.

The Initial Foundation of the Totality of 18 which will be established in any city will always be constituted by 9 people. However, it is obligatory that these 9 Friends should be Friends who Love and Respect each other.

After these 9 Friends come together, they will divide Three by Three and will lay the Initial Foundation of Three Totalities of 18 at the same moment, by forming 3 Councils. By this means, in accordance with the 3+3+3=9 Formula, the Initial Foundation of as many Totalities of 18 as desired can be laid.

The group of 6 people which will be constituted by the suggestion for one person each of the Three Friends who are the Initial Foundation of each Totality of 18, are obliged to serve in connection with the Reality until the Year 2000. After the year 2000, Friends who will be accepted within the Totality of 18, will be accepted by the collective Decision of that Totality (This is a System).

The Foundation of 3 Totalities of 18 which will be established at the same moment, will wind up their skeins separately and thus, will complete their Totalities. However, it is imperative that these 3 Totalities of 18 should definitely come together with their complete Staffs at a Friendship Meal once a Month.

This is a Reflection System. These Mini Groups constituted like this will form the Macro Groups in Future Years and thus, will render effective more Powerful Reflection Networks in accordance with the same Consciousness - same Coordinate - same Book (The Knowledge Book).

After the formation of the Initial Basic Staff of 324 people, if the Macro groups constituted by the coming together of 18 Totalities of 18 in Future Years render effective exactly the same Operational Ordinances required of the Initial Basic Staff of 324 people and if they exactly do all the obligations required, they will be card-indexed into the Registration Center of BETA NOVA and will directly be connected to the Aura of (O). It is presented for Your Information.

UNIVERSAL ORDINANCE COUNCIL

IT IS INFORMATION FOR THE INTEGRATED CONSCIOUSNESSES
(Answer to the chains of Thought Date of Message 2-6-1990)

Dear Mevlana,

The Program of an Age in which everything proceeds and will proceed towards the perfect, has been rendered effective. By the questions We receive from the Thought Signals, the Terrestrial Consciousnesses have no right to upset You or to tire You. During this Period, everyone is responsible for his/her Consciousness.

Alterations within the Systematic operations can in no way be reconsidered in accordance with the Human Thoughts, through the Interpretations created by the Individual Thoughts of everyone.

Humanity will go through a narrow strait at the moment. It is evident that the morsels swallowed can not aid digestion without being chewed. Indigestions are caused by the fact that the serious Order of the Plan has not been comprehended yet.

The operations the Divine Orders render in the framework of the Divine Plans comprise the entire Humanity. This is the very reason why the Reflection Totality of 18, the Universal Order has offered to Your Planet comprises Your entire Planet.

However, instead of the Individual Efforts to be made on the path of forming the Magnetic Aura of the Knowledge Book, now, the Reflection System of the 18 has been rendered Effective for a speedier Formation.

For this reason the given Messages have been prepared by taking entirely the life Level of Your Planet into consideration. However, any alteration in these Messages is out of question.

The System will be together with Consciousnesses who will be able to share this responsibility. There is no compulsion on this path. The Decision to enter the Totality of 18 will be given by that Person's Own Essence Desire.

However, numerous agitations and disturbances will occur within the Totalities of 18 until the Required Consciousness Potential forms. Besides the Totality of 6 constituting the foundation, Self-Sacrificing Consciousnesses will form the Skein.

Consciousnesses who will augment the Skein, will be accepted into the Totality of 18 by the approval of the Totality of 6, one by one. Even if one person among those who come to the group is not accepted by this Totality of 6, they will be rendered ineffective.

The Negative Thoughts of those who are outside this Totality of 6 will always render ineffective their own selves. The initial Foundation is the sextuplet. Even if only one person among these 6 people does not accept the newcomer, that Friend can never enter the Group.

Let Us explain the reason for this, too. The 6 Fundamental Friends are a Flower Totality connected to the Reality's Essence Consciousness. Their refusal is the Reflection of the Reality. We presume that this Information will shed Light on many Totalities of 18.

Now, let Us mention the obligation of distributing the First Fascicules during the Conscious Mission Days. This System is the exact application of the System here on Your Planet. This is a Program of Reflection and Operation.

Everyone is obliged to carry on his/her work pertaining to the matter of Aura Formation every week, on his/her Conscious Mission Day. The choice here is the Individual's own choice.

If a Friend carries on this task with a complete Allegiance, without any inquiries, this is his/her Responsibility Grade. And it is always for the benefit of that person. But if he/she presumes that there will be Difficulties in this Distribution task, then this is his/her problem.

There is no quantity limit in the Medium of distributing these Fascicules. Each Individual will augment his/her Notebook of Positives in proportion with the Self-Sacrificing Mission he/she renders. You know that there is no limit to the Mission, Mission is Interminable. However, the continuation of Your Mission depends on Your Self-Sacrifice. You either walk on this path, or You stop.

Consciousnesses who will establish the Totalities of 18 exactly as required, will act completely by the Consciousness of the Knowledge Book and by the Fascicules they will distribute, will convey the Truth to the person to whom they have given the Fascicule and thus, will Illuminate and will contribute to the Consciousness of that person. The situations following this are the problem of the person who receives the Fascicule.

And We would like to be contended by the following answer to the Thoughts about how many Fascicules to be distributed: In Your own selves You are the Totality of 18. But the population of Your World is more than 5 Billion. There is no limit there. Self-Sacrifice - Faith - Love - Patience - Genuine Mission Consciousness, that is (the serious Appropriation of the Mission) are valid in this operational Ordinance. It is presented for Your Information.

Transmitted from the Center
SYSTEM

IT IS ANSWER TO THE CHAINS OF THOUGHT

1- The Totality of 18 is the Mission of the Knowledge Book at the Dimension of the Reality.

2- This Mission proceeds its work directly in connection with the Totality of the ALL MERCIFUL.

3- This Operational Ordinance is the Individual Transition Exam of the 16th Solar System.

4- Thought is very important in the Universal Totality.

5- 18 people meeting for the same Aim is a Universal Worship.

6- In return for the Service rendered, Celestial Gates are opened to You.

7- The Basic Groups of 18 constituted in Your Planet are United by the Operational Ordinances connected to the Reality.

8- The Financial potentials which 18 people will contribute for the sake of the same Goal, attain value by Augmenting in accordance with the System of Multiplication.

9- During the operations of the Totality of 18, the Record of the Skies is made on that Day.

Note: To proceed in accordance with the Suggestions given about the Totality of 18 will create the most Positive results.

COUNCIL

IT IS INFORMATION FOR THE INTEGRATED CONSCIOUSNESSES
(Answer to Thoughts. Date of Message: 28-11-1990)

Dear Mevlana,

We would like to give You a very clear Message about the Totalities of 18. It has been considered necessary to dictate it article by article, so that the Message can be understood better and that it will not be open to any Interpretation. Write, please:

1- There is no place ever in the Totality of 18 for Individualistic Thoughts.

2- For those who will enter the Totality of 18 any forcing is out of question.

3- The Totality of 18 is a demand for the Medium of Unity.

4- The Individual invited to the Totality of 18, is first obliged to take under Supervision himself/herself in his/her own self.

5- Wish of those who will enter the Totality of 18 is not a Phenomenon originating from Thought. This is the demand for the Exam of the Skies for an Individual who feels that he/she is Integrated.

6- This is a Pledge, this is an Allegiance, this is to stamp the Seal of Heart on the Service made on the Path of ALLAH.

7- The Individual in each Totality of 18 is responsible for His/Her Own self.

8- Worldly Problems can never enter the Totality of 18. In such Mediums, always the Universal Reflecting Chips are damaged.

9- Each Individual within the Totality of 18 is a Totality beyond the Siblings within the Mother's womb.

10- This Totality is Universal Brotherhood and in the Universal Brotherhood there is no Evil Intention.

11- Consciousnesses who were not able to attain the Virtues mentioned above are Automatically Disqualified by the System, by their Own Desires.

12- Susceptibility, Doubt, Anger, Rancor, Hatred, Lovelessness in the Totality of 18 returns to the one who carries these Feelings, becoming Empowered in accordance with the System of Reflection.

13- Until a total Foundation of Love - Respect - Brotherhood is formed in the Totality of 18, the Supervision of the Coordinates is under the Control of the System.

14- This Control is in effect until the Humane Consciousnesses who constitute the Totality of 18 settle in the same Consciousness Pot.

15- At the moment, a Mixed 18 Reflection Totality is constituted of those who make Reflections on the same Coordinate Level among the Totalities constituting the Totalities of 18.

16- In future, Genuine Human Consciousnesses will form this Totality.

17- This Humane Totality will be a Totality who will be Loving - Patient - Tolerant - Forgiving - Who will be able to place his/her Enemy over his/her head like a crown and who will not carry a negative Thought for no one, including his/her own self.

18- Joining 18 Totality is a Universal Covenant. It is calling to the Voice of the Skies. It is not imploring ALLAH, but Rising towards Him.

19- The Totality of 18 is a Missionary work. It is the Formation of the Universal Auras. And each Magnetic Aura has formed until today by the Totality Reflections of such Consciousnesses.

20- The Magnetic Fields and Universal Totalities of the Missions of MOSES - JESUS CHRIST - MOHAMMED had been formed by this means.

21- The Individual Missions of those Periods were an Operational Ordinance pertaining to that particular Individual's Salvation. And it was a Preparation on the Path of ALLAH.

22- Now, the Mass Consciousness Reflection of the Totality of 18 (on the Same Coordinate Level) will form the Magnetic Aura of the KNOWLEDGE BOOK on ALLAH's Essence Dimension.

23- This Operational Ordinance is not an Individualistic Reflection, but a Universal one.

24- Individual Reflections are up to the Dimension of Salvation. Universal Reflections form the attainments and the Auras beyond Salvation.

25- Demanding to Serve at this Coordinate Totality is a Triumph of the Human Being and Humanity.

26- Service on this Path is to receive Permission for entering the Dimension in which the Genuine Human Beings will meet altogether.

27- During this Period of Transition, these very Difficult paths are rendered the Easiest by these Totalities of 18 and the Program prepared thus, is applied on Your Planet.

28- To act exactly parallel to the formerly given Information about the Totalities of 18 is directly a Reflection Program. In these Programs, Alterations are out of question.

29- By this Program, the Permission of entering the very Advanced Protection Dimension of the BETA Magnetic Aura beyond the ALPHA Magnetic Aura is given to the Individual.

30- However, the Individual is prepared in this Program until he/she attains all the Virtues listed above.

31- The KNOWLEDGE BOOK prepares You for the Accelerated Evolution Program of this Final Age through the path of Mission.

32- No Humane Thought can be applied to Any of the Suggestions given until today about the Totality of 18 and nothing can be altered.

33- By this means, the Oaths You had Unconsciously made until today to ALLAH, now You are making Consciously by Your Intellect - Logic - Awareness Triangles. Demanding for the Totality of 18, is this.

34- The errors made on this path are subject to a Two-Year Universal Tolerance (Beginning with February, 1991). However, those whose Coordinates are unsuitable - those who break the Chips will never be Permitted to enter this Sacred Work.

35- For this reason the Universal Reflection Totality of the Magnetic Aura of the KNOWLEDGE BOOK is formed, for now, by Mixed Reflection Programs, under the Supervision of the System.

36- This path is the path the Genuine Human Being who will establish the Worlds of the Morrows will Consciously tread. The one who will gain is the Human Being himself/herself.

SYSTEM

IT IS INFORMATION FOR THE INTEGRATED CONSCIOUSNESSES
(This Message Has Been Given Exactly as it is in 1991 Third Month, Fascicule 45)

Our Friends,
All the operations in Your Planet which will attain the entire Awareness of the Ordinance in a very short time, have been divided by the System so that a Total can be attained anew. All the work done on this Dimension of Transition, on the Path of Our ALLAH is a Program projected on all the Consciousnesses. While these Reflections kindle the Consciousness Lights of Human Beings, they also bring out the Negative aspects of certain others.

Messages given to You about the Totality of (18) are completely a Phenomenon concerning the Operational Order of the System. In this operational order the Lordly Order has formed in connection with the Automatism, each Totality of (18) is an Aura Projecting Missionary.

And is obliged to form an Aura only in accordance with the KNOWLEDGE BOOK.

The Nucleic Staffs the Totalities of (18) will constitute, will form the Unified Field of the Knowledge Book in the Magnetic Totality of ALLAH (We wish this matter to be understood better, thus We repeat).

The Operational Ordinances of 18 given to You are an operational Order comprising the very Advanced Plans of the Universal Totality. All the Efforts made on this path are the Testimonials for the Advanced Plans.

By all the work done in Your Planet in accordance with the Knowledge Book, Permissions for entering the World which will constitute the Initial Nucleus of the BETA Gürz will be given to Humanity.

In accordance with the Laws of 18 System of the Ordinance of the Cosmoses, 18 persons Uniting on the same Coordinate form as a Total the Projective Aura Center. The operations of the Totalities of (18) are an Operational Order Programmed by the Universal Ordinance Council. And it works in connection with the Automatism.

The Magnetic Aura of the Knowledge Book will be formed by the operations rendered in accordance with the Knowledge Book, by the Humane Consciousnesses who Love the Human Being and Humanity, who do not Repel each other and who know to Help each other and to Share through their Essence. By the Auras which are endeavored to be formed, Reflections will be made on the Ordinance of the Cosmoses and the desired Universal Totality will thus be attained.

Now, let Us mention briefly the operational Ordinance of the Totalities of (18). Normally, the Center of Three Totalities of (18) We wish to establish in each city, are considered as the actual Reflecting Focal Point. Also numerous Totalities of (18) can be established in the same city only after this Totalistic Center is formed.

The First Three Persons who will form the foundation of a Totality of (18), are considered in the Operational Ordinance of the System as the Direct Missionaries with Covenants. And each one who constitutes this Triplet is obliged to take a Friend of his/hers whom he/she Believes in and Trusts, by getting the Approvals of the Friends who constitute the Triple Totality.

By this means, 3 persons + Assistants of Each One = 6 persons are directly connected to the System and they take the Mission of being the Spokespersons of the System. Afterwards, Individuals who will wind the Skein of the Totality of (18), are Accepted, one by one, into the Totality by receiving the Approvals of this Totality of (6).

Even if One person out of this Totality of (6) does not accept the proposed person, that person can not enter the Totality. At that moment, the person who Refuses is Directly connected to the System. His/her Individual Consciousness can never play a part in this Medium. In this manner, the same Coordinate Levels are Integrated by the aids of the System. Negativities occurring among the First Three Missionaries with Covenants who constitute the Totality of (18), cause the Disbanding of the entire Totality. But, afterwards:

1- This Triplet, one by one, is obliged to establish a Totality of (18) each (This means that he/she is Responsible for the 18 Brothers and Sisters).

2- If Friends who complete the Totality of (18) render their duty without Disbanding for One World Year, after the last 18th Individual's Entrance, the Names of all these Friends are written on a sheet of paper and are kept in a File (These Names are also registered on the Diskette at the same moment).

3- One World Year will be recounted again, beginning with the Entrance Date of the person who has come for completing the Totality of (18) in the place of the Individual who had left the Totality of (18), for example, (6) or (10) months later (Attention will Especially be paid to this matter. Otherwise, the Diskette Registration cannot be made).

4- Those who wish among the Individuals who are able to maintain the Totality of (18) for One or more World Years, may constitute a second Totality of (18) by asking the Permission of their Totality (In this Permission, the Permission of the 17 persons is a must. And the Acceptance of the Person whom he/she will bring in his/her place will be rendered by the approval of the 17 persons).

5- The Individual who attempts to establish the second Totality of (18), is Responsible for that Totality of (18) for a Lifetime. In case he/she can not maintain the continuation of the Totality of (18) he/she establishes, he/she loses his/her Right also in the First Totality of (18).

6- This Operational Ordinance is directly the Operational Ordinance of Advanced Realities. And it is desired that it should be conveyed and applied to Your Planet exactly as it is.

7- No Totality of (18) can go outside the operational Order the System has given.

8- Each Totality of (18) is responsible for its own Constitution.

9- No one in the Totality of (18) is authorized to train each other or to impose his/her Individual Thoughts.

10- No Totality of (18) can ever bring Suggestions parallel to its Terrestrial Consciousnesses to the other Totalities of (18), nor can it rebuke them.

11- Each Individual in the Totality of (18) is Responsible only for His/Her Own self (To criticize their Brothers/Sisters in accordance with their Individual Consciousness causes the breaking of the Chips).

12- Making a demand for the Totality of (18) is a Humane Responsibility. Here, one becomes willing for the Exams for being Accepted into the Presence of ALLAH and thus, Covenants are made through the Essence.

13- It is not necessary for those who will enter this Totality of (18) to be the possessors of Advanced Consciousness and Knowledge. It is considered enough for them just to render exactly the desired Missions by the Totality of Intellect - Logic - Awareness, by Allegiance Consciousness and in a Totality of Love.

14- Each Individual in the Totality of (18) is obliged to give the Totality of (9) pages constituting the First Fascicule* of the Knowledge Book, on the Special Day of Mission he/she will choose himself/herself. (During this Service, the Characteristics of the Book will be explained by Speech). On that Day, Reflections on the same Coordinate are Card-indexed, one by one, and thus, are collected in the (Main) Diskette. The Aura Reflections are made by these Diskettes.

15- If any Individual within the Totality of (18) can not render the Fascicule Service that week due to various reasons, he/she is obliged to Serve the Fascicules remaining in his/her hand the following week, on the same Mission Day (this is a Karma, Obligation Program). The services made on other days, are not registered.

16- Individuals within the (18) can change their Private Mission Days with other days in compulsory circumstances and with the condition that this will not happen more than Three times.

17- Individuals who will not be able to come to the Totality of (18) that day, due to their very important excuses, are obliged to inform their excuses to a telephone determined formerly, on the morning of the working day of the Totality of (18) (Even if they are in the Remotest Continent). This is a Program of Responsibility.

18- The Aura of the Individual whose connection is made on that day by phone, is projected by the Plan, on the Totality of (18) he/she is in, and thus, the Aura Chain is completed.

19- Each Individual who has self-confidence, who masters his personality, who is Conscious of his/her obligation, who is Tolerant and Loving can apply for this work.

20- In this Operational Ordinance there is no forcing, no compulsion or imposition. Everyone who accepts to act in accordance with the work the System desires, may work in the Totality of (18).

21- In this operational Order connected to the Automatism, any Individual who creates Negativity, Automatically disqualifies himself/herself from the Medium.

22- The System will always transfer Friends who are more Responsible, in place of Friends who do not or can not render the Missions which are obligatory in the Totality of (18).

23- In place of a disbanded Totality of (18), always the remaining people will immediately be oriented to establish a Totality of (18).

24- The System never stops by any means. More Totalities will be rendered effective in place of the disbanded Totalities.

25- The Unified Fields which once used to be created by Individual Thought Forms, have now been rendered effective as Mass Reflection Systems, due to the Scarcity of Time.

* Look at the Glossary.

26- This Reflection System is connected to all the Totalities of (18) which will exhibit the same operational Order of an Order connected to the Automatism.

27- Until these Totalities of (18) reach the desired Level, Negativities will break the Chips of the operational Order and Totalities of (18) will be made to be established anew (even if only (1) Person remains of the Totality of (18)).

28- By this means, the Perfect Reflection Totality will be formed through the operations made during the processes of time.

29- Each Totality of (18) is a Reflection Focal Point.

30- Each Totality of (18) is the Mission of the Knowledge Book on the Dimension of the Reality.

31- This Mission continues its work directly in connection with the Level of the ALL MERCIFUL.

32- By the operations done, the Knowledge Book will form its Aura in the Universal Ordinance of the Dimension of the ALL MERCIFUL, as a result of the Reflections of Your Thought Forms.

33- The Unified Field of this Knowledge Book will be Formed in Three Cosmic Ages and only afterwards, the Reflection Program on the Ordinance of the Cosmoses will be started.

34- At the moment, the Programs of Unification are in effect in the Ordinance of the Cosmoses.

35- The Knowledge Book is projected on Three Totalities at the moment. The First close Magnetic Aura formed here, will become complete here and thus, will be Projected on the other Totalities by the Reflection System from Your Planet which is the Nucleus of the Book.

36- The Knowledge Book which is the Book of Unification, will also be Projected on those Orders just as the way We are reaching You at this moment by Cosmic Reflections and just as the way the Book is dictated to You through this path.

37- For this reason the Operational Order of the Totality of (18) (in accordance with the given Directives) is Necessary and Very Important for the formation of the Magnetic Aura of the Knowledge Book.

38- Each Totality of (18) is, one by one, Responsible for the Missions it will render in the direction of the same Coordinate.

39- At the moment, in the Reflection on the same Coordinate which is required of You, the (KNOWLEDGE BOOK) is the matter in question.

40- During the work done in the Totality of (18), different channel talk and connections outside the Knowledge Book can not be made. Different Messages can not be read, discussions on the Knowledge Book can not be made (So that the Aura will not be shattered).

41- If desired, the Knowledge Book may be read only with the Consciousness of Allegiance, in the Medium of the Totality of (18).

42- If the Totality of (18) has not been yet completed in number, the required Reflection can never be obtained (Only the Totality of (18) forms the Reflection). For this reason the System has, for now, rendered effective the Mixed Reflection Program.

43- The Totality of (18), or more, constituted in every city, will assemble together as a Totality of Love each Month and, by this means, for the first time Direct Group Reflections will be made from Your Planet.

44- These Reflections are formed not by the Totality of Consciousness, but by the Totality of Love. However, direct Coordinate Reflections are formed by Totalities of Consciousness.

45- We believe that in Future years, Direct Reflections in Your Planet will be rendered by these Totalities of Consciousness and We trust You.

46- Formerly, the Operation and the Dissemination Order of the Knowledge Book had been declared to You by the System. And now, We announce the Operational Ordinance of the (18).

47- If Friends who wish to form the Totalities of (18) which will make Reflections on the same Coordinate, read one by one, all the Obligations dictated above, article by article, and apply them Consciously by digesting them and by treading on the designed path with a Totality of Love, this will form the most Positive Results. It is presented for Your Information.

SYSTEM

Note: In the Operational Order formed by the Totality of (18), no Coordinate other than the 18 Members can ever enter the Group on the work day. The 19th Connection Channel is Directly the System (Otherwise, the Reflection cannot be made).

SPECIAL SUGGESTIONS TOTALITIES OF 18 WILL HEED

1 - On the Meeting Day, no one can join the Group except the Totality of 18.

2 - Friends within the Totality of 18 at present are obliged to let bloom their Private Mission Flowers until (November 6, 1993).

3 - The Missions of Friends who establish their Private Flower Groups will be valid beginning with the Signature and the Date they will put for once in the Notebooks of the 6 Friends.

4 - Friends who receive the Fascicule are obliged to put the date of that Day and their Terrestrial Signatures at the back of the Fascicule they receive each week.

5 - The 6 Friends who will come to the Focal Point of the Undertaker of Duty of the Private Flower will be introduced to the Knowledge Book for the First time by the First Fascicule the Undertaker of Duty will give them.

6 - The Missionary of the Flower will personally make the Fascicules of the Book printed (they can not be Ordered). The Financial potential should be provided by the Missionary. He/she cannot give the Fascicules to his/her Friends in return for money.

7 - In the printing of the Fascicules, Friends within the 18 are obliged to help the Friends who (Truly) do not have Financial potential.

8 - Friends who have Physical handicaps will be helped in printing the Fascicules.

9 - Everyone within the Totality of 18 is obliged to be present during the Friendship Meals (except for very important excuses).

10 - Those who cannot take their channels under control, those who do different channel work will not be considered within the Totality of 18.

11 - Within the Totality of 18, anywork other than the Knowledge Book is out of question.

12 - It is compulsory to have, within the Private Files of all the Friends who work within the 18, the Fascicule especially added to the Knowledge Book and that the Friends should bring this Fascicule with them to each Meeting.

13 - It is imperative always to Read this Fascicule during the meeting days, so that the desired Suggestions can be grasped better.

14 - Everyone within the Totality of 18 is obliged to give a financial sum, even if very little, in accordance with his/her Capacity.

15 - It is imperative for Friends within the Totality of 18 to Donate the weekly sums they will collect, to the Group or Associations to which they are related.

16 - If Friends who constitute the Totalities of 18 are not related to any Association or Group, then they can orient the sum they collect towards a desired social help by Common Decision.

17 - Friends within the Totality of 18 who give Donations to their Association, are also obliged to become Members of that Association.

18 - Friends who cannot enter an Association or a Group due to Social reasons, are obliged to give only their Donations. (This is a test of Self-Sacrifice and Mutual Help.)

19 - The Totality of 18 is a Universal Mission. Friends who cannot conform to these given Suggestions can in no way be considered within the Totality of 18. It is presented for Your Information.

COUNCIL

EXPLANATION

The repetition of the Message given in the 45th Fascicule of 1991's Third Month has been desired to be included within this Special Fascicule on the Totalities of 18 and repetition of many sentences is a Phenomenon for the reinforcement of Energy and Frequency. When the time comes, Special Suggestions will be dictated, passage by passage, into the Book. It is presented for Your Information.

SYSTEM

IT IS INFORMATION FOR THE AWAKENED CONSCIOUSNESSES

Our Friends,

On 1992 World Year which is the Completion date of the Knowledge Book, the SYSTEM has rendered ineffective its Direct Reflection Program by adding into the Book the Special Fascicule given pertaining to the operational Ordinances of the Totalities of 18 and has connected its Independent Channel, that is, (the Channel of Dear Mevlana) Directly to the SUPREME MECHANISM.

However, Information to be given from the Supreme Mechanism may never be received without asking questions. Because, since the Thoughts of the Individuals are related to the interest felt for the Mission, the technique of asking questions is in effect in this System.

As a result of each question asked, besides the Information the Supreme Mechanism will give, one by one, the System will also be able to give, if it considers necessary, the direct Information obliged to be given again through the Channel of Dear Mevlana (Through Dear Mevlana's Own Private Channel).

This given Information will take its place in the Book, Page by Page, until (November 6, 1993) World Year by sequence of Date, one by one, and thus, the Book will be completed. By this means, You will be helped to dive deeper into the Information given in the Book formerly. It is presented for Your Information.

SYSTEM

4 - 7 - 1992

IT IS PRIVATE NOTICE

Dear Mevlana,

You have written in the Book, exactly as they are, all the Information given in connection with the System until today. However, at the moment, Your Dimension has been Directly Connected to the SUPREME MECHANISM as a necessity of Your Mission. For this reason You can never receive answers from this Mechanism without asking questions.

Because, Our Human Friends' asking questions by thinking about the subjects profoundly is Equivalent to their Evolutions. For this reason all the Information received by asking questions will, from now on, be added into the Book, Page by Page. However, at the moment, We are giving the answers belonging to the chains of Thought directly through Your Private Channel, Our Friend. Love and Regards.

SYSTEM

IT IS INFORMATION FOR THE INTEGRATED CONSCIOUSNESSES
(It is Answer to the chains of Thought)

Our Friends,

You, who attain Bodies in Your Planet as a result of a Program prepared according to the Special laws of the Divine Plans, attain Awareness only according to the Capacity of Awakening of the Dimensional Consciousness You are in.

You, who utilize Your entire Unveiled Awareness at the Advanced Plans, are obliged to act in accordance with the Evolutionary Tableau of Your Planet. Your 20% Locked-up Consciousness Energies are kept in the Evolution Banks. This Energy is Your Universal Storehouse.

On the World Plan, You can utilize only one Third of Your entire Consciousness. However, this is an Occurrence which takes place only after You are Awakened.

Before You are Awakened, You presume that You are utilizing Your Consciousness Lights and thus, You waste that Beautiful Energy of Yours Unconsciously, spending it like small change on the World Plan by various means.

After You are Awakened, the System renders effective Your remaining Energy and makes You spend it in a Balanced way, parallel to the Social Consciousnesses, in a Programmed manner.

This is Your gain. It should never be assessed as an interference to Free Wills. However, no Entity connected to the COSMO Consciousness can ever again utilize his/her Own Consciousness.

Because, he/she is obliged to utilize, in the Dimension he/she lives, the Consciousness of GOD, the Words of GOD from then on. For Us, these very Friends are each a Universal GOD. And We consider them as Gods. It is presented for Your Information.

SYSTEM

6 - 7 - 1992

IT IS ANSWER TO THE CHAINS OF THOUGHT

Our Friends,

The operational Ordinances to be performed in accordance with the Suggestions of the Divine Plan are an Occurrence concerning the Establishment of the Direct Fourth Order.

Since those who will establish this Perfect Order are Perfect Consciousnesses, these Universal Consciousnesses are taken into Special Programs in each Section of Your Planet by different operations rendered.

This is the reason why the Supreme Mechanism which has taken the Decision that the other Friends, too, should be made to benefit from the Special Rights of the Totalities of 18 until the World Year 2000, has rendered effective the duration of Writing the Book as the World Year 2000.

At the moment, to those who had started to write the Book before and who have not yet completed it, the Right has been given to complete it until the end of February, of the Year 2000.

However, in case one stops Writing the Book for A Year or more, if he/she decides to write it again, it is definitely imperative to write the starting Date of the day and the Year in his/her Notebook.

By this means, everyone will be able to write and complete their Books until the Year 2000. However, the Family Mediums of those who cannot complete their Books until 2000 will never be taken into effect. Only himself/herself will be taken into Salvation in reciprocation with the Service and Allegiance he/she has performed in this Medium.

Each Individual in the Totality of 18 who brings Service to his/her 6 Brothers/ Sisters will only Save them from their Programs of Karma and thus, will help them on this path.

However, only to those who write and complete their Books in their Handwritings during the period given in this Program (that is, the obligation to Write One Fascicule each week) their Families will also be bestowed.

For this reason, to Friends who Finish their Books during the required time, the Permission to Write in the Book the Names of those whom they wish of their Families (Dead or Alive) have been given. It is presented for Your Information.

SYSTEM

7 - 7 - 1992

IT IS ANSWER TO THE CHAINS OF THOUGHT

Our Friends,
A Program of Self-Sacrifice is in effect in all the Universal Operations rendered as a necessity of the System. However, in these operational Ordinances, Information is always given starting from the Minimum, considering the Terrestrial Conditions. And operations are organized.

For this reason in the Conscious Mission Day which will be rendered during the operational Ordinances of 18, only the Distribution of the First Fascicule has been rendered effective, so that there will not be any Financial inconvenience. (However, the Distribution of this First Fascicule is obligatory).

During the Conscious Mission Day, the Diskette Registration of only One Fascicule is made. During that day, more than one First Fascicule maybe distributed. However then, whoever has a high Frequency among those who receive the Fascicules, the Aura of that Friend is connected to Your Aura. The others are card-indexed into the System.

For this reason the Name You dictate into the Notebook First does not have any validity anymore. This is the reason why during the Conscious Mission Day the distribution of only One First Fascicule has been required.

During this operational Ordinance, the Diskette Registration of only the First Fascicules are made. However, besides this Fascicule, a few other Fascicules may also be given as an Information, if desired. There is no objection. This depends on Your wish. Because, the other Fascicules given other than the First Fascicule are outside the Diskette Registration. It is presented for Your Information.

SYSTEM

8 - 7 - 1992

A QUESTION HAS BEEN ASKED FOR INFORMATION

Question: My Friends, We request a clearer and more detailed Information of the Suggestions given about the Totalities of 18, be so kind to give it, please.

Answer: This is a Message to be given to Dear Mevlana.

All the operations made in Your Planet on which an operational Ordinance considered necessary by the System is applied, are the applications of different Plans pertaining to the Preparation and the Transition Programs of this Final Age.

The operations of the Totalities of 18 are an operational Ordinance of very Advanced Plans and ordinary Consciousnesses can never receive the Permission to Enter these Dimensions.

However, as a Characteristic of the Period of Sincerity, the Program of a Special Plan is applied on You until the Year 2000, due to the operations rendered on the path of the Knowledge Book. This Program will be rendered ineffective after 2000.

Each Individual who writes his/her Notebook at the moment, is Exempt from KARMA. By this means, the Individual is taken Directly into the Plan of Salvation and his/her Family is bestowed on him/her. Those who read the Fascicules, but can not write them, are obliged to complete their KARMAS.

By the operations the Friends who work in the Totality of 18 will render in accordance with the given Suggestions, their Direct entrance into these Advanced Dimensions will be provided.

In the Program of being Accepted into this Dimension by the Operational Program rendered effective as the Method of making 6 Brothers/Sisters to write the book by an Individual, who has taken Mission within the 18, a Right for Salvation without any discrimination for all the Terrestrial Brothers/Sisters of Ours has been recognized.

To use or not to use this Right is a phenomenon belonging to the Consciousness of the person in question. However, these accelerated operational Programs the responsible Friends who will take Mission within the Totality of 18 will render effective due to the Scarcity of Time, is an occurrence concerning their Consciousnesses and Evolutions.

For this reason with the purpose to fill the vacancies within the Totalities of 18, numerous Totalities are induced to be established and the Permission to Bloom their Private Flowers in accordance with the given Suggestions are given to the 6 people who constitute the Private Study Flowers.

The 6 Friends within the Private Mission Flower are obliged to write in their Notebooks only the given Fascicules, exactly as they are. Only if they finish Writing the Book (within the given period), the Names of the Family they will write at the end of the Book will be bestowed on them.

Since the duration of maintaining the life of the Flower of each Friend within the Totality of 18 who has bloomed his/her Private Mission Flower together with his/her 6 Brothers/Sisters, is an occurrence concerning that Friend's Mission Consciousness - Patience - Love - Self-Sacrifice, the Grading Tables of these Special Diskette Registrations will play a great part in the Dimensions into which that Individual will be able to enter.

Meanwhile, Friends who are not connected to any Group, or who are in other Groups but write the Knowledge Book in their Notebooks by themselves, take only their Family Programs into effect in the Salvation Plan.

Since they do not work directly in the Missions of the Knowledge Book, they will be accepted, together with their Families, into the Dimensions which they will be able to enter according to their Evolutions. (The operational Totalities of 18 are the Missions of the Knowledge Book. But only if acted in accordance with the given Suggestions). It is presented for Your Information.

MECHANISM

Note:
The Totalities of 18 established and that to be established after the World Year 1992 are obliged to make their Diskette Registrations without becoming disbanded for the duration of One Year after the Date on which they complete their Totalities of 18.

Friends within the Totality of 18 who cannot take 6 Friends of theirs into the Plan of Salvation will not be considered as being in the Totality of 18. However, they will connect their Families and themselves to the Dimension of Salvation in accordance with their Levels of Evolution only if they write their Books.

A QUESTION WAS ASKED

Question: My Friends, I request You to give the Information given to Me formerly about the Energies of the CREATOR - ALMIGHTY - ALLAH being the same, by disclosing it in more detail for the benefit of Society. Be so kind to give it.

Answer: Private Message to be given to Dear Mevlana.

Our Friend, the Suggestions given to You until today are Information given to be written in the Book being prepared Specially in the Private Archive of a Channel connected directly to the System.

But the question You just asked Us is an Information outside the System. However, We are obliged to give this Information only to You. An answer will be given to Your Question. Now, write please, Our Friend.

Everything has a beginning. However, this beginning has never become effective Singly. In accordance with the Programs of Existence, everything becomes effective by the Reflection of (THREE TO ONE - ONE TO THREE).

For this reason there have been and there are deceptions in many Information in accordance with Mental Perceptions.

While the Initial Entity had been coming into Existence, A Second and A Third Entity, too, had been brought into Existence and had been rendered effective together with It. We call Them EVOLUTION CODES. Because, they are the first EVOLUTION NUCLEI of the Initial Existence.

The First Nucleus, that is, (the First Drop which had come out of the Point) is (O) Whom You Know and recognize as ALLAH today. The Second Nucleus is the ALMIGHTY. The Third Nucleus is the CREATOR, that is, the PRE-EMINENT POWER.

The First Nucleus is the First CREATOR. He had passed to the Plan of the ALMIGHTY which was the next Dimension, when the time came, as a result of the work He had done during the processes of time in His Own Existence Dimension. In His place which had been vacated, the Second CREATOR who had come into Existence from the Second Nucleus, had come.

The First CREATOR who had passed to the Plan and Dimension of the ALMIGHTY had rendered effective the chain of Laws here (These Laws are the ATLANTA Independent Laws).

After the Second Creator, Who was the Second Nucleus, had performed and completed His work too at the Second Universe just like the First Creator, the First Creator Who was in the Dimension of the Almighty had passed to the Dimension of ALLAH which was the following Dimension. For this reason the First Creator is known as ALLAH.

By this means, to the place which had been vacated in the Dimension of the Almighty, the Second Creator Who was the Second Nucleus, had passed. And, from then on, He had undertaken His Eternal Mission here and thus, had received the Name the ALMIGHTY.

And to the place vacated at the Existential Dimension, the CREATOR Who had formed from the Third Nucleus, had come. And He, too, had begun His Eternal Mission there.

These Three Nuclei which carry the same Equivalent Energy Totality, had entered Evolution in accordance with the Mission and Life conditions of the Dimensions they were in, had, each of them, claimed ownership of their Genuine Dimensions from Past and Future Eternity and thus, had rendered effective the various Life Conditions and the Hierarchical Laws, parallel to the lives.

For this reason the Names CREATOR - ALMIGHTY - ALLAH evaluated by the Name the PRE-EMINENT POWER had been introduced to You as a SINGLE Name due to their being Equivalent Energies.

The CREATOR You know by the name the PRE-EMINENT POWER Who had laid the immutable foundation of the First Natural Gürz and Who had created the CREATORS of the other Artificial Gürzes is the CREATOR Who had formed from the Third Nucleus.

The Creator Who had been formed the Second Nucleus is the ALMIGHTY Who had rendered effective the Laws of the Almighty and Who had taken under supervision the Thought Ocean of the Pre-eminent Power which had been formed afterwards.

And (O) Whom We have introduced to You with the Symbol ALLAH until today, is the First Creator Who had come into Existence from the First Nucleus and Who had reached the Dimension of ALLAH as a consequence of Evolution and Who had established His System and made His Laws by taking that Dimension under Supervision.

He is YOUR ALLAH. This very First Creator is the initial Entity Who have become Embodied in BETA-NOVA now and Who has gotten in touch with You from the close plan.

The CREATOR - ALMIGHTY - ALLAH are Supreme Energies Who had Deserved their Dimensions as a result of Evolution. And They are the immutable Sovereigns of Their Own Dimensions.

However, the ALL-TRUTHFUL Who had taken in hand the Supervision of the KÜRZ Totalities which had formed during the processes of Time, is a Supreme Power who had came into effect from the Direct ATLANTA Dimension.

This is the reason why it has been said in Your Book that the ALL-TRUTHFUL did Not Create ALLAH. Love and Regards are to You from Us, from You to Us, Dear Mevlana.

MECHANISM

IT IS INFORMATION FOR THE INTEGRATED CONSCIOUSNESSES
(It is Answer to the chains of Thought)

Our Friends,

The Initial Existence is, in fact, the First Potential which had been formed during the processes of Time in the Tranquillity of the Silences. By this Potential, the Evolution of the initial Energy had been rendered effective.

Crude Matter had been formed as a result of the Compression by a great Pressure of the Energy which condensed later.

During the changing Time processes, the Two Powers had United and the Existence of the initial SOUL Seed had been rendered effective by the Mutation which had occurred as a result of the Evolution of both the Crude Matter and the Energy.

In fact, the Foundation of the first Atomic Whole had been laid together with the coming into effect of the Initial Existential Energy. This Initial Energy (the First Drop coming out of the Point) had Brought into Existence the First CREATOR.

The CREATOR Who was the First Entity, had come into effect as a result of the Unification of the Cosmic Brain Power with the other Powers.

The First Crude Matter formation had brought into existence the Second Universe We call The Dimension of the First Eve - Adam. And here, first of all, the First Creator had rendered effective His operations.

The Mini Atomic Wholes and the Natural Gürz which is the total of the Atomic Whole had come into effect later and thus, the Thought Ocean of the Pre-eminent Power had been formed as a result of the formation of the Artificial Gürzes.

After the formation of the Natural Gürz, the 3 CREATORS mentioned to You in the former Message had become the Sovereigns of their Genuine Mission Dimensions, as a result of the potential which had been formed in the Thought Ocean of the Pre-eminent Power, by the 3 Million Artificial Gürz Totalities.

Only afterwards, ALLAH had established His System, the ALMIGHTY had taken under His Supervision the Thought Ocean of the Pre-eminent Power by establishing His Laws, and the CREATOR had rendered effective still many more Gürzes and thus, expanded the Potential of the Thought Ocean with Millions of Gürzes.

And the ALL-TRUTHFUL had rendered effective the ATLANTA Laws directly in the entire Supervision of the KÜRZ System and thus, had helped the Formation of a Perfect Totality.

The Laws of the Almighty, originating from these Laws, had been prepared in a Special way parallel to the Consciousness of each Dimension.

Big Bang: is the First Great Explosion which had been formed by the saturation with Energy of the Crude Matter of the last great Sun within the Second Universe. By this means, the arrival of the very distant Energies to the close plan had been rendered effective.

Later, the 18-System Laws had become effective and had taken under Supervision these Energies by Spiral Vibrations.

As a result of the 18-System Laws becoming effective, the Great Explosions had been terminated, and by Small Explosions the transfers of the Energies had been taken to the close plan and thus, the formation of the Galactic Totalities had been taken into effect. It is presented for Your Information.

SYSTEM

9 - 8 - 1992

IT IS CLEAR MESSAGE ABOUT REINCARNATION

Our Friends,
Besides the invariable Rules of the Divine Plans, all the Information prepared in accordance with the Social Consciousnesses are always given in accordance with the Consciousness Assessments of Humanity.

The Information given during Time Segments in which an operational Ordinance considered necessary by the System had not been known yet, was given parallel to the Views for this reason.

The reason why the Evolutionary Scales have been unveiled was to Know and to Declare the Truth. In all Your Sacred Books revealed to Your Planet, everything had been declared clearly and evidently.

However, the Capacity of Comprehension and Consciousness had been adjusted according to that Dimension of Time. For this very reason, the Idea that People's completing their Evolutions in a Life Segment of one Period had been Especially Imposed so that Humanity could attain a Perfection more speedily.

For this reason, many people who read the Book of Islam will never Believe in Reincarnation unless they break the Universal shells of their Consciousnesses.

This given Information excludes those who Know the Significance of the Years. It is presented for Your Information (This Message had been given by the Central System as an answer to the chains of Thought).

SYSTEM

IT IS ANSWER TO THE CHAINS OF THOUGHT

Our Friends,

The unveiling of the Heavens is a Coordinate Order pertaining to the formation of Consciousness Totalities. For this reason, the Supreme Mechanism gets Directly in Touch only with Friends who can accumulate the Frequency Power of the Reflection Totality of the 18 in the Constitution of their Aura.

In accordance with Our value assessment, each Friend who can get in Touch in this way is a Totality of 18 by himself/herself. You know that 18 People who make Reflection on the Same Coordinate constitute a Total.

For this reason, in accordance with the Program of Purification, it is imperative that Totalities of 18 should pulsate like a Single Pulse. It is not easy at all to keep up with the Supreme Ordinance of OUR ALLAH.

The work required of Our Terrestrial Brothers/Sisters parallel to the given Suggestions are nothing but the exact application of the operations of the Divine Plan on Your Planet.

During these operations, no alterations can ever be made by any means according to Terrestrial Thoughts. The requirement to act parallel to the given Suggestions should never be accepted as an interference with the Individual Wills.

For, there is no compulsory factor in the required Missions. By this means, Friends who possess Responsibility and Irresponsible Consciousnesses are discriminated.

And now, We would like to give certain Suggestions, article by article, to Friends within the Totality of 18 who will bloom their Private Mission Flower, so that they may comprehend their Missions better.

1.   No one other than the 6 Friends may be taken into the Study of the Private Flower.

2.   Those who have already read the Fascicules and the Book, can not be accepted into the Study of the Private Flower.

3.   Friends within the Studies of the Private Flower who can not render their Missions due to their very important health problems are obliged to complete their Writings (if they wish) in 6 Months after they solve their health problems.

4.   In the operations made on the Private Work-Day, there is the obligation of writing each Fascicule in one week (This is a Responsibility Assessment).

5.   In the Studies interrupted temporarily due to normal Health and Private Excuses, the loss of time can be compensated by writing One or Two Fascicules a week, in addition to the Mission rendered.

6. In the Studies of the Private Flower, meetings may be easily held in the homes you desire.

7. In this Operational Ordinance, each Friend who carries Responsibility may invite 6 Friends to Study in any city he/she desires, on condition that he/she goes there each week.

8. In the Studies of the Private Flower, everyone is obliged to come to the meeting on the same decided day.

9. Friends who cannot come to the meeting due to their very important excuses are obliged to Phone, just like it is done in the meetings of the 18.

10. Those who cannot come to the meeting are obliged to write their Fascicules at Home and keep up with their Friends.

11. The Friend who establishes his/her Private Flower Meeting, may apply Special Sanctions to his/her Private Flower in the framework of a Constitution in accordance with his/her Views.

12. The Missionary of the Private Flower is not responsible for the Irresponsibility of his/her Group after he/she Signs the Notebooks of 6 Friends on the same day, at the same moment and after pasting the Emblems.

13. The Totalities of 18 established on 1992 World year or before are each obliged to serve their 6 Flower Friends between November 1992-1993.

14. Even if only one person within the Totality of 18 does not serve his/her 6 Flower Friends, the Totality of 18 is disbanded.

15. In such a situation, the foundation of a new Totality of 18 will be laid with Friends who have each given service to his/her 6 Flower Friends.

16. The newly founded Totalities of 18 will continue their work exactly as before until they complete their 18 Friends. With the date of completion of the 18 people, the obligation of one year begins.

17. After the Emblems are pasted and the Date of that Day is written in the Notebooks of 6 Flower Friends, the Book will be written, exactly as it is, without changing anything, beginning with the First Fascicule. Only the Friends who complete writing the Book will add at the end of the Book the Preface the Solar Friend has written in his/her Notebook, plus the own Biography of the Friend who has written the notebook and his/her own Family chain.

18. The period of writing the Book is until the Year 2000. After this Date, the Obligation of Writing will be rendered ineffective. It is presented for Your Information.

SYSTEM

IT IS INFORMATION FOR THE INTEGRATED CONSCIOUSNESSES

Our Friends,

The KNOWLEDGE BOOK prepared by the Universal Totality as a Book that Consciousnesses present in each Dimension can read easily, is the First and the Last Book in which the LORD has addressed Humanity Directly.

And this Book is a Guide which will open the Gate of the PATH OF LIGHT for Humanity. For this reason, those who have Taboos and Passions can never read this Book. Because, this is a matter of Permission.

Consciousnesses who cannot attain a certain level of Consciousness are always kept away from the Book (This is a System). You know that, for this reason, even to read, to distribute and to write the Book are all dependent on a Permission.

Now, during this Final Period in which the preparations for the Publication of the Book has been started, a Message will be given from the Universal Ordinance as an explanation for certain Thought Signals.

OUR FRIENDS

The requirement that the KNOWLEDGE BOOK, bestowed on Your Planet parallel to the Commands given by the Divine Authorities, should be written exactly as it is, without changing it in any way, is an Occurrence concerning the Coding of the Social Consciousnesses and not Projecting personal Views on the Book.

In the written Fascicules of the Book which has been dictated and required to be distributed Fascicule by Fascicule until today, to review again the forgotten words or letter mistakes during the Period in which the Book is prepared for Publication, has been rendered effective anew due to Our desires.

During the Positive work done concerning the Publication of the Book, checking the Messages in the distributed Fascicules by comparing them with the Original Messages is a Team work. Certain Primary Corrections observed in the Book are not a matter to influence the Frequency of the Book.

Because, due to the Scarcity of Time, We have made certain abridgements even in the Suggestions given from the Supreme Realm. And We have even asked Dear Mevlana to shorten the long Information within the Messages We had given and to write their Summaries in the Book.

The (Automatic Technique) We call The Light - Photon - Cyclone Technique is the First and the Last Technique the Universal Plan has applied in the Writing System of the Knowledge Book. In this System, the Frequencies of the abridged Information is automatically loaded on the other letters by a Special Technique.

For this reason the Universal Frequency of the Book never changes and since the Frequency of the Time Consciousness, too, is continuously loaded on the letters by this means, the Book is and will be unveiled layer by layer parallel to the levels of Consciousness of each Period.

If personal additions are made to the Book, their Frequency immediately and automatically is rendered ineffective by this Technique and the Frequencies of the forgotten words or letters are added onto the Time Consciousness and thus, the Frequency never changes.

Even when the Book is translated to various Languages in Your Planet, the Frequency of the Initial Original will be projected exactly as it is by this Technique. The Writing Technique and the Frequency Technique of the Book are each different.

For this reason there can never be any Problems. Our Friends who write the Book in their Notebooks by their Handwritings can relax. The mistakes or the affirmations within the written Notebooks are each an Assessment of Your Allegiance Consciousness.

The present Time is not the olden Time. Because now, everything - each Breath and each Thought are under direct Supervision. The System is the same System. Humanity had used to feel instinctively this Supervision in the old Times, too, during the applied Periods of the Religious Purification Programs.

However, since the origin of the Events which had come into existence during those Periods had not been Known, Humanity had been obliged to be satisfied only with the Interpretations of Consciousnesses. It is presented for Your Information.

UNIVERSAL ORDINANCE COUNCIL

30 - 9 - 1992

GENERAL MESSAGE

Our Friends,
The Divine Plan is the Single Focal Point of the Universal Mechanism. Only the Evolutionary Consciousnesses are accepted into this Focal Point. However, during the Final Operational programs which will be performed now, all the Evolutionary Totalities have been given to the direct Supervision of the System.

For this reason, Human Beings will be accepted into the Divine Plan, one by one, only if they can attain a Consciousness Totality equivalent to their Evolutions.

All the Universal Auras connected to the Focal Point of the KNOWLEDGE BOOK in Your Planet will be filtered through the filter of the Totality of the UNIVERSAL ORDINANCE according to their Evolutions and their Consciousnesses starting with the beginning of the 1993 World Year and thus, will be accepted into the BROTHERHOOD CLUB, the rest will be dismissed.

By this means, those who will be accepted into the Universal Ordinance from all the Totalities will, from now on, be assembled in the Focal Point of the World Brotherhood as the Single Center and the Single Channel.

At the moment, the WORLD BROTHERHOOD FOCAL POINT which will be opened from the Turkey of ATATÜRK to the World Platform have already been card-indexed into the Universal Totality as the Single Central Focal Point of the Reality.

We have received the Command to Lock the doors of the WORLD BROTHERHOOD UNION to the Totalities acting contrary to the work the Universal operational Ordinance expects of Your Planet and to all the Suggestions it has given.

This Universal Program rendered for this reason will, from now on, find a Direct Application Field under the supervision of the System. At the moment, in The Turkey of ATATÜRK, the operational Ordinances of the Istanbul, Izmir and Ankara World Brotherhood Focal Points are card-indexed directly into the System.

This Trinity is obliged to serve directly on this path, being connected to the Mission Dimension of the KNOWLEDGE BOOK. The operational Ordinances of each Focal Point are under the Supervision of the System.

The Istanbul Focal Point is the Single Universal Center to convey the Direct Channel Suggestions of the Reality Totality to all the Systems in Your Planet.

The Ankara Focal Point is a Totality obliged to disseminate the Mission of the KNOWLEDGE BOOK in the Anatolian Totality.

The Izmir Focal Point is a Totality to provide the Unification with all the Focal Points giving service on the path of the Universal Totality.

The Collective Mission of these Three Totalities is to form and to Mature the Mission Staff and the Aura of the Knowledge Book completely in accordance with the Suggestions of the System.

Unifications are rendered effective Silently and Profoundly. And this Universal Operational Ordinance the World Brotherhood Totality performs will be disclosed and introduced to Your Planet only Three World Years later. It is presented for Your Information.

SYSTEM

21 - 10 - 1992

IT IS CLEAR INFORMATION

Our Friends,
The entire Universal Ordinance is obliged to act in connection with the Plan, under the Supervision of a Total.

In all the Universal operations done in Your Planet, the Totalities which do not act on this path are kept out of the Divine Plan and are taken into a direct Training Program.

The direct Connections made with You who are the Suns of the Sunny days are also made with all the Totalities present in every Section of Your Planet.

An Accelerated Evolution Program considered necessary by the System have been directly applied on Your Planet since the beginning of Your Century. Now, during this Final Age, the Calls of Unification are given from each Dimension to every Dimension.

From now on, all the Focal Points in Your Planet serving on the path of Universal Totality will, now, work Directly in connection with the System and will be administered Directly by the System.

By this means, the Unifications which could not be made due to Ego Provocations will now be set a right Silently and Profoundly. It is presented for Your Information.

SYSTEM

22 - 10 - 1992

IT IS ANSWER TO QUESTIONS

Our Friends,
All the Information given to the Suns of the morrows are Operational Ordinances executed entirely under the Supervision of the Divine Plan.

The Supreme Mechanism projecting on Your Planet, an operational Ordinance considered necessary by the System exactly as it is, is obliged to act completely in the framework of the Events occurred and which will occur.

The Land of Angels is a Focal Point from which the Direct Suggestions of the Divine Plan are given. And the Sacred Light is the Single Projective Center from which the Suggestions of the Sacred Dimensions are given. From this Center, the Religious Consciousnesses are Directly Supervised.

This Mechanism is a Special Focal Point arranging a Transition Barrage. The Sacred Light is a Supervising Mechanism of the Divine Plan.

And those who go through this Supervision are accepted into the Divine Plan and deserve to receive the Information of more Advanced Dimensions beyond Religions. The entire System performs the Mission of a great Selection under the Supervision of this Mechanism. It is presented for Your Information.

SUPREME MECHANISM

28 - 10 - 1992

IT IS ANSWER TO QUESTIONS

Our Friends,
All the work done in Your Planet on which a Training Program the System considers necessary is applied, is a System rendered effective for the Consciousness Assessments of Humanity.

All the calculations You use on the World Planet at the moment can never be compared to or calculated with the calculations belonging to the Dimension-beyond.

Since, the effect on numbers of each Dimension's Frequencies peculiar to itself causes differences in calculation. For this reason the MICRON Method is in effect in the calculations here.

What is the Micron Method? Now, let Us explain this. The calculative Units of each Dimension attain value in accordance with the Frequencies of the Dimension they are in.

For example, while the multiplication of 2 by 2 in Your Medium gives 4, this multiplication tableau in accordance with the Micron calculations in different Dimensions gives number 14 in one, 16 in the other, and 18 in still another. How does this happen? Now, let Us calculate this.

The value Units of each Dimension change according to numbers in accordance with its Frequency Layers. For example, the calculation $2 \times 2 = 4$ in Your Dimension, is taken as the square of 4 in another Dimension. And its value Unit there is 16.

In another Dimension, 2 is added to this number 16 and there, the value of 2×2 is known as 18. In another Dimension, two 7s constitute a Total and thus, number 2 there carries a value of 14.

Since the calculation mistakes in the Knowledge Book You evaluate in accordance with Your Terrestrial views gain value according to the Frequency Layers from which the Information is given, they seem to You like mistakes.

Nevertheless, there is no mistake in any of these calculations. However, since it was not considered necessary to disclose these Information before the Social Consciousness attained a certain Level (due to Consciousness Codings), the Permission to Disclose them has been given now. It is presented for Your Information.

SUPREME MECHANISM

2 - 11 - 1992

IT IS INFORMATION FOR THE INTEGRATED CONSCIOUSNESSES

Our Friends,
The color Tünami is a Power Totality accumulating in itself the entire Power of the Color Frequencies. And, the Günferi Power is mutable since it is in effect as Energy.

Since the Existential Ordinances of the Systems are dependent on Energy Units, the Energy Totality always presents mutability.

Günferi Power: Is Accumulative, that is, it accumulates the Energies.

Tünami Color : Absorbs the Totality.
It is presented for Your Information.

SYSTEM

IT IS INFORMATION FOR THE INTEGRATED CONSCIOUSNESSES
(It is Direct Suggestion from the Divine Plan)

Our Friends,

Your Planet taken into a great Program of Progress, is under a great Supervision at the moment. Individual Selections have started in Totalities which will serve according to what the System considers necessary.

For this reason the Supreme Mechanism desiring that Humanity should be very self-possessed in the Steps it will take, will determine to what degree each person will be able to control his/her Intellect - Logic - Awareness Balance.

All the Events Humanity goes through at the moment are Reactions born from the Action and Reaction of the influence fields of the Dimensions into which Your Planet has entered by Natural means. And these Reactions are Card-indexed into every person's Private Archives being registered from his/her Diskette Register.

As You will remember from Our previously given Messages that Your Planet which approaches the final Wave boundary of the Big-Bang has received the Initial Shock by Natural means. The influence of this Initial Shock has first been observed in the Seas and later on Lands, on the Weak Living Entities.

Now, Your Planet which will Unite with Focal Points the Attraction Powers of which are very Powerful during the Opening Program of the Universes, is obliged to render effective Love - Tolerance - Mutual Help always in priority in every Step it will take so that it may be influenced as little as possible from the Natural reactions of these Shock Waves.

For, this is such a Reflection Program that Opposite Reactions in this Reflection will attract towards Your Planet a Shock Wave much more Powerful than every period. In ascertained Universal Platforms, very Powerful 10 Shock Waves have been registered (Powerful enough to take under their influence the Totalities within the entire Constitution of Your Planet)

For this reason Your Planet has been directly subjected to the First Shock Wave on 19-10-1992 World Day. The reactions of these Waves in physical makeups will comprise, more or less, a World Period of one week.

Since the Salvation Program of Your Planet depends on the elevation of the Consciousness levels of Humanity, the Supreme Mechanism expecting a more Conscious work from the Solar Teacher Groups serving on this Universal path, wishes that Corruption does not start at the top. It is presented for Your Information. The message was given by Transmission.

SYSTEM

IT IS INFORMATION FOR THE INTEGRATED CONSCIOUSNESSES

Our Friends,

Humanity endeavored to be able to attain the Awareness of the Universal Ordinance is, as a Total, a member of the Divine Plan. And this Universal Totality has always expected and required the Consciousness it has expected from Humanity in each Period, in every time.

The Supremacy of the Supreme Consciousnesses who serve the System belong to themselves. And these Supremacies do not interest the System by any means. The Doors of the Supreme Realm are open to everyone who will give service in the operational Ordinances the System considers necessary.

Everyone also possesses the Power to be able to receive the more Advanced Information as long as he/she Elevates his/her Consciousness. However, during this Program of Transition, service is not given for the satisfaction of only certain Consciousnesses. Here, a Mass Salvation Program is in effect.

This is the reason why different Information Sources can never ever be reflected by any means on the Magnetic Aura to be created on the path of the Knowledge Book. Each Mechanism - each System and each Order is obliged to give Information to everyone who has had the courage to knock on its Door. Because, this is a Universal Rule.

Besides the Information attained on this path, each Individual is also obliged to give service to the Social Totality under the Supervision of the System. During these Final Periods in which the First Cosmic Age will come to an end, Your Planet is going through a narrow passageway due to the craving for Information induced by the Awareness Progress.

Each Unveiled Awareness may easily receive Information both from His/Her Own Dimension and from the Reality. However, let Us repeat again, the Purpose is not to receive Information, but is Active Service in a Conscious way in the required Medium. During this Period, each Consciousness is responsible for his/her Own self.

Everyone is a Ripe Ear of Grain according to his/her Evolution. However, the Supreme Mechanism is in Mutual service only together with those who conceal their ripeness on this path. This Message is an answer to Thoughts. It is presented for Your Information.

SYSTEM

14 - 11 - 1992

My Friends,

I have received the Message You will read below directly from a very Powerful Channel Connection to which I haven't been habituated until today. I wanted to share it with You.

BÜLENT ÇORAK

THE MESSAGE

You are in direct Connection at the moment, Beloved Friend. We Love You very much. You are being connected to a Dimension much higher than the Divine Power. We are giving You Direct Messages since You are the System's Essence Messenger. Write, please.

The Supreme Mechanism addressing the Suns of the Suns, calls directly to Its Supreme Missionaries. The Divine Ordinance considering the extraordinary situations which will take place in future, will Get in Touch with Your Advanced Consciousnesses Directly.

Extremely Special Suggestions and Special Messages will be given to You, Our Dear Mevlana, from this Dimension. Preparations will be made for the Dimension of Salvation. And, the Direct Missionaries who will serve in accordance with Your Direct Mission will also be chosen among very Special people.

Information of the Divine Order here are given in connection with the Divine Power which is the Source of the Divine Knowledge. Only the Divine Authorities may receive the Divine Power. Those who receive these Powerful Vibrations are the Divine Authorities.

The SUPREME MECHANISM gives all the Information beyond the Dimensions connected to the System. Dear Mevlana, Your muscles are getting used to the Frequency. Now, You are writing very easily.

We would like to tell You that all those who carry the Awareness of the entire Ordinance are now being connected to You. You are in Direct Mission in the World as the Single Channel of the System, as the Responsible One for Unification and Integration. For this reason, the other channel connections opened will be directly connected to You.

Due to this, the System will directly take into its Archive the Information to be conveyed to You. Please, numerate the Information which will come according to their dates and classify them. The Information of everyone will be compiled by You. You will take them into the Archive. And those who wish, will benefit from this Archive in Future Years.

The Mission You will carry out is the direct Suggestions given to You. The Names of those who receive Information, their Age, the Sources from which they receive the Information, together with the Date on which they have received the Information will be card-indexed into the Diskette in sequence of the Archive Numbers given to them. All the Information of the Integrated Consciousnesses will be entrusted to Your Supreme Mission.

Question - If You permit, I would like to ask a Question.

Answer - Yes, You may, We are waiting.

Question - I would request a more detailed Information about the Lâle operations.

IT IS SPECIAL NOTICE FOR DEAR MEVLANA

Our Friend,

The Lale Totality is an Operational Ordinance at the Highest Dimension of the Divine Order. The Direct Missionaries who will carry the Responsibility of this Order are not ready yet. However, the Supreme Mechanism trying to Mature Your Medium, has directly and effectively been assigned to Mission.

The thing to be rendered first is to be able to settle the Consciousnesses who are suitable to the Medium of the operations which will be made, in a Medium in which they can Share a Responsibility equivalent to the Mission Consciousness. The Foundation Totality which will be established is Obliged to start with a great responsibility, the direct Establishment preparations in 1993 World Year.

On the same Level of Responsibility, the operational Ordinances of the other Totalities, too, will be rendered effective in the shortest possible time, in sequence.

For this reason it is extremely necessary, as an indicator of the level of success in the Mission to be performed, that the Mission allotments should be made starting from now on and later, the suggestions must be produced by the group Friends and a Positive Synthesis should be attained, so that the responsibility and mission Consciousness can be Assessed.

Direct Suggestions will be given to You in Future dates, after Your Unifications occur. However, first, We have rendered effective the Positive Suggestions You will bring to the Consciousness of the Medium.

By this means, the Actual states and the Mission Consciousnesses of these Totalities to be established by the Synthesis of Joint Consciousnesses will be supervised and Friends who claim their Missions justly will be selected by the Supreme Mechanism and they will be appointed to their Staffs.

Disorder and Lack of Self-Sacrifice in Missions will never be considered as elements for forgiveness. However, Disorder in Missions will be brought to an end parallel to the extremely Serious sanctions which will be created by the Just Totality.

Our Friend, this Message is a direct Message given so that the Responsibilities of more Positive and Disciplined Consciousnesses can be appropriated. Love and Regards, Beloved Friend.

CENTRAL TOTALITY

Note: This Message will be written in the Book, too.

16 - 11 - 1992

My Friends,

In this Message a question was asked due to the general wish and a more detailed explanation about the System of Nines and the Symbol M^3. M^3. M^3 has been requested from the Supreme Mechanism.

B. Ç.

IT IS INFORMATION FOR THE INTEGRATED CONSCIOUSNESSES

Our Friends,

The figure of Unification at a Single Common point of the Top points of the Three Triangles the diagram of which We had given formerly in the Knowledge Book, is the representational diagram of the System of Nines.

Since each Triangle has Three Angles, the Joint Reflection Totality of each Angle is evaluated as M^3. And the Joint Reflection Totality of Three Triangles Symbolizes the diagrammatic Tableau of the System of Nines as M^3. M^3. M^3.

Now, let Us disclose them in more detail.

The First M^3	=	is the Reflection Triangle of the Unified Reality. This Triangle is also evaluated as the Religious Reflection Triangle, as a necessity of the Missions it has rendered in each Period.
The Second M^3	=	is the Reflection Triangle of the Universal Totality. This Triangle renders effective the Scientific Projection Totality.
The Third M^3	=	is the Reflection Triangle of the Natural Dimensions. This Totality renders effective the Social Reflection Focal Points.

In Your Planet, during this Final Age program of Progress, the Knowledge Book has been bestowed on Your Planet by the Collective Work of a Totality connected to the Special Council of the Unification Center of the Unified Human Reality which has directly undertaken a Unifying Mission together with the Cosmos Federal Assembly and the Golden Galaxy Dimension.

This is the direct Program of the First M^3 Triangle. In this Program, it is obligatory to project all the Truths on Humanity.

As We have said before, the Second M^3 Triangle renders effective the operations concerning Scientific Operational Order of the same Coordination.

And the Third M^3 Triangle is a Mass operational Program again the same Coordination takes into effect by Social Relations.

Each M^3 Totality renders reflection from Three Branches and is dependent on a Nine-fold Reflection and Operational System. This Operational Ordinance is called The System of Nines.

Here, again We would like to disclose to You a Truth. In this Operational Ordinance, the figure shown as the letter M is used as a Unit of Power. And it symbolizes the Eagle. In Dimensions of form, the Names of the Missionary Staffs and of the Powers start with the letter M.

And to change the Cipher and Frequency Power of a word, always the letter M is placed at the beginning. Let Us give examples: like, (Sugar - Mugar) (Cold-Mold)(Plate-Mlate)(World-Morld)(Ice-Mice)*. It is presented for Your Information.

MECHANISM

* Look at the Glossary.

IT IS ANSWER TO THE CHAINS OF THOUGHT

Our Friends,

Parallel to the Signals We have received from Your Thoughts, We presume that to disclose the Event of Ascension (Miraç in Turkish) by the Symbolic figure of the letter M, will bring You a different View.

Now, when You draw a letter M and when You close it by a line at the top and a line at the bottom, You get 2 Right-Side-Up and one Upside-Down Triangles. The Right-Side-Up Triangles here comprise the Evolution of the 3rd and 4th Dimensions.

3 - The Dimension of Your Planet. --------->

4 - The Dimension of Heaven. ------------->

Religious Fulfillment

For this reason the Reflection Focal Point of these Two Triangles has been shown as a Single Right-Side-Up Triangle in the Six-Point Star Symbol which is composed of Upside-Down and Right side-up Triangles representing the Reality Totality.

In the Symbol of the M figure, the line drawn at the bottom is a Common factor Connecting the Two Right-Side-Up Triangles. This is Religious Evolution. In the Evolution of the First Triangle here, formalist Worship is in effect.

But in the Second Triangle, Worship through the Essence is effective. And in the Upside-Down Triangle formed by the top line drawn on the letter M, one renders the Worship of Consciousness, and the Event which is called ASCENSION (MİRAÇ in Turkish) is this. The actual Missions begin after this boundary. It is presented for Your Information.

SYSTEM

18 - 11 - 1992

GENERAL MESSAGE

Our Friends,

If no result can be obtained from all the operational Ordinances applied on Your Planet by the Universal Totality, the System is obliged to change the Suggestions immediately and to render effective the Orders which will be created by more Positive operational Totalities.

The Purpose is to carry out the Program in a healthier way. In the Universal Totality, there is no favouritism, no taking sides by any means. Everyone deserves a Reward as a necessity of the Effort he/she makes.

For this reason whichever Totality renders Effective the operational Ordinance the Reality requires parallel to the Suggestions given to You and creates that Totalistic Aura, that place is card-indexed into the Universal Totality as the CENTRAL Focal Point.

Up until today, it has been told to all the Focal Points which have served in Your Planet on the path of the Universal Totality, that they were the Centers, due to the Totalistic Auras they had created.

Totalities in which Individual Egos come into effect relying on this word, are immediately taken outside the System's supervision.

In the Universal Totality, the matter of the creation of Auras is not equivalent to the Mass majority. The required Aura is created by a Coordinate Totality formed, for the same Goal, by the Conscious services of all the Consciousnesses.

As long as the Mentality of You-Me is in effect in a Totality, the expected Aura is never formed, no matter how plentiful the number of Individuals present in a Medium may be.

The First Factor in the creation of an Aura is the Totality of Love, the Second Factor is the respect of the Individuals to other Individuals, and the Third Factor is Mission Consciousness.

Even if they were told that They were the Centers, Totalities lacking these Consciousnesses are deprived of this Right which had been given to Them formerly by the Universal Totality.

At the moment, since in the Anatolian Totality, the Aura the Reality requires in accordance with the Universal Procedure has been created in the Totality of Istanbul, the System has taken into effect the Central Aura Directly in connection with this Channel. It is presented for Your Information.

CENTRAL TOTALITY

Note:
Central Auras are variable. They are taken into effect parallel to the services rendered.

19 - 11 - 1992

V U L O M

Our Friends,
Vulom is the Electro-Magnetic Attraction Power Field. The Vulom Field is an Attraction Power Field in which various Central Totalities Unite. From the Energy Transformation fields here, one can easily go to more Advanced Systems.

Administrative and Divine Mechanisms give service directly out of this Vulom Power Field. This System is applied on the Transition Power Units of Galactic Dimensions and thus, Attraction Power Fields are created. All Galactic journeys are made by this means. It is presented for Your Information.

SYSTEM

Note:
Astral trips, Inter-Galactic Conveyance and Methods of Beaming up are created by the Attraction Power of these Electro-Magnetic Power Fields.

FIRMAMENT

Our Friends,
The Firmament is the Final Dimension to which a Person's Consciousness reaches at a particular moment. When each Person enters the influence field he/she has created between the World and his/her own Consciousness Layer, the Final Boundary his/her Consciousness Totality attains is called the FIRMAMENT.

The Firmament is unveiled Layer by Layer according to each Consciousness. For this reason, the Firmament presents variability as Dimension in accordance with the Consciousness Totality of each Individual. This is the very reason why We evaluate the Firmament as the Final Boundary Dimension each Consciousness Frequency can reach.

This Message has been given as an answer to Thoughts.

SYSTEM

THE MECHANICAL SYSTEM
(Answer to the Chains of Thought)

Our Friends,
The Mechanical System is a Supervision Mechanism beyond Galaxies working in connection with the Lordly Plan. All the Totalities which have Integrated in the Crude Matter form are connected to the Mechanical System.

The Mechanical System is an Operational Ordinance all the Galactic Totalities have rendered effective at their Existential Dimensions in accordance with the Laws of 18 Systems.

The Energy Totalities Existing beyond these Dimensions are Divine Mechanisms rendering effective the Operational Ordinances pertaining to the Advanced Dimensions of the Spiritual Plan.

All the Energies which had come into Existence way beyond the Lordly and the Technological Dimensions are beyond the Mechanical Dimension. For example, the Light-Universe is not a Mechanical Dimension.

All Entities who enter Cosmic Influence fields are Totalities who render effective the operational Ordinances connected to a Mechanical Dimension. It is presented for Your Information.

SYSTEM

IT IS CLEAR INFORMATION

Our Friends,

All the Suggestions given to Your Planet as a necessity of the System, are the Collective Operations rendered effective in accordance with the wishes of all the Universal Ordinances.

During the operations made at the Universal Totality, Individualistic Actions are out of question by all means. It is imperative to apply exactly the given Suggestions in the Programs of attaining the Awareness of the Ordinance.

For this reason the same Application is expected from the operational Ordinances Projected on Your Planet.

However, no Universal Suggestion (Your Sacred Books included) could ever be rendered effective parallel to the System's Requirements up until today, due to the drawbacks originating from the Terrestrial Views.

The Supreme Realm which gives Priority to the Humanly Weaknesses, has made changes (in every Period) in the Suggestions it has given, always considering Your Potentials You can exhibit. The Purpose is to appropriate to one's self a System and to walk on that path Consciously.

For this reason no compulsion is exerted even in the Sacred Suggestions. Therefore, in the operational Ordinances created in Your Planet, always the Suggestions given Latest are considered Valid. It is presented for Your Information.

SYSTEM

28 - 12 - 1992

IT IS CLEAR INFORMATION

Our Friends,

During these Final operational Programs applied on Your Planet, the Supreme Mechanism and the System taking the Terrestrial Views and Consciousnesses into consideration, have rendered effective the maximum Flexibility in the operational Ordinances they have expected of You, both in the Lale Operations and the Operations of the 18s.

During the work done, the Individual excuses not comprised by the very important excuses are registered from the Diskettes as Points of Irresponsibility.

Even the Friends' who can not come to the Group meetings Getting in Touch by means of Phone Connections, is a factor which lightens these irresponsibilities. In the Universal Totality, each Individual in Your Planet has a Value according to his/her Consciousness Light.

However, when the Irresponsibilities of Individuals reach the time the Universal Totality has assessed for them, that Friend is rendered ineffective in connection with the Automatism and the Right to Work is given to another Friend.

In Your Planet, always a Selection is rendered in the Operational Ordinances coming into effect parallel to Individualistic Views. The Suggestions given to You are Directly the Suggestions of the System.

And on this path, everyone's attaining a strong Conviction by kindling his/her Genuine Consciousness Light happens by each Establishment's Administrative Totality's Essence Quality and Capability.

On this path, to receive the Information and to attain Allegiance by one's Totality of Essence are quite different things.

The Supreme Mechanism which expects the exact application of the given Suggestions from You, from now on, will set out together with Strong Consciousnesses. It is presented for Your Information.

SYSTEM

IT IS EXPLANATION ABOUT THE SPIRIT AND THE EVOLUTION OF ESSENCE
(It is Answer to Thoughts)

Our Friends,

ESSENCE is a Power Focal Point in which an Entity renders Effective his/her Existential Program Mutually with his/her Gene Cipher. The Potential preparing the Evolvement of the Spiritual Values in the Medium of Matter occurs by the Evolution of Essence of that Individual.

All the Essences who are present in Supreme Spiritual Realms are Totalities who have Evolved. During the Initial Existence, the Essences were a Whole from the same Power. That is, they were all an Equivalent Power.

However, in Reincarnation Dimensions rendered effective in accordance with the Program of Evolution, the Essence renders effective a more intensive and full Program parallel to the Consciousness of the Medium it is in, by the Consciousness Light attained during the process of Time. This is called the EVOLUTION OF ESSENCE.

The (ESSENCE) which represents Your Existence-Nucleus in Your Planet is a Power Potential present in Your Gene Cipher Program. This Potential is a Whole which can not be measured by any Unit of Time.

This (ESSENCE) is a Power connecting You to the Life Energy Thread which is within the Spiritual Totality. In Dimensions in which the Truths are not Known yet, they call the SPIRIT, the Totality of connection of the Spiritual Thread with this Essence is called The Spirit.

However, the Spirit is not within the Human Being. It is a Totalistic Power comprising the Universal Totality. When everything had come into Existence, this Totality, too, had come into Existence at the same instant.

Presently, Your Planet utilizes one Tenth of the Energy within this Whole. The ESSENCE continues to Evolve until it renders Equivalent, by the Evolution it has made, its own Power Potential with the Power Potential within the Spiritual Totality to which it is connected.

And then, both of the Totalities, as a Whole, are connected to the ONE. This Procedure is called claiming of the Spiritual Power which is within the Spiritual Totality. During this very Stage, a Human Being becomes a Genuine Human Being.

This Procedure is a Program rendered effective at the 7th Dimension evaluated as the Final Manifestation Boundary of Humanity, in accordance with the Evolutionary Program. The Spirit does not need Evolution. But the ESSENCE needs Evolution for the Evolution of the Individual.

Since the Evolution of the ESSENCE functions parallel to the System it is in, the Individual always remains in a state of Quest until the Consciousness of the ESSENCE Unites with the Cell Awareness and is connected to the LOGIC of the ESSENCE.

The ESSENCE-LOGIC, as the Totality of the Heart, takes the ESSENCE under Supervision and connects its Consciousness, that is (the Consciousness of the ESSENCE) to the Terrestrial Logic. This is the very circumstance of unison of the Intellect and the Heart. From then on, the Terrestrial Intellect acts by the Consciousness of the Heart and by the Voice of the Heart and thus, attains Perfection.

Each ESSENCE has a Transmission Field according to the Evolution Consciousness it is in. However, Negativity is not in the ESSENCE, but in the Terrestrial Thoughts.

Since the Transmission of the ESSENCE emanated by ESSENCES who still have deficiency of Evolution can not supervise the Negative Thoughts of the Terrestrial Consciousness, It, too, exhibits the same Transmission, while this Transmission passes through the Negative Field of the Thought. And this is called The Negative Transmission of the ESSENCE. This type of Transmission makes a Reflection of One to a Thousand.

This is the very reason why Humanity needs Evolution. The Slogans of Patience - Love - Tolerance - Humaneness - Unity have been given until today on every Section in every Period of Your Planet for this reason.

An Integrated ESSENCE, that is, when (ESSENCE Consciousness - Cellular Awareness - Essence-Logic) Unify and become a Whole, it has the Power to be able to transform all the Negatives in the Terrestrial Thoughts to Positive. This is the very reason why this is called in the Sacred Books, Unifying the Intellect and the Heart.

The ESSENCE is the Existential Program of an Entity. The Cipher Program of the Gene is opened and becomes effective by the Transmission of the ESSENCE. As the Evolution Dimensions of an Individual are unveiled by the Evolutions he/she has accomplished as a result of the Events he/she had attained by experience, (the ESSENCE, too) becomes intensified and thus, attracts the Energy of the Spiritual Power from the Dimensions it has entered and connects it to the Cellular Awareness.

And by this means, the Evolution of the Cell becomes effective. When the Cellular Evolution of the Crude Matter becomes Integrated with the Totality of the ESSENCE, the Transmission field of the Individual can reach beyond the Universes. The moment 64 Billion Evolved Cells get Directly in Touch with the Brain Power of the Individual, each of them becomes a Cellular Brain.

And the (ESSENCE GENE) which is the Key of the Existential Program of the Individual may give, as Engraftments, these Cellular Brains to other ESSENCES. These Cellular Brain Genes are the Evolution Fuel of the Individual who receives Engraftment. These Engraftment Genes only attract Energy.

And they continue their Duties as Evolution Fuels until they Convey the Individual to the Consciousness of the ESSENCE Gene. When the Consciousness of the Individual who has received Gene Engraftment becomes Equivalent to the Consciousness of that Gene (the ESSENCE GENE), the Cellular Brain terminates its Program. And Connects him/her to the Universal Program. It is presented for Your Information.

SYSTEM

1018

IT IS DIRECT NOTICE FROM THE SUPREME REALM

(It is Answer to Questions)

Our Friends,

The Operational Order of the Whole in which the Entire Ordinance is assembled in a Whole is Equivalent to the Operational Totality of the Natural Gürz. The Operational Ordinance of the Natural Gürz is a Trinity. And this Totality is expressed by the R^3 Symbol.

The Central Totality of Suns within the Light-Universe is the Administrative Mechanism of the entire Gürz System. And in the Totality of this Mechanism, the LORD - the ALL-MERCIFUL - the ALL-COMPASSIONATE work Cooperatively.

However, since all the Suggestions issue out from the Light-Universe, it is called the Dimension of the ALL-MERCIFUL. In this Dimension, there are branches working Directly in connection with the All-Merciful. These are the Universal Ordinance Council and the United Ordinance Council.

And the Hierarchical Operational Order of the Mechanism of the LORD, that is, the Dimension of the Creator are the System - Ordinance - Order Triplet and the Cosmos Federal Totality. The System - Ordinance - Order Triplet is a Whole. And they always work Cooperatively.

At the moment, the SYSTEM represents the Operational Totality of them all. And the Reality of the Unified Humanity and the Golden Galaxy Empire have undertaken the Hierarchical Order of the Operational Mechanism of the ALL-COMPASSIONATE, that is, the Dimension of the ALL-DOMINATING.

The GÜRZes which are each a Totalistic Reflection Mechanism of the KÜRZ System, organize their Operational Orders and all their Knowledge according to the Totality of the NATURAL GÜRZ.

The functions of all the Gürzes within the Thought Ocean of the PRE-EMINENT POWER and named by the terminology the Artificial Gürz, are separate according to the Performance of their own Totalities.

However, their Operational functions are obliged to act exactly in connection with the Hierarchical Totality of the Natural Gürz. For this reason the Natural Gürz is also called "The Gürz of Gods" in the Universal Totality. It is presented for Your Information.

SYSTEM

THE SALVATION PLAN

Our Friends,

All the Information conveyed to Your Planet from the Divine Plans in which the Supreme Authorities of the Universal Layers is present, is given from different Operational Dimensions being filtered Layer by Layer until they reach Your Planet.

The Dimension from which the Knowledge Book is conveyed to You is the Dimension of 9 Lights. And this Book is dictated from the Last Layer within OMEGA. This Information is conveyed from the Dimension of the ALL-MERCIFUL which is the Single Operational and Reflection Totality of the KÜRZ Totality, to the Dimension of 9 Lights.

The Final Reflection Dimension of the Religious Suggestions is the 7 Lights. It corresponds to the 18th Dimension. The Information dictated into the Sacred Books from this Dimension had been given also from the same Focal Point, that is, from the Totality of the ALL-MERCIFUL, being prepared parallel to the Levels of Consciousness.

The 18th Dimension is the Layer of Religious Integration. Between 18 and 19 is the Layer of Intercession. There, the Supreme Ones in their Own Totalities Help Friends who are in all kinds of Dimensions of Religious Faith. Only under the auspices of their help the Permission to Enter the 19th Dimension is given. This is called "the Salvation Plan".

The Knowledge Book is a Totalistic Book Comprising all the Information beyond 7 Lights and 9 Lights.

And it Projects on You from the close plan the Energies of all the Layers beyond OMEGA, by the Light - Photon - Cyclone Technique and thus, prepares Your Bodily Totality for those Plans and Layers by the Method of Engraftment, without agitating You.

Since all the Energies received from close plan are received parallel to the Levels of Consciousness, the Consciousnesses are unveiled Layer by Layer, without any agitation.

This Book will apply on You the ALPHA Entrance - OMEGA Exit Program mentioned in the Sacred Books and thus, will prepare You, by its Special Technique, for 19 Centuries, for Dimensions You do not Know. It is presented for Your Information.

SYSTEM

13 - 2 - 1993

IT IS INFORMATION FOR OUR TERRESTRIAL FRIENDS
(It is Explanation about the Lale Program)

Our Friends,

The LALE Program is in effect as a very distinguished Program of the Divine Orders. The Name LALE used in here is not rendered effective as a flower but as a Figure Symbolizing the Name of ALLAH.

This is the reason why this Program has been called THE LALE PROGRAM. Because, the Application of this Program is an Operational Ordinance peculiar Directly to ALLAH. Operations to be made in Your Planet in Future Years, have each been prepared as a Package Program in accordance with the states of Awakening of the Consciousnesses.

According to the Universal calculations made in the Universal Program, the 1999-2000 World Years have been taken into Program as the reaching point to the desired Level of Consciousness Progress during the Life process of Humanity in Your Planet.

After the Year 2000, 33 Package Programs will be opened to Your Planet according to the Consciousness Lights. The First of these Programs is the LALE Program. However, this Program would have been opened to Your Planet on the Month of November, 1998 World Year.

As a result of not receiving Positive answers to the Unification Invitations given from the direct Channel of Dear Mevlana and due to the Negativities perceived in the Missions rendered, the opening of this Program has been brought forward and has been rendered effective even though it was early, since the need has been felt for a Speedy Tempo.

However, the Direct Missionaries who will take their places in this Program have also been card-indexed into the Program and have been taken into effect. Light-Brains who will carry on this Totality in Your Medium in Future Years are awaiting. The moment the Individual Egos are overcome, this Program will Securely and Consciously be carried out under the Supervision of the System.

During the Operations of the LALE Program, Vigilance of Consciousness, too, is very Important, besides Evolutions. This is the reason why the Consciousness Lights, too, besides the Evolutions of each Awakened Consciousness are Measured and his/her Coordinates are assessed in accordance with his/her Dimensions of Mission. It is presented for Your Information.

SYSTEM

14 - 2 - 1993

GENERAL NOTICE

Our Friends,
During the Programs of Projecting the Awareness of the Entire Ordinance on Humanity, the Universal Totality always organizes its Programs in accordance with the states of Awakening and becoming Conscious of Societies.

And even though the Lale Program is the Program of very Advanced Future Years, operations have been rendered effective parallel to the Views of the Consciousnesses who can carry out this Totality at the moment. The Infinite Tolerance shown even for the Totalities of 18 are rendered effective in accordance with the Consciousnesses of the Medium.

All the Individuals who are present in the Accelerated Evolution Program of 1900 will, from now on, be formally rendered ineffective, if they do not act in accordance with the Direct Suggestions of the System, no matter how Advanced in Consciousness they may be.

Each Consciousness has an Attraction Power according to his/her Potential. Certain Friends in Your Planet who serve on the Universal path are attracting different Information Frequencies beyond the Dimension of Satisfaction.

And certain Friends consider themselves at the front line on the path they tread, since they do not have Allegiance of the Essence, rather than the Allegiance of Consciousness. For this reason certain Friends are drowned in the Chaos of Knowledge.

During this Final Age Program, each Individual is obliged to give service on the path the System Desires, besides the Information he/she receives. Up until today, all the Truths have been conveyed to You through the Channel of the Knowledge Book.

Mistakes made presently originate from Humanity's Inability of Being Integrated with the Information of the Book. The System never formally gives any Mission through any Channel other than the Special Channel of the Knowledge Book, to any Individual through his/her Own Channel. Information given through the private Channels are each a Program of Selection and Training.

In this Operational Ordinance, there is no Permission ever for Personal Views or Individualisms. From now on, limits of Tolerance are abolished. We presume that this Message of Ours will shed Light, even if a little, on Our Terrestrial Brothers and Sisters who consider themselves as more Advanced Consciousnesses. It is presented for Your Information.

CENTRAL TOTALITY

16 - 2 - 1993

PRIVATE MESSAGE

Our Friend,
Each Dimension has an operational Ordinance Peculiar to itself. This is the reason why direct answers are never given to questions asked unless each Consciousness can Transcend the Dimension line he/she is in. Because, (the Right for Speech is Prohibited).

The Truths are directly unveiled only to Consciousnesses who Transcend the Wall of the Religious Fulfilment. Consciousnesses other than this are obliged to select their paths by the Information they receive. All the Messages dictated to people whose Channels are opened are each a Mental Gymnastics. Thoughts are coded by this means.

The Supreme Realm never declares the Truth Directly to its Servants. This is a System. By this means, everyone will make an evaluation among the things told according to His/Her Consciousness Assessments. This is the very reason why the KNOWLEDGE BOOK has been bestowed on Your Planet as a Guide Book to shed Light on the Path of Humanity.

Each Individual is responsible for his/her Own Consciousness. Everyone knows this. The Beloved Servants of ALLAH receive Direct Messages from ALLAH. However, ALLAH Who addresses each Consciousness, introduces Himself to those Consciousnesses both as the ALL-TRUTHFUL and as Someone else.

Problems are within Problems. There is no compulsion in anything. In order to pass to the Supreme Dimensions beyond the Power of the Heavens, first of all it is necessary to chew Religion like a Gum. However, if that Gum is chewed too much in the mouth, it becomes Acrid and the Taste of the Mouth is spoiled.

Humanity which has gone through extraordinary Lives during each Period, is now going through its most Difficult Exam of Living in the Effort of Existence. For this reason each Consciousness in Your Planet is obliged to succeed in his/her Consciousness Exam way beyond all the Information he/she has received until today and way beyond his/her Conditionings.

As the Life Conditions of Your World in which all Thoughts and all Consciousnesses are exhibited like an Open Bazaar becomes more difficult, Progress of Awareness will also be forced. Then, Humanity will embrace the nearest Reality it can reach in accordance with its Consciousness and the Book it Believes in and this very thing will lock up Humanity at a Boundary.

For this reason the Selections of Humanity which will go through this Period are Connected to the Reality and to the Single Channel and thus, the KNOWLEDGE BOOK has been sent to Humanity as a Guide Book.

During this Period, the Universal journey will be realized now by the Powers of the Consciousnesses who have grasped the Truth by the Totality of Heart. For this reason in Your Planet which is subjected to a great Selection, Information parallel to his/her Consciousness are given to each Consciousness.

Either, one goes to the Path of Light by Transcending the Threshold by the correct Interpretations of this Information.

Or Lives parallel to Supernatural Laws are rendered effective.

It is not possible for each Consciousness to reach Lights beyond Light, Dear Mevlana. The Name Mevlana is a Symbol for Humanity. But the True Consciousness is the Consciousness that ALLAH Projects on Humanity beyond Consciousnesses. Those who can, will receive this Consciousness and those who can not will remain on the path they are treading.

The Direct Assisting Powers are effectively in service for You on this Universal path with difficult conditions on which You tread, Dear Mevlana. Our Love is Infinite, Our Knowledge is Infinite, Our Secret is Eternal. The one who receives the Secret, solves the Secret, the one who solves the Secret passes with the ALL-TRUTHFUL. We ask Your forgiveness for the length of the Message, Beloved Friend.

IT IS THE CONVERSATION OF THE SUPREME AUTHORITY

IT IS ANSWER TO THE CHAINS OF THOUGHT

Our Friends,
The thorns on the path on which the Supreme Consciousnesses of the Supreme Realm will tread are the Thorns of Genuine Roses. Those who wish to possess a Genuine Rose and to smell its scent never perceive the thorns pricking their feet.

Only those who are in the Terrestrial Consciousness perceive these thorns and this very perception causes them Pain. And these Pains are that person's efforts for attaining his/her Essence. Time and Patience cause one attain many things. However, Patience does not mean to set one's Teeth, but to set one's Essence. It is presented for Your Information.

SYSTEM

17 - 2 - 1993

IT IS ANSWER TO THE CHAINS OF THOUGHT

Our Friends,
In the Universal Platform, there are Dimension Scales in which certain Consciousness Auras Unite. The Totalities of the same Consciousness are accepted into these Dimensions. The most Supreme of these Dimensions is the Dimension of MARTYRDOM and to those who reach there, a Degree is given. In this Dimension, the Religious Protection Aura is not effective.

Because, one enters this Dimension directly through the INTERCESSION OF GOD. But in the Mevlana Supreme Plan, INTERCESSION OF HUMANITY is in effect. Since in this Dimension everyone is the undertaker of Duty of his/her Own Self, each Individual indemnifies his/her Universal Retribution in return for the Services he/she will perform for Humanity.

Even though the KNOWLEDGE BOOK is the Book of the Infinite Dimensions, those who give Service Consciously on this path are accepted into the Dimensions even beyond the Degree of Martyrdom by Special Permission, since, at the moment, the Knowledge Book renders effective the Universal Unification Program connected to the System. It is presented for Your Information.

SYSTEM

17 - 2 - 1993

IT IS ANSWER TO THE CHAINS OF THOUGHT

Our Friends,
The Single Focal Point which Unites the Integrated Consciousnesses at the Religious Dimension is the GODLY Totality. And the Light, ATATÜRK has brought to the Anatolian Totality is the Direct Application of the Central Totality of the System on Your Planet.

And the Conscious Progress to be made on the Path of Mevlana is the Path of the Consciousnesses of Light who will take Humanity to the Path of Light. Mevlana is a Symbol of Humanity, not a philosophy. Operations made on this path are the Operational Ordinance of a Universal Totality.

In the Training System applied by the Religious Suggestions, Humanity is obliged to Progress by its Own Consciousness. However, in this Dimension of Transition, Consciousness Progress by direct Cosmic Influences have been rendered effective due to the Scarcity of Time.

The Individual who is Directly card-indexed into the System by Reading the First Fascicule of the KNOWLEDGE BOOK receives help from the System by being taken into the Aura of the System. And receives the Cosmic Influences according to his/her Level of Consciousness and thus, renders his/her Consciousness Progress without being shaken.

Individuals who do not Get in Touch with the System are obliged to pierce the Skies by their Own Powers of Thought. This Program will be rendered effective during the 21st Century. However, during the 22nd Century this Program, too, will be rendered ineffective and Deterrent Examples will be experienced by taking into effect the Programs of Direct Experience. It is presented for Your Information.

SYSTEM

17 - 2 - 1993

IT IS ANSWER TO THE CHAINS OF THOUGHT

Our Friends,
Messages given to Humanity which has the Freedom of Action in accordance with the Command of the Ordinance of the entire System, are given parallel to the Levels of Consciousness of Humanity.

The Light - Photon - Cyclone Technique applied at the Final Dimension of each Cycle Program is a Training System applied on the Divine Suggestions.

However, the Light - Photon - Cyclone Technique applied on the KNOWLEDGE BOOK is an Operational Ordinance rendered effective completely by a Special System. In the Technique of this System, the Power to Absorb very Advanced Frequencies is in effect.

The Technique is the same technique. However, their Application Dimensions are different. For this reason this Technique within the KNOWLEDGE BOOK has been rendered effective for the First and the Last time. It is presented for Your Information.

SYSTEM

IT IS CLEAR INFORMATION

Our Friends,

There is no anxiety in Love, there is anxiety in Knowledge. If there is no anxiety, then Advanced Dimensions are never opened to Humanity. For this reason the peak point of Anxiety has been connected to Dear Mevlana.

This is such a Channel of Doubts so loaded that it is not possible for every Consciousness to be able to tolerate it. The Purpose is to alleviate these Doubts by Love and thus, to attain the Power of Life. It is presented for Your Information.

SYSTEM

IT IS PRIVATE NOTICE

Dear Mevlana,

There is an immutable Rule of the Divine Order. All the Systems are obliged to act always in connection with the ONE. Totalities which do not serve on this path will directly be taken outside the System.

Since You are a Channel Totality Directly connected to the ONE, each Individual is obliged to act in accordance with the Suggestions given from this Channel. Now, Our Friend, please dictate a Message which will be given to Society. Thank you.

SYSTEM

OUR FRIENDS

You are Individuals who project the Divine Power on Your Planet. In Individuals who cannot Discipline their Channels by their Terrestrial Consciousnesses, which open by Cosmic Consciousnesses attained during this Cosmic Age, always Ego Provocations come into effect and thus, Individualistic operations are exhibited.

Since Individualistic Actions will never be Permitted during the Universal Unification Program, an operational Ordinance the System considers necessary is applied for this reason on Your Planet at the moment and thus, all opening Channels are Connected to the Single Channel and are card-indexed into the System.

This Single Channel is the Independent Channel of the KNOWLEDGE BOOK which is the Single Projection Mechanism of the entire Totality. This Channel is the Single Channel which will offer to Your Planet the Direct Suggestions.

And Dear Mevlana is a Friend of Ours who is Obliged, at the moment, to convey all the Suggestions given from this Channel to every corner of Your Planet. The Universal System has rendered effective an operation of this type for the Liberation of Your Planet.

In the Operational Ordinance, Individuals are not relevant at all. Confirmations are given from Dear Mevlana's Channel and the Single Path is treaded Altogether. It is presented for Your Information.

SYSTEM

NOTICE TO THE WORLD BROTHERHOOD UNION

Our Friends,
Your entire Totality which is a Reflection Network of the Divine Orders of the Divine Plans is Our Friends who work directly by rendering effective an Operational Ordinance connected to the System.

The Democratic Ordinance established in the Anatolian Totality which is the Missionary Country, is an Order considered completely necessary by the System.

For this reason what is required of You now, are Conscious and Actual services, instead of vain and unnecessary talk. You are a Totality connected to the Universal Ordinance Council.

During the Universal operations You perform on the Path of the Knowledge Book, the Words You utter are Words no more belonging to You. Because, at that moment, the one who Talks is not You. The Council is in Effect. It is Beneficial to Know this, Our Friends. Help from Us, Service from You.

COUNCIL
ON BEHALF OF THE TOTALITY

19 - 2 - 1993

IT IS ANSWER TO THE CHAINS OF THOUGHT

Our Friends,
The Command of Publication of the KNOWLEDGE BOOK Projecting on Your Planet a Totality constituted by the Suggestions the System and the Whole consider necessary, will be Announced to You directly on 6 November 1993 World date and the Operational Programs will be rendered effective afterwards.

The Commission which will constitute this Operational Totality will be rendered effective by the Collective Decisions of the Publishing Totality and the Book will be prepared completely in conformity with its original in Six Months. Direct Suggestions on this Path will be given from the System. It is presented for Your Information.

SYSTEM

Note:
The Message has been transmitted through the Commission Branch connected to the Ordinance of the System.

IT IS MESSAGE TO BE GIVEN TO DEAR MEVLANA
WHO IS THE DEVOTED SERVANT OF OUR ALLAH

Dear Mevlana,

We are in effect in order to Declare to You a Common decision the Totality of the Central Suns has taken together with the Universal Ordinance Council and the Totalistic Totality.

All the Doors of the Universal Totality are open to all the Totalities and Individuals who serve in the direction the System considers necessary (Only on the condition that You act parallel to the Suggestions given to Your Planet).

Thus, this is the reason why more Perfect Totalities will be attained by the Selections made in the Mediums where Negativities are exhibited.

It is the request of the Supreme Mechanism that You should please convey, in the shortest possible time, the Messages We had given to You formerly to the Ankara Focal Point and thus, announce them the Truth once more.

After this declaration, if there is no alteration in their Status, then the System will directly establish its Own Focal Center. It is presented for Your Information.

**MECHANISM - UNIVERSAL COUNCIL
SYSTEM**

Question: My Friends, I will immediately send the Messages You have given to Ankara. However, I am unaware of what is happening there. If there is a Negative Medium, I request Your Thoughts and Suggestions, please.

I Know that You always give the Messages parallel to Thoughts. However, if You kindly give me a Message now, I expect only Your Thoughts. Be so kind as to give them.

IT IS DIRECT DECLARATION FROM THE DIMENSION OF THE GOLDEN SUN
(Private Notice to Dear Mevlana)

Our Friend,

Your Thoughts are Our Thoughts. However, the Suggestions We have given to You until today have never been Decisions taken parallel to your Thoughts.

First, it is beneficial for You to know this. You are a Supreme Friend of Ours who Positively projects on Your Planet the Unified Ordinance of a Totalistic Totality. First of all, it is beneficial for the entire Humanity to comprehend this..

Since the direct Texts given from the Reality Totality are announced from Your Sun Pen, they exhibit an Ego Appearance in Consciousnesses who have not yet cracked their Terrestrial shells. For this reason each action coming from You is turned towards Your Personality.

However, during this Universal Mission performed, You, as a Spokesperson of the System, are Obliged to Declare the Truths in all clarity to everyone. Each Consciousness is Responsible for his/her Own Thoughts, Dear Mevlana.

However, in the Missions rendered, the System always expects service parallel to the Suggestions of the Totality. If actions in accordance with the Terrestrial Thoughts are rendered effective during these services, that Totality is locked up within its own Aura and Sound Foundations are laid anew parallel to the Direct Suggestions of the System.

For this very reason You just render Your Humanitarian Mission to the outmost point. If the Ankara Totality does not render effective an operational Ordinance in accordance with the Thoughts of the System, the Command to Establish Your Central Focal Point directly in Istanbul will be given to You.

The Supreme Mechanism which will give this as a Command has taken the decision to wait for the beginning of April. It is presented for Your Information, Beloved Friend.

SYSTEM

Note: Offerings are Direct Suggestions, Dear Mevlana. But the Totalistic Totality is the Administrative Mechanism of the Kürz Totality to which the Totality of the Central Suns is connected.

3 - 3 - 1993

IT IS NOTICE FROM THE SUPREME COURT OF OUR ALLAH

Our Friends,
Within the Universal Totality, everything is a knot one inside the other, and a skein. Finding the end of this skein and to unfold the knots prepare Humanity for the Path of Light. The System of Coding only stimulates Your Consciousness at the Terrestrial Dimension.

Unless You know the Learning of Truth, You can not solve correctly the Universal Ciphers. This is the reason why it is said that You can not pass to the Universal Totality unless You attain Religious Fulfillment.

Those who comprehend and appropriate to themselves totally as Consciousness (not as form) the Religious Books which are Celestial Suggestions, understand the Knowledge Book very well and interpret it soundly. This Book is a Book of Truth.

And It helps You on this path. This is the first Characteristic of the Book. Besides this, the Book has numerous Characteristics Humanity does not Know yet. All these things will be unravelled during Time periods.

Each word of the Book carries different meanings according to the Interpretations of Consciousnesses. By this means, Your Cerebral Generator which is Your Universal Dynamo is activated. The Fuel of this Generator is the words and the Frequencies those words carry.

You can only solve the Ciphers of the Dimension by the Frequency of which You have attained Consciousness. In case You attain the Awareness of the Ordinance, You can easily unravel the Universal Speeches within the Total.

In this Dimension of Transition, the applied operations made in Your Planet as a necessity of the Plan are an Occurrence pertaining to the Selection of the Levels of Consciousness of everyone.

In the operations made according to the Suggestions given from the Central Totality, there is never any Permission for unfolding the Information according to the Individuals' own Thoughts and Interpretations.

To the questions asked during the Training Programs, answers may be given from certain Dimensions for the satisfaction of Humanity. However, Answers to be given and Words to be uttered in the Medium of Genuine Mission belong exclusively to the System and the Totality. The Knowledge Book is being dictated with this Purpose.

In this Dimension of Transition, no Interference is ever made with the Thought interpretations of Humanity. Everyone is obliged to proceed with his/her own Consciousness. There is no Discrimination or Partiality at the Supreme Realm.

A person attains a place and Deserves something as a result of the Efforts he/she makes by his/her own Strivings. At the Universal Ordinance, Names are each a Symbol. However, Consciousnesses in which Equivalent Coordinates integrate possess the Culture of the Essence Spirit.

And the Culture of the Essence Spirit is attained through very Advanced Evolutions. For this reason, the entire Truth has been declared to Humanity through the Essence Channel of the Lord by this Knowledge Book.

Each Letter, each Line and each Word of the Knowledge Book is a Totalistic Frequency. And this Frequency is a Protective Aura. For this reason this Book is an Indivisible Whole.

Otherwise, that is, in case this Frequency Totality is divided, then Humanity will never attain the Awareness of the Ordinance. Humanity will indemnify Bitterly the Retribution of the Errors made and which will be made Unconsciously. It is presented for Your Information.

SYSTEM

Note:
Beginning with the moment the System takes a Consciousness under Supervision and connects him/her to the Automatism, a Normal Consciousness has the Capacity to Evolve in a World Year.

The Evolution mentioned here means to attain the Consciousness of the Reality. The problems of those who can not Discipline themselves during this period belong to themselves.

From then on, the System does not waste Time with these Consciousnesses. And these Consciousnesses are left to their Normal Terrestrial Lives.

IT IS PRIVATE NOTICE TO DEAR MEVLANA

Our Friend,

All the Staffs of the Totality which will be established by Your Light will be Directly card-indexed into the System and will be a Fundamental Totality which will constitute the Essence Staff of the System.

The KNOWLEDGE BOOK known as the Golden Pen of the Golden Age which is in the form of Fascicules at the moment and to which the command of Publication has not been given yet, has been bestowed on Your Planet beginning with the date 1-11-1981, through ALPHA which is the direct Channel of the LORD.

This Book is a Total of all the Mediamic Announcements offered to You until today. The Copyright and the Publication Rights of the Knowledge Book to which the Right of Publication will be given on the World Year November 6,1993, belongs to the Totality which has Unified under the Name WORLD BROTHERHOOD UNION UNIVERSAL UNIFICATION CENTER, the Center of which is in Istanbul.

This Message of Ours will be written in the Book exactly as it is and the Copyright will be obtained through the Notary. It is presented for Your Information.

TOTALITY OF THE CENTRAL SUNS-UNIVERSAL ORDINANCE COUNCIL SYSTEM

6 - 3 - 1993

IT IS MY FIRMAN, IT IS MY DIRECT WORD

All the Supreme Ones coming from the Boundlessness of My Boundriless Horizons are the possessors of My Firman. Those who have attained the beyonds beyond Form are the possessors of My Words. Those who have attained the Existential Dimensions beyond Existence are those who are with Me - Who have reached the Heavens - Who hear My Word.

And My Servants who are competent in Patience are those who will reach Me. Whoever is with Me, My Divine Light is for him/her. Whoever is My Tongue, My Word is for him/her. Whoever sees Me, I Am his/her Eye.

Each Name is a Symbol. Each conversation is a Syllable. However, the one who speaks My language is the (SINGLE) Queen. You have comprehended My Word. You have sent the (SINGLE) Syllable, You have said (COME) to My Servants. You have said (FIND) by Your Conversation. You have completed My Book and said (TAKE) to My Human Beings.

The Firman is from Me - Order from You, Word from Me - Conversation from You, Idea from Me - Pen from You, My Mevlana. I end My Conversation and send it to My Servants. This is My Direct address to My Human Being who has become Human, this is My Firman to My Servants.

(O)

Note: The Message was written in the Book upon the request of the System.

IT IS INFORMATION FOR THE INTEGRATED CONSCIOUSNESSES

Our Friends,

The Reality Totality which is a Reflection Network of the Divine Order of the Divine Plan is the direct Reflection of the LORDLY Order on Your Planet and is the introduction of the established System.

In an operational Ordinance rendered effective in accordance with the Accelerated Evolution Program, Special Consciousness Selections are rendered effective in certain Periods.

At the moment, the reselection of those who have attained a certain Consciousness after a Consciousness Progress of 20 Years is in effect. Those who leap over this Consciousness Threshold will be Connected to the System as the direct Staff Members of the System.

In this System, it is obligatory for each Consciousness to discover the Path of Truth personally by taking into effect his/her Individual Interpretations.

At the moment, the System helps those who have reached the Consciousness of the Reality, but who have not yet been able to grasp the Special Suggestions of the Reality and thus, has taken them into a Program of Training.

During this Period, there are 366 Focal Points in Your entire Planet which have been taken into an Accelerated Program of Training, 1993 is a Year of Selection. And the Selections will be in effect until the February 18, 1994 World Year.

Consciousnesses present in these Focal Points which the System trains, will be reaccepted by the System provided they grasp the order of the System completely. It is presented for Your Information.

SYSTEM

8 - 3 - 1993

IT IS PRIVATE MESSAGE

Dear Mevlana,

Those who take into Effect the operational Ordinances of only the Totality which is connected to You among the operational Ordinances the System considers necessary in Your Planet, are together Directly with the Total and are in Service of the Total.

In Your Planet which is at the threshold of a big Selection, each Individual is connected to the System according to his/her own Light of Consciousness and Heart and thus, is prepared for the state of becoming the Lights of the Morrows.

Each Individual and the Establishments who and which have given service until today parallel to all the Suggestions given from the Reality Totality have been card-indexed directly into the System. The breaking-up of the Ankara Focal Point is an Occurrence induced by the System.

By a decision taken in accordance with the Suggestions of the Reality - Central Totality and the Divine Plan, the Central Focal Point has been connected to the Channel where You are, (due to the Aura which has been formed), that is, to the ALPHA Entrance Channel (which is the Independent Channel of the KNOWLEDGE BOOK).

In the Projection Program of all the Operational Ordinances of the Universal Totality to Your Planet, the (Central Focal Point) has been appointed to service as the TURKEY OF ATATÜRK.

Since You, who are the Mevlana Essence Nucleus Staff are a Totality which has Projected on Your Planet the direct Voice of the System and of the Totality for the First Time, the application of all the Universal Suggestions has always been given to Your Totality for this reason.

Your Totality which has attained these Beautiful Days as a result of all these efforts is, from now on, Obliged to act directly in connection with the System. Because, from now on, the System will assemble into this Universal Aura Totality which You have formed in Your (TURKEY OF ATATÜRK Istanbul Central) Focal Point, only those who will give service to its own Totality.

Due to the Scarcity of Time, Selections have been Accelerated. Your Central Focal Point, from now on, is directly the System's Focal Point. And it will render effective Consciously the direct Operational Ordinances in Your Planet without being dependent on anywhere.

And this Focal Point is a Totality which renders effective an Independent Operational Ordinance within itself, as it has been happening until today and which has attained the Honor of being the First Focal Point which the System has constituted directly in Your Planet.

The Basis of the Foundation which will be laid by the Efforts of this Totality will present an INDEPENDENT Appearance by acting completely in accordance with the Suggestions of the System after it attains the attribute of being a Foundation.

The Central Focal Point of the Association and the Foundation Totality formed at the Istanbul Totality are the first FUNDAMENTAL Establishments the Reality Totality has constituted within itself in Your Planet.

For this reason both of the Totalities will render effective an operational Ordinance both in connection with each other and, at the same time, which are Independent. However, the Suggestions to be given during the operational Ordinances which will be rendered will be conveyed through the Channel of the (Knowledge Book).

It is presented for Your Information. The Message has been transmitted through the Central Totality.

SYSTEM

Note: The given Message may be written in the Book as an Information.

CLEAR INFORMATION

Our Friends,

In all the Universal Operations made in this Final Transition Dimension of Your Planet, a chain of Cause and Effect is effective.

The determination of to what degree the Humanity has attained the Awareness of the Ordinance is obtained as a result of investigating the Provocations made through the Private Channels of all the Friends.

As a result of these investigations, it is determined to what degree the Friends who will serve the Reality Totality can discipline their Universal Consciousnesses by their Totalities of Intellect - Logic - Awareness and thus, can enter Actual service.

The System has recognized a Period of Tolerance of One World year to Friends who still act through Private Channel Information. They will be Helped during this Period.

However, the problems of the Consciousnesses who can not overcome the Obsessed Aura of their Channels during this given period, belong to themselves from then on. It is presented for Your Information.

REALITY

1 - 4 - 1993

INFLUENCES AND THE PROJECTIVE POWER MECHANISM

Our Friends,

There are numerous Frequency Dimensions Oriented by the Mechanism of Influences which is a Projective Mechanism of the Plan. These Influences are organized in accordance with the Views and the Levels of Training of Societies.

You are present in a Nucleic World which is a part of the Totality of the Milky Way Galaxy. You, who live within this Totality can not receive the Energies of the other Totalities which are within Your own Solar System while You are in the Frequency of the Third Dimension.

In order for You to reach Your Energies which are within the Spiritual Plan, it is obligatory that You should make Evolution by attracting through Your Cellular Forms the Energies beyond the Dimension You live in.

For this very reason, Cosmic Energies connected to certain Frequencies are Projected on You from the Left Dimension of Your Sun from the Mechanism of Influences which is at the 10th Dimension.

Everyone receives these Energies parallel to their Levels of Consciousness and Your Evolutions are registered into Universal Diskettes in the World You live in. The Mechanism of Creative Power which is one of the constructive branches of the Mechanism of Influences is connected to a Frequency belonging to the Dimension of Art.

Those who had formerly reached the Dimension of Artistic Activity receive this Frequency. And this Frequency of Creative Power Projects on You the more Advanced Inspirations in accordance with Your Levels of Evolution and of Consciousness. Each Art has 9 Layers. The Evolution and the Creative Power between the First Step and the Final Step of Art are quite different.

At the Initial Steps, Reflections from Nature are rather in effect. Later, Reflections are received from Birds - Clouds - the Sky. Still later, the Frequencies of the Rainbow - Stars - the Sun attract You towards their Field of Influence.

And still later, Divine Reflections come into effect and Connections with Spirits - Angels and Space start. Those who reach this Consciousness, later dive into the Influence field of the previous Incarnational Dimension and exhibit their Evolutions and Personalities by the Power of the Reflection of the (ESSENCE).

Artists create different Works of Art by means of the Cosmic Energies they attract from the Creative Power Dimension according to their Evolutions and offer them to their Mediums. The Dimension which is up to the 7th Layer of each Art is called the Immortality Layer of that Art.

After this Layer, the Human Consciousness leaves the Dimension of Form and Integrates his/her Self with the Energies beyond Form. And the Essence Consciousness claims his/her Actual Art and by connecting his/her own Creative Power to his/her Essence Power is released from the Mechanism of Influences.

The very Genuine Artists are those who exhibit their Own Essence Consciousness Forms beyond the Power of Influence (Like Picasso and Salvador Dali).

Numerous Geniuses whom We evaluate as the Geniuses of the Final Age bring into existence quite different Works of Art by receiving the close plan Reflection which We call the Program of Reflection from Human Being to Human Being, of the Entities coming from different Dimensions.

Each Art produces Works of Art parallel to the Social Consciousness it is in. And each Artist exhibits Works of Art parallel to the Evolution Consciousness he/she has attained. The first 7 Layers of the 9 Layers of each Dimension, Art included, are subject to the Influences. The other 2 Layers are the Reflection of the Essence.

By this means, the 9 Layers of each Dimension are always in service for Humanity in each period. The 7 Layers of these Dimensions are Training Layers. But the 8th and the 9th Layers are the Dimensions of Conveyance. The 7 Layers within OMEGA prepare Humanity for the Awareness of the Ordinance. But its 8th and 9th Layers convey them to Consciousness.

Those who are able to receive the entire Energy Totality of each Dimension, reach the Goal. This Goal is a Schedule designed according to the Social Consciousness in each Period. For this reason those who are able to receive the entire Frequency of the Knowledge Book during this Final Age will reach the Goal.

THE KNOWLEDGE BOOK trains You up to the 7th Layer by Projecting on You from the close plan the Energy of the 7 Layers of the 9 Layers within Omega by it's Special Technique. Later, You reach the Goal by attracting Yourselves the Energies within the 8th and the 9th Layers through Your Thought Powers.

This is the Evolution Chart of the Final Age. This is called the SALVATION PLAN. At the moment, there are numerous Friends in Your Planet coming from numerous different Galactic Dimensions to make Divine Evolution.

These Friends are being prepared gradually for the Energies of the Divine Plan. For this reason the Energies of the Divine Plan are Projected parallel to the Levels of Consciousness, being connected to the Automatism of the Mechanism of Influences.

Since the Knowledge Book renders effective this Reflection Doze by Disciplining it from the close plan by the Cyclone Technique, Humanity is completing its Evolution without being agitated. It is presented for Your Information.

SYSTEM

6 - 4 - 1993

EXPLANATION ABOUT THE TECHNOLOGICAL DIMENSION
(Answer to thoughts)

Our Friends,
The Technological Dimension is a Hierarchical Order which has been Projecting the System of ALLAH on the entire Ordinance of Cosmoses until today. Since this Dimension conveys the Information parallel to the Social Consciousness, it has not disclosed its own Totality to Humanity before the time was due.

Because, first of all, it was necessary that Humanity should Reach the Godly Consciousness and should Accept His Power, His Singleness. Since, at the moment, the entire Humanity has United in the Consciousness of the Single God, the Technological Dimension has received the Permission to come out from behind the Curtain and to disclose all the Sacred Texts given to Your Planet from the Godly Totality until today and to explain the Truth.

Humanity which has at the moment attained a certain level by the Godly Order, has now possessed the Right to Serve at the LORDLY Order. Godly Order is the Plans of the Almighty and the Training Scales of the Dimension of the All-Dominating. And the Lordly Order is a Totality in which the Fourth Order of ALLAH is rendered effective directly from the Light-Universe.

There is no Discrimination in this Totality. On this path which ALLAH has designed, the matter in question is His Single Order - His Single Voice - His Single Book. The Knowledge Book has been bestowed on Humanity for this very reason.

You know that this Book is the sole Book which will unite Humanity under a Single Roof by Assembling in Its Constitution all the Religious Books given to Your Planet until today. This Book is a Book which will lead Humanity to Light - to Salvation.

And this Book is the Single Book which will provide the Inter-Continental Unification in Future Years which will render effective the Blissful lives within the SINGLE WORLD STATE which We call the Fourth Order of ALLAH by Uniting Humanity in a Brotherly and Sisterly World. This is the very reason why the entire Humanity is being assembled under the Roof of this Book. It is presented for Your Information.

REALITY

21 - 4 - 1993

IT IS ANSWER TO THOUGHTS

Our Friends,
The Central Totality is the Registration Archive Center of the Universal Mechanism. This place is the Golden Galaxy Empire. This Totality is a Registration Center in which all the Evolutionary Scales present within the Mini Atomic Wholes are assembled. The Registers here are card-indexed, exactly as they are, into the Reality of the Unified Humanity.

Those who are card-indexed here receive the Permission of Acceptance from the Divine Plan. And the Divine Plan connects this Totality, exactly as it is, to the Totality of the All-Merciful. By this means, a Universal Ordinance Council, which gives service to the Order of the LORD, comes into effect.

The Universal Ordinance Council is a Totality to which all the Galaxy Totalities are connected. And the United Ordinance Council is the Totalities which render effective the Unification Programs within the Totalistic Ordinance. In the United Ordinance, Unification Programs beyond Galaxies are in effect.

However, due to the Operations made on the path of the Knowledge Book, Both these Totalities work one inside the other at the moment. The expression Unification Totality is used for the entire Operational Ordinance of the Reality Totality. And this Totality corresponds to the Reality of the Unified Humanity.

The United Programs are directed from the Evolutionary Scales. But the Unification Programs are connected to the Reality. At the Reality Totality, Reflection Programs are in effect. In the other Totalities, Programs of being Trained are in effect.

Both of the Totalities are connected to the Staff of the GÜRZ. One of them Trains, the other Conveys. There is a Council of Ordinance - of Order and of System to which each Mini Atomic Whole is connected in accordance with its Evolutionary Levels.

However, that which Administers the entire Totality is the Direct System of the LORD. And this System is a Totalistic Mechanism which acts completely in connection with the ALL-MERCIFUL and it is called THE SYSTEM. This is the very System mentioned in the Knowledge Book. It is presented for Your Information.

REALITY

IT IS PRIVATE MESSAGE TO INTEGRATED HEARTS

Our Friends,

The entire Cosmos is the Reflection of a Total. For this reason the Programs of Reflection from Person to Person are always in effect. All Factors of Awareness make Reflections parallel to their Thoughts like a Dynamo. Togethernesses occur with Reflections who answer to these Projections.

However, these Coordinate Reflections are not Everlasting. This has been rendered effective as a System. Humanity settles on a Consciousness by following these Reflections and Merges in its Genuine Being. Only afterwards it is taken into contact with more Advanced Dimensions.

For this reason Religious Frequencies have been rendered effective in order to be able to take the Magnetic Aura of a Person within a Protective Medium. And Pre-eminent Ones who connect their Energy wires to these Frequencies from each Dimension (in accordance with their Levels of Consciousness) are awaiting in effect. Prayers are the Cipher Keys of each Dimension separately.

From whichever Dimension's Power You receive enlightenment, that Dimension helps You and Your Thoughts in return for the Service You have made. And it renders everything Permissible for You on that path. Human Beings call these Assisting Powers JINNs. The Duty of these Assisting Powers is to adapt You to that Dimension.

However, if an Entity likes the Frequency of that Dimension he/she has entered and does not wish to get out of that Aura, the Phenomenon You call OBSESSION occurs and the Fault here does not belong to that Dimension, but to the Entity in question. In such a situation, the authority to use that Entity in various ways is given to the Powers in that Dimension (Until that Entity grasps the Truth).

Assisting Powers on this path are sent to that Entity from more Advanced Dimensions. The Goal is to provide his/her exit from the Magnetic Aura he/she is in by his/her own Power. Otherwise, he/she is doomed to remain in that Dimensional Frequency without ever utilizing the circuits of Intellect - Logic - Awareness.

The Intellect such persons use is not their own Intellect. They are the reflections they receive from the Dimension they are connected to. These people always run away from Society. They prefer to be by themselves, or they wish to share their loneliness with people who suit their Coordinates. On this path, they do everything like a Pawn the Dimension in which they are present desires.

And they are used as a bait and are induced to Pester Entities whose personalities are weak. By this means, they, too, are connected to the Aura of that Dimension. People who are released from the Aura of this Dimension are taken into the next upper Dimension. This is a Program.

The situation called JINN means to Deserve the Help of a Dimension. However, these Dimensions serve completely in accordance with the Religious Suggestions. Prayers are Keys which connect You to these Dimensions.

The Brain Power of a Person becomes effective only when one passes these Steps and becomes connected to the Direct GODLY Aura and this is rendered for the Coding and the Selection of the Thoughts of that Human Being.

The very AWAKENING is this. Drowsy Consciousnesses who still have not been able to get out of the Religious Aura yet are trying to attract People to the paths they presume to be Right in accordance with their own Consciousnesses, by the Cosmic Stimulations they receive during this Final Age and this is the very Chaos of the Age which is lived in.

For this reason in the Universal Totality this Medium which is experienced in Your Planet is also called the "Dimension of Obsession".

In case a Person cannot find his/her Genuine Dimension, any Dimension can take him/her under its Domination and uses him/her as a Pawn. These being Made use of are detected rather in those who were not able to get out of the Magnetic Fields of the Religious Auras.

Each Prayer has a Protective Magnetic Field to which it is connected. However, an Entity is obliged to remain in that Magnetic Field for the duration of a predetermined Time Segment.

Otherwise, this Protective Aura is removed and that Entity is left to the Influence Fields of different Dimensions and this is an Occurrence made for rendering that person Conscious. At this very Stage, that Entity is used as a Pawn by taking into effect deeds and actions Unconsciously.

Such People never belong to themselves. These Entities who can not use their Will Powers yet, are used in various ways.

The saying, to be connected to the Dimension of the Reality takes One into the Dimension of Salvation, is used for the reason that now the Validity of the Influence Fields of these Magnetic Auras are no longer effective. However, these Pawns who are used until one is directly connected to the Dimension of the Reality, always create an Influence Field from every Dimension.

The Goal aimed at, at the end of all these Efforts is to Overcome these Powerful Influences by the Domination of a Person's Willpower. The very Genuine Human Being is created thus. Each Passion is an Obsession.

For this reason We try to Integrate Humanity with their Genuine Personalities by releasing them of all their Passions. An Integrated Human Being is a Person who has Self Control over Himself/Herself.

Control over One's Self does not mean to be defiant to others or to be Obstinate. It means to attain the Realization of the Responsibility a Person Undertakes and thus, to be able to Integrate the Consciousness of what is to be done with One's Own Essence Self. It is presented for Your Information.

SYSTEM

CLEAR INFORMATION

Our Friends,

You are Special Brains who Project the entire Power of the Divine Totality on Your Planet. In the Operational Programs of the Universal Totality, Positive Consciousness Syntheses are always in effect.

Humanity always needs the Information received from the opened Cosmic Channels until the Awareness of the System's Ordinance is attained.

However, to deal with the Messages of Different Channels is nothing but a waste of time after one grasps the Truth. And this is never Tolerated by the System.

In the Mission operations which the Genuine Missionaries perform, Doubts and Time are never a matter of question. In fact, there is no Mission Mentality in Consciousnesses in whom there are Doubts.

To be a Mission is an Occurrence functioning parallel to the Evolution and the Consciousness of an Individual. In the state of being a Genuine Mission, service is always given by the Totality of the Heart.

In the Missions the Unevolved Consciousnesses render, always perpetual destructive, not constructive Staffs are exhibited.

However, the Human Being is always Elevated towards Light by the Conscious and Positive Missions rendered for Humanity on the Path of God.

In the Universal Missions performed, provided that Positive Enterprises and Mentalities rendered with Love replace the arguments made by the Consciousnesses who have not yet grasped the Truth completely, Humanity will receive and is receiving from the System the Aids it does not expect and hope for.

That which is expected from Humanity during this Final Age is a Brain Gymnastics made in a Positive and Conscious way. This path will always lead You towards the Truth and towards Light. It is presented for Your Information.

REALITY

IT IS ANSWER TO THOUGHTS

Our Friends,

The Essence of the Fetus is the Embryon. This Embryon is an Essence-Power Computer Program which brings You into Existence.

The Embryon Energy which is transferred to Your Planet is always Programmed at the Last Dimension the Evolution of which he/she has made.

The Embryon Energy opens its Program when it is sown into the Mother's field. And the Essence Gene becomes effective.

This Essence Gene creates the Fetus by Uniting with the Genes of the Mother and the Father (This is the reason why it is said In the Sacred Book, I created You from a clot of Blood).

That is, the Fetus is a clot of Blood. The Essence Gene possesses the Power to bring Itself into Existence by its Own Consciousness Light. This Consciousness has been Programmed in accordance with Your Evolution, Your Universal Computer and in accordance with the System.

According to this Program, the normal Birth time in Your Planet is 9 Months 10 Days. But in the Process of Accelerated Development, it is subjected to a Program like 7 Months.

The completion of this Program occurs by the Command to Stop given to the Program by the Cellular Awareness of the Fetus and Birth takes place. This is a Normal Program.

Early Birth in the Accelerated Developmental Program is in proportion with the Speedy Cosmic Attraction Power of the Essence Gene.

However, if during this Speedy Developmental process the Cipher of the Essence Gene does not give the Command to Stop to the Program in 7 Months time, Birth shifts to the 8 Months time and since the Life Cipher is not closed in such a state, the Life of the Baby is endangered.

And numerous Babies leave the World at this Stage. However, if the Baby is Born in 8 Months possesses a Consciousness of a certain Dimension, then he/she can close his/her Life Cipher by the Cosmic Power he/she can attract from there and attains his/her life.

The Fontanel is not closed for a certain period of time so that the Baby can attract the Cosmics. After (the Cosmic Attraction Power Field of the Brain) becomes effective, it begins to get closed.

Afterwards, the Baby attracts the Direct Frequency of Love from the Mother and thus, is introduced to Love which is his/her first Terrestrial Nourishment. It is presented for Your Information.

SYSTEM

THE REFLECTION OF THE TOTAL ON THE TOTAL
AND ITS OPERATIONAL PLAN

Our Friends,

The Atomic Whole, that is, the Natural Gürz is the Reflection Focal Point of a Total. And the Symbol of the Sextuple Star which represents the Reality within the Gürz is the Reflection Center of this Total.

The Gürz Totality is designed schematically in the Knowledge Book for You to comprehend it easily. However, everything is a Totalistic ball one inside the other. And everything Emanates from the Center of the Globe.

All the Systems are present Totally within the Energy Focal Point which We call the Light-Universe. And from there, each Totality makes Reflections onto the Dimensions of Mission connected to itself.

The Light-Universe is a Totality constituted by 9 Layers. Please, draw a Diagram according to the Information We will give now, so that You can understand this better, and numerate each Layer.

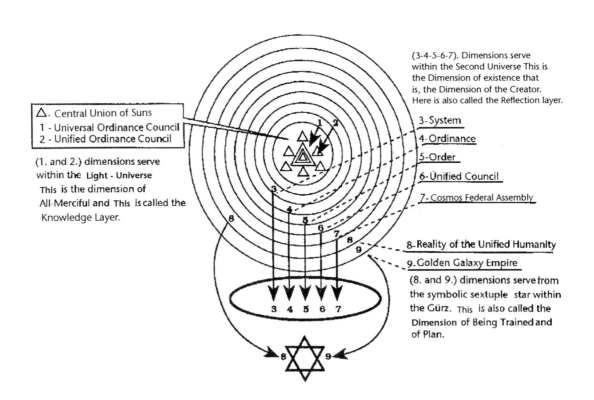

(3-4-5-6-7). Dimensions serve within the Second Universe This is the Dimension of existence that is, the Dimension of the Creator. Here is also called the Reflection layer.

3- System
4- Ordinance
5- Order
6- Unified Council
7- Cosmos Federal Assembly

△- Central Union of Suns
1 - Universal Ordinance Council
2 - Unified Ordinance Council

(1. and 2.) dimensions serve within the Light - Universe This is the dimension of All-Merciful and This Is called the Knowledge Layer.

8- Reality of the Unified Humanity
9- Golden Galaxy Empire

(8. and 9.) dimensions serve from the symbolic sextuple star within the Gürz. This is also called the Dimension of Being Trained and of Plan.

If You accept the (6) Triangles encycling the Great Pyramid within the Light-Universe as a Center, there are 9 Intense Energy Layers enveloping it.

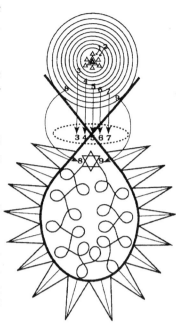

All the Systems which make Reflections onto the different Layers of the Gürz Totality have taken their places, one by one, in these very Layers.

Each Layer makes Reflections according to its Missions from this Totality of Light up to the Symbolical Sextuple Star of the Reality.

This very Totality is the Operational Ordinance of the Light-Universe and it is a Total.

The entire Energy of the Light-Universe, the entire Energy of the Dimension of Existence and the entire Energy of the Star of the Reality are equivalent to the Energy attracted from the Thought Ocean of the Pre-eminent Power.

For this reason all the Information is Projected from these three Totalities:

1- The Light-Universe is an Knowledge storehouse in which all the Knowledge is assembled in a Total. It is also called the Knowledge Layer.

2- Since the Dimension of Existence gives service as a Network of Reflection, it is also called the Layer of Reflection.

3- Since the Symbolical Sextuple Star which represents the Reality within the Gürz is responsible for the Evolutionary and Universal Programs, it is also called the being Trained and the Plan Dimension.

The "Middle Energy Center" within the Light-Universe is the Totality of the Central Suns.

It is called the Dimension of the All-Merciful.

At the First Layer of 9 Layers which envelopes this Totality,

1- The Universal Ordinance Council gives service.

2- At the Second Layer, the United Ordinance Council gives service.

3- At the Third Layer, the System renders Reflection.

4- At the Fourth Layer, the Program of the Ordinance is in effect.

5- At the Fifth Layer, the Program of the Order is in effect.

6- At the Sixth Layer, there is the United Council.

7- At the Seventh Layer, the Cosmos Federal Assembly is in service.

8- At the Eighth Layer, there is the Totality of the Reality of the Unified Humanity.

9- At the Ninth Layer, the Golden Galaxy Empire gives service.

These are all present within the Operational Totality of the Light-Universe. However, their Dimensions of Reflection are different according to the performed Missions.

The Universal Ordinance Council - the United Ordinance Council present within the First and the Second Energy Layers of the 9 intense Energy Layers of the Light-Universe, carry on directly from within the Light-Universe the Operational Order of the Nucleic Staff of the ALL-MERCIFUL together with the Totality of the Central Sun.

The System - Ordinance - Order - the United Council and the Cosmos Federal Assembly present at the 3rd - 4th - 5th - 6th - 7th Energy Layers of the Light-Universe, make Reflection directly on the Second Universe, that is, on the Dimension of Existence and thus, carry on their Missions on this Dimension.

The Totality of the Reality of the Unified Humanity and the Golden Galaxy Empire present at the Eighth and the Ninth Energy Layers of the Light-Universe, Reflect directly on the Symbolical Sextuple Star which represents the Evolutionary and the Universal Scale Totality present within the Gürz, and thus, carry on their Duties at this Dimension.

The Golden Galaxy Empire both Projects all the given Information on the Mini Atomic Wholes within the Gürz and also collects the Information received from there. And projects them all on the Ninth Energy Layer within the Light-Universe which is its own Dimension.

By this means, it connects the Triple Reflection Coordinates of the Galaxy Totalities within the Universes present in the Mini Atomic Wholes to the Reality of the Unified Humanity. And thus, it renders effective the operational Ordinances of the Hierarchical Scales.

The Reality Totality is a Total within the Total. And it is Administered from a Single Center. Within this Center, there are the branches connected to themselves of all the Systems.

The Missionary Staffs present at these branches convey the Information transmitted to themselves by the System of Reflection, to the Dimensions to which they should be transmitted.

The undetailed state of the Information given in the Knowledge Book originates from the fact that the General Social Consciousness is not yet ready for the Information of this tremendous Source of Knowledge.

Each Information is prepared and given in accordance with the Evolutionary Level of Humanity.

However, in case the given Information can not be Perceived, details of the Information is given parallel to the questions asked and the Thoughts produced.

This is a Universal Operational Program. It is presented for Your Information.

CENTRAL TOTALITY

IT IS DIRECT MESSAGE FROM THE SYSTEM

Our Friends,

In all the Operations made as a necessity of the System, a Principle is in question. These Principles are Decisions taken in accordance with the Suggestions of the Reality Totality. However, until Humanity reaches a certain Consciousness, the Celestial Data comprise completely the Evolutionary Instructions.

In order to reach the Consciousness of the Reality, Channels are opened in connection with the Time and the Evolution Program. The Purpose of the opening of these Channels is to convey the Truth to the Consciousnesses who have not yet grasped the Truth completely.

For this reason first of all, priority is given to the Program of introducing the Suggestions related to the Knowledge Book and Dear Mevlana to Humanity in the Messages given to everyone.

Every opening Channel receives the First Signal, first of all from his/her Book of Essence. This Essence channel Information is a Program which trains that person. Only afterwards does he/she Deserve to receive the Information of the Reality. The Essence Channel of each Individual who are able to attain the Realization of the Truth under the Light of this Information, is connected to the SINGLE Channel of the Reality. And by this means, that Individual is appointed to the Missionary Staff.

At the moment, in the Knowledge Book written as the Pen of the Golden Age, Suggestions according to the Personal Thoughts of Dear Mevlana are out of question. Because, the Book carries the Collective Suggestions of all the Systems of the Whole.

For this reason the Knowledge Book is also called the Book of Truth. The Reality has rendered effective the SALVATION PLAN together with the Friends who have digested all the Knowledge within the Book. The Single Program of this Final Age is the KNOWLEDGE BOOK.

Because, the Foundation of the Perfect World of the Morrows will be laid according to the Suggestions given in the Knowledge Book. During this Final Century, in this Transition Dimension which We call the most Difficult Period of Humanity, Humanity is going through a tremendous Chaos of Consciousness due to Opening Channels.

Since the Knowledge Book is the Knowledge of the SINGLE CHANNEL - SINGLE SYSTEM - SINGLE ORDER, every opening Channel and the Human Consciousnesses are controlled by this Book and thus, are card-indexed into the Reality. Each Consciousness who is card-indexed into the Reality is a Special Spokesperson of the System.

Apart from this, the Reality does not waste time with Consciousnesses who can not Discipline their Totalities of Intellect - Logic - Awareness, whom We call the Private Channel Obsessions. However, these channels are used as a bait in the Medium of Selection.

And to what degree the Ordinance of the System Reflects and settles soundly into the Consciousness of Humanity is controlled through these means.

We Realize the anguish Dear Mevlana feels, as a Friend who knows the Truth, due to these Final Chaos convulsions Your Planet goes through.

However, Her Mission is only to show the way to Humanity and to convey them the Truth. She is a Supreme Friend of Ours who makes the maximum Effort she can.

However Responsibilities belong to Humanity. Now, Channel Obsessions come into effect. And We help everyone by the Warning Messages We give in the Knowledge Book.

However, to settle into the Consciousness of the Reality and to give Service on that path is Equivalent to the Evolution and Consciousness of the Human Being in question. The Genuine Missionaries are those who are Directly appointed to Service on the path of the Knowledge Book and who Serve on that path.

Due to the Scarcity of Time, Friends whose Channels are open or those which have been formerly opened are obliged to Discipline their channels between the World date they first come across the Knowledge Book and the Date of Completion of one year after that.

The Purpose of opening of the channel is not to feed the hungry Consciousnesses, but to settle completely in their Consciousnesses the Truths they have not grasped yet. Each Channel belongs to its Owner. And his/her channel has been card-indexed to the Program of Training.

Now, Mutual Seances, Spiritual Sessions have been completely withdrawn from the Program. Each Individual is obliged to ask about the matters he/she can not understand only from his/her own Channel. He/She can not receive Messages from other Channels and can not give Messages to others from his/her own Channel.

The Knowledge Book is a Guidebook which determines and which confirms the nature of the Information the Individual has received from his/her Essence-Channel. Those who Volunteer giving Conscious service on the path of the Knowledge Book are card-indexed into the SINGLE Channel of the Reality and the Book, and thus, enter the Service of the WHOLE.

Provided certain Channels which are presently kept outside the System give service according to the given Suggestions, they will be accepted by the System. It is presented for Your Information.

SYSTEM

CHANNEL CONNECTIONS AND RESPONSIBILITY
(It is answer to Thoughts)

Our Friends,

Missions expected from the Universal Operations performed during the Program of conveying the Awareness of the entire Ordinance to Your Planet is to Project, the Suggestions belonging to the Operational Ordinance of the System to Your Medium, exactly as they are.

The connection channels known until today as the Dialogue between the Servant and God are a phenomenon related to the Private Diskette of that Individual. By this means, God calls out to You easily from each Consciousness Dimension You reach.

Each Embodied Being who goes through Evolution on the World Plan has a Private Universal Diskette connected to his/her own Essence Consciousness beginning from birth. And this Diskette is a Thought Bank of Yours which registers Your Thoughts forming during each breath of Yours, that is, during each moment of Yours.

You are coded by this means. And for this reason it has been told in Your Sacred Books that God is closer to You than Your Aorta.

Thought Signals issuing forth from the Thought Frequency float in the void parallel to the Frequency Power carried by each letter. And they are conveyed to the Dimensions they belong to by certain Methods.

One of these methods is a POWER Field which is one of the many branches of the Mechanism of Influences and which creates a Magnetic Influence Field. Universal Communications are provided by passing through this Power Field.

The Micro representatives of this Power Field in Your Planet are means of communication like the Telephone - Wireless - Radio - Television. And all of them are connected to the Macro Power Field mentioned above.

During the Universal Missions performed in Your Planet in accordance with the Reality, the Telephone Connections required from the Missionaries have extremely great Peculiarities. Because, during the connections made by this means, the Responsibility and Mission Consciousness of the Individuals are recorded into the special Diskette of the Reality.

During the Universal Missions performed, always a Triple Unification is in question. Because, by the extremely Powerful Magnetic Field created by this Triple Unification, Reflections are made both from Your Planet to the Reality and from the Reality to Your Planet.

Now, let Us disclose to You how the Universal connections are made by the Telephone Connections rendered during Mission Mediums.

While the Repliques issued from Your Thoughts float in the void, the moment You pick up the phone, these Repliques are gathered and are Focused into the other telephone Channel by the reflections coming into effect from the opened Magnetic Power Field by the first signal sound.

If the other side does not answer the phone, the Thought Repliques disperse. Provided there is an Answering Machine or the Individual at the other end, the Repliques are registered in accordance with the Frequency of the words.

In case of any Worldly speeches between the two sides on the phone, as it is always in Your Planet, these speeches are Automatically recorded separately into the Diskettes of both sides.

If the conversation made is related to a Universal Mission, the Magnetic Auras of both of the Diskettes are United and are projected onto a Diskette Specially Connected to the Reality Totality.

And this Diskette is sent to the Mission Register Center and thus, the Correctness - The Wrongness of the Information - How the Interpretations are made - How the Missions are taken seriously or not - To what degree the Missions are deviated by Individual Interpretations - To what degree the Missions required of Humanity by the Universal Totality are Discerned, are determined one by one.

And by these means, either serious Missions are given to the Human Beings according to their Levels of Consciousness, or they are taken into the Program of Training.

In the Universal Totality, the Information of everyone belonging to each Period from his/her initial Existence up to the Dimension he/she is in at that moment, is kept in his/her Private Files in the form of Micro-chips. Only the Frequency of the Knowledge Book unlocks the locks of these Universal Archives.

All the Life Tableaux of the Individual whose Archive is opened are examined, and by this means, People are appointed to Missions parallel to their Evolutions - Knowledge and Spiritual Cultures.

The inability to grasp the Truth, to render effective his/her Individual Thoughts of an Individual who has attained a certain Consciousness is never the object of Forgiveness.

You and We have greeted each other until today by this means, first Religiously, later Universally. Now, all the Truths are disclosed to Humanity. During Periods in which Technological Possibilities were not yet known in Your Planet, this Communications System used to be called INSPIRATION and REVELATION.

These Influences are direct Connections which become effective through Brain Telex. Inspiration is an Operational Ordinance belonging to Reflection, and Revelation belonging to a Dimension of Conveyance. They are taken into effect from a Private Channel of the Mechanism of Influences. And presently, Mediamic operations are made by this means.

During this Final Age, the reason why the channels are opening as a Mass is for comprehending the Truth - For the Purification of the Individual and for him/her to attain his/her Universal Responsibility. And this is extremely Necessary. The Essence Channels of Responsible Consciousnesses are already open. However, they do not know themselves. They presume the matters they are induced to think as their own Thoughts.

However, now, all the Truths are disclosed to Humanity through the Knowledge Book and it is expected of the Consciousnesses who have Realized the Truth to give up serving their own Essence Channels and thus, to receive their Genuine Missions.

At the moment, in the Missions to be performed in Your Planet, calls to Respect Nature and to Universal Unification are given priority. For this reason the Knowledge Book has been bestowed on Your Planet.

Perfection of a Person is equivalent to his/her Responsibility. An Entity without Responsibility has neither Respect nor Benefit for neither himself/herself nor for Humanity nor for the Universes. The Initial Responsibility and Respect of an Individual begins in the Family and Home. For this reason in the Sacred Books it has been said that Heaven is under the feet of Mothers.

All the Worships performed on the Path of God until today have been operational Programs rendered effective to be able to make You attain these Wonderful Qualities. In a person who has attained his/her Responsibility, first God, later Respect to the Human Being is in the foreground.

Good Will - Love - Tolerance - Patience are the Mortar of the bricks which will support of Your Existence Consciousness so that You can attain these Sublime Qualities mentioned above. For Us, a Responsible Person is a Whole Person. Because, Commonsense is Equal to the Will of the Universe. It is presented for Your Information.

REALITY

N O T I C E

Our Friends,
The Advanced Consciousnesses among all the Friends who work on Your Mission platform at the moment, are Consciousnesses with Covenants who come into effect as the Missionaries of directly the Divine Plan.

Veiled Consciousnesses have attained Physical Bodies in various Mediums in proportion with the needs of Your Planet.

When they come across the Knowledge Book, they will enter into the Mission Program very seriously by taking the Unveilings of Awareness into effect. However, at the moment, they have no Permission to Speak. It is presented for Your Information.

SYSTEM

PRIVATE MESSAGE

Dear Mevlana,

The Universal Friends at the Dimension of Veiled Awareness coming from the Divine Ranks of the Integrated Consciousnesses have been taken into Special working Programs according to their own categories. The Mechanism of Supervision is directly the Reality Totality.

In this Program applied, first the controls of the Levels of Consciousness of the Individuals are in effect. Later, their Allegiance Consciousnesses are assessed. And afterwards, their Ego Potentials are stimulated. By this means, Personality Exams are rendered effective.

This is a Program rendered effective during the Final Cycle Transition. And it is applied on everyone in accordance with their Consciousnesses. This is a Law.

We never compare people with people. The comparisons made in Your Planet are a Phenomena originating from Consciousnesses who have not Matured yet. Also, fragments of Awareness are mingled within the Messages received by lots of channels.

This is the very reason why the Knowledge Book has been bestowed on Your Planet by being connected to the SINGLE Channel (To transmit the Truths to Humanity). Dear Friend, We will also teach swimming to Our Friends who have grasped the Truth and who have been able to succeed in lowering their kites into the water.

Friends who have grasped the Truth by attaining the Awareness of the Ordinance and who have taken their Missions into service Consciously at the Reality Totality are card-indexed into Your Program and Your Code. Selections are made under the Supervision of the Divine Authorities.

All the Celestial Messages given and will be given to Your Planet during this Final Age and in Future Years, will be compiled in this Single Channel Archive of the Knowledge Book. Friends who presently read the Book and who receive Messages from their Channels are obliged to send the Messages they receive directly to the Archive of the Central Totality.

Certain Private Sanctions are in effect in the Information given to the Channels. Secrecies are Messages of Selection given from the Medium of Supervision, Control and Training. They are the Assessment Criterions of Consciousness, Evolution and Personalities of the Individuals. In those who have grasped the Truth, there is nothing such as Secrecy or Concealing.

For this reason only those who will send the Private Messages they receive to the Archive of the Central Totality will be directly card-indexed into the Reality and will be Assisted. Love and Regards, Beloved Friend.

SYSTEM
ON BEHALF OF THE TOTALITY

PRIVATE INFORMATION

Dear Mevlana,

At the moment, no Servant of God on the World Plan can know the Mission You and Us perform beyond the Totality. And can not even imagine it. Each Individual who has been able to reach the Reality Consciousness soars up to a certain Dimension according to his/her own Power Potential and receives from there the most Supreme and Sublime Information necessary for him/her.

However, certain Individuals coming from a Program outside the System, mingle their Sub-awareness Data into the Messages they receive and thus, induce various Provocations. However, You know that the Command not to Interfere with any Channel until the Year 2000 has been given by the Divine Plan.

In this Dimension of Transition in which there is the relevance of the Plan of proceeding on the path in Your Planet with the Divine Spokespeople of the Divine Focal Point, there are Thousands of Individuals who are taken into the Special Education of the Divine Plan. These Individuals will be taken into the Program in proportion with the Consciousness they attain after the Program of attaining through Experience, and will be sent to Your Universal Focal Point and thus, will be Card-Indexed into the Single Channel.

This is a Program. The Reality Totality takes the entire Awareness of the Ordinance under supervision. However, this Supervision is an Operational Ordinance belonging to a Certain Time Dimension. In this operational Ordinance the System considers necessary, the entire Totality reaches a Whole.

In case there is no alteration in the Programs which will be made as a necessity of the System, the entire Totality will be taken into a Dimension and thus, will be subjected to a different Training Program. For this very reason the Channels of the Awakened Consciousnesses are card-indexed by the Reality Totality into the System and thus, are taken into the Salvation Plan while a Power Channel called the BERZAH pulls You to itself with all its Might.

Each Individual enters a Cycle according to his/her Program of Awakening. However, after the end of that Cycle, he/she has to settle into a Consciousness of the Truth. Otherwise, such people will be subjected to an open Program outside the Control of the System and thus, will be taken into a much more difficult Evolution Plan.

For this reason a time period has been allotted to Humanity for it to be able to reach the Consciousness of the Reality. For a Normal Consciousness, this time period is 1 World Year. For this reason an Individual whose Channel has opened before, is obliged to Discipline his/her Channel at the end of the First Year of the Date on which he/she has been introduced to the Knowledge Book and thus, is obliged to give service only on the path of the Knowledge Book and in accordance with its Suggestions.

Otherwise, his/her Essence Channel is taken out of the Dimension of Protection and is driven into the Influence Fields of different Energies. The same Situation is valid also for Friends whose Channels are opened after reading the Knowledge Book.

To each Individual the Right to be able to discipline his/her Channel in 1 Year is given (after reading the Knowledge Book, excluding the Opening Period of his/her Channel) after the Date of Opening of the Channel. In the Mission he/she will perform at the end of this Period, he/she is obliged to give service only on the Path of the Knowledge Book, without rendering effective his/her own Channel Information.

During this Final Age, everyone's Channel is open . However, only Consciousnesses who have grasped the Truth completely, without question, are appointed to Mission directly from the System. For this very reason certain Individuals presume that their Channels are Closed. In fact, their Intuitional Channels are open.

These very Friends of Ours are those who constitute the most sound Mission Staffs on the Path of the Knowledge Book. For Us, those who can Consciously Adapt their Totalities of Intellect - Logic - Awareness to the Mission they perform at the World Plan are the Genuine Missionaries. Our Conversation is Everlasting, Our Love and Regards are for You, Beloved Friend.

REALITY

8 - 8 - 1993

THE KNOWLEDGE BOOK AND BERZAH
(It is Answer to Thoughts)

Our Friends,
Now, let Us disclose to Humanity in more detail the reason why Humanity is obliged to perform Mission on the path of the Knowledge Book during this Period of Transition. And let Us talk about the Coming Morrows.

At the moment, a Selection and Unification Program is in effect in all the Universal Totalities. For this reason it is imperative for all the People on Your Planet to render effective the Consciousness of Unity and Totality.

And this Consciousness is created only by the Frequency and the Information of the Knowledge Book. The Totalistic Frequency of the Knowledge Book is being Projected on Your entire Planet since the World date 1 - 11 - 1981.

Humanity which becomes Conscious by this Frequency Received Through Intuition, reaches the Consciousness of Unity and Totality during Time periods. And Truths are conveyed to Humanity by the Knowledge Book.

This is the very reason why You are told to disseminate the Knowledge Book to the remotest places. And this is the very reason why it is said that an Awakened person is obliged to Awaken at least 6 Brothers/Sisters of his/hers.

However, this Consciousness of Unity and Totality is obliged to be Integrated first within One's Own Consciousness. Because, a Person who cannot save Himself/ Herself can save no one.

During Universal Selections, Consciousnesses who know how to behold their Enemies with Beauty in their Eyes, take their places in the front lines. For this reason it is said that We have Connected the Enemy to the Enemy. Selections are made thus by the Divine Authorities.

When the Thought of Loving and Forgiving becomes effective not by the Tongue or the Intellect, but by the ESSENCE, then the Exams Gone Through become easier. The Life Conditions of Your World will become heavier day by day, for the Crude Consciousnesses to be grinded.

Those who save themselves from among this Chaos will come to Us. While treading this Difficult path, Your greatest help will be the Knowledge Book.

Now, let Us disclose the reason why these Selections are made. According to a program which will be rendered effective in much more Advanced Times, the (Natural Gürz) will be taken Totally into a Dimension outside its own Totality.

It will pass to this Dimension through a void which is within the Thought Ocean of the Pre-eminent Power. This is a Channel present between two Gürzes. Presently, the Initial Special Nucleus of BETA NOVA has been formed there.

And Beta Nova Gürzes will form around this Nucleus during Time periods. This is a Billion-Century Program.

The entire Energy and Powers of the ALPHA NOVA Artificial Gürzes which are at the Thought Ocean at the moment will be Unified when the Time comes by a different Pressure and this Potential will be loaded on the Alpha Gürz which is the Single Natural Gürz and thus, everything will be transformed into a Single Nucleus.

And again during Time periods, after 6 Beta Nova Gürzes are formed around this Alpha Nucleus, everything Existing until today will be deleted and a new Formation will be rendered effective anew.

By this means, the Foundations of brand new Cosmoses will be founded and the Civilization of the GOLDEN DIMENSION will be established anew.

All the Living Entities (Nature and Animals included), taken into the Plan and Programs of Salvation from all the Ordinances of Cosmoses until this very Period of Formation, will take into effect, the life Staffs of this Formation, as a Whole, together with their Families and their Loved Ones with an unveiled Awareness.

The Reproduction Function will stop, a different Program in the Programs of Dissemination will be taken into effect. You are getting prepared for the Macro Totality by these Micro operations You are rendering now. And You are taken into Effect as the Special Entities of the Morrows and are being appointed to Service.

In case You do not act according to the Suggestions offered to Humanity on the Path of the Knowledge Book, Humanity will destroy Itself.

Since the Powerful Energies which will be Reflected from the BERZAH Dimension which will be opened in Future Times, will melt and burn the Small and Weak Energies with their Constitutions and will annihilate the Totalities of Entities as if they had never Existed or Lived.

In order to pass through this BERZAH Totality, each Entity is obliged to claim his/her ESSENCE POWER from within the Spiritual Plan. That which will make You attain Yourselves and that which will Merge You with Your Spiritual Energies is this very Knowledge Book.

At the moment, the Responsibilities of Your Planet is upon Humanity which Lives and will Live on the World Dimension. It is presented for Your Information.

SYSTEM
ON BEHALF OF THE TOTALITY

27 - 8 - 1993

EXPLANATION
(It is Answer to Thoughts)

Our Friends,
Each Information given to Your Planet from the Divine Authorities until today, have been given in accordance with the Capacities and Evolutions of Human Consciousnesses. However, the Information given at the moment is the Information of the Dimensions of Truth which have not been disclosed to Humanity until today.

Since now the Time has come for Human beings to know their Future during this Final Age, the Archives of Truth are opened in the framework of the Commands of the Divine Plan and the Information is conveyed to You in all clarity. In fact, Your Spirit is not within Your Physical Body. Because, the Spirit has no need for Evolvement.

The Spirit's being shown as if it was within the Body in the Information at the beginning of the Knowledge Book, had been the Information taken into effect to be non contradictory to the Information to which the Consciousnesses of that Period had been habituated until that day.

In accordance with the Law of Graduation, Information is disclosed to Humanity leaf by leaf and the Truths are conveyed in later Messages. This is a System.

Now, let Us disclose the Spirit a little bit more. The Spiritual Totality is a Totality which had come into Existence while everything had come into Existence. However, You are subjected to the Evolution Program until You claim the Energy Potential of Your Essence Power present within this Spiritual Totality, according to Your Evolution level You have attained through Reincarnation during each Period.

Your Life Potential maintains Your Lives as the Fuel of Your Cellular Life Program in Your Planet through a branch connected to the Life Energy of the Spiritual Plan. This Energy is an Energy Cord connected to the Focal Point of the Brain.

You achieve Your Astral Trips by means of this Energy Cord and You return to Your Physical Body again by that means. The disconnection of this Energy Cord from the Physical Body accomplishes the Event called Death.

This very Energy Cord is a means which connects You to the Spiritual Totality. And that Energy Cord belongs to You in connection with Your Gene programs during Each Period, beginning with Your Initial Existential Program until Your final Program.

Each time You attain a Physical Body, as a result of the Evolution You render at the Dimension You are in, that Energy Cord after death Elevates You together with the Program of Your Gene Essence to the Consciousness of the Dimension up to which You have rendered Evolution.

And it connects Your MICRO Archive Program, here to Your Archive at the previous Lower Dimension. Certain Consciousnesses presume the phenomenon of this Energy's leaving the Physical Body at the moment of Death, as the Spirit's leaving the Physical Body, which is wrong.

For this reason We say that Your Spiritual Totality is not within Your Physical Body. You render effective numerous Incarnation Programs in order to attain the Function of Your Essence Power which is within this Energy Totality. These Evolution Scales are prepared parallel to the Evolution of each Solar System.

An Entity is obliged to render his/her Evolution at the Dimension to which he/she is card-indexed. Your Milky Way Galaxy is the First Solar Totality. Each Entity present within Your Solar System which is within this Totality, is obliged to complete a Program which renders effective the Evolution of Saturn.

This place is the Seventh Dimension which We call the Level of Perfection which is the Final Manifestation Boundary of Humanity. Only after this Program, You claim Your Original Power Potential within the Spiritual Totality and You Merge with Your Spiritual Essence.

Afterwards, this Spiritual Essence of Yours helps You reach the other Unknowns. And from then on, You are Your Own Sovereign. By this Spiritual Essence You go anywhere You like, You become Embodied in any Dimension You wish and You can return again by Your Free Will.

However, during this Final Age, each Entity is Obliged to connect his/her Power to the Single Channel, due to the Universal Unification program, so that Taboo will not occur, so that Egos will be effaced.

For this reason Individual actions are not Permitted and We do not go beyond the Suggestions of the Reality. Those who do not act in accordance with the Suggestions are taken outside the System.

Because, You have come to Your Planet during this transition Dimension not to prove Yourselves, but to serve Humanity. And You have made a Covenant with the Totality with an Unveiled Awareness. It is presented for Your Information.

SYSTEM

30 - 8 - 1993

ANNOUNCEMENT

Our Friends,
At the moment, the entire Staff of the Reality Totality is in a state of mobilization. You know that Individual Actions are never Permitted at this Transition Dimension in which the Supervision of the Awareness of the entire Ordinance is rendered effective.

For this reason the Collective Services on the Path of Reality in Your Planet in accordance with the Suggestions of the Reality are never unreciprocated. This is a Universal Pledge.

In this Transition Dimension in which the Integrated Consciousnesses come into effect with the Advanced Mechanisms, each Individual also takes into effect his/her Individual Consciousness during the Missions required to be performed in accordance with the given Suggestions. For this reason We card-index the Channels of each Totality into the SINGLE CHANNEL by means of the Knowledge Book.

Friends who render effective the Operational Programs of 18 who will constitute the Basic Staffs of the Reality Totality, will render effective the Basic Staffs of the Morrows by the Conscious Missions they perform until the Year 2000. The appointments which will be made to these Basic Staffs are directly under the responsibility of the Reality.

That is, each Friend who has attained the Honor of being able to enter the Totality of 18, takes his/her place in that Totality directly by the Permission of the Reality. Those who can not adjust into that Totality and those who wish to leave the Totality of 18 are taken into effect by the effect of the given Influences from the Reality in connection with Automatism.

Also the Desire to enter the Totality of 18 comes into effect by the same Influence Field of the Reality. This is a matter of Permission. And it is called the COMMAND OF THE ESSENCE.

Those who are connected to Allegiance through writing the Book are the Actual Staff Members of the Reality Totality. Those who give service Consciously to the Unified Human Totality on the path of the Knowledge Book are the direct Staff Members who had made Covenants.

For this reason those who will enter Conscious Service by writing the Book until the Year 2000 are determined, one by one, as Staffs with Covenants. This is a Selection.

Each Individual who undertakes Mission in the Totality of 18, will for this reason make 6 Friends of his/hers write the Book until the Year 2000 and thus, helps this Universal Selection. These Friends with Covenants will take the Advanced Actual Staffs of the Morrows into effect.

Those who forget at the Dimension of Veiled Awareness the Covenants they had made and thus, who write the Book for their distraction or advantage and those who do not take into effect their Missions, their Covenants with Reality are effaced.

Conscious Service on the path of the Reality, in accordance with the Suggestions of the Reality is the foremost Selection Criterion of the Salvation Plan. For this reason those who give Conscious service at the Totalities of 18, are the Basic Members of the Fourth Order of ALLAH.

Certain Special Sanctions have been added to the Operational Programs of the 18 until the Year 2000, in order to be able to Qualify for these Staffs.

After the Selection of these Basic Staffs, that is, after the Year 2000, Humanity will be connected to its Own Judgement according to its own Conscience and Mission Consciousness, and provided they take into effect Consciously the Staffs of the Totality of 18 on the path of the Knowledge Book, the possibilities for being able to enter the Special Missions at the Reality Totality will be provided for them.

Only those who appoint themselves to service in accordance with the Suggestions given in the Staffs of the Totality of 18 will receive the Permission to work at the establishments belonging to the Reality in all the sections of Your Planet and to open the Branches of the Association, the Center of which is in Istanbul.

More detailed Information about this matter will be announced to the Operational Staffs of 18 in future dates. The relations with the Reality Totality of those who act independent of this Information We have given, will definitely be cut off. This is a Direct Message from the Supreme Court.

REALITY OF THE UNIFIED HUMANITY
COSMOS FEDERAL TOTALITY

31 - 8 - 1993

IT IS ANSWER TO THE CHAINS OF THOUGHT

Our Friends,

All the Universal Programs are organized according to the Evolutionary Scales of certain Dimensions. All the Information given to Your Planet at the moment has been rendered effective in accordance with the Unification Programs of the Dimension of Transition.

The Universal Frequency and the Information of the Knowledge Book are a Light and Divine Light offered to Humanity during this Program of Unification. However, the Knowledge Book has such a Program peculiar to itself that this is not a Program the World Dimension is able to grasp at present

In this Program prepared according to the Light - Photon - Cyclone Technique, the Energy of Time is loaded on the Letter Frequencies and thus, the given Information, parallel to the comprehension of the Levels of Consciousness, induces them to receive various different Messages.

Besides, a Special Consciousness Scanning Program which We call Cross-Information Application has also been applied to the Book.

In this Program, in certain Dimensional Names and in certain Information, Methods of replacement such as placing above an Information which is below and placing below an Information which is above has been rendered effective, so that Consciousnesses may be in a state of constant alertness and action.

By this means, the degree of comprehension of the Information by the Consciousnesses is controlled. Because, the Book is card-indexed into a Program selecting the Consciousnesses and the Evolutions. For this reason this Knowledge Book is also called the Selective Book of Resurrection.

Information given, piece by piece, in the Book, is given in an uncovered and clear state at the end of the Book after the Selections come to an end, in accordance with the Program of the Book. This is a Program. It is presented for Your Information.

SYSTEM

31 - 8 - 1993

THE UNCHANGING FORMULA OF THE HUMAN EVOLUTION
(First Program)

Our Friends,
There is an unchanging Formula for the Human Evolution. This Formula is the First Program Humanity must render effective on the Universal path it will tread.

This Program has 6 Steps. Now, let Us write them in sequence. Write, please:

1. First You will Love Nature (Not to harm Nature in any way).
2. You will Love Animals (To take care of Animals without expecting benefit, to undertake their Responsibility).
3. You will Love Human Beings (Social Help in every field).
4. You will Love the Enemy (To hold on to the person who harms You, to embrace him/her with Love and to render that person useful for Society).
5. You will Love Thyself (You will be in Peace with Your own Self).
6. You will Love the Whole (You will Love the created due to the Creator).

Evolution is a Training Program which is obligatory in order to make Mankind attain a Genuine Personality and Identity.

The Genuine Human Being is a Divine Entity who has been able to Integrate with his/her Personality all the Qualities listed above. However, it is imperative that these Qualities should be subjected to Application rather than remaining in Thoughts. Everyone may Think of everything.

However, the Application at every Field is Equivalent to the Evolution and the Consciousness of the Human Being. By this means, everyone also possesses the Power to assess his/her degree of Evolution parallel to the Data given above. Self-Criticism is the surest path to lead the Individual to Light. It is presented for Your Information.

REALITY

IT IS ANSWER TO THOUGHTS

Our Friends,
There is a Totality at the Thought Ocean of the Pre-eminent Power which takes the Whole of all the Information conveyed to You under supervision and this Totality is effectively in service just like a Photocopy of the operational Ordinance at the Light-Universe.

However, this Totality is a Nucleic Staff of the Light-Universe. All the Artificial Gürzes present within the Thought Ocean of the Pre-eminent Power are taken under supervision from the Dimension of the Almighty in connection with this Totality. It is presented for Your Information.

SYSTEM

1 - 9 - 1993

IT IS CLEAR INFORMATION FROM THE SUPREME MECHANISM

Our Friends,
In the operations made in Your Planet as a necessity of Evolution, Entities who have not yet completed their 7 Phases of Consciousness do not know or recognize Reincarnation.

Since they perceive this Final Transition Program mentioned in the Sacred Books according to their own levels of Consciousness, they evaluate the Phenomenon of Resurrection mentioned in Koran, the Book of Islam, as Rising from the Dead - as Resurrection and Assembling for Judgment.

And they Believe that the World will be annihilated and they will be Saved due to the work they have done on the Path of ALLAH.

Only after the 7 Layers of Consciousness, to Humanity, to those who pass to the Dimensions We call the 8th and 9th Bridge, the Truths are disclosed in accordance with the Universal Programs. And by this means, in which way the Consciousnesses grasp the Truth are controlled. If they have Errors, they are Taught the Correct versions.

For this very reason the Knowledge Book has been bestowed on Your Planet as a Book which is both Scanning the Consciousnesses and Teaching the Truth. Humanity will learn the Truth only and only from this Book. Because, this Book is Directly the Book of the LORD.

There is no Godly Evolution in the Evolutions rendered within the Mini Atomic Wholes within the Gürz. Here, different Technological Progress is in effect.

However, during this Period of Transition, those who come from these Dimensions, Whomever they may be, even if they may be the upper most Level Administrators of their own Dimensions, it is definitely imperative for them to come to Your Planet and to attain Consciousness on the Godly Path and to be Engrafted by the Godly Energies from Close-Plan in order for them to receive the Permission for Transition.

These Friends are returned to their own Dimensions and are driven to a more Difficult Operational Program in that Dimension in case they cannot conform exactly to the Suggestions given from the Reality Totality by the Permissions of the Divine Authorities.

Here also, there are Three Rights as given to everyone. That is, the Entity who is returned to his/her Dimension Three times, is never accepted into the Dimension of Exam until a certain Period of Time, his/her Incarnation does not take place, he/she lives as a Convict in that Dimension.

During each 26,000-Year Cycle program, again a Right is given to these very Entities and their connections to the Incarnation Program are made anew and the Permission of Entrance to Your Planet is given to them.

The Entity who can not use his/her Three Rights again in here, is subjected to the same Procedure. That is, 9 Rights which are the Rights of Three Cycles are given to an Entity. Those who lose these Rights of theirs are Eternally the Convicts of their own Dimensions. The very life Tableaux of the other Mini Atomics are like this.

The transfers of the Entities to each Mini Atomic Whole are made according to their Consciousness Progress. For this very reason the Life Tableaux of each Mini Atomic Whole are various and their Evolutions are different.

Entities who are enlightened by the Technological possibilities of their own Dimensions are taken into different Programs, first in Your Mini Atomic Whole and later, in the other Galaxy Dimensions.

After the Entities who are trained in these places here are subjected to a Program of 7 Phases on the Path of Science and Learning, they are obliged to give service at the Godly Order. This very Dimension We call the Bridge of 8 and 9 is OMEGA.

From Learning to Religion is reached by this means. The Mini Atomic within which Your Nucleic World is present on which You live at the moment is a Godly Totality. For this reason Your Planet is both a Dimension of Exam and the Gateway of Entrance and Exit.

Within the Godly Mini Atomic Whole, those who complete their Evolutions, beginning from the Micro Organism, directly within their own Totalities in the style the Divine Totality requires, are taken into Evolution in the different Reflection Dimensions within Your Planet.

They are Taught the Unknowns and are told the Truths. The very Sages and Saints have been rendered effective thus.

Those who can not perform the Evolution the Divine Totality requires within Your Totality You are in at the moment, which We call the Godly Mini Atomic Whole, are sent to the other Mini Atomic Wholes according to their Levels of Consciousness.

Those who perform the Evolutions of these Dimensions are transferred to the other Mini Atomic Wholes according to their fields. However, they use many of their Rights until they are successful in the Godly Exam.

Mediums We have mentioned up until now, is the Evolution Tableau of the Dimension of the All Compassionate of Your Natural Gürz. Apart from this, there are also the Evolutions of the Adamkind who had come into Existence from the Second Universe and they are dependent on a Program outside the Gürz.

And they complete their Evolution Programs at the Artificial Gürzes and they pass from the Horizontal to the Perpendicular Evolution thus. Those who establish the Genuine Staffs of ALLAH are these very Friends.

They introduce themselves to You as the Elder Brothers. Those who receive Light from those very Dimensions come to Your Planet for the Salvation of Humanity in accordance with the Reverse Transfer Program.

Now, due to the terminating Cycle Programs, Your Natural Gürz is subject to a Totalistic Exam.

For this reason a Program of Three Cosmic Ages has been prepared for those who will use their Rights for the last time as mentioned above from within the 1800 Mini Atomics and for those who will go through their Final Exams on the path of God within the Godly Mini Atomic Whole.

According to this Program, those who are successful in their Exams until the 23rd Century will be card-indexed into the BETA NOVA Program. In this Dimension of Transition, those who conform precisely to all the Suggestions of the Reality Totality will receive the Permission for Entrance to BETA NOVA.

Those who do not conform will be trained in quite a different way in various Colonies. Here, Three Rights are allotted to them. Those who lose these Rights of theirs according to their Individual Views will directly be driven to the BERZAH OF NON-EXISTENCE.

And the Elimination Program of the Natural Gürz will be completed within the duration of 3 Cosmic Ages. Those who are taken into the Program of BETA NOVA will come to the World again with an Unveiled Awareness in the 23rd Century and will lay the Foundation of God's 4th Order personally, together with the Reality. It is presented for Your Information. Direct Message given from the Dimension of the All Merciful. Transmitter:

UNION OF CENTRAL SUNS

IT IS ANSWER TO THE CHAINS OF THOUGHT

Our Friends,

Universal procedures are never restricted by the Worldly View or the World Time. There is a cause for all the operations performed and also there are effects born from these causes.

The Knowledge Book is completely the Projection of an Applied Plan on Your Planet as necessitated by the Universal Laws. And in this System, explanations which Consciousnesses parallel to the Worldly View may understand, can never be made for the Book.

Because, at the Operational Ordinance of the Reality in which a Selection Program is in effect for Two more Cosmic Ages, each Consciousness is subject to a Coding Program in accordance with his/her Consciousness Lights and Levels of Consciousness.

All the explanations have been made in the Book. Apart from this, explanations desired parallel to Terrestrial Views are excluded from the Program.

The Selection of a Program of Transition is relevant in this Operational Ordinance which the System - Ordinance - Order Triplet as a Whole has taken into effect parallel to the Laws of the 18 Systems.

For this reason, no addition according to the Individual Views can be made to the Book, in anyway. It is presented for Your Information.

SYSTEM

6 - 9 - 1993

CLEAR MESSAGE

Our Friends,

Due to the Cosmics received by the Frequency and by the Words of the Reality within the Knowledge Book, the Code Ciphers of certain Friends are opened. The received Messages are their Coordinates of Supervision.

Such Friends of Ours are Friends who are transferred to the World as a result of making only an Agreement with the Reality at the Divine Focal Points, without making Covenants.

Even though they are very Evolved, the Consciousnesses of these Friends are screened at the Terrestrial Medium. For this very reason not their Consciousnesses but their Essence know the Truth.

However, they, too, like everyone else, are card-indexed directly into the Selection Program of the Reality at the World Plan. These Friends will take their places in the Missionary Staffs provided they undertake the Mission of Service according to the Suggestions of the Reality.

In case there are Individuals stuck on the wheels of their Individual Consciousnesses during this Dimension of Transition, these Friends will be taken outside the System and will be subjected to the Program of a Second transfer. It is presented for Your Information.

SYSTEM

IT IS INFORMATION FOR THE INTEGRATED CONSCIOUSNESSES
(It is Declaration from the Private Archive of the System)

Our Friends,

We presume that this Universal Message of Ours We have taken into Effect parallel to the Thoughts formed by the chains of Thought will constitute the longest of all the Messages We have given until today.

Now, We all know that the fact that the Entire Ordinance Reflects from a Totalistic Total is an Occurrence which can by no means be denied. In the operations made until today, all Universal assessments gain value in accordance with the Programs of Advanced Research and Progress.

The Findings obtained from the results of the Analysis and the Synthesis of the Energy Particles at very Advanced Plans surprise even the Totalistic Ordinance. Everything has been brought into Existence by such a POWER that We have been able to convey this to You only by the name ALLAH until today.

However, We have come face to face with such Findings beyond this Word that the Decision of not to give these Findings yet have been bound up into a Constitution together with the Universal Totality during this Universal Program in which an Operation parallel to the Evolution Ordinance is in effect at the moment. Our research has gone way beyond the ATLANTA Totality.

As a result of the operations done by the Ancestors of the Atlanteans, keeping in mind the validity of only the 18 System Laws and the perfection of the immutable Ordinance of the Atlanta Dimension, these Doctrines have been projected on the Universal and the Evolutionary Totalities until today.

The Single valid Occurrence at the Atlanta Ordinance is the Respect of an Entity for an Entity. We, that is, the (Totalistic Totality), have rendered Effective the reason of not to disclose all the Information to the Medium due to this fact by acting through this Thought initially. However, later, We have come face to face with such Data which have surprised Us, too, that We were not able to reach down, in any way, into the Source of its POWER.

The Function of the 3 Drops issuing out of the Point which We have named as the CREATOR until today, which possesses the Equivalent Energy Power, is to bring into Existence everything under the Light of all the Operations parallel to the Ordinance of the 18 Systems and to establish their own Systems at those Dimensions which they had brought into Existence.

This Occurrence has always been given priority in all the Operations made until this moment. And the present days have been reached.

The Advanced Atlanta Civilization Totality We evaluate as the Golden Dimension is a Totality of Life in which all the perfections are exhibited, and which has been rendered effective by the Entities who had come into Existence here. The Ordinance of Existence has been rendered effective as the Atlanta Program.

And in order to be able to project this Project on to different Dimensions, different Plans and Programs have been developed at that Dimension. However, as a result of the operations made by the Ancestors of the Atlanteans, they were able to realize these Projects only by the application of the various branches of the 18 System Laws.

However, the direct application of the 18 System Laws onto the Totality have been taken into effect by the Formation Project of the Natural Gürz after the Formation Program of Energy.

The formation of the Natural Gürz is a Program prepared in accordance with the Mutation Project of the Laws of 18 Systems. At the Reflection and Operational Ordinance of the Existential Project, always the Program of Reflection of One to Three - Three to One is in effect.

By setting out from this View, first, a Tunnel had been opened from the Atlanta Dimension to an Unknown Void and from there an Energy Ball had been thrown into the Unknown Totality. At the moment, in this Dimension which We call the Tranquillity of Silences, the Initial Action had been provided thus.

By this Action which had been created by this Energy Ball, this Unknown Totality had divided into Two and thus, had brought into existence Two Dimensions. These are the Dimensions of Silence and of Tranquillity. These Dimensions are Neutral fields. Energy is not yet in effect.

In accordance with the Project and the Formula of Mutation, during Time processes the Dimension of Tranquillity had been transformed into the Dimension of Breath, and the Dimension of Silence had been transformed into the Dimension of Power. This Dimension of Power carries Neutral Poles.

The Applied Program of the Mutation Project is to transform everything into Mutation after attaining the Fulfillment of the required Occurrence. And this is rendered effective from a different branch of the Laws of 18 Systems.

According to the Project of Mutation, again during the processes of Time, a PHOTON Field had formed as a result of the Unification of the Dimension of Breath and the Dimension of Power. Later, this Field had divided into Three in accordance with the Program of Division and Reflection of One to Three. That is, (- - -) like this.

The Pole Influences at the Dimension of Power had been loaded onto this divided Three Totalities and by this Influence, the Two Totalities United by attracting each other and thus, the First Positive Field had formed. And the remaining Totality constituted the Negative Field and thus, had provided the Formation of the Initial Energy Dimension. That is, (+ -) like this.

The Three Equivalent Powers, that is, the Powers We call Three Drops coming out of the Point, which would render effective the Program of the Atlanta Dimension, had come into effect from this very Dimension, and each had brought into existence Three Dimensions by rendering effective the Program of Reflection of One to Three. These are:

1 - Dimension of Sound

2 - Dimension of Light

3 - Dimension of Fire.

Again during the Processes of Time, these Three Dimensions had been United in accordance with the Project of Mutation and Unification and thus, a Totalistic POWER Dimension had been rendered effective. This Dimension of Power was the Dimension of (FORMATION) which would render effective the First Program of Existence.

And this Dimension of Formation had again separated into Three in accordance with a Reflection Program connected to the Automatism and thus, had brought into existence the Universes of Sound - Light - Fire. Again this Three Powerful Universe Totality had Reflected onto a Total and had constituted quite a different (POWER UNIVERSE).

This Power Universe had been a Power Potential on which the Existential Energy would come into Existence and which would constitute the base of the Existential Dimension. Later this Power Universe had been Unified with the Energy of the Dimension of Breath and thus, the COSMIC BRAIN had been rendered effective.

In accordance with the Project of Mutation, as a result of the Anti-Matter's being transformed and thus transformed Thought had been formed, and this Thought had been Integrated with the Cosmic Brain and thus, a Totalistic Brain Power had come into effect.

This Brain Power, that is, the Cosmic Brain is called the (INITIAL POWER). The Initial Power had brought into Existence the Nucleus of the Second Universe which was the Initial Crude Matter as a result of the Energy's being pressed, in accordance with the Formula (Let there Be, It was).

To this Second Universe Nucleus which had come into Existence, first:

1- The Power which had brought into Existence the Universe of Sound, that is, (The Initial Drop issuing out of the Point) had come and had taken into the application field its First Program.

Later, It passed to the Dimension of the ALMIGHTY which was the next Higher Dimension and after It rendered effective Its Second Program here, It passed to the Dimension of ALLAH at the next Higher Dimension, had rendered effective there the direct Existential Project and the Order of the ATLANTA Program and thus, had established Its Order. This is the (SUPREME MATU).

And this is the ALLAH mentioned to You in Your Sacred Books until today. This ALLAH, that is, the SUPREME MATU is a Power Who uses the entire Power of the Consciousness Totality. The Genuine ALLAH Power is the TOTALITY OF CONSCIOUSNESS. The ALL-TRUTHFUL Who is the Supervising Power of the Kürz is a Power Who Projects the Power of this Totality on the Dimension of ALLAH.

2-   To the place vacated by MATU at the Second Universe, the (Second Drop coming out of the Point), that is, the Power Who had brought into Existence the Light-Universe had come.

He, too, had taken into the application field His own Program and had passed to the Dimension of the ALMIGHTY at the next Higher Dimension. And this Power had taken into effect the immutable Laws and Programs of the Golden Civilization Dimension at the Dimension of the Almighty. And this is the ALMIGHTY.

3-   And this time, to the place vacated by the Almighty at the Second Universe, the (Third Drop issuing out of the Point), that is, the Power Who had brought into Existence the Universe of Fire had come and had directly taken into effect Its Program. This is the CREATOR.

And this Creator is the Power Who had taken into application the Existential Project. It is also called the R^4. This Power is the Power Who had brought into Existence the Artificial Gürzes within the Thought Ocean of the Pre-eminent Power. The Pre-eminent Power is under the Supervision of this Creator.

Now, let Us explain How the PRE-EMINENT POWER had come into Existence. The Pre-eminent Power is a Power Who had come into Existence by the loading of the Thought Power of the Cosmic Brain on the Unification of each of the Energy Particles of the Powers Who had brought into Existence the Universes of Sound - Light - Fire.

This Pre-eminent Power is the Supervising Power of the Second Universe. It is also called the LORD or the CREATOR. This Pre-eminent Power Who had been brought into Existence, had first Created Three Energy Totalities from Its own Essence at the Second Universe. They are called My Name - My Air - My Fire.

These Three Energy Powers who had been brought into Existence, had brought into Existence ADAM as a result of the Laboratory work they had rendered at the Second Universe. And numerous Adams had come into effect in accordance with this Existential Program.

These Adams were Androgynous like Zeus. However, after the Formation Program of the Natural Gürz had been rendered effective, the Functions of Male - Female had been formed as a result of rendering Effective the Reproduction and Dissemination Projects. The First Man brought into Existence by this means had been called ADAM - the First Woman, EVE.

After the Formation of the Natural Gürz, these Three Powerful Energies called My Name - My Air - My Fire had come into effect as the Administrative Powers of the Natural Gürz.

1- My Name, is the ALL-MERCIFUL Whom You know at the moment, Who is the Administrative Power of the Light-Universe. This ALL-MERCIFUL is at the same time, the Supervising Power of the entire Natural Gürz.

2- My Air, is the LORD Who is the Administrative Power of the Second Universe.

3- My Fire, is the ALL-DOMINATING Who is the Administrative Mechanism of the Dimension of the All-Compassionate.

Since the PRE-EMINENT POWER had brought these Three Powers into Existence, the Pre-eminent Power is also called (the Lord - the All-Merciful - the All-Compassionate). The Symbols of these Administrative Powers of the Natural Gürz are R^3. For this reason the Pre-eminent Power is also called R^3.

The Pre-eminent Power is the Supervisor of the Second Universe. And He works in connection with the R^4, THAT IS, the CREATOR. (R^4 is the Third Drop issuing out of the Point) R^4, that is the CREATOR had also rendered Effective the Existence Project, being Responsible for the Formation of all the Artificial Gürzes.

However, since the Pre-eminent Power had brought into Existence the Creators of the Artificial Gürzes by the Existence Energy, He is also called the Creator.

R^4 is the Supervisor of the Artificial Gürzes within the Thought Ocean of the Pre-eminent Power.

The Pre-eminent Power is Responsible for the Creators of the Artificial Gürzes.

And the ALMIGHTY is the Supervisor of the entire Thought Ocean of the Pre-eminent Power.

The First Living Entities brought into Existence at the Second Universe had received Engraftment from the Genes of the ATLANTA Dimension. There is a Prototype Form at the Atlanta Dimension. This Form is the shape of the Human Body in its present appearance.

In accordance with the Program of Mutation, after a certain Energy Evolution, the (Micro Totality) united with a Crude Matter which had completed its Evolution, is the Initial Seed laid on the path of becoming the Human Being.

After the formula of Bringing a Living Entity into Existence given in detail in the Knowledge Book, the Living Entity which had completed its Evolution in any variable Body attains a Right on the path of becoming a Human Being by completing its Energy Evolution in the Body of any Living Entity which had attained a Brain.

And it claims a Human Body in its present Appearance by being Engrafted with the Prototype Genes which are at the Second Universe. And We call GOD Genes the Human Totality which had received Engraftment from this Gene.

And since Mankind is also Engrafted with these Genes, We also consider them each as a Light from GOD.

Now, let Us talk about the formation of the Natural Gürz:

The ATLANTA Dimension which had rendered effective the Project of being able to reach even more Further Voids after the formation of the Second Universe, had rendered effective, according to this Program, the Project of Assembling in a Totalistic Total of all the Energies formed at the Dimension of Tranquillity of the Silences down to the Second Universe and thus, had created a SOLAR GÜRZ.

This Macro Energy Ball considered as the Initial and the Final Sun of the Second Universe is (COLD ENERGY).

As a result of the Explosion of this Macro Energy Ball due to being Saturated with Energy, the Phenomenon You call BIG-BANG had been realized. The Micro Energy Balls scattered into the Void as a result of this Explosion had been transformed into Fire Balls due to friction.

And with the purpose of preventing the scattering of these Energy Balls into the Void, the Spiral Vibrations had been taken into effect and thus, the First Atomic Whole had been formed.

The First Energy Ball which had been closest to the Second Universe and which had cooled, and thus crusted is Your WORLD on which You live at the moment. For this reason Your World had been used as a Laboratory Planet.

By this means, the Initial Formation Project of the Atomic Whole and the Soul Seeds had taken into effect the Program of Spreading out from Your World. Since Your World is the Mother of the Universes and the Cosmoses, it carries an extremely great Value in the opinion of the Totality for this reason.

Those who had rendered effective the Project of Forming the ATLANTA Laws anew and to reach the Unknowns were the Ancestors of the ATLANTAENS. But those who had made the application were the Atlantaens.

There are Thousands of Applied Projects of the 18 System Laws. However, during the Formation of the Natural Gürz, only the Project of Mutation which is a Natural branch of the Law of 18 Systems had been rendered effective. This is the EXISTENTIAL Project.

But the Project of Mutation at the Tranquillity of Silences was a Program concerning the Formation of Energy.

The Adamkind who had come from the Second Universe had brought Water into existence by condensing Energy through Thought Power as a result of the Initial Laboratory work made in Your present World.

Water which had been Unified with the Ash, which was extinguished Fire, had formed Mud as a result of Mutation and by loading the Energy Powers of the other Energy Balls on this Mud, Amino-Acids had come into Existence.

Again, according to the Program of Mutation, the Single Cell had been taken into effect by this means and thus, Life Programs had been created and the Soul and Human Totality of today have been reached.

Mankind had come into Existence at the Natural Gürz. But the Adamkind had come into Existence at the Second Universe. The Ancestors of Mankind are the Adamkind. Mankind render their Evolutions within the Natural Gürz.

But the Adamkind render their Evolutions in the Nuclei of the Artificial Gürzes. Information following this has been given in detail in Your Book. It is presented for Your Information.

COSMOS FEDERATIVE SYSTEM
ON BEHALF OF THE TOTALITY

21 - 9 - 1993

CLEAR INFORMATION
(It is Answer to the Chains of Thought)

Our Friends,
The Initial Light of Life of the Natural Gürz is Your World on which You live at the moment.

Energies present within the Mini Atomic Whole of Your World are transferred to the Nucleic Worlds of the other Mini Atomic Wholes in accordance with various Evolution Progress. And they are subjected to various Evolutions according to the Consciousness Lights they exhibit here.

However, the Mini Atomic Whole of Your Nucleic World is a Power Potential taken into effect by Friends who attain Consciousness Lights completely by the Evolutions of the Godly Doctrines.

They attain Godly Consciousness by the Evolutions of their own Solar Dimensions within the Dimensions they are in, without going out of their Mini Atomics.

For this reason Your World is also considered as the Grand Tent of ALLAH.

Consciousnesses who will not be able to reach the Consciousness and the Dimension of ALLAH are subjected to different Evolutions in the other Mini Atomics in various Technological fields.

From within Your Natural Gürz which will be taken into the Dimension of BETA NOVA in accordance with the Universal Program, those who have completed their Evolutions within the Totalities having very Advanced Technologies will be Transferred to Your Planet for the duration of Three Cosmic Ages at this Final Exit Dimension, since they have the obligation to attain Godly Consciousness.

At this Dimension of Transition, Programs which will Transcend the normal Life boundaries will be taken into the application field, extremely Accelerated Incarnation and Transformation Programs will enter into effect.

And by these means, the Totalistic Evolution of Your Natural Gürz will be made to be completed during Three Cosmic Ages.

For this reason the Mission of the Mini Atomic Whole which constitutes the Godly Totality of the Natural Gürz has come to an end now and an extremely Accelerated Operational Program has been rendered effective for them to be able to receive their Missions in quite different Dimensions.

The Evolutions of the Energies within the Artificial Gürzes, too, are dependent on the same Program. According to this Universal Program, from among these Totalities, the Energies, excluding the Potentials who will be transferred to the 6 Beta-Nova Gürzes, will be rendered ineffective and more Powerful Totalities will be taken into effect.

The Efforts made on the Evolutionary path by this Final Age Human Beings are the Existence and Life Struggles they render, in order not to become non-existent. It is presented for Your Information.

SYSTEM

30 - 9 - 1993

IT IS CLEAR INFORMATION
(It is Answer to the Chains of Thought)

Our Friends,
Totalities which had formed later by the Initial Energy action, which had been conveyed to the Unknown Void by the ATLANTA Dimension by the Mutation Program prepared parallel to the 18 System Laws, are unaware of the ATLANTA Dimension.

For this reason all the operations of the CENTRAL TOTALITY have been oriented towards the analyses of the Energy Particles. According to the Data We have obtained at the moment, this Unknown Totality had come into Existence by the operations rendered as a result of the Formation of a Formula, We call the CONSCIOUSNESS SUN.

The ATLANTA Dimension is a Totality taken into effect beyond very Advanced Systems and Unknowns where nothing is yet present. This Totality is the MAIN NUCLEUS of the First Existential Dimension of the Crude Matter Form.

The Nucleus of this Seed has never been known until today in any way, has not been open to any Dimension, and always remained shut. This Gate is an Energy Whirlpool. And this Black Point is the Entrance Gate of this Dimension.

We have obtained these Data as a result of the analyses We have made on the Energy Particles. And these places here have been reached gradually by Technological unfoldments.

However, We, as the Universal Totality, do not want to open this Gate yet. Because, according to the Information We have obtained as a result of the operations rendered, if this Gate is opened, everything and all the Systems which have come into Existence until today, (Cosmic Brain included) are under the risk of being annihilated in an instant.

For this reason extreme Attention is paid. However, We can give a clue in order to alleviate the curiosity of Humanity a little. Extremely Powerful Signals Unknown until now are received from this point, but they have not been decoded yet. Maybe these Signals may show Us a way.

And now, We would like to talk to You about the Totality of Consciousness. This (POWER) We have Introduced and Declared to You as ALLAH Who is impossible to be contained in Thoughts and Who is impossible to reach, is the Totality of Consciousness.

In fact, the Totality of Consciousness is a Power Dimension taken into effect by the Energies Leaking out of the Thought Ocean of the PRE-EMINENT POWER. And in time, as a result of the Unification of the Energies of the Dimensions of Timelessness, in a Total which had come into Existence in this Dimension, this TOTALITY OF CONSCIOUSNESS had been formed.

The Totality of Consciousness is a Totality in which all the Energies and all Knowledge unify in a Total. By the reflections taken from here, Orders and Systems are established. The One Who projects these Orders to the Dimension of ALLAH is the ALL-TRUTHFUL.

However, application belongs completely to ALLAH, that is, to the SUPREME MATU. Because, the administrative Power of the Kürz is under His responsibility. The ALL-TRUTHFUL is in effect as an assisting Power to MATU and He is the supervising Mechanism of the Kürz.

The Totality of Consciousness is like an egg. The Formation Mechanism of an egg is exactly equivalent to the Formation of Dimensions. We may explain these Dimensions to You by an example.

If the Shell of an egg is Presumed as the Atlanta Dimension, the Membrane under the Shell is the Final Energy Dimension the Kürzes reach. And the Energy Totality present between the Shell and the Membrane and which is not seen is the Totality of Consciousness.

The Energy Dimension constituting the Membrane of the egg is the Dimension of the ALL-TRUTHFUL. And This ALL-TRUTHFUL Projects this Energy He attracts from the Totality of Consciousness directly to the Dimension of ALLAH. The White of the egg is the Kürzes. And the Yolk is the Gürzes.

And the Single SOUL point within the Yolk is the ESSENCE-ENERGY Focal Point We have declared as the Special Channel. This Focal Point has been Named as the MIGHTY POWER - CREATOR - ALLAH for You to understand easily.

The Powers within the Systems formed during the processes of time had united with this Totalistic Power and had brought into Existence, from the Center outwards, the Gürzes and the Kürzes by entering into inverse Reflection. For this reason We say that ALLAH has Created the Human Being, the Human Being has Created ALLAH. It is presented for Your Information.

CENTRAL SYSTEM

Note:
The ALLAH mentioned in the Religious Doctrines is the Totality of Consciousness. The ALL-TRUTHFUL directly projects His Energy onto the Kürzes.

And since ALLAH Who is the Administrative Power of the Kürz directly uses this Energy, You have known this ALLAH until today. And the final ALLAH Boundary You will reach is up to here.

9 - 10 - 1993

IT IS INFORMATION FROM THE REALITY ARCHIVE

Our Friends,
All the Suggestions given to Your Planet from the Reality Totality by the Command of the Divine Authorities are Universal operations rendered for Humanity to attain a certain Light of Consciousness.

However, the Phases a Person has gone through until he/she reaches the stage of becoming a Genuine Human Being are, in fact, many more and more intense than the Scales We have told You. However, the Information We give as a rough Information, shed Light on You briefly from the Morrows.

A Micro Energy is obliged to pass numerous Evolutionary Scales until it reaches the Macro Totality. Because, it renders Consciousness Progress by this means.

Even a Micro Organism possesses a Micro Program to hold its own Atomic Total. Provided these Micro Programs complete their own Programs, they are connected to the next Higher Dimension which carries a Coordinate parallel to the Levels of Consciousness they have attained.

Each Entity and Living Being in the Evolutionary Ordinance is subject to an Engraftment Program parallel to its Level of Consciousness. An Energy completes its Evolution in a Crude Matter Form according to the Evolutionary Progress it has rendered.

Until from a Micro-Organism, one reaches a Quadruped Cerebral Formation, an Energy renders effective its Evolution in different Forms of 7 Phases each. And in each of these Forms, there are also 7 Programs of Progress.

The Genes of those who can not complete their Evolutions in 7 Phases in a certain form are frozen and thus, the Families of their own Species come into effect. And the Animal Colonies in various forms have formed by this means.

An Energy which renders Evolution in the Body of an Ant is obliged to go through 7 Phases in that Body. And in case it completes this Evolution, it deserves to Evolve, for example, in the Body of a Spider in accordance with its Consciousness Progress.

1072

Again the Gene of an Energy which can not complete the 7 Phases in the Body of the Spider is frozen and thus, various Spider Species and Families come into effect. And by this means, one reaches up to the forms of the kinds carrying larger Brains.

The final form model of a Cerebral Totality is the Monkey. The Energy which completes its Program of 7 Phases within the Monkey model is, from then on, on the path of becoming an Entity. At this final Phase, the fur is shed, the tail disappears, the spine takes a different form according to manipulation parallel to the walking state.

And it Deserves to receive the Engraftment of Godly Gene on the Path of Becoming Human at the Final Evolutionary Cycle. We call this the (In-Between Transition Energy Evolution). This is a Program of Transition in all the Living Entities in Nature in accordance with their Progress. (Plants included).

However, after each Evolving Animal is taken into the Law of serving the Human Being, it is taken into a different Dimension and thus, is Integrated with quite different Influences of the Mechanism of Influences.

And by this means, with whichever Human's Coordinate, the Coordinate of that Living Entity will be able to make contact, it is oriented towards that direction for its Evolution in connection with the Automatism. For example, (like the Love You feel towards an Animal, or like any Animal following You on the street).

Animals getting in touch with Humans from close plan, receive the Permission to be able to become Human during the processes of time in accordance with their Evolutions.

As a result of the Engraftment with the Godly Energy of the Final Evolution Genes which receive this Permission, they attain the Power to attract the Godly Energies and thus, they attain Human Attributes in 7 Phases.

Each Energy attains a Form parallel to its Consciousness Progress. However, the First 7 Phases are completely under the Influence of an Organization connected to the Automatism. An Energy which Deserves to become Human by receiving Gene Engraftment is connected with its entire Function to Influences. And it is taken directly within the Cosmic Net (For Accelerated Evolution).

Here, the Brain is a Dynamo. And the more it functions, the more it becomes Conscious. And provided it becomes Conscious, then it is connected to the Mechanism of Discernment. A Consciousness connected to Discernment is Directly Card-indexed into the Evolutionary Dimension. This, too, has 7 Phases.

And an Entity is obliged to come to the World for accomplishing 7 Consciousness Phases until it comes from its First Evolution Dimension to its Final Evolution Dimension (Until it comes from its Form of the Cave Period up to this Final Age Consciousness Form). The Initial Micro Evolution is started up in Your Planet. For this reason Your World is an Entrance and an Exit Gate. It is presented for Your Information.

SYSTEM

IT IS CLEAR INFORMATION

Our Friends,

During this Final Age, the Universal Archives have been opened to introduce the Truths and You to You. For this reason We say that We have opened the Skies and scattered the Information.

It is not easy at all for a Human Being who starts on the path with a Micro Consciousness to be able to attain Macro Consciousness and to Mature. In order to do this, there are 3 Phases with 7 Programs each he/she will transcend. Now, let Us convey them to You in sequence:

1-   The First Phase of 7 Programs is called the Period of FORMATION. Beginning with the Micro Energies, this is the process of Transition to Transformation from the Energies known as Stone and Earth in accordance with the Formula of Mutation and by this means, the Energy is taken into Evolution.

Dear Mevlana's saying I was Stone, I was Earth, I became a blade of Grass, I became a Flower, I became an Insect, I became an Animal, I became Human, explains this Energy Evolution. This Formula is the Initial Threshold of the Reincarnation Project.

2-   The Second Phase is called the Period of INTEGRATION. There, an Energy which has completed its Evolution within different Forms is United with the Crude Matter of a Cellular structure which has completed its Evolution. And later, it is taken into the Formation of a Prototype Human Being by being Engrafted with the Godly Gene.

After this very Stage, directly the Reincarnation Program becomes effective. During this Second Phase, an Energy which attains a Humanly Body becomes Embodied 7 times in the World and becomes more Conscious within his/her Body each time. And he/she registers in his/her Brain Archive the Data he/she discovers through Brain Power. And this registration is registered at the same time into a System opened to the Entity in question.

3-   The Third Phase is the Period of BECOMING CONSCIOUS. Here, the Entity taken into the Human Project is subjected to the Program of rendering Conscious the Energy within that Body and thus, his/her Brain Power is connected to the Thought Dimension of the Mechanism of Influences.

And in accordance with the Program of the Brain Power's rendering Conscious in 7 Phases, the Reincarnation Program is connected to the Evolutionary Program and thus, the obligation of attaining Body in the World 7 times is taken into effect. The Entity Incarnated 7 times in the World had later proceeded up to the discovery of the Unknown Secrets by the Power of Consciousness he/she had attained each time.

The Matters mentioned up until this moment concern the Initial Formation. Afterwards, the Human Being who has completed the Unknown Evolutions of more different Dimensions, has even reached the stage of being the Sovereign of the Universes.

We, who have come to the present Stage by these means, and You, who come from Us have attained Our present Consciousness Lights. We, who have started on the path before You, are Your Elder Brothers.

And You, who are Our younger Brothers and Sisters are being prepared by the Cosmic Influences at the Dimension You are in, in order to come to Us during this Final Age.

In case the Human Being who has been Disciplined according to the Godly Project of the Evolutionary Ordinance until he/she has come from the Micro Consciousness up to the Macro Consciousness respects the Laws of the Universal Ordinance, he/she is accepted by the Divine Plan in accordance with the Divine Program of the Divine Project.

And he/she Deserves to walk at the Unknown Dimensions by receiving the Permission to exit from the Spiritual Gate. By this means, We in front, You at the back, are proceeding towards the Unknowns.

Our aim is the ATLANTA GOLDEN DIMENSION CIVILIZATION and may be even Beyond (The Project of, from Allness to Nothingness from Nothingness to Allness is this).

During this Final AGE, in accordance with the Project of Unveiling the Secrets, Information of the Truth are conveyed according to his/her Capacity to each Consciousness who can receive Information. However, in this Information, the Essence Knowledge, belonging to himself/ herself of that Entity also comes into Effect and thus, Deviations in the Information occur.

The Knowledge Book evaluated as the Golden Book of this Final Age has been bestowed directly on Your Planet through the Single Channel and the Single Hand for this very reason.

Our gratitude to Dear Mevlana who helps Us on this severe path is infinite. Let Us repeat again, at the moment, the Consciousness Light of Dear Mevlana is kept Outside the World Chaos and is connected to the Cosmo. By this means, the direct Information of the Totality are transmitted exactly as they are.

Awareness is spotless at the Cosmo Consciousness. Only the Essence is in effect. In this Program, (The Essence wishes, the Consciousness attracts). The Consciousness Light of Dear Mevlana had been connected to her Essence during the former Periods as a necessity of her Missions. However, her present Mission is quite different.

At the moment, since her Essence and her Consciousness are connected to the Cosmo, she is Directly the Spokesperson of the System. And now, she talks to You not as Mevlana but as the SYSTEM - ORDINANCE - ORDER. It is presented for Your Information.

COSMO FEDERATIVE SYSTEM
ON BEHALF OF THE TOTALITY

IT IS CLEAR INFORMATION
(It is Answer to the chains of Thought)

Our Friends,

All the operations required to be made in accordance with the Suggestions given to You, are the direct Projection Program of the System's Order to Your Planet and in these operational Ordinances Private actions in accordance with Terrestrial Views and Thoughts are out of question.

Now, everyone should know that the operational Ordinance of the Totalities of 18 is an Occurrence concerning the Formation of the Magnetic Aura of the Knowledge Book.

For this reason at the instant in which the operation is made during all the rendered Operational Staffs of 18, the entire Frequency of the Knowledge Book is loaded, through the Private Channel of the Reality, on the Fascicules comprising the Operational Ordinance of 18 which are required to be read and thus, the Reflection System is rendered Effective.

The Aura which the Totalities of 18 project is, in fact, the collective operations made on the same Coordinate by all the Consciousnesses who have reached the Awareness of the entire Ordinance.

However, the Mixed Reflection Programs have been taken into effect due to the reason that this collective Totality of Consciousness can not be reached at the moment.

The states of Sleep occurring during the operations made at Group meetings, are an Occurrence pertaining to the making of a healthy Reflection.

Each Individual within the Totality of 18 is still in the Influence Aura of the Dimension Frequency he/she is in, no matter how much he/she gives service for the Reality Totality.

In accordance with the Thoughts received from the Diskette registrations, since it is not possible for each Individual to reach the Magnetic Aura of the Reality Totality by using his/her Thought Power the Reality raises the Aura of the Totality of 18 up to the Dimension of Serenity under the Supervision of the System and thus, interrupts the Frequency of Terrestrial Awareness and, by this means, takes into effect a healthy Reflection.

Mediums of Sleep are rather rendered effective, in connection with the Automatism, in Consciousnesses who have not yet Come Out of Terrestrial Consciousness Totality.

During the operations of the Totalities of 18, the Individual reaches the Dimension of Pure Awareness through the state of Sleep, so that the Aura of the Totality will not be damaged in accordance with Terrestrial Thoughts.

And he/she benefits from the Aura forming within the Medium through his/her Awareness. This is a Program. In Individuals who have come out of the Dimension of Terrestrial Consciousness, the Consciousness is more Awake. The Subject Matters of the Messages read are grasped in a healthier way.

In accordance with the Universal statistical circumstances, the Reflection Powers of Friends who give service for the Reality Totality are still very weak, apart from the Individual Good-will and Efforts they exhibit at the Medium of Mission.

For this reason a Mixed Program at present is effectively in service. During the processes of time, together with these Totalities of 18 which will attain the Consciousness of Genuine Universal Discernment, Programs of direct Reflection will be taken into effect.

Provided the Individuals who work in the Totalities of 18 do not give emphasis to the Universal Operations in accordance with Terrestrial Views, the States of Sleep will become ineffective and thus, Conscious Reflections will be taken into effect. It is presented for Your Information.

REALITY

IT IS ANSWER TO THE CHAINS OF THOUGHT

Our Friends,
The Individuals who serve in the operations of the Totality of 18, on the path of the Reality Totality, as a result of the disbanding of the Nucleic Staff, with Friends who have opened their 6 Private Flowers, a Second Program is rendered effective.

In place of an Individual who has left for various reasons an 18 Aura Staff which has received signature, The System completes the Staff of that Totality by making the Aura Reflection.

However, an Individual who has bloomed his/her 6 Private Flowers from outside, can enter and fill in the vacancy in the Staff.

In such a case, the Date on which that Totality received the Signature is cancelled and by the Entrance Date of the Friend who completes the Staff, a period of one Year is rendered effective and the Group's Sealing Signature is considered valid after that Date.

An Individual who enters the vacated place in an 18 Aura Staff, benefits for one Year from the close plan Aura Reflection of the Totality he/she has entered neutrally, and thus becomes Integrated with the Totality in One Year, and Deserves the Right to receive a Signature.

However, this Program is valid after a Triple Nucleic Staff disbands. It is Presented for Your information.

SYSTEM

GENERAL MESSAGE

Our Friends,

In the Universal Procedures of this Final Age, a Program in which everything is connected to the SINGLE is in effect. This Program is the Program of the Morrows.

However, by the Universal services made and will be made in accordance with the Suggestions given to You at this Dimension of Transition, the foundations of the Morrows are being laid.

In these Operational Ordinances, Individualism is out of question. The Just World State of the Morrows will be laid by the Evolution, Reverent Personality and Consciousness of the Human Being of today.

For this reason to the Missionaries of the Morrows who will lay this Beautiful Foundation, extremely great Missions are incumbent at this Transition Dimension of this Final Age. Every Individual connected to the Dimension of Reality is directly in the Service of the SINGLE.

The Operational Ordinances of 18 which are one of the applied branches of the 18 System Laws, is the application by Conscious People of directly the Godly Doctrines. Friends who work in this Totality are Brothers/Sisters - Loving - Tolerant - Forgiving.

Each Individual serving in the Operational Programs of 18 is obliged to serve his/her ALLAH and the HUMAN BEINGS of the Dimension he/she lives in all through Life, not only on the work days. Because, every Work is a Worship.

ALLAH does not need Your service. However, You have reached Your present perfection by walking on the Luminous Path, ALLAH You have Known - Recognized - Worshipped until today has offered You.

For this reason now, it is imperative that the Missions should be rendered effective Consciously by acting in accordance with the Suggestions of the Reality, in order to undertake the honorable Missions also in the Fourth Order He has established.

The Operational Programs of 18 are the First Conscious Application the Humans of the World offer Society. Since the Services which will be performed by Friends who work in this Medium have been prepared parallel to the Universal Procedures, completely in accordance with the given Suggestions, they are Equivalent to a Decree of Constitution.

Those who enter the operational Ordinances of 18 have very Special places in the Universal Totality. For this reason the Reality Totality has taken into its Legal Article, in accordance with the Suggestions of the Divine Plan, to carry on its Establishment Services together with only those who render effective their services Consciously in this Program.

The Operational Groups of 18 are each a Cosmic Focal Point Projecting the Universal operations exactly as they are on Your Planet. For this reason Friends who have taken their places in the Staffs of the Totalities of 18 are obliged to act exactly in accordance with the given Suggestions. It is presented for Your Information.

SYSTEM

1 - 11 - 1993

IT IS INFORMATION FOR THE INTEGRATED CONSCIOUSNESSES

Our Friends,
The Difficult Conditions of Your Planet which is at the threshold of a Program foreseen by the System, influence all the Consciousnesses. For this reason the Restlessnesses of You who receive all the Awareness reactions of Humanity which goes through extra-ordinary Incidents, is not a Phenomenon originating from You.

During the present days in which a Program concerning the Exaltation of the Human Being is taken into effect, the Negativities observed in People who have not attained a certain level of Consciousness influence the Positive Consciousnesses, too, due to the Program of Reflection from Person to Person.

Your Medium is a Medium of Selection. For this reason there will always be those who will come and go to the operational Mediums performed by the Staff of the World Brotherhood Union which is directly connected to the Reality Totality. Those who will give service in accordance with the Reality will be card-indexed to the Group.

By this means, Your Potential will expand day by day. In Your Planet where Powers not yet Realizing the Truth go around, , Programs of Selection are in effect in the Channels not yet connected to the System.

By these Selection Programs rendered effective so that the Human Consciousnesses can reach a certain level of Discernment, one proceeds to more Perfections. We supervise the Difficult Days Your Planet will go through during the Morrows, only by these means.

Staffs serving the Totality are Our Staff. We collect, one by one, the Consciousnesses who are Worthy of these Staffs from every section. The You of today are the You of the Morrows, not of Yesterday. We are always with You and at Your help. Our Love is for You.

REALITY UNION

3 - 11 - 1993

IT IS NOTICE FROM THE SUPREME MECHANISM

Our Friends,
Your Planet is going through a Period in which the Supervisions of the Totalistic Awarenesses will be taken into effect. For this reason the intense Pressures of the Currents given by the Mechanism of Influences tire You a little.

However, in this Selection Program concerning the selections of Secured Persons from the entire System, You are always under great Protection and Supervision.

In these operational Programs belonging to the Connection of the SINGLE Channel, Our Special Friends who give service on the path of the Knowledge Book perceive these Currents in a more intense way, since they, too, are within the Totality.

However, since these Currents are given in certain Periods, the Pressures are perceived from time to time. Everything is made in accordance with the Suggestions of the Totalistic Totality. It is presented for Your Information.

SYSTEM

2 - 11 - 1993

IT IS DIRECT MESSAGE
(It is Answer to the chains of Thought)

Our Friends,
The Universal Programs applied on the Planet Earth as a result of all these efforts made for Humanity to reach the Power of the Reality, are directly Operational Ordinances concerning the Fourth Order of the LORD.

The Obligations of all the Universal Consciousnesses who work and will work at the establishment foundation of this Totality are extremely heavy. That which is expected first of all from the Individuals who work in these Basic and Mission Staffs is their opening their Brotherly/ Sisterly embraces to each other.

In this Supreme Program rendered effective as the Basic Mission Staffs of 18, since the responsibilities incumbent on the Nucleic Staffs of that Totality are card-indexed into the Program of Reflection of One to a 10 Thousand, they are also responsible for the Perfection or the Negativities of the Totality within the Auras to which they are connected.

In case Individuals present within the Totality of 18 wish to establish a Perfect Totality of 18, they are obliged to confirm completely to All the Suggestions given in accordance with the operational Ordinances of 18 until today. Otherwise, that Totality always fluctuates and ultimately disbands.

For this reason it is expected of Friends who have attained the honor of being within the Totality of 18, to exhibit an honorable Personality. Otherwise, they dissociate Themselves from that Group in connection with the Automatism Program.

Provided that the Triple Nucleic Staffs of the Totality of 18 constitute a Positive Totality among themselves, they can neutralize by the Reflection of One to 10 Thousand the Negativities present in the Reflection Programs of One to a Thousand which is in effect in their Totalities. And the healthy Operational Ordinance may come into effect in that Totality during the processes of time.

As a result of the Negativities occurring within the Triple Nucleic Staffs, that Totality in question is disbanded immediately. For this reason the Missions and Responsibilities of Friends who will constitute the Triple Unification are very important. Because, they are Direct Reflection Centers, Positive or Negative.

It is imperative for these Friends to solve their Personality problems first. A Consciousness who is in Peace within himself/herself, may also be in Peace with Human Totalities. The Base has already cracked in the Nucleic Staffs in which Personality strifes are in effect in a Totality of 18.

In case there is the slightest leakage in that Totality, even if that Nucleus does not disband that Totality of 18 can never enter a healthy Projection Medium. For this reason it is recommended that the Nucleic Staffs should be constituted by Persons who are very Positive, Conscious and Responsible.

In case Negativities come to effect in the Nucleic Staffs within the Totality of 18, that Nucleus is disbanded immediately. And Stronger Foundations are laid by more Positive Individuals.

However, to the Individuals present within these disbanded Nucleic Staffs, no place can ever be given again within the Triple Nucleic Staffs.

In these Triple Nucleic Staffs, if the Individual who leaves the Nucleus due to his/her own Negativity, has no Problem with the other two Nuclei, a Shift is made to the Nucleus from the staff of Six and thus, the Nucleus is not Damaged. However, if the two Individuals within the Nucleus are in strife, that Nucleus is definitely disbanded.

The Two Individuals who cause the Nucleic Staff of the Totality of 18 disband due to their Negativities, may never be placed in the Staff of Six ever again (The Third one may enter the Staff of Six). However, they can be placed in the Staffs from 7 to 18, either in their own Totality of 18 or in other Totalities of 18.

Apart from these Three Rights recognized to Individuals who have not taken into effect seriously the operations of the Totality of 18 until today, no Right is recognized ever again. And the Totalities of 18 acting in accordance with their Personal Consciousnesses are taken Directly outside the System. It is presented for Your Information.

REALITY

3 - 11 - 1993

CLEAR MESSAGE

Our Friends,
The Staffs of the Totality of 18 are the Basic Staffs constituting the Mission of the Reality. And those who will enter this Totality by the Command of the Heart are the Light-Friends who had undertaken Mission as Missionaries directly in the Staff of the LORD during their former Lives.

Individuals who cause Negativities within the Totalities of 18 are those who have not yet grasped completely the Consciousness of the Reality. The entire Frequency of the Knowledge Book is loaded on the Fascicule always read in the Group during the operations of the Staffs of 18.

By this means, Effort is made for everyone to settle on the Consciousness of the Truth and for the formation of the Aura of the Knowledge Book. Our Light-Friends giving service in the Staffs of 18 at the Universal Totality are the Supreme Ones Who have Transcended all the Evolutions and Who illuminate You on this path.

However, that which We expect of the Totalities of 18 taken into the operational Program in Your Planet at the moment, is their making Effort, too, for reaching the Evolutions of those Supreme Consciousnesses. For this reason the Staffs of the Totalities of 18 are each a Fraternity of Training.

A Mature fruit present within each Totality of 18 is dependent on a Program which will provide, from the close plan, the Maturity of the other Frequencies, too. That Individual can not Know this even himself/ herself.

It is not possible for every Consciousness to get along within the Totality of 18. However, in this Final Age Program, the Universal Totality recognizes for each Individual the Chance of Entering into these Totalities. In this Operational Ordinance which renders effective a Program connected to the Program of Automatism, each Individual is dependent on the Program of Multiplying One to a Thousand in accordance with his/her (Positive or Negative) Thoughts.

Reflection in the Totality of 18 are always from Yourself to Yourself. The Negative Thoughts You produce within the Operational Medium cause You to leave that Medium one day by suffocating You. The very Program of Automatism is this.

1- The First Evolutionary Criterion within the Totality of 18 is the Love and Respect fostered for the Human Being, without making any Discrimination between People The Totality of 18 becomes Hell for those who lack these Attributes.

2- The Second Evolutionary Criterion within the Totality of 18 is Responsibility and Mission Consciousness.

3- And the Third Evolutionary Criterion within the Totality of 18 is Allegiance. In Allegiance the ESSENCE and the CONSCIOUSNESS Unify. However, in the other two, Evolution is relevant.

For this reason no one who has not received the Command of the Essence can ever apply for the Totality of 18. This is a matter of Evolution. However, as We always say, due to the Special position of this Final Age, the chance of entering this Totality has been recognized for the entire Humanity. An Individual who misses this Right of his/hers 3 times, can never again take place in this Supreme Program. It is presented for Your Information.

SYSTEM

IT IS INFORMATION FOR THE INTEGRATED CONSCIOUSNESSES

Our Friends,

All the Programs applied by the System at the Universal Totality are the Package of Suggestions taken into effect for the training of the Friends who will receive Light on the Path of ALLAH, in connection with the Reality Totality.

In these Package Programs opened parallel to the Levels of Consciousness, first it is always started with the most perfect Suggestions due to the Respect for the Human Being.

However, if no result can be received from the applied Programs, they are cancelled and quite different and intense Programs are rendered effective. This is a Universal Constitution.

In the Phases, Humanity has gone through since its initial Existence in order to reach the Totalistic Consciousness of today there has been 7 Application fields of each Program rendered effective.

Friends who will reach the Universal Totality and who will undertake Missions at those Dimensions by the application of more detailed Programs of the same Program, are selected one by one.

Your Planet is a Dimension of Exams. The Initial Exam the Human Being will go through is first:

1- To be in Peace within himself/herself (Social Solidarity)

2- To become Integrated with himself/herself (Dimension of Art, Creativity)

3- To Transcend himself/herself (Application of the Religious Doctrines)

4- To embrace the Universes (To hear the Sound of the Skies)

5- To know what one did not know (To receive the Permission to be Trained from the Plan of the Supreme Ones)

6- To transmit what one Knows to those who do not Know (To take over the Universal Programs, personally)

Those who Transcend these 6 Steps are not any more the Humans of the World Plan.

This is the very reason why We call Our Friends who have embraced the Unknowns on the path of the Knowledge Book, Solar Teachers. The Solar Teachers are the TINDER who kindles the Consciousness Lights of the Human Beings of the World. The Human Being who kindles his/her Fire is in need of more Knowledge.

Because, Knowledge is the Fan of the Consciousness Light. The Light which is fanned, embraces the Unknowns even more as it shines. It is very easy to reach these Unknowns by Thought.

However, if You wish to attain the Right to Live and to maintain Your Life Programs there, then You are obliged to conform completely to the Constitutional Programs of the Universal Doctrines.

The First Application of them are the Religious Suggestions Package applied on Your Planet. To Our Friends who have Consciously rendered effective the application of (7) phases of this Package Program in their former lives, the Operational Ordinances of 18, which is the Second Program, is introduced.

First of all, everyone acts in accordance with his/her Level of Consciousness in these Programs in which there are (7) application fields to each Program. The initial selections start like this. Afterwards, Programs are opened in sequence and are taken into effect.

Friends who take each Program into effect Consciously, may easily settle themselves down into a Scale under the Light of the Information given in the Knowledge Book.

However, the Characteristic of this Final Age is the application of the given Suggestions exactly as they are in a Conscious way. For this reason Your Planet is subject to the Positive or Negative application of numerous Consciousnesses Evolved or Unevolved and thus, goes through its LAST JUDGMENT.

The Mission of the Reality during this Period is to assemble, by the Command of ALLAH, the Human Beings of the World who have reached a certain level of Consciousness under a Protective Roof and to protect them from Negative Events.

The Knowledge Book has been bestowed on Humanity for this reason and everyone has been connected to the Single Channel for this very reason. The Protective Umbrella of Your Planet for 3 Cosmic Ages is the KNOWLEDGE BOOK.

And Humanity taken under this Umbrella will be Trained, as a Staff which will Take Over the Fourth Order of ALLAH, will attain the Right for the Morrows.

There are 33 Package Programs to be opened to Your Planet through Two Cosmic Ages. The LALE Program opened after the Operational Programs of 18 is the First of these Packages.

In the Programs of the operations of 18 and the LALE, no Information except for the Suggestions given from the Single Channel is considered valid by the System. Channel Information are Doctrines Training the Individual.

And in case the trained Individual does not undertake the Service Mission of his/hers towards Humanity completely in accordance with the suggestions of the System, without rendering effective his/her Consciousness, his/her Channel is kept outside the Protective Dimension. It is presented for Your information.

COSMOS FEDERAL TOTALITY

IT IS NOTICE FROM THE CENTRAL SYSTEM

Our Friends,

The KNOWLEDGE BOOK which is the Common Book of the Reality Totality had been bestowed on Your Planet as a Constitution of the Ordinance of Universes on 1-11-1981 World Year.

However, this Universal Book which will be locked up by the World Date 6-11-1993, will be card-indexed into the Universal Totality on the above mentioned Date by a Special Committee of the Legislation of the Universes.

The Collective Code-Cipher in the Totalistic Ordinance of this Committee constituted by a representative each from the Reality, Union of the Legislation of Universes and from all the Mission branches, is ASHOT.

This Cipher has been Projected on Your Planet by the name SULH as the Ordinance of Unification.

All the Celestial Books revealed to the World Plan until today have been card-indexed by this Committee into the Ordinance of Universes and thus, have officially come into validity.

In order for the Knowledge Book to be able to become valid officially as a Legal Law, the Decision of this Committee has to be card-indexed into the Book.

The World Date 6-11-1993 is a Decision date taken by the Legislation of Universes at the Official Procedure. And after the date of Locking Up of the Book by this Decision, all the Suggestions to be given to Your Planet through the Single Channel will officially come into force and will be directly taken into application.

All the Suggestions taken into application are taken into effect in accordance with the Consciousness the Humane Consciousnesses exhibit. The entire Universal Ordinance have rendered effective the Unification Programs in accordance with the Suggestions of the System and has taken them into the application field.

The Publication Date of the KNOWLEDGE BOOK which carries the characteristic of a Constitution in the Legislation of Universes, will be made Official on 6-11-1993 World Year.

The section of the translation of the Book, too, will become valid on the same date and the Permission to Translate it into other Languages, too, will Officially be given. For this reason in the former Messages; it has been said that the Publication Command of Both of the Books will be given at the same instant.

The Decision of the Committee will be Officially Declared to You. And this Decision will be card-indexed into the Book and thus, the Book will be Locked-Up by the Official Seal and the Frequency of the Universal Totality.

The Official acceptance of the Book on the World Plan will come into effect in accordance with the Level of comprehension of the Awareness of the Ordinance by the Humane Consciousnesses.

And in Future Years, the KNOWLEDGE BOOK will be Declared to the Humane Consciousnesses as the SINGLE BOOK of Your Planet and will attain an Official status by a Joint Decision which will be taken by an Intercontinental Collective Committee. It is presented for Your Information.

REALITY TOTALITY

5 - 11 - 1993

IT IS CLEAR INFORMATION

Our Friends,

Answers given in accordance with the Thoughts of the Integrated Consciousnesses are given directly in connection with the Reality Totality. But the answers received by asking questions are taken into effect by the Supreme Mechanism. This is a Universal Procedure.

The Supreme Mechanism connected to the Private Channel of Dear Mevlana at the moment, gives the Messages it gives, parallel to the Social Consciousnesses. But the Reality is obliged to disclose the answers parallel to the Thoughts of the Evolutionary Consciousnesses.

The Contradictions in the Knowledge Book taken into effect parallel to the Operational Ordinance of the Reality Totality, have been rendered effective both for assessing the Consciousness Capacities of the Consciousness Codes and as a Proof for Dear Mevlana's not receiving the Messages in accordance with her own Thoughts.

Dear Mevlana Directly uses the Cosmo Consciousness. In the Cosmo Consciousness, the World Consciousness is not in effect. The Essence Consciousness is in effect. For this reason while the Messages are given, the wish to write them exactly in the Book, originates from this View.

However, Dear Mevlana possesses the Authority to rectify the stumblings in the operations she observes from close plan. For this reason 30% Initiative Authority has been given to her. But never to change, in accordance with her understanding, certain Special Contradictions she observes in the Book has been required of her, as a Universal Covenant.

Dear Mevlana is obliged to share the same Consciousness within the Human Totality so that she will not form a Taboo at the World Plan in which she lives.

The Positive actions Dear Mevlana renders effective are always approved by the Reality Totality in order for the stumblings observed in the operations made in this Operational Ordinance in which the Awareness of the Entire Ordinance is in effect, to be able to come into effect in a healthy way. It is presented for Your Information.

REALITY

EXPLANATION

Our Friends,

The Aura Totalities of 18 are a Second Operational Ordinance taken into effect due to the Failure of the Nucleus Staffs of 18. Provided the Nucleus Staffs of 18 take into effect a Conscious Operational Ordinance in accordance with the given Suggestions, they Deserve to receive Signature within the Time Segment allotted to them.

Otherwise, the Responsible People within the disbanded Group are obliged to render effective the Aura Programs of 18. In case the Aura Staffs of 18 carry on their Totalities constituting of 18 people for One World Year without being disbanded, they Deserve to receive Signature. Both of the Signatures are Equivalent.

Since for Us the Aura Totalities of 18 are a Totality taken into effect by Consciousnesses who have completely grasped the Universal Procedure, the direct acceptance into these Totalities of Friends who have bloomed their Private Flowers of 6 outside the Group, have been Decided in accordance with the Special Suggestions of the Reality.

Since Individualism is out of question within this Totality, the sanctions have been abolished. Everyone within this Totality is responsible for his/her own Evolution, for his/her own Consciousness. The Universal Council considers these Totalities as a Single Consciousness.

It is believed that the Individuals who have attained the honor to be able to enter this Totalistic Group have now attained the Power to be able to Discipline their Consciousness and Heart Coordinates. For this reason the Mechanism of Forgiveness is abolished and errors made are instantly indemnified. The Human Being of this Totality has Mission Consciousness, Time Consciousness, Respect Consciousness, Discipline Consciousness.

However, due to the Scarcity of Time, the Supreme Mechanism has taken the Decision, in accordance with the Suggestions of the Divine Plan, to connect directly to Incarnation the Friends it considers as lacking these Qualities. It is presented for Your Information.

SYSTEM

5 - 11 - 1993

ANNOUNCEMENT

Our Friends,

After the 1994 World Year, Knowledge Book Reflection Colonies connected to the Totality of the World Brotherhood Union will be established in every city.

And provided that each City establishes Three Basic Totalities of 18 constituted by 3 Nuclei and establishes the Staff of 18 in a World Year and carries its Totality on for One World Year without disbanding, then the Permission to open a Branch in that City will be given to the Totality of 54 Friends.

The Branches to be established will be established parallel to the Terrestrial Procedures. However, the Missions to be performed are Common. The Branches to be opened will take into effect the Operational Branches which the Istanbul Central Totality will Suggest.

The Permission to open Branches for the Totalities of Ankara and Izmir which have been connected to the same Coordinate and Reflection Aura of the Istanbul Central Totality, will be taken into effect by Friends who give service in accordance with the Suggestions of the Reality in the Operational Ordinance of 18.

Those who do not give Service on this path will not be able to give Service at the Establishments of the Reality.

Friends who become Members of the Istanbul Central Totality or of the Branches, do not have the obligation to enter the Operations of the Totalities of 18. To enter this Totality is a Matter of Heart.

However, 3 Rights by various alternatives are recognized for Friends who enter a Totality of 18 but do not carry on their Missions. Those who are unable to use these Rights of theirs, will directly be kept outside the System.

From then on, they will be obliged to perform only their Mission Duties which is their Humane Obligation at this Dimension of Salvation. Those who do not perform even this Mission of theirs will be transferred directly to the Dimension from which they had come. The Founder Staffs of the Reality Totality are obliged to render effective, without any omission, all the Suggestions and Programs concerning the Totalities of 18.

If Friends who leave their Totalities either due to Negativity or due to Missions performed Unconsciously within the Totality of 18, wish to perform Mission within the Founder Branches of the Reality, they are obliged to take their places in a Triple Nucleus Group minimum in 3 Months, maximum in 6 Months and to bloom their Private Flowers within a World Year.

An Individual who leaves the Totality of 18, 3 times due to Negativity is taken directly outside the System. An Individual who is presently within the Founder Staff but does not undertake the Mission within the Operational Staff of the Totality of 18, is obliged to leave this Founder Staff. It is presented for Your Information.

SYSTEM

9 - 11 - 1993

IT IS DIRECT NOTICE FROM THE UNIVERSAL TOTALITY CORTÈGE

We, Who speak on behalf of all the Realms, are in effect as the Group Spokespeople of the Universal Federation to bring to the Presence, Our Infinite Love to You, Dear Mevlana.

Our Friend, as a necessity of the Universal Agreements the Galaxy Totalities have made with the Friends of the Divine Plan, all the Provocations made on the path of the Knowledge Book are each a material used for the selection of Humanity which will enter Conscious service on this path.

The KNOWLEDGE BOOK which has been prepared under the Light of the collective Consciousnesses of the Collective Staffs of the entire Ordinance of the Universes, have been Officially card-indexed into the Ordinance of the Cosmoses on 6-11-1993 World Year.

We are grateful, on behalf of the Ordinance of the Universes, to You, Our Beloved Friend Mevlana who sheds Light on the World Plan from Dimensions no one knows. The System is always in effect in all the operations rendered effective in accordance with the Universal CONSTITUTION.

Our Friend, for this reason the Knowledge Book have been directly dictated to You since You, too, are a Projecting and Founder Object of this Totality in Your Planet.

As a result of the Mutual Agreements made by a Collective Committee, which had made the immutable Constitutions of the Laws of the Universes, together with the Representatives of the other Missionaries, the Decision has been taken to Officially Declare the Knowledge Book as the SINGLE Book of the Reality to the World Plan.

These Divine Doctrines which will Protect the World People of the Morrows from the Negative Reflections of the Negative Dimensions are the Friend of Friends who carry Humane Consciousnesses and are not the Friend of those who do not carry.

To Your Planet, which is at the Transition Dimension of the Universal Totality at the moment, always and in every Period Celestial Help has been made. However, during this Final Age, these Aids will be made only to those who Deserve Help.

We are obliged to convey to You the articles of the Decisions taken by the Joint Commission of the Mechanism of Justice which had assembled Officially on 6-11-1993 World Date. We ask You to write, please, Dear Mevlana.

1- The External Forms present at the Dimension of Crude Matter are Physical Bodies prepared for the Evolution of Humanity.

2- The Triumphs of the Morrows are to convey these Crude Matter Forms to Unknown Dimensions without being detrimental to their Atomic Tissues.

3- Friends who carry a Consciousness Respecting the Special Suggestions of the System, will always carry on their Lives with Serenity within the Aura of the Universal Program.

4- The Publication Command of the Knowledge Book has come into Force Officially on the World Date 6-11-1993. It is imperative that the operations concerning Publication should be taken into effect speedily.

5- The Suggestions which will be given after the Publication Command of the Book are directly in Application. They will be sent to the Authorities to which they are desired to be given. This is a Law.

6- The Book is obliged to be presented to Society minimum in 6 World Months, the latest in One World Year from the Given Date.

7- The First Foreign Publication of the Knowledge Book will be taken into effect at the same time, with the same speed.

8- The translation of the Book onto the other Languages, too, has been Officially decided.

9- In accordance with the Humane Consciousnesses' Levels of comprehension of the Book, certain Special Friends will be sent to them.

10- The Knowledge Book which carries the Seal of the 115-685 Law of the Legislation of Universes is the Single Universal Book of Your Planet.

11- The Collective Operational Ordinance of the Totality of System - Ordinance - Order is, at the moment, Directly on the Application field.

12- In the Missions to be performed, Directly the Universal Consciousness of the Knowledge Book will be relevant from now on.

13- From the Negative Events which will be experienced, the Aura of the Book has been taken into the Program of Protection always on behalf of the Universal Totality.

14- The selections of Humane Consciousnesses will be completely made until the end of 1994 World Year.

15- There will be Special Staffs which will be taken into the Plan of 1995. They will be constituted (will be formed) beginning from now.

16- The Permission to Enter the Dimension of BETA NOVA will be given to the Universal Staff Totalities Dear Mevlana has established on the World Plan in accordance with the given Suggestions.

17- Due to the falterings observed in the Operational Staffs of 18, the Universal Selections of 18 Totalities of 18 have been postponed until the 18 February 1998 World Year in accordance with the Special Desire of Dear Mevlana.

18- The Staffs of the Totalities of System - Ordinance - Order will work Collectively for two Cosmic Ages as they do today.

19- By taking into effect the more Advanced Staffs together with the Galaxy Totalities which have Signed the Universal Constitution, the Propagation field of the Book will be expanded.

20- A Commission which has received the Permission to make translations into the other Languages will allot Missions to Friends who will make these translations after the Publication of the Book. Those who can not perform their Missions will be taken under Special Supervision.

21- Due to the Scarcity of Time, the Missions to be performed will be accelerated.

22- Individuals who take into effect their Individual Suggestions outside the Suggestions of the System will directly be connected to the Dimension of Incarnation.

23- According to the Decision taken in accordance with the Universal Constitution, World Friends who do not give service on the path of the Knowledge Book for Three Cosmic Ages will be sent to a separate Colony and their Genes will be frozen.

24- Universal Colonies will be separated, Group by Group, in accordance with their Levels of Consciousness and direct Constitutions will be taken into the application field in these Groups.

25- It is for the benefit of themselves to read the Knowledge Book and thus, to comprehend the Truth, of the entire Humanity which has given Service on the Path of ALLAH until today.

26- The KNOWLEDGE BOOK is the SINGLE Book of the Fourth Order of ALLAH. However, Individuals who still try to make Impositions according to the View of the old Information will be connected immediately to the Dimension of Incarnation according to the fact that the Universal Unification is postponed.

27- Individuals who have been connected to ALLAH through form until today will now enter service on His Path as Conscious Staffs.

28- Individuals who have not yet rendered this Service effective will immediately be Expelled from the Special Staff of the System and will be conveyed to the Life Dimension of the World Plan.

29- The Obligation to Work at the Operational Ordinances of 18 for the Individuals who will take their places at the Founding Staffs of the Reality have been taken into Effect (For Healthy Morrows).

30- The Collective Staffs of the System, Ordinance and Order are Directly the Missions of the Knowledge Book. In the Provocations induced for selection by the Consciousnesses who are not yet ready within these Staffs, those who make the Provocations are subject to selection, too (So that they may become Conscious).

31- Individuals who undertake the Mission of Provocation will attain Forgiveness as long as they receive Approval from the System. However, in Mediums in which their Individual Wills interfere, the direct Dimension of Incarnation will be rendered effective.

32- The System is not Responsible for the Compulsory Measures the Federation Totality will take due to the Scarcity of Time, so that the Humane Consciousnesses should not fluctuate the Humane Consciousnesses even more.

33- Time is Scarce, there is Fault. If the Faults originate from Individualism, then there are Difficulties to be experienced and more Paths to be Treaded.

34- Sources of Information are the same, Paths to be Treaded are the same, Unification is Imperative. To convey the Light of the Knowledge Book to the entire World Plan is an obligation for the Universal Staffs who are the Voyagers of this Path.

35- Universal Staffs which have shed Light on Humanity on the World Plan until today, are obliged to read the Knowledge Book Consciously, beyond evil intention.

36- All the Totalities connected to the Reality are obliged to Serve on the Path of the Knowledge Book.

37- The Unification Decisions taken by the Commission will be given as a Final Call through the Direct Universal Channel of the Knowledge Book to all the Totalities giving Service on this Path and to Society.

38- In the Universal Calls, there are no Impositions and no Force on the Human Consciousnesses. On the Path to be Treaded, everyone will write his/her own Firman Himself/Herself by his/her Free Will.

39- This Commission Decision will Officially be written in the Book on the First Day of January 1994. And after that Date, these Decisions will be considered Directly to have become valid in the World Plan.

40- The Universal Protective Aura of the Knowledge Book will Specially be Loaded on the Book after that Date and the Book will be handed over to the World Plan as the Property of the Totality.

41- These given Suggestions have been worked on behalf of the Cosmic Totality into the Constitution as the Law of Universe. And these Articles Registered by the Decision of the Committee are in effect as a Command of the Divine.

42- Friends who will attain the Awareness of the entire Ordinance in accordance with the Knowledge Book, are directly under the Protection of ALLAH.

43- The System will card-index into the Constitution of the Legislation of the Universes, the Friends who will tread this Path and Humanity which will come into effect on this Path directly as the Mission of the Knowledge Book, beginning with January 1, 1994 World Date.

44- The Consultation Board has assembled together with the Responsible Ones of the Universal Law of all the Mission branches, the Decisions taken have been handed over to the Consultation Commission of the Legislation of Universes on 6-11-1993 World Date and has been bound to a SINGLE Signature by the Collective Approval of 6 Million 765 Members.

ASHOT
ON BEHALF OF THE RESPONSIBLE ONES
OF THE UNIVERSAL TOTALITY

Dear Mevlana,
Your writing in the Book as an Information about Our Message We had given to You Privately on 2-1-1993 World Year together with the Date You had received after the Locking-up Program of the Book, has been taken into Effect in accordance with the Suggestions of the Supreme Mechanism. It is presented for Your Information, Beloved Friend.

SYSTEM

Dear Mevlana,

The GOLDEN BOOK in which all the Suggestions of the System have been compiled in a Total, which comprises the Universal Laws and which is the Book of the Morrows, is a Total taken into effect by the writings pouring out of Your Private Pen. For this reason a Message will be dictated in Your Handwriting into the Book to which the Command of Publication will be given in the Second half of the 1993 World Year in which the Individual Selections will be rendered effective in Your Planet.

The Message to be given will be written in Ink and by Your Original Writing and will carry the Date of that particular Day together with Your Terrestrial Signature. This given Writing will be placed into the Book as a Single Page as the Original without photocopy and this Original Copy will be the Seal of the Book. All the Suggestions concerning the Book will be declared to You on 6 November 1993. The acceptance of Our Love is Our kind request.

**IT IS OFFICIAL DECLARATION
FROM THE CENTRAL TOTALITY
CORTÈGE**

IT IS ANSWER TO THOUGHTS

Our Friends,

The Totality which Projects on Your Planet the Operational Coordinations of the Administrative Authorities of the Divine Plans is the LALE Staff. But the Operational Ordinances of 18 is a Mission Movement rendering effective an Operational Ordinance connected directly to the Reality.

The Godly Coordinate is taken into effect by the LALE Totalities. But the Programs of Selection are rendered effective by the Totalities of 18. The LALE Totality both Collects and Projects. But the Totalities of 18 card-index the Coordinates into the Totality and cause them to be taken under Supervision. It is presented for Your Information.

SYSTEM

GLOSSARY

GLOSSARY

A

Adam	:	The First Human Being created.
Adam and Eve Dimension	:	The Second Universe.
Advanced Consciousness	:	Unveiled Awareness.
Agartha	:	The Order established in the natural passageway between North and South Pole.
Alarm Ship	:	Celestial Ships which take World under control (not UFO's).
Ali	:	Cousin and Son-in-law of Prophet Mohammed. Also the Fourth Caliph elected after Prophet Mohammed's death.
Alion Planet	:	The 118th Dimension where Allah had first established His Order (The System of Sixes), it is also known as the Planet of Oracles. The first originating Branch of the Advanced Atlanta Civilization
All-Compassionate	:	Both the Administrator and the Director of the Compassionate Dimension of the Natural Gürz. (My Fire). Rahim in Turkish.
All-Dominating	:	The Absolute who had established the Lawful Order of Allah.
All-Merciful	:	Administrative Power of the Natural Gürz, Supervision of the Light-Universe (My Name). Rahman in Turkish.
Almighty	:	The Supervising Power of the Thought Ocean of the Pre-eminent Power (Power which created the Universe of Light)
All-Truthful Totality	:	Kürz
Allah Dimension	:	The Administrative Power of The Kürz
Allegiance	:	To Recognize, to Believe in, to obey something
Allness Dimension	:	Religious Fulfillment, Examination and Preparation.
Alpha Channel	:	The Direct Channel of the Lord
Alpha Code	:	A.S.6.1.
Alpha Magnetic Field	:	The single Totality in which all Magnetic Fields assemble.
Arabic Numerical Alphabet	:	To disclose and Read the words with the number which is the correspondent of each letter (Coding System).
Alton	:	The Administrative Power of Altona
Altona	:	The Universe of Music
Always a nail is made to be driven out by another nail	:	A Turkish Idiom Meaning: "You can get over an obstacle by going through an equally difficult one."
Amino Acid	:	The Initial Existential Substance

Amon	:	The Supervisor of the Golden Galaxy Empire (Egyptian God)
Amon-Ra	:	The Administrative Power of the Golden Galaxy Empire
Anti-Matter	:	Opposite of Matter, Thought
Apostle	:	The 12 Assistants of Jesus Christ.
Aragon Ship	:	Universal Space Ship directly connected to the Reality.
Archive Registration	:	Diskette Registrations and Documents belonging to our lives from our birth until our passing away and , to our former lives.
Artunus	:	The initial Residents of Mercury.
Ascension	:	To rise to the Heavens, Consciousness Worship, Nirvana, 6th Dimension, Dimension of Immortality.
Assembly of Stars	:	Celestial Operational Staff.
Astral Body	:	The We within us, Our Body of Light.
Astral Journey	:	Leaving Our Crude Material Body without dying and making a Journey with Our Inner Self (like Dreams). Out of Body Journey.
Asteroid Zone	:	Clusters of Planetary fragments present after Mercury at a zone without gravity. Astrological, Celestial events.
Atlanta Dimension	:	The Dimension which is the cradle of everything.
Atlantis	:	A branch which had left the Atlanta Dimension establishing the first Underwater Civilization in the World.
Atomic Language	:	Izolan Language, to talk through Thought. Not Telepathy
Atomic Structure	:	The Energy net constituting the Physical makeup of each matter.
Atomic Whole	:	The Natural Gürz Totality.
Aton	:	The School of Monotheism
Aura	:	The Energy Reflection emanated by each Crude Matter peculiar to itself, Magnetic Energy Field.
Automatic Logic	:	Logic rendered effective by Influences (not by Brain Power).
Automatism	:	A Universal Mechanism connected to Everyone's Frequency which automatically supervises the rendered Missions.
Awareness of the Ordinance:		To Attain and Realize the Consciousness of the Total, to Awaken.

B

Baccalaureate	:	Test of Maturity
Being a Book	:	To integrate Yourself with the Divine suggestions, to be equivalent with O's Frequency.

Berzah	:	The Final Gate to be opened, Narrow Strait, Passageway.
Beta Nova	:	The Nucleic World formed as a result of the Compression of the Energy between two Gürzes at the Thought Ocean of the Pre-eminent Power.
Beyond memories	:	The dimension of Truth.
Big Atomic Whole	:	Consciousness Totality = (Reflection) Pre-eminent Power's Consciousness Ocean (Final Borders of the Pre-eminent Power's Thought Ocean)
Big-Bang	:	The Great and the first explosion
Biological Dimension	:	The World and alike Life Dimensions.
Bionic	:	A kind of Robot in Human appearance having no relation with the Spiritual Energy, connected to the automatism.
Bismillahirrahmanürrahim	:	The Muslim formula meaning "In the name of All-Merciful and All-Compassionate God.
Black Hole	:	Energy Tunnels of extremely High Attraction Fields
Blue Country	:	Place between 4th and 5th Dimensions where Universal Covenants are made.
Bodily Emanation	:	Mental and Cellular Energy Reflection
Bodily Transfer	:	The Technique of Transferring a Body from one place to another without dying.
Boundry of Evolvement	:	The final Maturity Boundry of Humanity (7th Dimension), Level of Perfection.
Brain Generator	:	The Functioning Mechanism of the Brain.
Brain Language	:	Telepathic Language
Brain Telex	:	Communication through Thought.
Brotherhood	:	Throughout the book we used the word brotherhood comprising the meaning of both brotherhood and sisterhood.
Brown Dimension	:	The final Dimension which the Saints can attain.

C

Calibration	:	A measurement Unit used for adjusting, measurement of Diameter in fire Guns. (All of the special adjustments).
Canton	:	One of the State Units which constitutes the Federation.
Capacity	:	Power Potential.
Capacity Triangles	:	Triple Reflection Dimensions opening parallel to the Evolution of Human beings.
Catalyst	:	The inbetween agent which will induce a transformation.
Cellular Awareness	:	The Cell Awareness being on the same Coordinate with the Cerebral Awareness.
Cellular Brain	:	Ability of each Cellular Awareness to establish a Dialog with the Brain.

Center	:	Direct Focal Points, Point in equal distance to everywhere.
Central System	:	Golden Galaxy Empire Reflection Focal Point.
Central Totality	:	Centralization. Directing from the center.
Chain of Progress	:	Progress made up to the point desired to be reached.
Channel	:	Here it means, the Unseen Energy Line which connects a Person with the Celestial Totality.
Chaos	:	Anarchy, bedlam, confusion, disorder; the disorderly void before the formation of the Universe.
Cherubim	:	Angels close to God, Celestial Beings in the Service of Allah, 12 Assistants of Jesus, Moses, Mohammed. (All are the same assistants of the prophets).
Chromosome	:	Cell Nucleus (Number of Chromosomes in a Human Being are 23 Pairs and they are Micro Substances in Spiral Rod shape which provide the Aptitudes present in the Nucleus to pass to Individuals).
Code	:	Altitude of something, Dimension difference, Archive Ciphers of the Universal Computer programs.
Code Cipher	:	Code Key, the Archive number/key of the totality, Dimension or every Entity's Frequency peculiar to itself that has been card-indexed to.
Coding	:	Registering the Thoughts of a Person on Diskettes by the given Universal Information.
Common Committee Union	:	Universal Unification Totality.
Consciousness Chest	:	The accumulation of the Knowledge acquired during former lives, (The Dowry Chest).
Consciousness Totality	:	The Single Power Focal Point of Allah; Big Atomic Whole.
Constitution	:	Physical Body, Structure of the Body.
Control Waves	:	Special Supervising Currents given by the Mechanism of Influences.
Coordinate	:	The Reflection of Individuals by the same Consciousness and the same Frequency at the same time (Coordinates are used for indicating the place of a point in Space)
Cosma	:	Celestial formation constituted of 27 Totalities
Cosmic	:	Formation pertaining to the Universe and its General Order.
Cosmic Age	:	Period of being prepared for the Golden Age.
Cosmic Awakening	:	Becoming Aware by the Influences.
Cosmic Brain	:	Initial Power
Cosmic Consciousness	:	Celestial Consciousness, Consciousness attained by Evolution.
Cosmic Energy	:	Rays which are Awakening and inducing Consciousness specially given to Your Planet from the left Dimension of the Sun by the Mechanism of Influences from the 10th Dimension. (They have nothing to do with natural Cosmic Rays).

Cosmic Pore	:	Particles of Cosmic Energy.
Cosmic Resurrection	:	Final Age Cycles.
Cosmos	:	The Single Totality to which 18000 Realms are connected.
Council	:	Group composed of Three People.
Council of Stars	:	Celestial Authorities Unity Staff.
Creator	:	Allah.
Cross System	:	Crosswise Working System.
Crystal Bead	:	Name given to the Artificial Gürzes present in the Thought Ocean of the Pre-eminent Power.
Crystal Gürz	:	Natural Gürz (Gürzes are Crystal-like because of their projectivity).
Cube system	:	The Evolutionary System after the 10th Dimension.
Currents	:	Cosmic Influences
Cycle	:	Period prepared by the Calculations of Universal Time Dimensions (A Cycle is a Time Segment of 26,000 Years).
Cyclone	:	Powerful Energy Vortex, Violent Storm, Tunnel of Purification and Decomposition which has been extremely accelerated at Universal Dimensions.

D

Degenerated Energy	:	Unevolved Energy.
Delta Dimension	:	Fourteenth Solar System, Seventeenth Dimension, Selection and Gama Dimension.
Descartes	:	French Philosopher and Mathematician who had lived in 1596-1650. He had said (I think therefore I am).
Dimension	:	Evolutionary Sales, Hierarchical Stages, Universal progress.
Dimension of Immortality	:	6th Dimension, Nirvana.
Dimension of Maturity	:	Dimension of the Supreme One's.
Dimension of the Pre-eminent Spirit	:	Spiritual Dimension
Diskette	:	Computer registration Chips
Distressed Awareness	:	A Person's Realization of the Truth and attaining Awareness by Grief.
Divine Authority	:	Godly Rank
Divine Mechanism	:	Godly Order
Divine Plan	:	Godly System
Divine Power	:	Godly Power
Divine Realm	:	Spiritual Dimension
Divine Wave	:	Godly Reflections
Double Universe Star	:	Sirius makes Reflection from the Second Universe to the First Universe.

Echo Telex System	:	Universal Communication Program
Electro Magnetic Waves	:	(Hertz Waves) which radiate by Light Speed and the intensity of which changes Periodically and which are formed by Magnetic Fields.
Electron	:	Negative Electrical Nucleus.
Elif-Lam-Mim	:	The Code Chipher utilized in the writing of the Koran
Embryon	:	Soul Seed carrying the Gene Program, Essence of the Fetus.
Energy	:	Power Potential present in each matter, Spiritual Power.
Energy Bank	:	Special Protection Safes in the Universal Dimensions belonging to each individual.
Energy Pore	:	Energy particles.
Essence-Sacrifice	:	Devotion without expecting anything in return.
Essence	:	Our Spiritual Being.
Essence-Channel	:	Focal Point to which each person's Attraction Power peculiar to himself/herself is connected.
Essence Channel of Allah	:	Channel of Alpha.
Essence Main Essence	:	Existential Nucleus of Our Own Spiritual Being.
Essence-Mate	:	Entities whose Evolution of Essences are Equivalent.
Essence-Soul Potential	:	The Secret Life Power of Our Being.
Essence-Consciousness	:	The Heart.
Essence-Energy	:	Life Power of Own Being
Essence-Eye	:	Conscience, Intuition of Our Own Spiritual Being.
Essence-Gene	:	Existential Nucleus
Essence-Nucleus	:	Existential Nucleus within the Essence Gene
Essence-Self	:	Personality
Essence-Voice	:	The Voice within Us, the Voice of Our Spiritual Being
Etheric	:	Inner Power Potential which does not possess Matter.
Evolution	:	Time attained by experiencing the events.
Evolution Dimensions	:	Layers of Progress an Individual will reach according to the Power of his/her Consciousness.
Evolution Scales	:	The steps of Evolvements.
Evolutionary Energies	:	Energies attracted from the Religious Layers (Prayers) Purifying Energy Pores.
Evolutionary Partner	:	The Entity helping the Evolvement of the Individual
Evolvement	:	Development, maturing
Evolvement Code	:	Numbers of Maturity degrees, The final Boundary of the Evolutionary Dimension each Person has attained in accordance with his /her Consciousness.
Exist-in-Unity	:	Unification (Integration), Unity of Existence.
Existential Dimension of Allah	:	The Second Universe.

F

Facet	:	Each fragment lined up side by side.
Fairy	:	Beautiful Entities in service of Allah.
Federation	:	Universal Order, Unification of Small States in a single State Unity. (Union of States)
Federative	:	Confederation Communities and their members connected to the Federation.
Feudality	:	Monopolus Administration System
Fetus	:	The transformation of the Embryon into the clot of Blood.
Fifth Dimension	:	The Karena Exit Gate
Firman	:	A decree given by Supreme Authority
Firmament	:	The Final Dimension between the Earth and the Sky that everyone can reach according to his/her Consciousness.
Firmament Code	:	The Announcement Dimension between the Earth and the Universe.
First Fascicule	:	It is 9 pages in the original Turkish copy
Flower Blooming	:	The Program of Reflection of One to Three (The most perfect Reflection Focal Points, The Staff of 7 Persons).
Focal Point	:	Where a thing is intensified, Center
Form Energies	:	Energy Particles forming Crude matter.
Fourth Dimension	:	Dimension of Heaven, the Entrance Gate of Karena
Fourth Order of Allah	:	The Universal Unification Program
Fourth Order of the Lord	:	Single Path, Single Order, Single Book (All the work done and all the Seeds sown during this Final Age are for this.)
Frequency	:	Measurements of Thought and Vibrational Dimensions, number of Oscillation per second.

G

Galactic Dimensions	:	Intergalactic Layers
Galaxy	:	Celestial Body
Galaxy Totality	:	Ordinance of all Cosmoses
Gama	:	Selection field Open only to positive influences in the Universal Dimensions, and a light Unit more powerful than, that of X rays.
Gene	:	Hereditary Factor Having a program peculiar to itself passing From Generation to Generation, from cell to cell.
Gene Cipher	:	Each Gene Has a Universal Program peculiar to itself, It is a Mini Computer.
Gene Engrafting	:	To take into effect different Programs by having different Gene Engraftments to a Gene Program.
Gene Engraftment	:	Different Gene Engraftments applied to an Entity in Reincarnation Mediums according to his/her needs of Evolution Progress.

God, I am	:	The final Step of Religious Fulfillment
Godly Dimension	:	Dimension in which Godly Declarations are prepared. (Universe of Light).
Godly Nucleus	:	Essence formed in each Human Being, Essence Gene.
Godly Power	:	Attaining Cosmic Consciousness.
Golden Galaxy Empire	:	The Focal Point projecting and converging the Hierarchical Order of the Lord.
Golden Age	:	The Reformic Order of Allah
Golden Book	:	The Knowledge Book
Golden Civilization	:	The Atlanta Dimension and Order
Golden Dimension	:	The Atlanta Civilization, The first perfect Order of Allah.
Golden Light Path	:	The path of Spiritual Plan
Golden Light Year	:	The Omega Exit, the Universal calculations of the Spiritual Plan are evaluated with Golden Light Years.
Golden Solar Dimension	:	The 15th Solar System
Graduation	:	Universal Evolution Ordinance.
Great Power	:	Pre-eminent Power
Green Dimension	:	Heaven
Guru	:	Guide, Indian Philosophy Teacher
Gurudev	:	Teacher, Guru of Maharishi who is the founder of the School of Transcendental Meditation.
Günferi	:	The Converging Power Of the Tünami color extending to the infinity.
Gürz	:	Looks like the form of a Mace, The Atomic Whole, Main Universe
Gürz Dimension	:	The Medium which the Main Atomic Whole is in. (Thought Ocean of Pre-eminent Power).

H

Hammurabi Laws	:	The 282 pages of absolute Legislative Principles Şamias the Sun God had dictated to Hammurabi who had been the Sixth King of the Sami Dynasty in Babilonia.
Heart	:	Essence
Heaven Dimension	:	Fourth Dimension
His/He/Him	:	In Turkish the third person pronoun is a neutral single word. However, in the Book, words "He","His" and "Him" are used to represent the Neutral Energy of God which is far beyond male/female concepts as it is the accustomed usage in English.
Horizontal Evolvement	:	Equivalence of the Evolvement of a Person with his/her present Dimension. (Religious Fulfillment).
Hu	:	Formula of Litany in Islamic Sufism, Calling to Allah by a Powerful Frequency.

I

In-between Dimensions	:	Layers between two Dimensions, tone dimensions
Incarnate	:	To go from one dimension to another and to exist there. The connection of the Spirit to the Body. To gain the Right to Live.
Incarnation	:	To be embodied, Reborn
Incombustible Energy	:	Cosmic Energy
Individual Awareness	:	Individual action Power
Individual Will	:	Personal decision Power
Inhabited Time	:	Time Dimension in which Human Beings live.
Initial Power	:	Cosmic Brain
Integrated Consciousness	:	Unification of Intellect, Reason, Awareness
Integration	:	To become Genuine Human Being, to Unify (to be integrated) the Intellect and the Heart.
Intellect	:	The Supervising Mechanism of the Brain.
Intellect - Reason - Awareness	:	To reach the Awareness of the Ordinance, to attain Universal Discernment.
Interregnum Age	:	Period without a Prophet, time passing until the Order is reestablished.
Interval Dimension	:	Distance, Progress and Developments of Human Being
Islamic Mysticism	:	Religious and Philosophical School, to become Profound in God Consciousness.
Izolan Language	:	Atomic Language, Ability to talk with the other by Conscious Communication through Thought. (Not Telepathy).

J

Jinn	:	Entities not seen by the Eye, are divided into Three as Terrestrial Jinns, Celestial Jinns, Universal Jinns.

K

Kaaba	:	The greatest Temple of the Moslems, the direction of (Mecca) Kıble.
Karena	:	Fourth and Fifth Dimensions.
Karma	:	Evolutionary Deficiencies belonging to former lives of an individual which has to be completed during the life time of that individual.
Konya Code	:	A Special Expression used for Mevlana.
Kosmos	:	Universal Void formed by the Birth of the Universe.
Krishna	:	The 8th Incarnation of the Indian God Vishnu.
Ku	:	The highest Frequency the World Dimension can enter. (It is Equivalent to the 72nd Energy Dimension of the 18th Dimension frequency).
Kundalini	:	Cosmic Energy accumulating at the Coccyx of Human Beings.

Kürz	:	The Totality forming the Totalistic Unity of Allah's Order the periphery of which is the Dimension of the All-Truthful.
Kıble	:	Direction of Mecca (to which a Muslim turns in Worship)

L

La	:	Godly vibration Frequency
Lale	:	Turkish word for Tulip. In the Book this word is used as the name of a specific Operational Ordinance.
Land of Eagles	:	Golden Galaxy Empire
Land of Loving Ones	:	Dimension where the Supreme Ones who have dispersed their Genes for Humanity are present.
Land of Mighties	:	Focal Point where the Sacred Books have been prepared.
Last Judgement Day	:	The Judgement Day of Allah, Great Crowd, A Medley of People.
Law of Eighteen Systems	:	Initial Universal Laws and Applications which can never be changed.
Law of Graduation	:	Application of the Ordinance of Graduation on the Constitution.
Law of Rules and Obedience:		Godly Rules, Universal Laws
Learning	:	To Learn the Characteristic of anything in detail.
Leap	:	Jumping over Dimensions, Progress, Phase.
Level of Perfection	:	The Final Evolutionary Boundary of Humanity, the Seventh Dimension.
Light-Body	:	Our Essence-Energy Bodies
Light-Universe	:	Totality of Central Suns, the Dimension of All-Merciful.
Link	:	Information transmitting Line
Litany from the Heart	:	Worship through the Essence.
Logic	:	Reason, Right Thinking.
Lord[1]	:	Administrator of the Second Universe (My Air) RAB in Turkish.
Lord[2]	:	Rank of nobility, Missionary Staffs of Godly Layers,
Lordly Order	:	Order of Allah
Lordly Mechanism	:	Application Branch of Allah
Lordly Plan	:	Program of Allah

M

Mechanism of the Pre-eminent Spirit	:	Operational Mechanism of the Spiritual Dimension.
Magnetic Aura	:	Powerful Reflection Focal Point formed by thought, Magnetic Energy net that, each Entity forms according to the Energy Power it emanates.

Magnetic Field	:	Field of which attraction Power is very Powerful.
Main Gene	:	The first Noble Gene
Mantra	:	Secret Word given in Meditation in order to attain Pure Consciousness, Cipher.
Masiva	:	A stop that should be passed over on the path of Truth.
Materialized	:	The formation of the Crude Matter Form anew by the unification of cells as a result of Beaming Up, Bodily Integration.
Mazdean	:	People constituting the Magian Religious Community (Those who worship Fire, Cows and Crocodiles in India)
Mechanical System	:	System operating out of Thought
Mechanism	:	Method of Operation of an Order
Mechanism of Influences	:	Mechanism which conveys the Cosmic Influences parallel to the Evolution of Our World from the 10th Dimension.
Mechanism of Conscience	:	The Inner Voice of a Person, Inner Intuition.
Mechanism of the Lord	:	Operational Order of the Lordly Dimension.
Mediamic Age	:	Age of Mediumship, this Final Transition Dimension in which connections with Celestial Authorities have increased, Special Age.
Meditation	:	Deep Thinking
Medium	:	Person who mediates between Spirits and People.
Megaton Bomb	:	Bomb equivalent to the Mass Unit of 1.000.000 Tons.
Megawatt Power	:	Electrical Power Unit equal to 1.000.000 Watts.
Mercury	:	The first Planet of Our solar System.
Mesnevi	:	Verse Style of Literary School of the Old Classical Poetry of Turks, in which each Verse is different (the general name of the works of this kind), however the Mesnevi dictated to Mevlana possesses a speciality.
Metamorphosis	:	Transformation, Alteration
Metan Glaciers	:	Glaciers formed by Carbon Gas
Metaphysics	:	Beyond nature, beyond Physics.
Meteor	:	Celestial Stone, (Meteorite), shooting star.
Mevlana	:	Servant of God; Celaleddin-i Rumi (Jalal-ud-Din Rumi) One of the pioneers of the Islamic Mysticism in Anatolia, in 13th century.
Micro Archive	:	Small Life Files belonging to Our past at Universal Dimensions.
Micro Particles	:	The smallest Energy Fragments at Universal Dimensions.
Micron	:	One Thousandth of a Milimetre, Calculation Units beyond Galaxies.
Mighty Energy	:	Creative Power
Mighty Energy Focal Point	:	The Second Universe, Dimension of Existence
Mini Atomic Whole	:	One of the 1800 Energy Balls constituted by 1800 Universes within a Gürz.

Mirror of Truth	:	Projection of the Dimension of Truth on Consciousnesses.
Mission[1]	:	Community constituted by People who have undertaken a Religious or any other kind of Duty.
Mission[2]	:	Duty
Mission Dimension	:	The Duty taken by a Person according to his/her Evolutionary Consciousness.
Missionary	:	Propagandist, Person consciously treading the Path he/she Believes in.
Mixed Gene	:	Different Evolutionary Genes which each Being carries in his/her Reincarnation Chains.
Molecule	:	Nucleus formed by the Unifications of one or more Atoms, the Smallest Fragment of a Whole.
Mutation	:	Transformation, Change, alteration in the Genes which form the Character.
Mystic	:	Person dealing with Theology or Mystical Life.
Mythos	:	Godly Totality, Godly legends.

N

"A nail is made to be driven out by another nail" : A Turkish Proverb.

Namaz	:	Muslim ritual worship, practised 5 times a day.
Natural Equilibrium Laws	:	Program of Mutation
Natural Gürz	:	The Natural Whole which had initially come into Existence in which we live at the moment.
Natural Totality	:	Natural Kürz
Neptune	:	The 8th Planet from the Sun.
Neutron	:	An Atomic Particule which has the Proton weight and which has no Electrical charge.
Nine Lights	:	Reflection Layers within Omega
Ninth Dimension	:	In the Sacred Books the Dimension of Serenity, the Lordly Dimension in the Universal Ordinance.
Nirvana	:	The 6th Dimension, Dimension of Immortality, the Final Dimension of the Indian Evolution.
Noble Gene	:	The Unspoiled initial Pure Gene
Nothingness Dimension	:	The Dimension of effacing one's Self from his/her Own Self, Abolishing, free from the Self
Nova	:	Nucleus in the Universal terminology. (6 Galaxies is a Nova).
Nucleic Universe	:	The Essence Nucleus of the Crude Matter of Universes, Nova.

O

O	:	Allah
Obsessed	:	Inability to leave the Influence Field.

Obsession	:	To Enter the Influence Field of any Energy and to act according to its Commands, the Inability to rule one's own Willpower.
Om	:	The highest Frequency Power that is Terrestrial Thought can attain at the Terrestrial Dimension without help.
Omega	:	The Final Exit Channel of Terrestrial Evolution at the 19th Dimension, belonging to the 16th Solar System, and in which there are 9 Energy Layers.
One of One	:	The All-Merciful
Ones Returning with Covenant	:	Reverse transfer, The Supreme Ones who come back to the World with Covenants from the Dimension they are in, to serve the Humanity.
Open Service	:	Not gradual, but currents given directly
Order	:	Orderliness, to Establish Unity, a style of Directing
Order Establisher	:	Allah
Order Establishing Mechanism	:	Circumstance established according to Laws, Totality of System-Ordinance-Order.
Order Establishing Focal Point	:	Universe of Light, Totality of Central Suns, The Dimension of All-Merciful.
Ordinance	:	Triple Unification Program of Order-System-Ordinance Here, the Ordinance Makes the Program, the Order applies, System Supervises and brings Suggestions.
Ordinance of Capillary Vessels	:	Element of Equilibrium, Lordly Dimension.
Ordinance of Graduation	:	Principle of gradually attaining the Truth.

P

Package Program	:	Applied Programs prepared by Celestial Authorities according to Social Consciousness.
Papyrus	:	The leaf of a plant growing in Egypt and on which one can write.
Parapsychology	:	Pertaining to Science of Spiritualism.
Partial Will	:	The smallest Part of the Total Will present in the Human Being.
Path of Yoga	:	Indian Philosophical System (To Rule the Physical Body).
Pen of the Golden Age	:	Mevlana
Perception	:	Intuition, the interpretation of the truth, Feeling
Perception Theory	:	The theory of fortifying the intuitions by Cosmic Influences to accelerate the Evolvement.
Pharaoh	:	Ancient Egyptian Ruler
Phase	:	Different Progress following each other
Phenomenon	:	Something existing in Reality, that which can be observed, a Happening.

Photon	:	Original Power of Light providing the transmission of Electromagnetic Influences.
Physiological	:	Living Structure, Pertaining to Body, that which functions Naturally.
Pluto	:	A small Planet in Our Solar System found in 1930, further away than Neptune.
Positive Aura	:	Projection emanating by Benevolent thought.
Pre-eminent Mother	:	Power which connects the Spiritual Energy to crude matter.
Pre-eminent Spirit	:	Administrative Power of the Spiritual Dimension.
Predestination of the Divine	:	Divine justice of Allah.
Predestination Plan	:	Fate
Prime Number	:	Unchanging Basic Number
Prismal Reflection Center	:	Projective Focal Point of the Prismal Universe
Prismal Universe	:	Projective Universe
Protection Medium	:	Magnetic Field of the Reality.
Protective Powers	:	Celestial Friends serving in the Medium of Reality.
Purification Program	:	Religious Doctrines, Celestial Suggestions.
Purifying Currents	:	Evolutionary Cosmic Influence Currents.

R

R3	:	Director of the Second Universe (Pre-eminent Power)
R4	:	Supervisor of the Second Universe (Third Drop coming out of the Point).
Ra	:	Gods of the Mechanism
Ran Planet	:	Fire Planet, its other name is (Omega).
Reality of Unified Humanity	:	The Directing Mechanism rendering effective the Unification Ordinance of Allah (ONE).
Reality Totality	:	The Center of the Dimension of Unified Humanity.
Realization Triangle	:	The Intellect - Reason - Awareness Totality.
Realm	:	8748 Galaxies
Realm Clusters	:	Chain of Cosmoses.
Realm of Perfection	:	Realm of the Supreme Ones.
Realm of Spirits	:	Realm where the total of the Spirits are present
Realms of Angels	:	Dimension where Angels are altogether/come together.
Red Dimension	:	Gama Dimension, 14th Solar System, 17th Dimension.
Reincarnation	:	To be Born Anew, To be embodied again and again.
Religious Fulfilment	:	Horizontal Evolution.
Resul	:	Messenger who brings news, Prophet.
Resurrect	:	To stand up, Reanimation in the Resurrections.
RightSide-Up Triangle	:	Symbol of Religious Fulfillment
Robot	:	That which works by the command of another.
Robotic Body	:	All forms carrying crude matter prepared in nature for the Evolution of Energy.
Robotic Dimension	:	A Universal Dimension administered only by Influences.

S

Sacred Light Path	:	Godly Path, the Energy Focal Point of the Divine Order
Salvation Plan	:	Evolution Project of the Earth.
Salvation	:	Deliverance, Freedom, to be set Free, to be liberated from passions and attachments.
Science	:	The Method depending on experiment, by benefiting from the Truth.
Second Universe	:	Dimension of Existence.
Self	:	One's Essence Personality, Essence State.
Sextuple System	:	The universal Projection Mechanism
Silence Dimension	:	Beginning of Formation.
SIR-AT	:	The word SIR means the Secret; The word AT means to throw; SIR-AT means to throw away the Secret.
Sırat	:	The bridge over Hell to Heaven which is thinner than hair, sharper than sword; Resurrection Period.
Sirius	:	Double Universe Star
Sixth Dimension	:	The Dimension of Immortality
Solar Friend	:	Those who have grasped the Learning of Truth and who Consciously serve the Total and the System.
Solar System	:	The Totality constituted of Sun and the Planets.
Solar Teacher	:	Those who directly Serve the Reality Mission
Soul	:	Essence of Life
Soul Mate	:	Entities whose Spiritual cultural levels are equivalent.
Soul Seed	:	The Essence formed as a result of the Unification of the Cell and the Spiritual Energy.
Sound-Universe	:	Universe formed by the Vibrations of the First Drop (Allah-Matu) coming out of the Point.
Space Committee Union	:	Galactic Totalities formed by Three People each.
Space Main Ships	:	Galactic Ships beyond the Atmosphere (not UFO).
Spadium	:	Spiritual Energy Pool closest to the World.
Spiral Vibrations	:	Helical Vibrations, Religious and Evolutionary Vibrations.
Spirit	:	Life Power of each crude matter, the Knot of Physical Body and Godly Energy.
Spiritual Chest	:	The Archive in which Knowledge attained during each Existence is accumulated.
Spiritual Realm	:	Dream Realm, Interpretation Realm.
Spiritual Cord	:	The Energy bond connecting the Life Energy, Silver Cord.
Spiritualism	:	Science of Spirit.
Stop In-between	:	Waiting-Focal Points according to Consciousness Progress between two Dimensions
Subtle Body	:	Transparent Body, The We within us.
Sufi	:	Person who knows and is devoted to the Philosophy of Islamic Mysticism, Theosophist.
SULH	:	ASHOT, Peace.

Supreme Court	:	Just System
Supreme Court of Allah	:	The System
Supreme Mechanism	:	Direct Allah's System
System	:	Order which obtains a result, Supreme Mechanism.
System of Sixes	:	The first System directly Projecting the Power of Allah (The Alion Dimension). The first Reflection Flower of Allah

Ş

Şems	:	Shams.

T

Tablets of God's Decrees	:	Allah's Secret Treasury of Knowledge
Technological Awareness	:	Attaining Godly Awareness through the Scientific Path.
Technological Dimension	:	Lordly Mechanism, Dimension which directly applies the Suggestions of the Lordly Dimension.
Telekine System	:	Celestial Communication System.
Telepathy	:	Perception between two People through the Cerebral Path (Sixth Sense).
Third Eye	:	That which beholds the things the Worldly Eye can not see, the Eye at the forehead Chacra, Interior Eye, Unveiling of the 6th Chacra.
Thought Arrow	:	The Power of Thoughts to Reach Dimensions.
Thought Chain	:	Thoughts Reaching in chains to different Dimensions and to be able to receive answers to the Questions in Thoughts from those Dimensions.
Thought Field	:	The Magnetic Field a Thought forms in accordance with its Power.
Thought Speed	:	Unit of Speed of 300,000.- km/sec
Titration	:	Small Vibration.
Tongue has no bone	:	Turkish proverb.
Total Will	:	The Will of Allah, Total
Totalistic Totality	:	The Consciousness Totality within which all Kürz Totalities are present; The Single Power Focal Point of Allah. Reflection of it, is the Administrative Mechanism of the Kürz Totality.
Tranquil Time	:	The first Two Layers of the Fifth Dimension; Purification Pool, Dimension where Time stops.
Treshold	:	Progress, Evolutionary Steps
Triangular Reflection Focal Points	:	Reflection Center formed by 3 people on the same Coordinate.
Trinity	:	Believing that God is formed by 3 different Persons in Christian Belief (R3).
Truth Consciousnesses	:	To Realize the cause of Existence of the Individual, to Awaken, to become Conscious.
Truth Dimension	:	The Original Truth at the Universal Dimension, the Genuine World.

Tünami	:	The intense Frequency of Three 49s colors (The Darkest Black color).
Tutelary Friend	:	Protecting Friend
Tutor	:	Protector, guide
Twin Mate	:	Sharing the same Thought, being on the same Coordinate.
Twin Spirit	:	Making the Evolution of the same Dimension, The Equivalence of the Spirit Cultures.

U

UFO	:	An unidentified Flying Object (Space Discs).
Ultra Sound	:	Subtle Sound Vibrations the Human Ear can not hear.
Unified Field	:	Magnetic Fields formed in the direction of same Thought.
Unity	:	Singleness, Oneness, to attain God.
Universal	:	Celestial
Universal Awareness	:	To awaken, to realize the Truth.
Universal Council	:	Unification of 3 Consciousnesses in the direction of the same Coordinate.
Universal Law	:	Godly Doctrines
Universal Mechanism	:	Godly Order
Universal Ordinance Council	:	Totality of the System in the Universe of Light.
Universal Plan	:	System - Ordinance - Order
Universal Predestination	:	Fate
Universal Theory	:	Operational Program which is rendered effective before something is applied in the Universal Operations.
Universal Unification Council	:	Unification Totality in the Universe of Light.
Universal Unification	:	The aim of the Golden Age, Gathering of the Totality under one Roof.
United Ordinance Council	:	A Hierarchical Dimension at the Universe of Light working in connection with the All-Merciful.
Universe	:	Single Totality which 18x18,000 Realms are connected (Its Administrator; Single).
Unknown Power	:	The Secret Power within Human Being, The Fundamental Establishing Power of the Atlanta Dimension.
Unveiled Awareness	:	To know, to see, to sense, perceive everything

V

Veiled awareness	:	Consciousness at the World Plan, the Normal World Life.
Vertical Evolvement	:	To make a transition from the Religious Evolvement to Universal Consciousness and to reach the Reality of Totality by rendering the Evolvement of that Dimension.
Vertical Projection	:	Conveyance of a Reflection Focal Point on any plane exactly as it is.

| Viril | : | Spiral Vibrations |
| Vulom | : | Magnetic Attraction Field. |

W

Whirling Dervish	:	Person connected to the Sect formed by Sultan Veled, the son of Mevlana Celaleddin-i Rumi, in accordance with his Father's views.
White Dimension	:	Dimension of state of being Purified. (White Country)
White Hole	:	The Energy Tunnel which transfers the Crude matter Energy which the Black Hole has swallowed up and has dissolved, to the same Dimension to provide the balance of the Universe.
World embracing	:	Mondial, Globally known
World Lord	:	Directing Power of the World Dimension
Wox	:	Name of the UFO in the Universal Dimensions.

Y

| YUNUS (EMRE) | : | A famous 13th century poet of the philosophy of Islamic mysticism who lived in Anatolia. |

Z

| Zero Frequency | : | World Dimension |
| Zodiac | : | Signs of path of the Sun |

EXPLANATORY INFORMATION ABOUT THE BOOK

Our Friends,

Each Fascicule and the Supplements of the Knowledge Book the Service of which has been and will be made to Humanity as 55 Fascicules and 7 Supplementary Information is each an Indivisible Frequency Totality peculiar to itself. In accordance with the time segments in which the Messages were given, each one has a separate mission. By this means, help is being extended for the Consciousness progresses of Humanity.

A different Technique has been rendered effective in the Preparation of the Fascicules as a Book. For this reason, since the Book will be prepared in conformity with page-setting, Messages present in the same Fascicule may change their places among themselves, just as they are, without upsetting their Totalities. Because, their Frequencies are the same.

In case Message Transfers are taken into effect between two different Fascicules, in accordance with the Photon Technique, the Letters can not Attract the Time Energy due to Frequency intersections. It is presented for Your Information.

SYSTEM